The New World, 1939/1946

A History of the United States Atomic Energy Commission

Volume I
1939/1946

The New World

Richard G. Hewlett
Oscar E. Anderson, Jr.

University of California Press
Berkeley • Los Angeles • Oxford

University of California Press
Berkeley and Los Angeles, California
University of California Press, Ltd.
Oxford, England
First California Paperback Printing 1990

Library of Congress Cataloging-in-Publication Data

A History of the United States Atomic Energy Commission
    p. cm.
    Reprint. Originally published: University Park : Pennsylvania
State University Press, 1962.
    Contents: v. 1. The new world, 1939 / 1946 / Richard G. Hewlett,
Oscar E. Anderson, Jr.—v. 2. Atomic shield, 1947 / 1952 / Richard
G. Hewlett, Francis Duncan.
    Includes bibliographical references.
    ISBN 0-520-07186-7 (Vol. 1)
    ISBN 0-520-07187-5 (Vol. 2)
    1. United States.   Atomic Energy Commission—History.   2. Nuclear
energy—Government policy—United States—History.   I. Hewlett,
Richard G.   II. Anderson, Oscar E.   III. Duncan, Francis, 1922–
HD9698.U52H55   1990
353.0087'22—dc20   90-10902
                                                                                          CIP

Printed in the United States of America

The paper used in this publication meets the minimum requirements of American
National Standard for Information Sciences—Permanence of Paper for Printed
Library Materials, ANSI Z39.48–1984. ∞

CONTENTS

FOREWORD BY THE CHAIRMAN, HISTORICAL ADVISORY COMMITTEE

The Historical Advisory Committee of the Atomic Energy Commission hails the completion of the first volume of the History with enthusiasm. We congratulate both the authors on the fairness and clarity of their presentation and the Commissioners on their decision to publish an unclassified history and on their wisdom in leaving the authors a free hand subject only to the limitations imposed by national security. All of the members of the Advisory Committee are happy to testify to the scholarly world and to the general public that this book is a major, impartial and objective contribution to American history.

No other development in our lifetime has been fraught with such consequences for good or evil as has atomic fission. None has raised such challenging questions for the historian, the economist, the armed forces, the scientists and the engineers. The wartime scientific developments produced significant new techniques in public administration which came to be more widely used after the war, such as the enlistment of university and private contractors to perform new types of government activities. The fresh light this volume throws on the early history of these new techniques may prove helpful in clarifying current problems of conflict of interest in the "military-industrial complex."

Unlike the history of the proximity fuze the development of atomic weapons was an international achievement to which great contributions were made by European as well as American scientists and engineers. All were spurred by the agonizing fear that the Nazis were well ahead of the free world in the development of atomic weapons.

Among the wealth of new materials brought to light by Dr. Hewlett and Dr. Anderson, many of the most interesting papers came from a sealed safe containing the correspondence of Vannevar Bush and James B. Conant from 1940 to 1945. The ideas of these two scientific leaders became a part of the Interim Committee plan and of the Stimson proposals presented in September, 1945. They thus underlay the Acheson-Lilienthal plan. The materials from the sealed safe make possible for the first time a satisfactory account of the intricate wartime negotiations with Great Britain and Canada on atomic energy.

The authors have presented a clear account of the possible routes to the bomb, of the obstacles blocking each path, and of the tensions built up during the quest for solutions. Both the scientist and the lay reader will find this not only the fullest and best documented but the most balanced narrative of the greatest research enterprise of the Second World War.

James P. Baxter, 3rd

x

UNITED STATES ATOMIC ENERGY COMMISSION
HISTORICAL ADVISORY COMMITTEE

CHAIRMAN

JAMES P. BAXTER, 3RD
Williams College

JOHN M. BLUM
Yale University

FRANCIS T. MILES
Brookhaven National Laboratory

JAMES L. CATE
University of Chicago

DON K. PRICE, JR.
Harvard University

ARTHUR H. COMPTON
Washington University

GLENN T. SEABORG *
University of California, Berkeley

* Resigned February 20, 1961, to become Chairman of the Atomic Energy Commission.

PREFACE

The first public announcement that the United States had entered the atomic age followed the blinding flash over Hiroshima, Japan, on August 6, 1945. Until that moment only a few score of Americans had seen the major outlines of the wartime project which produced the bomb. Six days later, the Government released Henry D. Smyth's report, *A General Account of the Development of Methods of Using Atomic Energy for Military Purposes Under the Auspices of the United States Government, 1940–1945.* Dr. Smyth chronicled the administrative and the technical history of the secret enterprise. Although the report was devoted primarily to "all the pertinent scientific information which can be released to the public at this time without violating the needs of national security," Dr. Smyth saw fit to close with a broad, forward look at "The Questions Before the People." Some of his statements have grown more pertinent with the passing years:

> . . . Here is a new tool for mankind, a tool of unimaginable destructive power. Its development raises many questions that must be answered in the near future. . . . These questions are not technical questions; they are political and social questions, and the answer given to them may affect all mankind for generations. . . . In a free country like ours, such questions should be debated by the people and decisions must be made by the people through their representatives. This is one reason for the release of this report.

Despite Smyth's call for public discussion, the real issues posed by the exploitation of atomic energy failed to reach the American people during the succeeding decade. The fault lay partly in the continuing need for security restrictions, partly in the layman's disinclination to acquire the rudimentary technical knowledge necessary to understand the impact of this new force in his life. Politicians left technical details to the scientists; social scientists reacted with resignation or disdain to this newest manifestation of the scientific revolution in the twentieth century. The relatively few persons who were privileged to work behind the security barrier imposed by the Atomic Energy Act of 1946 found themselves ever more isolated in a world their fellow citizens had never seen.

Within the decade there were signs of a change. A new atomic energy law in 1954 liberalized security restrictions in the interests of international co-operation and civilian uses of atomic energy. The widening gulf between the physical and the social sciences caused growing concern. During 1957, the Atomic Energy Commission's tenth anniversary, one of the Commissioners remarked that he and his colleagues were making some of the most momentous decisions in American history without the benefit of an historian to record the events. The discussion resulted in a decision to employ two professional historians, give them complete access to the files, and permit them to write—with no restrictions other than those imposed by national security —the story as they saw it. The Commission also established an Historical Advisory Committee of distinguished, independent scholars in a variety of disciplines to give advice on policy matters and to review the work of the historians. Since most of the documentary evidence would not be available to the public for many years, the committee agreed to examine the sources and thereby provide a partial but effective substitute for independent scholarly criticism.

As the authors of the first volume in this series, we have tried to follow the lead of Dr. Smyth's closing sentences. From the outset it has been our intention to explain the effect of technological developments on policy decisions at the national and international level. Our uncomfortable proximity to the people and events we are describing has not deterred us from seeking the lofty perspective of the historian; on the contrary, it seems to make that approach especially important. The following pages are more often narrative than analytical, more often chronological than topical. The perspective is the highest appropriate level in the federal government. Whatever the subject, whatever the essential significance of the event, whether and how we relate that event depends on its relevance to the central perspective. We think this criterion makes for good history. Indeed, the complex interrelationships of modern science, industry, and government make it impossible to take any other approach if history is to be kept within reasonable bounds.

Yet the approach has the disadvantage of leaving voids in areas some readers would expect to be filled. From our chosen point of view we cannot write a comprehensive history of any single organization, project, discipline, or period. We cannot mention every important participant or even contend that those included are intrinsically more significant than those omitted. In many instances, we have been forced to depend on representative accounts. The greater technical detail on the electromagnetic separation process in Chapters 4 and 5 reflects the relaxation of security restrictions and our effort to use this project as an example of wartime research and development. Likewise, the description of contracting procedures and contractor relationships in Chapter 6 is but a small sampling of an incredibly voluminous record. Not that more exhaustive treatment would be unprofitable for some purposes. We, as historians, can but stake out the areas in which others with specialized interests may find rich ore.

Our approach has also required us to devote most of this volume to the Commission's inheritance rather than to the activities of the Commission itself. Without that inheritance, the Commission's history has no meaning. For this reason we have emphasized the development of key production processes, the construction of physical plant, the advent of nuclear weapons, the origins of the Atomic Energy Act of 1946, and the first steps toward international control. Important in its own right, this inheritance will serve as the foundation for subsequent volumes in this series.

We wish to emphasize (and it is a credit to the Commission that we can do so) that this volume represents a completely independent, unrestricted history within the limits of national security. In no instance have we been denied access to any records, facilities, or individuals sought in our research. The Commission and its operating staff have made no effort to establish the direction, emphasis, content, or conclusions of this volume. Even in the few areas where security restrictions apply, the effect has been only to eliminate detail; we have never consciously distorted the facts to accommodate security. In short, the Commission has authorized the preparation of this volume, but we must bear responsibility for its content. This book, like all historical works, should stand on its own merits and be judged in the light of subsequent research as the work of the authors alone.

In a work of this scope, we find it impossible to acknowledge our indebtedness to all those who have contributed to this volume. We must, however, mention those whose help more than warrants public recognition. First, we wish to express our deepest appreciation to the members of the Historical Advisory Committee, whose names appear elsewhere in this volume. From the initial proposals through the preliminary outlines, research, drafting, and redrafting, the committee proved a constant source of guidance and encouragement. The members not only fulfilled their responsibilities as scholars, but they also proved wise and patient friends. The opportunity to work with them over the past four years has been one of the joys of our task.

Within the AEC, we owe thanks to the various Commissioners who demonstrated their confidence in us by endorsing this project, and particularly the three men who have served as Chairman during these years: Lewis L. Strauss, John A. McCone, and Glenn T. Seaborg. Clearly indispensable was the direction and support provided by Woodford B. McCool, the Secretary to the Commission, who was among the first to see the need for this history, who helped to establish the project, and who resisted magnificently the temptation plaguing every administrator to divert historians from their primary task to the exigencies of daily deadlines and routine reports.

Literally scores of Commission employees, both in headquarters and the field offices, had a part in preparing this volume. Greatest thanks must go to our research assistants, Alyce M. Birch and Mary Lee McIntyre, whose industry, loyalty, and forebearance are reflected on every page of this book. Both Francis Duncan, who read the manuscript and helped to prepare the index, and Helen Anderson, who executed the drawings, performed services far beyond those required in their regular duties. Among the headquarters library and records staff, we wish to thank Elizabeth M. Cole, John L. Cook, Robert E. Devine, E. Jane Dossett, Velma E. Early, John E. Hans, William R. Johnson, Madeleine W. Losee, James D. Nuse, Jean M. O'Leary, Lillie B. Turner, Severina Tuttle, and Sara K. White. Murray L. Nash and Charles F. Knesel provided valuable guidance on classification problems; Clarence H. Little and his staff reproduced thousands of pages of manuscript, usually on short notice. Edward J. Brunenkant, J. William Young, and James D. Cape spent long hours on publication matters. Elton P. Lord provided many of the photographs.

Our research in the field was greatly facilitated by the following AEC managers: Samuel R. Sapirie at Oak Ridge; James E. Travis at Hanford; Harold A. Fidler at San Francisco; Joseph C. Clarke at New York; and Paul A. Wilson at Los Alamos. At Oak Ridge, Charles Vanden Bulck made arrangements to meet our many needs, James R. Langley helped us at the records center, and James E. Westcott searched his photographic files. At Hanford, Milton R. Cydell sought out many elusive facts; Ralph V. Button found many valuable documents in the records center. Among AEC contractor officials, we wish to thank Clark E. Center of the Union Carbide Nuclear Company, Oak Ridge; William E. Johnson of the General Electric Company, Hanford; Edwin M. McMillan of the Lawrence Radiation Laboratory, Berkeley; Norris E. Bradbury of the Los Alamos Scientific Laboratory; and Norman Hilberry of the Argonne National Laboratory. At Berkeley, Eleanor Davisson found many significant documents and Donald Cooksey permitted us to select photographs from his excellent collection. At Argonne, Hoylande D. Young and her staff searched dozens of laboratory files for documents of unusual interest.

Without the help of many other Government agencies and institutions, it would have been impossible to write this book. Special appreciation is due Sherrod E. East, Edward J. Reese, and Harold Hufford of the National Archives; E. Taylor Parks of the Department of State; Rudolph A. Winnacker of the Department of Defense; Herman Kahn of the Roosevelt Library; Philip C. Brooks of the Truman Library; Nathan R. Reingold of the Library of Congress; and Arnold A. Shadrick of the Army Map Service.

Many individuals graciously permitted us to use their private record collections: Herbert L. Anderson, Bernard M. Baruch, James F. Byrnes, John R. Dunning, Byron S. Miller, John A. Simpson, Jr., and Carroll L. Wilson. Just as valuable were the records furnished by the Federation of American Scientists, Iowa State University, the Stimson Literary Trust, Yale University, and the University of Chicago. To all we express our appreciation.

No less important was the assistance from those who subjected themselves to hours of insistent questioning during interviews. We thank them for their time and patience. Their names are listed in the note on the Sources.

Last of all, we wish to express our gratitude to the hundreds of scientists, engineers, officers in the armed forces, Government officials, and private citizens whose names appear in the following pages, and to the thousands not there recorded. They made this a stirring chapter in American history. Without them there would be no book; but more important, the United States might not have been the first nation to enter the new world of the atom.

Richard G. Hewlett

Oscar E. Anderson, Jr. *xv*

Germantown, Maryland
February, 1962

THE
INHERITANCE

CHAPTER 1

It was a dismal Thursday afternoon in Washington, the second day of January, 1947. Unnoticed among the hundreds of Government employees in the New War Department Building, ten men gathered at a conference table in a cramped office on the sixth floor. Looking southeast across Twenty-first Street toward Constitution Avenue, they could see the Washington Monument towering into the cold rain that was turning five inches of New Year's snow into a sea of slush. The four men on the far side of the table listened impassively as an aging graduate-school dean and a young Army colonel explained the intricacies of releasing wartime technical data without endangering national security.

The drabness of the surroundings and the pedestrian character of the discussion disguised the significance of the occasion. This was the first meeting of the United States Atomic Energy Commission since it had assumed control of the plants, laboratories, equipment, and personnel assembled during the war to produce the atomic bomb.[1]

Presiding that afternoon was the Chairman, David E. Lilienthal, a courageous lawyer and public servant who had risen to fame as head of the Tennessee Valley Authority. Nearby sat Sumner T. Pike, a hearty New Englander and experienced businessman who was returning to Washington after a term on the Securities and Exchange Commission. Next to him was William W. Waymack, an amiable gentleman farmer and newspaper editor from Iowa. The fourth Commissioner, Lewis L. Strauss, was a conservative investment banker with an interest in science and politics. Robert F. Bacher, the only scientific member, was on special assignment in Los Alamos, New Mexico, inspecting the nation's stockpile of atomic weapons.

Across the table was Carroll L. Wilson, a thirty-six-year-old engineer and former assistant to Karl T. Compton and Vannevar Bush. Just eight days before, President Truman had named him the Commission's general manager. With him were three other young men—Herbert S. Marks, the general counsel, George Fox Trowbridge, his assistant, and William T. Golden, administrative assistant to Commissioner Strauss. The elderly dean was Richard C. Tolman of the California Institute of Technology; the young Army officer, Colonel Kenneth E. Fields.

To the Commission the President had transferred "properties and an organization which, in magnitude, are comparable to the largest business enterprises of the country." In the days after the bombing of Hiroshima, journalists had described the more spectacular features of the Army's production plants, laboratories, and technical installations. Most American newspapers carried photographs of the huge buildings among the ridges of East Tennessee or the concrete monoliths in the desert of eastern Washington where materials for the bomb were made. Almost as many ran photographs of Robert Oppenheimer and other scientists who had constructed the first atomic weapons in a "super-secret" laboratory on an inaccessible mesa northwest of Santa Fe, New Mexico. The news services also described the research in the scientific laboratories which the Government had established at Chicago, Columbia, and California.

These, however, were just the highlights. Included in the transfer was a sprawling complex of men and equipment. The Army's transfer list ran to thirty-seven installations in nineteen states and Canada. With the facilities the Army would transfer 254 military officers, 1,688 enlisted men, 3,950 Government workers, and about 37,800 contractor employees. The entire project, representing a wartime investment of more than $2.2 billion, would cost an additional $300 million during the current fiscal year.

The Army could describe precisely the physical inheritance, but it was harder to measure the political and economic legacy, the temper of the times in which the new commission found itself. On New Year's Day, 1947, the President had taken a step toward ending World War II with a surprise proclamation recognizing the termination of hostilities. The sixteen months since V-J Day had been a chaotic period of transition. While Harry S. Truman struggled with the burdens of the Presidency, the nation moved from the flush of victory into the somber realities of reconversion and readjustment—inflation, strikes, and political strife at home and starvation, nationalism, and new power relationships abroad.

On the domestic scene, political fortunes were changing quickly. Franklin D. Roosevelt's death and the growing coalition between southern Democrats and conservative Republicans in Congress had undermined the majorities the President had carried to victory in 1944. In the face of such unpromising odds, his successor launched in September, 1945, a twenty-one-point reconversion plan as a return to the "progressive" tradition and the New Deal. Truman had to fight every inch of the way against the strong current of reaction to wartime controls, high taxes, and "government from Washington." A wave of strikes in major industries in 1946 alarmed business interests while the President's harsh action against John L. Lewis for his open defiance of the Government in the coal strike alienated some of the party's labor support. The Administration's efforts to extend price controls, rationing, and universal military training in peacetime met with failure. By the end of 1946, the Administration had made but two lasting achievements. One was the Employment Act, a mutilated version of the original Murray bill but still a step in the direction of economic controls. The other was the Atomic Energy Act, which passed only after a year of acrimonious debate by 9 votes out of 200 in the House of Representatives. Within the Administration itself, smouldering hostility ignited such explosions as the resignation of Harold L. Ickes as Secretary of the Interior and the dismissal of Henry A. Wallace as Secretary of Commerce. These awkward episodes, the President's failure to control Congress, and the inflation that occurred with the abandonment of price controls just before the November elections gave the Republicans their most effective slogan, "Had Enough?"

3

That 1946 would be a Republican year seemed certain, but few expected the landslide that occurred at the polls in November. Gaining twelve seats in the Senate and more than fifty in the House, the GOP took control of Congress and captured governorships in twenty-five of thirty-two non-Southern states. When the Eightieth Congress assembled on January 3, Arthur H. Vandenberg became president pro tempore of the Senate and Joseph W. Martin speaker of the House. Robert A. Taft, the Republican power in the Senate, stepped aside to permit Wallace H. White of Maine to serve as Senate majority leader. Taft was reserving for himself the chairmanship of the Senate Labor Committee, which would seek legislation to prevent recurrence of the strikes that had paralyzed the nation in 1946.

The character of the Senate, which would pass on the interim appointments to the Atomic Energy Commission, seemed transformed by the presence of such newcomers as Joseph R. McCarthy of Wisconsin, Henry Cabot Lodge, Jr., of Massachusetts, Irving M. Ives of New York, Edward Martin of Pennsylvania, Arthur V. Watkins of Utah, and John W. Bricker of Ohio. New members of the House included some young war veterans destined to make their mark: William G. Stratton of Illinois, Richard M. Nixon of California, and John F. Kennedy of Massachusetts.

Back in power after fourteen years, the Republicans were in a fighting mood as they talked of a 20-per-cent cut in federal taxes and appropriations, a drastic revision of the Wagner Labor Act, complete reorganization of the housing program, and a critical examination of reciprocal trade policies and foreign spending. Assuming that the Republican nominee in 1948 would succeed Truman as President, the principal aspirants were already engaged in a struggle for power. Robert A. Taft, Senate spokesman for the Midwest, seemed the leading contender. Thomas E. Dewey had bounced back from his defeat in 1944 with a resounding victory in the gubernatorial race in New York. Not out of the running were a dozen other hopefuls led by Harold E. Stassen of Minnesota, who had already announced himself a candidate.

Developments abroad looked no more promising for the Administration than did those at home. Though farm output in the United States hit a record high in 1946, millions of Europeans faced starvation. The devastation in Germany continued to tax the descriptive powers of American journalists. France was threatened by inflation and colonial unrest. The United Kingdom, for which the war had proved almost fatal, accepted indefinite rationing of consumer goods and transferred its coal mines to government ownership as a first step toward nationalizing basic industries.

The upheaval of war and the collapse of Europe stimulated political and economic aspirations throughout the world. In the Middle East, the British found themselves caught in the cross fire of Jewish and Arab nationalism. In India, Mahatma Gandhi sparked a new drive for independence. Southeast Asia was in tumult, and China remained an enigma. Despite a year of painful negotiation, General George C. Marshall had been unable to quench the fires of civil war which threatened to disrupt all Asia. In the Far East, only Japan, now under the firm hand of General Douglas MacArthur, seemed headed toward stability.

With the decline of Britain and France came the accelerated rise of the Soviet Union. In 1945, there had been confidence that somehow the victorious allies could establish a new era of peace and human freedom. But this dream grew dim in 1946, when countries bordering the Communist world from Germany to Korea felt the aggressive pressure of Soviet strength.

The United Nations had yet to prove itself. Secretary-General Trygve H. Lie warned that while the new association of states had laid a sound foundation on which to build peace, the state of the world left no room for "easy optimism." Certainly this judgment was borne out by the experience of the United Nations Atomic Energy Commission. After six months of negotiation, American delegate Bernard M. Baruch found the United States and the Soviet Union distressingly far apart on the requirements for effective international control.

The survival of western democracy seemed to depend upon the United States. Yet Americans were obviously uncomfortable with the responsibilities of world leadership. Europeans feared that the November elections might signal a withdrawal from overseas commitments. Their fears fed on Washington reports of a tighter attitude on foreign loans, of an end to support for the United Nations Relief and Rehabilitation Administration, and of open misgivings in the new Congress about the nation's foreign policy.

Undaunted by the universal uncertainty, Chairman Lilienthal prepared to enter the new world of atomic energy with an untried approach to public administration. The authors of the Atomic Energy Act themselves admitted that it was "a radical piece of legislation." They asserted that "never before in the peacetime history of the United States has Congress established an administrative agency vested with such sweeping authority and entrusted with such portentous responsibilities. . . . The Act creates a government monopoly of the sources of atomic energy and buttresses this position with a variety of broad governmental powers and prohibitions on private activity. The field of atomic energy is made an island of socialism in the midst of a free enterprise economy." [2]

The Act was no more revolutionary, however, than the forces that produced it. Never before had man exploited a new dimension of power so suddenly. Though the first reactions to Hiroshima now seemed exaggerated and hackneyed, there was no gainsaying the words of one congressman who declared the control of atomic energy "a matter for the ages." The Commissioners understood as well as other Americans the predicament in which they found themselves. Chairman Lilienthal reportedly said at the Commission's first meeting in November: "I have taken the oath of office several times before in my life, but the last four words never had the meaning to me they have today. So I'd just like to begin by repeating them—'So help me God.' " [3]

To their task Lilienthal and his colleagues brought many talents. All had held important posts in the Government. Together they possessed a range of experience touching many aspects of American life, but only Bacher had an intimate knowledge of the wartime atomic energy program. For the others, as for most of their fellow citizens, their inheritance lay in the secret recesses of a military enterprise. In the guarded language of the Smyth Report they had a glimpse into the past. They could not, however, recapture the human experience that lay behind the stiff prose of the official report. Time had already blurred the anguished moments of blind decision, the chance event, the unpredicted accomplishments upon which the success of the project depended.

Few men besides Vannevar Bush, James B. Conant, and Leslie R. Groves knew more than a fragment of the story. It began early in 1939 with the discovery of the fission of uranium and the first efforts to win support from the federal government for nuclear research. At a time when Nazi threats had only begun to raise questions about American isolationism, proposals for co-operation between government and science had already reached the White House. The idea was so new that only British confidence that fission could influence the outcome of the war and Bush's skillful leadership gave the United States the beginnings of an atomic energy program by the eve of Pearl Harbor.

In 1942, the lack of reliable information about fundamental processes paralyzed efforts of the Office of Scientific Research and Development to select the most promising method of producing fissionable material. June brought momentous decisions dictated not by experimental evidence but by the desperate race for the bomb. Then came the painful transition from research to process development and from OSRD to Army control. Through

5

the summer the project faltered in indecision and frustration until Bush won full Army support. In the meantime, Conant and his OSRD committee continued their search for the best route to a weapon. The prospects for the various approaches fluctuated from day to day. One process was dropped, another revived after a routine inspection trip by a reviewing committee, a third supported on the strength of an experiment not yet performed. The year ended with a climactic series of decisions which spelled out the nation's commitment to the atomic bomb as a weapon in World War II.

By 1943, the project had grown so rapidly in so many directions that no one individual could follow it. As the year began, earthmovers were already carving huge excavations out of the narrow Tennessee valleys for three plants and a new American city. Across the country a network of university laboratories and private contractors were designing and fabricating components to specifications unprecedented in mass-production efforts. Now, to follow the fortunes of the bomb, one had to observe physicists assembling vacuum tanks and high-voltage equipment at the University of California Radiation Laboratory, engineers laying precision-machined blocks of graphite within a concrete cube in Tennessee, chemists testing fragile pieces of porous metal in corrosive gases at Columbia University, scientists exploring the fundamentals of the fission process in New Mexico, and Army officers planning the transformation of a desert into an industrial city in the Pacific Northwest. Here one could feel the pulse of progress, share the moments of success and failure, watch hopes fade away one by one as Nature frustrated repeated attempts to solve the riddle of producing fissionable material and building an adequate weapon. No one who lived through the black days of June, 1944, could ever say that success was predestined.

But before the end of 1944, success was in sight. Engineers at Oak Ridge had devised an ingenious plan to operate the separation plants as a unit while taking maximum advantage of the peculiar capabilities of each. By the spring of 1945, the Oak Ridge complex was producing uranium 235 in significant amounts. The crisis at Hanford had passed, and increasing quantities of plutonium were being shipped to Los Alamos. Months of intensive research had made the bomb a certainty, though no one yet knew how powerful it would be.

Though the war was far from over in the summer of 1944, it was time to think about postwar arrangements, both domestic and international. Among the scientific men who shared this belief, Bush and Conant were in a uniquely favorable position to act. Believing that free interchange of scientific information under international auspices offered the only hope of averting a catastrophic arms race, they opposed any step that might bind the United States so closely to its British ally as to prejudice the chances for Russian co-operation. At Quebec in 1943, their views on a strictly limited form of Anglo-American technical interchange had prevailed, but in September, 1944, President Roosevelt and Prime Minister Winston Churchill agreed on full collaboration in the military and commercial applications of atomic energy after the defeat of Japan. Though not aware of the President's commitment, Bush and Conant knew the trend of his thought. They alerted Secretary of War Henry L. Stimson to the danger and urged the importance of naming a high-level policy committee to advise on the whole sweep of postwar problems. Then the fates intervened in the guise of distracting issues, the stress of war, and the death of the President. Not until the first week in May, 1945, did Stimson appoint his Interim Committee.

When the Interim Committee met, Stimson had turned his full attention to the Far East. For him, the issue was not whether to use the atomic bomb but how to end the war against Japan. If the bomb would foreclose the prospect of a long and bloody conflict, he was disposed to use it. Aware of the threat that atomic energy posed for the future, Stimson urged Truman to tell Stalin of American hopes for future international control before the United States dropped the weapon in combat. The President might have followed Stimson's advice had not Russian conduct at Potsdam discouraged both men about the chances for fruitful co-operation. By that time, the Alamogordo tests had shown that the atomic arm was more powerful than anyone had dared hope. With Japanese leaders offering little reason to expect an early acceptable surrender, the President simply told the Soviet chief that the United States was at work on an unusually powerful new weapon and allowed nuclear operations to proceed against Japan.

7

The bombing of Hiroshima made atomic energy a topic for public discussion. For weeks, the Truman Administration groped for a policy on domestic and international control. Not until his message to Congress on October 3, 1945, did the President establish the bare outlines of such a course. Even then, his position on international control did not clearly emerge until the November meetings with the British and Canadian Prime Ministers in Washington.

Meanwhile, a combination of parliamentary maneuverings in the Senate, organized opposition among the atomic scientists, and second thoughts in the White House had defeated the War Department's bill to establish an atomic energy commission. An alliance of scientists and senators now took control of legislation. Senator Brien McMahon organized his Special Committee and introduced a new bill excluding the military services from any real voice in developing atomic energy. While the scientists' lobby and pressure groups focused public debate on the civilian-military control issue, McMahon fought a losing battle with the conservative majority of his committee. The turning point came in late February, 1946, when Senator Vandenberg introduced an amendment to strengthen the hand of the military in atomic energy policy. Although McMahon denounced the amendment as a threat to civilian control, it proved a blessing in disguise. It captured the imagination of the American public and gave the McMahon bill the popular support it needed to pass the Senate. A long battle, waged for the most part behind closed doors in the White House and in Congressional committee rooms, was still necessary to win the House. Almost a year to the day after the Hiroshima attack, the President signed the act establishing the Commission.

Hopes for international control rose in late December, 1945, when the Soviet Union accepted the Anglo-American invitation to join in asking the United Nations General Assembly to establish a commission on atomic energy. Early in 1946 Secretary of State Byrnes started policy studies which resulted in the Acheson-Lilienthal plan for an atomic development authority. Now high principle, now sharp political infighting ruled in Washington conference rooms and executive offices. The proposal that Bernard Baruch presented in June was compounded in almost equal parts of imagination, prudence, and yearning for a certainty that many men considered illusory. In the summer and autumn of 1946, the prospect of international agreement faded as the Soviet Union insisted on outlawing the weapon before investigating controls. Some Americans, seeking to cast any beam from their own eyes, criticized Baruch's tactics and the substance of the United States plan itself. Yet by the time Lilienthal and his four colleagues took over the nation's nuclear program, one fact stood clear: the United States had offered to yield its monopoly of atomic weapons. True, it insisted on abandoning its favored position gradually, but it did not demand the right to dictate the timing of the transition process.

On that bleak afternoon of January 2, 1947, the Commissioners were gravely aware of their responsibilities and their opportunities. Six weeks of preparation had taught them how vast was their inheritance and how little they knew about how it came to be. They expected to learn more as the months advanced; their natural feelings of personal inadequacy would diminish. But many years would pass, they thought, before the story of their inheritance could stand forth in ample detail and just proportion. The Commissioners could not anticipate that when the passage of a decade and a half made this possible, mankind would be edging into the new frontiers of space. They did not realize that atomic energy so soon would appear as merely the first of a continuing series of revolutionary demands that twentieth-century science would make on the capacity of human nature to adjust to the physical universe. Had they been able to see into the future, the Commissioners would have believed even more strongly in the surpassing importance of their task.

IN THE
BEGINNING

CHAPTER 2

On the surface, there was nothing extraordinary about the first days of January, 1939. The American people were enjoying life's little diversions. They read in the newspapers that David O. Selznick had selected Vivien Leigh to play Scarlett O'Hara in *Gone With the Wind,* that Broadway was acclaiming Mary Martin as the season's musical-comedy find, that Brenda Frazier would make a $50,000 debut at the Ritz-Carlton. Many families contemplated a summer trip to New York's World of Tomorrow or San Francisco's Golden Gate International Exposition. Those in the market for a new automobile considered the Oldsmobile, advertised for as little as $777, or perhaps the Pontiac, listed at $862. Even business and politics, so long in turmoil, seemed to be returning to normal. The summer before, employment and production indices had begun to move up from recession lows. In November, 1938, the Republican Party won large gains in both Senate and House. Hard on President Roosevelt's failure to purge conservative members from his own party, the election returns suggested that the New Deal had run its course.

Yet no preoccupations of the moment, no mere redressing of the political balance, could still an underlying uneasiness caused by events abroad. Between 1935 and 1937, Congress had reacted to the signs of war in Europe and the Far East by passing a series of neutrality acts, laws which reflected a disillusionment with the results of American intervention in 1917. Hardly was the neutrality storm cellar complete, when the structure of international relations began to disintegrate at an alarming rate. In July and August of 1937, Japan expanded the incident at the Marco Polo bridge into a massive assault on China. During March of the following year, Nazi legions occupied and annexed Austria. Then late in September, 1938, Hitler's threats to take the Sudetenland intimidated Chamberlain and Daladier into appeasing him at the expense of Czechoslovakia.

Distressed by the Munich crisis, the President determined to make good use of the time that remained. Early in October, he announced an accelerated program of defense spending and projected plans for great increases in aircraft production. On Christmas Eve, his diplomacy bore fruit in the Declaration of Lima, which set up crisis machinery for assembling the foreign ministers of the American republics to take action in the common defense. Roosevelt was hopeful for a freer hand in countering the aggressors, but he recognized the difficulty of persuading Congress to revise the neutrality laws. Not that there was any significant pro-German or pro-Japanese sentiment in the United States. The absurd posturing of Hitler, the pogroms in Germany, the brutality of Japanese soldiers in China had forestalled that. But the overwhelming majority of Americans were resolved to take no action that might drag them into war.

The President's message to Congress on January 4, 1939, reflected the growing tension. With southern Democrats, whose support he needed for his foreign policy, no longer willing to follow his lead in domestic matters, Roosevelt rang down the curtain on the New Deal. He called for no new reform legislation and requested deficit spending only until recovery was complete. It was the international situation that now dictated the turn of events. In his address to Congress and in his budget message of the next day, Roosevelt recommended an augmented defense appropriation of almost $2 billion.

IMPACT OF FISSION

On a wintry afternoon twelve days after the President spoke to Congress, the liner *Drottningholm* was eased into its berth at New York. Aboard was the distinguished Danish theoretical physicist, Niels Bohr. Enrico and Laura Fermi were among those who met him at the pier. Their friend seemed to have aged perceptibly in the month since they had stopped off to see him at Copenhagen on their way to the United States from Stockholm, where the Italian physicist had accepted a Nobel Prize. There was good reason for Bohr's appearance. He was disturbed by the threat of war in Europe and by his knowledge of a recent scientific discovery of revolutionary implications. Late in 1938, Otto Hahn and Fritz Strassmann, working at the Kaiser Wilhelm Institute for Chemistry in Berlin, had discovered a radioactive barium isotope among the products resulting from their bombardment of uranium with neutrons. Hahn recognized the significance of this at once, but instead of proclaiming it himself, he chivalrously communicated his findings to Lise Meitner, an Austrian colleague who recently had been forced to flee Germany by the threat of Nazi racial laws. Fräulein Meitner and her nephew, Otto R. Frisch, concluded that the presence of barium meant that a new type of nuclear reaction had taken place—fission. They went to Copenhagen at once, where they advanced to Bohr the theory that the uranium nucleus had split into two lighter elements in the middle range of the periodic table. Part of the enormous energy required to hold the component neutrons and protons together in the heavy uranium nucleus had been released. Meitner and Frisch outlined an experiment to verify their hypothesis. Some days after Bohr arrived in the United States, he received a telegram from Frisch announcing that laboratory results had confirmed the theory.[1]

The word spread quickly. Bohr went at once to Princeton, where he was to spend a few months at the Institute for Advanced Study. Physicists there were greatly impressed by the possible implications of the discovery. Isidor I. Rabi, in Princeton on sabbatical leave, rushed back to Columbia University the next morning to talk with Fermi. On January 26, Bohr and Fermi opened the Fifth Washington Conference on Theoretical Physics with a discussion of the exciting developments abroad. Press reports now flashed to centers of physics research throughout the nation. Soon American scientists had the full story, for the *Physical Review* of February 15 carried an authoritative account by Bohr.[2]

11

The discovery of fission was stimulating enough from a purely scientific standpoint, but the finding had such a galvanic impact because it pointed to the possibility of a chain, or self-sustaining, reaction. Physicists thought it highly probable that fission released secondary neutrons. Should these be effective in splitting other uranium nuclei, which in turn would liberate neutrons, it might be possible to generate a large amount of energy. If the process could be controlled, a new source of heat and power would be available. If it were allowed to progress unchecked, an explosive of tremendous force might be possible.

By 1939, American physicists were in a strong position to exploit the breakthrough. True, physics had been slow to develop on their side of the Atlantic. At the turn of the century, American physics had been graced by a few great names—Henry, Gibbs, Michelson, and Rowland—but these few could scarcely compare with European giants such as Maxwell, Kelvin, Joule, Rankine, Helmholtz, and Planck. College instruction had then been poor despite the efforts of a few universities to improve. Even textbooks were translations of European works. Not until 1893 was the *Physical Review* founded. Not until 1899 was the American Physical Society established. The discipline progressed rapidly, however, in the years prior to the first World War, and by the nineteen-twenties universities such as California, Chicago, Columbia, Cornell, Harvard, Johns Hopkins, and Princeton were offering good training to increased numbers of students. To obtain the best advanced instruction, it was still necessary to go abroad, particularly to Germany. Fortunately, many young scholars received Rockefeller-financed, National Research Council fellowships for this purpose. At European universities American students felt that they had a better, broader education than perhaps 95 per cent of their European classmates. Yet from their experience on the Continent they gained an inspiration, a feel for their subject, that was more important than any considerations of factual knowledge or technique.

In the nineteen-thirties, physical studies flourished in the United States. The quality of graduate work was high. Probably the depression helped encourage advanced study and postdoctoral research. There was little else to do. Certainly the National Research Council fellowships enabled scores of young physicists to establish the habit of research. Europe may still have had more giants, but it could not compare in the number of lesser known physicists. As the decade wore on, American scientific ranks gained further as some of the most talented Europeans came to the United States, seeking refuge from persecution in their homelands.

Theoretical studies experienced a healthy development, but the great strength of the United States was in experimental physics. This interest led naturally to large-scale equipment. Americans played a leading role in the development of the mass spectrograph, essential in studying the isotopic forms of the elements. In 1930, Ernest O. Lawrence, an imaginative young experimenter at the Berkeley campus of the University of California, constructed his first cyclotron. This contrivance, which whirled charged particles to tremendous speeds under the influence of a steady magnetic field and a rapidly oscillating electrical field, soon became a research tool of vital importance. In 1931, Robert J. Van de Graaff, a National Research Fellow at Princeton, developed his electrostatic generator, another device for producing a powerful beam of subatomic particles. By 1939, the United States was pre-eminent in work requiring elaborate and expensive equipment.

Eagerly, American physicists followed Chadwick's work, which reached fruition in 1932 with his discovery of the neutron. They noted Cockcroft's and Walton's experimental demonstration of Einstein's proposition that mass and energy were equivalent. They read avidly of Fermi's uranium bombardments and the efforts of Joliot-Curie and Savitch to interpret them. But Americans did more than observe. The *Physical Review*, rapidly evolving from a provincial journal into one of the world's great scientific periodicals, bulged with reports of their own experimental and theoretical investigations. Fascinated by the possibilities inherent in neutron reactions, Americans believed that the world was on the threshold of nuclear power and that everything waited on some self-perpetuating mechanism. At the very time of the Hahn-Strassmann breakthrough, Philip H. Abelson, a Ph.D. candidate at Berkeley, was pursuing a line of investigation that in a few weeks would have led him almost certainly to the discovery of nuclear fission.[3]

The first experimental task facing scientists in the early days of 1939 was to confirm the Hahn-Strassmann-Meitner results. This came rapidly in the United States, as elsewhere. The issue of the *Physical Review* that carried

Bohr's letter contained reports of corroborating experiments at the University of California, Johns Hopkins, and the Carnegie Institution of Washington. The next issue related experiments undertaken at Columbia just after Bohr's arrival in which Fermi and John R. Dunning, joined by a number of younger collaborators, further demonstrated the validity of the results obtained abroad.[4]

This was only the beginning. Scientists throughout the world launched a comprehensive effort to throw light on the phenomena of fission. They published nearly one hundred articles on the subject before the end of 1939. All the great centers of American physical research took up the challenge. In the realm of theory, the prime achievement was a study carried out at Princeton by Bohr and John A. Wheeler. Their work, published in September as "The Mechanism of Nuclear Fission," was rich in insights destined to aid many another scientist in the years ahead.[5] In the experimental field, nothing was more immediately significant than the work being done at Columbia on the possibility of a chain reaction. It was an investigation for which Morningside Heights was well fitted. Here at the Michael Pupin Laboratory was Dunning with the cyclotron and other equipment he had acquired for neutron-reaction studies. Here were Herbert L. Anderson, a gifted graduate student, and Walter H. Zinn, a physicist at City College who did his research in the Columbia laboratories. Here were Fermi, who had no intention of returning to his native land, and Leo Szilard, a Hungarian scientist who had come without benefit of a faculty appointment to work with Fermi. Fortunately, this team was under a sympathetic if somewhat conservative administrator, George B. Pegram. A physicist himself, Pegram was now dean of the graduate faculties.

The men at Columbia had seen from the first that the key to the self-sustaining reaction was the release of neutrons on fission of the uranium atom. Like physicists generally, they had guessed that neutrons were emitted. Their experiments, along with others conducted both in the United States and abroad, soon indicated that this indeed was true. Once the neutron question was settled, another rose to demand attention. Was a chain reaction possible in natural uranium? At Columbia and elsewhere physicists disagreed over which isotope fissioned with slow neutrons, neutrons which traveled at the energies known most likely to produce fission. Was it the rare 235, considerably less than 1 per cent of the natural element, or the abundant 238? Dunning thought 235 was responsible, while Fermi inclined toward 238. Dunning was impressed by the small fission cross section—the physicists' term for probability—of natural uranium. He thought it indicated only a small chance for a chain reaction. But if uranium 235 was the isotope subject to slow-neutron fission, and if it could be concentrated, he considered the chain reaction a certainty. Fermi accepted his colleague's reasoning, but even if U-235 should prove the key, he was content to try for a chain reaction in natural, unconcentrated uranium because of the extreme difficulty and expense of separating the isotopes. To settle this debate, Fermi and Dunning agreed on a co-ordinated investigation. The Italian would try for a chain reaction in natural uranium, while the American would acquire small samples of concentrated U-235 and see if his views on its susceptibility to fission were correct.[6]

Fermi's first effort to ascertain whether the conditions of a chain reaction existed in normal uranium was to measure the number of neutrons produced per fission. By the middle of March, preliminary experiments indicated that the average was two.[7] The next objective was to discover how extensive was nonfission absorption. Fermi, Szilard, and Anderson knew that neutrons might be captured without fission and produce a radioactive isotope of uranium, U-239. If this happened on an excessive scale, too few neutrons would live to propagate a chain reaction. The experimenters placed a neutron source in the center of a large water tank and made comparisons, with and without uranium in the water, of the number of slow neutrons present. These measurements led them to conclude that a chain reaction could be maintained in a system in which two requisites were met. First, neutrons had to be slowed to low, or thermal, energies without much absorption. Second, they had to be absorbed mostly by uranium rather than by another element. Fermi and Szilard had doubts, however, about the proper agent for slowing down, or moderating, the neutrons. It would have to be some material of low atomic weight. Neutrons, common sense indicated, would lose speed more quickly by collision with light rather than with heavy atoms. Water, which Fermi had used because it was two-thirds hydrogen, had exhibited a tendency to absorb neutrons. On July 3, 1939, the same day the editor of the *Physical Review* received the Columbia results, Szilard wrote Fermi to suggest that carbon might be a good substitute. Szilard saw heavy hydrogen in the form of heavy water as another possibility, for it had less tendency to absorb neutrons than ordinary hydrogen, but he did not know if it could be obtained in sufficient quantity. A few days later, he was so convinced of the advantageous physical properties of carbon that he thought the Columbia group should proceed at once with a large-scale trial employing a graphite moderator without even awaiting the outcome of experiments to determine its neutron-absorption characteristics.[8]

FIRST APPEALS FOR FEDERAL SUPPORT

Publication of the results of the absorption experiments in the summer of 1939 marked a temporary halt to intensive work on the chain reaction at Pupin Laboratory. Fermi departed for the University of Michigan to study cosmic rays. Anderson, his assistant, devoted his time to finishing his Ph.D. investigations, while Szilard, though full of suggestions for accelerating the experimental work, concentrated on finding a way to alert the federal government to the significance of fission.

Actually, a branch of the government had already been approached. On March 16, Dean Pegram wrote Admiral Stanford C. Hooper, technical assistant to the Chief of Naval Operations, to say that Fermi, who was traveling to Washington on another matter, would be glad to tell Hooper of the experiments at Columbia. It was possible, Pegram wrote, that uranium might be used as an explosive that would "liberate a million times as much energy per pound as any known explosive." Pegram thought the probabilities were against this but that even the barest possibility should not be ignored. At the Navy Department the next day, Fermi talked for an hour to a group that included a number of naval officers, two civilian scientists from the Naval Research Laboratory, and several officers from the Army's Bureau of Ordnance. Fermi explained the Columbia efforts to discover whether or not a chain reaction could take place. He was not sure that the experiments would yield an affirmative answer, but if they did, it might be possible to employ uranium as an explosive. After some questioning, a Navy spokesman told Fermi that the Department was anxious to maintain contact with the Columbia experiments and undoubtedly would have representatives call in person.[9]

15

The most responsive of the listeners that afternoon were the scientists of the Naval Research Laboratory. They had a long-standing interest in a source of power that would permit protracted undersea operations by freeing submarines from dependence on tremendous supplies of oxygen. As soon as the news of fission broke in January, they had contacted the men at the Carnegie Institution who were checking the work of Meitner and Frisch. Just three days after the conference with Fermi, Admiral Harold G. Bowen, director of the NRL, recommended that the Bureau of Engineering help finance investigation of the power potential of uranium. The Bureau allotted $1,500 to the Carnegie Institution, which agreed to co-operate but for reasons of internal policy did not accept the grant. The NRL also approached Jesse W. Beams, a centrifuge expert at the University of Virginia, on isotope separation.[10]

The initiative for a new overture to the federal government in the summer of 1939 came in large part from Szilard, an impetuous, imaginative physicist who was at his best in goading others to action. The news of fission alarmed him, for he feared that it might lead to powerful explosives which would be dangerous in general and particularly so in the hands of Nazi Germany. Like many others, he hoped a bomb would prove impossible. But until this could be established, there seemed only one safe course: to pursue the work vigorously.[11] Szilard had been zealous on behalf of the Columbia experiments and had even borrowed money to rent radium for use in a neutron source.

Szilard was eager for some sort of federal action. At a June meeting of the American Physical Society in Princeton, he had consulted Ross Gunn, who, as the technical adviser of the Naval Research Laboratory, was at the center of the Navy's interest in the potential of uranium. On July 10, Gunn informed him that though the NRL was anxious to co-operate, restrictions on government contracts for services made it impossible to carry through any agreement that would be helpful.[12]

Frustrated, Szilard talked over the situation with physicist Eugene P. Wigner, also a native of Hungary. Szilard by now was convinced that the uranium-graphite experiment might quickly prove successful if only it could be carried out. More than ever, he thought it imperative to get on with the work. Besides, it was high time to take steps to keep the uranium ore of the Belgian Congo out of German hands. It occurred to the two physicists that Albert Einstein was the logical person to alert the Belgians, for he knew the royal family. They saw Einstein, who agreed to dictate a letter of warning, though to someone below that rank. Since this maneuver raised the propriety of communicating with a foreign government, Wigner suggested that they send the Department of State a copy with a note that Einstein would dispatch the letter in two weeks unless he received advice to the contrary. This, however, would do nothing to expedite research in the United States. Szilard believed that they should make some direct advance to the government in Washington. At the suggestion of Gustav Stolper, a Viennese economist and a friend of long standing, he went to see Alexander Sachs, a Lehman Corporation economist reputed to have ready access to the White House.

Quiet and unpretentious in appearance but curiously florid and involute in speech, Sachs prided himself on his skill in analyzing current developments and predicting the course of events. He specialized in "prehistory," he liked to say. Since 1936, when he had heard Lord Rutherford lecture, the work of the atomic physicists had intrigued him. Then early in February, 1939, while Sachs was visiting in Princeton, Frank Aydelotte, director of the Institute for Advanced Study, showed him a copy of a letter that Bohr had addressed to the editor of *Nature*. Sachs's excitement increased as the months went by and further experiments were reported. By the time Szilard called on him in July, he remembered some years later, he had already pointed out to the President the crucial character of the new developments. From Roosevelt, Sachs understood that the Navy had decided not to push uranium research, largely because of the negative attitude of Fermi and Pegram.

To approach the President successfully, Sachs believed it was necessary to counter the impression created by the Columbia physicists. This would require the testimony of a scientist more eminent than Szilard. The obvious solution was to enlist the name of Einstein. A letter should be prepared for his signature. Sachs could insure that such a communication, along with supporting scientific papers, received Roosevelt's attention.

The letter that emerged from conferences between Sachs and Szilard reported that recent work by Fermi and Szilard in America and by Joliot-Curie in France made a uranium chain reaction almost a certainty in the immediate

16

future. This would mean the generation of vast amounts of power and the creation of new radium-like elements. It was conceivable, though still not definite, that extremely powerful bombs could be constructed. These might prove too heavy to be dropped from an airplane, but they could be carried by boat and exploded in a port. The supplies of uranium ore in the United States were not extensive. Although there was some good ore in Canada and in Czechoslovakia, the Belgian Congo was the most important source. Something ought to be done to maintain contact between the Administration and the physicists working on the atom. Perhaps the President could assign someone, possibly in an unofficial capacity, to keep the appropriate government departments informed and make recommendations for action, particularly on raw materials. This agent might also seek to speed research by soliciting contributions from private individuals and by obtaining the co-operation of industrial laboratories. Closing the letter was a warning of German interest. The Reich had stopped the sale of uranium from Czechoslovakian mines.

17

At Sachs's request, Szilard drafted an accompanying memorandum. Seeking to explain more clearly the underlying science, the physicist stressed that a chain reaction based on fission by slow neutrons seemed almost certain even though it had not yet been proved in a large-scale experiment. Whether a chain reaction could be maintained with fast neutrons was not so certain. If it could be, it might be possible to contrive extremely dangerous bombs.

It was not hard to persuade Einstein to sign the letter, but before Sachs could take the completed dossier to Roosevelt, war broke out in Europe. Sachs delayed, for he wanted to present the case to the President in person, so that the information "would come in by way of the ear and not as a sort of mascara on the eye." He knew that Roosevelt, preoccupied with the international crisis and his fight to win repeal of the arms-embargo from a reluctant Congress, was unlikely to give the uranium recommendations adequate attention. But early in October, 1939, the time seemed more propitious, and Sachs arranged an appointment for the eleventh. At the White House, the President's secretary, General Edwin M. Watson, had called in two ordnance specialists from the Army and Navy, Colonel Keith F. Adamson and Commander Gilbert C. Hoover. After Sachs had explained his mission to them, he was taken in to see the Chief Executive. Sachs read aloud his covering letter, which emphasized the same ideas as the Einstein communication but was more pointed on the need for funds. As the interview drew to a close, Roosevelt remarked, "Alex, what you are after is to see that the Nazis don't blow us up." Then he called in "Pa" Watson and announced, "This requires action." [13]

This appeal for federal encouragement, if not support, of research touched a theme that went back to the Constitutional Convention of 1787. The powers expressly granted the general government seemed to imply a place for science, but just what this might mean awaited the resolution of constitutional issues that involved science only tangentially. As it worked out, Americans were slow to accept the idea that the federal government should have a permanent scientific establishment. Not until after the Civil War did a well-diversified corps of scientific bureaus evolve. By 1916, the process was largely complete. Since the several units had appeared at different times under widely varying auspices in response to the demands of society, there was no central organization. The emphasis was on applied rather than basic research.

This setup seemed reasonably well adapted to the day-to-day requirements of the government. All efforts had failed, however, to work out a satisfactory arrangement by which American science as a whole could serve in an advisory capacity in times of national emergency. The first attempt to achieve such an arrangement was the creation of the National Academy of Sciences. A group of scientists led by Alexander Dallas Bache made the Civil War the occasion for promoting their long-cherished plan to establish a self-perpetuating national academy which should serve the dual purpose of honoring scholarly attainment and of advising the government. Taking advantage of the end-of-session rush in March, 1863, they spirited the necessary legislation through Congress. Unfortunately, the wartime accomplishments of the National Academy were slight. Only through the efforts of Joseph Henry, the secretary of the Smithsonian, did the National Academy survive the crisis which saw its birth.

The first World War brought forth another effort to forge a working relationship between government and science. The National Research Council was organized in 1916 under the auspices of the National Academy to broaden the base of scientific and technical counsel. Not limited to members of the National Academy, the NRC sought the help of scientists generally, whether they were at work in government, the universities, private foundations, or in industry. Though it met the test of war by establishing cooperative research on a large scale and by serving as a scientific clearing-house, it left much to be desired. Never financed independently, the only effective way it could obtain funds from the military was to have its scientists commissioned. It was further handicapped by losing to the services the initiative of suggesting projects. After the Armistice, the NRC evolved into an agency for stimulating research by dispensing Rockefeller and Carnegie money. Though this was useful enough, the council lost the capacity to serve as an active scientific adviser. In many ways, a more significant development of the war years was the establishment of the National Advisory Committee for Aeronautics, an independent board of both government and private members with functions less advisory than executive.

It was not surprising that a new effort at establishing efficient liaison between government and science emerged in the summer of 1933. Isaiah Bowman, chairman of the National Research Council, used Henry Wallace's request for advice on the reorganization of the Weather Bureau as an opportunity to advocate a general review of government science. The result was a Presidential order creating a Science Advisory Board with authority under the National Academy and the NRC to appoint committees on problems in the various departments. This order named Karl T. Compton chairman. Compton, president of the Massachusetts Institute of Technology, promptly put subcommittees to work studying the government bureaus, but he had larger plans, plans which amounted to a New Deal for science. It was his idea that a large sum—in the final version $75 million in five years—should be spent to support scientific and engineering research. Programs would be formulated by the National Academy, the National Research Council, and a new advisory panel. Compton's dreams failed to win approval, apparently because of their scale and because of a reluctance to adopt a program that would support the natural sciences to the exclusion of other fields of learning. The Science Advisory Board itself did not survive for long. Thus was lost an opportunity not only to support science in the monetary sense but also to establish a rational basis for co-operation between the government and the great centers of investigation. There was still a hope that the National Resources Committee, which had its origin in the faith of social scientists in planning as the basis for sound governmental operation, might accomplish something. But although its science committee made a brilliant study of the federal research agencies and took the broad view that research was a basic national resource, it never gained the administrative position or the support from scientists that were essential for it to become an adequate instrument for mobilizing the nation's scientific strength.[14]

This, then, was the situation when Sachs talked with the President. Roosevelt's thinking must have been conditioned by the rather uneasy relations that had existed between the Administration and the scientific community. There was little basis for sentiments of mutual confidence. No adequate machinery was at hand. One alternative was to refer the matter to the National Academy of Sciences, but this was an unwieldy expedient, and there was little reason to believe it would be fruitful. Besides, every instinct would lead the President to conclude that security as well as policy dictated caution. Why not restrict consideration, for the present at least, to official circles? Whatever the reasoning, action came quickly. Roosevelt appointed an Advisory Committee on Uranium to investigate the problem in co-operation with Sachs. Its chairman was Lyman J. Briggs, a government scientist who had begun his career in 1896 as a soil physicist in the Department of Agriculture and was now director of the National Bureau of Standards. Other members were Commander Hoover and Colonel Adamson. This was a rational solution. Sachs later claimed he had suggested placing the Bureau of Standards in charge as a means of achieving a fresh view, a view uncomplicated by military prejudices. This may have been the case, but there

19

was a more obvious explanation for appointing Briggs. This, after all, was a problem in physics. Why not have it investigated by the Government's physics laboratory?

Briggs called a meeting at the Bureau of Standards for October 21, 1939. Joining the committee members and Sachs were two Washington physicists—Fred L. Mohler of the Bureau of Standards and Richard B. Roberts of the Carnegie Institution—and three physicists of Hungarian origin—Szilard, Wigner, and Edward Teller. The latter three were invited at Sachs's initiative. Sachs also had arranged for Einstein to be invited but the shy genius did not accept. Szilard focused the discussion by pointing out that it seemed quite possible to attain a chain reaction in a system composed of uranium oxide or metal and carbon in the form of graphite. The principal uncertainty was the lack of information on the absorption of slow neutrons by the graphite moderator. Szilard and Fermi had devised experiments for measuring this. If the absorption cross section should be either small or large, they would know at once whether the chain reaction would or would not work. If they obtained an intermediate value, they would have to conduct a large-scale experiment. Some of those present were openly skeptical about the chance for a chain reaction, but the three Hungarians were optimistic. In a sequence that bordered on comedy, the meeting drifted into a discussion of government financing, which was not the immediate objective. As Szilard recalled it, Teller referred quite incidentally to the amount of money that researchers could spend profitably in the months ahead. Colonel Adamson made this the occasion for a discourse on the nature of war. It usually took two wars, he said, to develop a new weapon, and it was morale, not new arms, that brought victory. These sentiments moved Wigner, who had been fidgeting in his chair, to venture the opinion that if armaments were so comparatively unimportant, perhaps the Army's budget ought to be cut by 30 per cent. "All right, you'll get your money," Adamson snapped.[15]

The Advisory Committee on Uranium reported to the President on November 1 that the chain reaction was a possibility, but that it was still unproved. If it could be achieved and controlled, it might supply power for submarines. If the reaction should be explosive, "it would provide a possible source of bombs with a destructiveness vastly greater than anything now known." The committee believed that despite the uncertainties, the Government should support a thorough investigation. It urged the purchase of four tons of pure graphite at once and the acquisition of fifty tons of uranium oxide in the event that the preliminary investigations justified continuing the program. To provide for the support and co-ordination of these investigations in different universities, Briggs and his colleagues advocated enlarging their committee to include Karl Compton, Einstein, Pegram, and Sachs.

On November 17, Watson wrote Briggs that the President had noted the report with deepest interest and wished to keep it on file for reference.

The President also wanted to be sure that the Army and Navy had copies. There was no further word from the White House until February 8, 1940, when Watson told Briggs he intended to bring the report to the President's attention again. Was there anything Briggs could add as a personal recommendation? Briggs replied on February 20 that the Army and Navy had transferred funds "to purchase materials for carrying out a crucial experiment on a satisfactory scale." He hoped for a report in a few weeks. It would show "whether or not the undertaking has a practical application." These brief sentences referred to $6,000 that the military services had granted for the purchase of supplies for experiments with the absorption qualities of graphite. By the time Briggs answered Watson, both the President and his aide had departed on a trip that would keep them away from Washington until about the first of March.[16]

The little group that had sought to interest the President the preceding autumn was dissatisfied. Early in February, Sachs obtained a copy of the November 1 report from General Watson. Now he could see what was wrong, he wrote Watson: the paper had been too academic in tone to make its practical point. Sachs asserted that Einstein thought the situation looked even better than earlier. Sometime during the coming month, the economist announced, he would submit a new appraisal.[17]

21

Meanwhile, Joliot-Curie reported his measurements of a uranium-and-water system. The Frenchman's encouraging results stimulated Szilard to greater confidence in his own uranium-graphite approach. Rumors that the Nazis had secretly intensified their uranium research made action seem especially urgent. Again Szilard saw Einstein. Resorting to pressure tactics in the hope of forcing Government action, he showed Einstein a manuscript on a graphite system that he was sending to the *Physical Review* for publication. Einstein reported the new developments to Sachs. On March 15, Sachs relayed the communication to the White House. In view of the brighter experimental outlook, he asked, would the President be able to confer on the practical issues it raised? [18]

The first response was disappointing. Watson replied on March 27 that he had delayed until he could speak with Colonel Adamson and Commander Hoover. They had come in that afternoon, and Adamson had said that everything depended on the Columbia graphite experiments. Under these circumstances, Watson thought "the matter should rest in abeyance until we get the official report." Within a week, however, there was encouraging news from the White House. On April 5, the President thanked Sachs for forwarding the Einstein letter. He had asked General Watson, he said, to arrange another meeting in Washington at a time convenient for Sachs and Einstein. Roosevelt thought Briggs should attend as well as special representatives from the Army and Navy. This was the most practical method of continuing the research. ". . . I shall always be interested to hear the results," he said.

The same day, Watson sent Briggs a copy of the letter to Sachs and asked for suggestions "so that this investigation shall go on, as is the wish of the President." [19]

March, 1940, had brought a new interest in uranium. The development that touched it off was the conclusive demonstration that uranium 235 was the isotope that fissioned with slow neutrons. While Fermi had been investigating the chain reaction in natural uranium, Dunning had organized his attempt to determine the fissionable isotope. He had persuaded Alfred O. C. Nier of the University of Minnesota, the country's foremost expert on the mass spectrometer, to prepare small samples of partially separated U-235. Dunning and his co-workers at Columbia, Eugene T. Booth and Aristid V. Grosse, made the necessary measurements. In the March 15 and April 15 issues of the *Physical Review*, they presented definite confirmation of what so many had suspected was the role of the lighter isotope.

This was an event of profound significance. If uranium 235 could be concentrated, there seemed no question that a slow-neutron chain reaction was possible. This meant power. A bomb, however, remained highly doubtful. Some physicists already saw that a bomb depended on fission by fast neutrons. If they had to rely on slow neutrons, the metal would tend to blow itself apart before the reaction had gone far enough. It was questionable if the resulting explosion would have sufficient magnitude to justify its cost. The Dunning-Nier experiments indicated that uranium 238 would undergo fission under fast-neutron bombardment, but it did not seem likely that the heavier isotope would sustain a chain reaction. The cross section or probability of fission was too small. What about U-235? Might not it be susceptible to fission by fast as well as slow neutrons? Some physicists thought it was probable. If this were the case, there was a good chance of an explosive reaction in a highly concentrated mass of the lighter isotope. Still, it was only theory. All that was known definitely was that fast neutrons had a lower probability of causing fission in U-235 than slow ones. In the absence of samples substantially enriched in 235, physicists could not determine its fast-fission cross section experimentally. [20]

Whatever might be the possibility of an explosive, the first task was to prove the chain reaction. On March 11, Pegram sent Briggs advance word on the role of U-235. On April 9, Briggs reported to Watson that it was "very doubtful whether a chain reaction can be established without separating 235 from the rest of the uranium." He recommended an intensive study of methods of isotope separation. By this time, interest in uranium 235 had spread widely. It found a focus at the meeting of the American Physical Society in Washington the last week in April. There Gunn, Beams, Nier, Fermi, Harold C. Urey of Columbia, and Merle A. Tuve of the Carnegie Institution discussed its significance for the chain reaction. The next step, they agreed, was to separate U-235 in kilogram quantities. Of the various possible methods, the centrifuge alone seemed to offer much hope. They decided to try to acquire the funds necessary to determine its potential.[21]

On Saturday afternoon, April 27, the Advisory Committee on Uranium met at the National Bureau of Standards. Joining Briggs, Adamson, and Hoover were Admiral Bowen, Sachs, and four university physicists— Pegram, Fermi, Szilard, and Wigner. Einstein again had declined to attend. Of the scientists, Szilard was the most optimistic concerning the chain reaction, though he could say nothing very explicit about the prospect for an explosive. Sachs urged prosecuting the work more vigorously. If the Government was not disposed to undertake it, he favored trying to finance it from private sources. Sachs was impatient with Fermi's conservative position. If the United States would plunge ahead, he thought, the difficulties experienced in the laboratory would tend to disappear. The Advisory Committee agreed on the need for investigation, but it was ready to proceed on only a small scale and a step or two at a time. As Briggs reported to Watson on May 9, the committee did not care to recommend a large-scale try for a chain reaction until it knew the results of the graphite measurements at Columbia. These were expected in a week or two. If the large-scale experiment was undertaken, the Army and Navy should supervise it at one of the proving grounds. As for methods of separating isotopes, the committee favored supporting the investigations of scientists in various universities but did not favor attempting such studies on a secret basis.[22]

Briggs made some progress in May. He spent the first day of the month at Columbia. On the sixth, Pegram reported the consensus of a conference with his colleagues Fermi, Urey, and Dunning. If support could be obtained from the Navy or elsewhere, they favored tests on a laboratory scale to determine which method appeared best for concentrating substantial amounts of U-235. They proposed to enlist the principal isotope-separation specialists and launch the work in June, when the academicians among them could escape their teaching duties. On May 8, Pegram explained to Briggs what was involved in proving the chain reaction in a uranium-graphite system. On May 14, Pegram announced that Fermi and Szilard had found the absorption cross section of graphite encouragingly small.[23]

As the outlines of a sensible program emerged, pressure for action intensified. Sachs had no intention of leaving everything to Briggs. He argued the cause in May letters to Roosevelt and Watson. Now that Fermi and Szilard had determined the characteristics of graphite, it was time to move. The Nazis were overrunning Belgium; something should be done to safeguard the uranium ore of the Congo. The research program should have larger financial support as well as a better and more flexible organization. Perhaps a nonprofit corporation with official status under the President could make the arrangements necessary to further the work.[24]

More important were the repercussions of the talks at the American

23

Physical Society meeting. Gunn at once recommended to Admiral Bowen that the Naval Research Laboratory foster a co-operative research effort. Apprised a few days later of the Columbia proposals on isotope separation, Bowen asked Urey to organize an advisory committee of scientific experts to counsel the President's Committee on Uranium. Urey conferred with Briggs and soon had a list of physicists and chemists he thought would be helpful.

The stirrings at the Naval Research Laboratory were echoed a few miles to the north at a private center for scientific research, the Carnegie Institution. Tuve prepared notes for the information of his chief, Vannevar Bush. Though Tuve thought submarine propulsion appeared more practical at the moment than a bomb, he judged that the interests of national defense justified trying to develop the centrifugal system of separation. His recommendations led Bush to call a conference for May 21. The discussion convinced him that the centrifuge deserved support. Bush telephoned Briggs that he would wait to see what funds the Government furnished. If there should be a gap, the Carnegie Institution might step in.[25]

Briggs was pleased at Bush's assurances that his only purpose in calling the conference was to determine how the Carnegie Institution might be helpful. This kept the way clear for the scientific subcommittee. Briggs and Urey soon settled on a membership consisting of Urey himself, Pegram, Tuve, Beams, Gunn, and Gregory Breit, a professor of physics at the University of Wisconsin. This group reviewed the whole subject at the Bureau of Standards on June 13 and advocated support for investigations of both isotope separation and the chain reaction.[26]

ENTER THE NDRC

A new force now appeared on the scene—the National Defense Research Committee. An effort to organize American science for war, it owed its existence to Vannevar Bush. A shrewd, spry Yankee of fifty—plainspoken, but with a disarming twinkle in his eye and a boyish grin—Bush was well known for his original work in applied mathematics and electrical engineering. During the first World War he had worked for the Navy on submarine-detection devices. Though he then turned to teaching, his talent for invention did not atrophy. From his fertile brain came many ingenious innovations, including an essential circuit for the automatic dial telephone. In 1939, he resigned the vice-presidency of the Massachusetts Institute of Technology to become president of the Carnegie Institution, a post that put him close to the nerve center of the embryonic defense effort. Soon he moved up from member to chairman of the National Advisory Committee for Aeronautics, and when war broke out in Europe, he cast about for some way of organizing American science for the test that lay ahead. After discussions with Karl Compton, with President James B. Conant of Harvard, with President

Frank B. Jewett of the National Academy of Sciences, and with his colleagues at the NACA, he evolved a plan for a committee that would have the same relation to the development of the devices of warfare that the NACA had to the problems of flight.

Early in June, 1940, when Nazi Panzer divisions were thrusting deep into France, Bush persuaded President Roosevelt to place him at the head of a National Defense Research Committee. Under the authority of the old World War I Council of National Defense, from which it was to draw its funds, the NDRC was to supplement the work of the service laboratories by extending the research base and enlisting the aid of scientists. Even more important, it was to search for new opportunities to apply science to the needs of war. It could call on the National Academy and the National Research Council for advice and on the National Bureau of Standards and other government laboratories for more tangible assistance. The NACA, already functioning well under Bush's leadership, lay outside the jurisdiction of the new agency. Not so the Committee on Uranium. It was to report directly to Bush, and the NDRC was free to support its work.[27] The NDRC did not owe its birth to uranium, but the pressure applied by those who had caught the vision of a chain reaction made Bush's organizational plan seem all the more attractive.

25

The new committee was an important factor in mobilizing the scientific resources of the nation. The NDRC did not have to wait for a request from the Army or Navy but could judge what was needed for itself. It was not limited to advising the services but could undertake research on its own. For the uranium program, its creation was an event of great significance. It freed uranium from exclusive dependence on the military for funds. More important, it rescued this novel field of research from the jurisdiction of an informal, *ad hoc* committee. By providing a place within the organizational framework of the defense effort of American science, the NDRC made it easier for nuclear scientists to advance their claims.

By the early autumn of 1940, Bush had reorganized the Committee on Uranium and adjusted it to its new place in the scheme of things. Guided by instructions from the President, he retained Briggs as chairman but dropped Commander Hoover and Colonel Adamson because the NDRC was now the proper channel for liaison with the military. To strengthen the scientific resources of the group, he added Tuve, Pegram, Beams, Gunn, and Urey. The new regime stressed security. One manifestation was the exclusion of any foreign-born scientists from committee membership, a policy adopted in deference to Army and Navy views and with at least one eye on future encounters with Congress. The other manifestation—arrangements for blocking the publication of reports on uranium research—originated with the scientists themselves. Szilard had sought in vain to accomplish this on an international scale back in February, 1939. In the spring of 1940, Breit sparked the establishment within the framework of the National Research Council of a reference committee to control publication of any research that had military significance. Uranium fell within its scope; indeed, the desire to control publication on fission phenomena prompted the ban.[28]

FORMULATING A PROGRAM

Though the NDRC would control the funds, it remained the duty of the Briggs committee to formulate a program. One of its concerns was uranium ore. There were no significant stockpiles in the United States, for the only commercial use of uranium was as a coloring agent in the ceramic industry. Of the 168 tons of oxides and salts American users consumed in 1938, only 26 came from domestic carnotite ores mined in the Colorado Plateau. The remainder was imported: 106 tons from the Belgian Congo and 36 from Canada. Early in June, 1940, Sachs urged Briggs to have someone make an overture to the Union Minière du Haut Katanga, the company that owned the Congo mines. He thought Union Minière might be persuaded to ship ore to the United States and, while retaining title, commit itself not to re-export without special permission. Briggs promptly authorized Sachs to make the necessary inquiries. The company showed no immediate interest in such a scheme, though later in 1940 its affiliate, African Metals Corporation, imported 1,200 tons of 65-per-cent ore and stored it in a Staten Island warehouse.[29]

Research, not raw materials, seemed the proper emphasis in June, 1940. Ore would become important when and if production was warranted, but with funds limited and with so little known about the defense potential of uranium, the Briggs committee did not deem it prudent to acquire large stocks of raw materials. There would be time enough when research had indicated the extent of the requirements.

The Committee on Uranium addressed itself to research on June 28. It accepted the findings of its scientific counselors that ample justification existed for supporting work on isotope-separation methods and for further efforts to determine the feasibility of a chain reaction in normal uranium. On July 1, Briggs gave Bush a report on his stewardship. He announced with gratification that the War and Navy Departments had approved a thorough study of separation. An allotment of $100,000 had already been made, which the Naval Research Laboratory would administer with the advice and assistance of the Committee on Uranium. That still left the chain reaction to be provided for. Briggs urged that the NDRC set aside $140,000 for two types of investigation: first, studies to determine more accurately the fundamental physical constants and, second, an intermediate experiment involving about one-fifth the amount of material judged necessary to establish the chain reaction.[30]

The NDRC approved the uranium recommendations in principle on

July 2 and asked Briggs to place them in definite form for consideration when funds became available. Briggs arranged for full presentations by Pegram and Fermi, and on September 6, Bush told him that the NDRC had agreed to assign $40,000. This was enough to finance the work on physical constants but not enough to undertake the intermediate experiment.[31]

RESEARCH: THE CHAIN REACTION

The chain reaction in natural uranium still had high priority despite the demonstration that it was only the lighter isotope 235 that contributed to slow-neutron fission. Many still thought that the expense made the isotope-separation approach impractical. To them it seemed essential to strive for a definite answer on unseparated uranium. If such a chain reaction did prove possible, to what use should it be put? In the summer of 1940, American scientists saw it first as a source of power. All of them, certainly, had thought of the possibility of a bomb. Some believed that in achieving a chain reaction they might gain understanding of what it took to make a bomb. But scientists in America did not direct their thinking primarily toward a weapon. When Pegram and Fermi outlined the research plans for the Columbia team in August, they listed their objectives only as power and large amounts of neutrons for making artificial radioactive substances and for biological and therapeutic applications.

27

More than a year of research had left the prospects for a chain reaction uncertain. The problem remained the same: to discover if enough of the neutrons produced by fission survived to keep the reaction going indefinitely. When one neutron produced fission, at least one of the neutrons emitted had to live to repeat the process. If this reproduction factor, which physicists were beginning to express by the symbol k, was one or better, the chain reaction was a fact. If it was even slightly less than one, the reaction could not maintain itself. In a uranium-graphite system there were three obstacles to a satisfactory reproduction factor. One was nonfission capture of neutrons by uranium. Another was their absorption by impurities such as might exist in the moderator. A third was escape from the surface. The larger the system, the less serious was the danger that the vital particles would be lost. This was so because the volume of the mass, where neutrons produced fission, increased more rapidly than its surface, where they escaped.

Fermi and his group at Columbia did not wait until the NDRC contract came through on November 1, 1940. First, they checked their work of the preceding spring on the neutron-absorbing characteristics of graphite. Their technique was to introduce a few grams of radon mixed with beryllium as a neutron source into a square column, or pile, of graphite a few feet thick. As the neutrons diffused through the column, they induced radioactivity in sensitive strips of rhodium foil that had been inserted as detectors.

This was work that Fermi especially enjoyed. Since the radioactivity in the rhodium was short-lived, the foil had to be placed under a Geiger counter within twenty seconds. Fermi would race down the hall to his office, where the counter had been placed to keep it from being disturbed by the neutron source in the laboratory, put the foil in place, and then delightedly tap his fingers in time with the clicking of the register. The measurements confirmed not only the suitability of graphite as a moderator but also led to a mathematical method for developing the life history of a neutron.

The second step for the Fermi team was to determine the average number of neutrons emitted by natural uranium when it absorbed a slow neutron. This was a value bound to be smaller than the number of neutrons emitted per fission, since not every absorption by a uranium atom produced fission. The experimenters rebuilt the graphite column to permit the insertion of a layer of uranium in a region where practically all of the neutrons had been slowed. Now it was easy to distinguish neutrons emitted by the uranium from those originated by the source. The value Fermi derived, 1.73, was so low that, although it did not rule out a chain reaction, it emphasized the necessity of keeping parasitic losses to a minimum. During the course of these experiments, Szilard brought forward the idea that if the uranium were arranged in lumps instead of being spread uniformly throughout the graphite, a neutron was less likely to encounter a uranium atom during the process of deceleration, when it was particularly susceptible to nonfission absorption. With heavy reinforcement from a new research group at Princeton, the investigators turned to explore the possibilities of Szilard's suggestion. By the spring of 1941, they had accomplished enough to gain a good understanding of the processes involved and of the arrangements most likely to minimize the unfavorable factors.[32]

While the basic work of measurement was proceeding, the physicists made plans to find out how large a pile with a given arrangement, or lattice, of uranium lumps should be in order to maintain a chain reaction. One way would have been to begin building a full-scale pile. When it started to react, they would know the necessary dimensions. If it should become impractically large without going critical, they could conclude that something was fundamentally wrong. But they had already rejected this crude and expensive technique, for it would delay reliable judgments until large quantities of materials had been amassed. A better method was to construct an intermediate-sized, or exponential, pile. This would make possible an informed, though not conclusive, opinion much earlier and at much less cost.[33]

It proved difficult to acquire suitable materials even in small quantities. Despite the co-operation of the Bureau of Standards, of Metal Hydrides, a producer of powdered metal alloys, and of the research laboratories of the Westinghouse and General Electric companies, the Briggs committee could find no dependable method of manufacturing either nonpyrophoric uranium powder or pure ingots. This disappointment forced the Columbia experimenters to turn to uranium oxide, even though the chances of success with this were less. Nor did it prove easy to acquire graphite low in boron, an absolute essential because of the strong neutron-absorbing characteristics of boron. By May, 1941, Briggs had placed orders for forty tons of graphite with the United States Graphite Company and for eight tons of uranium oxide with Eldorado Gold Mines, Ltd., of Canada. Not until these orders had been filled would it be possible to proceed with the intermediate experiment.[34]

The Fermi work at Columbia aimed at a uranium and graphite pile, but the Briggs committee considered other moderators as well. In November, 1940, Nobel Prize winner Arthur H. Compton, brother of Karl and chairman of the Department of Physics at the University of Chicago, suggested a beryllium moderator. Beryllium had not only the essential low atomic weight, he argued, but also the advantage that it would add rather than remove neutrons and thus contribute to a successful chain reaction. Two months later the NDRC let a contract for Samuel K. Allison to make the necessary measurements at Chicago. Meanwhile, it had not been forgotten that heavy water might be useful, both as a moderator and as an agent for removing the heat generated in a uranium-graphite pile. Early in 1941, Urey, the discoverer of heavy hydrogen, began to press for action. Urey, also the winner of a Nobel Prize, was interested in the experiments of Hans von Halban and Lew Kowarski. These co-workers of Joliot-Curie had fled to England at the fall of France with a few bottles of heavy water which constituted practically the world supply. Their studies now seemed to indicate a good chance of obtaining a chain reaction in a heavy-water and uranium-oxide system. Perhaps, Urey worried, the Germans were already ahead in this approach. Americans should study methods for producing large quantities of heavy water. By June, he had won Briggs's support and had done enough work himself to be able to submit a comprehensive report on the subject.[35]

29

RESEARCH: ISOTOPE SEPARATION

The big change in the uranium program after June, 1940, was the emphasis on isotope separation. The proof of U-235 fission by slow neutrons had dictated this second approach to the chain reaction. The scientists interested in isotope separation recognized the possibility of a bomb, but most of them, like the men working on normal uranium, were thinking mainly of a source of power.

Isotope separation appeared incredibly difficult. An isotope differed from its sister substances in mass—that is, in the number of neutrons in its nucleus—but not in atomic number. For most practical purposes, therefore, separation depended not on chemical methods but on some process involving a difference in mass. The task was especially troublesome in uranium, for the weight differential was slight, and uranium 235 was present in natural uranium in the ratio of only one part to one-hundred forty.[36]

To most scientists, the high-speed centrifuge seemed the best bet. The principle was as simple as that of the cream separator. Since the centrifugal forces in a cylinder spinning rapidly on its vertical axis acted more strongly on heavy molecules than on light ones, it was possible to concentrate them in the peripheral areas. If the principle was applied to the separation of a gaseous mixture of two isotopes, concentrations of the lighter isotope could be drawn off at the center and top of the cylinder. A high degree of separation could be attained by running these concentrations through a series, or cascade, of many such centrifuges. In 1919, Lindemann and Aston in England had suggested the centrifuge for isotope separation, but the early attempts had failed, for no one had been able to spin a tube rapidly enough. By 1939, however, Beams had developed at the University of Virginia a high-speed unit with which he achieved significant separation of chlorine isotopes. Beams had found some real difficulties. It was easier to spin a short tube than a long one, though long tubes were more efficient. Speed was limited by the strength of the rotating tube. Particularly troublesome were the vibrations encountered at certain critical velocities. It was necessary to accelerate rapidly through these zones before the machine shook itself to pieces. But no one thought these difficulties too serious. Purely mechanical, they would yield quickly to a concerted research effort.

Appropriately, Beams received an important share of the funds the Navy supplied for fiscal year 1941. He spun tubes of various sizes and tested methods of applying the principle. First, he worked with compounds of chlorine and bromine and with mixtures of gases. When uranium hexafluoride, the only gaseous compound of uranium, became available, he achieved concentrations of uranium 235. The yield, however, was not as high as theory had indicated. Another wing of the effort was located at Columbia under Urey, who had a long-standing interest in isotope separation. Its mission was to develop a centrifuge suitable for industrial operations, but Urey quickly concluded it was unwise to attempt specifications without additional exploration. Accordingly, he turned to Karl Cohen, an able young mathematician, and set him to work on theoretical calculations. By early 1941, Cohen had established a body of theory that made it possible to design a unit of encouragingly short length which the Westinghouse Electric and Manufacturing Company undertook to construct. Meanwhile, other workers at Columbia developed meters for determining the rate of gas flow. By May, the apparatus was about ready for the first experimental runs.[37]

Another possible method of separating the uranium isotopes was gaseous diffusion. A gas would diffuse through a porous barrier if there was high pressure on one side and low on the other. Since 1829, it had been known that the rate of diffusion was inversely proportional to molecular weight. It followed that if a gas was a mixture of two isotopes, the molecules of the lighter would pass through the barrier more rapidly and be present, for a while at least, in concentration on the low-pressure side. If this process could be repeated many times, a very high concentration could be achieved. Aston had used the principle in 1931 to effect partial separation of neon isotopes. Later, Harkins, a University of Chicago chemist, applied the method to chlorine, while the German physicist, Hertz, achieved almost complete separation of neon isotopes by recycling the gas through many stages.

During lunch at the Carnegie Institution conference on May 21, 1940, George B. Kistiakowsky, a professor of chemistry, suggested gaseous diffusion as a possible means of separating the uranium isotopes. At the time, he was thinking of a diffusion apparatus that Charles G. Maier of the U. S. Bureau of Mines had developed for separating mixed gases. The conference believed that Kistiakowsky should be encouraged to investigate this and other diffusion methods. During the days that followed, Kistiakowsky concluded that the Maier system had certain grave defects, but he found the simplicity of the diffusion principle so appealing that he decided to investigate the old Hertz method. Early in July, Urey suggested the possibility of making barriers of a special glass the Corning Glass Company had developed. Having independently thought of the same possibility, Kistiakowsky initiated efforts to procure samples. On October 14, he reported findings from his research on glass barriers that he judged extremely encouraging.[38]

31

By this time, others at Columbia besides Urey had become interested in Hertzian diffusion—the physicists Dunning and Booth, the chemist Grosse, and a professor of mechanical engineering, Karelitz. Pressed by other work, Kistiakowsky bowed out, and in the winter and spring of 1941, Morningside Heights became the center of research on gaseous diffusion. Reinforced by Francis G. Slack from Vanderbilt, Columbia investigated a number of potential barrier materials with favorable results and moved on to more comprehensive studies.[39]

The advocates of gaseous diffusion recognized that they faced formidable obstacles. The barrier—filter might have been a better name—would need billions of holes with a diameter less than one-tenth the mean free path of a molecule, about one ten-thousandth of a millimeter. A material so delicate at the same time had to be strong enough to withstand a considerable pressure differential and the mechanical strains of assembly. Like the centrifuge, a gaseous-diffusion system would have to process the devilishly corrosive uranium hexafluoride. This meant it would be difficult to prevent deterioration of the equipment, contamination of the gas, and plugging of the barriers. No leakage of air into the system could be tolerated, for the water vapor would react with the gas to form uranium oxyfluoride, which surely would clog the barriers and halt the operation. Nevertheless, the gaseous-diffusion method seemed fundamentally sound. Though a plant producing one kilogram of U-235 a day would require several acres of barrier area and thousands of stages, the process would be continuous, not batch. It offered less likelihood of mechanical difficulty than did the centrifuge.

Of several other separation methods that scientists considered in the spring and summer of 1940, liquid thermal diffusion was the most significant. The first thermal-diffusion process to attract attention used gases, not liquids. It was based on the tendency of the molecules of a mixed gas, when confined in a container having a marked temperature gradient, to concentrate in either the hot or the cold region. Experiments at Columbia and the University of Minnesota quickly established that this process was impractical for large-scale separation. But Philip Abelson, now working at the Carnegie Institution, thought of trying liquid rather than gaseous thermal diffusion. On the recommendation of Briggs, who had discussed the matter with Bush, the Naval Research Laboratory furnished funds to finance the research. Abelson did the actual experimentation at the Bureau of Standards, where facilities were better. The Navy, which hoped to concentrate uranium 235 in order to develop a nuclear power plant small enough for submarines, became enthusiastic about the prospects of the method. At the suggestion of Gunn, Abelson transferred in the summer of 1941 to the Naval Research Laboratory, where higher steam pressures and superior shops were available.[40]

The weakest part of the Uranium Committee's research program was the study of fission by fast neutrons. Workers at the Carnegie Institution reported measurements of the susceptibility of natural uranium to fission by fast neutrons in July, 1940. When theoretical physicist Edward Teller saw them, he thought they indicated a possibility for fast-neutron explosions. But on the basis of the most likely assumptions, he estimated that a uranium sphere of more than thirty tons would be necessary for an explosion. This was not very encouraging.[41] About the same time, Briggs brought Gregory Breit, now working at the Naval Ordnance Laboratory, into the picture. Breit served informally at first, then as chairman of a subcommittee to co-ordinate theoretical investigations. These included the slow-neutron chain reaction. Fast-fission studies received very little attention and were clothed with the deepest secrecy. They failed to have any direct impact on the course of the American uranium program.

DISCONTENT AND REVIEW

The year 1941 opened on a note of strident controversy. Americans had thrilled at the desperate air battles fought the summer before in English skies. They had rejoiced in the victories of Royal Air Force fighter squadrons. Yet the defeat of the *Luftwaffe* had eased the tension only briefly. By the end of the year, British credit was approaching exhaustion. The U-boats tightened their grip. To keep Britain in the war required heroic measures.

32

UNIVERSITY OF CALIFORNIA PHYSICISTS, 1938 / Staff of the Radiation Laboratory and associated physicists under the yoke of the 60-inch cyclotron magnet.

Left to right

row 1: J. H. Lawrence, R. Serber, P. C. Aebersold, F. N. D. Kurie, R. T. Birge, E. O. Lawrence, D. Cooksey, A. H. Snell, L. W. Alvarez, P. H. Abelson.

row 2: J. G. Backus, A. Langsdorf, J. G. Hamilton, S. J. Simmons, E. M. McMillan, R. R. Wilson, W. M. Brobeck, E. M. Lyman, J. J. Livingood.

row 3: D. H. Sloan, R. Cornog, M. D. Kamen, W. B. Mann, J. R. Oppenheimer, E. S. Viez, D. C. Kalbfell, W. W. Salisbury.

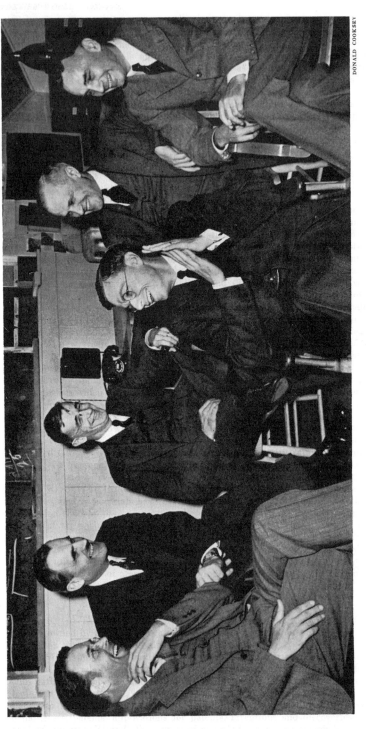

SCIENTIFIC LEADERS OF THE S-1 PROJECT / Considering the feasibility of the 184-inch cyclotron project at Berkeley, March 29, 1940.

Left to right

Ernest O. Lawrence, Arthur H. Compton, Vannevar Bush, James B. Conant, Karl T. Compton, Alfred L. Loomis. Karl Compton and Loomis served S-1 only occasionally.

These took shape in January when the Administration introduced the Lend-Lease bill in Congress. Though the measure passed both houses in March by substantial margins, the fight that marked its course was among the most bitter ever waged on Capitol Hill. Had it not been urged as a means of keeping the United States out of war, the majorities might have been much less. With Pearl Harbor nine months away, it was difficult for the American people to face the fact that they probably would have to intervene by force of arms.

During the long weeks of February and March, weeks fraught with anxiety and torn by controversy, a small, yet significant number of American scientists became extremely dissatisfied with the slow pace set by the Briggs committee. They were convinced that the crisis required vigorous, even ruthless, research on uranium.

The central figure in the growing discontent was Ernest O. Lawrence. The inventor of the cyclotron—now the hard-driving director of the Radiation Laboratory at the University of California—was more alert than many of his colleagues to the darkening war situation. A man known for his talent as a promoter, he found himself pressed to do something not only by restive American scientists but also by Ralph H. Fowler, the British scientific liaison officer in Canada. By March, 1941, Lawrence was ready to ask questions, even if it meant going out of channels. But his concern was not strictly a political matter. More than anything else, this many-sided man was a physicist. His involvement stemmed directly from achievements in his laboratory.

33

The most spectacular was the discovery of elements 93 and 94. When news of uranium fission reached Berkeley, Edwin M. McMillan, a young assistant professor of physics, devised an experiment to ascertain the energies of the main fission fragments. In making his measurements, he noticed the presence of another product—a radioactive substance with a half-life of 2.3 days. Since there was no evidence of energy release, he concluded that it was not a fission fragment. It seemed reasonable to suspect that it was an isotope of element 93, produced by the capture of a neutron by uranium 238 and prompt subsequent decay. In the spring of 1940, McMillan and Abelson (who happened to be west on a vacation) confirmed this interpretation with a positive chemical identification. Element 93, McMillan suggested, should be named neptunium after the next planet beyond Uranus, for which the ninety-second element had been named. The two investigators suspected that neptunium decayed to form an isotope of a ninety-fourth element with a mass of 239. Unfortunately, they did not succeed in proving it, for their work was interrupted by Abelson's return to Washington and McMillan's departure to assist in the radar program at the Massachusetts Institute of Technology. But early in December, 1940, Glenn T. Seaborg, an instructor in chemistry at Berkeley, obtained McMillan's assent to continue the effort to find and identify element 94. A few days later, Seaborg, in collaboration with Joseph W. Kennedy, another instructor, and Arthur C. Wahl, a graduate student, bombarded uranium with deuterons—the nuclei of heavy hydrogen atoms—and produced an isotope of element 93. In this, they observed evidence of 94. Before the end of February, 1941, they established chemically that they had indeed found an isotope of a new element.[42]

The significance of these discoveries, which depended so heavily on the cyclotron and its utility in making samples of significant size, lay in the possibility that element 94 would prove fissionable. Physicists the world over were free to speculate on this possibility, for McMillan and Abelson related their work in the June 15, 1940, issue of the *Physical Review*. Even though they did not report finding 94, their evidence left little doubt that it had been present. It seemed likely that the new element would fission easily. Even before the McMillan and Abelson article appeared, Louis A. Turner of Princeton had predicted both the way it was formed and its characteristics. In fact, as early as the fall of 1939 Bohr and Wheeler had forecast that it would undergo fission with slow neutrons. If 94 should prove fissionable, what would it mean? At first it was viewed as a means of utilizing all the metal in a natural uranium pile. The theory was that neutrons from uranium 235 would convert uranium 238 atoms into 94, which would be subject to slow-neutron fission. Soon, the idea took hold that element 94 could be produced in a pile and then separated chemically. Thus it would be possible to obtain a substance perhaps as fissionable as uranium 235 without the tremendous expense of building isotope-separation plants.[43]

Yet all of this was mere speculation. No policy decisions could come until there was experimental evidence of 94's fission characteristics. During the Christmas season of 1940, a number of scientists saw the best way to proceed: use one of the Radiation Laboratory cyclotrons for manufacturing enough 94 to measure its nuclear properties. Emilio Segrè, who had worked with Fermi in Rome and now was a research assistant at Berkeley, suggested the possibility to Fermi and Pegram during a visit to Columbia. About the same time, the Uranium Committee asked McMillan to undertake the studies. Committed to radar research for the immediate future, McMillan suggested asking Seaborg to do the work and enlisting Lawrence's personal support. Actually, the idea had occurred independently to Seaborg and Kennedy, and they had already planned their experiments. Meanwhile, the British were becoming interested in 94. When Fowler learned that Norman Feather and Egon Bretscher had been working on it at the Cavendish Laboratory in Cambridge, he urged Lawrence to prepare samples and make the necessary measurements. Before this suggestion reached Lawrence, Seaborg's crew, augmented by Segrè, had set to work. They bombarded uranium, this time with neutrons, and found the 94 isotope, one with a mass of 239, that McMillan and Abelson had predicted. By the middle of May, 1941, their tests proved that 94 was subject to slow-neutron fission. Before the month ended, Seaborg reported to Briggs that 94 was about 1.7 times as likely as uranium 235 to fission with slow neutrons.[44]

The cyclotron thus opened an exciting new approach, but early in 1941, Lawrence began to toy with another idea that made action seem all the more important. His new 60-inch cyclotron was operating well; why not convert his 37-inch model into a super mass spectrograph? The mass spectrograph depended on the principle that the lighter particles in a high-speed beam of ions—positively charged particles—were deflected to a greater degree than the heavier ones as they passed through a magnetic field. The device had proved valuable in determining the relative abundance of the isotopes of a substance and in obtaining the extremely small samples of concentrated uranium 235 used to prove that it was the fissionable isotope. The mass spectrograph and the cyclotron had some striking similarities. Both required a high-vacuum chamber and a large electromagnet. Conversion should not prove difficult. Lawrence thought it would open the way to separate larger, purer samples of uranium 235 for study and, eventually, to derive the lighter isotope on a large scale.[45]

35

On March 17, 1941, Lawrence conferred with Karl Compton and Alfred L. Loomis at Compton's office in Cambridge. Loomis was chief of the National Defense Research Committee's Division 14, the focal point of research in radar, while Compton had special responsibility in the same area as the NDRC member in charge of detection, controls, and instruments. Lawrence had known both men for many years, and in the last few months had done yeoman service in helping them staff the radar organization. This raw New England morning it was nuclear research that concerned him. In his infectious way, he told of his excitement. He was sure there was a reasonable probability of results useful in the present emergency. True, fission was not his NDRC assignment, but his physicist friends had urged him to investigate.

That afternoon Compton telephoned Bush, then wrote him a letter amplifying his analysis of the situation. The British, he thought, seemed farther ahead despite the fact that American nuclear physicists were "the most in number and the best in quality." More disquieting was the probability of active German interest. But most disturbing was the functioning of the Committee on Uranium. It had put to work only a few American physicists, and these were becoming more and more restive. The committee, which seldom met, moved with painful deliberation. The program was so shrouded in secrecy that even those who were participating could not find out what was being done in areas so closely related that they might well influence their own experiments. Harold Urey, himself a member of the Uranium Committee, felt deeply frustrated. Some of the most promising lines of investigation had received so little attention that the chances of developing an application for use in the current emergency were impaired. Part of the trouble was Briggs, who not only had heavy responsibilities in several directions—he was a member of the National Advisory Committee for Aeronautics—but by nature was also slow, conservative, and methodical. It was hard to know what to do, Compton realized, but he had some suggestions. Bush might appoint

Lawrence his deputy for ten days or two weeks with full authority to explore. Lawrence might be able to provide an impetus, just as he had done with radar. Another possibility was to set up a parallel committee to consider possibilities hitherto neglected. Perhaps Bush could make sure of more vigorous administration if he gave Briggs a deputy who would be free to spend practically his whole time organizing the work.[46]

Two days later, Lawrence presented his plea directly to Bush in New York. Bush, whose temper had a low boiling point, did not conceal his irritation. He was in a difficult position. His responsibility covered the whole range of the contributions science might make to national defense. He was anxious to support the uranium program to the extent it seemed likely to have military significance in the near future, but he did not want to have to cope with pressure tactics that might dangerously warp the scientific effort. He believed that Briggs had done well in a situation which required a balanced, reasoned approach. He proposed to back the Uranium Committee in its decisions unless a strong case developed for his personal intervention. Still, Bush was aware that there was considerable justification for some of the criticisms that had been voiced. In a gesture well calculated to help Briggs, to contain Lawrence, and to capitalize on Lawrence's gifts and enthusiasm, Bush arranged for him to become a temporary personal consultant to Briggs.[47] It did not take long for Lawrence to effect some changes. Soon the National Defense Research Committee, on the recommendation of the Uranium Committee, voted funds to support work on elements 93 and 94 at Berkeley and to enable Nier at Minnesota to produce five micrograms of uranium 235 with his mass spectrometer. This last appropriation owed something, at least, to British pressure. Fowler had urged Lawrence to do what he could to get a sample of 235 for the English physicist John D. Cockcroft.

By the middle of April, 1941, Bush had decided to seek a review of the uranium program by a committee of the National Academy of Sciences. After sounding out Frank B. Jewett, its president, he arranged for the National Defense Research Committee to authorize a formal request at its April 18 meeting. His motivation was partly political, for he saw the importance of maintaining good relations with the academy. He had already gone to considerable lengths to see that Jewett was appointed to the NDRC. After all, the NDRC in a sense had usurped the functions of the academy. But more important, Bush felt the need of a dispassionate review by a group of competent physicists not deeply involved in the subject. How much emphasis, he wondered, was justified? A great deal of money could be spent on uranium, but so far as he could see, no one had uncovered any "clear-cut path to defense results of great importance." Jewett selected what appeared to be a strong committee headed by Arthur Compton of the University of Chicago. Other members were Lawrence of California, John C. Slater of the Massachusetts Institute of Technology, John H. Van Vleck of Harvard—all physicists—and William D. Coolidge, a physical chemist who had just retired as director of the research laboratory of General Electric. Bancroft Gherardi, the retired chief engineer of the American Telephone and Telegraph Company, could not serve because of illness. The task of the committee, as Jewett defined it for Compton, was to evaluate the work already under way and to judge if larger funds and facilities and more pressure would serve the national defense.[48]

Compton's group met with Briggs, Breit, Gunn, Pegram, Tuve, and Urey at the Bureau of Standards on April 30. Briggs reported that the Committee on Uranium had been seeking to determine whether fission could be utilized successfully for explosive bombs, radiation bombs, and submarine power. Theory, he said, indicated that a bomb would require at least a ten-fold concentration of U-235 to be small enough to be carried in an airplane. Accordingly, a number of isotope-separation methods were under consideration. All methods for quantity separation would be difficult and expensive. When current studies revealed the most promising method, Briggs favored building a pilot plant. But Briggs spent most of the time discussing the Columbia work on the chain reaction in normal uranium. Compton came away with the impression that the Committee on Uranium was interested primarily in the generation of power. The National Academy delegation gained no clear understanding of the chances for a bomb. Compton and Breit were not able to get through to each other. A few months later, when an explosive was unquestionably the prime objective, Breit complained that the visiting committeemen exhibited only a polite interest in a bomb, while Compton declared with equal exasperation that he had been able to obtain only the barest outline of a report on the theoretical investigations into its possibility.

On May 5, Compton's committee met at Harvard. Here they discussed in some detail the relative merits of beryllium and graphite moderators and heard a report by Kenneth T. Bainbridge, a Harvard physicist just returned from an NDRC mission to England. The British, he said, took the uranium work very seriously and believed there was some possibility of developing an explosive within two years. In their efforts to establish a chain reaction, they were giving a great deal of thought to a heavy-water moderator. Halban, whose Cambridge investigations in this area they considered auspicious, was anxious to come to the United States to make closer contact with American research. In isotope separation the leading figure was Franz E. Simon of the Clarendon Laboratory at Oxford. He was hard at work on a gaseous-diffusion system and hoped to have a yes-or-no answer regarding it in July.[49]

Compton submitted a unanimous report on May 17 recommending a strongly intensified effort in the next six months. The committee saw military importance as depending on a slow-neutron chain reaction achieved with a heavy hydrogen, beryllium, or carbon moderator. It proposed three military applications. First came radioactive fission products which could be dropped over enemy territory. Since the development of such weapons would require about twelve months after the attainment of a chain reaction, they would not be available before 1943. In second place was an atomic pile which could generate power to propel submarines and other ships. Though this was a straightforward matter theoretically, the engineering difficulties were so great that it could not be important for three years after the first chain reaction. Listed last was the possibility of a bomb of enormous destructive power. It depended on a strong concentration of uranium 235 or of some other element subject to fission by slow neutrons. Viewing the problem optimistically, the committee thought it probably would take three to five years to separate adequate amounts of uranium 235. Possibly element 94, a potential substitute for the lighter uranium isotope, could be produced abundantly in a chain-reacting pile. Bombs made of 94 might be available twelve months after the first chain reaction, but they probably were some years away. All in all, Compton's group did not anticipate atomic explosives before 1945. It considered a chain reaction easy if enough uranium 235 were available, but to acquire this isotope in quantity meant erecting large, expensive plants of designs still undetermined. On the other hand, the prospects of a chain reaction in unseparated uranium were good. Perhaps eighteen months would suffice to achieve it.

What should be done? The National Academy committee saw the chain reaction in natural uranium as the most pressing concern. It recommended full support for the intermediate experiment on a uranium-and-graphite pile and for a pilot plant to produce heavy water. The committee urged emphasizing the beryllium project for the next six months. It favored continuing the isotope-separation studies but judged that they did not require such great stress. From an administrative standpoint, Compton and his colleagues had some improvements to suggest. The Committee on Uranium should be larger. It should pay more attention to the continuous interchange of research information. Only by sharing information and conferring on mutual problems could investigators make much progress. Finally, Halban should be brought over at once. He could help American research along and in turn take back to England information that might prove of value there.[50]

Bush and the National Defense Research Committee found the report hardly the solution to their problems. Its emphasis on power did nothing to allay fears that uranium had little military significance. Eventually atomic power would revolutionize naval warfare, but the NDRC's responsibility was to prepare the United States for possible involvement in the current war, not in some future conflict. The report mentioned bombs, but to discuss bombs in terms of slow neutrons was to admit one had no very clear idea if and how they could be made. And while Compton's review was good in regard to experimental physics, its bold estimates on weapons and time schedules were undocumented. Conant, a chemist and perhaps the most influential NDRC member, was decidedly unimpressed. Bush put it tactfully when he wrote Jewett that the NDRC, troubled at the thought of spending a large amount of government money on uranium, wanted to know "how far and how quickly results could be put into practical use." He wanted the study reviewed by one or two first-rate engineers.[51] Jewett, himself a member of the NDRC, promptly added Oliver E. Buckley of the Bell Telephone Laboratories and L. Warrington Chubb of Westinghouse to the National Academy committee. Since Compton had left for South America, Coolidge acted as chairman.

On July 11, 1941, the reconstituted committee reported that it had reviewed the earlier recommendations from an engineering standpoint and could endorse them. The discovery that element 94 was subject to slow-neutron fission had strengthened them. The uranium program should have support, not on the basis of definite plans for applications but simply because a self-sustaining reaction was bound to have tremendous import. Nothing more had been learned about separation methods to indicate early success, but because even moderate increases in concentration were important, the effort should continue at its present intensity. Even more than in May, the chain reaction in natural uranium promised success. A demonstration was needed. This would reveal its potential and call forth such an increase in scientific and engineering effort that practical utilization would follow rapidly. The experiments under way sufficed for ascertaining fundamental data, but any practical appraisal demanded investigations on a larger scale. These should start immediately under a project type of organization devoted exclusively to proving the chain reaction and exploiting its possibilities for national defense.[52]

39

This report was no more helpful than the first. It placed no greater stress on the possibility of a bomb. This was strange, for Lawrence had prepared a "Memorandum Regarding Fission of Element 94," which Coolidge had attached as an appendix. The text mentioned the slow-neutron fission of 94 and referred to the appendix, but it did not point up Lawrence's observation that a fast-neutron chain reaction was likely if large amounts of 94 were available. Bush was disappointed because this second report did not give him the information he had requested. He acknowledged to Jewett that some additional information on physics had been furnished, but he had wanted engineering advice. What was the outlook for military applications? Should he decide to push ahead, what did he have to face in terms of time, of money, of difficulties? All these questions were taking on added significance, for Congress had cut funds. It did not seem likely that enough money would be available to finance a year's work.[53]

While the National Academy was reviewing the program, Briggs was preparing the Uranium Committee's budget recommendations. He made his plans in the light not only of the committee report of May 17, 1941, but of the uranium work in the United Kingdom. In April, 1940, the British had established a committee of scientists under the chairmanship of George P. Thomson of the Imperial College of Science and Technology to examine fission phenomena.

Operating under the code name, the MAUD Committee, this group had launched an effort quite similar to that in the United States except, as might be expected in a country fighting for its very life, it was pointed more directly toward a weapon. In the fall of 1940, the British established liaison with the American committee. Fowler and Cockcroft met with Briggs's group at the Bureau of Standards. Later a number of British papers, including minutes of the MAUD Committee, were sent to the United States, while certain American reports were delivered to Fowler for transmittal to England. Briggs was working on his budget when he received the minutes of a MAUD Technical Committee meeting held April 9, 1941. Two matters discussed were of much interest. First, Rudolf E. Peierls of the University of Birmingham believed that the fission cross section of uranium 235 was large enough to make practical the construction of a bomb of reasonable size. Second, Halban reported it would take a year to transmute one one-thousandth of the uranium 238 in a graphite-uranium pile into transuranic elements. It would be so difficult to extract element 94 in such low concentrations that a graphite pile did not appear at all interesting as a means of producing it.[54]

Briggs submitted his recommendations to the National Defense Research Committee on July 8. The basic objective, he stated, was to ascertain whether a chain reaction was possible. A second was to determine through intermediate piles at Columbia and Chicago and through associated theoretical studies the most promising dimensions, arrangement, and materials to be used in the full-scale experiment on power production. Finally, the aim was to continue work on separating uranium isotopes in quantity. Briggs now urged isotope separation primarily for military purposes. He argued that a ten- or twenty-fold increase in the concentration of uranium 235 was required to produce a chain reaction in a mass small enough to be carried in an airplane.

Briggs proposed a grant of $167,000 for the chain-reaction work. About two-thirds of this was to support studies in progress at Columbia, Princeton, and Chicago, while the remaining third was to finance a contract for the construction of a pilot plant and the development of suitable catalysts for the production of heavy water. The centrifuge project should receive $95,000 and the Columbia gaseous-diffusion experiments $25,000. Nier required $10,000 to analyze the isotope separation attained in the various trials and to improve the mass spectrograph so that better samples might be available for measuring nuclear properties. A number of miscellaneous investigations—on the chemistry of uranium compounds, on proposed separation methods, and on element 94—needed $30,000, and a like amount should be available to cover administrative expenses and theoretical studies.

These budgetary plans showed clearly the influence of British thinking. Investigation of element 94, which the National Academy committee had mentioned so hopefully, was to have only $8,000. Since this was to go to study its production "by bombardment of U-238 and the subsequent contribution of 94 to the chain reaction by fission," Briggs evidently was not impressed by the American suggestion to separate it and use it as a substitute for uranium 235. On the other hand, the separation of uranium 235, which the National Academy reviewers had de-emphasized, was to have almost as much financial support as the chain reaction. Heavy water, it was true, had received support from the Compton group, but this program also owed its existence to British optimism.[55]

Actually, by the time Briggs had drawn up his proposals, the National Defense Research Committee had lost authority to act. The NDRC had been a great step forward, but a year's experience had revealed certain imperfections. Because it was a research organization, it was not well adapted to fill the gap between research and procurement orders that engineers called development. Another disadvantage was that the NDRC ranked equally with the laboratories of the military services and with the National Advisory Committee for Aeronautics. There was no easy way to correlate the research of these three agencies. Moreover, there was a crucial need for stimulating research in military medicine.

The Office of Scientific Research and Development, which Roosevelt established by Executive Order on June 28, 1941, was Bush's effort to remedy these defects at a single stroke. Located within the Office for Emergency Management of the Executive Office of the President, under a director personally responsible to the Chief Executive, the OSRD was to serve as a center for mobilizing the scientific resources of the nation and applying the results of research to national defense. The NDRC would continue, but within the OSRD. Its function was to make recommendations on research and development. The OSRD directorship went to Bush, and Conant replaced him as chairman of the NDRC. The Committee on Uranium became the OSRD Section on Uranium, soon designated cryptically as the S-1 Section.

The uranium program had not been the primary inspiration for these organizational changes. Nonetheless, they had profound significance for its future. Now the work was under the protective arm of the President. Should Bush decide that an all-out effort was in the national interest, he could go directly to the White House for support. The prestige and power of the Presidency would sustain him in dealing with other agencies of the executive arm, particularly the military, on whose co-operation the success of the project would so heavily depend.[56]

TURNING POINT

July, 1941, was the turning point in the American atomic energy effort. Two factors made for a basic change in the attitude of those who bore prime responsibility. One was the better prospect for using element 94. At Berkeley, Seaborg and Segrè measured its fission cross section for fast neutrons on five micrograms obtained by bombarding uranium in a cyclotron. They derived the value, admittedly uncertain, of 3.4 times that of natural uranium. This was encouraging, the more so because Coolidge of the National Academy committee had sent in a report from Fermi which discussed specifically the technical problems involved in a uranium-graphite pile. For the first time, Bush told Conant, he had something like engineering data, and it seemed to be "good stuff." [57]

The other factor, more important in effecting a new approach, was news from Britain. On July 10, Charles C. Lauritsen, an NDRC armor and ordnance specialist just back from London, talked with Bush in his office at the corner of Sixteenth and P Streets. Eight days earlier, he had attended a meeting of the MAUD Technical Committee at which Chairman Thomson presented a preliminary draft report. Unanimously, the committee had recommended pushing a uranium 235 bomb project with all possible speed, the necessary isotope separation to be accomplished by the gaseous-diffusion method. Some days later, Bush and Conant received a copy of the draft report forwarded from the NDRC office in London on July 7. Its basic premise was the conviction that if pure 235 were available in sufficient mass, any neutron produced—not just slow ones—could cause a fission. Since the bulk of the neutrons would be fast, the chain reaction would develop so quickly that an explosion of tremendous force would take place. How much uranium 235 would be needed for an efficient bomb depended mainly on the probability of its fission by neutrons in the energy range of 500,000 to 1,000,000 electron volts. The magnitude of this cross section was uncertain, for when working with natural uranium, one could not be sure that some of the fission produced by neutrons with energies below 1,000,000 electron volts was not due to 238. Measurements made at the Carnegie Institution in the United States, combined with those of Frisch at Liverpool, indicated a minimum critical mass—the smallest size that would maintain a chain reaction—in the neighborhood of five kilograms. Since the nuclear element in a bomb would have to be larger than its critical mass for good efficiency, ten kilograms seemed a reasonable estimate of its size. Clearly, such a weapon could be carried in a number of existing airplanes. Besides, it could be ready in time for use in the present war, say, in two years.

There was a remote possibility, the drafters of the report believed, that element 94 produced in a slow-neutron pile could be extracted and used in a bomb, but they considered it a much surer bet to separate uranium 235. Thermal diffusion was impractical. It was out of the question to suppose that the electromagnetic method would yield even a few grams. Centrifuging was based on principles that long had been understood, but it required precision machinery of a type that so far had been attained only in a laboratory instrument. This left gaseous diffusion by far the most promising method of separating uranium 235 on a large scale. To judge from the report, Simon had gone further in developing a system at Oxford than Dunning and his colleagues had at Columbia. All of this indicated that British scientists believed uranium to have military significance worth a major effort. The best proof of their serious intentions was that they raised the question of whether the gaseous-diffusion plant ought to be built in England or in Canada or the United States.[58]

This report gave Bush and Conant what they had been looking for: a promise that there was a reasonable chance for something militarily useful during the war in progress. The British did more than promise; they outlined a concrete program. None of the recommendations Briggs had made and neither of the two National Academy reports had done as much.[59] The scientists at work in the United Kingdom were no more able or advanced than the Americans. Fundamentally, the trouble was that the United States was not yet at war. Too many scientists, like Americans in other walks of life, found it unpleasant to turn their thoughts to weapons of mass destruction. They were aware of the possibilities, surely, but they had not placed them in sharp focus. The senior scientists and engineers who prepared the reports that served as the basis for policy decisions either did not learn the essential facts or did not grasp their significance. The American program came to grief on two reefs—a failure of the physicists interested in uranium to point their research toward war and a failure of communication.

43

On July 18, 1941, the National Defense Research Committee recommended negotiating contracts to carry into effect the research proposed by the Section on Uranium. This, however, was only an interim measure. The United States was going to have to decide quickly whether it should launch the industrial effort necessary to manufacture the bomb. The immediate problem was to determine the direction and scope of the preliminary investigations and to win support for the program, which would be expensive and which had to be secret, from the only authority who could assure it, the President of the United States.

While Bush and Conant were making their first moves, news of the British intentions reached other American leaders. One channel was Marcus L. E. Oliphant, an Australian physicist working on radar at the University of Birmingham, who made a summer visit to the United States. At Schenectady, he saw William D. Coolidge, the author of the second National Academy report. Coolidge was amazed to learn that the British were predicting that only ten kilograms of pure 235 would be required and that the chain reaction could be effected by fast neutrons. So far as he knew, this information had not been available in the United States when he submitted his report. Oliphant's story, Coolidge told Bush, made a further study of separation by diffusion look more important than the work based on the action of "slowed down neutrons" that the committee had recommended. Oliphant also visited Berkeley. Lawrence was so impressed with what Oliphant told him that he insisted that the Australian prepare a statement summarizing the report of the MAUD Committee. About the middle of September, Lawrence attended the celebration of the fiftieth anniversary of the University of Chicago. One evening he met with Conant, Pegram, and Arthur Compton by the fire at the Compton home, reported on what Oliphant had told him, stressed the importance of element 94 as an alternate route to a weapon, and gave vent to his dissatisfaction with the slow pace in the United States. Conant, who already knew the British plans, put on a show of needing to be convinced. Then he sought to make Lawrence realize that an all-out effort, the only kind that would yield significant results, would take the next several years of his life. Compton listened avidly and went to bed that night seeing clearly the military potential of uranium.

Yet there was an even more important result of Oliphant's visit to Berkeley. It inspired Lawrence to begin plans for converting his 37-inch cyclotron into a giant mass spectrograph. First, he intended to produce samples. A visit to Minneapolis convinced him that Nier did not have the equipment to turn out the needed uranium 235 rapidly enough. But beyond this, Lawrence had his eye on electromagnetic separation on a larger scale. Physicists quite generally believed that what they called the space-charge limitation made this method impractical. They assumed that a large beam of positively charged ions, repelled from each other by their like electrical charges, would scatter hopelessly and disrupt any separating effect. Lawrence, however, suspected from his experience with cyclotrons that the presence of air molecules in the vacuum chamber would have a neutralizing effect. Sensing that he was on the right track, he determined to put his intuition to the test.[60]

Another courier through whom information from Britain reached American scientists was George Thomson himself, chairman of the MAUD Committee. On October 3, he delivered to Conant a copy of his final report. In essentials it was the same as the draft Bush and Conant already had. Thomson had discussed its substance freely with both the National Academy committee and with the Section on Uranium, though he had avoided telling them that the British scientists were exhorting their government to take up uranium in a big way. The Briggs committeemen were impressed with the optimistic British attitude toward the bomb, as Bush, Conant, Compton, and Lawrence had been. They listened intently to Thomson's discussion of gaseous diffusion. It confirmed their plans to send Pegram and Urey to investigate at first hand.[61]

ROOSEVELT MAKES A DECISION

Meanwhile, Bush and Conant were making progress. They took their initial step, strengthening the Section on Uranium, before the first of September, 1941. To the section itself they added Allison, Breit, Edward U. Condon of the Westinghouse Research Laboratory, Lloyd P. Smith of Cornell, and Henry D. Smyth of Princeton. They dropped Gunn in accord with the NDRC policy not to have Army and Navy personnel as members of the sections, but they expected him to continue to perform a liaison function. Tuve they relieved so that he might devote his entire efforts to another vital war project, the proximity fuze. They retained Briggs as chairman and Pegram as vicechairman. They established a subsection on power production under Pegram and one on theoretical aspects under Fermi, while they put Urey at the head of groups devoted to isotope separation and heavy water. They assigned panels of consultants to the subsections. Now the uranium work had more representative leadership and broader participation.

Next, Bush asked the National Academy committee to review the situation once more. He had already strengthened the committee by arranging for the appointments of Warren K. Lewis, the dean of American chemical engineers, of Harvard's George B. Kistiakowsky, one of the country's foremost explosives experts, and of Chicago's Robert S. Mulliken, an authority on isotope separation. Bush spelled out for Arthur Compton just what he wanted. Most important was information on a uranium 235 bomb, particularly its critical mass and its destructive effect. He also needed tentative design data on a gaseous-diffusion plant. Less important, he would like a review of available data about a heavy-water pile. He had no desire, he said, to limit the efforts of the reviewing committee, but one thing should be understood. The question placed before it was the technical one. What should or should not be governmental policy was outside its sphere. If the committee could come through with the information Bush had requested, he would have an independent check on the British work. He would have as well the data he needed concerning the scope and direction of an intensified American effort.[62]

45

Bush did not wait for Compton's committee to report before seeking support at the highest level. Urged on by Conant, whose initial doubts had vanished, he had already decided that the United States had to expand its research and discover what was really involved in building a production plant. Back in July, 1941, he had briefed Henry A. Wallace on the status of American uranium research. He wanted to keep the Vice-President informed, for he was one man sitting in high councils who had the scientific background to grasp the subject readily. Now, the morning of October 9, the same day he sent Compton his instructions, Bush conferred at the White House with Roosevelt and Wallace. He outlined the British conclusions, mentioning the amount of uranium necessary for a bomb, the cost of a production plant, and the time needed to achieve a weapon. He explained that this did not add up to a proved case but depended primarily on calculations backed by some laboratory investigation. Hence, he could not state unequivocally that an attempt would be successful. At some length the three discussed the sources of raw material, the little that was known about the German program, and the problem of postwar control. From this meeting emerged a number of understandings. Most important, Bush was to expedite the work in every possible way. He was not, however, to proceed with any definite steps on an "expanded plan"—on construction as opposed to research and planning—until he had further instructions from the President. When the time came to build, some direction independent of the current investigative framework would have to be devised. It would be best if the necessary construction were done jointly in Canada. Roosevelt, who understood that a great deal of money would be required, said he could make it available from a special source at his disposal. Bush was to prepare a letter that would serve to open discussion with Britain, "at the top." Finally, the President emphasized that Bush should hold the matter closely. He restricted consideration of policy to himself, Wallace, Bush, Conant, Secretary of War Henry L. Stimson, and Army Chief of Staff George C. Marshall. He told Wallace to follow up on any details that required attention.[63]

This White House conference was an event of prime importance on the journey that ended at Hiroshima and Nagasaki. Bush now had the authority, not to make a bomb, but to discover if a bomb could be made and at what price. When this investigation should point the way to a production program, he would need further Presidential sanction. Until then he had virtually a free hand.

Arthur Compton, who knew nothing of the October 9 decision, went to work at once on a third National Academy report. At Columbia he talked with Fermi and Urey. Fermi had estimated that the critical mass of uranium 235 could be as little as twenty kilograms, but thoroughly conservative in temperament, he would not exclude the possibility that it might be as high as one or two tons. These estimates did not give anything very definite to go on, but Urey, as well as Dunning, was optimistic about the chances for separating the isotopes. At Princeton, Wigner was confident that a uranium-graphite pile was a feasible method for producing element 94. And Seaborg of California, to whom Compton talked in Chicago, was confident he could work out large-scale chemical methods for extracting 94 from uranium bombarded in a pile.[64]

To focus the attention of his committeemen, Compton drafted a tentative report for discussion at an October 21 meeting at the General Electric Research Laboratory in Schenectady. This was a useful technique which produced a full review. Lawrence led off by reading Oliphant's summary of the MAUD Committee report. J. Robert Oppenheimer, a young Berkeley physicist who had been invited at Lawrence's insistence, took an active part in the talk on the physics of the bomb. Though he recognized the uncertainties in the case, he thought that about one hundred kilograms was a reasonable estimate of the uranium 235 needed for an effective weapon. Consideration of the methods of separation centered around a comprehensive review of the subject by Robert S. Mulliken, who had visited the various centers of research. From discussion at the meeting, written comments submitted later, and his own calculations, Compton fashioned a draft which, after some changes, became the final document. Lawrence had been concerned by the tone of the Schenectady meeting. There had been a tendency to emphasize the uncertainties and the possibility that uranium would not be a factor in the war. This attitude was dangerous, he thought. "It will not be a calamity if when we get the answers to the Uranium problem they turn out negative from the military point of view, but if the answers are fantastically positive and we fail to get them first, the results for our country may well be a tragic disaster." His fears, however, were assuaged by the final document. He thought it "an extraordinarily good statement." [65]

The basic conclusion of the report, which Compton submitted to President Jewett of the National Academy on November 6, 1941, was that a "fission bomb of superlatively destructive power" would result from assembling quickly a sufficient mass of uranium 235. "Sufficient" could hardly be less than two kilograms or more than one hundred.[66] These were wide limits, but they stemmed from the prevailing uncertainty about the fission cross section of the lighter isotope, an uncertainty that could not be remedied until larger and better samples were at hand. Speed of assembly was essential. A bomb would be fired by bringing together parts, each less than the critical mass, into a unit that exceeded it. If a stray neutron triggered a reaction before the parts were thoroughly put together, a fizzle, not a powerful explosion, would result. Since uranium had some spontaneous fission, which meant that neutrons would be present, this was a possibility, but it did not seem likely to cause serious difficulty. The bomb would have tremendous destructive force, but just how much was still uncertain. Since only a small part of the energy locked in the uranium could be released before the mass blew apart and the reaction stopped, the available explosive energy per kilogram of uranium would be equivalent to no more than a few hundred tons of TNT. Besides, it was known that fast explosions involving small masses were less effective than slower explosions of the same energy involving larger masses. Following the judgment of Kistiakowsky in this matter, the report estimated that one kilogram would have a destructive effect equivalent in TNT to only about one-tenth of its available explosive energy. Though this was significantly lower than the estimate on which the British were proceeding, Compton, as he indicated in a footnote, thought even this might be too high.

The separation of isotopes could be accomplished in the necessary amounts, the National Academy committee concluded unhesitatingly. There was not enough information available to judge the British version of gaseous diffusion, but the Columbia system looked feasible, even though it might be slow in development. The centrifugal method appeared practical and was further advanced than gaseous diffusion. It was important to study both from an engineering viewpoint. Other methods deserved investigation, but these seemed further from the engineering stage. One possibility was the mass spectrograph. At the moment, it should be used to obtain samples for experimental work. Any estimate of the time needed to develop, engineer, and produce fission bombs could only be rough, but given all possible effort, they

47

might be available in significant quantity in three or four years. The separation process would probably be the most time-consuming and expensive part of the work. This too could be estimated in only the roughest way, but something in the range of $50 million to $100 million seemed reasonable. Other costs in connection with producing the bombs would probably be around $30 million.

How should this analysis be translated into action? Certain work, comparatively modest in scale, had to be done immediately. Trial units of the centrifugal and gaseous-diffusion systems had to be built and tested. Samples of separated uranium 235 had to be obtained for tests on its nuclear properties. While this was being done, engineering of the separation plants should start in order that plans would be ready when more exact information about the requirements was known. So much for the tasks directly ahead. The time had come for some organizational changes. Since isotope separation was at the development stage, a competent engineer should direct it. His efforts, of course, would have to be co-ordinated with the research program. To make the best progress in research, the major tasks should be assigned to key men, men of ability and integrity who had proved themselves. They should have adequate funds to use according to their best judgment.

The report was clear, concise, and as unequivocal as the circumstances permitted. Yet it omitted altogether the possibility of using element 94 as a substitute for uranium 235. Compton had referred to it in the draft he prepared after the Schenectady meeting. Even if a 235 bomb should prove impossible, he had stressed the importance of proceeding with isotope separation and the chain reaction. This would lead to the development of valuable power sources and to the production of 94, "which may itself become a practical means of producing a fission bomb." But that section was dropped from the final report. Just why and at whose initiative was not apparent, but to omit it was good tactics. Bush had emphasized that he was primarily interested in the possibilities for a uranium 235 weapon. He and Conant felt justified in striving only for military results useful in the current war. It was the failure to point out definite prospects for a bomb that had so long delayed an intensive American effort. Nothing had happened to make general references to a source of power or of other interesting by-products impressive now. Element 94, which depended on the chain reaction, seemed to offer hope for a weapon, but in November, 1941, it was hope alone. In September, Fermi at last had made a test of the chain reaction with his intermediate pile, a graphite column eight feet square and eleven feet high, through which lumps of uranium oxide were dispersed in a lattice arrangement. Disappointingly, his measurements gave a value of only 0.87 for k, the reproduction factor. There was promise that by improvements in purity, in geometry, and in density of uranium, k could be raised above 1, but it had not been proved.[67] Until it was, there was no way to make large quantities of 94. Besides, it was not even known that 94 emitted neutrons on fission. Men like Compton and Lawrence might feel in their bones that the 94 program was practical, but their faith would not have seemed very convincing in the cold print of a report.

The National Academy report gave Bush information he needed. Though more conservative than the British recommendations in highlighting uncertainties, it confirmed the conclusion of scientists in England that uranium 235 could be separated and made into an effective bomb. The report made valuable suggestions on how to proceed and how to organize the work. Yet it was not responsible for the decision to go ahead with an intensive investigation. The President had made that decision on October 9. On November 27, Bush sent the report to Roosevelt, pointing out in a covering letter that he was forming an engineering group and accelerating physics research aimed at plant-design data. He also reiterated his understanding that he would await Presidential instructions before committing the United States to any specific program. The report required no action at the White House. Not until January 19, 1942, did Roosevelt send it back with a note in his own handwriting: "V. B. OK—returned—I think you had best keep this in your own safe FDR." [68]

49

PLANNING THE ATTACK

The main task now confronting Bush was to reorganize the uranium program for a quick decision on a production plant. The basic idea, which had taken shape before the end of November, 1941, was a product of the recommendations of the National Academy committee and of conferences with Compton, Briggs, and Conant. Those with Conant were especially important, for he and Bush had become a smooth team, each respecting and trusting the judgment of the other. In essence, the new organization called for a planning board to make engineering studies, for the designation of scientific personnel to lead the research effort, and for Bush himself as OSRD director to co-ordinate research and engineering. [69]

Working out the details came next. On the recommendation of Warren K. Lewis, Bush recruited Eger V. Murphree, a young chemical engineer now vice-president of the Standard Oil Development Company, to become chief of the Planning Board. Bush assured him that this was a temporary assignment only and instructed him to recommend other persons for the board, stressing that he wanted it staffed by chemical engineers of standing. That Bush should turn to chemical engineers was significant, for in this specialty the United States was strong. Thanks largely to Lewis' teaching at the Massachusetts Institute of Technology and to the demands of the oil industry in the years between the wars, the United States had a corps of engineers well grounded in basic physics and highly skilled in developing and operating large industrial chemistry complexes. Bush continued to keep the Uranium or S-1 Section informed. He had Briggs tell a December 6 meeting that though the committee's concern was science and not broad policy, it could rest assured that the matter would be pushed. Then Briggs outlined the organizational plans that were taking shape.[70]

It was more than just organizational machinery. Information kept rolling in that had to be weighed in determining the direction and scope of the effort. Urey, just back from England, sent Bush on December 1 a preliminary report on the British work. He and Pegram agreed with the British that the Simon method of gaseous diffusion looked most likely to succeed and should have first priority. The Columbia system was not far enough along to evaluate properly. It might become the best method, but no one thought this probable. The second best approach to isotope separation appeared to be the centrifuge. It promised, though, to be about twice as expensive and to require more time after it was built before it could turn out product. The French scientist Halban, Urey reported, was convinced that the best chance for a chain reaction useful for power production lay in employing metallic uranium and heavy water.[71]

Fully as significant as Urey's report was the thinking of Lawrence and Compton on the possibilities of element 94. Early in December, Lawrence sent Compton a letter reporting that measurements by Kennedy and Wahl at Berkeley indicated a spontaneous-fission rate in 94 no higher than in uranium 235. This was heartening, and Lawrence emphasized that 94 might prove the shortest route to a weapon. Compton saw Conant and Bush and made a strong case over lunch at the Cosmos Club for the chain reaction in natural uranium. After convincing them the objective was a bomb and not power, he won their support.[72]

Lawrence had suggested the importance of 94, but his primary concern was an electromagnetic process for separating isotopes. On his own initiative, first with laboratory funds and then with a grant from the Research Corporation, he had diverted some of his best men from the 60-inch and 184-inch cyclotrons and assigned them to converting the older 37-inch unit. Briggs promised financial support and sent Nier out to Berkeley to help. Nier sent back encouraging reports on the enthusiasm at Berkeley. He was convinced that the Radiation Laboratory would be able to achieve its immediate objective, the preparation of U-235 samples.[73]

In the rush of the first week after Pearl Harbor, Bush completed his plans. In letters of December 13 to Briggs, Murphree, Urey, Compton, and Lawrence he spelled out the details. The Planning Board, Murphree at its head, would be responsible for engineering aspects. It would make engineering planning studies and supervise all pilot-plant experimentation or enlarged laboratory-scale investigations. Its job, in short, was to see that the plans were available when the time came to enter the production phase. The active direction of physical and chemical research would be divided among three program chiefs. Urey would be in charge of separation by both the diffusion and the centrifuge methods and of heavy-water investigations. Lawrence would take responsibility for small-sample preparation, electromagnetic separation methods, and "certain experimentation on certain elements of particular interest involving cyclotron work"—less cryptically, element 94. Compton would be concerned primarily "with the fundamental atomic physics and particularly with the measurement of constants and properties." Translated, this meant his spheres were weapon theory and the chain reaction for producing 94. The S-1 Section would continue under Briggs, and all research chiefs, along with Murphree and Conant, would sit with it. The section would meet frequently to interchange information, review the work of the program chiefs, and co-ordinate the scientific attack.

In the new organization Bush assumed a central role. The Planning Board was to recommend contracts to him as director of OSRD. He would take responsibility for integrating the engineering studies with the fundamental research. Bush would place the contracts for scientific research on the basis of recommendations from S-1, though·it was not expected that the full committee would have to pass on each one. Normally, these would be channeled through Conant. When quick action was required, any program chief could communicate directly with Briggs and Conant and the three make recommendations directly to Bush.[74] This arrangement made Conant, chairman of the National Defense Research Committee, more important than ever, but it left no place for the committee itself. A few days later Bush explained formally to Conant that the entire uranium program would henceforth lie entirely outside the NDRC. He had received "special instructions" which made this desirable. This was a reference to Roosevelt's insistence that policy considerations be restricted, apart from Conant and Bush, to Wallace, Stimson, and Marshall. To continue the uranium program under NDRC auspices would have extended knowledge of the effort to a degree that the President never was willing to permit.[75]

Three days after Bush's letters were sent to Briggs, Murphree, and the program chiefs, a top-level conference called by Wallace reviewed the whole situation, including the reorganization and the report of the National Academy committee. Joining the Vice-President at the Capitol were Stimson, Bush, and Director of the Budget Harold D. Smith, who was there at Wallace's invitation. General Marshall had been called away on other business, and Conant was down with a cold. The entire group felt that the fundamental physics and engineering planning, particularly the construction of pilot plants, should be expedited. (Later, after the conference, Smith offered assurances that if OSRD resources proved too low, he could supply money from funds the President controlled.) Bush stated his view that when full-scale construction started, the Army should take over. To this proposal no one objected. Bush favored assigning a well-qualified officer to the program at once so that he might become thoroughly familiar with it. Finally, Bush saw that all understood that relations with Great Britain on matters of general policy

51

were in the hands of the President and that the existing liaison was of technical and scientific information. This evoked no dissent, but the desirability of a joint Anglo-American plant in Canada was the subject of some discussion.[76]

END OF THE BEGINNING

Now the arrangements were complete. Back in October, Bush had won White House sanction for a full-scale effort to explore the possibilities for an atomic weapon. After a review by top scientists and engineers, he had reorganized the program and marked out the main lines of endeavor. A panel of the President's most trusted advisers had approved the preliminary steps. The time had come to act. On December 18, the full S-1 Section met at the Bureau of Standards to learn the new disposition. The way was open for letting contracts. A start came that day. After hearing Lawrence's plea for large-scale electromagnetic separation, the committee recommended assigning him $400,000.[77]

To achieve this much had been slow and painful. It was easy for younger men to complain that senior scientists and engineers had been slow to comprehend the meaning and potential of fission. It was easy to blame preoccupation with security. While secrecy was imperative in a world already at war, it was sometimes misdirected and self-defeating.

But it was also easy to fail to appreciate the position of men who held high responsibility. No scientist, no engineer held as much as Bush and Conant. Conceivably, they might have moved earlier. But Bush had assumed a tremendous burden in June of 1940: the creation of an entirely new relationship between science and government in the interests of national defense. He had to think of personalities and politics as well as technology. He and Conant had to look at uranium in the light of the entire role that science might play in the emergency. They had to turn a deaf ear to blue-sky talk of nuclear power plants and think of weapons. They had to navigate between the Scylla and Charybdis of excessive pessimism and soaring optimism. They had to set a course by the Pole Star of fact.

Two weeks after Pearl Harbor, all this was ancient history. The United States was at war. The goal Bush and Conant had seen so long was clear to everyone. Gone was the confusion of objectives. Gone too was the old day of leisurely research with its almost mystical faith that society could depend on the largely undirected, unplanned, and capriciously financed efforts of lonely toilers in the scientific vineyards. Gone was the hesitation, so pronounced just two short years before, to spend public money on the theories of a few research men. American science would never be the same. The United States would never be the same. The world would never be the same.

EXPLORING THE ROUTES
TO THE WEAPON

In 1941, Bush and Conant had succeeded in focusing atomic energy research on the development of a weapon for the present war. They had created the necessary organization under the OSRD and had obtained the President's approval of their plans to investigate the possible routes to a weapon.

Now the fate of S-1 rested with the working scientists and engineers led by the three program chiefs and the chairman of the Planning Board. Few men seemed better qualified for this assignment. Compton and Lawrence were accomplished directors of research enterprises; Urey, a scientist of extraordinary prestige; Murphree, a seasoned executive in industrial engineering. But their task was not easy. Devising an atomic weapon would be difficult enough. Doing it quickly would take all the experience and ingenuity at their command.

MAN WITH A MISSION

Arthur Compton left the meeting of the S-1 Committee in Lyman Briggs's office on December 18, 1941, fired with a missionary zeal. He was responsible for the theoretical studies and experimental measurements necessary for producing element 94 and the bomb. Important as these were, however, the demonstration of the chain reaction was far more urgent. If the production of 94 was to receive fair consideration, Compton knew he would have to prove its feasibility within six months.[1]

The next day, Compton discussed his job in greater detail with Bush and Conant. For research at Columbia and Princeton on exponential piles and measurements of physical constants, he would need eighty men and $340,000 for the next six months. Corresponding figures for Chicago were fifty-eight men and $278,000. These projects, plus the preparation of uranium

235 and plutonium samples at Berkeley, added up to 150 men and $650,000. On top of this, Compton wanted another $500,000 for pile materials. A few months earlier, the same request would have seemed fantastic. Now, after the momentous events of the previous ten days, Bush and Conant thought the plan reasonable.

Back in Chicago, Compton faced the stern realities of organization. Unlike Lawrence and Urey, he did not have a centralized project on his own campus. The news of the Hahn-Strassmann discovery had spawned hurried studies of nuclear reactions at a dozen universities, several of which were deeply engaged in experiments on the possibilities of a chain reaction. So diffuse were these activities that Compton could never concentrate them all in one laboratory, but some degree of consolidation was mandatory. Before the Christmas holidays, Compton invited the research teams at Columbia, Princeton, and California to a planning session in Chicago.

The Chicago meetings beginning on January 3, 1942, demonstrated the need for organization.[2] Compton found the several groups in disagreement even on the results of research already completed. The physicists soon reconciled the discrepancies in experimental data concerning the pile but found it harder to agree on specifications and procurement methods. As for future assignments, Compton could do little more than approve for the time being the projects already started at the various sites. Fermi would build a new exponential pile at Columbia. Allison would construct a pile using beryllium as a moderator at Chicago. Wigner and the Princeton group would concentrate on the theory of the chain reaction, and Oppenheimer would direct paper studies of the fast-neutron reaction at Berkeley. Norman Hilberry and Richard L. Doan would help Compton organize the project with special attention to procurement.

A second meeting, at Columbia on January 18, went more smoothly than the Chicago sessions.[3] The discussion on Sunday morning rambled, but it finally drifted back to events at Columbia. The group formed by Robert Bacher at Cornell in 1941 had, since the Chicago session, discovered an error in the intensity ratings assigned to some of Fermi's neutron sources. As a result, Fermi had underestimated the poisoning effect of boron. The corrected values now indicated much more rigid purity specifications for pile graphite and uranium. The Princeton group also had some interesting theoretical points to offer. Quickly assimilating the new information, Fermi explained its effect on his plans for a new exponential pile.

After lunch, the physicists inspected the Columbia pile experiments in Schermerhorn Laboratory and returned to Pupin, where Compton outlined his time schedule:

By July 1, 1942, to determine whether
a chain reaction was possible.

By January, 1943, to achieve the first
chain reaction.

By January, 1944, to extract the first
element 94 from uranium.

By January, 1945, to have a bomb.

With this timetable no one could quarrel, but there were differences of opinion about Compton's efforts to procure uranium metal. He explained that with Bush's permission he had written the members of the National Academy committee for their advice on purchasing thirty tons of metal for pile experiments. He had also approached Murphree, whose Planning Board was responsible for procuring materials. Szilard, always impatient with bureaucratic machinery, suggested bypassing the Planning Board. Bush settled the question the next day in Washington. He would approve the thirty-ton purchase, but Murphree would retain the procurement function.[4]

55

As often happened, Compton's hardest decision had human as well as technical implications. Late in the afternoon, the Columbia meeting had disintegrated into a free-for-all discussion of the merits of centralizing research at one site. As he listened to the argument, Compton realized he would have to decide soon. The issue was already distracting the scientists. After returning to Chicago, Compton analyzed the technical considerations with Lawrence. They agreed that as a minimum all research on the chain reaction should be conducted at one site. There would be added advantages in centralizing all work on producing uranium metal and separating element 94 from irradiated uranium. It seemed hardly practical, however, to concentrate all the basic nuclear research already under way in the universities.

Since concentration of the entire project was impossible, the solution was to find the best combination of personnel and equipment. Compton and Lawrence first concluded that Berkeley was the best choice mainly because it would be impossible to move the giant cyclotron magnets. Objections from Washington and Columbia reopened the question, which was not settled until Saturday afternoon, January 24, when Compton, sick in bed with influenza, decided to bring the Columbia and Princeton groups to Chicago.[5] The transfer of men and equipment would occur over a period of months so as not to disrupt experiments already in progress. Most of Fermi's group would not come until spring, when, Compton hoped, experiments would demonstrate a favorable value of k.

In the final days of January, 1942, Compton organized the Metallurgical Laboratory and authorized experiments at Chicago, Columbia, and Princeton.[6] Until other groups could be moved to Chicago, Compton found adequate working space by appropriating most of Eckart Hall, part of the large cyclotron room, and the area under the West Stands of Stagg Field. To co-ordinate the dispersed activities of the laboratory, Compton designated Doan as director with Fermi, Allison, and Wigner as co-ordinators of the research, experimental, and theoretical aspects of the chain reaction. Breit would continue to co-ordinate fast-neutron research at a half-dozen universities, while Szilard would be in charge of the supply of materials. For the time being, Seaborg would keep his research on plutonium chemistry at Berkeley. With this organization and the small supply of uranium oxide and graphite Compton hoped to show by April 15 whether a chain reaction would in fact be possible.

Initially, Compton was relying on the exponential pile which Allison was constructing in the racquets court under the West Stands. The stacking of high-purity graphite and uranium-oxide units continued during February until Allison had a block ninety inches on a side resting on a twelve-inch wooden base. Two horizontal channels at right angles in the bottom four inches of the pile permitted the insertion of radium-beryllium neutron sources. By the first of March, Allison was ready to begin the complicated measurements which might indicate the possibilities of a chain reaction.[7]

What the results would be, no one knew. But even Compton did not let his enthusiasm hide the realities. On February 10, he urged Conant to order one or two tons of heavy water and a kilogram of uranium 235 in case the experiment with natural uranium and graphite failed.

HOPES FOR A SHORT CUT

Even more spectacular than the pile project was Lawrence's electromagnetic method of separating the 235 isotope. Late in November, 1941, Lawrence had assembled a special task force of his best scientists and technicians to convert the 37-inch cyclotron. The flat cylindrical vacuum tank was rolled out of the eight-inch gap between the magnet poles, and the cyclotron equipment within the tank was replaced by hastily built components of a mass spectrograph. Controls for the ion source, which closely resembled Nier's, pierced one side of the tank. Electrical heaters vaporized solid uranium chloride in the source. The vapor then flowed to a second chamber, where electrons from a heated cathode ionized the gas. A slit two inches long and 0.04 inch wide permitted a ribbon of positively charged ions to escape into the vacuum tank. An electrode with a very large voltage just in front of the chamber accelerated the ion beam. In a plane perpendicular to the magnetic field, the beam would follow a circular path about two feet in diameter to the receiver on the opposite side of the vacuum tank. After traveling through a 180-degree path, the heavier 238 ions could be expected to hit the receiver a small fraction of an inch farther from the center of the tank than would the 235 ions. Between the source and receiver, a movable shield with a narrow defining slit permitted the operator to select the best part of the beam. The receiver was a small metal cylinder with a long slot in one side. The operator could control the position of the slot so that the beam would pass through it and hit the collector.[8] (Figure 1)

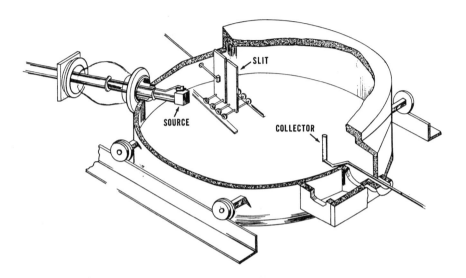

Figure 1. The first mass-spectrograph components in the 37-inch cyclotron tank, November, 1941.

When the device was first operated on December 2, 1941, a very small beam of about five microamperes reached the receiver. Lawrence was elated. The beam was ten times as large as Nier's. Although only a small fraction of the vaporized charge was ionized, at least half the ions leaving the source were singly charged, the best type for isotope separation. The succeeding experiments in December were largely attempts to attain stable operation. Most of the receivers were designed to measure beam current and not to collect separated isotopes, but before the end of the month beams as large as fifty microamperes showed a small enrichment to about 3-per-cent uranium 235. This performance was hardly significant even for the production of samples in microgram quantities, but there were important implications for the future. The experiment showed that Lawrence's hunch had been correct: the space charge would not spoil the beam. Apparently the beam ionized enough residual gas in the vacuum tank to neutralize much of this effect.

It was also evident that with a few simple refinements and adjustments, the apparatus could produce the uranium 235 samples for both American and British experiments. With OSRD support, this hope was realized early in 1942. By January 14, a nine-hour run with a beam of fifty microamperes produced eighteen micrograms of material enriched to 25-per-cent uranium 235. Improved techniques and a larger ion source made it possible early in February to get good resolution of a beam as large as 1,400 microamperes. By the middle of the month, three samples of about seventy-five micrograms each, containing 30-per-cent uranium 235, had been prepared for the Metallurgical Laboratory and the British.[9]

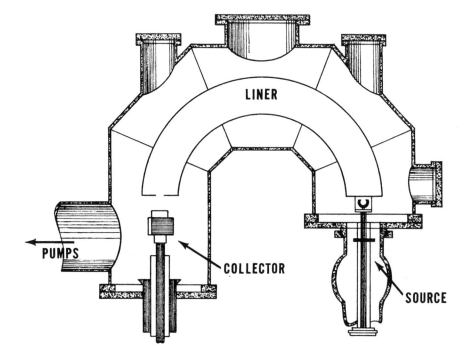

Figure 2. The first "calutron:" the original C-shaped tank in the 37-inch cyclotron, February, 1942.

In part, more people were needed to exploit fully other methods of using electromagnetic forces to separate isotopes. Theoretically, if a uniform kinetic energy was applied to an ionized gas containing two different isotopes, the lighter ions would travel a greater distance than the heavier in a given time. A series of very high speed shutters or high frequency electrodes at precise intervals along the ion path could trap one isotope and permit the second to continue to the target. This technique eliminated the need for a sharply focused beam; in fact, the ionized gas could radiate in all directions. Once the ions were in motion, they could move by free flight to the target; the difficult process of bending them into a precise circular path could be eliminated.

In 1941, Lawrence's group had already built a linear chopper that used mechanical shutters geared up to very high speeds. Other groups took advantage of recent accomplishments in electronics, particularly in the development of very-high-frequency, high-power oscillator tubes. At Princeton, a group under Henry D. Smyth and Robert R. Wilson developed a device which they named the "isotron." Using the principle of the klystron tube, they accelerated a cylindrical ion beam and then bunched the isotopes by applying a very-high-frequency voltage to a set of grids part way down the linear tube. Lloyd P. Smith and others at Cornell studied a radial source using the principle of the magnetron tube. In the devices they built at Berkeley in the early months of 1942, the ion source was in the center of a circular vacuum tank. Electrodes surrounding the source accelerated the ions radially into a magnetic field. The heavier ions would be collected at the periphery of the tank; the lighter ions would eventually return to collector plates in the center. An elaboration of the magnetron separator was the ionic centrifuge proposed by Joseph Slepian at Princeton. Experiments with all of these methods demonstrated that they could separate isotopes, especially of the lighter elements, where the relative difference in weights was large.[10] No one method, however, seemed to have the capability of the mass spectrograph to produce large quantities of uranium 235 in the short time available.

59

Even as the operation of the unit in the 37-inch magnet improved during February, Lawrence was preparing a better model. He planned to replace the cyclotron tank with a new vacuum chamber shaped like the letter C to conform to the semicircular path of the ion beam. (Figure 2) The smaller volume might eliminate some of the persistent leaks in the 37-inch system. A new ion source capable of producing a ten-milliampere beam replaced the original one-milliampere unit. This was installed in one end of the C, while the other end held the collector. In contrast to the small probe-type collectors used in the cylindrical tank, the new receivers had a boxlike appearance. (Figure 3) Two narrow slits carefully machined in copper or tungsten received the beams, which penetrated pockets within the box where they were trapped by the bevelled edges of the openings. To prevent the high-energy beam from melting the components, the collector contained a water cooling system and was insulated to operate at high voltage. A water-cooled copper liner inside the tank between the source and the receiver was insulated so that it could be maintained at the high negative voltage of the accelerating electrode and thus keep the ion path free of electric fields which would distort the beam.

The new unit, now called a "calutron," was installed in the 37-inch magnet in February. Within a week it was producing somewhat more than rated capacity. As Lawrence excitedly told Bush by telephone, the new unit measured up to expectations in every way.[11] He was already planning to build a 100-milliampere source and had broached with the university administration his long-cherished idea of using the 184-inch magnet for the great cyclotron to provide the field for ten calutrons, each rated at one-tenth of an ampere.

Lawrence's progress had indeed been spectacular, but even more impressive was his style. His daring, courage, and irrepressible optimism were contagious. He inspired his staff to sweat over tedious jobs with no thought of time, his superiors in the university to cut red tape, and his seniors in Washington to see heady visions of an early weapon. When Bush visited Berkeley in February, he found the atmosphere in the laboratory "stimulating" and "refreshing," and he thought it advisable to warn Lawrence that he should not let his group's enthusiasm for this project slow up efforts along other lines.[12]

60

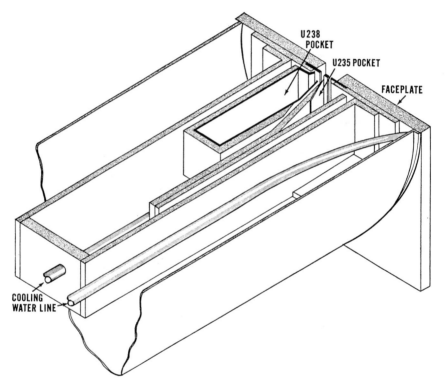

Figure 3. An early box-type collector for the 37-inch calutron with separate pockets for the two beams, April, 1942.

BRIEF REIGN OF OPTIMISM

The excitement at Berkeley was the inspiration for the special report which Bush sent to the President on March 9, 1942. After surveying the prospects and uncertainties of other production processes, Bush saw that recent work at Berkeley might mean a short cut to the bomb. "If full success is attained in certain crucial experiments now under way, there is a possibility of production of fully practicable quantities of material by the summer of 1943, with a time savings of six months or more." [13] He also noted that the United States was strong in research on electromagnetic processes.

Bush placed his greatest emphasis on what he saw as new reasons for being optimistic about the power and efficiency of nuclear weapons. Here he relied on a report from Arthur Compton. In fact, Bush chose simply to translate Compton's report into the layman's language which the President would understand. The size of the critical mass now appeared close to the lower end of the broad scale suggested in the report of the National Academy committee. As Compton explained, Norman P. Heydenburg, an expert in neutron measurements at the Carnegie Institution, had discovered with the aid of better samples from Nier that more than 80 per cent of the fissions produced by fast neutrons occurred in uranium 235. This meant that the fission cross section for the 235 isotope was near the middle of the range estimated in the Academy report. New cross-section data from Breit and Oppenheimer gave a critical mass for a sphere of uranium 235 between 2.5 and 5.0 kilograms, compared to the 2- to 100-kilogram range in the Academy report.

61

Bush also thought the efficiency of the fission weapon would be greater than that suggested in the Academy report. Oppenheimer's calculations showed that 6 per cent of the theoretical energy available would be liberated in the detonation. This could be compared to 2 per cent in the Academy report. Because the mass of a nuclear weapon would be much less than that of a TNT bomb, the destructive effect of the energy liberated would be only about one-tenth that of a conventional weapon of the same power. In a footnote to the Academy report, Compton had suggested that the destructive effect might be much lower. In January, Bush had asked Kistiakowsky to re-examine the data and both were now convinced that the higher value was correct.[14] Therefore Bush felt it justifiable to tell the President in layman's terms that the "estimates of the efficiency are now higher, by a factor of three, than they were at the time of the previous report." In other words, the bomb might have a destructive effect of 2,000 tons of TNT, as against the 600 tons estimated earlier.

Bush was also more confident about detonating the weapon. The Academy committee had doubted whether the chain reaction could be delayed until the fissionable material was completely assembled. As Compton admitted, he could not answer with certainty until physicists had determined the amount of spontaneous fission in uranium 235. But the smaller critical mass of the weapon now estimated by Oppenheimer would make possible a shorter assembly time and thus reduce the probability of predetonation.

Bush might have added another reason for optimism: the strong possibility that element 94, even more fissionable than uranium 235, might be produced in the chain reaction. Yet he omitted this possibility which fired the imagination of Compton and his staff at the Metallurgical Laboratory. Probably Bush hesitated because the chain reaction had not yet been demonstrated. However radiant were Compton's predictions of the future, they somehow seemed pale and elusive beside the solid accomplishment of Lawrence's super mass spectrograph, the gaseous-diffusion process, and the centrifuge. Certainly Bush and Conant could not be accused of taking an overly conservative position. Only in a few minor instances did Bush scale down for the President an estimate made by his scientific advisers. In most cases, he took the more optimistic position and added a note of caution that the "estimates depend upon the calculations of theoretical physicists, based on difficult measurements on exceedingly small quantities of materials." Even these caveats scarcely conveyed to the reader the extent to which the conclusions of the report were based upon great masses of postulation held together by a thin thread of experimental fact. In terms of the new information acquired, there was little justification for the March 9, 1942, report. It reflected not so much new knowledge as a greater confidence in the conclusions hastily drawn in November, 1941, and a growing optimism that fissionable material could be produced in a relatively short time. As Bush told the President, the project was rapidly approaching the pilot-plant stage and he believed that by summer the most promising methods could be selected and production plants started.

THE PLANNING BOARD

The work of Eger V. Murphree's Planning Board was indeed prosaic when compared to the excitement at Berkeley, Columbia, and Chicago. Murphree's assignment, however, was no less important to Bush and Conant, who saw something reassuring about the fact that isotopes had been separated in the laboratory long before uranium fission had been discovered. With their guidance, Murphree selected for his committee four outstanding engineers, two of whom had previously been associated with S-1. Both Warren K. Lewis and L. Warrington Chubb had served on the National Academy committee. Chubb, as director of Westinghouse Research Laboratories, had also been responsible for experiments on high-speed centrifuges for isotope separation. Percival C. Keith, a dynamic young Texan who like Murphree studied under Lewis, had gained practical experience with several engineering firms since leaving Cambridge. As vice-president of the M. W. Kellogg Company, he had already tried gaseous diffusion to separate hydrogen from methane. One of the nation's largest chemical engineering corporations, Union Carbide & Carbon, was represented on the board by George O. Curme, a specialist in hydrocarbons who had served with Lewis' chemistry section in the NDRC.

With the direct approach of the engineer, the Planning Board took up its duties early in January, 1942. Its assignment was to determine whether the table-top methods used at Columbia and the University of Virginia could serve as industrial processes for separating uranium isotopes on a massive scale. At their meeting on January 7, Murphree and his associates saw their job in four parts.[15] The first was to build at least one experimental centrifuge and one gaseous-diffusion unit of industrial size for engineering tests. The second was to design pilot plants which would use a number of separative units to demonstrate the feasibility of the process. The third task was to secure adequate supplies of uranium oxide, metal, and hexafluoride. A fourth concern was to produce a modest supply of heavy water for the nuclear pile in the event graphite proved an unsatisfactory moderator.

GASEOUS DIFFUSION AND THE CENTRIFUGE

What the Planning Board knew about gaseous diffusion had come from Kistiakowsky's investigations and from research at Columbia University in 1940 and 1941. By the latter part of that period, Dunning, Booth, Slack, and others were producing and testing barrier materials, including naturally porous substances, various metal alloys, and metal powders.[16] They had tested samples no larger than a coin in laboratory equipment that separated carbon dioxide from hydrogen. Similar samples they subjected to a stream of hexafluoride gas to check corrosion resistance and flow. Before the end of 1941, the Dunning team had tried to achieve some separation of the uranium isotopes, but they did not have a pump even of laboratory size which could operate with the corrosive gas. By the time the Planning Board first met, Dunning could report no positive results.[17]

63

At its first meeting the board approved research at Columbia on a single gaseous-diffusion unit and an engineering study of the process. Keith would direct a study of a pilot plant at Kellogg and would analyze the requirements for a large commercial plant. But Keith soon found he would have to develop components before he could start pilot-plant design. In the following months he sent Kellogg men to Columbia to investigate barrier development and the design of separative units. Keith also had to work from the ground up on high-speed pumps which would operate with the process gas over long periods without leaks. He supplemented research on pumps by Henry A. Boorse and others at Columbia by contracts with major pump manufacturers.[18] Columbia continued more fundamental studies on the corrosion resistance of materials and the properties of potential seal and lubricating substances under the OSRD contract. The result was that Keith was not ready to give serious thought to pilot-plant design until the late spring of 1942.

Engineering development of the centrifuge had started even before the first meeting of the Planning Board. When, at the time of his appointment in December, Murphree learned of the Columbia development contract with Westinghouse, he requested the company to submit a proposal for additional studies. At its first meeting the board recommended that Bush authorize

Westinghouse to obtain aluminum forgings and parts for twenty-four additional centrifuges to be installed in a pilot plant. To expedite matters, Murphree agreed to undertake the necessary engineering studies for the plant at the Standard Oil Development Company.

As engineers, the members of the Planning Board could see the difficulties in scaling up the centrifuge process to a production capacity of significance to the war effort. The basic design for a single unit was difficult enough. Even if one such unit were successful, there was no certainty that a plant would be feasible on the scale contemplated. Urey and Cohen estimated that, for a plant producing a kilogram per day of very pure uranium 235, they would need between forty and fifty thousand centrifuges with rotors one meter in length. The possibility of keeping so many high-speed units in continuous operation seemed almost incredible. The Columbia group estimated that if four-meter rotors could be built, the number of centrifuges could be reduced to something on the order of ten thousand,[19] but the longer rotors would be more difficult to accelerate through the critical vibration frequencies. Westinghouse investigated the long rotor during the spring of 1942.

A second possibility was to build a smaller centrifuge plant, at least initially. A plant producing a hundred grams per day would require only about six thousand one-meter centrifuges, which Westinghouse estimated they could produce at a rate of a thousand per month, beginning six months after the Government placed the order. Late in January, when Lawrence was troubled about the need for uranium 235 even in small quantities, he had urged the S-1 Section to support the construction of the smaller centrifuge plant. To this appeal Compton added the plea in his February 10 report for at least one kilogram of uranium 235 in the event a chain reaction proved impossible with normal uranium. Late in February, the board recommended engineering studies at Westinghouse on the hundred-gram plant, but in view of more fundamental problems encountered during the winter, the decision had little significance.[20]

The fact was that in both gaseous diffusion and the centrifuge, engineering development was going to take time. In gaseous diffusion Keith found it possible to concentrate research, for a time at least, on metal barriers. However, variables in the process and materials were so great that he could not think of specific plans for large-scale barrier production. Uranium isotopes had been separated only a few times on a laboratory scale with very low enrichment of uranium 235, and the design and construction of an industrial-size separator was just beginning five months after Kellogg started work. Results were no more encouraging with the centrifuge. Beams at the University of Virginia had completed two runs with uranium hexafluoride through a one-meter tube of the simple flow-through type. The degree of enrichment, from 0.72- to 0.73-per-cent uranium 235, was said to be consistent with theory, but was too small to indicate definite results.[21] At

Bayonne, New Jersey, Westinghouse had hardly begun to solve the problems of designing and constructing a single centrifuge of industrial size. In the meantime, the company had to delay work on four-meter rotors and the twenty-four units for the pilot plant.

PROCUREMENT OF MATERIALS

The Planning Board's responsibilities for procuring key materials included the purchase of uranium oxide. As the board surveyed the potential sources in January, 1942, the situation seemed favorable. The largest readily available supply was the 1,200 tons of Belgian ore stored on Staten Island. The Belgians also had 100 tons of oxide at the Port Hope refinery operated by the Eldorado Gold Mines on the north shore of Lake Ontario. Eldorado had 300 tons of its own concentrate at Port Hope and could produce 300 tons per year from its mine on Great Bear Lake near the Arctic Circle. The only sources in the United States were on the Colorado Plateau, where at least 500 tons of oxide remained in sludges from the vanadium refineries operated by the Vanadium Corporation of America and the U. S. Vanadium Corporation, an affiliate of the Union Carbide and Carbon Corporation. The board estimated in January it would need not more than 250 tons of oxide per year to operate a plant producing one kilogram of uranium 235 per day. Thus, unless other demands arose, not more than 150 tons of oxide would be required before the summer of 1944. This amount was small in comparison with the more than 2,000 tons then known to exist in North America. In February, the board recommended purchasing 200 tons of uranium oxide from Eldorado. From this amount, 45 tons would meet Compton's requirements. The purchase would also insure operation of the Eldorado mine in the summer of 1942.[22]

65

At the time the Planning Board was established, virtually no uranium metal meeting nuclear specifications had been produced in the United States. The Lamp Division of the Westinghouse Electric and Manufacturing Company had prepared small quantities for speciality items, but the process involved a photochemical reaction of the uranium oxide with potassium fluoride, which could be accomplished only by sunlight. With large vats installed on the roof of its plant at Bloomfield, New Jersey, Westinghouse estimated that it would be difficult to produce more than one ton of uranium metal per month, even under ideal weather conditions.[23]

A second and more promising source of metal was a process developed some years earlier by Peter P. Alexander of Metal Hydrides, Inc. In 1941, Alexander had succeeded in producing uranium metal in pound quantities in his plant at Beverly, Massachusetts, by reacting uranium oxide with calcium hydride. The process seemed susceptible to large-scale production, and the Columbia laboratory in January, 1942, had ordered six new furnaces for the

Beverly plant. The process had its disadvantages. First, the product was finely divided powder which was highly pyrophoric and therefore very difficult to melt and cast. Second, as a result of Compton's January 18 meeting in New York, Murphree lowered the permissible boron content in the metal from four to two parts per million. The calcium hydride which Alexander had already procured was now unusable. The distillation of extremely pure calcium was finally achieved with help from Clement J. Rodden of the National Bureau of Standards and from the Union Carbide & Carbon Corporation after many months of experimentation.

Final development of the process had to wait until new equipment could be procured for large-scale production in the two plants. Westinghouse did not receive the equipment for its Bloomfield plant until late in April, and Metal Hydrides could not install the last of nineteen new furnaces until the middle of May.[24] In the meantime, the two companies could produce metal only in pound quantities rather than in the tons needed for the pile program.

Uranium was also needed in large quantities as hexafluoride, the only stable compound known to exist as a fluid at ordinary temperatures. This unique property made its use mandatory in the centrifuge, gaseous-diffusion, and thermal-diffusion processes, despite its many disadvantages. Gram quantities of hexafluoride had been produced as early as 1931 for Aston's gaseous-diffusion experiments by fluorinating small samples of uranium metal. A more practical process resulted in 1940 from Philip Abelson's work at the Naval Research Laboratory on the thermal-diffusion process.[25] Abelson found he could make the material more easily and safely by fluorinating uranium tetrafluoride rather than metallic uranium. His process was much more economical in the consumption of fluorine and made possible the use of natural uranium compounds which were easily converted to the tetrafluoride. Since early 1941, Abelson's small plant at the National Bureau of Standards had provided all the hexafluoride for the isotope-separation experiments at Columbia, Virginia, and the Navy laboratory. Before the end of 1941, Gunn and Abelson had placed a small order with the Harshaw Chemical Company at Cleveland, Ohio, to acquaint it with the process. The Planning Board supplemented this early in 1942 with a contract to build and operate a pilot plant producing ten pounds of hexafluoride per day. By spring, the Harshaw plant was operating, and du Pont was also experimenting with the process. Both companies expected soon to produce hexafluoride on a limited scale and then rapidly expand production.[26]

The Planning Board had also to honor Compton's request for one or two tons of heavy water. Both Urey at Columbia and Hugh S. Taylor at Princeton had already investigated production methods. Knowing that Taylor had one of the few laboratory supplies of heavy water produced in the United States, Urey had invited him early in the summer of 1941 to study large-scale production techniques. Taylor experimented first with a hydrogen-water exchange process at Princeton. In such a plant, there would be an advantage in using hydrogen produced by the electrolytic process, which in

66

itself achieved a small enrichment of the heavy isotope. A British subject, Taylor knew that the Consolidated Mining & Smelting Company at Trail, British Columbia, was the largest producer of electrolytic hydrogen in North America. Before the end of 1941, he visited Trail and convinced the Consolidated management that it would be practical to operate the heavy-water equipment as a loop in the Trail ammonia plant. Thus, the heavy-hydrogen isotope would be extracted from the hydrogen supply to the ammonia plant without any appreciable consumption of hydrogen.

Experiments with the exchange process showed by early 1942 that it would work well, but entirely too slowly to produce heavy water in the quantities required. After studying other processes until spring, Taylor suggested using steam at atmospheric pressure in place of water in the exchange process. This idea proved feasible. Standard Oil of Louisiana studied the process in its pilot plant, and the Princeton and Columbia laboratories turned to the further development of a catalyst. Taylor discovered that the best catalyst was platinum on charcoal. Platinum not only worked well but was easily prepared. The valuable metal could be recovered simply by burning off the charcoal. In May, Taylor prepared cost estimates for constructing a heavy-water plant at Trail.[27]

67

For all their work, the Planning Board could conclude by May, 1942, that the road ahead for isotope separation would indeed be long. Engineering studies of the two main approaches had not revealed any short cuts comparable to that which Lawrence anticipated in the electromagnetic method. Instead, the investigations authorized by the board uncovered many problems which previously had not received attention. Five months of experiments had failed to produce a single operating centrifuge or gaseous-diffusion unit of practical size. The procurement of key materials had also proved to be time-consuming. By the first of May, the board had obtained no additional supplies of uranium oxide, no uranium metal in more than pound quantities, and no more than experimental amounts of hexafluoride. Conversion of the Trail plant for heavy water production was still in the early blueprint stage. To be sure, it seemed that all these uncertainties could be overcome in time, but time was the most precious commodity of all. In the midst of the war, when prompt decisions were essential, Nature itself seemed to be concealing the facts on which selection of a separation process should be based. The gnawing question was, how long could the decision be postponed?

MOVING TOWARD DECISION

While Murphree and the Planning Board were struggling with isotope separation in the spring of 1942, Conant was occupied with decisions on the pile project. In addition to the ever-present question of feasibility, Conant was forced to reconsider using heavy water as a pile moderator.

Strictly on the basis of theory, there was no question that heavy water was a better moderator than graphite, but the fact remained that nothing but graphite was available for the exponential pile experiments. Compton's February request for a few tons of heavy water at least acknowledged the possibility that he might need the more expensive material as a substitute for graphite. When Simon and Halban visited the United States a few weeks later, they predicted that a natural-uranium pile would require heavy water as a moderator. They suggested that Halban bring to the United States the small amount of heavy water which he had smuggled from France. Added to their appeal was the voice of Harold Urey, the indefatigable champion of the heavy-water approach.

On April 1, Conant sat down with Briggs and Compton to settle the question. He had to admit that heavy water had attractive features. If five tons were available, they could build a small pile to produce a few hundred grams of element 94 in a short time. If thirty tons were on hand, there would be no question of designing at once a pile which would produce a kilogram of 94 per week. But the point was that no heavy water was then to be had in quantity. Murphree estimated that five tons could not be produced until June, 1943; thirty tons, not until July, 1945. Conant also felt certain that Halban's small stock of heavy water could have no effect on the decision. Thus, the group decided they would use heavy water only as a substitute for graphite. As a protection against that contingency, the process would be developed on a small scale.[28]

Perhaps interest in heavy water would have been greater had it not been for encouraging experiments with the graphite piles. None of the exponential experiments had yet shown a value of k greater than 1, but they were close enough to make Compton confident of ultimate success. By the middle of March, 1942, Allison's experiments with the first Chicago pile had given a value of $0.94 \pm .02$. Then he shipped the neutron sources to Columbia, where Fermi had constructed a new experiment.[29] The Columbia pile was an eight-foot cube of graphite in which Fermi embedded pressed cylinders of uranium oxide about three inches in diameter and three inches high arranged in an eight-inch lattice spacing.[30] He had shifted from cubes to cylinders to gain certain theoretical advantages. Since he suspected that water vapor in the pile was swallowing up neutrons, he hoped to increase the value of k simply by extracting from the pile as much water vapor as possible. This he accomplished by preheating the uranium cylinders prior to installation and then by heating and evacuating the entire assembled pile. With these precautions, Fermi could for the first time report a k value greater than 0.9 for his graphite pile. In Compton's mind, the Fermi experiment demonstrated his contention that the all-important value of k would increase just by refining experiments and using better materials.

After his conversations with Compton, Conant reported to Bush that he found the pile project "well worth supporting, at least until June 1." He recommended additional expenditures totaling more than $250,000. This did not mean, however, that the OSRD would concentrate all effort on the pile project. To Conant, it was equally probable that by July 1 Lawrence's progress would justify authorization of a full-scale electromagnetic plant. Would it be prudent to spend another $1.5 million to demonstrate the feasibility of producing element 94? Would there be sufficient reason at that time for eliminating the gaseous-diffusion and centrifuge projects? And, if there were no exceptional developments in any of the projects within the next few weeks, was it possible to consider continuing all of them into the enormously expensive phase of engineering development and construction?

The day of reckoning on all these questions was May 23. Conant asked the program chiefs to meet with him, Briggs, and Murphree for a last-minute review of all the projects before they made a recommendation. As the day approached, Conant could see the outcome, and he was not pleased.[31] In place of the two methods selected for engineering development in December, there were now at least four on equal footing and a number of other ideas which had to be considered as long shots. All would be entering the expensive pilot-plant phase within the next six months. Furthermore, to save time, the production plants should be ready for design and construction before the pilot plants were finished. But to proceed with all approaches would involve the commitment of at least $500 million, to say nothing of the expenditure of scarce equipment, scientific manpower, and materials.

69

The real question in Conant's mind was whether S-1 was sufficiently important to the war effort to warrant a commitment of this size. If, on the one hand, the new weapon was not actually a determining, but a supplemental factor, there was no compelling reason for haste or for risking so much on the bomb. If, on the other hand, the possession of the new weapon in sufficient quantities would be a determining factor in the war, then it was paramount that the United States have it first. If there were five possible approaches to the bomb rather than two, was there not a greater probability that the Germans eventually would succeed? Since Germany, Britain, and the United States had started from the same point in 1939, was it not possible that the Germans had proceeded at least as far as the Western powers? In view of known German interest in nuclear research and the slow start of the United States program, was it not even possible that the Germans were in the lead? If all these questions could be answered in the affirmative, then every minute counted. It would no longer be a matter of which process was technically most promising, but which could produce a bomb first. By eliminating two or three methods at once, one might unconsciously be choosing the slowest. To proceed with all approaches would involve an awesome decision, but if the program chiefs could not come up with a clear-cut choice, what other decision was possible?

On May 23, a cool spring Saturday, the leaders of the S-1 Section assembled in Conant's office. Briggs, Murphree, Compton, Lawrence, and Urey listened as Conant presented the committee's assignment from Bush.[32]

They were to outline a program for each approach, covering both development and construction, together with a budget for the next six months and the ensuing year. They were to recommend how many programs should be continued and how rapidly these could be expanded, on the assumption that an all-out effort would be made, regardless of cost. They were to consider which parts of the program should be eliminated in the event of a limitation on men, money, and materials.

The logical starting point was to review recent progress. Murphree said the Planning Board was unable to draw any conclusions about the relative merits of gaseous diffusion and the centrifuge.[33] Their studies seemed to indicate an investment advantage for the diffusion process, but this might disappear if the enrichment now indicated per separator unit was not realized in a full-scale plant. They could make no sound conclusions without pilot plants, which could not produce results before the end of 1942. The board believed that if the production from a hundred-gram-per-day plant was essential, work on a centrifuge plant of that size should start at once. If such small quantities of uranium 235 were not absolutely necessary, development should start at once on a one-kilogram plant. Meanwhile, development would continue on the centrifuge and gaseous-diffusion pilot plants and on a full-scale diffusion plant.

Lawrence reported that the first calutron in the great cyclotron magnet would begin to operate in June. Then, as Lawrence phrased it in his own optimistic way, he would be in a position to say that there were no fundamental difficulties in building a large-scale electromagnetic plant. The jump from laboratory equipment to a full-scale plant was great, but Lawrence was confident that by fall the giant magnet containing a number of calutrons could be producing four grams of uranium 235 per day. If parallel development could start at once on a hundred-gram-per-day plant, the first product would appear in one year.

Compton was not to be outdone. He admitted that to gain the tremendous psychological advantage of first possession of the bomb, the nation might have to rely on isotope separation. But for quantity production the pile seemed to hold the greatest promise. There was no longer any question in his mind that the pile would work. Not ten days before the meeting, Fermi had obtained a value of k as high as 0.995 with essentially the same configuration he had used in April. Most of this increase had resulted from better experimental techniques and the refinement of calculations. Could anyone doubt there would be an additional improvement when high-purity graphite and uranium oxide were used, to say nothing of uranium metal? Purer materials were expected within a matter of weeks. If all went well, the pilot plant would be in operation before the end of 1942; gram quantities of element 94 would be available by April, 1943; and some kilograms before the end of that year. From a rough assumption of the amount of element 94 per bomb, Compton estimated he could produce bombs in numbers in 1944.

70

Urey and Murphree then reported on the production of heavy water as a back-up for the graphite pile. They estimated that studies on catalysts at Standard Oil of Louisiana would continue into 1943 and with good priority ratings they could complete the Trail plant about the end of 1942.

In the afternoon session, Briggs, Murphree, Lawrence, Compton, and Urey knuckled down to formulating recommendations, which Conant drafted on yellow tablet paper.[34] As an all-out effort, they recommended: construction of the hundred-gram-per-day centrifuge plant by January, 1944, at a cost of $38 million; construction of the gaseous-diffusion pilot plant and engineering work on a production plant at more than $2 million in the coming year and an undetermined amount thereafter; construction of a hundred-gram-per-day electromagnetic plant, to be completed by September, 1943, at $12 million; one or more piles producing element 94 on an intermediate scale by January, 1944, at $25 million; and conversion of the Trail plant to produce a thousand pounds of heavy water per month by May 1, 1943, at $2.8 million. Thus, at a total construction cost of at least $80 million and an annual operating cost of $34 million, the project would produce a few atomic bombs by July 1, 1944, and about twice as many each year thereafter. The group concluded with some general recommendations for possible cuts, should an unlimited program be impossible; but they favored proceeding on all methods at full speed.

By five o'clock, the meeting was over. Conant assembled his notes for the extraordinary report he would submit to Bush on Monday morning.

ENTER THE ARMY

The implications of the report from the S-1 Section were already clear to Bush and Conant. In its next phase, the project would involve large-scale design and construction, but the research teams operating under the program chiefs were not prepared in experience or skills for this job. Neither could they expect the Planning Board to accept such an assignment, since it consisted of a group of senior engineers who had agreed to serve only on a temporary basis.

In fact, Bush and Conant had assumed that they would have to transfer the gigantic task of design and construction to the Army. Bush had mentioned this possibility to Roosevelt in 1941 and had included it in his March 9 report. The President replied that he had no objection if Bush was satisfied that the Army had made adequate provision for absolute secrecy. The paramount importance of security, on which Roosevelt, Bush, and Conant all agreed, made it essential to limit the responsibility to one of the armed services. The possibility of construction projects of unprecedented size suggested assignment to the Army, and Bush knew the President's wishes. Roosevelt by this time was quite out of patience with the Navy for its lack of initiative and enterprise in the Pacific and with Secretary Knox for failing to control the intransigence of some of his officers.[35] Conant had seen research performed satisfactorily in a military organization during World War I. In discussing the matter with Bush earlier in May, he suggested that some of the top scientists would have to enter the Army as officers in the new specialist corps.

Bush had approached the Army's construction experts soon after the President's approval of the March 9 report. General Marshall had appointed Brigadier General Wilhelm D. Styer, Chief of Staff for General Brehon B. Somervell's newly created Services of Supply, as principal contact for S-1. Styer had experience as Deputy Chief of Construction in the Quartermaster Corps and had played a major part in the reorganization of the War Department which led to the creation of the Services of Supply in March, 1942. At Bush's invitation, Styer attended the meeting of the S-1 Section in March. He was present on May 23 and thus knew Conant's intentions. He began at once to calculate the impact which the S-1 project would have on other war construction. Styer and Bush both met with General Marshall on June 10 and obtained Army support for at least half the program outlined in Conant's report of May 25. Although Marshall understood the implications of S-1, he was also aware of the alarming shortage of critical materials and equipment which faced the nation. Thus, the Chief of Staff was unwilling to go beyond the authorization of the electromagnetic and pile projects. Both Bush and Styer realized this decision was incompatible with the findings of Conant's committee. Conant had insisted that success depended upon the continued development of all four processes. In the end, Marshall agreed to withhold any decision on gaseous diffusion and the centrifuge until Styer could determine the extent to which these would interfere with other essential projects.[36]

This stay kept all four projects alive, but it placed a burden on Styer. The OSRD appropriation was due to expire in twenty days with the end of the fiscal year. By that time, funding for both Army and OSRD contracts had to be arranged and the Army organization established. One consolation for Styer was that he could now seek the support of others in the Services of Supply. He conferred with General Lucius D. Clay, who was Somervell's priority chief. Clay found it difficult to predict the impact of S-1 without a detailed bill of materials, but it was obvious to him that the S-1 plants would use equipment and materials similar to those required for installations producing high-octane gasoline, toluol, ammonia, and synthetic rubber. As a temporary expedient, Clay suggested that OSRD start engineering studies at once on all four processes in order to draw up reasonably accurate bills of materials. At the same time, the Army could let contracts for the construction of all four pilot plants. As soon as detailed plans and designs had progressed sufficiently, Clay would assign the highest priority to the project which had the smallest impact on supplies of critical materials.

Clay's suggestion seemed to miss Conant's point entirely, but at least it implied the possibility of testing all four processes in pilot plants. When Styer reported back to the Chief of Staff, Marshall agreed "to go ahead with the whole program modified as might be necessary to meet the limitations which might be imposed by critical materials." This statement, recorded by Styer, was a model of equivocation but it was the only authority available. On June 12, Styer dashed off some rough notes which Bush could use as a guide in drafting his report to the President.[37]

It fell to Bush to encompass in one set of recommendations the conflicting views of Clay and Conant. Considering the fundamental impossibility of the task, one can scarcely imagine a more masterful reply. Bush stated both the Army and the OSRD positions, but with proper emphasis he gave Conant the advantage. He lifted verbatim his colleague's recommendation for the construction of four plants. Admitting that S-1 could not be prosecuted rapidly without interfering with other wartime demands, Bush suggested balancing the final military results against the interference. Then he justified Conant's argument that pursuit of all four methods was imperative. When he turned to the details, Bush used Clay's language. The OSRD should award design contracts at once to permit the preparation of bills of materials for all four plants. Then "the highest priority should be assigned to the plant or plants which at that time show the most promise of success and which in the demands for critical materials will have the least serious effect on other urgent programs." Between Clay's words, Bush slipped the ideas that more than one plant might be built and that promise of success would be a factor in selecting the processes to be employed. One further bow to Clay was Bush's acknowledgement that pilot-plant construction would fall under the eagle eye of the Army's procurement staff. Technically, the report was ambiguous and inconsistent, but it accomplished its purpose. Both Marshall and Conant could sign it in good conscience since all were agreed on its objectives. There was simply no time to iron out the technical details which might well resolve themselves during the summer. It was a tribute to Bush's administrative skill and to Marshall's forbearance that this delicate transfusion of authority from OSRD to the Army was accomplished without the skip of one heartbeat. There was, however, an element of finesse in Bush's action. It remained to be seen whether the Army would some day call his bluff.

73

The remainder of the report described the division of funds and responsibilities between the Army and the OSRD. In terms of proposed appropriations, the Army would control more than 60 per cent of the entire program—$54 million out of $85 million in fiscal year 1943. This included the construction of three plants for uranium 235 and one for element 94. A qualified officer designated by the Chief of Engineers and reporting to him was to be in charge of the entire project. The former program chiefs or members of the Planning Board would assist this officer on a full-time basis, preferably as Army officers. The Army would let contracts, prepare bills of materials, and select sites as soon as possible.[38]

Styer did not wait for Presidential approval of the report to begin organizing the Army effort. The selection of a commanding officer was his first task and by no means a simple one. As the Army's construction agency, the Corps of Engineers had drawn the assignment, but the fact was that the Engineers had only recently acquired this responsibility. Prior to September, 1940, the corps' construction experience had been limited to rivers and harbors projects and to overseas facilities, which for the most part were in the Panama Canal Zone and the Caribbean area. The transfer from the Quartermaster Corps had been gradual, with the Engineers assuming responsibility only for the construction of Army air bases and other Air Corps projects in November, 1940. The Quartermaster Construction Division, under General Somervell, had received the brunt of assignments for training camps and other projects of unprecedented size, such as the Pentagon in Washington. Not until December, 1941, had all remaining construction been transferred to the Engineers.[39] It was not surprising, therefore, that in selecting an Engineer officer for S-1 Styer chose a man with experience both in the Canal Zone and on air base projects.

On Wednesday, June 17, 1942, the day Bush forwarded the report to the President, Styer telegraphed orders to Colonel James C. Marshall of the Syracuse Engineer District to report to Washington. Marshall, a West Point graduate of 1918, had served in the corps since World War I, had spent three years with the 11th Engineers in the Canal Zone, and was at the time completing a major assignment for the construction of air base facilities and ammunition depots in the Syracuse District. When Colonel Marshall reported on Thursday morning, Styer outlined the project and told him of his appointment. On Friday, Styer introduced Marshall to Bush, who promptly opened his S-1 files. Later the same day, Styer forwarded to Colonel Marshall a letter from Bush indicating the President's approval of the June 17 recommendations. Marshall began at once to organize his command, which he called for the time being the "DSM Project."[40]

At the same time, Conant was planning to reorganize the S-1 activities of the OSRD. Although the greater share of the work had now been transferred to the Army, a vitally important segment remained within the scientists' responsibility. In addition to general supervision of research at the universities, Conant's committee would supervise the pilot-plant studies of centrifuge, gaseous-diffusion, and electromagnetic methods, including the construction of a five-gram-per-day electromagnetic pilot plant. They would also take over from the Planning Board the construction of the heavy-water plant at Trail. Thus, the committee would continue to maintain contact with those parts of the project on which, Conant hoped, the paramount decision would be based: the selection of the shortest route to the bomb.

74

The old S-1 Section, both from the organizational and security stand-point, had been too large for action as a group. Conant had not found it necessary to call a meeting of its full membership since March. When he needed expert advice for the May decisions, he had not called on the S-1 Section, but on a smaller group representing the program chiefs and the Planning Board. A few days after the May 23 meeting, Conant had recommended to Bush that the same group become a new S-1 Executive Committee, which would supervise all future OSRD work. On June 19, with the Presidential approval in hand, Bush had authorized the appointments: Conant as chairman, Briggs, Compton, Lawrence, Murphree, and Urey as members.[41] The group would meet regularly and survey the technical outlook. The Army would take over process development, engineering design, procurement of materials, and site selection.

75

CONFUSION IN THE RANKS

The new arrangement created confusion from the start. As both the Army and the Executive Committee soon learned, it was virtually impossible to separate pilot studies from engineering development and plant design. Yet, as the organization was now established, the OSRD and the Army would negotiate separate contracts with different companies for related work on each project. Such an obstacle between the pilot-plant and engineering phases of any development effort would at best have been trying, but for the Army, which had no technical experience in the project, the barrier was insurmountable. Perhaps the gap might have been bridged if the Planning Board or some of its members had become officers in the Corps of Engineers. But in fact, none of the scientists whose names were proposed ever received a commission, and the Army never directly employed the Planning Board.

Certainly Colonel Marshall had hardly had time to prepare for his assignment. For his immediate staff he could draw on the complement of his Syracuse office. The most valuable among these officers was Lieutenant Colonel Kenneth D. Nichols. Just thirty-four years old, Nichols had built an impressive record since his graduation from West Point. He had studied civil engineering in American and European universities, completed a doctorate in hydraulic engineering at the State University of Iowa, taught at West Point, and gained practical experience in two large-scale government construction projects in Marshall's command. His strong academic background made it easy for him to work with the scientists; as a competent, ambitious young officer, he understood the inner workings of the Corps of Engineers. Still, relatively few officers in the corps were qualified for the S-1 assignment in the turbulent summer of 1942, and none of them, of course, had a working knowledge of atomic energy. Except for Nichols and a few others, Marshall was not permitted to recruit career officers for DSM. The Corps of Engineers was assigning most regular officers to field commands. For the most part, Marshall had to rely on civilian employees, many from the Syracuse District, who were given reserve commissions. Their knowledge of corps procedures and their established relationships within the organization made them especially valuable.

Marshall also recognized the need for a much larger force to provide architect-engineer and management services. For this job he wanted an experienced contractor. A discussion on June 18 with General Eugene Reybold, the Chief of Engineers, and his Washington staff resulted in the selection of the Stone & Webster Engineering Corporation as the principal contractor for the DSM project, with the understanding that the company's role would be defined more specifically later.[42]

Time served to demonstrate still another weakness in the June reorganization: the project's lack of authority and prestige within the Army. Whatever may have been Colonel Marshall's engineering abilities and experience, he could not carry much weight with general officers at Army headquarters as a field officer commanding a new district in the Corps of Engineers. To be sure, Bush and Conant were experienced in working at the highest levels in the War Department; but now that the project was part of the Army and they were not, it was difficult to handle routine matters from the outside.

By far the worst fault in the reorganization was the division of responsibility without the provision of any higher authority to resolve honest differences promptly. The Army would control its contracts and priorities and the S-1 Executive Committee theirs. But who would co-ordinate? Who would handle assignments that seemed to fall outside the charters of both groups? Who could prevent hot issues from being passed back and forth as in a long tennis volley in which both players hope for a placement? If Bush and Conant had this authority, they were slow in using it. Perhaps a summer of frustration was necessary to demonstrate the need for a change.

SELECTION OF THE TENNESSEE SITE

A good example of how the new arrangement failed was the tedious process of selecting a site for the production plants. The Planning Board had first discussed the subject in April, when the board was primarily concerned with a site for either the gaseous-diffusion or centrifuge plants. Since the primary requirement was a large and reliable electric power supply, Murphree had approached the War Production Board for information about the most promising power areas in the country. Later that month, Zola G. Deutsch of Murphree's Standard Oil Development Company, Thomas V. Moore of Compton's Metallurgical Laboratory, and Milton J. Whitson of Stone & Webster visited a number of sites in the area recommended by WPB in the heart of TVA territory west of Knoxville, Tennessee. With some thoughts of a large water supply for cooling the piles, the group inspected several sites on the Tennessee River in the still-water reservoir area above the Watts Bar Dam, but they found the surrounding terrain too rugged and inaccessible for convenient railroad or power connections. On their way back to Knoxville they explored the Clinch River valley well above the Watts Bar reservoir. Their initial impression was that the area provided a less desirable water source since the flow of the Clinch would produce sediment. However, these doubts evaporated when the group came to the area just below Elza, where the Louisville and Nashville Railroad crossed the river. The Elza site, Deutsch reported, seemed almost ideal. "The topography is such that a number of operations could find reasonably flat areas divided by protective hills, the driving distance to Knoxville is less than 20 miles, and service from two important railroads is immediately available. Water from the Clinch River is regulated to a minimum of 200 sec. ft., and because of the nearby Norris Dam is relatively free of silt. A relatively small part of the land is under cultivation, indicating that a small number of families would have to be moved, and the land as a whole is fairly cheap." [43] As Murphree pointed out in discussing the report at the Planning Board meeting on May 6, the potential power resources of the site were excellent.

77

The selection of the Elza site seemed to be the one decision which the Planning Board could recommend with confidence. When Conant received the report late in May, he forwarded it to Styer and recommended to Bush that the Army proceed at once to acquire the site.[44] Just before Bush sent his report to the Top Policy Group (Wallace, Stimson, and Marshall) on June 13, he read a lengthy study from Compton, who had inspected the site with his staff and had found it equally as acceptable for the pile project as a site in the Dunes area south of Lake Michigan. Bush sent Compton's study to Styer with the comment that he favored the Tennessee site because it offered greater isolation and security.[45] He included the need for immediate selection of a site in his recommendations to the President and added a copy of Deutsch's report as if to imply what the decision would be.

With these firm recommendations, Styer was ready to act. He told the S-1 Executive Committee on June 25, 1942, that the Army would acquire the Elza site at once. But Colonel Marshall was not to be stampeded. First he ordered a detailed study by Stone & Webster, which had been a party to the original recommendation to the Planning Board. On July 1, he and Nichols met with Stone & Webster personnel at Knoxville and proceeded to retrace the steps the Deutsch group had made almost three months earlier. Then Marshall submitted a complete set of site criteria to the committee for review, requested detailed site requirements from the program chiefs, and asked the committee members to submit comments on the Stone & Webster report. By the end of July, the committee's patience had run out. Conant told Marshall that the committee had discussed the request for comments and agreed that construction should proceed where the greatest speed was possible. The Tennessee site seemed logical from this point of view.[46]

By this time, Colonel Marshall had convinced himself that there might not be a need for any site whatsoever. The day after the S-1 meeting, Marshall and Nichols called on the Assistant Chief of Engineers in Washington. Marshall told General Thomas M. Robins he was unwilling to proceed with site acquisition or construction until Compton's process seemed to justify a large-scale plant. The first pile would not be in operation until late fall; in Marshall's opinion even such a delay would postpone completion of the project by only a few weeks. With the support of his superiors, Marshall decided to delay acquisition for several months.[47] The S-1 Executive Committee and the Army were at loggerheads. Only higher authority could resolve the disagreement. But what authority?

78

STRUGGLE FOR PRIORITIES

In the earlier experimental period, the OSRD had encountered relatively little difficulty in securing conventional materials for S-1. But, when Bush and Conant formulated their new program calling for large construction projects, the procurement of both manpower and materials became crucial. It was entirely a coincidence, and by no means a happy one, that priorities became critical at precisely the same time in the S-1 project and in the nation's war effort at large. In the opening days of 1942, the President had challenged American industry to produce 60,000 planes, 45,000 tanks, 20,000 antiaircraft guns, and 8,000,000 tons of shipping in the coming year. The wheels of industry started slowly as government procurement officials awaited proper authorizations before awarding contracts. By spring, industry had signed contracts for more than $100 billion, or more than the total production of the entire national economy in its most prosperous and productive prior year.[48] To make matters worse, the unprecedented volume of orders resulted in a greater use of high priorities, a trend which wiped out any controls which the priority system might have exercised on the economy. In the ensuing period of severe priority inflation, chaos reigned. All semblance of balance disappeared in the national production effort, as orders for one program robbed critical items from the next and precious materials were diverted from essential projects for the construction of plants or equipment which could not be used.

In one sense, Bush's new alliance with the Army was a most fortunate arrangement for S-1. It placed the atomic energy project close to what little authority remained in the national priority system. Roosevelt's laissez-faire approach to economic controls in 1940 and 1941 had presumably been supplanted by a strong central authority in the appointment of Donald M. Nelson as chairman of the War Production Board. Nelson, however, refused to risk slowing the production effort by overhauling the existing machinery or, more specifically, by taking over the procurement and contracting functions of the armed forces.[49] The significant reorganization came not in Nelson's office, but in General Somervell's. The March, 1942, reorganization of the War Department brought to Somervell's Services of Supply not only the Corps of Engineers and the Quartermaster Corps, but also the Army and Navy Munitions Board. By Nelson's leave, the board continued to control the nation's productive capacity through its power to assign priorities for all military procurement. Thus, to the extent that Bush could establish a direct line through the Army to the Services of Supply, S-1 could be assured that its priority needs would receive due consideration.

The difficulty was, of course, that the tie between S-1 and Somervell's organization was at best tenuous. In preparing the June report to the President, Bush and Conant must have had some sense of what was in the wind. They had been able to win Army support only by pretending to accept Clay's "least-effect" principle. The Army's position was understandable as it struggled to equip and house the thousands of recruits pouring into induction centers each day, to push life-giving supplies and equipment to beleaguered allies abroad, and to mount the North African offensive, which was just a few months away.[50] True, the bomb might win the war someday, but the Army had to be sure that the war was not lost in the meantime.

An even greater handicap was the organizational cleavage between Marshall's DSM project and the S-1 Executive Committee. At the S-1 meeting on July 9, the committee agreed that the OSRD would seek its own priorities on its own contracts and that it would appeal to the Army only when all else failed. In other words, any possible advantage in the association with the Army was to be exercised only in an emergency. The committee soon found the arrangement impossible. Very few companies could attain the quality required, and most of these were heavily engaged in other war work carrying a AA-3 priority rating, for which orders had been placed months earlier. For S-1, at least AA-1 or even AAA priorities were essential. Better ratings would obviously interfere with other war work and thus would require a decision by higher authority. But who was that authority—Bush, the Army and Navy Munitions Board, the War Production Board, or the President? In the chaotic summer of 1942, no one seemed to know.

By the end of August, the S-1 Executive Committee realized that if some action were not taken soon, the atomic bomb would never be a weapon in the present war. In Conant's Washington office on August 26, the committee almost in desperation explored possible ways out of the priority dilemma. They agreed that the electromagnetic method would probably be the first to yield fissionable material, although it might not be the best. They wanted to proceed with engineering of a large-scale plant while the pilot plant was being constructed. The next question followed logically: In view of the priority situation, might not the best chance of success lie in the all-out development of the electromagnetic method at the expense of all other approaches? With the committee tottering on the brink of decision, Conant raised a steadying hand. He had said in June that no sound basis existed for eliminating any process, and he was convinced that none existed now. To bet on one project and lose might cost the war. The committee agreed to stick with the earlier choice.[51]

This action by the S-1 Executive Committee left the Engineers with no alternative but to seek a higher priority. Colonel Nichols, after checking with General Styer, saw General Clay on August 29.[52] As Deputy Chief of Staff for Requirements and Resources in the Services of Supply, Clay as much as any man in the Government controlled the flow of critical materials to the military and civilian economy. Nichols conveyed to Clay some of the committee's determination to proceed at least with pilot-plant development of all four approaches at higher priority and was careful to mention that if necessary Bush would approach the President directly. Clay recommended the more usual route through the Joint Chiefs of Staff to the Army and Navy Munitions Board, but he quickly added that such priorities should not be granted and that it was never contemplated to grant a AA-1 priority to DSM. The most Clay could do was to grant a blanket AA-3 priority for the entire project.

This concession was unacceptable. As Nichols found out later the same day, the AA-3 rating was extremely difficult to use. It was high enough to arouse stout resistance among Army procurement officers and yet not sufficient to impress them. As Bush understood the matter from Conant, the AA-3 rating simply would not get the job done in time. In an impassioned letter to Harvey H. Bundy, special assistant to Secretary of War Stimson, he pointed out that the difference between the AA-3 and the AA-1 rating was at least three months in the completion of the pilot plants.[53] This was exasperating in view of the small amount of material involved, not exceeding $250,000 in value. Bush had understood in June that the experimental and pilot-plant work would be expedited to the utmost; he now felt that with the present attitude of the Army and Navy Munitions Board, the entire project would be badly delayed unless some changes were made. The Army had indeed called his bluff. He concluded: "From my own point of view, faced as I am with the unanimous opinion of a group of men that I consider to be among the greatest scientists in the world, joined by highly competent engineers, I am prepared to recommend that nothing should stand in the way of putting this whole affair through to conclusion, on a reasonable scale, but at the maximum speed possible, even if it does cause moderate interference with other war efforts."

General Somervell. Under this barrage, Army resistance soon crumbled.

While Bundy carried the alarm to General Marshall and Secretary Stimson, Bush complained to Under Secretary Robert P. Patterson and General Marshall would sign a letter to Donald Nelson, chairman of the War

Production Board, urging that ample priorities be provided for S-1. Bush knew that with Marshall's and Nelson's endorsement, the Army and Navy Munitions Board could not refuse to act.

GROVES AND THE MILITARY POLICY COMMITTEE

The delay on site selection and priorities was more than enough to convince Bush by early September that the June reorganization left much to be desired. Army participation was of little value if the military were not subject to direction from the scientists. Either through indecision or honest doubts, Colonel Marshall had delayed selection of the Tennessee site through the summer and still seemed far from action. Furthermore, Marshall had established his headquarters in New York with the appropriate title: Manhattan Engineer District. He was a good field officer, but he was all too willing to leave the paper pushing and priority haggling in stuffy Washington offices to Nichols, who, though only a lieutenant colonel, seemed to do a remarkable job. Bush realized that what the project needed most was clear-cut authority at the highest level and the sort of authority which could make itself felt within the Army. It also needed a guarantee that the Army would not swallow up the entire S-1 organization. He had discussed with General Marshall and Bundy the creation of a high-level military policy committee, on which the civilian scientists would be well represented.

81

Bush's recent conversations with Somervell were the cause of his concern about Army domination. These revealed that the General was aware of the deficiencies in the S-1 organization. Now that speed was essential, Somervell thought it best to place the entire S-1 project under the protective wing of the Services of Supply. He casually mentioned to Bush that he knew "a Colonel Groves" who would be just the man to take over all aspects of the Army program. Since Bush assumed the new military policy committee would select the commanding officer, he was deeply disturbed when Colonel Leslie R. Groves presented himself on September 17 with the news that Somervell had given him the full-time job of directing the Army project. Mustering all his self-control, Bush listened to the confident, vigorous stranger who seemed to assume that the future of S-1 already lay firmly in his hands.[54]

Somervell had been able to act quickly because he had the right man for the assignment. He had found Groves one of the ablest members of his construction team in the Quartermaster Corps. Although the Colonel's contentious spirit, heavy humor, and sharp tongue sometimes annoyed his fellow officers, Somervell was impressed by Groves's intelligence and ability to get jobs done. These qualities the Colonel had demonstrated on big construction projects. The reorganization of the War Department earlier in 1942 had placed Groves back in the Corps of Engineers as Deputy Chief of Construction. There he had watched the organization of the DSM project and had reviewed the orders establishing the Manhattan Engineer District in August. He had learned about the Tennessee site as early as June and had grown increasingly concerned about Colonel Marshall's delay in acting as the summer wore on. In June, he had participated in selecting Stone & Webster. By August, Groves had requested Marshall to submit weekly reports and urged the selection of sites and the start of construction as the best justification for higher priorities.[55]

When Somervell first informed Groves of his impending assignment, the Colonel was not happy about the prospect, since he had long been counting on going overseas. After a closed-door session with General Styer, however, he knew there was no escape. His orders, signed by Styer on September 17, directed him "to take complete charge of the entire DSM project," and to arrange at once the necessary priorities and the immediate acquisition of the Tennessee site.[56] Groves's new command was not officially announced until his appointment as brigadier general on September 23, but he had already taken up his duties. On September 19, he signed a directive for acquiring the site. Then he discarded the letter which Nichols had drafted for General Marshall's signature requesting Donald Nelson to authorize AAA priorities. In its place he prepared a short letter addressed to himself. He walked it through Styer's office and went directly to Nelson, who signed it with only a show of resistance. Thus, within forty-eight hours of Groves's assignment, the Army resolved the two problems that had plagued the project all summer—site selection and priorities.[57]

In the meantime, Bush was trying to establish a policy committee which would assure the continued participation of the scientists. This he would do not by giving the scientists a dominant voice but by carefully circumscribing and balancing Army initiative. Presumably the appointment of a Navy member would give this balance, reduce the possibility of Navy interference with priorities through the Army and Navy Munitions Board, and provide access to Navy facilities for weapon development. Apparently Bush also hoped to restore Styer to his former position as the Army's chief policy representative on the S-1 project. Bush and Conant would speak for the scientists. The result would be an organization resembling the large corporation. In a way, Bush thought of the military policy committee as a board of directors with General Groves the vice-president in charge of operations.

This new pattern emerged during the week following Groves's appointment. Discussions with Patterson, Somervell, Styer, and Groves allayed many of Bush's initial fears, and he could see that a workable arrangement was evolving. The final decisions came at a meeting in Secretary Stimson's office on September 23, attended by General Marshall, Bush, Conant, Somervell, Styer, Groves, and Bundy. After Somervell assured the group that he had taken the necessary action on priorities, Stimson brought up the question of the military policy committee. All agreed on top-level representatives from the Army, Navy, and OSRD, but Groves insisted upon limiting the committee to three members. To give both Bush and Conant a voice, Stimson proposed Bush as chairman and Conant as his alternate. Admiral William R. Purnell would serve for the Navy. After Groves left the meeting for his first trip to the Tennessee site, Stimson appointed Styer as the Army member.[58]

The effect of the reorganization and of Groves's dynamic leadership was clearly in evidence at the meeting of the S-1 Executive Committee on September 26. Now that he could make definite plans for the Tennessee site, Groves was anxious to have from each program chief a statement of needs. For each project he wanted a schedule for all critical materials, sketches of laboratory layouts, estimates of water requirements, and needs for fire protection. He assured the committee he had solved the priority problem, and he outlined the criteria which Colonel Marshall would use in processing requests. Captain John R. Ruhoff of Groves's staff reported that Metal Hydrides was at last producing satisfactory lots of uranium metal. Colonel Nichols described his successful negotiations to secure additional quantities of uranium oxide, and Colonel Marshall explained his plans for improving security procedures. The emphasis was now shifting rapidly from exploratory research to the development of a production enterprise.

83

How the project was to be organized had been determined in September. Still in doubt were the processes to be used. The S-1 Committee did not believe the Army should pursue all approaches into full-scale construction. With Groves in command, they saw they would have to act quickly to narrow the field. Another complete program review was in order, this time an agonizing process which took most of the fall of 1942.

COMMITMENT

CHAPTER 4

Since the outbreak of war the previous December, Bush and Conant had probed the possibilities of a quick route to an atomic weapon. By the autumn of 1942, they felt more confident that such a weapon could be ready in the present war. Project leaders like Compton, Lawrence, and Urey saw in the experiments in their laboratories new hope for success. But was this optimism based on solid fact or did it feed on the excitement of the chase? Perhaps the irrepressible enthusiasm so obvious in Compton and Lawrence was distorting scientific judgment throughout S-1. Conant might have recalled an exchange in his correspondence with Compton earlier that year. In urging Conant's continued support of the pile, the Chicago physicist had ended a letter with the thought: "Now is the time for faith." Conant had replied, "It isn't faith we need now, Arthur. It's works." [1]

In October, 1942, Conant was still looking for works, for the scientific evidence upon which he could base a commitment of men, money, and materials. In June, he had insisted that it was too early to rely heavily on any one of the approaches. Now time was running out. He had to make a commitment.

BUILDING SUPPLY LINES

Although research and development were concentrated on four processes for producing fissionable material, the success of these efforts rested in a real sense upon the procurement of vital supplies, specifically high-purity graphite and uranium oxide, metal, and flouride compounds. The mushrooming requirements and the more rigid purity specifications transformed the modest efforts of the Planning Board in February, 1942, into a project of first importance before the end of the summer.

The graphite in the early experimental piles had been of ordinary commercial grade, secured for the most part from the United States Graphite Company. Although graphite could be produced in large quantities by heating a putty of petroleum coke and coal tar in an electric furnace, the product had poor neutron properties unless very pure materials were used and the process carefully controlled. The Metallurgical Laboratory rather than the Planning Board had undertaken the procurement of graphite during the spring of 1942. Norman Hilberry, formerly a physicist at New York University and now Compton's right-hand man, explored the situation and did not find it promising. He learned that the International Graphite and Electrode Corporation produced very pure graphite, but the small quantities needed for electrodes were insignificant in comparison with his needs. To secure the great quantities for the pile, he approached the National Carbon Company and persuaded them to take the order. Hilberry then shocked the staff of the War Production Board by asking for an A-1 priority on a material which had never been rated higher than C. By July 1, he had resolved the priority issue and placed orders with both companies for all the graphite needed for the first critical pile experiment.

85

The OSRD followed the Planning Board's recommendations on uranium oxide in April, 1942. On the strength of a prospective OSRD contract, Eldorado Gold Mines, Ltd., before the first of May flew an advance party to its mine site on Great Bear Lake, near the Arctic Circle. As the pale sunlight of spring crept into the frozen wastelands of the Northwest Territory, additional men and supplies were flown to the isolated camp. Assembling heavy equipment and pumping out the flooded mine progressed so slowly that it seemed unlikely much ore could be removed before the close of the Arctic summer.

The short mining season was not the only obstacle. Since uranium mining was a highly speculative venture at best, there could be no assurance that control of Eldorado would always remain in the hands of reliable business interests. Bush's contract officers at OSRD had also run afoul of Canadian export regulations in attempting to buy uranium from Eldorado through an American purchasing company. At the same time, there was no question that the Eldorado uranium was essential to both the American and British programs. By early June, C. J. Mackenzie of the Canadian National Research Council had proposed that his government quietly buy up a controlling interest in Eldorado so that American purchase of Canadian ore would become an intergovernmental matter. Thus the Eldorado purchase became a pawn in the complex negotiations with the British and Canadians on such problems as patent rights, export controls, and the exchange of scientific information. Mackenzie's plan was not approved until Roosevelt's conference with Churchill late in June, and another month passed before the Canadian government could begin the purchase of Eldorado stock.[2]

Strangely enough, neither the Planning Board nor the S-1 Executive Committee had shown any interest in the much larger stocks of Belgian ore already above ground in the United States and the Congo. The lack of firm requirements and the fact that 1,200 tons were already under export controls in the United States presumably made its purchase less pressing. Acting either on OSRD instructions or from ignorance of the ore's significance, officials from the State Department and defense agencies were cool to offers by Edgar Sengier of the African Metals Corporation during the spring of 1942. Sengier had brought the ore to the United States to keep it out of enemy hands. Now he could find no market for his investment in the American government. If Bush and Conant knew of Sengier's growing frustration, they did nothing to alleviate it. On July 9, 1942, the S-1 Executive Committee confirmed the earlier conclusion of the Planning Board that there was no immediate need to bring additional ore under S-1 control. Nothing happened until late August, when Bush learned that Eldorado, still a private company, was attempting to purchase 500 tons from Sengier's Staten Island supply. Bush alerted the Army and suggested the imposition of export controls.[3]

Early in September, Colonel Nichols took charge of ore procurement. With the approval of the S-1 Executive Committee, he arranged through the State Department for export controls on all 1,200 tons of the Belgian ore. On the eighteenth, he called on Sengier in his New York office and quickly reached the basic agreement which was later written into a series of contracts. The United States would purchase the ore and arrange for its refining at Eldorado's Port Hope mill. About 300 tons would be shipped to Port Hope in hundred-ton lots. The 1,000 tons above ground in the Congo would be shipped to the United States, which would have first option on its purchase. Before the end of September, Nichols had ordered the shipment of the first 100 tons to Port Hope and for the transfer of the remaining 1,100 tons from the Staten Island dock area to the Seneca Ordnance Depot. The S-1 Executive Committee accepted the Army's recommendation not to reopen the flooded Belgian mine at Shinkolobwe.[4]

Difficulties in dewatering the Eldorado mine made it impossible to produce more than a few small shipments of oxide in 1942, but enough could be recovered from ore already above ground to meet the needs of the first experimental pile. If production units were built later, the contracts negotiated by the Corps of Engineers in the fall of 1942 assured sufficient supplies of uranium oxide for the war effort.[5]

The purification of uranium oxide from the Port Hope refinery, and later from refineries in the United States, was developed with relatively little difficulty. The key to the process was the unique solubility of uranyl nitrate in ether, a fact which had been well known for over a century. The nitrate was easily formed by dissolving the crude oxide in nitric acid. As experiments at the National Bureau of Standards showed, virtually all of the impurities were left behind when the nitrate was in turn dissolved in ether. The uranium could then be easily recovered, concentrated, and reduced to uranium dioxide. The difficulty came in scaling up the laboratory experiment to an industrial process, an assignment for which Arthur Compton approached the Mallinckrodt Chemical Company in St. Louis on April 17, 1942. Mallinckrodt, with experience in working with tricky materials like ether, had the process going on an industrial scale by early summer and was able to meet all immediate requirements for oxide in the production of uranium metal or hexafluoride.[6]

Producing uranium metal continued to be difficult even after the essential processing equipment was placed in operation at Westinghouse and Metal Hydrides. The Westinghouse process gave a product of sufficient purity but the photochemical step was so slow and expensive that it was abandoned in favor of using uranium tetrafluoride, which became more readily available in the summer of 1942. Experience at Metal Hydrides was just the opposite—the production rate and costs seemed practical, but metal quality and purity were unacceptably low. Even with assistance from other S-1 laboratories, Metal Hydrides was unable to force production above 200 pounds per day, and by early September scarcely a ton of usable metal had been delivered to Chicago. So discouraging, indeed, was the situation that Nichols seriously proposed that Metal Hydrides stop all production until the company could deliver a better product. Only the desperate needs of the pile program convinced Nichols to permit production to continue at least until 5,000 pounds of metal had been delivered.[7]

The fact was that the Hydrides process was not going smoothly. Although Rodden found it possible to produce pure calcium by vacuum distillation, output continued to be low during the summer of 1942. Much more involved were the melting and casting of the finely divided uranium metal from the Hydrides process. The metal powder was so pyrophoric that it could be removed from the reduction furnaces only with special precautions. Even when packed in metal cans, the powder would become red hot unless refrigerated. As a temporary expedient, the powder was pressed and sintered. But for a satisfactory product, the metal would have to be melted and cast. Experimental work was started on such a process during the spring of 1942 at the Massachusetts Institute of Technology and at Iowa State College, Ames, where Frank H. Spedding established a branch of the Metallurgical Laboratory.[8]

The troubles encountered in getting good castings of high-purity uranium led Spedding, H. A. Wilhelm, and others to consider alternative methods which would produce the metal initially in massive rather than powder form. Experiments on such a process had been performed as early as 1926 by J. C. Goggins and others at the University of New Hampshire. A steel bomb, charged with a mixture of uranium tetrachloride and calcium metal, had been evacuated and heated to the ignition temperature. When the bomb had been cooled and opened, a massive lump of uranium weighing about three pounds had been recovered. The process had been abandoned, however, for lack of good-quality tetrafluoride. By the summer of 1942, there

87

was new interest in the process. High-purity calcium was now made at Metal Hydrides, and the first uranium tetrafluoride in more than experimental quantities was coming from the Harshaw and du Pont plants built under Planning Board contracts. Spedding at Ames and Rodden at the National Bureau of Standards independently repeated the 1926 experiment in August, 1942. Both were encouraged. By the end of September, Spedding was talking of producing a ton of metal per day by the new process.

The Ames process did not, by itself, provide enough metal for Fermi's critical experiment. Much more work would be necessary to develop the process on an industrial scale; larger supplies of calcium would be needed; and the Harshaw tetrafluoride process would have to be improved and production expanded at other plants. Then, as soon as possible, Ames would begin using magnesium rather than calcium, a modification which appeared to have significant cost and purity advantages. In the meantime, heroic effort was pushing production at Metal Hydrides as high as 300 pounds per day, with a goal of 8,500 pounds in November. Even at that, it seemed impossible that there would be enough metal for Fermi's experiment before the end of the year.[9] For Compton, there was consolation only in the fact that adequate supplies of uranium metal would be available for larger piles in 1943.

PILE

The same sort of optimism which permitted Compton to predict a reproduction factor as high as 1.14 at the time of Conant's program review in May helped to carry the pile project during the summer of 1942. Compton, Fermi, and others at the Metallurgical Laboratory were resigned to the fact that they could not demonstrate a chain reaction until they had sufficient supplies of pure uranium metal and graphite. In the meantime, the scattered research groups at Princeton, Columbia, and Berkeley had been assembled on the Midway in Chicago, and the measurements begun in the spring could be continued as the first dribbles of material arrived. Even these experiments, which Compton complained were "important but non-essential," provided ground for greater confidence of ultimate success.[10] The first of these showed that the reproduction factor k probably would be greater than one; the second demonstrated the possibility of separating element 94 from uranium and other fission products.

The elusive value of k was pursued during the summer of 1942 under the direction of Enrico Fermi, Martin D. Whitaker, and Walter H. Zinn. Their experiments confirmed rather dramatically Compton's prediction that higher values of k would come with better materials. Before the end of July, Whitaker and Zinn had constructed an exponential pile identical in design to that built at Chicago during May, except that very pure uranium oxide from Mallinckrodt was used in place of commercial-grade material. The effect appeared to be that k would increase from 0.995 to 1.004 in a critical pile. In August, when the first uranium dioxide was available from Mallinckrodt, the estimated value of k rose as high as 1.014, and further experiments in September with a pile about twice as large tended to confirm these results.[11]

The value of k was again thrown into doubt in October, when an exponential pile was constructed with the first pure uranium metal from Metal Hydrides. The value of k determined in this experiment indicated that Fermi and his group had overestimated the beneficial effect which pure metal would have on the chain reaction. Apparently, the first chain-reacting pile would have to be 15 per cent larger than originally planned.[12] Fortunately, this note of discouragement had come almost too late to have any damaging effect on the pile program. Materials were at last arriving in Chicago in significant quantities, and it seemed certain that the decisive experiment would be possible before the end of 1942. The regular notes of encouragement from Chicago during the summer had helped to establish confidence in Compton's dream both among members of the S-1 Executive Committee and the Corps of Engineers. The October results did no worse than restore the uncertainty accepted in the June decision; now only complete failure could cause abandonment of the project.

89

Equally important in the Chicago optimism was Glenn Seaborg's work on the isolation of element 94. Seaborg had moved quickly to explore the new world of transuranium chemistry. With great drive himself and an ability to inspire work in others, Seaborg had organized around his former graduate students, Joseph W. Kennedy and Arthur C. Wahl, an exceptionally capable research team. While still at Berkeley during the spring, they had continued to study the chemical properties of the new element which they proposed to call "plutonium," a name appropriate for the element following neptunium in the periodic table.[13] Perhaps the most interesting fact they discovered was that the new element had two oxidation states. That is, in chemical reactions with other elements, plutonium was found to form ions by giving up either 6 or 4 planetary electrons. In the higher oxidation state ($^{+6}$ion), plutonium would have a completely different chemical behavior than in the lower oxidation state ($^{+4}$ion). Furthermore, Seaborg and Wahl discovered that by treating plutonium with certain reagents they could change its oxidation state. These properties might be useful in separating plutonium from uranium and a host of fission products. For example, in the first separation step, plutonium in the lower oxidation state could be precipitated; then it could be "oxidized" to the higher state so that it would remain in solution in the second precipitation. The plutonium would then be "reduced" to the lower state for the third step and the "oxidation-reduction" process continued between precipitations until the desired purity was obtained.[14]

Actually, Seaborg's problem was more complicated. The oxidation-reduction process might work in plutonium solutions of reasonable concentration, but hardly for the infinitesimal quantities in irradiated uranium. Seaborg proposed to overcome this difficulty by using a "carrier" which would precipitate with plutonium in the lower oxidation state and act much like a sweeping compound in aiding the recovery of the microscopic plutonium precipitate. Certain rare earth compounds such as lanthanum fluoride had been used as "carriers" in plutonium chemistry since the experiments which led to the discovery of the element in early 1941.

On his thirtieth birthday, April 19, 1942, Seaborg arrived with some of the Berkeley group at the Metallurgical Laboratory. Older, more experienced chemists like Samuel Allison immediately recognized in Seaborg the drive, ambition, and ability which were to characterize his work in Chicago. Soon they saw the rough edges of inexperience disappearing as Seaborg learned how to blend administrative responsibilities with his scientific activities. A competent compiler of voluminous reports, the young chemist soon impressed the Chicago staff with the quantity and quality of his research.

90

The primary assignment of the Seaborg group was to develop a chemical separation process for plutonium within a matter of months. This would have been no mean task even with adequate supplies of the material to be separated, but it seemed virtually impossible with the microscopic traces of plutonium produced by cyclotron bombardment. To carry out complex chemical reactions with microgram quantities of material at normal concentrations required accurate measurement of incredibly small volumes and weights. Finely calibrated capillary tubing was developed to measure volumes as small as 0.1 milliliter and balances to weigh solids as small as 0.1 microgram. So minute were such operations that they had to be viewed through a microscope. Indeed, it was scarcely inaccurate to say that invisible materials were being weighed with an invisible balance.

The use of these ingenious techniques made it possible for Seaborg's staff to isolate a visible amount of pure plutonium compound, free of all carrier and foreign matter, on August 18, 1942.[15] Within six weeks, Burris B. Cunningham, with help from Seaborg at Chicago and Wahl at Berkeley, had isolated weighable amounts. These samples, though microscopic, were concrete proof of feasibility. To an experienced chemist like Conant, who understood all too well the difficulties of Seaborg's assignment, this was a truly momentous accomplishment. To an engineer like Groves, who could conceive of the problems in scaling up the laboratory experiment by a billion times, there were doubts whether an industrial process could be developed in time.

Producing plutonium on an industrial scale had troubled Compton and Colonel Marshall as early as June. Compton had already encountered "near rebellion" among his staff at the Metallurgical Laboratory when he suggested that an industrial organization familiar with large-scale operations be given the task of constructing and operating the production plants. Some of the Chicago physicists, many of whom were younger men with no industrial experience, believed that their accomplishments thus far had earned them the right to carry the project through to completion. Furthermore, they reasoned, why should time be wasted in teaching to a second group the knowledge which they had already created and mastered? Compton, with his experience in science and industry, had a better sense of the organization which would be necessary to procure materials, administer subcontracts, co-ordinate scattered design and development work, and supervise construction.[16] He also realized the fallacy of many scientists in assuming that the objective was to build just one bomb which would provide an overwhelming psychological victory in the war. As Colonel Marshall had pointed out to him, a weapon was no more important than a nation's continuing ability to use it. The job was to produce not just one weapon but weapons in quantity in assembly-line fashion.

The future organization of the pile project became clear at the first meeting of the S-1 Executive Committee on June 25, 1942. In line with Marshall's thinking, the committee agreed that Stone & Webster would be prime contractor on the Tennessee site. The next day, in a meeting with Marshall and Nichols, Compton accepted Stone & Webster as the design contractor for a pilot plant.[17] During the summer, Stone & Webster began to assemble information for a small graphite and natural-uranium pile and a plutonium-separation plant, to be located in the Argonne Forest Preserve southwest of Chicago, but by fall plans changed. The Argonne site could be used for Fermi's first critical experiment but would not be large enough or remote enough for a pile of the size then contemplated for the pilot plant. Likewise, General Groves was quick to recognize a fact which Compton's staff had been reluctant to admit—namely, that the scale and complexity of the plutonium-separation process would be a challenge even to the most experienced chemical engineering organization. Before Groves had been on the job two weeks, he had approached the du Pont Company to take over the design and development of the separations pilot plant, now to be constructed at the Tennessee site.[18] Compton recalled that Conant had admonished him in August for trying to hunt elephants with peashooters. In the swift movement of events in the fall of 1942, scientists at the Metallurgical Laboratory, as elsewhere in the atomic project, had to make a quantum jump in their thinking about the task ahead.

91

CALUTRON

During the summer of 1942, results from Berkeley were just as encouraging as those from Chicago. The use of the 184-inch magnet for the giant cyclotron had made possible a series of experiments with calutrons several times larger than those in the 37-inch magnet.

Late in May, when the magnet windings had been completed, William M. Brobeck and others had installed two vacuum tanks in its great jaws. As in the 37-inch device, the tanks were flat on the top and bottom and had the shape of a large C when viewed from above. As the operator faced the open end of the C, he had on his left the controls which permitted him to adjust the ion source. He could regulate the temperatures of the heaters which vaporized the uranium chloride, the temperature of the charge chamber, and the power supply to the cathode which ionized the vapor. He could change the position of the cathode in the chamber or replace it through an air lock without shutting down the calutron. Mechanical controls enabled him to move the arc or accelerating electrodes in all directions, to tilt them, or to change the width of the gaps. Through a vacuum-tight window the operator could observe the adjustments and their effect on the beam. In the right-hand end of the C were the controls and instrumentation for the boxlike collectors which received the ion beam and trapped the uranium isotopes. Within the vacuum tank, between the two ends of the C, was the metal liner, supported on two heavy insulators so that it could be held at a very large negative voltage. (Figure 4)

92

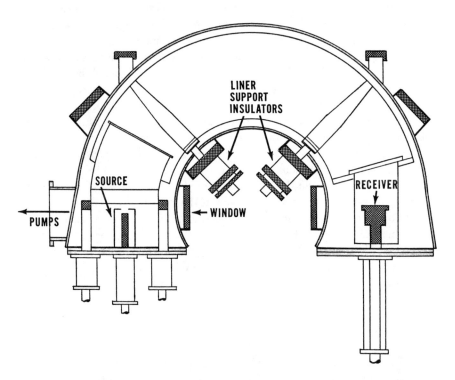

Figure 4. The C1 tank for the 184-inch magnet, June, 1942.

The first of these tanks, called C1, was placed in operation on June 3, 1942. Except for one experiment on July 20, C1 was not operated to produce uranium 235 but to explore the possibility of using a number of sources in one tank simultaneously. After a good beam was attained from a single source early in June, a source containing three beams, 1.25 inches apart, was installed in the tank. When no clearly definable beam could be produced at the receiver, the middle of the three beams was blocked off. Even with two beams, 2.5 inches apart, reception was far from satisfactory. Lawrence found that good sharp beams were produced when either source was operated alone or when both were run together at very low power. Simultaneous operation at full power produced nothing but a blob of scrambled ions at the receiver. Only with the aid of some complex electronic equipment did Lawrence discover that the sources generated a series of very high frequency oscillations, called hash, which smeared the beam. Painstaking adjustments of the source produced some reasonably good beams by the first weeks of September. They were hardly good enough to guarantee the successful operation of multiple sources in one tank, but Lawrence was hopeful. He now understood the cause of the interference and was beginning to learn how to overcome it. Multiple sources might alone bring a practical electromagnetic plant within reach. In any case, Lawrence was now convinced that if all else failed, the calutron could be operated on a large scale with a single source.[19]

93

Late in July, 1942, experiments began with the second tank, called C2. Installed back-to-back with C1 in the 184-inch magnet gap, C2 was devoted primarily to focusing problems and receiver design. The tank contained two sources which were a somewhat simplified version of the single source originally designed for C1, but for most of the focusing experiments, only one source was used at a time.

In earlier experiments some of the fine points of focusing had been successfully ignored, but they had to be faced before a pilot plant could be designed. Most of the trouble came from the fact that the ions never emerged from the source in exactly parallel paths. No matter how fine the slit in the arc chamber, many ions not directly in line with the slit would slip through and blur the beam at the receiver. One way to overcome this blur was to make slight variations in the magnetic field. If carefully contoured metal sheets or "shims" were attached to the top and bottom of the vacuum tanks, the width of the magnet gap would vary slightly across the pole face. In this way, the strength of the magnetic field could be varied enough to pull the wayward ions into focus. (Figure 5) The first set of shims, designed according to rather simple magnetic theory, was found to be unsatisfactory early in August. A second set was not completed until late September. Only then did Lawrence's staff begin to produce a beam sharp enough to resolve the two isotopes at the collector. The study of shims would continue well into 1943, but once again Lawrence had just enough evidence to convince him that he was on the right track.

Equally impressive were the improvements in collector design during the summer of 1942. While many of the collectors were simply instruments for measuring beam currents, more were serving the primary function of trapping the uranium 235 in a recoverable form. With the higher voltages and more intense beams produced in the 184-inch magnet, the design of a good collector was not easy. Collector parts, whether of metal or graphite, were quickly burned away by the high-energy ions. With greater velocities, the ions also tended to bounce out of the narrow pockets in the collector. This resulted in loss of product, contamination of the enriched material, and false readings on the instruments. The use of multiple sources complicated the process. Multiple collectors, of course, were needed to catch multiple beams, and many of the problems of beam interaction had to be solved at the collector end of the tank. The use of magnetic shims introduced even greater complications. The first shims tried in Tank C2 in late July bowed the flat plane of the ribbon-like beam so that it struck the face of the collector not as a straight line but as a curve. There was no way, however, to perfect the design of a new collector until a better set of shims had been made for the tank. Thus, the collector used in the first runs on September 23 was purely an experimental model. It had curved slots approximating the shape of the beams, but each slot was divided into three segments so that portions of the beam could be analyzed separately. Then, by carefully studying the beam segments and by photographing the impact of the beam through the collector window, the Berkeley scientists could reshape the collector slots and try again.

94

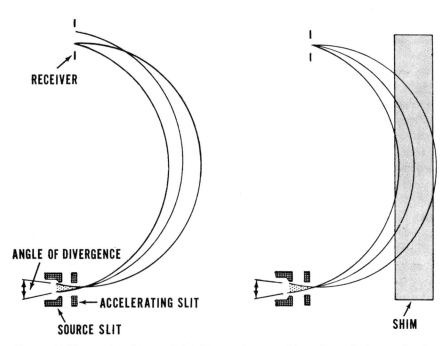

Figure 5. Precision machining of the shims made it possible to focus the beams sharply at the receiver.

This cut-and-try approach to collector design led to an important discovery early in October. Results were much better if the face of the collector was set at a 45-degree angle rather than perpendicular to the beam. The first receiver of this type (Figure 6), placed in Tank C2 on October 5,

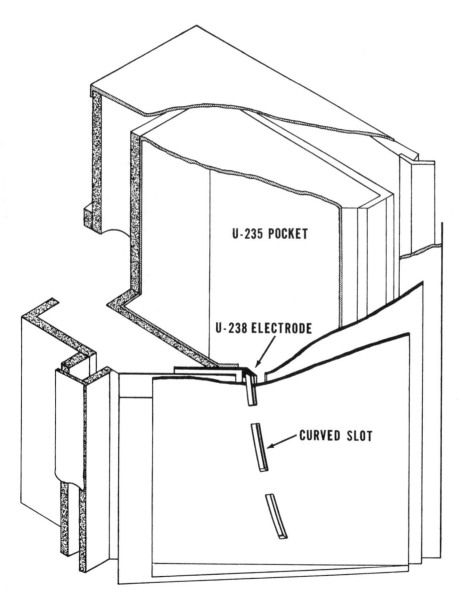

U-235 POCKET

U-238 ELECTRODE

CURVED SLOT

Figure 6. The first collector with its face at a 45-degree angle to the plane of the beam was tested in the C2 tank on October 5, 1942. Note the curved slots for experimental analysis of the beam.

operated successfully during the last three months of 1942. With its slots divided into three segments like its predecessor, this collector was nothing more than an experimental model, but it did represent a noteworthy accomplishment in the design of the calutron.[20]

Although Bush had assumed in June that development of an electromagnetic pilot plant would be the responsibility of the S-1 Executive Committee, the assignment was gingerly shifted to the Army, and then by Colonel Marshall to Stone & Webster. August C. Klein, the company's chief mechanical engineer, visited Berkeley in July and soon caught the enthusiasm which was sweeping Lawrence's laboratory. He urged that while experimental work continued, the design of the calutron should be frozen long enough to permit the development of a pilot plant consisting of five vacuum tanks at Berkeley. Klein's interest, the growing confidence of Marshall and Nichols, and the successful experiments with the C tanks were all part of the background for the S-1 Committee's meeting on August 26, when they considered concentrating all their resources on the electromagnetic process as a solution to the priority dilemma.[21] Although Conant's judicious logic prevented such a drastic step, the committee was excited enough to make the long trip to the West Coast. On September 13, they watched experiments with the C calutrons in the cyclotron building high above the Berkeley campus. At the Bohemian Grove, Lawrence summarized recent achievements. He emphasized that the pilot plant could now be built on the basis of sound experimental evidence. He now knew how to produce hash-free beams; and he knew that when the hash had been eliminated, two beams could be operated within a few inches of each other. Lawrence also found encouragement in the fact that the remaining problems did not involve basic theory but details of engineering and chemical extraction of the uranium 235. He did not favor going ahead on a full-scale plant if it meant eliminating the other approaches, but he did believe that fissionable material could be produced more quickly by the electromagnetic method than by any other. The S-1 Executive Committee recommended expediting work on the five-tank pilot plant and on a two-hundred-tank section of a full-scale plant, both of which would now be constructed at the new Tennessee site.[22]

CENTRIFUGE

Following their preoccupation with the Chicago and Berkeley projects in the summer and early fall of 1942, the S-1 Committee set out to see for themselves what had been accomplished in research on the centrifuge and gaseous diffusion. In Pittsburgh on October 23, they found the outlook for the centrifuge far from hopeful. In order to secure experimental results more reliable than those in the spring, Beams had succeeded in running a sample of uranium hexafluoride three times through his experimental centrifuge at the

University of Virginia. The degree of enrichment was then substantially greater than the experimental error in the measurements. When samples of the enriched material were sent to Nier for analysis, he found that the separation was only 60 per cent of that predicted from theory. If true, this fact alone seemed virtually to destroy the possibility of using the process. It meant that even for the small one-hundred-gram-per-day plant, the number of centrifuges would have to be increased from 8,800 to about 25,000, while the hold-up of uranium in the plant would rise from four months to about one year. There remained, however, two slender hopes for success. First, it was possible that the separation factor would increase if a significant number of obvious, if small, improvements could be made in the design and operation of the centrifuge. Second, as Harold Urey was quick to point out, there remained the possibility of using the theoretically more efficient countercurrent system rather than the flow-through principle. Although the more complicated countercurrent design had earlier been · passed over as much too complex for rapid development, its theoretical advantages could not now be overlooked. Karl Cohen had calculated that it would reduce the number of centrifuges required by 20 per cent, and the smaller quantity of gas used would make it possible to employ smaller equipment.[23]

97

Early in July, Beams began some experiments with the countercurrent system, but its eventual utility seemed doubtful in light of the severe difficulties which Westinghouse had encountered in developing one full-scale model centrifuge of the flow-through type. Test operation of this one-meter unit revealed severe instabilities at critical vibration frequencies. Repeated efforts to develop a gas-tight, corrosion-proof seal were unsuccessful, and all too frequent failures occurred in motors, shafts, and bearings at the high speeds required. Because of the high stakes involved, installation of auxiliary equipment in the pilot plant at Bayonne, New Jersey, continued during the summer despite the failure to perfect the model centrifuge. But obviously no work could be done on the twenty-four centrifuges for the pilot plant until the model ran successfully. Nor was it feasible under the circumstances to undertake the design of a full-scale plant or the development of longer tubes.

By the time of the S-1 Committee's visit to the Westinghouse laboratories in October, the experimental centrifuge at Virginia had been operated on the countercurrent system only for short periods, but long enough to dispel any hope for a reliable unit in the near future. Westinghouse continued to struggle with the model centrifuge, but the possibility of using the pilot plant seemed to fade with the weaker sunlight and shorter days of autumn.[24]

GASEOUS DIFFUSION

From Pittsburgh the S-1 Executive Committee traveled by overnight train to New York. There they found that research on the gaseous-diffusion process had spawned an experimental enterprise which was already causing Columbia officials to seek space outside Pupin Hall. The M. W. Kellogg Company had been assigning its ever growing research staff both to the Columbia campus and to its Jersey City laboratories.

98

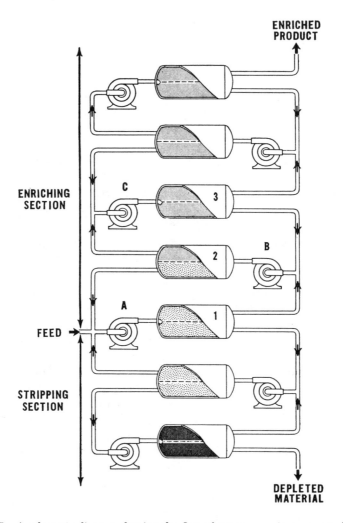

Figure 7. A schematic diagram showing the flow of process gas in a gaseous-diffusion cascade.

On the morning of October 24, John R. Dunning summarized progress in the first ten months of 1942.[25] With a drawing (similar to that in Figure 7) he explained the operating principle of the gaseous-diffusion cascade. First, it was necessary to understand the flow of gas at any one of the thousands of typical stages in a production plant. The uranium hexafluoride in Pump B, for example, would be propelled into the high-pressure side of the converter at Enriching Stage No. 2. About half the gas would diffuse through the barrier, indicated by the dashed line. This gas, containing a slightly higher concentration of the lighter 235 isotope, would be transported to Enriching Stage No. 3 by Pump C. The gas which did not diffuse through the barrier in Stage No. 2 would now contain a slightly higher concentration of the heavier 238 isotope and would be transported by Pump A to the next lower stage, No. 1. Theoretically, if this process could be repeated through thousands of stages, virtually pure uranium 235 would be drawn from the "top" of the cascade and virtually pure 238 from the "bottom." Since the proportion of 235 isotope in the gas near the bottom would be much less than the 0.7 per cent found in natural uranium, the feed point would be somewhere between the top and bottom. It would also be possible to draw off material of any desired concentration or to add feed of any concentration simply by tapping into the cascade at the appropriate stage.

The possibilities for theoretical, and especially statistical, analysis of the cascade were apparent. Some of these were explained by Karl Cohen of Columbia and by Manson Benedict, who advised Percival C. Keith of Kellogg on theoretical problems. One complication was introduced by the fact that natural uranium was more than 99-per-cent uranium 238. In the stages of the plant near the feed point, therefore, very large quantities of hexafluoride gas would have to be pumped through the converters. The quantities of gas to be pumped would be somewhat smaller near the bottom of the cascade and very much smaller near the top. Cohen had calculated the quantities of gas at each stage in the cascade and had plotted these values on a graph (similar to Figure 8). Obviously, in an ideal cascade, each of the thousands of converters and pumps should be of slightly different size. But for a practical design, Keith and his engineers would have to settle for just a few sizes of equipment. Cohen and Benedict had the task of determining how best to approximate the theoretical curve with the equipment sizes to be manufactured.

The most persistent difficulty continued to be the production of a suitable barrier material. Francis G. Slack, a physicist on leave from Vanderbilt University, explained to the S-1 Committee the conclusions his group had reached after hundreds of tests of many materials. Slack believed that certain metals might lead most quickly to a barrier for a pilot plant, if not for final production equipment. During the summer of 1942, Slack had selected many materials and had tested them in separating helium from carbon dioxide. Keith had arranged through Kellogg for the American Brass Company to produce the best of these in quantity. American Brass had developed a number of techniques which produced much better material than had been made in the laboratory. Likewise, continued research by Willard F. Libby and others at Columbia had resulted in a vastly improved product. The chem-

99

istry group had also studied the corrosion rate of uranium hexafluoride on various barrier materials and investigated ways of stabilizing them against corrosion.

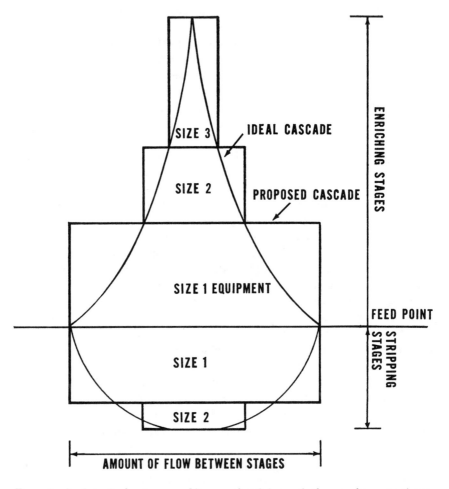

Figure 8. A schematic drawing resembling one that Cohen and others used to approximate the ideal gaseous-diffusion cascade with only a few sizes of equipment, October, 1942.

Despite these accomplishments, it was evident by the end of the summer that the metals tested would provide scarcely more than a makeshift barrier. The corrosion rates were high, the material brittle and fragile, and the separative quality far from uniform. Fortunately, other members of the gaseous-diffusion team were studying new barrier materials which seemed to offer success in the long run. Since it seemed certain that nickel would best resist corrosion by process gas, attention was turning to various types of nickel barriers. Foster C. Nix at the Bell Telephone Laboratories had already experimented with fine nickel powder. Edward O. Norris of the C. O. Jelliff Manufacturing Corporation and Edward Adler of the College of the City of New York had still another idea for metallic nickel. Both types of nickel barrier, however, were far behind those employing other metals in terms of process development, and there was doubt that either would be ready before the end of the war.

Design of the converter in which the barrier would be used was primarily Kellogg's responsibility.[26] Designs considered at this time were dictated by the physical properties of the metal barrier. Keith envisaged the converter as a long rectangular tank in which several pieces of barrier would be placed.

Next to the barrier, the toughest problem was the design of pumps. Pumping of relatively heavy, highly corrosive gas at high velocities, with no leakage into or out of the system was an imposing assignment. Because Keith had decided that centrifugal pumps would be required in the larger, lower stages of the plant, Kellogg had subcontracted their development to Ingersoll-Rand. During the summer of 1942, Ingersoll-Rand reported excellent progress on the design of both pump impellers and shaft seals. By September, the company was ready to begin test operation of a full-scale pump with freon gas. Meanwhile, Henry A. Boorse and others at Columbia were designing various types of reciprocating pumps which might also serve in the cascade. Here design of the seals was the principal concern among the usual problems of corrosion resistance, efficiency, and reliability.

101

Columbia and Kellogg were making progress, but for Conant and his committee, the proof of the process lay in the production of more than test-tube quantities of uranium 235. The New York research combine had not yet succeeded in doing that. During the summer, Rex B. Pontius had operated a laboratory apparatus consisting of one small converter and one pump, which tested small barrier samples with a mixture of carbon dioxide and helium. A group under Eugene T. Booth had built a twelve-stage system, which they operated in Pupin Laboratory, first with the same gases and later with uranium hexafluoride. By the time of the October meeting, they could report a very small separation after a five-hour run. Nothing resembling a production run could be anticipated, however, until Keith could complete the ten-stage pilot plant for which ground had just been broken in Jersey City.

In short, the S-1 Committee found some reason for encouragement in New York. Positive results were coming from the design and testing of components. On the debit side were the failure to produce a satisfactory barrier and the lack of evidence that the process could produce uranium 235 in practical quantities. Progress inspired limited confidence, if not enthusiasm, among the S-1 Committee members.

was there the usual problem of keeping the experimenters on the narrow path of investigation which led most directly to the project's objectives; there was also the much more exacting task of reconciling widely divergent results and trying to make some meaning out of them. Before many weeks had slipped by, Oppenheimer was convinced that the critical problems lay not in theory but in the lack of good experimental data. He found that theoretical studies took no time at all, compared to the slow, painstaking process of accumulating cross-section data.

The neat answers which Conant needed had to come from the theoretical group at Berkeley. There Oppenheimer assembled a group of theoreticians, including John H. Van Vleck, Robert Serber, Edward Teller, Emil J. Konopinski, Stanley P. Frankel, Hans A. Bethe, Eldred C. Nelson, and Felix Bloch. At a meeting late in June, the group reviewed the theoretical and experimental results and concluded that there were no major gaps in the theory of the fast-neutron reaction.[31] Nevertheless, the precise calculation of the amount of fissionable material needed for the weapon, the efficiency of the reaction, and the destructive effect of the weapon was not so easily accomplished. The discrepancy in experimental results made it impossible to do more than select possible ranges for these values. It was significant, however, that by the fall of 1942 the group's estimate of the amount of fissionable material needed for a weapon was moving toward a value twice as large as that stated in the March and June reports to the President.

102

This discouraging result was more than balanced by a startling conclusion by the theoretical group. Its discussions and calculations suggested that a much more powerful reaction than nuclear fission might be produced by the thermonuclear fusion of deuterium, the heavy-hydrogen isotope. So breathtaking was this new possibility that in July Oppenheimer made a special trip to Compton's summer retreat in Michigan to tell him the news, which soon spread among the scientists at Berkeley and Chicago despite the conscientious efforts of most to suppress any accidental reference to the possibility of a powerful weapon using a more easily attainable material. Oppenheimer arranged for basic nuclear studies of the very light elements using the cyclotrons at Harvard and Minnesota; members of the S-1 Executive Committee with straight faces evinced a new interest in the priorities assigned to the heavy-water plant at Trail, British Columbia; and a special meeting to plan research on the thermonuclear reaction was held in Chicago before the end of September.[32]

SEARCH FOR A SHORT CUT

The new results from Berkeley had important implications for Conant in his efforts to select a production process. From the beginning, he insisted that all planning be done strictly in terms of a weapon which would be ready

1944, the physicists and chemists might have by the end of that year the first kilogram which they needed to determine specifications for a nuclear weapon.

NEW WEAPON REQUIREMENTS

Ultimately, the selection of a production process would depend upon weapon requirements, a subject which had received little attention before the summer of 1942. Before much could be done to refine the crude estimates which Compton had made in January of critical mass and weapon efficiencies, it was necessary to compile data on basic nuclear reactions which required not only the use of cyclotrons, fast-neutron sources, and other scarce equipment but also the services of exceptionally skilled experimentalists. Early in 1942, Compton had given Gregory Breit the responsibility of co-ordinating the basic experiments on fast-neutron reactions at several universities and research institutions. With little authority and virtually no priority for his project, Breit found it difficult to mount the kind of effort he knew would be necessary to design the weapon. As a theoretical physicist, he did not find the administrator's role congenial, particularly after personality frictions developed at the Metallurgical Laboratory. A disagreement with Compton on security practices and a growing skepticism about the project resulted in Breit's resignation on May 18.[28] Having anticipated this event, Compton lost little time in choosing Breit's successor. His choice fell on Robert Oppenheimer, the California physicist who had assisted him in estimating weapon efficiencies earlier in the year. Oppenheimer accepted the assignment on the condition that he have as assistant someone with more experience than he had in experimental physics.[29] Compton selected John H. Manley, a physicist from the University of Illinois who was already engaged in cyclotron work at the Metallurgical Laboratory.

103

An organization meeting in Chicago on June 6 convinced Oppenheimer and Manley of the need for changes. They agreed that Oppenheimer would establish a group on theoretical physics at Berkeley, while Manley would use a firm hand in directing experimental work from Chicago. Heydenburg would continue his measurements at the Carnegie Institution on fission cross sections for both slow and fast neutrons in uranium 235 and 238. John H. Williams at Minnesota would continue his studies of analytical methods and the calibration of neutron sources. Joseph L. McKibben at Wisconsin would concentrate on scattering cross sections for fast neutrons. Several groups at the Metallurgical Laboratory would work on both measurements and instrumentation, while others at Berkeley, Cornell, Rice Institute, and Stanford would perform special measurements.[30]

Co-ordinating the efforts of this loose confederation of scientists was more than a full-time job for Manley during the summer of 1942. Not only

CONANT'S APPRAISAL

The last week end in October gave Conant time to reflect upon the things he had seen and heard during the two strenuous days in Pittsburgh and New York. On Monday morning, October 26, 1942, he outlined his conclusions for Bush.[27] No one process had yet emerged as superior to all the others, but the centrifuge was definitely the weakest. The S-1 Executive Committee on November 13 would have to decide whether or not to discontinue it. Gaseous diffusion still looked feasible but might be extremely difficult to complete in the time available. The pilot plant would not be ready until June, 1943, and no significant results from its operation could be expected before September. Conant could see no chance that either a centrifuge or gaseous-diffusion plant could be in operation before January 1, 1945. Still, Conant had not discarded the idea of a full-scale gaseous-diffusion plant.

There were, however, some aspects of gaseous diffusion which impressed Conant. Keith was convinced that the process was feasible on an industrial scale, and Conant had come to respect his judgment as practical and down to earth. Furthermore, Conant's trip to New York had led him to question the necessity for the pilot plant, which would require almost a year of effort. The very nature of the plant made it incapable of producing any appreciable amount of material before it was ready to turn out uranium 235 at full capacity. For this reason, a full-scale plant could be completed almost as soon as a pilot plant. He also recognized that the so-called pilot plant which Kellogg was building at Jersey City would not actually produce any uranium 235, but would only demonstrate the units for a large-scale plant. This realization of the limited value of the Jersey City pilot plant would have an important effect on impending decisions.

On the pile, progress during the summer seemed to be a reasonable basis for continued optimism. Conant noted that Lawrence, Compton, and Oppenheimer all had great hopes for the Chicago project. Compton, in fact, was now thinking of full-scale production by the spring of 1944. Conant, however, remained sufficiently skeptical about both the ultimate success of the pile and the time schedule to offer to buy the entire S-1 Committee a champagne dinner if the project attained full production by January 1, 1945.

All this deliberation led Conant to conclude that Lawrence's method remained the best bet for producing fissionable material before the end of 1944. True, there were more difficulties in the process than he had imagined earlier; the amount of equipment involved and the complexity of operation, Conant thought, staggered even Lawrence. Yet it still seemed conceivable if unlikely that the electromagnetic process would yield a kilogram of fissionable material by January 1, 1944. Conant recognized that the process might never be practical for large-scale production, but if it could be made to produce 100 grams of uranium 235 per day fairly regularly by the spring of for the present war. The production of the weapon was primarily a race against time, and now that the fissionable-material requirement for the weapon seemed to have doubled, time was even more important. It would no longer be possible to think of building small-scale plants which might produce a few kilograms of material. Scores of kilograms now seemed necessary either for fission or fusion weapons. More scientists were accepting the Army's plea for an industrial complex which would produce weapons in numbers. If the bomb were to have any use in the war, quantity production of fissionable material would be necessary within the next year. Certainly the possibilities were not good in late October, 1942. Could Conant dare to hope for some short cut to the weapon? Could he presume to suggest a giant stride over pilot plants and all intermediate steps, from laboratory experiments to full-scale plants? If there were reasonable chances for success, he would not hesitate. But what were the chances? Conant moved fast to find out.

In many ways Conant thought that the pile was the wildest gamble of all. As he suggested in his October 26 memorandum to Bush, he had strong reservations about its feasibility. He found Compton's time schedule unrealistic, and he doubted whether Chicago could do the job, particularly the large-scale separation of plutonium from irradiated uranium. If Compton disagreed with Conant on feasibility and the time schedule, he shared the concern over the plutonium separation process. Since June, Compton had consistently attempted to broaden the base of his organization by contracting parts of the work to experienced companies. Over the protests of his colleagues, he had welcomed the contract with Stone & Webster to design and construct the experimental pile facilities in the Argonne Forest. During the summer, he had urged Colonel Marshall to select an operating contractor promptly so that the company selected could have the benefit of participating in the development of the plant.

The most obvious need for outside help lay in the construction and operation of the plutonium separation plant. In August, Compton had arranged to borrow Charles M. Cooper, an experienced chemical engineer, from the du Pont Company. Cooper's presence in Chicago demonstrated the possible advantages of Compton's suggestion that du Pont be selected as operator of the experimental plant. Stone & Webster by this time was growing more uneasy about the scope of its assignment as plans for the Tennessee site evolved on an ever increasing scale. Perhaps du Pont could be induced to supply additional engineers to assist Stone & Webster.[33]

General Groves seized on this suggestion when he took command of the Manhattan project. He had frequently worked with du Pont in the construction of military explosives plants. He was impressed not only by the experience and competence of the company but also by the fact that du Pont had its own engineering department which built the plants the company was to operate. Why could not du Pont help Stone & Webster on design and construction of the plutonium separation plant and then take over as operator?

On the industrial scale, Seaborg's method would lend itself to some of the processing techniques which du Pont had used in its own chemical plants. After discussing the idea with Stone & Webster's executives, Groves presented it to E. G. Ackart, du Pont's chief engineer, on September 28. Ackart was inclined to believe that du Pont would prefer to assume full responsibility for a distinct portion of the work as a prime contractor rather than to be a jack-of-all-trades as a Stone & Webster subcontractor. But he agreed to carry the request back to the du Pont executive committee in Wilmington. Before the end of the week, du Pont officials returned to Washington to negotiate a contract covering design and procurement of equipment for the separation plant. A letter of intent was signed on October 3, and the additional du Pont personnel appeared in Chicago early the next week.

For Groves, the October 3 contract was but a beginning of his plans for du Pont. Within a week, he was back in Ackart's office with a request that the company take over the design and procurement of certain equipment for the pile. Ackart could not see how this assignment was related to du Pont's experience and suggested several other companies which the General might contact.[34]

Conant agreed that the pile project needed one of the nation's largest and most experienced industrial organizations, and he thought du Pont would be the best choice. He had been a du Pont consultant and was a friend of Charles Stine, a member of the executive committee. Groves called Willis F. Harrington, a du Pont vice-president, and asked him to come to Washington on Saturday, October 31. There would be no objection if Harrington brought Stine.

Groves pulled no punches in his discussions with the du Pont officials. Without speaking specifically of weapon uses, he emphasized the importance of the pile project to the war effort. He was convinced that du Pont could do the job better than any other company and that the task was beyond the capacity of any other company. The outcome of the war might well depend upon du Pont's willingness to take over the design, construction, and operation of the full-scale pile project.

The news which Stine and Harrington carried home to Wilmington troubled the du Pont executive committee. If the stakes were what Groves claimed, the company could not easily refuse. If the disadvantages were what they seemed to be at first glance, the company could not easily accept. The process, particularly the chain reaction, went far beyond the company's experience. The project would cause a heavy drain on du Pont's already short supply of technical personnel. Above all, Stine and Harrington were alarmed by the incredible specifications of Seaborg's process for plutonium separation. The company needed time and information to reach a decision. The executive committee notified Groves that, before giving an answer, du Pont would have to inspect the research in progress at the Metallurgical Laboratory.[35]

The group which arrived in Chicago on November 4 represented some of the best engineering talent in the du Pont organization. Stine, an organic chemist, had worked his way through the explosives and dyestuffs departments to the executive committee. Elmer K. Bolton had a similar background and was now general manager of the chemical department. Roger Williams, assistant general manager of the ammonia department, had twenty years of experience in the design and operation of chemical plants. At the other extreme was Crawford H. Greenewalt, a young chemical engineer who was director of research in the Grasselli department. Three members of du Pont's engineering department, including Tom C. Gary and Thomas H. Chilton, brought to the group their knowledge of industrial construction. Within a week, they observed every aspect of the research activities in Chicago and returned to Wilmington.

On November 10, less than two weeks after Stine and Harrington had gone to Washington, du Pont was ready to talk. Groves, Nichols, Compton, and Hilberry met with the du Pont executive committee in Wilmington. Prior to the meeting, Groves gave Walter S. Carpenter, Jr., the du Pont president, assurances that the President, the Secretary of War, and General Marshall considered the project of utmost importance to the war effort. Groves also admitted to Carpenter that under normal circumstances, the scientific knowledge available would not have been considered sufficient even to go into the design stage, but the paramount importance of the project made imperative the design, construction, and operation of the plants at the earliest possible date.

107

Then the du Pont officials presented their evaluation of Compton's project.[36] They emphasized that there were no positive assurances it would be successful. The self-sustaining chain reaction had not been demonstrated; nothing was known about the thermal stability of the reaction; no workable pile design seemed to be available; and the recovery of plutonium from highly radioactive material had not been demonstrated on more than a microchemical scale. By making all favorable assumptions, the du Pont staff estimated that it might be possible to produce a few grams of plutonium in 1943, a few kilograms in 1944, and to attain regular production in 1945. They could make no final decision, however, until the project had been compared with the other approaches to fissionable material production. Du Pont recommended that comparable feasibility reports be prepared on the other projects. In effect, the du Pont group admitted the outside possibility of meeting Compton's time schedule but insisted that the odds for doing so were extremely poor. If the report tended to confirm Conant's skepticism about the pile, Groves was encouraged that du Pont did not withdraw. He thought the company would probably accept the assignment if the process appeared to be the fastest route to a weapon.

When Groves returned from Wilmington after the November 10 meeting, he and Conant were ready to decide on the uranium 235 separation processes. They agreed to bypass the electromagnetic pilot plant in favor of the immediate development of at least a portion of the full-scale plant.[37] They had already agreed to a similar approach on gaseous diffusion. Since the end of October, Kellogg had been drawing up plans for a section of a full-scale gaseous-diffusion plant. The centrifuge could be eliminated.

The Military Policy Committee ratified these decisions on November 12. Du Pont and Stone & Webster would develop full-scale pile and electromagnetic plants. The gaseous-diffusion pilot plant was not to interfere with either. Depending on Kellogg's report, the committee might authorize a six-hundred-stage gaseous-diffusion plant.[38]

On November 14, the S-1 Executive Committee met in Conant's office in Washington. Conant, Briggs, Compton, Lawrence, Murphree, and Urey attended. Keith summarized the lengthy Kellogg report.[39] He thought he could complete the six-hundred-stage plant in ten months. It could later serve as the lower portion of a cascade capable of producing fully enriched uranium 235. After Keith left, Groves pointed out that this project might interfere with the electromagnetic and pile efforts, but he thought the plant could be in operation within fifteen or sixteen months after orders were placed. In its priority list, the committee placed the six-hundred-stage plant below the electromagnetic plant but above a second pile. During the afternoon session, the committee canceled the electromagnetic pilot plant and asked du Pont to recommend a process for producing an additional two and one-half tons of heavy water in the United States. All of these actions were routine; they represented nothing more than scientific approval of the decisions taken by the Military Policy Committee two days earlier.

A CRISIS FOR COMPTON

The November 14 meeting had its surprises. Before the day ended, both Conant and Groves were shaken by two disquieting developments in the pile program. The first came during the morning session when Compton blandly stated that he would build the first chain-reacting pile under the university stadium on Chicago's south side rather than in the Argonne Forest Preserve. Compton later recalled that Conant turned white at this news and that Groves rushed to the telephone to satisfy himself that the Argonne site could not be used.[40] Labor disputes had delayed the pile building scheduled for completion by October 20. When Fermi had seen that he could begin to assemble the pile before that date, he had convinced Compton that his calculations of the delay of neutron emission in the chain reaction were reliable enough to rule out the possibility of a runaway reaction or explosion. Not daring to seek approval from either the Army or the university administration, Compton had taken it upon himself to authorize the construction of the pile in the racquets court where Fermi had performed the exponential experiments. First there had been the downward revisions in the value of k; then the decision to enlarge the pile by 15 per cent; then the failure to complete the pile building; now the gamble with a possibly catastrophic experiment in one of the most densely populated areas of the nation!

If this disclosure did not weaken the S-1 Committee's faith in Compton's judgment, the news during the luncheon period shook the committee's confidence in the pile process to its foundations. Wallace A. Akers, the British technical chief, who joined Conant for lunch, informed him of Chadwick's recent conclusion that plutonium might not be a practical fissionable material for weapons. He reasoned that alpha particles emitted by the plutonium would produce neutrons in light-element impurities, which in turn would fission the plutonium and spoil the weapon before it could be completely assembled. Scarcely able to believe what he had heard, Conant checked Akers' statement with Lawrence, who confirmed the possibility.

That evening, after the S-1 meeting, Conant asked Lawrence and Compton for an explanation. He did not know that the scientists both at Berkeley and Chicago were aware of the danger. Early in October, 1942, Seaborg had discussed with Oppenheimer the possibility of spontaneous fission. Later, Seaborg had calculated that neutron emitters like boron could not be present in more than one part in a hundred billion of plutonium. On November 3, he had written Oppenheimer that he was "disturbed" about developing a chemical process to meet this specification. Before the two scientists could agree on any precise values, the issue had erupted at the S-1 meeting. Thus when Conant summoned Lawrence and Compton, they could only acknowledge the danger but offer no positive solution.[41]

109

Conant alerted Groves, who assembled a special investigating committee consisting of Lawrence, Compton, Oppenheimer, and Edwin McMillan. The committee's reply four days later overflowed with confidence in the plutonium process.[42] The new purity requirements the committee suggested would tax du Pont and the scientists at the Metallurgical Laboratory, but both Lawrence and Compton were confident they could be met. Almost before the report could reassure Conant, however, he received a study by Chadwick, who estimated that the total amount of impurities should be less than ten parts in a million by weight. When Conant compared this figure with those in the special committee's report, he was more disturbed than ever.[43] He thought it would be extremely difficult to meet Chadwick's specification, which would permit less than one-tenth the amount of impurities deemed allowable by the special committee. What concerned Conant just as much was the possible implication that the Berkeley and Chicago scientists could not produce accurate information. If this were true, it would not speak well for American science, which, Conant thought, would be judged for decades on its performance in the war projects. He hoped that the record would not show that in the enthusiasm of the chase, American scientists had lost their critical acumen and had failed to be realistic.

Additional studies at Chicago and Berkeley during the following weeks restored Conant's confidence in the feasibility of the pile. Compton countered du Pont's unenthusiastic report with an impassioned defense of the Chicago project. In his opinion, producing plutonium in 1943 was 99 per cent certain and fabricating bombs with this material a 90-per-cent probability. He defended the scientists at the Metallurgical Laboratory as unmatched in ability by any other group in the world. They were far better qualified, he insisted, to judge the feasibility and safety of the project than were the du Pont engineers, however talented they may have been. The Chicago group, he said, understood the responsibility of its position and believed that abandoning the plutonium project would be a national blunder. Lawrence agreed. He had stopped at Chicago with Oppenheimer and McMillan after the special committee meeting. After visiting the laboratory, Lawrence thought an all-out effort on plutonium was justified. As for purity requirements, Oppenheimer explained the apparent discrepancies between the special committee's report and Chadwick's conclusions. Compton in the meantime sent still another letter to Conant. Security barriers rather than a lack of scientific competence or acuity had caused the purity crisis.[44]

110

REAPPRAISAL

Groves and Conant, however, did not wait for time to resolve questions raised at the S-1 Committee meeting on November 14. The events of that day suggested a reappraisal of the entire S-1 project.[45] Du Pont had recommended such a survey in its report on the Metallurgical Laboratory, and some of those who attended the meeting in Wilmington sensed that the company would be more likely to accept the assignment after being permitted to inspect the work at Columbia and Berkeley. It was not surprising, therefore, that du Pont had strong representation on the committee appointed by Conant and Groves. To head the review, they turned to Warren K. Lewis, the chemical engineering professor who had served a year earlier on the National Academy committee. All the members of the group had at one time or another attended Lewis' classes at the Massachusetts Institute of Technology. The three du Pont members represented the three major aspects of the project: Greenewalt for research, Gary for engineering and construction, and Williams for plant operation. The fifth member was Murphree, who became ill at the last moment and was unable to serve. The du Pont members were concerned about the lop-sided composition of the group, especially after Murphree dropped out. But there was no time for additional appointments; Groves insisted that the review start at once.

Groves announced the appointment of the Lewis committee on Wednesday, November 18. Compton hurried back to Chicago that night and called a special meeting of his staff on Thursday morning. The situation was critical. In exactly seven days the committee would be coming to Chicago to determine the fate of the pile project. Unless it could be led to share the optimism at the Metallurgical Laboratory, the work and dreams of the past year might be discarded. Wasting no time, Compton asked members of his staff to prepare sections of a feasibility report which would bring together all relevant data on the pile, plutonium separations, and the weapon. In the meantime, the experimental group under Fermi did all in its power to complete the pile and demonstrate the nuclear chain reaction.[46] By recruiting all available help, Fermi and his assistants proceeded with the arduous task of machining the forty thousand blocks of graphite, unpacking blocks of uranium metal and oxide, and assembling them in the pile. Compton and his staff were convinced that the chain reaction was a certainty; perhaps this last great effort would justify the months of faith and work.

The Lewis committee assembled in New York on Sunday evening, November 22. The following day, the members discussed the gaseous-diffusion project with Urey, Dunning, and Keith. Then they inspected the experimental equipment in the Columbia laboratories. From what little they knew of the Columbia project before leaving Wilmington, they had been impressed with the possibilities of gaseous diffusion. Their New York visit confirmed this impression. The process seemed similar to some perfected before in the chemical industry. Even the work on barrier bore some resemblance to the development of catalysts for chemical processing. The committee was confident that, given enough concentrated study, the gaseous-diffusion process was sure to succeed. On the other hand, it was equally certain that the Kellogg-Columbia alliance as then constituted could not do the job. Far from being a united team dedicated to practical goals, the Columbia group seemed to be an informal association of academic scientists primarily interested in basic research. Since Keith seemed to have no voice in the work at Columbia, the Kellogg group was apparently pursuing an independent course on engineering and design. The committee agreed that gaseous diffusion was a most promising approach, but they saw a need for better organization and direction.

On Wednesday afternoon, November 25, the committeemen left Wilmington by train for Chicago. They arrived Thanksgiving morning and spent the day with Compton and his associates. Since the three du Pont members had inspected the Chicago project three weeks earlier, the stop was primarily for Lewis' benefit. Compton, however, did not miss his opportunity. Hilberry's hundred-page report reflected the determination of the Chicago group.[47] Capital letters on the first page proclaimed that the production of plutonium in quantities of military value was feasible. With full support for the project, the first 500 grams of plutonium could be produced in 1943 and the first bomb ready in 1944, with regular production in 1945. Appendices showed the chain reaction could be sustained and controlled, that sufficient materials for full-scale operation could be obtained, that plutonium could be produced and separated in quantity, and that it could be safely processed into weapons. But the fact remained that Fermi had not yet demonstrated the chain reaction. With neither enough high-grade graphite nor pure uranium

111

metal for the pile, Fermi was surrounding an inner core of superior materials with a shell of commercial graphite and uranium oxide. Despite the devotion and labor of Fermi's group over many weeks, the pile was not ready for operation before the committee took the train that same night for Berkeley.

When the committee arrived in Berkeley on Saturday afternoon, Lawrence launched at once into a briefing on the electromagnetic process. After the long train ride from Chicago, Lewis and his associates were too tired to enjoy the dinner which Lawrence had arranged at Trader Vic's, but they gamely returned to Berkeley for a full evening of presentations by Lawrence's enthusiastic staff. On Sunday morning they observed the operation of the calutrons in the cyclotron building. Everywhere they felt the impact of Lawrence's dynamic leadership, but the visit did not dispel their doubts that Lawrence could develop a full-scale electromagnetic process. Before the day was over, the committee boarded the train for Chicago, where they hoped to find Fermi's pile in operation.

In Chicago, the Lewis committee officially devoted the morning of December 2 to discussing the advantages of a heavy-water pile, but most thoughts were on the bizarre structure of uranium, graphite, and wood which Whitaker and Zinn, the night before, had completed under the stadium. By 9:45 that morning, Fermi had removed the first of the control rods from the pile, and before noon, summoned Compton to witness the final phases of the experiment. Greenewalt, as a representative of the reviewing committee, accompanied him. From the balcony of the racquets court, where Fermi and about twenty of his group were monitoring the array of instruments and observing the course of events, Compton could see the massive structure of the pile containing almost 400 tons of graphite, 6 tons of uranium metal, and 50 tons of uranium oxide. As the hours passed, Fermi repeated the tedious procedure of removing short lengths of the cadmium control rods and reading his instruments. Finally, at 3:20 P.M., the counters indicated a sustained chain reaction. In a few minutes, after an energy release of less than one watt, the increase in radioactivity in the room required Fermi to shut down the pile. Sustained operation would not be possible until the pile could be moved to the Argonne site, but the long quest was over. Greenewalt returned to his colleagues with the glow of success on his face. And after Compton had bid farewell to the committee, he called Conant at Harvard. "Jim," he said, "you'll be interested to know that the Italian navigator has just landed in the new world." [48]

LEWIS COMMITTEE REPORT

Significant as the December 2, 1942, experiment was in the history of technology, it was not in itself the key link in the closely ordered chain of events during that fateful month. Unlike the discovery of fission, the first demon-

MELVIN A. MILLER '46
ARGONNE NATIONAL LABORATORY

THE STAGG FIELD PILE, DECEMBER 2, 1942: AN ARTIST'S CONCEPTION / This first self-sustaining chain-reacting pile contained almost 400 tons of graphite, 6 tons of uranium metal, and 58 tons of uranium oxide. The figure in the foreground is withdrawing a control rod.

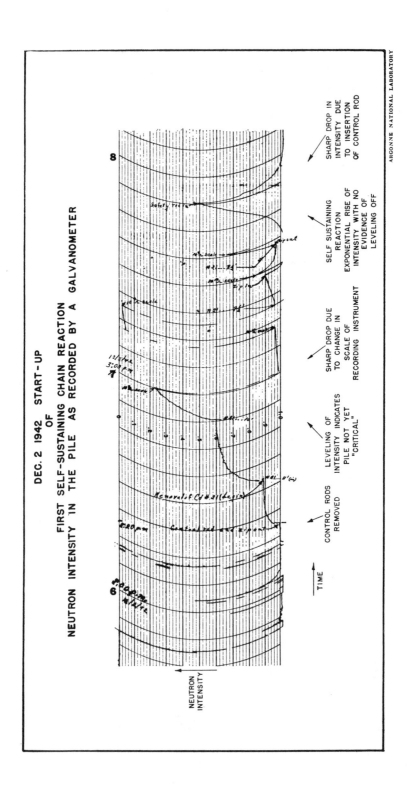

RECORD OF FIRST SELF-SUSTAINING CHAIN REACTION, DECEMBER 2, 1942 / Neutron intensity in the pile as recorded by a galvanometer.

stration of the chain reaction did not come as an unexpected burst of knowledge which staggered man's comprehension. It was rather the capstone of a structure which Fermi and others had been patiently building since the first weeks of 1939. To those most closely related to the work at Chicago, the final experiment verged on the anticlimactic. The famous bottle of Chianti which Eugene Wigner provided for the occasion had been purchased almost a year earlier in confident expectation of the event. Strictly speaking, the decision did not await the event; the event confirmed the decision already made. Before the Lewis committee members arrived in Chicago on their return trip, they had drafted their report which recommended continuing the pile project. The day before the Chicago experiment, Groves had.sent du Pont a letter of intent authorizing design and construction.

The most significant feature of the Lewis committee report concerned not the plutonium process but gaseous diffusion.[49] The committee concluded that "of all three methods, the diffusion process is believed to have the best over-all chance of success, and produces the more certainly usable material." Its recommendation was to design and construct the entire, full-scale gaseous-diffusion plant. Thus, after many months of neglect, diffusion regained the place it had held just a year before.

For the electromagnetic process, the committee recommended intensive development work on the experimental units at Berkeley to see whether the capacity of the calutron could be increased. With the equipment then available, about 22,000 calutrons would be necessary for a full-scale plant, a number considered too large to be practical. In the present state of development the committee did not believe that the electromagnetic process could produce fissionable material in quantities of military significance. The committee was less certain whether it should take advantage of the fact that the calutrons could produce a small amount of uranium 235 in a relatively short time. This advantage had impressed Bush and Conant in March. The committee recommended construction of a small plant consisting of 110 calutrons, which could produce a total of 100 grams of uranium 235 for physical measurements. Nuclear tests, it believed, required enough material for a weapon, and that meant a full-scale production plant. Since that possibility had already been ruled out, the committee could see no need for anything larger than the hundred-gram plant.

This recommendation drew virtually all the fire leveled at the report by the S-1 Executive Committee at its meeting in Washington on December 9. Murphree, still sick, wrote that he believed the electromagnetic process should be pushed harder. Lawrence thought that the committee's cost estimates did not reflect recent improvements. He thought he might get enough uranium 235 from the calutrons for the first weapon by July, 1944. Conant supported Lawrence in his opinion that the Lewis committee had overemphasized the difficulties and underestimated the value of having a weapon within eighteen months.[50] Since bomb design was becoming more

113

complicated, Conant wanted enough material for one test explosion. If the Germans should explode atomic weapons before the American plants came into full production, it would be of great psychological value to know whether the American bomb design would work, even though production by the electromagnetic process continued to be small. A plutonium weapon seemed much less certain than the uranium bomb, and Conant could not forget the fact he had uncovered during his October trip to New York; namely, that the entire diffusion plant would have to be completed before enough material could be accumulated for one weapon. He admitted that the electromagnetic process would look much less promising if several stages were needed to produce fully enriched uranium 235 or if the minimum amount of material for a weapon turned out to be several times the present estimates. In his opinion, it was essential to build an electromagnetic plant of 500 or 600 calutrons, which would produce at least 100 grams of uranium 235 per day.

114

DECISION

During the afternoon session on December 9, the S-1 Committee considered a report Groves had drafted for the President. As revised, the report carried the Lewis committee's recommendations with one exception: the pile was to be developed at once at full-scale without any intermediate plant. This did not mean, however, that Conant had abandoned his fight for the electromagnetic process. His sharp attack on the Lewis committee report required him to spend several hours with that group on December 10. He ended by admitting that his comments might have conveyed some false impressions about the report, but the meeting did not change his original conviction that the production of at least one weapon in 1944 was of supreme importance.[51] When Conant met with the Military Policy Committee later that day, Groves's report was revised to provide for the construction of an electromagnetic plant to produce 100 grams per day,[52] a compromise between a full-scale plant and that recommended by the Lewis committee to produce a total of 100 grams.

The report Bush sent to the President on December 16, 1942, approached the issues in terms of bomb size.[53] The new estimate doubling the amount of fissionable material for the bomb would not only increase the size and cost of the production plants, but would require a longer period to obtain the first bomb, which might end the war if the enemy were wavering. Also, the S-1 Committee had reduced the number of approaches to the weapon from four to three, rather than to one or two as originally hoped. It would now be necessary to build with utmost speed and the highest priorities full-scale gaseous-diffusion and plutonium plants costing $150 million and $100 million, respectively; a smaller electromagnetic plant which might later be expanded to full size, at a cost of $10 million; and heavy-water plants at ordnance works in the United States capable of producing 2.5 tons per month, at $20 million. Thus, the total effort would cost about $400 million, $85 million of which had been authorized in June.

There was a small chance, in the opinion of the Military Policy Committee, that bomb production could begin before June 1, 1944, a somewhat better chance before January 1, 1945, and a good chance during the first half of 1945. It was extremely difficult to estimate whether this schedule would beat the Germans. It seemed to the committee highly improbable that the Germans would have an atomic weapon in 1943, but it was possible that they might be six months or a year ahead of the United States.

Presidential approval on December 28 marked an important step in the transition from exploratory research in the scientific laboratory under the OSRD to an all-out production effort by private industry under Army supervision. Even before President Roosevelt initialed the December 16 report, General Groves had entered into contract negotiations with a half dozen of the nation's largest corporations for designing, constructing, and operating a giant industrial complex. Within a matter of days, Groves set his half-billion-dollar enterprise in motion on a scale which would have been beyond the wildest dreams of the S-1 Committee in the days after the Pearl Harbor attack just one year earlier. Now that the commitment had been made, the S-1 Committee could begin to liquidate its operations. By the first of January, 1943, Conant and Richard C. Tolman had in effect replaced the committee as Groves's scientific advisers, although the change was not formally ratified until March, when the committee transferred to the Army all their OSRD research and development contracts on the basic processes. The committee would continue to supervise several specialized research projects such as the centrifuge and the isotron until the fall of 1943, but the main current had now shifted decisively from the laboratory to the production plant.

115

The nation's reaction to the dramatic act of war by the Japanese one year earlier had been one of stunned disbelief. Confusion, indecision, and frustration marked the early months of 1942, but by spring a discernible plan of action had begun to emerge. By fall, those plans were taking material shape in the arsenals of war, and by the end of the year the nation was at last moving to the offensive. In a smaller way, the same pattern could be seen in the newborn atomic energy program. Bush and Conant had translated the confusion, false optimism, and indecision of the previous winter into a reasonable plan of operation by June. They had transferred authority to the Army during the summer and hammered out decisions on production processes and the scale of operation during the closing months of the year. As 1943 opened, the immense cradle of a revolutionary industry was being hastily carved out of the red soil of eastern Tennessee, and plans were being laid for two new communities in the desert wastes of the western United States. The race was on, and no effort to win would be spared. In the minds of those responsible, the haunting question remained: could the Americans beat the Germans to the atomic bomb?

RACE FOR THE BOMB:
URANIUM 235

CHAPTER 5

CITY IN THE WILDERNESS

On a muggy morning in September, 1942, General Groves stood at a vantage point near the hamlet of Elza, Tennessee, and looked southwest over the terrain where the race for the atomic bomb might well be won or lost. To his left, the main line of the Louisville & Nashville Railroad crossed the Clinch River. On his right, roughly paralleling the river's meandering course to the south and west was Black Oak Ridge and beyond that, through the haze, the outlines of the Cumberland Plateau. Between the river and the ridge from Elza to Gallaher Ferry, sixteen miles to the southwest, lay a rectangular area of roughly ninety square miles. Precisely folded by geologic forces, its system of long parallel ridges and valleys had served as avenues for American settlement a century before. Generations of farming had exhausted the bottom lands in the narrow valleys between the wooded ridges. Not even the monumental projects of the Tennessee Valley Authority had yet dispelled the cloud of depression which had settled over the area in the thirties. Few more than 1,000 families remained to be evicted from their homes by the Manhattan project.

In the weeks following the General's visit, local residents abandoned their churches, homes, schools, and roads, as the Army quickly acquired the entire area as a military reservation. Sealed off by fences, signs, and road-blocks, the site was closed to all but the tens of thousands of laborers, contractors, and Army engineers who were to build the production plant and town which would house the scientists and operating personnel. With no thought of building a permanent or ideal community, the Army set out to construct a temporary, low-cost housing development which would use a minimum of critical construction materials and on-site labor.[1]

Stone & Webster, the Army's general contractor, drew preliminary plans for the town during the summer of 1942 in its Boston offices. On the assumption that the production plants would require a town with a population of 13,000, Stone & Webster planned for 3,000 houses, 1,000 trailers, several dormitories, a guest house, cafeteria, administration building, and central laboratory. The contractor presented these plans to the Army on October 26. The same day, the Army opened the offices of the Clinton Engineer Works in the Andrew Johnson Hotel in Knoxville.

Before any construction could begin, extensive site preparation was required. Stone & Webster, with the help of the Harrison Construction Company, removed existing structures and utilities, cleared and graded building sites, and erected fencing and guard towers. From the beginning, poor roads hampered construction. Except for some winding trails and paths, only five country roads traversed the site—one along each of the three main valleys and two cutting across the ridge-and-valley system from Scarboro and White Wing Bridge on the south. None were paved with an all-weather surface except that part of Route 61 which crossed a corner of the reservation near Elza. Within a few months, construction crews had transformed some of these narrow rural roads into four-lane highways carrying more than 10,000 cars per day. Almost 100 miles of paved streets would be required for the town of Oak Ridge and another 200 miles of pavement were planned to reach the production plants isolated in outlying valleys. To this network the Army planned to add a central railroad system with thirty-seven miles of track connecting the site with the main line at Elza.

117

The town and central facilities would lie just beyond Elza gate on the slopes of Black Oak Ridge and in the broad valley drained by the East Fork of Poplar Creek. Down the center of the valley ran the new four-lane Oak Ridge Turnpike, which was to become the central artery of the community. On a rise to the left, facing the ridge, Stone & Webster began constructing the main administration building on the Sunday before Thanksgiving in 1942. In the absence of good roads and communications, progress was slow. One rural telephone in a nearby farmhouse served as the only direct line to Knoxville until December, when a three-position switchboard was set up on the second floor of the Blue Moon Cafe on the turnpike where the town steam plant was later constructed.

One of the first structures to be completed in 1943 was the administrative building. Soon dubbed "the castle" by the new residents, the rambling edifice dominated the expansive rise like a fortress, belied only by its flimsy wooden barracks-type construction. The building served first as headquarters for the Clinton Engineer Works, the formal name for the entire area, including the town, within the security fence. Later, in the summer of 1943, Colonel Nichols transferred the headquarters of the Manhattan District from New York to "the castle" when he succeeded Colonel Marshall as District Engineer. As the control center for the Manhattan project, "the castle" was second only to General Groves's liaison office in Washington.

Starting with Stone & Webster's general layout of the town, Skidmore, Owings & Merrill began to prepare detailed plans for housing and commercial facilities early in February, 1943. For family housing, they developed plans for nine types of homes and three apartment buildings, all of wood frame construction covered with cemesto board panels. Dormitories and commercial facilities were to be low, rambling wooden buildings closely resembling Army-camp architecture. In order to overcome the shortage of local construction labor, Stone & Webster adopted the policy of keeping as many contractors on the job as possible. As a result, more than sixty contractors, selected by competitive bidding for lump-sum or unit-price contracts, participated in town construction.

From the newly completed administration building, Colonel Robert C. Blair and his town planning staff could look out during the spring of 1943 on a forest of half-completed structures arising from a sea of mud. Clustered around the turnpike at the bottom of the valley were fourteen new dormitories. Beyond, on the lower slopes of the ridge, the town business center, later called Jackson Square, was taking form. Around the two-block area were the post office, supermarkets, drugstores, shops, movie theater, central cafeteria, and laundry. Higher on the slope were the guest house and the site for the high school. Festooned on the ridge both east and west of the town center were the cemesto homes and apartments for more than 3,000 families. A few to the east nestled among the shade trees of prewar Tennessee, but by far the majority of the new homes were unceremoniously wedged on the scarred contours of the ridge. In the low area on the opposite side of the turnpike were temporary housing facilities for construction laborers. Almost 5,000 workers lived in the boxlike prefabricated hutments of plywood grouped around central washhouses and mess halls. Federal housing agencies gathered more than 1,000 trailers from all parts of the United States for supplemental housing.

By the first days of summer in 1943, trucks were struggling through the mud with the household goods of the first permanent residents. Housewives learned again how to live without telephones, central heating, and spotless floors. Newcomers from every state in the Union began pouring into the stores on Jackson Square before the buildings were completed, and the flood seemed to have no end. A booming frontier town with a Klondike atmosphere, Oak Ridge never grew fast enough. But the dislocations and inconveniences of life in the mushrooming community were balanced by the excitement and quickened tempo of the town.

Some of the hardships and much of the color of early Oak Ridge were reflected in a letter to the townspeople in one of the first mimeographed issues of the *Oak Ridge Journal:* "Yes, we know it's muddy. . . . Coal has not been delivered. . . . The grocer runs out of butter and milk. . . . Your laundry gets lost. . . . The post office is too small. . . . There are not enough bowling alleys. . . . Your house leaks. . . . The water was cold. . . . The telephones are always busy. . . . The dance hall is crowded. . . .

The guest house is full. . . . Employees are inexperienced. . . . The roads are dusty. . . . You would have planned it differently." [2] The letter went on to assure the readers that some improvements would be made by the Roane-Anderson Company, the new organization formed by the Turner Construction Company specifically to manage the town. Other complaints such as food shortages would go unanswered until the end of the war, and some complaints recurred with the skyrocketing growth of the town. In the fall of 1943, the Army planned additional homes for 5,000 families. Based on designs developed by TVA, most of the homes were prefabricated in sections in many distant cities and trucked to Oak Ridge. For other housing needs, FHA provided 2,000 additional trailers. Local construction contractors threw up an additional 55 dormitories and 500 hutments and barracks. Skidmore, Owings & Merrill planned additional schools, shopping facilities, and churches as total population forecasts rose to 42,000. New concentrations of stores several miles down the Oak Ridge Turnpike at Grove Center and in the trailer area at Middletown Center were but modest predecessors of a new commercial institution that was to transform suburban America in the postwar period.

119

The town existed merely to serve the mammoth production sites which would soon rise in isolated portions of the reservation. The long ridges shielded the narrow valleys from prying eyes and would help to contain the effects of bombing or any cataclysmic accident which might befall these first efforts to produce fissionable material. Closest to the town but separated from it by East Fork Ridge was the site for the electromagnetic plant. Known as the Y-12 area, it was a long strip of flat terrain within Bear Creek Valley. The first plutonium-producing pile and its associated chemical separation buildings were to be located further to the south and west in Bethel Valley, in an area called X-10. At the far southwest end of the reservation, on the old Gallaher homestead was the K-25 area, where the gaseous-diffusion and thermal-diffusion plants were to be built. Construction on the first two sites started early in 1943, and all three had taken on the appearance of a giant industrial complex before the end of the year. By that time, working estimates had climbed to $24 million for the town and central facilities and $492 million for the production areas.

This investment was for one purpose only: to beat the Germans in the race for the bomb. There had been great progress since the days of Pearl Harbor, and the pace was ever quickening. But Bush, Conant, and Groves could never forget that the Germans had an eighteen-months' lead. The American leaders knew that prominent German physicists were investigating the process of nuclear fission in 1939. After the fall of Norway, the Germans had tried to increase the production of heavy water in a plant at Rjukan. The fear that the Germans might be collecting heavy water for use as a moderator in a pile to produce plutonium led to the British commando raid on the plant in March, 1943. The evidence of German activity and the slow start of the

American project alarmed Secretary of War Stimson. He told the President late in February that he was deeply concerned. Roosevelt offered to provide more money.[3] But more than money, Stimson needed tangible accomplishment in the form of operating plants for the large-scale production of fissionable material. That was the mission of K-25, Y-12, and X-10 at Oak Ridge.

K-25 PRODUCTION TEAM

On December 10, 1942, the Military Policy Committee agreed to immediate construction of a full-scale gaseous-diffusion plant. That decision reflected the Lewis reviewing committee's conviction that gaseous diffusion was the most straightforward approach to isotope separation and thus the most likely to succeed. Certainly the progress made by the Kellogg Company and the Columbia University laboratory was not the basis for that favorable verdict. The New York team had not yet built anything remotely resembling a pilot plant. In fact, they had scarcely demonstrated the feasibility of the process by the few laboratory experiments completed in 1942. Even more disconcerting was the failure of the Kellogg-Columbia team to transform itself into an efficient development organization. The company had made little impact on the informal, academic methods of the university. The erratic fluctuations between optimism and despair which pervaded the reports from Columbia in 1942 had dulled the reactions of the leaders in Washington. Groves and Conant learned to discount such reports as the sincere but momentary opinions of brilliant but unpredictable scientists.

One source of confidence in gaseous diffusion was Percival C. Keith. Although sometimes impetuous, the blustery Texan fully understood the requirements of an industrial process. When he saw during the autumn that technical difficulties would long delay the completion of a pilot plant, he had sold the S-1 Executive Committee on the six-hundred-stage plant.

Events moved swiftly. On Saturday morning, December 12, 1942, Keith and other Kellogg officials met with General Groves and his lieutenants to discuss a contract. A letter of intent was to be negotiated with Colonel Marshall on Monday morning, December 14. As Keith outlined the project for the General, he must have felt for the first time the full weight of the assignment. He was to direct the construction of a tremendous plant using an untried process. Such a plant, containing thousands of pumps and electric motors, would require more electricity than most American cities. The task would have been extraordinary even if it had involved a conventional technology. No wonder some of the Kellogg executives were less than enthusiastic about risking the reputation of the company on such an enterprise. Even with their wholehearted support, Keith knew he could not hope to recruit even his senior staff from the Kellogg organization.[4]

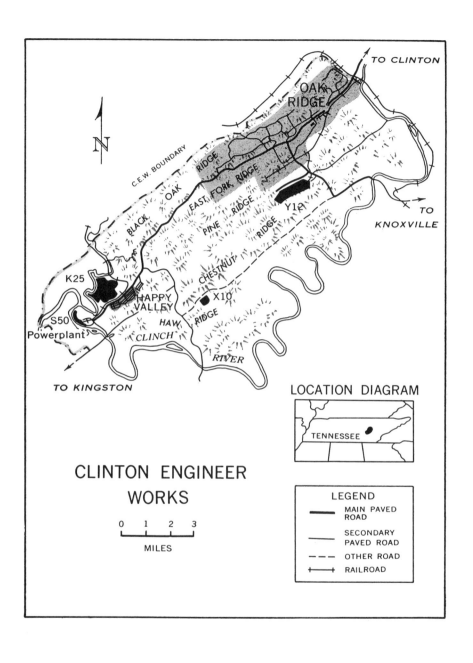

TO CLINTON

OAK RIDGE

C.E.W. BOUNDARY

N

BLACK OAK RIDGE

EAST FORK RIDGE

PINE RIDGE

CHESTNUT RIDGE

RIDGE

Y12

TO KNOXVILLE

K25

HAPPY VALLEY

X10

S50
Powerplant

HAW RIDGE

CLINCH

RIVER

TO KINGSTON

CLINTON ENGINEER
WORKS

0   1   2   3
MILES

LOCATION DIAGRAM

TENNESSEE

LEGEND

MAIN PAVED
ROAD

SECONDARY
PAVED ROAD

OTHER ROAD

RAILROAD

The corporate complications were resolved by creating a new company especially for the gaseous-diffusion job. Completely owned by Kellogg and staffed with virtually the same officers, the Kellex Company would be a separate entity with its own accounts and name to bear the stigma of possible failure. In addition to performing the research and development functions assumed by Kellogg a year earlier, the new corporation would design and procure the thousands of components, prepare detailed plans of the entire plant, supervise its construction, and direct the installation and assembly of equipment.

Personnel needs were not so easily met. Keith could recruit a few men from the Kellogg organization, like John A. Arnold, who served as his executive officer, or Albert L. Baker, Kellogg's chief mechanical engineer on refinery design, or Manson Benedict, a theoretical chemist who could cope with the more complicated aspects of design, or Clarence Johnson, an excellent process engineer. For most of his staff, however, Keith had to comb the engineering world, which by 1943 had been well picked over for other war projects. Even when Keith found a rare specimen, he could not always coax his quarry into the Kellex net. Many of the design problems facing the Keith team were sufficiently novel to require the very best of engineering skill and imagination. At the same time, nagging little engineering puzzles often proved poor fare for men of this caliber, especially when they were not aware of the larger significance of the project. Keith even used the great cathedrals of Europe as recruiting propaganda. To those who seemed reluctant to join his ranks on a tedious but vital task, he would extol the European artisans who had been content to devote a lifetime to the creation of a stained glass window at Chartres or to the intricate figures sculpted on the doors of the Baptistry in Florence. With these and other enticements, he succeeded in assembling a topflight group of engineers.

Harder for Keith to control was the organization beyond his own household. Since Kellex would not operate the plant, a second prime contractor had to be selected, and, as far as Keith was concerned, the sooner the better. He suggested several companies to Groves at the December 12 meeting. A good operating contractor, he thought, could help in many ways during design and construction. Upon the recommendation of Keith and several du Pont officials, Groves arranged a meeting with executives of the Union Carbide and Carbon Corporation. He proposed that Carbide start work at once, not only to prepare for operation of the plant but also to assist Kellex and the research group at Columbia. James A. Rafferty, a Carbide vice-president, agreed. The Carbide engineers would supply at once a group of trained technical personnel to study the data amassed by Kellogg during the preceding year; they would, where necessary, investigate the design, operation, engineering, and construction of the plant; they would serve both Kellex and the general construction contractor as consultant and inspector of equipment installation. On January 18, 1943, Rafferty signed a letter contract

121

for the Carbide and Carbon Chemicals Corporation, the Carbide operating subsidiary. Through this contract Keith could now call upon the resources of the Carbide empire, including the Electro Metallurgical Company, the National Carbon Company, and the Linde Air Products Company. Here was impressive talent, but the bonds uniting it with the rest of the project were tenuous at best.[5]

At the same time, Keith never let his eye wander from Columbia. There the struggle for a gaseous-diffusion process would be decided, and to a businessman like Keith, that fact was not particularly reassuring. For all their brilliance, the scientists at Columbia were not a reliable source of support. They, like most academicians, seemed to Keith unpredictable and ineffective, prone to wander off the straight paved road of practical progress into interesting but irrelevant theoretical byways. John R. Dunning was, perhaps, the most realistic of the group. Still the effective leader, if not the nominal head of the Columbia project on gaseous diffusion, Dunning seemed to many to be more an engineer than a physicist. He had been known to suggest that possibly a scientist could have too much knowledge, that too many facts would make him overly sensitive to the obstacles in the path of technical advances. He grew impatient with theoretical proofs of what would not work; he could feel in his bones that gaseous diffusion would be practical for large-scale separation of uranium isotopes.

Dunning's research organization had grown to an impressive size by 1943. Having appropriated all available space in Pupin Hall on the Columbia campus, the gaseous-diffusion group had overflowed into Schermerhorn. Before long Dunning was arranging for additional space at Princeton University, the Bell Telephone Laboratories in New York, and the Kellex Plant in Jersey City. By the spring of 1943, Francis G. Slack's section on barrier research was approaching fifty members, and there were about thirty scientists and technicians assigned to each of the other five groups. Henry A. Boorse continued to direct the development of pumps and other mechanical equipment. Eugene T. Booth was in charge of the cascade test units. The many problems requiring the chemist's skill fell on the broad shoulders of Willard F. Libby. The development of analytical techniques was the responsibility of Alfred O. C. Nier, a true master of the art. Hugh C. Paxton provided the multitude of engineering services needed to support the activities of the laboratory.

On the campus, research continued in the same informal, loose-jointed way which had characterized earlier investigations at Columbia. But administrative activities had taken on a new dimension as the Army, then Kellex, now Carbide joined the work. Early in January, Keith began calling weekly staff meetings at the Kellex office in the Woolworth Building on lower Broadway. Dunning usually represented Columbia, George T. Felbeck attended for Carbide, and at least one representative of the Army, usually Colonel James C. Stowers, acted for General Groves. Soon Carbide had offices in the same building. Dunning provided desks and books for the Columbia scientists as an inducement to make the trek from Morningside Heights for consultations with the engineers.[6]

FIRST BLUEPRINTS

The combined research forces first considered the general design of the plant. Keith and others had made rough estimates of the magnitude and probable requirements for a full-scale plant in 1942, but in 1943 it was time to be more specific. The first step was to fix once and for all the general "shape" of the cascade. As Cohen and Benedict had explained to the S-1 Executive Committee the previous summer, the gaseous-diffusion process ideally required an infinite number of stages and equipment sizes. They had shown the committee how to approximate the ideal cascade with a reasonable number of stages and a relatively small number of equipment sizes. It was one matter, however, to suggest how this might be done and quite another to produce a design that could be employed with confidence in a $100 million plant. By the end of 1942, Cohen had completed more detailed calculations. He was now confident that the shape of his pyramid was correct. He found that without seriously impairing production or increasing the inventory of uranium in the cascade, he could reduce the number of stages and equipment sizes in the plant, lessen the possibility of leaks, and simplify operational procedures. Working from Cohen's calculations, Benedict and the Kellex design group in March, 1943, completed a plot plan and general arrangement for the plant. They conceived of the main production area as a series of contiguous buildings in the shape of a U, occupying three sides of a rectangle 2,000 feet long and 1,900 feet wide. Warehouses and railroad sidings would occupy the fourth side and the central area would contain the powerhouse, electrical substation, cooling towers, pump houses, and central control rooms. They established the number of stages, the number of equipment sizes, and the general specifications for each size and type. From these, Kellex draftsmen prepared sketches of typical sections of the plant. Keith gave all these data, assembled in a thick orange book, to Columbia and Carbide for their guidance.[7]

For all the theoretical analysis and drawings, the Kellex report could hardly serve as the basis for final engineering designs and plant construction. So tentative were the designs of most components that it was impossible to conceive what the most elementary configuration of cascade equipment might be. Construction in the Y-12 and X-10 areas at Oak Ridge started early in 1943, but Kellex could not think of starting the gaseous-diffusion plant until its basic components had been developed.

K-25 COMPONENT DESIGN

One matter that worried Keith was the chemistry of the process. The day after the December, 1942, decision by the Military Policy Committee, Keith met with Dunning, Slack, and Libby in Jersey City. He was concerned about the consumption of uranium hexafluoride as it passed through the cascade. If the gas reacted even at an extremely low rate with the materials in the pumps, converters, and pipe, there might well be nothing left to emerge from the top of the cascade after the gas had traveled hundreds of miles through this mechanical labyrinth. Even if not this severe, losses might be sufficiently large to reduce the production of uranium 235 substantially. Keith also emphasized the importance of correlating experiments using mixtures of carbon dioxide and helium with those employing hexafluoride. It was much easier to experiment with the nontoxic, more common gases, but Keith was not sure that such results could be translated accurately into reliable data on diffusion. Correlation studies were critical for barrier materials, which would receive ever increasing emphasis. Several types of barrier had been subjected to the flow of hexafluoride for a period of hours or even days, but Keith wanted to know how it would stand up to weeks or months of exposure. In January, he gave Zola G. Deutsch the job of investigating the consumption of process gas by various types of barrier and put Clarence Johnson to work on correlation studies.[8]

As an engineer, Keith was no less impressed with the importance of developing suitable pumps to transport the process gas through the cascade. Next to barrier, pumps were clearly the most critical component of the plant. Moving parts were always susceptible to wear, and it was almost impossible to seal them against leakage. In the summer of 1942, Keith had agreed to leave the development of the reciprocating types to Boorse. At the same time, Keith assigned the initial development of the larger centrifugal pumps to Ingersoll-Rand. By early 1943, however, that arrangement came to an end. Ingersoll-Rand, now faced with the monumental task of developing a final design and manufacturing thousands of large pumps, found its facilities and manpower unequal to the task and withdrew from the project.

Ingersoll-Rand's withdrawal left Keith without a pump contractor and without any real solution to the critical problems of pump design. He erased the first deficiency in February, 1943, when he succeeded in securing the services of the Allis-Chalmers Manufacturing Company, which had already accepted a large contract in the electromagnetic project. The Army engineers under General Groves negotiated a contract with Allis-Chalmers and arranged the necessary priorities for construction of a new plant near Milwaukee.

It was easier for Keith to find a contractor than a good pump design.

The preliminary studies in 1942 by Ingersoll-Rand and Columbia pointed to seals as the primary obstacle in the development of centrifugal pumps, especially for small, high-velocity models. For this reason, Boorse had concentrated on reciprocating pumps. The rotary shaft seals developed by Ingersoll-Rand for their models of larger pumps were far from satisfactory when Allis-Chalmers entered the scene. Their first approach was to minimize the seal problem by enclosing the entire unit—both pump and motor—in a vacuum-tight enclosure filled with inert gas. A somewhat different application of the same concept was developed by Boorse, Gilbert F. Boeker, and John R. Menke at Columbia. Allis-Chalmers abandoned their suggestion when they found it impossible to find motors which would operate in the sealed unit, but the Columbia approach showed promise. Westinghouse built several test models which the Columbia scientists later used successfully in the laboratory for pumping uranium hexafluoride gas. But before Columbia could develop a production model for the gaseous-diffusion plant, they found a new seal which revolutionized the design of centrifugal pumps.

The new seal had its origins in Boorse's interest in pumps for the upper stages of the cascade. The design of a centrifugal pump for this application seemed especially difficult, but Boorse was not one to overlook possibilities. He asked for help from Ronald B. Smith of the Elliott Company of Jeannette, Pennsylvania. There, after an extensive investigation of sealing devices late in 1942, Judson S. Swearingen, one of Smith's scientists, hit upon a promising design. Swearingen after a series of experiments reported in March that his apparatus was mechanically stable and would almost completely contain the process gas. The Sharples Corporation in Philadelphia then built a test model of the seal under Swearingen's direction. This model, taken to Columbia for testing late in the spring of 1943, contained in prototype form most of the essential elements of the seal used in the K-25 plant.[9]

By far, Keith's biggest hurdle was to find a barrier material susceptible to large-scale production and capable of maintaining its separative qualities over long periods of continuous operation. For the moment, he would have settled for a material with just the latter property, but a year of research had not yet come even close to meeting that specification. The trouble was that so many of the desirable properties of barrier were contradictory. The holes in the barrier had to be submicroscopic but not susceptible to plugging. The material thus had to be porous but strong enough to stand large-scale assembly methods and extremely severe operating conditions. By the end of 1942, Keith was convinced that most of the metal barriers tested would never be satisfactory. During the fall he had reluctantly agreed to more research on the slim chance that a makeshift barrier could be developed for pilot plants. Since then, he had concluded that for the production plant the barrier would have to be in tubular form, and he believed that the original metal barriers could never be manufactured as tubes. In the

125

closing days of 1942, Dunning and Keith began formulating a new research program which would place greater emphasis on nickel barriers.

The relatively brief experience with nickel barriers during the fall of 1942 demonstrated that no simple solution lay in this direction. The nickel barriers first prepared by Norris and Adler seemed much too brittle and fragile for production in quantity. The barrier formed from nickel powder by Foster Nix of the Bell Telephone Laboratories showed very poor separative qualities. But of the two, the Norris-Adler barriers seemed more likely to be successful. The process was not a simple one. It usually involved as many as eight or ten steps. It did seem possible, however, that all these steps could be combined in a continuous process suitable for large-scale production. A second advantage was the infinite number of variations or combinations which could be tried. Experiments in 1942 had already shown that one slight variation in any step in the process could completely alter the separative qualities of the product. Until more of these variations and combinations could be tested, it would be impossible to rule out the production of a satisfactory barrier. The result was that literally hundreds of different nickel barriers were developed, tested, and discarded. In time, however, the barrier samples fell into certain general classifications and for purposes of communication were arbitrarily given names. By the end of 1942, the most promising type was known as "Norris-Adler" barrier.[10]

The large number of variables in the barrier manufacturing process might have appealed to the ingenuity of a temperamental chef, but to process engineers the recipe was a nightmare. How could one be sure that an individual accent here or a personal touch there did not spell the difference between a good and bad product? Indeed, so empirical was the method that success was likely to depend on just some such intuitive innovation. The cookbook approach did raise some perplexing questions. Was any one sample representative of the product as a whole? If so, was it good barrier? If good, could the process be duplicated on a production scale to make large amounts of uniform quality? Answering these questions placed a burden on those scientists engaged in analytical research at Columbia. In the spring of 1943, several groups were running tests on a laboratory scale. Robert T. Lagemann was using inert gases to measure porosity against certain standards. Clifford K. Beck was responsible for mechanical testing for tensile strength, elongation, bending properties, and fatigue resistance. Rex B. Pontius tested barrier performance in the single-stage unit, and a group under Willard F. Libby tested barrier for corrosion and plugging resistance. Begun as a series of informal laboratory measurements, barrier evaluation soon took on the proportions of a full-scale production control program. To guide this effort, Urey enlisted the aid of Hugh S. Taylor, the Princeton scientist who had been instrumental in developing the heavy-water process for the plant at Trail, British Columbia. In June, 1943, Taylor cleared his laboratory at Princeton to help in barrier evaluation.

126

The production of Norris-Adler barrier was limited to laboratory techniques in 1942. Obviously, the development of a continuous production process was a matter of high priority. In January, 1943, Norris and Slack laid plans for the construction of a pilot plant which would produce the barrier in a continuous process. With assistance from Kellex, they arranged for the necessary machinery to be designed and constructed by the New Jersey Machine Company. On February 4, they began clearing an area in the basement of Schermerhorn Laboratory at Columbia for installation of the pilot plant. Design, assembly, testing, and modification occupied most of the following five months; the plant was not operated until July.

By that time, the construction of a full-scale barrier production plant had been started in Illinois. On April 1, 1943, the Army had approached the Houdaille-Hershey Corporation to produce several million square feet of barrier by the end of the year. Accepting the job, the company at once made plans to construct a new building for the purpose next to its Oakes Products Plant in Decatur. Before the end of the summer, Houdaille-Hershey had set up its own pilot plant in the new building to experiment with various steps in the barrier manufacturing process.[11]

127

Operation of the pilot plants was not altogether discouraging. By mid-July, 1943, the Schermerhorn plant was running round-the-clock with some sections performing continuously for periods up to seventy-five hours. Although some minor adjustments and refinements were necessary, the original designs of the equipment were fundamentally sound. Within a short time, the plant produced enough barrier for testing purposes. Then the trouble began. Mechanical tests showed the old defects of brittleness and structural weakness. Libby's chemistry group found the material susceptible to corrosion and plugging. Performance in the single-stage test unit was far from satisfactory. Most distressing of all was the lack of uniformity of the material, especially in separative quality. For no apparent reason, one section of barrier would rate high; another from the same batch would be poor. Pinholes and other imperfections cropped up without explanation. Under the heavy pressure of time, Columbia continued to test samples in hopes that some modification in the process might somehow give a better product.[12]

Although barrier production occupied the center of the stage during the summer of 1943, there were other important activities in the New York area during that period. At Columbia, one of the largest supporting activities was in chemistry under Libby's direction. Even at this late date, there was much to learn about the chemistry of uranium hexafluoride. The results of such basic research directed by Homer F. Priest were utilized in the study of corrosion rates and the mechanism of corrosion for various materials. From these studies, Libby was able to determine some of the important factors in barrier corrosion and plugging. He also developed methods of making plant components resistant to such effects. A logical complement of this chemical research was the study of the whole family of fluorocarbons which might possibly be used as lubricants or coolants in the process-gas system.

The construction and operation of gaseous-diffusion test units continued to be a sizeable activity in 1943. All efforts to build a pilot plant even remotely resembling production equipment were abandoned in accordance with the decisions of the Military Policy Committee in the fall of 1942. Construction of the ten-stage pilot plant at M. W. Kellogg's Jersey City site was not halted abruptly but soon languished as more pressing assignments attracted available manpower. Eventually, the pilot plant area was used as a test floor, where single full-size converters or other cascade components could be tested under simulated operating conditions. At Columbia, Pontius continued to operate the single-stage unit. Chaloner B. Slade supervised the operation of the twelve-stage test unit in Pupin Hall. The apparatus consisted of twelve pumps mounted in a double bank and driven from a common crankshaft. The converters were short cylinders about four inches in diameter, between the faces of which a small square sample of barrier was sandwiched. The entire unit was mounted in a wooden cabinet about eight feet square on the front face and three feet deep. In the fall of 1942, the unit was used to check various aspects of cascade theory. Mechanical failures immobilized the equipment during the winter of 1943, but by May it was placed in steady operation for testing small barrier samples. During the summer, Eugene T. Booth and Clarke Williams began constructing a new six-stage unit in the Nash Building on Broadway at 133rd Street. Designed to test barrier in production sizes, the unit was not completed until May, 1944.[13]

CUTBACK IN K-25

As the summer of 1943 advanced, Urey grew more pessimistic about the future of gaseous diffusion. In May, when the Army had taken over the OSRD contract, Groves had appointed Urey Director of Research for what was now called the SAM Laboratory (the initials for the code name "Substitute Alloy Materials"). In this capacity, Urey found himself in charge of all work on gaseous diffusion in addition to his own projects for the production of heavy water and other isotopes. He attempted to tighten up the rather informal organization of Dunning's group, approved Dunning's plan to expand to an off-campus site, and instituted a series of bimonthly reports to keep tabs on the project. At first encouraged by the operation of the barrier pilot plants and by Libby's progress in stabilizing the Norris-Adler barrier against plugging, Urey was increasingly troubled by frequent snags in the process. A little dynamo of a man, sparked with fiery emotions, Urey was one to exaggerate failure as well as success. He was profoundly depressed by Keith's remarks at a co-ordination meeting on August 3. Keith confessed that despite all the good intentions and hard work, they had not yet produced a barrier which could be used in the plant at Oak Ridge. Bringing the news back to his associates on Morningside Heights the following day, Urey looked on the next four to six weeks as the last chance for gaseous diffusion. Unless the SAM Laboratory could produce a satisfactory barrier, work on K-25 would be drastically curtailed.

It was significant that Urey expressed these somber thoughts just at the time General Groves was re-evaluating the Manhattan project for the Military Policy Committee and the President. By contrast, Lawrence at that moment was playing a bold hand in attempting to double the size of the electromagnetic plant, despite the fact that Oak Ridge had not yet operated one production model of the calutron. No doubt the contrast in the two leaders' outlook was a subtle but powerful influence on Groves and the committee. With this psychological advantage, Lawrence could make his point. He had taken pains to explain to Groves in May that the production of uranium 235 in the electromagnetic plant could be greatly accelerated if partially enriched material from K-25 could be used as feed for Y-12. This would eliminate the need for the top of the cascade.

129

The idea of eliminating the upper stages of the gaseous-diffusion plant had long since occurred to the Columbia scientists. Cohen had spotlighted the idea in his studies of the squared-off cascade in January, 1943. In February, Eger Murphree had proposed substituting the centrifuge for gaseous diffusion in the upper stages of the cascade. Boorse's difficulties in the design of pumps and seals for the top of the cascade also suggested the advantages of limiting the plant to the larger quantities of material at lower levels of enrichment. Slow progress during the summer and Urey's lack of enthusiastic leadership all contributed to the decision to cut back the plant. On August 13, Groves reported to the Military Policy Committee that the gaseous-diffusion plant would be limited to a product enriched to something less than 50-per-cent uranium 235, which would be used as feed at Y-12. Two weeks later, Urey met with Lawrence, Oppenheimer, and Bacher in Berkeley to discuss the possibilities of producing enough uranium 235 for a bomb. After listening to Urey's pessimistic views, the western scientists were convinced that the electromagnetic process was the only hope. The first section of the Y-12 plant was nearing completion but ground had not yet been broken for the process buildings at K-25. Urey as well as Lawrence welcomed Groves's decision to double the size of the Y-12 plant.[14]

GALLAHER FERRY

Soon after the K-25 contractor team was organized in the first weeks of 1943, Kellex engineers began to investigate possible sites for the gaseous-diffusion plant.[15] Since the Army had made tentative plans to locate the plant in the Clinton Engineer Works, Kellex and Carbide officials visited that area on

January 18. Later they considered sites on the big bend of the Columbia River in Washington and in the Sacramento River Valley of California, but the advantages of these locations were not sufficient to revise the Army's plans. Within the Clinton reserve, the contractors found a promising area on the western boundary near the confluence of Poplar Creek and the Clinch River. Here, the narrow ridge-and-valley system broadened out into an area of some five thousand acres in which elevations did not vary more than fifty feet. A flat area was essential for the acres of buildings which would house the cascade. Roads and railroads would have easy access, and the river could provide water for the power plant and cooling towers. Another advantage was the isolation of the spot. McKinney Ridge screened the site from the mushrooming atomic village, eleven miles away. A worn-out farming area, the site was traversed by a few gravel roads to the hand-pulled Gallaher Ferry on the Clinch.

130

The transformation of this sleepy valley into an industrial complex began at the ferry site. On May 31, 1943, the first survey party arrived to lay out the huge power plant which would supply a portion of the electrical energy for the cascade. The powerhouse would be started first, partly because of the long lead-time required for generating equipment and partly as a hedge against failure of the gaseous-diffusion process. Keith later recalled he took comfort in the fact that if all else failed, the power plant could be sold to TVA.

On June 2, the J. A. Jones Construction Company, under a cost-plus-fixed-fee contract with the Army, began grading work in the power-plant area. The next step was to sink forty concrete-filled caissons some thirty feet to bedrock as a foundation for the boiler house. While this job progressed, Jones began hauling in the heavy structural steel by truck over the gravel road from a railroad siding thirteen miles away. Slowly from the red Tennessee clay there emerged during the fall of 1943 the brick and steel structure which was to be the world's largest steam-electric power plant to be constructed in a single operation up to that time.

From the beginning, the contractor was plagued by the deplorable access roads into the isolated area. Under the incessant pounding of trucks and heavy construction equipment, the pleasant country lanes became quagmires of mud or dusty, rutted infernos during the summer of 1943. While struggling to keep existing roads open, Jones hurried the construction of hard-surfaced roads east to Oak Ridge and west to U. S. Route 70 near Kingston. A larger, motor-propelled ferry was subsequently replaced by Gallaher Bridge to provide access from the south. During the summer, Jones pushed construction of the railroad spur to the Southern branch line at Blair Junction.

Ground was not broken for the main process buildings until September. The blueprints prepared by Kellex called for a cascade building truly gargantuan in scale. The rough drawings prepared the previous winter had now evolved into a plan for a series of fifty-four contiguous four-story buildings constructed in the shape of a U, almost a half mile long and more than 1,000 feet in width. The enormous area of the buildings (almost 2,000,000 square feet) and the weight of the process equipment they would contain required an extraordinary amount of earth-moving and unusual techniques in constructing foundations. The conventional method of excavating foundations only under load-bearing walls and columns would have required the design and setting of several thousand columns of many different lengths. As a short cut, Kellex decided to level the whole area and fill in the low spots with scientifically compacted earth. Since, over the half-mile length of the U, original elevations differed by as much as fifty feet, it was necessary to move almost 3,000,000 cubic yards of earth. The slow job of earth-moving and compacting fill continued into the fall of 1943, and it was not until October 21 that the first of 200,000 cubic yards of concrete were poured in the process area.

Other construction in the plant area was on an equally grand scale but more conventional in design. In September, Ford, Bacon & Davis started construction of the first of many auxiliary buildings in the area surrounding the U. The pressure on the contractor was great since these buildings would house special rigs for the pre-installation testing and servicing of process equipment. Jones also began work on the administration building in September, but the Army deferred construction of the cafeteria, laboratories, and other auxiliary buildings until 1944.

The isolation of the site forced the two principal contractors into the construction of housing facilities as well as industrial buildings. Two days after work started on the power plant, Jones began erecting 450 huts accommodating 5 men each. Central washing facilities and a mess hall were also constructed during the summer, but the lack of a filtration plant made it necessary to truck all drinking water from Oak Ridge until November, when additional housing was ready for 5,000 workers. The Jones camp, sardonically called "Happy Valley" by its inhabitants, grew with the rising tide of employment. By the end of 1943, when Jones's forces had passed the 10,000-mark, about 3,000 workers were living in hutments and 1,000 in barracks and trailers. Eventually a school, commercial center, theater, three recreation halls, and other buildings were added as total camp population climbed to about 15,000. Just to the west of Happy Valley was the Ford, Bacon & Davis camp which provided housing for about 2,000 workers. Even with these facilities, more than half the construction employees at K-25 made the gruelling daily trip by bus, truck, or dust-caked, aging car from surrounding communities.

131

ONE LAST TRY

Back in the congestion and civilization of upper Manhattan, Urey was girding himself for one last assault on the barrier problem. In July, 1943, he had established a special steering committee of senior members of the SAM staff to identify bottlenecks in the K-25 project and see that they were removed promptly. The most pressing problem of all—fabrication of a good barrier—had not been resolved even by the concentrated attention which the committee could bring to bear. In a tone of profound discouragement, Urey noted at an early September meeting that the six weeks' grace granted by the Army had long since expired without the production of any significant quantity of uniformly satisfactory barrier. By great effort, Norris, Slack, and Willard R. Ruby slowly untangled the kinks in the operation of the barrier pilot plant. By autumn, they could perform all but one step in the process with reasonably consistent results and had shown that the basic design of the processing machinery was sound. As for uniform quality, however, the barrier was far from acceptable. The evaluation group at Columbia was now using better techniques. The use of statistical sampling (which Taylor had encouraged) on Norris-Adler barrier showed wide fluctuations in quality. Pinholes, in barrier the equivalent of bullet holes in a vacuum tank, were all too prevalent, and the delicate surface tended to crack during processing. Except for a few tests performed by Libby and Dixon Callihan at Columbia, there was no reliable evidence that the barrier would withstand continuous exposure to the flow of process gas. In any event, it was impossible to consider the immediate mass production of Norris-Adler.[16]

There were hopes that a different type would in time prove acceptable, but the chances of mass-producing it for a plant to be in operation during 1944 diminished in the fleeting weeks of 1943. News of satisfactory progress was the norm for research projects, but during the fall unusually persistent reports of optimism filtered through to Urey from off-campus research on nickel-powder barriers. Although the early nickel barriers prepared by Foster Nix at the Bell Telephone Laboratories had shown very poor separative qualities, Urey, with encouragement from Carbide, had extended the contract with Bell in July. Taylor's group found little improvement in the Bell barrier evaluated at Princeton during the summer, but there were new reasons to be hopeful. Through the Carbide-Kellex organization, the Bakelite Corporation, a Carbide subsidiary, learned of Nix's attempt to fabricate barrier from nickel powder. It was clear to Frazier Groff and others at Bakelite's Bound Brook, New Jersey, laboratories that Bell was not utilizing the latest techniques for this kind of process. A series of experiments directed by Groff at Bound Brook, beginning in May, 1943, led to a promising material which the International Nickel Company subsequently produced in somewhat larger quantities at Huntington, West Virginia. By October, both Bell and Bakelite were sending powdered nickel barrier to Taylor for analysis. Taylor's team noted some gradual improvements in both types, but they considered neither a practical barrier.

This was not, however, the end of the search. In the fall of 1943, Clarence A. Johnson, a young engineer working for Keith in Kellogg's Jersey City laboratory, was experimenting with the Bakelite process. An old hand on barrier studies, Johnson was a frequent visitor at the Columbia laboratories. He knew the Norris-Adler process and some of the tricks the Columbia scientists had devised. Pooling all this knowledge, he hit upon a method that appeared to yield a barrier better than either the Norris-Adler or the Bakelite. So complex by this time was the intertwining of ideas in Johnson's formula that no one person could take full credit for the discovery. If the new barrier proved successful, Slack, Norris, Adler, Groff, Nix, Johnson, and many others would deserve the credit.

When Richard C. Tolman visited the Jersey City laboratory on October 6, he was impressed by the quality of the material Johnson was producing, but he noted that no continuous process had yet been developed for its production. How could millions of square feet of this material be produced in a few months without a continuous process? [17]

Now Keith was becoming impatient. With Johnson and others from the Kellex staff to back him up on technical details, he broached the question of barrier production on October 20, 1943, at a meeting with Columbia, Houdaille-Hershey, and Army representatives. If the K-25 plant were to have any value in the war effort, Keith believed that at least part of the cascade would have to be in operation by January 1, 1945. Allowing three months for production of barrier tubes by Houdaille-Hershey, Keith guessed that the Decatur plant would have to be in full operation by June 1, 1944. The many snags which continued to impede the refinement of the Norris-Adler process led him to fear that the June 1 date would not be met. From what he knew of the Norris-Adler method, he doubted that it would ever give a satisfactory product. On the contrary, he found the kind of barrier Johnson had exhibited to be much more promising. True, it had not been subjected to extensive testing, and there were some minor obstacles to be overcome. But Keith thought it might be wise to develop the new barrier as an alternative to Norris-Adler.

Urey agreed that in the long run the new nickel barrier might well prove to be superior, but for the war effort he considered Norris-Adler the best hope. A new untested type always looked promising in the initial stages of development. Look how long it had taken to overcome the "few minor difficulties" with Norris-Adler. The switch from other metal barriers to Norris-Adler had been disconcerting enough. Urey feared that a second shift would destroy the morale at the laboratory. But Keith refused to drop the

133

question. On November 3, he called attention to the continuing failure of the pilot plant to produce good barrier. Urey just as firmly refused to divert the resources of his laboratory to the new barrier.

As often happened in the Manhattan project, the thorniest problems were left for General Groves to resolve. He listened to both points of view at a meeting on November 5, 1943, but it appeared that he had already reached a decision after a thorough briefing by his subordinates in New York. As he saw it, the job was to make Norris-Adler work and then produce a better barrier for use later. Columbia would continue to give its first attention to Norris-Adler. On the other hand, every effort would be made to develop a second type as insurance against failure of Norris-Adler. Keith claimed that the most promising type was the new barrier being studied in Jersey City, provided that enough high-quality nickel powder could be obtained for its production. Groves asked Keith to investigate the sources of nickel powder at once so that other ways of making the material could be explored if necessary. Thus did Groves adopt compromise as a temporary expedient. If a choice between the two barriers was impossible, he proposed to develop both until a decision could be made.[18]

As usual, compromise pleased no one. Urey, especially, was disturbed by Groves's decision. Since July, he had been struggling to obtain sufficient scientific personnel to accelerate the improvement of the Norris-Adler process. Now Keith was planning to take over a floor in the Nash Building and assign forty men under Taylor to study the new barrier. How could Urey hope to continue the work on Norris-Adler in the face of this competition for men and equipment? Libby assured him that with all-out effort, the Norris-Adler process could be pushed through in six to eight weeks. Why had Keith insisted on switching to a more difficult shape when he knew, even in 1942, of the brittleness of the Norris-Adler surface? Why did he wait a year to decide that the barrier was unsatisfactory? Explosive questions such as these punctuated the meeting of Urey's steering committee on November 10. Thoroughly angry and depressed, Urey returned to his office and dictated an impassioned letter to General Groves. The previous spring, Urey recalled, Groves had insisted that he take personal command of the K-25 work at Columbia. Reluctantly, he had accepted Dunning's decision that the laboratory should be greatly expanded. He felt at that time that any war project which required such an expansion of research effort should be abandoned. Keith had now decided that Norris-Adler was hopeless and planned another major expansion. Urey could only conclude that K-25 had no further importance in the war effort and that no more funds should be expended on it until after the war. If any full-scale diffusion plant were to be built, it should be based on British design and technology.[19]

Although Groves did not look upon the British diffusion project with Urey's optimism, he thought the British might have some good ideas. He had watched the research on nickel powder with growing interest during the summer. Early in October he had asked Tolman to inspect the K-25 projects in the New York area in preparation for the California scientist's visit to England to discuss the resumption of interchange. Tolman's evaluation, though favorable, was hardly more encouraging than news from the British, who had reported some success in fabricating the powder into barrier. Groves was also impressed by the British cascade design, which allegedly would require much less barrier than the American plant. Before the November 5 meeting in New York, Groves cabled London to expedite the departure of a British diffusion team for New York. As he explained at the meeting, the purpose of the visit was to get British help, not to exchange information. The British plant might be better, but the Americans had at least come to a firm decision to proceed with construction.

Fortunately, it seemed, the groundwork had been laid for British participation in the American project. Throughout the fall of 1943, the British had brought constant pressure to bear for a resumption of interchange on all aspects of the Manhattan project as well as on gaseous diffusion. Groves succeeded in clearing details through the Combined Policy Committee by mid-December. Three days before Christmas, Wallace Akers and fifteen of his experts appeared at the Woolworth Building for a full-dress review. On hand to greet them were Groves and his two scientific advisers, Conant and Tolman. George T. Felbeck, Clark E. Center, and Lyman Bliss represented Carbide. Keith, Baker, Arnold, and Benedict led the Kellex delegation. Urey, Dunning, and Lauchlin M. Currie (recently transferred from the National Carbon Company) spoke for the SAM Laboratory. They presented the most comprehensive review of gaseous-diffusion technology since the visit of the Lewis committee a year before. Armed with these data, the British rolled up their sleeves to study the problems that had haunted Keith, Urey, and Dunning during all those months.[20]

135

While expediting the arrival of the British, Groves could hardly overlook within the K-25 project the strained relations which had come to the surface in the November 5 meeting. Perhaps most men could not have written as vehement a letter as Urey's and resisted the temptation of adding a resignation. Nevertheless, Groves could no longer expect Urey to bring aggressive leadership to K-25 research. Just before the meeting with the British, Groves arranged with the National Carbon Company to borrow Currie as associate director of the SAM laboratories. He would supervise all research except that being directed by Taylor, who had assumed full authority for the work on the new barrier. Thus was Urey relieved from any real responsibility for a project he believed would surely fail.[21]

Whether or not Urey's prediction proved correct, Groves understood only too well that the Government's commitment to the Manhattan project was irrevocable. The investment in K-25 alone was already too large to be abandoned, except in the face of incontrovertible proof that the process was impossible. In New York, Kellex had 900 employees on K-25 design and procurement. The SAM Laboratory at Columbia had more than 700 on K-25 research assignments with several hundred more at universities and industrial laboratories throughout the East. Houdaille-Hershey was erecting a $5-million plant at Decatur for the production of barrier, and Allis-Chalmers a $4-million plant in Milwaukee for pump manufacture. Chrysler was converting its Lynch Road plant in Detroit for the assembly of converters. At Oak Ridge, more than 10,000 workers were toiling on the gigantic plant in which this equipment would be used to produce uranium 235. Much more important than the investment, however, was the ever-present threat of Germany in the race for the bomb. Until that threat could be eradicated, Groves could not relax for a moment. It was still possible that, for all its disappointments, K-25 might prove the quickest route to the bomb. The first attempt to operate the electromagnetic plant had ended in demoralizing failure. The first of the great plutonium piles was still in the early stages of construction. Murphree's report on recent progress on the gas centrifuge convinced both Conant and Lawrence that this method had no practical use in the war. But could K-25 save the day without a breakthrough on barrier? [22]

DECISION ON BARRIER

Keith began the year 1944 with some problems on his mind. If the K-25 plant was to be in operation in early 1945, acres of barrier would have to be produced before the end of the summer. The November 5 meeting with Groves had secured greater support for the development of the new barrier, but the Army was still planning to produce a barrier which Keith thought would never be ready in time. Groves had rushed over the team of British experts to lend a hand, but Keith feared they would be more trouble than help. Akers and his group seemed to have little more than an academic interest in barrier. They seemed preoccupied with matters such as the optimum design of a cascade, questions which had been settled for a year as far as Keith was concerned. Even more serious in Keith's mind were the British attempts to involve the Kellex and Columbia groups in design problems which the British were facing in their own plant. Keith was trying desperately to forge the last link in the design of a plant which might, with luck, win the war. He had little patience with the detached, unhurried approach of his British colleagues.[23] The squeeze was on. Every week that slipped by without progress on barrier brought Keith closer to the deadline which Groves held remorselessly over him.

Keith's feeling of being trapped was probably the reaction Groves intended. But the purpose was to stimulate maximum effort, not to create a scapegoat. Groves had already taken action behind the scenes to accelerate the production of the new barrier. He had discussed the matter with Felbeck, who as head of the Carbide organization had quietly but persistently sup-

136

JACKSON SQUARE, THE OAK RIDGE SHOPPING CENTER / Across the Oak Ridge Turnpike in the background is "the castle," headquarters of the Manhattan Engineer District.

LAUNDRY FACILITIES AT OAK RIDGE / Wartime Oak Ridge had all the bustle and inconvenience of a frontier boom town.

TRAILER CAMP AT OAK RIDGE / More than 1,000 trailers served as supplemental housing.

K-25, THE GASEOUS-DIFFUSION PLANT, UNDER CONSTRUCTION / The U-shaped building contained thousands of pumps and converters for concentrating uranium 235. Service facilities are in the center.

ported research on nickel-powder barriers. He had been instrumental in interesting two Carbide subsidiaries, Bakelite and Linde Air Products Company, in the barrier problem. Felbeck talked to Keith and tactfully suggested that Carbide might be willing to accept full responsibility for the production of the new barrier. His approach to the conscientious, blustery Kellex executive was perfect. On January 4, Keith wrote Groves that Carbide should have full responsibility for producing the new barrier. The Army should procure sufficient nickel powder, and Houdaille-Hershey should produce the barrier tubes at Decatur.[24] Presumably Groves had this plan firmly in mind when he met the next day with the British to hear their comments on the American program after a fortnight in New York.

In his customary fashion, Groves used the meeting with the British and American scientists as a check on the plan which he, Felbeck, and Keith had tentatively accepted. Never was a cause for confirmation more justified. In the preceding eighteen months, Groves had made some daring decisions, but few as risky as this one. In essence, he was proposing that two years of work on barrier be set aside and that the fate of K-25 and perhaps the whole Manhattan project be placed on the mass production (within six months) of millions of square feet of a new barrier which had scarcely been tested. At the other extreme were the British, who looked on barrier production as but one element in a long-term development effort. No wonder it took four hours of discussion to reach a meeting of minds.

From the beginning of the conference, the British agreed that eventually the new process would produce a better barrier, but they considered the months of research on Norris-Adler to be an important advantage if speed was the governing factor. Keith disagreed. He believed that only the new barrier could be produced in time. Decisions in the past had been based on the assumption that only a continuous, assembly-line method could produce barrier in the quantities needed. Keith had come to the realization that this assumption was not necessarily true. Kellex had produced the new barrier in the laboratory by a very simple hand process; if production could be multiplied by the use of thousands of employees doing piece-work, there would be no problems of translating a laboratory process into an industrial one. This approach might be expensive, but it might produce barrier on time.

Keith's suggestion startled the British. If the new barrier could be produced more quickly than Norris-Adler despite the extensive research done on the latter, nothing should stand in the way of research on the new process. Beyond this, the British refused to go. They would not say which of the two barriers was superior; there was not enough evidence on the new barrier to make such a judgment. Couldn't development continue on both until the evidence was available? Keith assured them that with the limited resources and time at hand, this was impossible.

From this point in the discussion, Carbide led the way. Bliss of Linde Air Products suggested the possibility that research could be continued on

137

both barriers, but that a full-fledged production effort be limited to the new barrier alone. The British expressed cautious acceptance of this suggestion. They could not yet say that the new barrier was better, but they felt certain some sort of nickel-powder barrier would prove to be the best. Then Felbeck made his point: the only possible hope was to rip out all the carefully designed machinery in the Decatur plant and install the new process. The British faltered. What if the new process failed? Would there be time to reinstall the Norris-Adler machinery? Keith assured them there would not. The decision had to be made now, and it would stand, come what might.

To the British, this was nothing short of reckless. Even after full pilot-plant studies, it was customary to spend two years constructing chemical processing facilities much less complicated than a gaseous-diffusion plant. Here the Americans were proposing to build a fabrication facility for an untested barrier in four months, produce all the barrier needed in another four months, and have the plant in operation, all within one year. Would it not take a year just to get the works in operation? With incredible luck, the British estimated, the plant might be in production by the summer of 1946.

Groves was careful to be unimpressed by the proposals made by Keith and Felbeck. Whatever process they used, he would not relax one day on Keith's commitment to have the barrier plant in production in May. Nor was he even willing to acknowledge the possibility that both the Norris-Adler and the new plants could not be in operation by that time. Keith was confident there was a chance with the new barrier. Felbeck would guarantee that the gaseous-diffusion plant would be in operation before the last unit was completed. There was no reply to such unrestrained optimism. If the Americans met their schedule, as one member of the British delegation put it, "it would be something of a miraculous achievement." [25]

If miracles were required, there was little time to lose. The following week, amid the clash of organizational gears, Currie and Taylor struggled to divert the momentum of the SAM Laboratory into the new direction dictated by the January 5 decision. Keith carried the news to the Kellex forces in the Nash Building. By the end of the week, Groves was ready to loose his bombshell on Houdaille-Hershey. On Saturday, January 15, 1944, he took the train with Felbeck to Indianapolis. Around midnight, Groves commandeered an Army car which bounced them over the country roads of western Indiana. They arrived in Decatur on Sunday morning just in time to snatch a roll and coffee before the meeting began. Groves broke the news. The plant would be stripped for the new process. Carbide would have general responsibility for barrier production, with Leon K. Merrill of Bakelite serving as Carbide representative in Decatur. Houdaille-Hershey would convert and operate the Decatur plant and would send some personnel east to work with scientists at the SAM Laboratory. This much accomplished, Groves hurried back to Washington. Now it was up to Felbeck and Keith to meet the deadline. [26]

Whatever may have been the production strategy drafted at the January meetings, the first battle was to develop the new barrier. This task fell squarely on the shoulders of that shrewd, independent Princeton professor, Hugh S. Taylor. Dragged by Urey into the barrier crisis late in 1943, the rugged British scientist was expected as associate director of the SAM Laboratory to bring some order out of the confusion in barrier development. Refusing to sever his ties with Princeton, he resigned himself to a life filled almost entirely with lectures at Princeton, meetings in New York, and interminable hours on dingy commuter trains.

In New York, Taylor's first concern was the Kellex research on the new process. Appointed by Keith as an associate director of research in the Kellex organization, Taylor was in constant demand at the Nash Building, where Johnson struggled during the first weeks of 1944 to set up a pilot plant for the new barrier. Using the first experimental material produced at the International Nickel plant in Huntington, Johnson tried to fabricate a suitable barrier. Production was dishearteningly small during the winter, and when Taylor took samples to Princeton for analysis, he found not more than 5 per cent up to plant standards. What Taylor needed was more effort on the new process and larger quantities of high-quality nickel.

139

Prospects of getting more men improved as spring approached. In an effort to speed development of the Norris-Adler process, Urey had recruited Edward Mack, Jr., from Ohio State University to direct research on the barrier pilot plant in Schermerhorn Laboratory. Taylor was encouraged by Mack's progress early in 1944. By the middle of March, Mack had overcome most of the obstacles in the process and had demonstrated that it could be used as an alternate for the new barrier although it was admittedly much more complicated than the method Johnson was developing. As soon as Mack could complete the drafting of manufacturing and control specifications for the Norris-Adler process, he could swing his entire SAM division into the work on the new barrier.[27]

The production of good nickel barrier depended almost entirely upon the procurement of high-quality nickel powder. With a characteristic sharp eye for future requirements, General Groves had ordered Nichols a year earlier to broach the subject with the International Nickel Company. After discussing his requirements with the company, Nichols concluded that the best procedure would be to finance the construction of necessary equipment at an International plant. Thus, when Groves decided to switch to the new barrier, he had merely to place in effect the arrangements already made. International Nickel had eighty tons in storage and could begin regular shipments at once. Improvements in the International process provided the New York pilot plants with the first reasonably good nickel during the last weeks in April.[28]

Now with two barrier pilot plants and a reliable supply of nickel, Keith anticipated some significant production of the new barrier. Both Johnson at the Nash Building and Mack at Schermerhorn Laboratory set out with confidence to meet Keith's request for substantial production from each plant during April. At first the product was almost entirely below standard, mostly because the nickel tended to warp during processing. But by the first of May, things looked better. Deliveries of nickel had more than doubled and the percentage of acceptable barrier had risen from 5 to 38 per cent. Of all the barrier produced in the pilot plants during the last two weeks in April, 45 per cent met the specifications for separating properties.

If the new barrier could now be produced in the laboratory, it was a long way from production on an industrial scale. Early in February, Walter L. Pinner of Houdaille-Hershey began to plan for converting the Decatur plant. His first goal, which Taylor approved, was to complete 20 per cent of the plant as quickly as possible as a pilot run for full-scale operations. Even this modest aim was difficult to achieve as Pinner and Merrill improvised to make the equipment and parts on hand serve in the new process. During the spring, Taylor was constantly in touch with Pinner, Johnson, and Mack as he tried to smooth the way for completion of the Decatur plant. Not until June, however, was the first barrier produced, and this was far below plant standards. An art like barrier fabrication could not be transmitted in engineering specifications. As box after box of unsatisfactory barrier arrived, Taylor turned once again to his old techniques of statistical sampling and quality control. Urey's dire prophecies had not yet been laid to rest.[29]

By the end of June, time was running out on barrier production. Groves's May deadline had long since slipped by, and new pressures were coming to bear on Taylor's task force. Under the direction of Albert L. Baker at Kellex, the wheels of industry were beginning to turn out incredible quantities of special equipment and parts for the Oak Ridge plant. Chrysler had completed the conversion of a tank factory in Detroit and was prepared to assemble the thousands of converters for the gaseous-diffusion cascade. The new Allis-Chalmers plant in Milwaukee was producing the thousands of pumps which would propel the process gas through the barriers. A variety of special service pumps were being fabricated by the Elliott Company, the Valley Iron Works, Pacific Pumps, Inc., and the Beach Russ Company. Thousands of coolers to remove the heat of compression from the cascade were rolling off assembly lines at the A. O. Smith Company and the Whitlock Manufacturing Company. Bart Laboratories, International Nickel, and the Midwest Piping and Supply Company were using a new process developed by Bart and the Republic Steel Corporation to produce three million feet of piping which was resistant to corrosion by uranium hexafluoride. The Crane Company was fabricating about a half million valves varying in size from one-eighth of an inch to thirty-six inches with special seating materials developed by the British. Tens of thousands of recording instruments, gauges, mass spectrometers, pressure indicators, flowmeters, thermometers, and control panels were being produced by General Electric, Taylor Instrument, Republic Flowmeter, and Fisher Governor.

The equipment produced by these and scores of other contractors was beginning to converge on the plant at Gallaher Ferry. As the gigantic U-shaped building was enclosed, the J. A. Jones Company raced to install process piping, valves, pumps, and converters. By the middle of April, 1944, the first six stages (without acceptable barrier in the converters) were given mechanical and vacuum tests. The next objective was to complete a section of fifty-four stages in the same building. Delays in the delivery of equipment, especially valves, forced a postponement of mechanical tests of this section beyond the June deadline. All the same, the K-25 plant was assuming a staggering size. With more than one-third of the work on the main process buildings completed, construction labor forces were already beginning to decline from the April peak of 19,680. By the end of June, 1944, estimates of total construction costs for the K-25 project had climbed to $281 million.[30]

141

The full weight of this commitment fell on Keith, Taylor, Merrill, Pinner, Mack, and Johnson. Without barrier, the millions invested in K-25 would come to naught. Chrysler was already clamoring for barrier tubes to install in the converters in Detroit. With none to send, Merrill suggested shipping about 10,000 unacceptable tubes to Detroit for training Chrysler employees on assembly and testing techniques. As production at Decatur continued to founder during the first week of July, Currie called in Mack and Johnson. Perhaps by an extraordinary effort for a brief period, they could increase production in the pilot plants. Mack was already producing substantial quantities of barrier on a two-shift basis. With a few minor improvements in equipment and the use of three shifts, it might be possible to triple daily production. Johnson was able to produce some barrier in the Nash pilot plant. Since the Schermerhorn plant seemed to hold the best prospects for expansion, Mack would attempt to maximize the output of his plant during the last week in July. On this grim but determined effort might rest the hopes for K-25 and the bomb.[31]

Y-12 AT BERKELEY

By the end of 1942, Lawrence's research team at the Berkeley laboratory had determined what they needed to build an electromagnetic plant. They had demonstrated the validity of the mass spectrograph method early in the year with the magnet from the 37-inch cyclotron. The two tanks installed during the summer in the giant gap of the 184-inch magnet enabled them to study the process on a scale closer to that of a production plant. The erratic performance of these two tanks might seem hopelessly insignificant in comparison with the uninterrupted operation of the hundreds which would be necessary to produce enough uranium 235 for a bomb. With this unwieldy equipment, however, the Berkeley scientists could explore the elementary techniques of their new art—and in those days it often seemed more an art than a science. Lawrence had swept his laboratory clean of the customary patient research into Nature's laws; now he demanded results above all else. Like scouts on a vital mission through unexplored territory, Lawrence's subordinates could not wait for maps to be prepared for their journey; they would have to strike out for their destination and hope that they would stumble upon the shortest and easiest route. Experiments, not theory, had been the keynote at Berkeley. The magnetic shims, sources, and collectors that gave the best results were used, although no one could explain their superiority.

As the Berkeley group repeated experiments, however, they accumulated a body of knowledge. In these data they could detect some order which often in turn suggested a profitable theoretical approach. Lawrence, with his extraordinary scent for scientific game, was succeeding in his gamble to get quick results by unorthodox methods. In the closing weeks of 1942, discussions on the hill above the Berkeley campus turned toward those conceptions and assumptions that would fix the design of the plant at Oak Ridge.

Research on magnets had perhaps the greatest influence on the general plan of the plant. Fortunately, the theory was already well understood. It could be assumed, for example, that a large magnet with a great many gaps would be used. Physicists in Lawrence's laboratory could demonstrate with equations that, as the number of gaps increased, the weight of steel required for the magnet yoke, the weight of the coils, and the power required per gap all decreased to a constant value. Indeed, the limitation (r the maximum size of a single magnet of this type seemed to be dictated by the amount of electric power available, the size of the building, and the risk in production loss in the event of a single magnet failure. Several smaller magnets might theoretically require a larger quantity of already scarce construction materials than would one large magnet, but the failure of one coil would not shut down the entire plant. Thus, for a full-scale plant, Lawrence could expect to build more than one but perhaps not more than a few magnets.

It would also be necessary, for magnets of such great size and so many gaps, to change the direction of the magnetic field from that furnished by the cyclotrons. That is, the field would be horizontal rather than vertical, and the tanks within the gaps would stand on end so that the ion beams would be in the vertical plane, perpendicular to the magnetic field. The gross specifications for the magnet could be calculated once the size of the ion beam was determined. To achieve proper resolution of the 235 and 238 beams in the collector, it seemed that the radius of the beam paths should be about four feet. Thus the cross section of the magnet core would be about eight feet. In a properly shimmed field, the width of the magnet gap could not be much greater than about half the beam radius, or about two feet, and the best value for the magnetic field was calculated to be 3,410 oersteds.[32]

The next step was to determine the number of gaps and the general configuration of the magnets. Performance of the 184-inch calutrons in the fall of 1942 suggested that about 2,000 sources and collectors would be required to separate 100 grams of uranium 235 per day. Since it was not safe to assume that there would be more than one source and collector per tank, plans had to be made for 2,000 tanks. Matching this figure with the general specifications for the magnet, the Stone & Webster engineers were able to define the basic production units for the electromagnetic plant. It seemed practical to design electrical power equipment and other facilities to serve two magnets, each containing about 100 tanks. If each gap contained two tanks, the magnet would have fifty gaps. Actually, forty-eight was chosen since the larger number of common denominators in that figure would provide the greatest flexibility in the use of the elaborate power supply.[33] To minimize the amount of precious steel required for the core, the magnet was given an oval rather than a linear shape. Thus, from above, the unit would have the shape of a racetrack with each of the forty-eight gaps containing two tanks. During the autumn of 1942, a model of such a magnet was built on a $\frac{1}{16}$ scale at the Berkeley laboratory. The power supply for the 184-inch magnet could be used for the model, but the cooling system for the coils was so inadequate that the magnet could be operated only for short intervals. Even so, it was possible to measure variations in field strength and flux in different sections of the model racetrack and thereby to design the full-scale magnet more accurately.[34]

Vacuum systems, like magnets, were commonplace in physics laboratories in 1943, but industrial applications were rare. Although Lawrence and his associates had learned as much as anyone about vacuum technology in building the cyclotrons at Berkeley, it was an achievement even for them to hold a good vacuum in the 184-inch magnet tank. They also realized that the volumes contemplated for the Oak Ridge plant probably exceeded by many times all the evacuated space in the world at that time.

The vacuum specifications were rigid. Pressures in the calutrons had to be less than 0.00005 millimeter of mercury. Because the tanks would be opened after each run, the pumps had to be capable of restoring the vacuum quickly. Cold traps were required to remove every trace of water vapor, which would react with the uranium chloride charge material. Gaskets and welds would have to withstand large temperature fluctuations and long periods of operation. It was even possible that getters or bake-out procedures would be needed to extract residual gases trapped in components. In the absence of pilot-plant experience, the final design of the vacuum system would have to evolve from test runs of full-scale calutrons.[35]

With almost 200 sources per building, it was conceivable that as many as ten buildings would be required to reach the plant capacity established by the Military Policy Committee. A relatively large number of buildings would have certain advantages. It would limit each building to not more than a fraction of the total production capacity of the plant. Also, if all the buildings were not designed and constructed simultaneously, it would be possible to profit by experience gained along the way. On the other hand, it was hardly realistic to expect that ten buildings incorporating a series of design changes could be constructed within a year. One hope lay in increasing the production of the individual calutron. In the closing weeks of 1942, that possibility became increasingly more promising.

144

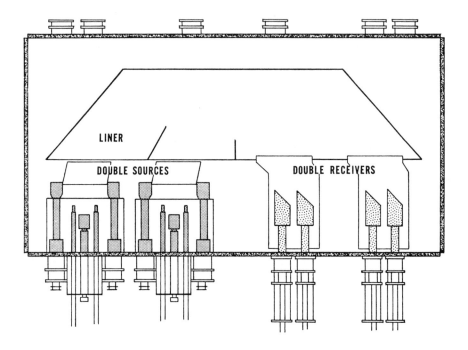

Figure 9. The R1 tank, installed in the 184-inch magnet in November, 1942, contained two sets of double sources and receivers.

Lawrence was very much encouraged by experiments with the new calutron which had replaced C1 in the 184-inch magnet on November 18. The new tank, designed during the fall of 1942 with an improved set of magnetic shims, was rectangular in shape and contained two sets of double sources and collectors. Thus R1, as the new unit was called, would combine the multiple-source capability of C1 and the magnetic shim feature of C2. (Figure 9) Operation of R1 during the last six weeks of 1942 was not all that Lawrence could hope for. Only one attempt was made, in early December, to operate all four sources simultaneously, and most experiments after that were limited to two sources. With the new set of shims, however, it was possible to bring two small beams into focus simultaneously. A much larger beam would be required for truly reliable data, but these experiments seemed to be an important first step toward the use of multiple sources.

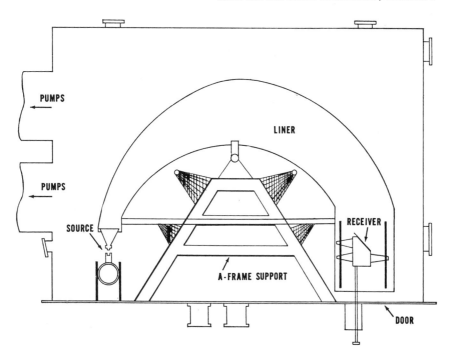

Figure 10. The D1 calutron, installed in the 184-inch magnet in January, 1943, had all its components mounted on the faceplate or "door" for easy installation in the tank.

Equally heartening were the improvements in the design of sources. In the first days of January, 1943, another new calutron was installed on top of R1. Although its external shape was also rectangular, the calutron was called D1 because the source, liner, and receiver were all mounted on one long metal plate or door so that they could be installed in the vacuum tank as one unit. (Figure 10) This innovation proved to be a significant step in the evolution of calutron design, but for the moment all eyes at Berkeley concentrated on the new type of sources to be tested in D1. Until November, 1942, all of the sources had just two accelerating electrodes or slits. The first, called the J slit, served as the face of the ionization chamber and was held at ground potential. The second electrode, called the G slit, was held at a negative potential of 50,000 volts. The new sources first tested extensively in the D1 calutron contained a third electrode, called the C slit, which was placed just beyond the G slit and held at a negative potential of 35,000 volts. (Figure 11) Although the C slit had a slightly decelerating effect on the ions in the beam, it gave promise even in the earliest tests of producing a much sharper, stronger beam at the collector. These experiments with the new calutrons suggested that the capacity of the electromagnetic plant might be greatly increased without adding more tanks or buildings. Successful operation of two sources and collectors in each tank might alone enable Lawrence to produce 100 grams of U-235 per day with just 1,000 tanks in five buildings.[36] Any one of the other design improvements then being investigated might again halve the number of tanks required.

These hopes for increasing production were more than offset by the shallow foundations upon which the process rested. However much the Berkeley scientists may have learned in 1942, what they did not know about the process was surely alarming. Perhaps only a scientist of Lawrence's skill and temperament could have seen a clear path through such a forest of obstacles.

146

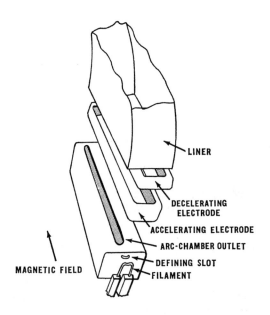

Figure 11. An exploded view of the three-electrode source installed in the D1 tank early in 1943.

As the year 1943 began, not one calutron even remotely resembling a production model had yet been built. A team of engineers from the Radiation Laboratory and Stone & Webster were designing such a unit, but not more than a few would be tested before the electromagnetic plant was ready for operation. In the race for the bomb, all thoughts of a pilot plant had been abandoned. Basic research, engineering development, and plant construction would all be telescoped into one great effort. Thus, the unfinished experiments with the horizontal tanks in the 184-inch magnet would have to be basis for the design of 500 vertical tanks for the Y-12 plant. Stone & Webster would launch the design and construction of the buildings at Oak Ridge with only the roughest idea of what equipment those buildings would contain.

The heart of the calutron—the sources and collectors—was only beginning to be understood. Experiments with the three-electrode sources had just started. No one knew why the third electrode improved the beam, and months of experimentation would be needed to find the optimum positioning of the slits simply by trial and error. For every part of the sources and collectors, the small group of scientists at Berkeley were probing new realms of research. They made thousands of studies for the design of the ionization chamber, the basic research on the behavior of ionized gases in electric and magnetic fields, the testing of materials for the filament and cathode which ionized the charge material, the design of the cathode and the positioning of the arc which it created, the design of the faceplate or J slit, and the removal of chlorine compounds and other "crud" which plugged the J slit. The collectors in use at the turn of the year were only a crude approximation of the devices which could be installed in the production plant. Again entirely by empirical methods, the Berkeley scientists were able to design a collector to fit the beam, but they had not yet considered ways of retaining the separated material in the collector, increasing the life of collector parts, measuring and controlling the intensity of the ion beam, or making fine adjustments in the positioning of the collector pockets. Until they explored such matters, there would be little hope of operating two beams in one tank.

147

What then did General Groves and his army of supply, construction, and equipment contractors know about the enormous plant they were to erect in Bear Creek Valley? They knew the general size, shape, weight, and power requirements of the magnet. They could guess the number of racetracks and buildings that might be needed. They had some idea of the size, weight, and shape of the tanks, but they had only the roughest specifications for the sources and collectors.

RECRUITING THE Y-12 TEAM

The Stone & Webster organization had been alerted to the possibility of an emergency construction program late in November, 1942, when the Lewis reviewing committee was making its grand tour of S-1 projects. On December 12, two days after the decision of the Military Policy Committee, Groves, Marshall, and Nichols met with John R. Lotz in Stone & Webster's Boston offices. Either anticipating the improvements which Lawrence spoke of making in the calutron or intending to build the Y-12 plant in large segments, Groves told Lotz that he had reduced the electromagnetic plant to 500 tanks. On the time schedule then contemplated, this would be a challenging assignment for Stone & Webster. Lotz could take some comfort in learning that his company would no longer be responsible for constructing the full-scale production piles, which were now being planned for a site other than Oak Ridge. However, Groves suggested that the company might be required under its general contract to serve as the prime construction contractor for both the gaseous-diffusion plant and the Oak Ridge community.

As with the gaseous-diffusion and pile projects, Groves was anxious to transfer design responsibilities from the universities to experienced engineering organizations. He was dissatisfied with progress at Berkeley and requested Lotz to attend a meeting with Lawrence in California. There, on an afternoon two days before Christmas, the three plenipotentiaries of the Army, university, and industry hammered out the agreement which was to govern the design and construction of the electromagnetic plant. The Radiation Laboratory would continue to supply Stone & Webster with experimental data, but the company would have the final authority in design and construction. The goal was to build a 500-tank plant as quickly as possible. The company was to order all materials for the entire plant at once but could use its discretion in determining the sequence and size of construction steps. Lotz remarked that the first step would probably be one racetrack of ninety-six tanks. Stone & Webster would also direct all procurement and expediting of materials, the negotiation of contracts with equipment manufacturers, and the preliminary testing of the plant. The university was clearly expected to take a secondary but still a vital part in its design and construction.[37]

The selection of an operating contractor had no less priority in the mind of General Groves. For the same reasons which led to the swift negotiations with Union Carbide for the gaseous-diffusion plant, Groves solicited the advice of Lawrence and Lotz at the Berkeley meeting. Apparently Groves was using his associates merely to check a decision he had already made. The following morning, he placed a long-distance call to James C. White, vice-president and general manager of the Tennessee Eastman Corporation. Groves was familiar with the company's accomplishments in constructing an explosives plant at the Holston Ordnance Works near Kingsport. White at once expressed his concern that the novelty of the process might rule out his company, which was primarily an operating unit for Eastman Kodak and did no fundamental research. Groves assured White that he was not looking for "long beards." He already had the pick of the academic brains and "so many Ph.D.'s that he couldn't keep track of them." What Groves wanted was a company with experience in industrial production. On January 5, after a long discussion with Groves in Rochester, White accepted the assignment. Like Union Carbide, Tennessee Eastman would serve as consultant during construction, undertake research on special problems as required, train operating personnel, and operate the plant. Before departing for Washington, the General announced that he was leaving Chicago on January 11 for a planning session in Berkeley; he expected Tennessee Eastman to send a delegation.[38]

The day before the Rochester meeting Groves had completed negotiations with four contractors to provide most of the equipment for the electromagnetic plant. From the contractor's point of view, the prospects were uninviting. Specifications were vague, the air swarmed with questions, and there was an impossibly short time to find answers. But the General's conviction and drive carried the day. The Westinghouse Electric and Manufacturing Company took the brunt of the job: to manufacture the tanks, liners, sources, and collectors. The General Electric Company accepted a scarcely smaller and in some ways more difficult load: to provide the tremendous amount of high-voltage electrical equipment to supply the magnets and tanks. The Allis-Chalmers Manufacturing Company, soon to be involved in the gaseous-diffusion project, agreed to fabricate the huge magnet coils, and the Chapman Valve Manufacturing Company accepted an order for the hundreds of precision vacuum valves. This, at least for the present, was the Y-12 team.

Groves and his entourage of contractors arrived in Berkeley on January 13, 1943. White and the Tennessee Eastman group spent the morning with Lawrence and Groves, who explained the process in detail and its relation to the bomb project. After lunch they returned to the cyclotron building on the hill and watched the operation of the new tanks in the 184-inch magnet. The following morning they met on the Berkeley campus with other members of their own staffs and with representatives of Stone & Webster, Westinghouse, and General Electric. Groves wanted the first racetrack in operation by July 1, 1943, and additional tanks to be delivered at a rate of fifty per month so that all 500 would be in production by the end of the year. Roy E. Argersinger, the Berkeley representative for Stone & Webster, insisted that this schedule was impossible. Design of the tanks was not yet complete, and he believed that it would take at least ten days to collect enough information just to start scheduling. Then all the purchasing, expediting, and design work would have to be done in Boston. Groves insisted that the schedule could be met. Perhaps it would be necessary to begin wholesale procurement without attempting to work out a well-geared delivery schedule. No doubt mistakes would be made by proceeding in this fashion, but the risk had to be accepted. What Groves would not excuse was indecision or delay in order to achieve perfection. What the contractors insisted upon was freezing designs as soon as possible so that manufacturing of components could begin. No one agreed with this aim more heartily than Groves, but he was, for all his talk about schedules, never one to be stampeded into premature decisions. Other questions were looming on the horizon, and detailed design of the plant would not be fixed for six weeks.[39]

149

The participants in the January 13 meeting, however, did carry away with them a general conception of the Y-12 plant. They could envisage the five racetracks, each containing ninety-six tanks housed in three long buildings. The racetracks would be massive, steel, elliptical structures 122 feet long, 77 feet wide, and 15 feet high. Since two tracks would be placed end-to-end on the second floor of each building, the structures would be nearly 450 feet long, of reinforced concrete and masonry. The forty-eight magnet coils would be connected by a huge bus bar running along the top of the racetrack and would be energized with direct current from motor generator sets at the ends of the building. Each of the forty-eight gaps would contain two tanks placed back to back, half facing the outside and half the inside of the tracks. All the internals of the tank—the sources, collectors, and liner— would be fastened to a huge vacuum-tight door which would be installed in the tank by special lifts. More than half the floor area in the building would be occupied by auxiliary and control equipment. Two-story bays on each side of the racetrack rooms would house the elaborate electrical equipment to supply carefully regulated high-voltage power for the electrodes, liners, and receivers. In these rooms would be located the control panels for each tank, to be manned by hundreds of young women from the surrounding Tennessee countryside.

150

The entire ground floor would be occupied by the massive vacuum pumps and by cooling equipment which would service the tanks above. It would also be necessary to build separate chemistry buildings, where the uranium tetrachloride charge material would be prepared from uranium oxide and placed in pyrex or stainless-steel bottles for the sources. Following operation of the tracks, the small amounts of uranium 235 would have to be recovered from each of the collectors by chemical extraction. Most of the charge material would be splattered over the inside of the liner, collectors, and sources and would be recovered by scrubbing and washing in the racetrack buildings. Facilities in the chemistry buildings would be used to recover the natural uranium from the wash. Thus the plant was conceived in broad outline. The details were yet to emerge from the hectic activity in Berkeley, Boston, Rochester, Pittsburgh, and Schenectady.[40]

On General Groves's instructions Lawrence called weekly co-ordination meetings of the representatives of all the major contractors. In the academic surroundings at Berkeley, Lawrence patiently listened to the questions, complaints, and suggestions. With his tact, good humor, and boundless enthusiasm he calmed troubled waters and proposed compromises. Transcripts of these conferences were sent to General Groves and the contractors' home offices. For important decisions, Groves went to Berkeley himself, and after a thorough briefing by Captain Harold A. Fidler, more than held his own in ironing out engineering problems. Hundreds of administrative and technical questions were settled quickly at the Berkeley meetings. They were to be the focus of the Y-12 project until the first racetracks at Oak Ridge were put in operation.[41]

During the winter of 1943, Tennessee Eastman quickly emerged as the chief co-ordinator of equipment manufacture and procurement. On January 23, White announced that the company would assume direct responsibility for the preparation of feed and for chemical processing, two matters to which Lawrence admittedly had given little attention. Lawrence was even more anxious to have the company's help on electrical equipment. Tennessee Eastman set up an office in Berkeley to serve as a clearinghouse for technical information and as a headquarters for operating personnel who would be trained on the full-size test calutrons to be constructed in the cyclotron building. With Stone & Webster fully occupied with design in Boston, Tennessee Eastman established an office there in February, and within a month began to gear research and design to equipment manufacture.[42]

The risk of undertaking construction without a pilot plant had been accepted as one of the hazards of war, and this fault harassed the electromagnetic project from the start. As soon as each group turned to the detailed design of a component, they inevitably found ways of enhancing its operation. When these improvements could be utilized without affecting other specifications, they were quickly adopted. But more often than not, their use would trigger a chain reaction of modifications which would upset decisions already regarded as final. It was startling to add up all the changes that purportedly would double the output of the plant. At the very first coordination meetings, Lawrence was advocating an increase in the height of the tanks from twelve to fifteen feet. Hardly had his suggestion of using two sources in each tank been accepted when he warmed to the possibility of using four; and eight or even sixteen were not beyond the limits of his imagination. Others on Lawrence's staff, notably Edward J. Lofgren, were convinced of the advantage of building a second stage, especially designed to use the enriched material from the first five racetracks. Lawrence was not sure that the second stage would be needed, but by the middle of February Groves found the idea attractive. His cool realism told him that a second stage might be required, not only for Y-12 product but also for that from the gaseous-diffusion plant. Resolving problems such as these required much more than technical knowledge; it demanded an intuitive sense or "feeling" for the process, a boldness and yet a reasonableness which Groves seemed to possess in the right proportions. Lawrence was inclined to be carried away by his enthusiasm. Colonel Marshall was too quick to shut off the flow of new ideas. Groves resolutely kept the situation fluid until a decision was in order; then he forced the decision regardless of the possible consequences.[43]

By the middle of March, 1943, Groves knew he had reached the time for decision. In the Stone & Webster offices in Boston on March 17, he reviewed the evidence. On the design of the first five racetracks, Colonel Marshall carried the day. All five would be identical, and no changes would be permitted except those which could be made without postponing the completion of the plant. A decision on the second stage was more difficult. The Radiation Laboratory had completed only the most preliminary studies of the equipment and only a few Stone & Webster personnel had seen the drawings. The calutrons in this second, or "Beta" stage, as it was now called, could be much smaller than those in the first five racetracks, or "Alpha" plant. They would be only large enough to process the relatively small amount of material from the first stage. Thus, all the product from Alpha could be handled by a Beta plant consisting of two magnets, each containing thirty-six tanks and seventy-two sources. In most dimensions, the Beta calu-trons would be half the size of the Alpha. The smaller volume of the tanks would make it easier to maintain vacuums, but the shorter running time with each charge would require more rapid pump-down of the vacuum system. The greatest risk in Beta was the possibility of losing the Alpha product. Since the accumulated product of several Alpha runs would be needed for one Beta charge, every loss in Beta would amount to a multiple loss in Al-pha. Despite the risk, Groves thought the second stage was necessary. When he had assured himself at the Boston meeting that the plant could be built in time to receive the first product from Alpha, he gave his approval.[44]

INITIAL Y-12 CONSTRUCTION AND PROCUREMENT

152

Long before the March meeting in Boston to fix the design of the plant, con-struction had started at the Oak Ridge site. Soon after the first of the year, Stone & Webster began assigning construction personnel to the project from its Knoxville recruiting office, and site-clearing was begun. The company broke ground for the first Alpha building on February 18, 1943, when only the foundation drawings had been approved. Within a few weeks the Boston office sent additional drawings and the tempo of construction increased. Workers on the site could not escape the impression that the whole valley was being torn up and transported en masse by scores of cranes, shovels, tractors, and road-grading machines. Before the end of the month, the con-tractor started foundations for the Alpha and Beta chemistry buildings, and this was weeks before any formal decision had been made to build the Beta plant. Score upon score of modifications would be required as the detailed designs were completed, but if the plant was to be in operation before the end of the year, construction could not be delayed even by the absence of plans. Sometimes the consequences were bad. For example, in May, when the Y-12 layout had been established by construction on two Alpha buildings, the chemistry buildings, administration building, cafeteria, and a score of service buildings, excavations for the third Alpha building revealed a layer of shat-tered limestone. The large irregular boulders and deep rock crevices made an uneven foundation. Because it was impossible to change the location of the building, the entire area had to be excavated, the crevices dug out by hand labor, and a solid mat of concrete placed over the irregular sections.

The magnitude and special features of the plant made labor recruit-ment difficult. Stone & Webster could recruit key personnel from its Boston office, but for general labor and especially the skilled trades the contractor had to rely on outside sources. The company's employment office in Knoxville produced enough labor for the early stages of construction, but Stone & Web-ster soon turned for help to the U. S. Employment Service, the Building Trades Council, and various national craft unions. Recruiters stationed in the larger labor centers throughout the South sent a steady stream of workers to Oak Ridge in the spring of 1943. Even when sufficient numbers of skilled laborers were on the job, they were not always able to meet the high specifications for the plant. Special tools and jigs were built, fully equipped shops were constructed, and groups of mechanics were trained for specific tasks for which they were moved from building to building.

Procurement of materials and equipment was scarcely easier than the recruitment of labor. Stone & Webster established one purchasing department in Boston for process equipment and another at Oak Ridge for structural materials. In terms of quantity, the procurement of structural materials was the more impressive. In one four-week period, sixty-three rail cars of concrete blocks were unloaded at Y-12. In an eleven-week period, 1,585 cars of lumber arrived. Almost 38 million board-feet of lumber, 5 million bricks, and 13,000 windows were delivered. Inspector-expeditors had to rush raw materials to equipment fabricators. At the peak of construction, in the spring of 1944, Stone & Webster had more than 100 men following thousands of suborders placed by contractors and vendors as well as the purchase orders placed by their own company.[45]

The Army had assumed responsibility for one of the largest procurement items in the summer of 1942. Even at that early stage in the evolution of the electromagnetic plant, Marshall and Nichols saw that tremendous quantities of copper would be needed for the magnet windings. Since the plant would probably be a temporary installation, they hit upon the idea of using the large stocks of silver bullion in the Treasury rather than copper, which was in desperately short supply. Early in August, Nichols learned from Daniel W. Bell, Under Secretary of the Treasury, that 47,000 tons of silver were already available to the defense program and that another 39,000 tons could be released with proper Congressional authorization. Nichols concluded arrangements for the transfer before the end of August, 1942. The first of 14,700 tons of silver were hauled from the West Point Depository to the Defense Plant Corporation at Carteret, New Jersey, on October 30. There the bars were cast as cylindrical billets, which were extruded and rolled into strips by the Phelps Dodge Copper Products Company at Bayway, New Jersey. The strips, 5/8 inch thick, 3 inches wide, and about 40 feet long, were wound on the magnet coils by Allis-Chalmers in Milwaukee. The huge bus bars of solid silver, roughly a square foot in cross section and running around the top of the racetrack, were fabricated at Oak Ridge.[46]

For most components, however, procurement could not be so methodically planned. No contracts for process equipment were signed until 1943, and even then the supplier had no definite specifications for the equipment he was to produce. With nothing more than the rough drawings and experimental results from the Berkeley laboratory, commitments had to be made on designs, production methods, and delivery dates, in full knowledge of the fact that changes would be required as more detailed designs were completed.

153

Westinghouse had to proceed with the production of 500 calutrons before one full-scale unit could be built and operated in the laboratory. General Electric had to place orders for electrical equipment before power requirements were clearly understood. To the lack of specifications were added the overwhelming priority problems faced by suppliers at all levels. Probably General Electric felt the priority pinch most severely as a result of the extreme shortage of electrical equipment and the large demands for Y-12. Late in February, 1943, Groves's lieutenants in Washington warned that electronic tubes were in such great demand for the war effort that the Army and Navy Munitions Board would force them to fight for every tube needed for the electromagnetic plant. Tube requirements were far from established at that time, but General Electric could estimate that as many as 5,000 high-voltage rectifier tubes, each more than two feet high, would be needed for the initial installation. No one knew what the expected life of the tubes might be, but it seemed possible that 1,000 replacements a month might be necessary. Six weeks later the outlook was far from good. In addition to the tube shortage, new bottlenecks were experienced in procuring high-voltage transformers, generator sets, switching gear, current regulators, and operating panels. By spring, delays in the production of electrical equipment were fast becoming the most serious threat to completion of the plant on schedule.[47]

154

Early in May, 1943, Lawrence made the rounds of Y-12 construction and equipment manufacturing projects in the East. In Pittsburgh at the Westinghouse plant he saw a large number of vacuum pumps already completed, about a dozen vacuum tanks being assembled, and one tank being vacuum tested. He inspected the assembly lines for the manufacture of sources and receivers. One liner assembly was complete and ready for shipment to Berkeley. In Boston he visited the Stone & Webster offices, where he saw hundreds of engineers, draftsmen, and procurement officers at work. He left a meeting of General Electric vice-presidents in Schenectady on priority problems with an air of optimism. He toured the Tennessee Eastman plant at Kingsport and the Holston Ordnance Works before going on to Oak Ridge. Everything before had been impressive, but this sight was awesome. He saw miles of new roads, acres of railroad track filled with trainloads of materials and equipment, rows of warehouses and barracks, and hundreds of new homes on the rolling hills. From the town, he climbed to the top of the ridge where he could look down on the Y-12 plant. He found it hard to adjust to its vast scale; the high-voltage transmission lines coming over the hill, the big switchyard with its mammoth transformers, the great expanse of excavations and building foundations. On that scale even the size of the racetracks, which seemed so large in comparison with laboratory equipment, was insignificant. Lawrence for once had difficulty in getting his bearings. He told his colleagues in Berkeley: ". . . When you see the magnitude of that operation there, it sobers you up and makes you realize that whether we want to or no, that we've got to make things go and come through. . . . Just from the size of the thing, you can see that a thousand people would just be lost in this place, and we've got to make a definite attempt to just hire everybody in sight and somehow use them, because it's going to be an awful job to get those racetracks into operation on schedule. We must do it." [48]

NEW RESEARCH ON THE Y-12 PROCESS

Although Lawrence justifiably emphasized the early operation of Y-12, he never lost sight of the many improvements which further research might make possible. During the winter and spring of 1943, he used the new tanks in the 184-inch magnet for such experiments.

Among all the possibilities, Lawrence took greatest interest in the "hot source." Rather than hold the ion source at ground potential or "cold," it was theoretically possible to run the source at a high positive voltage, or "hot." On paper at least, there were several advantages in the hot source. If the source were at a positive potential, the accelerating electrode would be at ground, and the decelerating electrode at a relatively small negative potential. The use of voltages both above and below ground potential would permit about the same spread of voltages between the electrodes as in the cold source, but the maximum potential with respect to ground would be reduced from 50,000 to perhaps 20,000 volts. The lower maximum voltage would reduce insulator failures in the power supply, and both positive and negative voltages would make for more efficient use of power. A second advantage seemed to grow in importance after experiments with cold sources: if the accelerating electrode were at ground potential, the liner and receiver could be at ground also. In fact, there was no reason why the cumbersome heavy liner suspended on insulators could not be eliminated altogether.

155

As often happened, the theoretical advantages were not immediately realized in the laboratory. Hot sources had first been tried in the C2 tank in August, 1942. Insulator breakdowns within the source were severe enough to indicate that the hot type could not be developed without further research. Lawrence, therefore, turned the main effort to the cold source for the initial electromagnetic plant. In March, 1943, however, he approved installation of a single hot source in the R1 tank. Results were excouraging almost from the start. Performance of the first experimental unit was low, but a new single hot source installed a few weeks later produced a beam of 110 milliamperes. The first double hot source installed in D1 in June gave a sustained total output of 175 milliamperes. These values were small, to be sure, but they convinced Lawrence that the best hopes for the future lay in multiple hot sources. [49]

At the same time, Sidney W. Barnes, Bernard Peters, and others at the Radiation Laboratory were making impressive advances in the design of receivers for the Alpha plant. The designs evolved slowly as a succession of experimental models was tested in the R1 and D1 tanks. In May, 1943, Barnes came up with a design which closely resembled the receivers later produced in quantity by Westinghouse. (Figure 12) Because he did not consider it worthwhile to recover the uranium in the 238 portion of the beam, Barnes did not incorporate a 238 pocket in his collector. Instead he let the beam strike an electrode called the Q carbon. To capture the 235 beam, he perfected the design of a deep cavity, called the R pocket, in the bottom of which were a series of tilted carbon plates. Known as the "footscraper," this unit trapped the 235 ions and was insulated so that the magnitude of the R beam current could be measured. On the 45-degree face of the receiver were the R and Q defining carbons which could be adjusted to optimize the reception of the beams. A door was installed over the R pocket to prevent the entry of contaminating materials during periods of start-up or adjustment.

156

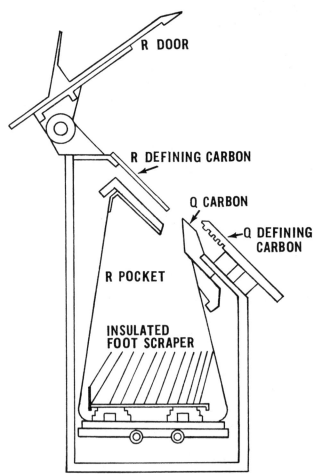

R DOOR

R DEFINING CARBON

Q CARBON

Q DEFINING CARBON

R POCKET

INSULATED FOOT SCRAPER

Figure 12. A cross section of the Alpha receiver developed in the spring of 1943. The Q electrode received the U-238 portion of the beam. The "footscraper" in the R pocket trapped the U-235 portion.

Every dimension and specification of the collector was determined in a long series of painstaking experiments, which had been telescoped into a few months of intensive study.[50]

The March 17 decision to build the Beta plant swept over the Berkeley project like a tidal wave. Before the basic design of Alpha was completed, research had to start on a new process. From the beginning, Lawrence planned to use multiple hot sources for Beta. Since the Beta calutrons were to be half the size of the Alpha, it would be necessary to build sources which would produce multiple beams operating very close together without interference. Although liners would not be required for electrical operation of the calutrons with hot sources, some sort of liner would be needed to facilitate the recovery of the enriched Alpha product, which would be used as feed for Beta. When efficient chemical recovery became the primary factor in design, substantial modifications in the liner could be expected. Receivers, too, would require some changes. Pockets to capture both the enriched and depleted material were now essential, and the more intense beams produced on the shorter radius in the Beta units would call more attention to methods of prolonging the operating lifetime of receiver parts.

157

In contrast to the initial electromagnetic plant, the general layout of Beta was not determined by experiments at Berkeley but by engineering studies at Oak Ridge. Months of mental, if not actual, wrestling with the calutrons for the Alpha racetracks revealed the changes that should be incorporated in any additional plants. First among these was the elimination of the oval racetrack in favor of a rectangular magnet. Tennessee Eastman had already discovered how hard it would be to hoist the heavy calutrons over the racetrack from the "infield." The alternate arrangement of tanks within the track unnecessarily complicated the electrical and vacuum supply lines. Fortunately, the rectangular arrangement was facilitated by the smaller number of tanks required. Tennessee Eastman concluded that the Beta building should house two tracks of thirty-six tanks. The tracks would be divided into two banks, the tanks in each bank facing the same way to simplify supply lines. If Lawrence's scientists were not called upon to make these decisions, they were required to incorporate them in research on the Beta calutron with the 37-inch magnet.

By far the greatest impact of Beta was on process chemistry. For Alpha, the chemical requirements seemed simple enough to be studied in a routine way at Berkeley. The preparation of uranium tetrachloride feed from uranium oxide was a straightforward process which was incorporated into the design of the chemistry building at Oak Ridge. The recovery of product seemed simple, if only in terms of scale. In early 1943, there were no plans for the complete recovery of the large proportion of uranium which did not enter the receiver pocket. The very small amount of enriched uranium in the pocket could be recovered by washing and scrubbing the receiver and then by separating the impurities from the uranium by chemical methods. The advent of Beta, however, caused Lawrence to see the chemistry in a new light. The implications for Beta were clear enough, at least in general terms. The feed for Beta would not be prepared from natural uranium oxide but from the valuable Alpha product. Thus, all steps in the preparation of feed had to minimize losses. Once the Beta units had been operated, the utmost care would have to be exercised to recover not only the traces of fully enriched uranium 235 but also the rest of the charge, which would be spewed over the liner, source, and receiver. This portion of the charge, containing virtually all the original, would have to be reprocessed in the chemistry buildings.[51]

Lawrence's acceptance of Beta reflected a much less optimistic view of Alpha, and this attitude had its effect on Alpha chemistry. When there arose some doubts whether the process developed at Berkeley would produce enough feed for Alpha, Lawrence arranged for research on an alternate process at Brown University. At the same time, he expanded chemistry activities at the Berkeley and Davis campuses of the University of California and encouraged Tennessee Eastman personnel in Rochester to take a greater part in the design of process equipment for the chemistry buildings at Oak Ridge.

Another drain on Berkeley talent was the effort required to build the first full-scale experimental models of the Alpha and Beta calutrons. During the first weeks of 1943, Lawrence ordered the construction of a small section of the Alpha racetrack in the cyclotron building. The unit was full-size, with twelve-foot magnet coils and vacuum tanks. There were, however, but three coils and two gaps, with only one tank in each gap. The calutrons were closely modeled after D1, the sources, collectors, and liners all being mounted on the door which sealed the tank. To approximate Alpha operating conditions in these first vertical tanks, the source was placed on the top of the door in the first tank and on the bottom in the second. Each tank contained double cold sources and two single-pocket receivers of the type developed by Barnes. The unit was quickly built and first operated in March, 1943. In production runs during May it was found capable of producing material enriched to 9-per-cent uranium 235, but production was unimportant except to the extent that it indicated success of the full-scale plant. The experimental unit was used to detect faults in the Alpha calutrons, to test different types of sources and receivers manufactured both at Berkeley and Pittsburgh, and to train senior operating personnel sent to the West Coast by Tennessee Eastman. During the first few months, both tanks were used mostly for experimental runs, but later the second tank was usually reserved for training until similar units could be completed at Oak Ridge.

Even by utilizing the Berkeley units around the clock, Tennessee Eastman officials saw that they were rapidly falling behind their training schedule. The company made a tremendous effort to complete the first Alpha experimental units at Oak Ridge. Ground was broken on April 13, 1943, for a building to house experimental Alpha and Beta units. The superstructure of the building was completed in three weeks. Within a few weeks more, Stone

& Webster was ready to install the three mammoth magnet coils, each weighing 330 tons, for the Alpha unit. By that time, Tennessee Eastman and the Army were clamoring for the calutron parts and electrical equipment needed to put "XAX" into operation.[52]

DECISION TO ENLARGE Y-12

These accomplishments in the spring of 1943 in large measure justified Lawrence's unflagging confidence in the electromagnetic process. By early summer, hundreds of engineers and draftsmen in Stone & Webster's Boston offices were completing the last of thousands of drawings which were being used in scores of manufacturing plants to produce equipment for Oak Ridge. For this enterprise, General Groves had authorized more than $100 million. Five Alpha racetracks, two Beta tracks, the Alpha and Beta experimental units, the chemical processing buildings, and scores of auxiliary and service structures were in various stages of construction. Heartening news came also from the experiments at Berkeley with the new tanks in the 184-inch magnet and with the experimental Alpha unit. Operation of the latter led Lawrence to predict that each Alpha tank at Oak Ridge would produce 300 grams of enriched uranium per month. This rate could be doubled, he believed, by installing double hot sources of the type tested successfully in Tank D1 during June. True, the contractor team had not met Groves's demand that the Alpha experimental unit at Oak Ridge be completed by July 1, but it was ready for initial tests during the first week of August. Although it did not seem likely that all five Alpha racetracks would be in operation by the end of 1943, Lawrence had not given up hope of having the first track running by early September, as Groves insisted.

But events elsewhere were moving even more swiftly. Lawrence's hopes for greater Y-12 production were more than offset by newer and higher estimates of the amount of uranium 235 needed for the bomb. In July, Robert Oppenheimer, director of the new weapons laboratory at Los Alamos, New Mexico, reported that the median estimate of his scientists had roughly tripled. This three-fold increase prompted Conant to admit to his diary that it was now nip and tuck whether Y-12 would ever produce enough material for a weapon in the present war. At the same time, Conant was not ready to write off the electromagnetic process. If the plant could be completed in 1943, a few kilograms of uranium 235 would be available early in 1944. These would be invaluable for weapon experiments; and with all the breaks, it might be possible to have one bomb by the fall of 1944. In view of the discouraging reports from New York on barrier development, it seemed to Conant unlikely that gaseous diffusion would produce even one gram of material by that time. Lawrence did not miss this opportunity to suggest that Y-12 might well be the only hope for a uranium-235 weapon. When the barrier crisis led Groves to speak of eliminating the top of the K-25 cascade, the California scientist was quick to calculate how it might be possible to reach the cherished goal of one kilogram of uranium 235 per day by using the partially enriched material from K-25 as feed for Y-12. Groves reported this suggestion favorably to the Military Policy Committee on May 5, 1943. During the summer, Lawrence relied on this idea as the main justification for proposals to enlarge the electromagnetic plant.[53]

Lawrence began his campaign at a Chicago meeting with Groves on July 8. Pointing to the recent success with the double hot source, he challenged the Army's decision to make all five Alpha tracks identical. He was sure that hot sources would double production. He was just as certain that double sources would work, and he could see no reason why four, or even eight, beams could not eventually be run in each tank. With such prospects within reach, was it not foolish to continue the construction of the Alpha tracks with the original cold source? Groves did not oppose plant improvements, but he was wary of any changes which might delay completion of the plant thus far approved. The best Lawrence could get was a compromise. The first four Alpha tracks would be completed as planned, but the fifth would use double hot sources. Any decision to convert the other Alpha tracks to hot sources was to be postponed until August 15; the question whether to build additional Alpha tracks would not be decided until the end of that month.

By the end of July, Lawrence was ready to try for two double hot sources in each tank. At a special meeting in Berkeley on August 5, 1943, he took the stump for such a four-beam source. One had been installed in Tank D1 the previous week and was already giving excellent results. Despite a minor error in the design of the electrodes, the source had produced a total beam of 300 milliamperes. Lawrence had no doubt that 400 milliamperes would be obtained when this error was corrected. From the standpoint of physics, the four-beam source was sure to be a success, and the engineers from Stone & Webster and Tennessee Eastman agreed that it would be as easy to install as the double source. After a few more probing questions, Groves was convinced. He authorized the four-beam source for the fifth track on the conditions that the change did not delay completion of the plant and that a fully successful run was achieved with the test unit in D1. Bubbling over with enthusiasm, Lawrence was determined to produce that evidence within a few weeks. On August 19, he admitted that the test runs were not all he had hoped for, but he was certain that he understood the reasons for inadequate performance. For Lawrence, this was good enough. The fifth track would use the four-beam source.[54]

Now only a few days remained before Groves had to make the big decision—whether to increase the number of racetracks in the plant. He had one mission, to produce the bomb in the shortest possible time. With that goal constantly before him, he was predisposed from the start to approve the expansion, but he insisted on being convinced by Lawrence and the others who advocated the step. Thus he could be sure that they considered every factor and put their decision in the record. Although he did not reveal his sentiments to the Y-12 group, he was optimistic about the project. He knew enough about the work at Los Alamos to see that estimates of bomb size were anything but certain. Therefore, no one could say when the plant might produce enough material for a bomb—any time from September, 1944, to early 1945. While he continually complained to his contractors about delays in construction, Groves told the Military Policy Committee that the job was on schedule. He was pleased when, after a week of start-up difficulties, the experimental Alpha unit at Oak Ridge was operated successfully for the first time on August 17, 1943. There was no question now that the plant would operate, and Groves felt certain that the electromagnetic process was the shortest route to the bomb.

Before making a final decision, Groves called the laboratory and con- 161 tractor representatives to an all-day meeting in Berkeley on September 2, 1943. He reviewed the series of decisions made on the fifth Alpha track and the impact those changes were having on the design and manufacture of equipment. He nailed down the decision to put any additional Alpha tracks in a completely new set of buildings. He explored the still preliminary designs of the Beta plant and the laboratory's plans to build test units. Then, late in the morning, he turned to the design of the new plant. How many sources would be used in each tank? How many tanks per magnet gap? Would rectangular magnets be used? How many Alpha and Beta tracks should be built? How many auxiliary buildings would be necessary? The wily general was getting a feel of the situation and by the end of a long day he liked what he felt.

Groves presented his plan to the Military Policy Committee on September 9. The new plant, which he designated Alpha II, would consist of two buildings each containing two tracks of ninety-six tanks each. The magnets would be rectangular, with all tanks facing the same side of the magnet. Four hot sources would be installed in each tank. Since liners would not be required, the sources and receivers could be mounted on separate doors to make maintenance easier. Groves estimated that Alpha II would cost about $150 million. To this figure, he would have to add the cost of perhaps another Beta building and additional chemical facilities. Thus the General placed a heavy bet on the Y-12 process.[55]

SHAKEDOWN

During the summer of 1943 the center of activity began to shift from Berkeley to Oak Ridge. With construction in full swing, Stone & Webster's payroll hit 10,000 employees by the first week in September. As soon as overhead cranes were set and roof slabs installed on the first Alpha building, workmen began unloading the massive magnet coils which had been shipped from Allis-Chalmers' Milwaukee plant. Then began the seemingly endless job of placing and grinding the heavy core castings. Meanwhile, pipe, valves, pumps, motors, cable, vacuum tanks, electrical equipment, control panels, and calutron parts began to inundate the construction site. Often the equipment to be first installed was the last to arrive, and carefully prepared installation procedures had to be revised on the spot. Because there had been no real pilot plant, the first Alpha building had to serve that purpose for many of the details of design and installation. No matter how careful the preparations, delays had to be accepted in the construction of a completely new kind of plant. With one last great effort, Stone & Webster succeeded in completing the magnet for the first track by the first week in October. Then, as the final calutron parts and electrical equipment were delivered, the contractor strained to complete the plant by November 1, 1943.

162

Tennessee Eastman had in the meantime been assembling and training its operating force. Early in the year, the company had estimated that it would need 1,450 people to operate the first track and 2,500 for all five Alpha units. The addition of the Beta buildings and Alpha II had by summer multiplied those requirements several times. Recruiting offices were established in a number of cities, but the best results were obtained in the Knoxville area. An initial cadre of operating personnel had gone to Berkeley during the spring for training on the Alpha experimental unit. Others went to the Berkeley and Davis campuses and to the Eastman plant in Rochester for instruction in chemical processing. Many members of these groups served as instructors for the large numbers of operating and maintenance personnel recruited during the summer. When the experimental Alpha unit at Oak Ridge was completed in August, the development building was swarming around the clock with would-be operators and maintenance crews. By the time the first Alpha track was ready for operation in November, Tennessee Eastman had 4,800 operating personnel on its rolls.[56]

The first notes of trouble began to filter through the hubbub of activity in late October, 1943. When the first magnet coils were tested, it was found that resistance to ground was no more than a few ohms. Because the leakage seemed to be distributed throughout the entire coil, it was assumed that moisture in the circulating oil which cooled the coils was effectively shorting out the system. If this were true, the leakage could be expected to disappear as the moisture was driven off by operating temperatures. In the meantime, there were other faults to correct. Testing of the vacuum tanks revealed many small leaks which had to be closed. Some of the welds in the magnets gave way and spilled oil on the operating floor. Under the stress imposed by the tremendous magnets, some of the vacuum tanks pulled loose and moved several inches out of line. The failure of rectifier tubes and other electric equipment constantly plagued the early attempts at operation. Even

EXPERIMENTAL RACETRACK (XAX) AT Y-12, OAK RIDGE / This unit was built in the summer of 1943 to test the Alpha tracks for the electromagnetic process and to train operators. Workmen are preparing a tank for insertion between the magnet coils.

ALPHA I UNIT IN WASHSTAND / Part of the process of recovering the uranium-tetrachloride charge that did not reach the receiver.

ALPHA I TWO-BEAM UNIT / This unit rests on its door on a storage dolly. The covers have been removed to show the double source at the right and the two receivers at the left.

ALPHA I CONTROL ROOM / Each operator tends two control panels, one for each tank. By the spring of 1945, almost 22,000 workers were required to keep Y-12 in operation.

ALPHA I RACETRACK / The reason for the name is obvious. The protruding ribs are the silver-wound magnet coils. The boxlike cover around the top contains the solid-silver bus bar.

BETA RACETRACK / Compare with the Alpha I racetrack, noting the rectilinear arrangement and the smaller scale of the equipment.

when enough faults could be eliminated to permit some semblance of operation in a few tanks, frequent shorts in the calutrons and clumsy adjustments by inexperienced operators made the attainment of a sustained beam an unusual event.

Under the weight of these failures, the operation of the first Alpha track ground to a halt in the first days of December. The worst problem was the shorts in the magnet coils. When a few of the coils were opened, it was discovered that the shorts were caused not by moisture but by millscale, rust, and other sediment in the cooling oil. The word flashed to Berkeley: Y-12 was in trouble.

When General Groves arrived on the scene on December 15, 1943, morale at Y-12 had hit bottom. The General inspected the opened coils and then met with his contractors to devise a solution. Westinghouse engineers assured Groves that there was nothing wrong with the magnet design. The coils could be expected to operate satisfactorily if the cooling oil could be kept clean. The only hope for the first Alpha track was to ship all the coils back to Allis-Chalmers, where an attempt would be made to clean them without complete dismantling. Having ascertained the facts, Groves ordered return of the coils at once. Then he turned to ways of preventing such failures in the future. From the divided counsels presented, the General selected the most likely, if not certain, preventive measures. The oil piping would be carefully cleaned before installation, and special oil filters would be added to the system.[57]

163

With the first Alpha track (Alpha 1) out of operation for weeks, Stone & Webster and Tennessee Eastman concentrated every effort on Alpha 2. All oil lines and coils were inspected, oil filters were ordered, and final adjustments were made on calutrons and electrical equipment as soon as they could be installed. By January 15, 1944, the first few tanks were evacuated, and the calutrons started. Within a week virtually all the tanks had been operated, although most of them for only a very short time. At first it seemed that routine performance would never be possible with the temperamental equipment. Electrical failures occurred by the hundred, chemical equipment broke down, and many tanks were turned off for lack of spare parts. Maintenance crews, often on double shifts, were so harried that repair work lagged. An improperly assembled source, a damaged receiver, a cracked insulator, a clogged accelerating slit, a vacuum spoiled by a dead mouse, a corroded chemical tank—thousands of little faults all added up to frustration and disappointment. Only in these first production runs was it fully apparent how damaging minor faults could be. The smallest failure inside a tank could require breaking the vacuum seal, a quick repair, and thirty or more hours of pump-down and bake-out before the operating vacuum was restored.

Lawrence, however, did not let this swarm of breakdowns cloud his view of what had been accomplished. Although only a few tanks were operating at any one time, their individual performance was improving. Early in

February, Lawrence found that the Berkeley scientists who were experimenting with eight tanks in Alpha 2 could maintain productive beams during 90 per cent of each operating cycle. For all other operable tanks in Alpha 2, the figure was approaching 40 per cent, and in many cases the inexperienced young women from the Tennessee mountains excelled the scientists in manning the tank controls.

By the end of the month, about 200 grams of material enriched to about 12-per-cent uranium 235 had been produced in Alpha 2. A portion of this product was shipped early in March to Los Alamos for fast-neutron experiments. The remainder would be used as feed for the first Beta racetrack.[58]

NEW LOOK AT Y-12

Lawrence's burst of optimism in early February, 1944, proved to be a momentary flicker in an otherwise darkening sky. The appalling rate of minor equipment failures experienced in Alpha declined slowly as additional tracks were completed. The rebuilt Alpha 1 track was not ready until March, and all four of the original Alpha tracks (Alpha I) were not in operation until well into April, almost four months behind schedule. Even then, the epidemic of breakdowns kept production far below what Lawrence had anticipated. Contributing to this general discouragement was the failure of the calutrons in the Beta building, first operated on March 11, 1944. A few attempts to achieve a good beam led to the unhappy conclusion that the Beta source would have to be completely redesigned.

The darkest shadow, however, was cast by the barrier crisis in the K-25 project. The abandonment of the Norris-Adler barrier after a year of all-out research had a deep psychological effect which spread far beyond the limits of the Columbia campus. Some, like Urey, were ready to discount the gaseous-diffusion process altogether. Even hardheaded people like General Groves were forced to scale down their expectations drastically. In August, 1943, Groves had anticipated that K-25 would produce material enriched to something less than 50-per-cent uranium 235. The following January, Oppenheimer called to his attention the fact that uranium of this enrichment would be of no value for weapons. Perhaps Carbide could accelerate K-25 production by enriching the material to just a few per-cent uranium 235 as feed for Y-12. Groves already had that idea in mind, and he was prepared to adopt it if necessary. Some weeks later, in the midst of the barrier crisis, he told the Y-12 contractors at an Oak Ridge meeting that if K-25 produced at all, the product might not be enriched more than a few per cent. Taken together, the outlook for Y-12 and K-25 scarcely seemed to indicate the possibility of producing enough material for a bomb in 1944, or even in early 1945. But adversity had not changed the paramount aim of the S-1 project.

Regardless of the odds, Groves had to take whatever action would produce the bomb in the shortest possible time.[59]

One course was to use any combination of isotope-separation processes which would result in the earliest production of uranium 235. It was this avenue which Groves chose to follow in 1944. This decision had profound implications for Y-12. If, according to the latest estimates, the product from K-25 were only slightly enriched, it would have to be fed to the Alpha rather than the Beta plants. In the original Alpha plant the use of enriched feed was difficult enough. The receivers would have to be replaced with new models containing pockets for both beams, but the research already done for Alpha II and Beta made this a fairly simple adjustment. Greater care would also be required in washing the liners and recovering the now valuable charge material in the chemical processing building. In Alpha II, however, the changes took on major proportions. Since Alpha tracks 6 to 9 were designed to operate on natural uranium with hot sources, the tanks would contain no liners, and washing facilities would be provided only for source and receiver parts. Now the tanks and doors would have to be redesigned to accommodate liners, and the washing areas in the Alpha II buildings would have to be more than doubled. In the new Alpha chemistry buildings, better recovery methods would be necessary and some of the equipment would require redesign to eliminate the possibility of accumulating a critical mass with the enriched material. For this reason, Tennessee Eastman and the Radiation Laboratory began an intensive campaign in the spring of 1944 to redesign calutron components and to enlarge and improve chemical processing facilities.[60]

165

The second course of action was to place increased reliance on the electromagnetic process. The successful operation of the first three Alpha tracks and experiments with the first Beta calutrons convinced Lawrence that Y-12 would soon be producing uranium 235 in quantity. The only question in his mind was whether the plant would be large enough. Before the end of March, Lawrence began agitating for a second Y-12 expansion, which would add four new Alpha tracks to the nine already under construction. Oppenheimer, who had seen the Berkeley calutrons the previous October and had only a fragmentary knowledge of K-25, agreed with Lawrence. Groves, too, looked upon Y-12 as the best chance for success, but he was not sure that additional racetracks could be built in time to be effective during the war. The General was also concerned about balancing Alpha and Beta requirements. He was therefore inclined to postpone a decision until these details were clarified, but he was ready to be convinced.

Consequently Groves, Oppenheimer, and Lawrence all went to the meeting of the Military Policy Committee in Chicago on March 30, 1944, fully expecting the expansion of Y-12 to be the issue of the day. For some strange reason, however, expansion was never mentioned specifically, as the discussion centered around the problems of using the gaseous-diffusion product in Y-12. Apparently, each assumed that silence on the part of the others indicated a loss of enthusiasm for the expansion. The truth of the matter burst upon Lawrence six weeks later in Oak Ridge when he received a letter from his old friend Oliphant. The Australian scientist reported a rumor that both Oppenheimer and Groves had gone to the meeting prepared to back Lawrence on the expansion and were disappointed that Lawrence had opposed it. Oliphant expressed the opinion that Groves was uneasy about the decision, but he had also heard that plutonium had now been found so superior for weapons that uranium 235 would be abandoned once the piles were completed at a new site on the Columbia River in Washington. Lawrence immediately telegraphed Oppenheimer for his understanding of the events. He assured his former colleague that he continued to support the Y-12 expansion and had failed to raise the issue on March 30 only because he understood that a decision against expansion had already been reached.

166

Oppenheimer's reply spurred Lawrence to action. There was no truth to the rumor that uranium 235 would be abandoned. Furthermore, Oppenheimer admitted, he had come to the meeting prepared to support the Y-12 expansion and had reluctantly dropped the idea only after hearing Lawrence's comments on the difficulties involved. Lawrence now saw the situation clearly.[61] On May 31, 1944, he wrote Conant: "The primary fact now is that the element of gamble in the over-all picture no longer exists. The electromagnetic plant is in successful operation and the experimental developments at Y [Los Alamos] leave no doubt that the production can be used as an overwhelmingly powerful explosive. It is only a question of time and indeed it is the time schedule that indicates need of at least two more alpha two buildings." [62]

Lawrence grew even more concerned the following week. He stayed on in Oak Ridge to keep his finger on operating problems with the fifth Alpha track. In addition to the usual shortage of equipment and spare parts, there were frequent power failures, and operating procedures seemed deficient. He also learned that his was not the only project in trouble in Tennessee. From Felbeck and Bliss of Union Carbide he obtained a depressing picture of K-25 barrier. Their words led Lawrence to doubt that K-25 would be useful in 1945. In fact, he wondered whether the plant would even be operative during the next year. Since the outlook for plutonium seemed no more certain, Lawrence looked to Y-12 as the only hope for the bomb in 1945. To him, the minimum was to convert the original Alpha plant to four-beam sources, Alpha II to eight-beam sources, and to build two more Alpha racetracks. These views the California physicist pressed on Conant and Groves with, he believed, some effect. Meanwhile, Oliphant was bombarding the Army from California. He wrote Colonel Nichols that he could no longer assume that K-25 would have any significance in 1945. British experiments with gaseous diffusion had demonstrated that. The only hope was to adopt Lawrence's expansion plan at once.[63]

On June 16, 1944, Lawrence was back in Berkeley, where he could examine in detail the various proposals for Y-12 expansion. He concluded that he could do nothing with the original Alpha plant to increase production before July, 1945. He might better put all laboratory and engineering talent on developing improved equipment for the new Alpha tracks and for a tenth track not yet authorized. These recommendations he telegraphed to Groves for his use in a major policy meeting at Oak Ridge on June 30. There, with the senior executives from Stone & Webster and General Electric, Groves quickly got down to facts. Any thought of converting Alpha I was dropped at once. As for Alpha II, the plan seemed ambitious enough. The Radiation Laboratory would attempt to develop a completely new type of calutron consisting of a cold source producing thirty beams simultaneously. The beams would move through a two-foot radius to the receivers, where the enriched segments would be caught by individual pockets and the depleted segments by a common electrode. Groves's only concern was whether it would be possible to complete the conversion in time to increase production before the middle of 1945. He gave the contractors four days to find an answer.

167

The group reassembled on the Fourth of July. The contractors were ready to go to work. The Radiation Laboratory would begin research at once on the thirty-beam unit. Westinghouse would shift all its development personnel from the four-beam to the thirty-beam equipment. General Electric would assign five physicists and two engineers to the Berkeley laboratory and would start design at once on electrical power equipment. No one mentioned additional tracks. General Groves accepted the proposal. With time running out, there was nothing else to do.[64]

In July, 1944, the production of enough uranium 235 for an atomic weapon looked far off indeed. Four Alpha tracks were in operation but they were producing only a fraction of the material expected. Minor operating difficulties continued to plague the fifth track, and the first attempts to operate the new Alpha II tracks had met with an unprecedented rash of insulator failures.[65] There was little hope now that Y-12 alone could produce enough fissionable material for a bomb by the middle of 1945.

Even more discouraging were the somber reports from K-25. Originally expected to carry the brunt of the uranium 235 requirements, K-25 had been cut back to a feeder process for Y-12 in the summer of 1943. The next spring there was still a chance that K-25 could supply slightly enriched feed. Now that hope seemed to be fading fast. Obviously, if Groves had any cards left in his hand, he would have to play them quickly.

THE LAST CARD

As early as 1942, the Military Policy Committee had thought exclusively of an isotope-separation process which could produce fully enriched uranium 235. By the summer of 1943, however, the committee had come to realize that it would probably be necessary to use a combination of processes to reach the goal. This seemed even more likely as the prospects for K-25 and Y-12 worsened in the spring of 1944. Perhaps one of the processes discarded earlier as impractical could be used as a stopgap to produce enough slightly enriched material to supply Y-12 until K-25 could be completed. It was just this kind of suggestion which Oppenheimer dropped in Groves's lap late in April, 1944.

168

Sometime during the winter, Oppenheimer had received from Conant two reports of Philip Abelson's work at the Naval Research Laboratory on liquid thermal diffusion. The reports interested Oppenheimer, but they convinced him that it would be almost impossible to produce fully enriched uranium 235 by this method. During the spring, Captain William S. Parsons, a division leader at Los Alamos, visited the Philadelphia Navy Yard. There Parsons discovered that Abelson was building a small thermal-diffusion plant to produce uranium 235 for the Navy. Abelson told Parsons he expected the plant to be producing five grams of material enriched to 5-per-cent uranium 235 per day about July 1, 1944. Parsons also reported to Oppenheimer that there was enough steam capacity at the Navy Yard to operate a plant three times as large as Abelson's. Now Oppenheimer was really interested. He saw that if the 100 columns in the plant were operated in parallel rather than in series, the plant theoretically would produce daily twelve kilograms of material enriched to about 1-per-cent uranium 235. Perhaps the Philadelphia plant would serve as the last card in Groves's hand.[66]

The thermal-diffusion project was an old and not altogether pleasant story to Bush, Conant, and Groves. Dating back to 1940, Abelson's research was among the first directed specifically to the separation of uranium isotopes. The process sounded simple. Abelson's idea was to introduce uranium hexafluoride under pressure in liquid form into the small annular spacing between two concentric vertical pipes. If the outer wall was cooled by a circulating water jacket and the inner heated by high-pressure steam, the lighter isotope would tend to concentrate near the hot wall and the heavier near the cold. Then the ordinary process of convection would in time carry the lighter to the top of the column. The taller the column, the greater would be the separation effected.

This consideration influenced Abelson's decision to transfer his research in the summer of 1941 from the National Bureau of Standards in Washington to the Naval Research Laboratory in Anacostia. The small supply of steam at the Bureau laboratories limited his experiments to columns twelve feet high. In Anacostia, he had a new twenty-horsepower, gas-fired boiler which could supply sufficient steam for a thirty-six-foot column. Procurement problems delayed operation of the first column until November, 1941. The column was ruined in an early experiment, and positive results from operation of the second were not obtained until February, 1942.[67]

By that time, Abelson had lost all contact with the S-1 Section of OSRD. In 1941, Bush and Conant had received rather general reports on Abelson's work from Ross Gunn, who was a technical adviser at the Navy laboratory. But with no positive results, Gunn could hardly impress the S-1 Section. Then, when Abelson's data were ready, Gunn was no longer in effective liaison with the S-1 organization. Furthermore, after the March 17 report to the President, Bush and Conant took the first steps to bring in the Army. At that time, Roosevelt had made it clear to Bush that the Navy was to be excluded from S-1 affairs.

S-1 contact with the thermal-diffusion project, therefore, lapsed until late July, 1942, when Urey mentioned Abelson's experiments to Conant. Nier, who was at that time analyzing isotopic samples for both Urey and Abelson, reported that Abelson's columns had succeeded in increasing the uranium 235 content of hexafluoride by 10 per cent. Conant was concerned about the Navy's independent ways, but Bush was more relaxed. The Navy's insistence on pursuing isotope separation independent of S-1 might be irregular, but it had done no harm. At Bush's request, Briggs called Gunn at the Naval Research Laboratory for news about Abelson's research. Briggs reported early in September that Abelson had completed many experiments with six different thirty-six-foot columns and was convinced that the process was practical. He estimated that seven such columns in series would double the enrichment of uranium 235 in the hexafluoride. The disadvantage was that the time required to increase the enrichment even as high as 50 per cent would be impractically long. This report was not one to inspire action in Bush and Conant, who were aware of recent progress in the electromagnetic and pile projects.[68]

Groves first learned about thermal diffusion on September 21, 1942, when he and Nichols visited the Anacostia laboratory. Gunn was quite willing to give the Army officers any information they desired; but Groves, remembering Bush's explanation of the President's order to exclude the Navy from S-1, said nothing about the recent expansion of the S-1 project under his direction. In his own mind, he discounted the Navy project because it lacked a sense of urgency.

There was no further contact with the Navy until December 10. The day before, while the S-1 Executive Committee was discussing the Lewis report, Briggs suggested that to complete their assignment, the Lewis group should visit the Naval Research Laboratory. Accordingly, Groves and Lewis presented themselves with the three du Pont members at Gunn's Anacostia office. They learned that Abelson now had two forty-eight-foot columns

169

operating in series. In processing about two kilograms of hexafluoride per day, the columns achieved a small but significant separation of the uranium isotopes.

The S-1 Executive Committee was impressed by this report and conveyed the information to Bush. Bound by the President's directive not to bring the Navy into the S-1 program, Bush elected to suggest to Admiral Purnell, the Navy member of the Military Policy Committee, that the Naval Research Laboratory be given all the support necessary for Abelson's experiments. Bush himself visited Anacostia on January 14, 1943, explained the Presidential directive, and assured Gunn of the action he had taken through Admiral Purnell. Gunn was not so easily satisfied. The Navy was interested in nuclear power for submarine propulsion. Abelson had a practical method of producing uranium 235; all he needed was data on nuclear constants, which, Gunn understood, were being produced by a large group under Arthur Compton at Chicago. Bush must have been relieved to know that the momentous events at Stagg Field the previous December 2 had not yet seeped through to Anacostia.[69]

Under the circumstances, Bush could not honor Gunn's request for information, but he did act to obtain more support. Gunn had told him of very recent results which were much more encouraging than any before. Bush would discuss the organizational problem with the Military Policy Committee the next week. Meanwhile, Conant had received from Purnell copies of Abelson's latest reports. He had referred them at once to the S-1 Executive Committee, which had requested Briggs, Murphree, and Urey to review them. With the help of Karl Cohen and W. I. Thompson of the Standard Oil Development Company, they inspected the experimental columns at Anacostia the following week. They found that since September Abelson had obtained much higher separation by increasing the difference in temperature between the two walls of the column. They were impressed by the simplicity of the plant which had no moving parts and no valves in the hexafluoride system. The process liquid moved by natural convection. The temperature and pressure conditions of the hexafluoride made it possible to stop its flow simply by "freezing" the supply pipe with a handful of dry ice. A rough calculation showed that to construct a plant producing one kilogram of fully enriched uranium 235 per day would require eighteen months and $75 million. Unfortunately, there were some big items on the debit side. The time required for such a plant to reach equilibrium was estimated at 600 days. This meant that, if work were started at once, the plant would not be in full production until early 1946. Briggs, Murphree, and Urey were disturbed by the fact that no product had yet been withdrawn from the columns, all production estimates being the result of measuring the difference in concentration between the top and bottom of the column and completing the necessary calculations. Thus, they could recommend only that the work be accelerated by having a large industrial organization prepare preliminary design studies for a production plant.[70]

A year earlier, this recommendation would have given Abelson the kind of priority which the gaseous-diffusion and centrifuge projects had enjoyed. But in January, 1943, it was hard to imagine a more equivocal suggestion. Murphree himself realized this almost as soon as he had submitted the report. Two days later, he wrote Briggs that the equilibrium time, construction period, and cost would be very much less if the plant were designed to produce 10-per-cent rather than fully enriched uranium 235. On second thought, he believed that the thermal-diffusion process had been as well demonstrated as gaseous diffusion. Why not consider it as a substitute for K-25 for the lower stages of enrichment? Briggs, as chairman of the subcommittee, sent off such a recommendation to Conant on January 30. Within forty-eight hours, Groves dispatched all the relevant documents to Warren K. Lewis and his committee of du Pont executives.

171

Within a week, Crawford Greenewalt had the committee's reply in the mail. There was no question that experimental work at the Naval Research Laboratory should be expanded, but the committee did not agree that the process could be considered as a substitute for gaseous diffusion. In contrast to gaseous diffusion, the theory of thermal diffusion was not sufficiently well known to permit the extrapolation of Abelson's data over the whole range of concentration to fully enriched uranium 235. The long equilibrium time and the extraordinary steam requirements were disadvantages. The committee would recommend nothing beyond more research and preliminary engineering studies. This recommendation was confirmed by the S-1 Executive Committee on February 10. Before the end of the month, Groves sent Purnell a description of the experiments to be completed before plant design could be started. In the future, Briggs would be the S-1 contact with Anacostia.[71]

A complete break with the Naval Research Laboratory came late in the summer of 1943. At Conant's request, Lewis, Briggs, Murphree, and Urey reviewed Abelson's work again just before Labor Day. The following Wednesday, they submitted a report which did not differ much from that prepared by Greenewalt in February. After discussing the report with the S-1 Executive Committee, Conant sent the bad news to Purnell in a firm but polite letter. He would consider it most unfortunate if the Navy drew away from the Manhattan project any of the scientists now engaged in S-1 work. No additional supplies of uranium hexafluoride would be given to the Navy for its experiments, but the Navy was requested to exchange any material enriched at Anacostia for hexafluoride of normal concentration. When Groves refused a Navy request for additional amounts in October, the Navy was constrained to remind him that Abelson had developed the original process for producing hexafluoride, which the Navy had given to the S-1 project. Only then did the Army reluctantly agree to fill the order. On this sour note, all exchange of information between the two projects ended. Not until Groves received Oppenheimer's suggestion the following April did thermal diffusion again become a factor in the race for the bomb.[72]

Although isolated from S-1, Abelson could continue his work on thermal diffusion now that he was assured adequate supplies of hexafluoride. He knew that the best way to reduce the equilibrium time was to increase the temperature difference between the cold and hot walls. Any such temperature increase in the forty-eight-foot columns, however, would require large amounts of high-pressure steam. A survey of naval installations revealed that sufficient steam capacity was available at the Naval Boiler and Turbine Laboratory at the Philadelphia Navy Yard. In November, 1943, Abelson got Navy authorization to build a three-hundred-column plant in Philadelphia. Construction started in January, 1944, on a hundred-column plant which would be operated as a seven-stage cascade before the larger plant was built. It was this plant which Oppenheimer reported would be completed in July, 1944.

172

Oppenheimer's letter could not have reached Groves at a more propitious time. Early in May, the General obtained the permission of the Military Policy Committee to re-establish contact with the Navy. A review committee consisting of Lewis, Murphree, and Tolman visited the Philadelphia plant on June 1. They found Oppenheimer's report to be essentially correct, although they considered his estimate of production with the columns in parallel to be somewhat optimistic. It would be possible, as Oppenheimer had suggested, to add 200 tubes to the Philadelphia plant, and the Navy believed that this could be done in two months. Immediate construction of the additional columns, however, would interfere with experiments on the hundred-tube unit. Without further improvements, the Philadelphia plant would consume large amounts of uranium and probably would not produce a significant portion of the feed requirements for the electromagnetic plant.[73]

In the light of these considerations, Groves and his advisers could quickly conclude that a full-scale thermal-diffusion plant might be the best answer. On June 12, 1944, Murphree put Cohen and Thompson to work on estimating the cost and construction time for a plant to produce fifty kilograms of slightly enriched hexafluoride per day. Groves reported to the Military Policy Committee nine days later that such a plant could be built at reasonable cost and be in operation well before January 1, 1945. Furthermore, there seemed to be an ideal source of steam. The thermal-diffusion plant could be built at Oak Ridge next to the K-25 powerhouse, which would be completed within a few weeks. Groves intended to operate the thermal-diffusion plant only until K-25 could be finished. At that time the steam could be turned back into the turbines to produce electrical power for the gaseous-diffusion plant. Six days later, Groves signed a letter contract with the H. K. Ferguson Company of Cleveland to build next to the K-25 powerhouse a plant containing twenty-one exact copies of the one-hundred-column plant in Philadelphia. The entire plant was to be in operation within ninety days. In his usual style, Groves wrote to Colonel Mark C. Fox, his representative on the project: "After considering the various factors involved, I feel that my statement to you as to the schedule of completion of the work under your charge is reasonable. . . . I think you can beat it." [74]

The thermal-diffusion plant was the last card in Groves's hand. If some combination of Y-12, K-25, and the thermal-diffusion plant did not produce sufficient uranium 235 for a weapon, all hopes would rest on the plutonium project.

173

RACE FOR THE BOMB: PLUTONIUM

CHAPTER 6

In their classic experiment on December 2, 1942, Fermi and his associates demonstrated the possibility of a self-sustaining nuclear chain reaction. They had erected an impressive landmark in the history of science, but they had not devised a practical method of producing plutonium. To accumulate enough for a weapon, Fermi would have had to operate his Stagg Field pile for thousands of years. That assembly yielded a few watts of power; a production pile would have to generate hundreds of millions of watts. Such a device would require an elaborate cooling system, an array of sensitive and positive controls, and some means of containing the unprecedented amounts of radioactivity produced in the chain reaction. All the radium sources in the world could not generate more than a small fraction of the radiation emitted by one nuclear pile. Fermi's exponential piles had neither cooling systems, control rods, nor radiation shields. No one ever considered them the forerunners of a production apparatus.

The plutonium-producing pile, then, did not stem directly from the Fermi experiments but from related research at the Metallurgical Laboratory that had begun in the spring of 1942.

SEARCH FOR A PILE DESIGN

When the scientists began to assemble on the Chicago campus in the spring of 1942, Arthur Compton established an engineering council to guide the laboratory's study of a production pile. Thomas V. Moore led the group as the laboratory's chief engineer. Schooled by many years in the petroleum industry, he had been among Compton's first recruits and had participated in the initial selection of the Tennessee site for the production plants. Accompanying Moore was Miles C. Leverett, a thirty-two-year-old chemist with ten years of industrial experience. An even younger member was John A. Wheeler, the Princeton physicist who earlier had caught the eye of Niels Bohr and had helped him develop the basic interpretation of the fission process. Allison and Fermi brought to the group not only decades of research experience but an intimate knowledge of the exponential pile. Norman Hilberry, Richard L. Doan, Glenn T. Seaborg, and Frank H. Spedding contributed their respective talents for administration, chemistry, and metallurgy.[1]

The council faced a tough assignment. In effect, Compton was asking the members to conceive the design of a production plant based on a principle not yet demonstrated in the laboratory. They knew nothing of the conditions that would exist within the chain-reacting pile. What effects would heat and radiation have on the fission process and the pile itself? How could the engineers sketch the roughest outlines of the cooling and control systems until they had determined the arrangement of graphite and uranium within the pile? And how could they establish the internal configuration until they knew what pattern would produce the optimum value of the reproduction factor k? The scientists' frequent reference to k led Fermi quickly to see the big stumbling block in pile design. In building exponential piles, the physicists were necessarily preoccupied with maximizing k. In designing production piles, they had to give their attention to practical engineering features, all of which would tend to reduce the value of k. By their very nature, controls would reduce the efficiency of the reaction, and even the best cooling system would have a similar effect. Until the designers could precisely measure k for a given pile, they could not determine how much reactivity might be sacrificed in the interests of a practical design.

175

It was only logical that the Engineering Council should first consider how to arrange the uranium and graphite. This it did on June 18, 1942.[2] Since the fissionable material and graphite were not to be a homogeneous mixture, Fermi had devised for his exponential experiments a three-dimensional lattice, in which cylinders of uranium metal were uniformly spaced throughout a solid graphite block. For a production pile, however, the lattice arrangement had disadvantages. It would be almost impossible to remove the irradiated uranium cylinders without dismantling the pile. It would be equally difficult to concentrate the cooling system at each of the cylinders.

Simply from logic again, there seemed to be three solutions. The first was to find some ingenious way of preserving the lattice arrangement while overcoming the engineering handicaps. Walter H. Zinn thought it might be possible to devise continuous chains of uranium in graphite cartridges. As the chains moved through the graphite block, the cartridges would assume the optimum lattice arrangement. If the chains moved at about three feet per second, Zinn estimated it would be possible to cool the cartridges outside the pile. Wheeler suggested stationary alternate layers with intervening uranium-bearing layers connected to a common horizontal shaft which would draw them out of the pile for external cooling. Both these suggestions seemed utterly impractical to the engineers, but they indicated the physicists' great reluctance to abandon the lattice arrangement. In fact, until k could be measured precisely, there could be no assurance that anything less than the optimum arrangement would maintain the chain reaction.

A second solution was to maintain the optimum lattice, introduce some sort of internal cooling, and run the pile until nuclear poisons formed by the fission reaction stopped the process. Then the pile would be destroyed, the irradiated cylinders removed, and a new pile constructed. Moore questioned the feasibility of demolishing the pile after each loading. On the technical side, Spedding thought disposition of the highly radioactive graphite from the pile a touchy procedure. Fermi wondered how to keep fission products out of the graphite. Wheeler noted that the operation might not be economical unless the pile would run for a long period before fission products stopped the reaction. Another obvious disadvantage of the one-run pile was that no samples or test quantities of plutonium could be removed during the run. On the whole, the council did not find this approach promising.

The third possibility was to abandon the optimum lattice in favor of a more practical design. A perfectly obvious modification was to use rods of uranium extending through the graphite block. With adequate shielding, it seemed feasible to push the rods through the pile and concentrate the cooling system in straight channels or pipes adjacent to the rods. A hopeful augury was Wheeler's estimate that the use of rods would reduce k less than 0.5 per cent.[3]

On June 25, 1942, the Engineering Council discussed cooling systems.[4] Conceivably the members might restrict the first experimental piles to power levels which would not require internal cooling, but they would need such a system in any pile producing significant quantities of plutonium. As always, the first thought was to minimize the losses in k. This meant considering not only the configuration of the cooling system but the nuclear properties of the coolant and the pipes or channels containing it. Scarcely less critical were the thermal and physical properties of coolant materials and their effect on the cost of pumps and other components. Gases, for example, had relatively poor thermal properties. To remove large quantities of heat would require large volumes. This would mean high pressures, which in turn would complicate design of the pile and increase pumping costs. Unless confined by pipes within the pile, the gas would diffuse through the graphite and pick up radioactive fission products, thus creating a radiation hazard. On the other hand, several common gases had excellent nuclear properties. Helium and hydrogen absorbed few neutrons, and air not enough to prohibit its use. Hydrogen had the disadvantage of reacting chemically with both uranium and graphite. Helium, although expensive and scarce, seemed to be the best choice.

Liquids in general had better thermal properties than gases, but the Engineering Council was impressed by their drawbacks. To use liquids, the engineers would have to insert pipes in the pile and accept a loss in k. With a liquid coolant, an internal leak might well destroy the pile or even cause a violent explosion as the coolant vaporized within the hot graphite. Furthermore, the difficulty of transferring heat from the uranium metal to the coolant might more than offset the superior thermal properties of liquids. An added disadvantage was the limited choice among liquids. Water, the classical material for heat-transfer systems, did not have especially good nuclear properties and corroded uranium rapidly. Some organics such as diphenyl had good nuclear properties, but there was little experience to support their use in a high-power cooling system. Theoretically more promising and technically more remote were metals like bismuth, which had a low melting point and excellent nuclear properties.

Balancing all these factors, the Engineering Council concluded that helium cooling had the edge, at least for the moment. It could hope that liquid cooling would be possible in a large production pile. But until the chain reaction had been achieved and k determined, it would be wiser to concentrate on the helium-cooled pile. Compton, after consulting his colleagues, had already concluded that a logical first step would be to build a 100,000-kilowatt pile. The council agreed that it should be cooled with helium.

177

Thus during the summer of 1942, Moore and his engineers concentrated on a helium-cooled pile. With Stone & Webster, the contractor selected for construction of the pilot plant in the Argonne Forest Preserve, Moore developed plans for the huge vacuum-tight shell which would surround the pile. Leverett pondered the internal design. He conceived of a large block of graphite pierced with vertical channels about five inches in diameter on an eleven-inch square pattern. In these channels he would stack graphite cartridges, each consisting of thin vertical grills or plates of uranium, through which the helium would flow. The uranium plates would be spaced at proper intervals within the vertical columns to maintain an eleven-inch cubical lattice. By maintaining the lattice arrangement and using helium as the coolant, Leverett was optimizing the nuclear if not the engineering properties of the pile. Consciously cautious in this first try, he was willing to sacrifice engineering efficiency in order to assure achieving a chain reaction.

Completion of the Moore-Leverett design actually rested upon the solution of relatively conventional engineering problems.[5] The uranium-graphite cartridges would not be easy to fabricate, and here the engineering team sought outside help. Spedding at Iowa State College devised a method of casting the thin uranium wafers in graphite molds. Edward C. Creutz, a physicist who had specialized in uranium metallurgy at Princeton before coming to Chicago, demonstrated the possibility of casting uranium in various shapes using an argon atmosphere in an electric furnace. The National Carbon Company studied designs of the graphite units and suggested improvements.

Meanwhile, Leverett was exploring the thermodynamics of the cooling system. He had to know the rate of heat transfer from the uranium metal to the helium coolant. Then he had to balance out such factors as the helium pressure drop through the pile, the temperature increase in the helium, the maximum uranium and graphite temperatures, and the rate of helium flow. For this purpose he planned a small helium cooling system consisting of tanks, pumps, heat exchangers, and full-scale models of the uranium-graphite cartridges. By September, 1942, Leverett had obtained the necessary components and had hired a contractor to assemble them in an unheated area under the North Stands of Stagg Field. With autumn coming on, he hoped to complete his experiments before freezing weather set in.

178

The preliminary design which Moore and Leverett submitted to Compton on September 25 closely resembled the plan conceived in June.[6] The heart of the reactor would be a twenty-foot cube of graphite weighing 460 tons. In the graphite would be 376 vertical columns, each containing twenty-two uranium-graphite cartridges. To remove the specified 100,000 kilowatts of heat, Moore and Leverett planned to pump 400,000 pounds of helium per hour through ducts into the bottom of the pile. The heated helium at the top would pass through heat exchangers requiring 900 gallons of water per minute. Until the experimental helium plant could be operated, these figures were tentative, but the engineers estimated they would need 12,000 kilowatts of electric power to operate the helium compressors and auxiliary equipment.

Moore and Leverett planned to surround the pile proper with several feet of graphite to act as an internal radiation shield. The entire assembly would be enclosed by a steel shell about twenty-eight feet in diameter and sixty-eight feet high. Following the advice of the Chicago Bridge & Iron Company, Moore and Leverett planned the shell as a series of spherical segments rather than a simple cylinder in order to provide greater structural strength. This configuration quickly inspired the nickname "Mae West pile." The upper section of the shell provided access to personnel loading the pile; the center section surrounded the pile itself; the lower section contained the dump mechanism which collected the irradiated cartridges. Actually, if the pile were ever constructed as planned, the shape of the shell would hardly be apparent since the entire assembly would be immersed in a huge cylindrical concrete tank filled with water.

Despite the activities of Moore and Leverett in developing their preliminary design, other scientists at the Metallurgical Laboratory were by no means satisfied. Early in July, 1942, Szilard and Wheeler expressed their growing concern that Compton had placed no equipment orders for the helium-cooled plant. Since the large helium compressors would take many months to procure, Compton should place orders at once. So uncommitted was Compton to the helium pile that the two physicists were constrained to remind him of the June 25 decision, but they got little satisfaction. Apparently, Compton interpreted that action as a priority for the helium-cooled plant and not as an exclusive selection of the type for development.[7]

Szilard, always impatient with what he considered red tape or indecision, looked back in September on a summer of aimless drift. In a scorching memorandum entitled "What Is Wrong With Us?", he complained that no decision on the cooling system had yet been made and that none seemed forthcoming in the near future.[8] This unfortunate situation he attributed partly to Compton's desire to avoid controversy and partly to security restrictions imposed by the Army. The result was that Moore and Leverett had attempted to develop the helium pile without any clear directive or priority. Similarly, he said, Wheeler and Wigner had explored the possibilities of a water-cooled pile, while Szilard himself had struggled to assemble a research team to study the bismuth-cooled pile.

Those who knew the impetuous Szilard no doubt discounted some of his statements, but he had expressed a growing sense of frustration among his colleagues. Its origins lay not so much in the leadership or the scientists themselves as in the situation they faced. The design of a production pile involved so many complex factors that there was no hope of a quick and easy answer. In the final analysis, Fermi's observation still hit the main point: until the precise value of k was known, how could the engineers get down to the details of design?

Compton understood Fermi's argument and did not intend to decide prematurely. Back in June, 1942, Compton had seen the first plans for a water-cooled pile drafted by Wigner and Gale Young. Both were experienced physicists—Wigner, the leader of the nuclear physics group at Princeton until the project was centralized at Chicago; Young, a former member of Compton's own department who had returned to the Midway for the pile project. Impressed with their hastily prepared report, Compton asked them to complete within two weeks as much work as they could on plans for a 100,000-kilowatt water-cooled pile. The plan they delivered to Compton during July called for a graphite cylinder about twelve feet high and twenty-five feet in diameter. The uranium would be cast as long pipes and placed vertically in the graphite block. The pipes would suspend from a water tank above the pile, pass down through vertical holes in the graphite, and discharge into another water tank beneath the pile. The cooling water would circulate through heat exchangers and return to the top tank. To prevent corrosion of the uranium pipes, Wigner and Young contemplated spraying or coating the interior surface with some material like aluminum or beryllium which would absorb few neutrons. If this were not sufficient, they

179

proposed to line the pipes with aluminum tubing. After studying the proposal, Compton admitted that water cooling looked promising enough to justify further planning.[9]

Even more speculative but still too attractive to be disregarded were Szilard's investigations of a pile cooled by liquid metal. Several metals such as bismuth were known to have exceptional thermal properties. Szilard believed that a cooling system using bismuth would be so efficient that the size of the pile could be reduced substantially. He was also intrigued by the possibility that a bismuth pile could use the electromagnetic pump which he had developed in a preliminary way with Albert Einstein. Since the pump depended upon electromagnetic forces set up within the liquid metal, it would require no moving parts and would not be subject to leaks. The disadvantage was that such metals were distinctly exotic materials. Although their basic properties were known, they were not commonly used in power systems. There was enough novelty in a nuclear pile without adding the complications of employing unusual metals at high temperatures. For Szilard, the new and unusual held no cause for hesitation. Hoping to initiate experiments during the summer of 1942 as a part of the work of his Technological Division, Szilard began recruiting metallurgists and investigating sources of bismuth. The crisis in the procurement of uranium metal forced the postponement of most of this work. Deeply discouraged, by September, Szilard had little more than paper studies to show for his intentions.[10]

DECISION ON PILE DESIGN

In October, 1942, Conant and Groves began to push the scientists toward decisions in all parts of the S-1 project. While Conant took the S-1 Executive Committee on an inspection of isotope-separation projects in the East, Groves headed for Chicago to break the deadlock in the pile program.

Certainly, decisions were overdue at the Metallurgical Laboratory. Week after week, Compton had met with his Technical Council (as the Engineering Council was now called) and listened to hours of earnest discussion to no avail. True enough, the lack of a precise value for k beclouded the issue. Much more confusing, however, was the disagreement over the number and size of the steps to be taken from the exponential experiments to the production pile. In the spring of 1942, the council had proposed two big steps, one to a 100,000-kilowatt pilot plant and the second to the full-scale pile. More recently, Compton had requested designs for a 10,000-kilowatt unit. Moore and Wigner studied adaptations of their original helium- and water-cooled piles. Fermi analyzed a lattice arrangement of uranium lumps cast directly in the graphite blocks with occasional cooling pipes. Charles M. Cooper, recently arrived from the du Pont Company, explored the feasibility

180

of filling metal pipes in a graphite block with small uranium shot and pumping through a helium coolant.

The scientists presented the results of their studies at a meeting of the Technical Council on October 5, 1942. While all the schemes had points in their favor, each had its weaknesses. In water cooling, there was the danger of corrosion; in helium cooling, the threat of a leak and radioactive contamination. Neither the Fermi nor Cooper schemes seemed capable of attaining 10,000 kilowatts. Fermi was fast coming to the conclusion that the first step should be short but sure. He suggested building a small pile generating only a few hundred watts, which could depend upon simple external cooling alone. Allison and Wigner were convinced that bigger steps were necessary if the bomb were to be a factor in the war.[11]

Quickly sensing the discord, Groves launched into the speech which was to become his trademark. He wanted speed. A wrong decision that brought quick results was better than no decision at all. If there were a choice between two methods, one of which was good and the other promising, build both. Time was more important than money, and it took time to build plants. He wanted a decision in Compton's hands by the end of the week.

The impasse, however, was not to be surmounted by exhortation. After Groves left, one of the members of the council remarked that it was well and good to emphasize the construction of buildings, but more important was what went inside. While the discussion that afternoon did not settle anything, it at least clarified some of the issues. Fermi, believing that immediate production of plutonium samples had priority over the cooling design, favored constructing a small, low-power pile. Allison and Wigner wanted to aim at once for a pile which would lead directly to large-scale production. Wheeler interjected the note of compromise. Would it be possible to build a simple pile of moderate size which would produce some plutonium samples but also have a few tubes in its outer edges for testing coolant systems?

Compromise proved the answer. As the debate dragged into the following week, Compton could see that one pile could not meet all requirements.[12] Fermi needed relatively simple, low-power piles to study control systems and develop operating procedures. At the same time Compton needed plutonium samples and data for designing high-power, plutonium-producing units. He believed the helium-cooled pile was certain and thus the best choice for an experimental unit of moderate size. Water cooling was more speculative, but the design held such great promise for large production that it could not be overlooked. From these premises Compton made his decision. Fermi's critical pile would be completed and operated before the end of 1942. A second pile generating a few hundred watts with no internal cooling system would be completed in the Argonne Forest and operated continuously until June 1, 1943, when it would be torn down for plutonium extraction. If

181

necessary, the pile could be rebuilt by August 1, 1943. In the meantime, Moore would start work on the Mae West pile, a helium-cooled plant designed to produce 100 grams of plutonium per day. To be completed by November 1, 1943, the pile would be used for experiments for one month and then be placed in full operation to produce ten kilograms of plutonium by March 1, 1944. Compton also directed his staff to continue their studies of the liquid-cooled pile. For the moment, water, diphenyl, and bismuth were all in the running. More definite plans would have to await the results of Fermi's exponential experiments.

CHEMICAL SEPARATION PROCESSES

182

Without a process for separating plutonium from irradiated uranium, the efforts to design a production pile would be in vain. Seaborg's chemistry group at the Metallurgical Laboratory had taken the first steps toward such a process in the summer of 1942. The isolation of weighable amounts of pure plutonium compound from samples containing not more than one part in a billion of the new element was an extraordinary achievement in chemical research. In many ways, however, this research bore little relationship to the problems Groves faced in producing plutonium on an industrial scale. Seaborg and his associates were still exploring the basic chemistry of the new element. Their oxidation-reduction process using lanthanum-fluoride carrier was nothing more than a laboratory demonstration. Its application on an industrial scale was just an incidental possibility in view of the fantastic scale-up required to obtain quantities of plutonium of significance for weapons.

During that first summer at the Metallurgical Laboratory, the lanthanum-fluoride process was but one of several which had possibilities for industrial application.[13] Isadore Perlman, Seaborg's assistant, embarked on a study of the peroxide method with William J. Knox, a June graduate from the University of California. The process depended upon the fact that most elements formed soluble peroxides in neutral or slightly acid solutions. Plutonium, they discovered, was an exception. They could precipitate it when they added hydrogen peroxide to a dilute uranyl nitrate solution. With these promising clues, Perlman and Knox explored the many variables involved in the reaction. Although they accomplished some separation in the laboratory, they found the size of the precipitates much too large. Translated to an industrial scale, the weight of the precipitates would be more than a ton, compared to a few pounds in the lanthanum-fluoride process.

A second approach was adsorption. John E. Willard from the University of Wisconsin found that certain materials, such as silicates and diatomaceous earths, tended to adsorb plutonium more readily than other elements in a solution. Willard had some success during the summer with small columns a few centimeters in diameter, but he found later that with larger columns he could not recover more than half the plutonium in solution.

Nor did Seaborg overlook solvent-extraction methods. He gave this assignment to two former students at California, Theodore T. Magel and Daniel E. Koshland, Jr. The method involved the use of two immiscible liquid solvents, one of which held plutonium and uranium in solution and the other fission products. After a series of experiments with various solvents, Magel found some grounds for optimism, but he saw little hope of developing the process quickly.

Somewhat more encouraging were the studies of volatility processes by Harrison S. Brown, a twenty-five-year-old chemist from Johns Hopkins, and his assistant, Orville F. Hill. They found that when they subjected irradiated uranium to dry reactions in a stream of fluorine, the uranium volatilized first. As temperatures increased, the plutonium followed. Brown at the Metallurgical Laboratory and Clifford S. Garner at Berkeley studied the best conditions for the reaction during the autumn of 1942. The process looked feasible on a large scale if some of the novel engineering techniques could be mastered in time.

Seaborg supplemented these process studies with a variety of basic research projects. Burris B. Cunningham, another California colleague, and Michael Cefola from the College of the City of New York undertook a systematic study of the chemistry of plutonium. To obtain samples, they continued to perfect the lanthanum-fluoride process. Arthur C. Wahl performed similar experiments at Berkeley in the chemistry group directed by Dean Wendell M. Latimer, whose department had produced a majority of the chemists then associated with the project. By September, 1942, both the Chicago and Berkeley chemists had the advantage of relatively large samples containing the long-lived plutonium 239 isotope produced in the cyclotron at Washington University, St. Louis. Prior to that time they were forced to use traces of what they believed to be the 238 isotope with a half-life of fifty years.

Somewhat removed from the main stream of process development but still critically important were the studies of fission-product and radiation chemistry. The fission reaction would produce a host of isotopes, some of which might conceivably bear enough chemical resemblance to plutonium to follow it through the separation process. Bertrand Goldschmidt, a French refugee scientist, and Perlman made a brief survey of fission products in the summer of 1942. Later, Charles D. Coryell and his group began a series of experiments to determine the chemical and radioactive properties of these materials. The effects of radiation on chemical processes involved a whole new field of research which was supervised at Chicago by Milton B. Burton and James Franck, an eminent German scientist who had left his homeland to teach at Chicago.[14]

Compton had no trouble convincing Seaborg and the chemists that

183

developing an industrial process was beyond the resources of the Metallurgical Laboratory. For one thing, Seaborg and most of his associates were American born. They had been educated in the ways of the new chemistry, which was closely allied to chemical engineering and industrial processing. They did not share the fears of men like Fermi, Wigner, Franck, and Szilard, who were accustomed to the more traditional, academic ways of European science. Not only backgrounds but also the apparent size of the challenge made a difference. In their designs the physicists were thinking of production piles ten to twenty times the size of experimental models. The chemists knew they would need a separation plant a billion times as large as their laboratory apparatus.

In chemistry, the transition from research to engineering started early and continued smoothly. Charles M. Cooper arrived in Chicago from Wilmington on August 3, 1942. After recruiting a small group of industrial chemists from du Pont and elsewhere, Cooper studied the experimental evidence which Seaborg's group had collected. At the moment, Seaborg could not rule out any of the four processes. All seemed capable of extracting plutonium, but he was not sure that any of them could be developed in time. Although Seaborg saw no clear-cut choice, he was impressed by the volatility methods. They would be easy to operate at a safe distance from radioactivity and seemed likely to achieve good separation. A drawback was the large requirement for materials and equipment. Cooper observed that the separation would be simple were it not for radioactivity. The equipment had to be designed to operate without maintenance behind six to eight feet of concrete. Cooper and Seaborg concluded that, while research should continue on all approaches, the lanthanum-fluoride method should serve as the principal guide in developing an industrial process.[15]

Cooper's decision followed du Pont practice. Without ruling out any of the possibilities, he gave a sense of direction and purpose to his assignment by selecting one approach for emphasis. Whatever the final decision, Cooper would proceed as if lanthanum-fluoride were the choice. He made his selection on conservative grounds. It was not the process with the greatest theoretical advantage but the one supported by the largest body of data. Until something better appeared, he would concentrate on lanthanum fluoride.[16]

By looking over the shoulders of the chemists, Cooper's engineers soon learned the experimental techniques. In a few weeks they were designing laboratory equipment which would permit them to study the processes on a small scale. With gram quantities of precipitates and cubic centimeters of solutions they simulated runs with lanthanum fluoride. Before the end of 1942, Cooper was encountering trouble. The process required large amounts of hydrogen fluoride, which quickly corroded even stainless-steel equipment. Cooper found it difficult to maintain plutonium in its higher oxidation state in fluoride solutions. The precipitates were also difficult to recover either by filtration or centrifugation.[17]

While the engineers were uncovering these obstacles, Seaborg was charting alternate courses. He knew that the phosphates of many heavy metals were insoluble in acid solutions. Was it possible that a phosphate might prove a better carrier than lanthanum fluoride? Another California colleague, Stanley G. Thompson, investigated this question. Thompson and his assistants methodically plodded through tests of the heavier phosphates —thorium, uranium, cerium, niobium, and zirconium. For a few days, zirconium seemed to have the properties of a good carrier, but further study eliminated that hope too. Almost against his better judgment, Thompson turned to bismuth phosphate. All his previous experiments indicated that bismuth would never carry plutonium in its lower oxidation state, and his first tests early in December seemed to confirm that prediction. On December 19, however, he attempted the precipitation of a relatively large amount of bismuth as phosphate. The process was slow but virtually complete. Thompson was surprised to find that the phosphate had carried with it more than 98 per cent of the plutonium in solution. Additional experiments by Cunningham and Cooper confirmed Thompson's results. The new process appeared to offer good insurance against failure of the lanthanum-fluoride method.[18]

185

Cooper was now ready to take the next step. After six months of experiments he could safely reduce the choice to lanthanum fluoride and bismuth phosphate. Since both were precipitation processes, he thought it possible to test both with the same kinds of equipment. In January, 1943, he began constructing a small semiworks in the New Chemistry Building, a row of low prefabricated structures along Ingleside Avenue, a block from Stagg Field. Designed for the lanthanum-fluoride process, the equipment would handle gallons of solution and pounds of precipitate. If necessary later, Cooper could convert the plant for bismuth-phosphate tests.

BEYOND THE LABORATORY

While the Chicago scientists struggled with pile design and the development of a chemical separation process in the autumn of 1942, Groves and Compton laid plans to expand the project beyond the confines of the university. They needed more space and more manpower.

During the spring, Compton had proposed to complete the exponential experiments on campus and to build a pilot plant at the Argonne site. As plans for the pile and separation plant evolved during the summer, he realized that such novel and potentially dangerous experiments should not be performed in the heart of one of the nation's population centers. In September, the S-1 Executive Committee recommended that Fermi's pile be moved from Stagg Field to Argonne. They likewise suggested that Compton abandon his plans to build the pilot plant at Argonne and use instead the proposed Tennessee site. Only when Groves took command and issued the order to acquire the tract near Knoxville did Compton agree to the change. Working closely with Stone & Webster engineers, Compton began to modify the Argonne designs to meet the requirements in Tennessee. He gave Martin D. Whitaker, one of Fermi's assistants, direct responsibility for supervising the design of research facilities at both locations.[19]

Groves also proved a willing ally in Compton's campaign to bring in a full-fledged industrial organization. Despite the bitter opposition of some of his colleagues, Compton had supported the selection of Stone & Webster as engineering and construction contractor. In August, he brought Cooper to Chicago to study designs for a chemical separation plant. Groves used the informal agreement with Cooper as an opening wedge for du Pont participation. On October 3, 1942, du Pont accepted the contract to design and build the chemical separation plant. Groves continued to blandish the company during the fall. The invitations to Wilmington executives to undertake the feasibility study of the pile project and to serve on the Lewis reviewing committee had the advantage of further involving du Pont in the enterprise.

The visit of the Lewis reviewing committee to the Metallurgical Laboratory on Thanksgiving Day, 1942, not only determined the future of S-1, but also convinced du Pont to accept a full partnership in Groves's organization. Through its representation on the reviewing committee, the du Pont high command had enjoyed an unprecedented view of the entire project. They could evaluate not only the feasibility of producing plutonium but also the relative merits of all approaches to the bomb. Before yielding to Groves's relentless pressure, the du Pont leaders had the satisfaction of determining for themselves the chances for success. They could also make sure they would participate in a way that would allow the company to make its maximum contribution to the war effort. The construction and operation of the plutonium production plant would tax du Pont's technical manpower resources, but personnel shortages were expected to decline in 1943. Having passed the employment peak in the construction of explosives plants, the company could count on transferring large numbers of engineers and technicians to S-1 work early in 1943.

Du Pont's broad responsibilities began formally on December 1, 1942, when Groves issued a letter of intent which was later superseded by a cost-plus-fixed-fee contract. Although the technology was new, the contract form was not. To set the wheels of American industry in motion for war mobilization, Congress had sanctioned the cost-plus contract in the First War Powers Act in December, 1941. Without a clear knowledge of future requirements, production costs, or wages, American manufacturers could not be expected to guarantee prices on Government orders. On procurement items, specifications were so often unusual that there was no basis for determining fixed prices. On construction projects, the contractor more often than not had to break ground for a new plant before the first sketches were off the drawing boards. In such instances the Government had resorted to the cost-plus-fixed-fee (CPFF) contract. The fixed fee, in contrast to the percentage-of-cost principle, presumably removed opportunity for the featherbedding which had disgraced the cost-plus device in the investigations after the first World War. With this safeguard, the CPFF contract became the principal instrument for procuring novel or expensive items such as aircraft, heavy ordnance equipment, and ammunition. Before the end of World War II, the Army CPFF commitments would exceed $50 billion and amount to more than one-third of all Army purchases.[20]

Groves, as an Engineer officer, and du Pont, as one of the Army's largest contractors, were thoroughly familiar with the CPFF form, and there was good reason to apply it in this instance. The technology was new and unpredictable. Groves had not established even the fundamental specifications of the plant and could not begin to estimate probable costs. Yet, without a week's delay, du Pont would have to start translating laboratory experiments into full-scale plant designs. The S-1 project provided a perfect example of the situation the CPFF contract was designed to meet.

187

There were, however, extraordinary considerations which caused du Pont to introduce special provisions. The tremendous military potential of the atomic weapon posed a possible threat to the company's future public relations. The du Pont leadership had not forgotten the "merchants of death" label slapped on the company during the Nye Committee investigations in the thirties. Certainly it was clear that the company had not sought the S-1 assignment; but, to keep the record straight, du Pont refused to accept any profit. The fixed fee was limited to one dollar. Any profits accruing from allowances for administrative overhead would be returned to the Government. Walter S. Carpenter, Jr., the du Pont president, disavowed not only profits but also any intention of staying in the atomic bomb business after the war. In his opinion, the production of such weapons should be controlled exclusively by the Government. The contract provided that any patent rights arising from the project would lie solely with the United States. In return, the company was indemnified against any losses or liabilities it might incur.[21]

Because of its size and experience, du Pont could fit the S-1 project into its existing pattern of operation and organization. Actually, the company was organized as a confederation of individual enterprises responsible only on the broadest policy and financial issues to the Executive and Finance Committees. The focus of operations lay within the industrial departments. The general manager of each department was responsible for his own budget and for all decisions on manufacturing, research, development, and sales. For plant construction, he called upon the Engineering Department; for special staff services, he could rely on other auxiliary departments. But the industrial department always remained in control. The organization was designed so that all the complex activities of the company were oriented around the manufacture of products. The S-1 project was forced not only into this organizational framework but also into conformance with this operating philosophy. In both respects, the impact of du Pont on the pile project was to be profound.

On the organizational level, the pile project was placed within the Explosives Department, which directed the construction and operation of the many explosives plants assigned to du Pont by the War Department. As general manager, E. B. Yancey had general responsibility. Roger Williams exercised direct authority as assistant general manager and director of the TNX Division, in which all S-1 activities were isolated for security and administrative reasons. Williams, a veteran chemical engineer at du Pont, had participated in the November feasibility study and had served on the Lewis reviewing committee. From the company's Ammonia Department, Williams brought R. Monte Evans, who would direct operation of the plutonium plant. From the Grasselli Chemicals Department, Williams welcomed Crawford H. Greenewalt, the young engineer who had served as secretary of the Lewis committee. As director of the research division in the Explosives Department, Greenewalt would be responsible for liaison with the Metallurgical Laboratory. In accordance with du Pont practice, construction activities were managed by the Engineering Department, most of whose principal officers had taken part in the November feasibility studies. E. G. Ackart served as chief engineer and Granville M. Read as his assistant. Tom C. Gary was director of the Design Division, and Thomas H. Chilton directed research. John N. Tilley had a vital job as Ackart's liaison officer with the Explosives Department.[22]

As for operating policy, du Pont had from the first insisted upon complete control. In the months of negotiations with Groves, the company had refused to consider any sort of joint venture. This approach appealed to both Groves and Compton. Du Pont's firm hand at the helm not only assured rapid progress toward the bomb but also relieved the two leaders from the many headaches of co-ordination and administration which plagued most joint enterprises between university research groups and industry. Groves and Compton wanted action and they got it. Before the end of January, 1943, Groves, Compton, and Williams made a series of decisions which completely altered the course of the pile project.

SEARCH FOR A NEW SITE

The first step was to find a new site for the production plant. Now that Groves had seen some of the preliminary designs, he knew that the Tennessee location was inadequate. The X-10 area itself was not large enough and was too close to Knoxville. The available electric power was not sufficient for the electromagnetic, gaseous-diffusion, and plutonium plants. Early in December,

1942, Groves made the search for a new site a top-priority assignment for the Corps of Engineers, du Pont, and the Metallurgical Laboratory. In two weeks he had a list of areas scattered from the Great Lakes to the West Coast.

Compton and the scientists established the criteria. They assumed that the plant would require three or four helium-cooled piles and two separation plants. Compton saw little need to isolate each pile as a precaution against an operating accident, but he suggested that the piles might be spaced at least one mile apart to reduce the danger of sabotage. The greatest hazard appeared to be the accidental release of radioactive materials from the separation plants. To provide an exclusion area, the scientists prescribed a four-mile safety distance around each separation plant. They likewise determined that the nearest town, railroad, or highway should be ten miles distant, and the laboratories at least eight miles away. Around this exclusion area of roughly 225 square miles, they recommended a six-mile strip in which residential occupancy would be prohibited.

189

Although a number of sites could meet these space criteria, only a very few of these could satisfy the requirements for a large dependable supply of pure, cool water and 100,000 kilowatts of electric power. The Corps of Engineers at once thought of the large river systems like the Columbia and the Colorado. Both provided large amounts of water and hydroelectric power and had the added advantage of being independent of coal or fuel-oil supplies. Both traversed great desert areas which would provide the necessary isolation. Both were far enough inland to be safe from coastal air attack. The corps ordered its district engineers in these areas to collect data on possible sites.[23]

On December 16, 1942, Colonel Franklin T. Matthias, a civil engineer serving as a reserve officer on Groves's staff, set out for the West Coast with two engineers from the du Pont construction division. They inspected two locations around Mansfield, Washington, near Grand Coulee Dam. Moving south along the Columbia, they stopped at the broad, flat valley in the big bend of the river at Hanford. Then they traveled south to a site on the Deschutes River in Oregon and two locations on the Colorado in southern California.

Among all the sites considered, Hanford appeared clearly the best. The great Columbia, with its dams at Grand Coulee and Bonneville, more than met the power and water requirements for the plutonium plant. The level valley between the west bank of the river and the foothills of the Cascades formed an uninhabited tract of the majestic dimensions required. The underlying basalt formation with its overburden of shale and sandstone would make an excellent foundation for the mammoth concrete structures and could provide enormous quantities of gravel for roads and concrete aggregate. Although the isolation of the site posed labor and transportation difficulties, these did not seem insuperable. A branch line of a transcontinental railroad crossed a corner of the site, and compared to other parts of the nation, the labor supply was relatively ample in the Pacific Northwest. During January, 1943, Matthias and his associates carefully weighed these and other factors. By the end of the month, Groves was ready to make his decision for Hanford.[24]

NEW PLANS FOR TENNESSEE

Selection of the Hanford site disrupted the Metallurgical Laboratory's plans for the X-10 area near Oak Ridge. As long as the Army had intended to construct the plutonium plant as part of the Clinton Engineer Works, Compton could see some advantages in building the laboratory and pilot plant there; but with the production plant in the Northwest, there seemed to be little reason to move any part of the pile project to Tennessee. Compton's scientists could perform more efficiently at Argonne any research and development studies required for Hanford. Early in December, 1942, they began to design a small water-cooled pile to be built at Argonne. Though the pile would bear little resemblance to a production model, they thought it would make enough plutonium for Seaborg's and Cooper's experiments. Du Pont could build the Hanford plant; the Metallurgical Laboratory would conduct its experiments in Chicago or at Argonne.[25]

To Yancey and Williams, this sort of thinking was unacceptable. They were convinced that a semiworks was necessary, and they knew that site limitations at Argonne would not permit the construction and operation of a plant on a large enough scale. No doubt just as important if not explicit was their conviction that the independent course which the Metallurgical Laboratory proposed to follow could not be reconciled with du Pont's operating philosophy. In their view, the scientists at Chicago were no different from the research division attached to any of the company's industrial departments. The research team existed only to serve the department. It neither dictated policies on plant design and operation nor determined independently its own research program. Thus the Metallurgical Laboratory was expected to provide the basic scientific data for design of the production plant. If, in the company's opinion, that required a semiworks in Tennessee, the scientists could not be permitted to follow an independent course at Argonne.

It was equally evident to du Pont officials that the Metallurgical Laboratory was indispensable. The company had not one official or employee who yet had a working knowledge of nuclear physics. Speaking to the Technical Council in Chicago on December 28, 1942, Greenewalt emphasized that du Pont was in no way taking over development of the processes. Here, he said, the company would serve as the laboratory's handmaiden; du Pont would do no more than contribute specialized techniques and talents. Greenewalt assured his new associates that he understood the problems of translating laboratory methods into production processes. He had gambled $20 million in a six-year period to develop a commercial process for the production of nylon. He was confident that a similar translation could be accomplished to produce plutonium.[26]

What Greenewalt said made sense to the Chicago scientists and they accepted the need for a co-operative enterprise. The critical point was control, and Greenewalt had wisely de-emphasized that issue. The scientists had worked for months on the assumption that they would direct the activities of the en-gineering contractor. Now they feared that control was shifting to Wilming-ton. They did not intend to become a field station of the du Pont Explosives Department.

Yancey and Williams faced a quandary. They could not proceed with-out the support of the Metallurgical Laboratory; nor could they afford to re-lax control. They could not build the Hanford plant without a semiworks of reasonable size, and only the scientists in Chicago had the knowledge and experience to design and operate such a plant. When Yancey and Williams took their problem to Groves, he threw it right back at them. If they needed a full-fledged semiworks, they would have to build it themselves with the laboratory's help. The du Pont officials reluctantly had to admit the General was right. On January 4, 1943, Groves gave them a letter contract for de-signing and constructing the semiworks. Two days later, Colonel Nichols met with du Pont representatives in Wilmington, and they agreed that the com-pany would construct the semiworks at the Tennessee site. Du Pont engineers would prepare the blueprints in Wilmington and send them to Compton, who was to approve them for the Government.[27]

John Wheeler, the laboratory's ambassador in Wilmington, did not have good news for Chicago. There was now no doubt at the Metallurgical Labo-ratory that du Pont intended to take control. Nichols hurried to Chicago to calm the storm. There he found even Compton objecting to the plan. Compton insisted the Argonne site was suitable and entirely safe for the semiworks. He did not have enough scientists to support activities in Chicago, Clinton, and Hanford. Certainly the Army-du Pont plan would affect morale. Sensing the cause was hopeless, Compton then suggested that he be permitted to build at Argonne a plant perhaps one-tenth the size of the semiworks. He had not misjudged the situation; there would be no sop for Chicago. After a full-dress review of the issues on January 12, Compton, Groves, and Williams agreed that du Pont would build the semiworks at Clinton.

Having been pushed this far, Compton fully expected du Pont to take responsibility for operating the semiworks. With Groves's support, Compton maintained that the company, having selected the site and agreed to build the plant, should operate it as well. Williams demurred. He would have to consult the du Pont Executive Committee.

Back in Wilmington, Williams analyzed the situation with Yancey. From the du Pont point of view, it was natural to expect the Metallurgical Laboratory to operate the plant. The company built experimental plants; the research group operated them. Du Pont had no one technically qualified to operate the semiworks. Why, then, was the laboratory reluctant to accept the assignment? One reason, no doubt, was the hostility engendered among the scientists by the semiworks decision. Du Pont had made their bed; let them lie in it. Williams also thought that Compton was sincerely concerned about his lack of engineering personnel. Yancey agreed that Compton might accept if they made a definite offer to supply the necessary supervisory, technical, clerical, and service personnel. When Compton and Nichols arrived in Wilmington on January 16, 1943, Williams proposed that the Metallurgical Laboratory accept the responsibility of operating the semiworks.[28]

Williams' suggestion shocked Compton. To his mind, the decision to build the plant in Tennessee clearly removed the Metallurgical Laboratory from the scene. The University of Chicago had been heavily involved in Government research projects since 1941. So rapidly had these grown that a large portion of the university's administrative staff under Vice-President Emery T. Filbey spent all its time on war contracts. But Williams' suggestion seemed out of bounds. How could the university, an educational institution, justify operating an industrial plant 500 miles from the campus? True, during the war, university scientists found themselves ever more involved in applied research, but how could operation of a plant be remotely related to the university's primary purpose? Furthermore, did the university have any guarantee that the laboratory would be able to operate a plant it had neither designed nor built?

Deeply troubled, Compton pondered the decision with Filbey and William B. Harrell, the university's business manager. They shared his misgivings, but if Compton believed the university's participation was essential to the war effort, they would support that decision. Compton turned the arguments over in his mind during the following weeks. He had to act soon, but first he wanted Conant's views. When he met with Conant in Washington on the morning of March 4, 1943, Compton did not get much moral support. Should Chicago accept the contract to operate the Clinton semiworks? Conant at first evaded the question by reminding his visitors that this was to be an Army, not an OSRD, contract. Harrell persisted. If this were an OSRD contract, would Conant ask the university to accept it? Conant admitted he wouldn't. Would he have been willing to accept such a contract at Harvard? Conant said he wouldn't touch it with a ten-foot pole. Why?, Compton asked. In the first place, Conant replied, the work was hazardous. This was obvious from the fact that du Pont, already in the project, refused to accept responsibility. Secondly, the university trustees would be signing a blind contract and putting all their faith in one A. H. Compton without any knowledge of the nature or hazards of the work. Conant admitted that the Army might put pressure on the university to sign in wartime a contract they would not otherwise accept, but he would not advise his friends either to accept or reject the request.

Compton realized that neither Conant nor anyone else could decide for him; he could act only from his own judgment and conscience, and these dictated that he accept the assignment. Back in Chicago, he found the support he needed. Filbey, now certain that the university must answer the call as a patriotic duty, took the issue to President Hutchins, and together they carried the decision through the university board of trustees. Now Compton could go back to work.[29]

FROM HELIUM TO WATER

The design studies completed at the Metallurgical Laboratory in the fall of 1942 were a real accomplishment. Though tedious and protracted, the animated October discussions had produced a definite plan for pile development and construction. The Technical Council agreed that when Fermi completed his critical experiments, he would construct a second pile at Argonne. Without an internal cooling system, the pile would be operated at a few hundred watts to provide basic data on neutron physics and to produce small samples of plutonium for separation experiments. Since helium cooling seemed to offer the best hopes for achieving the chain reaction on a production scale, Compton planned to begin final design and construction of the Mae West pile in 1943. Until Fermi could complete his experiments, Compton would not know whether k would be sufficiently large to permit liquid cooling. In view of the substantial engineering advantages, however, Compton ordered more study of liquid-cooled systems.[30]

When the du Pont feasibility team visited the laboratory in November, they immediately favored the helium approach. Though they doubted that the Mae West pile would work as designed, they saw it had definite possibilities. In examining the liquid coolants, the du Pont officials at once eliminated water because of its corrosive effect on uranium. Diphenyl seemed to have few advantages; bismuth was more promising but would require extensive research. So advantageous were the properties of heavy water as a moderator that it seemed clearly superior if sufficient quantities of the rare isotope could be produced in time. Thus du Pont ranked the designs in the following order: helium, heavy water, bismuth, and water. As Greenewalt told his Chicago associates, du Pont would "go hammer and tongs" for a helium-cooled pile and would urge the Army to construct four heavy-water plants in the United States.

Fermi's successful achievement of the chain reaction profoundly affected both Compton's and Greenewalt's plans. Fermi found k to be much larger than he had dared hope. To the Chicago scientists, this new information was a decisive argument for the water-cooled pile. Wigner and Young stepped up their work on designing an experimental unit of this type. Greenewalt, still strongly supporting helium cooling, saw a different advantage in Fermi's

193

results. It now seemed possible to design an experimental pile using air cooling. The substitution of air for helium would greatly simplify the design and accelerate the completion of the unit. For this reason, Greenewalt felt he could obtain plutonium samples most quickly from an air-cooled pile. Because it would resemble the full-scale helium pile in many ways, the experimental unit at Clinton could be expected to contribute to the design of the Hanford plant.[31]

Following du Pont practice, Williams organized the pile design group at Wilmington. For technical knowledge he relied on Moore, Whitaker, and Wheeler, who had gone to Wilmington on special assignment in November, 1942, to present the preliminary design of the helium-cooled pile to the du Pont staff. Early in December, the triumvirate had helped Williams' team make the decision to emphasize the helium approach. When Fermi's measurements of k reached Wilmington, the three men served as the nucleus of the group which designed the air-cooled pile.

194

In January, 1943, the design group established the general specifications of the pile. To provide enough plutonium for the chemical separation semiworks, it decided to fix the power output at 1,000 kilowatts. The pile itself would consist of a huge block of graphite surrounded by several feet of high-density concrete as a radiation shield. The graphite block would be pierced by hundreds of horizontal diamond-shaped channels, in which rows of cylindrical uranium slugs would form long rods. The cooling air would circulate through the channels on all sides of the slugs. After a period of operation, fresh slugs could be pushed into the channels from the face of the pile and the irradiated slugs would fall from the back wall through a chute into an underwater bucket. After weeks of underwater storage to permit the decay of short-lived, radioactive fission products, the bucket would be transported a short distance through an underground canal to the separation plant. A series of cells with thick concrete walls would contain chemical equipment operated by remote control. Beyond the separation plant would be large underground tanks for storing the highly radioactive wastes. The entire facility, from the pile to the storage tanks, would be located on a slope to make the best use of gravity flow. (Figure 13)

From this general plan, the design group turned in February to the specifics. Charging and discharging slugs remained a tricky operation, even though facilitated by the use of horizontal channels rather than the vertical ones incorporated in earlier designs. The design group thought it necessary to devise equipment to protect the operators from exposure to radiation when the channels were opened to replace slugs. They would have to mount this equipment on an elevator which would give the operators access to all parts of the huge face of the pile. The hazards at the rear of the pile were even greater, since the slugs would be highly radioactive as they fell from the channels. The entire back face had to be shielded by concrete, and every step of the discharge process tested to assure that remote operation and maintenance would be possible over a long period.[32]

The design group could plan many of the mechanical features at Wilmington, but for the detailed dimensions of the pile and lattice arrangement it looked to the Metallurgical Laboratory for help. The first thought was to select a lattice which would best assure the chain reaction. It was almost as important, however, to consider possible economies in the use of high-purity graphite and uranium metal, both of which were still scarce. At the Metallurgical Laboratory on February 16, 1943, the design group selected a plan which would emphasize operating reliability and metal economy. Wigner, with the help of Alvin Weinberg, a Chicago physicist, calculated that the graphite block would measure twenty-four feet on a side and weigh about 1,500 tons. The block would contain 1,248 channels on eight-inch centers. The uranium slugs, canned in aluminum jackets, would be 1.1 inches in diameter and 4.1 inches long. The pile was then estimated to reach criticality with about sixty tons of uranium, or half its capacity.

195

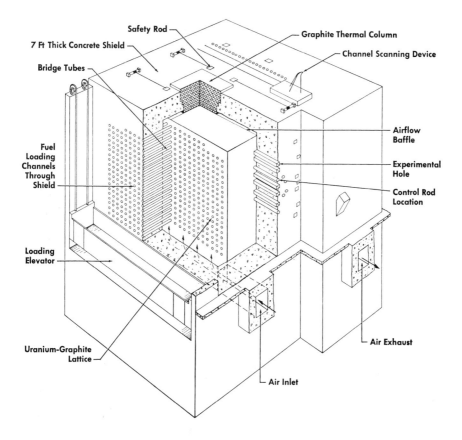

Figure 13. The air-cooled pile constructed in the X-10 area at the Clinton Engineer Works in 1943.

Once the design engineers had agreed on these fundamental specifications, they could begin to develop other features of the pile.[33] If their first concern was to assure that the pile would operate, their second was to make certain that they could control it. After further discussions in Chicago, they concluded that under ordinary conditions they could control the reaction with two boron-steel rods in the right side of the pile. To slow down the reaction, they could insert more of the rods, and the boron would soak up the excess neutrons. To shut down the pile entirely, they planned four additional rods in the right side. During start-up, the rods could be withdrawn only at a predetermined rate. A hydraulic system was designed to suspend two heavily weighted pistons which would fall and drive the rods into the pile within five seconds in the event of a power failure. As a second line of defense, four rods would be suspended above vertical holes in the pile. They would drop into the graphite block when the trip mechanism was energized. As a last resort, two hoppers would be filled with small boron-steel balls to be released into vertical columns in an emergency.

Design of the cooling system involved few difficulties. Air would enter the pile through a duct in the foundation and would be pumped inside the concrete shield to the channels at the front face. After traversing the graphite, the air would be conducted from the bottom of the pile, through a filter system, and out a two-hundred-foot stack beside the building. Fans were the one limiting factor in designing the cooling system. Since the largest commercially available fan had a capacity of 30,000 cubic feet per minute, du Pont immediately placed a special order for a 50,000-cubic-foot fan. A fan house was designed to contain one fan of each size and a small steam-driven unit for emergency use in the event of a power failure.

By April, 1943, the design group was approaching the last stages of its assignment. Instrumentation was certain to be complex, not only to assure safe operation but also to obtain the maximum amount of experimental data. Thus the design included thermocouples and other devices to measure the temperatures of slugs, graphite, and cooling air in various parts of the pile, a Pitot tube to measure the flow of cooling air, and ionization chambers to measure radiation intensities. All this information was to be channeled to a nerve center in the control room, where the data would be monitored by automatic recording instruments and tied into the pile control system. In developing this complex system, the design group obtained expert advice on both instrumentation and electronics from the Metallurgical Laboratory and equipment manufacturers.

The pile had a secondary but vital purpose as a powerful source of neutrons, other radiation, and fission products. For this purpose the design group planned a battery of test holes and chambers, mostly in the top and left face of the pile. These included slots for indium foils to measure neutron intensity, test holes for irradiation of sample materials, two tunnels for exposing small animals to radiation, a pneumatic system for very brief irradia-

196

tion of small samples, three aluminum tubes for experiments with water cooling, two holes for neutron spectrometers, and two columns of graphite blocks for exposing samples to slow neutrons.

While the du Pont group concentrated on the air-cooled design at Wilmington, Wigner and his Chicago associates grew more enthusiastic about water cooling. They had earlier recognized the superior heat-transfer properties of water. Now Fermi's experiments permitted them to believe that k might be sufficiently high to compensate for the losses of neutrons to coolant water. They could start with the rough sketches which Wigner and Young had hastily assembled the previous spring. Admittedly, the designs now looked a bit unsophisticated. The idea of an overhead tank supplying cooling water to vertical uranium pipes was simple enough at first glance, but the engineers had been quick to indicate fundamental weaknesses in the scheme. It would take some good engineering to design a large, flat tank to withstand the pressures required, especially with the bottom pierced by hundreds of holes for the uranium pipes. Extremely reliable seals between the tank and the pipes would be necessary to keep the cooling water from leaking into the graphite. Without easy access to the bottom of the tank, it would be difficult to maintain precise control of water flow to each pipe or to replace any of the pipes while maintaining water flow in the others. Nor was there any assurance that the inner surface of the uranium pipes could be satisfactorily coated or lined with aluminum to prevent corrosion.

By the end of 1942, Wigner and his associates had adopted the horizontal design which du Pont had selected for the air-cooled pile. If they placed horizontal aluminum tubes in the graphite, they could use a header and manifold system to distribute cooling water to each of the tubes. Uranium slugs could be sealed into aluminum cans with a small enough diameter so that they would be surrounded by cooling water within the tube. Instrumentation and valves on the pile face would permit the operator to regulate the water flow to each tube. Inoperative tubes could be easily sealed off.

Wigner's proposal early in January, 1943, envisioned a cylinder of graphite with horizontal aluminum tubes running parallel to its axis. Containing 200 tons of uranium metal and 1,200 tons of graphite, the pile would require almost 75,000 gallons of cooling water per minute to dissipate the 500,000 kilowatts of heat generated by the reaction. After examining the losses in reactivity caused by the introduction of aluminum tubes and graphite, Weinberg concluded that he had a 1-per-cent safety margin in k.[34]

Greenewalt received the water-cooled design on January 20, 1943. The plan looked appealing on first glance, but he worried about the inherent instabilities in the water system.[35] What would happen, for example, if the water flow in some of the tubes were reduced sufficiently to permit the temperature to reach the boiling point? Even if this could be prevented, corrosion and erosion of tubes and slugs still seemed critical. Greenewalt knew what such forces could do in high-velocity, high-temperature systems. Who could tell to what extent radiation might accelerate the destructive effects? Nor could he overlook the small safety margin in k and the obvious hurdles in developing a slug-canning process.

At the same time, Greenewalt's confidence in helium cooling had waned. Pushing a million cubic feet of helium through the pile each minute would require large compressors of special design. He was not certain that the forty or fifty units needed for the Hanford plant could be manufactured in time. Even more fundamental were the complications in designing the huge steel shell which would confine the helium within the pile. It would take some extraordinary welding to fabricate a vacuum-tight shell of such size and complexity. Loading and unloading operations looked extremely difficult, and Greenewalt doubted that the design would assure the proper flow of helium through all the channels in the pile.

Considering all these factors, Greenewalt did not see any immediate choice between helium and water cooling. First he needed answers to these technical questions, and for that he drew upon the engineering resources of du Pont. In the following weeks, he learned that procurement of compressors for the helium pile would be touch and go; that the chemists were still looking for a foolproof method of separating the irradiated uranium from the graphite cartridges when the helium pile was unloaded; that purification of the tremendous amounts of helium after circulation through the pile looked ever more formidable. The water-cooled design was still far from perfect, but at least Chicago was making some headway. By the middle of February, Greenewalt was convinced that helium was not the answer. While he took the news to the Metallurgical Laboratory, Williams shifted the du Pont forces from the helium-cooled to the water-cooled design. After three months of study, du Pont was ready to stake its reputation on the water-cooled pile.

NEW ROLE FOR CHICAGO

The series of technical decisions and organizational changes from October, 1942, to February, 1943, transformed the character of the plutonium project. In the fall, it centered about Compton and his academic scientists on the Chicago campus. Then came the du Pont contracts, the selection of the Tennessee and Hanford sites, and the design decisions on the experimental and production piles.

During this transition from laboratory research to industrial engineering, the initiative shifted from Chicago to Wilmington. By February, du Pont was firmly in command. Whether the Chicago scientists liked it or not, the Metallurgical Laboratory had become a vital, but distinctly subordinate affiliate of the du Pont organization. More than any other event, that shift in authority engendered the undertones of discontent which pervaded the laboratory until the end of the war. In part, the attitude was that of the parent whose child had been lured away by a rich uncle just as the promising youngster approached maturity. In part, it was the realization that the exciting quest for the atomic weapon had moved to Oak Ridge, Hanford, and Los Alamos, leaving the laboratory with little direct part in the war effort.

But most of the Chicago scientists anticipated a stimulating and rewarding future at the Metallurgical Laboratory. Many realized that they stood on the threshold of a new world of scientific investigation. Fermi's experiments marked the beginning, not the end, of the search. Most of the Chicago scientists, still in their twenties or thirties, had themselves participated in the 1942 experiments, had heard Fermi lecture, and had been infected by his enthusiasm and imagination. The pile, as the source of the chain reaction, seemed to lie closer to the heart of the new science than did the techniques of isotope separation. Where could a young scientist find greater opportunities to make his mark in basic research in early 1943 than at Chicago?

As a research organization, the Metallurgical Laboratory had much to commend it. It was, first of all, an integral part of the university, not a temporary, artificial appendage. At the beginning of the mobilization period, the Chicago administration had agreed that war research projects would be woven as much as possible into the fabric of university organization and practice. Although physically isolated for security reasons, the Metallurgical Laboratory was established on this principle. Compton as project director was also dean of the university's physical sciences division. Other Chicago professors like Allison continued to function as members of the faculty. The many visitors like Fermi, Wigner, and Szilard, became a part of the Chicago academic family. They worked in university buildings; they employed the customary research and teaching techniques of the classroom. They keenly sensed the pressures and restrictions which the Army brought to bear, but still the Metallurgical Laboratory retained the essential features of academic research.

If the university's first aim was to keep the scientists in the familiar surroundings of laboratory and classroom, the second was to relieve them of unusual administrative responsibilities imposed by the contract. Under Filbey's direction the university made every effort to lift this burden. Doan, the chief administrative officer for the Metallurgical Laboratory, reported not to Compton but to Harrell, the university's business manager. Filbey and Harrell negotiated the initial contract with the OSRD late in 1941. Under this no-fee cost contract, the university was reimbursed for salaries, materials, power, travel, insurance, and administrative overhead within certain limits. The contract also provided that the Government would have sole power on patent actions and the assignment of patents arising from work under the contract. Doan's group and the university's administrative office maintained fiscal, property, personnel, and procurement controls for the laboratory and prepared vouchers for payment by the Government. When the project was transferred from OSRD to War Department support in April, 1943, the

199

Chicago area office of the Manhattan District under Major Arthur V. Peterson provided additional administrative support and controls. Although more detailed, the Army contracts for the operation of the Chicago and Clinton laboratories contained essentially the same provisions as the OSRD instrument. Thus, transfer from the OSRD to the Army involved more formal and detailed procedures rather than any fundamental reorganization.[36]

As project director, Compton had full responsibility for laboratory operations. In determining policy and in allocating research facilities and talent he could rely on the advice and support of the Laboratory Council, which included Allison as associate director, Hilberry as assistant director, Doan as chief administrative officer, and the directors of the four research divisions. In external relations, however, Compton was on his own. No one else could speak for the laboratory when General Groves swept into Chicago with an impatient query or abrupt request. Only Compton could assure Greenewalt that the data needed for design work in Wilmington would be forthcoming. A scientist of extraordinary prestige, infinite patience, and Christian forbearance, Compton succeeded in harnessing the diversified talents and interests of his staff.

200

NUCLEAR PHYSICS IN ECLIPSE

Perhaps least at home in the 1943 version of the Metallurgical Laboratory were the members of Fermi's Nuclear Physics Division. Little more than an informal academic organization, the division was a tenuous alliance of Fermi's experimental group and the theoretical physicists under Wigner.

The Fermi team moved rapidly in 1943 to exploit the Stagg Field pile. They were impatient to begin a series of tests which would determine more precisely the value of k and especially the effects of temperature changes within the pile. This impatience grew when General Groves, with du Pont support, ordered moving the pile from the West Stands to the Argonne Forest. Fermi hoped to complete his measurements of the fundamental constants in the chain reaction by building several zero-power piles at Stagg Field, or at least to operate the original pile until a new unit could be constructed at Argonne. Bowing to higher authority, however, Fermi shut down the Stagg Field pile in February so that the graphite and uranium metal could be used at Argonne.[37]

The new pile, completed in March, 1943, was called CP-2 (Chicago Pile 2). Somewhat larger than CP-1, it had essentially the same lattice arrangement. Because it was surrounded by a five-foot concrete shield, Fermi could operate it for long periods without exposing his staff to dangerous radiation. Although the lack of an internal cooling system limited the power level to a few kilowatts, Fermi and his associates measured the probability of neutron capture by various materials, determined the effectiveness of control systems and radiation shielding, and tested the reliability of instruments. These data, plus the operating experience, all contributed to the design of the Hanford plant. But CP-2 would not long be in the limelight. By fall, most of the Hanford experiments would be completed, and the modest research facilities of CP-2 would soon be surpassed by the Clinton pile. Unless Compton could obtain funds for new pile facilities at Argonne, the future for nuclear physics at the Metallurgical Laboratory was hardly promising.[38]

Wigner's theoretical group fared even less well in the winter of 1943. In January, Young, Ohlinger, and Weinberg enthusiastically joined Wigner in completing the basic design of the water-cooled pile. The favorable reception of their report in Wilmington was encouraging, but in the following weeks Greenewalt made no move to invite Wigner or his associates to join the du Pont design group. Although Greenewalt consulted Chicago on isolated theoretical problems, Wigner realized that du Pont had no intention of giving the Metallurgical Laboratory a free hand in designing the Oak Ridge or Hanford piles.

201

Failing to appreciate the size or complexity of du Pont's assignment, Wigner, Fermi, and their colleagues grew more exasperated with what appeared to be needless indecision and delay in Wilmington. It had taken three precious months to come to the decision on water cooling which Wigner's group had reached in 1942. Without so much as consulting the Metallurgical Laboratory, du Pont had adopted the air-cooled design for Clinton. In view of the subsequent shift to the water-cooled design for Hanford, the air-cooled pile was at best an interesting research tool. At worst, it seemed to some a waste of time, money, and talent.

By February, 1943, Wigner had lost all hope. Du Pont seemed to be floundering, but Greenewalt steadfastly refused all offers of help. If he was to be frozen out of the pile project, Wigner saw no vital work left for him at Chicago. Willing to accept the possibility that his presence might alone be responsible for du Pont's aloofness, he offered his resignation. Compton persuaded Wigner instead to take a month's leave of absence. Then he set out to find a new project which would hold the interest of his physicists.[39]

A NEW LOOK AT HEAVY WATER

Compton saw one possible answer in the renewed interest in heavy water. The project had been shoved into the background in the spring of 1942 but had enjoyed a revival before the end of the year. In their November feasibility report, the du Pont high command had rated the heavy-water-moderated pile second only to helium cooling. Du Pont's interest had stirred General Groves to look for ways to expand the production of heavy water. The result was a contract with du Pont to construct heavy-water plants in connection with ordnance works which the company was building near Morgantown, West

Virginia; Montgomery, Alabama; and Dana, Indiana. Unlike the Canadian plant at Trail, the American plants would use the water-distillation process, which depended upon the very slight difference in the boiling points of heavy and ordinary water. Although considerably more expensive than the Trail process, the water-distillation method would permit du Pont to bring the plants into production quickly by utilizing excess steam capacity and other existing facilities at the ordnance works. With Trail, the three new plants were expected to raise production to three tons per month by October, 1943.[40]

The prospects of larger supplies of heavy water stimulated scientific interest both at Columbia and Chicago. Harold Urey, who had continued to encourage heavy-water research on both sides of the Atlantic, renewed his campaign with the S-1 Executive Committee. Using the results of Halban's earlier experiments in England, Urey estimated that it might be possible to build a homogeneous system with as little as ten tons of heavy water. The potential simplicity of the homogeneous system was too tempting to be ignored. If Halban's data were correct, it might be possible to replace the complex assembly of machined graphite, aluminum tubes, and jacketed uranium slugs in the graphite, water-cooled pile with a simple pot-pump-pipe device. Heavy water, serving as both neutron moderator and coolant, could be circulated through a large tank, where a slurry of uranium would have the proper configuration to produce the chain reaction.

202

Urey called a meeting in his office on March 9, 1943, to evaluate the homogeneous pile. At the last minute, the British had refused to let Halban attend, but Urey and Fermi analyzed the data as best they could. They concluded that a full-size homogeneous system might require as much as 300 tons of heavy water. There was some possibility, however, that a small experiment might reach criticality with ten tons. Groves and Conant could see no reason for increasing heavy-water production at the moment, but they agreed to ask Halban to re-examine some of his data in Montreal, where the British and Canadians were establishing a small laboratory to investigate the heavy-water reaction.

Never one to worry about consistency, Urey continued to blow hot and cold on the heavy-water idea. He severely tried Conant's patience during the spring with a series of letters which dredged up every decision on heavy water as far back as 1940. After a visit to the Metallurgical Laboratory in June, Urey was even more excited. Fermi had received from Trail fifteen kilograms of heavy water which he had irradiated in the CP-2. He found that the material absorbed almost no neutrons. This news gave Urey enough leverage to reopen the question of a full-scale heavy-water effort.[41]

In the meantime, Compton had been using the new interest in heavy water to utilize some of the excess energy of his Chicago staff. The heavy-water project fitted neatly into the basic research plans which Compton had emphasized by bringing Henry D. Smyth to Chicago. As head of the Princeton physics department, Smyth could be expected to organize a sound research program and give Wigner a feeling of reassurance. With a newcomer in charge, Compton would have greater confidence that basic research, however significant in the long run, would not interfere with the more prosaic but still vital tasks of the laboratory in giving du Pont technical support for Hanford.

Whatever value the heavy-water project may have had as a diversion for the Chicago physicists was quickly cancelled by other effects. The more the physicists studied the heavy-water pile, the more they were convinced it would work. Their doubts that du Pont could build the water-cooled piles continued to grow. They believed that the project was mired in the inflexibility and red tape of corporate bureaucracy. They judged the design to be over-engineered in terms of safety measures, too complicated and elaborate for a hasty wartime effort, and much too costly. To these fears was added the antagonism caused by du Pont's insistence that the Metallurgical Laboratory review all the blueprints for Hanford. To snatch the physicists' own invention from their hands and give it to du Pont was reason enough for hostility. Now they were asked to pore over reams of drawings in search of errors which would never have been made if they had been permitted to design the piles in the first place.[42]

203

Before the end of July, 1943, Compton knew he had a crisis on his hands. The pressure of discontent had mounted so high that complaints were beginning to seep through the tight seams of the security barrier. A young physicist on temporary assignment with Wigner's staff pieced together enough of the story to convince himself that blundering in the pile project might lead to a German victory in the race for the bomb. A letter to Mrs. Roosevelt resulted in an interview with the President, who promptly called Conant. Before the Harvard president could arrange a meeting, the troubled physicist had related his fears to Felix Frankfurter and Bernard M. Baruch, neither of whom had any connections with the Manhattan project.[43]

To calm these troubled waters, Groves turned to a well proved device. He asked Warren K. Lewis to serve as chairman of a special reviewing committee with Eger V. Murphree, E. Bright Wilson, and Richard C. Tolman. Officially, their job was to evaluate the various proposals for heavy-water piles and to recommend the future level of effort. This they did with dispatch and authority. Urey, with the last measure of his confidence in the gaseous-diffusion process rapidly draining away, looked on the heavy-water pile as the only hope for the bomb. After talking with Compton and the du Pont high command, however, the committee voiced its confidence in the Hanford project. Closely following Compton's recommendation, they suggested continuation of fundamental research on heavy water at Chicago, construction of a low-power, heterogeneous heavy-water pile at Argonne, and study of a high-intensity heavy-water pile for possible construction at Oak Ridge.[44]

Unofficially, the committee served an equally important function as a more proper sounding board for the discontent at Chicago. While discussing the technical problems of the heavy-water system, Wigner and Fermi did not overlook the opportunity to express their dissatisfaction with du Pont. With unfailing confidence in Compton's judgment, neither Bush, Conant, Groves, nor the committee contemplated a shift in policy, but the reciting of grievances seemed to clear the air. Wigner, with Smyth's encouragement, returned to his onerous duties. Fermi, lending a hand on the heavy-water pile to be known as CP-3, helped to solve new technical problems for Hanford before he left for Los Alamos. The physicists had not succeeded in regaining control of the pile project. They had, however, wrung from Groves the funds for an experimental heavy-water pile, which would be the center of the laboratory's research program until the end of the war period.[45]

PROGRESS IN CHEMISTRY

204

The dissension which plagued the physicists at the Metallurgical Laboratory was for the most part absent in the New Chemistry Building. Superficially the situation seemed the same. The independent groups of the previous summer had been organized by early 1943 in a division under the nominal direction of Franck. Like Fermi and Wigner, Franck was a distinguished refugee scientist. Having acquired the same sense of responsibility for the technical elaboration of his scientific discoveries, Franck found it equally difficult to accept the role to which the du Pont contract seemed to relegate the professors at Chicago. In actual operation, however, the dynamics of the Chemistry Division were quite different from those indicated on the organization chart. Seaborg had completed his critical preliminary work on the lanthanum-fluoride process and established a smooth relationship with Cooper before Franck took the center of the stage. In practice each of the chemistry sections pursued an independent course—Seaborg on plutonium chemistry, Franck on radiation chemistry, Coryell on the chemistry of fission products, and George E. Boyd on analytical chemistry. Frank H. Spedding, who served nominally as associate director, confined most of his activities to his own laboratory at Iowa State College.

In the winter of 1943, the spotlight fell on the combined efforts of Cooper and Seaborg to develop the small semiworks for the lanthanum-fluoride process. Additional space in the New Chemistry Building permitted them to set up stainless-steel equipment which could process thirty-five-gallon batches of lanthanum-fluoride carrier containing both uranium and a trace of cyclotron-produced plutonium. Joseph B. Sutton and a group of du Pont engineers found the semiworks capable of performing the oxidation-reduction steps which heretofore had been accomplished only on a test-tube scale. With help from Seaborg's staff, Sutton learned how to reduce the corrosion of equipment by the fluoride carrier. The test runs also showed that centrifuges would be more effective than filters in the precipitation steps.[46]

By April, 1943, Sutton had most of the information du Pont needed to design a lanthanum-fluoride plant and had converted the semiworks for test runs with bismuth-phosphate carrier. Taking advantage of additional studies by Seaborg's group, he completed two runs before the end of the month. Although he had not investigated most of the variables, Cooper was ready to admit that the chances of success were about as good with bismuth phosphate as with lanthanum fluoride.

It was encouraging to have two feasible approaches, but there were also disadvantages. Du Pont was impatient to start the larger pilot plant at Clinton. On the eve of the June 1 deadline established by du Pont, the Laboratory Council met in Chicago. Cooper reiterated his conviction that there was no sound technical basis for a choice between the two. Both Seaborg and Cooper stressed that success on a laboratory scale did not guarantee that a full-scale plant would work. Franck urged that research on both processes continue at the laboratory. Though sound, this suggestion did not give du Pont the answer it needed. If no determining data were at hand, intuition and courage would be as important as judgment in the decision. When Seaborg ventured to guarantee at least a 50-per-cent recovery of plutonium from the bismuth-phosphate process, Greenewalt was willing to act. Worried about possible equipment failures caused by the high corrosion rates with lanthanum fluoride, the du Pont official chose bismuth phosphate.[47]

205

Once the laboratory had made its decision, du Pont launched an intensive campaign to design the Oak Ridge pilot plant. In Chicago, Seaborg's group explored the infinite variety of chemical concentrations, process temperatures, and reaction times for each step in the operation. Sutton tested these data in the semiworks until September, when the equipment was transferred to Clinton for further experiments. By the time the Chicago chemists were settled in their new barracks-like laboratory in Tennessee, the pilot-plant structure was taking recognizable form.

A NEW TECHNOLOGY

Designing the chemical separations plant was but a small part of the work assigned to Cooper's Technical Division at the Metallurgical Laboratory. If scientists like Fermi and Seaborg were the discoverers of the new world of nuclear energy, engineers like Cooper were its first explorers. The scientists' basic knowledge was essential, but the engineers had to struggle with the stubborn little quirks of the workaday world which would be just as important as the majestic formulations in the race for the bomb.

In one respect, the technical problems in Chicago were no different from those which confronted the gaseous-diffusion project at Columbia or the electromagnetic at Berkeley. The severe specifications imposed by the need for great reliability in operation, extreme operating conditions, and the magnitude and complexity of the equipment were common to all three approaches. Overcoming corrosion, fabricating metals, purifying materials, understanding thermodynamics, building auxiliary equipment, developing special tools, using new materials, and testing models made up the engineers' day throughout the Manhattan project.

The unique factor at the Metallurgical Laboratory was radiation. The unprecedented production of radioactive materials in the chain reaction introduced a new dimension in the Chicago technology. To build a pile, the engineer had to know the effect of radiation on corrosion rates, on the properties of metals, on chemical reactions, on instruments and other equipment, and on man. He would need years to revise his handbooks. In the meantime, he could but resort to trial and error, leaving the systematic compilation of data to less critical times.

206

The engineering in 1943 was relatively simple, but it determined the path for the future. The mechanical design of the water-cooled pile rested with the development engineering section under Miles C. Leverett. Drawing on his original analysis for the Mae West pile, he established rough specifications for the cooling system, control rods, shielding, and loading and unloading devices. While Sutton supervised the operation of the semiworks, Waverly Q. Smith was responsible for other chemical engineering assignments. The fabrication of uranium metal as slugs, the canning of slugs, and the design of aluminum tubes extended beyond the Midway to Iowa State College, the Battelle Memorial Institute, the Bureau of Mines, the Grasselli Chemicals Department of du Pont, Westinghouse, and the University of Wisconsin. These widespread activities were co-ordinated by a committee under Doan. The complex electronics of control systems and instrumentation were explored by a group under Volney C. Wilson. Skipping quickly from one assignment to the next, Cooper's division toiled to keep du Pont supplied with engineering data for the Hanford blueprints.

So pervasive was the significance of radiation in all these studies that it clearly deserved investigation in its own right. Although radiology by this time was an established discipline, the implications of the chain-reacting pile as a radiation source swamped the limited experience of the X-ray specialist. Aware of the industrial hazards, Compton decided to establish a health division at the Metallurgical Laboratory in July, 1942. As a temporary measure, he asked Ernest O. Wollan from the Chicago Tumor Institute to make a radiation survey of the laboratory. In organizing the division, Compton consulted Kenneth S. Cole, a biophysicist from the College of Physicians and Surgeons at Columbia. On the advice of Cole and others, Compton selected Robert S. Stone of the University of California, Berkeley, as director. Stone, an advisor to Lawrence on radiation hazards in cyclotron operation, was one of the few persons in the country with practical experience in applying nuclear physics to medicine. To lead the medical section, Compton selected Simeon T. Cantril, head of the radiology department at Swedish Hospital in Seattle. Cantril worked with Wollan, chief of the health physics section, in collecting radiation exposure data on all laboratory employees. For the first time, pocket ionization chambers and film badges were issued to all personnel working in high-radiation areas. From the meager experimental data then available, they fixed maximum permissible exposures at 0.1 roentgen per eight-hour day for gamma radiation and 0.01 roentgen for fast neutrons. In biological research, Cole took responsibility by initiating a series of experiments on the toxicology of radioactive substances. Other institutions inaugurated research on radiation hazards in 1943, but the pile project in Chicago was the natural focus of activity. Thus, Stone's group was to have a special influence on the biomedical programs to be established at Oak Ridge and in the Manhattan project at large.[48]

In 1943, as the pile project expanded beyond the Chicago campus, Compton made a series of organizational changes. Often reflecting the shifting pressures of a wartime enterprise, the changing patterns of organization were complex and not always significant. The important trend was the creation of independent laboratories of equal rank. Whitaker became director of the new Clinton Laboratories established in the X-10 area near Oak Ridge. Fermi supervised the facilities at Argonne as a division of the Chicago organization until May, 1944, when he became director of the independent Argonne Laboratory. Spedding likewise became director of Ames Laboratory and Allison of the original Metallurgical Laboratory in Chicago. Compton, as director of the Metallurgical Project, co-ordinated the activities of all the groups with the help of Hilberry and the laboratory directors who periodically came to Chicago for policy discussions.

207

CONSTRUCTION AT X-10

When Groves selected the Tennessee site in September, 1942, Compton at once launched his plans for pile facilities there. Whitaker participated in the initial planning for Oak Ridge, including the first laboratory behind the administration building. Du Pont's assumption of command and the attendant policy changes in the pile project in the last weeks of the year disrupted Whitaker's efforts to anticipate Compton's needs at Oak Ridge. When the Hanford site was finally selected in January, 1943, the Oak Ridge plan was to build the air-cooled experimental pile, the chemical separations pilot plant, and supporting laboratory facilities on the isolated tract in Bethel Valley, known as X-10.

Since du Pont was charged with both design and construction of X-10, only a few weeks elapsed between the decision to proceed and the ground-breaking for the first building.[49] Du Pont started the first temporary buildings on February 2, 1943, and completed these and most of the utility installations before the end of March. Early that same month, Cooper supplied enough data on the chemical separations plant so that the construction crews could start excavations. They needed more than two months to complete the foundations for the six large underground cells in which the plutonium would be separated from the irradiated slugs. With concrete walls several feet thick, the cells would extend one story above ground and would be covered with mammoth concrete slabs which could be removed when replacing equipment. The first cell, linked to the pile building by an underground canal, would contain a large tank in which the uranium slugs with their aluminum jackets would be dissolved. The next four cells were designed for the large stainless-steel tanks, centrifuges, and piping for the successive oxidation-reduction cycles. The last was a spare which could be used for storing highly radioactive equipment removed from the processing cells. Stretching along one side of the row of cells, a one-story frame building was erected to house the operating gallery and offices. By June, du Pont had started pouring the cell walls. Once Greenewalt had decided to use the bismuth-phosphate process, Wilmington could accelerate equipment design. The installation of piping and cell apparatus began in September. The testing and extensive modification of process equipment took most of October, but the plant was ready to operate when the first slugs were delivered from the pile.

208

The du Pont construction forces could not begin excavations for the pile building until April 27, 1943, when the design group in Wilmington completed the plans. Work fell somewhat behind schedule when a large pocket of soft clay was discovered directly beneath the pile site. Despite the additional foundations, du Pont was ready to pour the front face of the pile in June. Composed of seven feet of high-density concrete, the shield was pierced by hundreds of tubes through which the uranium slugs would be inserted. The side and rear walls were poured during July.

In the meantime, du Pont had begun to procure graphite for the moderator block.[50] Late in December, 1942, the du Pont design group met in Cleveland with officials of the National Carbon Company to plan the fabrication of graphite bars. The extremely severe specifications on purity and density limited the size of the bars and hence influenced the design of the pile. In January, the two companies agreed on bars forty-eight inches long and four inches square on the ends. While National Carbon was firing up its furnaces for production, the design group surveyed graphite-machining techniques at the Metallurgical Laboratory and other installations. Each of the bars had to be carefully machined to remove surface impurities and to attain the precise dimensions required for a tightly fitting graphite block. Late in March, 1943, the design group completed plans for a graphite-fabrication plant to be located at X-10 next to the pile building. Du Pont began construction at once and had the plant running before the end of May. It was not easy to meet the 0.005-inch tolerance in machining, but with concerted effort the company finished almost 700 tons of graphite and carefully stored it until the four walls of the pile shield were completed. On September 1, the graphite crew began stacking the first of seventy-three layers of the heavy, slippery material within the shield. As the V-shaped bars and other precisely machined pieces were set in place like a giant three-dimensional puzzle, the thousands of fuel channels, experimental holes, and control-rod openings took shape within the block. Before the end of September, the construction crew could begin to install the steel girders that would support the heavy top shield.

The most critical item by far was the uranium fuel.[51] Thanks to research during the previous year, it was now possible to produce pure uranium metal in large quantities. But the scientists had found no reliable method of canning or coating the metal. Without a protective coating, the uranium would rapidly corrode in the presence of coolant, and fission elements produced in the uranium might escape into the coolant system. Under the direction of Doan's committee in Chicago, several laboratories had tried to spray, coat, dip, or can uranium metal. Results were inconclusive, except for the obvious fact that canning would provide the most positive protection but would probably be the most difficult to achieve.

209

Slug production on an industrial scale involved not just technical considerations but also some elaborate procurement and contracting procedures. Du Pont would receive cast uranium billets from Mallinckrodt, Metal Hydrides, and other producers operating under Army contracts. The billets had to be extruded or drawn and rolled into cylindrical slugs about an inch in diameter. The next step was the tricky procedure of precision machining. Then came the canning or coating process. It was du Pont's job to find companies that could perform these steps according to unusually rigid specifications, negotiate contracts, procure equipment, establish schedules, and maintain controls. So important was this assignment that du Pont created a special procurement group in the Engineering Department with complete authority for all aspects of slug production.

Initially, du Pont hoped to avoid canning the slugs for the X-10 pile. Corrosion would be less critical in the air-cooled pile, and there was less time to fabricate the slugs for Clinton. Du Pont requested the Grasselli Chemicals Department in Cleveland to experiment with a hot-dip process. In the meantime, the procurement group found several companies to study the canning method.

By June 1, 1943, the situation was critical. Grasselli had failed to perfect hot-dipping, and all but the Aluminum Company of America had given up on canning. The company had made several important improvements, particularly in the use of fluxless welding, which was necessary to preserve the purity of can and slug. Even so, the process was far from reliable. However, the deadline for 60,000 slugs by the end of June left du Pont no choice but to order full speed ahead.

Alcoa started production on June 14, 1943. The process seemed relatively simple, since there would be no bonding material between the slug and the can. Standard testing techniques indicated that 97 per cent of the cans were vacuum-tight. More rigorous tests at Clinton in hydrogen or nitrogen atmospheres at high temperatures showed that not more than 50 per cent were satisfactory. Most of the failures seemed to occur at the weld between the can and the end cap. With help from General Electric, the Metallurgical Laboratory developed an improved welding method. The equipment was built and tested in Chicago before shipment to the Alcoa plant, where it was installed in the production line in October, 1943. By that time, however, the X-10 pile was virtually complete. It was still uncertain when Clinton would have enough acceptable slugs to begin operations. No one could guess whether the slugs would withstand the prolonged exposure to high temperatures and intense radiation. Nor could anyone say confidently that the failure of one slug would not ruin the entire pile. Nothing but actual operation could provide the answer.

210

CLINTON LABORATORIES

When Compton reluctantly agreed to operate the Clinton pile and pilot plant in March, 1943, he already had the nucleus of his organization on the scene. A small group under Whitaker had been in Oak Ridge since the previous fall and had witnessed the start of construction in the X-10 area. The same group continued to represent the operating contractor during the early construction period. At the same time, Whitaker was preparing to operate the facility under a new organization which was officially named the Clinton Laboratories in April, 1943. Although most of his principal staff would come from the Metallurgical Laboratory, Whitaker could rely on strong support from du Pont. The research divisions, staffed largely from Chicago, reported to Doan, who joined Whitaker as associate director. Du Pont transferred several hundred engineers under S. W. Pratt to Oak Ridge to perform the industrial and managerial functions of pilot-plant operation. From sixty-four employees during July, 1943, the laboratory staff grew to almost 1,000 by the end of the year.[52]

The chemists were the first large contingent to arrive. As soon as du Pont completed the rambling, frame laboratory building, Warren C. Johnson and Harrison Brown came with many of the chemists and much of the equipment from the overcrowded facilities on the Midway. Oswald H. Greager, a du Pont chemist, supervised the shipment and reassembly of the semiworks for the bismuth-phosphate plant. By September, the semiworks was again producing data for Clinton and Hanford.

The research chemists arrived a few weeks later. Perlman's group continued laboratory studies of the various separation processes which had first been investigated in the summer of 1942, on the chance that some aspect of these methods might contribute to the plutonium production enterprise. As soon as larger amounts of plutonium were available from the Clinton pile, some of Perlman's group, under the supervision of Vance R. Cooper, Louis B. Werner, and Bernard A. Fries, concentrated on isolating the product from the pilot plant as a pure plutonium nitrate. Coryell's group, in addition to research on fission-product chemistry, operated the new "hot laboratory," which was equipped for chemical experiments with highly radioactive materials. The section under Boyd continued working on analytical methods and on alternate separation processes.[53]

Important as were the related research activities at Clinton, the primary purpose of the laboratory could not be realized until the pile was operating. During the last week in October, 1943, du Pont completed the final mechanical tests of the pile after last-minute modifications to improve the loading-unloading operation. With enough slugs on hand for a critical mass, Whitaker summoned Compton, Fermi, and others from the Chicago physics group. On the afternoon of November 3, two teams of scientists recruited from various parts of the laboratory began the monotonous task of loading thousands of slugs into the channels in the central portion of the pile. Introducing a little friendly competition to make the long hours of the night pass more quickly, the loading teams found themselves nearing the criticality point long before dawn on November 4. They did not fail to appreciate their unintentional joke on the "brass" when Compton and Fermi were hastily summoned from the guest house at five o'clock on a gray fall morning to witness the initial operation of the world's first power-producing pile.[54]

211

From the first, the Clinton pile was an obvious success. It had gone critical with less uranium than had been anticipated—about thirty tons, placed in roughly half the 1,200 channels. After a week's shutdown for testing and modification, the loading was increased to thirty-six tons which raised the power to 500 kilowatts, or half its design capacity. Before the end of November, five tons of metal containing 500 milligrams of plutonium were discharged for pilot-plant tests. In December, the empty channels were blocked off with graphite plugs to concentrate the cooling air on the fuel. This modification permitted the pile to reach 700 kilowatts. Further small increases in power level and steadier operation in January and February, 1944, resulted in a substantial rise in plutonium formation. A new loading in March not only put more uranium in the pile but also distributed the fuel more evenly throughout the graphite block. Then, as improved slugs were introduced during the spring, the power level was raised as high as 1,800 kilowatts, almost double its design capacity. The pile was now producing plutonium in significant quantities for research purposes, and Compton was already talking of fan modifications which would enable him to double the power once again.

As the pile came into operation, the chemists had their first real chance to test their separation processes. In December, 1943, they introduced the first slugs into the pilot plant and treated them in small batches. Before the end of the year, the first sample, a fraction of a milligram, was shipped to Chicago. Yields at first were low, but the plant operated extremely well for one backed by less than a year of laboratory tests. In February, new equipment was installed to remove bismuth-phosphate carrier which was collecting on the walls of processing tanks. With this change, the pilot plant processed twenty-six batches of uranium of about 700 pounds each, with a yield of 73 per cent. Further refinements during the spring of 1944 boosted that figure to more than 90 per cent. Higher yields and shorter processing times all meant greater production. The first dribbles of plutonium samples to the laboratories were steadily supplemented during 1944 by ever larger quantities. With these, the scientists began to assemble more accurate data on the physical and chemical properties of plutonium and other fission products. As gram quantities were produced during the spring, Clinton began shipping samples to Los Alamos, where basic studies of the fission properties of plutonium had started. In the summer of 1944, these first samples of pile-produced plutonium caused revolutionary changes in weapon development.[55]

212

By that time, the evolution of the Clinton Laboratories was complete. Originally conceived as a necessary step in the development of the Hanford plant, Clinton had met many of the immediate needs and was quickly transforming itself into a well-rounded institution for nuclear research. If Clinton represented the summation of all that had gone before in that new branch of science, it was even more the precursor of new patterns and methods. The pile, an incredibly complex and costly instrument for research, was the central and indispensable feature of the nuclear laboratory. It provided an abundant supply of neutrons for basic research in physics. In produced radioactive isotopes and other fission products which promised to have countless uses in science and industry. As a radiation source, the pile offered unprecedented opportunities for research in biology and medicine. The thousands of kilowatts of heat dissipated through the stack were a mute reminder of the eventual possibility of controlled power from the chain reaction. Devised in the exigencies of war, the pile was, even in the summer of 1944, becoming a powerful instrument for the betterment of mankind.

HANFORD

Scarcely ten days before du Pont broke ground for the first building at the X-10 site, the company and the Army reached their decision to construct the plutonium-production plant at Hanford, Washington. On January 23, 1943, Groves and Nichols met with Yancey and Williams in Wilmington for a final review of the site data which Colonel Matthias and the du Pont engineers had been collecting since their December trip to the West Coast. During the first weeks of the new year, radiological hazards had become ever more important. Discussions with the scientists in Chicago seemed to confirm that a sudden **release** of radioactivity from the plant under certain atmospheric conditions

FACE OF THE CLINTON AIR-COOLED EXPERIMENTAL PILE (X-10) / This natural-uranium-and-graphite pile went critical early on the morning of November 4, 1943. Visible on the pile face are the ends of the 1,248 channels in which the uranium slugs are inserted.

LOADING X-10 / The worker is inserting the aluminum-clad, natural-uranium slugs.

might create a hazard as far as forty miles away. The isolation of the Hanford site was thus an advantage, but Groves wanted to be sure that du Pont carefully examined this factor in recommending the amount of land to be acquired.[56]

While du Pont was completing this and other studies, Colonel Matthias set about the task of transforming a desert wasteland into an industrial community of more than ordinary size. In the broad valley within the big bend of the Columbia River, he found facilities insufficient even for an advanced operating base. Driving scores of miles over the few roads that traversed the site, he noted few signs of civilization. About fourteen miles from the railroad town of Pasco, he crossed the Yakima and passed through the village of Richland, with a population of 200. Twenty-three miles farther up the river was Hanford, a hamlet of barely 100 souls. The village stood on the river bank, where the State of Washington operated a free ferry connecting with the grazing lands to the north and east on the Wahluke Slope. A few miles beyond Hanford was White Bluffs, no larger than Richland, which served as the center of the Priest Rapids irrigation district. Surrounding the town were a few farms struggling to survive on irrigated orchards or carefully watered fields of mint or asparagus. Standing in White Bluffs, the Colonel could scan in every direction the vast sea of sagebrush and cheat grass which provided scanty forage for sheep during the winter and spring. Along the eastern side of the river he could see precipitous cliffs rising three or four hundred feet to the grazing land which sloped, gently at first, back to the crest of Saddle Mountain. Looking off to the south and west, he scanned the profile of Gable Mountain, a low volcanic outcrop in the middle distance and some twenty miles away the barren slopes of the Rattlesnake Hills, whose crest marked the proposed boundary on that side.

213

When Matthias set up a temporary land office in Prosser on February 22, he had orders to acquire almost 500,000 acres, an area roughly circular in shape with a diameter of about twenty-nine miles. Divided into more than 3,000 tracts held by 2,000 owners, the purchase was among the most complex ever accomplished by the federal government.

Almost from the start, the Army encountered trouble.[57] Associations of property owners in the irrigation districts became the natural rallying point for those seeking higher values for their land. Although the Army could acquire options with relative ease, final settlements were hard to negotiate. To encourage the harvesting of crops and to ease the impact on local residents, the Army did not insist on immediate possession. By the time the Government was ready for settlement in late summer, many of the landowners were thoroughly aroused and organized. The tight security regulations bred disturbing rumors alleging misuse of the right of eminent domain, collusion between du Pont and the Army, waste of Government funds, and favoritism in appraisals. As a result, the Army found it hard to negotiate settlements even after properties had been reappraised at substantially higher values. Nor was court action favorable to the Government since sympathetic juries often awarded settlements twice as high as the appraisals. In the end, the Army was forced to relax its negotiating standards to get settlements out of court. Although the Army could not complete the major portion of the settlements before the end of 1944, the total cost was not much above the estimate of $5.1 million.

In the grim race for the atomic bomb, Matthias knew that he would have to prepare for immediate construction. Under the best conditions, this would have been a challenging assignment, but in early February, 1943, it bordered on the unreasonable. At that time, du Pont could give him only the vaguest description of basic requirements. From the few conferences since the turn of the year, Matthias had learned that du Pont was toying with the idea of building six helium-cooled piles along the river, where water could be used in heat exchangers for cooling the helium. Spaced at three-mile intervals, the piles would be safe from a common catastrophe. There was also talk of building four separation plants some distance from the river, perhaps south of Gable Mountain, to give a natural barrier against explosion. About the only other fact Matthias could be sure of was that the plant would produce unprecedented amounts of radioactivity. First, this meant an exhaustive series of meteorological studies, which had already been started, and a careful survey of the area for deposits of gravel and aggregate for the extraordinary amounts of concrete which would be used as radiation shielding in both the piles and separation plants.[58]

Without more definite plans, neither the Army nor du Pont could do much at the site. There were soil studies to find good load-bearing locations for the piles, plans for gravel pits and concrete batch plants to provide the most economical scheme for producing and delivering concrete, and chemical analyses of river water to determine the nature of purification required. Tentative plans were made for road and railroad networks in the area and for a power-distribution system tying to the main transmission line between Grand Coulee and Bonneville Dams at Midway Substation near the western border of the site. There was no hope, however, of beginning actual construction before spring.

In the meantime, the Army and du Pont set about procuring the tremendous amounts of scarce materials and construction equipment required for the job. Far from the nation's manufacturing centers and a latecomer in the competition for priorities on materials, the Hanford project was difficult to supply. One approach was to canvass manufacturers and suppliers on the West Coast to stimulate the flow of equipment and materials. This was the special task of du Pont's Hanford field office. Even without blueprints, the du Pont engineers could draw on their experience in preparing tentative lists of equipment and materials. More specialized items, particularly processing equipment, were the responsibility of the Wilmington office. Groves's group of experienced Army officers in Washington fought the big battles on priori-

214

ties with the Army and Navy Munitions Board and the War Production Board. Colonel Matthias and his staff at the Hanford Engineer Works kept Groves informed of Hanford's needs and negotiated with other Government agencies in the area. Quickly establishing this division of responsibility, the Army-du Pont team began to place large orders for materials and construction equipment before Wilmington had even preliminary drawings of the plant.

Before the end of March, 1943, the general arrangement of the Hanford site emerged. The decision to build water-cooled piles made it possible to reduce their number from six, at first to four and then to three. These were to be placed at six-mile intervals along the south bank of the river, near White Bluffs. The four separation plants would be paired in two areas south of Gable Mountain, almost ten miles from the nearest pile. A third area, about midway on the Richland-Hanford road, was selected for a plant to fabricate uranium slugs and to test pile materials. Rather than have a separate construction camp at each of the sites, the Army and du Pont agreed to build one central camp on the Hanford town site. Because this location would be too close to the plants for safety, a permanent town for operating personnel would be constructed at Richland.

Hanford was an excellent site for the construction camp. Reasonably close to the plant areas, it occupied fairly level terrain near the river. There were existing secondary roads to Pasco and White Bluffs. A branch line terminating in Hanford connected the town with the Chicago, Milwaukee, and St. Paul Railroad. Existing residences, community buildings, and public utilities would serve as the nucleus of the housing effort.

In the first days of April, du Pont engineers began to lay out the town site and prepare for construction.[59] The initial step was to be a camp housing and feeding 2,000 workers. This would require ten four-wing barracks for men, two two-wing barracks for women, a mess hall and a commissary building. Until the first units could be completed, however, construction workers had to live in existing town buildings and pyramidal tents, which the Army furnished. During the summer of 1943, Hanford was more a tent camp than a town. With poor living quarters, complete isolation, few recreational facilities, and the heat and dust of the desert summer, workers quit in large numbers. The damaging effects of dust storms on the workers' morale led the hardier inhabitants to refer to the dust as "termination powder." The rapid completion of camp facilities became a critical factor by fall, when the first large-scale construction in the plant areas began.

As the Hanford camp grew slowly, du Pont and the Army were making a combined effort to find the thousands of laborers and craftsmen who would work and live there. The Army cleared the way through the War Manpower Commission to submit requests for specified numbers of workers in various craft classifications directly to manpower regions throughout the nation. With du Pont agents in each region, the War Manpower Commission organized advertising campaigns and recruiting centers. Prospective workers

215

were advanced railroad tickets to Hanford and were greeted in Pasco by welcoming committees which provided temporary housing and saw that the workers reached their assigned jobs. Incentive plans were introduced to keep workers on the job, and special recruiting efforts were made as far away as Alaska and the Mexican border.[60]

The best inducements, however, were adequate living quarters, good food at reasonable prices, and a variety of recreation for leisure hours. By the end of 1943, Hanford could lay some claim to all of these. With more than 25,000 workers on the job, 131 of the planned 135 barracks for men were completed, as well as 45 of the 64 planned for women. Two camps accommodating 1,200 trailers were already open, and seven of the eight mess halls were in operation. A weekly meal ticket entitled the worker to all he could eat. Since nearly everyone ate at the mess halls, food preparation was on a scale surpassing all but the largest army camps. A post office, bank, hospital, commissary and other stores provided the usual community services. For recreation, there were beer halls, dances and variety shows in the auditorium, bowling, movies, and sports. The long working hours, monotonous rows of ugly temporary buildings, dusty streets, and lonesome stretches of desert were undeniably part of the Hanford scene. But there was also good pay, good food, interesting companions from all parts of the nation, and a spirit of camaraderie bred by the obvious importance of the job.

Construction forces could not begin work on the piles until the basic design drawings were released in Wilmington on October 4, 1943.[61] In the meantime, however, there was much that could be done on conventional facilities. On the basis that each pile would produce 250,000 kilowatts of heat, the du Pont engineers could calculate the size of the facilities necessary to bring cooling water to the piles. For all three units, water consumption would approach that of a city of 1,000,000 persons. In fact, the design of the water supply for each of the pile areas resembled that of a large municipal plant. Each would have a river pump house, large storage and settling basins, a filtration plant, huge motor-driven pumps for delivering water to the face of the pile, and facilities for emergency cooling in the case of a power failure.

Construction in the first pile area, designated 100-B, began on August 27 with the water-cooling facilities. During the fall, the rough outlines of the river pump house, storage basin, filter building, and main pump house began to take shape. Not until October 10 did the du Pont engineers drive the first stakes marking the location of the pile building. Even then, the foundations were not fixed until the area immediately under the pile had been excavated and carefully load-tested. Then work gangs began to lay the first of 390 tons of structural steel, 17,400 cubic yards of concrete, 50,000 concrete blocks, and 71,000 concrete bricks that went into the pile building. Starting with the foundations for the pile and the deep water basins behind it where the irradiated slugs would be collected after discharge, the work crews were well above ground by the end of the year. Soon a windowless concrete monolith towered 120 feet above the desert.

Progress through the winter of 1944 was slow on B pile. There was a continual shortage of workers in all crafts, but especially among the carpenters, millwrights, welders, and electricians. On February 20, with 4,000 workers in the area, du Pont reported shortages of 850 laborers, 550 carpenters, 200 rodsetters, 125 pipefitters, 31 welders, 133 electricians, and 60 millwrights on B pile alone. Even when skilled workers were hired, they could not always be assigned to the pile area. Only those with security clearances could be employed in the restricted areas within the pile building. The unusual skill and experience demanded for many of the tasks excluded workers with normally acceptable qualifications. Welders, for example, were required to present work records and references going back as far as fifteen years and pass a welding test which rejected more than 80 per cent of the applicants. Most of the 50,000 linear feet of welded joints would be inaccessible when the pile was completed. With success possibly hanging on the integrity of every weld, du Pont believed exceptional standards were mandatory. They did, however, make for slow going, especially on the first pile.

Assembly of the pile itself began in February, 1944, after most of the rough concrete work was completed. Piping and instrumentation in the bottom of the pile had been encased in a second concrete pour on the first foundation. On February 1, workmen began laying the steel liner which would eventually be welded to similar sections in the sides and top of the pile to form an airtight unit. Then began the ticklish job of grouting the cast-iron base of the pile in a third concrete pour. The base had to be set within 0.003 inch and have a flatness tolerance after grouting of 0.005 inch. Before the third pour on March 6, laborers began setting the first rows of cast-iron blocks, which would provide a thermal shield, and the ten-ton sections of laminated masonite and steel blocks, which would form a biological shield within the thick outer concrete walls. Prefabricated with precision in another area, the laminated blocks were carefully cleaned and set in place. Each had to fit perfectly, particularly on the front and rear faces of the pile. On those faces, the blocks were drilled to receive the aluminum tubes, and they had to match corresponding holes in the concrete shield and graphite block within $\frac{1}{64}$ inch.

Placement of the shield was not completed until May 19. The next day, specially trained crews began the critical task of laying the graphite blocks within the shield. Precision and cleanliness were the chief concerns. The graphite crews were required to wear special uniforms. Handling the graphite carefully with gloves, they laid each piece by number according to a detailed plan. They used plumb bobs and guide wires to stay within the tolerance of 0.005 inch from the centerline of the pile. They carefully vacuumed each layer to remove any traces of dirt. On June 11, the crew laid the last piece of graphite, and others began installing the top shield.

217

By the first of May, mechanics, pipefitters, welders, and electricians were swarming over the area to install the jungle of machinery, piping, wiring, and instrumentation which converged on the pile. The arrays of control and safety rods, with their intricate operating mechanisms, were installed and tested. The huge water pipes from the pump building were connected to risers on the front of the pile. The risers were tied to crossheaders, and they in turn were connected by short loops of flexible piping called pigtails to each of the aluminum process tubes. A similar assembly was installed on the rear face to carry the cooling water to a retention basin, where the short-lived radioactivity would be allowed to decay before the water was returned to the river. Large trenches carried the thousands of pipes and cables which tied the swarm of instruments in the pile with the great panel boards in the control room. By the middle of August, B pile was complete.

218

To understand the full story of pile assembly, however, the observer had to look beyond the pile building itself. Behind each piece of equipment brought to the assembly area in the pile building lay months of research, engineering development, and fabrication. For anything as novel in 1944 as a nuclear pile, this was not surprising. What was striking was the realization that many of the major components had been fabricated on the desert at Hanford.[62] Following its Clinton experience, du Pont decided to finish every piece of graphite on the site. A special air-conditioned building to exclude dust and impurities was constructed near the Hanford camp. Wood-turning machinery was set up with special jigs for each step in the operation. Here again the tolerances required were exceptional. The allowable deviation in cross-section measurements was 0.005 inch; in length, 0.006 inch; in the diameter of longitudinal holes for the process tubes, 0.003 inch. About 17 per cent of all the graphite was tested in a small 30-watt pile constructed at Hanford. Du Pont followed a similar procedure in producing the huge laminated shield blocks. In special shops, skilled workers fabricated 2.5 million square feet of masonite and 4,415 tons of steel plates into blocks with tolerances comparable to those in other components.

Supporting activities at Hanford extended from these specialized operations down to a host of mundane but essential services. Not only all the concrete but also all concrete blocks were manufactured on the site. The central shops located between the two chemical separation areas offered virtually every repair and maintenance service available in a large industrial community. In addition to large warehouses containing everything from steam locomotive parts to safety shoes, the area had individual repair shops for heavy equipment, pumpcrete equipment, cranes, valves, batteries and radiators, tires, heavy trucks, automobiles, electrical equipment, transit mix equipment, railroad gondolas, and locomotives. Machine shops, training schools, and engineering offices also dotted the area. Though perhaps less dramatic, these varied services were as vital to the success of the project as any of the construction activities at Hanford.

CANYONS IN THE DESERT

Just a few miles east and west of the central shops area in August, 1943, the visitor with proper credentials could find groups of temporary buildings clustered around several immense excavations in the desert floor. These were the beginnings of the two areas where plutonium would be separated chemically from the irradiated slugs.[63] Superficially, the Hanford separation plants would bear little resemblance to the small concrete structure huddled next to the pile building at the Clinton Laboratories. Actually, the processes were to be similar, but the much greater scale of the Hanford plant gave it a completely different appearance. In both plants the irradiated slugs would be collected in the deep water pools behind the piles. But instead of being transported a few score feet through an undeground canal to the separation building, the buckets of Hanford slugs would be loaded into heavy shielded casks placed on special railroad cars by remote control and moved to storage areas about five miles from the piles. Here the buckets would be suspended in water inside low concrete structures isolated in the desert. When a sufficient amount of the short-lived radioactivity had been allowed to decay, the buckets would be transported by railroad car to the separation plant.

219

Each separation plant was designed to include a separation building, where the bismuth-phosphate process would be performed; a concentration building, where the plutonium would be separated from the phosphate carrier and other gross impurities; a ventilation building, for disposal of radioactive and poisonous gases from the process buildings; and a waste storage area, where the highly radioactive sludges of uranium, aluminum, fission products, and process materials could be stored. Original plans called for two plants in each area, but operating experience with the pilot plant at Clinton later permitted du Pont to reduce this number from four to three—the T and U plants in the 200-West area and the B plant in 200-East.

Under the extreme pressure imposed by Groves's schedule, du Pont made an effort to start construction in both the pile and separation areas during the summer of 1943. In the 200 areas, however, nothing more than the excavations for the separation buildings had been completed when work came to a standstill. Facing acute shortages of construction labor in the fall of 1943, du Pont had no choice but to concentrate on the pile areas. Besides, the plans for the separation plants did not go much beyond the fact that a precipitation process would be used in the major steps. The selection of the bismuth-phosphate method on June 1 had scarcely been reflected in Hanford designs. The pilot plant at Oak Ridge was itself in the early stages of construction, and no one yet knew what process would finally be employed in concentration and final purification of the plutonium.

As a result, no work of significance was performed in the separation areas until 1944, and even then most activity was concentrated in 200-West.

During January, the massive outlines of 221-T, the first separation building, appeared as the foundations were poured for the cells and heavy concrete walls of the structure. The building itself, more than 800 feet long, 65 feet wide, and 80 high, looked like a huge aircraft carrier floating on a sagebrush sea. Inside, it had roughly the same plan as the pilot plant. A row of forty concrete cells, most of them about fifteen feet square and twenty feet deep, ran the length of the building. Each cell was separated from its neighbor by six feet of concrete and would be covered by concrete blocks six feet thick. Since the cell openings were designed in step fashion to provide adquate shielding, the thirty-five-ton concrete lids with a corresponding configuration had to be poured with extremely accurate dimensions. Only by using machined cast-iron forms was it possible to maintain the one-eighth-inch tolerance specified.

220 Along one side of the cell row and separated from it by seven feet of concrete were the operating galleries on three levels, the lowest for electrical controls, the intermediate for piping and remote lubrication equipment, and the upper for operating control boards. The entire area above the cells was enclosed by a single gallery sixty feet high and running the length of the building. Its five-foot concrete walls and three-foot roof slabs were designed to prevent the escape of radiation when the cell covers were removed. Even with all covers in place, radiation levels in the gallery would be too high to permit the presence of unprotected personnel. Once operation started, this huge gallery, or canyon as it came to be called, would become a silent, concrete no-man's-land shut off from the outside world, its cold walls and hook-studded floor illuminated only by the long rows of glaring light bulbs.

The insensible but deadly powers of radiation influenced every feature of this strange man-made world. The great masses of concrete in the canyons, the completed cell covers standing on the desert like lopsided sarcophagi testified to the presence of this new force. Perhaps less picturesque but equally novel was the equipment the buildings would contain. Radiation meant remote control, which in turn placed a premium on simplicity of design, mechanical perfection, maintenance-free operation, and interchangeability of parts. To avoid servicing pumps and valves, steam jets were developed to transfer process materials from one tank to another. Centrifuges, considered more reliable than filters, were specially designed and subjected to a series of rigorous tests. Liquid-level and density meters were developed to trace the progress of each operation.

The first thought in designing cell equipment was to facilitate maintenance and replacement. Once the plant was operating, the only access to the cells would be by means of the huge bridge crane which traveled the length of the building. From the heavily shielded cab behind a concrete parapet above the gallery, operators could look into the canyon with specially designed periscopes and television sets. They could use the seventy-ton hook to lift off the cell covers and lighter equipment to work within the cell. With special tools and impact wrenches, they could remove connecting piping, lift out the damaged piece of equipment, and place it in a storage cell. They would then lower a new piece of equipment into the operating position and reconnect the process piping.

To perform such an operation successfully at sixty feet or more without direct vision required extreme accuracy in the dimensions of cell components, in the positioning of equipment, and in the location of piping within the cell. Because the final details of the process had not been firmly established, all the equipment and connections were standardized so that any two kinds of apparatus could be operated in any cell in the plant. Distinctive color codes were used on all units to assist maintenance crews, and all concrete surfaces were coated with a paint which was corrosion-resistant, easily washable, and adequately adherent to concrete.

In building the separation plants, du Pont found nothing more critical than procuring stainless steel for the hundreds of precipitators, catch-tanks, centrifuges, and dissolvers as well as for 700,000 feet of piping. Because many of the chemicals were highly corrosive, du Pont had to use a special grade of columbium stainless steel. Since this type of steel had never been manufactured in commercial quantities, du Pont had trouble placing orders for such large amounts, all to be produced according to rigid specifications. Welders, for the most part, had to be trained to use the high-temperature techniques required, since seamless pipe of this material was not then available. The final step in fabrication of the stainless steel was heat treatment, for which a special furnace was built in the 200-East area.

221

By carefully scheduling construction and the fabrication of equipment, the contractor made good progress during the spring of 1944. As soon as a portion of the long canyon was roofed over, equipment was installed with watchlike precision. By the middle of September, the end wall of 221-T had been sealed off. Construction of 221-U, also started in January, 1944, had been delayed for three months to speed up work on the D pile and was not completed until the end of the year. Work on 221-B followed about three months behind 221-U.

Excavations for the concentration buildings (224-T, U, and B) were not started until late in the winter of 1944. Since the great bulk of the uranium and fission products would be eliminated in the 221 buildings, the concentration units could be designed for smaller amounts of less radioactive materials. The possibility of smaller buildings, less shielding, and direct maintenance permitted some postponement of construction until the chemists at Chicago and Clinton could investigate the various processes which might be employed.

The main purpose of the concentration process was to remove the relatively large amounts of bismuth phosphate which carried the plutonium through the separation steps. At Chicago, Seaborg's group had found it easy on a laboratory scale to dissolve the phosphate carrier in hydrochloric acid and precipitate the plutonium with a rare-earth fluoride. However, the acid was so corrosive on stainless steel that the process was impractical for the production plants. Following a suggestion by L. C. Peery, the Clinton pilot plant tried the original lanthanum-fluoride process for the concentration step. The extensive studies of that process already completed made it possible to adapt it to the 224 buildings without delay. The real value of the combination of the two precipitation processes did not appear until later, when it was discovered that fission products not well separated by the phosphate steps were efficiently separated by the fluoride steps. The big construction effort on the 224 buildings came in the summer of 1944. The two plants in the West area were completed on October 8. The 224-B plant in the East area was not finished until February 10, 1945.[64]

The final step in plutonium recovery was isolating the material from the last traces of fission products, carrier, and other undesirable elements. Here the quantities of material and the radiation levels were so small that the process could be performed in a relatively conventional laboratory, only the great value and high toxicity of the product requiring special precautions. In selecting the process, du Pont could draw on the months of basic research which Perlman's group had conducted at Chicago and Clinton. On Seaborg's recommendation, du Pont selected the peroxide method, which Perlman had investigated in the summer of 1942. The process rested upon the fact that virtually all nitrates, except those of uranium, thorium, and plutonium, were soluble in hydrogen peroxide. Since the last traces of uranium and thorium had already been extracted, the plutonium could be isolated by separating it from the lanthanum-fluoride carrier, converting it to a nitrate, and adding peroxide. The product would be a pure plutonium nitrate, which could be sent to Los Alamos for reduction to metal.

Although the basic chemistry of the process was well understood, all the details of the equipment for the isolation building (231-W) were not known when du Pont broke ground in the West area on April 8, 1944. During the summer the Metallurgical Laboratory revised its estimates of the critical mass of plutonium, and this change affected the layout of the isolation building. Some of the mechanical processes were revised several times as the Chicago and Clinton laboratories tested various steps. Only with the greatest effort was du Pont able to complete the isolation building before the end of 1944.

SLUG CRISIS

Despite the remarkable achievements of du Pont and the Army at Hanford, no one in a position of responsibility in the summer of 1944 could look on the status of the project with confident optimism. The rough, energetic spirit of the Hanford camp with its 50,000 temporary inhabitants, the magnitude and intricacy of the three pile areas along the river bank, the combination of daring and precision in the huge canyons could not fail to leave a deep impression on those who saw them. But those in command knew that true progress had to be measured in terms of the bomb. In that respect, the value of Hanford was very much in doubt. Only one of the piles could be considered complete, and not one unit in the two separation areas was ready for operation. Disconcerting as these facts were, they by no means represented the greatest threat to Hanford. There was every reason to believe that the tempo of construction could be increased, but without adequate supplies of reliable uranium slugs for the piles, the massive structures in the desert might well stand as a monument to the folly of American engineering.

The slug crisis was nothing new. It had begun in the summer of 1943 with the first attempt to prepare the charge for the experimental pile at Clinton. Fortunately, the more moderate operating conditions anticipated at Clinton permitted du Pont to meet that first requirement with an unbonded slug, which was relatively easy to fabricate. The Clinton experience, however, provided a warning which no one overlooked. In a status report in October, 1943, Compton saw the development and production of slugs as the most critical job facing the project.[65]

A series of conferences in the last two weeks of October laid the groundwork for a three-pronged attack. Greenewalt agreed to build a small slug-production unit at Wilmington in an effort to translate the more promising canning techniques into a process which would be practical on a large scale. Compton was prepared to enlist every available hand in Chicago to build a canning semiworks in the old icehouse and stables on University Avenue. While Wilmington concentrated on the development of equipment for the production line, Chicago would study the chemical and physical reactions occurring in the various processing steps. Du Pont's Grasselli Chemicals Department in Cleveland would support the Metallurgical Laboratory with specialized research on bonding techniques. In the meantime procurement teams in du Pont's Engineering Department would expedite the production of uranium slugs and aluminum cans.

For the moment, du Pont was willing to let research follow its natural course. Several bonding schemes showed promise, and even Greenewalt was not ready to discount the possibility of developing an unbonded, canned slug or even a coated slug which would withstand the extreme operating conditions in the Hanford piles. During the last weeks of 1943, Grasselli and the Metallurgical Laboratory investigated a variety of bonding methods. The two principal approaches involved using an aluminum-silicon alloy as the bonding material between slug and can and incorporating a zinc bond in a special canning technique. In each process there were hundreds of variables in applying the bond and inserting the slug in the can, any one of which might determine the success of the method.

By the beginning of 1944, du Pont was determined to narrow the

223

field. Although only a few full-sized Hanford slugs had yet been canned with any of the processes, some line of development had to be established if the company was to have enough slugs to start the B pile in August. At a meeting in Chicago on January 4, 1944, Greenewalt examined the evidence. It was obvious from the outset that none of the bonding methods was yet ready for use in large-scale production. Even the preliminary evidence from a few experiments suggested that the bond greatly complicated welding the cap on the can. It was also extremely difficult to achieve a uniform distribution of the bond, which was necessary to avoid hot spots on the slug surface. In fact, some of the best minds at Chicago, including Wigner and Creutz, were convinced that the unbonded slug would be the most easily fabricated and the most reliable. Wigner doubted that the bond would withstand the effects of thermal expansion. Creutz was determined to circumvent the complications of bonding by perfecting a double-weld which would provide greater insurance against leakage. Greenewalt readily admitted the complications of bonding, but he saw its distinct advantages too. Not only would the bond facilitate heat removal from the slug, but the bond itself would protect the uranium from corrosion and swelling even if the can did leak. The du Pont engineer was greatly impressed with the properties of the aluminum-silicon alloy. He did not consider it impossible that a simple alloy dip might some day replace the canning process altogether. The Chicago scientists might continue some modest studies of zinc bonds and double-welds; Greenewalt intended to concentrate on the aluminum-silicon bond, now commonly called Al-Si.[66]

224

By this time, du Pont could begin to use the extensive slug-fabrication facilities at Hanford. Construction had started in the spring of 1943 on the third production site, designated the 300 area, about midway between Richland and the Hanford camp. There du Pont planned to concentrate operations which involved relatively small amounts of radioactivity and therefore no massive shielding. In addition to the slug-fabrication buildings, the 300 area contained the small thirty-watt pile in which finished graphite bars were tested, a general technical laboratory, instrument shops, and a semiworks of laboratory size for the chemical separation process. The plan was to perform eventually all the fabricating steps from uranium billets to finished slugs at Hanford, but initially work would be limited to experimental canning processes. Before the end of 1943, the construction forces had completed the simple concrete-block building in the middle of the 300 area. Early in 1944, du Pont began shipping equipment developed in the Wilmington test unit for the first experimental runs at Hanford.

Despite the intensive experimentation at Wilmington, Cleveland, Chicago, and Hanford, progress was discouraging during the winter of 1944. In some respects, the widely dispersed groups of engineers and scientists seemed to be learning more and more about less and less. They were amassing data but not developing a process. Was it possible that, despite all the good intentions, work tended to drift from the central purpose in isolated laboratories?

300 AREA AT HANFORD / Here du Pont manufactured uranium slugs and tested materials for the production piles. Slugs were fabricated in the one-story masonry building in the center background. Materials were tested in a 30-watt pile in the large vented building at the upper left.

FILTER PLANT FOR THE HANFORD D ➝ʼILE, JUNE 20, 1944 / The water-treatment system for each of the three production piles was comparable to a large municipal plant. The power plant is in the background and the pile building out of view to the right.

HANFORD D PILE AND SUPPORTING FACILITIES, JUNE 20, 1944 / The pile building, which towered 120 feet above the desert, is the concrete structure in the center. Behind it lies the water-treatment facilities. The Columbia River and the Wahluke Slope are in the background.

CHEMICAL SEPARATION BUILDING UNDER CONSTRUCTION AT HANFORD / Here the bismuth-phosphate process was used to separate plutonium from irradiated uranium. The completed building was 800 feet long, 65 feet wide, and 80 feet high.

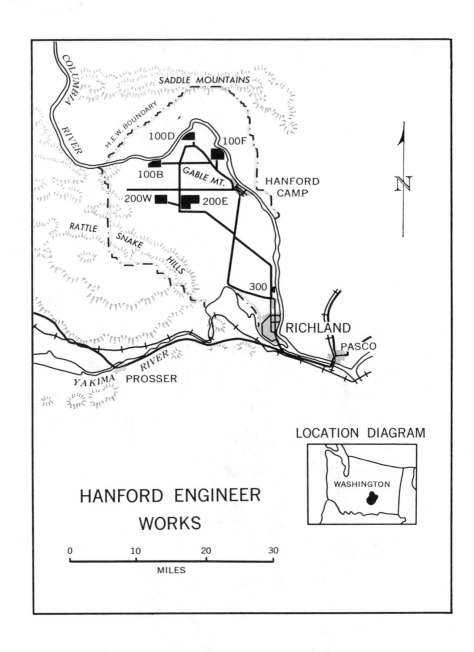

COLUMBIA RIVER

SADDLE MOUNTAINS

H.E.W. BOUNDARY

100D

100F

100B

GABLE MT.

HANFORD CAMP

200W

200E

RATTLE SNAKE HILLS

300

RICHLAND

PASCO

YAKIMA RIVER PROSSER

N

LOCATION DIAGRAM

WASHINGTON

HANFORD ENGINEER
WORKS

0   10   20   30

MILES

Williams and Greenewalt guessed there might be a psychological, if not a practical, advantage in centralizing all slug-development activities at Hanford. Accordingly, in March they transferred to Hanford all Wilmington slug operations and most of the du Pont engineers assigned to the semiworks in Chicago. The Metallurgical Laboratory and Grasselli would continue research on specific portions of the process.[67]

The first experimental canning operations started in the 313 building at Hanford on March 20, 1944. Nothing could have been further from assembly-line techniques. The development line consisted of little more than a series of open tanks in which scores of operators dipped clusters of machined slugs. Starting with a series of degreasing and pickling baths to remove dirt and oxidation, the slugs were successively dipped in molten bronze, tin, and Al-Si. Since the temperature, composition, and duration of each dip were extremely critical, the operators had great difficulty in achieving uniform results or detecting faulty slugs. After the final dip, the slugs were forced into the aluminum cans with hydraulic presses, a tricky process which produced a large number of rejects. The next step involved end-trimming and the complicated task of arc-welding the aluminum cap in an argon atmosphere. Completely a manual operation, the welding step required weeks of training to achieve reasonable results. When the end had been faced and machined, the slugs were subjected to a series of tests to detect weld failures, pinholes, or lack of bond uniformity.

225

With so many variables and so many opportunities for error, the Hanford operating crew considered it an accomplishment to can three or four slugs per day, even when working on double shifts. In the first two weeks they succeeded in canning a total of thirty-six slugs, and none of these looked acceptable. It was hard to imagine how the tens of thousands of slugs needed for the first pile loading could be completed by August 15. It was probably too late to take advantage of recent encouraging experiments with zinc bonding since nothing had been done to develop a production process for this method. The du Pont leaders had but two choices. They could lower their acceptance standards and hope to produce a sufficient number of aluminum-silicon-bonded slugs, or they could fabricate an initial loading of unbonded slugs for the first pile.

During the last two weeks of April, the du Pont operators found it possible to keep the experimental line going for several hours without a breakdown. Slug production jumped from units, to tens, to hundreds per week. These results were encouraging, but in terms of the number of slugs required and the time available, they seemed insignificant. Reluctantly, on May 2 du Pont agreed to the emergency production of unbonded slugs. The Quality Hardware Company in Chicago, with help from Alcoa, geared up to meet the August deadline. Only by the greatest effort was Quality able to begin regular production by the middle of June.

Meanwhile, Hanford was enjoying steady if not startling progress.

With the arrival of the first production press from Grasselli, the first true production line was started on May 11. Production quickly increased as additional dipping lines and presses were brought into action. With four lines in operation by the middle of June, it seemed possible that an adequate number of slugs for the first loading might be produced in time, but no one could yet predict how many of these would be acceptable. Until the pile was completed and the slugs installed, the success of the whole pile project would hang in the balance.[68]

By the end of June, 1944, Hanford was little more than half complete. Not one pile or separation plant was yet ready for operation. By concentrating labor and materials du Pont was hastening the completion of the first plants of each type (100-B and 221-T). The second pile (100-D) and the second canyon (221-U) were less than half complete, and the third pile (100-F) and separation plant (221-B) were barely started. Slug fabrication in the 300 area was just beginning on a production scale. Du Pont operating crews were only then taking over the first administrative offices, machine shops, and maintenance buildings in Richland and at the plant sites.

With a portion of the electromagnetic plant in operation and the first stages of K-25 ready for testing, Hanford was just reaching the peak of construction activities. At Hanford camp, work was almost complete on the last of 131 men's barracks, 912 men's huts, and 64 women's barracks which would accommodate more than 39,000 workers. Completion of a second trailer camp would raise the number of trailer spaces to more than 3,600. In the permanent community for operating personnel at Richland more than two-thirds of the 3,800 family units were ready for occupancy. The steadily increasing momentum of construction suggested that most of Hanford would be complete by early 1945. No one could yet foretell when the first significant quantities of plutonium would be produced.[69]

A LABORATORY
SET ON A HILL

The sprawling separation plants in the long valleys that stretched south-west from Oak Ridge and the massive piles that rose on the desert banks of the Columbia were spectacular achievements. In the summer of 1944, their success in time was still a matter to doubt, but even if they exceeded the rosiest expectations of their designers, they would produce only fissionable material, not a weapon. To turn uranium 235 or plutonium into a bomb required in its own right a prodigious research, design, and engineering enterprise. In 1942, no one had been able to visualize the magnitude of the effort that would be necessary, but several leaders had seen that even the theoretical work on weapons could not remain indefinitely an adjunct of the Metallurgical Laboratory.

NEEDED: A SPECIAL WEAPONS LABORATORY

The germ of the decision to create a special weapons laboratory was active as early as May 26, 1942, when Conant recommended to Bush the creation of a joint OSRD-Army committee to develop plans for constructing the bomb. Perhaps Conant was influenced by a letter he had just seen from Gregory Breit to Lyman J. Briggs. On resigning as co-ordinator of fast-neutron research at Chicago, Breit was distressed at the attitude toward secrecy there. Some of the influential scientists flatly opposed the system of dividing the work into tight little units and of allowing no one to know more than he needed to do his job. Just as a man-of-war was compartmentalized to prevent a single torpedo from sending the vessel to the bottom, the S-1 project had been subdivided to prevent some indiscreet or disloyal individual from revealing the whole enterprise to the enemy. Breit reported that though the Metallurgical Laboratory observed compartmentalization to a degree at a weekly colloquium, much information escaped the narrow confines that good security practice seemed to dictate. Many of the Chicago researchers considered this altogether fitting and proper. They judged it wiser to allow free exchange of ideas and data in the interest of more rapid progress. Compton himself held that no impenetrable barrier could exist between fast-neutron research and the slow-neutron pile program. Breit concluded that the S-1 leadership should edge Chicago out of the work on the bomb and centralize experimentation in two or three laboratories. Going a step further, he raised the question of placing weapons development directly under one of the armed services.[1]

Conant's suggestion found favor with Bush. Their June 13, 1942, recommendations to Wallace, Stimson, and Marshall called for a special committee to take charge of all research and development on the military uses of fissionable material. This committee—it might be subdivided into two or three—would serve under the jurisdiction of the Joint Committee on New Weapons and Equipment of the Joint Chiefs of Staff. The idea survived the hectic organizational plans and maneuvers of late summer. When Groves took over on September 17, his instructions included the injunction to arrange for "a working committee on the application of the product." The Joint Committee on New Weapons remained sufficiently a part of the thinking for its members—General Raymond G. Moses as well as Bush and Admiral Purnell —to sign the memorandum of September 23, 1942, that detailed the functions of the Military Policy Committee.[2]

Meanwhile, some of the scientists active in the fast-neutron program had convinced themselves that a special laboratory was the only way to achieve a co-ordinated effort. Spokesman for this point of view was Robert Oppenheimer, who had accepted responsibility for fast-neutron research after Breit's resignation. Oppenheimer found the disjointed character of the work alarming. Toiling in their widely separated laboratories, the experimenters knew very little about work elsewhere. In the vital field of cross-section measurements, confusion prevailed; there were as many values as laboratories. Oppenheimer concluded that dependable results awaited bringing the team together. Then the researchers could compare findings and correct each other's errors. As his experience deepened, Oppenheimer settled in the conviction that the weapons work would have to be divorced from the Chicago project. There was too much compartmentalization there, not too little. Constant bickering and, worse, a certain irresponsibility were the consequences. The trouble appeared in sharp focus early in the fall of 1942, when it was rumored that the weapons work would follow the Metallurgical Laboratory contingent to Clinton.

Not long after Groves assumed command, Oppenheimer suggested establishing a special bomb laboratory. He stressed the necessity for free internal communication and conceded this meant tight controls to prevent leaks to the outside. The idea was attractive. Everyone recognized that ordnance experiments eventually would require an isolated proving ground.

Why not make the arrangements at the outset, particularly when there were such obvious security advantages in isolating the work on military applications at some secluded hideaway? This prospect appealed to Groves, who was instinctively security-minded. A separate weapons laboratory seemed especially desirable because news of the possibility of using deuterium to make a hydrogen bomb had spread beyond the fast-neutron group. The threat to secrecy was no chimera but a clear and present danger.[3]

CHOOSING A SITE

Inaccessibility was most important in selecting a site. There had to be some rail and road facilities, of course, but since the weapons work was not expected to require a large installation, convenience could be sacrificed for the benefits of isolation. The objective was a laboratory in the wilderness, a remote inland site where the Army could apply the most rigid of external security measures. The search soon narrowed to the southern Rockies and a string of five possibilities stretching for 200 miles across northern New Mexico from Gallup on the West to Las Vegas on the East. Surveys by the United States Engineer Office in Albuquerque reduced the choice to two locations roughly fifty miles north of that city—Jemez Springs and the Los Alamos Ranch School, a private academy for boys near Otowi.

229

One day about the middle of November, 1942, Oppenheimer set out on horseback to inspect Jemez Springs with Lieutenant Colonel W. H. Dudley of the Manhattan District and Edwin M. McMillan, just released from his radar work at Cambridge. McMillan did not think the area suitable for the new laboratory. Located deep in a narrow valley, Jemez Springs did not offer enough space for a rational layout. Besides, it was vulnerable to floods. When General Groves arrived later in the day, he agreed that the valley was unsuitable. The four proceeded by automobile to the Los Alamos School. There they found themselves on the cone of a gigantic, ages-extinct volcano. Just to the west loomed the Jemez Mountains—the rim of the ancient crater. Radiating from this jagged line of rock were dozens of deep canyons cut in the soft yellow tuff by centuries of rain and melting snow. From where the group stood, on a mesa between two canyons, their eyes followed the land eastward as it sloped down to the Rio Grande. Beyond, far in the distance, rose the majestic snow-covered peaks of the Sangre de Cristo Range. It was a spot to stir the imagination.

Santa Fe, the nearest railhead and community of any size, lay, barely visible, twenty miles to the Southeast. Leading up from the antique capital was a road so poor that, as someone remarked, it made the back-country roads of Alabama and Georgia seem like the Merritt Parkway. The water resources were questionable, and power supply caused some concern, but other factors counterbalanced these. It would have been difficult to find a place more inaccessible than this mesa with its steep rock walls and execrable roads. Plenty of space for safe testing lay deep in adjacent canyons. Most of the land required was public domain, while the rest, valuable only for grazing, would cost little. Even the rustic buildings of the school counted in the balance as a head start on housing.[4]

Groves decided quickly that this was the place. On November 23, he acquired right of entry to the lands and property of the school. Two days later, he obtained authority to acquire the site. Before the end of the month, he had assigned supervision of initial construction to the district engineer in Albuquerque. By the end of December, Groves had persuaded the University of California to take responsibility for procuring supplies and employing personnel.[5]

230

MILITARY OR CIVILIAN?

It had taken only a few weeks of search for Groves and the Military Policy Committee to conclude that Oppenheimer was the man to head Los Alamos. Only thirty-eight years of age, Oppenheimer had a distinguished career behind him. On graduating from Harvard in 1925, he journeyed abroad to pursue advanced physical studies at Cambridge, Göttingen, Leyden, and Zurich. Back in the United States, he entered an academic career and by the mid-thirties attained professorships at the California Institute of Technology in Pasadena and at the Berkeley campus of the state university. He won a reputation as a brilliant teacher. His students helped fill the ranks of American physicists. Primarily a theoretician, he reported his work on the particles of the nucleus—the mesotron was his particular interest—in some fifty notes and articles in the *Physical Review*. He had no administrative experience, but his peculiar talents for leading a group of scholars offset this disadvantage. He understood scientists, their methods, their prejudices, their temperaments. His professional stature, open manner, precision of thought, and articulate yet temperate speech equipped him admirably for the task ahead. Groves, who wanted Oppenheimer in spite of his left-wing political associations, always insisted that he did a magnificent job.[6]

The assumption at the outset was that Los Alamos would be a military laboratory. The narrowly martial, supersecret mission appeared to demand it. Conant, now scientific adviser to General Groves, had acquired no prejudices against military laboratories from his World War I duty in the Chemical Warfare Service. Oppenheimer went along with the idea and even visited the Presidio in San Francisco to take the first steps toward becoming a commissioned officer. Just how the laboratory would operate was not apparent. According to plans, the director would be perhaps a lieutenant colonel and the heads of the scientific divisions majors. Thus, there would be a chain of command, but no one spelled out the process of making scientific decisions in this military environment.

The events that frustrated these plans and assured the civilian character of Los Alamos began with Oppenheimer's efforts at recruiting. The fast-neutron group, plus McMillan, provided a somewhat lopsided cadre, but there was no easy way to bring the company to strength. Most men with the requisite skills had already taken war jobs. Oppenheimer would have to pry them away. He wanted particularly to enlist Robert F. Bacher and Isidor I. Rabi, two outstanding physicists in the Radiation Laboratory at MIT.

Conant and Bush sought to clear the way, but Alfred L. Loomis and Karl T. Compton were reluctant to part with two such irreplaceable men. Ultimately, Loomis and Compton acquiesced, but Oppenheimer still had to convince Bacher and Rabi that they ought to come.[7]

Here he ran into trouble. Bacher and Rabi feared that a military laboratory could accomplish nothing significant. Differences in rank and between commissioned and civilian researchers would breed friction and bring on a collapse of morale. They believed that military organization would introduce a dangerous rigidity. Would not an Army officer find it difficult to be wrong, to change a decision? What assurance was there that he would act on scientific grounds? The laboratory must be civilian in order to retain scientific autonomy. In the realm of security, they insisted that the scientists must decide what measures should be applied. The military should only administer the regulations. Bacher's and Rabi's attitude was a real obstacle, Oppenheimer reported to Conant. Perhaps he could make the laboratory go without meeting their objections, but at best he would encounter dangerous delay. Physicists had such a sense of solidarity that the project would fail to attract the men from MIT. Those who already had planned to come might reconsider or bring misgivings that would reduce their usefulness.[8]

It was clearly necessary to assuage the fears of scientists. Conant's reaction was to draft a letter Oppenheimer could show the men he was trying to enlist for service at Los Alamos. Signed by both Conant and Groves on February 25, 1943, the letter stated the objective as the development and manufacture of a secret instrument of war, "Projectile S-1-T." The laboratory would first undertake certain experimental studies in science, engineering, and ordnance; then it would conduct some difficult large-scale trials involving highly dangerous material. During the period of laboratory experiment, organization would be strictly civilian. Personnel, procurement, and other arrangements would proceed under a contract between the War Department and the University of California. When the time for the final phase arrived (not before January 1, 1944), the scientific and engineering staff would be commissioned officers. This was necessary because of the inherent hazards and the need for special conditions to maintain secrecy. Although the Army would offer commissions to many civilians employed during the first period, no one obligated himself to become an officer.

The Conant-Groves letter explained that the laboratory was part of a larger project which the President had placed in a special category and had assigned the highest priority. General Groves had over-all executive responsibility under a Military Policy Committee. Oppenheimer was accountable for the scientific work. It was his duty to maintain strict secrecy among the civilian personnel. In determining policies and courses of action, he would be guided by the advice of his scientific staff. He was to keep Groves and Conant informed. Conant was available at any time for consultation on policy and research. Through him, the staff had complete access to the scientific world.

Los Alamos would have a military post, but its function would be ancillary to that of the laboratory. The commanding officer, who would report directly to Groves, was to maintain suitable living conditions for civilian personnel, prevent trespassing, and maintain what internal secrecy precautions Oppenheimer considered necessary.[9]

The letter of February 25, which served as a sort of charter for Los Alamos, seemed only a partial victory for the protesting scientists. It promised a civilian laboratory for ten months—no more. Neither Bacher nor Rabi were happy about final military control. Bacher answered the call to Los Alamos with a letter of acceptance which he stated was also his resignation, effective the day the laboratory became a military installation. Rabi did not join the staff but, pleased with the way the system worked in practice, he served as a consultant. In the long run, the advocates of a civilian laboratory won a complete victory. Groves never acted on the plans to militarize.

STARTING POINT

During the first three months of 1943, while contractors struggled to put the most essential facilities in shape, Oppenheimer faced a tremendous administrative task. Recruiting topflight scientists was a mission he could not delegate. To university, government, and private laboratories he went, trying to convey the interest, urgency, and feasibility of the work at Los Alamos. Planning the laboratory was a duty he could share. On organization, buildings, equipment, and all the countless details incident to creating a research center in the middle of nowhere, John H. Manley, Robert Serber, Edward Teller, and Edwin McMillan gave important help.

On March 15, Oppenheimer arrived at Santa Fe with a few members of his staff. During the next two weeks, the team assembled. The hard core was the fast-neutron group—from California, Minnesota, Stanford, and Purdue. Princeton sent the largest contingent, released by the cancellation of the isotron. California furnished the next largest increment and the Metallurgical

Laboratory the third. Columbia, Iowa State, MIT, and the National Bureau of Standards were among the other laboratories that lost valued workers to Los Alamos.

Despite recruiting difficulties, the people were ready before the housing on "the Hill." Scientists and their families crowded together in dude ranches near Santa Fe. Each day staff members had to reach the site over the miserable road. They could not yet obtain food there. They could communicate with the project office at Santa Fe only over a noisy Forest Service line. The laboratories were unfinished. Even the most basic equipment was not ready, and minor structural changes meant maddening delays. But soon the specialized equipment for nuclear research began to arrive. From Princeton came three carloads of apparatus, from Wisconsin two Van de Graaff generators, and from Illinois a Cockcroft-Walton accelerator. Harvard contributed a cyclotron. When the contractor laid the bottom pole piece of its magnet on April 14, the physicists could feel that a laboratory actually was in the making.[10]

233

More important than equipment was the technical understanding the assembling scientists brought with them. They knew that theory and experiment had thrown considerable light on the properties of uranium 235, even though important areas of uncertainty remained. Although they were aware of the scant data on plutonium, the new element fired their hopes. A plutonium bomb promised to require less metal, and it seemed possible to produce plutonium more rapidly than uranium 235. The greatest gap in the staff's understanding was the nuclear explosion itself—its nature, the methods of initiating it, and its destructive effect. Here Los Alamos had to rely entirely on theory. Experiments had been impossible.

An explosive chain reaction depended on each fissioning nucleus emitting a sufficient number of neutrons. Experiments with slow neutrons had indicated that an average of 2.2 was to be expected from U-235. Physicists considered this value essentially accurate, but they wanted to check it by bombarding samples with the fast neutrons important in the bomb. For proof that plutonium emitted neutrons, they would have to wait until a sample large enough to permit measurements was available. However, deductions based on the nuclear structure of element 94 led them to anticipate confidently that the essential particles would be released and in sufficient number.

A second factor controlling inherent explosibility was the speed with which the reaction developed. The critical measurement here was the time elapsing between the collision of a neutron with a nucleus and the emission of daughter neutrons. If this interval were not incredibly short—less than one hundred-millionth of a second—the mass would blow itself apart and the reaction would be quenched before the liberation of enough energy to make it all worthwhile. Theoretical calculations indicated that neutron emission occurred with sufficient speed, but no one had proved it experimentally.

Even if a favorable number of neutrons were released rapidly enough, no chain reaction and no explosion could take place unless the piece of metal was so large that neutrons could not escape from its surface at a rate that would thwart the breeding of successive generations. To determine this critical mass, Los Alamos would have to ascertain not only the number of neutrons per fission and the density of the metal, but the details on the probable fate of a neutron in a piece of uranium 235 or plutonium. Specifically, what were the relative probabilities that a neutron would cause fission in a nucleus, be absorbed without fission, or simply bounce off? In the latter case, what would be the speed and distribution of the recoiling particles?

The physicists thought they could find ways to reduce the critical mass. Possibly they could incorporate uranium 235 in some compound that would facilitate the chain reaction. Perhaps they could surround the fissionable material with a tamper, a case of some very dense substance that would reflect neutrons back into the active mass. Success for some such device seemed especially important, for since the first of 1943, measurements at Minneapolis and Madison had brought a doubling of the critical-mass estimates for U-235. This threatened to force enlargement of the isotope-separation plants or to delay the day when there would be enough metal for a bomb.

While dependable calculations of critical mass were fundamental, the theoreticians saw that building a useful bomb called for a more sophisticated concept, the effective mass. They recognized that good efficiency—liberating an appreciable amount of the total energy before the reaction stopped—required using more than just enough metal for a chain reaction. The shape of the metal was a factor, too, for the critical mass would be smallest when the active material was spherical. Should it be necessary to depart from this conformation, more than the theoretical critical mass would be required just to attain a minimum effect. Sound decisions on how much metal each bomb must contain demanded much work on basic nuclear constants, much theorizing.

Given a critical mass, the chain reaction would start. Physicists saw that the active material would have to be kept in separate, subcritical pieces until the moment an explosion was desired. Then the pieces would have to come together almost instantaneously. But could this be accomplished quickly enough? A stray neutron might set off a reaction during assembly—after a critical mass had been attained, but before the optimum configuration had been reached. An ineffective, wasteful fizzle would result. This possibility was real, for neutrons were abundant. Enough were present in cosmic rays alone to cause detonation in any supercritical mass within a fraction of a second. Besides, neutrons were known to appear spontaneously in both uranium 235 and plutonium. The gravest danger lay in the fact that all fissionable materials gave off alpha particles. Should these minute bodies collide with the nucleus of some light element present as an impurity, neutrons would be emitted. Should the impurities be too abundant, the number of neutrons would rule out an explosion.

Two ways of countering the threat of predetonation came readily to mind. One was to purify the metal and thus reduce the neutron background. The other was to bring the subcritical parts together so rapidly that the chance of a premature reaction would narrow to the vanishing point. The best way of accomplishing this lightning-like assembly seemed using an artillery field piece to fire one less-than-critical part into another. The scientists were reasonably certain that a gun would work for purified uranium 235. Indeed, they thought its neutron background might become so low as to delay the moment of detonation. To counter this possibility, they considered it necessary to develop an initiator. Such a device—consisting, perhaps, of an alpha-emitter and a light element like beryllium—would release a burst of neutrons when the mass reached its most favorable shape. For plutonium, a very strong alpha-emitter, the worries all lay in the direction of predetonation. The gun would work for 94 only if fantastically high purity specifications could be attained and only if the projectile could be fired at the extreme upper limits of practical artillery velocities.

235

Thinking centered around the gun method of assembly for both metals. Another alternative, however, offered some promise. Why not surround a mass of metal subcritical in shape with a layer of high explosive in such a way that when the charge detonated, it would burst inward and compress the active material into a critical conformation? Unfortunately, this concept— descriptively called implosion—was new, and no one knew much about its theory and application.

Nor did anyone understand very well the effects of an atomic explosion. The great difficulty was to know how to extrapolate available data on small high-explosive bombs. Of course, one way of achieving immense destructive power was to develop a hydrogen bomb. The energy liberated by a thermonuclear weapon would dwarf the power of a mere uranium or plutonium device. A hydrogen bomb was no closer to reality than in July, 1942, but careful calculations had set to rest fears that it might ignite the atmosphere. In any event, the super weapon depended on perfecting a nuclear bomb to trigger it.[11]

PLANNING THE WORK

The first task was to block out the research needed to fill the great gaps and uncertainties in the technical picture. A planning board began to meet at Los Alamos on March 30, 1943. One of its first acts was to sanction a short course of lectures to indoctrinate the scientific personnel. The talks, delivered by Serber early in April, reviewed comprehensively the nuclear-physics background. The planning group devoted the last half of the same month to a series of conferences designed to complete the technical orientation and to prepare a program of research. Three consultants imported for the occasion took part. So did a reviewing committee appointed by Groves after a check with Oppenheimer. Headed by Warren K. Lewis, it was a distinguished group, well versed in the problems that confronted the laboratory—Edwin L. Rose, an ordnance specialist, John H. Van Vleck, a theoretical physicist, and E. Bright Wilson, a Harvard chemist and explosives expert. Richard C. Tolman served as secretary. A physicist, Tolman had for some weeks been working with Conant as an adviser to Groves.[12]

The conferees hammered out research schedules for the next few months. Fermi, above all a great experimentalist, contributed substantially to the plans for physical investigations. These had to center around tests to confirm the explosive potential of uranium 235 and plutonium and to furnish data for calculating their critical masses. As soon as samples were available, as soon as equipment was operating, this work would have to be pressed to a conclusion. One of the advantages expected for a special laboratory was better co-ordination. To make sure this materialized, the planning board outlined an auxiliary program to ascertain and standardize the best techniques of measurement. As for chemical research, the board decided to direct it largely to study of alpha-neutron reactions and the methods of analyzing, purifying, and preparing active and tamper materials for experimental use.[13]

Supplementing the planning work at the April conferences was the report Lewis' reviewing committee submitted on May 10. The committee found progress satisfactory, and it approved the preliminary experimental schedule. The work in the offing, however, required considerable expansion of personnel and facilities. For one thing, Los Alamos should take over the purification of plutonium, since metal used experimentally at the site would have to be repurified. The Los Alamos chemists might as well assume responsibility for the entire process. The committee stressed the importance of metallurgy in preparing materials for fabrication. Since the methods used should not impair purity but even contribute to it, the metallurgists should work closely with the chemists. Perhaps the most important recommendation was the call for an engineering division. The Lewis reviewers recognized that detailed specifications of the final weapon were still distant, but they believed that the scientists already had indicated sufficiently the questions demanding answers. Engineering research was necessary for design selection and development of safety, arming, firing, and detonating devices. Oppenheimer had seen as early as March that ordnance engineering needed special emphasis. Now his views had support from men who saw the situation in all its ramifications.[14]

Groves accepted the Lewis recommendations in substance, thus destroying the original concept of Los Alamos as a small physical laboratory. Purification would require a considerable force of chemists, analysts, and helpers. Metallurgy would involve still others, while engineering would demand at least as many men as comprised the entire original staff. Had this expansion been fully foreseen back in November, the choice might not have fallen on that lonely New Mexican mesa.

ORGANIZING THE LABORATORY

By the middle of the summer of 1943, laboratory organization was almost complete. Four divisions were to share the technical work. Heading the Theoretical Division was Hans A. Bethe. Born in Strassburg, Germany, in 1902, Bethe had joined the physics faculty at Cornell in 1935. Now an American citizen, he was fresh from the Radiation Laboratory at MIT. The Experimental Physics Division had Bacher as its chief. Three years the junior of Bethe, he too came by way of Cornell and radar. Chemistry and Metallurgy was led by Joseph W. Kennedy, an able young disciple of Glenn T. Seaborg. Cyril S. Smith, an industrial scientist glad to escape irksome Washington duty with the NDRC, had immediate responsibility for the division's metallurgical work. Partly because of Kennedy's extreme youth—he was only twenty-six— and partly because the chemical and metallurgical problems at Los Alamos had so close a relation to those of the pile project, Groves and Conant persuaded Charles A. Thomas to co-ordinate the work at Los Alamos, Chicago, Berkeley, and Ames. Thomas, who directed research for the Monsanto Chemical Company, had the industrial experience that the operations at Los Alamos would require.[15] Navy Captain William S. Parsons was in charge of the fourth division, Ordnance, which would carry the engineering burden. Parsons had participated in the early development of radar, had served as staff gunnery officer of a destroyer command, and had been experimental officer at the Naval Proving Ground at Dahlgren, Virginia. Most recently, he had seen duty as a special assistant to Bush on the combat use of the proximity fuze.

237

Responsibility for over-all direction remained with Oppenheimer. His primary duty was to make the technical program succeed, but there was a discouraging mass of nontechnical administrative detail to claim his time. It was important to order housekeeping arrangements so that they facilitated research and development, but it hardly required the attention of a man whose talents were needed in a larger sphere. Oppenheimer's position became more difficult when Edward U. Condon, who had been brought from the Westinghouse Research Laboratories to be associate director, clashed with the military authorities and left the project. Recognizing that something would have to be done, the Lewis committee recommended the establishment of an administrative office under some competent individual reporting to Oppenheimer. It took more than six months to find the right man, but in the meantime the most urgent needs were met by special assistants who took charge of personnel, construction, and liaison with the post administration. By July, 1944, this arrangement had expanded into a competent staff which managed the nontechnical phases of administration.

For counsel, Oppenheimer could turn to a Governing Board consisting of division leaders, general administrative officers, and persons who served important technical liaison functions. Though this body at first spent perhaps two-thirds of its time on housing, construction, security, and personnel, its main concern was the planning and conduct of the technical effort. It served as a means for seeing the laboratory's work as an entity and for relating it to that in progress elsewhere under the aegis of the Manhattan District. It considered the data of the experimentalists and the calculations of the theoreticians, translating these into specifications for the chemists, the metallurgists, and the ordnance specialists. The Governing Board became more than an advisory group. It functioned as a directorate in which Oppenheimer and his principal staff members collaborated in making decisions.[16]

Two more organizations took shape in the first months at Los Alamos. One was the Co-ordinating Council, which consisted essentially of group leaders from the various divisions. It would keep the members of the laboratory informed of current developments, administrative and technical, and provide communication between the staff and the Governing Board.[17] The other organization was the Colloquium. At the May 6 meeting of the Governing Board, Bethe suggested regular colloquia for the entire staff once every week or two. This idea met with favor, and weekly sessions began in June. Oppenheimer led off at the first meeting with a comprehensive review.

The Colloquium was the antithesis of compartmentalization. It alarmed General Groves. He could appreciate the value of having perhaps twenty or thirty top scientists see the weapons work in the entire, but a wholesale dropping of the barriers was quite another thing. When he spoke to Oppenheimer about it, the physicist not only avowed his commitment to the policy but defended its principle. Information should go, he argued, to anyone who could work more effectively with it or maintain better security if he knew the significance of his labors. But in deference to Groves's views, Oppenheimer restricted the number eligible to attend the Colloquium and established a vouching procedure. It addition, he tried to maintain an academic tone in the discussions and to avoid matters that, whatever their importance in other ways, were of little scientific interest.[18]

The concern over security touched off by the Colloquium went straight to the top of the atomic energy project. On June 24, 1943, Groves raised the issue with the Military Policy Committee. The committee decided that Bush, if he found opportunity, should persuade the President to send Oppenheimer a letter emphasizing security. That very day, the President called Bush in for lunch and questioned him closely on progress. Bush seized the chance to suggest a letter, not just to Oppenheimer but to the other scientific leaders as well. Roosevelt thought this an excellent idea. Two communications from the White House were the result. One, drafted by Conant, went directly to Oppenheimer for relaying to the scientists at Los Alamos. The other, essentially the same, went to Groves with the request that he convey its contents to the other project leaders. In both, Roosevelt stated that he had ordered every precaution to insure security. He was certain that the scientists recognized the need for extraordinary restrictions. Coupling this polite injunction with praise, he expressed his appreciation of the willingness to accept dangers and personal sacrifices and his confidence that American science would be equal to the challenge it faced.[19]

Compartmentalization always applied, quite logically, with greater rigor against the interchange of information between sites than to discussions between workers on different facets at any one installation. Groves adopted this practice on security grounds but also because it kept the scientific leaders concentrating on their own responsibilities. The Manhattan project was so packed with scientific interest that he found compartmentalization a useful device for preventing men like Lawrence, Compton, and Oppenheimer from "frittering from one thing to another." [20]

Since, however, Los Alamos was to fashion the output of Clinton and Hanford into a weapon, a certain amount of liaison was necessary, particularly in the case of plutonium, if the job was to be done on time. Groves spelled out rules for exchanging information between Chicago and Los Alamos on June 17, 1943, just at the time of the Colloquium crisis. He informed Compton and Oppenheimer that the only justifiable purpose for interchange was to benefit the work at both laboratories. So imperative were the demands of military security that some information, even though it might further the work, was not subject to intersite transfer. In this category lay certain kinds of data on production piles, weapons, and time schedules. All contact was to be between authorized persons by specified procedures, though there was provision for any changes that time proved warranted. The contact authorized with Oak Ridge was even less extensive. In October, 1943, Oppenheimer asked Groves for permission to detail someone from the Los Alamos staff to report on the pile and the electromagnetic plant. Since operations would start at both facilities before long, and since the rate of production would determine much of the schedule at Los Alamos, it was important to have good information. No amount of paper estimates, he argued, could replace first-hand reports on actual operating conditions and prospects. This led to an arrangement the next month under which Oppenheimer himself visited the Tennessee plants. His visit served the purpose, and by the spring of 1944, when the flow of fissionable material actually started, scheduling difficulties became less bothersome.[21]

Scientists tended to criticize the restrictions on intersite liaison. In practice, the limitations were less severe than on paper, for when workers transferred to Los Alamos from other laboratories, they carried with them their accumulated information and experience. Wartime leadership had to strike a balance between speed and security. Criticism from both extremes was to be expected, but the procedures for exchanging information between the sites were understandable in view of the relaxation of the customary barriers at Los Alamos.

239

DETERMINING THE NUCLEAR SPECIFICATIONS

Once the details of staffing and organizing were in hand, at least for a time, and the rudiments of a laboratory were in place, the real labors could begin. Priority went to the fission bomb, not the super, as the hydrogen weapon was dubbed cryptically and familiarly. Nevertheless, a small group of physicists continued to investigate the super. They could do much, particularly the first year, without interfering with the main chance. When the unknowns were still so great that it was difficult to predict what might be useful, it seemed worthwhile to explore. Earl A. Long, a chemist from the University of Missouri, set up a cryogenic laboratory and studied the liquefaction of deuterium. The Ohio State University accepted a subcontract to investigate the properties of the liquid. By February, 1944, the theoreticians had concluded that heating deuterium to its ignition temperature would be more difficult than anticipated. To find a way would take so much time that they no longer could consider the hydrogen weapon a possibility for the war. Oppenheimer restricted the work, though he did not drop it completely. As Tolman reported to Groves, "super cannot be completely forgotten if we take seriously our responsibilities for the permanent defense of the U. S. A." [22]

240

The logical start for work on the fission bomb was to remove the remaining uncertainty about intrinsic explosibility. This was a matter of particular concern in the case of plutonium, for despite the enormous construction effort under way by the summer of 1943, it had not been established that plutonium emitted neutrons on fission. In July, John H. Williams' Electrostatic Generator Group conducted the first nuclear experiments at Los Alamos on a sample of less than 200 micrograms which Seaborg had brought from Chicago on the Santa Fe in his suitcase. Measurements by different methods indicated not only that neutrons indeed were emitted, but that their number was greater than in uranium. While the promoters of plutonium had been sanguine all along, it was comforting to see theory confirmed in the laboratory. Another result contributing to peace of mind came in November, when Robert R. Wilson's Cyclotron Group established that most of the neutrons from uranium 235 were emitted in less than one-billionth of a second. This provided ample margin for a weapon of good efficiency. Now there could be little doubt that a bomb was feasible.[23]

With practicality confirmed from the standpoint of basic physics, it was necessary to set precisely the nuclear specifications for each type of weapon. First, an estimate had to be made of the amount of active material that would be required. This information was vital to those responsible for planning the production plants and for estimating when the bomb might be used against the enemy. Next, those who were to design the weapon itself needed information on the sizes and shapes of the active parts and on the velocities at which they would have to be assembled. These factors also de-

FOUR LOS ALAMOS SCIENTISTS
Hans A. Bethe
George B. Kistiakowsky

Enrico Fermi
John von Neumann

CAPTAIN WILLIAM S. PARSONS / Naval officer who headed the Ordnance Division at Los Alamos.

RICHARD C. TOLMAN / Dean of the Graduate School, California Institute of Technology, and special adviser to General Groves.

termined the external conformation of the bomb, a set of dimensions needed to select the type of airplane to be used for delivery and to plan any bomb-bay modifications that might be necessary.

Determining nuclear specifications was a job for the experimental physicists. One of their most valuable findings came in December, 1943, in connection with studies of uranium spontaneous-fission rates. Emilio Segrè obtained results on natural uranium in reasonable agreement with those he had derived at Berkeley, but in the case of uranium 235, the number of fissions recorded at Los Alamos was much higher. This was encouraging, not alarming. The only possible explanation for the increased activity in the lighter isotope was neutrons from cosmic rays, which were more intense at Los Alamos, 7,300 feet above the sea. The phenomenon had been concealed in natural uranium because cosmic-ray neutrons were too slow to cause fission in 238. Now it was clear that much of what had been thought spontaneous fission was attributable to another source. This simplified the construction of a uranium bomb. Find some way to screen out the cosmic rays, and you could reduce materially the velocities required for assembly.[24]

241

Measuring cross sections was the most laborious of the tasks that fell to Bacher and his lieutenants—Williams, Manley, Segrè, and Wilson. Calculations of critical mass and efficiency depended on the probabilities for fission, capture, and scattering. It took an incredible amount of effort to determine these. Since a small difference in neutron energy sometimes meant a large difference in cross section, dependable values had to be ascertained for all the energies at which there were appreciable numbers of fission neutrons.

Indispensable to such measurements was the ability to produce neutrons of known energies. Ingeniously, the experimenters perfected the techniques of bombarding light-element targets with particles from their accelerators—the cyclotron, the Van de Graaffs, and the Cockcroft-Walton. They developed photoneutron sources, in which a deuterium compound or beryllium exposed to gamma rays liberated neutrons. Before they were through, the Los Alamos physicists could obtain fairly well-defined velocities over the whole energy spectrum up to 3,000,000 electron volts. Just as important was instrumentation for detecting the reactions and recording the results. The principal method was to count pulses in an ionization chamber. Since neutrons themselves did not produce much ionization, it was necessary to depend on the ions yielded by secondary particles. An electric current moved these to collecting electrodes, where they registered minute electrical pulses which then had to be amplified and fed into a counter. Because the frequency of the pulses was too high for recording by mechanical means, they had to be consolidated by an electronic device to a rate within the capability of the counting equipment. Under the leadership of Darol K. Froman, Hans H. Staub, and Bruno B. Rossi, much resourceful work was done in this area made so difficult by the scale and speed of the processes.

By the winter of 1943–44, the physicists had accumulated a substantial amount of helpful data. The first results on fission cross sections were comparative, for it was easy to expose uranium 235 and plutonium foils of known masses to the same neutron flow and to measure the relative reaction. At the outset, absolute values for even uranium 235 were in question, but as the techniques of producing neutrons of known speed advanced, it was possible to achieve reliable measurements at numerous points across the energy spectrum. Capture cross-section measurements yielded essential information on the characteristics of the fissionable substances and of the materials that might be employed in the tamper or other parts of the bomb assembly. One very encouraging outgrowth of this work was a strong indication that more neutrons might be emitted when high-energy neutrons caused fission. The Experimental Division also pursued studies of scattering phenomena. Since it was important to select the tamper material early, the first investigations were to determine the capacity of possible materials for reflecting neutrons back into the core. Later, when back-scattering measurements were complete for a large number of substances, the physicists concluded that neutrons which scattered inelastically—which recoiled with lessened energy after colliding with nuclei—would play a more appreciable role in the explosive chain reaction than they at first had believed. This led Bacher to set up experiments to study scattering as a function of neutron energy.[25]

242

The data provided by the experimental physicists were fundamental, but it remained for Bethe and his theoreticians—Teller, Serber, Victor F. Weisskopf, Richard P. Feynman, and Donald A. Flanders—to set the nuclear specifications for a bomb. Here their most difficult task was to understand the diffusion of neutrons in a mass. They could write an integral equation which would take account of the variations in neutron speed, the dependence of the scattering and fission cross sections on velocity, and the anisotropic nature of scattering. If they could solve it, they would know the exact neutron distribution. They could derive an answer of sorts by assuming that the diffusion of neutrons was analogous to the diffusion of heat, but this was highly inaccurate. While the equation as it stood had no exact solution, the theoretical physicists obtained better results by postulating certain restrictive conditions—single-velocity neutrons, no energy loss from collisions with nuclei in core and tamper, and isotropic scattering. Another responsibility of the Theoretical Division was efficiency calculations. This was infinitely complex, for the theory of efficiency required following the life histories of neutrons in a mass of fissionable and tamper material while it was being transformed in the unbelievable speed of the explosive reaction.[26]

By the summer of 1944, substantially more was known about the nuclear characteristics of a bomb than twelve months before. Experiments had shown that a tamper was the best method of reducing the mass and had indicated the most suitable materials from which to fashion it. Though detailed investigation of damage and other effects of a nuclear explosion had not progressed far, confidence prevailed that the destructive effect would be great enough to justify the effort.[27]

Just how much fissionable material would be needed for an effective weapon continued a matter of considerable uncertainty. On February 4, 1944, General Groves reported to the President that the amount was unknown and must remain so until Los Alamos had enough for physical measurements. Meanwhile, research was constantly changing the estimates. At the moment, it appeared that an efficient bomb would require from eight to eighty kilograms of uranium 235. Though the General did not mention plutonium, it was always assumed that less of that metal would be necessary. In June, after a visit to Los Alamos, Groves made estimates to the Military Policy Committee that lowered the maximums considerably—so much so that some present considered him too optimistic. Actually, the fairly wide range of his forecasts reflected not the inability of the scientists at Los Alamos to make reasonably close estimates but rather their doubts about the method of assembly. If they could make implosion work, the amount of active material required would be quite small. They knew enough about the nuclear requirements of a uranium 235 gun weapon in March to state its specifications with some assurance. Unfortunately, this type of bomb, inherently wasteful, would need comparatively large quantities of the precious metal. The more uranium it took, the longer the time before it was ready. To the men responsible for decision, men who saw completed weapons in terms of national security and the lives of fighting men, it was important to know how small a quantity of fissionable material would be effective and when. The physicists had furnished specifications for one type of weapon. The spread in the estimates was primarily a reflection of the desire to achieve a bomb more quickly.[28]

243

CHEMISTRY AND METALLURGY

While the physicists were seeking to determine the size and shape of a bomb, Kennedy's men, reinforced by the microchemical and micrometallurgical studies of Seaborg's researchers at Chicago, were hard at work on techniques of processing active and tamper materials. There were two major tasks here: purifying the output of Clinton and Hanford and reducing it to metal. Purification was the most difficult operation as well as the most crucial, for on it rested the hope of coping with the predetonation menace.

The purity requirements for uranium, only one-third as rigorous as for plutonium, caused little concern. As a consequence, the chemists did not work intensively on uranium until December, 1943. Even then, it was plutonium that called forth their efforts. With gram amounts from the Clinton pile expected to arrive in two or three months, it seemed wise to curtail the exacting microchemical studies of plutonium purification then in progress and to gain experience with a uranium stand-in. The resulting investigations, done to plutonium rather than uranium standards, threw light on several methods, all based on a series of wet and dry chemistry steps. Gradually, the chemists acquired information and experience against the time when large-scale operations would be the order of the day.

Intensive direct work on plutonium became possible in the late winter and spring of 1944, when significant quantities began to arrive from Clinton. This product, as well as that which came later from Hanford, was a viscous mixture of decontaminated and partially purified nitrates. Like uranium, it had first to go through a wet process. The chemists investigated many procedures and by July, 1944, had this stretch of the road to purity in good shape. They had settled on a series of precipitations dependent on oxidation states, an ether extraction step, and then a final precipitation. Summer also saw the erection of apparatus on a one- and eight-gram scale, completely enclosed to guard against the extreme toxicity of plutonium. Thus, the chemists had completed a large part of their assignment. The dry process, necessary for final purification, was still in its formative stage, but confidence ran high.

Reducing uranium 235 and plutonium to metal was in itself an arduous task. The Los Alamos metallurgists investigated electrolytic and centrifugal methods but finally settled on a stationary-bomb technique similar to that developed for natural uranium at Iowa State. Though the two processes were basically the same, the work at the weapons laboratory had its peculiar features. Since plutonium was so reactive a material, it was difficult to find suitable crucibles and liners. Smith and his men had to devote an appalling amount of time to finding refractory materials that would not introduce contaminants. During the summer of 1944, cerium sulphide, which the chemistry group at Berkeley had studied, seemed best. It had, however, a weakness—susceptibility to thermal shock. Another difficulty unique to Los Alamos was the high degree of metal recovery required in handling the precious uranium 235 and plutonium. A major step toward achieving close to 100-per-cent recovery was the discovery that an iodine booster increased significantly the heat attainable in the reduction bomb.

Once significant quantities of plutonium metal became available in April, 1944, the metallurgists could begin studying its physical properties. There was confusion here, for samples of different densities had been detected earlier at the Metallurgical Laboratory. For a while, the presence of slightly different alloys appeared responsible, but Los Alamos soon established that the real explanation for the inconsistent data was that plutonium existed in varying allotropic forms—forms with different crystalline structures and other distinguishing characteristics. Shortly, two such states were identified, but it took some time fully to appreciate the complexity of the situation and the trouble it would cause.[29] In June, 1944, the chemistry and metallurgy situation looked good. On the thirteenth, Charles A. Thomas sent Groves and Conant a report that exuded confidence. Groves was so encouraged that he reported to the Military Policy Committee that progress was "quite satisfactory and fully up to expectations." It seemed that one of the major objectives, pure plutonium, had been all but attained.[30]

PROBLEMS OF ASSEMBLY

One of the first decisions at Los Alamos was what emphasis to give the various methods of assembling a supercritical mass. At the April, 1943, conferences, Seth H. Neddermeyer, a CIT physicist, offered specific proposals for developing implosion. Though convinced by theoretical analysis of its superiority, he was unable to convey his enthusiasm to others. This was not surprising, for to depend on implosion meant proceeding in an area where there was no experience and where many unforeseen and perhaps insoluble difficulties were sure to arise. The gun method was a much better risk. Men had been manufacturing and firing artillery for centuries. A vast accumulation of ordnance data was at hand, and the experienced craftsmen in the nation's arsenals needed only orders and blueprints to turn to their lathes. Not surprisingly, priority went to the gun. It alone seemed sound enough to justify proving and engineering. The laboratory did not ignore implosion, but it did not support studies at a level commensurate with the obstacles to be surmounted. Captain Parsons, an experienced gunnery officer, maintained that implosion would never be reliable enough for field use. For several months, the faith of Neddermeyer alone kept this novel approach alive.[31]

245

To put the gun program in motion, it was necessary to acquire some cannon for testing. Despite the many unknowns, bold guesses made it possible to formulate specifications for two howitzers, one for a uranium bomb and the other for a plutonium weapon. The performance requested was in the range of standard ballistic practice, but some requirements were outside previous experience. One of these was tubes of unusually light weight. This was at odds with the demand for high velocities, but Edwin L. Rose, who had been introduced to Los Alamos as a member of Lewis' reviewing committee, made a number of suggestions that indicated success for a gun built to fire very close to the limit of its strength. Most important, designers did not have to worry about durability. They did not have to plan a field piece rugged enough to be safe after hundreds of firings in battle. They only needed a gun that would hold together for one shot.

Since the predetonation phenomenon imposed an extremely high velocity on the plutonium gun, the laboratory decided to concentrate first on that type. If the staff could make a plutonium gun work, a uranium model would be simple. No time was lost. Tolman procured data through his NDRC connections. The Naval Gun Design Section went into action. Forgings were ordered in September, 1943, and not long after, the Naval Gun Factory in Washington, D. C., took up the task of fabrication.[32]

While the guns were being manufactured, Los Alamos made arrangements for testing them. The laboratory sought out additional workers and equipped a proving ground. In September, the Ordnance Division began test firing with a naval anti-aircraft gun. This permitted the researchers to try the behavior of various propellants and to perfect their methods of observing and recording. The work moved forward quickly after March, 1944, when the first two plutonium guns arrived. McMillan, deputy for Parsons on the gun, led studies of propellants, pressures, strains, and velocities. By early July, he had established conclusively the soundness of the design. The testing crews had been able to deform the tube only by running the breech pressure far beyond the requirements.

Meanwhile, reports from the physicists on the nuclear qualities of uranium permitted setting specifications for a uranium gun that were considerably less exacting than the original. In March, 1944, Ordnance requisitioned two such units from the Naval Gun Factory. With the requirements relaxed, there was even less concern than before.[33]

246

Implosion research began immediately after the April, 1943, conferences, when Neddermeyer visited the Navy's Explosives Research Laboratory at Bruceton, Pennsylvania, to familiarize himself with the techniques of studying high explosives. Back at Los Alamos, he celebrated the Fourth of July by beginning tests in an arroyo in the mesa just south of the laboratory. His procedure was to detonate masses of tamped TNT packed around steel of various shapes. Since the only way of analyzing the results was to recover the imploded object, there was a sharp limit on the amount of explosives that could be used and, consequently, on the velocities that could be attained. Nevertheless, the early shots were sufficient to indicate the difficulty of achieving a symmetrical implosion and of controlling the ultimate conformation of the metal. Unless this could be done, performance would be uncertain and efficiency dubious.[34]

In the summer of 1943, implosion lay outside the main stream at Los Alamos. Neddermeyer was discouraged. A lone-wolf type, he did not fight back effectively. Not until autumn did implosion begin to seem more attractive. The change came during a visit by John von Neumann, a native of Budapest currently in residence at the Princeton Institute for Advanced Study. A noted mathematician, he had been studying shock waves for the NDRC.

Von Neumann's experience with the shaped charges employed in armor-piercing projectiles had convinced him that a more predictable result could be obtained with higher implosion velocities. Besides, would not great speeds of assembly wipe out all worry about predetonation? The more the men at Los Alamos considered von Neumann's ideas, the more promising they seemed. Teller suggested that fissionable material, subjected to the almost infinite pressure of a successful implosion, would attain such compression that its density would be substantially higher than normal. This meant that a quantity of metal subcritical at normal pressure could sustain an explosive chain reaction.

Neddermeyer's pet project now appeared in a most enchanting light. Implosion would require less active material. The first bomb would be ready earlier and reserves to support it accumulated more rapidly without making any changes in the capacities of the plants at Oak Ridge and Hanford. If Los Alamos could perfect implosion, it could abandon the difficult and perhaps impossible efforts to achieve extremely pure plutonium. Before the end of October, 1943, Oppenheimer and the division chiefs had decided they must push implosion aggressively. Groves and Conant agreed. The advantages of abandoning the plutonium-purification work were evident. The chance to get by on less metal justified the decision to go ahead with the costly electro-magnetic plant despite its limited output. It meant, if all went well, saving months in the drive for the bomb.[35]

Unfortunately, it did not seem possible to accelerate the implosion effort by merely expanding the existing organization. Though the men involved were somewhat short on knowledge of explosives, the real difficulty was tension between Neddermeyer and his chief, Parsons. Misunderstandings had developed early out of the Captain's lack of confidence in implosion. Though now he had committed himself to a vigorous try, some doubted that he believed it would be successful. The men in the implosion group, academic in background and accustomed to independent work, chafed under the naval officer's detailed supervision. Parsons, in turn, thought them unco-operative and impractical. No one was particularly at fault, but it was not a happy situation.

Oppenheimer concluded that the only hope for getting implosion off dead center was to find some new man who could ease the tension. George B. Kistiakowsky was the obvious choice. The Kiev-born Harvard chemist had made explosives his special field. He possessed not only superb technical knowledge and experience, but the qualities of personality the situation demanded. He was reluctant to leave his post as chief of the NDRC Explosives Division, but Conant convinced him he was needed. Already a consultant to Los Alamos, Kistiakowsky joined the staff in February, 1944, as Parsons' deputy for implosion. It was a good arrangement. Kistiakowsky could work with the scientists, while Parsons was free to look after the nonnuclear features of the weapon.[36]

Despite the new emphasis on implosion, nothing much happened in the winter of 1943–44. The theoretical physicists sought to analyze what occurred within the imploding mass. Though by the first of March they were deep in a promising effort to solve the equations that would elucidate this phenomenon, they were not yet able to predict the results of an implosion or to say how to make the assembly symmetrical. Since expanded work on implosion required large quantities of high explosives of varying shapes, it was

247

necessary to build facilities for casting and trimming. Construction began promptly, but when the February deadline rolled by, the plant was not complete.

Everyone concerned with planning the intensified program had seen that the development of implosion would require extraordinary testing techniques. It would be necessary to discover what was happening inside a violent reaction in an interval so brief that finite human senses were helpless. At first, the experimenters could do no more than continue imploding steel dummies and trying to draw conclusions from the recovered objects. In search of more satisfactory results, they spent the winter in applying intricate electronic and photographic techniques. These yielded much helpful information, but Oppenheimer told his staff in February that no experiment so far suggested would replace testing a full-scale implosion device. Since no one could guarantee a satisfactory nuclear reaction, much thought went into devising some means of recovering the precious fragments a fizzle would strew about. A steel shell heavy enough to withstand at least the blast of the high-explosive charge seemed the best bet, but in May Oppenheimer doubted that "Jumbo" could be made in time if at all. In that event, he toyed with the idea of setting off a test device above the ground in some sandy place and then putting the sand skimmed from a circular area below through placer operations to mine what plutonium fragments might be imbedded there.[37]

When Tolman drafted an implosion status report for Groves and Conant on March 1, 1944, he found both theoretical and experimental investigations vigorous and sensible. He considered further effort well justified. This was a wise and accurate analysis, but it did not conceal the sharp contrast between the gun and the implosion programs. The one was proceeding smoothly at a constant level of activity. There was every reason to believe it would be successful. The other was beset by growing pains and confronted by technical terrain so unexplored that some of the difficulties could not yet even be identified. Parsons' deputy for implosion understood the uncertainties as well as anyone. On March 5, Kistiakowsky drew up a detailed "Provisional Schedule of the Work on the Implosion Project." Day by day, he blocked out the rate of hoped-for progress. Then came his final entry, one for the months of November and December, 1944: "The test of the gadget failed. Project staff resumes frantic work. Kistiakowsky goes nuts and is locked up!"[38]

Oppenheimer pursued into the spring and summer of 1944 the only policy that made sense—to continue both implosion and the gun, with the edge in priority to the former. Implosion promised such great advantages that it had to be pressed. The time might come for dropping the gun, but to abandon an almost sure bet in favor of a superior but uncertain approach would not have been responsible, even though the men released could have been used to reduce that very uncertainty.[39]

In one sense, implosion began to look more hopeful. Rudolph E. Peierls, the British physicist, visited the laboratory in February, 1944. His

248

report on methods used in England to integrate complex blast-wave equations suggested a new analytical approach. Then in April, a number of IBM machines arrived. They made it possible to solve equations too difficult for hand calculations. The first results, available shortly, were encouraging in that they established the theoretical possibility of attaining an effective assembly by implosion.[40] In other ways the picture remained dark. The high-explosive program bogged down when it proved almost impossible to find experienced workers. Conant came through with some men from the NDRC, and the Army assembled from the ranks a staff with some experience or training, but the goal of a casting plant in full operation by April could not be met. The experimental studies were slow to yield regular and reliable results, and the data that did come in were depressing, for they showed that the test shots were not producing symmetrical implosions.[41]

The Los Alamos scientists did not give up on implosion as the days of June, 1944, ran out. They had little doubt that they could make the method work for both uranium and plutonium. The uncertainty, rather, was as to how efficient such bombs would be and how quickly they could develop a moderately efficient weapon.[42] This meant that the gun method remained the surest hope. If it alone came through, there would be bombs, though not so many nor so soon.

249

TOWARD A WEAPON

The first year at Los Alamos, perforce, had to be spent in determining nuclear specifications and in devising systems of assembly. This activity led the laboratory deep into basic scientific research, but the leadership always kept in mind that the ultimate goal was a combat bomb, not just some interesting explosive device. This meant that arming and fuzing mechanisms had to be developed, equipped with suitable wiring systems, and incorporated with the active components and assembly equipment in a housing that would have sound ballistic and aerodynamic characteristics. It was to take charge of this effort that Captain Parsons came to the project. He established at Los Alamos an engineering group on which rested responsibility for designing an integrated weapon. He arranged for the off-site development and manufacture of numerous vital components. Throughout, he maintained close liaison with the Army Air Forces.

Nothing went very smoothly. The work at Los Alamos was particularly trying, for theory and experiment forced frequent changes in specifications. This imposed a difficult adjustment on design engineers recruited from industry, accustomed as they were to less fluid situations. The necessity for doing so much development, fabrication, and testing away from the site brought co-ordination headaches that were the more troublesome for security requirements. Then as 1944 wore on, a new hazard emerged. American industry tended to feel that the crisis in war production had been passed. No longer were businessmen impressed by high priorities, especially when they could not see them leading to large-scale production.

Despite these annoyances, Parsons' division had accomplished much by the summer of 1944. It had pushed design to the limit that available data permitted. It had begun fuze development in the summer of 1943 and had a unit ready for major tests the following February, when the theoretical physicists indicated that the optimum height for detonation was perhaps six times as great as originally contemplated. This forced a new search, but by June, 1944, the fuze specialists had discovered a device developed for the Army Air Forces that they could adapt satisfactorily. Engineers of the Ordnance Division had worked out two basic bomb models, the Thin Man (Franklin Roosevelt) for the plutonium gun and the Fat Man (Winston Churchill) for the implosion weapon. In March, 1944, they put dummies through a series of tests at Muroc Air Base with a modified B-29. The drops revealed that the Thin Man was stable, but that the Fat Man was subject to violent yaw and rotation. When one bomb dropped and damaged the bomb-bay doors, the trials were suspended. Meanwhile, the staff assembled new models, a Little Boy for the uranium gun and a new Fat Man, a unit so complex that some 1,500 bolts were required to hold it together. When the tests resumed in June, stability in the Fat Man was achieved only when a young AAF captain, David Semple, suggested a simple field modification.[43]

250

MIDSUMMER CRISIS

Constantly hovering in the background the first year at Los Alamos was the specter of predetonation. Fortunately, the rate in uranium 235 turned out to be lower than expected—well within the margins of practicality. But despite the elaborate purification research, the development of the high-velocity gun, and the endeavor to solve the riddle of implosion, all the talent of the laboratory was unable to exorcise the threat to the plutonium bomb.

Disquieting intelligence had reached the Hill in June, 1943. Arthur Compton had heard from Pierre Auger, the French physicist, that Joliot-Curie had discovered neutron emission in polonium that he could not explain by the well-known reaction of alpha particles with light-element impurities. A reasonable hypothesis was that a process of neutron production existed which was associated with alpha decay. Since plutonium, like polonium, was an alpha-emitter, it appeared that there might be another source of neutrons to fear in addition to spontaneous fission and impurities. If this were true, it would probably preclude assembling plutonium by the gun method. The men at Los Alamos suspected that it was not true, however, and that Joliot-Curie's neutrons were to be explained by impurities which he had not eliminated from his polonium. To test this evaluation, they developed highly sensitive neutron counters and built a plant to produce radon, the most easily purified alpha-emitter. When results showed that Joliot had been mistaken, they could dismiss the particular danger he had pointed out, but the episode made them sensitive to the possibility that something else might appear to frustrate their plans.[44]

The real danger lay in a different quarter. In March, 1943, Seaborg had suggested that a new radioactive isotope, plutonium 240, might form in the production piles. Should this turn out to be a strong spontaneous fissioner, the neutron background in the separated plutonium could jeopardize the plutonium gun. Los Alamos developed similar concern, for measurements on uranium 235 suggested the existence of sizable radiative capture of neutrons at certain resonance energies. If this should prove true for plutonium 239, the longer it was irradiated, the more chance that it would pick up an additional neutron and the greater would be the concentration of 240 in the separated plutonium. When Segrè ran tests on plutonium from the Clinton pile, he confirmed these fears. Since the amount of spontaneous fission appeared proportional to the number of neutrons to which the plutonium had been subjected, extrapolations to the Hanford piles, where the neutron flux was much greater, indicated that the product there would have a neutron background several hundred times greater than the specifications for chemical purification permitted.

251

These results, which Oppenheimer communicated to Conant July 11, 1944, were the subject of conferences at Chicago on the seventeenth. Conant, Oppenheimer, Thomas, and Compton canvassed the situation and then conferred with General Groves, Colonel Nichols, and Fermi at an evening meeting. They reached the inescapable conclusion: to abandon the gun method for plutonium. The neutron background of 240 ruled it out.

Conceivably, the Manhattan District could build an electromagnetic plant to separate plutonium 239 from the undesirable isotope, but to surmount the great inherent difficulties would postpone the weapon indefinitely. There was no point in an intensive effort at the final purification of plutonium when 240 was there to smother the benefits. On July 22, Thomas reported to Groves that he was demobilizing his co-ordinating staff. Conant expressed the general disappointment when he scrawled his lament across Thomas' optimistic June 13 report: "All to no avail, alas!"[45]

Those July days at Los Alamos were on the discouraging side. With the gun method out for plutonium, implosion remained the only hope for using the Hanford production. When Conant talked privately with Oppenheimer at the Chicago conferences, he found him pessimistic about the chances of developing it quickly. Conant suggested that the laboratory make plans for a low-efficiency implosion bomb suitable for both uranium 235 and plutonium. It seemed to him an almost certain way of utilizing some atomic energy, even if only the equivalent of a few hundred tons of TNT. Should the Los Alamos staff develop this bomb to the point where it seemed a fairly sure thing, they could set it aside as Mark II (the uranium gun being Mark I) and go to work with less nervousness on Mark III, an implosion weapon that would require less metal and be more powerful. Oppenheimer agreed that this was a distinct possibility but thought it too early to tell.

Amid all the discouragement, one reassuring factor was the success of the "water boiler" in early May. This chain-reacting system, consisting of uranyl sulfate enriched in uranium 235 and moderated by ordinary water, went critical—became self-sustaining—almost exactly at the point predicted. As Groves reported when announcing the event to the Military Policy Committee, none of the experimental work had disclosed serious errors in the theoretical calculations.[46] This was cheering; so long as theory appeared sound, an enterprising scientist could not become unduly discouraged by the mechanics of application.

252

TIME FOR FAITH

The developments of the late spring and summer of 1944 forced a change in the time schedule for atomic weapons. In the middle of April, General Groves reported to Secretary Stimson and the top representatives of British and Canadian interests that there had been no essential modification in the estimates of weapon availability since the fall of 1942. There was a "chance" that the first bomb could be produced by the end of 1944, a "reasonable chance" for one soon after New Year's Day, and a "good chance" for one during the first part of 1945 that could be followed by others. In substance, this was what Bush had told the President ten months before.[47] But on August 7, 1944, Groves presented a new weapons timetable to General Marshall. It rested, he was careful to point out, "on the basis of our present schedule for the production of material and assuming reasonable success with experiments yet to be conducted. . . ."[48]

Groves told the Chief of Staff that several implosion bombs (of the model Conant had designated Mark III) would be available between March and the end of June, 1945. They would be the equivalent of several thousand tons of TNT and capable of "Class B" destruction—damage beyond repair—to 75 per cent of the buildings over an area of two to five square miles and of lesser damage to an area ten times as large. After July, Groves expected delivery of this type to accelerate. But "if experiments yet to be conducted with the implosion type bomb" did not fulfill "present expectations" and it was necessary to rely on the gun alone, a new schedule would apply. Under this, the General promised "with assurance" that a bomb—uranium, of course—would be ready by August 1, 1945. Its destructive effect would be roughly twice that envisioned for the implosion bombs. Since, however, the gun assembly was less efficient in the use of fissionable material than implosion models, it would be possible to complete only one or two additional units in the remaining months of 1945.

Groves's revised timetable meant that in all probability the first atomic weapons would be used against Japan. The bomb project had begun as an effort to overcome a Nazi head start. As fears eased that German scientists would win the race, American thinking turned toward Japan. In May, 1943, the Military Policy Committee concluded that the Japanese fleet concentration at Truk would be the best target for the first bomb. Later the same year, Groves approved arrangements to modify a B-29 for operations with nuclear weapons.[49] The choice of the B-29 over the British Lancaster, the only other plane sufficiently large, reflected the disposition to use the bomb against Japan. Had Germany been the primary target, the choice would hardly have fallen on an aircraft never intended for the European theater. Grove's availability estimates of August 7, 1944, all but settled the question. When General Marshall examined them, American soldiers were victorious in France. In the last week of July, Bradley's First Army broke through at St.-Lô and smashed south to the base of the Normandy peninsula. There at Avranches on August 1, Patton's Third Army went into action, fanning out to the west and south and east. By the middle of August, British, Canadian, and American forces had captured eight German infantry divisions and two Panzer divisions in the Falaise-Argentan pocket. Patton's armor was racing into central France. Marshall had every reason to believe that by the time atomic weapons became available in the spring and summer of 1945, the Reich would be breathing its last.

253

The bomb would come too late for the German war. It would be ready for Japan, but even for this, General Groves's timetable was optimistic. Though his report duly noted the elements of uncertainty, both Groves and Conant were strong in their faith that the effort would be successful. They knew as well as anyone that unforeseen difficulties might rise to confound them, but the summer of 1944 was no time for faint hearts. They needed courage, for success was anything but assured in the twelve or eighteen months directly ahead. The promise of a gun-type bomb in August, 1945, depended for fulfillment on successful production at Y-12 and K-25. Even if the most optimistic estimates turned out to be justified, the inability of the Oak Ridge plants to supply uranium for more than three gun weapons in 1945 raised a basic and very disturbing question of policy. Was it wise to drop the bomb in combat without the capacity to deliver others at frequent intervals?

It was the necessity of giving up the plutonium gun that put the matter of an adequate stockpile in such sharp relief. The discovery of 240 meant that plutonium was useless unless implosion proved feasible. While almost everyone was confident that Los Alamos could develop implosion bombs of a sort, at least, this confidence flourished unsustained by successful experiment.

And even if implosion should be perfected, there was good reason for doubting that the Hanford piles would turn out plutonium in sufficient quantities and on schedule.

August, 1944, was a time for faith. It offered comfort to the men who bore responsibility for the nation's grand strategy, but the bomb remained a promise for the future, not a ready weapon in the arsenal.

AN UNEASY
PARTNERSHIP

Just fifteen days after Pearl Harbor—December 22, 1941—the *Duke of York* dropped anchor at Hampton Roads. The mighty man-of-war, latest to fly the Union Jack, bore a distinguished visitor. Winston Churchill had thrust aside the many cares that demanded his presence in London. All else paled in importance to the task of working out a complete understanding with Britain's new comrade-in-arms. The plan had been to steam up the Potomac, but the Prime Minister, weary after nearly ten days at sea, decided to fly to Washington that night. The President met him at the airport, and the two then drove to the White House, where Mrs. Roosevelt welcomed her guest.

Military fortunes were at low ebb. Guam was in Japanese hands. Hong Kong was about to succumb. Washington expected momentarily a last message from the tiny garrison at Wake Island. In the Philippines and Malaya, large task forces assembled under the Rising Sun to strike south toward the rubber and oil of the Indies. Naught save Admiral Hart's puny Asiatic Fleet and a few Dutch and British cruisers remained to oppose them. The *Prince of Wales* and the *Repulse*, the only capital ships in the area at war's onset, lay on the ocean floor, victims of Japanese torpedo bombers.

Churchill spent much of the next three weeks at the White House. Prime Minister and President saw each other several hours each day. Both inveterate workers in bed, they conferred sometimes in the chamber of one, sometimes in that of the other. At lunch, Harry Hopkins joined them for business sessions. Only before dinner, when the President mixed cocktails, was the atmosphere more social.

Out of the exchanges between the two leaders, out of almost countless discussions between the British and American staffs came plans for a common military effort. The two partners agreed to pool their munitions and place them at the disposal of a joint Munitions Assignment Board. They established a Combined Chiefs of Staff in Washington and a British, American, and Dutch command in the Pacific. In full agreement that the war against Germany must have first priority, they planned the movement of American divisions to Northern Ireland and looked toward a descent on North Africa sometime in 1942. On New Year's Day, Roosevelt and Churchill, joined by the representatives of the Soviet Union and China, signed the Declaration of the United Nations, a pledge to devote their resources to the defeat of the Axis powers and not to make a separate peace.

ALLIES IN SCIENCE

Close collaboration between the United States and Britain had not waited on American entry into the war. In February and March of 1941, staff officers of both countries met in Washington and drew up a joint war plan which assumed that the Atlantic and Europe were the decisive theaters. On March 11, Roosevelt signed the Lend-Lease Act, a response to Churchill's appeal for help. In the months that followed, Roosevelt ordered the Navy into deeper and deeper involvement in the Battle of the Atlantic. In November, Congress voted to allow American merchantmen to arm and pass through the war zone to British ports.

The interchange of scientific information had been one of the most remarkable features of Anglo-American co-operation. Early in 1940, Lord Lothian, the British Ambassador in Washington, urged his government to offer to exchange scientific data. At first, the London authorities hesitated. They thought they had more to give than receive and doubted the ability of neutral Americans to keep secrets. But the fall of France made such considerations inconsequential, and in July, 1940, Lothian proposed to President Roosevelt an immediate and general sharing of secret technical information, particularly in the ultrashort-wave radio field. Britain did not make this offer subject to any bargain, Lothian declared, although she naturally hoped that the United States would reciprocate by discussing secret technical information needed in the beleaguered kingdom. As a first step, Lothian suggested that a small, secret mission come to Washington to confer with Army and Navy experts. The mission would bring over full details on recent technical developments, particularly in the new field of radar. More than anything else, the British were anxious to employ the resources of the American radio industry to obtain the greatest possible power for the emission of ultrashort waves.

Lord Lothian's proposition found favor with both the services as well as with the President. Roosevelt had the Department of State reply that the United States was in general agreement with the plan provided it did not interfere with its own procurement program.[1]

Sir Henry Tizard arrived at the head of the British mission in September, 1940. Rector of the Imperial College of Science and Technology and scientific adviser to the Ministry of Aircraft Production, Tizard led a group of representatives from both the British and Canadian armed forces and the National Research Council of Canada. Conversations between the visiting Britons and the Army, the Navy, and the National Defense Research Committee established at once the value of interchange. Each side was in a position to help the other. Particularly important to the Americans was information about the resonant-cavity magnetron, the key to the great wartime advance in radar.

On September 27, Tizard presented the NDRC with a plan for continuing the exchange of scientific information throughout the emergency. Bush and his committee heartily approved the idea, though they found themselves in a quandary when it came to specifics. The Army had authorized free discussion of all problems relating to national defense, but the Navy had imposed restrictions on a number of subjects. Some topics that fell within the Navy ban were important to the Army. If the NDRC followed the Navy view, it might fail to provide for all the interchange that the interests of the United States required. Bush could do nothing but ask General Marshall and Admiral Stark to work out a common policy. Marshall and Stark took the issue to Secretaries Stimson and Knox, who soon arrived at a joint position. On October 24, they informed Bush that they would make information available on all devices in use or under development except the Army bomb ballistic tables and the Navy bombsight and two-way-firing antenna mine. They authorized Bush to furnish data on the existence and operation of particular devices. Should the British Government want to put these in production, it would have to make appropriate arrangements with the patentees or original manufacturers.

Now Bush could proceed. On October 25, the NDRC approved a detailed agreement drafted by Carroll L. Wilson, a member of the NDRC staff, John D. Cockcroft, head of the British mission when Tizard returned to England, and Ralph H. Fowler, then serving England as scientific liaison officer at Ottawa. According to the plan, Fowler would become the channel of communication between the NDRC and the corresponding establishments in England and Canada. The NDRC would have to limit itself to transmitting information that fell within its cognizance, but the arrangements would supplement and not supplant other forms of exchange, such as that by military and naval attachés. Though the October 25 understanding did not mention the subjects which the Army and Navy had excluded, Bush and the NDRC considered themselves bound by these restrictions.[2]

The British and Canadians promptly approved the mechanics set forth, but interchange by way of Canada proved clumsy. Bush thought the NDRC should have a London office and shared Cockcroft's view that there should be a British scientific office in Washington. In December, 1940, he sought an invitation to send a mission to England. London suffered a recurrent attack of hesitation, but on January 20, 1941, it cabled the necessary overture.

257

Early in March, James B. Conant arrived in London as head of a mission that included Carroll Wilson and Frederick L. Hovde, a chemical engineer, former Rhodes scholar, and assistant to the president of the University of Rochester. Roosevelt had done well to choose Conant. One of the first American leaders to state frankly that he thought the United States should enter the war, Conant had recently testified strongly in favor of Lend-Lease. He had, moreover, sought the opportunity to go to London. He was anxious to overcome British reluctance and to get on with the exchange of information.

Conant's task did not prove difficult. Any lingering British misgivings evaporated when Lend-Lease became law shortly after his arrival. Virtually a declaration of war on Germany, it made a deep impression in England. Significantly, it covered information as well as munitions. Conant met a ready welcome wherever he went. He studied the organization of the British scientific endeavor. This was something that Bush would want to know. Conant discussed the division of research responsibilities and found ready agreement that the British should concentrate on immediate, short-run objectives connected with the defense of Britain, while the United States should do the larger share of long-range projects. He took up the intricacies of linking the two efforts. He reached no formal agreement on the extent of interchange, but three assumptions governed his approach. First, the purpose was to win the war. Second, the NDRC would exchange basic scientific research conducted under its auspices, but it could make no commitments on work originating in Army and Navy laboratories. Third, there were certain areas of even basic scientific research in which the British were not ready to turn their findings over to the Americans.

258

Conant and Wilson returned to the United States in April, 1941, leaving Hovde behind to operate the London mission. The same month, Charles G. Darwin, director of the National Physical Laboratory, arrived in Washington to establish the British Central Scientific Office. Now the machinery for collaboration was complete.[3]

Uranium had figured in interchange since the days of Tizard. The British mission had barely arrived when Cockcroft asked about fission. Bush first checked with the Navy, then authorized Cockcroft to meet with the Briggs committee. The first of a series of British reports arrived in November, 1940. Conant did not bring up uranium during his talks in England in the spring of 1941, for he knew that it was a special, highly secret phase of the NDRC. Nor did the British raise the question in any pointed way. Hans von Halban told Conant of his heavy-water experiments entirely in terms of a power plant. Professor Frederick Lindemann, the eccentric Christ Church physicist who had become Churchill's most intimate adviser, mentioned atomic power one day at lunch. When Conant expressed his skepticism over its value as a war project, "the Prof" agreed but said that a uranium explosive was barely possible. Conant regarded Lindemann's comments as private and unofficial.

The scheme seemed so vague and highly speculative that he did not even report it on his return.[4]

Information from England did not influence the American uranium program until the summer of 1941. Bush used the MAUD Committee report on the military importance of U-235 to win Presidential support. At their October 9 conference, both Roosevelt and Bush agreed that when the time came for construction, the job ought to be done jointly in Canada. Just as Bush rose to leave that Thursday morning, Roosevelt told him to prepare a letter for his signature to open discussion "at the top." The resulting communication proposed that the two heads of government exchange views soon "in order that any extended efforts may be co-ordinated or even jointly conducted." [5]

Churchill responded enthusiastically: "I need not assure you of our readiness to collaborate with the US administration in this matter." He spoke as the leader of an enterprise already under way, for the MAUD Committee report brought action in Britain as well as in America. Churchill had referred uranium to the Chiefs of Staff Committee at the end of August, 1941, observing that "although personally I am quite content with the existing explosives, I feel we must not stand in the path of improvement. . . ." The Chiefs of Staff recommended immediate action with maximum priority. Churchill at once set up a directorate to prosecute the work within the Department of Scientific and Industrial Research. Imperial Chemical Industries released one of its principal engineers, Wallace A. Akers, to take charge. Sir John Anderson, Lord President of the Council, supervised at the Cabinet level.[6]

Neither Roosevelt nor Churchill recorded that they discussed collaborating on uranium during the Prime Minister's visit in late 1941 and early 1942. Perhaps in the press of other decisions, they assumed that their letters sufficed for the time. If in some informal moment they did turn their attention to S-1 or Tube Alloys (the British code word), Roosevelt probably offered genial but vague assurances. All was harmonious. Although doubts about the wisdom of a joint production plant in Canada had risen at Bush's December 16 meeting with Wallace, Stimson, and Harold Smith, these misgivings had not reached the lofty levels where the President and the Prime Minister drew up their blueprints for the future.

UNDER TWO FLAGS

As 1942 opened, scientists on both sides of the Atlantic welcomed help from any quarter. Americans read avidly the reports on British research, and Conant intervened personally to see that they received better distribution than in the past. Conant himself was keen to have Eger V. Murphree fly to England to witness the trials of twenty diffusion units scheduled for March. British leaders shared the American concern for close collaboration. Akers braved winter seas to visit the United States with Rudolph E. Peierls, Franz E. Simon, and Halban—all members of his Technical Committee.

Eager as British and Americans were to exchange information, some of the difficulties of integrating an international research effort soon appeared. Simon and Peierls made a poor impression on the American gaseous-diffusion team. They seemed to assume the superiority of their approach; Peierls lectured rather than conferred. When Halban asked to come to the United States as head of an English heavy-water unit, Conant rejected the idea. It promised too many snarls, both in science and in personnel.[7]

Neither Bush nor Anderson, his English counterpart, knew just what direction the uranium work would take in his country. Each was satisfied with the progress of interchange for the time being, but with the technical situation so fluid, neither was ready for a final commitment. Anderson wrote Bush on March 23, 1942, to assure him that the British would like collaboration to be as complete later as it was then. Bush's reply on April 20 stressed the importance of adequate interchange when pilot plants went into operation. When the pilot-plant studies were complete, it would be appropriate to consider jointly what action was in order.[8]

Two months later—on June 19—Bush was able to be more specific. The President had just approved an intensified effort on all four routes to a bomb. In order that Anderson would know the scope and direction of the American program, Bush sent him a copy of a memorandum to Conant outlining the new arrangements. As for the British schedule, Bush wrote that he knew something about it from recent discussions with M. W. Perrin, secretary to Akers' Technical Committee. Bush thought it likely that when he and Sir John compared the two national efforts, they would find that they could easily adjust any conflict or unnecessary overlap.[9]

Just as Bush was preparing his letter to Anderson, a Boeing flying boat landed Prime Minister Churchill on the broad reaches of the Potomac. It was an urgent, two-fold mission that impelled him to cross the Atlantic at the height of the battle in the Libyan desert. His most immediate concern was Allied strategy. As Churchill saw it, he had to satisfy the American desire to engage the *Wehrmacht* before the end of 1942. But at the same time he wished to block a Stimson-Marshall plan for a strike across the English Channel, a project that raised in British minds the nightmare of a new and possibly bloodier Dunkirk. More important in the long run was Tube Alloys. Churchill believed the time had come for definite agreements with the United States.

On the morning of June 19, 1942, the Prime Minister flew to Hyde Park. Roosevelt met him at the airfield in his Ford touring car, a vehicle equipped with hand controls so that he could drive himself. Churchill had more than one anxious moment as his host maneuvered casually on the grassy bluffs overlooking the Hudson. The next day, after lunch, they took up the uranium question. With Harry Hopkins, they talked in a small first-floor room on the east side of the rambling Dutchess County home. Mustering his ample powers of persuasion in the intense heat of the summer afternoon, Churchill urged that the two nations pool all their information, work together on equal terms, and share the results. Then came the critical question: where should the "research plant" be located? Churchill and his advisers had already considered building it in the British Isles. But this plan did not appear practical, for it would force an alarming diversion of human and financial resources from the rest of the war effort. Besides, it would court disaster to erect the necessary factories under the eyes of German aerial reconnaissance and in defiance of the threat of bombing attacks. The Prime Minister was relieved when Roosevelt said he thought the United States would have to do the job. This made it unnecessary for Britain to undertake the venture under her own power in Canada or in some other part of the Empire.

In recounting the understanding in *The Hinge of Fate*, Churchill declared: "We therefore took this decision jointly, and settled a basis of agreement." In February, 1943, only eight months after the event, he was more explicit. The partners were to be equal; they were to share fully in the results. Churchill had every reason to come to this conclusion. Three weeks after the discussion, Roosevelt wrote in a note to Bush that he and the Prime Minister were "in complete accord." However, there was no written agreement and no effort to spell out the details of the joint effort. The discussion was in general terms, partly because neither leader was in a position to conceive of the complications that would arise in practice. Partly, no doubt, the lack of precision reflected Roosevelt's habit of avoiding inflexible commitments.[10]

261

If the Tube Alloys issue was dispatched in a genial but foggy atmosphere of good feeling, the disagreements on strategy were discussed bluntly and in hard detail. Roosevelt and Churchill took the train back to Washington, where, on June 21, the Prime Minister and General Marshall clashed head-on. Their prolonged debate ended in a standoff. The Americans would continue to increase their strength in the United Kingdom, but a firm decision to invade the continent would have to wait a few months. If the choice should go against a landing in France or the Low Countries, French North Africa lay open as the most likely spot for an assault in 1942.[11]

Britain tried first to give substance to the Hyde Park understandings on uranium. On August 5, 1942, Anderson sent two closely written letters to Bush. The Lord President was not a man to be taken lightly. A big Scot with black beady eyes, sparing of words and keen in mind, he had a long career of government service behind him—Under Secretary in the Home Office, Governor of Bengal, Member of Parliament for the Scottish Universities. A chemist by training and a director of Imperial Chemical Industries, he watched over the British uranium effort with calm assurance.

Anderson devoted one of his letters to co-operation in the immediate future. The British gaseous-diffusion program, he reported, was lagging. The two prototype units that had been scheduled to operate in the spring would not be ready before December, 1942. To compound the delay, engineers responsible for the full-scale plant had concluded that their final designs would have to wait until fifty to one hundred such units were operated in a pilot-scale assembly. Assuming the highest priority justified in hard-pressed Britain, this would take two years and probably longer. The data Bush forwarded in June, however, suggested a solution. The Americans apparently planned to build four plants on a similar scale in a substantially shorter time. Why not build the British diffusion pilot plant in the United States? If this could be arranged, Anderson suggested, he would send over Simon and Peierls, members of their research teams, as well as representatives of the industrial firms involved. And since this proposal would mean adding a fifth project to the American effort, why not add British members to Conant's S-1 Executive Committee?

262

Less immediate was the question of what to do with Halban's group. Here, Anderson admitted, there was not the same case for incorporation in the American program, for Compton's graphite pile promised the quickest, though probably not the most efficient, production of element 94. But were there not advantages in transferring the heavy-water-pile project to Canada? Both the Compton and Halban groups would benefit from interchange. Anderson said he was negotiating with the Canadian Government on the shift. If Bush had any strong views, he would like to have them.

The knotty issue of control during and after the war Sir John reserved for a separate letter. Nuclear energy, he wrote, required a special and powerful system of international curbs. In his view, the United States and the United Kingdom should consider them on their own merits at the highest level. It was not safe to rely on any general solution covering other fields in which American and British inventions had been pooled for wartime use.

For the duration of the current conflict, Anderson suggested that Britain and the United States develop a common patent policy. A firm base already existed, for in both countries patents arising from work with public funds automatically became government property. Since this suggestion implied some machinery, Anderson proposed a joint nuclear energy commission to work out the details. The commission would also examine the case for bringing other United Nations into the system, perhaps the British dominions or Russia, and for suggesting the conditions under which they might be admitted. The British, Anderson reported, had just acquired the rights of Halban and Kowarski and had taken steps to obtain the interests of their associates in France.

A joint patent policy would be a start toward a rational postwar plan, but it would have to be supplemented by other devices, such as control of raw materials and some method of supervising research and operation. Perhaps postwar restraints should be the subject of new international legislation or of provisions in the peace treaty. In any event, the proposed joint nuclear energy commission might bridge the gap between the end of the war and the establishment of peacetime arrangements.[12]

Anderson's letter arrived at a bad time. When Bush sat down to answer it, the fight for adequate priorities was at its peak. Priority difficulties, he told Sir John, had interfered with the pilot-plant program. Until American leaders knew where they stood themselves, they were in no position to cope with Britain's gaseous-diffusion dilemma. Bush hastened to add that he hoped for even more scientific interchange than in the past, welcomed further visits from British scientists, and considered desirable, on the whole, the prospect of interchange with Halban in Canada. He judged, however, that British engineering visits and membership on the S-1 Executive Committee must await a decision on the diffusion pilot plant.

Bush was even less ready to push the United States into any commitments on international control. He could agree that each country ought to own a substantial part of the patent rights arising within its borders. Such ownership would prevent private rights from complicating the task of arriving at sound international relationships. He thought that a joint nuclear energy commission deserved careful exploration, even though he considered it somewhat too early to take just this step. If the President and the Prime Minister were in full agreement, as he understood they were, appropriate arrangements would follow in due time. Although Bush thought the immediate technical problems more pressing than the international question, he promised Anderson to explore it and write as soon as he had something definite to propose.[13]

263

AN END TO INTERCHANGE

The events of September, 1942, put an entirely new face on the American program: Groves took command; Somervell cut the Gordian knot on priorities; and Bush arranged for the Military Policy Committee to assume general responsibility. All these moves cleared the way for construction. Confidence charged the atmosphere at the organizational meeting in Stimson's office on September 23. When co-operation with the United Kingdom came up for discussion, the premium on speed made the complications of an international venture seem unattractive, especially since the United States was doing ten times as much work as Britain. It was not hard to postpone any attempt to establish an international working arrangement until Stimson had the opportunity to ascertain the President's desires. For the present, this meant that the United States would hasten into the production phase without the British yet not definitely excluding them.[14]

On October 1, Bush wrote Anderson in the light of the changed situation. After a succinct review of the new organizational arrangements and the decision to construct the electromagnetic plant, he turned once more to Sir

John's August 5 questions on the British diffusion process. American technical people, he reported, now thought they would be able to choose between the two diffusion systems by comparing the British prototype machine and the American pilot plant expected to be ready in April or May, 1943. The whole effort was so urgent, however, that the Americans would have to construct large-scale plants on minimum data. They would not wait for the pilot-plant operations. Therefore, the problem of locating the British pilot plant was not likely to arise. Everyone was anxious, said Bush, to utilize scientific talent on both sides of the water to the maximum, but the most opportune time for a decision on further integrating the two programs would come when the British and American diffusion processes had been tested. In the meantime, close liaison was essential. The Americans were planning to send some men to see the British prototype in operation. Bush hoped, further, that Akers would soon be in America. He would like to explore with him the best method of putting the scientific resources of both countries to work. The letter did not misstate a single fact, but as Conant said after looking over the draft, it was a "masterly evasive reply." [15]

Bush and his colleagues had not misjudged the chances for support when they adopted a go-slow approach to further collaboration. After Cabinet meeting on October 29, Stimson discussed S-1 with the President. He told of the accelerating progress. The United States was doing 90 per cent of the work, he said, and Bush and the others were anxious to know what formal commitments the President had made. Roosevelt replied that he had talked with no one but Churchill and with him only in a general way. Stimson proposed going along for the present without sharing any more than necessary. Roosevelt concurred, though he suggested that sometime in the near future he and Stimson ought to speak with the Prime Minister. [16] The fact was, neither President nor Secretary felt much obligation at this time to go out of the way to help the British. Churchill and his Chiefs of Staff had hardly returned from the June conferences in Washington when they concluded there was no hope for a cross-channel attack in 1942. Weary of decisions that did not stay made, Stimson and Marshall considered Churchill's pet alternative, a North African invasion, a dangerous diversion from the main chance. It reminded Stimson of "the fatal decision to go half-baked to the Dardanelles" more than a quarter-century earlier. In the end, the United States went along on North Africa, but the dispute left a legacy of resentment. [17]

Meanwhile, word arrived from Anderson that Akers would be in Washington early in November to discuss linking the national efforts. Bush decided that Akers should talk mainly with Conant, whose role as chairman of the S-1 Executive Committee corresponded most nearly to the position Akers held in the United Kingdom.

As Bush and Conant prepared for Akers' visit, they found themselves in close agreement. Though both believed firmly in Anglo-American co-operation, they considered the exchange of scientific and technical information justified only when it advanced the war effort. They could see little but trouble in a joint project. It would complicate the Army's production job. Besides, moving the British diffusion work to the United States would save no time. Should the United States decide to adopt the Simon system in the spring of 1943, that would be the proper juncture to bring over the scientists and engineers who had developed it. In any case,. the scientists who had worked on diffusion would be welcome once their work in the United Kingdom was complete. Neither American leader would have objected seriously to Anderson's desire for a British scientist on the S-1 Committee had all projects been developed on both sides of the Atlantic. Since, among the production processes the British had done significant work only on diffusion and the heavy-water pile, Bush and Conant were reluctant to admit them to the centrifuge, the electromagnetic method, and the graphite pile, all strictly American in origin and development.

265

Reinforcing these considerations were the more rigid security arrangements that would prevail now that a weapon was in sight. Liaison would have to be more restricted than in the past. It would be unfair to compartmentalize American scientists while allowing their English counterparts to travel about picking up information from all projects. In short, Bush and Conant wanted the bomb quickly. Did it make any difference, they asked themselves, which partner manufactured the munitions? [18]

Conant talked informally with Akers on three occasions in November. He explored the mechanics of future arrangements, paved the way for assigning Halban the first heavy water from Trail, and offered to go on record to quiet Akers' fears that after the war the United States might claim the whole project as an American invention and demand international royalties. The two men did not really come to grips, however, until December 11, when Akers had returned from a trip to Canada and the Military Policy Committee had decided to construct full-scale plutonium and gaseous-diffusion plants.[19]

Lingering long over lunch that Friday, Conant and Akers set forth their positions. They found themselves far apart, and at times the talk was blunt. Conant explained the American stand on restricting interchange to information Britain could use in the current war. Akers inveighed earnestly against such restrictions. The closest possible connection should prevail not only in research but also in production. The President and the Prime Minister always had intended a co-operative effort, regardless of the origin of the ideas and of the country in which the plants were built. But Akers did more than appeal to a promise. British scientists had to have complete access to all large-scale American developments, he argued, for information on the progress of one method bore directly on decisions involving the others.

The fundamental difference on principle narrowed the chances for agreement on details. Conant ruled out interchange on the electromagnetic process because the British were not working on it. Akers held out for full access. Conant favored co-operation between the American and British firms studying diffusion-plant design but did not consider anything necessary beyond the exchange of experimental results on models. Akers insisted that the United States employ British engineers and scientists in the actual erection and operation of the full-scale factory. When it came to the manufacture of plutonium and of heavy water, Conant admitted interchange of scientific results but not of plant design. Akers, on the other hand, argued that British and Canadian engineers should participate in designing, constructing, and operating the final production unit. The United States could permit no interchange on research and development in its secret bomb-design laboratory, Conant said. British theoreticians might exchange data with Americans not isolated at Los Alamos, but that was all. Akers had no use for this plan. Secrecy was important, but on a matter like this, one had to compromise for the sake of efficiency.

266

Conant reviewed Akers' position with Bush the next day, December 12. One thing was clear: the Military Policy Committee would have to ask the President for a directive on future relations with Britain. Over the week end, Conant put his views in writing. Monday, he took up his statement with Bush and Groves. The place to begin, he thought, was to explain to the President that only one reason justified the free interchange of secret military information: prosecution of the war. A two-way flow was essential when both British and Americans were developing and manufacturing the same or similar devices. Uranium 235 and plutonium differed from most areas of joint endeavor. The British had said that neither England nor Canada could build production plants now. Since they did not intend to manufacture fissionable material during the war, passing data to them would not further the military effort.

The great advantage of cutting off the flow was to make it easier to maintain secrecy, no mean consideration now that the project had definite military significance. Conant argued the fairness of such a policy. The two diffusion processes had been pushed independently but with frequent exchange of ideas; he could not say which group had borrowed most. The United Kingdom had done more on a heavy-water moderator, though until American scientists discovered that plutonium probably would be explosive, the approach had only a low priority. But would it be expedient to end interchange on S-1? Conant admitted that the men building the diffusion plant could benefit from knowing British progress. Since, however, the United States was going ahead without waiting for the trials in England, the absence of information would not embarrass them materially. The heavy-water method of manufacturing plutonium was similar. The Metallurgical Laboratory could use the talents of Halban's group in Canada, but it would not suffer greatly if it had to get along without them. Of course, if the President should stop the transmittal of S-1 data, Canada might refuse to allow heavy water from Trail to cross the border. This would slow down but not cripple the effort here, for domestic plants would be producing substantial quantities by January, 1944. Canadian ore was a more difficult matter. Pending further exploration of supplies in Colorado, Conant hesitated to estimate the effects should Canada impose an embargo on oxide shipments.

As Conant defined the issue, the President had three choices. At one extreme, he could end all interchange. At the other, he could direct it not only in research but also in development and production. Or he could take a middle ground and permit restricted exchange along the lines of some carefully delineated plan such as Conant had spelled out for Akers. Conant naturally favored the last course, but if it should come to a choice between extremes, he would prefer cessation.

Bush incorporated this analysis and recommendation into his December 16, 1942, report to the President. For the sake of perspective, he reviewed the background of interchange. Then taking the long view, he stressed that the question of postwar international relations had not been settled. The development of atomic power held out both a threat and a promise. Though "an exceedingly difficult matter with which to deal wisely as between nations," it might be "capable of maintaining the peace of the world." In any event, the Military Policy Committee would make no decision without definite instructions.

Bush, Conant, and Groves wanted a Presidential ruling on interchange, but they did not want one based on anything less than a complete understanding of the facts. On Friday, December 18, Conant received a long letter from Akers setting forth his case in great detail. On checking with Groves, Conant discovered that Stimson and Marshall had already signed the Military Policy Committee report. Only Wallace among the Top Policy Group had not seen it. Though Conant and Groves thought Akers had furnished no new information, they believed that Stimson, Marshall, and Wallace should see the letter before the report went to Roosevelt. Accordingly, Bush drew up a summary of the British and American positions in parallel columns, added a note challenging the accuracy of some of Akers' facts, and took them, along with the Akers letter, to Harvey Bundy. Bundy promised to bring it all to Stimson's attention. Then Bush reviewed the report and supporting documents with Wallace, and the Vice-President questioned him closely on British relations. Saying he was quite in accord with Bush's approach, he added his signature. Two days before Christmas, after Bundy had checked with Stimson, Bush sent the report, the Akers letter, and the summary of the two positions to the White House. The British undoubtedly would object, he warned, if the President did not extend interchange to include plants and production. For that reason, he should have their position in mind.[20]

Any doubts Roosevelt may have had about the wisdom of restricting interchange vanished on Sunday morning the 27th, when Stimson talked to him at the White House. The day before, Bundy had brought in a copy of a September 29 Anglo-Russian agreement for the exchange of new weapons,

267

both those in use and those which might be discovered in the future. Up to now, Stimson had known nothing of this nor had the President. The situation was serious, Stimson observed. This agreement endangered the future of any new weapons confided to the British. John G. Winant, U. S. Ambassador to Great Britain, was flying to Washington at that very moment to urge that the United States also exchange such a pledge with Russia. Roosevelt noted the presence of an escape clause which he thought vitiated the effectiveness of the agreement, but he agreed with Stimson that it would be bad policy to enter a similar understanding.[21]

The following day, December 28, Roosevelt wrote to Bush saying that he would approve the recommendations.[22] Thus the United States embarked on a policy of limited interchange, which meant no sharing of information concerning the electromagnetic method and the bomb-design work at Los Alamos. It was assumed that there would be interchange between British and American firms designing and constructing the diffusion plant but no more than an exchange of scientific research on the manufacture of plutonium and heavy water. Finally, if Britain would make available all the information Halban developed in Canada, the United States would divert enough of the initial heavy-water production from Trail to permit him to pursue his experiments.

The next move was to inform the British and the Canadians. On January 2, 1943, Conant wrote C. J. Mackenzie of the Canadian National Research Council to tell him of the decisions as they related to Halban's group. On January 7, Conant prepared a broader memorandum setting forth the rules and regulations that would apply to the whole project under the new dispensation. Enunciating once again the use-in-the-current-war principle, Conant listed the areas closed to interchange. No further information would be forthcoming on the production of heavy water or on the fast-neutron reaction. The manufacturing details of uranium hexafluoride, uranium metal, and other materials were under the jurisdiction of General Groves; as a rule, he would not transmit information. Conant indicated that Groves also would control all interchange on gaseous diffusion, even basic scientific data. The Canadian group at Montreal and the American group at Chicago would share scientific information on chain reactions, but the Metallurgical Laboratory would report on neither the properties nor production of plutonium. This ban included pile design and extraction methods. The Canadians would provide du Pont engineers with scientific information, but du Pont would give Montreal only the minimum engineering design data necessary for fundamental research.[23]

Conant's memorandum was only a working paper. He never presented it officially to the British, though Akers early learned of its contents. On January 26, the memorandum became the subject of a stormy conference between the British leader and Conant and Groves. The General asked Akers to send experts to the United States for three or four days to discuss the design and construction of a diffusion plant. He emphasized that this implied no guarantee to continue exchange on large-scale design and construction. That depended entirely on the impression he gained at the meetings. If he concluded that further interchange would really help the Kellex Company, he would sanction it. Akers replied that it would be difficult to spare the right people at this time, especially when he had no assurance they would remain in the picture. Perhaps to make the meeting idea more attractive, Groves said it would provide an opportunity to discuss manufacturing data on uranium hexafluoride and metal.

Akers bitterly protested Conant's proposal to stop the flow of information on heavy-water production. To lessen the hurt, Groves indicated that the Americans would probably be willing to reinstate exchange in this area if they became satisfied that the British could use the information on a significant scale during the war.

When it came to the heavy-water pile itself, Conant and Groves refused to make arrangements until the Anglo-Canadian group indicated it would conform to the conditions specified in Conant's letter to Mackenzie and in his January 7 memorandum. Beyond this, they made construction of a pilot-scale pile in Canada contingent upon du Pont's agreement that such an experiment would help in designing a full-scale plant. Groves would not commit himself to supply either graphite or metal to Montreal unless the Hanford contractor made an express request. Akers asked Groves if he would revise the decision against interchange on the chemistry of plutonium. That would depend on du Pont, replied the General.

269

Groves reported that preparations for isolating American experimental physicists to work on the bomb were well advanced, but he repeated an earlier invitation for James Chadwick and Peierls to come to the United States for final discussions before confinement began. Akers was not impressed by Groves's argument that security demanded this arrangement and said that Chadwick would not come under such conditions. Peierls probably would take the same attitude.

At this point, Akers—a keen and wily antagonist—delivered a sharp counterthrust. The British, he said, were working on powdered nickel barriers. W. T. Griffiths was now in America and about to attend a discussion between International Nickel, Bell Telephone, and the Columbia group on nickel powder and its use in barriers. If the relations between British and American workers had remained as they were, Griffiths could have described his work on barriers. Under the new regulations, this seemed impossible. If Akers thought this threat would shake Groves and Conant, he was mistaken. Conant simply agreed with him. Griffiths should confine himself only to the production and properties of nickel powder. He should not discuss barrier manufacture.[24]

On that note the conference ended. A day later, Conant offered to send a half-ton of uranyl nitrate and three tons of Mallinckrodt oxide to Canada for Halban, but supplies of metal and graphite were so short, he told Mac-kenzie, that the United States could not spare any in the months directly ahead. Early in February, Conant wrote Akers renewing the invitation for a Chadwick-Peierls visit and holding out the hope of later conferences. But by then the authorities in London had decided to hold off. They did not send Chadwick and Peierls, and they did not allow Halban to go to New York for a March conference on the future of the heavy-water pile. Interchange slowed to a standstill. On March 30, 1943, the Military Policy Committee decided that in view of the British attitude, it was no longer necessary to deliver the first Trail heavy water to Montreal.[25]

THE PRIME MINISTER TAKES A HAND

270

Sir John Anderson felt deep concern when he learned from Akers the arrange-ments Conant had proposed in his January 7, 1943, memorandum. Churchill had just left for the Casablanca Conference. Anderson wired the Prime Minis-ter, and Churchill spoke to Roosevelt and Hopkins. From the President he elicited the usual hearty assurances and from Hopkins a promise that all would be put right as soon as Roosevelt returned to Washington. When Churchill saw a problem, he worried it with the energy of a bull terrier. Back in London, he jogged Hopkins, saying that the War Department was asking for information on the British experiments but refusing to disclose any re-ports on American work. Hopkins replied February 24. His inquiries—he had seen Bush—revealed that the Americans in charge believed there had been no breach of agreement. But he wanted to investigate thoroughly. Could An-derson send a full statement concerning the present misunderstanding? [26]

Sir John could, of course, but this was a subject the Prime Minister thought required his personal attention. Though he had barely recovered from a ten-day bout with pneumonia, he sent Hopkins two personal messages on February 27. One was a long historical review which concluded with Conant's January 7 statement of the principle that the recipient of informa-tion must be able to use it during the war. The restrictions Conant outlined were logical applications of this principle, Churchill admitted, but they de-molished Roosevelt's original concept of "a co-ordinated or even jointly con-ducted effort between the two countries." In the shorter message, the Prime Minister denied alleging any breach of agreement. He merely wanted Hopkins to review the American position and restore the original policy of joint work. Churchill maintained he would have little difficulty justifying his request on grounds of fair play, but he preferred to let it rest on his conviction that a return to the old conditions was necessary in order to employ the resources of both countries most efficiently. There had to be a firm decision on American policy soon, he admonished, for British decisions on programs in the United

Kingdom and Canada depended on the extent to which the United States reinstated full interchange.[27]

Hopkins did nothing very aggressive until March 20, when Churchill sent another reminder. Then, after dashing off a note promising that he would let the Prime Minister know just as soon as he had something definite, Hopkins saw Roosevelt and had him send Bush the Churchill correspondence. Bush, who understood that he was to suggest a reply, canvassed the situation with Conant, the Military Policy Committee, and Stimson. When he found that all shared his belief that the American position should remain unchanged, he prepared a long analysis. There was nothing new or unusual, he declared, in the policy of restricting information to those able to use it in furthering the war effort. Certainly there was nothing discriminatory about it. The OSRD operated on the "need-to-know" formula, essentially the same thing. The British followed the rule themselves. To make an exception on S-1 would decrease security without advancing the war effort.

Bush found it hard to believe that the British really objected to the policy. They were outraged, he told Hopkins, because the United States was withholding information that might be valuable to them after the war. For the first time he made explicit to the White House something that had long troubled himself and Conant: a suspicion that Britain was looking primarily to its postwar commercial advantage. Doubts about British motives had risen in the summer of 1942. They took deep root during the discussions with Akers, whom Bush, Conant, and Groves all judged to be an Imperial Chemical Industries man at heart, more interested in nuclear power plants than a bomb. The United States, Bush pointed out, was eager to transmit information when it would further the joint war effort. But it should not encourage Britain's postwar aspirations merely as an incident to developing the bomb, particularly when this threatened the security of the weapons program. If Britain expected the United States to yield findings produced at such great expense and effort for a purpose other than prosecuting the war, the question ought to be considered on its merits.

What should Hopkins say to Churchill? Bush picked up Churchill's disclaimer that he was charging a breach of agreement. That meant the British objection must be either to the policy adopted or to the method of applying it. Here was the crux. Bush recommended that Hopkins make no final reply but state the case and ask for a specific objection. If the British were thinking primarily of the period when Germany and Japan had been defeated, S-1 interchange could be considered in due time in connection with the broad question of postwar relationships.[28]

Churchill kept spurring Hopkins. On April 1, 1943, he cabled his concern at the lack of news. It would be "a sombre decision," he said, should the two countries work separately. Shortly before the middle of April, Foreign Secretary Anthony Eden added his urging. Seeing the many ramifications,

271

Hopkins delayed decisive action. Very likely, he hoped, Mackenzie, then on his way to England, could ease the situation. Bush thought the Canadian considered the American decision reasonable and would counsel the British to withdraw their objections.[29]

The matter dragged on through April without event. By the end of the month, Churchill had decided to make a third visit to Washington. The British and American staffs met in the President's oval study on May 12, 1943, and set themselves to hammering out a set of strategic decisions embracing the entire war effort. While the discussions dragged on almost interminably, Bush stood by. Finally on May 25, the last day of the talks, he received a phone call from Hopkins. Churchill had raised the question of S-1 interchange. Would Bush come over to the White House, talk with Churchill's adviser, and see if there could be a meeting of the minds?

Bush arrived at Hopkins' office at 3:30. He found himself confronted by two able men, each of whom wielded great influence because of his close relationship to a national leader. There was Hopkins—sick, emaciated, but still quick and sharp of mind. With him was Frederick Lindemann, now Lord Cherwell. He was a big man with rather heavy features, the son of an Alsatian father and an American mother. To look at him, Bush never could have guessed that he subsisted entirely on egg whites, stewed apples, rice croquettes, cheese (only Port Salut), and startling quantities of olive oil. Since the latter was virtually unobtainable in wartime Britain, one of the headaches of the Washington Embassy was to see that a case for the Prof went forward each week in the diplomatic pouch. Like Hopkins, Cherwell was the object of much public distrust, but the Prime Minister felt a need for his ruggedly independent thought.[30]

Hopkins introduced Bush to Cherwell, who at once asked why the United States had altered its policy. In reply, Bush traced the organizational history of the American effort, observing that the OSRD's concern had been scientific. When S-1 went into production under the Army, a new policy was required. Moving nimbly along the path he had suggested earlier to Hopkins, Bush outlined the use-in-this-war principle and its applications. Did the British disagree with the principle or with the application?

Cherwell said it was the principle itself. Bush was ready for this. Security, he said, demanded restricting information to those who could use it. There was nothing anti-British about this. The S-1 leadership was withholding reports from the Naval Research Laboratory on the same ground. The Army was restricting each contractor to the data necessary for his part of the work. Tactfully, Bush pointed out that Britain would have to assign its production effort to Imperial Chemical Industries. If the United States were to furnish manufacturing information to the British Government, ICI would be privy to the entire project. How then could the United States justify compartmentalizing American firms? And if it could not, what about security?

Bush was a worthy antagonist for Cherwell, who seldom met defeat

ROOSEVELT AND CHURCHILL AT QUEBEC, 1943 / Photograph taken August 18, the day before the President and the Prime Minister signed the Quebec Agreement. Canadian Prime Minister Mackenzie King is in the background, while in the foreground is the Earl of Athlone, Governor-General of Canada.

in a dispute on which he had a well-thought-out position. Bush questioned Britain's ability to use manufacturing information until the Oxford don rather freely admitted that his government wanted the information at once so it could manufacture the weapon promptly for itself after the war. Cherwell disclaimed any interest in the commercial aspects of nuclear energy. It would be five or ten years before such applications became practical. A little study, and the British would have no trouble taking up that phase.

Now Bush had the issue isolated. Supported by Hopkins, he maintained that delivery of information to the British for after-the-war military purposes was a subject that needed to be approached on its own merits, for one reason, because it was tied to long-term international relations. Cherwell countered that there was a definite connection with the current war, for in order to make their island's position secure in the years immediately following, his countrymen might have to divert some of their present effort to building production facilities for nuclear weapons.

273

Hopkins closed the exchange by explaining how difficult it was for the United States to make a long-range covenant. Except by treaty, one administration could not bind its successor. But for the first time, he said, he had the dispute definitely in mind. He understood exactly the point at issue. As Bush left, Hopkins told him not to act until he heard something further. Bush returned to the OSRD believing that Hopkins intended to talk with the President.[31]

Early the next morning, Churchill and his party took off for Gibraltar. As the huge flying boat thundered along its great-circle course, the Prime Minister thought that at last he had resolved the Tube Alloys tangle. He sent Sir John Anderson a message saying that the President had agreed the enterprise was joint and the exchange of information should be resumed. The President's ruling would be based "upon the fact that this weapon may well be developed in time for the present war and that it thus falls within the general agreement covering the interchange of research and invention secrets." Lord Cherwell, who did not accompany the Prime Minister to Gibraltar, learned the news when he arrived in England. He sent Hopkins a note saying he understood the interchange matter had been concluded satisfactorily. He was sure Hopkins was largely responsible. The restoration of the old conditions, he rejoiced, would benefit everyone. Back in Whitehall on June 10, the Prime Minister himself wrote to thank Hopkins for his help and to urge that the two countries promptly carry the understanding into effect. As soon as the President gave the necessary instructions, Churchill hoped Hopkins would telegraph him so he could have the right people on the spot in Washington.[32]

On June 17, Hopkins informed Churchill that he expected complete disposition of the Tube Alloys matter by the first of the week. Bush, however, heard nothing, and as chairman of the Military Policy Committee, he would have to know of any change. Then on Thursday, June 24, the President invited him to lunch. How was S-1 progressing, he wanted to know. Bush reported that the United States was still riding three main horses and supporting one or two auxiliary matters. The President was full of questions. What was the timetable? Where did the enemy stand? Would it be a good idea to invent a cock-and-bull story to quiet the rumors generated by the construction at Hanford? What about the control of raw materials? Finally, Roosevelt reached his most important question. What was the status of relations with the British?

Wondering where to begin, Bush asked the President if Harry Hopkins had reported the conversation with Lord Cherwell. At the negative reply, Bush recounted the exchange. The details made a strong impression. Roosevelt thought it "astounding" that Cherwell had placed the whole matter on an after-the-war military basis. Several times the discussion turned back to the British position, and FDR repeatedly seemed amazed, murmuring on one occasion that Cherwell was "a rather queer-minded chap." His last words as his guest departed were a reference to the extraordinary nature of the British stand. Bush understood that he was to "sit tight." He had suggested this in so many words, and the President had nodded rather vigorously. Even though Roosevelt knew that Bush was leaving shortly for England for discussions on antisubmarine warfare, he gave him no instructions. Bush concluded that the Chief Executive had no intention of going beyond his December, 1942, position.[33]

Sometime during the May conferences at the White House, probably on May 25, Roosevelt had made Churchill a sweeping promise on interchange. Perhaps he offered it when the Prime Minister first broached the subject. Perhaps he did so later in the day. Hopkins knew of the assurances tendered the British leader, but for some reason he did not see fit to brief his chief on the discussion between Bush and Cherwell. Roosevelt probably intended to tell Bush of his pledge to Churchill when he asked him to lunch June 24. When he discovered that he had acted on an incomplete understanding of the situation, he drew back. If this was indeed the way it happened, the President remained sufficiently adroit to conceal the true extent of his discomfiture. Bush judged that the President had not thought about interchange since March.

Roosevelt procrastinated for two weeks, but if he thought he could wear Churchill down, he was mistaken. On July 9, the Prime Minister demanded action once again. The President turned to Hopkins, but his adviser could suggest no way out of the dilemma. "I think," he wrote, "you made a firm commitment to Churchill in regard to this when he was here and there is nothing to do but go through with it." Finally on July 20, almost a month after his promise to Churchill, Roosevelt wrote Bush at his P Street office and directed him to "renew, in an inclusive manner, the full exchange of information with the British Government regarding tube alloys." While aware of the vital necessity for security, he felt that the understanding with the British encompassed "the complete exchange of all information." At the same time Roosevelt sent a personal message to his friend, "the Prime": "I have arranged satisfactorily for tube alloys. Unless you have the proper person in this country now, it might be well if your top man in this enterprise comes over to get full understanding from our people." [34]

Meanwhile, Bush had gone to London. On July 15, 1943, he attended a meeting of the War Cabinet Anti-U-Boat Committee. Just before the session began, Sir Stafford Cripps took him to see the Prime Minister. Churchill was incensed at the trouble over interchange. The President had given him his word of honor that the two nations would share equally in the effort, but every time he got an agreement to modify the present arrangements, somebody in the American organization knocked it out. He had been at this for months, he complained, adding urgency to his plea by alluding darkly to "the threat from the East." The spunky little Yankee did not quail before this broadside; on the contrary, he returned some hot shot of his own. Churchill was asking not just for scientific data but for commercial manufacturing information as well; this was a threat to security. Besides, it was unfortunate that the British were approaching the war and postwar aspects of the subject together. The Prime Minister interrupted; he did not give a damn about any postwar matter. He wanted to be in shape to handle the affair in this war and that alone. If that was the case, Bush retorted, there would be no disagreement. The policy the United States had adopted would serve. Secretary of War Stimson, who was senior to him in the American organization, was in London. Churchill, he ventured, should take the matter up with him. [35]

275

Bush at once sought out Stimson's aide, Bundy, to make sure Stimson had the issues firmly in mind when Churchill approached him. On Saturday, July 17, the Prime Minister took Stimson and a small party to Dover in a special train. Late in the day, he drew the Secretary aside and poured out his troubles on Tube Alloys. Stimson listened sympathetically, but he promised only to submit the issue to the President for decision. [36]

Churchill scheduled a full-scale conference with Stimson for the afternoon of July 22. That morning Bush went to Claridge's and talked for an hour with Stimson and Bundy. Bundy gave him a voice at Stimson's elbow. An able Boston lawyer, he shared Bush's opposition to settling postwar problems as an incident to the present struggle. He saw interchange in constitutional terms. For Roosevelt's own protection as well as a matter of principle, he wanted him to stay within his war powers. It was not proper that the President encourage by executive action the creation of a great new British industry with unforeseeable economic and commercial implications.

As Bush and Bundy presented their arguments, Stimson voiced his opinion that Churchill had a strong case. He believed that good postwar relations between Britain and the United States were essential. He considered it quite impossible to isolate the war effort. The constitutional argument was too legalistic. Stimson's position stemmed from a deep-seated conviction that the two English-speaking nations must co-operate not only during the war but after. Stimson had just been fighting to hold Churchill to the decision to invade France in 1944. Though Churchill and Roosevelt had reached an understanding on this at the White House just two months before, the British leader again was inveighing against the plan. Stimson did not want to disagree with him on everything. But any desire to make Churchill feel better by supporting his views on interchange was secondary. Stimson already believed that atomic energy had created a new order in international relations. It made Anglo-American collaboration all the more imperative.[37]

After lunch, Stimson, Bundy, and Bush went to 10 Downing Street. There they found the Prime Minister flanked by Lord Cherwell and Sir John Anderson. Ironically, neither side knew that Roosevelt had already decided the issue in line with the British claims. Churchill spoke first, reviewing Roosevelt's repeated promises. He told of the chagrin wrought by Conant's January memorandum and of his inability to turn the President's agreement into action. The snarl was reaching the point where it might affect adversely relations between the two countries. Britain could not stand by and allow the United States to claim the right to sole knowledge. She was not interested in commercial advantage, Churchill stoutly asserted. Something more important was involved: her independence in the future as well as success in the present war. Unless Americans and Britons worked together, Germany or Russia might win the race for a weapon they could use for international blackmail. The United States could not contend at the peace conference for sole control of atomic energy. Unless the Americans agreed to full interchange, he threatened, Britain would launch a parallel development, even though this was an unwise use of wartime energies.

When Churchill subsided, it was Bush who spoke. Just before entering the meeting, Stimson had told Bush to take over—a way of saying he was going to follow his advice. Though Bush could not resist the temptation to correct the Prime Minister's views that the British had started the whole enterprise, he was more conciliatory than the week before. He doubted that the Conant memorandum was the final American position. It had placed the matter in a rather negative light, while the document that the Military Policy Committee and the President had sanctioned set down a formula that was completely adequate for winning the war. Again he reasoned that the difficulties on complete interchange related to postwar considerations. Now the British moderated their tone. Churchill again stated that he placed no importance on any hope of commercial advantage, and Anderson offered his opinion that American concern stemmed from Akers' using commercial possibilities as camouflage for the real objective.

After Stimson had read a brief memorandum in which he sought to state the issue precisely, Churchill proposed that he and Roosevelt agree to a set of propositions: first, the enterprise would be completely joint with free interchange; second, neither government would employ the invention against the other; third, neither would pass information to other powers without consent of its partner; fourth, use in war required common assent; and fifth, the President might limit the commercial or industrial uses of Great Britain in such manner as he considered fair and equitable in view of the large additional expense incurred by the United States.

Stimson replied that while he could not speak for the United States, he would present Churchill's suggestions to Roosevelt. The meeting adjourned with the understanding that Churchill would make his proposals by letter to the President. Cherwell, with Bundy's assistance, would prepare a draft. Stimson was relieved. The discussions, he noted in his diary, produced a "satisfactory atmosphere." [38]

Bush was rather pleased at the turn of events. While Churchill's propositions meant interchange, they included a strong commitment on commercial applications. On July 27, 1943, news arrived that disturbed these sanguine thoughts. One of Anderson's aides called to say that the President had sent the Prime Minister an encouraging message. Bush said he suspected it had been inspired by a Stimson report on the good progress July 22. Privately, he thought it might be Roosevelt's response to Hopkins' report. The next day Bush received a cable transmitting the President's July 20 instructions. Garbled in decoding and paraphrased, it directed him to *review* full interchange.

277

Bush was worried, and he would have been even more worried had he known that the President's instructions really were to *renew*. Might not Churchill refuse to make the overture he had suggested? Might not interchange be resumed without the Prime Minister's fifth proposition as a safeguard? [39] Actually, Bush had nothing to fear. Roosevelt's cable to Churchill had not been nearly so explicit as his instructions to Bush. On July 28, the Prime Minister wrote Stimson to say he had telegraphed the President and had dispatched Anderson to Washington with the draft heads of agreement. The draft understanding, a copy of which he enclosed in the letter to Stimson, was essentially the same as he had outlined at the July 22 meeting. In addition to affirming that any postwar advantages of an industrial or commercial character should be dealt with as Roosevelt should specify, Churchill disclaimed expressly "any interest in these industrial and commercial aspects beyond what may be considered by the President of the United States to be fair and just and in harmony with the economic welfare of the world." [40]

QUEBEC

When Bush returned to Washington the week end of July 30, 1943, he finally discovered that Roosevelt had instructed him to *renew* full interchange. Since the President was inaccessible at Shangri-la, Bush conferred with Stimson and Bundy, who agreed that he should begin discussions on arrangements. On August 3, Bush and Conant called on Sir John Anderson at the British Embassy, reviewed with him the December, 1942, report, and asked how he thought it should be extended in order to speed the war effort.[41]

The following day Sir John sent Bush an expanded version of Churchill's draft agreement, suggesting that they try to reach accord on a document for submittal to the Prime Minister and the President. Anderson's draft began with a Churchillian preamble stressing that a joint effort was vital in order to bring the project to the earliest possible fruition in the present war. Then followed the pledges never to use the weapon against each other and never to communicate it to or employ it against a third party except after mutual agreement. Anderson incorporated the Prime Minister's disclaimer on postwar commercial advantages and added a section specifying arrangements to assure full and effective collaboration. To provide for co-ordination at the top, he proposed a combined policy committee, a body that would agree on the work to be undertaken in each country, keep all sections of the project under constant review, allocate materials in short supply, and settle any questions about the interpretation or application of the agreement. In the field of scientific research and development, full interchange should prevail between those engaged in similar endeavors. In design, construction, and operation of large-scale plants, interchange should be regulated by such *ad hoc* arrangements as might appear necessary or desirable to speed the effort. Such details would be subject to approval by the combined policy committee.[42]

278

From the American point of view, Sir John's proposals were highly satisfactory. Conant's reaction to them was a test. Conant had been alarmed when Roosevelt's July 20 letter arrived at the OSRD. He was convinced that restricted interchange would best serve the war effort, the United States, and the future peace of the world. He did not change his mind on learning that Bush and Stimson had wavered, though he began to wonder if he ought not to join the staff of the Chicago *Tribune*. When he saw Sir John's views, he relaxed. Renewed interchange under the suggested arrangements, he thought, was tantamount to British acceptance of the American offer of the preceding winter. Anderson had pressed somewhat beyond it by providing for interchange of general information at the highest level, but American thinking had never precluded that. Conant did not think that the six-month interruption had delayed the project, but he was glad to see interchange resume, for the diffusion program needed all the help it could get.[43]

Working closely with Conant, Bush spent much of Saturday, August 4, preparing a reply. After conferring with Stimson, Marshall, and Purnell and incorporating changes they suggested, he sent it to the British Embassy Monday morning. Bush restricted himself to the arrangements for collaboration, since the political propositions were beyond his sphere. Anderson's memorandum, he was happy to say, brought the two countries to a position where all misunderstandings could be cleared away and effective collaboration restored. Once the combined policy committee was in being, it could work out the details. The great value of the committee, Bush thought, would be to provide for a thorough understanding of the status of the effort at the top level in the two governments. Committee members would have access to general information about all phases, but the American leadership understood that interchange on the final weapon would require special arrangements. They wanted it clear, moreover, that the existence of the combined policy committee would not interfere with control of the American program by the Army Corps of Engineers.

Anderson closed the negotiation that same Monday. He agreed that the combined policy committee should not interfere with Army control. He thought committee members should have all the information necessary to satisfy themselves that they were making the greatest possible contribution to success. Their work finished, Bush and Anderson submitted the draft to their respective chiefs. Churchill and Roosevelt, they knew, would meet within a fortnight.[44]

Bush was worried lest Roosevelt weaken under the influence of the persuasive Churchill and throw away the commitments he had wrested from the British. When Bush sent the President copies of his correspondence with Sir John, he recorded once again his conviction that all present steps should be solely for winning the war quickly. At the same time, Bush told Bundy he hoped Stimson would try to make the President understand the implications of proceeding beyond the Anderson-Bush draft. Bundy did his part, and when Stimson went to the White House Thursday afternoon, August 9, he carried a note reminding him to tell the President that Bush and Conant were trying to protect him from charges of abusing his war powers.

279

Stimson did not record that he actually made this point to the Chief Executive, but whether he did or not, the fears that Roosevelt might go too far proved unjustified. In a few days, the American and British staffs converged on Quebec. On August 19, 1943, in the Citadel that overlooked the Plains of Abraham, Roosevelt and Churchill signed "Articles of Agreement Governing collaboration between the authorities of the U. S. A. and the U. K. in the matter of Tube Alloys." They approved the arrangement on interchange spelled out by Anderson and Bush and the four political articles as well. Only in one sense did they alter the section on interchange: they added their choice for members of the Combined Policy Committee. Stimson, Bush, and Conant were to serve for the United States and Field Marshal Sir John Dill and Colonel J. J. Llewellin for the United Kingdom. Canada received representation through the appointment of its Minister of Munitions and Supply, the U. S.-born engineer, Clarence D. Howe.[45]

The Quebec Agreement was an effort to resolve a basic conflict of interest, a conflict as intricate and divisive as any in the long annals of Anglo-American discord. Fortunately, the dispute took place behind the ironbound doors of wartime secrecy, and popular passions were not a factor. Even so, the issue threatened the smooth and efficient functioning of the alliance against the Axis. It menaced it at a most inconvenient time for the United

States—when Roosevelt and Stimson were trying to mount a cross-channel attack in face of their ally's deep misgivings. More than that, they were preparing to insist that an American commander lead British troops in an operation that even so stout a warrior as Churchill feared would repeat the horrors of Passchendaele. Yet the Quebec Agreement was no mere concession to sweeten the pill the United States was asking its military partner to swallow. The understanding was the product of a year of hard negotiation. Both Roosevelt and Churchill knew that the stake of their diplomacy was a technological breakthrough so revolutionary that it transcended in importance even the bloody work of carrying the war to the heartland of the Nazi foe.

INTERCHANGE RESUMED

280

The Combined Policy Committee met for the first time at the War Department on September 8, 1943. Presiding at the conference table, Stimson faced a group assembled on short notice. Bush and Howe were not even in Washington. Stimson himself had only a few hours' warning. The day before, Roosevelt had told him that the Anderson-Bush draft had been signed. On the morning of the eighth, just as Stimson was leaving to lunch with the President and the Prime Minister at the White House, a copy of the agreement arrived. To his dismay, Stimson saw that he had been named chairman of the Combined Policy Committee. After lunch, he drew Roosevelt and Churchill aside and told them he could not undertake the routine work the responsibility imposed. Both leaders insisted that he serve but agreed to have General Styer act as his deputy and assume the administrative burden.[46]

The committee met under considerable pressure, for a distinguished group of British scientists—Simon, Chadwick, Peierls, and Marcus L. E. Oliphant—stood in the wings, eager to proceed with interchange. No amount of pressure, however, could conceal the necessity for much detailed staff work. Accordingly, the committee asked Styer to form a subcommittee with Tolman, Chadwick, and Mackenzie—men thoroughly familiar with the American, English, and Canadian programs. The subcommittee would prepare directives for exchanging data on scientific research and development and recommend *ad hoc* arrangements on design, construction, and operation of production plants. Where there was unanimity, the subcommittee might act without consulting the CPC.[47]

On September 10, the subcommittee met at the Pentagon. Styer outlined a plan that the Military Policy Committee had approved the day before. Drafted by General Groves, it set forth the arrangements he considered desirable. In weapons development, it envisaged Chadwick and Oliphant going to Los Alamos, but it insisted that the same restrictions placed on American scientists prevail. To get things started would require a conference set for the following Monday between the British fast-neutron experts and Oppenheimer and Bacher. The MPC plan suggested scientific exchange on the gaseous-diffusion, centrifuge, and thermal-diffusion methods of isotope separation as well as on the heavy-water pile. It made no provision for the electromagnetic process and the graphite pile. Interchange here, the argument went, would jeopardize security without serving a legitimate purpose, for engineering design had reached the stage at which any changes meant costly delays.

The American proposals did not go very far along the road to full interchange. Chadwick protested, and before the long session had ended, he succeeded in making some modifications. The subcommittee finally agreed to extend co-operation on gaseous diffusion and the heavy-water pile beyond scientific research and development to production plants. It settled on special committees to function in each of these areas and on another to consider the desirability of continuing work on the centrifuge and thermal diffusion. Chadwick was not able to force any immediate action on the graphite pile, but he did persuade his colleagues to have Groves, Tolman, and Oliphant take a detailed look at the merits of transferring scientific information on the electromagnetic process.[48]

281

Yet committees were not the answer. The British members could indicate what they were able to bring to the joint effort. They could make tentative arrangements. But they could not speak with finality, for every decision, every assignment of a scientist, had a long-run impact on the British program. In October, Chadwick and Tolman went to England to discuss details, and the work in Washington fell to General Groves and to Colonel Llewellin of the Combined Policy Committee. On December 10, Groves finally submitted a blueprint for interchange sanctioned by Sir John Anderson. The Styer subcommittee approved it the fourteenth as did the Combined Policy Committee a few days later.

Under the new policy, Chadwick was to be the immediate scientific adviser to the British members of the Combined Policy Committee with access to all American and British work on both research and plant scale. Chadwick was also to help direct the experiments at Los Alamos. A small party of scientists would accompany him there. Peierls was to assist at Kellex. Though he could discuss Los Alamos theoretical problems with an appropriate member of the staff, he was not to visit the laboratory. Oliphant and about six assistants were to join Lawrence at Berkeley for as long as they could make contributions that could be incorporated in the plant. Thereafter, they would go to Los Alamos to help on ordnance, but Oliphant was to keep in close contact with Lawrence and the full-scale plant operation. Akers and a mission of about fifteen experts would visit Columbia and Kellex to exchange all information on British and American diffusion methods. The arrangements for Montreal were less definite. Halban and his group were to investigate the physics and chemistry of the heavy-water pile in full collaboration with those making similar studies in the United States but in a program yet to be agreed upon.[49]

These arrangements went a good deal further than Groves liked. Though he was eager for British help when he thought there was a chance that it might advance the American program, as in the case of diffusion, he detested the joint enterprise. After the war, he boasted that he dragged his feet. Certainly he did not go out of his way to expedite interchange. He was carefully and unenthusiastically correct.[50]

Actually, interchange did not wait upon formal approval of the Groves-Llewellin agreement. Machinery for exchanging technical reports was in operation, and British scientists already were at work in the United States.

The most extensive exchange then under way was on gaseous diffusion. Akers had arrived in New York with his fifteen experts, a team that included not only theoreticians Rudolph Peierls and Klaus Fuchs and experimentalist Franz Simon but also specialists on instruments, corrosion, pumps, and barriers. They had already embarked on discussions with Manhattan District contractors that covered the entire effort to build K-25. Early in January, 1944, they took part in the full-scale review conference that eventuated in the decision to manufacture the new nickel barrier. A number of more specialized conferences followed, but by the end of January, most of the Akers group had returned to England to continue developmental studies on plant components. Peierls and Fuchs, however, remained in New York to help Kellex on theory. In February and March, 1944, chemist Harold C. Urey and physicist Eugene T. Booth visited England, but their report on the work there contained nothing to make further interchange seem worthwhile.[51]

December, 1943, also saw the first two British scientists arrive at Los Alamos. Early in 1944, when others had come, Chadwick went out to head the mission. Later, Peierls took over so that Chadwick could be available in Washington. Eventually, more than twenty British scientists joined the laboratory. Though subject to the same isolation as their American co-workers, they did not have to wait until the end of the war to brief their superiors on the details of weapons technology. Peierls sent Chadwick weekly reports that gave him a good picture of developments on the Hill.

Oliphant meanwhile had gone to Berkeley. It was too late to try to impose his ideas for electromagnetic separation on the plant at Oak Ridge, but Lawrence welcomed the Australian physicist and his colleagues as additional hands and brains. Second only to Lawrence in enthusiastic support of Y-12, Oliphant remained at Berkeley until the work was done in March, 1945. His collaboration was unfailingly harmonious.

While Britons and Americans were working together on gaseous diffusion, the electromagnetic process, and the bomb before the end of 1943, interchange between Chicago and Montreal encountered a long delay. Neither Groves nor Conant was eager to agree on a program, for there seemed little or no chance that a joint undertaking on a heavy-water pile would contribute to the war effort. They might have let the matter drift indefinitely had not Chadwick raised it at a Combined Policy Committee meeting on February 17,

282

1944. The English physicist urged the advisability of building a large-scale heavy-water pile in Canada to produce plutonium. He recommended that Great Britain and the United States finance it jointly, use the heavy water produced in the United States, and admit Canada to control. Chadwick's proposal raised several technical questions. Was the project militarily advisable? How soon could it completed? How much would it drain the resources of the participating countries? After considerable discussion, the committee referred the proposal to Chadwick, Groves, and Mackenzie.[52]

This special subcommittee reported seven weeks later, after canvassing the technical situation with the leaders at Chicago and Montreal. It had agreed on certain premises: the Hanford plant would produce enough plutonium for the current war; heavy-water piles probably would have no appreciable influence on the outcome; their marked technical advantages and promising postwar applications argued against neglecting such piles completely. Therefore, both Chicago and Montreal should continue their present efforts to develop fundamental information. The United States, the United Kingdom, and Canada should construct jointly a pilot pile in Canada. When adequate information had been obtained, it would be time to consider a large production unit. In the meantime, somebody should be named to oversee the project. On April 13, the Combined Policy Committee approved these recommendations and asked Chadwick, Groves, and Mackenzie to supervise.[53]

It took another five weeks for Groves and Chadwick to set the ground rules, but on May 20, 1944, the General was able to give Compton a tentative draft of the regulations and authority to begin interchange. The guiding principle was to exchange only information essential to constructing and operating the Canadian pilot plant. This meant—Groves and Chadwick spelled it out—data on the operation of the graphite pile in Tennessee as well as the piles in the Argonne Forest. It included the fundamental physics of a heavy-water pile and such findings on corrosion, water treatment, and properties of materials as were necessary to design and construct the one in Canada. It specifically excluded, however, all construction details on Hanford, the methods of separating plutonium, and plutonium chemistry and purification. The techniques of interchange were to be transmittal of reports and visits of scientists. To see that the needs of the British-Canadian group were met promptly and that irrelevant information was not exchanged, General Groves would establish a liaison office in Montreal.[54]

The scientists in Canada were upset when they learned they were denied data on the chemistry of plutonium. As a gesture in their direction, Groves agreed to permit a limited amount of irradiated uranium in the form of slugs from Clinton to go to Montreal so that the group there could work out independently the methods of plutonium separation and purification. With but this addition, the tentative rules became final.[55]

The Canadian work gradually gathered momentum in the last half of 1944 under the direction of the English physicist, John Cockcroft. While re-

283

search proceeded at Montreal, construction began at Chalk River, the pilot-plant site three hours by train north of Ottawa. Meanwhile, Groves agreed with Chadwick and Cockcroft on the erection of a zero energy exponential pile (ZEEP) to seek data on such questions as lattice dimensions, sheathing materials, and control rods. Groves promptly fulfilled his pledge to establish a liaison office at Montreal, the Evergreen Area, and placed William W. Watson, a Yale physicist from the Metallurgical Laboratory, in charge. The transmittal of reports, the exchange of visits, and the shipment of materials (including loans of heavy water and uranium rods) went forward as planned. Groves made every effort to restrict the flow of information to the subjects that had been agreed upon, but it was a losing battle. When British and Canadian scientists came to work at Chicago, it was inevitable that they should acquire a fairly comprehensive picture of the operations there and some understanding of the difficulties encountered in the production piles at Hanford.[56]

PATENTS

As time went on, the Combined Policy Committee assumed responsibilities that had not been fully foreseen. One of these was patents. The three countries represented on the committee had a common policy: to develop a clear and comprehensive control of the new art. Each required its employees to transfer their rights to the government. It helped to have a common policy, but the exchange of information, ideas, and inventions meant complications. For one example, it was difficult to draft patent documents which would be noninterfering yet comprehensive when an invention made in one country was affected by information received from another. Nor was it clear where lay the initiative for instituting patent action when workers employed by more than one government made a joint invention or when an employee of one nation made a discovery while working in the establishment of the other. A further consideration was security. The three governments wanted to help each other obtain secrecy orders for applications in which they had no direct interest deriving from any contribution to the invention.

The Combined Policy Committee inherited these concerns when Arthur Blok and Robert A. Lavender, the British and American experts, concluded that the uranium field lay outside the scope of the August, 1942, Anglo-American agreement on interchange of patent rights. Bush brought this to the attention of the Combined Policy Committee on April 13, 1944, by pointing to the need for protecting purely British inventions made by United Kingdom scientists working in the United States. The committee referred the whole patent situation to its joint secretaries, Harvey Bundy and W. L. Webster. On September 19, after consulting with Blok, Lavender, and others, they reported a detailed outline of procedures. This agreement, which the committee approved unanimously, was not intended to be a general and final settlement. It was understood that a clarification and settling of interests would be in order later.[57]

ORE: THE LONG VIEW

Uranium ore was another responsibility in which the Combined Policy Committee soon found itself deeply involved. General Groves had summarized the situation in an August 21, 1943, review of the entire project. This report, which he had Colonel Nichols rush to President Roosevelt at Quebec, offered the reassuring conclusion that sufficient ore for expected needs was on hand, under contract, or available in the United States and Canada. Not so heartening was Groves's analysis of long-range prospects. After the war, he told the President, supplies in North America would be well on the way to exhaustion and the United States would face the dilemma of having no control whatever over the major world supply in the Belgian Congo.[58]

285

For some months past, Groves had been worried. In May, 1943, he found a contractor to determine and evaluate the uranium resources of the world. On June 24, the Military Policy Committee approved his recommendation that the United States allow nothing to stand in the way of achieving as complete control as possible.[59]

During the autumn of 1943, Groves tried to persuade Union Minière to reopen the flooded Shinkolobwe Mine and to sell the entire output to the United States. When these efforts did not bring results, the Military Policy Committee concluded that the best hope for obtaining a commitment for Congo ore was to enlist the United Kingdom in a joint approach to the Belgian Government-in-Exile. Not only did Britain normally exercise a large influence on Belgian policy, but British interests also owned perhaps 30 per cent of Union Minière stock. The British also were anxious to open the question of uranium supply, and when the matter came up at the Combined Policy Committee meeting on December 17, everyone agreed to launch the studies necessary to formulate recommendations.[60]

A move to secure ore supplies required approval at the highest level. Groves reported to the President on February 4, 1944, the Military Policy Committee's recommendation that the United States and the United Kingdom take what steps might be necessary to obtain long-term exclusive rights to the Belgian Congo uranium and to deposits involving similar considerations. On February 15, Bush discussed the matter with Roosevelt. So interested that he asked for a map of the Congo with the mines marked, the President indicated his general agreement with the plans. Armed with White House approval, Stimson, Bush, and Conant met the British members of the Combined Policy Committee at Stimson's office on the afternoon of February 17. There they settled on a tentative draft agreement for reference to the governments of the United States, the United Kingdom, and the Dominion of Canada.[61]

The draft agreement envisioned a corporation or other appropriate business agency functioning under the general direction of the Combined Policy Committee. Its board of directors would consist of three Americans, two Britons, and one Canadian. The three nations would split the expenses of operation, with the United States paying one half and the British and Canadians the other. At the end was a bow in the direction of the American Constitution: when hostilities ceased, the heads of state would recommend that this wartime emergency agreement be extended and revised to cover postwar conditions and that it be formalized by treaty or other proper method.[62]

At this point, the scene shifted to London, where Sir John Anderson, now Chancellor of the Exchequer, still presided over the large-policy decisions affecting uranium. Secretary Stimson had the President assign to Ambassador Winant the negotiations with Sir John. With Stimson and Bundy following each step closely from the Pentagon, weeks of drafting and redrafting culminated June 13, 1944, in an Agreement and Declaration of Trust. Signed by Franklin Roosevelt and Winston Churchill, it established a Combined Development Trust of six persons to function under the direction of the Combined Policy Committee. Though it had the same intent as the February 17 proposal, the final document introduced some important changes. For one thing, it created a trust, not a corporation. This reflected American second thoughts about the appropriateness of the corporate form. For another, it dropped Canada as a signatory. This made for consistency with the Quebec Agreement. And while the paper of June 13 was more precise in defining responsibility, it referred simply to "certain areas outside the control of the Two Governments and of the Governments of the Dominions and of India and Burma." [63]

Perhaps the most important change was the injunction that the Trust work to control and develop the production of thorium as well as uranium. As early as 1942, Glenn T. Seaborg had established that when the nucleus of thorium, the ninetieth element, underwent neutron bombardment, it absorbed neutrons and decayed to form a fissionable uranium isotope of mass 233. This was interesting, for it might prove easier to separate uranium 233 from thorium than plutonium from uranium. Besides, it appeared that U-233 might be considerably easier to purify. Nonetheless, Conant and Tolman had to conclude in the summer of 1943 that U-233 was not a program for the current war, for the Hanford piles could not make enough of it unless they were completely redesigned. Then late in April, 1944, Thorfin R. Hogness of the Metallurgical Laboratory called on Conant to report some exciting news. The Chicago group believed that after a pile containing thorium had been started with uranium, it might produce enough U-233 to permit the reaction to sustain itself without the addition of anything but more thorium. Thus thorium

—estimated about ten times as plentiful as uranium—assumed great strategic importance. After checking with Arthur Compton, Conant had General Groves see that the negotiators in London inserted thorium in the agreement. This addition made even broader the world-wide mission of the Combined Development Trust.[64]

The uranium ore of the Belgian Congo had already been the subject of extended negotiations. On March 27, 1944, Sir John Anderson and Ambassador Winant had met the ministers of the Belgian Government-in-Exile at the Chancellor's chambers on Great George Street and canvassed the situation. Stressing the need to keep the ore from falling into the wrong hands, they asked for an option to buy the entire uranium output of the Congo. Though the Belgian ministers were not unreceptive, they would not negotiate in the absence of Edgar Sengier, the principal official of Union Minière, who was in New York. So the British asked Sengier to come to London, and at a series of meetings in early May, Anderson and Winant again pleaded their case. Sengier was reluctant to enter a long-term arrangement, but Belgian officials agreed in principle to grant the right of first refusal on Congo uranium. They were willing to guarantee a contract for reopening the Shinkolobwe Mine and for supplying 1,720 tons of uranium oxide. Any further amounts needed for military purposes they were willing to deliver at cost plus a reasonable margin of profit.

Anderson and Winant quickly submitted draft articles to clinch the understanding, but the Belgians did not submit counterproposals until July 14. They not only raised their price for co-operation during the war but insisted that discussion on the postwar period be limited to exploring means for collaboration with the United States and Britain in acquiring and using the uranium and thorium of the Congo. Anderson and Winant sought vainly in two long conferences to prevail against this position, but the Belgians took a strong stand for a ninety-nine year agreement on three-power control and utilization.[65]

Following the negotiations from Washington, Henry Stimson saw the danger that the impasse might delay acquisition of the first 1,720 tons. On August 25, he briefed the President on the situation. Roosevelt agreed on the wisdom of negotiating the short-range contract alone in order to get quick action in developing the Congo supply. On September 26, 1944, the United States and the United Kingdom finally reached agreement with the Belgian Government that African Metals (acting for Union Minière) would contract with the Combined Development Trust for the 1,720 tons of uranium oxide. While the American and British negotiators did not attain their full postwar aims, they won a right of first refusal on all the uranium and thorium ores for a period of ten years after the conclusion of the first contract. This was at least a start. When the Combined Policy Committee considered the matter a few days before the agreement became final, Stimson, Bush, and Conant expressed their satisfaction that the arrangement promised important supplies for some years. Besides, they consoled themselves, complete pre-emption of raw materials probably was not practical.[66]

The Combined Development Trust began to function in July, 1944, when General Groves and Sir Charles Hambro, the principal American and British members, undertook to negotiate the Shinkolobwe contract with Sengier. The Trust assumed control of the uranium and thorium supplies liberated by the advancing allied armies. Most important, it surveyed for the Combined Policy Committee the present and potential sources of raw material throughout the world. At the end of November, Groves, who served as chairman of the CDT, sent Stimson a report that depended heavily on the work done for the Manhattan District. It found the uranium situation encouraging. If Britain and the United States could augment their own resources with the ore of the Congo, they would have over 90 per cent of the world's likely supply. Thorium was so scattered throughout the world that such complete control was virtually impossible, but the two governments could obtain a dominant position by controlling sources in India and Brazil. If they could supplement these with the thorium of the Dutch East Indies, Ceylon, and Madagascar, so much the better. In short, the Anglo-American raw-material position was strong. But the United States and Britain should not fall into a false sense of security. Groves told Stimson that until the Combined Policy Committee instructed otherwise, the Trust would assume it should purchase major uranium deposits and remove them to safe storage. Its stockpile of uranium should be as large as possible. It probably was not yet wise to purchase thorium, but the Trust should seek options and political agreements to assure control should the mineral become as important as it seemed it might. Thus the Combined Development Trust arrived at a program of aggressive action.[67]

MIDSUMMER HARMONY

The Anglo-American partnership appeared to be working very well indeed in the summer of 1944. The Combined Policy Committee encountered no differences too difficult to resolve. Both countries were moving quietly to strengthen their control of the essential raw materials. British scientists were at work in the laboratories at Berkeley and Los Alamos. Groves, Chadwick, and Mackenzie finally had completed arrangements for Chicago-Montreal collaboration. Bush was so pleased that he wrote warmly to Sir John Anderson: "There is complete harmony, and rapid progress, and we certainly can ask for no more than this." [68] Relaxing for a moment in the satisfaction of having overcome great obstacles, neither man fully recognized the potential for discord that remained.

RACE FOR THE BOMB:
HOMESTRETCH

CHAPTER 9

On Friday morning, June 9, 1944, Secretary of War Stimson with his customary dedication was struggling with the intricacies of global warfare. The first American troops had hit the Normandy beaches on Tuesday and were driving toward Cherbourg. In Italy, Allied forces were advancing north of Rome. In New Guinea, Army units were consolidating positions on Biak Island. Nearing the end of one of the most momentous weeks of the war, the Secretary looked forward to the few hours of relaxation the week end promised.

CONGRESS AND APPROPRIATIONS

Under the circumstances, Stimson was hardly pleased when General Somervell brought him the news that the Senate Appropriations Committee would consider at once the War Department bill which was about to pass the House. Since General Marshall was out of town, Stimson faced the prospect of spending Saturday morning on Capitol Hill. Someone would have to explain the huge appropriation for S-1 which the Army had buried in the bill and clear the way for Senate action without public discussion of the sensitive items. Fortunately, the session would be a repeat performance for Stimson. On February 18, he had gone with Marshall and Bush to Speaker Sam Rayburn's office on a similar mission. In a secret session with the Speaker, Majority Leader John W. McCormack and Minority Leader Joseph W. Martin, Stimson revealed to members of Congress for the first time the purpose of S-1. Without hesitation, they assured him that the House would act swiftly without giving more than a partial explanation to a few members of the Appropriations Committee.

On Saturday morning, June 10, Stimson rode to the Senate Office

Building with Bush and General George J. Richards, War Department budget officer. In addition to Senators Alben W. Barkley and Wallace H. White, the majority and minority leaders, Senators Elbert Thomas and Styles Bridges, ranking members of the Appropriations Subcommittee, were present. Stimson told them the bill contained a large appropriation for S-1. He explained how the Germans were believed to have had a head start in the race for the bomb. Since Pearl Harbor, S-1 had expanded to an enterprise of vast proportions. Army expenditures had risen from $16 million in calendar year 1942 to more than $344 million in 1943. Expenditures in 1944 had already exceeded the 1943 figure and were approaching $100 million per month. Stimson estimated that before the end of the next fiscal year, the nation would have close to $1.5 billion invested. The costs were staggering but so were the anticipated results. With the funds he was requesting, Stimson expected the Army to produce a bomb small enough to be carried in a single plane and powerful enough to be a decisive factor in the outcome of the war. After stressing the need for absolute secrecy, Stimson yielded to Bush.

290

The OSRD chief touched on the technology of S-1. He explained that "there was now no scientist either in Britain or the United States associated with this matter that did not believe that the program would be successful." He described the Stagg Field experiment as but one confirmation of the scientific theory postulated in 1939. With great care and precision, the thousands of scientists and engineers under Army contract were coming in sight of their goal. Not only were they on the homestretch; Bush was convinced they were now well ahead of the Germans.

It remained to General Richards to reveal the budgetary camouflage. He had smuggled a $600 million appropriation for S-1 into the carry-over from 1944 for "expediting production." The Senators were impressed. Pledging their complete co-operation, Barkley and his colleagues assured Stimson that the carry-over item would pass the Senate without a word of discussion.[1]

In the full context of events, Bush was justified in glossing the facts a bit. What he had said was true: there was little doubt that a bomb could be produced. What he neglected to say was whether the bomb would in fact be completed in time to play its decisive part in the war. The remarkable achievements in constructing and equipping the plants at Oak Ridge and Hanford dispelled most doubts of eventual success. But how long would it take? The electromagnetic plant, months behind the original construction schedules, had scarcely begun to operate. The gaseous-diffusion plant was but half finished with no guarantee when mass production of an acceptable barrier might begin. Operation of the Hanford piles was threatened by the failure to develop a satisfactory slug-canning process. New facts from the Clinton pile about the properties of plutonium had disrupted weapons research at Los Alamos. To use Conant's analogy, the United States had three horses well out in front in the homestretch, but no one could yet say confidently that even one of them could clear the remaining hurdles in the required time.

URANIUM: FROM MINE TO PLANT

Procurement of uranium ore in quantities significant for large-scale production of fissionable materials began with Colonel Nichols' aggressive activities
in September, 1942. Two conferences with Edgar Sengier of the African Metals Corporation resulted in a basic agreement giving the Army the option to
buy some 1,200 tons of Belgian ore already in the United States and about
3,000 tons above ground in the Congo. Before the end of the year, Nichols'
staff in New York had negotiated the purchase of the entire amount. A few
hundred tons had been shipped to the Eldorado mill at Port Hope, Ontario,
for refining as pure uranium oxide, the remainder having been stored at the
Seneca Ordnance Depot at Romulus, New York. Meanwhile, African Metals
was preparing to transport Congo ore in several-hundred-ton lots from West
African ports. Sea transport over the U-boat infested waters of the South Atlantic was a dangerous enterprise, but by using sixteen-knot ships, the company brought through all but two cargoes. Since deliveries from the Congo
far exceeded the capacity of processing plants in 1943, the Army leased a
warehouse in Middlesex, New Jersey, where storage, sampling, and assaying
facilities were established close to the Port of New York. By the end of 1944,
the Army had received Congo ores containing approximately 3,700 tons of
uranium oxide.

Also in September, 1942, Nichols began negotiations with Eldorado
Gold Mines, Ltd. (later called Eldorado Mining and Refining, Ltd.), both
for producing ore in their mine on Great Bear Lake and for refining Canadian
and Belgian ore at Port Hope. Under an OSRD contract, Eldorado had reopened the mine during the summer of 1942 and moved a small quantity of
ore to the refinery. In December, the Army negotiated a new contract which
brought the total amount of refined oxide on order to about 700 tons.

Canadian ore deliveries to Port Hope rose sharply in 1943, the first
year of full-scale operation. No longer depending on the three short months
of open water on the Mackenzie's tributaries, Eldorado could now use an airlift of United States and Canadian military planes to haul ore from the mine
to a new RCAF field at Fort McMurray. The airlift moved almost 300 tons
of ore during 1943 to the railhead at Waterways for shipment to Port Hope.
By the end of 1944, the refinery had produced about 400 tons of uranium
oxide, and Eldorado had above ground enough ore for 500 additional tons.[2]

Within the United States, uranium occurred in carnotite ores on the
Colorado Plateau, but the few deposits of high-grade ore had long since been
mined for radium, and to a lesser extent for vanadium and uranium. The
heavy demand for vanadium early in the war gave the industry a new lease
on life and provided a small but practical source of uranium as a by-product
of vanadium production. The process used by the Vanadium Corporation of
America at Naturita, Colorado, could produce a vanadium-uranium sludge

291

containing about 50 per cent uranium oxide. The United States Vanadium Corporation had stockpiled at its Uravan, Colorado, plant tremendous quantities of vanadium tailings containing unconcentrated uranium oxide. Early in 1942, the company built a small pilot plant which could concentrate the tailings in a sludge of 20-per-cent oxide. Late in the year, the Army arranged with another Union Carbide subsidiary, the Linde Air Products Company, to build a pilot refinery at Tonawanda, New York, to produce uranium oxide from the USVC sludge.

A survey of activities on the Colorado Plateau in December, 1942, led to Manhattan District contracts with both USVC and VCA. By the end of 1944, USVC had produced from its stockpile almost 150 tons of uranium oxide in a 20-per-cent sludge in its Uravan plant and had provided tailings for almost 400 tons produced in the Government-owned plant at the same site. At Durango, Colorado, where USVC operated a Government vanadium plant, the company produced about eighty tons of oxide of 20-per-cent concentration before purchasing the Government-owned sludge plant in August, 1944. The 20-per-cent sludges were further concentrated in the central refinery which USVC operated for the Government at Grand Junction, Colorado. During the same period, VCA concentrated about eighty tons of oxide in a 50-per-cent sludge at its Naturita plant and sold tailings to the Government for refining at Uravan. All the domestic ore in process by the end of 1944 would yield not more than 800 tons of oxide.

Adding up all his sources in late 1944, Nichols could see that he had in various concentrations almost 6,000 tons of uranium oxide, which then appeared to be enough to operate all the S-1 plants until the fall of 1945. Two-thirds came from high-grade Congo sources, a little more than one-sixth from Canadian pitchblende, and one-seventh from the Colorado Plateau. By 1944 standards, the domestic enterprise was small and relatively expensive, but it would serve as the nucleus for a domestic uranium industry if significant ore reserves were later discovered.[3]

By the summer of 1943, the Army supply line included three refineries for processing ore to pure uranium concentrates, uranium oxide (U_3O_8) or sodium diuranate. Eldorado had greatly expanded its Port Hope refinery to handle most of the high-grade African ores and all the Canadian deliveries from Great Bear Lake. The Vitro Manufacturing Company processed a substantial portion of the high-grade Congo ores and all the VCA 50-per-cent sludges at its Cannonsburg, Pennsylvania, plant. Linde, drawing on its experience with the pilot refinery, began processing the 20-per-cent sludges from USVC, its Carbide affiliate, at Tonawanda. Late in 1943, the plant was converted to processing low-grade African ores until the end of 1944.

The next step was to reduce the concentrate to lower oxides. The Mallinckrodt Chemical Works produced two-thirds of all the orange (UO_3) and brown (UO_2) oxides at its St. Louis plant with the solvent-extraction process which the company developed on an industrial scale in 1942. The second largest producer of brown oxide was du Pont. The company began production in the plant at Deepwater Point, New Jersey, in June, 1943. More than half the du Pont product came from scrap and by-product materials from other steps in the production chain. Linde, as part of its Tonawanda plant, produced a small amount of black oxide before that section of the plant was placed in stand-by in the spring of 1944.

At this point the supply line branched to furnish uranium in the various forms required for the production plants. Mallinckrodt shipped orange oxide directly to the electromagnetic plant at Oak Ridge, where it was converted to the tetrachloride (UCl_4) for separation in the calutrons. In a building adjacent to its St. Louis plant, Mallinckrodt constructed the facilities that produced most of the green salt (UF_4) for the project after the spring of 1943. The fluoride was shipped to the Harshaw Chemical Company in Cleveland, where Abelson's process was used to produce the hexafluoride (UF_6) for the thermal- and gaseous-diffusion plants at Oak Ridge. Early in 1943, Harshaw supplied some green salt for the reduction process which Frank Spedding developed at Iowa State College for producing uranium metal. But after metal production began on a large scale, Linde and Mallinckrodt produced most of the green salt for the reduction process. By late 1944, Harshaw was using its green-salt facilities to develop a two-step method of producing hexafluoride.

293

All of the uranium metal used in Fermi's Stagg Field experiment came from Westinghouse in Pittsburgh, Metal Hydrides in Beverley, Massachusetts, or the pilot plant at Ames, Iowa, which Spedding built to perfect the calcium reduction of uranium tetrafluoride. Before the end of 1942, Spedding and his associates had concluded that none of these methods could produce uranium metal of the quality and quantity needed for full-scale plutonium piles. Gambling on the ultimate superiority of magnesium reduction, the Ames group turned all its efforts to that process in February, 1943.

The key to the new process lay in the fact that magnesium reduction required a higher reaction temperature than did the calcium method. The higher temperature was attained at Ames by placing the steel bomb containing the mixed charge of magnesium and tetrafluoride in a heat-soaking pit until the temperature of the charge was raised to the point of spontaneous ignition. The reaction developed sufficient additional heat to fuse the products, the dense liquid uranium metal collecting in the bottom of the bomb and the magnesium fluoride slag on top. The bomb was then allowed to cool and the solidified metal was removed as one large mass or "biscuit." The biscuits, weighing from 40 to 125 pounds depending on the size of the bombs, were melted in a vacuum induction furnace and poured into graphite molds to form ingots about four inches in diameter and some thirteen inches long.

So thoroughly did the Ames group investigate the magnesium process in early 1943 that no other method was considered for the production plants constructed that spring. The largest was that built at Niagara Falls, New York, by the Electro Metallurgical Company, the third Carbide affiliate in the ore-to-metal production chain. Electromet produced the first ingot in its new plant in July. Just a few days later, Mallinckrodt began production on the floor above its green salt plant in St. Louis. Du Pont operated a small reduction facility at its Deepwater Point plant until August, 1944, and Spedding expanded the pilot plant at Ames into a respectable production facility. Both Metal Hydrides and Westinghouse continued metal production during the summer of 1943. The Westinghouse electrolytic plant was shut down during the fall after producing sixty-five tons of high-grade uranium metal. Metal Hydrides, du Pont, and Ames gradually shifted their operations to recovering the ever increasing amounts of uranium scrap and turnings from the slug fabrication plant at Hanford. From time to time, there were minor fluctuations in the uranium supply lines, but this general pattern prevailed from the fall of 1943 until the end of the war.[4]

294

U-235: COMPLETING THE PLANTS

The supply lines were ready but the plants were not. Surveying his sprawling empire in July, 1944, General Groves could not yet foresee with certainty when the first significant quantities of uranium 235 or plutonium would be produced for weapons. In Chicago on the seventeenth, Groves and his scientific advisers had reluctantly concluded that Oppenheimer should abandon attempts to use plutonium in a gun-type weapon. Unless the much more complicated technique of implosion were perfected, the nation might have to rely on uranium 235. Unfortunately, the prospects for fissionable material in quantity were poor.

Since the summer of 1942, Groves and his aides had counted on the electromagnetic process for quick if not the most economic production. Stone & Webster had started to build the Y-12 plant at Oak Ridge in February, 1943, four months before J. A. Jones broke ground for the gaseous-diffusion plant in the K-25 area. Faltering production in the oval Alpha racetracks began in January, 1944. Sporadic runs with the first four tracks yielded a few samples of slightly enriched material which were shipped to Los Alamos during the spring of 1944. But even after five months of frenzied maintenance, repair, and modification, Tennessee Eastman had not achieved anything resembling routine operation.

Some of this discouraging performance could be discounted by the fact that the four original Alpha tracks, with only two cold sources in each tank, were no longer expected to bear the main burden. The great hope rested in the new Alpha II and Beta calutrons which would employ the more compact high-voltage double sources. Attempts to operate the new calutrons, however, created the same sort of maddening frustration that had gripped Y-12 six months earlier during the first Alpha runs. In Alpha 5, the first track to use the double "hot" sources, equipment failures occurred in such numbers that no more than a small percentage of the calutrons could be operated at any one time. Failures of the insulators supporting the hot sources alone accounted for a quarter of the breakdowns at times, but operating errors and defective workmanship also took their toll. Tennessee Eastman could only hope it could straighten out most of the kinks before Alpha tracks 6 to 9 were ready for operation.

Even more crucial was the performance of the Beta tracks, which were to enrich the product of the Alpha plants from about 15-per-cent uranium 235 to something more than 90 per cent. By the end of June, 1944, both tracks in the first Beta building were operating, one devoted to production, the other to training personnel and experimentation. Not even General Groves could expect the initial output from the first track to be large, but one could reasonably anticipate output approaching design capacity within a few weeks. Nothing of the kind materialized. The best efforts of the Beta operators could not produce fifty grams of uranium 235 in June. When there was little sign of improvement in July, the General made two trips to Oak Ridge to investigate.[5]

295

The probable causes seemed obvious. Beta, like Alpha II, was suffering from insulator failures in the hot sources. There were the usual water and vacuum leaks, assembly errors in components, and mistakes by inexperienced operators. The Tennessee Eastman staff also recognized the possibility of losses or hold-up of uranium in the complicated chemical equipment. Not until late August, however, did Groves have a precise appraisal of the situation. At a meeting in the Manhattan District offices in New York on August 25, J. H. Webb of Tennessee Eastman presented a detailed analysis of Beta performance. After almost three months of operation, he said, the plant was running at less than 50-per-cent efficiency. Judging from the amount of charge material fed to the Beta calutrons, he estimated that the tracks themselves were operating at an efficiency of 83 per cent. Most of the trouble seemed to lie in chemical processing.

Those associated with Y-12, including Lawrence, had early recognized their preoccupation with physics rather than chemistry, but they had never successfully overcome that bias. The prosaic techniques of chemical processing could hardly compare with the novelty and magnitude of the electromagnetic plant. Alpha chemistry appeared to be simple from the start, and experience had shown that estimate to be correct. Lawrence sparked the first research on Beta chemistry in the spring of 1943, but not until a year later did the Y-12 team knuckle down to the details.

The physicists understood the technical intricacies of Beta, but they never fully appreciated the effect of the second stage on production. Feed for Beta came from the Alpha tracks at great expense in time and money. During the first months of 1944, not more than 4 per cent of the uranium 235 in the Alpha charge bottle reached the receiver. This pinch of material had to be recovered, purified, and accumulated for Beta. Then the process was repeated with no better efficiencies than in Alpha. During April, 1944, less than 5 per cent of the uranium 235 in the Beta charge found its way to the receivers. Refining this product was hard enough, but most of the scientists had underestimated the task of recovering the preponderance of the charge which failed to vaporize or ionize, coated electrodes, splattered the liner, or missed the receiver pocket. The internals of the tanks had to be scrubbed, the enriched material recovered from the wash and repurified for another low-efficiency run in the Beta tanks. The complexity of the processing cycle caused some losses of the valuable Alpha product, but more important were the growing inventories of material in the chemistry recycle and the loss of time.

The first reaction at Y-12 was to minimize losses in the recycle equipment. Small but significant amounts of enriched material were imbedded in calutron parts. Traces were left behind in the wash tanks. Still larger quantities were trapped in the glass-lined tubing, stainless-steel centrifuges, filters, tanks, and rubber gloves. But after tearing down and dissolving some of the equipment for chemical analysis, the Tennessee Eastman engineers were convinced that the losses themselves were of minor importance. More urgent was the need to reduce inventories in the recycle by speeding up processing time. They would replace the glass-lined tubing with pyrex, straighten out some of the bends, study different solvents, use more graphite parts which could be burned for uranium recovery, and even resort to electrolytic stripping of metallic parts. In this way, they hoped to reduce recycle holdup from about six days to two. All these improvements seemed reasonable, but until they were accomplished, there would be no significant production of uranium 235.[6]

Scarcely less critical during the summer of 1944 was the status of the gaseous-diffusion and liquid-thermal-diffusion projects. While Houdaille-Hershey rushed the production of barrier for the K-25 plant, the H. K. Ferguson Company threw its full resources into constructing the S-50 plant next to the K-25 powerhouse at Oak Ridge.

On June 27, 1944, the Ferguson management signed a War Department contract to construct the thermal-diffusion plant within ninety days. The day before, Admiral Ernest J. King had ordered blueprints of the Philadelphia pilot plant sent to the contractor. After studying these drawings and examining Abelson's one-hundred-tube plant at the Navy Yard, the Ferguson engineers concluded that they could do little more than build twenty-one exact duplicates of the Philadelphia plant and tie them together with steam lines running to the K-25 powerhouse.[7]

The one critical procurement item was the 48-foot columns in which the thermal-diffusion process occurred. It was one thing to make 100 columns in a Navy shop and something else to fabricate more than 2,000 of them commercially. Extremely uniform tubing was required to maintain the critical annular spacing between the inner nickel and outer copper tubes. Perfect roundness and a tolerance of 0.002 inch was difficult to attain especially when copper and nickel tubing could not be drawn in 48-foot lengths. Only after

INTERIOR OF S-50, LIQUID-THERMAL-DIFFUSION PLANT / A few of the 2,142 identical 48-foot process columns that were housed in a building 522 feet long, 82 feet wide, and 75 feet high.

BETA SOURCE UNIT / During operation the two beams of ions were projected from the vertical slots. At the conclusion of a run it was necessary to wash off and recover the uranium-tetrachloride scale.

INSIDE THE U AT K-25 DURING CONSTRUCTION / The partially completed gaseous-diffusion plant presented a cluttered appearance in September, 1944.

J. E. WESTCOTT

K-25 POWERHOUSE AND S-50 / The power plant (rated capacity: 238,000 kilowatts) stands beside the Clinch River. Behind the power station is the S-50 complex: the main process building, the supplementary boiler plant, and the fuel-oil tank farm.

Y-12, THE COMPLETED ELECTROMAGNETIC PLANT / The town of Oak Ridge lies in the distance to the left.

K-25, THE COMPLETED GASEOUS-DIFFUSION PLANT / This four-story structure was almost one-half mile long and almost 2 million square feet in area.

canvassing twenty-one manufacturers did Ferguson find two contractors willing to accept the assignment. The Mehring & Hanson Company of Washington, D. C., and the Grinnell Company of Providence, Rhode Island, quickly devised methods of welding and soldering shorter lengths of nickel and copper tubing. They also learned how to maintain the critical annular spacing between the tubes by welding small nickel buttons to the inner tube to act as spacers. Fastening the tubes together was a tricky process requiring the use of hot nickel and cold copper to reduce thermal stresses during operation. Using trial-and-error methods, the fabricators were soon able to reduce the number of failures and increase production in each plant to fifty columns per day.

On July 9, four days after awarding the contracts for column fabrication, Ferguson began clearing the site on the banks of the Clinch. By the end of the month foundations were complete. On these, the various subcontractors erected the maze of steel racks, heavy cooling-water pipes, steam lines, valves, and ventilators. The whole was enclosed in a huge barnlike structure of black-coated metal siding more than 500 feet long, 80 feet wide, and 75 feet high. Ferguson co-ordinated the design and fabrication of special pumps for the cooling-water system and a novel desuperheating process for reducing steam from the K-25 powerhouse to the conditions required for S-50.

297

Ferguson had little time or opportunity to prepare for plant operations. To avoid possible disputes with labor unions, the company early obtained permission from the Manhattan District to establish a wholly-owned operating subsidiary called the Fercleve Corporation. About the end of August, four Fercleve employees and several Army enlisted men went to Philadelphia to be trained as operators on Abelson's pilot plant. On September 2, the mechanical failure of a tank containing uranium hexafluoride killed two operators and injured several others. It did not take Abelson long to make repairs, but by that time the first rack was nearing completion in the S-50 plant.

At Oak Ridge, riggers and steam fitters began installing the first process columns during the first week of September. With welders, carpenters, sheet metal workers, and electricians swarming over the plant, the operators introduced the first steam in Rack 21 on September 15. From that day on, they learned to work amid the hissing clouds of escaping high-pressure steam that drowned out all conversation and enveloped the racks. The S-50 plant surpassed the wildest dreams of the cartoonist Rube Goldberg, but Abelson, the Ferguson engineers, and the Army and Navy officers were confident it would work. General Groves had asked that operation begin on September 16, just sixty-nine days after the start of construction. On that day, one-third of the process building was complete, the fabricators had delivered 320 columns, and preliminary operations had started in Rack 21. This was an extraordinary achievement, but the future did not look good. Ferguson would have to develop a new type of connector between steam lines and the columns to eliminate excessive leakage. Column fabrication was falling behind schedule. The operators were far from ready to place hexafluoride in the columns. September passed and most of October, and only the thin stream of material from the Alpha racetracks was available to feed the Beta plant, still stumbling through shakedown runs at Y-12.

In September, the K-25 plant was still too far from completion to be a predictable source of uranium 235. Although the massive U-shaped structure was more than half finished, Kellex had received just two complete models of the thousands of converters that would comprise the cascade. Carbide operators were performing test runs in one section of the plant with fifty-four converters containing dummy barrier tubes and operating on nitrogen gas. The test unit provided valuable information on instrumentation and leak-testing, but it was impossible to simulate true operating conditions. The great question mark was still barrier production. By the end of August, Houdaille-Hershey had shipped a few thousand finished tubes to the Chrysler assembly plant in Detroit, but even they failed to meet minimum standards. Carbide had expected to begin production runs with the first 400 stages on January 1, 1945. The failure to produce satisfactory barrier threw those plans in doubt. In October, Nichols reported to Groves that initial operation of K-25 might miss that date by as much as ten weeks unless the barrier crisis ended soon.[8]

U-235: PLANNING FOR PRODUCTION

Although none of the Oak Ridge plants had approached full operation, Nichols realized it was time to make detailed production plans. The existence of three plants, each with unique advantages and disadvantages, made possible a variety of operating schemes. To determine which pattern would most quickly yield the uranium 235 for a bomb, Nichols appointed a production-control committee in September, 1944. Under Lieutenant Colonel Arthur V. Peterson, the group included contractor representatives from each of the projects.

The plan Groves had formulated in August, 1943, was to use the Alpha racetracks at Y-12 and the K-25 plant for the lower stages of enrichment, in which the amounts of process material would be large. At that time, the General abandoned plans to build the top portion of the K-25 cascade, thereby fixing the plant at something less than 50-per-cent uranium 235. When the barrier crisis threatened to limit the enrichment capability of K-25 to a few per cent of the 235 isotope, Groves had authorized the last-minute construction of S-50. Now, Nichols told the committee, the method of producing the maximum amount of material would depend upon proper combinations of feed for the three plants. The relationships between capacities, losses, and construction schedules could be solved only by careful study and mathematical analysis.[9]

Nichols' timing was good. Just as gloom and frustration marked the record in September and October, the closing weeks of the year brought solid accomplishment. At Y-12, November production equalled that of all previous months combined. Output from the original Alpha I tracks was small but steady. As Tennessee Eastman overcame insulator and operating failures in Alpha II, production increased erratically but sharply. There was also evidence that the bottleneck in Beta chemistry was breaking up, not suddenly from one single action but gradually over the weeks as the contractor completed minor refinements in equipment and operating techniques. The statistics were also reflecting the steady addition of Alpha II and Beta tracks. All of the four Alpha II tracks and the two Beta units authorized in September, 1943, were now complete. Even more impressive was the progress on the third Beta building containing tracks 5 and 6. The plant, intended to handle increasing amounts of partially enriched material from K-25, was not started until May 22, 1944. Six months later, most of the calutrons in Beta 5 and 6 were operating. To sum up, all nine Alpha and three Beta tracks were in production on December 15, 1944. Beta 4 and 6 were processing unenriched Alpha feed, and Beta 5 was devoted to training operators. Y-12 was far from its potential, but production was at last gaining momentum.[10]

299

S-50 was hardly operating but it was nearing completion in December, 1944. Colonel Mark C. Fox's courageous effort to have a section of the plant running seventy days after the start of construction had been successful but not significant in terms of production. At best, the summer campaign at S-50 was a device to accelerate construction to an unprecedented pace; at worst, it was another example of the Army's emphasis on gross construction progress even at the expense of systematic process development. The fact was, however, that hard work had built the plant in less than six months. Fercleve delivered a token sample of slightly enriched hexafluoride to Y-12 in October; regular deliveries seemed still some months off.

The mediocre performance of both S-50 and the Alpha I racetracks made K-25 look even more important by the end of 1944. Only the stubborn barrier problem stood in the way of quantity production. K-25 had staggering dimensions, but from what engineers now knew about the idiosyncrasies of operating calutrons and thermal-diffusion columns, the simplicity of pumping gas through pipes and filters looked more inviting than ever. Automation, not art, seemed the key to large-scale operation.

Nichols could not yet be sure Kellex had broken the barrier impasse, but there were encouraging signs. By December, 1944, Chrysler was receiving in Detroit enough barrier tubes to assemble a large number of converters each month. Carbide already had many converters in place at K-25. Though a negligible portion of the entire plant, these few units could be the foundation for the production effort if properly utilized. From the beginning, Carbide's philosophy had been to plan assembly of the plant in such a way that each converter could be operated as soon as it had been installed. With the cooperation of Kellex, Carbide followed this plan. As quickly as the converters were connected to the assembly of pipes, pumps, and instruments in the K-25 building, Carbide-Kellex teams began operating them in groups with nitrogen and other test gases to detect leaks and other defects. As soon as the segments passed inspection, they could be charged with hexafluoride gas and hooked together in a small cascade. Proceeding in this way, Carbide anticipated that most of the plant would be in production weeks if not months before the last unit was completed.

Testing and modification necessarily marked the closing weeks of 1944. So vast was the plant and so rigorous the vacuum requirements that the contractors employed hundreds of technicians solely in leak detection. These tests required special mass spectrometer equipment since the leak rate for the entire cascade could not be as large as that permitted by a single small hole. The large number of stages also made the smallest modification of equipment a big job.

300   On January 20, 1945, the first stages were charged with hexafluoride. Because the process gas was recycled through the stages, it was technically accurate to say that K-25 had started to separate the uranium isotopes. Pump troubles plagued Carbide's efforts to start up additional stages during the next three weeks. But by late February, the shakedown runs seemed to be approaching an end. Hundreds of components were being modified and adjusted according to new specifications. The chances seemed good that Carbide could add new sections as quickly as the manufacturers could deliver pumps and converters.

By the first of March, S-50 and Y-12 were also picking up speed. For the first time, all twenty-one racks in the S-50 plant were in production; March output would be more than twice that of all previous months. Now the S-50 product was having a measurable effect as feed for Y-12. Together, the two plants were making impressive gains in producing highly enriched uranium 235.

Transporting the precious material to Los Alamos involved all the melodrama of an undercover operation. Since air travel seemed too risky, the Army shipped the product by rail. The containers of uranium tetrafluoride were packed in special luggage. At 10:30 A.M. on specified days, armed couriers wearing civilian clothes took the shipments to Knoxville in an unmarked Chevrolet sedan with Tennessee license plates. At 12:50 P.M., the couriers left for Chicago in a private compartment aboard the "Southland." Arriving in Chicago the next morning, the Oak Ridge couriers were met by security officers from the local Manhattan District office. At 12:01 P.M., Chicago couriers boarded the Santa Fe "Chief" for the long ride west. The next day at 2:10 P.M., a car from Los Alamos met the train at Lamy, a way station in the New Mexico desert. There was some danger that conductors, porters, and station attendants might come to recognize the couriers no matter how hard they tried to make themselves inconspicuous, but train transportation was cheap and relatively safe.[11]

As the production-control group analyzed the performance of the electromagnetic plant, they saw that Y-12 was weakest in the lower stages of enrichment, particularly in the inefficient and now obsolete Alpha I tracks. It was just in this range that they expected K-25 and S-50 to be at their best. The continuous operation of cascades seemed much more practical than the Y-12 batch method for processing the large amounts of material which contained only a small percentage of uranium 235. In the final stages of enrichment, involving a small amount of valuable material, the absolute separation of the Y-12 plant seemed clearly superior to the statistical principle of separation in the diffusion methods.

On these premises, the production-control committee mapped out a detailed plan in late February. They had to include several alternatives since the precise operating characteristics of K-25 were not yet known. For the most part, however, the alternatives involved dates rather than procedures. The general plan was that S-50 would operate at full capacity to enrich relatively large amounts of feed material from 0.71 per cent of natural uranium to 0.89-per-cent uranium 235. The S-50 product would be fed to the Alpha tracks at Y-12 until K-25 demonstrated that it could achieve an enrichment of 1.1 per cent and could handle the S-50 product. Then the chain would be from S-50 to K-25 to Y-12. The gaseous-diffusion plant would produce 1.1-per-cent material at maximum capacity until it could furnish material of 20-per-cent enrichment. Then K-25 would be gradually shifted to 20-per-cent production, and Y-12 would begin to shut down the Alpha I calutrons. It remained for the analysts to calculate the precise feed rates between plants.[12]

301

The start-up of additional units of K-25 early in March indicated the production campaign could be effected as planned. On March 12, three buildings were tied together in a cascade capable of generating a significant amount of feed. Now Groves was ready to commit himself on long-range construction. Since December, 1943, the production-control group had been toying with the idea of adding the top on the K-25 cascade, and Lawrence had renewed his pleas for a large addition to Y-12. Neither scheme, however, fitted the plan for tandem operation of the two plants. On March 16, 1944, the General cancelled the authorization for the K-25 addition. He had already formally rejected Lawrence's request for additional Alpha tracks at Y-12. Following the advice of the production-control group, Groves decided instead to build a second gaseous-diffusion plant which would increase capacity in the lower stages of enrichment and to add a fourth Beta plant at Y-12 for the higher stages. As Groves pointed out to Stimson, these balanced additions to the Oak Ridge plants would greatly increase the production of uranium 235 at a cost of about $100 million. Groves noted that the additions could not be in operation before February 15, 1946, but that would be soon enough. "On the assumption that the war with Japan will not be over before July, 1946, it is planned to proceed with the additions to the two plants unless instructions to the contrary are received."[13]

In the absence of a countermand, Groves authorized the construction of the new gaseous-diffusion plant, to be known as K-27, on March 31, 1945. Two days later, he issued a similar order for the fourth Beta plant. Except for a few minor additions, this completed the production complex which had been evolving at the Tennessee site since the fall of 1942. With the end of the war in sight, the construction phase was drawing to a close. Now it was up to the General to produce the bomb with the facilities at hand.

Shortly after noon on Tuesday, April 11, Groves arrived at the Knoxville airport by plane with Stimson and his military aide. After a late luncheon at the Guest House in Oak Ridge, the party drove to K-25. To save the aging Secretary's failing strength, the motorcade proceeded around the sprawling K-25 building, down the cluttered roadway to the bottom of the U, and then to the large service building where components were tested, assembled, and repaired. Entering the structure, the cars stopped for a few moments so that Stimson could examine some of the equipment. From K-25 the party drove over the back road to the X-10 area, where Whitaker was prepared with a short talk and demonstration at the pile building. On the way back to Oak Ridge, the group stopped on the ridge near the filtration plant to give Stimson a bird's-eye view of Y-12 and the town. That evening, Colonel Nichols entertained the Secretary at a small reception in his home on Black Oak Ridge. At six the next morning there was a briefing on the Y-12 plant at the Guest House, an inspection of trailer and housing units in the town, a tour of three process buildings at Y-12, and the long, bumpy drive to the Knoxville airport. The trip had been physically tiring but Stimson felt "immensely cheered and braced up." It had been a thrilling experience. He considered the Tennessee plant "the largest and most extraordinary scientific experiment in history." Its promise of a quick end to the war made the crushing burdens in the Pentagon seem, for the moment, more bearable.[14]

PLUTONIUM: LAST APPRAISAL

On Friday morning, July 21, 1944, Roger Williams and Crawford Greenewalt hurried to Washington for an urgent meeting with Conant and Groves. On Wednesday, they had learned from Charles A. Thomas the distressing news that Oppenheimer had abandoned all hope of using plutonium in a gun-type weapon.

Thomas' report meant first of all that the possibility of developing a plutonium weapon during the war was now small. Unless the Los Alamos scientists could design an implosion weapon within a matter of months, all the work at Hanford might be in vain. Even if they were successful, some guessed that the implosion device would not require more than a few kilograms of plutonium. Whatever happened, it looked as if the need for plutonium might be greatly reduced.

For Greenewalt and Williams, the news had obvious implications at Hanford. In an effort to produce experimental quantities of plutonium as quickly as possible, they had emphasized construction of B pile. Work on D was several months behind B, and F was not more than a quarter complete. If the plutonium requirements for the implosion weapon were as low as some scientists thought, there would be no need for F at all. If implosion did not work, there would be one less pile to scrap.

Groves saw the logic of their argument, but he wanted to be sure of the facts. Could B and D piles meet the minimum demand for plutonium? Greenewalt laid out his schedules for construction and operation of each pile. They indicated that two piles would more than meet the minimum. But the question in Groves's mind was whether he could count on using so little plutonium in an implosion weapon. Conant had his doubts. Research on implosion still gave a wide range of estimated requirements. Conant was not willing to bet on so low a figure. The General agreed. He asked the du Pont leaders to discuss the estimates with Fermi when they reached Hanford the following week. He did not intend to reduce Hanford capacity unless Oppenheimer and Fermi were positive the implosion weapon would work with the minimum amount of plutonium.[15]

303

END OF THE SLUG CRISIS

Williams and Greenewalt must have been pleased with what they saw when they arrived at Hanford on July 31. The entire project was now two-thirds complete, and Granville M. Read, the du Pont construction manager, estimated that the job would be finished on February 1, 1945, a month earlier than the previous forecast. Under Read's seasoned leadership, the project had gained momentum.

Du Pont crews and engineers were putting the finishing touches on B pile. They had performed pressure tests on the gas-tight steel liner and expected to turn the pile over to the operating forces of R. Monte Evans by the middle of August. D pile was more than half complete, and work was reaching the final stages on the first chemical separation building.

Subcontractors were rapidly transforming the hamlet of Richland into a bustling town for the permanent operating and administrative staff. Twenty-nine hundred of the 4,300 family dwelling units and 19 of 21 dormitories were ready for occupancy. Dominating the town square on George Washington Way were the administration building, the transient quarters, theater, post office, and stores—all resembling the Army architecture that prevailed at Oak Ridge. As Richland grew, Hanford camp declined. Construction forces had dropped from the June peak to 42,400. The days were numbered for the temporary city at the big bend of the Columbia.[16]

For all these accomplishments, the future of Hanford seemed uncertain as long as the success of the slug-canning process hung in the balance. As a safety measure, the Army had contracted with a Chicago manufacturer to fabricate one charge of unbonded slugs for B pile. When Williams and Greenewalt arrived, it was still not clear whether the unbonded slugs would be used. Du Pont had finally succeeded in concentrating at Hanford the last remnants of the canning operations previously located in Chicago, Cleveland, and Wilmington. Somehow, on the Washington desert a few miles from the piles themselves, it was easier to concentrate on the practical techniques of canning. Experience on both the production and testing lines in the slug-fabrication building provided new leads on improvements. As the weeks passed, the operators learned the fine points of their craft.

August, 1944, proved to be the turning point. Minor adjustments and changes on B pile as a result of preoperational tests delayed completion for several weeks. The additional time for fabrication seemed to assure that an adequate number of bonded slugs would be ready for the first pile charge. Two significant developments in August made that possibility more certain. First, operators on the test line discovered that certain slight modifications would greatly improve the process. At almost the same time, engineers found a way to eliminate entirely one of the most unsatisfactory steps. Adopted at once, these changes had a dramatic effect on canning statistics. Yields of acceptable slugs went up, and the number of failures in autoclave tests declined even more sharply. The slug crisis was over. Now the du Pont leaders could feel reasonably certain that they would have enough slugs to supply all three piles.[17]

304

DAY OF RECKONING

On Wednesday morning, September 13, 1944, the last of the construction forces left the B pile building. Operating personnel had already moved in and were busily checking instruments and controls. This would be the last chance for examining first-hand many of the intricate mechanisms incorporated in the pile. Once the chain reaction had been achieved, every piece of equipment within the thick concrete shield would become intensely radioactive. The charge-discharge crews were intent on their final inspection of equipment for changing the charge of slugs in the pile. The procedures were especially difficult on the rear face, where the radioactivity of emerging slugs required remote controls.

Late that afternoon, Compton, Fermi, Williams, Greenewalt, and Colonel Matthias arrived. Compton had been waiting for this moment since those exciting but confusing days after Pearl Harbor nearly three years earlier when he had used the full weight of his prestige and persuasive powers to keep the plutonium project alive. Fermi could contrast the occasion with a similar event which had fired Greenewalt's enthusiasm on December 2, 1942.

CHEMICAL SEPARATION BUILDING 221-U / The second chemical separation plant nears completion, September, 1944.

D PILE COMPLETED / This plutonium-production facility at Hanford operated for the first time with a full loading on December 17, 1944.

Williams could recall the many painful steps in converting a laboratory experiment into a production process. Matthias could remember the same spot as a trackless desert little more than two years earlier. In a real sense, the efforts and imagination of them all, and of thousands of other Americans, were bound up in that moment.

At five forty-three, Fermi inserted the first slug in the B pile. As the loading settled down to a routine, he stepped back to supervise. It would be a long process, not just because of the number of slugs to be loaded but because of the many tests to be performed. In many ways, this was an irreversible experiment which would give the nuclear physicist an extraordinary opportunity to observe the genesis of the chain reaction on an unprecedented scale. Proceeding slowly with alternate loading and testing procedures, the operating crews worked through Wednesday night, and all of Thursday. At two-thirty on Friday morning, they approached what the pile engineers called "dry critical," which meant there was just enough uranium in the pile to sustain the chain reaction with no cooling water in the tubes. Repeatedly the loading stopped while physicists checked the rate at which reactivity would increase. Then the control rods were inserted and loading resumed.

305

Fermi calculated how much uranium he would have to add to make the pile critical with cooling water flowing through the tubes. As the loading teams approached this value on Monday afternoon, they paused so that the physicists could make precise measurements. They found that the loading checked with the calculated value within 0.1 per cent. Every phase of the process seemed according to plan. From now on, the pile would generate heat whenever the control rods were withdrawn. As the loading crews continued to insert slugs, the operators prepared for a final test of the cooling system. Minor adjustments in cooling equipment, endless measurements, and rearrangements of the loading took the rest of the week.[18]

A few minutes after midnight on September 27, just two weeks after Fermi had inserted the first slug, the initial power run began. The operating crew withdrew the control rods enough to raise the power slightly. After about an hour at this level, they raised the power a bit higher. By two o'clock, the power level exceeded that of any previous chain reaction, but it was still a small fraction of the rated capacity of B.

All went well until about three o'clock when the operators noticed that the power level had declined slightly. Since they had made no changes in the controls, they feared that something strange was happening. Through the early morning hours the decline continued. Dropping faster as time went on, the power level fell to half its original value before four o'clock that afternoon. By six-thirty the pile had shut itself down completely. Nothing like this had ever happened at Clinton or Argonne. Could it be that in all their experiments the scientists had failed to uncover one fatal flaw in the design of the Hanford piles?

Most of those present in B pile building that evening were not thinking in such somber terms. It seemed most likely that an aluminum cooling tube was leaking water into the graphite block, but there was no evidence of moisture within the pile. Perhaps the cooling water had introduced some neutron "poison." Analyses of water samples and scraping of thin films from dummy slugs in the pile revealed no such phenomenon. In the meantime, some of the dummy slugs were pushed out of the peripheral tubes and neutron counters were inserted to measure the decline of reactivity below criticality. Early on Thursday morning, the counters showed that reactivity was again increasing, but at a very slow rate. By seven in the morning, the power level was near the middle of its previous operating range. Twelve hours later, with the pile still holding its reactivity, the power level was raised to Wednesday's maximum, and the same decline occurred.

306

Since there was no moisture in the graphite, the fault was clearly not a leak. Hilberry concluded that the phenomenon was either a very peculiar film deposition on the slugs or a true poisoning effect. Was it possible that one of the fission products absorbed enough neutrons to shut down the pile? Its behavior seemed to fit this hypothesis. During the power run, the fission process might have created enough of this unknown isotope to capture neutrons faster than the process generated them. Once the poison had shut down the pile, no more of it would be formed. Then as the radioactive poison decayed to another element, the flow of neutrons would be restored. Thus, the physicists reasoned, they could estimate the capture cross section of the isotope from the rate at which reactivity declined and its half-life from the length of time during which the pile was shut down by the poison. By Friday morning, September 29, close study of pile data yielded a half-life of about 9.7 hours. This information corresponded closely to the known decay chain of isotopes with mass number 135. Of these, xenon, with an estimated half-life of 9.4 hours fitted the data. That afternoon, Greenewalt telephoned Allison in Chicago. In guarded language he explained what had happened. Would Allison ask Zinn at Argonne and Doan at Clinton to see whether they could detect a similar effect in their experimental piles? [19]

It was late afternoon when Allison called Zinn. The small group of scientists and technicians on the outskirts of Chicago had closed down the pile and were about to leave for the day. Zinn could not believe the news. He had never noted such an effect even in the new heavy-water-moderated pile which had a neutron flux high enough to produce it. Allison assured him that B pile had shut itself down. Zinn hastened to call back his staff before they could leave the laboratory. He planned immediately to begin an extended run at full power in an effort to reproduce the effect.

The heavy-water pile, called CP-3, was housed in a factory-like brick building at Argonne. It consisted of a cylindrical aluminum tank six feet in diameter filled with 6.5 tons of heavy water. Through the top of the tank were suspended 121 uranium rods sheathed with aluminum. The pile was the result of a compromise in the battle over the heavy-water research program in the late summer of 1943. Essentially an experimental pile with some research fa-cilities, CP-3 was first operated in May, 1944, and achieved its full-power rating of 300 kilowatts two months later.

Zinn was not long in detecting the xenon effect in CP-3. Starting with a twelve-hour run at full power, he made a series of reactivity measurements which revealed a decay rate and capture cross section roughly consistent with the Hanford results. He concluded that "the agreement for the twelve-hour decay is quite satisfactory and that there can be little doubt that the high cross-section poisoning product is xenon 135." Doan could find no convincing evidence in the operating data for the Clinton pile, but neither did he find any reason for doubting the Hanford and Argonne reports. Presumably in the Clinton pile thermal effects overrode the small influence of xenon poisoning.

Compton presented these unhappy tidings to Groves in a special meet-ing in Chicago on October 3, 1944. The General was annoyed. The physicists had disregarded his explicit orders to run CP-3 at full power around the clock. If they had followed his instructions, they would have noted the xenon effect long before. The scientists admitted this possibility, but they emphasized that CP-3 was a research tool. They could not perform experiments with the pile operating at full power at all times. Compton confessed they had made an embarrassing mistake, but they had in the process made "a fundamentally new discovery regarding neutron properties of matter." He was confident the discovery had not been made too late. He was flying at once to Hanford to see what could be done.[20]

307

INCHING TOWARD PRODUCTION

When Compton arrived at Hanford the next day, he learned from Hilberry and Greenewalt that they had already taken steps to improve pile operation. The only way to maintain reactivity at higher power levels was to add more uranium slugs. By filling something more than 100 additional tubes on Oc-tober 2, they were able to increase the power level several megawatts without a drop in reactivity. So far so good, but several important questions remained unanswered. How much additional uranium was necessary to operate the pile at its full design power? Could this be provided by using all the remaining space in the pile? Even then, with a full loading, would the control rods be effective during the start of each run when there was no xenon to suppress the reaction?

None of the questions could be answered at once. There were so many conflicting factors affecting reactivity that no simple predictions were possi-ble. But it did seem unlikely that the pile capacity would prove too small. As at Clinton, du Pont had provided for a generous number of extra tubes. In fact, the excess was so much greater than the anticipated needs that many of the tubes on the periphery of the pile were not hooked to the water-cooling system. The scientists at the Metallurgical Laboratory had cited this feature as one of the best examples of extravagant conservatism in the du Pont design. Without the slightest reason for believing the additional tubes would ever be necessary, the du Pont designers had stuck to their guns as a matter of principle. Now it seemed that the incredible had occurred. More from luck than foresight du Pont was prepared to meet the situation.

The approach to full power would now be a matter of months rather than weeks. Before du Pont could make any definite plans to increase the capacity of the pile, the engineers needed a better understanding of its operating characteristics. Early in October, they increased the loading to about that originally anticipated for full-power operation. The pile was not producing significant amounts of plutonium, but only through continuous operation at this maximum stable power level could the necessary data be obtained. At first, operations were frequently interrupted by the thousands of instruments which could automatically touch off a shutdown. In such instances, the operating force began a feverish search for the fault so that the safety rods could be withdrawn before the poisoning effect made it impossible to restore the chain reaction without waiting several hours for xenon decay. In time, the operators learned how to reduce the number of "scrams" and to correct most of the simple faults or false signals within the "scram" period. Thus was a new word added to the nuclear vocabulary.

The final decision on loading came in late November. Fermi noted that reactivity followed a complex pattern during an extended run. This he attributed to the fact that many changes within the pile were exerting both negative and positive effects. Fermi himself could list nine factors, and for many of them he could make no precise estimate of their effect on reactivity. It seemed likely, however, that all 2,004 tubes in the pile would be needed to attain the design power level.

There was just one further test to make. D pile was almost complete. Before modifying B, du Pont decided to see whether the control rods in D were adequate for a full loading with no cooling water in the pile. This "dry critical" test was successfully completed during the second week in December. Meanwhile, all tubes in B had been connected to the water-cooling system. On Christmas day, several tons of irradiated slugs were discharged from the pile. Three days later, B pile operated for the first time with a full loading. D had been running on a full loading since December 17, and F would be ready in six weeks. At long last, plutonium formation was beginning at Hanford.[21]

PLUTONIUM SEPARATION

When the pile operators discharged the first batch of irradiated slugs from B pile in November, 1944, the chemical engineers in the 200 Area were about ready to receive them. That was no mean accomplishment in view of the fact that du Pont had postponed construction of the huge canyon buildings to accelerate progress on Hanford camp and the piles. As a result, all the experimental work and training of operators was performed in the pilot plant at Clinton or in the laboratories at Chicago. Among the first 100 operators who arrived at Hanford in October, thirty-five had had at least six months' experience at the other sites and sixty-five had completed a three months' training course at Clinton.

Operating personnel took over the first of the three canyon buildings (221-T) on October 9. Their first assignment was to replace all gaskets in the plant with a new type which would withstand the strain of tightening by impact wrenches operated by remote control. Then came the calibration of instruments and controls and testing of mechanical equipment. The lids on the dissolvers were found to be warped by steam and had to be ground to make a tight fit. The piping for the hydraulic controls on the centrifuges was inadequate, and the contact microphones used to detect mechanical failures had to be replaced. By the end of October, the concentration building (224-T) was complete, and testing had started. Construction forces were pouring the end walls for 221-U nearby.

309

In November simulated test runs were started with the dissolver units in 221-T. The first test was simply to heat nitric acid in them. On November 25, the first aluminum cans were dissolved. After several larger batches of cans were successfully processed, the dissolvers were charged with slugs rejected in the canning plant. Chemical runs (with unirradiated uranium) started early in December. These were followed by tracer runs of slugs first from Clinton and later from B pile in very dilute solutions. In all runs, the operators controlled the process with the remote procedures that would be used in actual production.

The first charge composed entirely of metal from B pile was dissolved in the 221-T plant on December 26. The first production runs through the bismuth-phosphate steps were completed early in January, 1945, with excellent results. Losses of plutonium in the process were much lower than expected. Some losses were encountered initially in the lanthanum-fluoride steps in the concentration building, but before the end of January these had been improved.[22]

By this time most of the equipment had been installed in the isolation building (231) where the last traces of carrier and other fission products were removed and the product precipitated as a pure plutonium nitrate. Before the end of January, the first material was processed in 231, thus completing the entire process from uranium ore to a new man-made element.

As the process improved, larger amounts of nitrate were accumulated. Early in February, Colonel Matthias completed arrangements to transport the material to Los Alamos. Because he considered air travel too risky and rail travel too slow, he decided on a motor convoy. The nitrate would be transported in a small truck especially equipped to carry twenty shipping cans.

Escorted by two radio-equipped patrol cars, the truck would travel from Hanford to Boise, Salt Lake City, Grand Junction, Pueblo, and Los Alamos.

On February 2, the first small sample of plutonium reached the laboratory on the New Mexico mesa. Charles Thomas enthusiastically reported that its purity was excellent. The only objectionable matter present was silica, undoubtedly picked up from the many silica filters then used at Hanford. The number of filtrations would be greatly reduced as Hanford straightened out the kinks in the process. The essential ingredients of the bomb were beginning to flow from Oak Ridge and Hanford. More and more each day, the fate of the project rested with Oppenheimer's talented staff at Los Alamos.[23]

REORGANIZATION AT LOS ALAMOS

310

Oppenheimer's staff was talented indeed. Strong at the start, the laboratory was even stronger in the summer of 1944. The presence of John von Neumann and George B. Kistiakowsky gave the original cadre a new dimension. Fermi's visits. always inspirational, became increasingly frequent as the pressure eased at Chicago. Lieutenant Commander Norris E. Bradbury, a Stanford physicist with four years' experience at the Dahlgren Navy Proving Ground, arrived to head the implosion field-test program. The mission from Britain lent an international atmosphere. Led first by James Chadwick and then by Rudolph E. Peierls, it numbered almost two dozen scientists. The most distinguished were hydrodynamics authority Sir Geoffrey I. Taylor, physicists Otto R. Frisch and Egon Bretscher, and explosives specialist William G. Penney. Among the many able men of less renown were electronics experts Ernest W. Titterton and Philip B. Moon and physicists James L. Tuck, Tony H. L. Skyrme, and Klaus Fuchs. Niels Bohr was in a special class. Like Taylor, he did not take up residence at Los Alamos but made several extended visits. He showed a vigorous interest in both theory and design and acted as a scientific father confessor to the younger men.[24]

Los Alamos had its troubles, to be sure. One was the shortage of skilled technicians and junior scientists. Here the laboratory had to compete with the all but inexorable demands of the selective service system. The Army sought to help by creating the Special Engineer Detachment, a device for channeling technically trained enlisted men into the Manhattan project. This was not an ideal solution for Los Alamos, committed as it was to a civilian establishment. There was no alternative, however, and the laboratory took SED's and a few assignees from the Women's Army Corps as well. By August, 1944, enlisted men constituted almost one-third of the scientific staff.[25]

Another difficulty lay in the fact that the unquestionably beautiful scenery never compensated completely for the physical inconveniences of marginal housing and the psychic strain of living in an isolated, artificial community under security regulations that seemed fantastic. Nor did the Au-

gust talk of an early peace help. It was natural to wonder if any desirable civilian positions would remain when the laboratory shut down. Yet complaints
and doubts had little effect on the men most responsible for success. Those in
a position to recognize the importance of the work welcomed its challenges
and its opportunities. Research morale was high.[26]

Los Alamos needed all its genius and an ample measure of good fortune. Prior to the summer of 1944, the laboratory had viewed implosion as
an interesting but extremely difficult alternative to the gun. With the discovery that the neutron background of Pu-240 ruled out the plutonium gun, the
implosion program took on an aura of grim desperation. If the Hanford piles
were not to be a total loss, Los Alamos had to make implosion work. But
much more was at stake than success of the plutonium project. If the Hanford
product were useless, the United States would have to rely on the U-235 now
beginning to trickle from the Beta tracks at Oak Ridge. So long as this material had to be assembled by the inefficient gun system, weapons would be
so few in number as to raise major doubts about their military utility.

To speed the work on implosion, Oppenheimer effected a sweeping
reorganization. Early in July, 1944, he had sought to provide more effective
direction by abolishing the Governing Board, assigning the innumerable
housekeeping headaches to an Administrative Board, and leaving a new Technical Board free to grapple with the central scientific issues.[27] But more was
required than reshuffling at the top. An organic change was necessary, one
that would make possible an intensive, co-ordinated effort to develop an implosion weapon before plutonium arrived in quantity. Oppenheimer accomplished such a change in a series of conferences during late July and early
August.

Now Robert F. Bacher and Kistiakowsky accepted the implosion assignment. Bacher headed a Gadget Division which would investigate implosion experimentally and eventually design a bomb. He drew his staff primarily from the Experimental Physics Division, now renamed Research, and
from Captain William S. Parsons' Ordnance Division. Kistiakowsky led a
fresh division, derived principally from Ordnance, devoted to the high-
explosive components. These two task forces collaborated in the closest possible way. Both depended heavily on Hans A. Bethe's Theoretical Division for
the essential analyses of how matter behaved under the extreme conditions of
implosion.

The reorganization concentrated work on the uranium gun in an Ordnance Division group directed by Commander A. Francis Birch, a Harvard
physics professor turned naval officer. While Edwin M. McMillan remained
Parsons' deputy for the gun program, he now had responsibilities under
Bacher for developing test methods that pre-empted most of his time. Unen-
cumbered by the complexities of implosion, Parsons concentrated on turning
devices into weapons and arranging to deliver them in combat.

Serving both the gun and implosion were the Research Division under

311

Robert R. Wilson, the Chemistry and Metallurgy Division led by Joseph W. Kennedy and Cyril S. Smith, and a consolidated shop group directed by Earl A. Long. An F Division was reserved for Fermi, who arrived in September to stay for the duration. It would explore the possibility of a thermonuclear bomb and take over the water boiler (a small research pile, valuable as a strong neutron source).

The laboratory still worked as a unit. The Co-ordinating Council and the Colloquium continued to meet. Divisions and groups collaborated freely across organizational lines. *Ad hoc* committees tackled problems of common concern. With Parsons and Fermi serving as assistant directors, the top leadership had added assurance that it saw things in the whole.[28]

IMPLOSION: THE GREAT QUESTION MARK

When the reorganized laboratory turned to its tasks in August, 1944, Commander Birch of the Gun Group found himself in a fortunate position. The abandonment of the plutonium gun had simplified his job. Even more important, the calculation and experimentation on this high-velocity device had left no worries about projectile, target, and initiator design or internal ballistics. The remaining anxiety as to the critical mass of Y-12 metal eased early in October when John H. Williams and Alfred O. Hanson of the Research Division ran tests on the multiplication of neutrons in small spheres of Beta material. Happily, their results conformed closely to existing Theoretical Division estimates by Robert Serber. Assuming that Los Alamos could count on Y-12 product having a high degree of isotopic enrichment, Birch's principal task now was to devise a unit that would be absolutely dependable. Not that this was a small assignment; the U-235 entrusted to the gun would represent an investment of roughly a billion dollars.

Assuring reliability meant an almost infinite amount of testing. Trials with full-size components were not possible, for the guns ordered in March, 1944, did not arrive until October, and even then, it was necessary to wait for special mounts. In the meantime, Birch could develop satisfactory target units. Natural uranium was a perfect stand-in for U-235, for it had the same mechanical properties. All through the autumn, the canyons echoed with the test firing at Anchor Ranch, two and three-quarter miles southwest of the central Technical Area. By December, when the first shots were fired from a full-size tube, the gun method seemed sure.[29]

For implosion, the essential puzzle remained the same: how to achieve the symmetry necessary for a reasonably efficient nuclear reaction. Complicating the research situation at the same time that they offered encouragement, certain new possibilities were much in the thoughts of the Los Alamos directorate.

Explosive lenses were one of the possibilities. The principle had been studied in England and at the U. S. Navy's Explosives Research Laboratory at Bruceton, Pennsylvania. Los Alamos did not try to apply that principle until the summer of 1944, when von Neumann and Peierls worked out a design that looked promising. Kistiakowsky and his Explosives Division had inherited an idea, but if it were to be useful, they had to devise both the precise geometric design and the actual technique of manufacture.[30]

Throughout the fall of 1944, the Gadget and Explosives Divisions explored this and other hopes. The development of better methods for studying test implosions had high priority. Four of Bacher's group leaders—McMillan, Seth H. Neddermeyer, Bruno B. Rossi, and Darol K. Froman—directed this effort with the ingenious help of William A. Higinbotham and his Electronics Group, who provided the novel and complex instrumentation. Rossi's method was ready first, but the data it yielded on test shots in October and November furnished no grounds for optimism. Not until a December 14 test did Rossi find definitely encouraging evidence. But time was running short.[31]

313

A few days after the December 14 test, Groves and Conant visited Los Alamos. Though the gun weapon would not be ready before August 1, 1945, everyone was confident it would work. Conant bet Oppenheimer it would be used before implosion. He probably was taking advantage of the sporting spirit to spur Los Alamos, for a bet on the gun was hardly a daring wager. The implosion program still looked bad. Conant thought the chances very much against an implosion of relatively high efficiency in 1945. A bomb looked possible, but Conant judged it would yield less than 850 tons TNT equivalent and perhaps only 500 tons. Privately, Groves and Conant were so discouraged they gave up all thought of using the first U-235 in an implosion weapon. Instead, they would assign it to the certain but terribly wasteful gun. The best they dared hope for was enough progress in implosion to permit a proof firing in the spring of 1945 and a few low-power bombs in the second half of the year.[32]

FROM RESEARCH TO PRODUCTION

While the physicists pondered the riddle of implosion, Los Alamos experienced a fundamental change. For the first fifteen months on the Hill, research necessarily was the dominant theme. After the summer of 1944, while research remained important, it had to yield to the stern task of making sure that nuclear weapons were ready in time. Now the emphasis was on the development of sound, dependable components. It was essential to provide for their manufacture, often before final specifications were known. It was equally as important to integrate all parts into assemblies that were truly weapons, not mere laboratory devices, and to perfect arrangements with the Army Air Forces for dropping them on the enemy.[33]

In short, the laboratory had to shift from research to development and production. In September and October, the transition was well under way. Many of the components could be manufactured under contract, but Los Alamos itself had to determine specifications, reduce the Y-12 and Hanford product to metal, work uranium and plutonium into the proper shapes, and perform many intricate manufacturing jobs, especially the production of high-explosive castings for the implosion research.

The Los Alamos site also served as headquarters for weapon design. There, George Galloway's Engineering Group and Norman F. Ramsey's Delivery Group could plan, design, and modify. While outlying areas were suitable for some physics and engineering trials, the main testing efforts centered at Wendover Field, an isolated air base in western Utah. In September, the 393d Bombardment Squadron (VH) arrived under the command of Colonel Paul W. Tibbets, a veteran airman who had proved his mettle in European skies. The 393d was the nucleus of the 509th Composite Wing, a unique organization scheduled for activation in December so that the combat unit might have the greatest possible independence and security. As soon as the squadron received its specially modified B-29's in October, Los Alamos teams began the essential test drops. In the months that followed, Ramsey, Birch, Commander Frederick L. Ashworth, Robert B. Brode, Edward B. Doll, Kenneth T. Bainbridge, Lewis Fussell, and Maurice M. Shapiro led studies on the ballistic behavior of bomb cases and on the design and performance of fuzes, detonators, and aircraft release mechanisms.[34]

Los Alamos faced severe handicaps in adjusting to its new role. For one thing, there were personnel shortages—in the shops, in the explosives plant, and in the laboratories. Plenty of chemists were available, but physicists were in scant supply, particularly men qualified to work in the Gadget Division.[35] Another handicap was that Los Alamos remained essentially an academic community. The imagination and flexibility this assured were vital, but they did not remove the need for the experience and judgment of a first-rate industrial engineer.

Added to these troubles was a distressing procurement situation. In February, 1943, Oppenheimer had met with Army and University of California representatives and worked out a plan whereby the university would conduct operations from a special purchasing office in Los Angeles. The project procurement officer at Los Alamos would make his requisitions by mail or teletype, ordinarily dealing only with Los Angeles and not with the branch offices to be established in Chicago and New York. Supplies would flow first to Los Angeles or Chicago and then be transshipped to Los Alamos under fresh bills of lading.

This complicated procedure served well its purpose of concealing the movement of strange supplies to a secret New Mexican destination, but it did not promote efficiency. Fortunately, some of the most essential items came through Manhattan District and other Army and Navy channels. The system never worked well. Even for standard catalog articles, there were frustrating delays and shipments that did not meet specifications. As the laboratory began to demand more and more specially fabricated items, a major crisis loomed.

The Los Alamos scientists tended to blame the purchasing office in Los Angeles. At times, their charges of inefficiency rang true. Contrary to instructions, Los Angeles shipped by rail instead of air freight a piece of equipment on which an important experiment depended. Yet there were reasons more fundamental than human failure. Los Alamos had to meet its requirements—greater in variety than those of the Bell Laboratories—in a market depleted by years of war. Isolated in its mountain fastness, Los Alamos would have had some difficulty in time of peace. Under wartime security regulations that prevented direct contact between the laboratory and its suppliers, troubles were all but inevitable.

Groves had foreseen some of the complications. Early in 1943, he had opened an area engineer office in Los Angeles to supervise and expedite the University of California operation. Within this unit, he organized an engineering procurement division responsible for utilizing available machines and shop time in the Los Angeles vicinity. In the fall of 1943, a special office in Detroit took over procurement activities in that area for the Ordnance Division. This was not always effective, but in June, 1944, when Lieutenant Colonel Robert W. Lockridge took charge at Detroit, an improvement was in prospect. Meanwhile, Oppenheimer struggled with patch-work measures—clearing the chief purchasing agent at Los Angeles for visits to the laboratory and persuading the University of California to improve the organization and staff of its purchasing arm. But for all the effort, the situation remained distressing, and when Conant visited Los Alamos on October 18, 1944, he was alarmed. Unless something were done about engineering and procurement, he feared the wreck of the whole billion-dollar enterprise.[36]

With time so short, no administrative change could suddenly transform Los Alamos into a rational, efficient unit for developing and producing weapons. It was necessary to adopt emergency measures, to piece together whatever expedients were available. To make up staff deficiencies, Los Alamos recruited scientists freed by the reduced requirements at Chicago and Oak Ridge. It launched a concerted drive to find civilian machinists to man the shops. It accepted Army enlisted men in ever larger numbers. Soon soldiers constituted over 90 per cent of the working force at the explosives plant. The time was approaching when nearly one-half the laboratory workers would wear uniforms.[37]

In November, 1944, Los Alamos acquired the industrial-engineering experience it so badly needed. At Conant's suggestion, Groves persuaded Hartley Rowe to review the engineering situation at the laboratory. Chief engineer and vice-president of the United Fruit Company, he had headed an NDRC division and had just completed a tour as technical adviser to General Eisenhower. When he had finished his study, Rowe stayed on as consultant,

315

informally supervising the transition to production and trouble shooting on some of the more critical procurement bottlenecks.[38]

Another way of helping Los Alamos was to take advantage of any suitable resources that might become available outside the Manhattan project. Parsons was able to arrange for the Naval Mine Depot in Yorktown, Virginia, to join the Bruceton Laboratory in backstopping the explosives program. More important was an alliance with the rocket-development team led by Charles C. Lauritsen at the California Institute of Technology. Scientists at CIT had developed rocketry under an OSRD contract to a stage at which the Navy was prepared to assume the major share of the work. Watching from his OSRD command post in Washington, Bush saw that Los Alamos could use CIT talent and facilities. At his suggestion, Lauritsen went to Los Alamos in mid-November, 1944, and talked with Groves as well as Oppenheimer and other laboratory leaders. The conversations confirmed Bush's view on the value of collaboration. A special NDRC committee promptly allotted $1 million as a beginning. At this point, the Navy's Bureau of Ordnance objected that the new project would affect CIT's continuing responsibilities adversely. December saw quick efforts to quiet such fears, and early in January the OSRD established a special project at Pasadena and at the Inyokern Naval Ordnance Testing Station. The OSRD supplied funds for technical work and the Manhattan District money for construction.

With Lauritsen and Oppenheimer conferring frequently, the CIT project devoted itself to developing components for the implosion weapon's high-explosive system, nonnuclear metal parts, and handling equipment. The project assumed complete responsibility for the development and production of practice bombs. Assisted by AAF crews from Wendover Field, it also conducted drop tests on the range at Inyokern and at the Naval Auxiliary Air Station at Sandy Beach, California. The Sandy Beach range, located on the Salton Sea, afforded opportunity to test fuzing in drops to very low altitudes.

The alliance with CIT was a stroke of good fortune. CIT supplemented Los Alamos with scientists trained in the special techniques needed in the climactic drive for the bomb. Fully as important, CIT possessed an established, well-tested procurement organization. Headed by Trevor Gardner, this unit not only served the work at Pasadena and Inyokern but also facilitated the Los Alamos efforts of Colonel Lockridge, who in December accepted leadership of a new group responsible for all Ordnance Division procurement.[39]

The emergency tactics adopted in the closing months of 1944 put the laboratory on the track. Yet for all its growth and change, Los Alamos remained an informal, highly adaptable, catch-as-catch-can endeavor, hardly systematic but brilliant in improvisation.

316

FREEZING WEAPON DESIGN

Early in December, 1944—a fortnight before the first encouraging implosion test—Samuel K. Allison took charge of a new advisory body, the Technical and Scheduling Conference. An experienced physicist just arrived from the Metallurgical Laboratory, Allison could look at Los Alamos from a fresh, detached point of view. The plan was for the conference to schedule experiments, facilities, and materials. To this end, Allison held meetings, each session devoted to some particular subject, the personnel in attendance fluctuating with the business of the day. This procedure necessarily led the conference beyond mere scheduling duties to consideration of the most critical technical issues. In large part, Allison's group replaced the Technical Board. In January and February, 1945, it was the nerve center at Los Alamos.

The gun caused little concern. On January 1, 1945, Commander Birch appeared before the Technical and Scheduling Conference and explained at length what his group was trying to accomplish in its experimental shots and drop tests. Pointing to the time required for a change in gun design, he warned that the critical mass of U-235 would have to be determined quickly. He was optimistic, nonetheless. In all probability, he said, the Gun Group would have a reasonable model ready in July. The conference already had anticipated Birch and made arrangements for multiplication tests on sizable metal spheres. Williams' research group had favorable results in February, and that month it was possible to freeze design of the gun.[40]

317

The year 1945 opened with encouraging developments in implosion. The Research Division reported neutron-multiplication studies run on a small sphere of Clinton plutonium (0.9 inch in diameter) which confirmed quite convincingly the current estimates of critical mass.[41] Luis W. Alvarez reported the development of an electric detonator that gave consistently good test results. His group in the Gadget Physics Division had fired sets with a time spread less than a microsecond. The prospect was for an even higher degree of simultaneity. Los Alamos had the capacity to load explosives in about 200 detonators a day. If the implosion tests were not to suffer, it would be necessary to establish loading facilities at CIT. Fortunately, techniques had been sufficiently standardized for transfer.[42] Charles L. Critchfield told of promising work on initiators. This device remained a stubborn puzzle, as Critchfield's January progress report made plain, but early in February, Niels Bohr clarified what had to be done.[43] The best news came from the implosion testing ground; on February 7, Rossi's method was used to observe a test fired with electric detonators. It showed a distinct improvement in the quality of the implosion.[44]

For all the good omens, the implosion program lacked direction. The danger in this stood out at a four-hour meeting of the Technical and Scheduling Conference on Saturday, February 17. The limited high-explosive casting capacity at S Site was imposing a sharp limit on experimental efforts. Lauritsen argued that Los Alamos would have to decide on a definite line of development if it were to meet its schedule: an implosion device ready for a test with active material on July 4. Allison pointed to the only design he thought could be ready in time. While Oppenheimer agreed with Allison, he favored a more conservative approach. If Allison's method should fail, implosion would lose four months. Peierls thought as Oppenheimer, and Allison conceded the merits of their views, though he believed their plan meant missing the July 4 date by six weeks. Whatever the laboratory decided, warned Lauritsen, it would have to make a clear-cut choice. Los Alamos did not have the resources to spread itself over two designs.

No decision was possible the seventeenth, but Oppenheimer asked Allison to help him estimate time schedules for the two designs that seemed most promising. Later that month, General Groves came to Los Alamos, and a special conference decided in his presence that the laboratory would have to adopt the model Oppenheimer and Peierls had favored. The July test date, it judged, could still be met. On March 5, Oppenheimer announced the decision to the Co-ordinating Council. As insurance against failure at Los Alamos, CIT would develop the alternate device.[45]

GIRDING FOR THE FINAL EFFORT

With the design of the implosion weapon set in principle and the July deadline fast approaching, Oppenheimer mobilized the laboratory for the critical months ahead. He assigned over-all direction of implosion to Allison, Bacher, Kistiakowsky, Lauritsen, Parsons, and Rowe. Dubbed the Cowpuncher Committee, they were to "ride herd" on implosion.

At the same time, Oppenheimer arranged for Bainbridge to take charge of Project Trinity, a new organization with division status that would conduct the July implosion test. Oppenheimer and most of the division and group leaders considered a test with active material essential. The step from theory and experiment to a practical weapon was so great that they were unwilling to risk a first try over enemy territory. If the bomb should fail, the United States would lose the advantage of surprise and quite possibly present the foe with a large amount of plutonium in recoverable form.

Bainbridge, a Harvard physics professor with a three-year stint at the MIT Radiation Laboratory, had carried responsibility for the test since March, 1944, as a group leader under Kistiakowsky. In September, he could point to two accomplishments. First, General Groves had approved his recommendation for locating the test site in the Jornada del Muerto Valley in the northwest corner of the Alamogordo Bombing Range about 100 miles south of Albuquerque. Second, one of his section leaders, Fussell, had made preliminary plans for measuring blast, ground shock, neutrons, gamma rays, nuclear efficiency, and for photographic and radar studies of general phenomena.

In the fall of 1944, Bainbridge had to turn his attention away from test preparations and throw all but two of Fussell's section into the work on the Fat Man (implosion weapon) detonating system. Despite this, Bainbridge was able to accomplish a few things—design and contract for Jumbo, the 214-ton steel tank that would permit recovering the plutonium in event of a nuclear failure; establish a camp at the Alamogordo site; obtain and calibrate instruments; and plan a few of the measurements. This was all the testing program could legitimately demand when the plight of implosion seemed so desperate.

With the February, 1945, decision to concentrate on a specific design, it was time to give Bainbridge the men and priority he needed. At the head of a new organization, staffed largely by physicists from the Research Division, he was in a position to rush preparations for his first task—a trial run on an explosion of 100 tons of high explosive scheduled for May. He had a demanding assignment, but it was eased at the outset by a decision to dispense with Jumbo. The chances for successful implosion looked sufficiently good to risk losing the plutonium in the interest of better measurements.[46]

319

Beyond the test lay combat. Oppenheimer's third effort at more effective organization in March, 1945, was to create Project Alberta, soon abbreviated to Project A. Organized under Parsons as a loose co-ordinating body independent of any existing division, it was an attempt to integrate all work on the preparation and delivery of a combat bomb. Ramsey served as Parsons' deputy for scientific and technical matters and Ashworth as his operations officer and military alternate. Project A needed its strong staff—Bradbury and Roger S. Warner in charge of the Fat Man assembly, Birch the Little Boy (uranium gun), Brode fuzing, Fussell the electric detonator system, and Philip Morrison and Marshall G. Holloway the active material and tamper. Project A would complete the design, procurement, and preliminary assembly of the nonnuclear components. It would continue the Wendover tests to confirm the adequacy of the bombs in flight. Finally, it would prepare for overseas operations.[47]

As Los Alamos girded for its final effort, the Chemistry and Metallurgy Division occupied a position of signal importance. Everything depended on its ability to take Y-12 fluoride and Hanford nitrates, reduce them to metal, and prepare the shapes the physicists specified. Since the start of the project, Kennedy and Smith had been hard at work to make sure they would be able to go into production as soon as the Oak Ridge and Hanford product reached the Hill. Any delay, they knew, would be measured in the lives of American soldiers and sailors.

U-235 caused no sleepless nights, even though its extreme value demanded an accounting system far more rigid than a goldsmith's and despite the need to guard against assembling a critical mass. It was plutonium that remained the great challenge. Kennedy's chemists concentrated on simplifying the purification process, establishing an efficient production routine, and controlling the health hazard that constantly menaced. Smith's metallurgists found plutonium extremely difficult to fabricate. Part of the trouble was its extreme toxicity. Breathing even traces of plutonium dust exposed a worker to dangerous radiation. Another complication, a major threat to success, sprang from the fact that plutonium existed in several allotropic states. Smith's men succeeded in identifying five phases between room temperature and the melting point, each with a different density. These unusual characteristics raised the possibility that the metal might powder like gray tin. On the other hand, there was the comforting thought that at least one phase ought to be malleable.[48]

320

Kennedy and Smith carried an especially heavy load in February and March of 1945. In addition to the division's regular service functions, Oppenheimer had to ask them to take on implosion assignments that bordered on the impossible. On top of everything else, they had to supervise the design and construction of a new plutonium works at the DP Site, a mile and one-half east of the existing facilities in the Technical Area. The health hazards and limited capacity of the old plant in D Building justified the new construction, but what really brought General Groves to approve it was a fire in the shops the night of January 15. Should such a fire break out in D Building when any considerable amount of plutonium was in process, it might contaminate the entire Los Alamos community.[49]

March and April saw increasingly firm specifications, and Kennedy and Smith assured the laboratory they could do anything with uranium and plutonium that needed doing. Word arrived from Groves that Hanford would start quantity shipments in May. On April 27, Kennedy met in Chicago with Charles A. Thomas, Colonel Matthias, and a delegation from du Pont. Without difficulty, the conference agreed on upper limits for impurities in shipments from Hanford. Now the long period of preparation was over. Kennedy returned to Los Alamos, relieved that the time had come for the chemists and metallurgists to put their skill to the proof.[50]

APRIL PROSPECT

April, 1945, was a good month throughout the laboratory. Work on the gun moved smoothly and surely forward. Frisch's group in the Gadget Division achieved the first critical assembly of metallic U-235 on April 13, thus demonstrating its critical mass experimentally. Wilson's Cyclotron Group reported on its efforts to establish the amount of metal the gun projectile and target should contain. While these experiments were not yet conclusive, they induced Birch to draw up plans for a modification. On April 5, the Technical and Scheduling Conference assigned high priority to obtaining more definite data. Yet there was no sense of crisis. When Birch and Serber, the expert on gun theory, spoke at Colloquium a few days later, they emanated confidence.[51]

The outlook for implosion was very much better than at the freeze six weeks before. Oppenheimer reported the good news to Groves on April 11. Bacher and Kistiakowsky seemed to have overcome their greatest enemy, the asymmetrical implosion. Test results, favorable beyond expectation, had shown compressions that agreed with theory. Oppenheimer's report did not mean that all reason for anxiety had vanished. The explosives factory was short on critical facilities and the detonating circuit—marginal at best—lagging in production. Yet these disappointments did not preclude success. Neither did the uncertainty about the initiator. Though no one could say positively that the several types under development would work (categorical proof short of trial with active material was impossible), it seemed likely that three varieties would prove satisfactory. By the end of April, Bethe's Initiator Advisory Committee was ready to name its first choice.[52]

321

General Groves could look back proudly on the estimate of weapons availability he had presented Chief of Staff Marshall the preceding summer. His prediction of a uranium gun by August 1, 1945, still stood. There had been some anxious moments, but now it was certain that the Oak Ridge production complex would meet its schedule. There never had been any real doubt that Los Alamos would have a gun assembly ready in time.

Groves's promise of several implosion bombs between March and June, each the equivalent of several thousand tons of TNT, had not fared so well. Based on the hope that Los Alamos would come through with a high-efficiency implosion, it had to be revised in the fall of 1944. By December, the best Groves could anticipate was a few weapons in the second half of 1945. Though these would improve in power, the first models were expected to yield the effect of considerably less than 1,000 tons of TNT. In the late winter and early spring, the prospects improved. While the timetable for combat weapons did not accelerate (in fact, the full-scale implosion trial had to be postponed from spring to early July), there seemed a good chance for higher yield. If every component worked as hoped, Bethe's theoretical physicists anticipated that the first weapon would rate slightly under 5,000 tons.[53] In short, April, 1945, confirmed the August, 1944, estimates on power but not on availability. Though combat bombs were roughly five months behind schedule, this was a reasonable margin of error in a field so unexplored, so pocked with unforeseeable pitfalls.

Far surpassing any pride which Groves felt at that time was his gratification that atomic weapons would be available in time to use against Japan. The bomb would justify the years of effort, the vast expenditures—yes, the judgment of everyone responsible—by bringing the war in the Pacific to a fiery end.[54]

THE QUEST FOR POSTWAR PLANNING

CHAPTER 10

Bush and Conant—like other scientific men—had seen from the first that the development of atomic energy might be a turning point in the history of civilization. They knew it would require extraordinary means of control. It was because they recognized the revolutionary character of atomic weapons that they had resisted policies which might shape the future as a mere incident of the war effort. Neither Bush nor Conant had been in a rush to precipitate postwar issues, but late in the summer of 1944, they concluded the time had come for earnest thought about arrangements for both domestic and international control. Their minds had been much on these subjects since the spring, but the events of the summer supplied a sense of urgency. In France, the eastward dash of the Third Army brought the end of the war within sight. In Chicago, scientists of the Metallurgical Laboratory raised searching questions about the future.

THE CHICAGO STIMULUS

Chicago was the most immediate stimulus to action. As early as the fall of 1943, it was apparent that the Metallurgical Project was nearing the end of its assignment. In the first days of 1944, the scientists' natural concern for the future of nuclear research reached a peak when rumors swept across the Midway that 90 per cent of the personnel would be released by June 1. Director Arthur H. Compton denounced this gossip as baseless and sought to allay the surging discontent. On February 16, he told his council that while the immediate aim remained the early and successful production of plutonium, it was time to think about post-Hanford objectives. As a start, he had asked Henry D. Smyth to draft long-range plans. On April 10, Compton sent General Groves a report advocating three major tasks for the coming fiscal year, 1945. First, the project should support Hanford; second, it should co-operate with Los Alamos; third, it should investigate new possibilities. These included the study of pile concepts, thorium, and the military, scientific, industrial, and medical applications of radiation. Compton also suggested basic research in nuclear physics, chemistry, biology, and metallurgy. National safety justified such investigations even though they lay beyond current military goals. If the United States was to maintain its leadership after the war, it must launch vigorous explorations.[1]

General Groves and his Washington advisers thought it both unnecessary and unwise to begin extensive postwar research amid the grave uncertainties of the hour. Early in June, orders went down through Colonel Nichols. While approving the Chicago suggestions in principle, they imposed definite limitations on work of long-range significance. Compton was not to recruit new personnel for such activity. Neither was he to permit major construction or detailed design efforts without prior approval. The most he could do was to use men held in stand-by for Hanford and Los Alamos on new research whenever time permitted. When Compton explained the orders on June 7, 1944, the Project Council received them with restrained approval. Smyth thought the directive reasonable. Samuel K. Allison wondered if the exponential experiments on a homogeneous heavy-water pile could continue. Compton's reply that he believed so afforded Allison a measure of reassurance.[2]

323

The tension eased for less than a month. On July 5, Compton informed his chief lieutenants that Groves had asked him to consider a 25- to 75-per-cent reduction in staff after the project went on stand-by status about September 1. Thorfin R. Hogness and Richard L. Doan outspokenly opposed the whole idea. The psychology of stand-by was deadly, they argued. It would be almost impossible to keep the ablest young scientists from drifting away. Zay Jeffries, a General Electric executive whom Compton had brought in as consultant, opposed any retrenchment until Germany was beaten. One never knew when some piece of basic research might become important in meeting current needs. Smyth and Major Arthur V. Peterson suggested trying to set definite goals. Win recognition for these from higher authority, and the project would gain a sense of purpose to hold it together. Compton saw the uses of this tactic at a time when support for postwar research was out of the question. When a few days later Jeffries advocated preparing a prospectus on "nucleonics" (his word for the new industry he saw just over the horizon), Compton named him head of a committee to do the job. Meanwhile, Compton had urged each division director to prepare a suitable program and personnel plan for the difficult phase ahead.[3]

The Chicago scientists were still dissatisfied on Friday, July 14, when Bush called Compton by long distance. Complaints had reached OSRD, he said, that the University of Chicago had sought to lure Enrico Fermi away from Columbia with the suggestion that only by joining the Chicago faculty could he become director of the Argonne Laboratory after the war. Bush did not accept this at face value, but he wanted to know the facts. The charges suggested that Chicago was exploiting the war effort for its own aggrandizement. Compton admitted he had offered Fermi a professorship and had indicated the university would welcome him as director of Argonne. At the same time, Compton recognized that no one was in a position to assure anything about the postwar operation of the laboratory. Bush accepted Compton's explanation and was willing to dismiss the episode as a misunderstanding. He was glad to learn that Compton would be in Washington on August 7. He thought it would be a splendid opportunity to discuss the relationship between the universities and the Government, not only for the present but also in the years of peace.[4]

324

On August 7, Compton stressed the importance of a minimal research effort that would develop information needed at the peace table and lay the foundation for rapid progress under postwar conditions. Both Bush and Compton agreed that while they must look to the future, the planning process should proceed within the Manhattan project. Both pledged they would give careful thought to the future but would prevent general discussions that might detract attention from the primary objective, prosecution of the war.

Bush wanted to make sure he had relieved the fears of the Chicago scientists. On August 10, he wrote Compton that the Military Policy Committee had authorized Richard C. Tolman to head a study of postwar needs, particularly the characteristics of the future program. Tolman would give some attention to possible industrial applications. Compton might tell his staff the study was under way and that those with important ideas would have a chance to express them. On August 28, Bush replied to a letter James Franck had written voicing the alarm of the Chicago rank and file. Bush offered his assurance that the Army would not permit a disastrous break at the end of the war. There was such a thing as timing, however, and postwar proposals would stand a better chance at some significant date, such as the defeat of Germany or the collapse of Japan. Planning certainly was in order now. Both Conant and he were most anxious to reflect accurately the opinions of the scientists who had been so deeply engaged in the enterprise.[5]

NUCLEAR FRONTIERS

During the fall of 1944, the Jeffries and Tolman committees scouted the frontiers of nuclear energy. The Jeffries team—Fermi, Franck, Hogness, Robert S. Stone, Charles A. Thomas, and Robert S. Mulliken—moved quickly. Acting as secretary, Mulliken solicited views throughout the Metallurgical Project and had a rough draft ready before the end of September. October saw revision and refinement. On November 18, the "Prospectus on Nucleonics" was complete. After a review of the history of nuclear science and an analysis of the current program, Jeffries and his colleagues outlined the applications they anticipated in the near future and speculated on the possibilities of nuclear power. They did not limit themselves to the technical potential. Pointing to the threat of atomic war, they argued that a world-wide organization was necessary to prevent the atom from becoming the destroyer of nations. They believed it vitally important—both before and after establishment of such an organization—for the United States to keep the lead in nuclear research and its industrial applications. They hoped for a future marked by happy collaboration between the universities, the Government, and an independent nucleonics industry.[6]

Tolman's Committee on Postwar Policy was a more ambitious undertaking with a more definite objective—technical recommendations on the research and development policies the Government should pursue. In October and November, the committee held meetings in Chicago, New York, and Washington. Its members—Warren K. Lewis, Rear Admiral Earle W. Mills, and Henry D. Smyth in addition to Tolman—conducted forty-four direct interviews with scientists representing the Manhattan project's principal research centers. On the basis of this oral testimony, supplemented by thirty-seven written memorandums, they prepared a report which concluded that the need to maintain military superiority controlled planning for atomic energy. The United States must continue work on the separation of U-235, the production of Pu-239 and U-233, and the development of weapons. It must adapt nuclear power to naval propulsion. In addition, it should encourage fundamental research and industrial development, both of which were essential to maintaining the advanced scientific and technical position that national defense demanded. The Tolman committee did not venture an opinion on international control, but for the domestic scene it envisioned a national authority which would distribute its funds among military and civilian laboratories of the Government, academic institutions, and industrial organizations.[7]

325

The Jeffries and Tolman reports had two things in common: first, they called for national support of a comprehensive nuclear energy program after the war; second, they had no immediate impact. This did not mean that the Army shoved them into pigeonholes and promptly forgot about them. It meant only that the reports were ready before anyone could use them. Bush and Conant were alert to the need for planning. They knew the value of scientific research. They did not require reports to tell them it was crucial to devise effective arrangements for national and international control. In a unique position to think in terms of both science and high policy, they were not neglecting their opportunities. But until they could interest the officials who had to make these essentially political decisions, the detailed analyses of the working scientists had little utility.

THE HYDE PARK STIMULUS

As soon as they had reassured the Chicago scientists, Bush and Conant turned to stimulating postwar planning at the policy-making level. On September 19,

1944, they addressed a letter to Secretary Stimson which stressed the approaching need for releasing basic scientific information and enacting national legislation to control atomic power. In the same communication, they urged the importance of a treaty with the United Kingdom and Canada that would insure domestic controls similar to those contemplated for the United States, put interchange on a permanent basis, and determine satisfactorily the future industrial rights that the Quebec Agreement had left in the hands of the President. On the broader international questions raised by the bomb, Bush and Conant warned that it would be dangerous for the United States to assume that security lay in holding secret its present knowledge.[8] Actually, these two leaders had ideas not yet sufficiently crystallized for formal expression. They were thinking in terms of an international control agency, one that would have Russian membership. While they looked with favor on joint Anglo-American efforts to acquire raw materials and contemplated extending interchange into the years of peace, they did not want the United States to commit itself so completely to Britain as to prejudice its relations with Russia. They wanted to avoid precipitating a nuclear arms race before the United States had made a reasonable approach to international control on a multilateral basis.[9]

326

On Friday, September 22, 1944—three days after the letter to Stimson—the President called Bush to the White House for a long conference that brought to fever heat the concern he shared with Conant. Roosevelt had not talked S-1 with Bush for a good many months, and he did not know that Bush had been giving a great deal of thought to postwar problems. For his part, Bush did not know that the President had been thinking—and acting—on the same subject.

Some weeks before, Justice Frankfurter had called at the White House and told the President he was much worried about the handling of the secret project after the war. He wanted the President to see the Danish physicist, Niels Bohr, who had some striking ideas on the subject. Roosevelt was taken aback to learn that Frankfurter had heard about S-1. While pretending not to know what the learned justice was talking about, he agreed to see Bohr. Late in August, Bohr had a short talk with the President, a talk he used to urge that Britain and the United States tell the world about the bomb in an effort to achieve international control and head off a fateful arms race. Bush and Conant had not contemplated so immediate an overture, but the Dane and the two Americans were moving in the same direction.[10]

The next person to turn Roosevelt's attention to the postwar aspects of atomic energy was Winston Churchill. On Sunday, September 17, 1944, the Prime Minister, accompanied by Mrs. Churchill and their daughter Mary, left Quebec to pay a visit to the Roosevelts at Hyde Park. As the train rolled south, Churchill could reflect with satisfaction on the work of the week just passed. The second great wartime conference at the frowning Citadel above the St. Lawrence had opened in "a blaze of friendship." Flushed with success, the President, the Prime Minister, and their military advisers quickly adjusted their views on the final assaults against the Reich and laid plans to join in forcing the Japanese to surrender. Roosevelt and Secretary of the Treasury Henry Morgenthau, Jr., had shown their growing understanding of the economic troubles Britain would face once Germany collapsed. Having liquidated her overseas assets to finance the fight against Hitler, Britain had to rebuild her export trade quickly. Morgenthau's plan for restricting German industry was in part a measure of his concern for Britain's problem and the threat that German competition would pose to her recovery. Roosevelt's favorable attitude toward Churchill's proposal for continuing Lend-Lease after Germany's defeat stemmed from his realization that the United States could not allow its ally to collapse in the hour of victory.[11]

Roosevelt and Churchill had not made any commitments on Tube Alloys at Quebec, but the Prime Minister would have his opportunity in the quiet, informal atmosphere of Hyde Park. The time must have seemed unusually propitious. Churchill's interest in atomic energy had never been narrowly commercial, but he could not close his eyes to the economic advantages the new technology might offer Britain with her sick coal industry and her desperate need for exports. The only interests in industrial and commercial aspects Churchill disclaimed in the Quebec Agreement of 1943 were those that lay "beyond what may be considered by the President of the United States to be fair and just and in harmony with the economic welfare of the world." With the President taking a larger view of Britain's economic crisis, this disclaimer meant very little.

On September 18, the two heads of government talked atomic energy. They considered Bohr's suggestion (he had also brought his views to Churchill's attention), but neither thought it time to break the news of the bomb to the world. When the discussion turned to industrial applications, Churchill found the President liberally inclined. To record their common views, Roosevelt and Churchill initialled an *aide-mémoire*. Flatly rejecting Bohr's approach, they concurred that the project should continue to have the utmost secrecy. When a bomb finally became available, "It might perhaps, after mature consideration, be used against the Japanese, who should be warned that this bombardment will be repeated until they surrender." Finally, both men agreed on what amounted to an Anglo-American approach to the postwar world: "Full collaboration between the United States and the British Government in developing Tube Alloys for military and commercial purposes should continue after the defeat of Japan unless and until terminated by joint agreement."[12]

Roosevelt had the talks with Churchill much on his mind when he called Bush in on September 22. After introducing Admiral William D. Leahy, who had just learned about S-1, and Lord Cherwell, who had come down from Quebec, the President told Bush about Frankfurter and Bohr. He was much disturbed at the thought there might have been a security leak. But Bush reassured him, and the President began to talk quite generally. Should the bomb, he asked, actually be used against the Japanese or should it be tested in the United States and held as a threat? Bush replied that this question warranted careful discussion but could be postponed for quite a time in view of the inadvisability of making a threat until the United States was in a position to follow through. Roosevelt agreed.

Then the President turned to the postwar situation, affirming his belief in the necessity of keeping the British Empire strong. Economic aid was one way, and atomic energy was another. There should be complete interchange on all phases after the defeat of Japan. Although he did not mention the *aidemémoire* he had signed at Hyde Park, the President made it clear that he had talked to Churchill along these lines. Bush spent an uncomfortable hour. Paying no heed to Cherwell's presence, Roosevelt was discussing matters he had never considered with his own advisers. Bush could not say what was uppermost in his mind—that collaborating too closely with the British without considering the world situation might lead to most undesirable relations with Russia. He managed, however, to work in the observation that there would be free and open publication of the scientific aspects of the subject after the war and that he hoped the Russians would participate.

When the President mentioned commercial use and the necessity for domestic control, Bush told him of the letter he and Conant had just written to Stimson. Of course, he discreetly refrained from mentioning its suggestion for a treaty with Britain. Grasping for a chance to get the ear of the President under more favorable circumstances, Bush offered to tell Stimson the President would like to talk with him. Roosevelt allowed that this would be desirable.[13]

Thanks to Harvey H. Bundy, Bush had a conference with Stimson after lunch the following Monday. Still upset, he reported the exchanges of Friday. The more he thought about it, the more it seemed that the President contemplated an Anglo-American agreement to hold S-1 technology closely after the war and thus to control the peace of the world. The trouble with this, Bush told Stimson, was that it might well lead to extraordinary efforts by Russia to develop the bomb secretly and to a catastrophic conflict, say twenty years hence. Might not another policy head off such a disaster? Bush said he felt that if there were complete scientific interchange among all countries, it would minimize the danger of a race on military applications as the art changed. One might even hope, he thought, for an international organization that would permit all nations to share control. Someone ought to analyze this possibility carefully. Stimson agreed specifically to this last suggestion, and Bush gained the impression that the Secretary concurred in much he had said. But Stimson was most pessimistic about holding the President's attention long enough to get to the bottom of the subject. He had been trying in vain to discuss a number of things with his chief. Still, he thought that the S-1 leadership ought to make the effort, if only for the record.

Stimson, harassed by the cares of directing the greatest war machine in the world, had just entered his seventy-eighth year. As Bush looked at him, he saw that he had neither time nor energy to give the matter the attention it deserved. So he suggested that he and Conant draft a brief statement of what they considered a reasonable approach to international control. Stimson seized the offer. He thought that some such brief statement ought to go to the President and that it might bring at least a pause for further study.[14]

PLEA FOR PLANNING

Five days later, September 30, 1944, Bush and Conant sent Stimson two papers, one setting forth their views on future international handling of atomic bombs, the other covering the same ground in more detail. The memorandums had been carefully contrived to make it easy for Stimson to grasp the essentials. To be certain they got their ideas through to the Secretary, Bush and Conant forwarded the documents under a covering letter that reduced the argument to a few sentences. There was every reason to believe, they reported, that atomic bombs would be demonstrated before August 1, 1945. The type then in production would be equivalent in blast damage to from one to ten thousand tons of high explosive. This was frightening enough, but not far in the future lay the hydrogen bomb, perhaps a thousand times more powerful. It promised to place every population center in the world at the mercy of the nation that struck first. The present advantage of the United States and Britain was temporary. Any nation with good technical and scientific resources could overtake them in three or four years. It would be folly for the two English-speaking countries to assume they would always be ahead. Accidents of research might give another nation as great an advantage as they currently enjoyed.

Such was the alarming situation. What were the possibilities? It was foolhardy to attempt to maintain American security by preserving secrecy. Physicists knew all the basic facts before development began. In view of this, Bush and Conant advocated disclosure of all but the manufacturing and military details of the bombs as soon as the first was demonstrated. "This demonstration might be over enemy territory, or in our own country, with subsequent notice to Japan that the materials would be used against the Japanese mainland unless surrender was forthcoming." Fully as unwise as reliance on secrecy was dependence on the control of raw materials. The two powers could not count on this, particularly should a hydrogen bomb be developed. The supplies of heavy hydrogen were essentially unlimited.

Bush and Conant considered that the best chance of forestalling a fatal competition lay in proposing free interchange of all scientific information on the subject under an international office deriving its power from whatever association of nations was developed at the end of the war. As soon as practical,

329

the technical staff of this office should have unimpeded access to scientific laboratories, industrial plants, and military establishments throughout the world. This course was bound to encounter heavy resistance. There were those in the United States who would oppose it stubbornly. Russia would be more reluctant than any other nation, but since the United States and Britain held an advantage, even if only temporary, they would be offering the Soviets a valuable consideration. Whatever the opposition, the magnitude of the danger warranted the effort. Such a system offered the great advantage of laying before the people of the world the true state of the armament situation. If that were done, there was reason to hope that the weapons never would be employed. One could even dream that their existence might decrease the chance of another major war.[15]

Some three weeks later, Stimson spoke to Bush about the memorandum. He did not say what he was going to do, and Bush concluded he had not yet decided. Privately, Bush thought Stimson should add his own comments and place the document in the hands of the President. Ultimately, Roosevelt should have a solid group of men to study the implications of atomic energy and to advise him on possible moves.

Though Bush judged it was not yet time to advocate an advisory committee, he was becoming more and more hopeful about the outlook for international control. The recently concluded Dumbarton Oaks conference was encouraging, he told Conant on October 24. It had gone much further than he had thought possible at this stage of the war. The planners of international organization had done more for co-operation on economic subjects than on scientific, but it was not too late to correct the deficiency. Perhaps biological warfare was the place to start. Biological weapons would be a terrible threat should some aggressor develop them in secret and suddenly spring them on the world. But if there were interchange among biological scientists everywhere, especially if it took place through an international organization, the chances for clandestine development would be much less. The United States and Britain had just begun exchanging information. Suppose they offered Russia a chance to share? Might it not be most instructive? Might it not be the opening wedge for a similar approach to atomic energy? Perhaps a document outlining the biological-warfare issue would serve as a beginning. A talk with Secretary of State Edward R. Stettinius might be helpful in deciding how to proceed. Three days later, Bush and Conant sent Stimson a memorandum on biological warfare.[16]

November saw a lull in the quest for postwar planning. Bush had to go to Europe for consultations on using the proximity fuze against the Germans. Not until early December did Conant and he have opportunity to press for top-level consideration of impending problems. On the eighth, they conferred with Bundy and Assistant Secretary of War John J. McCloy. Urging that planning begin at once, Bush brought forward his idea for an advisory committee. Stimson should suggest that the President nominate such a group. The scope of its responsibility would range from drafting news releases and legislation to giving advice on any current experimentation that a well-rounded postwar approach demanded. Bush and Conant judged that technical research had little bearing on the international issues. Everyone agreed that the latter required bringing in the Department of State. There would, of course, be interrelationships between domestic and foreign policies, and that department should have representation on the planning committee.

Bundy brought these considerations to Stimson's attention on December 9, and four days later Bush himself had a chance to review them with the Secretary of War. Stimson did not commit himself on the planning committee, but he agreed that the time had come to inform State. He intended to propose this to the President. When the discussion turned to international exchange after the war, it was evident that Stimson still was mulling the question over in his mind. The decision was exceedingly difficult, he said. So great was its moment that arriving at a policy demanded enormous care.[17]

331

DIVERSION

Just at this juncture, Stimson learned from Bundy, Harrison, and Groves that a storm had blown up over a portentous development—the flow of S-1 information to liberated France. Recognizing the potential for trouble, Stimson had Bundy come in on Friday, December 29, 1944, and review with him a long report from General Groves.

It was a tangled story. In May, 1944, Pierre Auger, a French physicist working on the pile project at Montreal, resigned and indicated his desire to return to France. Groves considered this a threat to security. He discussed the request with British representatives in the United States, and they agreed on the necessity of preventing information from leaking to France. London, however, saw things differently, and Auger returned to France shortly after the St.–Lô breakthrough. About the middle of October, another of the French nationals employed at Montreal, Jules Guéron, asked to return to France to settle some personal affairs. This request was disturbing. Guéron had learned a great deal about the American program. He indicated he intended to talk with Joliot-Curie, who, it was known, had joined the Communist Party. Groves asked London to delay, but the authorities there replied that they had promised to permit Guéron to visit his homeland. The French scientist arrived in London about October 15 and a few days later went on to Paris. Groves determined to try to protect security by having American agents shadow Guéron. But when his men in London sought to make arrangements, a first-class controversy developed.

Both Sir John Anderson and Ambassador John G. Winant became involved. At Winant's request, Anderson submitted an *aide-mémoire* reviewing Britain's relations with the French scientists who had escaped in 1940. Auger.

Guéron, and another—Bertrand L. Goldschmidt—were French civil servants. Britain had promised Auger that he could leave the Tube Alloys work in May of 1944. As for Guéron and Goldschmidt, they had agreed to work in Montreal until August, 1944, at least, with the understanding that they could pay a short visit to France if this seemed desirable in connection with their scientific position in the French Government. Halban and Kowarski, who had brought Joliot's heavy water to England, had a special relationship. After prolonged negotiations, they had assigned their rights in past and future inventions to Britain. Halban further undertook to try to have the French Government assign Britain all rights in the patents it held. In return, Britain pledged herself to reassign to France all rights for metropolitan France and the French Empire in the Halban-Kowarski patents, in patents that the physicists might apply for on information which they brought with them from France, and in future patents they might obtain which were dominated by any of the others.

332

Sir John argued that the United States and Britain could not treat the French scientists as prisoners. Besides, whatever was done, the information eventually would reach Joliot and the French authorities. By virtue of the pioneering researches of her scientists and their help during the war, France had a better claim than any fourth country to participate in postwar arrangements. How far that claim should be recognized, if at all, was a matter for the signatories of the Quebec Agreement to decide at an appropriate time. Meanwhile, it seemed unwise to take action which might give French officials a sense of grievance and lead them to raise their claims prematurely.

When Groves saw the *aide-mémoire*, he was astonished. He had never heard of these British obligations. Neither had Bush. In August, 1942, Anderson had written to Bush that Britain had acquired the rights of Halban and Kowarski and had taken steps to acquire the rights of other French inventors associated with them, but he had not indicated that Britain had agreed in return to extend certain rights to the French Government. The situation was awkward. At Quebec in 1943, Churchill had proposed and Roosevelt had agreed that neither partner should pass information to third parties without obtaining the consent of the other. Yet no one on the British side had taken that occasion to make clear the fact that prior obligations existed.

The issues raised by the Guéron episode had not been resolved when, early in November, Halban himself went to England. Groves understood from British representatives in America that their government would not allow the French physicist to go to the Continent. Yet as soon as Halban arrived in London, Sir John Anderson raised the question of his proceeding to France to talk with Joliot. The Chancellor did not approach the Combined Policy Committee, which was the arbiter of the interpretation and application of the Quebec Agreement. Instead, he turned to Ambassador Winant, with whom he had worked on the Congo ore negotiations. Anderson thought Halban should be permitted to visit his mentor, Joliot, for Halban needed to report on the patent arrangements he had made. He could take advantage of the opportunity to persuade Joliot that France should not yet raise her claims on the future. To deny Halban a visit to France, the Chancellor argued, would threaten both security and the chance of acquiring the patent rights held by the government there. To make sure Halban did not pass an undue amount of information to Joliot, the British would furnish him written instructions on what to say, instructions setting forth in barest outline the progress made since 1940.

Anderson, a hard-driving negotiator, put pressure on Winant. Knowing Groves's opposition to the Halban visit, the Ambassador tried to persuade the General to come to London to talk with Sir John. But Groves could not break away, and Winant gave Anderson his assent. The Chancellor's contention that any different course would create an even more difficult situation convinced him, although it did not convince Groves. As he interpreted the Quebec Agreement, the disclosure of information required the consent of the President. Sir John, be believed firmly, had violated Churchill's pledge. He had sent to France information developed by American scientists with American money. Such were the fruits of interchange.[18]

333

Viewed in broad perspective, the French imbroglio argued the necessity of international control and the importance of prompt planning to that end. But coming when and as it did, it tended to divert attention from the central issue. Talking with Bundy on December 29, Stimson could see that the mess demanded Roosevelt's attention since it was more than a breach of military security. France was in a position to play power politics—to bring or threaten to bring Russia into the picture. All through Christmas week Stimson had sought an appointment with Roosevelt. Finally, about eleven o'clock on Saturday morning, December 30, General Watson called to say the President would see him in an hour. Stimson summoned Bundy and Groves at once and prepared to give his chief "the works on S-1."

A WHITE HOUSE LOOK AT THE FUTURE

When Stimson arrived at the White House, Groves at his side, the complaint that the British were allowing information to leak to the French dominated the conversation. Reminding Roosevelt of the Quebec Agreement pledge, Stimson accused Chancellor Anderson of hoodwinking "poor old John" Winant. Roosevelt listened to the story, fascinated. What were the French after, he wanted to know. Stimson did not profess exact knowledge but declared Sir John was putting them in a position to claim full partnership. Stimson had expected the President to take a dim view of this development. He was right. Roosevelt observed that the unstable political situation made France an unsuitable confederate at present. But even if her government were completely satisfactory, he saw no reason for cutting France into the atomic partnership.

Stimson now turned the President's attention to other issues. He told him that impending raw-materials negotiations as well as the French situation made it advisable to admit Secretary of State Stettinius to the little group of top officials who knew about the bomb. The President agreed. Stimson also pointed to the British vacancies on the Combined Policy Committee. Roosevelt suggested that Lord Halifax was the right sort of man for the post.

The President showed great interest throughout the interview, particularly in the implications of the leaks to France. Was Churchill in on all this? No, not so far as Stimson and Groves could tell. Anderson, a man dominated by the "imperial instinct," seemed to be running the show. Groves proudly defended his tactics in protecting information developed by American men, money, and effort. In response to Roosevelt's query, he said there was every evidence the Russians were spying on the bomb project, particularly at Berkeley.

334

Finally, Stimson showed the President a report Groves had prepared for Chief of Staff Marshall outlining current expectations on the availability of nuclear weapons. A gun-type bomb yielding the equivalent of a 10,000-ton TNT explosion and not requiring a full-scale test should be available about August 1, 1945. A second should be ready by the end of the year and others at somewhat shorter intervals thereafter. Scientific difficulties had dissipated previous hopes for an implosion bomb in the late spring. For weapons of this type, it would be necessary to use more material less efficiently than had been expected. Sometime in the latter part of July there would be sufficient metal for a unit with the effect of about 500 tons of TNT. It would be possible to produce several additional implosion weapons during the remainder of 1945. Their effectiveness should increase toward 1,000 tons each and, as some of the problems were overcome, to as much as 2,500 tons.

According to Groves, the plan of operations was based on the more powerful gun weapon with provision for employing the implosion type when it was ready. The target was Japan. Since nothing but the scientific difficulties themselves should be allowed to affect the time schedule adversely, the 509th Composite Group had been organized and put into training. The time had come to supply information to the Army, Air Force, and Navy officers whose co-operation was necessary in combat operations.

Roosevelt indicated that he approved the Groves report. By now, Stimson and Groves had stayed far beyond their allotted half-hour. But the President remained much interested, and when Stimson asked for another appointment, Roosevelt told him to call the next day at noon.[19]

The President was still in bed when Stimson saw him Sunday. Roosevelt reported he had already broached S-1 to Stettinius. Eventually, the conversation turned to the impending conference with Churchill and Stalin at Yalta. Russia was increasingly intransigent. Only the day before, Roosevelt had written Stalin to protest Russia's determination to recognize the Lublin Committee as the Provisional Government of Poland. Stimson took occasion to tell the President of General John R. Deane's warning from Moscow that further easy concessions would gain nothing, that the United States should be more vigorous in insisting on a *quid pro quo.* The Secretary observed this had a bearing on S-1. He knew the Russians were spying on the American atomic project, even though they had not yet obtained any real knowledge of it. He was troubled about the effect of withholding information from them but was also convinced that it was essential not to take them into confidence until the United States was sure of getting something for its frankness. Stimson admitted that he had no illusions about keeping the secret permanently. Still, it was not yet the time to share with Russia. Roosevelt said he thought he agreed.[20]

MARKING TIME   335

Bush was disappointed to learn from Bundy on January 2, 1945, that Stimson had failed to discuss with the President either the planning committee or postwar international safeguards. Bush, however, had long since become an experienced bureaucrat, not easily discouraged by the frustrations of Washington. About the planning committee, he would continue to prod Bundy. As for international control, he understood that Stimson wanted to talk to Marshall about it. Besides, that subject might well come up in discussing the French situation with Stettinius. So it happened. On January 3, Stimson and Bundy outlined the atomic project to the Secretary of State. Stettinius was much impressed, and the three agreed that State's James C. Dunn should devote his attention to S-1. This paved the way for a Bush conference with Dunn on January 30. Bush outlined the international approach he and Conant had suggested to Stimson. Dunn thought Bush and Conant ought to present their views directly to Stettinius.[21]

Stimson delayed asking Marshall's views on international control, but he hurried to work out a joint Anglo-American policy on the French scientists and their double loyalties. With the bomb project nearing completion, security of information on dates and production possibilities was especially critical. Even had he been so inclined, Stimson could not have delayed, for Sir John Anderson told Winant he was under considerable pressure. For one thing, Goldschmidt wanted to pay a short visit to France. For another, Joliot was pressing to come to London. Anderson promised to block discussion of Tube Alloys with Joliot or any other representative of the French Government until there was agreement on policy. But, he warned, it was necessary to reach an accord within a reasonable time, for he could not put off Goldschmidt and Joliot indefinitely.[22]

Bundy and Groves reviewed the whole dispute for Stimson on Friday, January 19, in preparation for the Combined Policy Committee meeting the following Monday. Bundy took the lead, stressing the importance of postponing any French demand for immediate participation. He suggested arranging to have Sir John Anderson tell Joliot it was inadvisable to attempt detailed discussion until the end of hostilities, but at that time the United Kingdom and the United States would take up any French claims relating to commercial or industrial application of nuclear power. Stimson agreed with the general idea but insisted on dropping the reference to the United States. There must be no American commitment of any kind to the French. Bundy then brought up preventing the disclosure of further information. Groves had been studying this with Chadwick, an Englishman with whom he had always worked effectively. The two men were not far apart on how to handle three of the Frenchmen still at Montreal—Goldschmidt, Guéron, and Kowarski. They would extend their contracts, keep them under close security, and allow Goldschmidt to go to Paris for a brief trip if prior commitments made it unavoidable. Halban's case was more difficult. There were several alternatives that required further discussion.[23]

336

Stimson felt so strongly that the United States should make no promise to France that he did not wait until Monday. He had Bundy telephone Sir Ronald Campbell, currently the ranking Briton on the Combined Policy Committee, explain the American position, and suggest the text of a statement for Sir John to make to Joliot. Campbell agreed to send Anderson the instructions, and when the committee assembled Monday morning, the issue had been pretty well decided. Stimson simply reported where he stood, what he had done, and then gave Sir Ronald the opportunity to explain why the British attached so much importance to the French patents. The discussion dragged on, but the committee at last concluded that it would be undesirable from the security standpoint to have discussions with the French go beyond the statement proposed to Sir John Anderson.

Stimson was glad that the final decision was unanimous. He was further gratified that no important differences erupted when Groves and Chadwick reported on the French scientists in Canada. The slight disagreement narrowed down to Halban, and the committee asked Clarence D. Howe to work out some solution that would safeguard security to the satisfaction of all concerned.[24]

Stimson's quick action restored harmony and the crisis passed. Sir John saw Joliot. Definite arrangements about the French scientists replaced the confusion engendered by Britain's conflicting international obligations. Yet the affair struck an ominous note. It suggested the complexity of the issues that faced the United States and Britain in the months ahead. Such a sobering reminder was useful. Unfortunately, it did more than emphasize that the stakes were high and that the bargaining would be sharp. It added tension to the mistrust and misunderstanding that had accumulated through the years. It made it more difficult for the wartime partners to face the future in wisdom as well as strength.[25]

BUSH STRIKES AGAIN

Just as Stimson stabilized Anglo-American relations, Bush saw two excellent opportunities to press the Secretary of War to further deeds. The first was a resurgence of the previous summer's concern for the future of the Metallurgical Project. Bush had postponed rather than settle the dispute in August, 1944, and by November, it was again crying out for attention. Hanford was almost 92 per cent complete. One pile was functioning successfully, another was ready for inspection and testing, while a third would be finished in February. Plutonium chemical operations would begin in the T canyon about the first of the year. Compton could see that Hanford needed very little more support. Anticipating the crisis, he told Colonel Nichols that although the project's reason for being had practically disappeared, there was much it could contribute to the national security. Nichols was sympathetic as usual. Judging it would be possible to terminate Chicago's Hanford contract at the end of June, 1945, he asked for recommendations which he could pass on to higher authority. It was his reassuring opinion that present laboratories should conduct any future investigations.[26]

337

When Bush learned that the postwar-research issue had risen once more, he seized it as ammunition in his campaign for a high-level advisory committee. On February 1, 1945, he told Bundy that Groves should not turn to the Military Policy Committee for advice on the Chicago plans. The General should go to Stimson himself. The Secretary, of course, would need counsel. It should come from a new committee concerned entirely with postwar matters. George L. Harrison, president of the New York Life Insurance Company and special consultant to Stimson, would make an excellent chairman. There should be scientific members, but Bush excluded Conant, Compton, Lawrence, and himself. The project scientists would be more favorably inclined if the committee were staffed by men of the stamp of Tolman and Smyth. Though well informed, they did not bear direct line responsibilities. Bush urged action at once. Time was running out. At last, his representations were successful. On February 13, Bundy told him that Stimson had approved establishing the committee.[27]

For the immediate future, Bush's point that Groves should turn to Stimson for direction on postwar research was more plausible than practical. It would take time for an advisory committee to set out guidelines. Groves faced a dilemma. If he could not put off the scientists indefinitely, neither did he have authority to spend money on distant objectives, however worthy. There was only one solution: give the scientists the bitter truth. After gaining the concurrence of the Military Policy Committee, he wrote Compton. The Manhattan District must limit itself to winning the present war, he explained. Nor could the MPC assume responsibility for work that looked beyond that goal. Accordingly, the General announced he was restricting the Metallurgical and Argonne Laboratories to supporting operations at Hanford, helping Los Alamos, and conducting such research—not development engineering, he warned—as was necessary to determine the value of thorium. As for the Clinton Laboratories, he would find some commercial firm to relieve the University of Chicago.[28]

Bush's second opportunity came toward the end of the second week in February, when the Yalta communiqué reported the success of the meeting in the Crimea and announced the April conference in San Francisco to draft plans for the United Nations. Bush could not afford to let this pass. He thought the United Nations Charter ought to provide for a scientific section charged with communication between nations on scientific matters, particularly those with possible military applications. This was no patent cure-all, but it offered hope of preventing an aggressor from developing some devastating secret weapon and of forestalling a clandestine armament race. Bush told Conant he thought they ought to place a memorandum on this subject directly in the hands of the President instead of depending on an approach to Stettinius.[29]

Thursday morning, February 15, Bush saw Stimson and showed him a draft letter to Roosevelt. Stimson considered the plan along the right lines, but he found Bush so delighted with the news from Yalta that he was anxious to be "chivalrous" toward the Russians on S-1. The Secretary was still inclined to tread cautiously. He thought it inadvisable to put Bush's plan into full force until the United States had obtained all it could in the way of liberalization from Russia in exchange for S-1. As the two men talked, Stimson observed that it might be a good idea to start with one form of scientific research. This thought had occurred to Bush months before, and he brought out his plan for trying bacteriology. There was no conflict here. Stimson "is a very wise man," Bush told Conant, "and I only wish he had more of the vigor of youth when he is so badly needed."

Bush went back to his office and revised his draft. As he sent it to Conant later that day, it urged that the United Nations Charter provide for an international scientific section. In order that no peace-loving nation have reason to fear the secret research activities of another, this agency should establish full interchange of information on all scientific subjects which had evident military applications. To curb aggressor nations, it should recommend ways of policing their scientific activities. If the attempt to secure peace by international organization went well, it should recommend ways to extend interchange to the actual military applications of science. This could be done subject by subject. Ultimately, the time might come when the United Nations, in the interest of peace, could assume control of excessively powerful weapons. Sometime in the next few weeks, Bush sent his letter to the White House.[30]

Though Stimson had accepted the idea of an advisory committee, he had done nothing to bring it into being. Bush and Conant, impatient, cornered Bundy on Saturday, March 3. Many matters demanded attention, they said:

public statements, draft legislation, international control, the postwar technical program. Unless something were done, confusion would fill the vacuum when the bomb became public knowledge. The various executive departments would fight for control. Something akin to mass hysteria was a possibility.

Bundy was impressed. On Monday afternoon, he spent two hours laying before Stimson the whole sweep of impending issues. From domestic regulation to international control, the story captured Stimson's imagination. The implications touched the basic facts of human nature, morality, and government. How fine, he thought, if someone like Phillips Brooks could head the international control agency—a man who could touch the souls of mankind and bring about a spiritual revival on Christian principles. Then in a more somber mood, he thought of the base emotions the war had stirred and how ill-prepared was the world for coping with the great discovery. When Bundy had gone, Stimson walked over to General Marshall's office. The Chief of Staff was just leaving for home, but Stimson talked to him for some time in an effort to start him thinking on these imponderables.[31]

339

STIMSON'S LAST TALK WITH FDR

Now that Roosevelt had returned from Yalta, it was time, Stimson thought, for directing his attention to the issues that Bush, Conant, and Bundy had been raising. Besides, the Chief Executive should know the delicate situation in Congress regarding Manhattan District appropriations. In mid-February, 1945, Under Secretary of War Robert P. Patterson appeared before the House Deficiencies Subcommittee, explained that the War Department was short of "Expediting Production" funds for the Manhattan District, and asked leave to transfer other department appropriations to that item. The subcommittee indicated no opposition, but Congressman Albert J. Engel, a Republican member of the Subcommittee on Military Appropriations, learned of the request and wrote Stimson a long letter of protest. Unless the War Department furnished a justification in detail and granted him permission to visit the plants, he would ask the House for a thorough investigation. He even indicated that he might take the floor to move striking the crucial amendments from the deficiency bill. Engel posed an alarming threat to security. On February 26, Stimson met with him in the company of Congressman John Taber (Speaker Rayburn was out of town), appealed to his decency and loyalty, and persuaded him to hold his objections in abeyance. This quieted matters for the moment, but it was apparent that extraordinary measures would be necessary to win Congressional approval of fiscal year 1946 appropriations.[32]

Stimson needed no special excuse to see the Chief Executive, but he had one nonetheless in the form of a March 3 memorandum Roosevelt had referred to him from Director of War Mobilization James F. Byrnes. As Byrnes understood it, Manhattan expenditures were approaching two billions with no definite assurance of production. While the Administration might be able to maintain Congressional co-operation for the duration, there would be relentless investigation and criticism if the project proved a failure. Byrnes admitted he knew little about the enterprise save that it was supported by eminent scientists. But even eminent scientists, he warned, might be unwilling to concede a failure. Therefore, he proposed an impartial investigation and review by a small group of scientists whose pride was not involved. If nothing else, such a tactic would make it clear that the Administration was mindful of the tremendous expenditure of men and materials.[33]

340

Stimson spent Thursday morning, March 15, preparing for an interview with the President. No date had been arranged, but he expected it would be soon. Shortly before noon, Roosevelt called and invited him to the White House for lunch. While they ate, Stimson talked S-1. First, he disposed of the Byrnes memorandum by producing a list of the scientists actually engaged on the project, pointing out that it included four Nobel Prize winners and practically every physicist of standing. Then Stimson explained the timetable for the bomb and how important it was to get ready. On the question of future control, he said, there were two schools of thought. One favored a secret attempt at control by the United States and Britain. The other proposed an international effort based on free interchange of scientific information and free access to the laboratories of the world. Stimson told the President these things had to be settled before the first bomb was used and that the White House must be ready with a public statement at that time. Roosevelt agreed. The international question covered, Stimson reviewed the dispute with Engel and explained his plans for arranging the next annual appropriation. He would lay the project before Rayburn and probably would send four congressmen to Oak Ridge so they could say they had been through the establishment.

Stimson considered the talk successful. Yet it accomplished nothing. Perhaps the Secretary did not present his thoughts specifically enough. Probably the President was too exhausted to act. Whatever the case, Stimson never saw his chief again. Postwar planning had advanced no further when on April 12 the news flashed from Warm Springs that Franklin Roosevelt was dead.[34]

DESPERATION ON THE MIDWAY

In Chicago meanwhile, Compton had been distressed at Groves's order eliminating most of his research program. He protested that the continued safety of the nation depended on the rapid and uninterrupted development of nuclear science. His remonstrance brought assurance that Washington fully recognized the validity of his argument; it was a question of ways and means. On March 20 and 21, 1945, Compton explained the situation at meetings of his top staff. The entire Metallurgical Project faced heavy personnel cutbacks, with the laboratory at Chicago due for the greatest loss. Bush and Groves had asked the War Department to establish a committee on matters vital to the nation's safety. Compton admitted he did not see how this group could act quickly enough to relieve the immediate distress. On the other hand, he thought the Government would support nuclear research after the war. Until that time, the present policy would at least permit the University of Chicago to retain some key men at the Metallurgical Laboratory and to keep Argonne in operation. Walter H. Zinn and Warren C. Johnson asked how it would be possible to retain good men when the future seemed so nebulous. Franck inquired about the make-up of the advisory committee. Smyth wondered if the President would have a hand. He noted that Bush and Groves had taken the position that their authority was limited to the war. Yet they were the only channels through which scientists could approach the President. Compton argued for giving Bush and Groves a chance. If nothing happened, the scientists would be justified in going directly to someone with power to act.[35]

341

For almost a year, the restless scientists of the Metallurgical Project had been contending that the national interest demanded a continuing research effort. Though this was their main theme, a secondary strain was their concern with the international implications of atomic weapons. Compton himself had set the pitch in August, 1944, when he told the Project Council that the war would not be over "until there exists a firm international control over the production of nucleonic weapons." In early November, twenty-two of the most prominent scientists prevailed on Compton to forward a memorandum advocating that the United States issue a general statement on the new weapon in an effort to allay any suspicions that might exist among its allies. The Jeffries report with its call for international control was yet another manifestation of the sentiment that was current, particularly in the laboratories on the Midway.[36]

The secondary theme began to come through more clearly in February, 1945, after publication of the Yalta communiqué. Among the Chicago scientists sensitive to political issues, there was general agreement that the United States should take a strong position at the San Francisco conference to avert a secret race in nuclear arms. This was the time to capitalize on the nation's advantage and win what they considered the best guarantee of peace—a strong international research center with full access to the scientific activities of all nations.[37] Their concern reached the point of desperation in March when they judged the news from Washington to mean that Groves and the Military Policy Committee were taking a short-sighted view on even the research that the security of the nation required. Though there was talk in the capital about a committee to study future policy, this was vague and indefinite. Besides, the committee might be dominated by men who did not understand the imperatives of the hour. Not aware that Bush and Conant had been thinking and acting on international control, a growing number of scientists concluded that it was their duty to act.

No one was more inclined to take matters in his own hands than Leo Szilard. As early as September, 1942, he had suggested that the Metallurgical Laboratory give more attention to the political necessities bound to arise from its work. By January, 1944, he was so convinced of the necessity for international control that he wrote Bush and urged him to expedite the work on the bomb. Unless high-efficiency atomic weapons were actually used in the present war, he argued, the public would not comprehend their destructive power and would not pay the price of peace. Sometime in March, 1945, Szilard prepared a long memorandum explaining how vulnerability to atomic attack made it essential for the United States to seek international control. Presumably, the most favorable opportunity for presenting the matter to Soviet leaders would come immediately after the United States had demonstrated the potency of its atomic arm. In the interim, it was important to press American development. Scrambling his technology to cloak his reference to the hydrogen bomb, Szilard divided atomic development into two stages. The first was reaching fruition. If the United States were well along on the second when it approached Russia, the better the chances of success. If international control proved a vain hope, the worst possible course would be to delay developing the second stage. Mindful of his successful tactics in the summer of 1939, Szilard persuaded Einstein to write a letter of introduction to the President. Einstein did so on March 25, but this time nothing happened.[38]

While Szilard was pulling strings to gain a Presidential hearing, his more conventional colleagues were organizing seminars and speculating on the machinery of international control. When Roosevelt died, their hopes sank. Compton tried to find a vent for the desperation that gripped the laboratory. On the eve of the San Francisco conference, he took Franck to Washington to see his old friend Henry A. Wallace. They discussed the situation over the breakfast table, and on departing, Franck left behind a memorandum stating the views of the Chicago scientists. Its argument was that of the "Prospectus on Nucleonics" made more urgent by the events of March. Scientists, it warned, found themselves in an intolerable situation. Military restrictions were tearing them between loyalty to their oaths of secrecy and their consciences as men and citizens. Statesmen who did not realize that the atom had changed the world were laying futile plans for peace while scientists who knew the facts stood helplessly by.[39]

STIMSON BRIEFS THE NEW PRESIDENT

Unknown to the breakfast conferees at the Wardman Park, Stimson was preparing to brief President Truman on S-1.[40] On Monday, April 23, 1945, he had Groves and Harrison come to his office with a status report Groves had prepared. He spent most of Tuesday studying it. Late in the afternoon, Bundy joined him, and together they drafted a paper on the political significance of the bomb. Wednesday morning, Stimson revised it in consultation with Bundy and Harrison and later with Marshall and Groves.

While the Chicago scientists fretted, Bush and Conant attained their long-sought goal. Stimson would tell the President the fears that all scientific men shared. His memorandum was a forceful statement of their central thesis that the United States could not retain its present advantage indefinitely. Although Russia probably was the only nation able to begin production during the next few years, the future held the real danger that a wilful nation—even a small one—might construct the weapon secretly and unleash it without warning against its unsuspecting neighbors. The very existence of modern civilization was at stake. As American leaders approached the new world organization, they must appreciate the bomb's awful power. Effective safeguards meant unprecedented inspection and controls. A primary question was whether the United States should share this weapon with other nations and, if so, on what terms. American leaders had a moral obligation they could not shirk without incurring responsibility for any disaster that might follow. On the other hand, could they but use the weapon properly, they had an opportunity to establish a pattern which might save the peace of the world and civilization itself. The memorandum concluded by announcing that a committee would be appointed to recommend early steps in anticipation of postwar problems and to furnish advice on policies that would be appropriate once the bonds of secrecy had been loosened.

343

At noon on Wednesday, April 25, Stimson went to see the President. He wanted Groves to be present, but in order to prevent reporters from putting two and two together, he had the General proceed by a separate route. At the White House, the staff spirited Groves through underground passages to a room in the west wing. Stimson first showed the President the memorandum he and Bundy had prepared. Truman read it with care, evincing much interest. Then Stimson produced Groves. With Truman reading one copy and his visitors the other, the three men examined the General's report together. The whole story was there: the genesis of the project, its current status, and a forecast of weapons availability. A gun-type bomb would be ready about August 1 (no test was necessary). A second should be on hand before the end of the year. Early in July, Los Alamos should be able to test an implosion weapon. If necessary, it could hold another trial by the first of August. Less than a month after that, it could have a Fat Man ready for combat. Unfortunately, this model would require more material and yield less explosive effect than had been hoped. Japan had always been the target. A special Twentieth Air Force group was about to leave for its overseas base. For three quarters of an hour, the President listened. Stimson returned to the Pentagon convinced that he had accomplished much.[41]

SUCCESS AT LAST

The same day Stimson briefed President Truman, Bush raised a new question: what was the best time to tell Soviet leaders about the bomb and the hopes for its control? Niels Bohr had turned up at OSRD headquarters with the memorandum he had used to guide his conversation with President Roosevelt the previous summer and an addendum inspired by the conference about to assemble in San Francisco. What a great opportunity would be lost, he thought, if planning for the postwar world did not include the atom. In long, Germanic sentences that did scant justice to the clarity of his thought, he explained how a system of international control might actually work without stifling the advance of nuclear science. But it was important to act quickly.

Without mentioning the Soviet Union by name, he warned that Russia might soon fall heir to whatever work the Germans had accomplished. It was important to raise the question of international control while it could be done in a spirit of friendly advice. If the United States delayed to await further developments, its overtures might seem an attempt at coercion no great nation could accept. Indeed, it was important to start consultations before the weapon made its debut in actual warfare. This would permit negotiation before public discussion aroused passions and introduced complications. How fortunate if, when the atomic weapon was announced, the peoples of the world might be told that science had helped create a solid foundation for an era of peaceful co-operation among nations.[42]

Bush sent Bohr's memorandum to Bundy with a strong endorsement. He quite agreed with its general thesis that immediate steps in the international field were advisable. Like Bohr, Bush did not mention the Soviet Union specifically, but he left no doubt of his intent. Time was growing short. Preliminary discussions before the bomb became public knowledge were more likely to produce the correct atmosphere than were subsequent talks. Some of the best minds in the country should be put to work on international policy. It was important to name the advisory committee and set this matter before it promptly.[43]

Harrison and Bundy saw Stimson the morning of May 1 and pressed him to organize the advisory committee. While the memorandum they brought with them did not mention an early approach to the Soviet Union, it paid ample attention to international implications. "If properly controlled by the peace loving nations of the world this energy should insure the peace of the world for generations. If misused it may lead to the complete destruction of civilization." Harrison and Bundy recommended that Stimson himself chair the committee and that Harrison serve as his alternate. The other members should be Bush, Conant, Karl T. Compton, Under Secretary of the Navy Ralph A. Bard, Assistant Secretary of State William L. Clayton, and a special representative of the President. Appointed by the Secretary of War with the approval of the President, the committee should organize panels to aid in its work—scientists, military men, congressmen, legislative draftsmen, and others. Stimson approved these proposals and then checked with Marshall, who also sanctioned them.[44]

Stimson met with the President on May 2. Truman accepted the suggested membership, saying that it was satisfactory even without a personal representative for himself. When Stimson indicated he preferred that the President have some close confidant on the committee, Truman said he would try to think of someone. The next morning, Stimson had an idea. Byrnes, who had just resigned from his OWM post, would be just the man. He phoned Truman, who called back that afternoon to say Byrnes had consented to serve. On May 4, Stimson sent out the invitations. He was calling the advisory group an "Interim Committee," he said, because Congress probably would wish to appoint a permanent commission to supervise, regulate, and control.[45]

When Conant received his notice, he was troubled. He doubted that Bush and he should represent the scientists who had been actively at work in in the laboratories. There was a growing restlessness among this group, he wrote Stimson on May 5. Many were deeply concerned about the international impact of the weapon. They were particularly worried about relations with Russia. They feared that soon the United States and the Soviet Union would be locked in a secret armament race, particularly if the United States should use the bomb in battle before notifying the Russians of its existence. Conant had two requests: first, he would like permission to show the Bush-Conant memorandum of September 30, 1944, to a few of the interested scientists and assure them that Stimson had conveyed the substance of some of its arguments to President Truman; second, Conant hoped the Secretary would favor having the Interim Committee ask a few of the leading scientists to present their views on international relations either through the committee or directly to the President. This was important. The Government needed full support from the scientific community. There should be no public bickering among experts. Conant still doubted that he should serve on the committee, but if Stimson could reassure him on these points and still wanted him, he would accept and do his best.[46]

Stimson replied that he did want Conant. The Harvard president might tell some of the more important scientists that the committee no doubt would wish to hear their views sometime soon. Though Stimson had no personal objection to acquainting a few with the September 30 memorandum, Conant might wish to defer this until he knew more definitely about committee plans for meeting with the scientists. Meanwhile, there had been talk of forming a scientific panel. Conant checked with Bush and then recommended that Stimson invite Arthur Compton, Ernest Lawrence, Robert Oppenheimer, and Enrico Fermi to serve on this panel. This group, Conant understood, would have opportunity to express their views on any subject. In addition, he hoped the Interim Committee might decide to ask other scientists their views on

345

political issues. The panelists, chosen for their technical standing, might not give the best advice on general policy.[47]

At last, just as the European war drew to its close, Bush and Conant succeeded in their efforts to start active planning for the years of peace. It had been a long and frustrating endeavor. They had begun back in August and September of 1944. Twice—when Stimson saw Roosevelt in December and again in March—they had success within their grasp only to have the prize elude them.

At the root of their difficulties were the issues themselves. Stimson's advisers judged that research for postwar objectives lay beyond the authority of the President and the War Department. As a matter of fact, it had taken the exigencies of war and all of Stimson's personal force and prestige to keep funds flowing to the Manhattan gamble. Perhaps greater ingenuity might have shown a way to turn the scientists to long-range research targets, but international control was something else. Here were substantive questions of the most baffling complexity. Should the United States make the best of a bad situation and seek its security in Anglo-American atomic solidarity, or should it take daring measures to allay Soviet distrust and win Russian cooperation in a system of postwar safeguards? With Russian policy in eastern Europe inspiring little confidence, there was no easy answer.

Complicating the hard choice on international policy was the fact, still unknown to Stimson and Bush, that at Hyde Park the previous autumn Roosevelt had committed himself to what amounted to an Anglo-American approach to the postwar world. He could hardly have intended to preclude some form of multipower control, and his promise did not bind Truman. Nevertheless, he had signed the *aide-mémoire*. If the United States, pursuing every chance of heading off competition with the Soviet Union, held back on the pledge of continued collaboration for military and commercial purposes, Britain would feel betrayed.

Of course, the refractory nature of the subject was no reason for inaction. It made planning all the more important. Why was there so long a delay? In large part, the reason lay in the character of the President and his Secretary of War. Roosevelt was subtle, temperamentally indisposed to commit himself in matters of policy and thereby limit his freedom of action. The definite, written assurance to Churchill in September, 1944, had been out of character. Stimson was cautious, by lifelong habit disinclined to move until sure of his footing. Both men could be bold and decisive, but both had been slow to conclude the time was ripe. Compounding their natural proclivities was the strain of four years of war. In failing health, exhausted by the autumn's fight for a fourth term and the rigors of the trip to the Crimea, Roosevelt was not at his best. Neither was Stimson.

But the long winter was over. The sweet news of victory made the month of May all the more inspiriting. Bush and Conant were far from discouraged. Aware of the snares ahead, they were eager to see how human wisdom could cope with the bomb they both wished had been impossible.

TERRIBLE SWIFT
SWORD

In the dark morning hours of May 7, 1945, the German High Command surrendered unconditionally to the allied armies of General Eisenhower. Henry L. Stimson shared the general rejoicing of the day of triumph. He was entitled to a special measure of pride, for it was his cross-channel invasion strategy that had brought the victory. But the Secretary of War could not relax in the spring sunlight of success. Not until the Empire of Japan bent its knees in surrender could he lay down the responsibilities he had assumed in 1940. Stimson had responded gladly to Franklin D. Roosevelt's call to active service. Though he had never been entirely at ease on the late President's staff (disorderly administration was his despair), he found compensation in Roosevelt's sound strategic sense and his foresight in foreign policy. It would be hard for Stimson to face the battle in the Far East without his leadership, but the aging warrior had been encouraged by the calm, decisive demeanor of Harry S. Truman, the new Commander in Chief.[1]

For Stimson, the surrender of Japan meant far more than fulfilling his personal mission or even saving the lives of American fighting men. An early end to the war in the Pacific was essential to national security. Only when the conflict ended could the United States work effectively to create the conditions for a stable peace—not only in the Far East but also in Europe. Stimson could face the months ahead with confidence. The atomic weapon, if all went well, would assure a quick victory. The bomb raised the gravest questions for the future, but for the next few years, its existence would shift the balance of power massively in favor of the United States. It would give American leadership time to build a decent world.

President Truman bore the ultimate responsibility for the hard decisions that impended, but for questions concerning the Japanese war and especially the atomic bomb he would rely heavily on the counsel of his Secretary of War. More than any other man, Stimson was in a position to influence the advent of nuclear energy.

THE CENTRAL ISSUE

Stimson knew that the fortunes of war had turned disastrously against Japan. From their bases in the Marianas, B-29's rained fire on the teeming cities of the Island Empire. With the better part of the Imperial Navy disintegrating at the bottom of the Pacific, American submarines and aircraft easily severed the lifeline that bound the homeland to its resources beyond the seas. From any rational military point of view, Japan was defeated. But the United States Tenth Army and the First and Fifth Marine Divisions could testify that her fighting men remained capable of tenacious resistance. After five weeks and many casualties, American troops were still slugging it out on Okinawa.

348

The United States, Great Britain, and China were committed to forcing unconditional surrender on Japan. By the summer of 1944, the American Joint Chiefs of Staff had concluded that this objective demanded invading the empire's industrial heart. At Quebec in September, the British chiefs concurred, and both President Roosevelt and Prime Minister Churchill endorsed the plan. Now the prospect of the Soviet Union entering the war took on fresh luster. A Russian drive into Manchuria would neutralize the powerful Kwantung Army and prevent Japanese war lords from reinforcing the defenders of the home islands.

In January, 1945, the eve of the Yalta Conference, the United States had assurances that Russia would enter the war against Japan about three months after the defeat of Germany—provided certain Soviet objectives in the Far East were guaranteed. In the Crimea the next month, American negotiators sought a confirmed early date for Russian entry and arrangements for efficient collaboration. Though Yalta produced no written understandings in regard to the details of the military effort, the Russians renewed earlier pledges of co-operation. During the course of the discussions, Marshal Stalin brought forward the political conditions he desired. President Roosevelt recognized them in the agreement of February 11. Russia would begin hostilities two or three months after the end of the European war provided the status quo in Outer Mongolia was preserved, the Kurile Islands were transferred to the Soviet Union, and the rights Japan had seized in 1904 were restored. Specifically, this last demand referred to the southern part of the island of Sakhalin, the naval base at Port Arthur, and the pre-eminent Russian interests in the port of Dairen and the railroads of Manchuria. It was understood that the clauses on Outer Mongolia, the ports, and the railroads required the concurrence of Chiang Kai-shek. When Stalin said the word, Roosevelt would take measures to obtain his consent.[2]

Since early April, Washington planners had viewed the Far Eastern war with a growing sense of urgency. A number of interrelated issues demanded decision. Together, they would absorb much of Stimson's time and strength in the months ahead.

At bottom, it was a matter of military judgment. Admirals Leahy and King now thought intensified air bombardment and naval blockade sufficient to bring Japan to unconditional surrender. To further that strategy, they favored gaining lodgments along the Asiatic coast or on islands in the Tsushima Strait area. General Marshall believed that an early invasion of the home islands would be quicker and cheaper. Bolstered by support from General Douglas MacArthur and Admiral Chester W. Nimitz, the Army Chief of Staff could argue that even the massive air offensive against Germany had been insufficient to force her capitulation.

The Joint Chiefs of Staff were aware that the demand for unconditional surrender complicated the military situation. They recognized that a war of annihilation was in prospect unless the allies offered assurance they did not intend the extinction of Japan. Expounding surrender terms, however, was the responsibility of political leaders. As a matter of fact, they had already acted. On May 8, Navy Captain Ellis M. Zacharias launched an Office of War Information propaganda offensive by quoting from the President's VE Day proclamation. While reaffirming unconditional surrender, Truman defined it as an end to both the war and the influence of the militarists who had led Japan to disaster. It did not mean, he pledged, extermination or enslavement of the Japanese people.

What of Russia? Collaboration with the Soviet Union seemed less necessary than at Yalta three months earlier. At the end of April, the Joint Chiefs cancelled the lengthy negotiations for a Siberian air base. They lost interest in a supply route through the Kuriles. But they did not abandon their hopes for Russian action against the Kwantung Army. As Marshall explained to MacArthur, Russian entry was a prerequisite for landing in Japan in 1945.[3]

Yet no one could be certain Russia would keep her promise to join the fight. Even before Roosevelt's death on April 12, the Soviet Union's evident determination to make Poland a satellite raised doubt as to the value of all the Yalta engagements. The Polish question had come to an early crisis on April 23, when Truman called a hurried meeting of his top advisers. The Russians, he told them, had refused flatly to honor the understanding to seat a mixed Polish delegation at the San Francisco Conference. They were insisting on their Lublin Government. Secretary of State Stettinius did not welcome a break, but he believed it necessary to tell the Russians that the United States stood for a free and independent Poland. Secretary of the Navy James V. Forrestal argued that if a showdown was necessary, it had better come then than later. Stimson had seen such attitudes developing in the past few weeks, and they troubled him. He believed the United States must exercise infinite patience. Now he urged caution. Though American leadership should have been much firmer on minor matters in the past, this was no time to take chances. The only man to support Stimson was General Marshall. He explained his hope that the Soviet Union would enter the war against Japan on a schedule useful to the United States. The Russians could very well delay

349

until American forces had done the dirty work. In view of this, risking a break was a very grave step. Be this as it might, President Truman was in no mood for forebearance. Agreements with the Soviet Union could not remain a one-way street, he said. He intended to proceed with the plans for San Francisco. If the Russians did not care to co-operate, they could go to hell.[4]

While Russo-American relations deteriorated, the day approached when the President would have to inform Chiang of the Yalta accord. On May 12, Acting Secretary of State Joseph C. Grew sent a memorandum to Stimson and Forrestal raising three fundamental questions about American policy in the Far East. Was Russian help in the Pacific war so important as to preclude an attempt to obtain Soviet agreement to desirable political objectives in the Far East? Should the United States carry the Yalta Agreement into effect? Should it accede to any Soviet demand for a share in military occupation of the Japanese home islands? In the opinion of the Department of State, said Grew, the United States ought to obtain certain commitments and clarifications before keeping its Yalta promises. It should have assurances on the unification of China, the return of Manchuria to Chinese sovereignty, an international trusteeship for Korea, and aircraft landing rights in the Kuriles.[5]

On the second Sunday afternoon in May, Stimson arrived in Washington after a week end at Highhold, his Long Island home. He was barely settled when Assistant Secretary John J. McCloy brought in Grew's memorandum. Stimson was delighted that Grew had raised the policy issue and given him a chance to be heard. But as he mulled over the questions Monday with McCloy and Marshall, he changed his mind. At a meeting of the Committee of Three (the Secretaries of State, War, and Navy) on Tuesday morning, May 15, Stimson said the queries were premature. What he really thought he did not feel free to state. As he understood it, the President had promised to meet Churchill and Stalin on July 1—two weeks before the atomic bomb would be ready for testing. If the Far Eastern settlement was discussed, Truman would have to gamble for high stakes without the royal flush that might well be his should the game be delayed a few more weeks. Now was the time to avoid unnecessary quarrels. Americans should not talk too much. They should let their actions speak.[6]

Later that day, Stimson reviewed the strategy of the coming campaign with Marshall and McCloy. He had learned that T. V. Soong, Foreign Minister of China, had been at the White House trying to convince the President the United States should fight Japan to a finish on the Asiatic mainland. This was the very thing Stimson had sworn to avoid. It would drag out the war indefinitely and exact an appalling cost in American lives. Marshall's plan to invade Japan meant heavy casualties, but it was a straightforward drive for a quick decision. Stimson thought the Chief of Staff right in pushing forward. Nonetheless, he found it comforting that they would know if the bomb worked before the time to launch the assault. He was thankful for the two great uncertainties—the bomb and the Russians—that promised a speedy end to the fighting in the Pacific.

Stimson took advantage of a conference with the President on Wednesday, May 16, to register his views on the disturbing events of the past few days. He argued against committing American troops to fight the Japanese in China, assuring Truman that the Joint Chiefs' plan for ending the war would prove less costly and more acceptable to the American people. He advised against hurrying to settle the political issues raised by the price Russia had exacted for entering the fight. American forces would not be deployed for several months. There was more time for the necessary diplomacy than some of the President's hasty advisers realized. Stimson urged delay. If the S-1 test went off as expected, American negotiators would have a stronger hand.[7]

The whole spectrum of American policy assumed sharper definition in the remaining days of May. On the twenty-fifth, the Joint Chiefs issued a directive setting November 1 as the target date for invading Kyushu. Though the President had yet to approve the operation, the order marked an important step in the evolution of strategy.[8]

351

Relations with Russia took on a brighter cast. On May 21, Stimson replied to Grew's questions. He was not eager for Russia to join in occupying Japan, but he thought it unnecessary to discuss the possibility at present. While he would welcome Soviet assurances on such matters as the unification of China and the restoration of Chinese sovereignty in Manchuria, he doubted much good would come from early conferences on the Yalta concessions. With the possible exception of the Kuriles, the Red Army had the power to make good its claims whether the United States approved or not.[9] This response reflected Stimson's opposition to rushing into negotiations, but both he and the President still hoped for Russian co-operation. Soviet help in the campaign against Japan and in the quest for a decent peace was a prize well worth the most earnest effort.

Such an effort materialized on May 23, when Harry L. Hopkins departed for Moscow in the company of Ambassador Averell Harriman. Roused from his sickbed, Hopkins traveled as a special representative of the President. If any American could assuage the fears that might be motivating Stalin and relieve the strains that had tortured Soviet-American relations since Yalta, Hopkins could. He told the Russian leader his purpose at their first meeting on the twenty-sixth. He wanted to arrange a meeting of the Big Three, review the Polish tangle, discuss the future relations of the United States and Russia with China, and learn the approximate date of Soviet entry into the war against Japan.

Stalin promptly affirmed his interest in conferring with Truman and Churchill and suggested the Berlin area as a meeting place. No agreement was possible on Poland and other European questions, but on May 28, there was real progress on the Far East. Stalin said the Red Army would be ready to strike by August 8. The actual date of hostilities depended on Chinese acceptance of the Yalta conditions. Foreign Minister Soong was expected in Moscow after the San Francisco Conference; this would be an appropriate occasion for the negotiations. Stalin's assurances on the future of China were all that Hopkins and Harriman could ask. Russia had no territorial claims against China. The best of her leaders, Chiang was the man to create a unified nation that should include Manchuria. Stalin even favored the American policy of the Open Door. In addition to these friendly affirmations, he had some interesting news about Japan. So-called republican movements were attempting to court the Soviet Union in the hope that they could split the allies. The Japanese might attempt a conditional surrender to save their army, navy, and political leaders. As for the eventual occupation of Japan, the Soviet chieftain told the Americans that Russia expected to share.[10]

352

Truman was pleased with the news Hopkins cabled from Moscow. He accepted Berlin as a site for the meeting and, thinking of the latest estimates from Los Alamos, suggested July 15. The Soviets acquiesced despite their surprise at so late a choice. Highly encouraged by Stalin's views on China, the President arranged to talk with Soong in Washington and then have him flown to Moscow for the necessary conversations.[11]

The only factor that did not become more definite in the closing days of May was the possibility of offering Japan further assurances as an inducement to surrender. On May 28, Grew called at the White House and told the President that the Japanese were capable of resisting to the last man. To avoid sickening losses, the United States should consider any steps that might make it easier for the enemy to yield unconditionally. The greatest obstacle was fear for the Emperor himself and the throne as an institution. A statement promising the Japanese they could determine their own political structure would improve the chances of averting a fight to the death. Truman said his own thinking had been running along these lines. Would Grew discuss the prospect with Stimson, Marshall, Forrestal, and King?

The next day Grew followed through on the President's suggestion. He called the Committee of Three into session and read a draft statement which coupled a warning of impending destruction with a promise of self-determination. Stimson told Grew he was sympathetic to modifying the unconditional-surrender formula but thought the time not yet appropriate. Since some of those present were not supposed to know about the atomic bomb, Stimson could not reveal the real reason he considered the timing wrong. First Marshall and then the others supported Stimson, and Grew reported the consensus to his chief. For the time being, his own plan went on the shelf.[12]

The meeting over, Stimson lingered with Marshall and McCloy. They discussed the situation in Japan and how to employ S-1 when it was ready. The subject had preoccupied Stimson in recent weeks. For him, the issue was not whether to use the new weapon. Rather, it was how to end the war against Japan and safeguard the true interests of the United States throughout the world. The prospect of a long, bloody war in the Far East weighed heavily upon him. If the atomic lightning could shorten it, he would not hesitate to hurl the bolt.

THE INTERIM COMMITTEE CONVENES

Concerned as Stimson was with the immediate military implications of the bomb, he had not forgotten the shadow that atomic energy cast across the future. Shortly before ten on the morning of May 9, 1945, Bundy at his side, he greeted the Interim Committee at his office in the Pentagon. Their mandate was broad, he told his visitors. It ranged from a report on temporary wartime controls and publicity to recommendations on postwar research, development, and control, including whatever legislation they judged necessary. After Stimson explained the basic facts of S-1 for the benefit of James F. Byrnes, Ralph Bard, and William L. Clayton, Deputy Chairman George L. Harrison led the company into another room. There he and General Groves presented the situation in greater detail.[13]

On Monday, May 14, the Interim Committee met informally. All but Stimson, Conant, and Karl Compton were present, and Harrison had invited General Groves to join the discussion. After approving the Bush-Conant suggestions for a scientific panel, the committee turned to the public announcements. It decided that content would depend on the test scheduled for July at the Alamogordo Air Base in New Mexico. If results were poor, it would suffice for local military authorities to state that an explosives dump had blown up. If the results expected should materialize, a more complete, Presidential statement would be necessary. This should explain the general nature of the weapon, trace the history of its development, and indicate that the United States contemplated both national and international controls. These general considerations outlined, the committee agreed that William L. Laurence of the New York *Times,* whom Groves already had under contract, should draft the statements. Arthur W. Page, Stimson's old friend and aide, should review them.

The committee had no trouble reaching a consensus on the research program at Chicago. Groves and Bush explained the nature of the work and brought up the question of its future. The committee favored continuing the current limited operations. Long-term status could wait until the weapon was used in combat.

On its other responsibilities, the committee made only a start. Bush passed out copies of the September 30, 1944, memorandum on international control. While specific, he said, it did not represent a rigid position on the part of either himself or Conant. They had been trying to demonstrate the need for close thinking on the future. Copies of the Jeffries "Prospectus on Nucleonics" were also on hand, and Bush urged Harrison to talk with Niels Bohr for further insight into the views of working scientists. As for domestic

353

legislation, discussion ranged from needs to proper scope. Harrison announced he planned a study, while Bush promised to furnish documents that reflected opinions at OSRD.[14]

Four days later, the Interim Committee was ready to get down to cases. The meeting of May 18 examined the draft releases Laurence had prepared. There was no trouble in sanctioning the content of two versions for issue by the Commanding Officer of the Alamogordo Air Base, but the committee was not satisfied with the Presidential statement, a long, seventeen-page document designed for release after the bomb had been used against the Japanese. Conant considered it too detailed, highly exaggerated, even phoney. The committee decided that after a successful test, the President should make only a short announcement concerning the general nature of the weapon and its military and international implications. A more complete and detailed press release would follow. The committee asked Page to see to reworking the drafts. The next day, Harrison assigned to Page the President's statement and to Lieutenant R. Gordon Arneson of his office that of the Secretary of War.

The press releases had been the main scheduled business, but international issues took most of the time. They especially interested Byrnes, who knew that he soon would become Secretary of State. Experienced in every branch of the Government and a confidant of the President, he was the most influential member of the committee. He had read the September 30 memorandum, he said, and was particularly impressed with Bush's and Conant's judgment that the Soviet Union could catch up in three or four years. This was an important point in determining whether or not the President should tell the Russians about the weapon after the July test. General Groves disputed the three-to-four-year premise. Taking a very low view of Russian ability, he considered twenty years a much likelier figure. Bush had not been able to attend the meeting, but Conant was there to defend their views. He stated plainly that it was highly unsafe to count on twenty years; four seemed more reasonable.

This debate led naturally to the Quebec Agreement. Byrnes wanted to know what the United States had received in exchange. He was not satisfied when Groves pointed to the arrangements on Congo ore, and Conant had to put the agreement in better perspective. Byrnes thought Congress would question the clause requiring the United States to obtain British assent before using the bomb against a third power. On this note, the committee adjourned to meet again on Thursday, May 31. Stimson would be present then and, it was hoped, at least three members of the Scientific Panel. Perhaps a few industrialists and military men could also be heard that day or the next.[15]

The last few days of May saw intensive preparations. Stimson met with Truman on Sunday the twenty-seventh and said that he was going to devote all his time in the coming week to S-1. On Monday, he consulted Bundy, Harrison, and Marshall and arranged to relieve himself of as much routine as possible during the next few months. He wanted to give his primary attention to atomic energy. Tuesday, he explored the use of the bomb with McCloy and Marshall. Wednesday, Memorial Day, he spent entirely in girding for the morrow's encounter with the scientists. During the morning, he restudied important papers and talked with Bundy, Harrison, Groves, and Marshall on how the bomb might be employed to effect Japanese surrender. After lunch, Stimson conferred again with Harrison, who had returned with a letter from O. C. Brewster, a Kellex Corporation engineer. Dated May 24 and addressed to the President with copies for the Secretaries of State and War, the letter had been forwarded through Manhattan District channels.

Aware of the bomb project through his work on the gaseous-diffusion plant, Brewster was as worried as any nuclear physicist about the dangers the nation faced. Other great powers would never permit the United States to enjoy a monopoly, he warned. Sooner or later, the inevitable race for atomic weapons would turn the world into a flaming inferno. Brewster proposed that American leaders announce that the United States had the bomb and would demonstrate its power. They should proclaim that the United States was foregoing its chance to dominate the world and propose arrangements for making sure that no nation could ever produce fissionable material in a form suitable for destructive purposes. Brewster saw no reason why materials already available should not be used against Japan, but he advocated halting further production as an evidence of good faith. Stimson considered this a remarkable document—so remarkable that he sent it to General Marshall with a note saying he was anxious for him to have the impress of Brewster's logic before the next day's meeting. He would take the President's copy to him personally or send it through Byrnes.[16]

Meanwhile, on May 25, Leo Szilard and Walter Bartky of the University of Chicago's Division of Physical Sciences called at the White House. They did not see the President, but Truman's secretary, Matthew J. Connelly, arranged a visit to Byrnes, who had returned to South Carolina for a few days. On May 28, Szilard and Bartky—joined by Harold C. Urey, ever eager for a cause—saw Byrnes at his home in Spartanburg. Szilard handed Byrnes the memorandum he had originally prepared for Roosevelt's attention. According to Szilard's memory in 1949, the question of using the bomb arose. Byrnes did not argue that it was necessary for the defeat of Japan; his concern was the Soviet Union. He thought American possession of the bomb would make Russia more manageable in eastern Europe. In Byrnes's recollection, the talk centered on Szilard's belief that he and other scientists should discuss atomic energy policy with the Cabinet. Whatever transpired, two attitudes emerged from the encounter. Byrnes acquired a distinctly unfavorable opinion of the physicist, while Szilard was convinced that Byrnes did not grasp the true significance of atomic energy.[17]

355

LISTENING TO THE EXPERTS

At ten o'clock on May 31, the Interim Committee met in the Pentagon with the four members of the Scientific Panel and Marshall, Groves, Bundy, and Page.[18] Stimson opened the meeting by explaining that the committee would make recommendations on temporary wartime controls, public announcements, legislation, and postwar organization. Recommendations on military aspects of atomic energy were a responsibility that he and General Marshall shared. That was why Marshall was present; it was important that he learn at first hand the views of the scientists. Stimson wanted it understood that neither he nor Marshall considered the project in narrowly military terms. They recognized it as a new relation of man to the universe; they acknowledged it must be controlled, if possible, to make it an assurance of peace, not a menace to civilization. Stimson hoped the meeting would take a look at the future and consider weapons, nonmilitary developments, research, international competition, and controls.

First on the agenda was a technical briefing. Arthur Compton explained the work then under way, estimating it would take a competitor perhaps six years to overtake the United States. Conant pointed to the possibility of a thermonuclear bomb, which Oppenheimer estimated would require three years to develop.

These considerations gave Lawrence an opportunity he could not resist. If the United States was to stay ahead in atomic energy, he declared, it must know more than any other power. Research must proceed unceasingly. New methods and materials cried out for investigation. The Government should initiate a vigorous program of plant expansion and stockpiling. Only by such a strenuous campaign could the United States hold its lead. Karl Compton advocated making every effort to encourage industrial progress; this was basic to strengthening fundamental research. Having listened intently to the discussion these views occasioned, Stimson summarized the sense of the meeting: the United States should keep its industrial plant intact, stockpile materials for military and industrial use, and open the door to industrial development.

The prospect of continuing under wartime pressure did not appeal to Oppenheimer. This was not mere personal preference. The current effort, he pointed out, had simply plucked the fruit of earlier discoveries. To exploit the potential of this field to the full, it was important to establish a more leisurely and normal research environment. Bush agreed with Oppenheimer; as many as possible of the present staff should be released for freer and broader inquiry. Arthur Compton and Fermi seconded their fellow physicist. Only thorough, fundamental research could realize the tremendous promise of nuclear energy.

Apart from purely military uses, Stimson inquired, what were some of the possibilities? Oppenheimer's reply ignored the specifics. He saw the basic goal as the advancement of human welfare. The United States should offer the world free interchange of information with emphasis on peacetime uses. The nation would strengthen its moral position if it acted before it used the bomb. The idea of interchange and co-operation was not new to Stimson. He remembered the Bush-Conant memorandum. But what kind of inspection would be effective against abuse? And how would democracies fare against totalitarian states under a regime of international control coupled with scientific freedom?

The scientists were confident the advantage would lie with the democracies. Bush pointed out with pride that British and American scientists had outstripped the Germans, though he confessed some doubt that they could remain ahead of the Russians if they turned over the results of their research without reciprocal exchange. Both Comptons thought it impossible to conceal the secrets of nature for any length of time; Karl stated flatly that Americans could share their knowledge and still remain ahead. Conant believed that international control demanded inspection. Both he and Oppenheimer thought the fraternity of interest among scientists would contribute to its effectiveness. Marshall and Clayton, however, were not convinced; they cautioned against putting too much faith in inspection.

357

About this time, Stimson had to excuse himself. He was due at a White House ceremony awarding the late Secretary of the Navy, Frank Knox, a posthumous decoration. While he was gone, the talk drifted deeper and deeper into a troubling question: should the United States tell the Russians about the bomb? Oppenheimer observed that Russia had always been friendly to science. He thought it might be wise to broach the subject in tentative terms and express a hope for future co-operation. Americans should not prejudge the Russian attitude. General Marshall offered some measured judgments. He had found that the seemingly unco-operative attitude of the Soviet Union in military matters stemmed from the necessity of maintaining security. While he considered himself in no position to express views on postwar problems not purely military, he inclined toward building up a combination of like-minded powers that would bring Russia into line by the very force of the coalition. If the Soviet Union was informed about the bomb, he did not fear it would disclose the news to the Japanese. Would it be desirable, he wondered, to invite two prominent Russians to visit the Alamogordo test?

Now Byrnes intervened decisively. He feared that if the United States gave information to the Russians, even in general terms, Stalin would ask to come into the partnership. Bush pointed out that even the British did not have blueprints of production plants, but this did not alter Byrnes's judgment. He concluded that the best policy was to push production and research and make certain that the United States stayed ahead. At the same time, he favored making every effort to improve political relations with Russia. Such a strong statement by a man of Byrnes's prestige was not to be dismissed lightly. All present indicated their concurrence.

As the hour for lunch drew near, Stimson rejoined the committee, and Arthur Compton tried to recapitulate the morning's discussion. It suggested a three-fold program, he said. First, the United States should permit as much freedom of research as was consistent with national security and military necessity. Second, it should establish a combination of democratic powers for co-operation in atomic energy. Third, it should seek an understanding with Russia.

At lunch—everyone was there but Marshall—Byrnes asked Lawrence about a suggestion the physicist had made briefly during the morning: give the Japanese some striking but harmless demonstration of the bomb's power before using it in a manner that would cause great loss of life. For perhaps ten minutes, the proposition was the subject of general discussion. Oppenheimer could think of no demonstration sufficiently spectacular to convince the Japanese that further resistance was futile. Other objections came to mind. The bomb might be a dud. The Japanese might shoot down the delivery plane or bring American prisoners into the test area. If the demonstration failed to bring surrender, the chance of administering the maximum surprise shock would be lost. Besides, would the bomb cause any greater loss of life than the fire raids that had burned out Tokyo? [19]

Luncheon finished, the talk turned on the bomb as a weapon. Oppenheimer assured the group that an atomic strike would be quite different from an air attack of current dimensions. Its tremendous visible effect would be supplemented by radiation dangerous to life for a radius of at least two-thirds of a mile. After further discussion of targets and effects, Stimson offered a conclusion which commanded general agreement: the United States could not give the Japanese any warning. While it could not concentrate on a civilian area, it should seek to make as profound a psychological impression on as many of the inhabitants as possible. Conant suggested and Stimson agreed that the most desirable target would be a vital war plant employing a large number of workers and closely surrounded by workers' houses. Someone brought up the desirability of attempting several strikes at once. Oppenheimer considered this feasible, but Groves doubted its wisdom. Such a plan would require a rush assembly job, lessen the opportunity to learn from using the weapon, and obscure the unique character of the attack.

About three-thirty, Stimson left the meeting. The committee had covered his agenda and more. If Stimson was satisfied, Arthur Compton was not. He was determined that the group understand the Chicago situation. In conformity with the directives of General Groves, he said, the Metallurgical and Argonne laboratories were assisting Hanford and Los Alamos, studying health problems, doing research on a thorium pile, and making preliminary investigations of advanced uranium piles. While the last two activities did not bear directly on current war use, they comprised only about 20 per cent of the work, and the Chicago scientists considered them desirable in terms of future development. Such matters lay beyond the ken of most members of the committee. They called on Bush and Conant, who recommended that all present programs, including Chicago's, be continued at existing levels until the end of the war. The committee then asked Harrison to transmit this recommendation to Stimson.

Now it was time to bring the meeting to an end. Harrison explained that the Scientific Panel was free to present its views at any time. The committee was particularly anxious to have the scientists' opinion on what sort of organization should be established to direct and control atomic energy. Would Compton, Lawrence, Oppenheimer, and Fermi prepare a memorandum on this subject?

Compton asked what he and the other panelists could tell their staffs about the Interim Committee and their testimony before it. His question led to the understanding that they could say that the Secretary of War had appointed the committee to consider control, organization, legislation, and publicity. While they could indicate that Stimson was chairman, they should not identify the other members. They could explain that they had met with the committee and enjoyed complete freedom to present their views on any phase of the subject. They should make it clear that the Government was taking a most active interest.

359

Later that day, Stimson indulged in a moment's reflection. He had felt miserable when he came to work after a sleepless night. But the interplay of fresh, keen minds had stimulated him, and he had thrown off his lethargy. Stimson thought Marshall and he had convinced the scientists they were thinking like statesmen, not mere soldiers anxious to win the war at any cost. The scientists had impressed the Secretary as a fine lot of men. Oppenheimer, he mused, though not a Nobel Prize winner, was really one of the best of the group. So far, so good. The next morning, Stimson and the Interim Committee would meet with a panel of industrialists.[20]

The Friday, June 1, session began at eleven.[21] Instead of four scientists, a quartet of business leaders confronted the committee—Walter S. Carpenter of du Pont, James C. White of Tennessee Eastman, George H. Bucher of Westinghouse, and James A. Rafferty of Union Carbide. Stimson again opened the meeting, assuring the visitors that he and Marshall were aware that the potential of atomic energy extended far beyond immediate military purposes. Then he went directly to the point. When could other nations overtake the United States? Interpreting Stimson's question to mean the Soviet Union, each man spoke in the area of his special competence. Their estimates lay between the two extremes but much closer to the three-to-four years of Bush and Conant than the twenty of Groves. Carpenter judged the Russians would need at least four or five years to duplicate Hanford, even if they had the basic plans. Should they acquire the services of a large number of German scientists, progress would be more rapid. White did not attempt a specific estimate of the time required for a Russian electromagnetic plant, but he doubted that the Soviet Union had the necessary highly skilled personnel and capacity for manufacturing precision equipment. Bucher agreed, though he thought that Russia might build a pilot plant in nine months if she had the help of German scientists and technicians. Even so, he estimated it would take three years to put the electromagnetic process in operation. As for gaseous diffusion, Rafferty guessed it would take ten years to build the plant from scratch. If the Russians should gain the barrier through espionage, he judged they still would require three years to start production.

RECOMMENDATIONS

In the afternoon, the committee heard the businessmen give their views on postwar organization and then dismissed them with thanks. Stimson having bowed out, the committee went into executive session in Harrison's office. When a discussion of appropriation problems had run its course, Byrnes brought up the bomb. While recognizing that the final selection of the target was a military decision, he thought the committee should inform Stimson that it believed the bomb should be used as soon as possible and without warning against a Japanese war plant surrounded by workers' homes. The committee adopted this recommendation and turned to the first public announcements. There was still much to be done, Harrison reported. The conclusion the day before that the bomb should be used without warning had already made obsolete a draft Presidential statement Arthur Page had prepared.[22] And since the question of actual targets was still under review, considerable uncertainty remained as to what the statements should include. In view of all this, Harrison obtained authority to confer informally with available members and have new draft statements ready for the full committee at its next meeting.

Only one matter remained: domestic legislation. Since there was an obvious need for some point of departure, the committee asked Harrison to prepare an outline of the major points a bill should include. This done, the committee decided to meet again in three weeks to consider both legislation and publicity.

On Wednesday, June 6, Stimson called on the President. The Interim Committee, he reported, had decided that S-1 work should not be revealed to Russia or anyone else until the first bomb had been used successfully against Japan. But suppose the Russians should raise the subject at the Big Three conference? Truman said he had succeeded in postponing the conference until the fifteenth of July to give the United States more time. Stimson heartily approved, but he pointed out there might still be delays. If the Russians should ask to come in as partners, Stimson thought Truman might turn the query aside with the simple statement that the United States was not quite ready.

Then Stimson took up international control. The Interim Committee's only suggestion was that each country promise to make public all work being done on atomic energy. To assure fulfillment of this pledge, it favored constituting an international control committee with complete power to inspect. Stimson recognized this proposal was far from perfect. He realized that Russia might not assent to it. Yet he thought the United States could accumulate enough fissionable material to provide insurance against being caught helpless should the attempt break down. Stimson was emphatic in recommending a policy of no disclosures until control was established. Before the meeting ended, both men were canvassing the possibility of negotiating quick protocols with the Russians as considerations for taking them into partnership on S-1. Truman mentioned the same objectives that had occurred to Stimson— settlement of the troubled situations in Poland, Rumania, Yugoslavia, and Manchuria.[23]

361

JUNE THOUGHTS ON THE SURRENDER OF JAPAN

For more than a week, Stimson had given his primary attention to the bomb. He had resolved the immediate questions it raised and set in motion the machinery of long-range planning. For the next fortnight he devoted his flagging energies to his central objective: forcing the surrender of Japan. The bomb was one means of achieving this. Stimson saw three others: bringing Russia into the war, modifying the unconditional-surrender formula to induce an early capitulation, and invading Japan itself. The Secretary of War recognized the importance of continued air bombardment and naval blockade, but he believed these tactics alone could not bring an early victory.

Russian participation in the struggle was President Truman's goal in talks with T. V. Soong during the second week of June. On the ninth, he described in general terms the price the Soviet Union had exacted at Yalta. On the fourteenth, he told the Chinese Foreign Minister of the benevolent intentions Stalin had expressed to Hopkins and Harriman. He emphasized his desire to see the Soviet Union come into the Far Eastern war early enough to shorten the conflict and save countless American and Chinese lives. While thus encouraging Soong to confirm the Yalta understanding, Truman assured his visitor he would do nothing to harm the interests of China.[24]

The unconditional-surrender formula took the center of the stage on June 12. Secretary of the Navy Forrestal remarked at a State-War-Navy meeting that he considered it one of the most important questions confronting the nation. Stimson subscribed fully to his colleague's view. Although he found universal agreement that the United States should demilitarize Japan, he knew of no one who favored subjugating Japan permanently or dictating her form of government. Grew, still Acting Secretary of State, announced that his department was attempting to formulate a precise definition of war aims and find some means of affording the Japanese an escape from their desperate dilemma.[25]

Though the three secretaries—indeed, all the world—knew that Japan was in trouble, they had no means of following the moves and countermoves of the contending factions within Premier Kantaro Suzuki's ministry. When Suzuki came to power in April, 1945, a definite campaign to end the war took shape despite the threat of military violence and the enigmatic course of the Premier himself. The end-the-war advocates were by no means ready for peace at any price, but they hoped to negotiate a settlement short of unconditional surrender, a settlement that would save the Emperor and preserve the integrity of the nation. At Foreign Minister Shigenori Togo's initiative, Koki Hirota, a former premier, approached Soviet Ambassador Yakov Malik on June 3. Hirota's immediate mission was to improve Russo-Japanese relations and prepare the way for a formal understanding that the Soviet Union would remain neutral. Unfortunately for Japan, Malik's noncommittal response yielded but scant grounds for optimism. On June 6, 7, and 8, a series of conferences at the highest level sanctioned Army plans to fight on and engage the enemy on Japan's own shores. Suzuki supported the military men; only Togo warned of the consequences. Fearing that delay in seeking peace threatened the imperial house and the nation's form of government, Marquis Kido, Lord Keeper of the Privy Seal, went directly to the Emperor and proposed that he attempt by personal letter to open negotiations through the Soviet Union. Hirohito accepted this idea, and Kido spent the next ten days in an effort to obtain backing from important members of the government.[26]

While Kido was trying to foster a realistic attitude among Japanese leaders, both Forrestal and Grew carried their views to President Truman. Forrestal saw the President on June 13. The Chief Executive said that before he left for Berlin he wanted to hold a meeting with the Joint Chiefs and the Secretaries of State, War, and the Navy in order to arrrive at a clear understanding of American objectives in Asia.[27]

Grew made his play on June 16 when he sent to Judge Samuel I. Rosenman, the President's assistant, a memorandum suggesting a public statement calling on Japan to surrender. Grew considered it plain common sense to give the Japanese a clearer idea of what the United States meant by unconditional surrender. He emphasized two points. First, once their country was demilitarized and genuinely committed to the cause of peace, the Japanese should be permitted to determine for themselves the nature of their future political structure. Second, they should have a reasonable, peacetime economy that would allow them to work their way back into the family of nations. Grew favored spelling out these assurances. The sooner the Japanese started thinking about surrender, the better the chances of saving American lives. Grew considered the impending fall of Okinawa a favorable opportunity. Delay until the United States had suffered heavy casualties in a landing on Japan, he warned, and American public opinion would tolerate no concessions whatever. The only recourse then would be to let the fight proceed to its bitter end.

362

Grew had a conference with the President himself on the morning of June 18. Truman had read his memorandum, it developed. But while he liked the idea, he had decided to wait and discuss the tactic at the approaching Big Three meeting. The President's decision ended the matter, but Grew explained he had wanted to satisfy his conscience by omitting no recommendation that might save American lives. He conceded that his proposal might not speed Japanese surrender, but neither would it cause delay.[28]

The last and most undesirable means of compelling Japan to surrender —an invasion of the home islands—had moved closer to reality on June 14. Admiral Leahy told the Joint Chiefs that the President had scheduled a full briefing on the Japanese campaign for the eighteenth. Truman wished to be thoroughly informed when he saw Churchill and Stalin. Forced to a definite recommendation, the military leaders decided in favor of making an invasion of Kyushu the main effort. They also agreed on the desirability of encouraging Russian entry into the Japanese war in accord with the conditions set at Yalta.[29]

363

Each of Stimson's hopes for the defeat of Japan received a hearing before the President on Monday, June 18. It was a tumultuous day in Washington. General Eisenhower had returned in triumph, and the capital's multitudes showered their greetings on him. As the day wore on, Stimson developed a migraine headache and asked McCloy to take his place at the meeting scheduled for three-thirty at the White House. Home at Woodley, however, worries beset the Secretary. He dragged himself out of bed and back to town. At the President's office he found Generals Marshall and Ira C. Eaker (the latter representing Henry H. Arnold), Admirals Leahy and King, and Secretary Forrestal as well as McCloy.

Truman opened the proceedings by asking Marshall for his views on the campaign against Japan. The Army Chief of Staff advanced the case for a November 1 invasion of Kyushu. If the Japanese were ever to capitulate short of complete military defeat, it was necessary to make them face a landing in Japan itself and a Russian attack (perhaps the threat alone would suffice) in addition to the destruction already wrought by air bombardment and naval blockade. Kyushu would exact a heavy price, but there was reason to believe that the cost of the first month would not exceed the 31,000 casualties the nation had paid for Luzon. Marshall thought Russian participation might well bring capitulation either at the time of Soviet entry or shortly after the American landing. He was convinced that air power alone was not enough to put the Japanese out of the war. Confirming this judgment, Eaker recalled that the air arm had not been able to break German resistance. Next, Admiral King came to Marshall's support. Kyushu followed logically on Okinawa, he said. Once that campaign was successful, there would be time to judge the effect of possible operations by the Chinese and Russians. At the same time, he favored starting preparations for the ultimate assault on the Tokyo Plain. Finally, the President said that as he understood it, the Chiefs still believed that the Kyushu operation was the best of all possible alternative plans. This was so, agreed the military leaders.

Stimson had said nothing all the while, and now the President asked for his opinion. The Secretary of War concurred in the thinking of the Joint Chiefs; there was no choice but to proceed against Kyushu. Personally, he felt more responsible for the political side of the decision. He judged that there was a large submerged class in Japan which did not favor the war and had never made its weight felt. If attacked on its native soil, this class would fight stubbornly. Something ought to be done to develop any influence it might have before committing American troops to the assault. Stimson still hoped for some approach more promising than actual invasion. He told Truman he would like to present his views more fully at another time.

Though Stimson's remarks were general, they pointed to some clarification of unconditional surrender. Blunt sailor that he was, Admiral Leahy denounced the Casablanca formula. For an unnecessary shibboleth, he said, the United States risked making the Japanese desperate and lengthening its own casualty lists.

As the meeting broke up, the President walked over to McCloy. No one was going to leave the room without expressing himself, he said. What did the Assistant Secretary of War think? The entire discussion had struck McCloy as fantastic. Since the President wanted his opinion, he would let him have it. Why not use the atomic bomb? McCloy sensed the chills that ran up and down the spines assembled there, but the President replied that this was a good possibility. In fact, it was just what he wanted to hear about. Then he called everyone back to discuss it. McCloy thought the United States with its tremendous military might and prestige could win the war without invading Japan. The atomic bomb made American power all the more effective. He favored warning the Emperor that the United States had the bomb and would use it against Japan unless she surrendered. McCloy's suggestion had appeal, but a strong objection developed which no one could refute—there was no assurance the bomb would work.

Reiterating earlier remarks, the President stated he had hoped to prevent an Okinawa from one end of Japan to the other. The meeting had clarified his thinking. He was quite sure the Joint Chiefs should proceed with Kyushu. Admiral King had a final word. It might be desirable to have the Russians in the war, but they were not indispensable. He thought realization of this should strengthen the President's hand in the coming conference. He believed it poor policy to beg them to come in.[30]

The Joint Chiefs had had their say on the war against Japan. It remained for Stimson, who had Forrestal's support, to press the importance of avoiding a fight to a finish. Forrestal had to miss the State-War-Navy meeting on June 19 for an appointment on Capitol Hill, but Stimson met with Grew and one of Forrestal's aides. Stimson called for a joint stand by the three departments. Grew brought out his proposal for a warning, explaining that the President wanted to wait. This did not disturb Stimson particularly. To him, the only fixed date was the last-chance warning which had to be given before American armies landed in Japan. Fortunately, he thought, there was enough time to bring up sanctions for that warning in the shape of conventional air attacks and the atomic bomb.

After the meeting of the Committee of Three, Stimson reviewed the situation with Marshall, who reminded him of a third sanction—a Russian declaration of war. This would co-ordinate all possible threats, Stimson thought. That afternoon, refreshed by a little reading, he began dictating a memorandum for the eyes of the President.[31]

THE BOMB AGAIN

While Stimson centered his thoughts on the surrender of Japan, others pondered how the bomb should be employed. At the military level, it was a matter of target selection. Late in April, a committee had set to work under the direction of Groves and his deputy, General Thomas F. Farrell. A month later this team of scientists and Army Air Forces officers had concluded that Kyoto, Hiroshima, and Niigata were the best targets. They further decided not to try to pinpoint industrial zones but to shoot for the center of the city. These recommendations had troubled Stimson, particularly the choice of Kyoto, an ancient capital and cultural shrine. He positively forbade an attack on Kyoto, and on June 14, Groves handed General Marshall a revised recommendation which tentatively selected Kokura, Hiroshima, and Niigata. All were manufacturing centers, and Hiroshima was a port of embarkation, convoy assembly point, and the site of an army headquarters. Groves reminded Marshall that the Quebec Agreement required British consent for the use of the weapon and the release of any information about it. He was asking the Secretary of War to make the necessary arrangements.[32]

About the same time these plans took definite form, the Scientific Panel of the Interim Committee found itself involved in the question of whether the bomb should be used in combat at all. Arthur Compton, Lawrence, Oppenheimer, and Fermi had left the May 31 meeting with the understanding they should give Bush, Conant, and Karl Compton their suggestions on postwar organization, research, and development. Before they returned to their posts, they had submitted a preliminary memorandum on the organization of an atomic energy commission. The main job they postponed to the week end of June 16, when they planned to assemble at Los Alamos.

The ferment at Chicago made Arthur Compton particularly sensitive to the importance of giving the working scientists some contact with the policymakers. He had already furnished the Interim Committee with a forty-two-page memorandum in which he had sought to present a composite picture of Metallurgical Project views. This was a fair, full statement, but Compton recognized that morale required a sense of personal participation. At a meeting of laboratory leaders on Saturday afternoon, June 2, he explained the Scientific Panel's interest in suggestions for the future of nuclear energy. He was leaving June 14 for a meeting of the panel and would appreciate having as much information as possible before his departure. To assure systematic treatment, it was decided to establish committees to explore clearly defined areas. Bartky would head a unit on organization; Zinn one on program; Mulliken a group on education, information, and security; Szilard one on production problems; and Franck a committee on social and political implications.[33]

The Chicago scientists responded to Compton's invitation with a will. During the next two weeks, the reports piled up—not only the formal committee presentations but the statements of individuals as well. One of the first to be finished was from the Committee on Political and Social Problems, submitted June 11 and signed by Franck and six colleagues: Hughes, Nickson, Rabinowitch, Seaborg, Stearns, and Szilard.

Stripped to essentials, their argument depended on two propositions. First, it was futile to try to avoid a nuclear arms race by throwing a cloak of secrecy over the basic scientific facts or by cornering the supply of raw materials. Second, when such a race developed, the United States would be at a disadvantage compared to nations whose population and industry were less centralized. The only hope for safety lay in international control. Since this was the case, it would be unwise to use nuclear bombs without warning against the Japanese. Such a course would cost the United States support throughout the world, precipitate a fatal competition, and prejudice the possibility of reaching an international agreement on control. A demonstration of the power of the bomb in some uninhabited area would create more favorable conditions for agreement. Besides, it would not preclude using the weapon later against Japan with the support of other nations. In any event, the decision should not be left to military tacticians alone. It involved national policy, a policy which had to be directed to achieving international control.

A sense of urgency ran powerfully through the Chicago laboratories that June. Fed by distrust for scientists turned administrators, it led some of the more impetuous spirits to prevail on Franck to take the report directly to Washington. They feared it might not work up through the Scientific Panel in time. Compton met Franck in the capital on June 12 and tried to arrange an appointment with Stimson. The Secretary of War was not available, but Compton saw Lieutenant Arneson of Harrison's office and gave him an unsigned copy of the report along with a letter to Stimson which explained he was submitting the document at the request of the Metallurgical Laboratory. The Scientific Panel had not yet considered it but would do so in a few days. Compton summarized the argument forcefully and succinctly—the scientists were proposing a technical as distinct from a military demonstration in the

366

belief that this was the best prelude to an American proposal for a firm international agreement to outlaw nuclear weapons. In conclusion, Compton added an observation of his own. The report did not mention two possible consequences of failing to make a military demonstration: prolongation of the war and loss of the opportunity to impress the world with the national sacrifices that enduring security demanded.[34]

Arneson reported to Harrison, and on June 16, Harrison telephoned Compton at Los Alamos. He wanted to know the Scientific Panel's thoughts on the immediate use of nuclear weapons. He thought the Interim Committee should consider the views of the Chicago scientists only after the panel had given its comments. Compton promised to make these available in time for the next meeting of the Interim Committee.[35]

On June 16, the Scientific Panel finished three reports which Oppenheimer forwarded under a covering letter to Harrison. One dealt with future policy. It proposed that the Government spend about a billion dollars a year to support a broad and active program ranging from fundamental studies to military, industrial, scientific, and medical applications. It hoped that the responsible national authority would avoid bureaucratic inbreeding, reduce secrecy to the absolute minimum, and develop this new frontier in co-operation with other powers so that it might become a force for peace. Another report looked to the months immediately ahead and recommended extending the authority of the Manhattan District to permit it to undertake work of postwar importance to the extent of $20 million a year.

367

The Scientific Panel directed a third report to Harrison's desire for comment on the use of the weapon. The four scientists believed the bomb should be employed in a way that would promote international harmony. At the same time, they recognized the obligation to save American lives. They pointed out that their colleagues differed. Some advocated a purely technical demonstration on grounds that military use would prejudice future attempts to outlaw atomic weapons. Others were impressed by the opportunity to avoid the human cost of invading Japan. Viewing war, not the bomb, as the fundamental problem, these scientists thought a military demonstration might be the best way of furthering the cause of peace. Compton, Lawrence, Oppenheimer, and Fermi found themselves closer to the latter view. Unable to propose a technical demonstration likely to end the war, they saw no acceptable alternative to direct military use. They believed, however, that the circumstances of military use made a difference. They advocated that the United States approach its principal allies before employing its new arms—not only Britain but also Russia, France, and China. It should advise them that considerable progress had been made on atomic weapons and welcome suggestions on how the powers might co-operate in making this development contribute to better international relations.[36]

The Interim Committee assembled in executive session on Thursday morning, June 21.[37] Stimson had gone to Highhold to escape the pressures of

Washington, but every other member was there. Harrison began by submitting news releases which Major William A. Consodine of Manhattan District Headquarters had drafted for issue after the July test. The committee quickly agreed that the commander of the Alamogordo Air Base should report that a remote ammunition magazine had exploded. If necessary to evacuate the area, he should explain the operation in terms of gas shells. Harrison next introduced Page's draft of a Presidential statement for issue on use of the bomb. After careful consideration, the committee decided against a sentence that virtually committed the President to seek an international agreement on control. Judging that this was a matter Truman alone could decide, the committee settled on wording that did no more than affirm interest in making the weapon "a powerful and forceful influence towards the maintenance of world peace." Finally, Harrison presented Arneson's draft of a statement for Stimson. The committee had a good many suggestions to make. It pointed to the importance of acknowledging the prewar activity of American scientists, the assistance of the Navy Department, and the outstanding contribution of General Groves. It decided against making any specific reference to the Quebec Agreement and to the various arrangements for acquiring ore. Its review finished, the committee asked Page and a representative of General Groves to incorporate its suggestions and submit the revised drafts to Stimson.

368

While this action took care of the first announcements, it did not provide for the more general and continuing flow of information the public would demand. On Harrison's suggestion, the committee assigned responsibility for preparing news releases to Groves and Page. Present by invitation, the General indicated he would draw up a list of rules to govern such publicity and present them to the Interim Committee for approval.

Groves already had responsibility for a report summarizing the technical achievements of the wartime program. Conant, Arthur Compton, and Henry D. Smyth had discussed the possibility in the autumn of 1943. In Conant's view, a technical report would at once provide a basis for rational public discussion and make it easier to maintain the essential military secrets. When Bush independently suggested a technical history in March, 1944, Conant proposed assigning the task to Smyth. Groves was agreeable to all this, and a few weeks later he informed the Military Policy Committee that the work was under way. Now Groves explained Smyth's efforts to the Interim Committee. Guided by carefully drawn criteria, the Princeton physicist was almost finished. Other project scientists were checking his manuscript for accuracy.[38]

After lunch, everyone except Karl Compton returned to discuss the three reports of the Scientific Panel. The committee approved the recommendation that the Manhattan District have authority to devote as much as $20 million a year to work of postwar importance, but Bush argued against tackling the larger problem of future research and development. He saw planning for a national authority to replace the Manhattan District as the proper sphere of the Interim Committee. This view had a strong appeal, and at Harrison's suggestion, the committee assigned responsibility for draft legislation to a small subcommittee.

Harrison next brought up the Scientific Panel's recommendations for using the bomb. By way of explanation, he related that Arthur Compton had sent him a report from a group of Chicago scientists who believed the United States should limit itself to a purely technical test and that he had referred the document to the Scientific Panel for comment. Since the panel offered no acceptable alternative to direct military use, the committee reaffirmed its position that the weapon should be used at the earliest opportunity, without warning, and against a war plant surrounded by homes or other buildings most susceptible to damage.

The one positive point in the Scientific Panel's report on the bomb made a sharp impression: the call for the United States to notify its principal allies before making a combat drop. There was no question about informing Britain; the Quebec Agreement required that. France and China seemed irrelevant. The real issue was international control, and Russia was the great imponderable. From the first, Bush and Conant had opposed any policy that unnecessarily risked prejudicing relations with Russia. For the past two months, they had been convinced that the United States ought to bid for Soviet co-operation before dropping the bomb. Now they had the best possible opportunity to make their point. After a lengthy discussion, the committee concluded unanimously that considerable advantage lay in having the President advise the Russians at the coming Big Three meeting that the United States was working on the bomb and expected to use it against Japan. The President might say further that he hoped for future discussions to insure that the weapon become an aid to peace. Should the Russians press for more details, the President could say he was not yet ready to furnish them. With the understanding that Harrison would tell Stimson of this judgment, the meeting adjourned.

COUNSEL FOR THE COMMANDER IN CHIEF

Stimson had spent four days resting and thinking in the quiet, substantial comfort of Highhold. On Sunday, June 24, he flew back to the capital. Monday noon, Harrison and Bundy came in with the details of the June 21 meeting. Stimson was much impressed, and the next day Harrison explained the details in writing: the Chicago scientists feared that dropping the bomb might impair the chances for international control; the Scientific Panel was unable to see any acceptable alternative to direct military use; and the Interim Committee favored telling the Russians about the bomb and American hopes for future talks on how to make the bomb a force for a peaceful world.[39]

Like the good staff officer he was, Harrison kept his chief informed of every significant detail. During the past few days, he had had several talks with Under Secretary of the Navy Bard. Bard was disturbed at dropping the bomb without warning. On June 27, he put his concern in writing. As he explained to Harrison over the telephone, his memorandum was an effort to think out loud, not to make any specific recommendations. Bard wrote of his feeling that the Japanese Government might be searching for some opportunity to surrender. Might it not be possible to arrange a conference with representatives of Japan somewhere on the China coast after the Big Three conference? At such a meeting, emissaries from the allies could warn Japan of Russia's intention to enter the war and the impending use of atomic power. At the same time, they could deliver whatever assurances the President might care to make with regard to the Emperor and the treatment of the Japanese nation following unconditional surrender. Bard thought no one could estimate accurately the chances for success. The only way to find out was to try.

370

He could not see that the United States had anything in particular to lose. Recommendation or not, Harrison had a courier deliver Bard's memorandum to Stimson on June 28. He wanted Stimson to know that the June 21 advice from the Interim Committee was no longer quite unanimous.[40]

Meanwhile, Stimson had met with Forrestal and Grew on Tuesday morning, June 26, and raised the question that weighed most heavily on his mind: how to force the Japanese to surrender without invading their homeland. Arguing that the American people would not be satisfied unless their leaders made every effort to shorten the war, he urged pounding Japan—possibly with the atomic bomb—and then offering her an opportunity to surrender. Stimson read a draft memorandum to the President which proposed that the allied powers warn Japan of the destruction that faced her should she continue to resist. While asserting determination to stamp out militarism, the allies would disavow any attempt to destroy the Japanese race or nation. On the contrary, they would promise favorable economic opportunities and withdrawal of occupying forces on the establishment of a government that was peacefully inclined and representative of the masses of the Japanese people. If it would add substantially to the chances for acceptance, Stimson favored indicating that the allies did not rule out a constitutional monarchy under the present dynasty. Success depended on the potency of the warning. Since the Japanese fought to the death when actually engaged, it was important to issue the ultimatum before launching the invasion and before destruction had reduced them to fanatical despair. If Russia were a part of the threat, the Russian attack, if actually under way, must not have progressed too far. For the same reason, American bombing should be confined as far as possible to military objectives.

Forrestal and Grew approved Stimson's plan and the substance of his memorandum. After a long, thorough discussion, they set their aides to drafting the text of a warning. While no one was sure Stimson's program would bring Japanese surrender, all considered it worth trying. If the Japanese rejected the offer, their action would at least consolidate American opinion for an all-out struggle.[41]

Stimson arranged to see the President at eleven o'clock, Monday, July 2. He was at the Pentagon early that morning for last-minute consultations with Groves, Bundy, Harrison, and McCloy. At the White House, he told the President he was concerned about two subjects: plans for the war against Japan and proper arrangements for defeated Germany. Confessing that both troubled him, Truman welcomed Stimson's views. Encouraged by the President's attitude, the Secretary of War brought out three documents: the memorandum he had read to the Committee of Three on the twenty-sixth, a draft warning, and the Interim Committee draft of a Presidential statement for issue after dropping the first bomb.

The warning followed the argument of Stimson's memorandum. While affirming allied determination to prosecute the war until Japan capitulated unconditionally, it set forth the terms Japan must accept to avoid complete destruction of her armed forces and utter devastation of the homeland. These terms made it clear that the allies would insist on demilitarizing Japan, limiting her authority to the home islands, and punishing war criminals. On the other hand, they would preserve Japan as a nation and permit the Japanese to work out their economic salvation and establish a peaceful, responsible government. Stimson's hope was made specific: the Japanese might choose a constitutional monarchy under the present dynasty if they could convince the world that such a government never again would aspire to aggression. Finally, the warning called on those in authority to proclaim the unconditional surrender of all the armed forces of Japan. This draft was necessarily tentative, Stimson told the President. It could not be completed until they knew what would be done with S-1.

371

Truman read the three documents carefully. Since he seemed to acquiesce in the suggestion on Japan, Stimson turned to the Interim Committee's views on telling Russia about the bomb. By now, however, his allotted time had expired, and the President's assistants were signalling from the door. Truman told his visitor that the matters he had brought up were so important he wanted him to come back the following day, when there would be plenty of time. As he rose to leave, Stimson observed that both Germany and Japan would be issues at the approaching conference with Churchill and Stalin. Had the President failed to ask him to attend out of concern for his health? When Truman laughed and said yes, Stimson indicated both his ability and desire to go to Berlin. The President, he said, ought to have advice from the top civilians in the War Department.[42]

That evening Stimson and Bundy sat on the porch at Woodley and discussed S-1. The next day at three-fifteen, the Secretary entered Truman's office. The two men sat down, and Stimson began to speak without notes, observing that the subjects which concerned them required long talks by the fire. Stimson turned once again to Russia and the bomb. If the President judged the opportunity favorable, he should tell Stalin that the United States was working on the bomb, intended to use it against Japan, and would like to discuss afterwards how the new weapon might make the world peaceful and safe rather than destroy civilization. Should Stalin want details, the President could say that the United States was not yet prepared to supply more information. Truman listened attentively and said he understood. He thought Stimson had outlined the best way to proceed.

Having accomplished one objective, Stimson turned to his second: warning Truman against counsels of vengeance that might prevent laying foundations for a new Germany that would be a proper member of the family of nations. Here too, Truman's attitude was reassuring, and Stimson departed with Presidential permission for McCloy and himself to proceed to Berlin.[43]

372

A CHECK WITH THE BRITISH

Stimson spent the next two days in last-minute arrangements for the long journey. But even in the midst of packing, there was an important job to do: obtain the clearances the Quebec Agreement required prior to using the atomic bomb or disclosing information about it. Neither side anticipated trouble. The British had learned it did not pay to be assertive, and the Americans had every reason to believe that London did not differ fundamentally on how to use the bomb. On June 25, conversations in Washington led to the conclusion that a minute of the Combined Policy Committee was the best instrument for recording British assent.[44]

On July 4, the Combined Policy Committee met in the Pentagon.[45] It was a distinguished group of Americans and Britons who conferred on that 169th anniversary of the Declaration of Independence. Stimson and Bush represented the United States, Sir Henry Maitland-Wilson the United Kingdom, and Clarence D. Howe Canada. Present by invitation were Lord Halifax, Chadwick (now Sir James), Groves, and George Harrison along with Harvey Bundy and Roger Makins, the joint secretaries. Field Marshal Wilson required only a moment to announce that the British Government concurred in the use of the weapon against Japan. The Prime Minister, he added, might wish to discuss this matter with the President at Berlin.[46]

The disclosure of information proved harder to resolve. A week before, Bundy had submitted the draft statements of Truman and Stimson to the British members of the CPC. They had promptly offered certain suggestions, which Bundy now said raised no real difficulty. Lord Halifax, however, had late word from Sir John Anderson and the Prime Minister. They questioned the technical disclosures in the Secretary of War's statement. Bush had little patience with this. The object, he said, was to release as much scientific information as possible without aiding the rest of the world. Once competent scientists knew that the atomic bomb was a fact, they could easily acquire more information than Stimson's announcement contained. Chadwick agreed with but one qualification: the statement revealed the certain success of the electromagnetic process.

Bush observed that the same issue was bound to arise over the scientific report Smyth had prepared. It was impossible to keep the development of atomic energy secret once the weapon had been employed. On balance, the advantage lay in publishing as much scientific information as possible without actually disclosing technical data which would help other powers. The normal development of the field depended on permitting customary scientific interchange. Halifax thought the British Government ought to have a summary of the Washington views on the degree of secrecy desirable or attainable. As he saw it, the greater the amount of information released to other countries, the less incentive they had to accept any measures of international control Britain and the United States might suggest.

The British Ambassador's comment turned Stimson's mind to the events of the previous day. Stimson said an even more immediate problem concerned him: the Berlin meeting. If the President said nothing about the weapon to Stalin and used it against Japan a few weeks later, it would have an adverse effect on relations among the three great allies. For that reason, he had advised Truman to watch for a chance to broach the subject to Stalin.

373

No one was more interested in this than Bush, but he brought the meeting back to the subject—the scientific report. Finally, the committee decided that Chadwick, Groves, and Bush should draft a statement of the principles and conditions governing the release of scientific information. After consultation with London, the CPC should approve the statement informally. Then Groves should review the scientific report with Chadwick, who would certify that it conformed to the rules and was acceptable to the British.

ATLANTIC CROSSING

On July 6, Stimson boarded the Army transport, U. S. S. *Brazil,* bound for Marseilles. For a week or more, he could enjoy the salt air and restore his strength. The two months since the end of the war in Europe had been as exacting as any in his long and strenuous life. But they had been worth it. He had every reason to hope American armies would not have to enter Japan across flaming beaches. The Russians were committed to join the fight if China fulfilled the Yalta conditions. Even now, T. V. Soong was in Moscow. There was even the possibility that badly beaten Japan might surrender if she were offered a decent future under a peaceful government of her own choosing. A formal offer was in draft, and the President thought well of it. Finally, there was the bomb, the ultimate sanction. It threatened the very future of civilization, but there were those who believed it might be the instrument that would make mankind recognize the futility of war. Though Stimson never adopted that sanguine view, he believed that using the bomb in combat did not preclude its ultimate control. Of course, it was important to have the confidence of the Soviet Union. With this in mind, he had advised the President to take the first step toward enlisting the co-operation of Russia before dropping the weapon on Japan. Stimson had done all he could. Now he waited on news from Alamogordo.

HARVEST TIME AT OAK RIDGE AND HANFORD

As the *Brazil* steamed eastward, Stimson knew that the production efforts at Oak Ridge and Hanford had been splendidly successful. At the time of his visit to Oak Ridge in April, the Alpha II tracks at Y-12 were working their first batches of feed from S-50 and K-25. During April, K-25 demonstrated its capacity to produce 1.1-per-cent material. This was the signal for Fercleve to discontinue shipments to Y-12 and send the entire S-50 output to K-25. In May and June, the great gaseous-diffusion plant came in with a rush. The number of stages operating doubled in May. June saw another big increment. On May 12, Carbide discontinued withdrawing the 1.1-per-cent concentration. On June 10, it started supplying 7-per-cent material to the Beta tracks at Y-12. A week later, Beta calutrons began working the K-25 production, and June statistics showed a rise in Beta output. For July, the prospects were good. K-25 engineers expected the number of stages to grow by a third and the shipments to Y-12 to increase in volume and enrichment. The final push was up to Beta. After conferring with Oppenheimer at Los Alamos on June 27, Groves sent Colonel Nichols instructions to expedite the work. Nichols appealed to the patriotism of all Tennessee Eastman workers: the war material they were producing would save lives in the battle against Japan.

The Hanford story was just as encouraging. April plutonium shipments were only a beginning, though they looked substantial alongside the driblets from the Clinton pile. May production was greater by more than five times. With June output even better, there was no reason to worry about results in July. On the fourth, just as Stimson was making his last-minute preparations for the trip to Berlin, Groves ordered Colonel Matthias to increase shipments to Los Alamos the coming week.[47]

STATE OF THE WEAPON

The latest technical developments at Los Alamos were also favorable. As from the start, the uranium gun seemed sure. Early in June, the Critical Assemblies Group completed tests which, while falling short of conclusive proof, made it seem most likely that the designed U-235 projectile and target were safe against criticality prior to detonation. On Monday morning, June 4, the

Technical and Scheduling Conference drew up a timetable for casting the active material. The Chemistry and Metallurgy Division promptly went on a three-shift basis to reprocess the U-235 that had been out for experimentation. By the end of June, S. Marshall's group had finished part of the target and almost all of the projectile. A casting planned for July 3 would put the projectile well ahead of schedule.[48]

Implosion began to look much better. May, to be sure, was a trying month for Samuel K. Allison and the Cowpuncher Committee. For one thing, the theoretical physicists, particularly Philip Morrison, found reason for fresh worry about predetonation. For another, detonator troubles cropped up. Though Edward J. Lofgren's group completed specifications for a rugged, reliable, combat-service detonator, tests on the first units revealed an alarming failure rate. Extensive changes were necessary if the probability of malfunction were to be reduced to the desired one chance in ten thousand. These hitches were distressing, but a comforting thought mitigated them: Los Alamos probably could dispel them by its own efforts. Not so two other concerns—firing circuits and molds for casting the full-scale explosive charges. The contractor supplying the critical circuits fell behind. This meant inadequate testing for a component that Los Alamos already recognized had design weaknesses and was not as dependable as it should be. The shortage of molds was particularly frustrating. Just when completed construction enlarged the capacity of S Site, the lack of satisfactory molds hampered the study of production techniques and the tests of high-explosive performance.[49]

375

Fortunately, Chemistry and Metallurgy proved equal to the task of processing the first sizable shipments of Hanford plutonium.[50] Good news also came from the men working on initiators. On May 1, the Cowpunchers gave priority to the most promising model. Fabricating it proved a ticklish task, but tests by Lyman G. Parratt's group in the Gadget Physics Division confirmed reasonably well the performance expectations. It would take a test with active material to know for certain.[51]

June was a much happier month for the men responsible for implosion. Molds finally arrived in quantity. This was a great relief; the late deliveries had already delayed the Alamogordo test by a week or two. While the firing circuits were still in desperately short supply, modifications in the detonators made the chances of their failure negligible. Moreover, the technique of making initiators was in hand. It was only an accident that the first complete unit nearly bounced down an open sewer pipe when a nervous metallurgist dropped it on the floor.[52]

On Sunday evening, June 24, the Cowpunchers gathered in the Technical Area to consider the results of critical-mass trials that Louis Slotin and other members of Frisch's group had made the day before at Omega Site deep in Los Alamos Canyon. On the basis of this information, Allison and his colleagues established the size of the active Trinity shape. Now Eric R. Jette could manufacture it. The Cowpunchers, their assignment virtually complete, were confident of success. The only real question was how successful. The many unknowns made prophecy a precarious business. There were some purely theoretical grounds for expecting a very large yield. But assuming that all components functioned perfectly, the Cowpunchers counted on no more than about 5,000 tons of TNT.[53]

While Allison rode hard on the implosion range, Captain William S. Parsons led his Project A hands in a last drive to make sure that the ingenuity of the Los Alamos scientists resulted in a combat bomb. Designers had more than enough to do supplying the numerous details necessary for a practical weapon and rectifying the faults that became apparent in the tests at Wendover. For the Fat Man, the task was not very rewarding. At so late a date, the project was committed to a design based on early guesses and compromises. Now, when Project A knew enough to plan a less clumsy, more reliable model, it had to bend all its efforts to patchwork expedients. In some matters, it was too late even for patchwork. Slow deliveries so hampered trials that it would be the end of July before it was possible to confirm that the firing circuit was safe with high explosives.[54]

Parsons was also responsible for Los Alamos operations overseas. In March, he froze construction requirements at North Field, Tinian, the base assigned to Colonel Paul W. Tibbets' 509th Composite Group. Construction at Tinian began in April. Back in the United States, Project A prepared special kits containing handling equipment, tools, scientific instruments, and other supplies. May saw the first batch of kit materials and components for test and combat units begin the long sea voyage to the Marianas. On June 18, the first Los Alamos personnel departed for Tinian. The 509th had already arrived to complete its specialized training. The stage was set. Operations waited on the test and the availability of weapons.[55]

ALAMOGORDO

Alamogordo was only weeks away. At the establishment of Project Trinity in March, July 4 was the target date. In April and May, hopes grew dim for meeting the Independence Day deadline, and on June 9, the Cowpuncher Committee formally postponed the test until July 13, with a dress rehearsal July 8. On June 30, the Cowpunchers again reviewed the situation and changed the date to July 16 or as soon thereafter as weather conditions permitted. This postponement allowed the inclusion of some important experiments and still enabled Oppenheimer to make good on his commitments to Washington.[56]

Project Trinity had been hard at work. On May 7, Kenneth T. Bainbridge's task force fired 100 tons of high explosives spiked with 1,000 curies of fission products from a Hanford slug. The test served admirably as a trial of observation methods and administrative procedures. It familiarized the

CONFERENCE ON THE SMYTH REPORT / Henry D. Smyth (left) confers with
Ernest O. Lawrence at Berkeley, autumn, 1944.

ARRIVAL OF ACTIVE MATERIAL FOR JULY 16, 1945, TEST / Sergeant Herbert Lehr delivers the plutonium core to the assembly shack at the Trinity test site, about 6 P.M., July 12.

UNLOADING THE SHELL OF THE TRINITY DEVICE / At the test site. When everything was assembled except the detonating system, the device was hoisted to the top of the tower.

staff with the tribulations of field work miles from the laboratory. It provided an opportunity to calibrate instruments, particularly for blast measurements, and threw considerable light on the techniques of gauging radioactivity. Even more important, it revealed some of the defects. Too much of the test equipment failed to operate, often due to human error. By common agreement, one of the most important corrective measures was setting a date after which further apparatus, particularly electrical equipment, could not be introduced into the experimental area. This would allow plenty of time for dry runs and would reduce the risk of last-minute damage to electrical connections.[57]

The tempo of the Trinity preparations accelerated in May and June. Under the cloak of supreme secrecy, a great laboratory grew in the desert, absorbing a large part of the brains and skills of Los Alamos. Save Bainbridge, no man bore a larger share of the preparations than John H. Williams, whose Services Division provided the wiring, power, transportation, communication facilities, and construction. In planning the test itself, Bainbridge had the help of a council which met each week to correlate and schedule the work and especially to review proposals for new experiments.[58]

377

By the first of July, plans were complete. Working in shelters at three stations 10,000 yards south, west, and north of the firing point, teams of scientists would undertake to observe and measure the sequence of events. The first task was to determine the character of the implosion. Kenneth Greisen and Ernest W. Titterton would determine the interval between the firing of the first and the last detonators. This would reveal the degree of simultaneity achieved. Darol K. Froman and Robert R. Wilson would calculate the time interval between the action of the detonators and the reception of the first gamma rays coming from the nuclear reaction. From this value they hoped to draw conclusions as to the behavior of the implosion. With Bruno Rossi's assistance, Wilson would also gauge the rate at which fissions occurred.

The implosion studies were only a start. The second objective was to determine how well the bomb accomplished its main objective—the release of nuclear energy. Emilio Segrè would check the intensity of the gamma rays emitted by the fission products, while Hugh T. Richards would investigate the delayed neutrons. Herbert L. Anderson would undertake a radiochemical analysis of soil in the neighborhood of the explosion to determine the ratio of fission products to unconverted plutonium. No one of these methods was certain to provide accurate results, but the interpretation of the combined data might be very important. The third great job at Trinity was damage measurements. John H. Manley would supervise a series of ingenious arrangements to record blast pressure. Others would register earth shock, while William G. Penney would observe the effect of radiant heating in igniting structural materials. In addition to these specific research targets, it was important to study the more general phenomena. This was the responsibility of Julian E. Mack.

His group would use photographic and spectrographic observations to record the behavior of the ball of fire and its aftereffect.

As Los Alamos faced the Alamogordo test, the only real concern from a safety standpoint was the distribution of the radioactive by-products. While the fission products introduced into the May 7 shot behaved as expected, they did not permit a detailed prediction on what would occur in the actual test. For that reason, Project Trinity relied heavily on the forecasts of its meteorologist, Jack M. Hubbard, so it could fire under circumstances that would allow the cloud of active material to rise high in the atmosphere and drift away from the nearest towns. If anything should go wrong, the Army was prepared to evacuate the threatened communities.[59]

On July 2, just as Bainbridge was completing the final test plans, the Chemistry and Metallurgy Division finished the plutonium to be imploded at Trinity. Clad in the impervious coating the metallurgists had applied to prevent corrosion and protect the health of those who handled it, the metal was beautiful to behold. Unfortunately, its surface already was undergoing a change which threatened the success of the whole effort. Cyril S. Smith gave the job of finding some corrective measure to Samuel I. Weissman, Morris L. Perlman, and David Lipkin. These close friends—the three musketeers, Los Alamos called them—had a suggestion by July 9. No one knew for sure whether it would work, but work it did.[60]

On Thursday afternoon, July 12, Slotin and Morrison carried the plutonium core to Alamogordo in the back seat of an Army sedan. At midnight, a convoy left Los Alamos with the nonnuclear components. July 13 was devoted to assembly operations. At three-eighteen in the afternoon, Robert F. Bacher's "G Engineers" brought the core to the white tent at the base of the hundred-foot steel tower where Commander Norris E. Bradbury was supervising as Oppenheimer looked anxiously on. Late that evening, everything was in place except the detonating system. Saturday morning, Bradbury ordered the hoist operator to remove the tent and lift the device to the galvanized-iron shed at the top of the tower. Now Greisen's group installed the detonators and the firing circuit. By five o'clock that afternoon, the gadget was complete.[61]

Sunday was reserved for last-minute inspection and—Bradbury's suggestion—hunting rabbits' feet and four-leaf clovers. It was also the day for distinguished visitors to check in. Groves arrived at the Trinity base camp with General Farrell. Bush, Conant, and Tolman were also on hand. At five-thirty Sunday evening, those members of the Los Alamos Co-ordinating Council not already at Trinity left the Technical Area gate in three buses and headed south. Sedans picked up Charles A. Thomas in Santa Fe and Ernest O. Lawrence, Sir James Chadwick, New York *Times* reporter William L. Laurence, and other visitors in Albuquerque. At three o'clock Monday morning, the caravan arrived at Compania Hill, twenty miles northwest of the steel tower. It had been raining in defiance of Hubbard's Sunday morning prediction of clear weather. Would the shot be fired on schedule at four? Finally the party learned over the radio in an MP car down the road that there would be an hour or two's delay. Some tried to sleep on the ground. Thomas, Joseph W. Kennedy, and Laurence sought slumber in one of the sedans, but the reporter's stentorian snores soon routed the two chemists.[62]

At S-10,000, the observation post due south of the tower, Groves and Oppenheimer had been debating what to do. The rain which began shortly after midnight upset their plans. At three-thirty, they decided they probably could fire at five-thirty. About four, the rain stopped, and their decision became more firm. Shortly before five, they cast the die. Bainbridge, George B. Kistiakowsky, and a small arming party had been standing by at the tower until the last moment to prevent any possible misadventure. Now they made the final electrical connection and drove away to S-10,000—contrary to later rumor, at speeds not over 35 miles per hour. At five-ten, Groves left Oppenheimer to join Bush and Conant at the base camp, another 7,000 yards away.

At S-10,000, Allison began a countdown which reached the shelters over a public-address system and the base camp by FM radio. Forty-five seconds from firing, Donald F. Hornig actuated a mechanical timing device which alerted the complex system of instrumentation. Just as Allison cried "Now," a brilliant, warm, yellow light suffused the whole landscape. Virtually every observer felt the sensation of heat and suffered momentary blindness. Those who recovered first saw a ball of fire like a half-risen sun but much larger. Almost immediately it transformed itself into a swirling column of orange and red, darkening as it rose until it looked like flames of burning oil. Suddenly, a narrower column rose and mushroomed into a parasol of billowy, white smoke surrounded by a spectral glow of blue. Within a second or two, the blue vanished, leaving an outline of gray smoke faintly illuminated by the yellowing streaks of the dawn's early light. Seconds after the first flame— more than a minute and a half on Compania Hill—came the blast and thunder. This was much less impressive than the extraordinary pyrotechnic display, but five minutes later, the hills still echoed with a faint, continuous rumble.

At the base camp, where all lay prone, feet toward the explosion, Conant and then Bush reached over and shook Groves's hand. The General remembered how Blondin had crossed Niagara Falls on a tightrope and thought to himself that his personal tightrope had been three years long. Fermi, ever the experimenter, was quickly on his feet, dropping small pieces of paper to estimate the force of the blast wave. Greisen's reaction was more typical: "My God, it worked." At S-10,000, Oppenheimer's face relaxed into an expression of tremendous relief. Kistiakowsky, who a few days earlier had bet a month's salary against ten dollars the gadget would work, put his arm around the director's shoulder and said, "Oppie, you owe me $10." At the Co-ordinating Council's vantage point, far to the northwest, some felt let down that the display was over so quickly. But soon the significance of what they had seen and heard made its impression. When the observers climbed back into their buses shortly before six, a curious sense of elation tempered with solemnity was in the ascendant.[63]

It would take many weeks to correlate and interpret the Trinity measurements, but it was apparent at once that the implosion weapon was a tremendous success. The ball of fire and other data immediately available indicated that the yield had not only been more than the Cowpunchers' 5,000 tons but greater than the most optimistic predictions of the theoretical physicists. So favorable an outcome gave Groves sensational news to report to Stimson in Berlin. It justified setting the fuze for both the Little Boy and the Fat Man at a higher and more effective altitude. It confirmed the judgment that implosion was by far the most efficient way of using fissionable material.[64]

More than ever, speed was the order of the day. Groves telephoned the news to Harrison in the War Department at eight o'clock Eastern time. By the afternoon of the seventeenth, he was in Washington giving Harrison a verbal report and preparing his own message to the Secretary of War. The Los Alamos scientists rushed back to the Hill. On July 23, Chemistry and Metallurgy delivered the plutonium shape for the first weapon. The following day, forty-eight hours ahead of schedule, the division finished the target for the uranium gun.[65]

380

POTSDAM

Secretary of War Stimson arrived in Berlin at ten minutes to four, Sunday afternoon, July 15, 1945. His sea voyage had been pleasant. The *Brazil* had passed through the Straits of Gibraltar Saturday and sailed on to Marseilles, where Stimson boarded a plane. Sunday morning, the cruiser *Augusta* had docked at Antwerp with the President and his party. Stimson was just in time to be on hand when his chief flew into Berlin. After Truman had inspected a unit of the 2nd Armored Division drawn up to greet him, the American leaders proceeded by automobile caravan through troop-lined roads to Babelsberg, twelve miles southeast of Berlin. A summer resort and the site of the Reich's motion-picture colony, Babelsberg lay in the Russian zone. Here the Soviets had assigned luxurious quarters in beautiful villas bordering tree-ringed Griebnitz Lake. Only a little farther down the road from Berlin was Potsdam, seat of the Kaisers, where Truman would confer with Chruchill and Stalin.

Nothing happened while Stimson was at sea to change the prospects for the atomic weapon. The implosion test was still almost eight hours away when he landed at Gatow Airfield. However, developments of high significance had occurred on two other matters that deeply concerned Stimson—Russian participation in the campaign against Japan and the possibility of combining threats and assurances in an effort to induce an early surrender.

The Russo-Chinese talks in Moscow struck an ominous snag. Although Stalin promised Soong he would support the Nationalist Government, not the Sinkiang insurgents and the Chinese Communists, he went far beyond his Yalta price. He insisted that the military zone under Russian control include the port of Dairen as well as Port Arthur and that Dairen have a naval base. Moreover, he demanded arrangements which meant full Soviet control of the Manchurian railroads. Soong could not accept such terms. Finding that Stalin would not give way, he announced he would fly back to Chungking for consultation and return to Moscow whenever Stalin wished. Ambassador Harriman had been checking with Soong and reporting his progress to Truman and Byrnes. On July 13, he informed them of Soong's hopes that they would be able to persuade Stalin to accept the Chinese position or at least work out some compromise to which Chiang Kai-shek could assent.[66]

The effort to clarify the meaning of unconditional surrender was caught in conflicting cross currents. The draft warning received its finishing touches just in time for Grew to hand it to Byrnes—since July 3 the Secretary of State—as he left his office for the trip to Germany. While Grew took satisfaction in a mission accomplished, he was not confident of final success. He feared that some of the people accompanying the President—Charles E. Bohlen among others—would torpedo the warning on grounds the Russians would construe it as an attempt to end the Japanese war before their entry. Grew faced formidable opposition within the Department of State itself. At the meeting of the Secretary's Staff Committee on Saturday morning, July 7, Assistant Secretaries Archibald MacLeish and Dean G. Acheson asked questions reflecting their doubts about the wisdom of preserving the imperial institution. The militarists had manipulated the throne in the past. If it survived, what would prevent them from doing so in the future? While admitting the power of the argument that the Emperor alone could surrender, they believed it had to be balanced against long-range considerations. Green H. Hackworth, legal adviser to the department, wondered why the warning could not state simply that the allies would eliminate military control and then give the Japanese opportunity to develop a government of their own choosing. Grew asked Hackworth to put this formula in writing and suggested that James C. Dunn bear the morning's discussion in mind when he took up his duties as chief political adviser to the American delegation at Berlin.[67]

If the policy planners in State had misgivings about modifying the demand for unconditional surrender, military planners were coming to view modification as a most attractive tactic. The Combined Chiefs of Staff Intelligence Committee estimated on July 8 that the Japanese rejected unconditional surrender as the equivalent of national extinction. It judged, however, they might yield all conquered territory and agree to practical disarmament in order to assure survival of the throne. The problem was not simple, to be sure. The Japanese Army would not accept a surrender that discredited the warrior tradition or precluded the ultimate resurgence of a military Japan.

381

Nevertheless, the chance for an early surrender was too inviting to ignore. A few days later, the Operations Division of the War Department completed its guide for the Army delegation at Berlin. It pointed to the advantages of avoiding an invasion and settling affairs in the western Pacific before too many of the allies had committed themselves and made substantial contributions to the defeat of Japan. It concluded that the United States was justified in making any concession which might appeal to the Japanese as long as it did not affect adversely realistic American aims for peace in the Pacific.[68]

Intelligence estimates were remarkably accurate. No Japanese leader could contemplate unconditional surrender, but the end-the-war advocates were growing bolder. On June 22, the Emperor acted on Kido's advice and summoned the six most important members of the Supreme Council for the Direction of the War. It was the imperial wish, he indicated, that the ministers seek peace through the Soviet Union. Hirota resumed his talk with Malik, but again he was unable to inspire any sense of urgency. On July 7, the Emperor told Suzuki he opposed wasting any more time on Malik. Would the Premier send a special envoy to Moscow with a message from the throne? On July 12, Foreign Minister Togo radioed Ambassador Naotaki Sato in the Russian capital. Pained by the sacrifices of the citizens of the belligerent powers, His Majesty desired a swift end to the war. So long as America and England insisted on unconditional surrender, however, Japan had no alternative but to fight on for the sake of survival and the honor of the homeland. In the interest of restoring peace, the Emperor intended to dispatch a special envoy, Prince Fumimaro Konoye, with a personal letter. Togo instructed Sato to convey this information to Foreign Minister Molotov and arrange for the Soviet Government to admit Konoye and his suite. American monitoring services intercepted and decoded this message. It confirmed the view that Japanese leaders knew they had lost the war and were troubled by the demand for unconditional surrender.[69]

Stimson scarcely had time to unpack when he heard the latest word on the Far East. Harriman called early Sunday evening with Ambassador Robert D. Murphy, political adviser for Germany. Alarmed by the Soviet pressure for new concessions in Manchuria, Harriman wanted Stimson's help. The next morning, Stimson received an important report on Japanese peace maneuvers.[70]

PLANS FOR ACHIEVING THE SURRENDER OF JAPAN

The conference did not open Monday, July 16, as planned, for Stalin was late in arriving. This had no effect on Stimson's activities; he had come to advise, not negotiate. With McCloy and Bundy, he spent the morning drafting memorandums on the subjects that preoccupied him—the administration of Germany and the conduct of the war against Japan. The first paper emphasized his view that while Germany must be demilitarized, it was essential that she become a productive member of the family of nations.[71]

The paper on the Far East began by underlining the importance of early Japanese capitulation.[72] So long as the Pacific war continued, it would be difficult politically and economically for the United States to contribute substantially to re-establishing stable conditions abroad. The warning Stimson had proposed July 2 offered a strong hope for ending the war. The psychological time was at hand. The news that the Japanese were trying to approach Russia made prompt delivery all the more important. Therefore, Stimson urged warning Japan during the course of the conference, the earlier the better. In the meantime, military operations should continue. If the Japanese persisted, the full force of newer weapons should be brought to bear. At this stage, another warning should be dispatched, backed by the new weapons and possibly by Russia's entry into the war.

Whether the United States should notify the Russians in advance depended on reaching a satisfactory agreement on the terms of their participation in the fight against Japan. What were acceptable terms? Assuming continued control of the Pacific islands, Stimson thought the Yalta stipulations should not cause the United States any concern from a security point of view, provided they were interpreted consistently with the Open Door and Chinese sovereignty over Manchuria. The United States could permit Russia commercial access to Dairen and the naval base at Port Arthur. But it could not allow the Soviet Union to control or prohibit trade through Dairen or any other commercial port in Manchuria. The Manchurian railroads must be operated without discrimination against the trade of any nation.

Stimson also set forth his views on the important collateral issues. If the Russians should seek joint occupation of Japan after playing a creditable role in the conquest, the United States could hardly refuse a brief, token share. Should the Kuriles be ceded to Russia, the United States must retain permanent landing rights. As for Korea, the only way to avert a Far Eastern Poland was to press for an international trusteeship in which a small force of soldiers or marines would manifest the interest of the United States.

The memorandum on the Japanese war finished first, Stimson sent two copies over to the yellow-stucco villa the Secretary of State shared with the President. He would like to discuss the subject with Byrnes and Truman at their earliest convenience, he wrote in an accompanying note.

Stimson had put in a profitable day, but the excitement was yet to come. At seven-thirty that evening, a message arrived from Harrison in Washington:

> Operated on this morning. Diagnosis not yet complete but results seem satisfactory and already exceed expectations. Local press release necessary as interest extends great distance. Dr. Groves pleased. He returns tomorrow. I will keep you posted.

383

This was what Stimson had been waiting to hear. Though the report was preliminary and vague, there was no mistaking its import. The atomic bomb was a reality. Stimson at once took the message to the President's house and showed it to Truman and Byrnes. They proved as interested as he.[73]

Early Tuesday morning, July 17, Stimson was back to confer with Byrnes. It did not take him long to discover that the Secretary of State disagreed on the wisdom of an early warning to Japan. Byrnes had been exposed to another point of view. The day he left for Berlin, he had called his influential predecessor, Cordell Hull, and asked his opinion of the draft warning, particularly its assurance that the Japanese might choose a constitutional monarchy under the present dynasty. Hull had immediately voiced doubts, and on July 16, he sent Byrnes his views through State Department facilities. The issue, he said, was whether the allies should *now* declare that they would preserve the Emperor. Hull admitted the possibility that this might save allied lives, but no one really knew. The Japanese militarists would try hard to interfere. Should the warning fail to bring surrender, it would encourage the Japanese and bring on terrible political repercussions in the United States. Would it not be well to wait the climax of the bombing attacks and Russian entry into the war? Byrnes promptly assured Hull that he agreed the warning should be delayed and should contain no commitment concerning the Emperor.

The news from Harrison lent force to Stimson's early-warning idea, but Byrnes continued to oppose and outlined a timetable to which the President apparently had agreed. Recognizing that he had lost, Stimson pressed the matter no further and turned to other subjects—the importance of maintaining the Open Door in Manchuria and of preventing the dismemberment of Germany.[74]

That noon, Stimson dined with Churchill, Lord Leathers, and Deputy Prime Minister Clement R. Attlee. The talk ranged over economic issues— the distribution of the German merchant marine and the coal situation in both Britain and the United States. When it was time to part, Churchill walked his guest down to the gate. Stimson took advantage of the opportunity to report that the implosion test had been successful. The Prime Minister had not heard, and his spirits soared. He took a strong stand against Stimson's suggestion that the Russians ought to know—so strong that Stimson felt it necessary to argue at length the dangers of a secretive course.[75]

While Stimson made his rounds and waited on further news from Alamogordo, there were interesting developments in other quarters. The United States Joint Chiefs of Staff met at ten o'clock to review the draft warning from a military standpoint. General Marshall was impressed with the role the Emperor might play in inducing Japan's armies overseas to lay down their arms. He thought it important to refrain from any language that might indicate removal of the Emperor. After discussing the issue, the Joint Chiefs directed their secretary to draft a memorandum incorporating their views. The result was a communication to the President which the military leaders put in final form at their meeting the next day. The Joint Chiefs took the position that the draft warning needed clarification. Paragraph 12 promised the Japanese "a peacefully inclined, responsible government of a character representative of the Japanese people" but then went on to say: "This may include a constitutional monarchy under the present dynasty. . . ." Might this not be construed as a pledge to depose or execute the present Emperor and install some other member of the imperial family? On the other hand, might not radical elements in Japan interpret the phrase as a commitment to continue the institution of the Emperor and Emperor worship? The Joint Chiefs favored deleting the reference to a constitutional monarchy under the present dynasty and adding the simple but noncommittal promise: "Subject to suitable guarantees against further acts of aggression, the Japanese people will be free to choose their own form of government." Such wording, while more likely to appeal to all elements in Japan, avoided any statement that might make it difficult or impossible to utilize the Emperor's authority in effecting surrender in outlying areas as well as the home islands. Thus, the Joint Chiefs of Staff advocated making no commitment in regard to the Emperor out of the same desire to effect a surrender without invasion that had moved Stimson, Grew, and Forrestal to favor a specific reference to the survival of the throne.[76]

385

No man could guarantee how the Japanese would react to a warning, however it might be phrased. A surer way to cut American losses was a properly timed Soviet drive into Manchuria. The outlook for this improved when Stalin, now Generalissimo, called on President Truman Tuesday noon. While Stimson lunched with Churchill two blocks away, Truman and Stalin closeted themselves with their foreign ministers and interpreters. Stalin came bluntly to the point. Soviet armies would be deployed by the middle of August, but he wanted agreement with the Chinese before ordering them to strike. Important differences remained on Dairen, Port Arthur, and the Manchurian railroads, he said. Soong was returning to Chungking to confer with Chiang. Stalin asserted he had pledged that the Soviet Union considered Manchuria a part of China and would recognize the authority of the central government alone. At Byrnes's request, Stalin gave his version of the points of disagreement. When Truman asked what effect Russian plans for the administration of Dairen would have on the rights of the United States, the Russian leader answered that Dairen would be a free port, open to the commerce of all nations. Byrnes observed that if the Manchurian arrangements were in strict accord with the Yalta agreement, it would be all right; if they were in excess, there would be difficulties. Stalin replied that Russian objectives were really less than the Yalta guarantees. The Soviet Union did not wish to go beyond the Yalta agreement or to deceive China. Chungking just did not understand horse trading; that was the trouble. At this, Truman and Byrnes emphasized that the main interest of the United States was a free port.

After Stalin stated that Soong expected to return to Moscow at the end of July, the group adjourned and joined Admiral Leahy for lunch. The hour's talk had been highly instructive. Truman and Byrnes concluded that a Sino-Soviet agreement was unlikely. This, however, did not rule out Russian help against Japan. They judged that concessions or not, Stalin was determined to enter the war. Truman, at least, was quite pleased at the prospects for Manchuria. That evening at dinner he told Stimson he thought he had clinched the Open Door there.[77]

A NEW ORDER OF POWER

On Wednesday morning, July 18, Stimson received another report from Harrison:

> Doctor has just returned most enthusiastic and confident that the little boy is as husky as his big brother. The light in his eyes discernible from here to Highhold and I could have heard his screams from here to my farm.

These were some of the details Stimson had been waiting for. And what sensational news! The cryptic sentences could only mean that the Trinity device had been much more powerful than anticipated. The flash at Alamogordo must have been visible for 250 miles, its thunder audible for 50. Groves was confident the plutonium bomb was as potent as the uranium gun. The power available to crush Japan had taken on a new dimension. Stimson sped the cable to the Little White House. The President was delighted. His confidence noticeably reinforced, he said how glad he was Stimson had come to the conference.[78]

Shortly after one that afternoon, Truman lunched privately with Churchill at the Prime Minister's quarters. He brought out the Harrison cables and asked his host what he thought ought to be done about telling the Russians. Churchill judged that Truman was determined to inform them and that his real question was on timing: would not the end of the conference be best? Reassured by Truman's resolve to withhold all details, Churchill did not oppose divulging the simple fact that the United States and Britain had the weapon. As for timing, Churchill favored making the test itself the occasion for talking to Stalin. Truman had just learned that the bomb worked. This would give him a good answer if Stalin should ask why he had not been told earlier. Truman seemed moved by this reasoning and said he would consider it.

If Truman had news that noon, so did the Prime Minister. The night before, Stalin had told him of the peace overtures the Japanese Government had made through Sato in Moscow. Churchill had advised the Generalissimo to send Truman a note on the subject before the next plenary session, but

Stalin was reluctant. He did not want the President to think the Soviet Union was trying to influence him toward peace, but he had no objection if Churchill wanted to mention it. Churchill told Truman he too would abstain from saying anything that might indicate reluctance to go on with the war. Nevertheless, it was important to reckon the tremendous casualties that would be suffered in thrusting unconditional surrender on Japan. Would it be possible to express the concept in some less offensive way, some way that would give the allies all the essentials for future peace and security but yet afford the Japanese some show of saving their military honor and some assurance of continued existence as a nation? Truman's first reply was tart: in view of Pearl Harbor, he thought the Japanese had no military honor. However, Truman mellowed when Churchill commented that at least they had something they were willing to die for in large numbers and that this might be more important to them than to anyone else. The President spoke with feeling of his terrible responsibility for the lives of American soldiers. The Prime Minister was relieved at these confidences. They confirmed his surmise that American leaders would limit themselves to punishing Japan for her treachery and obtaining the essential guarantees of world peace and security. They would not rigidly insist on unconditional surrender.[79]

387

When Truman and Churchill finished lunch, they joined Byrnes and Anthony Eden to call on Stalin. Though it was only three o'clock, the Russians had prepared a sumptuous buffet. After politely addressing themselves to the repast and the inevitable toasts, Truman and Byrnes had a few moments of private conversation with Stalin and Molotov. Announcing that the Soviet Union had received a communication from the Japanese, Stalin handed Truman a copy of a note from Sato relating the Emperor's desire to dispatch Prince Konoye to Moscow in the interests of peace. Was it worth an answer? Truman's first reaction was to say he had no respect for the good faith of the Japanese. Stalin suggested that since the Soviet Union had not yet entered the war, it might be a good idea to lull the enemy to sleep. Perhaps a general, unspecific answer would suffice. He could easily point out that the Japanese had not made clear the exact character of the Konoye mission. The alternative was to shut the door, either by ignoring the communication or by definitely rejecting the proposal. Truman said he thought Stalin's first suggestion would be satisfactory. After some discussion of previous peace feelers during which the President mentioned some activity in Sweden, Truman and Byrnes departed for Potsdam, where the second plenary session was scheduled to convene shortly.[80]

SHADOW OF THE KREMLIN

Thursday and Friday, July 19 and 20, were busy days for President Truman. In the high, dark-paneled conference room at the Cecilienhof, he grappled with the tough, central problems of the European settlement. At the Little

White House Thursday evening, he entertained Churchill and Stalin at a lavish state dinner. Stimson took part in neither the negotiations nor the festivities. For him, these were days of marking time. Though he knew that the Trinity test had been successful and that the 509th Composite Group was poised on Tinian, he needed a full report from Alamogordo and even more, a fresh, firm estimate on the timing of operations. While he was waiting, he had plenty of opportunity to reflect.

At noon on Thursday, Lord Cherwell called at Stimson's quarters. Stimson and Bundy sat under the trees with their British guest and talked about the bomb. Cherwell, they discovered, doubted the wisdom of notifying the Russians. Stimson himself had developed doubts during the past few days. He had observed the cold efficiency of the Russian security forces. He had sensed the heavy atmosphere of repression which Army officers reported prevailing throughout Russian-occupied Germany. Though he had cherished no illusions about the Soviet Union, this firsthand experience made him rethink relations between Russia and the West. In the last analysis, he concluded, the friction stemmed from the differences between a free society and a police-dominated state that did not permit the essential civil liberties. Permanently safe relations with such a state were impossible. As for atomic energy, had the Interim Committee been thinking in a vacuum when it recommended an effort to enlist Russian co-operation in its control?

Late Thursday afternoon, Stimson explored the whole question in a long talk with McCloy and Bundy. Then he dictated a memorandum to organize his thoughts and serve as a possible basis for action. In the finished paper, atomic energy emerged as the central issue. It emphasized the essential dilemma and offered the best hope for resolving it. No world organization for controlling the atom could function effectively if it had to depend on a nation which did not permit its citizens free speech and whose governmental action was controlled by the autocratic machinery of secret political police. Therefore, the United States should ask itself if it dared share atomic energy with Russia under any system of control until the Kremlin put into actual effect the liberal Constitution of 1936. Should American leaders decide that a free society was indeed necessary for successful control, they ought to proceed slowly in making any disclosure regarding atomic energy or agreeing to Russian participation. At the same time—and herein lay the hope—they should explore constantly how the United States could use its head start to remove the basic difficulty—the character of the Soviet state.[81]

The next day, July 20, Stimson invited Harriman to stop by for a talk about Russia. Harriman read Stimson's memorandum with much interest. He quite agreed with its analysis. He had spent four years in Russia, however, and was pessimistic about the chances of persuading the Kremlin to change its system in any way. The two men chatted earnestly for a long time. Stimson was depressed to know that a man of such experience, intelligence, and capacity had been forced to so despairing a view.[82]

388

THE IMPACT OF ALAMOGORDO

For all his concern about the future, Stimson could never forget his immediate objective: ending the war against Japan. On Friday, July 20, he sent the President his views on the latest draft of the warning. As always, he wanted to make it easy for Japan to accept. Now for the first time, the wording of the second paragraph struck him. He was disturbed by its assertion that the allied nations were determined "to prosecute the war against Japan until her unconditional capitulation." The "unconditional surrender" in paragraph 13 was enough. Besides, the dictionary defined "capitulation" as "conditional surrender." It was confusing to call in effect for an "unconditional conditional surrender." It was better to say the allies would fight Japan "until she ceases to resist." The other paragraph that attracted his attention was number 12. Though Stimson had originally favored including a specific reference to "a constitutional monarchy under the present dynasty," he found himself persuaded by the Joint Chiefs' July 18 recommendation that it be eliminated. He concurred, he informed the President.[83]

389

Stimson's long hours of waiting ended on Saturday, July 21. At eleven-thirty that morning, a special courier arrived bearing General Groves's account of the test at Alamogordo. Groves had not attempted a concise, formal, military report but had set down what he would have told Stimson had he been in Washington. The result was a personal narrative of remarkable force. Stimson read it eagerly. The test had been successful beyond the most optimistic expectations of anyone—by a conservative estimate, the device had generated energy equivalent to from fifteen to twenty thousand tons of TNT. The details were fantastic: the brightness of several suns at midday, the massive cloud, the steel tower that turned to gas, the shattered window 125 miles away. Everyone realized that the true goal still lay ahead, said Groves. In the war with Japan, it was the battle test that counted.[84]

When Stimson learned at three o'clock that Marshall had returned from a Joint Chiefs of Staff meeting, he hurried to the General's quarters and had him read Groves's letter. Then Stimson went to Truman's villa, saw the President and Byrnes, and read them the report in its entirety. Their pleasure was immense. Truman said the news gave him an entirely new feeling of confidence, and he thanked Stimson again for coming to Germany. The American leaders informed, Stimson picked up Bundy, and the two went to Churchill's villa to see the Prime Minister and Lord Cherwell. Churchill began reading the document, but in a few minutes he laid it aside to hurry to a Big Three meeting at the Cecilienhof. He asked Stimson to return the next morning so that he could finish.[85]

Saturday evening, Stimson received two new cables from Harrison. One reported that Stimson's military advisers in Washington favored striking Kyoto. They wanted to give it priority if local weather conditions were right.

The second reported that the uranium bomb would be ready for use the first favorable opportunity in August. The complicated preparations for the mission were proceeding so rapidly that Washington must know of any change in plans no later than July 25. Stimson replied to the first message at once. He saw no reason for reversing his decision on Kyoto. Quite the contrary, new factors tended to confirm it. For the present at least, the second message required no answer, but Stimson would have to show it to the President and to Generals Marshall and Arnold.[86]

At nine-twenty Sunday morning, Stimson called on the President. Truman was pleased to learn of Harrison's report that the schedule for the first operation had been advanced. As for Kyoto, he strongly endorsed Stimson's refusal to make it a target. The President also had a word about the Secretary's memorandum on relations with Russia, which Stimson had left with him the day before. Truman had read it overnight and concurred in its analysis.

Stimson's next stop was British headquarters. There he and Bundy talked with the Prime Minister and Lord Cherwell until almost noon. Churchill read Groves's report through and then recounted how Truman had stood up to Stalin so emphatically the day before, refusing to countenance Polish occupation of eastern Germany or to recognize the governments established in Rumania, Hungary, and Finland. Churchill could not understand it at the time, but now he could see the President had been fortified by the report on Alamogordo. Churchill said he felt just as encouraged. His very attitude, Stimson thought, bore out his words. The Prime Minister no longer feared telling the Russians. In fact, he was inclined to use the bomb as an argument in the negotiations. Be that as it might, both Stimson and Churchill as well as Bundy and Cherwell agreed it was important to inform the Russians of the work on the bomb and the plans to use it if the project proved successful.[87]

Stimson had still another mission to perform. Back at his headquarters, he summoned General Arnold and showed him the report from Groves and the two cables from Harrison. What were Arnold's views? The airman concurred in Stimson's judgment on Kyoto. Organizing the operations required lots of hard work, he said. General Carl A. Spaatz, commander of the Strategic Air Forces, should make the actual selection of targets in co-ordination with General Groves. Arnold would order his special courier, Colonel John N. Stone, back to Washington with a memorandum covering the matter. Stimson approved these arrangements. A little later, Marshall dispatched a message to General Thomas T. Handy, Acting Chief of Staff. Stone was on his way to Washington with additional information, he reported. After conferences with Stone, Spaatz, and Groves, Handy was to prepare a tentative directive, and send it to Potsdam for Stimson's and Marshall's approval.[88]

While Stimson discussed operational plans with Arnold, Churchill called at the Little White House—at the President's invitation—and presented his views on the bomb. To the Prime Minister, the weapon was "a miracle of deliverance." It made invasion unnecessary. It could end the war in one or two violent shocks. Its almost supernatural power would give the Japanese an excuse that would save their honor and release them from the samurai obligation to fight to the death. Moreover, the bomb made Russian participation unnecessary. There was no need to beg favors of Stalin. With the war over in the Far East and the balance of power redressed, the United States and Britain could face European problems on their merits.[89]

American leaders were already thinking more concretely of the political dividends the bomb might pay. For one thing, it strengthened their hand in the Far East. On July 20, Chiang Kai-shek sent Truman a message declaring that China had already gone beyond the Yalta formula in an effort to satisfy Stalin. Would the President talk to the Russian chief, impress on him the reasonablenesss of the Chinese stand, and persuade him not to insist on the impossible? Truman replied he had not asked Chiang to make any concession beyond the Yalta terms. If there was any difference on their interpretation, he hoped Chiang would arrange for Soong to return to Moscow and continue efforts to reach complete understanding. This reply may have been more an attempt to delay than to bring about agreement. At any rate, Secretary of State Byrnes called on Churchill Monday morning, July 23, and reported that he had advised Soong not to give way on any point but to return to Moscow and keep on negotiating pending further developments. Churchill concluded from his conversation with Byrnes that the American leaders no longer desired Russian assistance in the fight against Japan.[90]

Had Churchill been with Stimson and Truman that Monday morning, he would have been even more convinced that the bomb had sharpened American thinking. Ambassador Harriman had called on Stimson, McCloy, and Bundy at ten-fifteen and told them about the plenary session the preceding afternoon. Throwing off restraint, the Russians had demanded bases in Turkey and trusteeship rights in the Italian Mediterranean colonies. This intelligence was fresh in Stimson's mind when he saw Truman at eleven. He ought to know what happened at the late afternoon and evening meetings, he told the President, particularly now that S-1 was tying into what the United States was doing in all fields. The President agreed to see Stimson every morning. This settled, Truman confirmed Harriman's account of Russian demands. The United States was standing firm, he said, and Stimson concluded that the President's confidence stemmed from a conviction the Russian claims were largely bluff and from his knowledge that the bomb was a success. Stimson reported that he had just asked Harrison for more exact information on the timing of operations. The President said he had approved the latest change in the draft warning and would send it out as soon as he learned the definite date of the first strike. One matter continued to disturb him. Did the United States still need Russian help against Japan? He was anxious to know what General Marshall thought. Would Stimson find out?

After lunch, Stimson summoned Marshall and Arnold. For Arnold, he had some questions about the bomb and its effect. For Marshall, he had Truman's query about needing the Russians. Precisely and cautiously, the Chief of Staff thought out loud. He had wanted the Soviet Union in the war that it might contain the Japanese forces in Manchuria. Now that Russian divisions were massed on the border, his objective had been accomplished. The United States might go ahead without the Russians, but that would not prevent Soviet legions from marching into Manchuria and taking whatever they wanted. Marshall had not answered the question specifically, but Stimson was sure he believed the new weapon made Russian assistance unnecessary.[91]

In the evening, two more messages came in from Harrison. One informed Stimson that Hiroshima, Kokura, and Niigata—in that order—were the targets favored in Washington. The other announced that the strike might come any time from August 1 on, the exact time depending on two variables—the weapon and the weather. There was some chance the bomb would be ready between August 1 and 3 and a good chance for August 4 and 6. Barring something unexpected, August 10 was almost certain. This information was helpful, but it applied only to the uranium gun. Stimson shot back a quick inquiry: when would the plutonium bomb be available? It was still Monday night in Washington when Harrison sent Stimson his answer: August 6.[92]

THE TWENTY-FOURTH OF JULY

On Tuesday, July 24, all the intricate parts of Stimson's plans finally meshed. The day—perhaps the most momentous in his long career—began at nine-twenty, when he was ushered into the President's room at the Little White House. Truman told of Monday's plenary session and seemed well satisfied with the way things had gone.

Stimson had important information for the President. First, he reported the conference with Marshall and his inference that the General believed there was no need for Russian help against Japan. Then Stimson showed Truman the latest news from Harrison on the dates for S-1 operations. The President was pleased. It gave him his cue for the warning to Japan, he said. He had just sent the draft to Chiang Kai-shek for approval. As soon as he had heard from Chiang, he would release the warning. It would fit nicely into the timetable Harrison had outlined.

Mention of the warning gave Stimson the opportunity to discuss again the advisability of giving the Japanese some assurance of continuing their imperial dynasty. Stimson had concurred in the Joint Chiefs' recommendation that the reference be eliminated, but now he reverted to his first position. Though he knew from Byrnes that the decision had gone against any commitment in regard to the Emperor and that it was too late to make further changes in the draft since it was now in Chinese hands, he asked the President

STIMSON ARRIVES IN BERLIN, JULY 15, 1945 / The Secretary of War at Gatow
Airfield. Accompanying him is his aide, Colonel William H. Kyle.

AMERICAN LEADERS AT THE POTSDAM CONFERENCE / President Truman, Secretary of State James F. Byrnes, and Admiral William D. Leahy in front of Hitler's chancellory, July 16, 1945.

to watch the situation carefully. If the Japanese held back on that one point, Stimson thought he might offer verbal assurances through diplomatic channels. Truman said he would carry out the Secretary's suggestion, should such a contingency arise.

Stimson stated once more his reasons for striking Kyoto from the list of targets. If Kyoto were bombed, such a wanton act would bring on bitterness which might rule out what American interests in the Far East demanded—a Japan sympathetic to the United States, should Russia indulge in any aggression in Manchuria. To Stimson's gratification, Truman was unusually emphatic in agreeing with him.[93]

Though the bomb held out the promise that Japan would have to surrender within a few weeks, it was still important to finish the plans for conventional operations. For all the optimism, prudence dictated being ready for any eventuality. At eleven-thirty the morning of the twenty-fourth, the American and British Combined Chiefs of Staff met with Truman and Churchill at Truman's headquarters. Their final report, CCS 900/2, reaffirmed the premise that it was necessary to defeat Japanese armed forces in their home islands in order to compel unconditional surrender. British and American forces were to attack the Japanese will to resist by every device, but they would concentrate on the invasion with the preliminary assault on Kyushu set for November 1. To further the over-all strategic objective, Russia would be encouraged to enter the war. The President and the Prime Minister examined the report paragraph by paragraph, made minor changes, and then directed that copies of the revised version be prepared for their signatures.[94]

This action completed the plans for Anglo-American co-operation. What of Russia? There had been no definite word from the Soviet leaders other than Stalin's personal assurances to Truman on July 17. Marshall thought it might bring a decision one way or the other if Truman told Stalin that since the British Chiefs of Staff were leaving the conference, he might as well let the American Chiefs leave too. Truman thought Marshall's suggestion wise, but at the tripartite military meeting the afternoon of July 24, General Alexei E. Antonov said that Soviet troops were massing in the Far East and would be ready to commence operations during the last half of August. The actual date depended on the negotiations with the Chinese. Russia's objective, he said, was to destroy the Japanese army in Manchuria and to occupy the Liaotung Peninsula. When Japan had been defeated, the Soviet Union intended to withdraw its forces from Manchuria. This information was no more specific than that which Stalin had given Truman. Neither the British nor the Americans pressed further for an exact date, though on July 26, the U. S. and U.S.S.R. Chiefs of Staff agreed on arrangements to facilitate and co-ordinate their operations in the Far East.[95]

While British and American military leaders revealed their plans for invading Japan at the meeting with the Russians, they said nothing about the

393

bomb. That required attention at the highest level. Truman and Byrnes had given the matter their careful thought. They had checked with Churchill; they had listened to Stimson. Finally, they decided to inform Stalin as casually and briefly as possible. When the plenary meeting adjourned early the evening of the twenty-fourth, Truman strolled around the conference table to where Stalin was standing. Playing his part in low key, the President did not even have Bohlen, his interpreter, accompany him. He simply reported that the United States had a new weapon of unusual destructive force. Stalin showed no special interest, saying only that he was glad to hear it and hoped the Americans would make "good use of it against the Japanese." Truman had taken the minimum step necessary to warn Russia of the advent of the bomb. Technically, he forestalled a Russian charge that the United States and Britain had not dealt frankly. Actually, he did not go far enough to have much chance of winning Russian confidence as a prelude to an effort at international control. The President said nothing about the bomb as a power for peace, nothing about later talks on how to make this dream a reality.[96]

Stimson had no part to play in the day's military and diplomatic conferences. His job was to conclude the final operational arrangements. In the afternoon, he went to see Arnold, but Arnold told him they could do nothing more until they heard from Washington. In the evening, a message arrived from Harrison. General Handy was sending the draft directive for Spaatz. In Harrison's judgment, Stimson should approve it the twenty-fifth, even if he thought modifications might later be necessary. That same evening, Handy's message arrived by radio. It enclosed two directives. One removed an earlier Joint Chiefs injunction against attacking Hiroshima, Kokura, and Niigata and released them for attack by the 509th Composite Group alone. The other directive had been drafted by General Groves with the concurrence of Harrison and Colonel Stone. It ordered General Spaatz to have the 509th Group deliver its first special bomb as soon after about August 3 as weather permitted visual bombing on one of four targets: Hiroshima, Kokura, Niigata, and Nagasaki. The 509th was to deliver additional bombs on these cities as soon as they were available. Field commanders were to release no information; that was the prerogative of the President and the Secretary of War. Prepared for the signature of General Handy, the draft specified that Stimson and Marshall had directed and approved the instructions. Spaatz personally was to deliver one copy to General MacArthur and another to Admiral Nimitz.[97]

Handy's message ended Stimson's vigil. He approved the directive to Spaatz, and early Wednesday morning, July 25, Marshall wired word to the Pentagon. Later that day, Handy issued the orders. Since Stimson had finished his work at Potsdam, he flew to Munich in the afternoon for a visit with Generals Patton and Clay. On Friday, he took off for New York, arriving on Saturday, July 28.[98]

THE POTSDAM PROCLAMATION

Back at Potsdam, Truman and Byrnes waited anxiously for news from Chiang Kai-shek. As soon as they heard from him, they could issue the warning to Japan. Churchill had returned home the twenty-fifth to await the outcome of the general election, but before he left, Truman and Byrnes accepted certain minor British textual suggestions, and Churchill himself approved the final document.[99]

The Big Three meetings suspended in the Prime Minister's absence, Truman and Byrnes flew to the Frankfurt headquarters of the American zone of occupation on the twenty-sixth. When they returned to Potsdam shortly before seven, they found two messages awaiting them. One reported the stunning news of Churchill's defeat. The other was from Chiang. He concurred in the proposed warning with but a single change: as President of China, he should be listed ahead of the Prime Minister in the opening sentence. Truman and Byrnes immediately released the warning. A few hours later, American transmitting facilities in San Francisco began beaming the full text across the Pacific in Japanese.[100]

Basically the same document that Stimson had shown the President July 2, the Potsdam Proclamation reflected the various considerations that had motivated the American delegation. Paragraph 12 promised Japan "a peacefully inclined and responsible government" established in accord with "the freely expressed will of the Japanese people," but there was no reference to the possibility of a constitutional monarchy under the present dynasty. The confusing "unconditional capitulation" had disappeared from paragraph 2, replaced by Stimson's suggestion that the allies prosecute the war against Japan "until she ceases to resist." Paragraph 13, however, the heart of the warning, had gone through all revisions essentially unchanged. The President of the United States, the President of China, and the Prime Minister of Great Britain called "upon the government of Japan to proclaim now the unconditional surrender of all Japanese armed forces, and to provide proper and adequate assurances of their good faith in such action." The alternative was "prompt and utter destruction."[101]

There was no effort to clear with the Russians in advance. Byrnes simply sent Molotov a copy with notice that the proclamation had been given to the press for release and publication the next morning. Molotov fired back a request for a two or three days' postponement, but he was too late. The next day, Byrnes suavely explained that the President had decided for political reasons to issue an immediate appeal for Japanese surrender. He had not consulted Russian leaders in advance because the Soviet Union was not at war with Japan. He did not wish to embarrass them.[102]

The Japanese Government spent all day Friday, July 27, considering

395

the allied ultimatum. As Stimson had suspected, fears for the future of the imperial house were the obstacle. The end-the-war party had only one prerequisite: it must save the throne. Though disconcerted by the omission of any reference to the Emperor, its leaders finally concluded the proclamation did not rule out a peace that satisfied this basic condition. The military—those who wanted to fight on through an invasion and exact additional terms from the allies—argued that the failure to mention the throne meant that the enemy was determined to destroy the very basis of the Japanese nation. Facing an opposition armed with so powerful an argument, the best Foreign Minister Togo could do was persuade the Cabinet that the Government should not answer the proclamation for the time being and limit itself to ascertaining Soviet intentions. Saturday morning, Tokyo papers carried an expurgated version of the Potsdam manifesto along with the comment that the Government would "mokusatsu" it. Premier Suzuki's word "mokusatsu" might have meant "withhold comment" in the context of Cabinet discussion. Standing alone, it meant "treat with silent contempt," "take no notice," or "ignore." Even this was not strong enough for the military leaders, and they called for a more positive stand against the ultimatum. Saturday afternoon, Suzuki told a press conference that the Government did not consider the proclamation "a thing of any great value"; it would "just ignore it." It would "press forward resolutely to carry the war to a successful conclusion." Radio Tokyo began broadcasting Suzuki's statement on the morning of July 29, Potsdam time.[103]

396

A TIME OF WAITING

Truman and Byrnes could only conclude that the warning had failed. Yet they knew that Japan was eager to end the war. With the return of Attlee, now Prime Minister, the plenary sessions had resumed. At the tenth meeting late Saturday night, July 28, Stalin announced that the Soviet delegation had received a new proposal from Japan. Assuming an air of injured rectitude, he said that he was informing the United States and Britain, even though they had not given him prior notice of their proclamation. His translator then read a communication from Sato stating more precisely the proposed mission of Prince Konoye. The Prince had special instructions from the Emperor to convey His Majesty's desire to avoid further bloodshed. He would ask the Soviet Government to take part in mediation to end the war and would present the complete Japanese case in this respect. Konoye would further have power to negotiate on Soviet-Japanese relations during and after the war. When the translator had finished reading, Stalin said there was nothing new in this communication except that it was more definite. That being the case, his answer would be more definite than the last time. It would be negative.[104]

Truman's only response was to thank Stalin politely and turn to the business of the evening. Actually, Stalin's information was not news to Truman and Byrnes. American signal intelligence had intercepted the messages passing between Togo in Tokyo and Sato in Moscow. Taken together, these exchanges made it clear that while Japan would not accept unconditional surrender, she would yield if her national polity were assured, if she had a guarantee of the nation's existence and honor. Honor, however, was so elastic a concept that to guarantee it might only give the Japanese an escape clause. And while the Potsdam Proclamation called for unconditional surrender, it permitted the Japanese to establish a peaceful and responsible government of their own choosing. The President and the Secretary of State must have felt they had given the Japanese every reasonable, prudent assurance.[105]

With the bomb ready and the Japanese wavering, Truman and Byrnes had lost all interest in Russian aid. On July 28, Secretary of the Navy Forrestal, just arrived from Washington, called on Byrnes. After telling him about the Togo-Sato messages, he quoted General Eisenhower as saying Truman had told him his principal objective at Potsdam was to bring Russia into the war. Forrestal thought this was beside the point; it would take an army to keep the Russians out. Byrnes quite agreed, but he doubted that the President still wanted Soviet help. Speaking for himself, Byrnes said he was anxious to end the Japanese affair before Stalin declared war. He was particularly worried about Dairen and Port Arthur. Once the Russians were there, it would be difficult to get them out.[106]

Such was the attitude of Truman and Byrnes when Molotov called on them shortly before noon on Sunday, July 29. Announcing that Stalin had caught cold and could not leave his quarters, Molotov mentioned Soviet entry into the war. His government thought the best procedure would be for the United States, the United Kingdom, and the other allies to address a formal request. The refusal of the Japanese to accept the recent ultimatum and the importance of shortening the war provided ample basis. Of course, he added, the Soviet Union was assuming that the Chinese would sign an agreement before Russian armies went into action.[107]

Truman stalled for time. He would examine the Soviet request carefully, he told Molotov. The Russian had created a nice dilemma for the American leaders. No longer desiring help, they certainly did not want to beg for it and let the Soviet Union appear the decisive factor in the victory over Japan. On the other hand, it would serve no useful purpose to tell the Russians their assistance was no longer wanted. Benjamin V. Cohen, Byrnes's assistant, came up with a shrewd, lawyerlike solution—a letter suggesting that the Charter of the United Nations (though not yet ratified) imposed obligations which made it proper for the Soviet Union to consult and co-operate with the powers fighting Japan with a view to joint action to maintain peace and security on behalf of the community of nations. On July 31, Truman sent such a letter to Stalin as an unsigned draft. If Stalin wished to use it, he should notify him, and Truman would wire the request and forward a signed copy by courier. If Stalin preferred not to use the letter and to base his action on some other grounds, Truman had no objections.[108]

The loose end in all these complicated maneuvers was the Sino-Soviet negotiation, temporarily in suspension. Even though the United States no longer desired Russian help against Japan, a satisfactory understanding between the Soviet Union and the Republic of China was an important prize in its own right. It would bolster the National Government and preserve Chinese sovereignty and the Open Door in Manchuria. The impending demonstration of American atomic might would tend to strengthen Chinese diplomacy. In the closing days of the conference at Potsdam, Ambassador Harriman urged on Byrnes his view that the United States would have to help China resist exaggerated Soviet demands. Harriman wanted authority to tell Stalin that the United States opposed any departure from the strict terms of the Yalta Agreement and to propose a protocol that would reaffirm in writing the Russian leader's verbal assurances to observe the Open Door in Manchuria. On July 28, Byrnes sent Soong a message designed to bring a prompt resumption of the talks with Stalin. On August 5, while en route back to the United States aboard the *Augusta*, he sent Harriman the instructions he desired. Now Byrnes could relax. For a few hours, at least, the diplomat's work was done.[109]

FINAL ARRANGEMENTS

Stimson's prime purpose in rushing back to Washington was to conclude preparations for the public announcements. Work on the Truman and Stimson statements had been completed shortly after the American delegation departed for Germany. On July 6, the Interim Committee considered the British suggestions. It adopted all the recommended changes in the President's statement and made important concessions on the Secretary of War's. While seeing no point in trying to conceal the mere fact that several production processes were being employed, it omitted the sentences identifying them. In deference to British views that the summary of background scientific studies was misleading because it was incomplete, the committee decided to refer only to the universality of knowledge in the field of nuclear physics before the war. Harrison sent the revised drafts to the British representatives in Washington, who made a few minor textual changes which the Americans accepted. The British forwarded the drafts to London for approval. Then came delay. As late as July 28, Roger Makins could tell Harrison no more than that the Prime Minister's advisers had approved the statements and that he assumed Bundy would be able to report on the attitude of the Prime Minister himself when he returned from Potsdam.[110]

On Monday afternoon, July 30, Stimson sat down with Bundy, Harrison, Page, and Groves and revised the Presidential statement in light of the successful test and the Potsdam Proclamation. Stimson was surprised to realize what a change Alamogordo had made in his own psychology. The result was changes that added "pep" (Stimson's word). The revision accomplished, emergency action was in order. Word had come in from Tinian that, weather permitting, the weapon would likely be used as early as August 1, Pacific Ocean time. Stimson therefore sent Truman a message asking authority to have the White House release the revised statement as soon as necessary. The next day, he dispatched Lieutenant Arneson to Berlin with two copies of the message. The President approved the draft just before he left the conference. Stimson also reviewed his own statement, but the revisions made in his absence did not offend him.[111]

Tuesday the thirty-first, Spaatz radioed that captured Japanese soldiers reported an allied prisoner-of-war camp one mile north of the center of Nagasaki. According to the same sources, which aerial photographs did not corroborate, Hiroshima was the only one of the four target cities that did not have camps containing allied prisoners. Did this intelligence influence the choice of objective for the initial strike? It was rather late for changes. General Handy replied that Spaatz's previous instructions still held. If, however, he considered his information reliable, Spaatz should give Hiroshima first priority among the four. On discretion, he might substitute Osaka, Amagasaki, and Omuta, but these were much less suitable. Should he decide on any one of them, Spaatz was to consult with General Farrell, Groves's representative on Tinian.[112]

On Wednesday, August 1, Groves brought a sheaf of papers to Stimson's office. Originating in the Metallurgical Project, they were but additional manifestations of the ferment at the University of Chicago. Leo Szilard had circulated a petition during the first two weeks of July. In final form it argued that a nation which set the precedent for using atomic bombs might have "to bear the responsibility of opening the door to an era of devastation on an unimaginable scale." If the United States should drop the bomb, it would so weaken its moral position that it would be difficult for Americans to lead in bringing the new forces of destruction under control. In view of this, the petition asked the President to forbid the use of atomic bombs unless the terms imposed on Japan had been made public and Japan had refused to surrender. Even in that event, it called on him to make the decision in the light of all the moral responsibilities involved.[113]

Sixty-nine of Szilard's colleagues had joined him in signing the petition, and Compton had forwarded it through channels to Washington. But the accompanying agitation inspired counterpetitions, and Compton had asked Farrington Daniels, the new director of the Metallurgical Laboratory, to poll his scientists in an effort to obtain a fair expression of opinion. Daniels announced the results to Compton on July 13. Fifteen per cent of the 150 who took part favored using atomic weapons in whatever manner would be most effective militarily in bringing prompt Japanese surrender at the minimum

399

cost to American armed forces. Forty-six per cent held for a military demonstration in Japan followed by a renewed opportunity to surrender before full use of the weapons. Twenty-six per cent advocated an experimental demonstration in the United States before Japanese representatives as a warning. Eleven per cent preferred a public demonstration and nothing more, while two per cent believed the United States should forego combat use and keep the entire development as secret as possible. At a request from Washington relayed by Colonel Nichols, Compton had forwarded the results of the poll on July 24. His own sentiment, he said, was with the 46 per cent that leaned toward a military demonstration.[114]

Nothing could have seemed more irrelevant to Stimson and Harrison on August 1 than further expositions of scientific opinion. Scientists had been given opportunity to express themselves, and the current arguments added nothing to what had already been said. The responsible authorities had considered how best to use the bomb and had reached a decision. Even had the President been in the country, it would have served no useful purpose to send the papers to the White House. With the President and Byrnes away, Harrison simply deposited them in his S-1 files.[115]

Stimson was much more concerned at that time about whether to issue Smyth's scientific report. The Secretary of War spent much of the day discussing this with Harrison, Bundy, and Groves. The British had been reluctant to see the document published, and the clearance arranged at the Combined Policy Committee Meeting July 4 had not been accomplished. However, a conference with Chadwick and Makins was scheduled for Thursday, August 2. Neither Stimson, Harrison, Bundy, nor Groves wanted to issue the report for its own sake. On the other hand, they recognized that news of the bomb was bound to generate a tremendous amount of excitement and reckless statement by independent scientists. Groves, whom Stimson considered a very conservative man, argued that the report was the lesser evil. Carefully contrived not to reveal anything vital, it would permit the War Department to seize the center of the stage from irresponsible speakers.

Conant joined Stimson's advisers for the meeting with the British Thursday morning. Conant argued that so many people knew about the project that some sort of technical release was necessary. If nothing were done to make the scientific facts available, political pressure would build up and a troublesome commotion would follow. Smyth's report made it possible to hold the line on information with little sacrifice. Any power could acquire the data it contained in less than three months. Chadwick, Conant's scientific counterpart, said that the British would never consider the release of such a report, but he understood that the situation was different in the United States. In any event, he thought it would give the Russians scant help.

Stimson had grave misgivings about the whole venture. He had started out, he said, full of hope that international control would be possible, but his recent contact with the Russians discouraged him. He thought no country

STALIN, TRUMAN, AND CHURCHILL CHAT INFORMALLY, JULY 17, 1945 / The first session of the Potsdam Conference was about to begin. Earlier the same afternoon, Stalin had assured Truman that his objectives in the Far East were less than the Yalta guarantees. Truman concluded that Stalin, concessions or not, was determined to enter the war against Japan.

"LITTLE BOY," THE URANIUM BOMB (GUN) / Nuclear weapon of the "Little Boy" type, the kind detonated over Hiroshima, Japan. The bomb is 28 inches in diameter and 120 inches long. The first nuclear weapon ever detonated, it weighed about 9,000 pounds and had a yield equivalent to approximately 20,000 tons of high explosive.

"FAT MAN," THE PLUTONIUM BOMB (IMPLOSION) / Nuclear weapon of the "Fat Man" type, the kind detonated over Nagasaki, Japan. The bomb is 60 inches in diameter and 128 inches long. The second nuclear weapon to be detonated, it weighed about 10,000 pounds and had a yield equivalent to approximately 20,000 tons of high explosive.

infected with the OGPU could become part of an effective system of international control. He said he had returned from Potsdam more conservative than even Groves had been. Now he questioned the wisdom of making any scientific information public. He believed that the Russian people, living in an atmosphere of repression, could not be as alert as a free people. If the Russians did not have the spark of initiative, he did not want to supply it.

Conant and Groves hastened to assure Stimson that the report contained nothing that would help a Russian industrial effort in atomic energy. Conant thought that *Time* magazine could discover everything it contained in a short time, and Groves warned that if the Smyth report were pigeonholed, a scientific battle would start that would end up in Congress. Stimson finally announced that he would approve release if the report divulged no industrial secrets. Of course, publication would have to wait until the President returned and saw Stimson's recommendations. Furthermore, the Secretary wanted British concurrence, for he knew Truman would want to satisfy himself that the Quebec Agreement had been kept. Makins promised that he would have an answer in twenty-four hours. He observed that Stimson's judgment gave great weight to the proposal, and Chadwick reported Sir John Anderson's opinion that this was primarily a responsibility of the United States. Friday, August 3, saw more conferences between Stimson and his advisers. Assistant Secretary of War Robert A. Lovett opposed publication bitterly, but Stimson decided to proceed with his recommendation to the President.[116]

401

HIROSHIMA

Stimson had been expecting the atomic strike from day to day. Everything that man could control had gone well on Tinian. Parsons had flown there after Trinity, and his deputies for Project A, Norman F. Ramsey and Commander Frederick L. Ashworth, had seen that the assembly and testing facilities were complete. Beginning July 23, they supplied four dummy Little Boys which B-29 crews of the 509th dropped in a series of reassuring tests of the fuzing system. On July 26, the cruiser *Indianapolis* had delivered the gun and its U-235 projectile. On the night of July 28–29, three Air Transport Command C-54's had flown in, each bearing a part of the U-235 target component. By the time General Farrell arrived on July 31, the combat Little Boy was ready. Then the weather intervened. Since radar bombing had been ruled out, it was necessary to wait until visual sighting was possible. The twenty-four-hour advance forecasts continued to indicate unsatisfactory conditions over Japan, and Stimson withdrew to Highhold to rest and await developments.[117]

Stimson awoke Monday morning, August 6, to a steady Long Island rain. At seven-forty-five, the telephone rang. It was Marshall calling from the Pentagon to report that the mission had been flown successfully. The Chief of Staff then put Harrison on the wire, and as Groves looked on, Harrison talked from a memorandum the Manhattan District chief had just finished. Hiroshima had been attacked visually through a one-tenth cloud cover a little more than twelve hours before. It had not been possible to observe structural damage, for the city had been covered with a layer of dark gray dust, turbulent with flashes of fire. But there was no doubt that the results were clear-cut, successful in every respect. A swirling cloud of smoke had mushroomed to 40,000 feet. Parsons and other observers thought the strike awesome even in comparison with the test at Alamogordo.[118]

It was time to break the five years of silence. Stimson authorized Harrison to notify the President and release the prepared announcements. In Washington, Lovett cautioned against claiming the destruction of Hiroshima, and Groves rewrote the first paragraph of the Presidential statement to report only that an American airplane had dropped a bomb with more power than 20,000 tons of TNT on Hiroshima. At eleven, just as Truman was receiving official word aboard the *Augusta,* American radio stations began broadcasting the President's statement. A little later that afternoon, they turned to the Secretary of War's. By design, Stimson's release was a sober report to the American people on how the War Department had brought the bomb project to fruition and had made a start on planning for the future. The President's declaration was short and vivid. Though it promised recommendations to the Congress on domestic control and explained that atomic power could become a potent influence in maintaining world peace, its main appeal was not to the American people, not to the world at large, but to the Japanese. It announced that the bomb dropped on Hiroshima was an atomic bomb which had loosed, against those who had brought war to the Far East, the force from which the sun drew its power. The United States was prepared to obliterate every productive enterprise above ground in any city of Japan. The July 26 ultimatum from Potsdam had been designed to spare the Japanese people from utter destruction, but their leaders had rejected it. If they did not accept American terms now, they could expect a rain of ruin the like of which the earth had never seen. Vast and powerful sea and land forces stood ready to follow the assault from the skies.[119]

The United States had struck a fearful blow, but whether it would be sufficient to force Japanese leaders to surrender depended on how well it was exploited. The Potsdam Proclamation had not mentioned the atomic weapon specifically. If that had lessened its effect, Truman's ultimatum of August 6 corrected the deficiency. It left no doubt as to the character of the force available to the United States. To help drive home this awful fact, Stimson authorized General Farrell on Tinian to blanket Japan with invitations to surrender. If the Japanese leaders should lag, there were further sanctions to apply. The components of a plutonium bomb had already arrived on Tinian and the final shipment for a second would soon leave Los

Alamos. The first Fat Man was originally scheduled for use August 11. On August 7, Parsons and Ramsey saw they might have it ready by the tenth. Colonel Tibbets of the 509th asked if they could not advance the schedule two days instead of one in order to avoid the five-day stretch of bad weather that had been forecast. Parsons and Ramsey agreed to try to meet the accelerated schedule.[120]

CATASTROPHE AND SURRENDER

The campaign to end the war had gone as Stimson planned. The progression was logical: first the warning, next the atomic shock, then the warning again. Other nuclear blows would follow automatically unless the Government of Premier Suzuki acted quickly to surrender.

But Japan no longer possessed the capacity for quick, decisive action. The attack on Hiroshima severed communications with Tokyo. It was almost evening on August 6 when the capital received official word that a small number of enemy planes had wrought appalling damage with what appeared to be a new type of bomb. Not until the next morning did a report make it clear that a single bomb had destroyed the entire city instantly. Suzuki and Togo sought an audience with the Emperor, related what had happened, and advised that the time had come to accept the Potsdam Proclamation. The military, however, were not ready to yield. Interpreting President Truman's announcement as scare propaganda, they dispatched an investigating team to Hiroshima.

It would take additional disasters to shock Japanese leaders into decision. The Soviet Union's declaration of war came first. The Sino-Soviet negotiations had resumed on August 7. Stalin's demands on Soong reflected his continuing determination to gain control of the port of Dairen. But the events of August 6 had changed his mind about waiting for the Chinese to meet his price. Late in the afternoon of August 8, Ambassador Sato called on Molotov to advance Japan's plea for Russian mediation. The Foreign Minister greeted him with a stunning announcement. On Japan's refusal to accede to the surrender demand of the United States, Britain, and China, the allies had approached the Soviet Government with a proposal that it join the war against Japanese aggression and assist in the prompt re-establishment of general peace. Faithful to its obligations, the Soviet Government had accepted the proposal and adhered to the Potsdam Proclamation. As of August 9, it would consider itself at war with Japan.

To suggest that the allies had made a fresh appeal for Russian help since July 26 was thoroughly misleading, but even had the Japanese known the truth, it would have made no difference. When the news reached Japan early in the morning of August 9, it dealt military leaders a staggering blow by ending all hope of dividing the allies. Coming on the heels of the disaster

403

at Hiroshima, it gave the end-the-war advocates opportunity to come into the open. At a seven-o'clock conference with the Emperor, Suzuki decided that Japan should accede to the Potsdam terms. The six regular members of the Supreme Council met at ten amid rumors that Tokyo was scheduled for an atomic bombing on August 12. Suzuki, Togo, and Navy Minister Mitsumasa Yonai were ready to accept the Potsdam Proclamation if it were understood that it did not alter the legal position of the Emperor. But War Minister Korechika Anami and the Army and Navy Chiefs of Staff, Yoshijiro Umezu and Soemu Toyoda, held out for further conditions. They wanted themselves to disarm and demobilize the armed forces, assure a Japanese trial of war criminals, and either prevent or greatly restrict an allied occupation. Whatever thinking may have inspired these conditions, they could easily have become the foundation for a later myth that the imperial forces had never been defeated.

404

The meeting ended in deadlock, as did a session of the full Cabinet that lasted until eight in the evening. Even word of the day's second great catastrophe—the atomic attack on Nagasaki shortly before eleven that morning—failed to resolve the differences.[121] In this extremity, Suzuki arranged for the Inner Cabinet to confer with the Emperor. The meeting convened in Hirohito's personal bomb shelter shortly before midnight. It was after two the morning of the tenth when Togo and Anami finished stating their opposing views. Premier Suzuki then rose and asked the Emperor to indicate his wishes. This was an unprecedented maneuver, but Hirohito knew it was coming. He responded with a short speech declaring that he agreed with Togo and had decided the war should be stopped. As the Emperor made his way from the room, Suzuki said that the imperial decision should be the conclusion of the conference. By silence, the ministers indicated assent. The Cabinet met at once and ratified the decision. At seven the same morning, word went to the United States through Switzerland and Sweden that Japan accepted the Potsdam terms provided they did not prejudice the Emperor's prerogatives as a sovereign ruler.[122]

Washington learned of the Japanese decision from Radio Tokyo broadcasts about breakfast time on August 10. Though this first word was unofficial, Truman called Leahy, Byrnes, Stimson, and Forrestal to his office for a conference at nine. Should the United States accept the Japanese condition? Stimson spoke first. Except for a brief period at Potsdam, he had stood consistently for some specific assurance regarding the Emperor. Indeed, just yesterday he had urged Byrnes to make it as easy as possible for the Japanese to yield. Now he argued his case again. It was advantageous to retain the Emperor, the only symbol of authority that all Japanese acknowledged. Leahy also favored accepting—if only because the Emperor could facilitate the surrender. Byrnes took an opposing view. Since the Japanese were obviously eager to yield, it was no time to weaken. Besides, the allies had adhered to the unconditional-surrender formula. If the United States retreated now, there would be delay while it tried to gain their acquiescence. Forrestal advocated a middle ground. The United States might indicate willingness to accept, he said, yet define the terms in such a way that they would assure the intent and purpose of the Potsdam Proclamation if not its actual words.

Truman asked Byrnes to prepare a reply along the lines of Forrestal's suggestion. In the meantime, American armed forces in the Pacific would keep the war effort at its present intensity with but a single exception—the third atomic bomb should not be dropped without express Presidential authority. As a matter of fact, Truman expected the negotiations to be complete before the second Fat Man was ready for use.

Byrnes had the reply ready for a two o'clock Cabinet meeting. While reiterating the Potsdam thesis that the utlimate form of government should be established by the freely expressed will of the Japanese people, it made a specific gesture to the Emperor. From the moment of surrender, his authority to rule should be subject to the Supreme Commander of the Allied Powers. The Cabinet found this device acceptable, and Truman sent the draft to London, Chungking, and Moscow for approval. The British and Chinese answers came promptly and caused no difficulties. The Soviet reaction suggested a desire to delay and assure itself a share in the occupation. Since Truman was prepared to proceed without Russian concurrence, Harriman took a strong line. When Molotov amended the original Soviet response, the way was clear. The United States dispatched its answer to the Japanese on the morning of August 11.[123]

The military chieftains of Japan remained unwilling to yield. The American note, they held, was unsatisfactory with respect to the position of the Emperor. War Minister Anami even raised once more the issues of disarmament procedures and occupation. On the morning of the fourteenth, Suzuki went to the Emperor privately and asked him to call an imperial conference. Shortly before eleven, the Emperor met his assembled ministers of state in the royal air-raid shelter. Anami, Umezu, and Toyoda argued that the Government should ask for a more definite reply, but everyone else favored acquiescence. Hirohito said that his view was the same as five nights before. He judged the American answer acceptable. He desired his ministers to prepare an imperial rescript he might broadcast to the nation. The Cabinet returned to its headquarters and formally subscribed to the terms of the allies. The war was over.[124]

STIMSON AND THE BOMB

At seven o'clock on Tuesday evening, August 14, President Truman announced that he had received a message from the Japanese Government which he deemed unconditional surrender—a full acceptance of the Potsdam

Proclamation. Resting 400 miles north in the Adirondacks, Secretary of War Stimson could feel that his work was done. The atomic bomb had been the coup de grâce. Unnumbered thousands of Americans—and Japanese— would live to see the peace. Freed from a bloody holocaust in the Pacific, the United States could turn to rehabilitating its war-ravaged friends and foes and establishing the foundations of a decent and lasting peace. For the present at least, the bomb had tipped the balance of power in favor of the United States. Yet Stimson had not seen the problem narrowly. He knew that the United States could not maintain its monopoly indefinitely and that American security demanded some form of effective international control. He knew the argument that dropping the bomb in combat would impair America's ability to lead the nations in a co-operative effort to remove this threat to civilization itself. But he also knew that given the frailty of mankind, international control was perhaps the greatest illusion of all. With all this in mind, he had used his great prestige and personal force to urge employing the atomic weapon should it be necessary to compel Japan to surrender.

That was the question men would ask as soon as word of victory flashed round the world. Were Hiroshima and Nagasaki necessary? Certainly Japan was badly beaten and looking for a way out. That was not the point. The true issue was this: had the United States refrained from using its atomic arm, could the allies have forced Japanese military leaders to surrender within an acceptable time on acceptable terms without fighting a climactic battle in the home islands? Perhaps they could have. Perhaps a demonstration could have been devised that would have impressed the militarists sufficiently. Perhaps more specific assurances with regard to the Emperor would have deprived the last-standers of their most powerful argument against the men who were trying to end the war. Against these possibilities was the extraordinary intervention of the Emperor. For all the talk about the imperial will, the concept had little meaning and few adherents. The militarists were accustomed to dictate to the Emperor, not heed the wishes of the throne. As it was, Hirohito had to assert himself on two different occasions. Would the militarists have yielded but for the awful fact of Hiroshima and Nagasaki? The question was insoluble. Yet down through the years, Stimson would have the advantage. It was impossible to prove what might have been.[125]

RELIEF FOR A LONELY RESPONSIBILITY

On August 9, 1945, Stimson had gone to the White House with Bush, Conant, Groves, Harrison, and Byrnes to present the case for publishing the Smyth report. The British had wired their assent, but Stimson wanted the President to make the final decision. When Truman had heard the views of his callers, he unhesitatingly approved immediate release.[126] The Sunday morning newspapers of August 12 carried summaries and excerpts from the lengthy document.

Smyth's classic *General Account of the Development of Methods of Using Atomic Energy for Military Purposes* might not have been published but for the argument that it was the only way to hold the line on the release of information. The covering War Department press bulletin stated the point bluntly: "The best interests of the United States require the utmost cooperation by all concerned in keeping secret now and for all time in the future all scientific and technical information not given in this report or other official releases of information by the War Department." Yet the report had another and more important purpose, which Smyth stated in his preface and in the text itself. The ultimate responsibility for the nation's policy on the questions raised by atomic energy rested with its citizens. Heretofore, military security had restricted their consideration to the scientists and a few high officials. Now the great political and social questions that might affect all mankind for generations were open for the people to debate and decide through their elected representatives. Men of science, Smyth hoped, would use the present semitechnical account to explain the potentialities of atomic bombs to their fellow citizens and help them reach wise decisions. "The people of the country must be informed if they are to discharge their responsibilities wisely." [127] Here lay the real significance of the Smyth report. The President and his chief advisers would still face torturous decisions. They could never escape the necessities of secrecy that national security demanded. But never again was atomic energy likely to impose such a vast and lonely responsibility as it did that fateful summer of 1945.

407

CONTROLLING THE ATOM:
SEARCH FOR A POLICY

CHAPTER 12

July 6, 1945, was an arduous day for Harry S. Truman. Visitors and decisions confined him to his office from early morning until well into the dinner hour. The President allowed himself a few moments of relaxation that pleasant summer evening at a band concert on the south lawn of the White House. Later, as the throb of traffic died away in war-weary Washington, a motorcade sped from the Executive Mansion down Pennsylvania Avenue to Union Station. There, on Track 2, at the entrance to the tunnel under the Mall, the President and his party boarded a special train for Newport News. Before most Virginians were up the next morning, the cruisers *Augusta* and *Philadelphia* slipped through Hampton Roads. Few knew that Task Force 68 was carrying the President and his new Secretary of State to Europe for the Big Three meeting at Potsdam.[1]

Truman and Byrnes took with them the question of how to use the bomb, which had distracted the Interim Committee since May. Now Harrison hoped that the group could at last turn to its primary task of postwar planning. With the pace of the war quickening, there was little time left for the thorough study of international and domestic control which Bush and Conant had been urging on Secretary Stimson since September, 1944. The committee could not do much about international control until the framework of postwar policy emerged from the Potsdam meetings. The domestic scene was more nearly in focus. Unless the committee acted quickly, it might not have a bill ready to introduce in Congress when atomic energy first became a public issue.

DOMESTIC LEGISLATION

Fortunately, the committee did not have to start from scratch on domestic legislation. The early preoccupation with postwar problems at the Metallurgical Laboratory and the foresight of Bush and Conant had already stimulated some study of the principles if not the details of legislation. Harrison had a copy of the Tolman Committee report and a lengthy document prepared by Norman Hilberry with the help of the Chicago scientists. But by far the most influential was a file of OSRD speculations dating back to the previous summer.[2]

As a result of earlier discussions with Bush, his deputy Irvin Stewart and Conant completed a two-page summary of a domestic control bill in July, 1944. They conceived of a twelve-man commission on atomic energy appointed by the President. Five members would be scientists or engineers nominated by the National Academy of Sciences to serve five-year terms. The President would appoint three other civilians for one-year terms, and the military services would name two Army and two Navy officers. The commissioners would have unprecedented peacetime powers. They would regulate all transfers of special nuclear materials, the construction and operation of all production plants, and all nuclear experiments involving significant amounts of these materials. They would also have authority to conduct all these activities in their own facilities or through private contractors.

409

A discussion with Bush on September 15, 1944, brought out a new facet. He and Conant concluded that the commission should control not only large-scale production, but also experiments involving very small amounts of material. It was conceivable that an overenthusiastic or irresponsible scientist might cause an explosion that would wreck a city block and spread poisonous radioactivity over a wide area. Here was a unique type of health hazard not only to the individuals immediately involved but to an entire community. This danger of even small-scale experiments pointed up the need for comprehensive federal control. Perhaps a treaty would have to serve as the basis for federal legislation.

As Bush suggested in his conversation with Stimson a few days later, the emphasis in atomic energy legislation should be on control and regulation. For Bush, this was not a job for political hacks or even for well-intentioned laymen. The commission he recommended would consist largely of technical specialists selected by the National Academy and the Army. The President would appoint only three of the twelve commissioners outright, and there was no mention of Senate confirmation. Serving part-time without compensation, the civilian members would be virtually independent of government controls. In fact, the proposed commission smacked of the quasi-governmental bodies which had been a feature of federal research in two world wars. For such a group Bush was willing to recommend powers which seemed to surpass those ever granted to an executive department or agency.

During the fall of 1944, Bush applied the same principles in his plans for continuing research on other military applications. With war research activities nearing an end, Bush saw that there was no time to delay. As a member of the Wilson committee appointed by the military services, he recommended replacing OSRD with a Research Board for National Security. Composed of Army and Navy officers, an equal number of civilian scientists and engineers appointed by the National Academy of Sciences, and members of Army and Navy organizations, the board would keep abreast of new scientific developments. Stimson and Forrestal established the board early in 1945, only to be frustrated when Budget Director Harold D. Smith refused to release funds for its support. The Navy responded by drafting a bill to establish the board by act of Congress, but that abortive effort missed the main point at issue.[3]

Smith was not just being obstinate, as Stimson and Forrestal seemed to think. He had long been concerned with postwar organization of the Executive Branch, particularly that of keeping the activities of the sprawling federal establishment consistent with Administration policy. Now that science had become a touchstone of national security, strong federal support would have to continue in the postwar period. It was obvious that the Government could never return to prewar levels of scientific support. From 1938 to 1944, federal research expenditures had jumped more than ten-fold from $68 million to $706 million, or from 20 per cent to 75 per cent of the total national expenditure for that purpose.

The issue was not whether but how the Government would support science. Bush wanted to guarantee the scientists' freedom of research by insulating them from political pressure. Smith believed that large-scale federal support required, if it did not indeed depend upon, effective controls through the regular channels of government.

Smith was not alone in his position. Senator Harley M. Kilgore and his Subcommittee on War Mobilization had throughout the war sought ways of mobilizing scientific and technical manpower. In January, 1945, Kilgore published a detailed survey of the Government's wartime technical program. During the spring, Bush learned that the committee was preparing a second report and a bill to create a National Science Foundation. It was already clear that the Kilgore bill would follow Smith's approach rather than Bush's. It would provide a new Government agency under a full-time director responsible to the President. Furthermore, Kilgore favored a clean break with American patent policy by requiring that the results of research supported by Government funds be free from patent restrictions. As an engineer and inventor, Bush believed the patent system provided the necessary incentive for private organizations to participate in Government research.[4]

Early in 1945, Bush put his OSRD staff to work on a counterproposal. Shortly after the President left for Potsdam, Bush gave the Interim Committee a copy of his plan, soon to be published as *Science, the Endless Frontier*. Like his two earlier proposals, it called for an agency (the National Research Foundation) to be directed by a large, part-time board of technical experts. The board would establish national research policies which

410

would be administered by the foundation staff. Committees appointed from National Academy lists would supervise the staff divisions, and military officers would serve on the committee within the division of national defense, which was Bush's substitute for the Research Board for National Security. Once again Bush was trying to guarantee that scientific research would be controlled by the scientists without interference from the politicians.[5]

As Bush informed the Interim Committee on July 9, his proposals for the foundation and the commission had to be considered together.[6] While the commission's chief functions would be to control the uses of atomic energy and advise the President on policy, the foundation's main duty would be to encourage and promote independent research. Bush admitted that Congress might attempt to consolidate all these functions in one agency, but he was prepared to defend the proposition that the commission's powers of control should not be combined with the foundation's promotional activities. He thought that atomic energy legislation was most urgent, but he also realized the danger that the dramatic imposition of atomic energy on the American scene might obliterate any interest in the foundation and the basic sciences. As it happened, the course of events favored the foundation, at least initially. On July 19, Senator Warren G. Magnuson introduced Bush's bill to establish the National Research Foundation. Four days later, Senator Kilgore presented his bill for a National Science Foundation. By that time, the Interim Committee's staff had just completed the first draft of its bill, and the whole subject of atomic energy was still shrouded in secrecy.[7]

411

LAST CHANCE FOR PLANNING

When the Interim Committee met on July 19, 1945, there was a new note of urgency in the air. The implosion device had been successfully tested at Alamogordo, and all the members knew that combat use of the weapon was not far away. Whatever was to be done on postwar planning would have to be done quickly.

Bush and Conant were eager for the Interim Committee to begin thinking about international control. To facilitate the process, they proposed that the committee recommend their plan for a scientific office under the United Nations Organization. As they now conceived it, this agency would insure complete publication of all research in nuclear physics and free access of scientists to all laboratories where such work was proceeding. For at least five years, the agency would have no jurisdiction over American facilities concerned with the technical details of current methods of manufacturing fissionable materials and bombs. The United States, however, would keep the world informed on the number and power of the bombs in its arsenals. Should this arrangement go into effect, Bush and Conant admitted, the United States would be giving Russia and the rest of the world technical information that might shorten their road to a weapon by two years. On the other hand, the plan seemed the best hope for avoiding an armament race. To move more rapidly by proposing complete interchange was Utopian. A limited offer had the merit of testing Soviet good faith. The committee accepted all this as food for thought, but like Bush and Conant, it favored deferring consideration until the other members had returned from Potsdam.[8]

The main business of the day was the first draft of the atomic energy bill.[9] Several weeks earlier, Harrison had recruited two experienced lawyers on duty with the War Department. Kenneth C. Royall had practiced law in North Carolina for twenty years before returning to the Army in 1942. He rose to brigadier general as deputy fiscal officer of the Army Service Forces and before the end of 1945 would succeed Patterson as Under Secretary. William L. Marbury, like Royall, was a Harvard Law School graduate. He had left his Baltimore practice to help Patterson set up the Army's procurement organization in 1940. That task accomplished, he served as chief counsel on War Department contracts.

412

In general outline, the bill resembled the proposal which Bush and Conant had submitted to Stimson the previous September. It would establish a nine-man commission, consisting of five civilians, two representatives of the Army, and two of the Navy. Unlike the earlier proposals, it did not require nomination of the civilian members by the National Academy of Sciences, but it preserved the concept of the part-time advisory commission. Commission members could hold other positions in the federal government and would receive no compensation.

Neither was there any doubt that the authors intended the commission to be dominated by experts securely insulated from political pressures. The terms of the commissioners would be indefinite, and the President's powers of removal would be limited to a few specific grounds. In addition to the commission, the bill would create four advisory boards on military applications, industrial uses, research, and medicine. Required to have technical qualifications, the advisory board members would be appointed by the commission and would serve without compensation. An administrator and deputy administrator appointed by the commission would direct the full-time staff. Since the commission could delegate all its powers and authority to these officials, the administrator and his deputy would in effect be the agency's executive officers.

In terms of powers granted to the commission, the bill also resembled the earlier OSRD proposals. It would give the commission custody of all raw materials and deposits, all plants, facilities, equipment, and materials, all technical information and patents, and all contracts and agreements related to the production of fissionable materials. For this purpose, the commission would have virtually unlimited powers of condemnation and eminent domain. The administrator would be authorized to conduct atomic research either in commission facilities or by contract. He could control all such activities in all other government agencies except for military research by the armed forces. He could acquire any property, facilities, or services required for commission activities. He could, with commission approval, license all property to other persons or government agencies. The commission would also establish and administer its own security, personnel, and audit regulations.

The bill would not only grant these sweeping powers; it would prohibit almost any such activities outside the commission's control. It would be unlawful for any person to conduct atomic research without its consent. Even then, the commission and the administrator would have "plenary authority to direct, supervise, regulate, and inspect" such activities.

If Bush and Conant were pleased to find their earlier suggestions in the bill, they did not get far into the specifics before they realized that the Army lawyers had, if anything, done too good a job.[10] In 1945, it was much easier to see the needs of the postwar world. Both Bush and Conant now felt that only civilians should serve on the commission. Royall suggested that strong military representation would be necessary for Congressional support. Both Harrison and Groves agreed with the scientists. Harrison believed that the advisory board on military applications would provide adequate representation for the services. Groves, perhaps recognizing that the real power would lie with the administrator, added that military experience was more important than formal representation.

413

As for the commission's powers, both Bush and Conant found them far too sweeping. Bush agreed that the commission should have freedom of action, but he warned it was possible to ask for more than was necessary and end up with something less. At OSRD, Bush had never sought exemptions from Civil Service regulations or from regular government audits. He had never seen the need for the unlimited powers granted by the bill on property condemnation or security regulations. How could the Interim Committee hope to justify such extraordinary provisions?

Most of the scientists' criticism centered on the research provisions. In contrast to his 1944 position, Conant no longer believed that the Government should control every phase of research. He knew some restrictions were needed, but could not the committee establish some quantitative limits below which independent research would be possible without commission regulation? Compton suggested a standard defined in terms of energy release. All agreed that the bill should contain some limitation on the commission's power over research in the universities.

Bush detected an even more fundamental flaw. He heartily disapproved of the provisions granting the commission authority to conduct research either by contract or with its own facilities and personnel. One might think from a quick reading of the bill that research was the commission's primary function. This approach he held faulty on two counts. First, research was incompatible with the commission's regulatory and control responsibilities. Second, research would be the job of the National Research Foundation operating through grants to educational institutions. Bush wanted the commission's research powers reduced, and he advocated adding a strong declaration that the universities would be expected to perform the basic research required in the nuclear sciences.

Despite these criticisms, the Royall-Marbury draft was not far from the pattern which Bush and Conant had established in 1944. Obviously, it stemmed from the same philosophy that underlay the Magnuson bill. It was also close to what the scientists themselves were thinking. The Hilberry proposal differed from the Royall-Marbury bill in some details, but it rested on the same premise of heavy federal support and control. Although Hilberry and his associates favored a full-time commission, they accepted the idea of military representation.

The proposed commission also bore similarities to the wartime organization. The Royall-Marbury conception of the commission, administrator, and staff seemed to be an extension of the roles of the Military Policy Committee, General Groves, and the Manhattan District during the war. Indeed, the parallels were so apparent that Groves would never live down the accusation that he had designed the bill to permit him to continue the working relationships he had established with Bush and Conant.

The Army lawyers took the committee's suggestions at the July 19 meeting not as a mandate but as a bargaining position for a compromise. General Royall, now in command of the drafting operations, had no intention of writing a new bill. He instructed Lieutenants George S. Allen and George M. Duff in the Manhattan District's legal office to make only minor changes without modifying "the basic approach of the document."[11] This meant, for example, that the refinements suggested in the audit, security, and condemnation provisions could be adopted. On more substantial matters, however, the Army was willing to go no more than halfway.

Apparently, there had been no sharp difference of opinion on the question of military representation on the commission. Conant had suggested a civilian body, and Groves saw no need for formal representation of the services. Royall could easily compromise with an amendment that four members of the commission be officers in the armed forces, either in active or retired status.

The sticking point came on the powers of the commission. Royall was willing to qualify the definition of the commission's plenary powers with the high-sounding declaration that "the Commission shall adopt the policy of minimum interference with private research and of employing private enterprise to the maximum extent consistent with . . . this Act." As for the commission's authority to conduct basic research, the Army offered no change other than a similar proviso declaring it the commission's policy "to utilize, encourage and aid colleges, universities, scientific laboratories, hospitals, and other private or non-profit institutions equipped and staffed to conduct research and experimentation in this field." [12]

The Army proposed a similar compromise on the section granting the commission unlimited supervision and control over atomic research in university and other private laboratories. In place of the precise limitations suggested by the committee, the Army substituted a provision outlawing research "involving the release of atomic energy in amounts deemed and to be prescribed by the Commission as constituting a national hazard or being of military or industrial value." [13]

Marbury assured Harrison that "perhaps 75 per cent of Bush's objections had been met in the redraft." This statement may have been true in terms of sheer numbers, but not in substance. Bush was pleased with the qualifying provisions, but he was still bothered by the general tone of the bill. He wrote Harrison on August 7 that the granting of broad and sweeping powers to the commission had been "greatly overdone." He urged a complete review of the bill "in order to provide for exemption from the usual governmental controls only when it is clearly necessary." [14] By this time, however, the bomb had dropped on Hiroshima. The time for long-range planning had run out.

415

THE WORLD IS CHANGED

Even for men like Bush and Conant, the Hiroshima attack meant the end of one era and the beginning of a new. Because they had lived for more than four years with the quest for the bomb and knew of its effects at Alamogordo, they were not, like most people, stunned by the news from Japan. For them, the psychological impact lay rather in the shattering of the little world of secrecy in which they had so long been confined. In an instant, the closely guarded secret of S-1 was swept into the merciless glare of the public limelight. Almost as quickly, new forces far beyond their control began to operate.

For most Americans, the news came in Truman's terse statement. The President told the nation of "a new era in man's understanding of nature's forces." Ordinarily, he said, both the Government and the scientists would have made public all technical data. But under the circumstances he did not intend to divulge the technical processes of production or all the military applications, "pending further examination of possible methods of protecting us and the rest of the world from the danger of sudden destruction." He would ask the Congress at once to establish a commission to control the production and use of atomic power in the United States, while he developed plans to make it a "forceful influence for world peace."

Secretary Stimson's statement gave the nation a glimpse of the hitherto secret activities of the Manhattan project, but any elaboration on policy issues had to await the President's return. Meanwhile, the press indulged itself in unrestrained sensationalism and speculation. Tabloid feature writers blithely supplied from their own imaginations the details of weapon design which the Army had denied them. Even responsible columnists were reduced to echoing hollow-sounding hopes for international and domestic control. The President's message was reassuring as far as it went, but what did he mean by "a commission to control the production and use of atomic power"? Would this agency interfere with research, as some scientists feared? Was there really any hope of international control? No matter how fantastic it seemed, was anything short of world government acceptable? Robert M. Hutchins remarked on the University of Chicago Roundtable's Sunday broadcast: "I do not think we shall be any better off because of the bomb. But the alternatives seem clear. Only through the monopoly of atomic force by world government can we hope to abolish war." [15]

President Truman was not so sure that the time had come for such revolutionary measures. Reporting to the nation on his trip to Potsdam on August 9, the President reiterated his determination to keep the secret of the bomb until means could be found to control it. "As far back as last May," he said, "Secretary of War Stimson . . . appointed a committee . . . to prepare plans for the future control of this bomb." The people could speculate, but the decision would come from the President, the Interim Committee, and Congress.

General Royall, for one, was not wasting time. The day after Hiroshima, he and Marbury had discussed the draft bill with the Attorney General, the Judge Advocate General, and the OSRD patent attorney. After making a few minor changes in the draft, they sent it to Stimson. With his approval, they would have a bill ready to introduce when Congress reconvened in the fall.[16]

Neither Stimson nor the nation was yet prepared to knuckle down to the business of domestic legislation. Stimson had returned from Potsdam exhausted in body and spirit. He had been unable to shake the specter of Soviet oppression which had haunted him since his European trip. Stimson felt none of the exhilaration which swept the nation with the news from Hiroshima. After a meeting at the White House on August 9, he returned to the Pentagon for his regular Thursday press conference. For a moment of triumph, he spoke in somber tones. "Great events have happened. The world is changed and it is time for sober thought. It is natural that we should take satisfaction in the achievements of our science, our industry, and our Army in creating the atomic bomb, but any satisfaction we may feel must be overshadowed by deeper emotion. . . . The result of the bomb is so terrific that the responsibility of its possession and its use must weigh heavier on our minds and on our hearts." [17]

Feeling the last ounce of his physical endurance fast ebbing away,

POSTWAR PLANNERS / George L. Harrison, General Leslie R. Groves, James B. Conant, and Vannevar Bush leave the White House, August 9, 1945.

THE "BUTTERFLY WINGS" CONFERENCE, CHICAGO, SEPTEMBER, 1945 / At the opening of the University of Chicago's Institute of Nuclear Studies, Samuel K. Allison warned that Army security restrictions might force scientists to limit their studies to butterfly wings.

Left to right

seated: W. H. Zachariasen, H. C. Urey, C. S. Smith, E. Fermi, S. K. Allison.

standing: E. Teller, T. R. Hogness, W. H. Zinn, C. Zener, J. E. Mayer, P. W. Schutz, R. H. Crist, C. Eckhart.

PRESIDENT TRUMAN AWARDS STIMSON THE DISTINGUISHED SERVICE MEDAL, JULY 21, 1945 / After this ceremony, many of those present attended a Cabinet conference to consider American nuclear policy toward Russia. Behind the President and Stimson, left to right: OWMR Director John W. Snyder, Secretary of the Treasury Fred M. Vinson, Secretary of War Robert P. Patterson, General Brehon B. Somervell, Mrs. Stimson, Assistant Secretary of War John J. McCloy. Behind and to the left of Somervell is Stimson's friend and aide, Harvey H. Bundy.

Stimson told Truman he would soon be forced to resign. The President, urging him to stay on, suggested that Stimson take a month's vacation and come back as soon thereafter as he could. Over the week end, he went to St. Huberts in the Adirondacks. There, in the rustic beauty and peace of a mountain retreat, the elder statesman soon recovered his enthusiasm. Perhaps the chances for a reliable agreement with the Russians were small, but certainly there was no hope at all unless the United States made a sincere effort to negotiate with its powerful ally. Within a fortnight, Stimson was formulating a proposal for such an attempt. John J. McCloy, one of his closest advisers in the War Department, flew up twice to help him with the draft. McCloy bolstered his spirits, but he also brought discouraging news from Washington. Harrison reported that Byrnes was taking a hard position on negotiations with the Russians. Byrnes thought "it would be difficult to do anything on the international level at the present time and that in his opinion we should continue the Manhattan Project with full force, at least until Congress has acted on the proposed Bill." [18]

417

Ironically, Byrnes's attitude had been strengthened by a report which Oppenheimer had drafted to support the case for international negotiation. Warning of the possibilities of a more terrible weapon in the thermonuclear reaction, Oppenheimer reported the Scientific Panel's "unanimous and urgent recommendation" that such developments be controlled by international agreement. When Byrnes read the report, he told Harrison to inform Oppenheimer that "for the time being his proposal about an international agreement was not practical and that he and the rest of the gang should pursue their work [on the hydrogen weapon] full force." [19]

Events were quickly coming to a head in those last days of August. Byrnes was preparing to leave for the foreign ministers' conference in London, fully determined, as Stimson put it, "to have the implied threat of the bomb in his pocket during the conference." Stimson asked McCloy to see Byrnes before his departure and telephoned Bundy in Washington to give him the latest version of his proposed approach to the Russians.

On the domestic front, McCloy and Harrison were busily planning their strategy for introducing the Royall-Marbury bill, now that Congress had decided to reconvene on the Wednesday after Labor Day rather than wait until October. Since Hiroshima, virtually all discussions of the bomb had been cast in the international context. This fact, plus Stimson's absence, gave Byrnes and the State Department the initiative. The War Department had drafted the bill, but now State was to sponsor it. And that, of course, meant State Department concurrence.

Benjamin V. Cohen, soon to be counselor in the Department, found several changes necessary. He urged that, in the interests of national and world opinion, the preamble state that atomic energy would be used not only for national defense but for promoting world peace. If the bill was to provide specifically for military officers on the commission, he suggested that one or two members be required to have experience in foreign relations. He thought the commission should be subject to the guidance of the Secretary of State in international matters, and suggested that the appointment of advisory boards be made discretionary rather than mandatory.[20]

Royall and Marbury were not inclined to accept these conditions, but Harrison saw no alternative. If the bill was to be ready when Congress met on Wednesday, he could not afford further negotiations with State. He had managed to turn aside some rather fundamental objections from Harold L. Ickes, the Secretary of Interior, and had restricted criticisms from other agencies to minor details. Working through the Labor Day week end, McCloy and Harrison made an appointment with Byrnes and Assistant Secretary Dean G. Acheson on Sunday, September 2. The Army accepted the revisions, and State agreed to sponsor the legislation.[21]

When Stimson returned to the Pentagon on Tuesday morning, he learned that he had been invited to attend the first of Truman's Cabinet luncheons. He was reluctant to accept, but when the President assured him that it was to be more a social than a business affair, the Secretary decided to go. For one thing, it would give him a chance to talk with Byrnes, who had delayed his departure for London. Chatting with Byrnes in the hall at the White House after the luncheon, Stimson found the Secretary of State as adamant as ever in his opposition to any attempt to co-operate with Russia. He was, in Stimson's opinion, thinking about other points which he hoped to carry at London with the help of the bomb. Byrnes described Stalin's perfidious acts at Potsdam which led him to discount any Russian promises. Stimson explained his proposal to negotiate international control of atomic energy with the Russians. The two secretaries were poles apart, but they understood each other. They parted for the last time as members of the Truman Cabinet, Byrnes for New York to catch the *Queen Elizabeth,* Stimson for the Pentagon to organize the last effort of his public career.[22]

LAUNCHING THE STIMSON POLICY

Back in the Pentagon, Stimson found that his communiqués from St. Huberts had stimulated a warm response among his immediate associates. Only Robert Patterson was reluctant to adopt his idea of an overture to Russia. His old friend Goldthwaite H. Dorr caught the far-reaching implications of his proposal in an analysis for McCloy. Was the bomb just another devastating military weapon which could be assimilated in the old pattern of international relations or could it be the first step in a new control by man over forces of nature too revolutionary and dangerous to be handled by conventional means? The conventional methods of diplomacy, Dorr suggested, would call either for pursuing secrecy and nationalistic military superiority or relying on mutual international caution to proscribe the weapon. A bold, new approach would be for the United States and Britain to make a direct offer to Russia of full partnership in further developing and controlling atomic energy, with the idea of eventually bringing the other nations of the world into the agreement. Unless the second course were adopted, Dorr warned, the Russians would surely begin an arms race which would destroy any confidence built up between the nations by their common suffering during the war. True, the Russians might have already rejected such a course, in which case the United States would in fact have no choice. But certainly the United States had to make the offer.[23]

Stimson followed much the same line of reasoning in the three-page memorandum which he took to the White House on the afternoon of September 12.[24] Giving the document to Truman, he took his time as he discussed each paragraph from his carbon copy. Stimson recalled the misgivings about the Russians he had expressed at Potsdam. These were still valid, but he had concluded that the United States could not use the bomb as a lever to accelerate the granting of individual liberties in Russia. Such changes would come slowly, and the United States could not delay its approach on the atomic bomb until that process was completed.

419

Stimson believed that the bomb had stimulated great military and political interest throughout the world. Certainly the Russians would be tempted to develop the weapon as quickly as possible. Unless the "Anglo-Saxon bloc" offered the Russians full partnership in the development of atomic energy, the Secretary feared that the Soviet Union would begin "a secret armament race of a rather desperate character." The primary consideration was not whether Russia got the bomb in four years or twenty, but whether they were "willing and co-operative partners among the peace-loving nations of the world." The United States might embitter relations irretrievably by failing to approach Russia on atomic energy. "The chief lesson I have learned in a long life is that the only way you can make a man trustworthy is to trust him; and the surest way to make him untrustworthy is to distrust him and show your distrust."

Explaining the details of his plan, Stimson told the President he favored a direct offer by the United States and Britain to control the bomb and encourage the development of atomic power for peaceful purposes. The United States might propose to stop weapons work if the British and the Russians would do likewise. It might impound its current stockpile if all three nations would forego the bomb as an instrument of war. Further, the United States might consider a covenant for exchanging information that would advance commercial and humanitarian applications. He emphasized above all that an international organization would take too long and would never be considered seriously by the Russians. As Stimson proceeded, Truman endorsed each paragraph and at the end told the Secretary he agreed with his approach that "we must take Russia into our confidence."

The following Tuesday, September 18, at the Cabinet luncheon, the

President, with Stimson's memorandum still very much on his mind, turned the conversation to atomic energy. As the discussion continued, he concluded that atomic energy should be the only item on the agenda for the Cabinet meeting on Friday. The luncheon was really an informal farewell for Stimson, who had already resigned. Would he stay over to give the Cabinet one last benefit of his wisdom and knowledge? Although Truman's request was a blow to his plans to leave for New York, Stimson said he would come "if I could walk on my two feet." [25]

Friday, September 21, 1945, was Stimson's last day of public service and his seventy-eighth birthday. At a brief ceremony in the White House rose garden, Truman awarded him the Distinguished Service Medal. Then the group moved inside. All the members of the Cabinet were there except Byrnes, whom Acheson represented. Stimson had invited Bush and Patterson, who was replacing him as Secretary. Kenneth McKellar, president pro tempore of the Senate, John W. Snyder, director of the Office of War Mobilization and Reconversion, and other war agency officials brought their special points of view to the meeting.

Speaking extemporaneously, Stimson argued that the future of atomic energy lay in its research applications and in the development of power. The scientific facts supporting these activities could not be kept secret. Therefore, the United States had everything to gain and little to lose by making a direct offer of a partnership to Russia. Stimson had used the same argument to win Patterson's support; he hoped it would have a similar effect on the President and the Cabinet.

The Cabinet divided on the Stimson proposal. James V. Forrestal, Secretary of the Navy, saw the bomb and the knowledge that produced it as "the property of the American people," which the Administration could not give away until it was very sure that the people approved. Pointing to the failure of the Japanese to live up to the 1921 naval agreements, Forrestal said the Russians, like the Japanese, were Oriental in their thinking. Until the United States had a long record of experience to test the validity of commitments made by the Russians, America should not try to buy their understanding and sympathy. It seemed to Forrestal that "we could exercise a trusteeship over the atomic bomb on behalf of the United Nations and agree that we would limit its manufacture for use on such missions as the United Nations should designate." [26]

Secretary of Commerce Henry Wallace disagreed. He was wholeheartedly in favor of giving scientific information to Russia. Like Stimson, he argued that basic facts of nature could not be kept secret and that an attempt to do so would embitter and sour people throughout the world. Secretary of the Treasury Fred M. Vinson and Attorney General Thomas C. Clark, opposed to giving away information about the bomb, saw no way to release part of the data.

With the group's sentiments moving away from the Stimson proposal,

Bush pointed out that it did not involve giving away the secret of the bomb. That secret rested in the details of bomb design and in the manufacturing processes. The question was whether the United States could trust Russia. Was it not reasonable to suggest that, as a test case, the United States could offer a *quid pro quo* exchange of the basic scientific information which could not be kept secret anyway? Until the Russians passed such a test, Bush believed that the United States should hold tightly the secret of the bomb.[27]

Truman, exhilarated by the exchange of ideas, asked those present to submit their views in writing. For the first time since his return from Potsdam, he was beginning to grasp the essential issues involved in atomic control. With written statements to study, he might be able quickly to formulate a proposal. Certainly, he could not much longer delay a clear-cut policy statement on international and domestic control. In the three short weeks since Labor Day, the basic policy issues had become hopelessly snarled in public and Congressional debate. Unless the Administration acted soon, the onrushing tide of public opinion might leave the President powerless to control its direction.

421

THE PUBLIC SPEAKS

The headwaters of this torrent of public controversy lay deep in the isolated domain of the Manhattan District installations. At the Metallurgical Laboratory, the Committee on Social and Political Implications continued to meet weekly during August and September. As the Chicago scientists picked up scraps of information about the Royall-Marbury bill and Byrnes's attitude toward international control, they became concerned that decisions would be made without adequate guidance in technical matters. This sort of pressure caused Compton to ask Groves that the scientists be permitted "to express their views on human applications." Compton also suggested that members of the Scientific Panel and those in the project who were members of the National Academy of Sciences be authorized to make semiofficial statements concerning technical subjects.

It was bad enough that the scientists were not being consulted; it was even worse that the Army was bridling them with security regulations even after the Japanese surrender. John H. Manley wrote Groves in August that he found much anxiety about future policy at Chicago and Los Alamos. The scientists were genuinely worried about atomic controls, and they resented being kept in the dark. Putting it bluntly, Manley said there was too little contact between those who had done most of the work and those who formulated policy. The scientists had little enthusiasm for government employment, and every day they were receiving attractive offers of academic positions. Unless they got better treatment, Manley feared that the more competent scientists would soon leave the project.[28]

The first public manifestation of this discontent came in Chicago on September 1. Seventeen atomic scientists, including Allison, Fermi, Cyril Smith, and Urey, assembled at the Shoreland Hotel on the South Side to announce their affiliation with the Institute of Nuclear Studies to be established on the Chicago campus. The event itself made good local news, but Allison's remarks gave it national significance. The outspoken Chicago scientist used the occasion to make a plea for free and unhampered research in the development of atomic power. Most arresting was his remark to the effect that, unless the Army removed security restrictions, the atomic scientists might resort to studying the color of butterfly wings. To this Fermi added: "It is not that we will not work for the government but rather that we cannot work for the government. Unless research is free and outside of control, the United States will lose its superiority in scientific pursuit." Allison's threat spurred Groves to action. He sent Nichols posthaste to Chicago with instructions that there be no more talk about butterfly wings. It might, the Colonel warned, jeopardize the Administration's legislative proposals. The scientists' reply was to be expected: they did not know what the legislative proposals were.[29]

422

In a strict sense, the retort was true. The scientists would not see a draft of the Royall-Marbury bill until it had been introduced in Congress. But they knew enough about it from hearsay to begin organizing an opposition. The week following the Shoreland luncheon, John A. Simpson, Jr., a twenty-nine-year-old physicist at the Metallurgical Laboratory, took the lead. At a meeting on September 4, his group began drafting the objectives of their organization from some material prepared in August by the Committee on Social and Political Implications. Here the emphasis was on "the urgent necessity of establishing international controls of atomic explosives," but the group was also thinking about political action on domestic legislation. The plan was to study the various bills introduced in Congress and to discuss their relative merits with senators and representatives. To guide their evaluation, Simpson suggested that they oppose any domestic control plan that would create vested interests which might later hamper the international exchange of scientific information. He urged opposition to all formal security regulations on the theory that the voluntary system adopted in 1940 would adequately protect the national interest. He advocated a full-time commission and a permanent Congressional committee. His last point was that most of the "atomic bomb secret" had been released at Hiroshima and in the Smyth report.[30]

The fact that Simpson emphasized these particular points reflected his fragmentary but accurate knowledge of the Royall-Marbury bill and the misgivings engendered by Congressional sentiment in the opening days of the September session. Within the first few hours of the session, members of both houses introduced atomic energy legislation. Brien McMahon, the freshman senator from Connecticut, rushed forward with little more than the skeleton of a bill proposing to create a control board composed of Cabinet officers and other federal officials. Moments later, Arthur H. Vandenberg introduced a resolution establishing a joint committee to investigate the development and control of atomic energy. In the House, George H. Bender of Ohio offered a bill making it a capital offense to disclose information on the bomb, and Louis Ludlow of Indiana presented a resolution urging the United Nations to ban the bomb as an instrument of war. In the following days, congressmen dropped additional bills in the hopper and larded the record with shallow speculations on the curses and blessings of the atomic age. All this was maddening for the scientists. It proved their contention that almost no one outside the Manhattan project had more than a superficial understanding of the atomic predicament and its consequences. This fact was alone enough to elicit a conscientious, if not self-righteous, response from the scientists. But they were also horrified to see Congress talking itself into a continuation of rigid wartime security measures.[31]

At Chicago, the response took two forms. One was the petition signed by James Franck and sixty-four other Chicago faculty members urging the President to share the secret of the bomb with other nations to avoid an armaments race. The petition received widespread newspaper coverage on September 10. The second was the formal establishment of the Atomic Scientists of Chicago. The executive committee included four signers of the Franck report and three new members of the Committee on Social and Political Implications. All the scientists and technicians at the Metallurgical and Argonne laboratories were invited to join. The purpose was "to explore, clarify and consolidate the opinion of the scientists . . . on the implications of atomic power, . . . to present this opinion before the National Administration, . . . and to educate public opinion." Through study, discussion, and association with similar groups elsewhere, they hoped to play an active part in formulating national policy.[32]

Similar organizations were already forming at the other Manhattan project sites. The scientists at Los Alamos asked Oppenheimer to help them secure a War Department release for a statement they had prepared on the significance of the bomb in the postwar world. Similar appeals for an end to secrecy and for international control were drafted at Oak Ridge and at Columbia University. In each case, the effort marked the effective, if not the formal, beginnings of the scientists' associations.[33]

423

THE ADMINISTRATION ACTS

In contrast to the rising tide of public opinion among the scientists on one hand and Congress on the other, the Administration remained strangely quiet. If the Army expected quick action on the War Department bill, it was disappointed. No move was made to introduce the bill in the opening days of the session. The President's special message to Congress on September 6 contained twenty-one specific recommendations for conversion to a peacetime economy, but not one reference to atomic energy.[34]

That same day, Harrison called Acheson's attention to the fact that the newspapers were already speculating on atomic energy bills being introduced by individual congressmen. Acheson seemed to think he needed more authority from Byrnes, who had just left for London. Harrison reminded the Acting Secretary of the agreement they had reached the previous Sunday that State would introduce the bill. Early the next week, McCloy raised the question again and got the impression that "Mr. Acheson was very timid about it." A few days later, Herbert S. Marks, a young lawyer serving as Acheson's assistant, contacted the War Department about discussing the bill, but there was no hint of impending action. When Stimson went to the White House on September 12, he left with the President a copy of Harrison's analysis of the legislative situation. According to Stimson, the President would direct Acheson to act.[35]

Acheson was still hesitant. He told Harrison that he feared the proposed bill because it would raise international questions which were still officially undecided. Resolution of those questions did not begin until the Cabinet luncheon on September 18. That same day, Acheson discussed the legislative tangle with the President. There were strong reasons for introducing the Administration's bill, but Acheson warned that once Truman had taken that step his freedom of action on international policy would become severely limited. Acheson emphasized the urgency of translating Stimson's proposal or the President's ideas into concrete terms. Then the Administration's international and domestic program could be introduced in some dramatic way which would crystallize public opinion.

Acheson then cleared the legislative channels. The following morning, September 19, he went to the Capitol to discuss the various bills with the Senate Foreign Relations Committee. There he learned that, unless the Administration acted quickly, atomic energy legislation would become hopelessly snarled in parliamentary red tape. Since no one committee had clear jurisdiction over the broad subject of atomic energy, Senator Vandenberg feared a battle between several committees "and a rush to get somebody's pet Bill reported." The Michigan senator had already taken steps to counter a move by Senator Elbert D. Thomas and his Military Affairs Committee to stake a claim on atomic energy. Vandenberg's solution would be to establish a special joint committee on atomic energy to which all bills on the subject would be referred. There was also a need to co-ordinate legislative and executive plans. This was accomplished at a White House meeting on September 20. The President would submit his proposals for international control to Congress; Vandenberg would try to establish the joint committee to speed action on legislation.[36]

The week following the September 21 Cabinet meeting and Stimson's farewell marked a renewed effort by the War Department to break the log jam. Quickly assuming his new office, Secretary Patterson organized his attack. Since domestic legislation would have to await formulation of international policy, Patterson concentrated on clearing the way for the Stimson proposal. In response to Vinson's and Clark's criticism, Harrison and Oppenheimer studied the possibilities of separating weapons information from basic scientific data. They helped Patterson and Acheson in drafting for the President specific proposals effecting Stimson's plan. Perhaps these would encourage Truman to commit himself.[37]

The next move was concerned with domestic legislation. On Friday, September 28, Patterson called Groves and the remnants of the Interim Committee to his office to map out legislative strategy. Groves was more worried with every day of delay. The demobilization fever which was sweeping the nation was taking its toll at the Manhattan District installations, where the scientists seemed willing to exchange the indecision and restrictions of government service for the opportunities and freedom of academic research. Companies were anxious to pull out too. The du Pont executive committee, which had accepted the Hanford project reluctantly, was already dunning Groves for a replacement. Until the new commission could be established, Groves could do little more than try to hold the line. The Manhattan District, strictly a wartime organization, could not last long on that basis. But just holding the line would carry the General far beyond his wartime powers.

Chafing under the State Department's procrastination, Patterson wondered whether he might not regain the initiative and introduce the Royall-Marbury bill through the Military Affairs Committee. If State did not act over the week end, the new Secretary was determined to make another appeal to the President.[38]

Patterson never had to make that appeal. That same week, Acheson had asked Herbert Marks to prepare a Presidential message to Congress on both domestic and international control. Marks began his draft by recalling that the bomb had shortened the war and saved the lives of "untold thousands of American and Allied soldiers." The bomb, he wrote, marked the beginning of a new era in civilization in which atomic energy might "prove to be more revolutionary . . . than the invention of the wheel, the use of metals, or the steam or internal combustion engine." [39]

Prompt decisions were necessary to preserve "the huge investment in brains and plant" assembled during the war and to control the development of atomic power for peace or war. To accomplish these aims, Marks described the sort of commission proposed in the Royall-Marbury bill, but he was careful to avoid committing the President to any specific measure. Thus, the President would suggest a commission to be "appointed by the President for a term of years" with the consent of the Senate. Marks noted also that the commission should be supported by a full-time administrator and special advisory boards. Much more carefully did he spell out the powers to be

425

granted to the new agency. The commission, in the traditions of a free society, "should be required to adopt policies involving the minimum practical interference with private research and private enterprise." Nonetheless, the commission would control all sources of atomic energy, all plants, materials, research activity, and production related to atomic energy, issue licenses for such activities by others, and establish security regulations. These measures might seem drastic and far-reaching, but atomic energy involved "forces of nature too dangerous to fit into any of our usual concepts."

Then Marks turned to international policy. Again following Stimson's argument, he wrote: "In international relations as in domestic affairs, the release of atomic energy constitutes a new force too revolutionary to fit into old concepts. We can no longer rely on the slow progress of time to develop a program of mutual control among nations." There was a paragraph about the futility of keeping the scientific secret. Then to the alternatives: either the bomb had to be renounced or the world would find itself in "a desperate armaments race." The President would propose to discuss with other nations an agreement "under which cooperation might replace rivalry in the field of atomic power." Marks's language was cautious and general. There was no mention of Russia. A disclaimer that weapons information would be exchanged during these discussions overshadowed a reference to exchanging scientific information. By comparison with other proposals which had been sent to Congress, the Marks draft was short, restrained, and tentative.

The War Department first saw the Marks version on Sunday, September 30. Going over a copy with Harrison, Marks had little difficulty in isolating the differences of opinion. In the first half of the message covering domestic control, Harrison suggested only minor changes. He deleted all references to the administrator or to the advisory boards and sharpened some of the technical language. However, the section dealing with international control gave him trouble. Primarily interested in securing passage of the Royall-Marbury bill, Harrison was reluctant to leave in the message references to international complications which might cause delay in Congress. He favored shortening the international section, not to remove the fundamental proposal of an agreement on international control, but to delete such gratuitous statements as that scientists agreed there were no secrets to keep, that foreign nations could soon catch up with the United States, that there were no effective defensive measures against the bomb, and that the power to destroy had outstripped the capacity for defense. At the end of the message, Harrison added what he hoped would be some insurance against delay on the War Department bill: "But regardless of the course of discussions in the international field, I believe it is essential that legislation along the lines I have indicated be adopted promptly to provide for the situation within the United States."

Accepting all of Harrison's changes except the deletions in the international section, Marks proposed that the revised draft contain both the War

Department and State versions. In this form, Marks sent the message to Judge Samuel I. Rosenman at the White House on Monday, October 1. The master speech-writer expertly trimmed the last remnants of fat from Marks's prose and inserted a few transitional phrases. When he discussed the international section with Patterson and Harrison, he found that they still preferred the War Department version; but, since they did not insist on it, he adopted Marks's language.

The only change was in the section proposing international discussions. In the spirit of the Quebec Agreement, the President would "initiate discussions, first with our associates in this discovery, Great Britain and Canada, and then with other nations." Acheson had the revision in the draft he cleared that afternoon with Lord Halifax, the British ambassador. Cabling the ambassador's reaction to Byrnes in London, Acheson told the Secretary that "the President has decided that he must send to Congress, probably tomorrow, the message regarding the Atomic Energy Commission." [40]

427

On Tuesday, Rosenman ironed out the last wrinkles in the message with Harrison and Marks. Late that afternoon, he joined Acheson, Patterson, and Harrison to discuss it with Senator Alben W. Barkley and Speaker Sam Rayburn, the Administration's leaders on the Hill. Again, the only question was whether the message should include the longer international section. Again Patterson and Harrison expressed their approval of its substance but not of the strategy of including statements which might create a roadblock for domestic legislation. After reading the message twice, Barkley and Rayburn agreed that the international issues had been so generally debated that this section of the message would help rather than hurt passage of the bill.[41]

Thus the message read in Congress closely resembled the first draft which Marks had prepared in the State Department. General in tone, it nevertheless put the President squarely behind the Stimson approach to international control and the War Department proposal for domestic legislation. The Administration had taken two months to formulate just the bare outlines of an atomic energy policy. For one brief moment, Truman had succeeded in fusing the international and domestic issues in one policy statement, but disruptive forces were already at work. Now the two streams abruptly diverged, the international into a long, inconclusive meander, the domestic into a plummeting torrent of public controversy.

CONTROLLING THE ATOM: FROM POLICY TO ACTION

CHAPTER 13

The President's message to Congress on October 3, 1945, laid down the broad principles the Administration would follow in its quest for domestic and international control of atomic energy. Though formulating that policy had been an agonizingly slow process during the summer, the results seemed substantial in retrospect. Meeting what some called the greatest challenge mankind had ever faced was not something to be done in a few hours or days.

Policy, however, was one thing and action another. Carefully skirting the shoals of controversy, the President had fixed the destination but he had not plotted the course. It remained for Byrnes, Acheson, Patterson, and Royall to discover how to translate policy into action.

THE ARMY IN COMMAND

When Rosenman and Acheson left the Capitol late on the afternoon of October 2, 1945, Patterson and Harrison stayed behind to ask the advice of Barkley and Rayburn on a matter close to their hearts. The President's message was a good start, but how could they be sure the Royall-Marbury bill would have a favorable reception in Congress? The legislative leaders suggested they call on Senator Edwin C. Johnson of Colorado, the ranking member of the Military Affairs Committee. Going at once to Johnson's office, the Secretary and his assistant were warmly received. The senator assured them he would be pleased to introduce the bill immediately after the message was read. Presumably, Rayburn would see that Andrew Jackson May, chairman of the House committee, had an opportunity to present the bill in the lower chamber. Now that the international issue was out of the way, Patterson intended to drive for passage of the bill with the aid of the smooth working relationships which the Department had established with the Military Affairs

Committees of both houses. Whatever arrangements Acheson had negotiated with the Foreign Relations Committee would no longer apply to domestic legislation.

If Patterson anticipated streamlined action on the bill, he was doomed to disappointment. True to his word, Senator Johnson introduced the measure and moved its referral to the Military Affairs Committee. Vandenberg objected. Maintaining that the bill went far beyond the usual competence of a standing committee, the minority leader argued the matter should be considered by the special joint committee to be established by his concurrent resolution which the Senate had approved on September 27. With Barkley joining Johnson, the three veteran senators carried the debate through most of the October 4 session. By a parliamentary maneuver, Vandenberg prevented referral of Johnson's bill to any committee pending House action on his concurrent resolution. Thus were the opposing forces stalemated before the battle had really begun.[1]

Beneath Vandenberg's outward concern for parliamentary proprieties, one could detect other motivations: a challenge to executive authority, distrust of the alliance between the Army and the Military Affairs Committee, defense of the prerogatives of the Senate and the Foreign Relations Committee, and support of the minority party position. Another factor was Senator Lucas' support of Vandenberg, a move strongly suggesting the influence of the Chicago scientists.

In the House, events moved more according to the Army plan. On October 3, May introduced the bill, which Rayburn immediately referred to the Military Affairs Committee. Vandenberg's concurrent resolution had been reported back to the House floor, but there seemed little chance that the measure would ever come to a vote. Representative Oren Harris, who had introduced the resolution in the House, told the press he understood the President was supporting the War Department bill, and he thought there was little reason to anticipate action on his resolution.[2]

May promptly scheduled hearings on the bill before the Military Affairs Committee. He wasted no time when the committee assembled on October 9.[3] In six sentences, he stated the purpose of the hearing and noted that all the witnesses were "very busy men, who like the committee, have to be at work all the time." Plunging ahead, he asked the Secretary of War to present his prepared statement.

Patterson maintained the chairman's pace. Quick action, he said, was necessary to bring this new force under control. The bill reflected the views of those who had developed the bomb; it embodied all the points on domestic legislation in the President's October 3 message; it had been reviewed by the appropriate executive departments and by the President himself. The nation should set its domestic house in order before tackling the far-reaching international issues. Thus, the War Department had "taken the initiative in proposing that it be divested of the great authority that goes with the con-

429

trol of atomic energy, because it recognizes that the problems we now face go far beyond the purely military sphere." The War Department bill, he said, would place control of this terrible force in the hands of men who "would be representative of all that is best in our national life—men of demonstrated wisdom and judgment who would accept appointment not because of any emoluments that might attend their membership but rather because of a profound recognition of the significance of atomic power to the future of civilization."

Even the Secretary's brief remarks did not seem to relieve the pressure of time. Since Groves had an early engagement, the committee deferred questioning Patterson until the General had testified. In a prepared five-minute statement, Groves hit the same note of urgency and the need for responsible action.

Only then did the pace slacken. Other members of the committee persisted in questioning Groves on security. Would the bill permit the commission or the President to give away the secret of the bomb? Could a leak give another nation a significant advantage? Should scientists and technicians in the Manhattan project be permitted to travel abroad? Groves handled these questions deftly and confidently. The only secrets, he said, lay not in the basic scientific information but in "the ingenuity and skill of the American worker and the American management."

Both Bush and Conant had anticipated the next turn of the discussion. Why was it necessary, the committee asked, to grant the commission "plenary supervision and direction . . . over all matters connected with atomic research, the production of atomic fission and the release of nuclear energy"? Had the General exercised such extraordinary powers during the war? Groves admitted he had not used them all. He was not sure they would be necessary in peacetime, but he thought the commission should have such powers to meet its overwhelming responsibilities.

Bush led off the afternoon session. Concentrating on research, he explained how the proposed legislation complemented Magnuson's bill for a national research foundation. The atomic energy bill, he said, emphasized control and regulation. It also encouraged research on special applications of atomic energy and would supplement the foundation's general support of research. Bush was convinced that, far from imposing crippling restrictions on research, the bill would encourage universities to resume the activities now languishing in the absence of federal support and direction.

The heart of the question was the commission's authority. Under persistent questioning, Bush admitted that except for power over appropriations and the basic act, Congress would divest itself of all control over atomic energy. The commission's powers would be extraordinary, but so was the situation the nation faced. As Bush explained: "I certainly, as a citizen living in this country after the war, want to see rigid Federal control of what is done in this area. I certainly do not wish to think that some group of experimenters might set up a laboratory half a mile from my house and family and experiment on atomic energy carelessly, poison the neighborhood, or possibly blow it up."

Conant reiterated Bush's warning. Somberly, he read from the first section of the bill: "The misuse of such energy, by design or through ignorance, may inflict incalculable disaster upon the Nation, destroy the general welfare, imperil the national safety, and endanger world peace." The Harvard president found it difficult to convey the deep feelings with which he read those words, but as one who had witnessed "the tremendous illumination that burst all over the sky" at Alamogordo, he was convinced that extraordinary controls were mandatory.

When Conant finished, Patterson returned to answer a few factual questions. At a little past four, Chairman May thanked the War Department witnesses. The committee would go at once into executive session to consider the bill. As far as the Military Affairs Committee was concerned, the hearings on atomic energy were over.

431

SCIENTISTS TO THE ALARM

Congressman May now anticipated no trouble in reporting the bill back to the House before the end of the week, but more discerning participants could detect some disturbing undertones in the day's proceedings. The committee's preoccupation with security and the broad powers proposed for the commission confirmed the War Department's fears that Congress might attempt to restrict the commission's freedom of action. It also seemed likely that this negative emphasis which had dominated the day's hearings would arouse the opposition of many scientists who were already sensitive about restrictions on research.

Nor was the War Department wrong. The publication of the "May-Johnson bill," followed by reports of the one-day hearing, aroused the scientists to opposition. Taking a cue from the physicists at the Metallurgical Laboratory, the Chicago *Sun* ran banner headlines charging that the Army was trying to muzzle the atomic scientists in order to "railroad" legislation through Congress. The new associations at Chicago and Oak Ridge issued press releases warning against the dangers of hasty legislation. Before considering specific bills, members of Congress should have ample opportunity to acquaint themselves with the facts in extensive hearings before a special nonpartisan committee.[4]

Privately, many of the scientists felt themselves betrayed. Their Washington representatives had assured them that the Royall-Marbury draft was a "good" bill, that its passage would assure rapid progress in developing atomic power. Dismayed by the vague, sweeping provisions of the May-Johnson bill, some chose to read into its clauses a crude attempt by Groves and the Navy to seize control of the project by placing military officers in the jobs of administrator and deputy administrator while Bush and Conant, too busy for full-time service, kept a hand on the project as part-time commissioners. Others found the security provisions frightening. Could they not be interpreted as enabling the commission to jail a scientist for ten years and fine him $10,000 for violating a security regulation he never knew existed? How could physics professors in their classrooms segregate scientific data according to arbitrary rules established by the commission? Herbert L. Anderson, a Chicago physicist, wrote to a friend at Los Alamos: "I must confess my confidence in our own leaders Oppenheimer, Lawrence, Compton, and Fermi, all members of the Scientific Panel, . . . who enjoined us to have faith in them and not influence this legislation, is shaken. I believe that these worthy men were duped—that they never had a chance to see this bill. Let us beware of any breach of our rights as men and citizens. The war is won, let us be free again!" [5]

432

The young physicist who wrote this letter was unaware of the turmoil these reactions were creating in Washington. That same morning, October 11, both Conant and Patterson had called Harrison and suggested a meeting of the Scientific Panel. There were also reports that Szilard had denounced the bill. Harrison sounded out Oppenheimer by phone. The Los Alamos leader was inclined to discount Szilard's criticisms as overly conscientious and not necessarily representative of the true feeling at Chicago and Oak Ridge. Oppenheimer believed a statement from the panel might set the record straight. Before the end of the day, he persuaded Fermi and Lawrence to join him in a telegram to Harrison urging prompt passage of the May-Johnson bill. Delay would be costly, the telegram read, but with wisdom atomic research could continue within the framework of the bill. The broad powers granted the commission were justified "by the importance and perils of the subject." The three physicists added: "We assure you that in our opinion the legislation as presented represents the fruits of well informed and experienced consideration." Hoping that publication of the telegram would momentarily stem the tide of opposition, Oppenheimer made plans to meet the Scientific Panel in Washington on Wednesday, October 17.[6]

Not until the panel assembled at the Pentagon were the true sentiments of its members known. As Anderson had guessed, the panel members had not read the May-Johnson bill carefully before their public endorsement was released. Only Compton had been cautious enough to withhold his judgment until he had studied the bill. Now all the members had reservations on the security provisions, especially those imposing heavy penalties for the unauthorized release of classified information. Letters from other prominent scientists supported the panel's sentiments. Lee A. Dubridge, writing for 300 scientists in the Boston area, raised similar objections. Karl Compton, while strongly supporting the bill, suggested that some revision of the security sections might be necessary.[7]

To some extent, the shift to a more cautious attitude among the Scientific Panel must have reflected the impact of the joint hearings before the Senate Military Affairs and Commerce Committees on the Magnuson and Kilgore bills to establish a national science foundation. Starting on October 8, the committee had heard a steady stream of prominent witnesses including Cabinet officers, renowned scientists, and university presidents. The common testimony was that such a foundation was necessary but that the dangers of federal control were to be avoided at all costs. Isaiah Bowman, president of The Johns Hopkins University, summed up the argument: "I am against federal support of scientific research if this brings political management and if the top command is to be appointed for reasons other than the highest available scientific competence and political disinterestedness." Some of these fears had been allayed by the testimony from Bush, Patterson, Oppenheimer, and a number of military officers earlier in the week, but certainly the nation's scientists were as a group deeply concerned about government control of research.[8]

433

President Truman was singularly unimpressed by the clamor among the scientists. He let it be known on Capitol Hill that he expected the bill to be reported in the House on October 17. But the reservations of the Scientific Panel, the uproar in the Manhattan laboratories, and the tenor of the Magnuson-Kilgore hearings caused Patterson to relent. He agreed to open the hearings for another day of testimony, this time by the critics representing the Chicago scientists. Royall drafted amendments to clarify the safeguards against the misuse of the bill's security provisions. Patterson was determined, however, to ram the measure through as quickly as possible. He could not forget the dangerous tendencies of the first hearing. Surely, the scientists "did not realize that by delaying action and raising all sorts of objections to the present bill, they may very well end up with a much more stringent measure than is now before the Committee." Oppenheimer volunteered to see Szilard, Urey, and Anderson before they testified on October 18. Perhaps it was not too late to head off a public wrangle.[9]

SECOND HEARING

The October 18 hearing before the May committee did little to heal the breach.[10] From the outset there was an air of hostility as the chairman announced that the hearings had been resumed "for the purpose of permitting a group of interested people, known as scientists, to present their views." Taking this cue, some members of the committee made an obvious attempt to embarrass Leo Szilard, the first witness, by questioning him about his long-standing patent controversy with the Manhattan District. Some of the scientists who attended the hearing were convinced that the committee had been coached by officers from Groves's staff.

Szilard's testimony was tolerated as the questionable opinion of an unorthodox individual. At times, his torrent of original ideas and insights captured the imagination of his questioners; but before Szilard finished, the committee was growing restless because of his inability to confine himself to simple, unqualified statements. The exchange with Herbert Anderson was even less gratifying. He took such an inflexible position against the commission's power to regulate nuclear research that he succeeded only in antagonizing Chairman May.

In the afternoon session, the atmosphere was friendlier. Arthur Compton exhibited the skill in oral exchange that came from many years of teaching and academic administration. He was firm but patient. His sweet reasonableness could not fail to win the committee. Compton found the bill essentially acceptable in its present form, though he regretted the tendency toward negative and repressive language. Compton agreed that both the control and development of atomic energy were important, but he wanted to emphasize development more than the bill did.

The last witness was Oppenheimer, who spoke frankly in defense of the bill. May served up the questions and Oppenheimer lobbed back the answers in a facile and confident style. He assured the chairman that the President should be able to find nine reasonably intelligent and conscientious men to execute the provisions of the bill. Oppenheimer admitted it would be better if the commission's powers could be more sharply defined, but he thought that impossible in such a new and rapidly changing science. He refused to share his colleagues' fears of military domination. The purpose of the bill, he reminded his listeners, was to get the Army out of the project, not to put it into the War Department. So forthright was this disclaimer that Chairman May could not restrain himself: "The War Department discovered the weapon. Why can they not keep the secret?"

Urey was to testify next, but he had wandered off to Senator Glen Taylor's office, which had become an unofficial headquarters for the scientists. May growled that Urey's statement could be printed in the record. With a bang of the gavel, he adjourned the hearing.

As a last attempt to allay fear and suspicion, Patterson issued a statement which Bush had suggested weeks earlier, encouraging the scientists as informed citizens to join in the public discussion of atomic control. The scientists had already recognized their obligation. During the last two weeks of October, criticism of the May-Johnson bill mounted. The most common charges were that the bill placed intolerable restrictions on scientific research and that it severely undercut efforts to establish international control.

Compton did his best to temper the extravagant statements from the Chicago and Oak Ridge laboratories. He stood by the May-Johnson bill with minor amendments. To the Army, he suggested small changes in the phraseology which seemed especially irritating to the scientists. But the gap between the two camps was widening day by day. Hastily formed associations of scientists, public figures, and university professors joined the chorus: "We urge withdrawal of the May Bill. We further urge full and extended hearings on this or any other legislation pertaining to atomic energy." [11]

Secretary Patterson had reason to be discouraged. Despite the weeks of study and planning which the War Department had invested in the bill, his worst fears were coming true. One of the most critical issues to face the nation was becoming entangled in political controversy and irresponsible emotionalism. But where did the fault lie? It took a man like Karl Compton, who had been on both sides of the issue, to see it in its full context. He was certain that "the bill was prepared and introduced with the wisest of motives and that back of it there is nothing of the sinister intent which some people, including a good many of our scientists have suspected."

At the same time, there was no question that the bill was badly handled. The War Department had underestimated public interest in the measure and the sudden shift in attitude toward the military and leaders of the war effort. The same men who could command unquestioned support for a two-billion-dollar secret project a few months earlier were now looked upon as power-hungry connivers. The decision to hasten the bill through the military affairs committees of Congress, the clumsy impatience of Andrew May, the badgering of witnesses, the indefinite powers which the bill granted to the commission were all elements of human shortsightedness, pettiness, and folly. No one person had set in motion this complex chain of events, and if anyone were to blame it was not Patterson. The Secretary of War, nonetheless, would bear the burden of the prolonged struggle. Indeed, new troubles were about to harass him.

435

IN SENATE AND WHITE HOUSE

While the May committee and the War Department were doing their best to expedite the May-Johnson bill, other forces were already at work in the Senate and the White House.

Early in October, Senator Vandenberg had succeeded in bottling up the May-Johnson bill by parliamentary maneuver. He hoped to force the House to act on his concurrent resolution establishing a special joint committee to study atomic energy legislation. During the following week, when the May committee held its first abbreviated hearing, Vandenberg knew his resolution was dead. The next best approach would be to create a special committee in the Senate alone. Senator McMahon had suggested such a measure on October 4. Five days later, he introduced a resolution establishing a special committee which would not only study the subject but also consider all bills and resolutions related to it. [12]

While the McMahon resolution ran the gantlet of committee clearance, the young Connecticut senator made his plans. Like others, he had been deeply impressed by the dramatic events of August, 1945. One of his favorite statements on the Senate floor was that the bombing of Hiroshima was the greatest event in world history since the birth of Jesus Christ. Profoundly moved, he began to ponder ways of integrating this new force into the fabric of national government and international relations. He had introduced the first bill on atomic energy in the Senate, a slapdash proposal that, although it received little attention, established his claim to Senate leadership in a new field of legislation. For a freshman senator, this was the opportunity of a lifetime.

McMahon hovered over the Senate debates like a hawk. Vandenberg had surprised him with his concurrent resolution, but the House had killed that measure. Now with his own resolution providing for a special Senate committee, McMahon cautiously approached Vandenberg and Kenneth McKellar, who as president pro tempore would appoint the members of a special committee. McMahon satisfied himself that Vandenberg had no personal interest in the question but was rather trying to prevent a fragmenting of the issue which would lead to irresponsible legislation. To McKellar, McMahon tactfully advanced his claim to the chairmanship of the committee on the grounds that he had introduced the legislation establishing it.

On the Senate floor, Johnson attempted to capture control of the committee by arguing for appointment on the basis of seniority. But with Vandenberg's and Barkley's support McMahon carried the day. On October 23, the Senate established a special committee of eleven members. Three days later, McKellar appointed McMahon chairman. The young senator had his work cut out for him. In addition to Johnson, McKellar named such veteran Democrats as Richard B. Russell of Georgia, Tom Connally of Texas, Harry F. Byrd of Virginia, and Millard E. Tydings of Maryland. All conservatives, they were no more so than the Republican members—Vandenberg, Warren R. Austin of Vermont, Eugene D. Millikin of Colorado, Bourke B. Hickenlooper of Iowa, and Thomas C. Hart of Connecticut. For McMahon, the odds were poor, but the prize seemed worth the effort.[13]

In October, 1945, there were already two sources of interest in atomic energy within the President's own staff. One of these was centered around James R. Newman, John Snyder's assistant in the Office of War Mobilization and Reconversion and former assistant to Secretary Patterson. A lawyer interested in administration, Newman had an extraordinarily broad background. An authority on the literature of science and mathematics, he had a genuine understanding of the principles of science. Like almost no one else in the Administration, he had some conception of the dismaying scientific discoveries which had suddenly overtaken the American people. Better than most scientists, he could comprehend the political and administrative barriers to atomic legislation. The struggle was much more than a political cat fight. It had broader implications. It represented the first attempt to incorporate an incredibly dangerous, mysterious force into the life of the nation. Newman understood how the American people could think of atomic energy only in terms of the bomb, but this was much too narrow a perspective. "This new force," he wrote, "offers enormous possibilities for improving public welfare, for revamping our industrial methods and for increasing the standard of living. Properly developed and harnessed, atomic energy can achieve improvement in our lot equalling and perhaps exceeding the tremendous accomplishments made possible through the discovery and use of electricity."

From this perspective, Newman found the May-Johnson bill inadequate. It overemphasized military uses and failed to stress the potentially more significant civilian applications. To realize its full possibilities, atomic energy would have to be broadly understood and utilized, not isolated and hoarded as a fearsome weapon of destruction. The commission should not stand in splendid isolation but should be part of the Executive Branch with a program consistent with Administration policy. The work of the commission should be expanded to include increasing man's understanding of atomic energy and its social, political, and economic effects. The commission should support a vigorous program of research and make applications of these new discoveries available to all the people. To carry out these aims, Newman saw the need for full-time commissioners of varied backgrounds. He suggested two members from public life, two from the armed services, and one each from the physical sciences, social sciences, management, labor, and agriculture. The administrator, he believed, should be a civilian.

437

As for the commission's powers, Newman was concerned that the May-Johnson bill contained no reference to the Magnuson and Kilgore measures. Showing his predilection for the Kilgore approach, Newman thought the bill should be tightened by providing expressly for a commission monopoly of all nuclear materials and production facilities. Likewise, he contended that all patents on devices developed in federally-sponsored research should be held by the commission, which would grant royalty-free licenses to private users. He also believed that the commission's power to dismiss any person from public or private employment for violating security regulations should be conditioned on conviction in a court of record.

These arguments Newman embodied in a memorandum which Snyder sent to the President on October 15. Receiving a favorable response, Snyder asked Newman to summarize for the White House the public criticism which was pouring into Washington from scientists and administrators. Under greatest attack, Newman reported, were the commission's plenary powers in many areas—to negotiate contracts, issue regulations and enforce them, control independent research, employ personnel, appropriate property and information, and establish security regulations and penalties. But the greatest danger of all was the tremendous power of the administrator, who would not be subject to control by the commission or the President. Newman suggested that it would be almost impossible to remove the commissioners for action taken by the administrator. "It is vitally important," he wrote Truman, "if you are to preserve the freedom of these United States that the Administrator be appointed by you and not by the Commission." [14]

If Truman was not moved to action, he at least recognized the need to formulate an Administration position. On October 18, he asked OWMR to co-ordinate executive action on the twenty-one points outlined in his reconversion message of September 6. Although the message to Congress did not mention atomic energy specifically, Truman saw fit to use it as a basis for assigning OWMR responsibility for atomic energy legislation. With this mandate, Newman could prepare for battle. [15]

In the Bureau of the Budget, Harold D. Smith felt some of the same fears that haunted Newman. Early in October, he had expressed his views before the Magnuson-Kilgore committees: "I believe that science has far more to gain than to lose by being brought into the main stream of public affairs as a more active force in our governmental system. For research requires the support that only our public resources can provide, and the power of science can be too far-reaching for it to grow in a state of irresponsible detachment." [16]

To keep track of such subtle threats to executive authority, Smith had enlisted the service of Don K. Price, a former Rhodes scholar who had come to Washington from the Public Administration Clearing House in Chicago. While reviewing War Department comments on various atomic energy bills, Price was struck by Patterson's stock reference to the May-Johnson bill as "representing the views of the Administration as well as of the War Department."

After studying the provisions of the May-Johnson bill, Price was not so sure the President should permit such an endorsement, and reported his misgivings to Smith. In a memorandum to the President, Smith claimed the bill would make the commission "virtually independent of Executive control." He noted the commission would serve only part-time and would be exempt from conflict-of-interest statutes. With nine-year terms, only three members would come up for reappointment during any Administration. The bill also would severely limit the President's removal power. Smith thought any force as far-reaching as atomic energy should be under the President's control. "Full control by the Executive," he concluded, "is the most effective means to insure control by the Congress, to which the President is accountable for the administration of the Government." [17]

Truman's reaction to the Smith memorandum was immediate. He informed Patterson that the May-Johnson bill did not represent his final views on the subject. Then the President wrote to Smith: "I think that before we definitely commit ourselves to the May-Johnson Bill there should be some conferences between the War Department and those who have submitted criticisms about it, including your own." [18]

Before Snyder could schedule a White House meeting, the Military

438

Affairs Committee completed its revisions of the May-Johnson bill. In a long executive session on October 24, General Royall presented a series of amendments which he had drafted after conferences with the National Academy of Sciences and other scientific organizations. Various sections had been amended "to make it absolutely clear that private research in this field can be carried on without interference from the Commission . . . and to bring out still further the Congressional policy that the Commission should encourage research and development." Other amendments reduced the broad, independent powers of the administrator and made that official in most cases a subordinate of the commission. The penalties for security violations were reduced, and other minor changes were made to remove some of the exceptions from standard Government procedures.

The committee approved these amendments quickly, but the members found it impossible to agree among themselves on a fundamental point of the bill. Representatives Chet Holifield of California and Melvin Price of Illinois were convinced that the commission should be composed of full-time, well-paid members; that they should be subject to the President's normal removal powers, and that the administrator should be a civilian appointed by the President. Failing to secure agreement within the committee, May submitted his majority report on November 5, 1945. Holifield and Price added a minority report as did the Republican members of the committee.[19]

439

MARSHALLING THE OPPOSITION

Once aware of the dangers implicit in the May-Johnson bill, the President had not hesitated to jerk the rug from under Patterson and May. He privately withdrew his endorsement of the bill, but he offered no substitute. That would have to come from those who sounded the alarm: McMahon's new committee, OWMR, the Bureau of the Budget, and the rapidly multiplying associations of scientists.

On Capitol Hill, Senator McMahon was trying to breathe life into his committee. Completely unversed in the fundamental issues facing him, McMahon knew that he could scarcely rely on help from his colleagues. They may have been steeped in the ways of traditional politics, but most of them probably knew even less than he about atomic energy. If McMahon were to survive politically as chairman of the committee, he would need the help of an experienced guide—someone who could understand the broad meaning of technical terminology and who had some conception of science legislation. It was not surprising that he thought of Newman, whom he had met the previous summer at the home of Helen Gahagan Douglas, a representative from California. Somewhat leery of Newman's New-Dealish tendencies, McMahon nevertheless liked his smooth, articulate manner and the broad sweep of his intellect. The senator had heard reports of Newman's work in

OWMR as liaison officer between OSRD and the White House and the enthusiasm with which he led the assault on the Magnuson and May-Johnson bills. A check with Newman's former boss, Secretary of the Treasury Fred Vinson, confirmed his appraisal. Vinson thought Newman possessed "a unique combination of talents" as an extremely able lawyer and a man of considerable scientific training.[20]

On the last week end in October, Newman left Washington to attend a conference in Rye, New York, sponsored by a group of social scientists and educators headed by Robert M. Hutchins and Robert Redfield of the University of Chicago.[21] Newman had been invited to attend because the purpose of the meeting was to organize opposition to the May-Johnson bill. When he arrived in New York City, he received a telegram from McMahon informing him that the special committee had been named and asking him to return at once to Washington. At breakfast at McMahon's home on Sunday morning, October 28, Newman found the senator facing the task with mixed emotions. He was tremendously pleased about his designation as chairman of the committee and terribly discouraged by the conservative bias of its membership. Newman agreed to serve as the committee's special counsel. In this position, he could give the committee the technical support it needed. He did not intend, however, to take over the usual administrative duties of an executive director. These would be given to Christopher T. Boland, a young lawyer McMahon had known for many years.

As Newman saw it, education should be the committee's first concern. How could the members hope to approach the questions of legislation intelligently unless they had some understanding of the nature of nuclear research and the problems peculiar to atomic energy? He believed that the committee members should first subject themselves to a period of self-education. Then, after a reasonable time, they could start hearings on the May-Johnson bill. There would be pressure from the War Department for immediate action, but Newman saw no need to hurry. Understanding the issues first was more important. More than a political body, the committee would be something approaching a seminar on science legislation. This emphasis would demand some expert talent to start the education process. Newman pondered the idea of establishing a panel of scientists or at least choosing one nuclear physicist to advise the committee on technical subjects.[22]

Over McMahon's name Newman sent letters to twenty-two scientists and educators asking for their recommendations. Many names were submitted, but high on the list was that of Edward U. Condon, who had just been selected to replace Lyman Briggs as director of the National Bureau of Standards. Newman had met Condon several weeks earlier, when Leo Szilard brought him to Newman's office. Szilard, in town for his appearances before the Kilgore and May committees, told Newman jokingly that he brought Condon with him because he had an honest, farm-boy face which reassured those who were made uncomfortable by Szilard's Hungarian accent. Newman was aware of Condon's work at Los Alamos during the war, though he knew none of the details. He had been captivated by Condon's sparkling personality and good humor. On November 6, he announced Condon's appointment as the committee's scientific adviser.[23]

Meanwhile, Newman had not neglected his OWMR responsibilities. Not able himself to bear the full burden of drafting legislation, Newman turned to Thomas I. Emerson, the OWMR general counsel. Emerson suggested Byron S. Miller, a young lawyer who had worked in his office at OPA. With Government experience during the war, Miller had both the precision and knowledge necessary to capture Newman's torrent of ideas and subject them to the strictures of legislative terminology.

In the weeks following release of the May-Johnson bill, the two lawyers spent hours discussing atomic energy legislation. Miller made an exhaustive analysis of the bill, which Judge Rosenman sent to the War Department. They had incorporated many of their ideas in the memorandums which had helped to alert the President to the hazards of the War Department bill.

441

These projects made it easy for Newman and Miller to cast their broad principles in legislative form during the closing days of October, 1945. As an opening declaration of policy, they wrote: "The effect of the use of atomic energy for civilian purposes cannot now be determined. But it is reasonable to anticipate that tapping this new source of energy will cause profound changes in our present way of life." The nation must, they reasoned, develop atomic energy not only for military security but also to improve public welfare, raise the standard of living, and strengthen free competition in private enterprise. To do this, the commission would require the constant services of experts with a variety of talents. Thus, Newman and Miller provided for a nine-man, full-time commission whose members would be required to qualify in the range of disciplines set forth in the October 15 memorandum to the President. Furthermore, the commission would be closely tied to the Executive Branch by provisions that the commissioners and administrator be appointed by the President and be subject to his normal removal powers.[24]

Newman and Miller had a second principle—to give the new commission the responsibility and power to encourage and support atomic research. It was one thing to use the vaguely permissive language of the May-Johnson bill and quite another to spell out such powers in positive terms. If some kinds of research were to be free from commission control, the limits on commission authority would have to be sharply defined. This sort of definition relied on a sound understanding of nuclear research and production processes.

For this sort of technical assistance, Miller depended upon the atomic scientists. His best contacts were with Chicago, where he had taken his law degree before the war. In Washington he had kept in touch with

Edward H. Levi, a member of the law faculty who served as special assistant to Attorney General Clark. Levi's Washington experience helped the atomic scientists after he returned to the university. Like Miller, he had been drafted by his colleagues to prepare critiques of the May-Johnson bill soon after its release. Patiently during the following weeks he tried to answer the endless questions which Szilard and other scientists posed in long evening sessions in his home. Guiding as best he could the impassioned but diffuse efforts of the scientists in legal draftsmanship, Levi completed in November a Chicago version of an atomic energy bill. Though covering all the proposed agency's functions in a general way, the bill reflected Chicago's special interest in providing for federal support of research with minimum controls.[25]

442

There was no evidence that specific sections of the Levi draft were incorporated in the Newman-Miller bill, but some interest in its research provisions must have rubbed off on Miller during his visits to the Midway. Certainly, the positive approach to the commission's research responsibilities was one of the striking features of the OWMR draft.[26] Section 3 authorized and directed the commission to encourage independent research by supplying fissionable material without charge to all persons meeting the standards of personal safety and military security established by the commission. Beyond these minimum standards, the commission was not to restrict or control independent research. The commission itself was empowered to conduct research either in its own facilities or through contracts or grants, the only restriction being that such awards be made in accordance with the policies of the proposed national science foundation. The bill also asserted the commission's absolute control of patents arising from such activities when financed by federal funds. Privately financed research in atomic energy presumably would be completely free, except for the commission's right of inspection to enforce safety and security standards.

With the research provisions strengthened, the bill also had to contain a distinction between the commission's research and production activities. So inadequate was the understanding of most laymen that few could then see the possibility of isolating within the area of military security the authentic secrets involved in production and fabrication techniques while leaving in the area of freedom the study of natural phenomena which were impossible to classify. While the commission would have limited powers to control research, its authority in production and utilization would be greater than that provided by the May-Johnson bill. Newman and Miller wished to make certain, as did responsible scientists, that the legitimate secrets of technology were protected. Their thinking was also dominated by strong antimonopoly sentiments.

The trick was to find some legal concept which would draw a practical line between the commission's proper responsibilities and all those other secondary activities in which control was not essential. The device Newman and Miller proposed was to give the commission complete control over the production and utilization of "fissionable materials" and then to permit the commission to establish some specific definition of that phrase. The draft completed on November 5 did not contain a precise definition, but it appeared to include uranium ores and concentrates, feed materials, enriched uranium 233 and 235, plutonium, special materials such as heavy water, and of course weapons. All these materials would fall under commission control. Title to all such materials would rest with the commission as would all patents on piles and other utilization devices. Production activities would be limited to the commission alone, while private industry could engage in utilization activities only under commission license.

This framework automatically circumscribed the commission's powers to impose and enforce security regulations. The vague limitations on these powers in the May-Johnson bill had drawn some of the heaviest fire from its critics. Under the Newman-Miller proposal, the contract and license became the instruments for controlling private activities within the security area; all others were either completely free or completely prohibited outside the commission according to the definition of "fissionable materials." The OWMR drafters relied on this formula rather than any reduction in the penalties for security violations to counter the scientists' objections to controls.

443

THE ISSUE JOINED

Whether the Newman-Miller draft would ever be introduced in Congress as a bill was not at all clear in early November, 1945, but it did serve an immediate purpose in helping OWMR to formulate recommendations for the White House conference which the President had requested on the May-Johnson bill. Newman and Miller prepared a lengthy analysis of the War Department bill which Snyder distributed within the Administration. Giving his colleagues a few days to study the OWMR comments, Snyder called a meeting in his White House office on November 7. The session quickly revealed that Patterson and Royall would oppose Ickes, Wallace, and Frederick J. Bailey, who spoke for the Bureau of the Budget. Lewis L. Strauss, representing the Navy, maintained his neutrality by saying little. Patterson, while not necessarily against every opinion of the civilian agencies, in every instance expressed his preference for the provisions of the May-Johnson bill.

The OWMR analysis reiterated most of the arguments which Newman and Miller had presented in their memorandums to the President and in the draft bill.[27] They concentrated their attack on two points in the War Department measure: the commission's independence from Presidential or Congressional control and its vaguely defined powers in regulating atomic energy activities. Ickes, Wallace, and Bailey agreed with Snyder that the President should appoint the administrator as well as the commission, with full powers of removal. They also agreed that military officers on active duty should not be permitted to serve as administrator. No one suggested, however, that the military be excluded from the commission.

The first major difference of opinion among the civilian agency heads occurred on the qualifications of the commissioners. Snyder asserted Newman's position that they should serve full-time and represent a broad range of disciplines. Here Ickes revived his earlier argument for a commission of Cabinet officers and other Government officials operating as an advisory body to the administrator, who would direct day-to-day operations. Both Wallace and Bailey supported Ickes, while Patterson maintained the War Department's advocacy of a part-time body. Snyder and Newman, however, were not alone in their stand for the full-time commission. The minority report by Holifield and Price on the May-Johnson bill suggested substantial Congressional support for the idea.

The meeting also revealed a difference of opinion on the scope of the commission's powers. On the one hand, all agreed that control over independent research should be limited to matters of public safety and military security. On the other, both Wallace and Ickes agreed with Snyder that the commission should own all supplies of fissionable materials and all patents on their production. Ickes and Snyder likewise approved of private patents on "atomic energy devices," such as piles and radiation sources. Wallace believed that such patents should be granted to private companies when the holders agreed to grant nonexclusive licenses for reasonable royalties.

All three civilian agency heads found the security provisions and penalties in the May-Johnson bill too extreme. Snyder proposed that all security regulations be subject to Presidential approval. His colleagues also agreed that commission employees should be dismissed for willful or grossly negligent security violations only after court conviction.

Beyond these specific objections, the civilian trio disliked the tone of the May-Johnson bill. Wallace later wrote to Truman: "It is important to place *much more* emphasis on the peacetime development of atomic energy. We must recognize that the development of atomic energy for industrial purposes may soon be of much greater concern to the nation and have greater effect on our economy and our way of life than the atomic bomb." Snyder suggested a general recasting of the bill to emphasize peacetime uses. Specifically, he favored a provision authorizing the commission to study the social, economic, and political effects of atomic energy, an idea that came straight from Newman.

Having led the Administration forces in the quest for atomic energy legislation, Patterson now found himself cut off with the May committee on the untenable ground furnished by the May-Johnson bill. First he had lost the support of the rank-and-file scientists in the Manhattan District laboratories by his excessive zeal in ramming the bill through the abbreviated hearings. Then the Senate had deserted him by demanding the Special Committee, which Vandenberg and McMahon had combined forces to establish. Now the heavy assault on the bill at the November 7 meeting served notice on the Secretary that he could not hope for Administration support without extensive revision. If he refused to pay that price, Patterson must have seen that the new McMahon committee would be in an excellent position to present an alternative. That, in fact, was the destiny Newman intended for the draft bill which he and Miller had completed just a few days earlier. The McMahon committee had not yet met, and the President had not yet publicly repudiated the May-Johnson bill. But, given the existing trend of events, both developments could be expected soon.

Whatever happened, Patterson now saw little hope of establishing an effective and powerful commission free from political entanglements. It seemed to him ironic that the scientists who stood to lose most by delay were largely responsible for the unhappy turn of events. Scientists like Bush, Conant, Oppenheimer, and the Compton brothers, with their broad experience in government, seemed to understand his position. It was the "little" scientist, full of idealism and overwhelmed by the monstrous threat he had created for mankind, who seemed unreasonable. "To my mind," the Secretary wrote Arthur Compton, "the bill merits real support from scientists rather than the well-nigh hysterical criticism it has received from some quarters." [28] Perhaps he was thinking of Urey's speech a few days earlier at Columbia University. Urey was quoted as saying that the May-Johnson bill was the "first totalitarian bill ever written by Congress. . . . You can call it either a Communist bill or a Nazi bill, whichever you think is the worse." [29]

Perhaps some of the criticism was exaggerated and unwarranted, but the conflict was now more than a misunderstanding of terms. A new alliance of scientists and senators had joined the issue. The May-Johnson bill could no longer be adopted without a fight.

THE RELUCTANT LOBBY

Patterson's ill-fated strategy also helped to drive the local associations of scientists toward national organization. At first, each group saw its task to be primarily one of education within its own community. For example, during September the Atomic Scientists of Chicago made no effort to contact groups at other sites and were scarcely aware of their existence. Pleased with the rapid growth of the Chicago organization, Simpson was shocked by the sudden threat of the May-Johnson bill. He realized that its introduction had taken him by surprise only because his group was not close enough to events in Washington. Reluctantly, he recognized the need for a listening post in the capital. The financial and professional sacrifices of such a move were more than he could ask of most of his colleagues. As a young bachelor and leader of the Chicago group, he decided to take the assignment himself. He would have to set aside his promising career as a research scientist and go off to Washington for an indefinite period, probably until his scanty savings were exhausted. The Chicago group had no funds to support him, but President Hutchins agreed to continue his salary.

After a few weeks in Washington, he found that by pinching pennies and living in a cheap hotel, he would be able to stay indefinitely. Certainly the experience was worth the sacrifice. He was encouraged to find scientists from the other laboratories in town with the same purpose in mind. During the day, they buttonholed congressmen on Capitol Hill or chatted with friendly reporters looking for a story. Later, they hobnobbed with Cabinet officers and ambassadors at teas or cocktail parties given by sympathetic socialites like Mrs. Gifford Pinchot. Remembering the harsh treatment dealt Szilard and Anderson at the May committee hearings, the young atomic scientists were pleased by the warm reception accorded them. No one in Washington seemed to know anything about atomic energy, but everyone was eager to learn. At the hearings on science legislation, the Kilgore committee sat in undisguised awe as Oppenheimer, with a charming combination of modesty and understatement, described the spectacular power of the fission process. Simpson and his friends may not have reached this height, but for a junior professor of physics, it was exhilarating to find oneself the center of attention among political leaders in Washington.

There was, however, more than excitement and entertainment. Simpson and his colleagues learned things about national politics that their fellows in the laboratories never dreamed of. Atomic energy had made a deep, initial impression on Washington, but it had not swept all other issues from the legislative calendar. The envoys from the laboratories saw that they would have to compete for the legislative ear with long-established trade associations, professional societies, and lobbies. Obviously, their personal appeals would have to be supplanted in time by some sort of sustained organizational effort. However, they were determined to avoid the pitfalls of the pressure group. They would hold themselves above the common bargaining of politics by cautiously eschewing alliances which might later commit them to causes not essential to their own. Lacking both financial support and authority from their local associations, the Washington representatives had to be careful not to move too far ahead of their colleagues at home.

Thus, the beginnings were modest. Sparking the organization meeting on October 31 were Simpson, Austin M. Brues, and Eugene Rabinowitch from Chicago. Irving Kaplan and Clarke Williams represented the SAM Laboratories at Columbia. Paul S. Henshaw and Spofford G. English spoke for Oak Ridge and William M. Woodward and Joseph Keller for Los Alamos. As an interim measure, they agreed that each group would keep at least one representative in Washington at all times. The Independent Citizens Committee of the Arts, Sciences, and Professions offered them a temporary office at 1018 Vermont Avenue.[30]

The formal organization inevitably involved a statement of principles. Their purpose, the scientists wrote, was to promote studies of the long-term implications of atomic energy, explain the dangers of atomic warfare, and help establish a spirit of world security in which the beneficial possibilities of atomic energy could be developed. They would study proposals for national legislation to see that there was no conflict with international policy. They would also have to carry their message to the people: since a continuing monopoly of the bomb was impossible, no nation could feel secure until world control of atomic energy had been established. This, the group concluded, would ultimately mean forming a world government.

Until the local associations ratified the charter, the Federation of Atomic Scientists would in fact be nothing more than the eight or ten representatives in Washington. But Simpson and his friends had no fear of being forgotten. As they anticipated, the news of the October 31 meeting brought offers of assistance and affiliation from a score of scientific, religious, and civic associations throughout the nation. Again fearing a dilution of their cause, the Washington leaders were cautious about new alliances. They could accept other groups of atomic scientists in the FAS, but to represent the broader interests they favored separate federations.

447

So heavy in fact was the pressure from other groups that within two weeks the atomic scientists had to face the problem of organization. Wisely, they chose to divide the hodgepodge into two federations. As Simpson reported to his colleagues in Chicago, "we must be sure that other groups which really have no scientific interests at heart and no more background do not join us openly." To organize the scientists in a distinctive body, the FAS leaders called a meeting at George Washington University on Sunday, November 16. In addition to the six atomic energy groups now in the FAS, there were representatives from scientific associations in Cambridge, New York, Philadelphia, Rochester, Dayton, and Washington and from the Allegheny Ballistics Laboratory. Under the leadership of William A. Higinbotham from the Association of Los Alamos Scientists, the assembly agreed to establish a national federation of scientists, which would "gather and disseminate information concerning developments in science insofar as they would affect world peace and the general welfare." This they would try to do by re-establishing the free interchange of scientific information between nations.

On the same Sunday, just ten blocks away at the Mayflower Hotel, the FAS leaders were attempting to guide the deliberations of the non-scientists. The organizations most prominently represented were the National Education Association, the American Association of University Women, the United Council of Church Women, the Catholic Association for International Peace, the Federal Council of Churches, the American Association for the United Nations, the ICCASP, the National Farmers' Union, the United Steelworkers, CIO, the National Council of Jewish Women, the

National League of Women Voters, the Disabled American Veterans, Americans United for World Organization, and the FAS. One of Bush's friends who looked in on the Mayflower meeting reported that "the attitude of most of these groups, as inferred from the statements read, seemed to be that 'the Atomic Bomb is just too dreadful, too awful, too-too-too—Everybody must do something about it quick. What are you doing? What am I doing? We must all get together right away and do more.' " [31]

Perhaps some ridicule was justified, but this observer probably did not realize how cleverly the atomic scientists had handled the situation. By placing their nonscientific friends in a separate organization, they would not be embarrassed by such naive enthusiasm. At the same time, they could count on the considerable influence and support which these groups could bring to their cause. Within a few weeks after the Mayflower meeting, the atomic scientists succeeded in creating the National Committee on Atomic Information. As a clearinghouse for atomic information, the NCAI could keep its member associations supplied with FAS news releases about the legislative struggle in Washington.

As *Newsweek* reported, the atomic scientists were the reluctant lobby. Part of their reluctance stemmed from their conviction that the cause of science should not be dragged through the political arena. To some extent, however, they were capitalizing on the sentimentality of Americans who had made the movie *Mr. Smith Goes to Washington* a hit before the war. What could be more appealing than to have the boy scientists challenge the giants of politics at their own game? The crew cuts, bow ties, and tab collars testified to their youth. They could not dispel the image by appearing too skillful in the ways of their adversaries. As Mrs. Pinchot remarked to the *Newsweek* reporter, "they're ideally inefficient." [32]

Behind the boyish faces were not only keen minds but also some astute politicians. A case in point was Higinbotham. Although at thirty-five he was somewhat older than his colleagues, his small stature, slight build, and unpretentious appearance concealed his age. During the depression, Higinbotham had learned the ways of the world working as chef, radio mechanic, and folk-dance leader to support his graduate studies at Cornell. An expert in electronic equipment, he had followed Robert Bacher to the MIT Radiation Laboratory and then to Los Alamos. Soon after coming to Washington in November, he became the spark plug of the new federation. In the capital, he was equally at home lecturing to Methodist ministers on atomic energy, chatting with congressmen, finding office space, gathering intelligence, and placing stories in newspapers. He seemed so openly honest, friendly, and good-natured that senators and bellboys called him Willie. He also possessed an innate feel for politics that made him an indispensable leader of the reluctant lobby. [33]

MILITARY AFFAIRS COMMITTEE, U. S. HOUSE OF REPRESENTATIVES, 1945

Seated, left to right: Carl T. Durham, Paul J. Kilday, John J. Sparkman, Overton Brooks, R. Ewing Thomason, Andrew J. May, Walter G. Andrews, Dewey Short, Leslie C. Arends, Thomas E. Martin.

Standing, left to right: Philip J. Philbin, Arthur Winstead, Chet Holifield, Robert L. F. Sikes, Melvin Price, J. Parnell Thomas, Ivor D. Fenton, J. Leroy Johnson, Charles H. Elston, Forest A. Harness.

EDWARD U. CONDON EXPLAINS URANIUM MINERALS TO SENATORS Mc-MAHON AND VANDENBERG, NOVEMBER 7, 1945 / Condon's appointment as scientific adviser to the Senate Special Committee on Atomic Energy had been announced just the day before.

ALEXANDER SACHS AND GENERAL GROVES / Chatting at a hearing before the Senate Special Committee on Atomic Energy, November 27, 1945.

THE AGREED DECLARATION OF WASHINGTON, NOVEMBER 15, 1945 / President Truman with Prime Ministers Attlee and King after Truman had finished reading their proposal for a United Nations commission on the control of atomic energy. Senators Vandenberg and Connally had left in a huff without waiting for photographs.

Standing, left to right: Vannevar Bush, T. L. Rowan (Attlee's secretary), Charles A. Eaton, Brien McMahon, Lester B. Pearson, James F. Byrnes, Sol Bloom, William D. Leahy.

COMMITTEE OFFENSIVE

Only occasionally did the scientists see McMahon, Newman, or Condon during the busy days of November, 1945. Though the two groups had similar aims, their missions were different. The new national federation of scientists was preparing to embark on a broad program of education which would disseminate a fundamental understanding of the atom among the public at large. The Special Committee would make the frontal assault on the Army positions which defended the May-Johnson bill. Simpson helped write speeches for McMahon, and Newman periodically discussed strategy with Higinbotham. But most of the time the scientists and the senators went their separate ways.

Early in November, Newman prepared for committee action. First he wanted to educate the Special Committee. The members had to understand the forces they were attempting to control by legislation. With the Smyth report as their text and Condon as their instructor, the senators began a study of nuclear physics and chemistry on the most elementary level. How much of the forbidding technical language in the first forty pages of the Smyth report made a lasting impression on the august students was hard to measure, but they no doubt became aware of how much there was to learn. The academic atmosphere which Newman and Condon were trying to create could also have a good psychological effect. It might induce some of the veteran senators to set aside their predilections for the May-Johnson bill and face the questions of atomic energy with a fresh point of view.

449

The study sessions concluded with a trip to Oak Ridge on November 20 and 21. As McMahon later explained in a speech, the committee's technical vocabulary took on reality when they saw the strange equipment and buildings nestled in the narrow Tennessee valleys.[34] They climbed through portions of the U-shaped building at K-25 and pondered the complexity of the Y-12 plant. At X-10, Senator Vandenberg provided a dime which was irradiated in the pile until it had become sufficiently radioactive to make a counter sputter excitedly. Newman arranged through the scientists to have members of the Oak Ridge associations on hand to answer questions, and Groves and his staff graciously accepted McMahon's invitation to have dinner with the committee at the Guest House. The congeniality of the occasion for the moment broke through the senatorial reserve. With the Army officers present, some of the more conservative members of the committee found it easier to talk with the brash, young scientists. McMahon was pleased with the Army's gesture of sociability.[35]

Time was to prove, however, that the dinner marked the high point of amity between McMahon and the Army. During the course of the evening, McMahon and Vandenberg suggested to Groves that the committee would need some highly classified information to complete its nuclear education.

The request made Groves uneasy. It had not been his habit to grant access to atomic secrets for the purposes of general education, but only on the basis of a clear "need to know." His worst fears were realized later in the week, when Condon sent him a request for the most sensitive top-secret information, including full details on Anglo-American relations during the war, raw material supplies, bomb stockpiles, production rates, and military intelligence.

Refusing the request point-blank, Groves warned Patterson of the impending conflict. He knew that McMahon would not hesitate to take the issue to the President, and he had no intention of giving the information to the committee on anything less than the President's authority. There was good reason to contend, as Groves did, that vital secrets were not kept by giving them to as large a group as the Special Committee. As the General reminded the Secretary, he had never revealed all the data Condon had requested to any human being. Groves was convinced that the top-secret information was more for the staff's edification than the committee's. He suspected that the questions had been drafted by someone who knew more about the classified aspects of atomic energy than did Newman or McMahon.

Groves's opposition to the request stiffened in a long, fruitless meeting with McMahon on November 24. The Senator appeared determined to give the information not only to the committee members but also to the staff. This meant revealing the nation's most vital secrets to Newman, Condon, and indirectly, perhaps to Szilard and Urey. The latter three had all clashed with Groves during the war over the necessity of compartmentalizing information. Without reflecting on the loyalty of any individual, could not Groves assume that differences in attitude might lead some recipients to accord the data less care than the Army thought necessary? The General urged Patterson to ask the President to invoke a wartime order permitting the Secretary to withhold military secrets.

From the committee's perspective, Groves's position was preposterous. Was the Army implying that information which had been given to foreign-born scientists during the war could not be entrusted to the elected representatives of the people? Newman and Condon believed that Groves had overstepped his authority. He had no purview over classified data on foreign policy or international relations. And what gave the Army exclusive rights to any atomic energy information, except perhaps to that which was related directly to weapons? In the last analysis, McMahon's advisers concluded, Groves was nothing more than the mouthpiece for Army policy. Final interpretation of the Espionage Act rested with the President and the Secretary, not with the General. McMahon, too, was determined to go to the White House.[36]

Tempers were raw when McMahon and Newman went to the Pentagon for a final appeal to Patterson. Sitting in the Secretary's outer office, McMahon looked at the ceiling light and wondered if it were "bugged." Once

450

inside, McMahon let Newman do the talking. Patterson, at first restrained and polite, soon showed his annoyance. Giving the information to the committee would be tantamount to a public release. He would fight the committee with all his strength. Then looking reproachfully at Newman, Patterson asked his former assistant whether he had been sent to OWMR to do this to the Army.

The President found little time to apprise himself on the controversy now raging in his official family. Since late October, he had been preoccupied with the international rather than the domestic aspects of atomic energy. Truman, as Newman observed, had never manifested any deep convictions on domestic legislation, but he had bristled when Newman and Smith pointed out the dangers to the President's constitutional position in the May-Johnson bill. Now, whatever the validity of the War Department's position, the Secretary was coming dangerously close to intractability if not insubordination. He had taken an uncompromising stand at the White House meeting on November 7. He had persisted in his defense of every provision of the May-Johnson bill in a Pentagon press conference a week later.[37] His flat refusal of the committee's request for classified information suggested that he was following a studied policy of intransigence.

451

Others beside Newman and McMahon saw Patterson's actions in this light. He was treading on sensitive senatorial toes. John Bankhead, for one, wrote McMahon: "I do not like the effort of Secretary Patterson to assume leadership for this administration on the most important subject pending before Congress. . . . I think Patterson ought to be put in his place. The Senate rejected his leadership and his idea when he sent his bill to the Senate." [38]

McMahon and Truman were ready to take Bankhead's advice. On November 28, McMahon issued his public challenge to the Army in a speech at the "Atomic Age Dinner" in the Waldorf-Astoria in New York.[39] The Senator was among friends since the dinner was sponsored by the Americans United for World Organization, a member of the newly formed NCAI. He described the committee's efforts to prepare for its heavy responsibilities. It intended to continue its education in atomic affairs during the hearings which had just started in Washington. It had invited scientists, military officers, economists, lawyers, government officials, and social scientists to testify. Only by bringing to light every pertinent fact consistent with military security could the committee write a satisfactory bill.

Above all, McMahon emphasized, "we must find a way of controlling the destructive power of atomic energy on a world level." Therefore, in drafting domestic legislation, the committee would have to keep a sharp eye on international implications. The provisions of the bill would have to be consistent with the purposes of the proposed international commission on atomic energy; it would have to provide for the necessary freedom in scientific research, for the full development of atomic power, for protection of the public from hazardous activities, and for adequate control of "all critical natural resources." Finally, military security regulations would be reviewed "so as best to protect the *individual* and the nation." Here was the committee's first public avowal of its intention to draft a substitute for the May-Johnson bill.

Meanwhile, Newman was devising a new attack on the War Department measure. He drafted a letter from the President to Secretaries Patterson and Forrestal informing them that the May-Johnson bill "in its present form contains a number of undesirable features and requires substantial amendment." Newman then specified ten changes needed to make the bill acceptable to the Administration. Most of these he lifted directly from the earlier analyses which he and Miller had prepared. The fourth point was entirely new and reflected the growing hostility to the military: "The specific provisions in the Bill permitting either the members of the Commission or the Administrator to be a member of the Armed Forces should be eliminated." [40]

True, the scientists had been beating the drums against military security since September, but their complaints had always been cast in terms of freedom of research. It was just an incidental heritage from the war that the security system which threatened that freedom was enforced by General Groves and his Army officers. Almost everyone had heretofore accepted the idea of military membership on the commission, provided the basic American tenet of civilian supremacy was recognized. Now, however, Newman was shifting his ground. Civilian supremacy was no longer sufficient. Complete military exclusion was now the order of the day. The President with a stroke of the pen confirmed the shift when he sent the memorandum to the military secretaries on November 30.

In this charged atmosphere the adversaries came face to face in the White House on December 4. McMahon, Newman, and Condon were there to present the case for the committee. Patterson, Forrestal, and Groves spoke for the military services. The discussion mainly concerned the committee's request for information, but there were overtones generated by the President's memorandum. Truman admitted that if the committee insisted on the data, he might find it hard to refuse their request. He believed, however, that to give such sensitive information to so large a group was to risk compromising it. He was at the moment trying to erect a system for international control through the United Nations, but he did not yet feel confident that the Russians or the French would live up to such an agreement. Under the circumstances, the President did not want to risk losing the advantages of secrecy. [41]

Patterson and Groves had carried the day, but they had by no means won the battle. They had first lost the initiative in October when the new alliance of scientists and senators made its surprise attack on the May-Johnson bill. The Army's opposition had then taken time to regroup and was now

452

ready to take the offensive. The Army was reduced to a last-ditch fight for the May-Johnson bill.

The immediate task was to answer the President's memorandum, which requested the Interim Committee to consider amendments to the bill. The committee had in fact been discharged early in November, but Harrison did not hesitate to ask Bush, Conant, Oppenheimer, and Karl Compton for their personal views. In the meantime, the Army's legal staff compiled an exhaustive analysis of the President's message. This and the comments from the former members of the Interim Committee were the basis for a full-dress strategy meeting in Patterson's office on December 11.[42]

The War Department was in no mood for concessions. Patterson and his advisers could accept only four of the President's ten points. They agreed that the formulation of commission policy, the appointment of the administrator, and the establishment of security regulations should all be subject to Presidential approval. They did not object to strengthening the sections of the bill providing for freedom of research, although they considered the present language adequate in that respect. On those points which represented the heart of the Newman philosophy, however, they voiced disapproval. Adequately qualified men could never be found for a full-time commission. To exclude military officers would needlessly restrict the President's discretion in appointments and weaken the national defense. An absolute monopoly of fissionable materials and their production by the commission was impractical and would prevent full industrial development of atomic energy. The same could be said for the compulsory licensing of private patents. To provide for the dismissal of employees for security violations only after a court conviction would hamstring the nation's security system. It was also unnecessary that the bill conform to the general patent policies for government-supported research to be established in national science legislation. The discussion furnished the basis for the reply which Royall's staff drafted the following day. But the Under Secretary seemed in no hurry to finish the unpleasant task. Not until December 27 did Patterson send the letter to the White House.[43]

453

With public opinion running against it, the Army suffered a telling blow of its own making. On November 25, news from Tokyo sparked the scientists to protest. General MacArthur's forces, acting on orders from Washington, had confiscated the cyclotrons at three Japanese universities and dumped the valuable research instruments into the Pacific. In a clipped reply to the scientists, Patterson declared the action in accord with War Department policy. While he recognized that a cyclotron could be used for non-military research, it was "of special value in atomic research which our Government believes should be prohibited to our enemies."

Patterson's statement seemed to justify the warnings of the scientists. The Army apparently intended to maintain full control of all atomic research, whatever its purpose. The continuing barrage from the laboratories forced the Secretary to elaborate. In a second statement on December 15 he admitted that the order to MacArthur had gone over his name but without his knowledge. Taking the responsibility himself, Patterson did not reveal that Groves's office had issued the order on November 7. No matter, the damage was done. The scientists would not soon forget the incident. Months later, Herblock gleefully drew for the Washington *Post* a cartoon depicting a swarthy gladiator leaning back in his swivel chair to assure the nation that he could manage research while his hobnailed boots shattered delicate scientific instruments on the desk.[44]

If the Army could find any consolation in the events of December, it lay in the dismal fizzle of the Special Committee hearings. Armed with high hopes and a list of questions which Newman and Condon had carefully prepared, McMahon embarked on a series of leisurely hearings which consumed the better part of thirteen days between Thanksgiving and Christmas. The scientists were happy with the long-awaited opportunity to speak their minds, and the committee members were presumably broadening their knowledge of nuclear matters. But the rehash of facts which were sensational in August had no news value in December. Alexander Sachs, the first witness, set the tone for the hearings when he consumed a whole day for an excruciatingly verbose account of his part in enlisting Roosevelt's support in the S-1 project. Most of what followed was aimless, repetitious, and speculative. There was no controversy, few differences of opinion, and only an occasional barb. Perhaps McMahon was not yet sure enough of his committee to draw attention to the hearings by striking directly at the Army. To make matters worse, the Pearl Harbor inquiry just a few doors away was badly outdrawing him. Even the revelations of the December 7 tragedy had heavy competition in most newspapers from news of strike threats, housing shortages, and American troop demonstrations abroad. In a telegram, Simpson urged his Chicago colleagues to express their "deep concern that news commentators, newspapers, and the radio are not bringing to the American people an adequate report on the hearings."[45]

If McMahon was marking time, he was doing it with a purpose. Behind the scenes he was working with Newman, Miller, Levi, and Emerson on the third draft of an atomic energy bill. Miller and Levi were doing most of the legwork in reconciling the views of Newman and the scientists. McMahon himself had little interest in the details. What he wanted was a bill he could support before the committee and the Congress.

Two weeks before Christmas, Levi almost despaired of producing an acceptable bill. After several exchanges of draft with Miller, he still felt that some sections needed further revision. The scientists, especially Szilard, were becoming restless. Without Newman's personal support, Levi doubted that he could bring the scientists to accept the draft, but he knew they would not back the bill if the committee introduced it without consulting them. Somehow, in the swirl of events Newman, Miller, and Levi reconciled their differences or swept them under the table. On December 20, Mc-Mahon introduced his bill in the Senate as S. 1717. He had not discussed it with his committee. In fact, he had hardly read it himself. But he was confident that Newman had provided him with a respectable piece of legislation. The committee and the public would have ample time to consider it after the holidays.[46]

In some ways, the exhilarating first days of the September session now seemed a long way off. Both sides began the task of drafting an atomic energy bill with hopes for swift, constructive action. But neither side had fully understood all the complicated issues involved. In American politics that spelled controversy, confusion, and delay. The issues were just as pertinent in December as in the summer of 1945, but no one could now pretend to see what the future might hold.

455

INTERNATIONAL CONTROL: A PLEDGE TO FULFILL

The President's slowness to muster the powers of his office in the struggle for domestic legislation had a parallel in his delay to carry out the October 3 promise of a quest for international control.

Not that atomic energy was ever far from the center of his thoughts that early autumn. On October 7, Harry Truman took a holiday in his native Missouri. Speaking extemporaneously before the throng attending the Pemiscot County American Legion Fair at Caruthersville, he pleaded for the co-operation of all Americans during the difficult months of demobilization. Beyond current trials, he saw a future of infinite promise. The force locked in the nucleus of the atom could be liberated for the service of mankind. He prophesied that when nations decided "the welfare of the world is much more important than any individual gain which they themselves can make at the expense of another nation, then we can take this discovery which we have made and make this world the greatest place the sun has ever shone upon." [47]

The next day, the President went fishing at Reelfoot Lake just outside the little Tennessee resort town of Tiptonville. In the evening, he invited reporters to the front porch of his lodge for "an old fashioned bull session" and a little hospitality. He surprised the newsmen by asserting that his remarks would be on the record. Taking advantage of the opening, one of the guests asked for clarification of his Caruthersville speech. Did the President mean the United States was refusing to share the atomic secret until nations put world progress ahead of their own immediate advantage? That was not quite the case, Truman replied, distinguishing between scientific knowledge and weapon technology. It was idle to talk of withholding the scientific knowledge. Already it had spread throughout the world. But engineering secrets were something else. The United States would not share them. As a matter of fact, no other country could use them. Only the

United States had the combination of industrial capacity and resources necessary to produce the bomb. While Truman had drawn the same distinction between science and engineering in his message to Congress the week before, he now seemed to be downgrading the importance of international control. He contributed further to this impression by indicating he did not intend to take a personal hand in the discussions with Britain and Canada. That was a job for the Secretary of State, he said.[48]

Byrnes had just returned from the London meeting of the Council of Foreign Ministers. Exasperated by weeks of wrangling, the Secretary found the prospect of negotiations on international control more distasteful than ever. He saw the President's message creating difficulties. He had visions of Molotov confronting him at future meetings and demanding to discuss control of the bomb. Byrnes thought too much attention was being paid to the views of scientists. Science might not know national boundaries, but Stalin and Molotov did. No control plan was safe without inspection. How did anyone expect to see Russian bomb factories when Americans could not even gain access to Poland and Hungary? Byrnes was convinced the United States should hold off until it made sure of a decent peace. On October 10, he told Forrestal and Patterson that he was going to urge the President to procrastinate.[49]

While powerful leaders within the Administration urged caution, a potent influence from abroad pressed the President to act. On September 25, Prime Minister Attlee had sent Truman a long letter pointing up the dilemma the new weapon posed for the nations of the world and suggesting discussions of the future of the atomic partnership. The President's message to Congress afforded the Prime Minister a measure of satisfaction, but when Truman replied personally on October 5, he set no date for the promised talks. Lord Halifax raised the matter at a meeting of the Combined Policy Committee on October 13. Chairman Patterson said he had no information on how the President intended to proceed, though he assumed the choice lay between the usual diplomatic channels and the Combined Policy Committee itself. He promised to ask the President at the first convenient opportunity.

Patterson's inability to supply details suggested that the United States was not likely to act quickly in the absence of some external stimulus. On October 16, Attlee moved to administer it. Acknowledging Truman's letter of the fifth, he reported he was facing insistent Parliamentary demands for a statement of policy. He was going to reply to a question the next day, but he wanted a conference with the President before making a further exposition. The view in Britain was that the bomb had overshadowed the recent meeting of the Foreign Ministers. Unless the wartime partners had a clear position, the atom might jeopardize the prospective meeting of the United Nations General Assembly. Mackenzie King of Canada shared this concern; he should be a party to the discussions. Warning that he could not put off Parliament for long, Attlee volunteered to come to Washington at once.[50]

In point of fact, the Labor Government was under strong pressure from Parliament and the newspapers to treat atomic energy as a world, not a national, heritage. The focal point of the argument was the effect of the bomb on relations with Russia. Whatever might be gained militarily in the five or ten years until the Soviet Union could manufacture the weapon for itself would be lost politically in heightened distrust and bad feeling. Why not use atomic energy for purchasing the good will of the Russian bear? Criticism of the United States followed as a corollary. Did not American policy statements indicate a desire to monopolize the bomb? Was this not the basic cause of the differences that were turning to ashes mankind's yearning for a better world? Truman's October 3 message to Congress brought few cheers in Britain. Influential journals emphasized the ban on disclosures of manufacturing processes as evidence of intent to play power politics with the atom. The Manchester *Guardian* scoffed at the suggestion of a pact renouncing the bomb. "That would add as much to world security as the Kellogg Pact for the renunciation of war did in its day." [51]

457

The clamor set up by the partisans of a radical approach to international control tended to obscure a solid, typically English unwillingness to rely completely on the chances for reforming the conduct of nations. Winston Churchill did not hide his belief that the United States, Britain, and Canada should retain the bomb secret until the United Nations had demonstrated fitness to take over. Lord Alanbrooke, Chief of the Imperial General Staff, argued in high councils that splitting the atom had undermined British security. He reasoned Russia would be loath to renounce a weapon that might mean control of the world. In the sad situation in which Britain found herself, "any international agreement that was not thoroughly efficient was, on the whole, worse than no agreement at all." The Labor Government had moved as rapidly as any Tory ministry in preparing the nation for the nuclear age. Early in October, it decided to set up a research station at Harwell near Oxford. The new establishment would include a pile to provide fissionable material for research. While the Government had not yet decided what to do about large-scale production, the fact that it assigned Harwell to the Ministry of Supply suggested the objective was chiefly military.[52]

Though the Prime Minister did not make it explicit in his letter to Truman, the plans for hurrying on with an atomic energy program were in themselves an urgent reason for meeting with the President. As the British looked forward to active work in the United Kingdom, they hoped to make use of the experience the Americans had gained during the war. But what was the basis for continued interchange? The Quebec Agreement was inadequate. For one thing, it rested solely on the necessities of the war against the Axis. For another, it was an executive agreement, binding only on the administration that negotiated it. Worst of all from the standpoint of British pride, it placed any postwar advantages of an industrial or commercial character in the hands of the President of the United States. The *aide-mémoire*

Roosevelt and Churchill had signed at Hyde Park in September, 1944, specified full collaboration after the defeat of Japan. But this informal document was even less substantial than the Quebec Agreement. When Sir Henry Maitland-Wilson of the Combined Policy Committee asked about it some two months after Roosevelt's death, the American copy could not be found. Some years later it turned up in the files of Admiral Wilson Brown, Roosevelt's naval aide. Apparently someone had looked at the heading, "Tube Alloys," and concluded the paper dealt with naval supplies. At war's end, the flow of information slowed to a trickle. Clearly, Attlee would have to see what he could do to restore it.[53]

458

Attlee's request for a face-to-face meeting could not be ignored, and the necessary invitation went forward. The first public hint that Anglo-American discussions were imminent came from Truman himself on Saturday, October 27. It was Navy Day and an occasion for pageantry in New York. Seven miles of fighting ships lay at anchor in the North River from Sixtieth Street to Spuyten Duyvil. The President arrived in the morning. Manhattan hailed him as a conquering hero during the ride to Central Park. There in the Sheep Meadow, against a backdrop of towering cumulus clouds, an audience of a million heard him deliver a major foreign-policy address. Standing hatless, his grey topcoat whipped by the strong winds, Truman sought to restate the established fundamentals of American foreign policy. The atomic bomb did not alter them, he said. It only made them more urgent. It meant the United States must act with greater speed, determination, and ingenuity. The American people must answer the menace of atomic explosives in partnership with all the peoples of the United Nations. Adverting to his message to Congress, the President stated once again that discussions with Great Britain, Canada, and later with other nations could not wait on the formal organization of the United Nations. They would begin in the near future. Once more he emphasized that the talks would look toward the free exchange of fundamental scientific information. They would not, he pledged, touch on the methods of manufacturing the bomb. With an eye on the criticism this promise had met abroad, he declared that American possession of the weapon threatened no nation. The people of the United States considered the new power of destruction "a sacred trust." The world knew they would execute that trust faithfully. The highest hope of all Americans was that "world co-operation for peace will soon reach such a state of perfection that atomic methods of destruction can be definitely and effectively outlawed forever."[54]

Formal announcements came the following Tuesday. Attlee told Parliament he and King would visit the United States. In Washington, the White House announced that the Prime Minister would arrive in time for the talks to begin November 11. At a press conference October 31, the President confirmed that atomic energy was the only subject on the agenda. Of course, he would be glad to consider any other matters the British and Canadian leaders might have in mind. When asked if the conference was a prelude to another meeting of the Big Three, Truman dodged. However, he did say that the next step was for the United States, Britain, and Canada to discuss control with other governments.[55]

BUSH ONCE MORE

Though Prime Minister Attlee would arrive in another ten days, no preparations had started within the American Government. In the Department of State, Under Secretary Dean Acheson and Counsellor Benjamin Cohen were alert to the need but unable to interest their chief. In the War Department, Secretary Patterson sensed the urgency of the situation. On November 1, he wrote Byrnes recommending a prompt, close, and thorough examination of the subject before the British leader arrived. Though his thoughts covered the entire sweep of the international question, his most immediate concern was the Quebec Agreement. Its implications deserved the most careful consideration now that the war was over. No one was more alarmed at the lack of planning than Bush. Yet in its absence lay a splendid opportunity. He saw a chance to intercede and help bring to fruition his long-maturing plan for a sound first step on the thorny road to international control. On Saturday, November 3, he called on Byrnes and stressed the need for some sort of policy. Byrnes proved receptive to suggestion and asked Bush to set out his views in writing.[56]

459

It meant a busy week end, but on Monday Bush had a seven-page statement ready. At the outset, he offered some advice on tactics. Once the President decided on general policy and objectives, he should appoint a small group to prepare for the approaching conversations. This should not be the Interim Committee but a new group including members from the Senate. Thinking no doubt of the last month's confusion, Bush argued the Administration should make no statements until this group had reviewed them. It was the only way to present the public with a consistent and united point of view.

Turning to substantive questions, Bush reviewed the Quebec Agreement. The rather informal secret understanding of 1943 would have to be replaced by an open, more permanent arrangement. The new understanding should conform to any more general agreements that might be in the offing. The coming conference was no place for the actual drafting labors. But the participants could explore matters of form and content. Were it up to him, Bush would supersede the Quebec Agreement by a compact providing for no more than sharing materials. Any political clauses and details relating to the dissemination of information should rest on a broader international basis.

Bush considered Russia the most important question facing Truman and his visitors. Secretive and suspicious by nature, the Soviet Union was the chief obstacle to moving down the road of international understanding, to averting a secret arms race and the catastrophe of nuclear war. If there were any way to remove this barricade, it lay in making agreements which the Kremlin would find advantageous to keep. This meant proceeding step by step, so that Russian leaders would face clear alternatives. They should have to choose between conforming to the plan and facing hostile public opinion throughout the world. The United States wanted no war; but if a conflict proved unavoidable, the nation needed atomic bombs and the ability to use them promptly if the enemy had stockpiles of his own. For that reason, the American program should avoid any premature outlawing of nuclear weapons. The national safety demanded realism.

Bush visualized the mechanics in greater detail than ever before. At the outset, the United States should announce that it proposed going "the whole distance" but that the steps must come in sequence, the success of one essential to the next. American leaders should conform scrupulously to their undertakings and be tolerant of minor irritations and infractions. The great hope was to open the Soviet Union. Everyone must realize it would take time.

The first move, Bush thought, was to go to Russia and invite her to join Britain and the United States in suggesting that the United Nations General Assembly create a scientific agency and charge it with the full dissemination of fundamental information in all fields, including atomic energy. As a prerequisite, every nation would give foreign scientists free access to its basic research laboratories, allow its own citizens to travel for such purposes without restriction, further the exchange of students, and encourage its researchers to publish. The primary objective was to start Russia down the path to collaboration. No policing would be necessary; the scientists themselves would soon know whether Russia was really opening her laboratories. This tactic would cost nothing. The chances were that the United States would make public what it was doing in pure science no matter what Russia did. The great value of the scientific-freedom approach was that it would tell the world whether Russia really intended to co-operate.

Assuming that the initial effort went well, a second would be to extend free interchange of information to the practical aspects of atomic energy, particularly to its industrial uses. A condition for this was the establishment of an internationally constituted inspection system under the United Nations. The inspection commission would have the right of visiting any laboratory or plant to determine such significant information as magnitude of operations and disposition of product. Since at present the United States alone had extensive operations, it would have to move gradually until it was certain the inspection system would really work. To reassure Russia, the United States should set out a definite schedule for extending the scope of inspection. The United States should commit itself to follow this, subject only to UN certification that the system was operating satisfactorily. The great hope was that inspection might be broadened to a point where secret preparations for war would be sufficiently difficult to rule out a covert arms race of any kind.

460

If the international commission should run into obstacles, it could place the facts before the world. That, at least, would serve as a danger signal.

The third and final step would be for all nations to agree on using fissionable materials only for the production of commercial power. Safeguarded by effective inspection, the United States would turn its bombs into power plants. All this was a task for many years, but the goal was worth a patient effort. Perhaps the control of atomic arms would pave the way for eliminating other weapons and finally war itself. "This," Bush concluded, "is the path that can finally lead to a climate of opinion in which a United Nations Organization fully implemented to regulate international relations of all sorts, and prevent war, can be brought to pass." [57]

Bush's letter arrived in time for Byrnes to have its argument in mind when he conferred with Truman on Wednesday, November 7. If either President or Secretary of State retained any lingering doubts about the wisdom of prompt action, a Molotov speech the same day must have dispelled them. Haranguing the party faithful in the Kremlin's Hall of St. Andrew, the Soviet Foreign Minister warned the West against setting up anti-Soviet blocs and using the bomb as an instrument of power politics. The weapon, he asserted, could not remain the exclusive possession of some one country or some narrow circle of countries. In a fiery peroration that brought the audience cheering to its feet, Molotov shouted: "We will have atomic energy and many other things, too." [58]

461

As Attlee's visit drew near, Byrnes pondered the Bush plan. On November 8, he called in both Bush and General Groves. Assuming that the United States embarked on the proposed step-by-step plan, he asked, "what would we do with our bombs in the meantime?" This was a puzzler, but the next day Bush and Groves tentatively advanced one answer. They assumed that the nation would continue manufacturing fissionable material for the present. Then, when the international discussions reached a favorable point, the President might announce we would not assemble this material into bombs. Instead, we would store it in bar form for later installation in industrial power plants. Once a workable inspection system was in operation, the President would invite the international commission to satisfy itself that the United States was honoring its pledge. Such an announcement, Bush and Groves reasoned, would be a partial proof of good will. It would show that Americans did not wish to hold an atomic sword over the world. If the gesture were made soon, it might have a salutary effect. In any event, its cost would be small—no more than making the material unavailable for bombs without a period of preparation.[59]

CONFERENCE ON THE POTOMAC

The British and Canadian Prime Ministers arrived in Washington Saturday morning, November 10. That night Truman and Attlee exchanged graceful toasts at a White House dinner. Shortly before eleven on Sunday, Armistice Day, the President and his guests drove through a drizzle to Arlington, where they stood silent before the tomb of the Unknown Soldier. After stopping down the hill to pay homage at the fresh grave of Sir John Dill, the party proceeded to the Navy Yard. There the three leaders boarded the *Sequoia*. Accompanying them were Secretary Byrnes, Lord Halifax, Canadian Ambassador Lester Pearson, Admiral Leahy, and Sir John Anderson. Shortly after noon, the yacht cast off and disappeared downstream into the mist. It did not return until eight-thirty that evening.

The Monday morning newspapers headlined stories that Attlee had brought over a plan for sharing the atomic bomb with the United Nations. Presumably, he had advanced his views aboard the *Sequoia*. Though the reports did not name a source, someone in the British entourage obviously had been talking. The Prime Minister, it was said, considered a firm understanding of Russian policies and objectives the prerequisite. The plan could go forward if the Soviet Union supplied an acceptable statement of its political, territorial, and economic desires and pledged to subscribe wholeheartedly to the UN. If she did not, Attlee believed the United States, Britain, and Canada should retain their secret but guarantee to use it only in co-operation with the United Nations. According to the papers, the Prime Minister hoped to internationalize scientific developments. But he regarded as impractical any formal inspection involving surveillance of thousands of topflight researchers. He saw no merit in outlawing the bomb. No rules applied when a nation was fighting for its existence.[60]

Bush was at his P Street office that Monday morning when he received a call from Secretary Byrnes. He hurried to the State Department where Byrnes received him at once and announced that the conference had already reached an agreement. Astonished, Bush asked for details. Byrnes outlined an understanding which followed almost exactly Bush's recommendations of the week before. Mindful of the morning headlines, Bush asked what proposals the British had made. None at all, said the Secretary. Hardly able to believe his ears, Bush came back to the question several times. The reply was always the same. Apparently, Truman and Byrnes had suggested the Bush plan, and the British had accepted it. Now Byrnes came to his main point. How about preparing a draft communiqué? Bush protested. How could he report on a conference he had not attended? Byrnes insisted. Protesting still but not too strongly, Bush agreed to try.[61]

Bush had been thinking so long about international control that he needed only an hour or so to strike off a draft. A short and very general statement, it began by asserting that the way to permanent peace lay in full support of the United Nations. Mankind could not reach its cherished goal at a single stride, but it could make substantial progress by preventing a secret arms race in atomic or any other major weapons. Toward this end, the United States, Britain, and Canada would propose that the UN establish an international body devoted to acquiring full information on the building of weapons in any part of the world. Its efforts should result in such full knowledge that all nations, convinced no secret development of atomic weapons could occur, would agree to use the atom only for peaceful purposes. Of course, it would be necessary to proceed with deliberation, defining relatively narrow areas of information at first and extending these as progress was attained. In order to make a start at once, the three conferring governments announced their willingness to effect complete interchange of fundamental scientific knowledge with any nation that would reciprocate.

The draft completed, Bush dashed over to the War Department and showed it to Harrison and Patterson. After making a few minor changes, he went back to State and handed it to Byrnes. The two talked for a while, discussing particularly the mechanics of putting the proposal into effect, but Byrnes suggested no changes.[62]

Tuesday morning, Byrnes again called Bush. This time he wanted him to come to the State Department and check with Ben Cohen, who was also at work on the communiqué. Bush was annoyed to discover that Cohen had discarded his draft for an entirely new document. While Cohen had summarized correctly the conclusions of the talks aboard the *Sequoia*, Bush thought the order and manner of his presentation weak in the extreme. Determined not to correct scientific language in a report he did not approve, he attacked Cohen's work fundamentally, criticizing practically every sentence.[63]

463

At four that afternoon, Byrnes phoned once more. He wanted Bush to see a draft Cohen had revised in light of the morning's exchange. A few minutes later, Bush was in the Secretary's office. Though he found Cohen had adopted most of his suggestions, he said quite directly he still thought his own statement covered the ground better. But Byrnes must not have been convinced, for at a general conference with the British at the White House an hour later, he presented the Cohen version. The British had prepared a paper of their own. Rapidly, the discussion drifted into a review of the entire subject. At one point, Admiral Leahy argued for outlawing the bomb. This threatened to throw everything off the track, but Bush, who had been summoned at the last minute, spoke forcibly on the dangers of premature outlawry. He was relieved when his remarks met with general consent. He had scotched the idea for good, he hoped. Despite all the talk, the conference adjourned with nothing more concrete to show than an understanding both parties would work on fusing the statements and meet again the next afternoon.[64]

Wednesday, November 14, was a busy day for Bush. He saw Byrnes in the morning, talked over the conference of the day before, and then joined Cohen to work on the communiqué. The document on which they settled was longer and more specific than Bush's draft of Monday. In this respect, it reflected the Department of State's natural concern with the mechanics of translating an idea into action. No doubt an improvement was a section which charged the international commission with making recommendations and draft conventions on four major aspects. The revision stated effectively the plan for starting with an exchange of fundamental scientific information, but it went further than Bush had gone in emphasizing the need for controls and safeguards prior to transmitting data on practical industrial applications. In doing so, it necessarily struck a somewhat more negative note. Yet on the whole, Bush was pleased. He thought it a good statement.[65]

At three o'clock that afternoon, the talks resumed in Truman's office. Now there were three drafts: American, British, and Canadian. The Canadians had limited themselves to certain sections, but the British covered the entire subject. Their version was more eloquent than the American in depicting the dilemma that confronted mankind, but in content it was substantially the same. Despite such agreement, it soon became apparent that so large a group could not settle on final phrasing. Accordingly, the conference named Bush, Anderson, and Pearson as a drafting committee. They went into session at once in the Cabinet room. Taking parts out of each of the three texts, adding some language here and there, they had a composite draft ready for the typist at six o'clock.

Lord Halifax entertained at dinner that evening in the British Embassy. Bush, Anderson, and Pearson left early to return to the White House and review the freshly typed statement in preparation for a final conference scheduled for ten Thursday morning. They had hardly begun when they learned that Truman, Attlee, and King had decided not to wait until morning. There was nothing to do but take the one copy and join their chiefs and the foreign secretaries in the President's study. It was ten-thirty. For an hour and a half the discussion proceeded. Bush acted as secretary, penciling the changes in his barely legible scribble. Finally, he read the draft aloud, making a few final corrections as he went. Now there was complete agreement. Well past midnight, Bush drove to his home in Spring Valley. Folded in his pocket was the only copy of the three-power declaration.[66]

Thursday morning, there was still work to do. At nine, Bush was back at the White House to supervise typing the official copies. He made but a single change. One phrase had been inserted twice. When he called Truman's attention to the slip, the President offered a practical solution: "Strike out one of them." Meanwhile, the White House summoned Congressional leaders and the press. Shortly after eleven, the reporters filed in. They found the President and the two Prime Ministers with drawn faces proclaiming a short ration of sleep. Behind them sat Senators Connally, Vandenberg, and McMahon and Representatives Bloom and Eaton. Byrnes, Halifax, and Pearson were nearby, while Bush stood quietly to one side. Truman carried the Agreed Declaration in his hand. Without preliminaries, he rose and began reading the two legal-size pages: "We recognize that the application of recent scientific discoveries to the methods and practice of war has placed at the disposal of mankind means of destruction hitherto unknown, against which there can be no adequate military defence, and in the employment of which no single nation can in fact have a monopoly."

The President read on hoarsely. The three leaders had met to consider international action for preventing the use of atomic energy for destructive purposes and promoting scientific advancements for peaceful and humanitarian objectives. As representatives of the countries that already knew how to use atomic energy, they were willing to make a first contribution. They would exchange fundamental scientific information, as well as scientists and scientific literature for peaceful ends, with any nation that would reciprocate fully. They believed that the fruits of research should be available to all nations and that free investigation and interchange of ideas were essential to the increase of knowledge. Already they had made available the basic scientific information essential to the development of atomic energy for the uses of peace. They intended to continue this practice and hoped other nations would do the same. This would create an atmosphere of reciprocal confidence in which political agreement and co-operation would flourish.

465

As Truman continued, Attlee and King sat slumped in their chairs, looking up only occasionally and blinking eyes that struck reporters as bloodshot. The newspapermen heard the President point out that the conferees had decided not to disclose detailed information on the practical industrial application of atomic energy at present. Since military exploitation depended on the same methods and processes required for industry, the immediate revelation of such data would not contribute to controlling the bomb. But the three governments were prepared to share details just as soon as effective, enforceable safeguards could be erected against diverting atomic energy to destructive purposes.

In his flat, Missouri accent, the President now recited the heart of the plan. The Anglo-American chiefs believed the United Nations should set up a commission to make specific proposals for (a) extending between all nations the exchange of basic scientific information for peaceful ends, (b) controlling atomic energy to the extent necessary to ensure its use only for peaceful purposes, (c) eliminating from national armaments atomic weapons and all other major weapons adaptable to mass destruction, and (d) setting up safeguards to protect complying states from the hazards of violations and evasions. The work of the commission should proceed by separate stages. The successful completion of one would develop the confidence necessary for the next. The commission might first devote its attention to the exchange of scientists and scientific information. As a second stage, it might turn to developing full knowledge of raw materials.

Truman was nearing the end of the declaration. He predicted that the application of science to destruction would make every nation realize more urgently the need to banish forever the scourge of war. "This can only be brought about by giving wholehearted support to the United Nations

Organization, and by consolidating and extending its authority, thus creating conditions of mutual trust in which all peoples will be free to devote themselves to the arts of peace. It is our firm resolve to work without reservation to achieve these ends." [67]

All week the newspapers had featured fact and rumor—mostly rumor —about the talks on international control. They did not guess that another facet of atomic energy was up for consideration—the future of Anglo-American co-operation. Indeed, this issue did not intrude until late in the negotiations. When Bush talked with Byrnes Monday morning, he asked about the Quebec Agreement. The Secretary reported that no one had even mentioned it. How extraordinary, Bush thought. Surely the British would raise the issue. If they did not, the United States should. Quebec was an understanding for the duration of the war. Unless some new arrangement were adopted, the Combined Policy Committee and the Combined Development Trust would be stranded. The War Department had been doing some detailed staff work in this area. Patterson had a very thorough memorandum. Byrnes ought to discuss it with him, Bush suggested, and see that the President knew its substance.

Bush was right in his conviction that the British would not ignore the issue. At the end of Tuesday's late-afternoon conference, Sir John Anderson stepped up to him and announced that the two of them were to work out a basis for future collaboration. The President and Prime Minister Attlee had just decided. Bush considered this a matter for Patterson, and he sought out Truman and told him so. "All right, arrange it," the President said in effect. At the State Department Wednesday morning, Bush interrupted the talk on the draft communiqué long enough to relate the incident to Byrnes. This latest turn of events was news to him. Though Byrnes thought it strange Attlee should have gone directly to the President, he agreed Patterson ought to take over.[68]

At ten o'clock Thursday morning, just as the White House was scrambling to put the declaration on international control in final form, the second set of negotiations began in Patterson's office. Flanked by his advisers, Harrison and Groves, Patterson greeted Anderson and a British delegation. Sir John at once brought up the fourth clause of the Quebec Agreement, the specification that the President should call the turn on any postwar advantages of an industrial or commercial character. The British, he reported, hoped to build pilot plants soon and needed to know where they stood. Patterson set Anderson's mind at rest by declaring he would recommend a solution that would not put the United Kingdom at a disadvantage. The air cleared, the delegations easily agreed on the need for continuing the Combined Policy Committee as a supervisory body and the Combined Development Trust as a device for acquiring ores. Both sides conceded that it was desirable to terminate the Quebec Agreement in its entirety and replace it with a new covenant reflecting the postwar situation. Such a document was no work for a hasty one- or two-day conference. The Combined Policy Committee was in a better position for considering the details of collaboration. For the present, the only requirement was agreement on a suitable directive. Anderson and Patterson asked their advisers to have a draft ready the following morning.

This meant a busy day for Groves, Harrison, and the two young officers who assisted them, Joseph A. Volpe and R. Gordon Arneson. They immediately adjourned to Harrison's office to devise some preliminary understanding concerning form and content with their British counterparts, Roger Makins of the Washington Embassy and Denis Rickett, Anderson's personal assistant. Groves and Harrison proposed two memorandums: one a short directive from the President and the Prime Ministers to the Combined Policy Committee; the other a more detailed instruction. Makins and Rickett accepted the plan and undertook preparation of the shorter document. Both sides agreed to try their hands at the longer one.

467

The afternoon saw drafting and redrafting in both camps. At six, Groves, Volpe, and Arneson met again with Makins and Rickett. They had no difficulty in giving their assent to the simple, three-sentence statement the Englishmen had composed. It did no more than have Truman, Attlee, and King affirm their desire for effective co-operation, agree that the CPC and CDT continue in "a suitable form," and request that the CPC recommend appropriate arrangements. The trouble came on the companion piece. Makins and Rickett wanted an informal statement of broad principle serving merely as a guide, while Groves held out for a paper specific on policy issues and binding on the committee. When discussion failed to produce accord on the force of the document, there was no resource but admit an impasse and concentrate on the contents.

After a short recess for dinner, the talks resumed. In a session that ran far into the night, the weary negotiators agreed on everything except information exchange. Finally, Makins and Rickett permitted Volpe and Arneson to write in a restrictive Groves formula with the understanding that the Englishmen would advance an alternative proposal at the general meeting.

It was a distinguished group that assembled in Patterson's office the next morning at nine. Sir John Anderson had brought Lieutenant General Sir Ian Jacob, Military Assistant Secretary to the War Cabinet, Nevile Butler, Under Secretary of State in the Foreign Office, as well as two Canadians long familiar with the work, C. J. Mackenzie and Clarence D. Howe. The two-memorandum approach must have struck Anderson as an American attempt at assuring the joint acquisition of raw materials before taking up the knotty and controversial section on interchange. At the outset, he insisted on amending the short directive to provide "full and effective," not just "effective" co-operation. Suspecting he was being outmaneuvered, Groves objected strenuously. But his arguments failed to make much impression on Patterson, who accepted the insertion after offering his opinion as a lawyer that it made little difference.

With the longer document, the Memorandum of Intention, still to be considered, time was running out. The visiting delegations were scheduled to depart for Ottawa that afternoon. Patterson cleared the way for speedy action when he yielded to the British contention that the instructions serve only as a general guide. If they did not bind, there was no point in having them signed by the three political chiefs. Now the Secretary could commission Groves to confer with Sir John, arrive at a final draft, and sign for the United States. Anderson and the General retired to Harrison's office. Patterson was free to take the amended directive with its pledge of co-operation to the White House. There, about ten-fifteen, Truman, Attlee, and King affixed the signatures that made it official.[69]

By noon, Anderson and Groves had concurred on a Memorandum of Intention. In conformity with the decision of that morning, it was only a set of recommendations for the Combined Policy Committee to consider in preparing a document that would supersede all wartime understandings except the 1944 Agreement and Declaration of Trust. These recommendations differed from the Quebec Agreement in four respects. First, they included Canada as a partner. Second, they said nothing about commercial and industrial rights. Third, they watered down the political obligations by requiring consultation, not consent, prior to decisions to use the bomb against third parties or to negotiate with or disclose information to other governments. Fourth, they subjected all raw materials, no matter what the source, to allocation by the CPC.

Otherwise, the recommendations followed the Quebec Agreement. They specified that the Combined Policy Committee continue its supervisory role. Most significant of all, they reproduced the essence of the 1943 understanding on interchange. They promised the same full and effective co-operation in the field of basic scientific research but once again imposed a qualification on the development, design, construction, and operation of plants. While recognizing such co-operation as desirable in principle, the recommendations provided that the CPC should regulate it by such *ad hoc* arrangements as might from time to time prove mutually advantageous. It was Groves who insisted on this. Sir John consented over the outspoken opposition of his aide Rickett. Perhaps the British leader thought recognition of the principle of co-operation was enough in a document that would serve only as a guide.[70]

On Friday afternoon, the Prime Ministers departed. The Union Jacks were lowered from the lampposts on Pennsylvania Avenue. The White House seemed strangely quiet as throngs of office workers, intent on the coming week end, scurried past it at five. For the first time in a week, there was opportunity for reflection. Few Americans could bring greater perspective to their musings that evening than Bush. He had long wondered how mankind

468

could save itself from the horrors of nuclear war. He had no illusions about human nature. He knew the path to international control would be long and difficult at best, perhaps impossible. But there must be a start: that was the great imperative.

Bush thought the week's talks had turned out well—remarkably well in view of the hasty preparations and the lack of co-ordination throughout. The United States, Britain, and Canada had taken the first step. They had embarked on the program Bush had urged so persistently. True, the November 15 declaration was silent on the direct approach to Russia which he considered essential. On the other hand, nothing that had been said or done precluded it. More disturbing was the state of the Anglo-American partnership. For years, Bush had opposed too close a tie to the United Kingdom for fear that it might impair American chances of negotiating successfully with the Soviet Union on the all-important question of international control. The directive of November 16, read literally, suggested that his fear had become reality. Still, the Anderson-Groves instruction to the Combined Policy Committee counterbalanced it. There remained room for maneuver.

469

In Bush's final analysis, the worst mistake of the entire week had been political. On the eve of the conference, he had urged bringing influential senators into the discussions, but his advice had gone unheeded. Truman and Byrnes had ignored the Senate until the morning the President announced the declaration on international control. Tom Connally, the powerful chairman of the Foreign Relations Committee, and Arthur Vandenberg, ranking minority member, arrived at the White House seething with resentment. When Truman had finished reading the declaration, they walked out, not even waiting for the usual photographs. Bush was worried. It was dangerous to risk alienating the Senate.[71]

A DIRECT APPEAL TO THE RUSSIANS

One thing Bush did not know that Friday evening: the United States would soon make a direct appeal for Russian co-operation by presenting the Washington call for international control to the United Nations. To judge by their public statements, the President and the Secretary of State did not contemplate this. Byrnes had left the conference in a rush to keep a November 16 speaking engagement at Charleston, South Carolina. Seizing the opportunity to explain the declaration of the day before, he rewrote his address on international trade, devoting the first half to atomic energy. He emphasized that responsibility rested with all governments, not the Anglo-American powers alone. The Truman-Attlee-King announcement had made the same point. But Byrnes said nothing about carrying the idea to its next logical step— giving the Soviet Union a special invitation to share the initiative. For a week or more, the Administration's position did not change. On November 20,

Truman told a press conference that the plan was to go before the first meeting of the United Nations General Assembly—scheduled for London in January, 1946—and request establishment of an atomic energy commission. The following day, Byrnes was more explicit. The United States, Britain, and Canada might offer the plan jointly, he told reporters. In response to a question, he stated that there had been no attempt to enlist Russia, France, and China as sponsors.[72]

However, forces already at work emphasized the importance of addressing the Kremlin leaders before the London meeting. For one thing, the false impression created by the Moscow press was cause for alarm and called for quick action; it distorted the news of the Washington meetings. With utter disregard for accuracy, it summarized the first six points with a single phrase: the means of production must remain a secret. The Soviet citizen was supposed to conclude that an Anglo-American bloc, bomb in teeth, intended to array the United Nations against Russia.[73]

470

Within the Department of State, the men who thought in terms of staff work began looking anxiously at the calendar. If the President and the Secretary of State intended to ask the General Assembly to set up a commission in January, it was time to buckle down. The basic plans for the establishment of the agency, its composition, and its frame of reference ought to be completed by early December. On November 24, Ben Cohen and Leo Pasvolsky, chief architect of the United Nations, joined in prodding Byrnes. It was most important, they declared, to check with the United Kingdom and Canada and gain agreement on a proposal. That done, Byrnes ought to try for Soviet concurrence. Since Stalin made all final Soviet decisions, discussions should proceed in Moscow. If at all possible, talks there should begin by December 10. Meanwhile, Cohen and Pasvolsky would be glad to take the lead in formulating the American position.[74]

Furthermore, there was pressure from Capitol Hill. On November 23, Representative Helen Gahagan Douglas of California introduced a resolution calling on the President to invite the leaders of Britain and the Soviet Union to confer on a joint proposal to the United Nations. Four days later, John W. Trischka and Richard N. Lyon of the scientists' lobby met with Senators Morse, Tobey, Taylor, and Alexander Smith. Would they introduce Mrs. Douglas' resolution in the upper house? At Smith's suggestion, the senators decided to recruit a bipartisan delegation to call on Truman and Byrnes and ask whether Russia had been invited to the Truman-Attlee-King meeting. If so, why had the Soviets failed to respond? If they had not been invited, why not? Unless Byrnes and Truman could give satisfying answers, the senators would introduce and support the Douglas resolution. True to their plan, Smith, Tobey, and Taylor, joined by Kilgore and Saltonstall, made their representations at the White House on the morning of November 29.[75]

Throughout the week that followed the tripartite talks on atomic energy, Byrnes had pondered the state of East-West relations. To him, the

Attlee-King visit was a diversion from the more immediate issue, the European peace treaties. The London meeting of the foreign ministers had ended in a discouraging deadlock. But Byrnes still hoped. Perhaps, he mused, there might be better progress in Moscow. There Molotov would have less excuse for delay. Why not remind the intractable Russian of the Yalta plan for a meeting of the foreign ministers every three months and suggest that the time had come for gathering in the Soviet capital? After checking with Truman, Byrnes dispatched a cable on November 23. As he had anticipated, the Russians extended an invitation. The conference was set for December 15.[76]

Byrnes may have had atomic energy in mind when he asked Molotov for a Moscow meeting. But not until November 29 did the Secretary take the first step toward enlisting Russian co-operation on its fearful challenge. At eleven o'clock that Thanksgiving Day morning—just a few minutes before the Smith-Tobey delegation called on the President—Byrnes sent British Foreign Minister Bevin a long message suggesting an agenda for Moscow. First on the list was the proposal for a United Nations commission to study control of the atom.

471

Later the same day, Lord Halifax called at the Department of State. The ambassador brought news that while His Majesty's Government doubted Russia's willingness to join in sponsoring the November 15 proposals, they would welcome Soviet co-operation. Would Byrnes consider asking Russia to act with the Anglo-American powers? Now the way was open. Byrnes showed Halifax the message he had just sent Bevin. On December 1, he formally notified the United Kingdom that he planned to discuss both the method of proposing the commission and the nature of its authority.[77]

His decision made, Byrnes authorized Cohen and Pasvolsky to begin policy planning. They lost no time organizing an interdepartmental working group. Its nucleus was a trio of able young men—Carroll Wilson, Bush's executive assistant in the OSRD; Herbert Marks, special assistant to Under Secretary Acheson; and Joseph E. Johnson, a Williams College history professor who had become chief of State's Division of International Security Affairs. Others—among them Volpe and Arneson—sat in from time to time, but Wilson, Marks, and Johnson shouldered the main burden. Though Wilson, an engineer, had a good grasp of the technology, none was a scientist. To make up for this deficiency, they depended on two old hands whom Cohen and Pasvolsky had brought to Washington as consultants—Henry Smyth and Robert Oppenheimer.

Driven by an inexorable deadline, the working committee turned quickly to both the policy and the technical features of its assignment. By December 7, it had draft proposals ready for consideration by a policy committee. Assembled in Cohen's office were Harrison for the War Department, Admiral William H. P. Blandy for the Navy, Bush for the OSRD, Pasvolsky, and Charles E. Bohlen, Russian specialist in the State Department. The dis-

cussion centered around tactics to follow at Moscow. Was it possible to limit
the talk to a simple request that Russia join the three western powers in proposing a commission on atomic energy? Or would Russia want to know more
about how the plan would work? If she did, how far could Byrnes go, particularly in discussing technical interchange? Gradually, something approaching
a consensus emerged which the working committee sought to express in a
revised draft of December 10.[78]

The plan called for Byrnes to begin by stressing the desire of the
United States to collaborate with other nations in preventing the destructive
use of atomic energy and other scientific advances and in utilizing those
advances for the benefit of mankind. As Russia was aware, the United States,
Canada, and Great Britain believed the UN should set up a commission to
study and make recommendations. Would the Soviet Union join in sponsoring such a proposal? In order that Russian leaders might know what was
involved, Byrnes would submit a statement embodying American views on
how to establish the commission and on its composition and terms of reference. Set forth in an annex to the draft proposals, this position was not
complicated. The General Assembly should create the commission and receive its reports. Each nation represented on the Security Council and
Canada should be members. The commission should inquire into all phases
of the problem including the four matters the Truman-Attlee-King declaration
had mentioned as subjects for specific proposals.

Having extended this invitation, Byrnes would admit the existence of
some difficult substantive questions. This meant that any international action
was likely to be highly complex and had to be based on careful, earnest
study. As the United States saw it, the subject divided naturally into a number of separate, though related, segments. Among these were (a) ever-
widening exchange of scientists and scientific information, techniques, and
materials, (b) development and exchange of full knowledge concerning
natural resources, (c) exchange of technological and engineering information, and (d) safeguards against and controls of methods of mass destruction.

Byrnes would explain that the United States believed mutually advantageous action might be undertaken promptly in some areas. Others
would require effective, reciprocal, and enforceable safeguards acceptable
to all nations. The difficulties were real, but the American Government
wanted to work with Russia and other nations toward establishing arrangements for full collaboration as rapidly as possible. It believed that successful
international action on any one phase was not necessarily a prerequisite for
beginning affirmative action on others. Such action should be taken wherever
it was likely to be fruitful. For this reason, the United States was anxious
to talk with the Soviet Union. It would consider Russian proposals on any
phase.[79]

The December 10 paper was a direct bid for Russian collaboration, not merely in presenting a plan of action to the United Nations but also in consulting on the knotty issues the international commission was bound to encounter. It differed from the Agreed Declaration of November 15 in yet another way: it would give Soviet leaders reason for hoping the western powers would move quickly beyond the mere release of basic scientific information. The Washington communiqué had offered an immediate exchange of such data with any nation that would reciprocate fully, but it ruled out disclosures of industrial applications until effective safeguards had been devised. Further, it seemed to require the successful completion of one stage of progress as a prerequisite to embarking on the next. While the draft of December 10 affirmed the necessity of safeguards in some areas, it made a special point that a beginning on any one stage did not necessarily wait on success elsewhere.

Although such a flexible position might facilitate negotiations with the Russians without unduly committing the United States, it invited opposition at home. General Groves put in writing his hope that American negotiators would offer no more than the interchange of basic scientific data. He had grave doubts about the wisdom of fostering international visits of scientists and was particularly anxious lest the forthcoming talks drift into the raw-material situation. Though Secretary of War Patterson refrained from endorsing these views, he forwarded them to Byrnes. More forceful was the protest from the Navy Department. Forrestal wrote to the Secretary of State objecting that the December 10 paper went too far. He opposed any discussion of the specific kinds of information the United States should release until there was a guarantee of genuine reciprocity. To emphasize his point, he submittted an alternative draft. According to this plan, Byrnes would begin by affirming a desire for collaboration to prevent the destructive use of atomic energy. Then he would simply submit a statement of American views on establishing the commission and inquire if the Soviet Government would associate itself with an overture along such lines.[80]

When Byrnes took off for Moscow on Wednesday morning, December 12, he knew that influential senators shared Forrestal's convictions. On the eve of his departure, he had summoned several members of the Committee on Foreign Relations and of the Special Committee on Atomic Energy. First, he introduced James B. Conant, announcing that the chemist would go to Russia in an advisory capacity. Then he talked of his trip, reading from the draft proposals of December 10. Connally, Vandenberg, and the others were in a mood for dissent. They resented this last-minute briefing—when Byrnes had already packed his suitcases. This was almost as bad as the treatment they received during the talks with Attlee and King. But it was more than procedure that bothered them. From the drift of Byrnes's remarks and the presence of Conant—Connally muttered something about bringing in "college professors"—they concluded the Secretary was going to disclose

473

scientific information during the coming conference. If not actually that, he would discuss and perhaps agree on the revelation of atomic data in advance of any arrangements for safeguards.

The senators made no secret of their dissatisfaction, turning their most intense fire on the section of the proposals that suggested discussing the various stages independently. What could that mean but the possibility of agreement on exchanging information before agreement on safeguards? They conceded that Russia could develop the nuclear science for herself in perhaps two years. They knew the facts of nature could not long remain secret; but they were determined not to make it easier for Russia until there was absolute, effective, world-wide inspection and control. Every senator spoke earnestly, but at the end of the meeting, none could see that the arguments had made any impression on Byrnes. So great was the concern, the Special Committee on Atomic Energy met and voted unanimously to ask President Truman to hear their views.

474

On Friday morning, December 14, almost the entire membership of the committee filed into the President's study, Connally and Vandenberg in the lead. When they had stated their case, Truman said at once he agreed. But he was sure they had misunderstood Byrnes. The Secretary of State had no intention of disclosing scientific information at Moscow. His primary objective was Soviet support in establishing the United Nations commission. On information exchange, all Byrnes planned was an exploration of the conditions under which the traditional freedom of international scientific discussion might be pursued in the field of atomic energy. The President stressed that no data on applied science, technical know-how, or ordnance was at stake. Byrnes was thinking only of pure research and scientific theory. This would soon be freely available in American journals and at learned-society meetings. Byrnes wanted access for American scientists to similar material from the Soviet Union. If he were successful, he would establish a basis for good will and mutual confidence. Besides, Truman said, Byrnes would refer any proposals to Washington before making a commitment. The senators could rest assured he was not going to disclose information about the bomb until there were satisfactory arrangements for inspection and safeguards.

But Truman's sweeping assurances did not dispel his visitors' concern. Vandenberg asked for the directive he had given Byrnes. The President readily produced a document and read it aloud. Was it the full draft proposals of December 10, a section of the annex dealing with mechanics, or a Presidential instruction based on the November 15 declaration? No matter, the senators were amazed. It seemed authority for the very thing they warned against—giving away half our "trading stock" in the process of seeking controls. They asked Truman to change the directive by radio, but they left the White House not knowing what he would do. For some reason, Vandenberg noted in his diary, the President had not grasped the point. The delegates concluded that both Truman and Byrnes planned a fairly frank approach at Moscow in the hope of allaying Russian suspicions of American bomb policy and of creating an atmosphere conducive to settling the other issues that disturbed relations with the Soviet Union. The gentlemen from the Senate viewed this tactic coldly. They insisted the United States could not assume Russian co-operation. They believed there should be no atomic energy disclosures until a rigid system of international control had been devised and until Congress had given its approval.

Truman did not change any instructions, but he had Dean Acheson, who had attended the meeting, send Byrnes a full report. Acheson prepared a lucid summary, which Truman approved before transmittal. On the seventeenth, Byrnes replied: any proposal he made would lie within the framework of the three-power declaration.[81]

Thursday, December 20, the New York *Times* carried a long James B. Reston article relating in detail Byrnes's stormy meeting with the senators the preceding week. The President's first reaction was to have a verbatim text rushed to Byrnes in Moscow. He wanted everyone fully informed. By the next morning, however, he had become rather anxious. He did not want Byrnes alarmed at the news from home. When Acheson came in, Truman told him to make it clear to Byrnes that the brush with Connally, Vandenberg, and company had not disturbed the President. The Secretary should know that he approved the plan to confine any offers to the November 15 communiqué. But Truman had not surrendered entirely the idea of a special effort at winning Soviet confidence. He had a suggestion for Acheson to forward. If Byrnes thought it helpful in promoting co-operation and useful discussion, he could say that the United States would be glad to consider any propositions the Soviet Union might make regarding any phase of the problem. The United States would discuss them with Russian leaders alone, as well as with other members of the UN commission.[82]

As it worked out, Byrnes did not find it necessary to offer any special inducements. At first, trouble seemed likely, for Foreign Minister Molotov insisted on placing atomic energy at the bottom of the agenda. Byrnes wondered why but eventually concluded it was no more than an attempt to give the impression that the Soviets did not consider the issue important. After the Secretary of State conferred with Stalin in the Kremlin on the night of December 19, the foreign ministers finally took up atomic energy. Byrnes and Bevin limited themselves to asking the Russians to join in recommending that the General Assembly set up a commission. As a working paper, Byrnes put forward the annex to the draft proposals of December 10. This was no more than a short statement of American views on the commission and its function. The section on the terms of reference, however, had been modified in two respects. First, it followed word for word the Truman-Attlee-King formulation of the four specific proposals the commission should make. Second, it included their November 15 recommendation that the work

475

"should proceed by separate stages, the successful completion of each of which will develop the necessary confidence of the world before the next stage is undertaken." The annex as prepared in the Department of State had dropped all reference to stages.

To Byrnes's amazement, the Russians showed little of their celebrated inflexibility. Molotov expressed concern over the relationship between the proposed commission and the Security Council. Byrnes and Bevin recognized some logic in his argument and agreed to a revision providing that the commission report to the Security Council rather than the General Assembly and that the Council issue directions to the commission in matters affecting security. Molotov occasioned some anxious hours by objecting to including the sentence on stages. He thought this was a matter for the commission's determination. But when Byrnes declared this was the heart of the proposal and insisted on retaining it, Molotov withdrew his opposition. Marvelous to relate, atomic energy occasioned less debate than any other item on the agenda. Byrnes felt like apologizing to Conant for having dragged him into the icy depths of the Russian winter for such an anticlimax.[83]

476

Byrnes, Bevin, and Molotov announced the results of their conference in a joint communiqué from Moscow on December 27. The three foreign ministers proclaimed their intention of recommending that the General Assembly establish a commission on the problems arising from the discovery of atomic energy and related matters. They had decided to invite the other permanent members of the Security Council, France and China, together with Canada, to join them in sponsoring a resolution to this effect at the first session of the General Assembly in January, 1946. The resolution as printed in Section VII of the dispatch was simply the paper Byrnes had submitted with the changes occasioned by Molotov's views on the role of the Security Council. The commission would have the same function that Truman, Attlee, and King had spelled out November 15. Proceeding by separate stages, it was to make proposals for exchanging basic scientific information, for confining atomic energy to peaceful purposes, for eliminating atomic and other weapons of mass destruction from national armaments, and for effectively safeguarding the states that complied.[84]

Secretary Byrnes had tried to do everything the senatorial delegation had requested. He had neither discussed scientific information nor agreed to discuss it. He had insisted on stages, and the Moscow resolution announced that the successful completion of each stage would "develop the necessary confidence of the world before the next stage is undertaken." Yet Vandenberg did not consider this sufficient. The communiqué alarmed him. He thought it said the work would proceed through four stages with disclosure first and total security last. Had Byrnes agreed to the very thing the senators had opposed? Vandenberg immediately protested to Acting Secretary Acheson, who arranged a meeting with the President just as soon as he returned from his Christmas visit to Independence. On Friday, December 28, the Michigan senator confronted Truman. Then he went to the Department of State and conferred with Acheson. Back at the White House a little later, he read a statement to the press. Apparently, the President had seen and approved it. Vandenberg told reporters he did not agree that international control could be achieved by separate and unrelated stages. For this reason, he had sought additional information about the policy announced at Moscow. Now he was reassured. "I am advised by the State Department that while the communiqué listed four separate objectives, with inspection and control listed last, it is not intended that these objectives should be taken in the order indicated but that it is intended that the four shall be read together and that each shall be accompanied by full security requirements—all being finally subject to Congressional approval." At last, it seemed, the White House had averted a break with the principal powers on Capitol Hill. The trouble had stemmed more from misunderstanding and faulty co-ordination than difference on policy. But it taught the fledgling Truman Administration a lesson. Henceforth it would be more sensitive to Congressional views on the atom.[85]

477

It was important that the Administration and the Senate travel together down the road to international control. Proceeding by different routes could end only in futility. No one was more aware of this than Bush. He was gratified that Truman and Vandenberg had reached a meeting of the minds. But he was even more delighted that Byrnes had won Soviet co-operation in proposing a commission on atomic energy. This was the first real sign that the plan he had urged so long might indeed be practical. Bush had not considered agreement on safeguards a necessary condition for the exchange of basic scientific information, but he was willing to bow to political realities. What really counted for the present was an accomplished fact. The United States had made a special approach to Russia. The Soviet Union had received it favorably.[86]

HOLDING OFF THE BRITISH

While the positive features of Bush's plan for controlling the atom were faring well in the closing days of 1945, the negative side remained unresolved. It still seemed possible that too close a relationship with the United Kingdom might jeopardize American hopes for a broad, multilateral understanding. Perhaps the chances for a successful control agency were not good, but with the stakes so high, it was important to play the game to the limit. As it happened—for good or for ill—events were moving to thwart close Anglo-American collaboration.

On December 4, the Combined Policy Committee had met to consider the Truman-Attlee-King directive of November 16 and the Anderson-Groves Memorandum of Intention. As Patterson explained, the committee's task was to prepare a formal document that would take the place of the

Quebec Agreement. General Groves, who had succeeded Harvey Bundy as the American secretary, pointed out that the Memorandum of Intention was not exhaustive and that there were one or two other questions which might have to be included in the final compact. Thereupon, Lord Halifax proposed appointing a subcommittee to draw up a document for submittal to the parent committee. This draft, the CPC decided, should be in the form of an executive agreement.[87]

The subcommittee—Groves for the United States, Makins for the United Kingdom, and Pearson for Canada—went to work. It decided the embarrassing fourth clause of the Quebec Agreement should be disposed of by a simple letter. The President would inform Prime Minister Attlee he had determined it was fair, just, and in harmony with the economic welfare of the world that there should be no restrictions on the Government of the United Kingdom in developing atomic energy for industrial or commercial purposes.

478

A draft Memorandum of Agreement sufficed to spell out the other arrangements. Subject to any wider agreements for the control of atomic energy, the President and the Prime Ministers would agree not to use nuclear weapons against other parties without prior consultation. Nor would they disclose information or enter into negotiations concerning atomic energy except in accord with agreed common policy or after discussion. Each government would take measures to control and possess all deposits of uranium and thorium within its borders and to acquire desirable deposits elsewhere. The Combined Policy Committee would allocate all raw materials. A reconstituted Combined Development Trust would serve as the agent of the CPC in raw-material matters. In regard to information, there was sweeping provision for full and effective exchange to meet the requirements of the respective national programs. The Combined Policy Committee would be responsible for taking the measures necessary to put this pledge into effect.

General Groves had no sympathy with the provision for full and effective interchange. While he consented to present the Memorandum of Agreement to the Combined Policy Committee, he hastened to alert Secretary Byrnes, now the CPC chairman, to its real significance. The new arrangement, he charged, was an outright military alliance. People in the United States might talk about the peaceful potential, but until international control was a reality, atomic energy would remain the most strategically important weapon in existence. The British were aware of this and intended to ask the United States for information that would help the United Kingdom develop a large-scale plant for producing fissionable materials. Groves argued that these considerations were particularly grave in view of the United Nations Charter. Article 102 required that every treaty and international agreement be registered with the Secretariat and published. The United States was fostering an international effort to control the bomb. Would not publication of the proposed agreement reflect on the sincerity of the effort? In short, the military, political, legal, and international implications of the pending alliance required the closest consideration by the highest authorities in the land.

The Combined Policy Committee turned its attention to the subcommittee report on February 15, 1946. Byrnes brought up the requirements of Article 102. Since the same point had occurred to Halifax and Pearson, there was no difficulty in deciding to seek advice on the form of any revised agreement from the legal authorities of the three governments. Someone raised the possibility of continuing under the Quebec Agreement, but Lord Halifax observed it provided for collaboration only in bringing the bomb project to fruition. As interpreted at present, it did not provide a sufficient basis, particularly for the exchange of information. The United Kingdom had been basing its plans on the Truman-Attlee-King pledge of full and effective co-operation.[88]

When the Combined Policy Committee met again on April 15, Halifax tried once more to activate the November agreement of the heads of government. He introduced a proposal (circulated in advance) to continue co-operation under the Quebec Agreement and the Declaration of Trust, making such amendments as were necessary to apply these documents to the circumstances of the postwar years. In substance, this would provide for the collaboration envisioned in the report of the subcommittee two months before. The American members of the CPC—Byrnes, Patterson, and Bush—objected. In the opinion of their legal advisers, it did not surmount the difficulty presented by Article 102. The United Kingdom members protested that this left the decision of November 16 without effect. Co-operation was neither full nor effective, and their country was not receiving the information it required to carry out its atomic energy program. Byrnes and his colleagues could only reply that nothing should be done which might in any way compromise the success of the discussions within the United Nations. For the first time, the Combined Policy Committee reached a hopeless deadlock. The British and Canadian members could do nothing but agree to Byrnes's suggestion that they refer the matter back to Truman, Attlee, and King and ask them to confer on the effect that their November 16 directive should have.[89]

Halifax reported to London so promptly that within twenty-four hours Prime Minister Attlee had dispatched a protest to President Truman. He was disturbed at the turn of events in the Combined Policy Committee. The joint directive of November 16 had pledged "full and effective co-operation in the field of atomic energy between the United States, the United Kingdom and Canada." This could not mean less than full interchange of information and a fair division of the raw material. It was by no means inconsistent with the Agreed Declaration of November 15. In that document the three national leaders had stated their willingness, subject to suitable safeguards, to share information with other states about practical industrial applications. The clear implication was that the three governments had already provided for sharing information among themselves. Attlee thought

479

the Combined Policy Committee should make a further attempt to work out a satisfactory basis of co-operation. If it failed, Truman, Attlee, and King themselves might have to issue instructions to assure the interchange of information.[90]

A few days later, Truman explained his position to the British leader. The November 16 statement about "full and effective cooperation" was very general. It had to be interpreted in the light of the intentions of those who signed it. Speaking for himself, the President did not understand that the memorandum obligated the United States to furnish the engineering and operating assistance necessary to complete another atomic energy plant. Had anyone told him that was the purpose, he would not have signed. As a matter of fact, Truman said, the Groves-Anderson Memorandum of Intention supported his argument. It showed that the men who prepared the directive for the heads of government meant that "full and effective cooperation" applied only to the field of basic scientific information. Co-operation in building and operating production plants, though recognized as desirable in principle, was to be regulated by such *ad hoc* arrangements as the Combined Policy Committee might from time to time find mutually advantageous. Truman judged it unwise to set up such machinery at present. The three governments had embarked on an effort to establish international control. He did not want it said that the morning after they announced their intention, they had entered into a new agreement whereby the United States would furnish Britain information that would enable her to build another production complex.[91]

The President had set the course. He did not deviate. Except in the field of raw materials, Anglo-American co-operation withered away. The men responsible for shaping Britain's destiny had made no secret of their intention to produce fissionable material. If the effort to control the atom through the United Nations was successful, they would conform, of course. In the meantime, they believed they could not hold their plans in suspended animation. The American position seemed manifestly unfair. Comparatively minor help would save time and money. This the United States refused, even though it was eager for British aid in controlling uranium and thorium supplies.

A desire to safeguard the chances of successful action in the United Nations was not the only reason for the stand which the American leaders took. Distrust generated during the war colored their thinking, unquestionably. So did the security issue. Congress had left no doubt of its zeal for protecting the nation's atomic secrets. In February, the Canadian Government had broken the news of the Gouzenko spy ring. Shortly thereafter, Ottawa announced that Alan Nunn May, a British nuclear physicist employed on the Montreal project, had admitted giving atomic energy information to Russian agents. These disclosures more than justified the wartime judgment that interchange was inherently a threat to security. By the spring of 1946, it had become practically if not legally impossible for American officials to give fresh authorization for the exchange of information.

Yet granting all these considerations, determination to make the best possible try for international control played the major part in the thinking of the Truman Administration. The President was resolved not to allow too close a relationship with Britain to spoil the game. Bush had seen the danger when Franklin Roosevelt had called him to the White House back in September, 1944. Bush's influence and the influence of those who felt like him— liberally assisted by the course of events—carried the day.

481

THE LEGISLATIVE
BATTLE

CHAPTER 14

In the fall of 1945, the combined forces of senators, scientists, and members of the President's official family had succeeded in blocking the Army's attempt to ram the May-Johnson bill through Congress. The alarm sounded by the coalition spurred the President first to disavow the bill as an Administration measure and then to repudiate many of its key provisions. In the meantime, Senator McMahon had succeeded in capturing the chairmanship of the Senate Special Committee. The strongly conservative bent of its membership neutralized much of his advantage as chairman, but he hoped that with help from Newman and Condon he could in time wean most of the committee away from the attractions of the Army bill.

Biding his time, McMahon watched the December hearings drift into aimless repetition. He failed thereby to capitalize on the opportunity to publicize his cause, but that price he was willing to pay in order to gain time. Not only did he need to organize and educate the committee; he also had to delay until Newman and his associates completed a substitute bill. That they accomplished by mid-December, and McMahon introduced their measure as S. 1717.

FIRST REACTIONS

The first reactions to the McMahon bill came from the scientists. Representatives of each of the Manhattan District laboratories met in Chicago during Christmas week to consolidate their views. Thanks to the earlier efforts of Miller and Levi to reconcile the differences between the Washington politicians and the Chicago scientists, the conference ratified every provision.[1]

The scientists were especially pleased with the strong emphasis on international control. Section 6 [2] forbade weapons research and development which proved contrary to international agreements. Until the objectives of the Truman-Attlee-King declaration could be realized, Sections 4, 5, and 6 would keep the production of fissionable material and the fabrication and stockpiling of atomic weapons strictly within commission control. This would prevent the military services from embarking on a weapons production effort that might jeopardize international negotiations.

On the positive side, the scientists liked the language of Section 3, which described the commission's research functions. Contrary to Bush's recommendations, the commission could finance private research in the physical, biological, and social sciences. It could also perform research and development work in its own facilities. Furthermore, there would be a minimum of restrictions on the flow of information. Section 9 drew a distinction between "basic scientific" and "related technical" information. The former would be completely in the public domain, and the commission was enjoined to disseminate as much of the latter as was consistent with national security. Some scientists were pleased to see that the only sanction for restricting the circulation of technical data was the Espionage Act, which seemed to apply only to official Government secrets and not to privately financed research.

483

The patent provisions also seemed reasonable. The commission would hold all patents relating to the production of fissionable materials and weapons, but those covering devices or processes utilizing atomic energy would be subject to compulsory, nonexclusive licensing. A patent royalty board would assure adequate compensation for the individual inventor, but compulsory licensing would prohibit private monopoly of vital patents.

The scientists had less interest in the administrative features of the bill, but these they found acceptable. There would be five commissioners appointed by the President with the consent of the Senate. Since they would serve indefinite terms at the pleasure of the Chief Executive, the commissioners were not insulated from political control as they would have been under the May-Johnson bill. Another feature was that the members would be required to serve full time. As for the commission's staff, Section 11 established four divisions—research, production, materials, and military application. Their directors would be appointed by the President. The high status of Presidentially appointed directors of statutory divisions convinced the scientists that these four key areas of commission activity would receive the attention they deserved.

It was not surprising that the first comments on the bill within the Government came from the Bureau of the Budget. Traditionally, the Bureau formulated the Administration's position on all legislation. The day after New Year's, Don K. Price made an appointment to discuss the bill with Newman and Miller. He was pleased with the clear lines of responsibility from the commission to the President, but he objected to some features of internal organization. Most glaring was the failure to provide for a general manager who would execute commission policy and direct the staff. Price also took exception to the Presidential appointment of directors for the statutory divisions. Although the commission could establish other divisions, Price believed that in practice the Presidential appointees would be independent of commission control. He saw a similar threat in the provisions establishing four boards to allocate fissionable material, fix patent royalties, disseminate information, and dismiss personnel for security infractions. The bill required at least one member of the commission to serve on each board, and all of the groups in one way or another seemed to have powers superior to the commission itself.[3]

484

Newman and Miller accepted the idea of a general manager and subsequently adopted Price's draft almost without a change. They likewise agreed to drop out the references to the boards. They insisted only on retaining the Presidential appointment of division directors on the grounds that officials with such important responsibilities should have the status of Assistant Secretaries in old-line agencies. Price agreed to draft, with Fred G. Levi's help, revisions for a dozen other sections. Most of these the committee later adopted.

Then came the big issue of Administration support. Newman and Miller had convinced McMahon to submit the bill to the Bureau of the Budget, OWMR, War, Navy, Commerce, Interior, and OSRD. They wanted the Bureau to gather the comments from these and other agencies and prepare a unified Administration position. This Price agreed to do, but he warned the OWMR officials that they must expect Budget Director Harold Smith to speak frankly when he testified on the bill before the Special Committee later that month. As Price reported to his superior, Newman's multiple role in the legislative effort was sometimes confusing. "I will continue my discussions with the OWMR staff, in hopes that Mr. Newman (in his OWMR capacity) will prepare for Mr. Snyder an adverse comment on certain aspects of the bill that was drafted by Mr. Newman (aide to Senator McMahon), especially the aspect that conflicts with the President's memorandum of November 30, which was drafted by Mr. Newman (ghost writer to Judge Rosenman)."

Just how the Army was reacting to the McMahon bill Newman and Miller had no way of knowing, but they could guess that the response would not be favorable. Patterson had taken almost a month to reply to the President's November 30 message and then had refused to accept its basic principles. There were also rumors that the Army had done nothing to carry out Truman's instructions for revising the May-Johnson bill. But the McMahon group would know the Army's position soon enough. A second series of hearings was scheduled to begin on January 22, 1946.

While Newman and Miller mustered support within Congress and the Administration, other forces were at work outside the halls of government. The public interest in atomic energy stirred by the Federation of Atomic Scientists in the Washington meetings on November 16 was now manifest in three groups. The broader organization of scientists sparked at the meeting at The George Washington University now largely eclipsed the original federation representing the Manhattan District sites. Reluctant to surrender the emphasis on atomic energy, the latter association preferred to retain its identity if only on paper. In fact, after the organization meeting in New York on January 5 and 6, the burden of the scientist lobby rested with the new Federation of American Scientists, of which the original atomic group was but one of the participating bodies. The FAtS and the FAmS maintained separate budgets and offices, but in day-to-day operations the two were indistinguishable. They occupied adjacent rooms in a fourth-floor walk-up at 1621 K Street. Higinbotham, a spark plug in the FAtS, soon became executive director of FAmS, and the transient representatives of the Manhattan sites used both offices indiscriminately.

The third group was the National Committee on Atomic Information, which had its origins in a second Washington meeting that same November week end at the Mayflower Hotel. Representing some sixty women's groups, labor unions, religious, civic, and peace organizations, NCAI lacked cohesion but proved a highly effective clearinghouse for information on atomic energy. Under the guidance of Daniel Melcher, the executive director, the NCAI staff sold information kits and provided a steady stream of feature stories for American newspapers and magazines. Since NCAI included a broad spectrum of interests and opinions among its membership, it could never take the partisan stands of a pressure group. But simply by explaining the issues, the organization helped the cause of those who advocated effective international and domestic control of atomic energy. The left-wing tendencies of a few in the NCAI group were a source of anxiety to some of the scientists, who were rightly convinced of the need to keep the movement respectable at all costs. No one was more sensitive to these dangers than Higinbotham. Since the NCAI offices were on the same floor, he could follow their activities closely and work to prevent Communist infiltration in the larger organization. For the most part, the three groups worked harmoniously in their common effort to keep the nation informed on atomic energy.[4]

485

Supporting the overt publicity campaign of the NCAI and the FAS were the subtler but persuasive efforts of the McMahon group. Newman early adopted the strategy of selling the philosophy of the McMahon bill to a select group of public figures, editors, and columnists likely to be sympathetic to the cause. The first such effort was a banquet at the Mayflower Hotel on November 29. The guests included eminent scientists like Conant and Du-Bridge, leaders of the NCAI organizations, and a few columnists.

A second dinner on December 18 concentrated on the press. Joining Senator McMahon and his associates were Walter Lippman, Marquis Childs, Bert Andrews of the New York *Herald Tribune*, Richard L. Wilson of the United Press, Paul Miller of the Associated Press, and—from the Washington *Post*—publisher Eugene Meyer and editor Herbert B. Elliston. To the smoker following the dinner, McMahon invited Joseph Alsop, Blair Moody, Raymond Swing, Drew Pearson, Raymond Brandt, Roscoe Drummond, and Thomas L. Stokes, among others. McMahon made a brief opening statement, Newman talked for an hour on the McMahon bill, and Condon added a few remarks on technical implications. Some noted that Meyer's head nodded during the speeches, but apparently the words did not go unnoticed. On January 4, the *Post* began running a series of articles by Marquis Childs on the fight over the May-Johnson bill. The following Sunday, the same paper featured an editorial supporting the McMahon bill and Elliston's six-point peace plan, which called first for stopping all production of atomic bombs.

The dominant theme in Childs's articles was the danger of military control of atomic energy. Taking his readers behind the scenes into the November controversy between the Special Committee and the Army over the release of secret information, Childs described how shocked certain Cabinet members were to learn that not even Secretary Patterson knew the location or size of the atomic stockpile. Only General Groves had this vital information. The reader could not fully appreciate this "dangerous abdication of civil authority" until he had read subsequent articles describing Groves's iron-fisted rule over the scientists during the war. Admitting that Patterson belittled the idea, Childs suggested that the May-Johnson bill had been written to keep Groves in power.

The Childs articles hammered at two sentiments that obsessed the McMahon group as well as some newspapermen and scientists. One was the fear of military control; the other was a deep personal antagonism for General Groves. The first was clearly a product of the postwar period. After six months of hectic peace, the flush of victory was gone. Americans read in their newspapers of the charge and countercharge of folly and brass-hat stupidity at Pearl Harbor. They raised their eyebrows at reports of 4,000 soldiers marching on a bitterly cold night to the Army headquarters in Frankfurt to join in a "We want to go home" chant. They saw the news of the struggle over unification of the armed forces and extension of the draft in peacetime interpreted as military greed for power.

In such an atmosphere, the implications of the battle over atomic energy legislation seemed clear. During the war, behind the cloak of military security, the Army had developed a new force that threatened to rock international alignments and modern technology to their foundations. Who needed to look at the facts to discover the Army's intentions? Was it not perfectly apparent that the generals would try to preserve their monopoly of atomic energy for military purposes? Presumably those who were too stubborn to accept the obvious had only to observe General Groves. A few men who knew him well, like Bush and Conant, could fully appreciate the extent to which his peculiar abilities contributed to the success of the wartime project. To most of the scientists, however, he was the legendary martinet who marched through their laboratories with more interest in clean floors and low inventories than in the complexities of research. The General reminded them of the wartime restraints and indignities they wanted to forget.

For Newman and McMahon, civilian supremacy was initially little more than a first principle of American government, but Groves quickly added the personal issue by defying the committee in refusing to release classified information. The controversy brought into the open his long-standing feud with Condon, who was now prominent on the Special Committee staff. Condon himself fanned the flames of discord. The stories went that he closed every telephone conversation with the sarcastic benediction, "God bless General Groves."

Whenever a few scientists and newsmen gathered together, the conversation turned inevitably to the growing folklore of anti-Groves stories. A case in point was the smoker which Edward H. Levi staged in the home of a Washington friend. Prominent columnists, a congressman, a few FAS members, and representatives of the McMahon group gathered to hear Urey discuss the implications of the bomb. His stirring words of warning quickly provoked some frank and outspoken opinions. Robert S. Allen, formerly co-author of the "Washington Merry-Go-Round" and himself an Army colonel, declared vehemently that the military were now in the saddle and had to be kicked out. No one disagreed with that statement, and many of the group accepted Urey's contention that world government was the only answer to the atomic bomb. The evening did not end, however, without the usual excoriation of General Groves. One of the scientists later noted in the FAS diary: "His nibs (G. G.) took quite a beating." [5]

487

Most but not all of the hostility to the military and General Groves was spontaneous. The smart politician or propagandist with a nose for issues could not fail to find one in these sentiments. Charles Calkins was so gifted. An old-time liberal and member of McMahon's staff, Calkins was an officer in the Democratic secretaries' club in Washington. In Capitol corridors, press-rooms, and hotel lobbies, Calkins prospected for rumors and new ideas. Soon after Congress reconvened in January, 1946, he thought he had struck pay dirt. The composition of the Senate Special Committee and the lack of interest in the December hearings convinced him that there was little chance that the McMahon bill would ever come out of committee. The only hope was to dramatize the one issue that would catch the public eye—civilian versus military control.

The first step was to pierce the armor of military security and expose the Army's mistakes during the war. McMahon could do this by subjecting the Army and industrial representatives to "merciless cross-examination." "Groves should not be questioned; he should be grilled relentlessly on many mistakes made by the Project." A subcommittee should visit every Manhattan site to uncover "the careless planning and the many evils of Army brass-bound thinking." Calkins admitted that such an open declaration of war might hurt the Administration. A better approach might be to induce the

President to endorse the McMahon bill publicly and use party discipline to force it through Congress. In any case, Calkins thought McMahon should be prepared for the worst. "If S. 1717 can be passed without a fight, then there should be no fireworks. If the issue is in doubt, then we've got to make a goddamdest fight we know how to make. There isn't any other way." [6]

DRAMATIZING THE ISSUE

If McMahon made any decision to follow Calkins' suggestions, it was not apparent at the Special Committee hearings beginning on January 22. The tenor of the discussion was, if anything, sympathetic to the armed forces. On the second day of the hearings, Secretary of the Navy Forrestal presented the services' first public appraisal of the McMahon bill. He criticized the idea of a full-time commission and the absence of any provision for a general manager, but his main target was the exclusion of the military. He believed that the War and Navy secretaries should have a voice in all policy decisions on atomic weapons. The commission should quite properly design and develop nuclear warheads, but the military services should be responsible for weapons systems. Forrestal suggested a commission composed of the Vice-President, the Secretaries of War, Navy, and State, and four public members. As Senator Byrd emphasized in his questions, Forrestal's suggestion preserved the principle of civilian control, if not military exclusion. [7]

The first replies to Forrestal's argument seemed to stem from FAS rather than committee sources. What little press coverage the story received suggested that the Navy secretary had attacked the idea of civilian control. When Robert M. Hutchins and his Chicago colleagues staged a discussion of the bill round-table style before the committee, the university president made the mistake of relying on such sources for his remark that Forrestal "seemed to feel that complete military control of this new power would be highly desirable." Senator Johnson was quick to point out that Forrestal had never implied anything of the kind. Although Hutchins and most of the witnesses the following week generally supported the McMahon bill and thus by implication the idea of military exclusion, the committee seemed far from convinced. Byrd, Hickenlooper, and Johnson quickly drew the distinction between civilian supremacy and military exclusion. Millikin especially voiced his doubts about taking the bomb completely out of the hands of the Army. That could be done, he reasoned, if international control became a reality, but what if the nation found itself involved in an armaments race? At present, atomic energy seemed to have no important applications other than the military. What harm would there be in leaving its control with the Manhattan District for another six months or so, until the chances of international control had been explored? [8]

McMahon chose what Calkins called the "velvet glove approach" rather than a direct assault on the Army. On January 18, a week before the hearings resumed, Newman drafted a letter from the President to Patterson informing the Secretary "that the recommendations contained in my memorandum of November 30 to you and the Secretary of the Navy should be adhered to without major modification." [9] The President would stress that the commission "should be exclusively composed of civilians." Military officers might serve in administrative posts during wartime, but under normal conditions, civilian control was "in accord with established American tradition."

Following his original philosophy on legislation, Newman emphasized two additional points. "An absolute Government monopoly of ownership, production and processing of all fissionable materials appears to me imperative." Controls would be difficult but would not outweigh the advantages of Government monopoly in dealing with international problems and distributing the benefits of atomic energy. Thus, Newman found it essential "that atomic energy devices be made fully available for private exploitation through compulsory, non-exclusive licensing of private patents, and regulation of royalty fees."

489

Newman mentioned specifically only these three points in the November 30 memorandum; but to prevent any misunderstanding, he added, "I deem substantial adherence to all the recommendations in that memorandum to be essential." On January 25, the day the Hutchins round table appeared before the committee, Truman signed the memorandum. That wedge completed the split between the President and the War Department over the May-Johnson bill.

All that remained for the McMahon group was to secure the Administration's public endorsement of S. 1717. Whether Newman and company tried to direct the course of events leading to that result was not clear, but certainly their actions did not delay the outcome. On Thursday morning, January 31, Henry A. Wallace testified before the Special Committee as the anchor man of Newman's relay team of witnesses supporting the bill. In some respects, Wallace was ideal for the job. As Secretary of Commerce, he could speak with authority on the economic implications of atomic energy. On the other hand, he bore the scars of old political conflicts. Despite efforts to play down the association, Wallace was known to be close to the McMahon-scientist coalition. He had spent four days at an informal conference on atomic energy which Hutchins conducted at the University of Chicago in September, 1945. Newman had selected Condon as scientific adviser to the committee within days after Wallace had appointed him director of the National Bureau of Standards. It seemed likely that Newman and Condon had had a hand in Wallace's carefully prepared statement. The Wallace testimony was the most complete summary of the views of the McMahon group.

Wallace insisted on the overriding importance of international control. The alternative was an atomic arms race and ultimate chaos. In considering any of the proposed bills, Wallace first wished to be sure that they were consistent with international policy. This meant civilian control, free international exchange of basic scientific information, exchange of technical information under international agreement, and early development of the best possible techniques for inspection of atomic energy activities.

As for the McMahon bill, Wallace noted (somewhat inaccurately) that it had the advantage of being drafted after the basis for international control had been enunciated at the Truman-Attlee-King conference. It established a civilian commission which had sole responsibility for the production and custody of atomic bombs and the duty of fostering the development of peaceful uses. In sharp contrast, the Secretary found the May-Johnson bill "defective with respect to all three criteria of consistency with our international program." It was designed "for promoting further military developments of atomic power." It vested "the real power" in the administrator, the one full-time official, who was given "sweeping powers" and was not subject to removal by the President. Furthermore, Wallace said, the bill placed little emphasis on research for peaceful uses and permitted the administrator and his deputy to be military officers. He found Senator Joseph Ball's compromise bill less objectionable on this score, but he noted it did not offer much guidance on specific points of policy.

On all counts, Wallace found the McMahon bill superior. Both the May-Johnson and Ball bills would make it difficult to administer international controls and promote peaceful uses. Only the McMahon bill had detailed patent provisions. Only S. 1717 provided compulsory licensing that would prevent private patent monopolies. Wholeheartedly endorsing the McMahon bill, Wallace concluded with a long list of imperatives. Of them all, one caught the public eye: "We must insist on adherence to the traditional principle of civilian control over military matters—and avoid any possibility of military domination or dictatorship." [10]

That same afternoon, the President held his usual Thursday press conference. A member of his Cabinet had all but denounced the May-Johnson bill as a threat of military dictatorship. What, the press wanted to know, were his views? If the President said anything about the dictatorship reference, it was off the record. But Truman did back up Wallace's advocacy of civilian control. He felt that the Manhattan project should be turned over to civilians when Congress had fixed the necessary responsibility. The statement was equivocal in that it did not say exactly how Congress should act, but perhaps the President was merely avoiding a positive commitment until he had consulted the McMahon group. [11]

Newman once again prepared the way for a Presidential statement. On Friday morning, February 1, he delivered a draft letter to Judge Rosenman. In it the President would thank Senator McMahon for "the thorough and impartial manner in which atomic energy hearings have been held before your Committee." He would reiterate the three cardinal principles in his letter of the previous week to Patterson. To these Newman added a fourth point, that legislation "must assure genuine freedom to conduct independent research and must guarantee that controls over the dissemination of information will not stifle scientific progress." [12]

The President signed the letter the same day and released it to the press the next morning. He had all but endorsed the McMahon bill explicitly, and with Wallace's help he had dramatized the one issue on which the McMahon group hoped to make its campaign. On February 3, for the first time in months, atomic energy grabbed the headlines of the nation's newspapers: "Truman Asks Atom Rule By Civilians." Having won the Administration's support, McMahon could now concentrate on his committee colleagues. [13]

STALEMATE

491

There were still big obstacles in the legislative path. Although McMahon and his advisers controlled most of the testimony before the committee in January, the hearings failed to kindle much enthusiasm for the bill.

For one thing, McMahon had no solid backing in the committee. S. 1717 was his bill, not the committee's. While none of the members were basically opposed to the measure, all avoided giving the bill any preference. Nor did McMahon have much support from members of his own party or from those who might have been expected to back his cause. Of the six Democratic members, only McMahon and Johnson regularly attended the hearings. During January and February, Russell and Connally were never present and Byrd appeared only twice. On the Republican side, Austin, Millikin, Hickenlooper, and Hart attended most of the sessions. Vandenberg, the one Republican who seemed genuinely sympathetic to McMahon's aims, was in London for the United Nations General Assembly with Connally and did not return to Washington until all the regularly scheduled hearings were completed. In one sense, McMahon was fortunate. The very members he was trying to "educate" were most faithful in listening to his witnesses. Presumably, in a strict party test, he could count on the support of the Democratic members. On the other hand, it was a psychological disadvantage to be alone in the fight. In the face of his colleagues' studied detachment, if not opposition, it was impossible to build into the hearings any sort of movement toward the McMahon bill. [14]

Outside the committee, the McMahon group and the FAS had some success in dramatizing the civilian-military control issue. Within the committee, the issue was ineffective. Not only were the conservative majority worried about the military applications of atomic energy; they were also offended intellectually by the patent absurdity of complete military exclusion. The very point which seemed most useful for publicity purposes was most vulnerable within the committee. Some journalists had tried to portray Forrestal as unreasonable in his stand on the question of military control. The hearings, however, suggested that McMahon was taking the dogmatic position.

The same pattern prevailed during the discussion of other subjects, which in fact occupied a far more prominent place in the hearings than did civilian-military control. While the conservative majority leisurely discussed the issues, McMahon alone seemed impatient and sometimes petulant. His frequent use of leading questions made him appear more interested in the fortunes of S. 1717 than in the fundamental issues. The fact was that McMahon had maneuvered into a stalemate. As chairman of the committee and sponsor of the bill, he enjoyed an unassailable position, but in the face of the conservative majority he was scarcely free to act. Until he or his adversaries could seize a decisive advantage, the hearings were destined to drag along an enlightening but inconclusive path.[15]

GROUNDWORK FOR LEGISLATION

Though of little news value, the testimony on subjects other than civilian-military control laid some vital groundwork for legislation. The very first witness, Budget Director Harold D. Smith, raised such central issues as the terms of appointments to the commission, its relations with the President and Congress, and the internal organization of its staff. Following closely Price's comments on S. 1717, Smith soon found himself opposed to the committee on several points. Neither McMahon nor Johnson seemed convinced of the need for a general manager, though both later conceded that just for the sake of efficiency one official should be responsible for executing the commission's decisions.

Johnson emphasized Congressional control. So far-reaching and unpredictable were the implications of atomic energy that he wanted a tight legislative rein on its development. Smith argued, as he had before when the May-Johnson bill was under discussion, that adequate Congressional control depended upon a firm hand of the Executive in the larger policy decisions of the departments and agencies. McMahon jibed that Johnson was suggesting that individual senators operate the atomic energy plants and lead armies in battle. Nevertheless, Johnson persisted. As he continued to question witnesses on the need for Congressional restraints, his concern grew. On February 9, 1946, he introduced in the Senate his own bill, providing a commission of five members from each house. The rest of the committee, however, seemed to think the terms of S. 1717 were adequate. In addition to its traditional powers over appropriations and appointments, Congress would have the benefit of quarterly reports from the commission and a period of ninety days to review any commission proposal to license commercial applications.[16]

POWERS TO CONTROL

Of far greater concern to the committee were the extraordinary powers which S. 1717 would grant to the commission. The bill provided for unprecedented government authority over technical information, materials, processes, and patents. So sweeping and complex were the probable effects of the provisions that they all but defied analysis within the format of a Congressional hearing, but the testimony of expert witnesses did help the committee members to explore in a rambling, informal manner the main outlines of domestic control.

Largely as a result of pressures from the Chicago scientists, Section 9 emphasized dissemination rather than control of information. It was much more liberal in this respect than the May-Johnson bill, and most of the scientists accepted it. The committee, however, reacted differently. Comprehensive controls seemed imperative, at least until the international picture was clearer. The section provided merely that the commission could by regulation adopt administrative interpretations of the Espionage Act. Early in the hearings both Forrestal and Ickes contended that this device would not protect technical information in peacetime. Since the Espionage Act appeared to cover only the dissemination of official Government documents, the commission could not rely on it to control information generated in private research not supported by Government contract.[17] Thus the commission could not hope to maintain the rigid security system which the Manhattan District established under the war powers and which the scientists had bitterly opposed. Even if the section were adopted as written, Senator Hickenlooper doubted that an executive agency should have the power to interpret a criminal statute in peacetime. Senator Austin disabused his colleagues of any idea of enlarging the scope of the Espionage Act. After long service on the Senate Judiciary Committee, he was convinced this was impossible. If the committee did not yet have a solution, it now saw the issues.[18]

493

The McMahon bill's provisions for controlling materials had even more critical implications. Within the realm of atomic energy, the bill seemed to contradict some of the most sacred traditions of the American economic system. That the bill created a state monopoly of atomic energy was unusual enough. What was even more surprising was that this did not seem to offend the conservative majority on the committee. Newman later wrote of "the curious paradox that conservative men, actuated by the most profoundly conservative of all emotions, the desire to achieve security, were forced to resort to the radical expedient of state socialism." [19]

Section 5 made the commission sole owner of all source materials after mining, all fissionable materials, all devices for producing fissionable materials, and all atomic weapons and weapon parts. The commission would acquire all existing materials and devices from other Government agencies by transfer and from companies or individuals by purchase or condemnation.

There were similar provisions in the May-Johnson bill, but S. 1717 went further in one respect. It declared that the commission should be "the exclusive producer of fissionable materials, except production incident to research and development activities." Section 4 provided that existing production contracts could continue in effect for not more than one year, by which time the commission would "arrange for the exclusive operation of the facilities employed in the manufacture of fissionable materials by employees of the Commission."

Those present at the hearings seemed to agree that extraordinary Government controls were justified, but was it necessary to give the Government sole right of ownership and to go so far as to require operation of the plants by Government employees? That depended upon how one interpreted the purposes of control. One aim was to keep atomic energy firmly under the Government's thumb until international controls were established. A second was to prevent the atomic revolution from swamping the free enterprise system. Virtually all the controversy occurred in the second context.

494

The classic approach to free enterprise was to minimize Government controls. George E. Folk, speaking for the National Association of Manufacturers, could not reconcile Sections 4 and 5 with the stated purpose of the bill "to insure the broadest possible exploitation of the field" of atomic energy. If the bill was to fulfill the stated policy of "strengthening free competition among private enterprises so far as practicable," Folk advocated that "the Commission should be given only such authority as is, or may become, conducive to public safety and public health, with the least possible Government interference." John C. Parker, representing the Association of Edison Illuminating Companies, agreed. "I think it would be most desirable that as much as possible in the active production be done under the thing that—for want of a better phrase—we call the free enterprise system and by a plurality of producers, but subject to the most extremely tight controls." [20]

The counterapproach to free enterprise was to inhibit monopolies. Specifically, this meant keeping Manhattan District contractors from cornering atomic energy technology and exploiting its civilian uses. Newman and Miller had criticized the May-Johnson bill for providing inadequate protection against this threat. They had emphasized the antimonopoly theme in drafting the McMahon bill, and no member of the committee had yet objected publicly to this feature.

What stirred the committee, however, to advocate unprecedented Government intervention in the economic process was the anticipation of substantial if not spectacular innovations in nonmilitary uses of atomic energy. Most of the scientists probably would have agreed with Oppenheimer's conclusion that technological advances in the foreseeable future would fall within the area of existing scientific knowledge; but lawyers and legislators had to allow for every eventuality, scientists only for the plausible. Who could be sure that someone would not invent a pill which could be dropped in a pail of water to heat a house or even a community for a year? Could the Government permit such a revolutionary invention to remain in the hands of a single individual or company? The committee was not yet prepared to rewrite the preamble of the bill which Newman and Miller had drafted in November: "The effect of the use of atomic energy for civilian purposes upon the social, economic, and political structures of today cannot now be determined. It is reasonable to anticipate, however, that tapping this new source of energy will cause profound changes in our present way of life." [21]

Section 7 clearly reflected the "pill in the pail" philosophy. Basically, the section prohibited manufacturing or operating any device utilizing atomic energy or fissionable material without a license from the commission. To this provision, Newman and Miller attached two long paragraphs describing the procedures for licensing civilian uses. "Whenever in its opinion industrial, commercial, or other uses of fissionable material have been sufficiently developed to be of practical value, the Commission shall prepare a report to the President stating all the facts, the Commission's estimate of the social, political, economic, and international effects of such utilization, and the Commission's recommendations for necessary or desirable supplemental legislation." Not until ninety days after the President filed the report with Congress could the commission license the manufacture of the device and the utilization of fissionable material on a nonexclusive basis. In case someone contrived a "pill in the pail" invention, Congress would presumably have time to pass appropriate legislation before the commission issued a license.

495

PATENTS

In one way or another, the committee's discussions of political and economic implications always turned eventually to patents. Like nuclear physics, patent law was a subject only experts understood. Even laymen could see, however, that atomic energy would profoundly affect the American patent system. Government control of materials and processes implied restrictions on the patent process. The original patent clause (Section 10) of the McMahon bill did not go much beyond recognizing the fact that a private inventor could not be permitted to patent a device for producing fissionable materials. Under Section 10, he would send his application to the Commissioner of Patents, who would assign to the commission all patents related to atomic energy. The bill also created a patent royalty board which would determine just compensation for the inventor.

The hearings demonstrated how dangerous a little knowledge could be in the patent field. William H. Davis, a former director of the Office of Economic Stabilization and veteran patent attorney, lectured the committee for an hour on the fundamentals of patent law. Looking at Section 10 as legislation supplementing the basic patent statute, he suggested minor changes to avoid inconsistencies and facilitate administration of the law. But Davis did not restrict himself to practical advice. Soon the discussion drifted into the philosophy of the patent system. What, after all, was the committee trying to accomplish in Section 10? Was it attempting to use patents to control information about technical devices for producing fissionable materials? Or was it seeking to forestall monopoly in the new industry by setting aside the patent system? If the latter were the aim, Davis objected. It was perfectly natural to think of patents as a monopoly and therefore to try promoting widespread development of atomic energy by abrogating the patent system. In fact, Davis contended, the patent system stimulated rather than retarded technical progress. It rewarded inventors, encouraged them to publicize their inventions, stimulated the investment of risk capital in new ideas, and promoted diversity in inventions. In the interests of public safety and national security, Davis believed Government ownership of patents as provided by Section 10 was essential. The great weakness in the section was the imposition of compulsory, nonexclusive licensing on patents acquired by the Government. This provision, in Davis' opinion, would cut off all risk capital from the atomic energy industry.[22]

As the hearings continued, the committee exhibited growing concern about the application of the patent section to the complex contractual relationships of modern industry. Suppose a contractor like Kellex had developed a pump which was a vital part of an isotope-separation plant but also had valuable commercial applications unrelated to atomic energy? Was it proper for the Government to acquire the patent under Section 10 and grant royalty-free licenses to Kellex's competitors? Was it any more proper to permit Kellex to retain exclusive rights to the commercial applications? Davis evaded the question by saying that the answer depended upon the terms of the contract. The question then became, what were the patent clauses in the OSRD and Manhattan District contracts during the war?

Testimony by Irvin Stewart and Captain Robert A. Lavender, the OSRD and Manhattan District patent adviser, outlined the wartime patent system in all its complexities. Stewart explained that OSRD research contracts contained one of two patent clauses. The first gave the Government full power to dispose of all patent rights developed under the contract. The second, modeled after Army and Navy practice, left with the contractor title to inventions under the agreement, subject to a license in favor of the Government for military, naval, and national defense purposes. The Manhattan District had used many patent clauses in a variety of contracts covering not only research and development but also procurement, construction, and operation of plants. Lavender explained that most of the patent clauses fell into one of four categories. For research contracts, the Army used the OSRD form granting the Government full rights. The second form granted the contractor a nonexclusive license for commercial applications while the Government retained all rights to atomic energy uses. The third form gave the Government the right to determine the disposition of all inventions but permitted the contractor to retain the sole license for commercial applications and the right to grant sublicenses. This form was used to procure equipment which required only a slight modification of an already existing product. The last form, incorporated in contracts for procuring standard items, provided that the contractor assume liability for patent infringement.[23]

Exploring these intricacies gave the committee many new insights. Particularly arresting was Lavender's description of Patent Office procedures for handling applications filed by the Manhattan District. These were reviewed by a limited number of examiners and filed in special safes. Despite Lavender's assurances, McMahon and Millikin were disturbed to discover that secret atomic energy data were in Patent Office files. They were even more alarmed to learn that detailed descriptions of the bomb were filed with patent applications. Lavender explained that, anticipating a flood of applications on bomb devices after the Hiroshima attack, he had filed the applications to protect the Government's interests. Apparently, under existing law Lavender had no other choice. Still, McMahon and Millikin regretted the action.[24]

497

The committee could not explore all aspects of the patent question in open hearings, but enough had been said to sketch in the issues. To protect the Government's interests, Lavender had filed applications on secret devices and processes. Under wartime powers, he could delay issuance of the patents and set aside interferences temporarily. But eventually, the Patent Office would have to act. Routine issuance of the Manhattan District patents to the commission was unthinkable because the atomic secrets would thereby be published. The issuance of secret patents would disrupt the American patent system and was considered a legal absurdity by most American patent lawyers. The one recourse not yet explored but consistent with American patent practice was to introduce an exception to the enumerated classes of patentable subject matter under the Patent Act. Many kinds of inventions were already excluded from the patent system by law. A similar exclusion for Section 10 of the McMahon bill would automatically protect the Government's interests while permitting it to maintain secrecy in atomic technology.[25]

These discussions during the hearings provided a firm point of departure for subsequent study in executive session. In the five weeks prior to March 14, the section was completely redrafted twice. The final version rested entirely on the principle of excluding large areas of atomic energy technology from the protection of the Patent Act.[26]

Since the commission was to have the exclusive right to produce fissionable materials and weapons, there was no hesitation in excluding these activities from the patent process. In its final form, the section provided that "no patent shall hereafter be granted" and "no patent hereafter granted shall confer any rights" for any inventions in these two categories. Furthermore, persons making such an invention or discovery would be required to report it to the commission unless an application had been filed at the Patent Office, which would be required to give the commission access to all such information.

More unusual was the exclusion of any invention or discovery "used in the conduct of research or development activities in the fields specified in section 3." Since that section embraced not only atomic energy research but also the many disciplines in which that research could be applied, the language of the bill seemed to remove from patent protection large areas of scientific investigation. On the other hand, as one patent authority observed, "the actual effect upon patent rights may be almost negligible, for few of the patents involved will be so clearly destined for research purposes alone that the patent right can be ignored." [27] Apparently, the purpose of the section was not to remove many classes of scientific devices from patent dominance but simply to assure that patent control would in no way restrain atomic energy research.

Except for the production of fissionable materials or for research and development, atomic energy utilization devices could be patented, but exclusive rights could not be retained by the inventor under certain conditions. The bill required the commission "to declare any patent to be affected with the public interest if (A) the invention or discovery covered by the patent utilizes or is essential in the utilization of fissionable material or atomic energy; and (B) the licensing of such invention or discovery under this subsection is necessary to effectuate the policies and purposes of this Act." For all patents so affected, the bill granted nonexclusive licenses to all persons authorized by license to manufacture equipment or to utilize fissionable materials. The first condition protected Government control of fissionable material; the second guarded against the revolutionary effects of a "pill in the pail" invention.

During twelve mornings since January 22, the Special Committee had heard almost twenty-four hours of testimony on the riddles underlying domestic legislation. For the first time, a Congressional committee had succeeded in breaking through the superficialities that had plagued earlier explorations of this novel subject. Coming at last to grips with the cumbersome political and economic issues which the bill raised, the committee forgot about political overtones and concentrated on the pedestrian tasks of the legislator. But this was only a brief interlude. From the turbulence of the Washington political scene there inevitably emerged the fleeting advantage which McMahon and his colleagues eagerly awaited. After all, successful political careers and even vital legislation were less the product of reflective statesmanship than the fruits of skill and dexterity in the political arena.

498

RETURN TO THE FRAY

The break in the stalemate came when Patterson testified on February 14, 1946. The Secretary had been on a world tour when the hearings began in January. As a result, the Pentagon's only official comments on the McMahon bill had come from Forrestal. He had struck a telling blow against the policy of military exclusion, but the main assault on the McMahon bill would come from the Secretary of War.

Patterson had launched his attack three days earlier. On the eleventh, he sent to the Executive Office a bulky document containing the Department's comments on S. 1717. A twenty-two-page analysis prepared by his legal staff in January, the Patterson report placed every section of the bill under the legal microscope. Every vague or ambiguous phrase, every inconsistency or omission was meticulously recorded. As for the larger policy issues, the report cited the defects already revealed by the hearings—the lack of a general manager, the anomalous position of the statutory divisions and advisory boards, the inadequacies of the Espionage Act, and the administrative difficulties involved in commission ownership and production of fissionable materials.[28]

499

Patterson struck his hardest blow at section 6 and the other clauses that excluded the Army from any part in developing atomic energy. "Except that the President may direct the transfer of atomic bombs to the armed services in the interests of national defense," he said, "the War and Navy Departments are almost totally excluded." He urged amending the bill to permit a military officer on active duty to serve as director of the division of military application, to permit the services to engage in research on atomic weapons, to direct the commission "continuously to consult and maintain close liaison with the War and Navy Departments," to require the commission to "secure the concurrence of the Joint Chiefs of Staff prior to the adoption of principles or policies affecting the utilization of atomic energy as a military weapon," and to establish an advisory board of national defense to guide the commission on military applications of atomic energy.

The War Department report was a competent and convincing critique of the McMahon bill. It was not soon destined, however, to be the subject of public debate. By Executive Order, all departmental comments on proposed legislation went first to the Budget Director to be certain that the views expressed were consistent with the position of the Administration. Harold Smith and Frederick J. Bailey did not have to study the Patterson report long to see the possibility of its contradicting the views the President had expressed in his February 1 letter to Senator McMahon. Truman's first point had been that the commission "should be composed exclusively of civilians." Literally, that might restrict military exclusion to the commission itself and still permit military officers to serve on the staff or advisory boards. Patterson had hung his argument on that interpretation, but his proposal seemed to violate the spirit if not the letter of the President's memorandum. Smith sent the document to OWMR, where presumably Newman would prepare a reply. Whatever Smith's intentions, his action was tantamount to killing the War Department report.

Thus Patterson was in a tight spot. He could not publicly oppose the President's position. Yet he could not support it in good conscience without repudiating the unequivocal stand he had taken in defending the May-Johnson bill. Since he could not use the written report at the Special Committee hearings, Patterson had no recourse but to clear his prepared remarks directly with the President. The night before his appointment with the McMahon committee, the Secretary discussed his statement with the President and Admiral Leahy. Though Truman would allow no compromise on the principles in his February 1 letter, he did not force his associate into a strait jacket. After avowing his agreement with the President's letter, Patterson could suggest the possible dangers of excluding the armed forces from all phases of research and development on military applications. Truman even went so far as to let Patterson advocate that the Army retain the existing supply of bomb components rather than transfer them to the commission. The Secretary was also permitted to advance his arguments against basing the control of information on the Espionage Act alone.[29]

The Secretary's towering integrity and forensic skill were evident during his testimony on February 14. He declared his views consistent with those in the President's letter. He carefully restricted his criticisms to those points mentioned in his prepared statement, and he refused the opportunity afforded by McMahon to introduce the specific recommendations in the suppressed War Department report, which provided greater military participation in atomic energy affairs. But even his exceptional dexterity in juggling the committee's questions could not save him from a few difficult moments. Senator Hart grilled him for his abrupt shift regarding the composition of the commission. In supporting the May-Johnson bill, Patterson had advocated a part-time, nine-man commission. Now he was accepting Truman's recommendation for a full-time, three-man body. By avoiding any reasonable explanation for the switch, he adroitly implied what his own views were.[30]

If the McMahon group planned to make any political capital out of Patterson's testimony, they were disappointed. Without violating his obligations to the President, Patterson managed to convey his own opinions to the committee. His confident manner and grasp of the subject made a solid impression. Unless McMahon could turn the tide, the fortunes of military exclusion seemed to be waning. For the following week he scheduled a few more witnesses who would concentrate on the arguments for civilian control. On Tuesday, February 19, he hoped to conclude the hearings and begin executive sessions on the bill.[31]

500

Over the week end the roof fell in. Saturday, February 16, brought news from Ottawa of the arrest of twenty-two persons in an investigation of the disclosure of secret information, reportedly about atomic energy, to unauthorized persons, including members of a foreign mission. Although Canadian officials at first denied that atomic energy data were involved, it was clear by Tuesday that some "bomb secrets" had reached the Soviet embassy. The news stunned Washington. To those who had come to think of the "secret" as the nation's most valuable possession, the reports represented a threat to American security. For others, the evidence of Russian perfidy shattered the hopes for international peace and understanding. Few agreed with Joseph E. Davies, former ambassador to the Soviet Union, who declared that the Russians in self-defense had a moral right to seek bomb secrets through military espionage if they were excluded from such information by their former allies.[32]

For most Americans the news was a psychological shock. From the FAS headquarters in Washington, Higinbotham sadly reported to the local organizations that the steady flow of correspondence supporting the McMahon bill had ceased the day the spy story broke. Disillusionment with the Russians, the impulse to protect even more carefully what secrets might remain, and elemental fear seemed in a moment to drown the sort of postwar idealism that prompted scientists to advocate the free exchange of scientific information. These reactions were understandable, but many FAS members were dismayed to see how many people saw in the spy case an argument for retaining General Groves's military security system. Already suspecting the Army of using the incident for this purpose, some of the scientists began telling newsmen and radio commentators that the spy stories were part of an Army attempt to force passage of the old May-Johnson bill.[33]

One element in the growing hysteria was the fact that very few people knew any of the details of the Canadian spy case. Not even the Special Committee knew how much, if any, weapon technology had seeped to Soviet intelligence agents or whether any American citizens were involved. On Thursday, February 21, McMahon assembled the committee to hear the facts in executive session. J. Edgar Hoover, director of the Federal Bureau of Investigation, appeared presumably to describe the spy ring itself. Secretary of State Byrnes assured the committee no Americans were implicated. General Groves explained what had not yet been released to the press, that Alan Nunn May, a British physicist assigned to the Canadian atomic energy project, had transmitted to Soviet agents some information about the American effort. During three visits to the Chicago Metallurgical Laboratory in 1944, May had seen most of the research and development work at the laboratory, learned something of the design, construction, and operation of the Hanford piles, and received very limited information about the production of fissionable materials and weapons.

During his testimony Groves made a deep impression on the conserva-

501

tive members of the committee. Confident of his skill in Congressional hearings, the General was not one to hide his superior knowledge of the Manhattan project. Nor was he reticent to express his opinion on related subjects if asked. Hearing the General for the first time since his brief appearance in November, the committee became engrossed in the discussion. Before the session ended, the members had invited Groves to testify at an open hearing to state his views on legislation.[34]

McMahon was annoyed when the committee convened to hear the General on February 27. He emphasized that Groves had already testified "a couple of times before" and that the committee, not the chairman, had invited the witness to speak on legislation. Having put those facts on the record, McMahon threw down the gauntlet to his adversary in his most pompous Senatorial manner: "Now, you go right ahead, General."

Groves accepted the invitation gladly. First, he went out of his way to explain that it was "rather unusual for an Army officer to be asked to appear before a Senate committee to give his personal views as divorced from the War Department." He referred to his unsuccessful efforts to secure a written invitation from the chairman. The implication was that an exceptionally qualified witness could not be prevented from testifying by a chairman's opposition or by ordinary rules of procedure. He also thought it necessary to add: "At the outset, I would like to make it perfectly clear that I have never sought nor do I now aspire to any appointment on or under any proposed commission on atomic energy." He proposed, in other words, to speak with all the independence of a private citizen.

Since Groves did not consider himself bound by Administration policy as Secretary Patterson had been, he launched a renewed appeal for a part-time commission. When asked, he did not hesitate to suggest the names of men to be appointed to the new body. He was equally frank when Vandenberg questioned him about military exclusion. National security depended upon the Army and Navy having a voice in developing "the most powerful military weapon in existence." And by service representation, he did not mean putting a civilian head of a department on the commission but a man with extensive military experience "who is not going to forget for one minute that . . . defense must come first and other things will have to come afterward until the international situation is resolved."

McMahon tried ineffectively to parry Groves's strong thrust. He cited a column by Roscoe Drummond reporting an interview with General Eisenhower in which the Chief of Staff advocated an all-civilian commission. Groves denied any knowledge of Eisenhower's views. He did not care whether the military representatives were active or retired officers so long as they had the proper background and ability. To this McMahon replied: "It seems to me you have drawn a bill of particulars here which you could pretty well fit."

Moving the discussion from personalities back to issues, Vandenberg probed Groves's arguments for military representation. He believed the commission should have the advantage of military experience. On the other hand, the Michigan senator was committed to civilian control. Any military officers serving on the commission should be permanently retired "to be absolutely free from domination" by the armed services. Groves did not disagree, but he made it plain that military representation was necessary in some form. "If any such bill is adopted which does not include men with military background on the Commission, the Commission should be required by law to submit to the Joint Chiefs of Staff all matters of policy prior to adoption and before publication."

This suggestion bore striking similarity to that included in the War Department report on S. 1717, which the Budget Bureau had not yet released. By emphasizing his role as an independent witness and by denying any intimate knowledge of the War Department report, the General was able to present its principal recommendation to the committee with impunity. If Newman had by chance chosen to overlook the report until the hearings were over, he had delayed in vain. Groves had succeeded in interjecting the one idea that would doom McMahon's plea for military exclusion.

503

McMahon seethed with rage. Assuming the air of a prosecuting attorney, he asked Groves for the date of every promotion since his graduation from West Point in 1918. The questioning served to emphasize the fact that he had been a first lieutenant for fifteen years, from 1919 to 1934. Other questions implied that Groves had had little experience in research and development activities and that he had deliberately challenged the Administration's position on the bill. Designed to embarrass Groves, the questioning gave him the advantage. McMahon, not Groves, seemed petty and unreasonable. Hickenlooper made a point of thanking Groves for testifying, and several members later told the General they regretted that "the Chairman's attitude had been so obviously unfair in every way." [35]

Desperation marked McMahon's actions. He had helped save the nation from the May-Johnson bill; he had organized the Special Committee; he had sponsored the new bill and patiently nursed it through weeks of hearings. Then with the fruits of victory almost within grasp, the Army had used the spy case to revive the May-Johnson bill. Groves had won a hearing and succeeded in capturing the support of the conservative majority, including Vandenberg, who might well hold the destiny of the bill and the committee.

In this frame of mind, McMahon could no longer see the issues clearly. Civilian control to him meant nothing less than military exclusion; anyone who opposed the latter was advocating military control of atomic energy. This was the message he would carry to the people. Speaking before the Overseas Press Club at the Waldorf-Astoria the evening after the Groves hearing, McMahon confined himself to the military-civilian control issue. The failure of the United States to transfer atomic energy to a civilian agency would be a signal to the world that the atomic armament race was on. Military control, as embodied in the May-Johnson bill, would violate not only the law and the Constitution but also the most sacred American traditions.

The reference to the May-Johnson measure was not just an idle attempt to dredge up old issues. Rumors were rife in Washington that the War Department was helping Congressman May plan a move to force the bill through the House. May as much as acknowledged this in a brief statement on the House floor on March 1. The news frightened the scientists. Higinbotham wrote the FAS locals of a last-ditch fight to save the McMahon bill. The Washington organizations were planning full-page advertisements in the New York *Times* and Washington *Post* and would hold a press conference on legislation before the end of the week. Higinbotham urged the FAS locals to begin a "strong campaign of letter-writing."

The combined efforts of McMahon, the Newman team, the FAS, and the NCAI soon produced results. Griffing Bancroft began in the Chicago *Sun* a series of articles reviewing the long development of the civilian-military struggle. George Fielding Eliot criticized Groves and the supporters of the May-Johnson bill in a syndicated article. Urey, maintaining a whirlwind pace in his speaking tour on the eastern university circuit, attacked both the bill and the Army. By insisting on military control, he said, the Manhattan District "has practiced and wishes to practice a whole number of things contrary to the Bill of Rights of the American Constitution." [36]

504

VANDENBERG AMENDMENT

As these alarms were sounding through the nation, the Special Committee was preparing to draft legislation. The first issue was where to begin. During the open hearings the conservative majority had studiously preserved the attitude that McMahon's bill was but one of several proposed. It was therefore something of a victory for McMahon when the committee after some discussion agreed to accept his bill as the basis for legislation. [37]

That the subject was debated was fair warning to the McMahon forces that they could anticipate extensive amendments. Vandenberg in particular was eager to find a sensible solution to the military-civilian control issue. Groves's testimony had set him thinking. At the executive session the following day, he emphatically denounced military exclusion. No one was more interested in civilian control than he, but the commission's decisions had to be subjected to military review when military considerations were involved. The civilian commission should have absolute freedom to make any decision it wished, but he believed the Army Chief of Staff should review any action on military questions.

So convincing was Vandenberg's proposal that McMahon's group again had to go to the White House for help. Unless they could smoke out the issue for public debate, they had little chance of stopping it in the committee. McMahon wrote the President asking for the War Department report on S. 1717. Newman, quickly changing to his OWMR hat, could then draft a memorandum to Budget Director Smith opposing Administration approval of the report. That gave Newman a chance to spike the idea of giving the Joint Chiefs of Staff power of review. To counter Vandenberg's only slightly different suggestion of Army Chief of Staff review, Newman drafted for John Snyder's signature a memorandum attacking that proposal in detail. At the end of the six-page statement, Snyder recommended that the President discuss the subject with Eisenhower before he testified before the committee. Whether or not Truman followed the suggestion, the committee soon learned that Eisenhower did not favor military review.[38]

McMahon had survived this threat, but he was now convinced he had no hope of selling complete military exclusion to the committee. As a compromise, he suggested a military applications advisory board, consisting of an equal number of military officers and civilians as determined by the commission. The board "would advise and consult with the Commission on all atomic energy matters relating to the national defense," would be kept fully informed by the commission, and would have the authority to make written reports to the commission. The commission itself would consist of four public members, plus the Secretaries of State, War, and Navy. However galling these proposals may have been to the McMahon forces, they had several points to recommend them. The commission would retain the initiative through its power to determine the composition of the board, decide what information the board needed to be fully informed, and accept or reject the board's recommendations. The proposal also avoided direct military representation on the commission or its staff.

505

The closed-door sessions during the first week of March, 1946, showed even this proposal to be an optimistic gambit on McMahon's part. The conservative majority, including Vandenberg, were not convinced the proposal was more than clever window dressing. The military, many members thought, should not only have a voice; they should also have some legal guarantee their voice would be heard. Late in the week, the majority proposed two amendments—that the President rather than the commission determine the size of the board and that the board have the right of appeal to the President on all commission decisions related to military applications.

Now fast losing ground, McMahon again appealed for outside help. The committee agreed to hear the views of Eisenhower and Fleet Admiral Chester W. Nimitz, the Chief of Naval Operations. McMahon arranged a private dinner party at the Metropolitan Club on Monday evening, March 11. In the congenial surroundings of the old club, everyone relaxed. The evening was far spent before the conversation turned at last to atomic energy legislation. Vandenberg was pleased to see the two war heroes exercise "amazing restraint" on the subject of military control. Not preoccupied as Groves was with the sanctions of military representation, they emphasized "their desire to establish civilian control to the last possible degree of national safety." At the same time, they believed the military services should have a strong voice on matters of national security.[39]

Superficially, the dinner meeting was inconclusive. Yet, when the committee reassembled on Tuesday, it was clear that the military leaders had impressed the conservative members. Vandenberg arrived with some new language. First, he would remove the *ex officio* members from the commission, in line with his interest in giving the civilian body complete independence in its deliberations. His proposed revision of McMahon's draft was subtle but fraught with significance. McMahon had placed the burden upon the military board to consult with the commission and keep itself informed of the commission's military activities. Vandenberg would direct the commission to consult with the board, which could make written recommendations to the commission. The board's right of appeal to the President would be broadened to apply not only to "military applications of atomic energy" but also "to all atomic energy matters which the board deems to relate to the national defense."

Here McMahon chose to make his stand. Vandenberg's amendment was tantamount to giving the military a veto over every decision of the commission. To call this civilian control seemed a mockery. McMahon protested as vigorously as he knew how, but the cause was hopeless. The committee by a vote of six to one adopted the Vandenberg amendment.

In this highly charged atmosphere, the news did not take long to spread through the capital. It happened that on the same day Secretary Wallace was opening an exhibit at the Department of Commerce dealing with the development of atomic power. Also scheduled to speak on the occasion were Condon and Byron Miller. By the time the ceremonies began, Wallace had news of the committee's action. He could not suppress his indignation. His voice rising angrily, he told his audience that the revised bill had the possibility of delivering the nation into the hands of "military fascism." He warned that "when the American people realize its significance, they will rise up in their wrath and let the Senate know what that action means." Before the end of the day, the scientists had joined Wallace. Two Washington societies wired McMahon that the amendment "would be a clear declaration to the world that the people of the United States will put their faith only in military might." [40]

Action quickly followed words. The next morning representatives of twenty member-organizations in the NCAI assembled at the offices of Americans United for World Organization. To get the widest possible discussion of the amendment, the group agreed to organize an informal committee which would serve as a clearinghouse for information and as a strategy board. By creating a special group rather than giving the responsibility to an existing organization like NCAI, they hoped to concentrate all its effort on "opposing any step leading to any degree of military control other than the strictly military applications of atomic energy." The delegates sent a telegram to McMahon urging him to reopen hearings on the amendment. Before adjourning, they agreed to call an "Emergency Conference on Atomic Energy" for the following week. Friends on the Hill had arranged to hold the opening session in the House Caucus Room. Rachel Bell, executive director of Americans United, would take over the planning details. With the conference only a week away, there was not a minute to spare.

An equally spirited reaction to the Wallace statement came from Vandenberg. The Michigan senator was furious because the McMahon forces had obviously attacked the amendment before anyone knew its details. "I am perfectly sure," he told the press, "Mr. Wallace did not know that the action of the committee leaves total and final authority over every phase of atomic energy in the hands of civilians." Determined to put the senator from Connecticut in his place, Vandenberg demanded an immediate meeting of the committee. He made sure that every member attended. To make the rebuke more painful without damaging the amendment, he supported a revision by Senator Austin, who liked the sound of the well-rounded phrase "common defense and security." Austin proposed to substitute it for the words "national defense," thus appearing to broaden the scope of the military board's right of appeal. The final vote, this time ten to one, was a stinging slap at McMahon. Vandenberg had demonstrated that every other member of the committee, including every other Democrat, had deserted the chairman. With that, he released the text of the amendment.

507

McMahon could take some comfort in the support that came from the President at his regular Thursday press conference, but on Friday the senator sustained new humiliations. Word leaked out that the commission's authority had been further circumscribed by the addition of two more committees. The first, growing out of Vandenberg's initial approach to atomic energy legislation the previous autumn, would create a joint committee, composed of five members of each House, to make continuing studies of the commission's activities and "of problems relating to the development, use, and control of atomic energy." That amendment had been added earlier in the week. On Friday, the committee accepted a proposal by Senator Hart to create a committee "to advise the Commission on materials, production, research and development policies, and other matters." This time the vote was four to two. McMahon refused to identify his sole supporter, but he angrily told the press the amendment was tantamount to deprecating in advance the power and prestige of the proposed commission.[41]

McMahon had indeed suffered humiliation, but there were compensations. Though he might not have chosen that particular battlefield, he had not lost the fight. The bitter struggle over the amendment had attracted great interest in his bill. Building on the preparations over several months, the FAS and NCAI had launched an extraordinary publicity campaign over the military-civilian control issue. No matter how little the average American knew about the McMahon bill, he was soon likely to learn that the Vandenberg amendment constituted a threat to civilian control in his government. It was also a stroke of luck that the McMahon group had been able to tack Vandenberg's name to the amendment. Coming up for re-election that year, the Michigan senator was susceptible to public pressure. Washington veterans like Dean Acheson had learned to rely on Vandenberg's habit of initially opposing a new idea and then moving through a period of "gestation" to final support of the cause. With Vandenberg's name on the amendment, McMahon had perhaps the best available insurance that his bill would ultimately pass in some form. Except for the controversial amendments, McMahon was pleased with the committee's action. By the end of the Saturday session, they had reached tentative agreement on twenty-two pages of the forty-page bill.

McMahon's strategy was to stimulate the public debate. The following Monday night he addressed a nation-wide radio audience on the CBS network. The vital issue was: "Are we going to have military domination or civilian development of atomic energy in this country?" The effect of the Vandenberg amendment "would be to so throttle the action of the civilian commission as to amount to the abandonment of all actual control to the military." The review powers of the military liaison board "would exalt the military to a position of authority in our national affairs unprecedented in our history. . . . Why not station a deputy chief of staff in the Attorney General's office, in the Interstate Commerce Commission?" [42]

Vandenberg could not permit this attack to pass unnoticed. Rising in the Senate on Tuesday afternoon, he disclaimed any desire to "precipiate a premature discussion of atomic energy controls," but he thought it important for the country to have an accurate understanding of pending legislation. He did not agree that an amendment supported by ten of the eleven members of the committee amounted to military fascism. Nor was it accurate to call it the Vandenberg amendment since he was "merely the draftsman who put on paper the consensus of the views" of the committee. The amendment assured that every member of the commission would be a civilian and that "civilians have the last word on everything." The liaison board would simply make recommendations; it had no vote and no veto. Perhaps the word "board" had too formal a connotation. Vandenberg was willing to substitute "committee," but he was "totally at a loss to understand the amazing adverse interpretations" placed on the proposal.

McMahon continued to argue that under the amendment the liaison board could "look into every single telephone call, every single file, every single action the Commission will take." But McMahon was standing alone. Senator Russell made that clear when, as ranking Democrat on the committee, he supported Vandenberg. On the Republican side, Hickenlooper went even beyond support. He noted that "we have heard eulogistic remarks concerning the sanctity of civilian control and the need for such control." But did the Senate know that one of the scientists who had access to top secrets in the

Manhattan project had been charged with treason? "He," Hickenlooper said, "was a civilian and a scientist." The Iowa senator disavowed any attempt "to indict any class or group of men in this country," but his dramatic revelation of Alan Nunn May's role in the Canadian spy ring produced that connotation in some newspaper headlines the following morning.[43]

If McMahon had no visible means of support in the Senate, he could take heart in what Senator Russell acknowledged was a "tremendous storm of protest which has been blowing across the Nation." For this he could thank the NCAI, the FAS, and especially the new Emergency Conference. Under the capable direction of Rachel Bell, the conference held its organization meeting in the House Caucus Room on Thursday morning, March 21. More than 300 delegates from a score of organizations heard Senator McMahon describe the status of the bill and make an appeal for organized help. The conference president, the Reverend A. Powell Davies of All Souls Unitarian Church in Washington, then explained that their aim was "to take control of atomic energy out of the hands of the military and to conduct a determined drive to vest control permanently in civilian hands." Several scientists and nine congressmen made brief supporting statements. Then Mrs. Bell outlined her plans for the campaign. Delegates were to secure commitments from their national organizations and local chapters to flood the President, members of Congress, and especially Senator McMahon with messages opposing the Vandenberg amendment, the May-Johnson bill, "or any other legislation which would mean military rather than civilian control." So they would not lose the advantage of the moment, the delegates then dispersed to call on their own congressmen. That evening, Davies and some of the same speakers addressed a public meeting in the F Street Auditorium of the Press Club Building. Now the campaign was in full swing.

509

In the meantime, the conference had not neglected the press. With the help of NCAI and FAS contacts, the new association got excellent coverage in some newspapers and magazines. Setting the pace for the newspaper press was the series of seven articles which Alfred Friendly wrote for the Washington *Post*. Beginning on March 20, Friendly apprised his readers of the struggle which had been developing behind the scenes since the previous fall to wrest the control of atomic energy from the military. The mass of detail, generously sprinkled with a choice selection of derogatory stories about General Groves, showed that the author had been well briefed by the Washington organizations. Taken together, the articles comprised a comprehensive if biased summary of the legislative battle.[44]

The efforts of the Washington groups brought quick results. Local FAS chapters served as the nuclei for "emergency committees" at the various sites. At Chicago, the university provided office space in the social science building, and a group of dedicated volunteers under the direction of Mrs. John P. Welling promptly organized letter-writing campaigns, canvassed Chicago civic leaders for funds, and maintained a steady flow of news releases to the press. The Chicago committee also encouraged the formation of groups in Michigan, especially in Vandenberg's home town of Grand Rapids. These activities, duplicated in a score of communities, brought Washington a torrent of mail. In the four weeks following the introduction of the Vandenberg amendment, the Special Committee alone received 42,189 pieces of correspondence, almost twice the volume delivered in the previous three months of committee activity. Many were bulky petitions containing hundreds of signatures, and there were the usual form letters. Most of the flood, however, was composed of individual letters from indignant war veterans or painstaking handwritten notes from conscientious housewives. There was no way of knowing the character and size of the correspondence delivered to the offices of committee members, but if it resembled that in the commitee's files it gave the desired impression of a widespread and sincere opposition to "military control" and the Vandenberg amendment.[45]

510

By the last week in March, there were signs that the atmosphere was clearing. Tempers had cooled. McMahon was beginning to feel the ground swell of public support. Vandenberg had begun his customary long pilgrimage from initial hostility to constructive action. Some of the scientists, after taking time to read the amendment and Vandenberg's remarks, were willing to concede the Michigan senator a point. The worst chink in McMahon's armor had always been his insistence on military exclusion. The Chicago scientists admitted their efforts "to rid themselves of military control and of security regulations have been identified in the public mind with international control of the bomb and with 'giving the secret to Russia.'" Perhaps by accepting a modification of the Vandenberg amendment, the scientists might eventually obtain an atomic energy act that was "40 to 50 per cent agreeable to us."[46]

McMahon sounded the note of compromise when he appeared with Helen Gahagan Douglas, Senator Johnson, and General Farrell on the March 28 broadcast of America's Town Meeting of the Air. Although he found a nation-wide demand for civilian control arising, he admitted that "our people realize that . . . we cannot and must not deny military participation in atomic energy until international controls are assured." He thought the military liaison board would be "an unworkable administrative monstrosity," but did not a feasible solution lie in the idea of a commission made up of four civilians and the Secretaries of State, War, and Navy? Senator Johnson joyfully acknowledged what he considered to be a McMahon concession. "I think that all of us are very happy that Senator McMahon is at last coming along and that he is now providing for consultation on the part of the War and Navy Departments. It is true, in his original bill that he introduced last September, that he advocated something along that line and then he got cold feet and introduced another bill that cut the military people clear out. Now he's kind of coming back again and we welcome him back home."

Vandenberg also was completing an intellectual journey. The personal pique engendered by the Wallace attack had given way to sober study of the issues. Now firmly committed to the idea of civilian control with military guidance on national defense, the Michigan senator was looking for a way to make compromise palatable. The opportunity came from an unlikely source. One of his callers that last week in March was Thorfin R. Hogness, who had come from Chicago to help organize the Emergency Conference. Hogness had succeeded in getting an appointment with the Army Chief of Staff. Like Vandenberg, Hogness found Eisenhower surprisingly flexible on the question of military representation. Showing some impatience with Groves's hard-headed views, the General said he was not fussy about the language of the amendment so long as it established reasonable liaison between the commission and the military services. Then, after talking with Vandenberg for a few minutes, Hogness realized that the views of the Army, the Vandenberg supporters, and the Emergency Conference were almost identical. Somehow, the specters of the previous fortnight had evaporated. Now there was reason to think the controversy could be settled quickly.[47]

511

When the Special Committee reconvened on Monday morning, April 1, the members had at their disposal a new committee print which consolidated the successive revisions during March. The print was, however, much more than a collation of changes. During the public debate of the previous two weeks, Newman, Miller, and the committee staff had found time to complete some major reorganizations which transformed the original McMahon bill into a measure more nearly resembling the committee's views.[48]

The most striking change was in Section 2. Once again the bill was back to five members appointed by the President. Now, however, they were to serve staggered terms of five years each. Added to Section 2 were the paragraphs previously in Section 11 on organization of the staff. These now provided for a general manager to be appointed by the President and the directors of the divisions of research, production, engineering, and military application, to be appointed by the commission. Also incorporated in Section 2 were the paragraphs establishing a general advisory committee, a military liaison committee, and a joint committee on atomic energy in the Congress.

Section 4, governing the production of fissionable material, completed the transition from the original idea of sole commission operation of production plants to sole commission ownership. The commission would be the exclusive owner of all such plants, but it was also authorized to make contracts for producing fissionable material in its own facilities. Under this provision, the commission could continue the system of contractor operation created by the Manhattan District.

Without specifically enlarging the role of the armed services in military applications of atomic energy, the revision of Section 6 shifted the emphasis away from exclusive commission activity on weapons research and development. The clause giving the commission control of the weapons stockpile was deleted, leaving only the provision that the "President from time to time may direct the Commission to deliver such quantities of weapons to the armed forces for such use as he deems necessary in the interest of national defense."

More substantial changes occurred in Section 10, previously titled "Dissemination of Information." Now bearing the effects of the Canadian spy case, the section was marked "Control of Information." In abandoning the attempt to distinguish between "basic scientific" and "related technical" information, the committee also deleted the declaration establishing free dissemination as the cardinal principle in the information field. Now the emphasis was on restrictions, including the right of the service secretaries to prescribe additional regulations on information concerning military applications. Revisions in other sections included expansion of the patent provisions (Section 11) to include qualifications and standards for patent compensation and stiffening of the penalty provisions (Section 15) for violations "with intent to secure an advantage to any foreign nation." The impact of the conservative majority was clear, but the original premises of the McMahon bill had not been totally obscured.

The first order of business at the April 1 session was the military-civilian control issue. McMahon had silenced some of the charges of military exclusion by softening the provisions of Section 6 on military applications. The remaining points in dispute were the composition of the commission and the Vandenberg amendment. The first consumed most of the session on Monday as Johnson and McMahon both made unsuccessful attempts to add *ex officio* members to the commission.[49]

The long-disputed amendment was reserved for Tuesday, when all the committee could be present. Vandenberg offered the compromise he had beat out on his own typewriter after talking with Hogness. The changes seemed minor. Having the service secretaries rather than the President appoint the military liaison committee seemed to subordinate it to the commission. This pleased McMahon. The scope of the committee's responsibility would be reduced from Senator Austin's sonorous "common defense and security" to "military applications of atomic energy." This pleased Hogness and the scientists. The burden of responsibility to keep the committee fully informed was placed on the commission. This pleased the Army. The committee would appeal commission decisions not to the President but to the service secretaries, who would decide whether to appeal to the President. This pleased both McMahon and the scientists. The situation was identical to that of March 14. Vandenberg moved adoption of the revised amendment, Russell seconded the motion, and the committee voted its approval, ten votes to none, with McMahon abstaining.[50]

Just how these seemingly minor changes could transform the hostility of March 14 into the harmony of April 2 was something of a mystery. The

New York *Times* suggested that the initial dispute could have been avoided if all the parties had come to the conference table and discussed the issues sensibly. Ernest K. Lindley in the Washington *Post* thought most of the scientists' fury was directed at the straw man of military control. He thought the fight could have been avoided by giving up the impossible idea of military exclusion from the beginning. Newman and Miller later concluded that the committee's action had all the markings of a genuine political compromise. Not in a legalistic analysis of the language but in a study of the political undercurrents did they find the meaning of the revision. An equally good key to the mystery was McMahon's desperate need for public support. The dispute had made atomic energy legislation a national issue. With the spotlight focused on the bill, McMahon could afford to compromise and move for quick passage in the Senate.[51]

513

VICTORY IN THE SENATE

After the dissension that raged in the committee during previous weeks, the remaining sessions were an anticlimax. On April 3, 1946, McMahon entertained a dozen minor revisions which were quickly adopted. The only notable change was the deletion of all references to commission research on the social, political, and economic effects of atomic energy. Thus died quietly one of the principles of the original Newman-Miller draft. After four months of conflict, no one relished a skirmish over that point.[52]

Thursday, April 4, brought an open hearing on a more substantial question. Apparently, Senator Byrd had doubted the necessity of exempting the commission from the standard Government contract and audit regulations enforced by the General Accounting Office. Someone volunteered that GAO had approved these sections of the bill, but Byrd wanted to find out for himself. A routine call to a fellow champion of Government economy brought a decidedly negative reply. Lindsay C. Warren, the Comptroller General, told the committee on Thursday morning that he had never seen these provisions and would never have approved them if he had. He could see no reason for permitting the commission in Section 3 to award research contracts and grants "without regard to the provisions of law relating to the making . . . of contracts."

As for the provisions relating to audit procedures in Section 12, Warren found them "a mockery and a fraud." First, the section prescribed a number of audit functions for which the Comptroller General already had authority. Second, there was no need to permit the commission to use its own system of administrative accounts and other business documents; one of the primary purposes of GAO was to establish uniformity in administrative practices. But the "joker" in the section, said Warren, was the sentence preventing the Comptroller General from disallowing the expenditure of funds for items to which GAO had taken exception. The following Monday, April 8, General Groves backed up Warren by testifying that GAO had audited all Manhattan District accounts to date according to the standard regulations. Warren suggested some alternate language which seemed to meet the committee's aim of freeing the commission from bureaucratic technicalities, and the committee promptly adopted it.[53]

The next day, the committee came to the last unresolved issue in the bill—how best to control the dissemination of information. The phrase itself carried the contradiction that caused disagreement. On the one hand, it was important to stimulate the exchange of scientific data on the basic laws of nature if the nation were to enjoy the continued benefits of scientific advancement. On the other, national security demanded full protection of the few remaining technical secrets involved in producing fissionable materials and the bomb. The trick was to find some way to separate the first from the second. The committee had early learned that it could not adequately protect the technology under the Espionage Act. It had more recently abandoned the attempt to write a foolproof definition of "basic scientific" and "related technical" information. On April 9 and 10, the committee threshed out the possibilities and finally settled on the legislative device Newman and Miller had employed to assure the commission absolute but clearly defined control of nuclear materials—to coin a new term, give it a special meaning in the bill, and then give the commission the authority to interpret the meaning of the general definition in specific cases. Thus, to replace the generic phrase "information relating to atomic energy or fissionable material, or the production or utilization thereof," the committee devised the phrase "Restricted Data." This they defined as "all data concerning the manufacture or utilization of atomic weapons, the production of fissionable material, or the use of fissionable material in the production of power, but shall not include any data which the Commission from time to time determines may be published without adversely affecting the common defense and security." The definition itself gave the commission discretionary authority to meet unforeseen circumstances. Under this legal definition, the committee could then elaborate the full range of penalties for criminal actions involving the unauthorized dissemination of Restricted Data.[54]

On Friday, April 11, the committee completed its final actions on the bill. The next week was devoted to preparing the report to the Senate. To the usual history and analysis of the bill, McMahon added an essay on the fundamentals of atomic energy by Condon, several historical documents, a glossary, a chronology, and a bibliography. "Because of the extreme importance of the subject," he told the Senate on April 19, "I believe Senators will find it helpful to study the report as well as the provisions of the bill." Thus the Connecticut senator endured his first great trial, but others were yet to come.[55]

Taking stock of the situation, the McMahon group concluded that their best chance of getting the bill through the Senate was to play down the issues and above all to avoid a fight on the floor. The agonizing experience in committee amply demonstrated that at least a half dozen provisions of the bill could stimulate enough debate to hamstring the measure indefinitely. Furthermore, anything less than a solid front in the Senate would make it almost impossible to force the bill through the May committee and the House.

One danger was that the scientists might bring pressure for amendments during the Senate debate. The FAS Council at a meeting in Pittsburgh on April 21 objected to the broad powers given to the military liaison committee, the sweeping provisions on security which went "far beyond the Espionage Act," and the restrictions which the security provisions would impose on independent nuclear research. The Chicago Committee for Civilian Control added to these criticisms their disapproval of the commission's "arbitrary" right to deny licenses for industrial applications developed in Government projects. These reactions, however, bred resignation rather than hostility. Higinbotham took this position in his report to the FAS locals. They could not publicly compromise on the bill's deficiencies, but "the people who have worked with the committee on the bill feel that in spite of everything, this is a fairly good bill and should be passed." The Chicago group concluded: "The bill is not ideal, but it is workable providing a competent Commission is obtained." It seemed the McMahon group could keep a rein on the scientists.[56]

515

There was less reason to believe McMahon could influence the Army's response. Fortunately, the War Department was in no mood for a fight. The first anniversary of the Interim Committee's initial attempt to draft a bill was fast approaching, and the Manhattan project was still an Army responsibility. Patterson's legal advisers found nothing but minor faults in the bill. Marbury wrote to his former chief that S. 1717 covered all the fundamental points the Interim Committee had considered in drafting the May-Johnson bill. Arneson thought it assured adequate military security. In fact, he said, the legislation with the Vandenberg amendment "*guarantees* greater military participation than does the May-Johnson bill." General Groves was satisfied with the security provisions. Arneson thought that by accepting the revised McMahon draft as providing adequate participation for the armed services, the Department could lay the ghost of "military fascism" and speed enactment of legislation.

Arneson warned, however, of the dangers of repudiating the May-Johnson bill outright. That, thought Patterson, would be "fouling our own nest." More important, it might antagonize the House committee. To avoid that possibility, Patterson drafted a cautious letter to Chairman May. Deploring the attack on the May-Johnson bill as "unwarranted and unjustified," the Secretary stated his support of the McMahon bill in a dead-pan style. The first aim was to secure immediate passage of an adequate atomic energy law. It would be fatal, Patterson wrote, to resurrect the May-Johnson bill. If that were done, the debate would "bog down once again over this nightmare of military control." His letter might give results, but Patterson still feared unfortunate repercussions. Laying the draft aside, he waited to see what happened in the Senate. The War Department remained silent, and the McMahon group understood the tacit agreement. If the scientists did not attempt to amend the bill on the floor, neither would the Army.[57]

Playing the atomic energy bill in low key had advantages, but there was also danger of losing it in the legislative jungle. Slow progress of the British loan bill during May put even greater pressure on the Senate calendar, which still included extension of the draft law and the Office of Price Administration. Talking with Mrs. Welling by telephone on May 17, Senator Barkley weighed the relative advantages of waiting for House action or passing the bill in the Senate first. To wait might not leave the House enough time to act. The majority leader made no promises, but he thought he could sandwich the McMahon bill between the draft and OPA measures.[58]

With no signs of Senate activity by the end of the week, the scientists made plans for another letter and telegram campaign. This, however, proved unnecessary, for Senator Barkley was as good as his word. On June 1, a relatively quiet Saturday afternoon in the Senate, Barkley moved postponing debate on the draft bill until Monday when more members would be present. It was just before three o'clock. Senator Vandenberg and the Republican members of the committee moved across the aisle to join Senator McMahon, who rose to present the bill. Proceeding with a description of the legislation, McMahon paused occasionally for a question. After an hour of routine debate, he moved a committee amendment to prohibit the export of facilities for producing fissionable material. Senator Joseph C. O'Mahoney proposed a technical amendment in the section reserving source materials in the public lands for the United States. By the time the amendments were adopted, there were forty or fifty senators on the floor. Without a pause, the presiding officer put the question, and the Senate passed the bill unanimously by voice vote.[59]

ACTION IN THE HOUSE

Prospects were not good for prompt action in the House. Nearing the end of the session in an election year, most of the members were anxious to complete vital legislation and return to the hustings. Some members could be expected to respond favorably to the Administration's call for action or to the Emergency Committee's plea to defend the principle of civilian control, but these supporters were more than counterbalanced by the known hostility of the Military Affairs Committee. To some extent, pride was involved. Chairman May and his associates could not forget the fact that they had rushed to comply with the President's October 3 request for legislation, only to be deserted when the tide of public opinion swamped the unpopular War Department bill. They had reported out what they believed an acceptable measure more than six months ago. Now they were expected to give preferred treatment to a bill written by the Senate committee which had untiringly attacked the May-Johnson proposal. Added to this important factor of committee rivalry was a genuine disagreement on public policy. Nine of the Republicans on the twenty-seven-member committee had already gone on record as opposed to Government control of atomic energy. Several Democrats consistently sided with May in advocating a stronger military voice in the commission. Ironically, some of the stanchest supporters of the McMahon bill would soon be leaving Washington to attend the Bikini tests in the Pacific.[60]

The only hope for passage seemed to be very strong pressure from the President and House leadership to overpower the opposition and secure a quick decision. There was even talk of passing the bill before Bernard M. Baruch presented the American plan for international control at the United Nations on June 14. But there was another reason for haste. So late in the session, delay could be as fatal as an unfavorable vote.

Fortunately, the Administration had a week to organize its campaign since the House calendar prevented any action before June 10. It was a week of achievement. On June 3, Speaker Sam Rayburn had his Monday-morning legislative conference with the President. As he left the White House, he told the press that Mr. Truman preferred the McMahon bill to the May-Johnson measure and expected House action the following week. John J. Sparkman, a member of the May committee, suggested the possibility of recalling the May-Johnson bill so that the committee could act at once on the McMahon proposal.

If statements such as these did not tell May which way the wind was blowing, he could not have missed the import of other events not yet in the public press. First, the President had taken a personal interest in the McMahon bill, even to the extent of asking Executive agencies to swallow a number of imperfections in the Senate version in the interest of some atomic energy legislation in the Seventy-Ninth Congress. The second was the rapid closing of the ring around May and his wartime relationships with certain defense contractors. On Tuesday, the Kentucky congressman testified at a secret session of the Senate Special Committee Investigating the National Defense Program. Although May explained his activities in the Cumberland Lumber Company owned by Henry M. Garsson, he denied that he had participated in transactions with other Garsson companies which Senator James M. Mead's committee was then investigating. Under the circumstances, May was hardly in a position to challenge the Administration on the McMahon bill.[61]

The following week, May exhibited a new fervor for atomic energy

517

legislation. When S. 1717 was referred to his committee on Monday, June 10, he at once scheduled hearings to begin the next day. Brushing aside Republican efforts to raise the issue of the May-Johnson bill, the chairman turned at once to Secretary Patterson, the first witness. "All I want to do," May said, "is to get it to the floor of the House so we can act on it." [62]

Patterson began as usual with a recounting of the history of atomic energy legislation during the previous year. Starting with the appointment of the Interim Committee, he followed the tangled chain of events through the summer and fall of 1945. This approach permitted him to extoll the contributions of the May committee in their prompt action on the War Department bill and thereby pave the way for more gracious acceptance of the Senate version. The review also enabled the Secretary to clarify the original objectives of the Interim Committee—to create a civilian agency whose activities would "be consistent with foreign policy and national defense." Then he could proceed to the judgment that S. 1717 "does not depart in objectives or in principal provisions from the program suggested last summer by the Stimson committee." The commissioners would be civilians, but the military would have a voice through the military liaison committee. Furthermore, the commission would have specific authority to engage in weapon development and production, and the President would have the power to transfer weapons to the armed forces. The provisions, Patterson thought, were adequate for national defense. In fact, he thought the McMahon bill went "further in dealing with the national defense aspects of atomic energy than the earlier bill did."

May was impatient. He asked Patterson a few brief questions to point up the issues and then gave the floor to R. Ewing Thomason, ranking Democrat on the committee and avowed advocate of the McMahon bill. The Texas congressman quickly set about establishing Patterson's belief that the interests of the armed services were adequately protected by the military liaison committee.

But the opposition was in no hurry. Dewey Short, the ranking Republican, wondered whether the bill made "proper provision for private industry to explore and carry on this work, or whether ownership and control are wholly going to be under the Government." When Patterson suggested that the licensing provisions opened the way for industrial participation, Short was not sure the bill adequately restricted the commission. He thought it possible the commission could use the bill to regulate industries whose products had some incidental application in atomic energy plants. Charles H. Elston of Ohio joined Short in asking: "As a matter of fact, does the bill restrict anybody except the American people, American industry and the War and Navy Departments of this country?" On this note, the committee rushed off to meet a roll call in the House on the military leave bill.

On Wednesday morning, June 12, May was determined to conclude committee action on the McMahon bill. He had a few questions for Secretary

518

Patterson, and the only other witness scheduled was W. John Kenney, Assistant Secretary of the Navy. May hoped to conclude the testimony early enough so that the committee could at once consider amendments and final action on the bill.

The Republicans upset that plan, however, when they persisted in grilling Secretary Patterson for more than an hour. J. Parnell Thomas, the most outspoken opponent of the McMahon bill, wanted to know how Patterson could advocate passage of the May-Johnson bill in October and take the same position on the McMahon bill eight months later. If the delay resulted in a better bill, as Patterson claimed, why should not Congress delay longer until a still better bill was produced? What was all the hurry? Patterson replied that the improvement had come only at the price of delay, which had threatened the vigor and progress of the atomic energy program.

Thomas E. Martin of Iowa was particularly concerned about excluding military representatives from the commission. Congressman Elston questioned the need to establish any restrictions on the armed services or private industry in developing atomic energy. He maintained that the bill was unconstitutional because it delegated to the commission the power to write regulations, the violation of which would be punishable as felonies. J. Leroy Johnson of California suggested that the bill gave the commission authority to give the "bomb secret" to the United Nations without Congressional approval. Clare Boothe Luce declared the bill "a radical new departure for the American people." The commission, she said, "is not even socialistic, it is a commissariat."

By the time the committee had questioned Assistant Secretary Kenney, the morning session was over. May was angry as he left the committee room. He told the press that, although he did not agree with the McMahon bill, he had hoped to report it out that day so that the House could fight out amendments on the floor. Now he was forced to seek committee action the following day in executive session.[63]

BEHIND CLOSED DOORS

If May contemplated trouble, events did not prove him wrong. Out of the glare of public opinion, it was easier for the opposition to stall. In fact, as some members of the McMahon group charged, it was also easier for May himself to drag his feet. The chairman, however, stoutly disclaimed any lack of diligence on his part. He later told the House he had tried to convince the committee to report the bill without amendment, just to get it on the floor. His colleagues, however, decided to read the bill section by section and make detailed amendments. As the executive sessions continued day after day, May adopted the only strategy available to him. He agreed to accept the three amendments designed to give the military a stronger hand in com-

519

mission affairs—the inclusion of at least one but not more than two military representatives on the commission, a requirement that the director of military application be an active military officer, and a provision permitting active military officers to serve in any position on the commission's staff. Then he proposed to fight off disabling amendments as best he could. The bill was endangered not only by the delay but also by amendments which would make reconciliation with the Senate almost impossible.[64]

No one could be sure what was happening behind the closed doors of the committee room. May protested he was doing all in his power to expedite the bill. Newman was convinced "that at all times enough votes could have been mustered to get the bill out of Committee." Not only, Newman said, had the committee dallied; they had adopted the unorthodox practice of bringing in witnesses to testify on sections of the bill even though the hearings were "officially closed." Newman reported that on June 26 the committee heard a witness "purporting to be a representative of the American Bar Association, which has expressed itself in strong opposition to the patent features. It was evident from the tactics of the Republican members of the Committee present this morning that there is a concerted effort on their part to kill the entire bill in Committee by stalling and filibustering." Newman thought May was "sufficiently alarmed by press reactions and by Administration leaders so that he is now very anxious to get the bill out of Committee," but he was enjoying little support from the Democratic side. Sparkman had gone off to Alabama to begin his campaign for the Senate, and Chet Holifield was attending the Bikini tests. Without proxies from other Democratic members, May could not muster a quorum without Republican support. Since under House rules a bill could not be reported without a quorum, the opposition was able to prevent action simply by staying away.[65]

Newman was convinced the bill was dead unless it could be blasted out of the committee. He urged the President to see Speaker Rayburn and ask him to contact each Democratic member personally. The members should attend the hearings or leave their proxies with Thomason. Just how the job was done remained shadowed in mystery. Perhaps a sharp reminder from the Speaker was enough inducement for most of the faithful. For May, there may have been an added incentive, as Miller later suggested. The Mead committee was collecting records on the Garsson munitions enterprises and was preparing to open public hearings which would implicate the congressman. Whether or not May knew the committee had written evidence of his calls to the War Department on behalf of the Garsson interests, he must have suspected the worst. On July 2, the day his name was first involved in the open hearings of the Mead committee, May announced that the McMahon bill had been reported out by a vote of twenty-four to three.[66]

The House committee report would not be published until the following Monday, July 8, but there was no secret about its contents. The Chicago Committee sounded the alarm in a form letter to more than 1,000 religious leaders. The McMahon bill, as finally passed by the Senate, had established civilian control. "Now the House Military Affairs Committee is changing this bill by amendments restoring *military control*." Miller reported to the President's staff that the committee had "added a large number of amendments, some of which directly raise the issue of military control by requiring military membership on the Commission, and a great many of which are picayune but troublesome because they were prepared without full knowledge of the subject matter and construction of the Bill."

Miller saw that the bill could never survive this swarm of amendments. Either it would die in the House or would become hopelessly snarled in conference with the Senate. Even if some version did pass after a prolonged conference, enactment might come too late to permit the President to appoint the commissioners and general manager and have them confirmed before the end of the session.

521

TRIAL BY AMENDMENT

Stripping the amendments from the bill looked like a very tough job in the House. Under the House rules, there was no way to slip the bill through some quiet afternoon as McMahon had done in the Senate. First the bill would go to the Rules Committee, which could sidetrack it entirely or establish the rules under which it would be debated in the Committee of the Whole House. Ordinarily in that parliamentary form, the chairman of the committee sponsoring the bill would have the right to assign half the time allowed for debate and the ranking member of the opposition would receive the other half—in this instance, Congressmen May and Short. This dismal prospect led the supporters of the bill to adopt a new strategy. They could not prevent May from assigning time as he pleased during the general debate, but they could control the situation during the next phase, when each member of the House was allowed to offer amendments under the five-minute rule for each section of the bill. Thomason, not May, would command the Administration forces at that point. As Miller noted, "if we are advised of the strategy in advance, we can do a good deal of spade work with other members of the House to help on the floor." [67]

The McMahon forces worked out their strategy as best they could during the first week in July. On the tenth, May set the irreversible process in motion when he reported the bill in the House and automatically to the Rules Committee. There, the McMahon group could count on the support of the chairman, Adolph J. Sabath, who as a representative from Chicago was sensitive to the appeals of the scientists. [68]

The Administration seemed to have enough votes in the Rules Committee to get the bill to the House floor, but they had not reckoned on the concerted effort by J. Parnell Thomas to kill the measure in committee. To prove that continued control of atomic energy by the War Department was essential to the nation's safety, Thomas introduced on July 11 a report by Ernie Adamson, chief counsel of the House Committee on Un-American Activities. On the basis of a recent investigation at Oak Ridge, Adamson reported that former Manhattan District employees had organized small groups in various cities and continued to correspond with the scientific societies "inside the reservation at Oak Ridge." Adamson said his final report would show that "these societies are devoted to the creation of some form of world government." Furthermore, the scientists were supporting international control of atomic energy, were "definitely opposed to Army supervision at Oak Ridge, and are just waiting for the day when military administration will be thrown out." "The security officers at Oak Ridge," Adamson warned, "think that the peace and security of the United States is definitely in danger." Adamson concluded that "the Army should exercise permanent control over the manufacture of atomic energy."

522

What started out to be a routine hearing ended in the worst case of sensationalism since the introduction of the Vandenberg amendment. The scientists' groups, led by the Atomic Scientists of Chicago, pounced on Adamson's charges as "naive and unfounded." The Oak Ridge organizations charged the House committee with "raising a red herring" to block action on the bill. Under questioning, the Oak Ridge security officers denied they had expressed a concern for the national safety. Letters poured in to Sabath and the committee from the NCAI, FAS, and civilian control groups. The flood of public reaction quickly drowned Thomas' charges. On Saturday, July 13, the resolution passed the Rules Committee by a narrow margin—an eloquent warning of the hard fight ahead. The National Committee for Civilian Control ran a full-page advertisement in the Washington *Post* on July 15, urging the House to "Place The Control of Atomic Energy In *Civilian* Hands *Now!*" [69]

The debate began the following Tuesday, the sixteenth. The lumbering procedures of the House first required adoption of Sabath's resolution establishing the rules—four hours of general debate, equally divided between the two sides and followed by reading the bill for amendment under the five-minute rule. Committing himself firmly for the resolution and the bill, Sabath maintained "the most thoroughly informed people in America . . . say that none of the amendments strengthen or add to the bill." He noted that the May committee was far from unanimous in supporting the amendments. Thomas' charges and the Adamson report Sabath refused to take seriously.

On the other side, Elston found the measure "one of the most dangerous bills ever presented . . . it will deprive the people of their liberties." Thomas thought the one man in the world most interested in the bill was Andrei Gromyko. "He is sitting in New York laughing up his sleeve, hoping that the Congress of the United States is going to pass the kind of a bill that will do the very thing he has been trying to get." Since May took no part in the debate, Thomason summed up for the Administration. After Sabath agreed to extend the general debate to two and one-half hours for each side, the resolution passed easily, 162–35.[70]

On Wednesday morning, Chairman May rose after the opening formalities to begin the general debate. Rambling over the history of the May-Johnson bill and defending his committee against the charges of filibustering (which Short agreed were "a dirty lie"), May had little time to speak for the bill. He was appealing to the House not necessarily to support his views but "to use their conscience and their judgment." He thought it would not hurt to have the legislation on the books. It ought to be enacted but not permanently, perhaps for a period of three years. May's remarks indicated his lack of enthusiasm for the bill; his assignment of the Administration's time during general debate confirmed this attitude as he gave the floor to friend and foe alike.

523

The debate wandered over the provisions of the bill on Wednesday and Thursday as May and Short assigned their allotted time in ten- and fifteen-minute intervals. Under the rules, any semblance of logical order in the discussion was impossible, but the jumble of remarks gravitated to three topics—military control, patents, and security.[71]

No portion of the McMahon bill was more bitterly attacked than Section 11 on patents. In the opening moments of debate, Short gave the floor to Forest A. Harness of Indiana, who denounced the bill for placing "in the hands of a five-man commission complete and absolute authority over American industry and the lives of our entire population." The compulsory licensing of patents in Section 11 (c) would destroy "one of the fundamentals of a free-enterprise system under a free government." Fritz G. Lanham, for twenty years a member of the House Committee on Patents, likewise struck at the patent section as an attempt to undermine the American system. Because "the subject of patents is a very technical and detailed one," it might be hard to appreciate the threat implied in the patent clause. To indicate the opinion of the "experts," Lanham read into the record letters from the National Patent Council and the American Bar Association denouncing Section 11.

Clare Boothe Luce continued the assault. Her principal weapon was the testimony of a former Assistant Commissioner of Patents, who told the May Committee in a sneak session on June 26 that the only parallel he could find to Section 11 was in the Soviet patent law. The bill, Mrs. Luce said, had "a politically revolutionary character" and "might have been written by the most ardent Soviet Commissar." Elston attacked the "soviet" patent section as unnecessary, dangerous, and unconstitutional. Leslie C. Arends of Illinois said he would vote for the bill if it were restricted to controlling the production of atomic energy, but he was convinced it "would also change our fundamental patent policies in a manner to remove the keystone of our technical and economic progress." The only words reminiscent of the Senate hearings came from Clyde Doyle of California. He quoted letters from the National Association of Manufacturers acknowledging the necessity for Government control and ownership of fissionable-material production facilities, with operations by private industry permitted only under adequate licensing. Existing laws were "ridiculously inadequate" to meet the requirements of national safety and security. But Doyle's was a lonely plea in the House. The McMahon group could do little to slow the momentum of the amendment which Lanham promised to introduce.

Many of the same voices criticized the provisions of Section 10 on the control of information. Harness thought the bill "would remove all security provisions that we now have against the disclosure of secrets that are in the national interest." John M. Vorys of Ohio agreed: "I could not find any place where there were criminal penalties that could be invoked against the Commission." For J. Parnell Thomas, Harness' contention was validated by considering the authorship of the McMahon bill. One author was Newman (apparently Thomas thought no comment was necessary). A second was Condon, "an appointee of Henry Wallace," who had been prevented at "the last minute" from leaving the United States for a scientific conference in Russia "in a Russian plane." The third author was Urey, whom Thomas quoted as saying: "I would personally like to see all the penalty and security violations deleted from the bill." After rehashing the Adamson report, Thomas closed with the warning: "If you want to get the cue of who is pushing hard for the passage of this bill, read the Daily Worker . . . or read, in the New York papers of last week, the suggestion of the Russian delegate, Andrei H. Gromyko."

524

Strong support for the scientists and the freedom of scientific information came from both sides of the House. Mrs. Luce found "two consoling features about this socialistic, though I repeat necessary, bill." It gave the scientist every freedom for investigation consistent with national security; it permitted integration of national control with a world plan for atomic control. Estes Kefauver of Tennessee soberly but firmly defended his constituents at Oak Ridge. To Helen Gahagan Douglas fell the main burden of defending Section 10. She denied that the bill was designed to "give away the secret of the bomb." More than merely giving the nation a temporary defense, the bill provided a much more durable form of security. It promoted the progress of research, which would enable the United States to maintain its pre-eminent position in science. The only enduring protection against the destructive use of atomic energy was to maintain peace. The President's message of October 3, his letter to McMahon urging civilian control, the Truman-Attlee-King declaration, the establishment of the United Nations Atomic Energy Commission, the Acheson-Lilienthal report, and the McMahon bill were all steps in that direction. President Truman, General Eisenhower, Secretaries Byrnes, Patterson, and Forrestal, Senators Vandenberg and Connally all supported the bill. It was the way to lasting security.

A third but definitely subordinate theme in the debate was military control. Early in the Wednesday session, Melvin Price of Illinois rose in defense of the Senate bill. The crux of his argument was that the President, the Army Chief of Staff, the Chief of Naval Operations, and the service secretaries all believed the armed forces had adequate representation on the commission through the military liaison committee. "Who is there among us," Price asked, "who would wish to be more militaristic than the military?" In due course, the answer came from both sides of the aisle. John E. Rankin of Mississippi was perfectly willing to leave the bomb in the hands of the military for five more years. "If the Communists had this bomb and we did not . . . they would use it to destroy everything that Christianity has built in the last 1900 years." He warned his colleagues: "You are not going to wreck my country if I can prevent it; you are not going to take the only weapon we now have to protect ourselves and give it to our enemies. God forbid." In a somewhat lower key, Thomas E. Martin of Iowa defended the amendments the Military Affairs Committee proposed. He did not advocate military control of the commission, but he could not "subscribe to any program that disqualifies each and every one of our armed forces from active responsible participation in the control of this greatest of all known potential weapons." Elston found the military liaison committee "nothing more or less than a sop handed out to convey the erroneous impression that our armed forces are given some recognition."

About noon on Thursday, July 18, the time for general debate ran out. As the clerk began to read Section 1 for amendment under the five-minute rule, Representative Rankin rose with a preferential motion to strike the enacting clause. "If my motion prevails, the bill goes back to the committee . . . for further consideration. The measure will be left there and we will still have the question before us at the next Congress." On the question, then, rested the fate of the McMahon bill. So close was the voice vote that Rankin demanded a division. The Chair counted 93 ayes, 102 noes. By 9 votes out of almost 200, the bill had survived.

Following this narrow squeeze, the Administration forces could lay their strategy for the final skirmish. The McMahon group dispatched about fifty telegrams in a desperate effort to draw back to Washington the most sympathetic of the 125 Democrats who had already gone home. Thomason was prepared to defend the bill during the amendment process. With this slim margin, he could not hope to do battle against the impending flood of amendments, especially those proposed by the May committee. Fighting a rear-guard action, he would try to hold down the number of amendments so long as some semblance of a bill ultimately passed. Then the Administration could try to drive a hard bargain in the House-Senate conference.[72]

The House plunged into the amendments on Thursday afternoon. At first the going was slow as congressmen who were not members of the

525

Military Affairs or Patents Committees presented *pro forma* amendments simply to gain an opportunity to present their views on the bill. Several minor amendments to the statement of policy in Section 1 were quickly defeated. Section 2, on the organization of the commission and its committees, was a major target of the Military Affairs Committee. Thomason objected to the committee amendment making mandatory at least one military representative on the commission. J. LeRoy Johnson offered as a compromise that the appointment of a military member be permissive rather than mandatory. Mrs. Luce supported Thomason, but Elston and Martin brought up the heavy artillery for the committee. The Johnson compromise was swamped and the committee amendment adopted, 115–87. The other two committee amendments requiring the director of military application to be an active military officer and permitting officers to serve without prejudice on the commission staff were adopted by voice vote. Thomason obviously had no hope of stopping the committee on these changes, which were primary recommendations of its report.

Before the end of the day, the Committee of the Whole completed its work on the first five sections of the bill. Two significant amendments were proposed for Section 3, and one was adopted. Charles R. Clason, a Republican member of the May committee, proposed to give the military specific authority to engage in independent research and grant contracts for weapons research. The Clason amendment was defeated, but not one offered by Frank A. Mathews striking the commission's authority to make grants-in-aid for research. In the closing moments of the session, several minor committee amendments were adopted in Section 4 (Production of Fissionable Material) and Section 5 (Control of Materials).[73]

The Friday session began with the crucial Section 6, which prescribed the commission's role in military applications. The principal committee amendment would authorize the armed forces to produce atomic weapons. Although Carl Hinshaw argued that the proposed change would contradict Section 9 granting the commission ownership of all fissionable material and weapons, the amendment was adopted, 63–38. Thus the committee carried all of its objectives for strengthening the hand of the military in the commission.

An hour's respite came as the clerk and May committee members plodded through a dozen technical amendments in noncontroversial sections. But the tempo quickened again as the clerk droned out the fourteen paragraphs of Section 11 on the control of information. Over the opposition of both May and Thomason, the Committee of the Whole accepted Elston's amendment striking the policy statement which declared the commission should share industrial information on atomic energy with other nations on a reciprocal basis as soon as enforceable international safeguards were established. In the same vein was Harness' proposal removing the commission's authority to establish information services. Section 10 (b), said Harness, would authorize the commission "to set up the biggest propaganda agency ever created by the Congress." In a matter of minutes, the House was striking down the entire structure for disseminating knowledge of modern science and technology, the keystone of the scientists' plan for international control and peaceful use of atomic energy. Thomason spoke with a tone of resignation and disgust. "I am opposed to the amendment offered by the gentleman from Indiana, but I am very frank to say that I think it is sort of a futile thing for me or anybody else to oppose it in view of the adoption of the amendment offered by the gentleman from Ohio. Judging from the last vote, it looks like isolationism is again in the saddle. I take it that most of you want no part in our international problems."

Thomason's sense of futility was born out by subsequent proceedings. In a few moments, the Harness amendment was adopted by a respectable margin. Then followed in quick succession amendments requiring FBI investigations of all commission employees, a minimum penalty of ten years' imprisonment and a maximum penalty of death for security violations with intent to injure the United States, and a unanimous vote of the commission to remove information from the Restricted Data category. Heeding the shrill warnings against "giving away the secret of the bomb," the House was adopting the very type of repressive legislation which the scientists and the McMahon group most deplored.

527

No happier fate awaited the Administration in the amendments to Section 11 on patents. The debate centered not on the original patent section which was already presumed dead but on the substitute drafted by Fritz Lanham and the patent interests. Carefully avoiding any infringement on the patent system, the proposal authorized the commission to purchase, by condemnation if necessary, all rights to inventions relating to the production or utilization of atomic energy. Inventors of such devices would file patent applications in the usual way and would be entitled to compensation for use of the invention by the Government. When the national security was no longer involved, all rights would revert to the owner, subject to a nonexclusive, irrevocable, nontransferable license to the Government. The debate involved the same arguments and same speakers of the previous day—Lanham, Elston, and Martin speaking for the substitute; Doyle and Thomason supporting the original patent provision. The vote was a foregone conclusion, 121–57 for the substitute.[74]

Thomason hoped the debate could be ended quickly on Saturday morning, July 20. The Committee of the Whole speedily adopted several amendments, making the commission subject to the Administrative Procedures Act of 1946, increasing the membership of the joint committee on atomic energy from nine to eleven, and requiring FBI investigations of all security violations. Tension mounted, however, as the debate drew to a close. When Lanham offered an amendment to Section 15 removing penalties for violations of commission regulations, Thomason denounced it as "just a part of the general plan to kill or recommit the bill or wreck it with crippling amendments." Though Elston denied the charge, J. Parnell Thomas did not. He detected a plan to get the bill to conference where the Senate conferees would try to force their version on the House. He believed the May committee should "keep the bill locked up until such time as we see what the world picture will be like." John W. McCormack in a last-ditch effort to stem the tide for recommittal succeeded only in involving himself in a heated wrangle with Harold D. Cooley of North Carolina. The exchange ended in an uproar around the rostrum.

Fortunately, the debate did not end on this rancorous note. Jerry Voorhis of California strode to the microphones and made a stirring appeal for the McMahon bill. Although he had opposed most of the amendments, he begged the House not to recommit the bill. As it came from the Senate, the bill was "absolutely clear to anyone who wants to understand it." Was the House, by recommitting the measure, going to admit that one year after the first atomic explosion Congress did not understand the general issues well enough to legislate upon them? "We must be able to deal with this our greatest problem if we are to prove that democratic parliamentary legislative Government can justify its continuance in the new and admittedly dynamic and in some respect fearsome age in which we live." As the galleries applauded, the atmosphere in the House seemed to change. The speaker's soaring phrases seemed to lift the members out of the pettiness, boredom, and selfishness of everyday politics. For a moment they would be statesmen. This was, Voorhis reminded them, "a matter for the ages."

Under the House rules, all debate ended when the Committee of the Whole rose. Except for one motion to recommit the bill, the House would vote immediately on the amendments and then on the bill itself. As soon as the amendments had been adopted, Short introduced his motion to recommit. The crucial vote was 146 to 195, defeating the motion and assuring passage of the bill. By exerting all its influence, the Administration had saved the measure by the small margin of 49 votes. Party discipline was an important factor in that only 18 Democrats out of the 168 present voted against the bill. On the Republican side, 128 voted against the measure, but without the support of 43 Republicans and 2 independents, the Administration's margin would have been too close to assure victory on the final vote. As it was, the House adopted the bill, 265 to 79.[75]

Early the next week, before the two houses appointed the conference committee, the supporters of the Senate bill mustered all their resources. Higinbotham wired the FAS locals for "an avalanche of telegrams to conferees Brien McMahon and Andrew May recommending Senate form of bill. Urge your sending two best contact men with American names arriving Monday for individual congressional contacts to insure passage of final conference report." Miller meanwhile was attempting within the Administration the preparation of public statements by the President, Secretary Patter-

PRESIDENT TRUMAN SIGNS THE BILL CREATING THE U. S. ATOMIC ENERGY COMMISSION, AUGUST 1, 1946 / Behind the President, left to right: Senators Tom Connally, Eugene D. Millikin, Edwin C. Johnson, Thomas C. Hart, Brien McMahon, Warren R. Austin, Richard B. Russell.

son, General Eisenhower, and Bernard Baruch. He thought statements by these men would be "of enormous importance in obtaining approval of the conference report" and would carry great weight with the House conferees.[76]

The members met for their first session on Tuesday, July 23. Although conferences were invariably held in the Senate wing of the Capitol, the members agreed to meet on the House side out of deference to May. McMahon, Russell, Johnson, Vandenberg, and Millikin represented the Senate; May, Thomason, Durham, Clason, and J. Parnell Thomas spoke for the House. In a mood befitting the location, the Senate members conceded to seven House amendments in the opening session, but all were minor points. Furthermore, the unanimity and decisiveness of the senators' action suggested a well organized strategy rather than retreat.

On Wednesday, the conferees met in a room nearer the Senate wing. As if to suggest some significance in that fact, the senators took a firmer position. The debate for the most part involved the control of information and the penalty clauses. The senators agreed to permit the Attorney General to prosecute violations of the act without consulting the commission, to adopt the death penalty, and to accept greater investigative powers for the FBI. The representatives on their part agreed to accept the exchange of information on industrial applications with other countries after Congress had determined by joint resolution that effective international safeguards against the atomic bomb had been established. This seemed a death-blow to what remained of the wartime arrangements for interchange with Britain and Canada, but it was an improvement over the House version.

529

Only at the final session on Thursday did the senators bring their full weight to bear. They had saved their fire for the two most important issues, patents and military representation.

Despite the publicity campaign the patent interests had mounted to support the Lanham amendment, the Senate had a distinct advantage in the conference. Lanham was not there to defend his proposal and the Senate could rely on the impressive abilities of Millikin. An avowed conservative, the Colorado senator had been slow to accept the novel approach to patents in the original McMahon bill. As a result of the Senate hearings and further discussion in executive sessions, he had been instrumental in perfecting the idea of patent exclusion, which lay at the heart of the final Senate patent section. Convinced of the soundness of the Senate version and solidly versed in the facts, Millikin proceeded in an hour's speech to win over the House conferees. Thomason as much as testified to that fact when he later spoke on the conference report in the House. May voted with Thomason and Durham to accept the Senate version without change.

On the vital question of military representation, Vandenberg played much the same role as had Millikin on patents. The force of his personality, his prestige, and his convictions overpowered the misgivings on the House side. The end result was consistent with Vandenberg's position at the time he introduced his amendment in the McMahon committee. He had no objection to military officers serving as the director of military application or in other positions on the commission's staff, but he stood firm against military men on the commission itself. He opposed two of the three House amendments in Section 2. Now on the verge of a heart attack, May could no more than whisper his assent, a melodramatic but understandable gesture at the end of a long but tragic career.[77]

A final flurry of resistance came in the House. Thomas, in an unusual move, refused to sign the conference report and charged that the House had never been given a chance by the Senate conferees. Thomason, however, seemed fully in control as he guided the report through the House. The final break came when Representative Clason, one of the Republican minority on the conference committee, announced that he would vote for the conference report. On Friday, July 26, both houses accepted the compromise.[78]

530

The following Thursday morning, August 1, the members of the Senate Special Committee assembled in the President's oval office to witness the signing of the Atomic Energy Act of 1946.[79] Surely no other group better deserved to be present on that occasion. The act bore the mark of every member present. Above all, it would be remembered as the work of Brien McMahon. Against overwhelming odds, he had persisted where many people had lost heart. With rare courage and good luck, he had won not only a great personal victory but also what seemed at least a momentary triumph over the bomb and its threat to mankind.

To trace all the threads woven into the new act, however, carried one far beyond the small group in the President's office. Just one year before the Interim Committee had been struggling with a draft bill to control the atom in the postwar world. Since that day many thousands of Americans had expended millions of words in public debate on domestic control. The final bill was not what any single one of them would have written. Yet, it was probably better than any individual could have produced. In this fact, perhaps, lay the secret vitality of American democracy. It seemed that Congress and the nation had answered Congressman Voorhis' stirring appeal "to raise our sights even for a moment . . . above the level of political slogans . . . to a vision of the stars themselves and the universe whence atomic energy has come."

INTERNATIONAL CONTROL:
LAST BEST HOPE

CHAPTER 15

The lines in the battle for domestic control were still forming on Monday afternoon, January 7, 1946, as Under Secretary of State Dean Acheson, ill with flu, rested at his Georgetown home. Since early October, he had had no responsibility for atomic energy. He knew little about the Administration's search for a policy besides what he read in the papers. A little after four, the telephone rang. It was James F. Byrnes, who was about to leave for London and the first meeting of the United Nations General Assembly. The Secretary of State said he was naming Acheson chairman of a committee to formulate American policy on the international control of atomic energy. The other members would be Vannevar Bush, James B. Conant, Leslie R. Groves, and John J. McCloy—nice fellows Acheson would enjoy working with. Acheson pleaded his ignorance, but Byrnes waved the protest aside, saying he had to run to catch his plane.

BIRTH OF THE UNITED NATIONS ATOMIC ENERGY COMMISSION

An hour later, Byrnes was airborne in the President's C-54. He had put in a full day. Anticipating that the General Assembly would act favorably on the proposal for a commission on atomic energy control, he had announced his committee to study "the controls and safeguards necessary to protect this government." Byrnes expected the group which Acheson was heading to serve two functions. Its work would benefit whoever might become the American representative on the UN commission, and its members would keep in touch with the appropriate Congressional committees.[1]

The Secretary of State's Committee had its origins in the continuing studies of the working group that Byrnes had established on the eve of the Moscow Conference. Carroll L. Wilson came to Bush with proposals for investigations that should be made before any UN commission convened. One matter that required attention was the term "stages" as used in the Moscow resolution. Another was controls and inspection, while a third was the relative strength of the American technical position. Bush agreed with Wilson. After checking with Conant, he urged Byrnes to initiate studies promptly.[2] Bush's suggestion carried an appeal that went beyond the obvious need for planning. Byrnes not only had to work with the senior watchdogs of American foreign policy; he had to hold off the aggressive Brien McMahon, who as chairman of the Senate Special Committee was threatening to begin hearings on the international aspects of atomic energy. The prospect of an incursion into an area the Executive guarded as its peculiar prerogative was disturbing, especially in view of the delicate nature of relations with Britain. This was hardly the time to risk telling the tangled wartime story. What would better keep the initiative in the hands of the Administration than to set a strong committee to work on policy studies? It probably was such reasoning that led Byrnes to replace his working and policy groups with a team more likely to inspire confidence on Capitol Hill.

532

His committee provided for, Byrnes had turned to the fears of Senators Vandenberg and Connally that the international negotiations might jeopardize American security. Ten days earlier—before the two had left for London to serve as members of the American delegation—the President had told Vandenberg there was no such danger. Now Byrnes issued a formal statement adding his own assurances. No international commission could compel the United States to release information, nor would its recommendations have force without the approval of the United States as a permanent member of the Security Council. The decisions of the American representative would in any case be subject to review when the resulting treaty came before the Senate for ratification.[3]

In London, atomic energy negotiations went smoothly. Byrnes invited Connally and Vandenberg to dinner and succeeded in quieting their last misgivings about the adequacy of the pending resolution. In the Political and Security Committee debate, Connally spoke for the United States. On January 24, the General Assembly took up the resolution. Byrnes expressed the hope that the Assembly would give its approval. "We who fought together for freedom," he declared, "must now show that we are worthy of the freedom that we have won." No nation raised its voice in dissent. The resolution adopted was identical to the proposal the three sponsoring powers had made at Moscow the month before. The United Nations Atomic Energy Commission, consisting of all members of the Security Council plus Canada, was to make proposals for exchanging basic scientific information, confining atomic energy to peaceful purposes, eliminating atomic and other weapons of mass destruction from national armaments, and effectively safeguarding complying states. Like the Moscow proposal and the Truman-Attlee-King Agreed Declaration, the resolution was specific in requiring gradual, step-by-step progress. "The work of the Commission should proceed by separate stages, the successful completion of each of which will develop the necessary confidence of the world before the next stage is undertaken." [4]

THE SECRETARY OF STATE'S COMMITTEE

In Washington, Acheson had been dismayed at the assignment Byrnes had given him. Nonetheless he had no choice but to begin. On January 14, Acheson—his special assistant, Herbert S. Marks, at his side—met the Secretary of State's Committee in Byrnes's office. A previous engagement prevented Conant from attending, but Bush was there. Though under no illusions as to the difficulties ahead, Bush was as convinced as ever that the United States had to make a vigorous, public effort at international control. McCloy, who had worked so closely with Stimson on his September 11 memorandum urging an approach to Russia, was down from New York. Groves was present too. For him, the issue was simple. If American leaders were truly realistic—not idealistic, as he considered them—they would permit only firm allies in whom they had absolute confidence to manufacture or possess atomic weapons. Should any other power try, the United States would protect itself by destroying that nation's capacity to produce them. Groves believed there was only one legitimate alternative: a hard-boiled, realistic, enforceable world agreement that would ensure the outlawing of atomic weapons. [5]

533

Acheson began the meeting by making it clear that the primary objective was a study of controls and safeguards for the information of the American member of the international commission. He thought the committee ultimately would want to submit a report to the President and Secretary of State along with draft instructions for the United States representative. As a first step, Acheson volunteered to arrange for a summary and analysis of the various proposals already advanced. This would serve as a point of departure. For the main part of the work, he suggested a board of consultants. A small group of specially qualified persons could investigate and report on all pertinent facts. It should pay particular attention to inspection. At least one man on the panel, Acheson argued, should be experienced in statecraft as well as familiar with technological and scientific matters. This would assure a review which would bridge the gap between technology and politics.

After considerable discussion, the committee decided to create a panel that would ascertain the facts bearing on the inspection question and appraise that matter as well as the relative potential of the United States and other nations in atomic energy. Who should serve? A number of names came to mind. Finally, Groves suggested and the committee agreed that Acheson should appoint a panel of up to five members with similar qualifications. [6]

Acheson spent the next few days in intensive recruiting, and when his committee met again on Wednesday, January 23, he was able to introduce the Board of Consultants. He had persuaded David E. Lilienthal to act as chairman. His fifteen years on the Wisconsin Public Service Commission and the Tennessee Valley Authority gave Lilienthal the broad view of both government and technology that Acheson knew was necessary. Robert Oppenheimer, now back at the University of California, had consented to serve. His presence meant that the consultants would have good counsel on physics. Charles A. Thomas also had accepted the call. Vice-president of Monsanto Chemical Company and an expert on plutonium chemistry, he could deliberate from the perspective of both science and industry. Lilienthal, Oppenheimer, and Thomas were all in their forties. To balance the board with the judgment of older men of varied backgrounds, Acheson had prevailed on Harry A. Winne and Chester I. Barnard. Winne, a Groves suggestion, was vice-president in charge of engineering for General Electric. He had helped direct and co-ordinate the manufacture of components for the electromagnetic and gaseous-diffusion plants. Barnard, president of the New Jersey Bell Telephone Company, had headed the United Service Organizations during the war. The Board of Consultants would have a staff of high order. Bush had loaned Carroll Wilson for secretary. Marks would assist as Acheson's representative.

534

Acheson and his committee spelled out the task of the consultants, but they drew back from rigid specifications on the form the report should take. Lilienthal's group, they thought, should first have opportunity for a preliminary review. It would require much information from the Manhattan District. Groves promised to make available the resources of his command, including the Technical Committee on Inspection and Control he had just established to make feasibility studies. After agreeing that Acheson would handle relations with Senator McMahon, and Groves with the Joint Chiefs of Staff, the committee adjourned with the understanding it would meet as often as the Board of Consultants considered worthwhile.[7]

THE BOARD OF CONSULTANTS: LEARNING AND LABORING

At two-thirty on the afternoon of the twenty-third, the consultants held a first, preliminary meeting. Conant was there to help them get started. No one had thought longer about international control. In his definition, an effective system of inspection was one which gave a danger signal—flashed a red light—when some power moved toward manufacturing an atomic weapon. He told the panel it should concentrate on devising such a system and on scheduling the packages of information the United States would have to disclose as the plan went into operation. Conant warned against getting bogged down in the subject of sanctions. Punishments were the domain of the Security Council.

Searching for analogies that might help, Lilienthal thought of the alcohol industry. The distillation of alcohol for industrial purposes had languished until denaturing was adopted as a means of preventing the diversion of a tax-free product to beverage uses. Might not fissionable materials be denatured and rendered useless for weapons without impairing their suitability for peaceful ends? The possibility of industrial applications appealed to Winne. Was this not the key to control? If a vigorous program to use the atom in industry were under way, might not it be the basis for inspection that would reveal illegal weapons activity?

What were the consequences of trying to maintain complete secrecy? How long would it take other nations to gain the bomb? Should the board present a plan for international control, what was a rational schedule of disclosures? At this early stage, discussing such questions was hardly profitable. Everyone saw the need for study. Only Oppenheimer and Thomas possessed the necessary technical understanding.[8]

535

The work of education began Monday morning, January 28, in quarters the OSRD had arranged—the loftlike top floor of the American Trucking Association Building across Sixteenth Street from the Carnegie Institution. The large room was drab. Each man had a desk or table and a kitchen chair. Telephones stood on the floor and the window sills. There for two days amid the cobwebs, Oppenheimer put his colleagues through a short course in nuclear physics. Except for Thomas, it was the first time the panelists had been exposed to the physicist's extraordinarily fluent, lucid speech. Starting with the most basic concepts, he told how plutonium was produced and how the neutron bombardment of thorium offered the prospect of deriving important quantities of the fissionable isotope U-233. He described the various isotope-separation processes and what it took to build a reactor (physicists were abandoning the colorful but imprecise wartime term, "pile"). He explained the physics and ordnance of the uranium and plutonium bombs, observing that the effort required here was relatively small. It was the fissionable material itself that demanded heroic exertions.

For expert analysis of the raw-material situation, the panel spent the morning of Thursday the thirty-first with George W. Bain, an Amherst College professor who was senior geologist for the Murray Hill Area, the exploration arm of the Manhattan District. Bain reviewed in detail the world deposits of uranium and thorium, while Captain Joseph A. Volpe of Groves's headquarters reported how the raw-material work had been organized during the war.[9]

With the raw-material picture in mind, the Board of Consultants was ready to grapple with its assignment. On the afternoon of January 31, Lilienthal defined the issue. The General Assembly resolution had called for recommendations on four objectives. Actually, he pointed out, these goals were so closely related they must be treated as a single package. Several alternative courses were apparent. The board might throw up its hands and say nothing would stop competition in nuclear arms. It might adopt a more hopeful approach and limit production of fissionable materials to the United Nations. It might recommend leaving atomic energy to national initiative under a policing system to make sure no power undertook to build nuclear weapons. Or the board might simply endorse a convention outlawing the bomb as the Kellogg-Briand Treaty had outlawed war.

Thomas and Winne voiced the sentiment of the entire group when they pictured the extreme alternatives: holding American atomic technology as closely as possible or abandoning all attempts at secrecy. Either policy, they were sure, would promote an armaments race. The only hope lay somewhere between, and this meant international control. But what form should control take?

This was Oppenheimer's moment. For some time, the outlines of an international control agency had been taking shape in his mind. He had not revealed his thinking at the first meetings of the consultants. It was better, he judged, to wait until his associates possessed the fundamental information necessary to understand his plan. Now he enthusiastically sketched a vision of an international agency that would have important developmental functions. Only a unit that was organic and alive could keep abreast of the changing technology and attract an able, imaginative staff. Atomic activities, Oppenheimer said, could be classified roughly as harmless and dangerous. A small reactor useful only as a laboratory instrument was harmless; it need not be operated by the international authority. But dangerous activities—the separation of U-235 or the operation of large reactors for generating power —must be its exclusive prerogative. The authority would have a monopoly of raw materials. It would exercise certain controls, to be sure, but its emphasis would be on positive, not negative, responsibilities.

Oppenheimer's idea had immediate appeal. Thomas began thinking of the form it should take. Why not an international corporation? The stockholders would be the participating nations, bound together for mutual advantage. Barnard agreed. People were accustomed to government corporations. The Bank of England was an example, and the idea was not even alien to Soviet Russia. Oppenheimer's suggestion was especially attractive to Lilienthal. He liked the idea of going ahead with peacetime development, of not retreating in the face of the obvious dangers. A corporate authority would give an incentive to development. Its positive, dynamic character would avoid too much stress on the negative, preventive side. It would reduce "the cops" to a minor role. Besides, the world would have more confidence in an agency that knew through its own activities what was going on.[10]

On the morning of February 1, the consultants assembled once more. There was general agreement that they should present an informative document to educate the American representative on the Atomic Energy Commission. The group further agreed that it was neither possible nor desirable to formulate one specific control plan. The board would limit itself to discuss-

536

ing the types of useful international machinery. It should advise, but leave freedom of choice to its parent, the Secretary of State's Committee.

Lilienthal had allowed the group to talk freely and reach a consensus. Now he split a tentative outline of the report into segments and assigned each man responsibility for drafting a section. The next morning, the committee met with Acheson, and Lilienthal related its progress. The report, he said, would be written as if the board were addressing the American delegate —a device that would avoid dogmatism. It would consist of a set of alternate proposals and an appraisal. Acheson was pleased. This was exactly the thing to do. Their plans thus blessed, the panelists adjourned to write, exchange memorandums, and reconvene in ten days.[11]

Each man did his homework diligently. When the five met as scheduled on February 12, they had a substantial collection of papers. If not quite a first draft of a report, it was at least a workbook, and so they came to call it.[12] Lilienthal had reserved for himself the first section, the introductory remarks. "Thinking made the bomb," he began. The underlying assumption of the present document was that thinking—the rational process—could help unmake it. He would advise the American delegate against sponsoring any particular plan or proposal. The recommendations of the Atomic Energy Commission should be the product of joint international discussion. Running through Lilienthal's draft was the theme that not only officials and scientists but also the public generally should understand the facts. The discussions within the Commission might have to be secret, but the American member should realize "that a wider understanding of the *affirmatives* of nuclear energy are an essential part of the process of eliminating its war-like uses." No recommendations would be effective unless they were palatable, understandable, and capable of stimulating the constructive impulses of mankind.

Four sections of the workbook were essentially factual. Oppenheimer had prepared "A Primer on Atomic Energy," a recapitulation of his lectures to the board. Wilson had drawn up a series of memorandums on raw materials and on mining and refining uranium and thorium, separating isotopes, and producing plutonium. Winne had composed an essay in which he analyzed the requirements of a satisfactory control system and evaluated specific proposals against his standards of security, acceptability, flexibility, and simplicity. Barnard had considered the merits of specific techniques of control: accounting and inspection systems, denaturing processes, and free association among scientists.

Two papers, one by Oppenheimer and the other by Thomas, argued for a world authority with positive functions. Thomas cast doubt on the adequacy of inspection alone. No nation would enjoy having a small army of inspectors descend on its laboratories and factories. And for all this obnoxious snooping, it would be easy to conceal small reactors among the intricacies of large oil refineries and chemical plants. Thomas thought it more practical to invest ownership of the world supply of uranium and thorium in an

537

international commission, a cartel, or a world corporation. This agency would refine the metal and lease it to reputable nations or individuals for peaceful purposes under careful accounting procedures. This would not eliminate inspection, but theoretically, at least, it would simplify it. Any breakdown would be a sign of gathering war clouds.

Starting from the same misgivings about inspection, Oppenheimer elaborated his case for an international authority that would develop as well as inspect. He was sure that constructive functions were essential in any effective system of safeguards. The international authority should have, first, a monopoly on the study and exploitation of uranium and thorium. An agency well informed about the location of deposits and the best means of working them would be in a strong position to detect and discourage illegal enterprises. Second, the international authority should do research in atomic explosives. Only by being in the forefront of research could the authority determine whether some discovery beyond its control threatened the world. A third function would be to develop atomic energy for industrial purposes and power. Some relatively safe applications might be assigned to national and private organizations under licensing arrangements. Certainly the authority would have to work closely with independent scientists, engineers, and industrialists. They would provide enlightened criticism and disseminate findings on beneficial applications. Should any nation abrogate its agreements, the question of sanctions would arise. But Oppenheimer thought it not profitable to discuss punishments at the moment.

The consultants spent February 12 and 13 considering the workbook papers, particularly the Lilienthal, Thomas, and Oppenheimer memorandums. Then they enplaned for a week's tour of Oak Ridge and Los Alamos. Never had there been any doubt they would recommend some form of international control. A mere treaty outlawing the bomb was too negative—a useless gesture. At the other extreme, leaving the bomb in national hands raised the threat of domination by the military. During the morning meeting on the twelfth, Lilienthal warned against abdicating control of foreign policy to the generals and admirals. Marks and Oppenheimer seconded him. When Barnard pointed out that many considered the alternatives either Russian or American imperialism, Oppenheimer admitted this might be the case but feared it would mean the ruination of the country. As the discussion proceeded, the board found the logic of Oppenheimer's proposal compelling. By the sixteenth, it had abandoned the idea of submitting mere appraisals of various methods of control and decided to recommend a dynamic, developmental, international authority. The staff undertook to make a draft. Marks set to work on a paper stressing that sound policy decisions depended on understanding the facts. Wilson sought to combine the Barnard, Winne, Thomas, and Oppenheimer papers into an integrated argument.[13]

Back in Washington, the board devoted Monday and Tuesday, February 25 and 26, to considering the Marks and Wilson drafts. This was no vague, general discussion but a detailed analysis of the mechanics of international control by men who were becoming experts. They made many additions and revisions, but by Tuesday noon they had an outline.[14] A meeting with the Secretary of State's Committee had been scheduled for March 7 and 8, only a week away. The remaining days were crowded. There was a hurried trip to New York to check with the Manhattan District Technical Committee. There were long drafting sessions at the loft on Sixteenth Street. To an unusual degree for the product of a committee, the report was a common effort. The basic idea was Oppenheimer's, and the technical sections owed much to his gift of clarity. The references to raw materials reflected Thomas' strong doubts on inspection. Lilienthal had helped give the passages on the international authority a ring of practicality. He had a surer feel than anyone else for how the agency would actually operate. More than that, Lilienthal had set the chatty, informal, deliberately repetitious tone that pervaded the entire document. Ideas that Winne and Barnard first put in written form found their place in the final version, but their major contribution had been at once less obvious and more important. In a sense, they were the outsiders, the hardheaded executives the others had to convince. They had helped make the report persuasive; their approval made it peculiarly impressive. Just as significant had been the influence of Wilson and Marks. As staff members, they had done much to set the broad outline and develop the main line of argument. They had borne a heavy share of the literary labors.

539

On the afternoon of March 6, the Board of Consultants met to settle their strategy for the morrow's meeting. Each man had a copy of the report, which had run to four substantial typed volumes. The first was the heart, the essay pointing the way to security through an international control agency. The second volume was Oppenheimer's primer, now entitled "The Scientific Basis of Atomic Energy Development." The third was the report by the Scientific Panel of Stimson's Interim Committee, "Proposals for Research and Development in the Field of Atomic Energy." The fourth was a survey of "Current Proposals for the International Control of Atomic Energy" by Carl McGowan. This was the staff study Acheson had promised his committee at its first meeting.

Lilienthal said that he had told Acheson the report should be published as a basis for informed public discussion. While Acheson did not reject the suggestion, he doubted the wisdom of publication without prior endorsement. If the document were attacked, there would be no one to defend it. Should his committee approve the report, Acheson thought the first step was to gain prompt acceptance by the President and the Secretary of State.

Lilienthal told his colleagues how strongly he felt about publication. Though their mandate was to prepare a guide for the American representative to the Atomic Energy Commission, he had concluded that the attempt at international control must be based on broad popular consent. The Administration should not repeat Woodrow Wilson's 1919 mistake of seeking support after he had committed himself. Oppenheimer and Marks believed just as firmly that the report should go to the people.

But the immediate objective was approval by the Acheson committee. What if that august body objected to the report's scope and emphasis? Or what if someone, Groves perhaps, persuaded the committee that the Russians were up to no good and had no intention of using the United Nations for anything but mischief? There could be no hard-and-fast answer to these questions, but Marks counseled against letting the discussion take the form of negotiations. He believed the board should not modify its report unless it was genuinely convinced. Moving on to the tactics of presentation, Lilienthal said Acheson wanted the first volume read aloud. To give everyone a chance to talk, he assigned each man a section. The plans as complete as they could be, the group adjourned for a good night's sleep before what more than one suspected might be quite a battle.[15]

DUMBARTON OAKS

Shortly before nine-thirty Thursday morning, the Secretary of State's Committee and the Board of Consultants assembled at Dumbarton Oaks in Georgetown. Acheson turned the meeting over to Lilienthal, who outlined the plan for reading the first volume aloud.[16] After speaking of the deep humility in which his group had approached its task, the TVA chairman, veteran of many a conference, read the letter of transmittal. For more than six weeks, the board had lived with the study. He admitted that absorption in the task did not assure the soundness of the recommendations. It did, however, measure the board's concern that the United States develop a rational and workable plan of international control. The consultants had become more hopeful as they steeped themselves in the facts. Eventually, they had reached complete agreement. This illustrated the importance of studying the technology. If others would repeat the process, they might have a similar experience. The board did not pretend its report was a final plan. Rather, it was "a place to begin, a foundation on which to build." Many questions had not been touched on at all. The necessity for winning the agreement of other nations would inevitably raise issues which hardly could be drawn precisely in advance of international negotiations. The Atomic Energy Commission of the United Nations would consider many of these in joint discussion.

The introductory remarks completed, Lilienthal gave Barnard the floor. He began to read Section I, "The Practicability of Systems of Inspection as Sole Safeguards of International Outlawry of Atomic Weapons." The first three pages disposed of the question implicit in the title. In the shock that followed Hiroshima, men the world over naturally concluded that nations should outlaw the bomb. On reflection, many had seen that mere international agreements were no answer to the quest for security. The trouble was that developments in atomic energy for peaceful and for military purposes were interchangeable and interdependent. While a nation might promise not to use nuclear energy for bombs, there was nothing but its own good faith to assure against diversion to the uses of destruction and terror. This realization suggested inspection by an international agency. The consultants had studied the question earnestly. Their investigations led them to conclude that inspection and similar policelike methods *alone* offered insufficient security.

The rest of Barnard's section explained the board's reasoning. Inspection operations would be staggering in magnitude. Even so, they would offer no guarantee against national managers diverting dangerous quantities of U-235 or plutonium. Inspection would involve countless irritations. It meant the presence of a large number of "foreigners." It meant checking not merely accounts and instruments but human beings as well. It would be a persistent challenge to the good faith of all nations. It could easily inflame emotions and become itself a threat to peace.

541

Oppenheimer, Winne, and Thomas joined in presenting Section II, "Principal Considerations in Developing a System of Safeguards." Oppenheimer read first. The introduction was an attempt to answer a basic question: what were the characteristics of an effective system of safeguards? The board judged that it should provide early, unambiguous, and reliable signals that a nation was taking steps toward atomic warfare. If safeguards failed or the international situation collapsed, each nation had to be left in a relatively secure position. It was imperative that the system cope with new dangers that technological advance might pose. Finally, the plan must involve international action and minimize rivalry between nations in the dangerous aspects of atomic development.

The first chapter reported that fortunately the task of building security had finite boundaries. Of all natural substances, uranium alone could maintain a chain reaction. It was the key to all foreseeable applications. Without uranium, there could be no plutonium. It might be possible to fuse light nuclei and produce a violent thermonuclear reaction, but the only way of attaining the necessary ignition temperature was to use atomic explosives based on uranium. What about thorium? Could it not be converted into the fissionable U-233? Not unless there was a fairly substantial amount of uranium to begin with. Theoretically, complete control of uranium was enough. But to provide an additional safeguard against significant amounts of uranium escaping the system, thorium should be included. Control uranium and thorium, and you could disregard all other materials. Although the two minerals were distributed with relative abundance throughout the world, although many new sources would be discovered, high concentrations occurred only under very special geologic conditions. This meant the areas to be surveyed and ultimately controlled were relatively limited.

Chapter II was an effort to correct the impression prevailing in some quarters that nuclear science was subject to such unpredictably rapid change that no account of the current technical situation had much validity. Actually, the chances were against future experience modifying current basic knowledge. Prophesies as to future discoveries must not be allowed to obscure the fact that firm anchor points existed throughout the field of knowledge. Around these it was possible to construct an effective system of control.

Now it was Winne's turn. The thesis of Chapter III was that man's spirit of inquiry, his driving force toward knowledge, was a clue to effective security measures. Give a control agency responsibility for developing the peaceful uses of atomic energy and it would attract men of the highest caliber, not the type that had staffed Prohibition squads. The beneficial possibilities were exciting. The Interim Committee had spelled them out: the generation of power, the research and medical applications of radioactive isotopes. Combine responsibility for control with these challenging opportunities and it would be possible to draw on "the best human resources of good will, imagination, and ingenuity."

Chapter IV, which also fell to Winne, was the core of the whole report. The rivalry between nations in atomic energy had introduced dangerous inflammables. Witness the highly secret Anglo-American contracts for the output of the Congo. Any other nation, say Russia, could make similar arrangements. It took little imagination to conceive of a nation seeking to upset an existing compact or fomenting revolutions to gain control of uranium ore. Rivalry in developing other phases of atomic energy was just as likely. If an international agreement banned plutonium in a bomb but permitted uranium reactors for heat and power, the temptation to divert the by-product plutonium to weapons would be almost irresistible.

The Board of Consultants had concluded that the only workable system of safeguards required eliminating the right of individual nations or their citizens to engage in activities intrinsically dangerous. If such activities were limited to an international authority, the control system would give clear danger signals. If only the international agency had authority to own and develop uranium ore, the mere fact of national or private mining or possession would be illegal, an unmistakable alarm. So it was with plutonium-production reactors. If they were designed and operated exclusively by an international body, building and operation by another party, or even a move in that direction, was a plain warning. Let an international authority be responsible for developing atomic energy as well as for enforcing safeguards against atomic warfare. Then its personnel would have the "power of knowledge," the "sensitivity to new developments," that would make it competent and effective.

It was left for Thomas to read the last chapter of Section II, a sug-

542

gestion on how to draw the line between dangerous and safe activities. Dangerous activities were those which, either in actual fact or by slight alterations, were essential steps in making atomic weapons. These were three: providing the raw materials; producing U-235, plutonium, or U-233 in suitable quality and quantity; and incorporating these fissionable materials in a bomb. The possibility of denaturing introduced a certain flexibility. Uranium in which the U-235 was below the concentration required for effective weapons was reasonably safe. The same was true of plutonium with a high concentration of Pu-240. While it was possible to remove the denaturants, the excess U-238 and Pu-240, this called for complex isotope-separation plants and considerable scientific and engineering skill. New developments might alter this judgment, but this was only a good example of the need for constant reconsideration of the boundary between dangerous and safe. Clearly in the safe area were radioactive isotopes for scientific, medical, and technological research and small nuclear reactors operated as radiation sources. More marginal from the standpoint of safety were high-power-level reactors using denatured U-235 and plutonium as fuel.

543

Now came the third and final section, "Security through an Atomic Development Authority." Winne read the introduction, which explained that the board had not tried to write a corporate charter. Rather, it had sought to show that such a charter was practical and that the organization it created would have decisive consequences for world security. Barnard then took over the first chapter, a discussion of the responsibilities of the proposed agency. These were both proprietary and regulatory. The first proprietary function would be control of the world supplies of uranium and thorium. Wherever these materials were found in useful quantities, the authority must either own them or hold them under effective leasing arrangements. Implicit in this function were continuous surveys and constant examination of new methods for recovering these materials from substances in which they existed in small quantities. The authority would have to conduct all actual mining operations. It would own and operate the refineries for reducing ores to metal or salt. It would own all uranium and thorium stockpiles, selling the by-products and providing the necessary supplies for the present limited commercial uses. International control of raw materials raised some extremely difficult policy questions. How should nations and individuals be compensated? How could a strategic balance be maintained so that stockpiles of fissionable materials were not unduly large in one nation and small in another?

The second major function would be construction and operation of primary production facilities. This meant separation plants and plutonium piles like those at Oak Ridge and Hanford. But since it was important to conserve the world's supply of fissionable material, it also meant plutonium reactors for breeding more plutonium and uranium reactors for converting thorium to U-233. Inasmuch as plants in this category yielded material suitable for weapons, critical policy questions were involved. Strategic balance here was even more troublesome than for raw materials. And how would an international administration distribute large amounts of by-product power?

A third proprietary duty was research. Only by preserving its position as the best-informed agency in the world would the authority be able to tell where to draw the line between the inherently dangerous and the safe. In addition to conducting its own research, the authority should encourage investigations in private or national hands.

The regulatory responsibilities would be discharged by two techniques —licensing and inspection. The uranium and thorium the authority mined and the fissionable materials it manufactured would remain its property. But under appropriate licensing arrangements it could lease denatured U-235, U-233, and plutonium for use in reactors designed for research or the production of radioactive isotopes and power. The other regulatory arm, inspection, still had a place, despite its inadequacy as a single tool for enforcing international agreements. The authority would inspect but frequently in a form that would be scarcely recognizable. The geological survey, for example, involved inspection, though its focus was a world-wide search for the essential raw materials. As the authority pursued its labors of research and development, it would become aware of the activities in various countries. Similar insights into what was happening throughout the world would flow from the operation of mines, refineries, and primary production plants. Indeed, inspection would be an essential part of the licensing function.

Lilienthal took over for the last chapter, an essay on the organization and policies of the international control unit which started from the premise that it was too early to seek definitive answers to the many questions in this area. To be valid, answers must be the product of international deliberation, not a unilateral statement of a detailed plan. It was possible, however, to illustrate the types of queries bound to arise and some of the possible replies. One obvious matter was personnel. The authority must be staffed on a truly international basis, with due weight given to geographical and national distribution. Another certain issue was the means of making the authority sufficiently accountable to the nations and peoples of the world. Some organ of the United Nations, perhaps the Security Council itself, would have to serve as overseer. The details remained, and any plan would require intensive further exploration.

Even more tentative must be present remarks about policies, Lilienthal read. The charter would deal with some of these. It should, for example, define the dangerous and safe areas and set the procedure for redefinition as new knowledge shifted the demarcation line. Probably, the charter would have to include a plan governing the strategic location of the operations in the interest of maintaining a physical balance among nations. These were two

544

of the more difficult matters, but there were others that had to be faced in the international negotiations: initial financing, compensation to nations and private agencies for raw materials, and allocation of the materials and facilities the authority would have to license or sell. One idea smacked of Lilienthal's TVA experience. The charter could provide specifically that the agency turn over all power at the bus bar, thus leaving transmission and use in national or private hands. No utility need fear international competition in the distribution of power.

Abruptly, without peroration, the report ended. It had been a long morning. Conant suggested discussing the first volume before proceeding to the other three. After a few congratulatory remarks, the meeting recessed for lunch.

At the afternoon session, the consultants at last had a chance to gauge the committee's reaction. General Groves had doubts about the practicality of raw-material control. If it turned out that certain low-grade ore deposits could be exploited, it would be difficult to achieve monopoly. Oppenheimer and Lilienthal were quick to counter that this made an operating authority, not a mere inspection system, all the more necessary. Though Bush pointed out that low-grade deposits required large and easily detectable operations, Groves remained unconvinced. Close Colorado to travelers, he said, and it would be a cinch to conceal that the United States was working carnotite ores. Conant then came to the General's support, asking the consultants if they had not played down too much the right to go anywhere and see anything. It was vitally important to have guaranteed freedom of access.

Bush observed that Russia had a large army and the United States only a small one. Should this country put itself in a position to lose the bomb immediately and throw the preponderance of power to the Soviet Union? It would be much better to present the plan as a goal toward which to work through a series of steps. If these were successful, the full objective could be gained in a few years. Lilienthal had reservations about this approach, but Oppenheimer, Thomas, and Winne joined to affirm that their plan did envision steps—the first, a raw-materials survey.

Bush had not finished. Control had to be sold at two levels, he said— national and international. The American people must know if the United States could withdraw with a minimum of danger should it become clear the plan would not work. Other nations must have answers to other questions: when would denatured material be available? when would plant-construction data be revealed? It was important for the United States to propose paths which other powers could follow. The prize was worth seeking. It would be a great thing if Stalin opened Russia. Lilienthal thought Bush was right on the need for a selling job. For that reason if no other, any United States proposal must be on the level. Unless businesslike and free of craft, it would not appeal to the American people. Groves added the

545

weight of his judgment. The United States had to make a first-class, honest gesture to the Russians. This meant saying what this country would do and what it would get in return.

Lilienthal saw a chance to bring the discussion to focus. Was the Board of Consultants plan a good, honest proposal? Groves said he would like to see the transition process spelled out. Winne pressed for a more definite commitment. Assuming that suitable steps could be devised for putting it into effect, was the plan workable? Yes, answered Groves, adding that everything depended on whether Russia really wanted to co-operate. Acheson had a question. Presumably, Russians would hold high places in the atomic development authority. Did not this present a danger? Lilienthal conceded risks. A Russian member of the board of directors could go back home and tell everything he knew. The agency must be alert to the consequences of such treachery. A successful surreptitious effort, however, would take much more than leaks. Bush injected a positive note. The control system was going to develop over a period of ten to fifteen years. During that time, he thought, a new class of international civil servants might come forward, men loyal to the organization.

The talk had gone on long enough to suggest the committee's reaction: qualified approval. It was time for Acheson to try his hand at crystallizing this sentiment. He had just conferred with Brien McMahon, he said. Back in January, the Senator had promised to hold off hearings in the international field until the Secretary of State's Committee had reported, but now he was getting restless. Acheson thought the committee ought to agree on a proposal of some sort and send it to the Secretary of State, the President, and the Senate. It might reject, modify, or adopt the consultants' plan, but something had to be done to instruct the American delegate to the Atomic Energy Commission. Along with this, it was essential to prepare public opinion. Perhaps the committee could adopt a technical paper to go to the Senate and the public and serve as a basis for discussion.

Acheson's remarks defined the issue. If the scheme under consideration were to be adopted, what did it require? For one thing, Conant said, a schedule of steps. Bush thought this need be no more than a general outline. The specific plan could come later. He would much prefer to put the proposition before the President and Senate in generalities than throw everything at them at once. Lilienthal was reluctant to take on the job of setting forth the specific stages of transition.. For this, the Board of Consultants was scarcely competent. It would be better to consider its report only one phase of the arduous task of preparing a document to guide the American negotiator. Acheson had been impressed by what Bush had suggested. Why not, he asked Lilienthal, add a section at the end? The report could conclude that while the plan was an entity and would be adopted as a whole, it would take time to put in effect. First it would cover raw materials, then plants. Lilienthal thought something like this might be possible, but the board, he reiterated, would not consider the details of negotiation.

It was after five now, and ideas began to fall into place. After satisfying himself that sterilizing—removing the classified data—would not destroy the sense of the report, Conant made his earlier position more specific. There was too much argument against inspection at the beginning. Lilienthal agreed. His group already had that change in mind. Bush was happy. "I am ready to endorse this plan right now," he said. The form of the additions could be discussed tomorrow. Conant too was pleased. Once more he emphasized that there should be more about inspectors going everywhere and seeing everything. If that were done, he was willing to go along with Bush. For a few minutes there was a general exchange on inspection. The crux was how to strike a balance between the irritation it admittedly entailed and the need for greater safeguards against diverting uranium to national uses. It was six o'clock when the meeting broke up.

Later that evening the Lilienthal group met in a fifth-floor room at the Carlton Hotel. All had serious misgivings about adding a section on stages. It was not that they had any illusions about Russia. They recognized that the shift to international control must come in orderly steps. But they considered it bad tactics to write in an implied distrust of other nations. Their report assumed the good faith of Russia. It permitted the concept of stages to evolve during the negotiations. It avoided giving the plan a made-in-America stamp that would prejudice others against it. Yet what could the consultants do? If they refused to write the fourth section, someone else would. Perhaps they ought to stick with the task and see it done well. Distinctly unhappy, fearing they were blighting the spirit of the work, they decided to undertake the revision.[17]

The Acheson committee and the Lilienthal board devoted all Friday, March 8, to exploring the implications of the control plan and determining the substance of the revision. McCloy, who had said very little the day before, voiced his admiration for the affirmative tone the report had struck. He warned against delay. The United States could not keep running its atomic energy plant and prevent other nations from developing their own. Emphasizing what Bush had said previously, he held that the United States proposal had to be written in a way that would appeal both to the American people and to the world.

When McCloy had finished, Conant asked a disconcerting question. Suppose a geological survey indicated there was no uranium in Russia. What then? McCloy thought Conant's question took everything back to the original issue: should we take international action? The Administration already had been through the torture of deciding that. The task now was to make it workable without being softheaded. But Acheson thought he saw what Conant was driving at and rephrased his question. If Russia did not

547

have sizable quantities of uranium, how much damage would be done after the international authority had built the most dangerous types of plants in the Soviet Union? Groves had no doubt the threat to American security would be substantial. For one thing, Russia would want nuclear materials stockpiled within her boundaries. Both Oppenheimer and Conant agreed it was folly to rely on Russia having no uranium. If she had none, Conant said it was only a matter of time until she made war to get it.

At this juncture, McCloy thought the meeting should explore the possibility of using international control to alter Russia's closed society. Or perhaps the United States could make disarmament the price for relinquishing its special position. This moved Acheson to say there was no use chasing a will-o'-the-wisp. It was impossible to settle the Russian problem in one fell stroke. You could not make a change in the Russian system the subject of negotiation. The United States was in for a long period of tension. It had to hope for Russia's gradual "civilization." Acheson drew a parallel with the Washington Disarmament Conference of 1921-22. The idea of heading off a naval race had been a good one, but the content of the treaties was wrong. Worse, the United States did not build up to treaty limits and the Japanese fortified their island bases. The present situation was much the same. Perhaps the present proposal was faulty. It was good to challenge it. But the mere presence of defects was not a valid argument for discarding the whole approach.

Acheson succeeded in directing the discussion back to the gradual steps of transition. For the rest of the morning, the talk churned. When everyone had had his say, Acheson tried to summarize. Reduced to simple terms, he said, the consultants' plan risked shortening the time other nations needed to overtake the United States against the chance of achieving a system of controls, operation, and management. This system would not make atomic warfare impossible, but it promised to warn the American people if another power started developing nuclear arms. Acheson thought the full plan should go into effect as rapidly as possible, but he recognized it would take time— five or six years perhaps. When the United States presented its plan, it would have to explain the process of transition. Then the nations would establish an international authority. As soon as the organization had completed the first transitional stage and everyone was "playing pool," it would turn to the next. If the first phase revealed bad faith, further progress was out of the question. The United States would not give everything away the day it agreed to institute the plan; rather, it would promise to do so. In the meantime, there would be crises in Russo-American relations. The United States must be prepared. Perhaps difficulties in the plan itself or other issues would wreck everything.

After lunch, Bush explained that it was not necessary to prepare a final, detailed schedule of transition. That was a job for the American representative. Acheson supported Bush; stages could be discussed in a speculative way. Lilienthal understood the new section was not to prove the United States could hold back but to give the report the ring of reasonableness.

Lilienthal now had a few final remarks. He was greatly encouraged. The committee had come to grips with what internationalization really meant. Similar discussions should go on throughout the country. The board's definite plan would elicit them. Acheson confined himself to saying his committee would report to Secretary Byrnes that the plan was sound, serious, substantial—the best it knew. Of course, the section on stages would have to be added and some editing was in order. Could the Board of Consultants be ready in ten days? Oppenheimer thought the work could be done by the sixteenth, so Acheson set that Saturday for the next session, once again at Dumbarton Oaks.[18]

REVISION   549

General Groves had sensed that the consultants were downcast at the prospect of another week at hard labor. They ought to take the week end off, he told them. Their task would seem lighter Monday morning. In theory a good idea, Groves's suggestion did not suit the mood of Lilienthal and his associates. They adjourned at once to their headquarters on Sixteenth Street, where Lilienthal moved quickly to dispel any gloom. He saw little reason for discouragement. The board had established a basis for public discussion. The Acheson committee recognized the need for this and judged the plan the best yet proposed. Was it reasonable to expect more? It remained to explore the process of launching the plan and guiding it to full operation. This was an important task.

Saturday morning, revision began in earnest. By noon, the board had set down the transitional stages in rough outline and determined that Oppenheimer, Marks, and Wilson should draft a revision. Sunday morning there was another session, this time to consider the larger dimensions of the new draft. All agreed with Marks on directing the report to any intelligent reader. It should keep the personal touch and be as simple as possible. With its instructions complete, the drafting team could go to work.[19]

Oppenheimer, Marks, and Wilson did their duty with dispatch. The letter of transmittal became a foreword. A thoroughly reworked Section I began with a short statement characterizing the report as a preliminary study to help clarify the position of the United States representative on the United Nations Atomic Energy Commission. Several new paragraphs reviewed why the United States had committed itself to the quest for international control. The passages on the inadequacy of inspection, de-emphasized by being moved back into the body of the section, were shorter. Finally, there appeared a fresh statement—underlined—asserting that the consultants did not underestimate the need for inspection as a vital component in any system of international controls.

In Section II, it was necessary only to eliminate the classified data. This included references to thermonuclear bombs, Anglo-American raw-material arrangements, and weapon characteristics. These had no place in a document the board hoped would be published.

While the new draft had touched on inspection in its early pages, Section III was the best place to insert the emphasis Conant had demanded. Five new paragraphs on the functions of the atomic development authority made clear that the board's objection was to relying on inspection alone. They stressed the peculiar advantages of the proposed authority as an inspecting agency. Nevertheless, except in the raw-material field, the plan did not contemplate systematic or large-scale inspection activities. It was the board's hope that a fully operating authority would need no elaborate and formal procedures.

An entirely new section, the fourth, put the question that had so troubled the Acheson committee. What conditions would prevail during the transition to international control? This query, the draft explained, rose from the fact that the United States had a monopoly of atomic weapons. While experts differed on how long it would last, virtually everyone expected a profound change in five to twenty years. Any plan for international control would shorten the duration of American primacy. The Board of Consultants believed that its plan, fully in operation, would furnish adequate security against surprise attack by atomic weapons. But what would happen should any nation try to cheat while the transfer was under way?

An answer required investigation of just how much and in what way the loss of monopoly would accelerate. If the dangers of bad faith during the transition period were sufficiently great, the plan might be unacceptable at the outset. It helped to realize that the special position of the United States rested on two different things: theoretical knowledge and physical facilities. Manifestly, this country must make sufficient technical information available at the outset so that other nations could evaluate its proposals. This might be more or less than had been available to the Board of Consultants, but once the development authority was established, the United States would have to supply all basic scientific information. This would happen before the security system was in operation; there was no blinking the fact. Fortunately, it posed no threat to the United States. Theoretical knowledge was one of the first things any other nation could attain on its own. To supply it might shorten another power's bomb effort, but only by a small portion of the total time required. It was safe to say that revelations in the Atomic Energy Commission and in the early planning of the authority would not alter American superiority essentially.

The real source of American strength was experience, technology, physical facilities, industrial plant and organization, and stockpiles along with the capacity to replenish them. It was here that sharing would affect national security. Here prudent and reasonable scheduling was in order.

While the scheduling of transition steps might be decisive in determining the acceptability of control, it was premature and unwise to set out the details now. They must be worked out in co-operation with other nations. In some areas, clearly, the international authority would have to operate from the outset. Its first major activities would be directed to controlling raw materials. Very likely, it would want to establish its own research agencies and planning boards. It might license the use of radioactive materials. Other operations would come later. The most careful scheduling was necessary for disposition of the raw-material stocks, the plants at Oak Ridge and Hanford, the stockpiles of bombs and fissionable materials, and the laboratory at Los Alamos. Throughout the transition period these facilities would be readily available. Should there be a breakdown at any time, the United States would be in a position relatively more favorable than when the plan was in full operation.[20]

551

DUMBARTON OAKS: ROUND TWO

The procedure at Dumbarton Oaks on Saturday afternoon, March 16, was the same as the week before. Lilienthal, Barnard, and Winne read the revised sections. When Winne had finished Section IV; Lilienthal declared that the board had gone about as far and in as great detail as it could. It had not produced a final plan or the only report possible. It hoped, however, its work would contribute to discussion and perhaps to clarity. Acheson hastened to voice his satisfaction. The additions of the past week had been most helpful to him. Conant was of the same opinion. The board had strengthened enormously what was already a strong report.

Bush also thought the board had accomplished much. He found the document convincing as it stood. But what happened next? The statement that it was "premature and unwise" to suggest a schedule jarred him. True, there could be no final schedule until there was a meeting of minds on the Commission, but the American negotiator needed a timetable satisfactory to the United States. Troubled by a "feeling of vacuum," Bush confessed to being puzzled. Oppenheimer had no such doubts. The essential elements of a schedule were in the report. It was easy to guess at specific times, but this left out of account the need for elasticity. Besides, who could define the minimum conditions for American security? McCloy was inclined to agree with Oppenheimer. The next considerations were strategic and political and beyond the scope of the report. Groves emphasized strongly the need for a more definite statement to guide the American negotiator. He did not care about specifying times, but he thought the report should state what steps the United States should take, what they did to its position, what the nation would do if Russia suddenly dropped out. The report should go right through the transitional period showing where the American people would come out if someone suddenly double-crossed them.

The committee had to report at once, Acheson said. Senator McMahon wanted hearings in April. It was unnecessary to develop the plan in all its detail now. If it were acceptable to the Secretary of State and the President, then the committee could get to work on scheduling. This clarified his thinking, said Bush, but when would the job be done and who would do it? Acheson explained what he thought would happen. Byrnes and Truman might say the report was all right or all wrong. Or they might say it was good enough to publish in order to get some discussion started. From this, it would become quite apparent what the American people would accept. Then, the Administration would go to work. It would appoint a delegate, and technical advisers would provide the detailed studies he needed to carry into the negotiations.

Acheson did not convince General Groves. He still held for tackling the schedule. Not so Lilienthal; setting out a schedule, he said, was another way of specifying the price the United States would pay for what it received. He would not want to put an answer down on paper until he had heard from the American people. Besides, what would other nations pay? He would not want to say until there were some preliminary discussions.

The meeting was making very little headway, so Acheson tried another tack. He suggested reviewing the report paragraph by paragraph. Byrnes, he said, was much attracted by the concept of control through development. Remove the "bugs" and devote some space to scheduling possibilities. Then the committee could submit the plan. Once Truman and Byrnes had decided what they wanted, the committee could go ahead with enthusiasm and assurance. Following Acheson's lead, the committee devoted the rest of the afternoon to detailed criticism.

Sunday morning, Acheson told the consultants his committee had conferred again the night before. It was troubled by the information disclosures the board's plan required. What effect would they have on American security, on the acceptability of the plan? The discussion centered on denaturing. Was it possible to bring it up without explaining the implosion method of bomb assembly? No one wanted to let this out in the coming negotiations, but there was considerable difference on the chances of avoiding it. Finally, Bush stated his position at some length. The board's plan was unquestionably attractive. The only danger was disclosing a great amount of data at the outset. He did not want this on his conscience if the whole effort broke down at the end of the year. It was not essential to divulge any details on denaturing. That could come later, when the authority was ready to undertake it. He thought the committee's qualms might be allayed by subdividing information into categories and laying down a schedule indicating when each class should be revealed.

This fourth meeting of committee and consultants was well along. Though the differences seemed fairly small, there was no consensus on what to do. Miss Anne Wilson, a perceptive young woman who had been recording the sessions in shorthand, passed up a note suggesting coffee. Acheson took the opportunity to break the tension. Coffee seldom tasted better than it did that cold, damp, gloomy morning. The meeting broke into little clusters of informal conversation. Acheson moved quietly about the room, making suggestions. When everyone had finished and resumed his seat, a new atmosphere was apparent. In a few minutes, Acheson put the decisive question: did the committee wish to transmit the report with a statement of approval or simply forward it for information and further instructions with the observation it was the best analysis the group had seen? Bush replied without hesitation. If the report stated that a schedule was feasible, the committee should transmit it with a strong endorsement. Then Acheson sketched in the details of a letter to the Secretary of State.[21]

That afternoon, March 17, the report and its letter of transmittal took final shape. The only major changes in the report came in Section IV. These made the discussion of information disclosure much more specific. The United States could not, should not, lose its monopoly of knowledge at once. A limited category must be released in the early meetings of the United Nations Commission. A more extensive class would come some years later when a charter had been adopted and the atomic authority was ready to start operations. Other information might be reserved until the agency was prepared for later stages of its operations, research on weapons for instance. The details required for the negotiations were largely theoretical and descriptive, dealing in the main with constructive applications. Once the international unit was undertaking operations in a given field, it would need all information bearing on them, practical as well as theoretical. To illustrate: if the authority were to obtain control of raw materials as its first major undertaking, the United States and other nations must make available all pertinent knowledge. The sequence and timing of the several stages would be fixed by negotiation and agreement among the nations. The United States would be committed to making the information available at the time and in the full measure required by operating necessities.

The letter of transmittal borrowed the words of the consultants and laid the report before Byrnes "not as a final plan, but as a place to begin, a foundation on which to build." The committee believed it the "most constructive analysis" it had seen, a "definitely hopeful approach" to international control. It recommended the plan for Byrnes's consideration "as representing the framework within which the best prospects for both security and development of atomic energy for peaceful purposes may be found."

To assist in evaluating the impact of the plan on American security, the committee stressed that disclosure of information and transfer of authority over physical things would proceed by stages. The first move would come when the United Nations Atomic Energy Commission took up its duties. The United States would have to make enough information available for other powers to understand its proposals. If this were made known to a

553

nation already equipped to develop atomic armament within five years, it might shorten that period by as much as a year. Whether any nation—excluding Great Britain and Canada—could achieve such an intensive program was a matter for serious doubt. If a nation's effort were spread over a considerably longer period, the initial disclosures would not shorten its labors appreciably.

The committee emphasized further that any detailed proposals for scheduling the remaining stages required additional study with the aid of a highly competent technical staff. This would be done, of course, within the framework set by high-policy decisions. One such decision was the duration of the period in which the United States would continue manufacturing bombs. The plan did not require the United States to discontinue manufacture upon either proposal of the plan or establishment of the international agency. At some stage, bomb making would have to stop, but the plan did not mean this should or should not be done at any specific time. That decision involved considerations of the highest policy and had to be made by the United States under its constitutional processes and in the light of the world situation.

The letter of transmittal closed with the announcement that the committee awaited instructions as to whether it was discharged or whether the Secretary wished it to proceed further. The letter was the work of a master committee chairman. Composing the crucial parts himself, Acheson had succeeded in saving the consultants' report and at the same time voicing the sentiments of his strong-minded committee.[22]

Two things the letter did not do. First, it did not advise Byrnes to adopt the report. The committee would do no more than recommend it for consideration as the best framework for international control. Second, it said nothing about publishing. A draft letter of transmittal had carried the observation, "it would seem desirable that the report be made available to broader circles both within and without the Government. It appears to us to be the most suitable starting point now available for the further study and the wide discussions that are essential factors in developing a sound solution." McCloy objected. He thought publication prior to review by the American negotiator most unwise. It might prove a serious embarrassment. The committee supported him and voted against any reference to publication. Acheson, however, reserved the right to advise the Secretary to publish, a right he intended to exercise.[23]

ENTRY OF THE GLADIATOR

Acheson and Lilienthal—indeed, every member of the Secretary of State's Committee and the Board of Consultants—knew that one day the President would nominate a representative to the United Nations Atomic Energy Commission. But when they completed the report Sunday afternoon, March 17, none knew that just the day before Truman and Byrnes had chosen Bernard M. Baruch. It was the most natural thing in the world for Byrnes to think of his fellow South Carolinian. For years they had been close political and personal friends. Byrnes frequently was a guest at Hobcaw Barony, the financier's magnificent seventeen-thousand acre estate. It was Baruch who had urged President Roosevelt to make Byrnes Director of Economic Stabilization. Sometime late in February, 1946, probably while visiting at Hobcaw, the Secretary sounded out his friend. Would he take over the UN atomic energy assignment?

Baruch must have had misgivings. This was a difficult, perhaps thankless assignment for a man in his seventy-sixth year. Yet unquestionably it was a flattering call to public service. To help decide, he procured a copy of the General Assembly's resolution establishing the Commission on Atomic Energy. As he studied it, he concluded there was no reason why nations should not exchange basic scientific information for peaceful ends, even though this raised some difficult patent questions. But he did not see how the Commission could proceed at present with the other proposals the January 24 resolution enjoined. If Russia would not permit newsmen and others to move freely, why believe she would permit inspection? How could the United States discuss eliminating the bomb unless the United Nations began to work better? He saw no point in going ahead unless it was understood that other countries, particularly Russia, would live up to their contracts and promises. There was no point in making new agreements unless the powers lived up to the old ones.

555

On March 13, Baruch sent Byrnes a letter reporting his reaction to the General Assembly's resolution. He wanted to know more of the Secretary's thinking, particularly on "the control of atomic energy to the extent necessary to ensure its use only for peaceful purposes." There were some things Byrnes himself should know. Baruch could only work from ten to twelve in the morning and from two-thirty to four-thirty in the afternoon. Should he serve, it must be understood that this would not prevent him from expressing his views publicly on any other question. Finally, he would need an alternate or assistant in addition to scientific advisers. If Byrnes still wanted him in the face of his views and his conditions, he would accept.[24]

Byrnes did want Baruch, and he talked to Truman about it on March 16. The Acheson committee was due to report any day, Byrnes said. The United States needed a spokesman who would command respect at home and abroad. Baruch was just the man. The suggestion appealed to the President. He was heavily involved in the fight for the McMahon bill. The struggle over the Vandenberg amendment was still in doubt. Moreover, the Senate Special Committee might report a bill that would make it impossible for the United States to participate in a plan for international control. In these circumstances, Baruch seemed the logical choice. The Senate held him in great esteem. His association with the effort at control of atomic energy might well remove some of the opposition to the McMahon bill and bring legislation that would not tie the Administration's hand in the UN. But it was more than the Senate that influenced Truman. Baruch was an international figure with many friends abroad. Far from the least among them was Winston Churchill, who had just made his Iron Curtain speech at Fulton, Missouri. Truman believed that Baruch's support would add weight to any proposal the United States put before the world.[25]

Monday, March 18, Presidential Secretary Ross announced that Truman had sent Baruch's name to the Senate for confirmation. The news was no sooner on the wires than reporters sought out the tall, white-haired elder statesman. Byrnes had persuaded him on Sunday to take the post, he said. "I felt it my duty to accept." Four associates would assist him: Herbert Bayard Swope, John M. Hancock, Ferdinand Eberstadt, and Fred Searls. "You know I never do any work myself," laughed Baruch. In addition, he said he would rely for scientific guidance on men like Conant, Bush, and Arthur Compton. On questions of manufacture, he would consult General Groves and the industrial pioneers in the field.[26]

556

The selection produced the expected favorable reaction on Capitol Hill. McMahon found it "highly pleasing." No member of his committee raised a voice in criticism. Vandenberg was especially gratified. He wrote Baruch he would like to avoid calling him as a witness before the Foreign Relations Committee. He could manage it, he thought, if Baruch would furnish a statement affirming his belief that there should be no agreement for atomic disclosures without prior dependable safeguards at every stage and that any international agreements on atomic energy were subject to the approval of Congress. Baruch supplied the necessary assurances at once. Satisfied, Vandenberg promised he would present them to the committee as a matter of record and move confirmation.[27]

Baruch's appointment unquestionably had a broad appeal. His reputation as a miracle worker had sunk deep in the public consciousness. Not everyone was pleased, however. Acheson saw problems, for Baruch might bottle up the Board of Consultants' report; the essential public discussion might never take place. Many scientists' were concerned. Given good advisers, they thought, Baruch might have been a valuable salesman, but Hancock, Eberstadt, and Searls were prominent figures in the banking business, while Swope, admittedly a successful journalist, had devoted most of the last fifteen years to heading the New York State Racing Commission. What did these men know about atomic energy? Nor did Baruch promote confidence by mentioning Conant, Bush, Compton, and Groves. In the minds of many supporters of the McMahon bill, advocacy of the May-Johnson measure was by itself enough to disqualify.[28]

On Thursday, March 21, Byrnes sent the Board of Consultants' report and the Acheson committee's letter of transmittal to the President, the

Secretaries of War and the Navy, the members of the Special Committee, and to Baruch. It was a paper of unusual importance, Byrnes stated in his covering letter, one that deserved the most serious study and consideration by the Government of the United States. Byrnes said nothing about publishing the report. But two days later, in letters of appreciation to the members of the Lilienthal board and the Acheson committee, he said he hoped it soon would be possible to make the document public. He considered it "the most suitable starting point for the informed public discussion which is one of the essential factors in developing a sound policy." [29]

It was no secret by now that the Acheson committee had reported. In their Sunday column of March 24, Joseph and Stewart Alsop guessed that the Board of Consultants had recommended vesting control in an "independent, government-owned corporation," but this was too general to mean much. Then on Monday morning Acheson went before an executive session of the McMahon committee. He explained the report and gave the senators to understand that State would delay its release for some days so that they might study it in advance of publication. That afternoon, accounts leaked to the press. Apparently, some members of the committee had talked to reporters. By Tuesday morning, newspapers across the country summarized the plan.[30]

Baruch had called the White House Monday. He would be passing through Washington on his way south the next afternoon and would like to see the President. When he arrived Tuesday, March 26, Baruch handed Truman a letter. He did not underestimate, he had written, either the honor or the responsibility of his appointment. But certain elements in the situation were causing him concern. As he understood his duties and authority, they consisted solely in representing United States policy on atomic energy as communicated by the President directly or through the Secretary of State. He did not see that he had any duty or responsibility in the formulation of that policy. The day's news stories had brought the situation forcibly to his attention. Byrnes's letter transmitting the report had stated that the Secretary of State's Committee had "unanimously recommended" it.[31] This brought it "pretty close to the category of the United States Government policy." "I have no doubt," Baruch continued, "that the public feels that I am going to have an important relation to the determination of our atomic energy policy." He said there was no legal basis for this view, and now that the report was public knowledge, it would greatly affect the determination of policy. He was convinced that the report would be the subject of rather violent differences of opinion. The leak did not make the situation less difficult. For these reasons Baruch wanted to talk with the President before reaching a final decision as to whether he could be useful. He needed more time to reflect. It would avoid embarrassment all around if Truman would ask Senator Connally to postpone action on his appointment until he had had a little more time to think things over.[32]

557

Baruch's letter was no model of clarity. He had coupled assertions that he had no duty or responsibility to participate in policy decisions with protests suggesting this was exactly what he wanted to do. Perhaps, as Arthur Krock wrote in the New York *Times*, Baruch feared that national policy was more unsettled than he had been led to believe and might materialize in a form he could not speak for. Just what the President said to him remained uncertain. When Truman recounted the interview ten years later in his memoirs, he had concluded that Baruch's real concern was whether he would receive public recognition. Truman remembered he had told Baruch that the report, plainly marked as a working paper, was not an approved policy document. As President, he would approve any policy presented to the United Nations. Of course, Byrnes probably would want Baruch's help in preparing a proposal for his approval, but Baruch was to have the same role as all other American delegates to the United Nations. When Baruch wrote his autobiography, however, he denied that Truman lectured him on the prerogatives of the President. On the question of who was going to draft the proposals, Truman's only comment was, "Hell, you are!" [33]

558

Whatever was the fact, Baruch had nothing to say as he left the White House. When reporters asked him about the Lilienthal report, he ostentatiously turned off his hearing aid and remarked, "I can't hear you." On the twenty-seventh, the Senate Foreign Relations Committee met, with its members prepared to confirm Baruch without dissent. Senator Connally startled them by announcing that the nominee had asked that action be postponed until he could confer with Secretary Byrnes. Sometime in the next few days, Baruch apparently received satisfactory assurances, for on April 3, the committee acted favorably. Two days later, the Senate itself approved the nomination.[34]

STAFF AND STATUS

The Department of State formally released the Acheson-Lilienthal report on March 28. Baruch was right in expecting sharp differences of opinion. At one end of the spectrum, the Chicago *Tribune* and the Washington *Times-Herald* denounced the report as a transparent scheme to give the bomb secret to Russia. Columnist Dorothy Thompson dismissed it as an "Elysian daydream." A larger number of observers, while conceding the plan was statesmanlike, questioned the validity of its scientific conclusions and the chance for winning Russian assent. But the predominant reaction was favorable. The New York *Times* welcomed it as a starting point based on the realities of the situation. Alfred Friendly of the Washington *Post* saw the report offering hope for lifting the "Great Fear" that had descended over the world the previous August 6. Newscaster Raymond Gram Swing, a World Federalist, hailed it as "one of the most significant pointers ever erected on the long road to world peace." The document proved capable of arousing an emotional response. Paul H. Appleby of the Bureau of the Budget was so excited the night he read it he could hardly sleep. "In my opinion," he wrote Acheson, "it is the *most important and most perfect governmental job that has been done in generations.* Anyone who had anything to do with it can feel that his life has an extraordinary and enduring significance." Countless less eloquent citizens felt the same. Senators Mitchell, Fulbright, Kilgore, and Morse introduced a resolution urging immediate negotiations to give effect to the Acheson-Lilienthal plan.[35] The Federation of American Scientists endorsed the report, and the National Committee on Atomic Information scattered reprints broadcast.

Even had the response been less favorable, Baruch would no doubt have wished to avail himself of the advisory services of the Acheson committee and its Board of Consultants. The ardent reception made it seem almost imperative. When Byrnes asked if he should keep his committee in being, Baruch replied affirmatively. He would like both committee and consultants to feel free to express their views to him, while he should like the right to call upon them. But when Byrnes transmitted Baruch's wishes in the name of the President and himself, there was no overwhelming rush to Baruch's standard.

559

The Acheson committee was divided in its response. McCloy and Groves replied that they were available. Bush and Conant were reluctant. Judging it better to rely on a strong working group within the Department of State, they questioned the wisdom of reconstituting the committee. Conant's responsibilities at Harvard made it difficult for him to help on anything but a strictly informal and personal basis. Bush's position was more complicated. While he advanced the press of his heavy OSRD and Carnegie Institution responsibilities, something more was troubling him. A few days later, he told Baruch what it was to his face. He was accustomed to working in "higher echelons." He didn't relish being a consultant to Baruch's group of "Wall Streeters." Baruch toyed with the idea of making Bush his alternate, but this, he learned, was politically impractical. Identified with May-Johnson and "military control," Bush had alienated McMahon and, apparently, Truman as well.[36]

There was no division among the Board of Consultants. Bound by a remarkable sense of unity, they conferred by telephone and sent Byrnes a single response. While they recognized the arduous responsibility that Baruch faced and expressed their desire to help, they doubted that the intermittent advisory services Byrnes had suggested would prove very useful unless there was some concentrated staff work. This reply was the product of conflicting emotions. The consultants knew how many questions their report left unanswered. They knew better than anyone else how much detailed study remained to be done. They thought it important to be as helpful as possible.

On the other hand, they wished to avoid being put in a position in which they could not speak out freely should Baruch advance proposals they deemed wrong.[37]

Baruch spent the week of April 15 in Washington. The Senate had confirmed him, but he still was unsure of his status. On Thursday morning, he had a long conference with Byrnes in the company of two of his aides, Hancock and Searls. Baruch called the Secretary's attention to a statute enacted the preceding December which specified that American representatives to the United Nations "shall, at all times, act in accordance with the instructions of the President transmitted by the Secretary of State. . . ." What did this mean? Did it imply he was to be a mere messenger boy carrying out the policy of other men, men who presumably would not be as well informed as he? Byrnes hastened to reassure him. Of course, he said, the President determined policy. But as a practical matter, the President would ask Byrnes for his views, and he in turn would ask what Baruch thought. Byrnes said that although the Acheson-Lilienthal report had impressed him favorably, he did not consider it the last word on the subject. On the contrary, he would give careful consideration to any views Baruch presented after he had opportunity to make a study. Baruch would not prepare a formal report. He and Byrnes would advise the President, who would determine policy. Truman, however, would not announce this policy. As representative of the United States, Baruch would make it public before the Atomic Energy Commission.

Once the Commission was in operation, Byrnes continued, there would have to be close co-operation between Baruch and himself. Baruch could exercise his own judgment in handling the unforeseen matters that would inevitably arise. There would be no trouble with the President. Byrnes had never had any difference with him that was not quickly reconciled. If Baruch needed help from the State Department, Byrnes was sure it would be granted without question.[38]

The next day Byrnes sent Baruch a letter setting forth in black and white what he had said the day before. Monday afternoon, the twenty-first, the two men conferred by telephone. Baruch now wondered where Acheson stood. When he had heard from Acheson, he said, he could reply more intelligently to Byrnes's letter.[39]

On April 30, Hancock called on Acheson and Marks. He was pleased to discover that Acheson did not have a large staff at work and expected Baruch to take the initiative. Acheson wanted the Baruch team to develop its views in outline as soon as possible and to discuss them with interested agencies— State, War, Navy—and with the President himself. Acheson would expect Baruch's group to draft all the necessary papers, including a tentative draft of a final report to the Security Council. He strongly urged drawing up a charter, a sound and fair-minded statement of policy and procedure. A good

LILIENTHAL BOARD OF CONSULTANTS AT OAK RIDGE, FEBRUARY, 1946 /
Left to right: Harry A. Winne, David E. Lilienthal, Colonel Kenneth D. Nichols (not a
board member), Chester I. Barnard.

LILIENTHAL BOARD OF CONSULTANTS AT OAK RIDGE, FEBRUARY, 1946 /
Left to right: Robert Oppenheimer, Charles A. Thomas, staff members Herbert S. Marks
and Carroll L. Wilson.

BERNARD M. BARUCH PRESENTS THE AMERICAN PLAN FOR INTERNATIONAL CONTROL, JUNE 14, 1946 / Baruch proposed that the United Nations Atomic Energy Commission recommend the establishment of an international atomic development authority. Seated at Baruch's right is UN Secretary-General Trygve H. Lie.

plan would test the good faith of the rest of the world, he said. That was the important thing at the present stage.[40]

This was what Baruch had been waiting to hear. He wrote Byrnes May 6 to express his pleasure at Acheson's thoroughly satisfactory assurances. Now he could say he was quite in accord with Byrnes's views on his relation to the making of policy. He too, Baruch wrote, had been impressed by the constructive and practical approach of the Acheson-Lilienthal report. That was why he had asked Byrnes to continue the Acheson committee and the Board of Consultants. Baruch put in writing his understanding that State would not build a large staff at present. As for himself, he would set up an adequate but small staff to develop the facts. Finally, Baruch would assume that his official work was done when the Atomic Energy Commission reported to the Security Council. The State Department would take over the further responsibility.[41]

Meanwhile, Baruch had begun to recruit his staff. As a nucleus, he had his personal team. Baruch had come to depend heavily on Swope, a member of the inner circle that had served on the War Industries Board in 1917 and 1918. Another old WIB man was Hancock. A naval officer who had worked effectively on price fixing, Hancock resigned his commission in 1919 to become vice-president of the Jewel Tea Company. This was the start of a new career that led him to a Lehman Corporation partnership. He had been associated with Baruch on the rubber survey during World War II and along with Baruch had been an adviser to Byrnes. Swope and Hancock were old friends who affectionately addressed Baruch as "Chief." Somewhat younger and more recent associates were Eberstadt and Searls. A lawyer by training, Eberstadt had moved into the investment banking business with conspicuous success. Throughout 1942, he had served ably on the War Production Board. Baruch was so impressed that had he become chairman of WPB, he would have made Eberstadt his deputy. Searls was a first-class mining engineer. An assistant to Byrnes in the Office of War Mobilization, he had just served on the Strategic Bombing Survey in Japan.

Confident as he was in the abilities of Swope, Hancock, Eberstadt, and Searls, Baruch knew he needed the help of specialists, particularly in the military and scientific fields. General Groves had indicated his willingness to assist, while General Eisenhower and Admiral Nimitz planned to make the American representatives on the UN Military Staff Committee available as advisers. But Baruch needed a full-time military man. He found one in Major General Thomas F. Farrell, who had become Groves's deputy in early 1945 and had headed the field operations in the Marianas. By April 18, Farrell had his first assignment: to see how long it would take other powers to manufacture atomic bombs.[42]

Even more urgent was Baruch's need for a scientific adviser. On April 5, he sounded out Oppenheimer. The physicist did most of the talking.

561

The consultants' plan, he said, was entirely incompatible with the present Russian system. The proper procedure for the United States was to make an honorable proposal and find out whether the Russians had the will to cooperate. He stressed the warning principle on which the Acheson-Lilienthal report was based and seemed to have great faith that the American people would act quickly if some foreign nation went back on its promises. Baruch and Hancock had doubts about this, but Oppenheimer was the man Baruch wanted. He called him in the week end of May 4 and offered to make him chief technical adviser to the American delegation. Oppenheimer did not jump at the opportunity. He was convinced in his own mind that Bush, Acheson, or Winne—any one of them—would be better than Baruch as top man and that Baruch's associates were not competent. Besides, he did not want to serve unless the President made what he considered the right policy decision. Oppenheimer did not refuse, but he revealed enough of his thinking to convince Baruch he would not do.

562

Baruch then telephoned Conant, who suggested he contact Richard C. Tolman. Sunday, Baruch put in a long-distance call to Pasadena. Would Tolman be chief technical adviser? Would he let Baruch know by Tuesday? Tolman hardly knew what to do. He recognized he could not recruit the necessary scientific assistance unless the major physicists, including Oppenheimer, and the Lilienthal Board of Consultants were in a mood to cooperate. A call to Oppenheimer did not put his mind to rest on this point, but Monday Farrell and Groves called and urged Tolman to accept. It was absolutely essential that he come, said Groves. If Tolman said no, he would put pressure on the Cal Tech trustees. By Tuesday, Tolman was enough convinced to phone Baruch he would come and see if he thought he could be helpful. As soon as he could arrange train reservations, he went east. Satisfied that he would have the necessary co-operation, he took the job.[43]

CONFERENCE AT BLAIR-LEE HOUSE

Baruch and his personal team had not waited to complete their staff. Conversations began at Baruch's Fifth Avenue house early in April and continued almost daily. From the very first, important objections to the Acheson-Lilienthal report figured prominently in the deliberations.

For one thing, there was the Acheson-Lilienthal emphasis on controlling raw materials. On March 31, Searls sent Baruch the draft of a letter to Byrnes which pointed out the magnitude of the task. At the turn of the century, the poorest copper ore it was profitable to mine contained only slightly less metal than Shinkolobwe uranium ore. Recently, however, the Utah Copper Company had been mining large tonnages containing less than one-fifth the content considered payable in 1900. The same pattern could be expected in uranium. How was the proposed atomic development authority to ride herd on such huge production? Slightly different doubts found emphasis April 4, when General Groves brought Edgar Sengier of Union Minière to a meeting at Baruch's house. While Sengier believed the authority should own uranium stockpiles, he opposed having it work the mines. The present owners should conduct operations under reasonable control. He feared an international administration would upset wages, dissatisfy people, and, on account of the different nationals involved, present tremendous management difficulties.[44]

Perhaps a more fundamental objection to the Acheson-Lilienthal plan was its failure to explain the source of the development agency's power. Searls had raised this question in his draft of March 31. Presumably, the fount was the Security Council of the United Nations. If that were the case, would not any act be subject to veto by one of the five permanent members? Were the plan adopted, the United States would disclose atomic information to other nations. There must be no veto, no loophole, to permit turning the expected good to evil. Searls's argument appealed to Baruch. Once committed to the atomic energy fight, Baruch was not inclined to accept half-way measures. His thoughts already ranged beyond the limited goals of Acheson and Lilienthal.[45]

563

By early May, Baruch unquestionably was in a difficult position. While he was moving toward an independent stand, public opinion had come to understand the Acheson-Lilienthal report as official policy. Even more alarming, Sir Alexander Cadogan, the British representative to the United Nations, had told Baruch he understood from Acheson that the United States would submit that document as a basis for discussion. Everything was made the more embarrassing by the failure of the Secretary of State's Committee and the Board of Consultants to continue in their former capacities. Byrnes being in Paris, Baruch and Hancock confronted Acheson May 9 and frankly voiced their dissatisfaction. Acheson was firm in denying that the President was committed to the Board of Consultants' plan. He had seen it and thought well of it, but no one had put pressure on him to accept it. Hancock tried to explain the dilemma that Baruch faced. Unless he went rather far in listing reservations, he might be condemned by silence to accepting the report as a statement of policy. On the other hand, there was danger in going so far with reservations as to appear to reject it in its entirety. This continuing concern made imperative a meeting between Baruch's team and the Acheson-Lilienthal groups. Acheson set it for the next week end in Washington.[46]

At two o'clock on Friday, May 17, an impressive group assembled at the Blair-Lee House on Pennsylvania Avenue. Baruch and his staff were there—the four associates, Farrell and Tolman, and John P. Davis, a young attorney who was serving as executive secretary. Conant and Groves could not be present, but Acheson attended with McCloy and Bush. Joining them was every member of the Board of Consultants and Marks and Wilson. From the Manhattan District came Captain Volpe and Colonel John R. Jannarone.

Acheson opened the conference by stating that his committee and its consultants were present to help Baruch in any way they could. Baruch expressed his appreciation and said he would like to have Hancock act as chairman. Before moving into the heart of the afternoon's business, Hancock reported that the Baruch group had been considering a preliminary raw-material survey. As Searls explained, it might take a year or two for the UN Commission to reach a decision. In the meantime, it would be advantageous to get a line on world ore deposits. Not only would the survey furnish information helpful in the negotiations; it would be an early first step in international co-operation. No member of the State Department group thought the survey a good idea. Lilienthal pointed out it would force the United States to disclose its arrangements for the ore of the Congo. Besides, it would appear that Americans were only fishing to find out what Russia might have. Acheson was even more categorical in his dissent. It was dangerous for the United States to suggest a general survey at an early meeting. Other countries would not appreciate its value and would fight it. Acheson was especially opposed if the purpose was only to test the good faith of other powers. Any good-faith test had to be conclusive. A survey based on an informal agreement or resolution could not be.

Startled by the unanimity of opinion, Hancock dropped the survey and turned to one of the main questions that interested Baruch. Did any member of the Acheson committee or the Lilienthal board wish to modify the report in the light of present circumstances? Lilienthal would change nothing. Barnard said he would modify only Section IV; it implied too much holding back by the United States. Oppenheimer had more second thoughts than anyone else. Like Barnard, he thought Section IV came too close to saying, "This is what the United States wants to do." It might have been better to stress minimum steps to be taken in some certain order. But there were other things that might be improved. The section on denaturing had stimulated too much hope. The report might have been more clear about the ownership or control of raw materials. Finally, it said nothing about the relation of the atomic development authority to the veto question (he was thinking of a veto on day-to-day operations, not punishment).

Now the talk turned to strategic balance, the authority's charter, personnel, interagency co-operation, relations with other delegates, and especially to the stages of information disclosure. Well on in the afternoon, Hancock asked about international stockpiling of bombs. Marks ventured to reply: the report said nothing explicitly one way or another on this, but stockpiling was inconsistent with its concept. If the plan were adopted and some power jumped the traces, there would be a year's warning—possibly more, possibly less—before the offender could release bombs in warfare. Stockpiles of ready bombs would offer too great a temptation. Some ruthless nation might seize them and drop them without warning.

Swope had said nothing yet, but at Marks's comments, he roused himself. Why did the report stop short of specifying a penalty for violations? Why should any nation join unless there was punishment for those who broke their covenant? And suppose the guilty party used a Security Council veto to thwart punishment? Acheson remarked that the question was very important. He recalled the thinking that lay behind the Charter of the United Nations. The drafters had concluded that no machinery could deal with a war between major powers. If a major power disregarded a treaty and wanted a test of strength, no treaty clauses would have any value. Complete security was an illusion. If a transgression occurred under the consultants' plan, the signatory countries would have a reasonable warning. Everything would rest on their intelligence, power, and preparations to meet the threat.

Thomas and Oppenheimer came to Acheson's support, but Baruch indicated that Swope's question was his own. Did anyone have any suggestions on what to do about a violation? Until the nations had reached the stage of automatic penalties, replied McCloy, this was not a very profitable line to pursue. Besides, sanctions were a matter of high state policy. It might be considered presumptuous for the Acheson committee and the Board of Consultants to suggest penalty provisions. It would not be presumptuous for the American representative on the AEC, Swope observed acidly.

Eberstadt had a question. Did he understand correctly that the Acheson-Lilienthal plan sought only to give a warning, release beneficent uses without encouraging the dangerous, and set a pattern for international co-operation? Yes, said Lilienthal. The consultants had set their sights higher —or was it lower?—than the unlimited-objective advocates. These were "a dime a dozen" because they only needed paper. A penalty was completely unintelligible when superpowers were involved. If the board's plan worked, it would control the bomb. Control means complete control, Swope said. What do we say to those who violate? There must be sanctions, retaliation. Now the antagonists pressed home their thrusts with ardor. Eberstadt said it was essential to state the truth about the plan: it did not eliminate the bomb. You do not eliminate the bomb merely by specifying a penalty for violations, Lilienthal replied. The public had the wrong impression, insisted Eberstadt. People thought the State Department plan was a system for controlling the bomb. Thomas asked what Eberstadt considered necessary. Outlawry and a penalty, he replied. The board's plan did have a penalty, said Oppenheimer —war. Marks pointed out that the United States would fight if Russia attacked Alaska. So under the proposed system: violation of the plan would be equivalent to violation of our boundaries.

Finally, Acheson declared there were only two ways to go further than the Board of Consultants had. One was a treaty requiring that an offender nation meet with an automatic declaration of war by all others. He thought this meant little. The other way was world government envisioning all wars as civil wars. This meant not a "damned thing." Winne had a few words to ease the tension. It had been a "hell of a job" to get the United Nations to its

565

present point. The State Department plan proposed to add greatly to its responsibilities. But an international stockpile, sanctions, and the like meant an international army—a whole new deal. The plan the consultants had drawn up provided a reasonable degree of safety and was still palatable. Then—it was ten minutes till six—the meeting adjourned.

When the conference resumed Saturday morning at ten, everyone was on his guard against another explosion. Each speaker was the soul of reasonableness. Hancock brought up the ownership of mines. While he favored international ownership and operation of manufacturing facilities, he considered it unwise to compel the development authority to own uranium ores in the ground. As an illustration of the difficulties involved, Searls pointed to mining operations producing uranium as a by-product. Suppose these employed 600,000 workers and represented 40 per cent of a nation's economy. He doubted such a nation would agree to international control of ore in the ground. A more practical plan was to restrict the authority to taking over the concentrates at the mill and conducting whatever mine inspections seemed necessary. Oppenheimer agreed that mining operations might be undesirable in certain circumstances. The agency ought to do as little as was commensurate with safety. However, it should decide for itself what was necessary.

This exchange set the tenor for the rest of the discussion. Barnard, Lilienthal, and Oppenheimer explained the report's section on stages, and Acheson pointed out that the atomic authority would be based on an independent treaty. While the authority would be related to the Security Council, the Council would not have a veto on its day-to-day functioning. But suppose, said Eberstadt, there was a warning, an act of aggression. Would not that bring in the Security Council? Yes, Acheson conceded, and in that case the veto power might become a factor.

Baruch had commented a time or two but not at length. When the talk seemed to have run its course, he expressed his appreciation. Everyone in the room bore a share of the responsibility; everyone could help. Most of all, he needed a statement of what the Acheson-Lilienthal report contained, or what its authors thought it contained. Acheson said it was important to act quickly. McMahon was on his heels. The Senator wanted to know when Baruch would talk to his committee. Baruch refused to go unprepared. The matter had not yet jelled in his mind. First he had to have a statement from the Board of Consultants. If McMahon complained, Acheson could put the blame on him. Baruch did not care whether the statement was ready early or late, but he wanted it well done. He needed a piece of paper before him. He would use a good deal of what Lilienthal's group had proposed, although he was inclined to be more generous and forthright. It was up to the board to help him know what he was talking about. Give him a chart, he said, and he could steer his way.[47]

By Sunday, the consultants had a summary ready. They had condensed their plan to twelve fundamental features which stressed the nature of control and the disclosures required in the period of transition. Their only concession to the discussions at Blair-Lee House was to emphasize more specifically that the plan was primarily a warning device. If a nation decided on a program of aggression and seized the plants or stockpiles of the international authority, it would need a year or more before it could produce enough atomic weapons to have an important influence on the outcome of war. Protection depended on the plan furnishing clear, simple, and unequivocal danger signals. This statement of May 19 contained both a word of caution and an offer. Baruch should realize that the summary could be understood and evaluated only in the light of the entire report. And if he wanted help in any way, the consultants were anxious to co-operate.[48]

FRAMING A POLICY STATEMENT

567

Sometime during the last week in May, Baruch decided definitely to support the Acheson-Lilienthal concept of an international agency with positive, developmental functions. Whatever thinking lay behind his choice, it was not due to the lack of an alternative. The distinguished legal subcommittee of the Carnegie Endowment's Committee on Atomic Energy had drafted a treaty for prohibiting all production, possession, and use of atomic weapons not specifically authorized by the United Nations Security Council. Punishment was to come through action by the Security Council or through immediate retaliation by other states. While there would be an international commission which might operate plants and laboratories, it would depend primarily on inspection to ascertain if the signatory powers were complying. James T. Shotwell, director of the Endowment's Division of Economics and History, had sent Hancock a draft. There were some grounds for fearing that the proposal would appeal to Baruch's staff, and Conant made a special effort to warn Baruch and Swope against it.[49] Perhaps the warning was not necessary. In any event, when on Memorial Day Baruch and Hancock called on Byrnes and Acheson at the State Department, Hancock had already prepared a working paper calling on the Atomic Energy Commission to establish an atomic development authority.

While Hancock's draft adopted the central idea of the Acheson-Lilienthal report, it differed substantively in some important ways. First, it specified definite crimes for which there should be prompt and certain penalties. Second, it recommended against mandatory mine ownership. The authority should have absolute dominion and control over ores containing source materials, but normally, the draft implied, licensing would be an adequate method of exercising it. Third, Hancock's paper recommended the initial raw-material survey he had suggested at the Blair-Lee House conference.[50]

Baruch did not bring out the Hancock draft. Instead, he asked Byrnes what his policies were. "Oh Hell," said the Secretary, "I have none. What are your views?" But when Baruch and Hancock began to question him, they discovered that the Secretary was being at least half-facetious. He felt strongly it was important to lay a working document on the table before a proposal was up for discussion. He had concluded that this was one way to keep the advantage when dealing with the Russians. On the other hand, it was very dangerous to use the verb "present" in offering documents. That implied a paper carried official validation. Nor were Byrnes's views confined to tactics. When Baruch pointed out that the General Assembly resolution of January 24 called for proposals on "all other major weapons adaptable to mass destruction," Byrnes said he thought it would be a mistake to try covering other weapons as part of the present assignment. He flatly opposed any preliminary raw-material survey. To propose moving on it before setting up the central plan would invite an early breakdown without furnishing a clear and adequate basis for it. Baruch spoke of the need for penalties. He had to be in the position of advocating something in which he believed. There was not enough time, however, for threshing out the issue. Since Byrnes had to leave for the Carter Glass funeral, he scheduled an after-dinner session at his apartment in the Shoreham.[51]

568

That evening, Acheson raised some organizational matters. First, he said, an interdepartmental committee ought to be set up under the Department of State to find answers to any questions the Baruch group might encounter during the course of negotiations. Second, he suggested reconstituting the Lilienthal Board of Consultants to advise the State Department. While Acheson did not press his suggestions to a decision, Hancock privately had some grave misgivings. He saw advantages in State having a staff group to dig up facts, but he wanted to keep direct lines of communication open between Baruch and the President. As for the Board of Consultants, Hancock opposed bringing it back into the picture. It might be all right if it were possible to keep scientists on purely technical matters. This was difficult, however, and Hancock thought scientists generally too inelastic in politics and negotiation.

The main business began when Hancock distributed the draft of his working paper. Since the earlier meeting, he had dropped its last point, the preliminary raw-material survey. After Byrnes and Acheson looked over the statement, they turned their attention to the call for automatic sanctions. Baruch was firm in arguing that automatic penalties were a must. Otherwise, the United States had to tell the world that the plan offered no more than a warning of three months to a year. In the American form of government, this meant nothing. Acheson quite frankly doubted the wisdom of Baruch's suggestion. But he presented his own position objectively and did not insist on it. Byrnes thought the penalties would be some deterrent. He would see the President about the statement of policy.

Acheson and Hancock then clashed on the control of raw materials.

The Under Secretary thought inspection could never be as effective as ownership. Besides, Russia would not consent to inspection. Hancock could see no advantage in ownership and thought inspection would be just as easy for the Soviet Union to accept. Furthermore, Hancock opposed ownership by an international authority on principle. What right did government have to seize a citizen's property and employ it as fuel in commercial power plants? The two men did not fight the issue to a conclusion. Acheson ended by saying he wanted the control unit to have responsibility for safeguarding uranium supplies and preventing diversion in any way it saw fit. For his part, Hancock did not demur to ownership in some cases and leases and licenses in others. He was willing that the authority be free to exercise its best judgment on means, but he still worried that it would exhibit bureaucratic tendencies and grab all the power it could.

Baruch raised once again the possibility of a reference to other weapons of mass destruction. Byrnes said that the only intent back of the General Assembly resolution was to control atomic energy and atomic bombs. Byrnes explained that there had been some mention of biological warfare; the broad term was used so that it might be included. As Hancock sized up the situation, Byrnes was trying to simplify the job by limiting it to atomic energy. In doing so, he was trying to picture the other-weapons reference in the instructions to the AEC as a bit of window dressing designed to win support. While Hancock agreed that the major effort ought to be on atomic energy, he thought Baruch correct in believing that the United States ought not to exclude the broader issue from its presentation.[52]

569

The next evening, a Friday, Baruch and Hancock met once again with the Secretary of State. Byrnes told them he had just reported to the President on the recent conferences. Truman had approved his recommendation that the penalty idea expressed in Hancock's draft become a part of the American position. Byrnes had mentioned that other minor points of difference existed between the Baruch and State Department groups, but he had assured Truman that these could be worked out in the ordinary course of things.

Then Byrnes handed Baruch and his aide a memorandum he said Acheson had dictated in about a half-hour.[53] He wanted Hancock to look it over so that he could put his own paper in a form more in keeping with accepted State Department practice. Hancock looked at the first sentence and saw something he did not like. The proposals were advanced "as a basis of discussion." This was too soft, he thought. He told Byrnes it would put Baruch in a stronger position, one less likely to be traded against, if he could always say that the statement was a definition of the American position. As he looked further, Hancock discovered to his astonishment that the memorandum was not a rewrite of his paper, as Byrnes seemed to think, but a slightly revised version of the memorandum the Board of Consultants had sent Baruch right after the Blair-Lee House meetings. When he pointed this out to Byrnes, the Secretary dismissed the matter lightly, emphasizing that the

Acheson draft "was written for form rather than content, though it was partly to inform the President." Hancock made it very clear that the content was substantially different—Acheson's paper, for example, had nothing on penalties. He and Baruch left with the understanding Hancock would try to put his own statement in briefer, more proper form.[54]

Saturday morning, Byrnes phoned Hancock. The talk the evening before had set him thinking. By emphasizing Baruch's general approval of the Acheson-Lilienthal plan, Byrnes feared he might have misled the President as to the extent of the differences between the two positions. Would Hancock explain how his memorandum differed from Acheson's? He wanted something in writing to show the President so that there would be no misunderstandings.[55]

Before nightfall, Hancock had a memorandum ready. As Byrnes already knew, one substantial difference was on ownership of ore in the ground. Another was penalties. The Baruch group was united in favoring penalties, and the provision Hancock had drafted looked toward some way around the Security Council veto. Licensing was a third discrepancy. Hancock had depended more heavily than Acheson on licenses. Denaturing was the heart of a fourth. Hancock had not put as much reliance on denaturing as seemed to lie in the background of the Acheson-Lilienthal report. Indeed, he thought the chances for commercial power plants operating under private control had been oversold. Hancock wanted operation of power reactors limited to the authority. Finally, he still favored trying for the preliminary raw-material survey at a later stage in the negotiations, providing it could be done smoothly without forcing a break.[56]

Hancock spent the first few days of June trying to fuse his working paper with Acheson's. By the fourth, he had it ready for Byrnes, who turned it over to Acheson for revision and comment. Acheson sat down with his assistant, Marks, and authorized liberal blue-penciling. The section specifying crimes would have to be deleted. While Acheson conceded the treaty would have to consider the crisis that collapse of the plan would precipitate, he considered the proposed system of penalties neither realistic nor effective. He also marked for excision a large section on the licensing of raw materials. He believed its tendency was to encourage other nations to insist on national or private operation of mines under inspection arrangements which the United States could never accept as adequate.

But this was only the beginning. Hancock had slipped in a phrase requiring the Security Council to approve the atomic authority's decisions in distributing intrinsically dangerous activities throughout the world. This specification had implications that the United States ought to consider very carefully before fixing its position. Out it came. So did a sentence declaring the agency should have power to decide what activities were dangerous or nondangerous and to change its decisions as conditions changed. The authority should have this power, Acheson agreed, but in so complicated a matter he believed the initial American position should remain more fluid. Acheson further favored eliminating a paragraph on management and licensing. This stressed the need for international control and inspection of dangerous activities, but it contained references to licensing that obscured the purpose and effect of the whole section.[57]

When Marks finished making Acheson's deletions—as well as a few insertions—on June 6, it marked a major step in the definition of policy. The first section of the revised document set forth the conclusions underlying the American proposals. First, adequate security did not lie in obligating nations to forswear atomic weapons and in relying solely on international inspection to detect evasions. Second, an international atomic development authority should be created. In connection with the greatest safeguards which could be established through this device, there should be "a clear statement of the consequences of violations of the system of controls, including definitions of the acts which would constitute such violations and the procedures and concerted action which would follow." (This was Acheson's substitute for Hancock's "immediate and certain penalties for certain defined crimes.") One of the objectives of the plan should be that no bomb stockpiles would exist when the system was fully in operation. (This provision Acheson had rephrased in the direction of caution.) The plan might also include a parallel statement on a system for controlling biological warfare. A third conclusion was that the international authority must have managerial control of all atomic energy activities intrinsically dangerous to world security along with power to control, inspect, and license all other activities.

571

The second section of the revised draft set forth the plan's fundamental features. The atomic development authority should exert control through various forms of ownership, dominion, licenses, operation, inspection, research, and management. One of its earliest purposes should be to bring world supplies of uranium and thorium under its dominion. The precise pattern of control would have to depend on the geological, mining, refining, and economic facts involved in different situations. The authority should conduct continuous surveys and constantly investigate new methods of recovering these metals from low-grade ores. It should exercise complete managerial control of the production of fissionable materials. This meant controlling and operating all plants manufacturing fissionable materials in dangerous quantities; it meant owning and controlling the product of these plants. That the authority might keep in the forefront of knowledge and be able to prevent illicit manufacture of bombs, it should have exclusive right to conduct research in atomic explosives. It should distribute the activities entrusted exclusively to its charge throughout the world. Above all, it must centralize stockpiles of ore and fissionable materials.

The authority should open safe activities—including "to some extent" the production of power—to nations and their citizens under reasonable licensing arrangements. It should furnish the necessary denatured materials under lease or other suitable arrangement. An essential function was to promote the peacetime benefits of atomic energy. Since there was no hard-and-fast dividing line between the dangerous and the nondangerous, machinery was necessary to assure constant examination and re-examination.

Assigning dangerous enterprises exclusively to the authority would reduce the difficulties of inspection to manageable proportions. With the international unit alone empowered to act in the hazardous field, operations by any nation or individual would be a danger signal. The authority would inspect in connection with its raw-material and licensing functions. While it should have the power to make special spot investigations, it would not pursue systematic or large-scale inspection procedures covering the whole of industry.

To conclude its outline of the American plan, the Acheson-Marks draft observed that the first step was to spell out the functions, responsibilities, authority, and limitations of the controlling agency. But even when the Atomic Energy Commission had drafted a charter and the nations had adopted it, the authority could not leap at once into full operation. The plan, therefore, would have to come into effect in successive stages. Either the charter should fix these stages itself or it should specify some other means for making the necessary step-by-step transition. During the deliberations of the AEC, the United States would have to be prepared to make available the information essential to a reasonable understanding of its proposals. In the interests of all, further disclosures must depend on effective ratification of the treaty. If and when the authority was actually created, the United States must be prepared to make available other information essential for the performance of its functions. As the successive stages were reached, the United States would have to yield its national control to the extent each stage required. Finally, it should be understood that any national agency would be subordinate to international direction and dominion to the extent necessary for effective operation of the control system.[58]

COMMAND DECISION

June 6, the day Acheson and Marks finished their revision of Hancock's memorandum, Baruch decided it was high time to force a final decision. With the schedule calling for the Atomic Energy Commission to meet June 14, there was little time under the best of circumstances. Baruch reached Byrnes by telephone. If the Secretary still favored laying the Acheson-Lilienthal report on the table as a basis for discussion without further comment, Baruch said he thought Acheson, Lilienthal, Barnard, or Winne could present it. Since they believed in it without limitations, deductions, or additions, they could advocate it more wholeheartedly than he. Speaking bluntly, Baruch declared he had lost confidence in being able to work this out satisfactorily with Truman and Byrnes. Only friction would result if he stayed in, and that would be bad for the goal they all wanted to reach. The Secretary of State, a past master at pouring oil on troubled waters, asked Baruch to come to Washington the next day. They would take the issue to the President.[59]

When Baruch arrived at Byrnes's office Friday afternoon, June 7, he carried a memorandum to guide his conversation. It stated his conviction that any declaration of policy which fell short of bringing the public a sense of security and of truth would be a gigantic error. He could not present such a statement and do justice to the job. The United States proposal must include "a statement of regulations, controls, and above all, punishment or sanctions." His only quarrel with the Acheson-Lilienthal report was that the authors were content with its limitations. These he regarded as dangerously restrictive. Not only did the report fail to provide punishments; it gave, its supporters admitted, no more than a warning of "from 3 months to a year." As time went on, even that factor of safety would be diminished. Baruch was particularly disturbed by the disposition he had observed to make the Acheson-Lilienthal report basic policy and to have further decisions grow out of committee meetings and negotiations. He doubted that this was the proper method. It might be the best course in the ordinary processes of diplomacy, but atomic energy struck at the "very heart of public thinking and feeling." Therefore, the United States "should be the first to proclaim an intention of reaching not merely a basis of negotiations but a formula of a secure peace."

573

Baruch listed two courses open to the United States. One was to go before the Atomic Energy Commission, offer the Acheson report as an approach to the subject, and hope that a fruitful meeting of minds would take place in the progress of discussion and negotiation. The other course was to state the necessity of an international atomic development authority and outline it in sufficient detail to permit others to grasp the nature of the control it would afford. It was important to point out all shortcomings and show the necessity of enforcing the engagements of the nations. Baruch considered penalties the *sine qua non*. He was quite aware this might bring the United States "athwart of the veto power," for war, the ultimate penalty, might be necessary. This meant changing the structure of the United Nations or establishing the control unit as a separate body operating outside the Charter. Baruch could not supply an outline of the punishment mechanism at the moment, but he believed it might be developed during the negotiations. One thing was certain: it would take true intent on the part of all nations to eliminate the atomic bomb and eventually abolish other instrumentalities of destruction with the ultimate objective of eliminating war.[60]

Byrnes had a ready answer: the State Department revision of Hancock's June 4 draft. For all the deletions and additions, Acheson and Marks had not altered the essential substance. Byrnes put it alongside the Hancock draft and explained the changes. Baruch made sure the Secretary understood his views. Penalties meant immediate punishment and elimination of any veto of it. Punishment for a major violation meant war. Denaturing had given rise to false hopes; the public should be set straight. As for the warning element in the plan, the American people should know how little it amounted to.

After these preliminaries, Byrnes and Baruch walked over to the White House. Anxious that the President assume responsibility for the necessary decisions, the Secretary handed him two documents—the memorandum Baruch had brought with him and the Acheson-Marks revision altered only in two particulars. One change called for a clear statement of "the *penalties* and concerted action" which would follow violations, not "the *procedures* and concerted action." The second simply restored the section stressing the importance of international management, supervision, and control of dangerous activities minus the confusing passage on licensing. Truman read the Baruch memorandum and signed it to indicate general approval. As he went over the statement of policy, he initialled most of the paragraphs in the right-hand margin. When he came to the paragraph on progress by successive stages, he wrote, "most important." At the bottom of the final page he penned an endorsement in his bold handwriting: "Above general principles approved June 7, 1946. Harry S. Truman."

574

Baruch made sure the President understood his position on punishment and the veto. To his satisfaction, the President agreed. A treaty without enforcement was useless. It reminded Truman of the Manchurian crisis in 1931 and 1932. If Harry Stimson had had power behind him then, he said, World War II would not have occurred. Finally, Baruch insisted that the United States show no preference to the United Kingdom and Canada. The negotiations in the Atomic Energy Commission required treating every country alike.

It had been a long fight, but Baruch had won. To clinch the understanding, the President dictated a letter formally transmitting the approved policy statement. The statement was solely for Baruch's guidance, he wrote. It was general in character because the President wanted him to exercise his judgment on the methods of achieving the stated objectives. If Baruch should conclude during the negotiations that changes were in order, he was frankly to state his views. Baruch, in short, would exercise his own discretion, subject only to the present statement of policy or any the President should transmit in the future.[61]

CLEARING FOR ACTION

There was only a week to go. Some rather considerable co-ordinating was in order before Baruch addressed the Commission. For one thing, it was important to check with the British. Byrnes had been unwilling to furnish information that would help them build their atomic energy plant at a time when the United States was seeking international control, but he saw no reason for not informing them of the American proposals in advance. Since international control was a joint venture, possible charges that the United States was forming a tight Anglo-American bloc did not concern him. On June 8, he called in the British Ambassador, Lord Inverchapel, and Canadian Ambassador Lester Pearson. Using the memorandum Truman had approved the day before, he explained the plan in detail. Baruch, Byrnes told them, would discuss the plan with the British and Canadian representatives in New York the next week.[62]

Baruch had already established contact with the Joint Chiefs of Staff. On May 27, Admiral Nimitz confirmed that General Groves would represent them on technical matters and secrecy requirements. On problems of national security or broad strategy, the Chiefs would be glad to furnish their views either directly or through the American members of the UN Military Staff Committee—General George K. Kenney, Admiral Richmond K. Turner, and General Matthew B. Ridgway.[63] On June 6, these three officers called at Baruch's New York office. Baruch stated his position, and his visitors declared it their personal judgment that a penalty clause was essential.[64]

575

More significant was Baruch's direct communication with the Joint Chiefs. On May 24, he had written General Eisenhower and asked for his views on an atomic-control treaty, automatic sanctions, and how to expand the present attitude into a movement for the elimination of war. Eisenhower replied that this was not a matter for him personally but for Admiral Nimitz and General Spaatz as well. Though Eisenhower thought the request should have come through the President, the Joint Chiefs went ahead, prepared comments, and submitted them to Admiral Leahy at the White House. Leahy sent them back saying the President had no objection but believed they should be co-ordinated with the position he had approved on June 7. This was not too helpful, for the Joint Chiefs did not know what that position was. Neither did Leahy, it developed; but he found out, and Eisenhower, Nimitz, and Spaatz composed separate replies.

The three military leaders agreed on the fundamentals. They considered the Acheson-Lilienthal principles the most promising first step. They believed the United States must maintain its pre-eminent position until effective control was assured. They all felt concern at taking action on atomic weapons, where the United States had the advantage. Eisenhower made it most explicit: to control atomic weapons and leave other weapons of mass destruction untouched could endanger the national security. All three believed the ultimate solution was to end war itself. It was on penalties that they disagreed. Spaatz believed a control agreement should provide for immediate, effective multilateral action. Eisenhower favored making provision for retaliation if other control or prevention devices failed, but he raised the practical difficulties of nerving the American people for this drastic step. Nimitz had grave misgivings about the effectiveness of any international agreement to take concerted action against violators. He advised against any national policy placing major reliance on such a compact.

The most interesting thing about Baruch's exchanges with the military was not the views of the Joint Chiefs but their apparent isolation from the process of decision making. Far from dictating policy, they had some difficulty in discovering what policy was. Though Baruch sought out the opinions of Eisenhower and his colleagues, though he unquestionably had a sure sense of where they stood, neither he, nor Byrnes, nor the President waited on their views. Eisenhower did not finish his statement until the very day Baruch formally announced American policy.[65]

More important at the minute than either the British or the Joint Chiefs was the Senate Special Committee on Atomic Energy. The Department of State had won delay after delay, but it was unthinkable to enter the impending negotiation without a check with McMahon's committee. Finally, Baruch was ready, and on June 12, just two days before he was scheduled to announce the American plan, he testified at an executive session. For an hour and forty minutes, he expounded his views. When he had finished, McMahon emerged and told waiting reporters that Baruch's proposal would incorporate many details of the Acheson-Lilienthal plan. This was true enough, but other senators emphasized that Baruch's approach included variations, both in spirit and in fact. For one thing, he proposed to go very slowly in revealing information to scientists of other countries; he believed it unnecessary to make any additional disclosures during the negotiations. Baruch might demand that all nations submit an inventory of their uranium and thorium ores as one of the first steps in the UN discussions. He did not favor having the world authority own ore deposits outright. Most important, Baruch indicated he would insist that the Big Five of the Security Council expressly waive their right of veto in atomic energy matters and that the plan specify sanctions for any nation refusing to abide by the rulings of the world authority. Without punishments, the whole scheme was not worth twenty-five cents.

Newsmen concluded the senators were highly pleased with Baruch's testimony, especially what he had said on the veto. They were correct. The only sour note had been sounded by Senator Connally. He had heard that Baruch had told some Russian friends that armies, not atomic weapons, should have priority in disarmament. With a show of temper, Connally warned Baruch to stick to his knitting—he would have his hands full getting an agreement on the bomb.[66]

BARUCH FOR THE UNITED STATES

At eleven o'clock on the morning of June 14, Trygve Lie, Secretary-General of the United Nations, took the rostrum in the gymnasium of Hunter College in the Bronx. There were assembled the delegates to the Atomic Energy Commission and their staffs—the representatives of Australia, Brazil, Canada, China, Egypt, France, Mexico, the Netherlands, Poland, the Soviet Union, the United Kingdom, and the United States. In the American section he could see Tolman sitting with the men he had persuaded to help him—Compton, Urey, Bacher, Thomas, and Oppenheimer. Perhaps Lie saw some special significance in the presence of the wartime chief of Los Alamos, the man who had built the bomb and then sought to find a means of controlling it. When Lie had finished his introductory remarks, he announced that the delegations assembled had agreed it would be fitting for Mr. Baruch, the representative of the host nation, to take the chair.

Baruch stepped smartly to his place. Six feet-four and lithe, he presented an imposing appearance in his dark, double-breasted jacket and striped trousers. He seemed the embodiment of the elder statesman. Here was the almost legendary figure who had mobilized American resources in the first World War, the counsellor of Presidents, the park-bench sage. Yet here too was a voice from another age. This son of a Confederate veteran had first seen the light of day in unreconstructed South Carolina. As a young man, he had known Diamond Jim Brady and seen John W. Gates bet a million dollars on a poker hand. On advance news of the Navy's victory at Santiago, he had hired a locomotive, rushed back to New York, and made a fortune. Now, forty-eight years later, he was at the center of the stage, wrestling with an issue that would set a pattern for the future.

577

"We are here to make a choice between the quick and the dead," he began apocalyptically. "That is our business." In sentences that read like a front-page editorial of the New York *World*—Swope had written them— Baruch dramatized the objective: a mechanism to assure that atomic energy was used for peaceful purposes and not for war. The men meeting today for the first time represented not only their governments but the peoples of the world. They must answer "the world's longing for peace and security." They were here "to test if man can produce, through his will and faith, the miracle of peace, just as he has, through science and skill, the miracle of the atom."

So much for the goal. Baruch came directly to the point. The United States proposed creating an international atomic development authority to which should be entrusted all phases of the development and use of atomic energy. The authority should exercise managerial control or ownership of all activities potentially dangerous to world security. It should have power to control, inspect, and license all others. It should foster beneficial uses and assume such research and development responsibilities as would put the authority in the forefront of knowledge. Baruch offered this "as a basis for beginning our discussion." But the peoples of the world, he warned, would not be satisfied with a treaty that did no more than outlaw the atomic bomb. "If I read the signs aright," he said, "the peoples want a program not composed merely of pious thoughts but of enforceable sanctions—an international law with teeth in it." The American plan meant that once an adequate system for control was in effective operation and condign punishments set up, the manufacture of atomic bombs should cease, existing bombs should be dismantled, and the authority should possess the entire sweep of nuclear technology. The United States was ready to make its full contribution.

Reassured by his conversation with the President, Baruch was far more explicit on punishments and the veto than either the Hancock draft or the State Department revision Truman had initialled. He did more than assert that the agreement creating the international agency should fix penalties for criminal actions; he listed specific infractions ranging from illegal possession or use of an atomic bomb down to operation of dangerous projects without a license. Punishments, he emphasized, lay at the very heart of the system. Not only that: "It might as well be admitted, here and now, that the subject goes straight to the veto power contained in the Charter of the United Nations so far as it relates to the field of atomic energy. . . . There must be no veto to protect those who violate their solemn agreements not to develop or use atomic energy for destructive purposes."

578

Throughout, Baruch had stressed that the ultimate goal of mankind was peace. It was this quest that had brought him out in the "late afternoon" of his life. As he reached the end of his remarks on penalties, he turned to this theme once more. "But before a country is ready to relinquish any winning weapons it must have more than words to reassure it. It must have a guarantee of safety, not only against the offenders in the atomic area but against the illegal users of other weapons—bacteriological, biological, gas— perhaps—why not? against war itself." Had they stood alone, these sentences would have suggested that control of atomic weapons depended on eliminating other weapons of mass destruction. Actually, they were intended to introduce the idea of outlawing war. "In the elimination of war itself lies our solution," Baruch continued, "for only then will nations cease to compete with one another in the production of dread 'secret' weapons which are evaluated solely by their capacity to kill. This devilish program takes us back not merely to the Dark Ages, but from cosmos to chaos. If we succeed in finding a suitable way to control atomic weapons, it is reasonable to hope that we may also preclude the use of other weapons adaptable to mass destruction. When a man learns to say 'A' he can, if he chooses, learn the rest of the alphabet, too."

It remained for Baruch to itemize the fundamental features of the plan for an atomic development authority. For this, he supplied an edited version of the June 7 policy statement.[67] The changes were slight and only two had much significance. One warned that "denaturing seems to have been overestimated by the public as a safety measure." The other stressed that "adequate ingress and egress for all qualified representatives of the Authority must be assured." On stages of transition, Baruch quoted directly from his instructions: "These should be specifically fixed in the Charter or means should be otherwise set forth in the Charter for transitions from one stage to another, as contemplated in the resolution of the United Nations Assembly which created this Commission." This made it as clear as language could that upon adoption of the agreement, the United States would surrender any claim to time the transitional steps at its unilateral discretion.

"And now I end," said Baruch. "I have submitted an outline for present discussion. Our consideration will be broadened by the criticism of the United States proposals and by the plans of the other nations. . . . The light at the end of the tunnel is dim, but our path seems to grow brighter as we actually begin our journey. We cannot yet light the way to the end. However, we hope the suggestions of my government will be illuminating." As a closing text, Baruch dramatically paraphrased Abraham Lincoln: "We shall nobly save, or meanly lose, the last, best hope of earth. The way is plain, peaceful, generous, just—a way which, if followed, the world will forever applaud." [68]

It was almost twelve-thirty. American policy had been two years in evolving. Bush and Conant had been first to see the need. Recognizing that the bomb could not long remain an American monopoly, they had called for an international agency that would spare mankind the dread of secret preparations and surprise attack. They had ventured to hope that success in controlling atomic bombs might point the way to success with other weapons and finally to the ultimate achievement, prevention of war itself. Though Bush and Conant had recognized that the transition to international control must be gradual, it was the insistence of Senators Vandenberg and Connally and of General Groves that made stages so specific and emphatic a feature of the American proposal. The Lilienthal Board of Consultants had contributed the idea of transforming the international agency from an inspection unit to an authority charged with the positive development of atomic energy. Baruch, dissatisfied with the limited objectives of Acheson and Lilienthal and convinced that a warning was not enough, had added the emphasis on penalizing violators and preventing them from finding protection in the veto. Now the policy of the United States lay before the world. It was the work of many men.

579

INTERNATIONAL CONTROL:
NO FLESH FOR THE SPIRIT

CHAPTER 16

BIKINI

William L. Laurence stood on the skydeck of the U.S.S. *Appalachin* and stared northeast across the Pacific, bright in the morning sun. At nine o'clock, a B-29 was scheduled to drop an atomic bomb over the great fleet riding at anchor in the lagoon of Bikini Atoll. It was July 1, 1946. Eleven and a half months before, the New York *Times* reporter had waited in the desert darkness for the blinding flash at Alamogordo. How different it had been then. The Army had taken the most elaborate pains to conceal the shot. Only a few scientists and officers were privy to the plans. Laurence was the only newspaperman, and he was on leave, assigned to the War Department. Now there were military experts, congressmen, scientists, foreign observers, and an entire shipload of accredited journalists. A good many of the latter had but tenuous connections with the press and had wangled the junket only for the spectacle. Among some, a lost-week-end atmosphere prevailed. Most observers, however, took a sober view, and many expected a preview of the day of doom. Back in the United States—it was almost six o'clock Sunday evening in Times Square—millions gathered around their radio sets to hear CBS correspondent Bill Downs, poised in the astrodome of *Dave's Dream*, describe the explosion.

Then it came. At thirty-four seconds after nine, Bikini time, Laurence saw smoke and a ball of fire shoot upward like a meteor going in the wrong direction. Suddenly, it seemed to puncture. Out burst great masses of flaming cloud that reminded him of a monstrous brain. Soon a column of white smoke emerged from the purple clouds and at tremendous altitude took the form of a cosmic mushroom. For all these spectacular pyrotechnics, the blast was a disappointment to many who observed it and to the public at large. The buildup had been too extravagant. Only three vessels, a destroyer and two transports, sank at once. Goats still munched their feed on warship decks. Even the Bikini palm trees stood unscathed. In the weeks that followed, detailed damage analyses corrected the initial underestimates. The beneath-the-surface explosion of July 25 with its mighty column of water was more visible and more impressive. It helped restore respect for the power of the bomb. Yet Bikini made a difference in the public mind. Before July 1, the world stood in awe of a weapon which could devastate a city and force the surrender of an army of 5,000,000 men. After that date, the bomb was a terrible but a finite weapon. To the extent the test dulled men's minds to the dangers that faced the world, the effect was bad. To the extent it supplanted emotionalism with realism, the effect was good.[1]

The first blast at Bikini took place just two weeks and two days after Baruch had unveiled the American plan for international control. Testing the bomb with one hand and seeking its control with the other was bound to lay the United States open to charges of conducting atom diplomacy. The scientists' lobby had seen this as soon as the tests were announced. Scott Lucas had raised the question in the Senate in January, 1946. "If we are to outlaw the use of the atomic bomb for military purposes, why should we be making plans to display atomic power as an instrument of destruction?" Two months later, on March 29, Lucas joined Senator Huffman of Ohio in submitting a resolution requesting the President to cancel the tests. Baruch, said the senator from Illinois, ought to have something to say about whether the experiment was in the best interest of the United States. Turn the situation around, he suggested. Suppose the United States had a big army but little or no air power, no fleet, and no atomic bombs. Would the Senate rest unperturbed should some other power undertake a nuclear display in the Atlantic or the Pacific? Lucas and Huffman got nowhere. Most of the few congressmen who questioned the tests were more concerned over the sacrifice of seaworthy warships than any international impact.[2]

581

The Russian reaction was predictable. *Pravda* charged that the United States aimed not at restricting but at perfecting the atomic weapon. Americans sought to maintain their monopoly as an instrument of international blackmail. The test, implied the Red journal, was timed to coincide with the meeting of the Atomic Energy Commission and to influence its deliberations.[3]

Whatever the wisdom of testing and negotiating simultaneously, the Soviet vision of a closely co-ordinated diplomatic and military offensive was an illusion. There was no connection between the proposals advanced at New York and the thunder in the Pacific. The origin of the Bikini tests lay in the Navy reaction to Hiroshima. What would such a missile do to a warship, to a fleet? Senator McMahon put the question publicly in a speech of August 25, 1945, and suggested testing the bomb against the surviving Japanese naval vessels. On September 18, General Arnold asked the Joint Chiefs of Staff to make a number of Japanese ships available to the Army Air Forces as targets for atomic bombs and other weapons. Admiral King countered by proposing that the Joint Chiefs control the tests and that both Army and Navy groups participate. He also suggested including a few modern American vessels in the target fleet. The Joint Chiefs promptly instituted the necessary staff planning, and on January 10, 1946—two weeks before the General Assembly adopted its resolution establishing the Commission on Atomic Energy—President Truman approved a detailed administrative and technical plan.[4]

The actual timing of the tests had no more relation to the Administration's plan for international control than their origin. Admiral Blandy, the task force commander, set the first explosion for May 15, 1946. His choice of so early a date was influenced largely by the need to act before civilian scientists returned to their university posts in September. Since there were formidable technical and logistical difficulties, Blandy might not have been able to meet his deadline. As it happened, a Presidential decision removed the pressure. On March 22, the matter of timing came up at Cabinet meeting. The President said it was essential for Congress to be in Washington May 15. He wished neither to have congressmen away then nor to hold the tests without inviting them. He had no objection, however, to beginning the trials July 1. Unless someone demurred, that would be his decision. Thus the date was set.[5]

FIRST REACTIONS TO THE BARUCH PROPOSALS

When the mushroom cloud rose over Bikini, the reaction to Baruch's June 14 address had already assumed a discernible pattern. The response of the American public was overwhelmingly favorable. Congratulatory messages deluged Baruch's headquarters. Commentator Hanson Baldwin found the American plan "thoughtful, imaginative and courageous" even though he judged it an attack on the symptoms, not the disease. His colleague Anne O'Hare McCormick did not qualify her praise. "The more its intent and implications are studied," she said, "the more epoch-making it appears as an instrument of world disarmament." On June 19, Bush encountered Lilienthal and Marks at the Cosmos Club. He was gratified to discover that they agreed the affair had been started down the right path. Yet the response to Baruch's presentation was by no means unanimous. The Hearst press labeled the proposal an "imbecilic," "New Deal" scheme to give away the national advantage. "The Truman administration is exhibiting both abject MORAL WEAKNESS and an inexcusable LACK OF FARSIGHTED STATESMANSHIP in its wilful efforts to devise a scheme for surrendering to FOREIGN MASTERS the AMERICAN SECRET of the atomic bomb." Other critics spoke from a more sympathetic point of view. In Washington, many informed people felt that Baruch had injected the veto question unnecessarily. Walter Lippmann thought that Baruch's treatment of the veto had taken the

United States up a blind alley. The decisions of a majority of governments, he wrote, could only be enforced by war. Since war was as punishing on the states keeping the law as on those breaking it, nations would apply such a drastic penalty only rarely and reluctantly. It was not safe to count on it.[6]

The first official reactions from other members of the Atomic Energy Commission came at a meeting June 19. First to speak was General A. G. L. McNaughton, president of the Canadian Atomic Energy Control Board and a distinguished soldier who bore the scars of Ypres and Soissons. He announced that the Canadian Government welcomed the American proposals and supported the principles on which they were based. When he had finished, four other delegates expressed their general approval—Sir Alexander Cadogan, the representative of the United Kingdom, Dr. Quo Tai-chi of China, Captain Alvaro-Alberto da Motta e Silva of Brazil, and Dr. Sandoval Vallarta of Mexico. All recognized that it was necessary to devote a great deal of study to details. McNaughton and Cadogan suggested trying to promote an atmosphere of mutual confidence by moving promptly to exchange scientific information. Quo Tai-chi raised a question about the composition of the atomic development authority, and Vallarta warned that managerial control of ore deposits required careful consideration. It was on the veto that the delegates differed. Quo Tai-chi and Vallarta supported it specifically, and while Cadogan avoided using the word, he endorsed the United States position on the need for immediate and effective penalties. McNaughton, however, made it plain that Canada had never liked the veto. He suggested that the Commission avoid this potentially divisive issue and concentrate on other aspects of the American proposals.

583

The big question mark was the Soviet Union. Its representative, the handsome Andrei A. Gromyko, only thirty-six years of age, also spoke on June 19. With a minimum of rhetoric, he proposed an international convention prohibiting the production and use of atomic weapons. This treaty should be followed by measures establishing methods of assuring strict observance. Gromyko read a draft which supplied the details. The signatories would obligate themselves to use no atomic weapons, prohibit producing and storing them, and destroy all existing bombs within three months of the day the convention went into effect. Within six months, the high contracting parties should pass legislation providing severe penalties for those who violated the statutes of the convention.

In addition to his basic proposal, Gromyko had a plan for organizing the work of the Commission. Two committees should be established. One would make practical recommendations for organizing the exchange of information specified in the General Assembly's resolution of January 24. The other would seek to prevent using atomic energy to the detriment of mankind. So far Gromyko had said nothing about the proposals of the United States. Then, when he had almost finished, he stated flatly that the Soviet Union rejected any tampering with the veto. Any attempts to undermine the unanimity of the Security Council in deciding matters of substance, he said, were incompatible with the interests of the United Nations.[7]

There were two quite different ways in which western observers might interpret Gromyko's statement. Those charitably and hopefully inclined might recall Russia's deep-rooted distrust of the outside world and conclude that pending clarification of the American proposals, she was pursuing a natural minority policy: determined opposition. Those who had steeped themselves in the realities of the Soviet system might conclude that the Kremlin was endeavoring to turn the tables on the United States. Certainly a mere convention was an ideal way to assure American disarmament and to permit the Communist leaders to develop an atomic arsenal undisturbed.

Neither of these attitudes prevailed in the conference Ferdinand Eberstadt held June 20 at the headquarters of the American delegation on the sixty-fourth floor of the Empire State Building. The three United States members of the UN Military Staff Committee were there along with Oppenheimer and Charles Fahy, formerly Solicitor General of the United States and now legal adviser to the Department of State. The meeting suspended judgment. Eberstadt observed that the Russians did not appear opposed to some form of sanctions. He even thought they might go along on the atomic development authority. In his view, the real conflict would come on the veto. Admiral Turner, supported by Oppenheimer, argued against trying to abolish the veto on sanctions. General Kenney doubted that anything less than world government would furnish adequate control. But what policy should Baruch pursue for the immediate future? General Ridgway advised against exerting too much leadership at this stage in order to protect the United States from adverse public opinion should the Commission fail to agree. All thought Baruch should make no further statement of position at this time.[8]

The remaining national representatives had opportunity to indicate where they stood at the third Commission meeting on June 25. After a polite nod to "long-range plans like that proposed by the United States," Oscar Lange of Poland supported Gromyko's call for a convention that would outlaw the bomb immediately. E. N. van Kleffens of the Netherlands expressed no preference. Finding the American and Russian plans by no means incompatible, he was anxious to begin work on a specific draft as soon as possible. Avoidable misunderstandings might easily arise should general discussion run on too long. At the same time, he favored stressing the positive, constructive aspect of the work and side-stepping for the present the questions of veto and penalties.

The Egyptian and French delegates upheld the American propositions. While Colonel Mohammed Bey Khalifa warmly applauded Baruch's remarks on the veto, "this fictitious distinction of States and super-States," Alexandre Parodi tried to minimize the differences between the two great powers. Like van Kleffens, the French diplomat considered it bad tactics to try to settle all issues of principle at the outset. Until a state knew what controls were possible, what they would involve, it could hardly pronounce any opinion on the obligations it was asked to undertake. What was needed, he argued, was a system of committees to investigate the two essential and related aspects of the work—the practical, technical, and scientific side and the legal and political side.

The strongest speech that June afternoon was that of Herbert V. Evatt, the Australian historian-jurist-politician who had been chosen to preside over deliberations for the first month. Evatt left no doubt that his country adhered to the principles Baruch had laid before the Commission. His essential point was that the Commission faced a highly complex problem which required consideration as a whole. It was not sound to deal with any one of its many aspects independently. This, he said flatly, was the trouble with Gromyko's proposals. Evatt stressed ordering each measure so as to create the international trust necessary to remove the dangers and seize the benefits. At the outset, however, he favored deferring detailed discussion of all the steps and stages. The Commission should first consider the fundamental principles of the proposed international authority and the obligations which all nations might reasonably be asked to assume.

585

At the conclusion of his formal statement, Evatt proposed setting up a working committee composed of one representative from each of the twelve members of the Commission. It should prepare a first draft of a general plan for a world authority and consider the proposals and suggestions made subsequent to Baruch's address. After Gromyko had elicited an understanding that the committee would indeed examine all proposals, not just the American, the Commission approved Evatt's suggestion.[9]

EXPLAINING THE AMERICAN PLAN

The Working Committee—in effect, the Commission sitting in executive session—met Friday, June 28. Knowing that Evatt had plans to take the initiative, Baruch urged speed. "Time presses. Each day finds the world more insecure. Let us proceed at once to find a way out." As a reference and study aid, he supplied a chart dividing control into twenty issues and indicating the position of the twelve nations on each. Gromyko conceded that this was a useful document, but he emphasized the importance of considering the substance of the proposals and observations that had been made. It seemed to him that the Working Committee should turn to a study of the Soviet proposition. It dealt with the "primordial subject," an international convention forbidding "the use of the atomic arm for the harm of humanity." Quick to oppose concentrating on a single feature of the task, Evatt brought out his own idea on the next step: a small drafting committee to work out in skeleton outline a system of control and development. This body would consider all plans and proposals advanced and pose issues for the Working Committee to decide at its next meeting. Gromyko thought the name "drafting committee" confusing and wanted it clear that the committee was merely to continue studies that would assist the larger group. Evatt was quite willing to call it Subcommittee No. 1—or Alpha, Beta, or Gamma for that matter. Reassured, Gromyko consented.[10]

The Soviet delegate revealed his uncompromising temper at the first meeting of Subcommittee No. 1 on Monday, July 1. Evatt was there as chairman, joined by representatives of France, Mexico, the Soviet Union, the United Kingdom, and the United States. Making their first appearances at the council table were Joliot-Curie of France and Eberstadt of the United States. The hard-driving Evatt proposed six principles for general discussion. In sum, they embodied the American plan for an international authority, including an effective system for preventing breaches of the agreed restrictions and controls. Evatt favored measures designed to preclude the use of atomic energy for war, but only as part of a general system of control. For Gromyko, this would not do. The first step was to outlaw the bomb. An international authority was a matter for later consideration. Besides, the Russian argued, the United States plan contained ideas that were incompatible with the functions and organization of the Security Council. So long as this was the case, he could agree to it neither in whole nor in part.[11]

586

So basic a disagreement was discouraging, but at least it furnished the occasion for elaborating the proposals Baruch had announced in his opening address. At the second meeting of Subcommittee No. 1 on July 2, Eberstadt outlined a treaty establishing the atomic development authority. The treaty was to include a charter for the agency, an organic act stating its purposes, functions, powers, composition, organization, and location. The suggested covenant must contain provisions defining the authority's relations with the various organs of the United Nations as well as with the control agencies of the signatory states. It must specify the rights and obligations of each member, govern the sequence and timing of the steps of transition to full control, and state the time and conditions for outlawing atomic weapons. The treaty must define the violations constituting international crimes and list the sanctions to be employed. Finally, it must contain provisions for its amendment and, more important, any necessary amendment of the Charter of the United Nations.[12]

The views of the United States on the functions and powers of the authority were the subject of a second memorandum, which Eberstadt circulated at a meeting, July 5. This document explained the American proposals in more detail than Baruch could employ June 14. Like that first presentation, it stressed that controls could not spring to existence full-grown upon the legal establishment of the authority. They would have to come into effect by stages specified by the treaty or charter.

Fully as informative as the memorandum itself were the exchanges it proposals advanced and pose issues for the Working Committee to decide at its next meeting. Gromyko thought the name "drafting committee" confusing and wanted it clear that the committee was merely to continue studies that would assist the larger group. Evatt was quite willing to call it Subcommittee No. 1—or Alpha, Beta, or Gamma for that matter. Reassured, Gromyko consented.[10]

The Soviet delegate revealed his uncompromising temper at the first meeting of Subcommittee No. 1 on Monday, July 1. Evatt was there as chairman, joined by representatives of France, Mexico, the Soviet Union, the United Kingdom, and the United States. Making their first appearances at the council table were Joliot-Curie of France and Eberstadt of the United States. The hard-driving Evatt proposed six principles for general discussion. In sum, they embodied the American plan for an international authority, including an effective system for preventing breaches of the agreed restrictions and controls. Evatt favored measures designed to preclude the use of atomic energy for war, but only as part of a general system of control. For Gromyko, this would not do. The first step was to outlaw the bomb. An international authority was a matter for later consideration. Besides, the Russian argued, the United States plan contained ideas that were incompatible with the functions and organization of the Security Council. So long as this was the case, he could agree to it neither in whole nor in part.[11]

So basic a disagreement was discouraging, but at least it furnished the occasion for elaborating the proposals Baruch had announced in his opening address. At the second meeting of Subcommittee No. 1 on July 2, Eberstadt outlined a treaty establishing the atomic development authority. The treaty was to include a charter for the agency, an organic act stating its purposes, functions, powers, composition, organization, and location. The suggested covenant must contain provisions defining the authority's relations with the various organs of the United Nations as well as with the control agencies of the signatory states. It must specify the rights and obligations of each member, govern the sequence and timing of the steps of transition to full control, and state the time and conditions for outlawing atomic weapons. The treaty must define the violations constituting international crimes and list the sanctions to be employed. Finally, it must contain provisions for its amendment and, more important, any necessary amendment of the Charter of the United Nations.[12]

The views of the United States on the functions and powers of the authority were the subject of a second memorandum, which Eberstadt circulated at a meeting, July 5. This document explained the American proposals in more detail than Baruch could employ June 14. Like that first presentation, it stressed that controls could not spring to existence full-grown upon the legal establishment of the authority. They would have to come into effect by stages specified by the treaty or charter.

Fully as informative as the memorandum itself were the exchanges it

586

tle all issues of principle at the outset. Until a state knew what controls were possible, what they would involve, it could hardly pronounce any opinion on the obligations it was asked to undertake. What was needed, he argued, was a system of committees to investigate the two essential and related aspects of the work—the practical, technical, and scientific side and the legal and political side.

The strongest speech that June afternoon was that of Herbert V. Evatt, the Australian historian-jurist-politician who had been chosen to preside over deliberations for the first month. Evatt left no doubt that his country adhered to the principles Baruch had laid before the Commission. His essential point was that the Commission faced a highly complex problem which required consideration as a whole. It was not sound to deal with any one of its many aspects independently. This, he said flatly, was the trouble with Gromyko's proposals. Evatt stressed ordering each measure so as to create the international trust necessary to remove the dangers and seize the benefits. At the outset, however, he favored deferring detailed discussion of all the steps and stages. The Commission should first consider the fundamental principles of the proposed international authority and the obligations which all nations might reasonably be asked to assume.

585

At the conclusion of his formal statement, Evatt proposed setting up a working committee composed of one representative from each of the twelve members of the Commission. It should prepare a first draft of a general plan for a world authority and consider the proposals and suggestions made subsequent to Baruch's address. After Gromyko had elicited an understanding that the committee would indeed examine all proposals, not just the American, the Commission approved Evatt's suggestion.[9]

EXPLAINING THE AMERICAN PLAN

The Working Committee—in effect, the Commission sitting in executive session—met Friday, June 28. Knowing that Evatt had plans to take the initiative, Baruch urged speed. "Time presses. Each day finds the world more insecure. Let us proceed at once to find a way out." As a reference and study aid, he supplied a chart dividing control into twenty issues and indicating the position of the twelve nations on each. Gromyko conceded that this was a useful document, but he emphasized the importance of considering the substance of the proposals and observations that had been made. It seemed to him that the Working Committee should turn to a study of the Soviet proposition. It dealt with the "primordial subject," an international convention forbidding "the use of the atomic arm for the harm of humanity." Quick to oppose concentrating on a single feature of the task, Evatt brought out his own idea on the next step: a small drafting committee to work out in skeleton outline a system of control and development. This body would consider all plans and evoked that Friday morning. In reply to questions by Evatt, Eberstadt emphasized that the United States did not recommend having the atomic authority take title to uranium and thorium deposits in the ground. The legal, practical, and financial obstacles were too great. It would be enough if the authority could shut down or take over property when the owners were not co-operating or were diverting uranium to improper uses. As for assuring an adequate supply, the authority could operate through pricing policies. Gromyko was full of questions. How would inspection work? Eberstadt explained how the American plan would reduce the volume of inspection to a minimum. How would facilities be distributed throughout the world? Eberstadt admitted the difficulties and suggested that the principle at least should be set forth in the treaty. It might be best to assign the authority the task of applying that principle. At this point, Joliot-Curie asked the views of the American representative on making cessation of weapons manufacture one of the first stages. Eberstadt replied by quoting Baruch. The United States was willing to stop producing the bomb whenever adequate systems of control had been put into effect.

587

Finally, Gromyko asked why the United States was unwilling to sign a convention outlawing atomic weapons. Eberstadt explained patiently that such a convention would not fulfill the mandate of the General Assembly. It would accentuate international suspicion. The Kellogg Pact had demonstrated the ineffectiveness of such treaties. Evatt observed that the Soviet Union was asking the United States to stop manufacturing atomic weapons, destroy existing stockpiles, and give the rest of the world its exclusive information on how to make bombs in return for a mere promise by other countries not to use them. Such unilateral action would hardly satisfy public opinion in the United States. In Evatt's opinion, the American proposal was a gift which should not be refused. Gromyko thought a better gift would be to outlaw the use of the bomb and destroy it. To put an end to the bantering, Evatt suggested that an even greater gift to the world would be for all countries to reduce their armies and stop manufacturing explosives.[13]

In view of the emphasis Baruch had placed on the veto, it was important to expound in detail American ideas on the relation of the atomic authority to the United Nations. Gromyko had suggested this at the July 1 meeting. He placed Eberstadt in a rather difficult position—then and subsequently—because the United States delegation had not finished its statement on the subject. At last, on July 12, it was ready. The memorandum came too late to help Eberstadt, but it went on the record as an official exposition of American views.

The United States based its position on three general considerations. First, the international agency needed a sound relationship to the various organs of the United Nations. Second, no existing UN body had the managerial, proprietary, inspecting, and licensing powers necessary for effective international control and development. Third, a considerable degree of finality must attach to the agency's determinations, orders, and practices. What did all this mean in application? For one thing, the General Assembly would receive periodic reports from the authority and might play a role in connection with its budget. For another, when a significant violation occurred (these would be specified in the treaty), the authority would certify it to the Security Council, General Assembly, and participating states. The Security Council would have full jurisdiction over these offenses. But as Baruch had said on June 14, no power that had signed the treaty could use the veto to protect itself or any other state that had violated its solemn commitments. This affected the veto only on questions relating to atomic weapons. It did not compromise the principle of unanimity in any other case. A third organ of the United Nations, the International Court of Justice, would not be fully available in the absence of an amendment to the UN Charter. The atom authority, however, could request advisory opinions.[14]

588

STALEMATE ON POLITICAL QUESTIONS

On Monday, July 8, Subcommittee No. 1 met for the fourth time. It had accomplished nothing more than to indicate the extent and character of the disagreement. Evatt could see that his committee of six could not attain even the limited objective he had set for it. At the close of the session, he proposed that he make a report to the Working Committee. Aware that his term as chairman was about to expire, he considered it his duty to explain the situation as he saw it and to recommend appropriate steps for coping with it.[15]

When Evatt addressed the Working Committee July 12, he stressed that his report was purely personal. Reviewing carefully the exchanges since the first of the month, he made it clear that while the subcommittee majority agreed on the soundness of the American proposals, it had not been able to work out any formula that would satisfy the representative of the Soviet Union. Gromyko's insistence on a convention that would do no more than disarm the United States, his doubts about an international agency, and his opposition to eliminating the veto in the Security Council were the obstacles. Was it not time, Evatt asked, to bypass these stubborn differences and to move on to the technical work? Break the subject into its parts, he urged, and then later on have another try at treating it as an integrated whole. He suggested four committees: a co-ordinating committee which would be an extension of Subcommittee No. 1; a controls committee which would examine questions associated with the control of atomic energy activities; a legal committee which would act as an assistant to other committees, examine the relationship between measures of control and the United Nations organization, and ultimately submit a draft treaty or treaties to the Working Committee; and finally, a scientific and technical panel which should consider exchange of information and proposals for the peaceful uses of atomic energy.

The Working Committee rejected Evatt's call for a co-ordinating committee. When both General McNaughton and Sir Alexander Cadogan joined Gromyko in urging that the Working Committee retain over-all direction, Evatt conceded the point. But it was not possible to dispatch so quickly the proposal for a controls committee. Gromyko called for a more precise statement of its functions, one that would include the Soviet idea of a proscriptive convention. Furthermore, the name ought to reflect the function. What about "Committee for the Prevention of the Use of Atomic Energy for the Detriment of Mankind?" Trying to meet Gromyko's objections, Evatt expanded his definition until it read: "To examine questions associated with the control of atomic energy activities, including all measures designed to insure the prevention of the use of atomic energy for purposes of destruction and other weapons of mass destruction and also including the subject-matters of possible conventions, sanctions, and observance, and to make specific recommendations on the said subjects." This should have provided something for everyone, but the committee had to adopt it over the opposing votes of the Russian and Polish delegates. Still hoping to reconcile the dissenters, Evatt proposed designating the new group simply as committee 2. Gromyko preferred a name, but in the absence of agreement, he considered it logical to use a number.

589

The rest of the session went much the same way. Gromyko would not admit the need for a legal committee; at present, the main questions were political. This committee too had to be created over his opposing vote. In deference to the Russian's protests, the scientific and technical panel became the Scientific and Technical Committee. "Panel," Gromyko argued, diminished the importance of exchanging information. Though he still preferred "Committee on the Exchange of Information," he did not vote against establishing the body under the other name. The afternoon had been on the harrowing side. It was six-fifteen before Evatt could announce that the business of the day was complete. There was every reason for his voice to have a special ring of sincerity when he said he would be very glad to see his distinguished friend from Brazil take over the chair.[16]

Evatt's hope that a system of subcommittees would subordinate the central disagreements proved vain. The functions assigned to Committee 2 were so broad that the effect was merely to transfer to another arena the issues which had frustrated Subcommittee No. 1. Besides, most members of Committee 2 were inclined to tackle the political questions at once and to delay what they called detail. On July 17, they agreed to an agenda that called first for considering the establishment of an international development authority and next for discussion of a convention to outlaw atomic weapons. John Hancock, sitting in as the American representative, was not hopeful. What a travesty, he thought, to expect that men who wasted so much time debating the name of a committee could ever agree on the draft of a treaty.[17]

It took no longer than the second meeting to bring the basic differences to the center of the stage. On July 24, Committee 2 took up the American memorandum of July 12, the essay on relations between the atomic authority and the organs of the United Nations. Gromyko attacked the American position. No new agency was necessary, he argued. The Security Council had full power to deal with atomic energy. Even if it were necessary, the proposed authority would have broad functions and powers not easily reconciled with the UN Charter provisions ensuring the sovereignty of member states. The activities, perhaps the very existence of the United Nations, depended on maintaining national sovereignty. Then there was the veto. The Soviet Union believed it wrong, perhaps fatal, to undermine the principle of unanimity among the permanent members of the Security Council. Gromyko rejected the American proposals categorically. As presented, the Soviet Union could not accept them "either as a whole or in their separate parts."[18]

On July 26, Gromyko made a second statement, this time in advocacy of the Soviet plan for a convention outlawing the production and use of atomic weapons for purposes of mass destruction. To those who hoped for some means of reconciling the American and Russian positions, it offered nothing. It contained no idea, no fact beyond what Gromyko had stated in his opening address five weeks before. Van Kleffens of the Netherlands, who had taken very little part in the deliberations thus far, put his finger on the defect of the Soviet proposal. It called for prohibiting atomic weapons without simultaneously putting in force a system of controls. Going back to 1868, he showed how similar conventions had failed to check small incendiary or explosive shells, dum-dum bullets, aerial bombardment, and poison gas. The Russian proposition, he concluded, needed considerable elaboration if it were to have practical effect. Hancock reiterated this theme for the United States. He rejoiced that despite differences on timing, every one agreed that outlawing atomic weapons was of first importance. He hoped that Gromyko would explain his plan further, that he would tell the committee how it could be made truly effective.[19]

The representatives of Canada and Australia added their demands for more information on the Russian plan at the July 31 meeting. McNaughton made every effort to be conciliatory. He for one believed that the Soviet proposal implied the establishment of safeguards. He hoped Gromyko would discuss the specific measures he had in mind. The Russian representative rose to the occasion. He observed that the question of guarantees applied not only to the Soviet convention on atomic energy. It was central to the general activities and even the very existence of the United Nations. Where was there a guarantee for any of the aims of the United Nations? The only real assurance lay in the genuine desire of all members to co-operate. Yet the Soviet proposal, he said, went beyond asserting general principles. It required signatory states to enact legislation providing severe penalties for violations. Furthermore, it envisioned that the Security Council would apply sanctions, if necessary, should the convention be violated.

Gromyko had no sooner finished than Luis Padilla Nervo of Mexico voiced his agreement that real co-operation was the only guarantee. There was a further requirement, however. It was necessary to distinguish between preventive action and sanctions. If atomic weapons were used, sanctions might come too late to do any good. Nervo thought it necessary to discover and punish violations in the different stages of the production process. Why not have the Scientific Committee inform Committee 2 of the kind of controls necessary? Parodi of France snatched at the suggestion. The discussion during the last month had centered on such questions as the veto and national sovereignty. He thought it wise to consider a more concrete approach. Why not obtain the advice of scientific experts on the possibility of controlling the production of atomic weapons, on how extensive control must be to be effective? The answer to these questions would condition the decisions regarding such issues as state sovereignty.

591

This turn took Hancock off guard. He had no advance notice and could only speculate on the Frenchman's motives in breaking into the discussion of the Soviet convention. He had two misgivings. First, he considered it futile to separate the scientific and political aspects. Second, it might take the scientists some months to prepare an adequate answer. Perhaps it would be better to ask the Scientific and Technical Committee to study specific matters that had come up in the Committee 2 discussions. Parodi's idea did not evoke enthusiastic response from anyone, but it was difficult to object to more information. Accordingly, Committee 2 agreed without dissent to ask its sister group, the Scientific and Technical Committee, for a report on the feasibility and methods of effective control.[20]

The next day, Thursday, August, 1, Baruch met with Hancock, Eberstadt, Davis, and Lincoln Gordon, a political scientist and former WPB official who had joined his staff as consultant. Baruch viewed the situation positively. He believed there was no real cause for disappointment. The work had come along as quickly and as well as anyone had a right to expect. The goal remained a unanimous report incorporating the principles of the American plan. The delegation was not considering any alternative objective, and no member should suggest that it was. The proper tactic, he insisted, was to draw out the Russians and their ideas as fully as possible. At all costs, the American representatives must avoid humiliating the Russians even if it involved absorbing some personal humiliation themselves. If any breach arose in the negotiations, it must not originate on the American side. It must be crystal clear that the United States had explored every possible avenue of agreement. The plan he had presented, Baruch declared, was generous and just. The United States had right as well as might on its side. He saw no reason to believe that the Russians would not come around when they had opportunity for complete understanding of the American proposals. Hancock then spoke of the lines along which work might progress. The American delegation should maintain informal contact with the representatives of other powers and make sure they understood its proposals. The staff should draft a treaty; indeed, Fahy already was at work on one. Finally, the staff should elaborate the stages of the transition period. For the present, this was the major substantive task.[21]

Hancock stated Baruch's policy in a memorandum to the entire staff. The single objective was to gain a workable treaty. Earnestly and patiently, everyone must strive for general concurrence. The situation reminded Hancock of a Joel Chandler Harris story he had read many years before. Uncle Remus had a pack of hounds chasing Brer Rabbit. Finally, he got his hero trapped inside a high board fence. Every possible opening was closed. He could not jump the fence and the hounds were closing in. Both the story and the rabbit were in danger of coming to an end. The resourceful story-teller then thought of having Brer Rabbit climb a tree. "But a rabbit can't climb a tree," the boy on his knee complained. "That's right, sonny," said Uncle Remus, "but this rabbit was just 'bliged to climb that tree." So with the American delegation. It was just 'bliged to get unanimous consent.[22]

On August 6, Committee 2 had another try at drawing out Gromyko. Hancock stressed that the goal of the United States was a workable plan. In accord with the instructions of the General Assembly, it wanted to prevent the use of atomic energy in war and provide safeguards for complying states. Within these limits, however, the United States did not insist on its plan without change. Hoping that he had quieted any misapprehensions, Hancock turned to Gromyko and the Russian proposal. Supposing a nation embarked secretly on aggression with atomic weapons. How would the Security Council learn of it? What would happen if it did? How could the Council be sure it learned in time? Would other nations consider the Security Council an adequate safeguard? Gromyko refused to come to grips with these questions. The United States, he said, was concentrating on the future. It viewed the present, in which atomic weapons could be produced and used without limit, as normal. The Soviet Union regarded the present as abnormal and saw no reason why other states should accept the American proposals without question. As for the Security Council, Gromyko only noted that the Charter gave the Council powers extending even to the use of armed force. The Council could direct this against an aggressor using atomic weapons.

Other delegates tried without success to persuade Gromyko to go beyond generalities. The meeting settled into utter deadlock. R. L. Harry of Australia accepted the facts of the situation. While he still considered it was time for detailed discussion on control, he thought it would be advantageous to call off meetings until the Scientific and Technical Committee reported. The chairman, Captain da Motta e Silva, recommended this course. It seemed more profitable than continuing discussions in the present framework. There were no objections, and Committee 2 prudently withdrew from the field.[23]

THE SCIENTISTS TAKE OVER

This decision centered all hopes for progress on the Scientific and Technical Committee. The scientists were already at work. At their first session on July 19, Tolman, the American technical expert, pointed out that his country had already provided substantially the information necessary to understand the possible peacetime benefits of atomic energy and to comprehend the difficulties of controlling its dangerous aspects. This included not only the Smyth and Acheson-Lilienthal reports but also "Background Information," a series of seven essays submitted on June 14, and "Beneficial Uses of Atomic Energy," four papers transmitted July 10.[24] The United States, said Tolman, would be glad to provide experts to discuss these documents and other available information. Of course, national policies on military security limited the information any delegate could exchange. But if anyone wanted further data in order to understand the reasons for provisions proposed for the charter, the United States would entertain his request.

At the same meeting Pierre Auger of France proposed that the Scientific and Technical Committee form a subcommittee to make a preliminary technical study of control. Hendrik A. Kramers of the Netherlands, who was serving as chairman, endorsed Auger's objective but favored a different approach. Kramers persuaded his colleagues to proceed through informal conferences of scientists rather than through a subcommittee. In such conferences, all agreed, the scientists would not act as representatives of their countries. The experts would simply explore the subject in their personal capacities. Should their discussions result in reports, these documents could be acted upon in formal session. This procedure proved a happy one, and on July 25 and 30, the scientists turned to constructing a flow chart which clarified their understanding of the scientific facts basic to both peaceful and destructive uses.

Thus, a framework had already been established. When the request for a report came from Committee 2, Padilla Nervo of Mexico suggested that the scientists ignore the political aspects of controls and limit themselves strictly to scientific and technical feasibility. Oppenheimer, who had been assisting Tolman, proposed organizing the facts relevant to control and avoiding commitment to any specific system. Agreement on these propositions made the work easier. The scientists held five more informal meetings in the first ten days of August. To assist Kramers in preparing a draft report, they discussed the principal matters at length. Kramers and Dmitrii V. Skobeltzyn of Russia were the chief interrogators. Tolman, Bacher, and Sir George Thomson did most of the explaining.

Kramers had his first draft ready on August 20. Eight sessions were devoted to criticizing this paper and its revisions. Perhaps the most important issue arose from the fact that on some subjects—denaturing, for instance—Tolman and Bacher could not supply full data, which some of the delegates found disturbing. Kramers thought the restricted areas of informa-

593

tion raised doubts as to the sincerity and equity of American statements. Such doubts and the irritations they fostered, he argued, tended to inhibit real progress, perhaps more than the actual lack of information. Yet this difficulty did not prove as stubborn as might have been expected. The introduction to the report, worked over carefully in group discussion, disposed of it neatly. Much of the information developed during the war, the passage read, had not been supplied in full nor had it been confirmed by full descriptions of experimental procedures. "It is equally true, however, that no scientific arguments would lead one to doubt the essential accuracy of this information. It represents an orderly extension of the pre-war science of nuclear physics, and there are no apparent inconsistencies with this pre-existing body of scientific fact."

594

On September 3, the report was ready. Its heart—essentially a diluted version of the Smyth and Acheson-Lilienthal reports—analyzed the different stages in producing atomic energy, exploring the elements of danger and the safeguards that might be erected against them. The scientists were hopeful that safeguards on mining operations would not be too difficult. They emphasized that particular attention should go to installations which produced concentrated nuclear fuel. As for Committee 2's basic question, whether effective control was possible, they did not find "any basis in the available scientific facts for supposing that effective control is not technologically feasible."

The final meeting on the report reflected the co-operative spirit that increasingly had marked the informal discussions. Skobeltzyn announced he had no objections to the document in its present form. Though he would not be able to attend the formal meeting on Friday, September 6, he assured Kramers that the Soviet representative who replaced him would take action. But disappointment was in store. On Friday, Pavel S. Alexandrov said he did not yet have clearance from the head of the Soviet delegation. He had no personal objection to the report, he explained, but Gromyko had been very busy with Security Council matters during the past week and had given him no instructions. In response to a question by Tolman, the Russian added that he expected to be able to take formal action on any day of the following week. That week, however, came and went. Nothing happened. Were the Russians determined to block even a strictly limited, negatively stated agreement on the technological facts? [25]

BARUCH ASKS FOR NEW INSTRUCTIONS

August was a quiet month for the American delegation. Tolman and his aides were busy. Hancock and Gordon Arneson were working on a counterblast at Gromyko. Eberstadt was drafting a treaty. No one else, however, was heavily engaged. On Friday, August 23, Baruch called in his entire staff.

Where do we go from here? he asked. Searls thought that soon it would be time to bring the basic political problems into sharper relief. Perhaps the delegation should present a draft charter along with a progress report. Eberstadt cautioned against dragging things out interminably. Groves added his urging against indefinite delay; it was important to maintain a favorable public reaction in the United States. Swope was eager for action. Too much patience means toleration, he said. Toleration leads to appeasement and appeasement to compromise. By prolonging the negotiations unduly, the United States would play into the hands of the Russians. Albin E. Johnson was the only one to urge moderation. He pointed out that the negotiations in the Atomic Energy Commission were only part of a much larger picture. This was not the time to force the issue. The spotlight was on Paris, where Secretary Byrnes was leading the American delegation in its quest for a lasting peace. It would be well to see how this turned out before stirring up too many difficulties in the Commission.[26]

595

Baruch must have been impressed by Johnson's advice. At any rate, when he met informally with members of the Canadian delegation the next week, he stressed how anxious he was not to force the pace. He did not want to drive Gromyko into a corner. He was convinced that a slower, educative technique was best; the present emphasis on the work of the Scientific and Technical Committee manifested this conviction concretely. The United States would not trade. Atomic energy was far too important for that. At the same time, it was essential to make every effort to reach agreement. Then he could face a break with a clear conscience. Baruch was encouraged to observe that the tide of public opinion was running strongly against the Soviets. Even many of "the so-called liberal groups" had said they could not support recent Russian actions.[27]

In September, the concern in the United States delegation deepened. The Russian failure to approve the report of the Scientific and Technical Committee, added to Gromyko's categorical rejection of the American proposals, meant total impasse. This had the most serious implications. In Baruch's judgment, it surrendered the lead to Russia. The longer the United States hesitated, the more other nations would shift away. There was real danger of alienating the nine nations who had been favorably inclined. Then there was the military situation. With the negotiations so unpromising, it was important to redouble American efforts to accumulate raw materials and bombs against the day the talks might collapse. Baruch and his associates recognized that they had no direct concern with the nation's military policy. On the other hand, they believed it was in their province to remind the President of the military implications posed by the progress of the negotiations.

With such thoughts in mind, Baruch and his staff met on September 10 to consider a draft letter to the President. Baruch announced his conviction that the delegation had a clear duty to report in writing how things stood.

Besides, he implied, the present American delegation might have outlived its usefulness. The negotiations in the Atomic Energy Commission had become a sideshow. They ought to be tied in with the main rings of the international circus. Perhaps the Baruch group should merely serve the Department of State in an advisory capacity. If a temporizing procedure was in order, it might better be carried out by the bureaucrats. For the greater part of two hours, Baruch, Hancock, Eberstadt, Searls, Swope, and General Farrell canvassed alternatives for suggestion to the President. In the end, they agreed to redraft the letter. Three days later, Eberstadt told his chief the letter should be completed and delivered to the President promptly. The responsibility for policy and tactics ought to emanate from the White House, he said. At the least, the White House ought to be a partner in their determination. Eberstadt stressed the importance of speed. Before long, many people were "likely to express the opinion that no progress is being made and to vent their spleen on the Commission generally and possibly on individual members." [28]

The letter from Baruch to President Truman, polished by Swope, was ready on September 17. It reviewed the original presentations, the opposition of Gromyko, and the Soviet failure to approve the report of the Scientific and Technical Committee. General McNaughton of Canada had proposed that Committee 2 consider this report. Baruch thought such discussion would help clarify the issues and promote understanding of the technical subjects. No one could be sure, however, that Gromyko would agree. If he did, the talks could last only a month or two. Then the Commission would have to face basic policy issues.

Baruch despaired of unanimity on fundamentals in the foreseeable future. Exactly when and how the Commission should act, questions intimately related to the larger course of international relations, were matters of high policy. Once the Commission had completed its short-term work, the American delegation could see only two possible courses of action.

One alternative was to recognize the difficulty of reaching unanimous agreement, press the matter to a vote, and send a divided report to the Security Council. The majority report would consolidate the American position and provide opportunity for a public statement on the inadequacy of the Soviet plan. Such tactics, however, would precipitate a bitter debate in the Security Council. Moreover, they might necessitate a premature decision about the treatment of atomic energy outside the Soviet sphere, a matter which involved vital diplomatic and military considerations. Baruch admitted he might not have the support of all friendly delegates in achieving prompt action. But if he could once force the issue to a vote, he thought he would have everyone on his side except the representatives of Poland and the Soviet Union.

The second alternative was to avoid a sharp break in the near future by recessing the Commission and permitting the delegates to consult at length with their own governments. The French representative had already made this suggestion informally. Should this tactic be adopted, the Commission might render an interim report to the Security Council summarizing the discussions and highlighting the issues without seeking to resolve them or create a break. Depending on the general state of international relations, the Commission might resume its sessions after a reasonable interlude, suspend them until there was a promise of success, or await advice from the Security Council or the General Assembly.

What policy did the American delegation recommend? For the short term, Baruch said he favored a continuing exploration of all aspects of the subject with special emphasis on the technical problems of effective control and safeguards. This tack, however, would hardly suffice for more than another thirty to sixty days. Of course, the Soviet delegate might at any time initiate a break. If he did, it would be necessary to counterattack at once. For the longer term, Baruch and his associates favored the first alternative, bringing the United States proposals to a vote within a reasonable time. This would show the American people and the world how the nations stood. If the President should choose this course, an early decision was essential. Three supporters of the American proposals—Egypt, Mexico, and the Netherlands—would leave the Commission on January 1, 1947. The General Assembly would replace them with three others. Belgium, Colombia, and Syria had been discussed as successors, but it was impossible to be certain what position they would take. In any event, considerable time would have to elapse before they could express themselves formally. Unless there was prompt action, the United States was more likely to lose present support than gain new. The American delegation was aware that considerations of general foreign policy might make the second alternative the better. That, however, was a matter Baruch could not now appraise.

In closing, Baruch emphasized the importance of being ready to take the necessary national measures should the effort for international control collapse. National security could not rest on the assumption that the negotiations in New York would prove successful. "Pending establishment of the national Atomic Energy Commission on a fully operating basis," the letter ended, "there must be assurance that there is no lack of decisiveness in any aspect of our atomic energy program. These considerations add further weight to the importance of a prompt appointment of very able men to that body." [29]

597

THE WALLACE AFFAIR

On Wednesday, September 18, Baruch and Hancock were in Washington to report to the President. When they awoke that morning, they found that atomic energy policy had become front-page news. The papers carried the full text of a letter Henry A. Wallace had sent the President on July 23. The Secretary of Commerce had expressed alarm at the growing tension between the United States and Russia. He was troubled to find many Americans feeling that the United States could do nothing but arm to the teeth. All past experience, he said, indicated that an armaments race led to war, not peace. Wallace feared American distrust of Russia and, even more, Russian distrust of the Western world. The United States should try to allay any reasonable Russian grounds for suspicion. It should act in both the diplomatic and economic fields and in the negotiations for control of atomic energy.

598

Wallace applauded Truman's objective of an effectively enforced atomic disarmament. But, he charged, the Moscow resolution of December 27, the Acheson-Lilienthal report, and the Baruch plan all contained a fatal defect. They proposed arriving at international agreements by easy stages. They required "other nations to enter into binding commitments not to conduct research into the military uses of atomic energy and to disclose their uranium and thorium resources while the United States retains the right to withhold its technical knowledge of atomic energy until the international control and inspection system is working to our satisfaction." While the United States was telling the Russians it might share knowledge of atomic energy if they were "good boys," it had set no objective standard for "good" nor specified any time for releasing its knowledge. Was there any wonder, asked Wallace, that the Russians had not shown more enthusiasm for the American plan? Russia held only two cards and both were weak— American uncertainty about Soviet science and technology and American ignorance of Russian uranium and thorium resources. In effect, the United States was asking the Soviet Union to show her cards at once, "telling her that after we have seen her cards we will decide whether we want to continue to play the game."

Wallace could see only deadlock if the United States insisted on its own rules. Russians would redouble their efforts to manufacture bombs. Americans might feel very self-righteous in refusing to compromise, but that would mean only that the atomic armament race was on in earnest. Wallace argued that the United States must abandon the impractical step-by-step idea presented to the United Nations. "We must be prepared to reach an agreement which will commit us to disclosing information and destroying our bombs at a specified time or in terms of specified actions by other countries, rather than at our unfettered discretion." The United States would lose nothing by adopting this policy. During the transition period, the United States would still retain its technical knowledge and the only existing production plants for fissionable materials and bombs.

Wallace believed that the United States should not pursue the veto question. While the veto had meaning in the general activities of the Security Council, it was irrelevant in a treaty on atomic energy. What action would be vetoed if a nation violated its commitments? "As in the case of any other treaty violation," Wallace answered, "the remaining signatory nations are free to take what action they feel is necessary, including the ultimate step of declaring war."[30]

Publication of this letter was only the latest reflection of a widening rift between the Secretary of Commerce and the President. In March, Wallace had proposed a special economic mission to try to convince the Russians that the United States desired peace sincerely. Truman ignored the proposal. The July 23 letter was another attempt to persuade the President he must quiet Russian fears. Truman read the twelve-page, single-spaced document but did nothing more than forward it to Byrnes.

Then at Madison Square Garden the night of September 12, Wallace attacked the Byrnes "get tough" foreign policy before a throng of Soviet sympathizers. His speech, he said, had Presidential approval. His claim was the more impressive because in response to a press-conference question earlier in the day, Truman said he had read and approved the Wallace speech. This was a serious slip; actually, he had not read the text, even in part. The morning of the fourteenth, Truman yielded to the demand for an explanation. He told White House correspondents he had meant to say he approved Wallace's right to speak his mind. Emphatically, he denied any intention of endorsing the address as a statement of American foreign policy.

599

Wallace, far from withdrawing, found encouragement in the outcry he had provoked. On the sixteenth, he marked his return to Washington with a statement that he stood by the New York speech and was continuing the fight. About midday the seventeenth, Drew Pearson's syndicated column was delivered to the Washington *Post*. Pearson had procured a copy of the July 23 letter, which he proposed to publish in installments. Reporters descended on Bruce Catton, Wallace's press representative, and then on White House Secretary Charles G. Ross. There followed a public-relations nightmare. Ross apparently misjudged the President's intention and despite Truman's express disapproval, he permitted mimeographed copies of Wallace's July letter to reach the press.[31]

Baruch was furious. He naturally concluded that Wallace was responsible for the leak.[32] Such a public attack during the progress of a delicate negotiation was bad enough. But Wallace had based his attack on a gross error. In his June 14 address, Baruch had said that the charter of the atomic development authority should either fix specifically the stages of transition or set forth the means for doing so. He had not suggested that the United States judge the timing unilaterally. After checking with their colleagues in New York the morning of September 18, Baruch and Hancock called on Acting Secretary Clayton at the Department of State and outlined what they were going to say to the President that afternoon. Clayton tried to reassure them. Truman would see Wallace at three-thirty. Very likely, he would issue a statement. Clayton was confident it would be satisfactory to both Baruch and the State Department.

With Clayton as escort, Baruch and Hancock next went to the White House. Baruch told the President there was not enough time now for his report on the negotiations. The release of Wallace's letter created a new situation. Baruch charged that the Wallace facts were wrong, that the Secretary of Commerce had not made any direct effort to establish the truth. Where was Wallace getting his information? The President should require him to reveal his source. "Quite obviously," it was someone trying to preach Red doctrine, divide public opinion, and undermine the American position. In a manner that Hancock considered firm but friendly, Baruch said he could see only three courses. The President could require a full retraction. He could repudiate the criticisms Wallace had made. If he did not adopt one of these alternatives, he would have to accept Baruch's resignation. Baruch was careful to say he was not giving the President an ultimatum. Nonetheless, these were the only possible lines of action. Don't be in a hurry about resigning, the President replied. He was going to see Wallace in a few minutes. He thought Baruch would find his action satisfactory. Once Baruch had seen what Truman had done with Wallace, Baruch could issue any statement he wished.[33]

Shortly after Baruch and Hancock departed, Wallace arrived at the White House. For almost two and one-half hours the President closeted himself with his errant Secretary of Commerce and Ross. Truman showed cables from American diplomats abroad asking if United States foreign policy was going to change direction. Wallace was free to speak his mind within the official family, Truman explained, but public criticism was another thing. At great length, the Secretary argued that Russia wanted peace but feared American intentions. Looking across the desk at his visitor, Truman saw his honesty and sincerity but questioned his judgment. Wallace had a following that was important politically. Perhaps it would be easier to check him in the Cabinet than out. Therefore, Truman explained Byrnes's difficult position at Paris and persuaded Wallace it was wise to forego foreign-policy criticism at such a time.

A little before six, Wallace emerged from the President's study. All smiles, he read a statement to the reporters and photographers who swarmed around him: "The President and the Secretary of Commerce had a most detailed and friendly discussion, after which the Secretary reached the conclusion he would make no public statements or speeches until the Foreign Ministers' conference in Paris is concluded." Wallace was not the least downcast. Was everything patched up? "Everything's lovely," he replied. Did he still stand on his New York speech? "Absolutely." Was he remaining in the Cabinet? "Yes, I am."[34]

Baruch and his associates found this performance utterly unsatisfying.

600

Wallace had not retracted a thing. He had submitted to no more than a month's muzzling. True, the New York *Herald Tribune* reported that Truman had given Baruch assurances that he stood behind the American plan for atomic energy control, but this was not strong enough. Hancock concluded that Truman either had misled Baruch or changed his mind when he faced Wallace.[35]

Truman had hoped to keep Wallace in the Cabinet, but it took only a day to change his mind. Official Washington and the press viewed the Truman-Wallace understanding as a truce which settled nothing. So did the Baruch group, and Hancock called Clayton shortly before noon on the nineteenth to tell him so. A little later, Truman conferred by teletype with Byrnes in Paris. He found the Secretary dismayed at the prospect of continued attacks after the conference. If this happened, Byrnes said he would ask to be relieved. Truman insisted that he supported Byrnes and had not promised Wallace he could resume his assault on Administration foreign policy.

What finally tipped the scale against Wallace was the afternoon edition of the Washington *Daily News*. HENRY SMILES, HARRY PHONES, JIMMY "BURNS" screamed the tabloid's front page. Truman had authorized Wallace to read only the one-sentence agreed statement. He was to say nothing more. Yet here was evidence that Wallace had revealed the intimate details of the interview. According to the *News*, Truman had coupled his request that Wallace keep silent on foreign policy with a plea that he help out in the Democratic congressional campaign. Wallace had refused to talk at all unless he could discuss foreign affairs. Hence the statement announcing no speeches of any kind until the Paris conference had ended. Truman was thoroughly exasperated. This was the sort of thing that could wreck the bipartisan foreign policy. The morning of the twentieth, he asked his Secretary of Commerce to resign. To the last, Wallace was difficult to manage. He was so nice about everything that the President almost changed his mind.[36]

While the Wallace resignation eased Truman's troubles, it did not relieve Baruch's. There were two things Baruch had to do at once. One was to make sure Wallace's arguments did not mislead the President. The other was to have Wallace himself correct the damage he had done Baruch and the American plan in the court of public opinion. On September 24, Baruch sent the President a long memorandum to set the record straight. Systematically, he quoted the Wallace statements to which he objected and then offered his rebuttal. First, he demolished the weakest point in a weak case—Wallace's charge that the United States was insisting that it judge the timing of the transition steps. Baruch easily showed this baseless by referring not only to his June 14 presentation but to the memorandums the American delegation had submitted to the Atomic Energy Commission's Subcommittee No. 1 on July 2 and 5. Next, Baruch denied Wallace's implication that the United

601

THE NEW WORLD / 1939-1946

States was asking the Soviet Union to yield information on its uranium and thorium while maintaining indefinitely its atomic monopoly. The United States, he said, had not yet made specific proposals on the content and sequence of transition stages. Any treaty obligation would be binding on all nations. Americans would not ask others to refrain from research on military applications unless they were prepared to do so themselves. It.was necessary to ban the veto in atomic energy matters in order to prevent wrongdoers from escaping punishment and hindering the day-to-day operations of the control agency. The American plan was an effort to extend the domain of effective international law by defining crimes, providing for judicial determination of guilt, and setting up machinery for appropriate punishments. It contrasted sharply with the view that the only sanction against international crime was war. Finally, to Wallace's argument that the United States should make its plan more acceptable, Baruch had an easy answer. The American delegation could not modify the fundamental principles which in its judgment must be maintained if the Atomic Energy Commission was to meet its mandate from the General Assembly.[37]

Baruch's effort to persuade Wallace to recant began September 19 with a telephone call. Baruch adopted a conciliatory tone. He was sorry to learn of the July 23 letter. Would Wallace come up to New York and review with him the public documents in which the United States position had been detailed? The American delegation was doing everything it could to understand the Russian point of view, but Wallace really should correct his errors of fact. When Wallace replied that the President had muzzled him and that he was in no position to make any public statement, Baruch was blunt. The decision was up to Wallace, but if he could not make the necessary corrections for himself, the American delegation would do it for him —and in its own words. Finally, Wallace indicated he might come. If he did, he would like to bring Edward U. Condon with him.[38]

The Baruch-Wallace confrontation took place Friday morning, September 27. Baruch had called in Hancock, Eberstadt, Swope, Farrell, Gordon, and Arneson, while Wallace had brought along not Condon but Philip M. Hauser, his assistant in the Department of Commerce. The discussion soon convinced Hauser that the Baruch group did not insist on the United States retaining unfettered discretion. Hauser could see that Baruch intended to conclude the agreement in a single package, which was what Wallace wanted. Much of the July 23 letter had been written before June 14. The references to the Baruch proposals were an afterthought.[39] But Hauser still had a question on the timing of stages. Had not Baruch proposed full disclosure of raw-material sources before the United States would be willing to share any technical and scientific information? It was true, said Hancock, that the United States had suggested dominion over raw materials as one of the earliest purposes of the authority, but it had not insisted that this be first. In fact, like the exchange of scientific and technical information, the revelation of raw-material sources involved questions of timing that would have to be settled by negotiation and set forth specifically in the treaty. Eberstadt added that the American delegation had not gone beyond declaring that the plan should be put in effect by a series of stages that would be fair, equitable, and applicable to all nations.

After Wallace had read the veto section in Baruch's memorandum to the President and announced his full agreement, the discussion turned to his view that Baruch should seek some face-saving device to induce the Russians to acquiesce. Wallace thought Soviet intransigence stemmed from deep distrust of other nations. What did he have in mind, Eberstadt wanted to know. Wallace replied that the United States could agree to stop manufacturing bombs and perhaps allow the Security Council to inspect and make sure it had. But when Eberstadt pointed to the disadvantageous position of the United States if negotiations broke down, Wallace agreed that it was not yet time to halt bomb production.

603

It was noon, and as he was about to leave, Wallace observed, "It is obvious I was not fully posted." Hauser stayed on, declaring he was going to suggest that Wallace bring the matter up to date. After lunch, Baruch's aides read Hauser the draft of a statement they wanted Wallace to issue. It was not only a recantation but a sweeping endorsement. Wallace was to say: "I have concluded that I was not fully posted on the position of the United States representative. In the light of information that I have received, I am in full agreement with the course pursued by Mr. Baruch."

Hauser doubted Wallace would accept this. Discussion, drafting, and redrafting continued the rest of the afternoon. Finally, the seconds settled on a statement Hauser thought he could sell to Wallace. According to this version, Wallace would pay tribute to the sincerity and reasonableness with which Baruch and his associates were approaching their difficult task. Most important, he would admit that when he wrote his July 23 letter, he was not fully posted on some aspects of the position of the United States representative. He now was in full agreement with the principles Baruch had outlined in his September 24 memorandum to the President. He attached particular importance—and so did Baruch—to certain points. First, any plans must be wrapped in a single package and agreed to in advance by all parties. Second, the specific sequence and substance of the stages should be negotiated freely. Third, the machinery of control should contain adequate inspection and other safeguards. There must be no loopholes whereby any nation could threaten the peace of the world and at the same time prevent concerted action to maintain peace. And fourth, satisfactory agreement on control of atomic energy depended on the development of mutual faith and confidence among nations.[40]

Hauser left the Baruch offices with a promise to see Wallace immediately. The week end passed with no word. Not until Monday afternoon, September 30, did Eberstadt reach Wallace by telephone. Wallace told Baruch himself that he had a statement Baruch would not like. The substitute text again acknowledged Baruch's sincerity and reasonableness. Now, however, there was no admission of error. Wallace said merely he was pleased to have assurances that many points of the policies Baruch was pursuing were identical with his proposals and had been in effect at an earlier date. But, said Wallace, the central issue remained—the absence of mutual trust and confidence between the United States and Russia. The current impasse in the Atomic Energy Commission demonstrated this. While Russia refused to agree to an international system of inspection, the United States wanted to continue producing and stockpiling bombs during the period of transition before international control. The United States could not hope for success until there was a plan which would assure Russia "by deed as well as by words, of our sincere desire to pay due regard to Russian as well as American security needs during the period of transition before international control of the atom." [41]

604

Baruch had just about reached his boiling point. Wallace had not corrected the July 23 letter. Worse, Baruch understood that Wallace planned to publish the letter in pamphlet form. The week end had shown how erratic an influence the former Secretary had become. Meeting at Chicago September 28, a conference of the Political Action Committees of the Congress of Industrial Organizations and the Independent Citizens Committee of the Arts, Sciences and Professions adopted Wallace's interpretation of the American proposals. Now Baruch could not possibly let Wallace off without a retraction.

Baruch's staff devoted Tuesday and Wednesday to efforts at bringing Wallace back to the position he had taken the preceding Friday. The closest they came was late Wednesday afternoon, October 2, when Hauser telephoned another revision. This time Wallace said it appeared that at the time of his July 23 letter Baruch did not support a procedure that would leave the succession of stages to the sole discretion of the United States. Wallace affirmed his general agreement with Baruch's statement that atomic energy control should be achieved "through an international authority responsible for the operation of all dangerous activities in the field of atomic energy, supplemented by a system of inspection and machinery for swift punishment of violations." Then, however, Wallace raised the question of the United States continuing to produce bombs. This time he extended its scope to the period of negotiation as well as transition. He reiterated his plea that the United States pay due regard to Russian security requirements. Americans should go as far as they could with safety in preventing an atomic bomb race. He felt sure that "approached in this spirit, agreement would be reached and the first long step toward freedom from atomic fear would be taken." [42]

Baruch could not accept Wallace's latest revision with its implication that the United States should stop producing bombs in an effort to make it easier for Russia to accept the American proposals. Taking matters into his own hands, Baruch released four documents in time to make the morning papers of October 3. The first was his September 24 memorandum to the President, the second the statement Hauser had accepted, and the third Wallace's alternate suggestion of September 30. The fourth was a Baruch-to-Wallace telegram of October 2. Ignoring his antagonist's last-minute revision, Baruch turned his guns on the proposal Wallace had telephoned Monday afternoon. It had disappointed and shocked him, he said. Wallace had not corrected his misstatements. He had failed to express approval of Baruch's course on the points he had originally criticized. Instead, he had proceeded to discuss other questions that had no bearing on the errors in his letter to the President. The errors stood uncorrected. They threatened the delicate negotiations now under way. They created confusion and division among the American people. "You have no monopoly on the desire for peace," Baruch concluded bitterly. "I have given thirty years of my life to the search for peace and there are many others whose aims have been the same." [43]

605

Wallace fired back in the newspapers of October 4. "Mr. Baruch has spoken," he began. "But he has not yet dealt with the central issue to which my letter of July 23 to the President was addressed." Wallace found no evidence that Baruch had come to grips with the disagreements which had deadlocked the AEC or with the fact that a frantic atomic bomb race had begun. He thought it regrettable that Baruch had chosen to reaffirm his stubborn and inflexible position. The danger of failure lay in his statement that "the United States delegation cannot consider modifications in those fundamental principles of its plan which, in our judgment, must be maintained to meet the mandate given the commission by the United Nations General Assembly last January." Baruch's "judgment" as to what "must be maintained" was precisely the cause of the impasse. The most important difference in the UN Commission was whether the United States should continue producing bombs during the negotiation of the treaty and the transition to full control. A second was the Russian refusal to agree to an international system of inspection. A third was the Russian refusal to waive its veto right. "I still feel that the veto question was unnecessarily raised in the American proposal and has served as a barrier to the successful negotiation of an international atomic energy treaty." Wallace was convinced that these issues demonstrated the major thesis of his letter of July 23—the absence of mutual trust and confidence. "Nothing in the recent statements of Mr. Baruch would cause me to revise the basic tenets of my letter to President Truman concerning the way to peace and atomic energy controls." [44]

Baruch found an appropriate forum for rebuttal on October 8, when he accepted an award from Freedom House for outstanding service in the cause of peace. Before an audience that included every member of the Atomic Energy Commission except Gromyko and Lange, Baruch defended the American proposals. "That program still stands—generous and just. And no amount of deliberately created confusion shall prevail against it." The United States asked nothing it was not willing to give. It was ready to proscribe and destroy the bomb, but only if the world would join in a pact to insure security from atomic warfare. Such a covenant must be realistic, "not merely a pious expression of intent, wholly lacking in methods of enforcement." The United States was working with all participating nations. All would have to agree on the specific stages of the transition to international control. As for the veto, it was one of the weightiest points in the American position. Once a treaty of prevention and punishment dealing with atomic energy had been agreed upon, the veto of the Great Powers must not be available to protect offenders. The entire speech was directed against the Wallace contentions, but only once did Baruch become personal. "Every man has the right to an opinion," he said, "but no man has a right to be wrong in his facts. Nor, above all, to persist in errors as to facts." [45]

606

Baruch thus closed the Wallace affair. It had been a sorry episode. Entirely apart from the impropriety of attacking the American representative in the arena of public opinion, Wallace did a poor job. Foolishly, he did not have his facts straight. Moreover, he failed to strike effectively at Baruch's stand on the veto. Here he might have made a respectable case and won important support. Though Wallace acted from pure motives, he created confusion which lent comfort to enemies and spread dismay among friends.

These consequences were apparent to any alert observer of the political scene. Another was not. The tempest had the effect of postponing the review of American policy Baruch had been about to urge. Baruch did not try to discuss the negotiations at the White House on September 18. The next day, he sent the President his September 17 letter on the subject. Truman asked Acting Secretary Clayton for comment, but the Wallace uproar seemed to overshadow the importance of Baruch's report. Perhaps the President was waiting for Byrnes to return from Paris. In any event, October came and approached its end, and still the White House did not act. [46]

OCTOBER OPTIMISM

Meanwhile, there was a flutter of hope in New York. At the Scientific and Technical Committee meeting on September 26, Chairman Kramers asked if the members were willing to take up the report on the technical feasibility of control. Every representative replied affirmatively. This was encouraging, but it still did not indicate the Russian attitude. Next, Kramers put the decisive question, and twelve hands went up. The decision to adopt was unanimous. Alexandrov then asked for the floor. Since the information at the disposal of the committee was limited and incomplete, he said, the majority of its conclusions were hypothetical and conditional. It was with this reservation that he had voted for the report. Kramers refused to consider this a restriction on unanimous approval, for the introduction stated the report's conditional character.[47]

On October 2, Kramers presented the report to Committee 2. General McNaughton observed that the next step was to examine the safeguards required at each stage of the production process. This task, which involved both scientific and nontechnical considerations, was a fitting undertaking for Committee 2. Thinking of the informal procedure that had served the scientific representatives so well, McNaughton proposed that a working group launch a series of informal discussions, meet frequently, and draw on the advice of appropriate experts. At the next session, October 8, a noticeable atmosphere of good feeling prevailed. Committee 2 agreed to sit informally and examine and report on the safeguards required to prevent the possibilities of misuse suggested by the Scientific and Technical Committee.[48]

The informal discussions began October 15, when the scientific and technical advisers turned to raw materials. Searls, the American mining expert, presented the report of the Carnegie Endowment's Committee on Inspection of Raw Materials as well as a paper the United States delegation had prepared on "Control Measures in the Mining and Metallurgical Recovery of Uranium and Thorium Ores." To the surprise of some of the representatives, Russia's Alexandrov made the first contribution. A geologist himself, he discussed Soviet practices, stressing the value of surveys as well as nationalization in production control.

In the next fifteen days, the experts devoted five more sessions to preventing diversion of raw materials at the mine, the concentrating mill, the refinery, and the chemical and metallurgical plant. C. S. Parsons of the Canadian Department of Mines and Resources reviewed the mining and concentrating procedures employed in the Eldorado Mine at Great Bear Lake. Searls commented on control at mines where uranium was a by-product. John E. Vance of Yale described some of the methods of controlling chemical processes involving uranium and thorium compounds. Throughout these conversations, the American delegation took the lead, presenting working papers which examined the thorium question and analyzed the principal types of safeguards. These, along with papers prepared by the Secretariat, served as bases for discussion. By the end of October, the committee had almost completed the raw-material sector of its investigations. It had begun to stake out areas of agreement. Soon it would be able to take up production reactors and isotope-separation plants.[49]

607

ATTACK AND COUNTERATTACK

For a brief season, the informal talks in Committee 2 created the impression that the Atomic Energy Commission was making steady if painfully slow progress toward the American objective of an international atomic development authority. Any hope, however, that the United States could depend on this tactic alone did not survive October. The Peace Conference at Paris adjourned on the seventeenth. The twenty-third, the United Nations General Assembly convened at Flushing Meadow. On Tuesday the twenty-ninth, Soviet Foreign Minister Molotov rose to deliver a characteristic harangue. The American plan "suffers from a certain amount of egoism," he charged. "It proceeds from the desire to secure for the United States of America the monopolistic possession of the atomic bomb." He attacked Baruch almost as if he were a private citizen carrying out some Machiavellian scheme of his own. "Is it not because there is a desire to give a free hand to the admirers of the atomic bomb that someone is raising such a hubbub around the veto?" There was no reason to postpone adopting the Soviet convention prohibiting the production and use of atomic weapons. "Only by taking such a decision shall we create suitable conditions for a free and fruitful examination of the questions relating to the establishment of control over atomic energy in all countries." Then Molotov made a shrewd bid for the initiative. Arguing that the time had come for a general reduction of all armaments, he introduced a resolution calling for the Security Council to arrange the necessary measures. As a primary objective, the resolution specified, this should include banning the manufacture and use of atomic energy for military purposes.[50]

608

Senator Warren R. Austin, chief American delegate, took the Molotov attack in stride. Eschewing any recriminations, he welcomed the Soviet proposal. It should have a place on the agenda, he said. It deserved full consideration and discussion. Indeed, it was highly appropriate for the Soviet Union with its formidable armies to advance this proposition, just as it had been fitting that the United States suggest measures to prevent the manufacture and use of atomic weapons. Austin reviewed the long-standing interest of the United States in disarmament. Since the end of the war in Europe and the Pacific, it had rapidly reduced its own military establishment. It would not, however, make the mistake of unilateral disarmament. As far as the United States was concerned, any general reduction of the arms burden depended on creating effective safeguards, establishing peaceful postwar conditions, and providing the Security Council with peace forces adequate to prevent acts of aggression.[51]

Baruch had no quarrel with Austin's response. He thought the Vermonter had handled the matter well. But Baruch had special responsibilities as the American representative on the Atomic Energy Commission, and Molotov's speech had touched a sensitive nerve. From the first, Baruch had believed general disarmament the only way to deal decisively with the bomb. Though Byrnes had ruled against striking for disarmament, Baruch's June 14 address had intimated that other weapons of mass destruction and war itself might be the ultimate objective. On June 23, right after Gromyko's first speech, Baruch had written Acheson that atomic weapons were just a means of killing people quicker than before. All wars were inhuman. Was no one going to say anything about the great Russian army? Acheson had replied that Truman thought the question of general disarmament would distract attention from the immediate task and confuse the public mind about the nature of the American proposals. Yet Baruch did not change his mind about what was best, and when Molotov captured the disarmament issue for Russia, Baruch was furious. This was the fruit of the Administration's failure to act on his September 17 letter. "The Soviets have taken advantage of our indecision," he wrote Acheson on November 2. "It is disheartening, to say the least, to see the moves that can and so apparently must be made, only to find that somebody else makes them, and we are fighting rearguard actions." [52]

Baruch concealed his dismay in the letter he sent Byrnes on November 4 asking for a policy decision. He contented himself with remarking incidentally that Molotov had made a neat political maneuver. For the moment, the Russian had the advantage, but Baruch thought "our people" would see through his stratagem. Baruch emphasized the need for choosing between the alternatives he had outlined in his letter of September 17. Pointing to the change in membership scheduled for the first of the year, he still advocated working for an early 10–2 vote. A prompt decision was necessary, he said. Otherwise, there would be a long delay—six months, quite certainly —before the American delegation could achieve even an interim report to the Security Council. [53]

This time Baruch got action. On November 5, Byrnes replied that although he had not talked with the President, he personally favored pressing for the 10–2 vote and a divided report to the Security Council. Shortly after, Byrnes checked with the President, and the instruction stood. [54]

Baruch set the machinery in motion. At a plenary meeting of the Commission on November 13—the first since July 18—Colonel Khalifa of Egypt suggested that the AEC report its findings and recommendations to the Security Council by December 31. He would instruct Committee 2 to complete a draft report by December 20. Baruch moved that the Commission adopt these suggestions. Ten members voted in favor. Poland and the Soviet Union abstained. [55]

The Administration responded more slowly to the broader though closely related issue raised by the Soviet disarmament proposal. Early in November, Acheson discussed it with Assistant Secretary John H. Hilldring and with his aides, Herbert Marks and Alger Hiss. This group concluded that Molotov had introduced his resolution to divert the West from focusing on Russia's position in the AEC. Should the General Assembly adopt the Molotov resolution, attention would center on outlawing atomic weapons and reducing the size of air forces and armies. Safeguards would be buried in a maze of generalities and technicalities. To guard against this, American delegates should emphasize that disarmament agreements were futile without

609

inspection, international operations, or other safeguards involving ready access by an international organization to the various nations of the world. The State Department planners saw, however, that the United States could not allow the Russians to take the lead in advocating so popular a goal as disarmament. While effective expositions of the American stand, complemented by Baruch's course in the AEC, would help, it might prove desirable to propose a specific measure to the General Assembly. One possibility would be a resolution reaffirming the importance of the directive of January 24, 1946, expressing the conviction that safeguards (including inspection) were basic to disarmament measures, and stressing how important it was for the Atomic Energy Commission to complete its assignment.

Acheson put this thinking in writing for Byrnes on November 7.[56] Byrnes concurred in the analysis but questioned the suggestion for a resolution. Not that he was opposed should it become necessary; he only thought the time not yet opportune. By the end of November, timing was no longer a question. The Political and Security Committee began debating the Soviet resolution on the twenty-eighth. The next day, President Truman told his Cabinet that he favored disarmament so long as it included adequate inspection; he was determined not to repeat the 1922 mistake of disarming unilaterally. On December 2, Senator Connally presented an American resolution which urged four actions to the General Assembly. First, it should recommend prompt Security Council consideration of practical measures for regulating and reducing armaments, measures that all nations would observe. Second, the Assembly should recognize that atomic energy control was essential to any real disarmament and recommend that the Security Council give priority to the report of the Atomic Energy Commission. Third, the Assembly should record its belief that disarmament depended on practical and effective safeguards. It should call on the Security Council to devise such safeguards for both atomic energy and other weapons. Finally, the General Assembly should appeal to all national governments to render every possible assistance to the Security Council and the AEC.[57]

PRIORITY FOR ATOMIC ENERGY CONTROL

Thus, one month after Molotov's speech, the United States had advanced counterpolicies in both the General Assembly and the Atomic Energy Commission. The issue was fought to a conclusion first in the General Assembly. During the debate in the Political and Security Committee on December 2, Connally told Soviet Vice-Foreign Minister Vishinsky that the United States would never agree to put disarmament questions at the mercy of the Security Council veto. To the surprise of the other delegates, Vishinsky declared several times that the American disarmament proposals deserved the closest study and attention. Observing at one point that "this is not simply a case of eating pancakes," he said the Soviet delegation needed more time before it could say whether it could accept all, part, or none of the American plan. The hope born of Vishinsky's conciliatory demeanor turned to genuine optimism two days later when Molotov told the committee that once the Security Council had established a control agency, the veto rule would have no further connection with its work. No country could use the veto to obstruct its operations. Molotov indicated that the Soviet Union was willing to accept the United States disarmament resolution as a basis for further discussion. Molotov by no means endorsed the American plan for an international atomic development authority, nor did he accept the prohibition of a veto on punishments. Still, he had announced agreement to a significant principle on which the United States had insisted.[58]

The Political and Security Committee appointed a subcommittee to draft a resolution. After frustrating Russian efforts to specify a world troop survey, the subcommittee submitted a text which the parent committee adopted with a few minor changes. On Friday night, December 13, Secretary Byrnes spoke in support of the resolution, stressing anew that priority must go to the international control of atomic energy. Demobilized divisions, he pointed out, could be recalled speedily. Meaningful disarmament must start with the major weapons of mass destruction. On the fourteenth, the General Assembly acted unanimously. The resolution it approved followed the American version of December 2. Molotov considered the wording acceptable because it reflected both the idea of reducing armaments generally and of prohibiting the use of atomic energy for military purposes. From the point of view of the United States, the resolution was satisfactory because it emphasized the importance of inspection and called on the Atomic Energy Commission to discharge expeditiously the General Assembly's mandate of January 24. The United States had succeeded in keeping the AEC, pending its report, at the center of the international stage.[59]

611

THE AEC REPORTS

Baruch's drive for a favorable report on the American plan began in earnest on Thursday, December 5, when he told the UN Atomic Energy Commission that it held primary responsibility for creating a system to protect the world against the bomb. The stakes were the peace and security of mankind. Who could doubt that if the nations controlled the atomic weapon, they could proceed to other instruments of mass destruction? The United States, Baruch said, would surrender the absolute weapon. Its only price was "a declaration of peaceful intent and of interdependence among the nations of the world, expressed in terms of faith and given strength by sanctions—punishments to be meted out by concerted action against wilful offenders." But the United States would not accept unilateral disarmament. It would not give up the bomb "to no result except our own weakening." In this great enterprise the United States welcomed the support of all countries. It sought especially the participation of the Soviet Union, which, to judge by the recent statements of its highest representatives, no longer regarded the original American proposals as unacceptable. "The time for action is here," Baruch declared in presenting a resolution which specified the heart of the report. Although he desired no immediate vote, he did want the chairman to call an early meeting at which the Commission would debate the findings and recommendations the resolution contained.

612

Baruch's draft resolution condensed the American plan to its essence. Under "Findings," the AEC would report that it was scientifically, technologically, and practically feasible to eliminate atomic weapons from national armaments and to provide effective safeguards against violation and evasion. The Commission would say that everything depended on effective control of the production and use of uranium, thorium, and their fissionable derivatives. Appropriate control mechanisms included inspection, accounting, supervision, licensing, and management. To be effective, these controls must be enforced through a single, unified, international system established by an enforceable multilateral agreement. While the agreement should outlaw atomic weapons, such a ban must be an integral part of a comprehensive plan. Outlawry would fail unless fortified by adequate guarantees and safeguards in the form of international supervision, inspection, and control.

Under "Recommendations," the American resolution would have the AEC outline a treaty establishing the international control agency within the United Nations and defining its rights, powers, and responsibilities, as well as its relations with the other organs of the United Nations. The treaty would prohibit the manufacture, possession, and use of atomic weapons by all participating powers and their nationals and provide for the disposal of any existing stocks of atomic bombs. It would specify the means and methods of determining violations, stigmatizing such violations as international crimes and establishing the nature of measures of enforcement and punishment. It would arrange for immediate reporting of serious offenses to the Security Council. "In dealing with such violations, a violator of the terms of the treaty should not be protected from the consequences of his wrongdoing by the exercise of any power of veto." If the enforcement features could be "rendered nugatory" by the veto, the provisions of the treaty would be "wholly ineffectual."

Baruch's resolution left no doubt on the point Wallace had raised. The treaty should set forth a program for completing the transition to international control "over a period of time, step by step, in an orderly and agreed schedule." The United Nations Atomic Energy Commission should supervise the transitional process. It should have power to determine when a particular stage or stages had been completed and subsequent ones were to commence. The United States would have no right of unilateral judgment.

When Baruch had finished presenting the American proposal, the current chairman—Parodi of France—was the first to comment. Since Baruch's draft contained conclusions, he thought it best to postpone discussion until Committee 2 had completed its work on the scientific and technical issues. Unless there were objections, Parodi would refer the resolution to one of the Commission's study groups. In the absence of any strong protests and in the face of Gromyko's desire for more time for study, the Commission adjourned without setting a date for another meeting.[60]

Baruch had not been able to push his colleagues into speedier action on December 5; but once the General Assembly had passed its disarmament resolution on the fourteenth, the outlook was better. Armed with the Assembly's call for AEC action and bolstered by a new Byrnes injunction to force a vote on the American plan, Baruch had the new chairman, Mexico's Vallarta, schedule a meeting for Monday, December 17. Baruch urged two claims upon the delegates. First, they should adopt and proclaim the basic principles. Second, they should act at once. The General Assembly had placed them under compulsion. A new spirit had come into being. Employing a favorite figure of speech, Baruch said it was their "privilege and duty to give flesh to that spirit."

Gromyko objected. The American proposals did not conform to the resolution of the General Assembly. Agreement had been possible there only because the veto question had been put differently. Baruch's call for dropping the veto on punishment would violate the United Nations Charter. Offering the prospect of a unanimous decision, Gromyko called for additional study and discussion. The Russian had struck a responsive chord. Baruch recognized the inevitability of a short postponement. In the hope that granting Gromyko's request for time might produce unanimity, the United States would agree to a short delay—no more than three days. This was not enough to suit Gromyko, but Baruch insisted on his deadline, Friday, December 20. "There may be more delays," he said: "time goes by and years pass, and then nothing is done." [61]

Thursday saw feverish maneuvering behind the scenes. General McNaughton of Canada, while supporting the American plan, thought Baruch was driving too hard. In an effort to keep a solid front, Eberstadt conferred at Canadian headquarters until three o'clock Friday morning. He came away with an understanding that McNaughton would offer an amendment to Baruch's December 5 resolution. This amendment was to affirm that the AEC approved and accepted the principles upon which the draft findings and recommendations were based. By its terms, the Commission would instruct the Working Committee to conform their relevant parts to the wording of the General Assembly resolution of December 14 and include them in the draft report to the Security Council.[62]

When the Commission met at 10:30 Friday morning, Gromyko was still not ready to discuss the Baruch proposals. He favored checking the ex-

613

tent to which they conformed to the resolution of the General Assembly. To this end, he proposed postponing discussion and action for six or seven days. This gave McNaughton his opportunity. He brought out his amendment, explaining that it endorsed only the principles on which the American resolution was based. It did not bind the Commission to adopt Baruch's proposal as it stood. Not impressed, Gromyko held out for the postponement. Baruch, who had called Byrnes on the telephone and obtained fresh approval for his course, accepted the Canadian amendment and insisted on a vote. By a 10–2 division, the AEC rejected Gromyko's call for delay. Then 10–0, it approved the American proposals as amended. This meant that the Working Committee—the Commission in executive session—would take the Baruch findings and recommendations, the Committee 2 draft, the General Assembly resolution of December 14, and from these three documents fashion a report to the Security Council that was consistent and unambiguous.[63]

614

Committee 2 had been hard at work. Throughout November, the informal sessions on safeguards continued. The experts spent long afternoons listening to American engineers—James H. Critchett, Harry A. Winne, Wilbur E. Kelley, Charles A. Thomas, and George T. Felbeck—discuss the control of reactors and chemical, metallurgical, and isotope-separation plants. They devoted many hours to reviewing working papers. By the middle of December, they had a draft ready for formal consideration. Meanwhile, the Secretariat, under the direction of Pendleton Herring of Harvard, had begun blocking out the report to the Security Council.[64]

When Committee 2 met formally December 18 to consider the report on safeguards, the impossibility of meeting the Security Council's December 20 deadline was apparent. It took another formal session the nineteenth and some heavy staff work thereafter, but the day after Christmas, the report was ready. Herring laid it before the full committee at a morning meeting. Part I was the Secretariat's account of the proceedings. Part II summarized the findings on safeguards, but it was incomplete. Its section on "General Findings" waited on Working Committee consideration of the American resolution. The same was true of Part III, "Recommendations." Part IV was the Scientific Committee's "A First Report on the Scientific and Technical Aspects of the Problem of Control," and Part V was Committee 2's own "First Report on Safeguards Required to Ensure the Use of Atomic Energy Only for Peaceful Purposes."

After several amendments had been suggested and approved, Chairman Vallarta put the issue to a vote. With Russia not participating and Poland abstaining, the representatives adopted the report, 10–0. Its most significant feature was the "Report on Safeguards." Twenty-six printed pages in final form, it was a detailed, dispassionate survey of the measures required to prevent the dangers outlined in the report of the Scientific and Technical Committee. To a gratifying degree, the report bolstered the essentials of the American plan. Most important, it concluded that a single international agency must be responsible for the system of safeguards and control. The agency must manage both isotope-separation plants and production and power reactors. Managerial operation alone could provide the necessary security and close supervision. It was largely in emphasis that the report departed from the position the United States delegation had sustained. It said nothing about ownership of ore deposits and mines; the American plan left open this possibility. The major departure was reliance on inspection alone during the early processes of production. The report depended on inspection of mines, mills, refineries, and chemical and metallurgical plants, while the American plan insisted on whatever control would assure the international authority ownership of all uranium and thorium actually produced. The report failed to specify that the authority should own all fissionable materials. Yet even this was not necessarily an adverse judgment. Committee 2 had not yet had time to discuss the issue.[65]

615

The Working Committee met Friday morning, December 27, behind closed doors in the Security Council chamber at Lake Success. General McNaughton proposed a revised version of Baruch's December 5 draft of findings and recommendations. This document reflected a behind-the-scenes effort to assuage Russian sensitivities. The American delegation had made some concessions. Eberstadt had worked over the revision with George Ignatieff of Canada and agreed on a number of textual changes. The types of safeguards the international authority would employ received a less inclusive definition. All members of the United Nations could participate "on fair and equitable terms" instead of "with the same rights and obligations." The treaty or convention establishing the international authority would contain a provision "setting forth" rather than "stigmatizing" the violations that constituted international crimes.

McNaughton's version included a revised section dealing with the veto on punishments. Here, the Americans and Canadians had been unable to agree. As submitted, the section dropped the Baruch draft's flat assertion that "a violator of the terms of the treaty should not be protected from the consequences of his wrongdoing by the exercise of any power of veto." The phrase it substituted said the same thing in language less heavily freighted with moral indignation—"there shall be no legal right, by veto or otherwise, whereby a wilful violator of the terms of the treaty or convention shall be protected from the consequences of violation of its terms." The obstacle to agreement was the four words, "by veto or otherwise," on which the Americans had insisted. The revised section on punishments also included a suggestion that wilful violation might involve the inherent right of self-defense recognized in Article 51 of the United Nations Charter.

When McNaughton had finished, the committee proceeded to discuss the document page by page. Captain da Motta e Silva of Brazil won acceptance for an amendment stating specifically that international ownership of mines and of ores still in the ground was not mandatory. Chairman Vallarta of Mexico proposed an amendment stating that the veto should not be applicable in the day-to-day work of the control agency. The committee accepted it in principle, leaving the precise wording until later. As always, it was the veto on punishments that kindled the fireworks. Parodi of France opposed the words "by veto or otherwise." It should be sufficient, he said, to include a statement that no violator should be able to protect himself by legal methods. Sir Alexander Cadogan spoke next, observing that the United Kingdom favored omitting the phrase if omission would aid in achieving unanimous acceptance of the principles. The British Commonwealth, however, did not present a united front. Hasluck of Australia favored the section as written. The hesitation to use the word "veto" reminded him of a game in which children sang a song, nodding their heads at certain words and keeping silent instead of pronouncing them. Eberstadt said that when the United States delegation said "no legal right," it meant "by veto or otherwise." Should the Commission omit the word "veto," it would be perfectly clear that the members had backed away from using it. In view of the great importance of the subject, he was turning his chair over to Mr. Baruch, who would restate the views of the United States.

616

Baruch spoke slowly and impressively, taking great pains to explain that the United States was not trying to violate the principle of unanimity among the great powers or the application of the veto as conceived in the UN Charter. There was no issue about the operations of the atomic control agency itself. As he understood it, all nations agreed that the doctrine of unanimity was not applicable there. The only question occurred in case of a violation. If some nation defied its treaty commitments, the international authority would be obliged to bring this to the attention of the nations and of the Security Council. Both the Security Council and the participating nations would already have accepted the responsibility to observe and enforce the provisions of the treaty. It was at this point that the United States maintained a violator should have no veto to protect him against the consequences of his wilful wrongdoing.

The American people, Baruch declared, believed that the United Nations stood for the sanctity of treaties. They would—and should—withdraw their support from an organization which became "no more than a debating society and a place to exchange pious-sounding documents." To refuse to take the course the United States delegation had advocated "would shock the moral, common sense judgment of the world. . . . If the violators of a treaty can legally and with impunity escape the consequences of a violation of an agreement voluntarily entered into, then every treaty executed under the auspices of the United Nations contains the fatal defect that it is binding only so long as the major nations want it to be binding." Baruch said he could neither recommend to the American people nor advocate before the Senate that the United States surrender the atomic weapon under any system open to nullification of punishment by subterfuge. His peroration was brief and uncompromising. "Gentlemen, it is either—or. Either you agree that a criminal should have this right by voting against our position (or you fail to take a stand on the question by refraining from voting), or you vote for this sound and basic principle of enduring justice and plain common sense."

Baruch did not succeed in forcing a decision. McNaughton and Cadogan indicated they still had some misgivings but would go along with the majority. Katz-Suchy of Poland supported Parodi on deleting "by veto or otherwise." Only da Motta e Silva of Brazil and Khalifa of Egypt spoke unequivocably for including the controversial phraseology. The chance for decision seemed slight. Finally, the delegates agreed that Chairman Vallarta should submit the report to the Atomic Energy Commission with a covering letter stating the disputed passages. Alexandrov, who had sat silent throughout the long, grueling session, asked that the letter note that he had not participated in the discussions.[66]

617

When the Atomic Energy Commission assembled in plenary session at eleven o'clock, Monday morning, December 30, there could be no doubt that Baruch was right in his Friday assertion that the veto on punishments was a prerequisite to American participation in the quest for international control. Over the week end, the Hearst newspapers pulled out all the stops in a lurid campaign against international control of any sort. Mustering statements from representatives and senators assembling for the Eightieth Congress, they charged that the "Baruch atomic control plan of the United Nations would place this country eventually at the mercy of any enemy." More impressive than such alarms was a Vandenberg-to-Baruch letter published in the Sunday morning papers. "In my personal opinion," said the man who soon would be chairman of the Senate Foreign Relations Committee, "the Senate would not ratify an atomic control treaty which leaves any possible chance for subsequent international bad faith to circumvent total and summary enforcement or for any subsequent disagreements regarding enforcements to paralyze even temporarily the application of effective sanctions."[67]

Vallarta turned the Commission to the only item on the agenda— consideration of the draft entitled "The First Report of the Atomic Energy Commission to the Security Council" and dated December 31. Gromyko spoke first, charging that the American position on the veto, despite Baruch's denials, defied the Charter of the United Nations. The Russian left no doubt as to his position. The Soviet Union would not be put off by mere modifications of phraseology such as France had proposed. The Commission should turn to prohibiting atomic and all other weapons adaptable to mass destruction. This would be the first important and practical step toward fulfilling the General Assembly resolution of December 14. To that end, Gromyko proposed an item-by-item consideration of Baruch's December 5 proposals in order to make the necessary corrections and proceed without delay to preparing a convention along the lines he had outlined the previous June.

Baruch was beyond rebuttal. Without commenting on Gromyko's speech, he quietly moved adoption of the report as forwarded by the Working Committee. One by one, delegates rose to support Baruch—Australia's Hasluck, Brazil's da Motta e Silva, Egypt's Khalifa, China's Quo Tai-chi, Canada's McNaughton. Baruch was anxious when Cadogan rose to speak for the United Kingdom. Just before they had entered the council chamber, the Briton had called him aside and said Whitehall could not accept the American position. It must have been a last-minute effort at bluff, for Cadogan's first words were, "My Government approves the report that has been submitted to us by the Working Committee." Having gone this far, Cadogan went all the way. He declared that the United Kingdom "attaches the greatest importance to the principle that there must be no 'veto' protection of violators of the convention." When the British representative had finished, Parodi announced that though France still had doubts about the veto, she agreed with the report as a whole and would support it. Only Lange of Poland spoke in opposition. Deploring Baruch's threat that the United States might withdraw from the United Nations, he suggested submitting the report without taking a vote but giving due notice of disagreements. If that proved unacceptable, he favored amendments to reduce the area of disagreement.

When the Commission resumed its deliberations at three after an hour's recess, Baruch demanded a recorded vote. Lange refrained from pressing amendments but suggested that the chairman indicate in his letter of transmittal that certain passages were not approved by all the delegations. He would not block a vote, but he would not vote for a report that stood no chance of being accepted by all the permanent members of the Security Council. The vote itself was anticlimactic. The entire report, including the findings and recommendations, received ten "ayes." The Soviet Union joined her satellite in abstention.[68]

OUTLOOK

A chapter had ended. A few days later, Baruch submitted his resignation to the President. The United Nations Atomic Energy Commission had completed the first phase of its work. Now that the Security Council would be turning actively to disarmament, the United States should have identic representation on both Commission and Council. Baruch was proud that he and his associates had carried out their orders. He thought they had lessened the difficulty of obtaining unanimity. While unanimous action was important, he warned, it must not be gained at the expense of principle. Baruch closed by expressing his belief that the work on the Atomic Energy Commission might prove the beginning of a broad program to govern weapons of mass destruction. In view of this, he saw no reason why the United States should not continue making bombs, at least until a suitable control treaty was ratified. It was important to preserve the nation's atomic secrets, particularly the designs, engineering, and equipment. The McMahon act provided authority; if inadequate, it should be broadened. "While science should be free, it should not be free to destroy mankind." [69]

The Truman Administration had embarked on a policy as unprecedented as the bomb itself. It had offered to abandon atomic weapons —its complete if temporary monopoly—in the interest of international control. Though this offer came at a time when it was reducing its conventional forces, the American Government was not blindly throwing away the atomic shield that offset the Soviet Union's puissant divisions. Maintaining that the control had to be effective, the Government insisted on moving carefully through specific stages. Though the United States did not demand the right of judging by itself the timing of the transition process, it envisioned a span of years during which American stockpiles would continue in being. This period of grace was important. It kept the balance of power stable for the immediate future. If things went well, disarmament might be extended beyond the atomic sphere. If things went poorly, what had been lost? The United States could not maintain its monopoly more than a few years in any event. The prize—elimination of all weapons of mass destruction from the arsenals of the world—made the effort imperative.

619

Hope for controlling atomic energy had not died, but it was failing rapidly. In December, 1945, the Soviet Union appeared ready to co-operate. A year later, it dismissed a plan whose merit had commanded overwhelming international support. In the Atomic Energy Commission, Gromyko talked about the threat to the veto power, yet was the principle of unanimity really the obstacle? Was it not more likely that the Politburo had decided to trust to Russian scientific and technical resources? If its proposals for outlawry first and control second were successful, it could look forward to a world in which Russia alone would have the bomb. If this was indeed the reasoning, the veto was not fundamentally significant. Certainly it was not responsible for the failure of the American plan. But was it good tactics? By insisting that there be no veto on punishments—a safeguard of debatable value at best—American leadership gave the Kremlin an opportunity to cloud the issue. The stand on the veto fed unjustified suspicions at home and abroad that the United States had been insincere in its efforts for international control. [70]

A TIME OF TRANSITION

CHAPTER 17

Throughout the legislative battle of 1945 and 1946, the contending factions had been able to agree on at least one principle: the members of the United States Atomic Energy Commission should be leaders of the highest caliber. Harlow Shapley called for "heroes" before the Senate Special Committee on January 29, 1946, men who were "willing to sacrifice their past and future . . . to take positions and responsibilities on the Commission." During the climactic House debate the following July, Representative Clare Boothe Luce lamented the poor chances for attaining this ideal. Concurring in a suggestion that the Commissioners ought to be of the stamp of Bernard M. Baruch, she cried: "how many Bernard Baruchs are there in the United States? If the mold made for that great public servant is not already broken, and if there are any more Baruchs you may be well assured that they have highly satisfactory, useful, remunerative jobs now. . . . How shall we find men to fill such gigantic shoes? Is not the danger that we shall be forced to put bureaucratic peewees into jobs that should be held only by supermen?" [1]

NAMING THE COMMISSION

That same July in the offices of the McMahon committee, two lawyers not accustomed to speaking in such hyperbole were thinking of possible nominees. James R. Newman and Byron S. Miller knew that Senator McMahon had won the right to speak powerfully to the President on this subject. On July 8, Newman gave McMahon a recommendation prepared on the assumption that the Commission should not include more than one scientist—or at most two. Heading his list was David E. Lilienthal, chairman of the Tennessee Valley Authority, followed by Sumner T. Pike, a former member of the

Securities and Exchange Commission, and Frank P. Graham, president of the University of North Carolina. Edward U. Condon of the National Bureau of Standards and Irving Langmuir of the General Electric Company were the scientists. Other suggestions were Judge Charles E. Clark, who had been dean of the Yale Law School, Lewis L. Strauss, a Kuhn, Loeb & Company partner, and two Washington newspapermen who had held important posts under President Roosevelt—Wayne Coy and Lowell Mellett.

As the stifling days of midsummer wore on, rumors swept through Washington. The morning newspapers of July 19 quoted "authoritative capital circles" as saying that Joseph P. Kennedy and General George C. Marshall were among the suggested candidates along with Coy, Robert Oppenheimer, and President Emeritus Charles Seymour of Yale. On July 28, a senator who asked not to be identified told a Washington *Star* reporter that President Truman had mentioned Marshall in preliminary discussions. Former SEC Chairman Kennedy still figured prominently in the speculation on Capitol Hill, but he was only one among several who were considered good possibilities—Condon, Langmuir, James B. Conant, Vannevar Bush, Edward R. Stettinius, and O. Max Gardner. Though his name was not always mentioned in the planted stories that flowered in Washington, many observers concluded that Lilienthal was the strongest contender.

621

The President was keeping his own counsel. Without fanfare, he called Sumner Pike to the White House for a July 29 interview and asked him to serve. Pike's prompt, unequivocal "yes" was appealing. The two men were delighted to learn they both had been artillery officers in the first World War and shared the dubious distinction of going broke in Kansas City. On July 30, Truman asked Lewis Strauss to come to Washington for duty with the Atomic Energy Commission. Strauss carried the blessing of Secretary of the Navy James V. Forrestal. One of the few Navy reservists to rise to flag rank, he had played an important part in the wartime ordnance program. With two commissioners in hand, Truman searched quietly for a chairman. First, he offered the job to Conant, who decided not to accept. Then he approached Karl Compton, but poor health—he was just recuperating from a heart attack—forced Compton to decline.

Meanwhile, support was building up for Lilienthal. On July 31, Bush wrote Truman to second his nomination. A man of judgment and ability, Lilienthal—like John McCloy and Dean Acheson—would make an excellent chairman. Observing that the President probably wanted to name at least one scientist, Bush volunteered to sound out opinion. It was especially important that the profession regard him as a man of good judgment. On August 2, Truman accepted Bush's offer to sample the thinking of scientists. As for Lilienthal, the President said, "I like him very much myself but he is doing a grand job where he is and I don't want to take the chance of getting a dud in that place." [2]

Lilienthal seemed more and more the logical choice in the weeks that followed. As chairman of TVA, he had become an adept practitioner of the art of public administration. As leader of the Acheson committee's Board of Consultants, he had identified himself with an imaginative approach to international control. He commanded the respect of Bush and Conant, the distinguished statesmen of American science, as well as the enthusiasm of the backbenchers of the FAS. Moreover, Lilienthal might not be indispensable in the valley of the Tennessee. When Byron Miller learned why the President was reluctant to name Lilienthal, he scouted the situation and reported to John R. Steelman, his chief in the Office of War Mobilization and Reconversion, that Gordon R. Clapp, general manager of the TVA, would be a suitable replacement.

On October 3, Truman launched a trial balloon by announcing that he might appoint Lilienthal to the Atomic Energy Commission. Senator Kenneth McKellar of Tennessee, Lilienthal's archenemy, promptly opened fire: "I will do everything that I can to see that he is rejected." The President, however, had already discounted McKellar's opposition, and he proceeded to enlist the TVA chairman.[3]

Only two places remained to be filled. Lilienthal submitted a list of names from which the President late in October selected William W. Waymack and Robert F. Bacher. Waymack was the editor of the Des Moines *Register and Tribune* and a public director of the Federal Reserve Bank of Chicago. He had won the Pulitzer Prize for editorial writing in 1937. Bacher, one of the most essential physicists at Los Alamos, had returned to Cornell and at the time was helping Richard C. Tolman present the technical case for control to the United Nations Atomic Energy Commission. Bush had endorsed him as a first-rate scientist high in the esteem of his colleagues.[4]

Now Truman had his five. He was proud that he had not mixed politics with the atom. He had not even asked the political affiliations of his appointees. As it turned out, Pike, Strauss, Waymack, and Bacher were Republicans, while Lilienthal considered himself an independent. Each man had distinguished himself in his own field. If the nonscientists knew little or nothing about atomic energy, they had Bacher to set them straight. Though Waymack had been a prominent sponsor of the National Committee for Civilian Control of Atomic Energy, none of the five had been scarred by the legislative fight for the McMahon bill. Lilienthal's role in the controversies that had swirled about the TVA made his name anathema to men as different as Senator McKellar and Harold L. Ickes, but his moderation and eloquence had won him admirers who more than compensated for the vulnerable plates in his political armor.[5]

The White House saved the public notices until Monday, October 28, when it could name the entire Commission. At ten that morning, the five appointees assembled in Room 220 of the State-War-Navy Building, where each man prepared a brief biographical sketch for press secretary Charles Ross. At eleven-fifteen, Lilienthal took Clapp, his successor at TVA, to see

Truman. For Clark M. Clifford, special counsel to the President, Lilienthal had two draft statements. One was on the Clapp appointment, the other on the Commission. Lilienthal had prepared the latter with the help of lawyer Herbert S. Marks, whom he had already recruited for his staff. At eleven-thirty, Waymack and Bacher arrived to meet the President for the first time. Truman had already called Baruch in New York to inform him of the AEC appointments and to regret that necessity compelled him to deprive Baruch of Bacher's services.

At three-fifty in the afternoon, all five Commissioners filed into the White House. At four, they sat inconspicuously to one side as the President read his statement to a large group of reporters. The nation was grateful, he said, that the Commissioners had been willing to set aside their personal interests and shoulder responsibilities as great as men had ever assumed in peacetime. There was no activity, public or private, upon which the security and enrichment of the United States depended more heavily. Trying to bind old wounds, Truman paid tribute to the Army and General Groves. During the war, they had directed the atomic project with brilliant success. Now that Congress had placed the Atomic Energy Commission in charge—here the President read with special emphasis—the enterprise would proceed with the complete co-operation of the Manhattan District and its contractors and with the full support of the Army and Navy. It might require several months to accomplish an orderly transfer of the functions and properties of the Manhattan District. During this transition, the Commission had asked the War Department to carry on so that there would be no interruption in the work. Secretary of War Patterson and General Groves had agreed to this arrangement.

623

The United States, said the Chief Executive, looked to the Commission to develop and pursue an ever-expanding program to realize the benefits of atomic energy. The nation recognized that the full measure of these benefits depended on the establishment of adequate international controls. Therefore, the most important step for the American people and the world was the successful conclusion of the negotiations in the United Nations. The President had come to the last sentence. "Although the way may not appear entirely clear, we must direct all our efforts to the end that neither this nation, nor any other nation, shall suffer the penalties of atomic warfare and that the great achievement of science and industry shall be instrumental in bringing a better way of life to all mankind." As he finished, Truman looked up from his paper and repeated the thought in his own words. The United States wanted the entire development of atomic energy to be devoted to peace and not to war.

The conference concluded, the President and the Commissioners stepped out on the White House lawn for pleasantries and photographs. Lilienthal quipped about "the homeless five" and "the quintuplets in a quandary." The next day, October 29, the Commission issued its first public statement, which announced the selection of a temporary staff of three and reaffirmed the President's remarks on transfer. The Commission needed time to study the present program, analyze the broad scope of the problems it faced, and lay plans for carrying out its great responsibilities.[6]

GROVES HOLDS THE LINE

General Groves had been waiting for more than a year to bring the affairs of the Manhattan District to a close. At the end of the war in September, 1945, he did not anticipate so long a delay. He expected speedy Congressional action on the War Department legislative proposals and looked for a civilian commission to take over in a few months. Assuming this course of events, he could see his responsibilities clearly. He must keep the Manhattan District sound in its essential parts, complete the construction already under way, and do everything he could to advance efficiency and economy.

624

Groves's most important charge was the production chain, especially the U-235 plants at Oak Ridge and the plutonium piles at Hanford. The Oak Ridge complex had been built in the days when cost was no object, when speed was the only consideration, and when no single process of isotope separation looked certain. With victory won, it was time to shut down the uneconomic facilities. First to go was S-50, the jerry-built, liquid-thermal-diffusion plant thrown up in the summer of 1944. As soon as the Japanese surrendered, Colonel Arthur V. Peterson's production-control section recommended placing S-50 in stand-by. S-50 had been useful when all-out production was the order of the day. During the drive for the Hiroshima weapon, it had accelerated by about a week the flow of weapons-grade U-235 from the Beta tracks at Y-12. Now, however, the K-25 plant was able to accomplish the entire first stage of separation much more economically. On September 4, the Manhattan District ordered S-50 to discontinue operations. By September 9, workers had stopped all racks and removed the last uranium hexafluoride for shipment to K-25.[7] The Alpha plant at Y-12 followed S-50 into stand-by the same month. Though the tracks were functioning better than ever before, it was obvious they could never compete with K-25. Shutdown began September 4. The last tank ceased operating September 22.[8]

The gaseous-diffusion plant flourished while its less efficient sisters expired. The final group of K-25 stages went on cascade August 15, and by the end of September, K-27 was 80 per cent complete. If all went on schedule, K-27 would be in full operation before February 1, 1946. Throughout the autumn, production of feed for the Beta calutrons exceeded expectations.

The production-control officers at Oak Ridge still depended on electromagnetic separation to bring the product to top enrichment. The new Beta chemistry building was finished November 17 and the new process building November 30. Every month, the statisticians were able to chart new output records. Partly responsible were the larger quantities of higher-assay feed from K-25 and the greater capacity provided by the last two Beta tracks, which went into full operation in November and December. But an explanation more gratifying to the designers and operators was a reduction in the outages that had plagued the process from the start.[9]

The production of plutonium at Hanford settled into routine. In the great concrete canyons, du Pont operators standardized their procedures and introduced minor changes in the interest of efficiency. On November 14, Hanford temporarily discontinued shipments to Los Alamos and began stockpiling the plutonium nitrates.[10]

Groves faced a special set of circumstances at Los Alamos. Unlike Oak Ridge and Hanford, it was a combined research and production establishment. For the immediate future at least, it seemed best to keep it that way. Groves judged that the only justifiable step toward a separation of functions was to begin centralizing weapon-assembly facilities at Sandia, the old Albuquerque airport, which had been an Army convalescent center during the war. The first technical group moved from Los Alamos late in September. By the end of October, the entire Wendover Field staff and facilities had been transferred to the new site.[11]

Groves also faced the imminent resignation of the scientific staff at Los Alamos. After Hiroshima and Nagasaki, many of the best men decided that their mission had been accomplished. Like their contemporaries in uniform, they wanted to go home. There were those who still savored the technical challenges at Los Alamos and gloried in its scenery and salubrious climate. Unfortunately, the uncertain future of the laboratory made it difficult for them to stay.

Groves did everything he could to provide reassurance. Oppenheimer, just back from Washington, briefed his principal aides on August 20. He told them that the War Department's legislative proposals to put the project on a peacetime basis would go to Congress in a few days. There was a stockpiling job to accomplish, so Los Alamos would operate for several years. While stockpiling meant production, the necessity for improving the weapon meant research—happily, on a more relaxed timetable. On September 18, Groves himself spoke to a meeting of division leaders. He announced that the legislation which President Truman was sponsoring called for a new federal agency to run the atomic project. While he could not predict its policies, he expected Los Alamos to continue as a weapons-research center. Secrecy would still be necessary, but it would not be so severe as during the war. Since Oppenheimer was returning to his post at the University of California, the laboratory needed a new director. Groves said he was appointing Norris E. Bradbury to serve in the interim; he would expect Oppenheimer and the division chiefs to select a permanent leader.[12]

Bradbury's interim appointment lengthened into a long-term responsibility. Early in October, he became director of the laboratory for six months

625

or until national legislation was enacted, should this occur sooner. Surveying his new job, Bradbury saw that the fundamental objective for the next few months had to be the establishment of conditions as nearly ideal as possible. This meant reasonable salary scales and employment practices. More important, it meant a program that would attract good men by virtue of its inherent intellectual interest. On October 1, he had outlined his views on what such a program should include. Los Alamos must produce implosion weapons, he told the Co-ordinating Council. It should re-engineer some of the more uncertain features of the Nagasaki weapon and try to develop a better model. Though Bradbury recognized that everyone hoped it never again would be necessary to use an atomic bomb, he pointed to the need for greater reliability, simplicity of design, and safety. There should be fundamental experiments to settle whether or not "super," the hydrogen bomb, was feasible. There ought to be additional Trinity tests. It was important to know everything about the pathology of nuclear energy, just as it was necessary to study cancer. The tests would serve as a goal to stimulate the staff. While weapons work necessarily would remain, for the foreseeable future, the central theme at Los Alamos, Bradbury believed that the laboratory needed research on the constructive applications of nuclear energy if morale was to hold at the level necessary for efficiency.[13]

Bradbury's views made sense, but to maintain an adequate staff, Los Alamos needed some tangible promises for the future. The authorities in Washington could do little to satisfy this requirement in the prevailing climate of uncertainty. Meanwhile, the staff melted away. Most of the old leaders departed by the end of the year. Lured by the call of opportunity outside and smarting under the irritations engendered by isolation, security restrictions, and poor housing, a great many of the scientific and technical rank and file also left. Though an able group of experienced men was willing to remain and assume leadership, the laboratory was short-handed. It was difficult under these circumstances for Los Alamos to move in even the channels that were open.[14]

At the close of 1945, Los Alamos fell far short of the ideal Bradbury had set. Though there was a large amount of U-235 on hand, a considerable backlog of unpurified plutonium-nitrate slurry, and some metallic plutonium scrap, only a very few weapon shapes had been fabricated. A campaign to acquire and stockpile mechanical and electrical components was under way. When it was completed, the supplies would be substantial. What seemed an adequate number of explosive charges for implosion weapons was in storage, but the production situation was disquieting. Cold weather had forced shutting down the plant at S Site. By the time operations could be resumed, the staff would be so depleted that routine manufacture of full-scale charges would halt casting for experimental projects. Although production of high-explosive charges at the Inyokern Naval Ordnance Testing Station had been authorized, that plant was finding it difficult to achieve adequate quality.[15]

All along the line, Los Alamos had time for only a beginning. Roger S. Warner's Ordnance Engineering Division had turned to making existing models more reliable and designing a radically improved implosion weapon. Physicists in other divisions undertook calculations and experiments looking to a still more advanced design. Meanwhile, Edward Teller's group in Theoretical Physics explored the feasibility of a thermonuclear weapon. The only work with important peacetime implications was on Philip Morrison's proposal for a ten-kilowatt power reactor, fueled by plutonium, and operating on fast neutrons. This project could easily be justified, for it would provide a useful tool for investigating nuclear reactions important in weapons. On November 10, Morrison had begun a series of design conferences.[16]

Throughout the Manhattan project, it was research and development that suffered most as 1945 dragged to a close without Congressional action on atomic energy legislation. In this field, where long-range considerations dominated present decisions, General Groves was more inhibited than in setting policies for the production chain. The laboratories faced the uninspiring task of ordering the loose ends left over from the wartime program. Under the circumstances, it was remarkable that they were able to spend any time on projects that looked to the future.

The Clinton Laboratories were under new management at the end of the war. Acceding to the University of Chicago's desire to withdraw, Groves had persuaded the Monsanto Chemical Company to become the operator. A special Monsanto division headed by Charles A. Thomas had taken over on July 1, 1945. Martin D. Whitaker stayed on as director. According to plans, Clinton would produce radioactive isotopes for experimental purposes, recover the large amounts of uranium from the extraction wastes being held in storage solutions, and continue investigating the effects of radiation on animals. The laboratory's directive also provided for work on a reactor using enriched uranium. One of the main objectives here was to learn more about converting thorium to U-233 and separating this fissionable isotope. Throughout the fall, the laboratories pursued the basic research these assignments demanded. The reactor project developed design data. At first, the objective was a ten-thousand-kilowatt homogeneous pile—that is, a reactor in which the active material was a U-235 salt dissolved in heavy water. This approach had the advantage of requiring the skills of chemists rather than metallurgists, who were in short supply. Before the end of the year, however, Clinton dropped the homogeneous pile in favor of the heterogeneous type, which relied on uranium metal. Some studies continued on subjects of general engineering interest, but it was clear that the homogeneous unit presented technical difficulties that precluded any early achievement of a practical prototype.[17]

The Metallurgical Project was caught in the confusion of postwar readjustment. Though Arthur H. Compton had become chancellor of Washington University in St. Louis, he remained at Groves's request as director of all project activities operated by the University of Chicago. Farrington Daniels became director of the Metallurgical Laboratory, and Walter H. Zinn continued as leader of the Argonne Laboratory division. This was only an interim organization, and in November, 1945, the Manhattan District launched a study of the future role of Argonne. In spite of the unsettled prospects, the Chicago physicists, chemists, and metallurgists had plenty to do. Hanford still made important demands on their time and talent, but Zinn's breeder reactor provided most of the intellectual stimulation. For many months, the Metallurgical Laboratory had been stirred by the challenge of a reactor that would breed—in either natural uranium or thorium—more fissionable material than it consumed. The fall of 1945 provided time for preliminary design sketches and the first experiments. By the end of the year, Zinn had reached some important conclusions. He would build a reactor operating primarily on fast neutrons. He would use highly enriched U-235 rather than plutonium fuel. He would seek to breed Pu-239 in U-238 rather than try for U-233 in thorium, whose physical and nuclear properties were virtually unknown.[18]

628

The Radiation Laboratory at Berkeley had the advantage of not being a child of war. Under Ernest O. Lawrence's aggressive leadership, it had been an important center of research since its establishment in 1936. As soon as the war ended, Lawrence was ready with a proposal that the Manhattan District support completion of his 184-inch cyclotron, interrupted back in 1941, and construction of the electron synchrotron, an improved accelerator based on the phase-stability principle Edwin M. McMillan had discovered at Los Alamos. Groves favored work along the lines of the Lawrence recommendations, but he thought there should be additional study as to the method and extent of federal subsidy for such tools of basic research. Pending the establishment of an atomic energy commission, he thought it advisable to proceed at a reasonable rate on pilot-plant studies only. But at the end of December, when he had seen a more definite proposal and cost estimate, Groves agreed to share the expense of completing the cyclotron to the extent of $170,000 and authorized Lawrence to proceed with construction of the synchrotron under the contract then in force.[19]

1946 COMMITMENTS: PRODUCTION

As the eventful year 1945 drew to a close, General Groves abandoned his hopes for prompt creation of an atomic energy commission. The opportunity for quick legislative action had been lost in September and October. With months of delay in prospect, he had to change his initial policy of merely holding the line. Now he had to make definite plans even though this meant commitments which would tend to restrict the future commission's freedom of action.

The production complex remained Groves's most urgent concern. He saw that he would have to extend the major operating contracts. As a rule, these agreements were to terminate six months after the end of active hostilities against the Axis. To assure uninterrupted production, Groves had negotiated supplemental agreements fixing June 30, 1946, expiration dates. Where possible, he had obtained options permitting the Government to renew for an additional one-year period. On March 11, 1946, he informed the Secretary of War that it was necessary to exercise these options. With Patterson's approval, Groves acted quickly to keep Carbide and Tennessee Eastman on the job at Oak Ridge.

Hanford was another matter. Du Pont had come into the program reluctantly with the understanding it did not wish to stay beyond the war emergency. In view of Congressional delay in determining atomic energy policy, du Pont promised to carry on until October 31, 1946, but it was determined to withdraw at that time. Groves explained the situation to Patterson in his letter of March 11. It was necessary to find another operator for Hanford. Du Pont's departure, he lamented, was "most unfortunate from the government's standpoint." He doubted that a new contractor could be found until legislation had crystallized. Patterson made a strong plea to Walter S. Carpenter, Jr., but the president of du Pont politely declined to continue.[20]

629

Even before du Pont reaffirmed its decision, Groves had approached the General Electric Company. It was a logical choice. Past Manhattan District experience justified confidence in the firm, and Groves felt that the possibility of future power applications might be an inducement. At first, General Electric was reluctant, advancing in explanation the uncertainty that surrounded the nation's atomic energy program and its own plans for reconversion. But in May, after renewed representations from Groves, the company accepted the Hanford assignment. According to the letter contract that confirmed the understanding, General Electric would operate the Hanford works, conduct research and development incident to process operations there, and take responsibility for the design and construction of alterations and additions. The company would also design and construct a Government-owned research laboratory at Schenectady. Here General Electric would pursue fundamental research and development. From the beginning, it was understood that the atomic power laboratory would be located at the Knolls, a former country estate five miles from the center of Schenectady, that the company had acquired for its own research establishment. By September 1, General Electric had substantially taken over the operations at Hanford. On September 6, the company accepted a formal contract which would expire September 30 unless approved by the Atomic Energy Commission. Since the Commission had not been appointed at the end of the month, Groves extended the contract until November 30.[21]

Groves found it necessary to make decisions on the production processes themselves. At Oak Ridge, it was the spectacular success of the gaseous-diffusion plants that forced his hand. K-27 came into operation in January, 1946, and on February 8, all its buildings went on cascade. Together, K-25 and K-27 were supposed to supply sufficient feed for Y-12 at the highest enrichment the electromagnetic plant could safely process. Pleased engineers recognized that increased power input had something to do with the splendid performance, but they knew that more fundamental explanations were better barrier quality and fewer losses due to operational disturbances than the designers had assumed.

Careful analysis of operations suggested strongly that K-25 and K-27 could achieve as high a concentration of U-235 as the Beta tracks at Y-12. Engineers saw two obstacles—the possibility of accumulating a critical mass in K-25 and the uncertainty as to the rate at which uranium hexafluoride consumed plant surfaces. Extensive studies provided reassurance, however, and in May, 1946, the Manhattan District authorized Carbide to raise product concentration on a trial basis. Now it was possible to check theoretical calculations by actual performance.[22]

630

Hanford presented Groves with less pleasant prospects. Eugene P. Wigner had predicted that graphite would expand when subjected to heavy neutron bombardment. Though Metallurgical Laboratory physicists had suggested various ways of coping with the phenomenon, they had found nothing that seemed a sure countermeasure. Should the "Wigner effect" appear on a significant scale in the Hanford piles, their operating lives would be in jeopardy.[23]

This threat dominated the Hanford scene. It was a factor early in 1946, when authorities there considered the possibility of adopting a new separation process that had been developed at the Metallurgical Laboratory. In 1944, Glenn T. Seaborg had conceived the principle of alternating between the plutonium ($^{+3}$ ion) oxidation state and a higher state or states as the basis for separating plutonium from uranium and removing the fission products with organic solvents. Developed almost furtively by the chemistry section in 1945, this "Redox" process promised great advantages over bismuth phosphate, including the recovery of uranium for reuse. Engineering and cost studies confirmed its soundness, but prudence dictated postponing installation until more was known about the possibility of graphite expansion. Not until August, 1946, did it seem worthwhile to start planning a semiworks for Redox developmental studies.[24]

Groves had to act most boldly at Los Alamos. As 1946 opened, the laboratory was in a crisis. To compound the discontent there, the water line from Guaje Canyon had frozen. For many weeks, tank trucks had to haul water from the Rio Grande. Housewives had to line up with buckets and pans for their daily ration.

At this juncture, Groves made a command decision. Los Alamos must remain active for at least the next few years. He must improve the existing establishment sufficiently to make that possible. Early in January, Groves told Bradbury that the major factors requiring improvement were utilities, housing, and community facilities. Planning had already started for the transition to a peacetime community. In the months that followed, Groves arranged for construction of wells, pipelines, and pumping stations to bring water to a new 1,000,000-gallon steel storage tank. He persuaded Secretary Patterson to authorize 300 units of permanent housing. Stimulated by this positive approach, authorities at Los Alamos turned to developing a master plan for transforming the hodgepodge laboratory into an ordered group of permanent structures, work areas, roads, walks, and utilities. Though it would take years to bring all these projects to fruition, Groves had made an important contribution by tangibly demonstrating his confidence in the future.[25]

The technical program at Los Alamos fell under the shadow of Operation Crossroads, the bomb tests at Bikini. These trials imposed heavy burdens on the laboratory's depleted staff. The Joint Chiefs expected Los Alamos not only to prepare the weapons but also to advise on the over-all character of the test, compile a technical handbook, furnish yield estimates, and prepare firing circuits and timing systems. Reduced to statistics, these responsibilities meant $1 million of additional procurement and the time of one-eighth of the staff for almost nine months. While Bikini provided a specific objective and a sense of purpose, its effect on the weapons program was adverse. With its senior personnel preoccupied with test preparations, the Ordnance Engineering Division's development efforts were severely handicapped.[26]

631

The unsatisfactory state of weapons development had grave implications for the nation's supply of nuclear arms. Despite the continued production of fissionable material at Oak Ridge and Hanford, not much metal had been fabricated for bomb use. A few powerful weapons would have been impressive had they been available for use on short notice. But they were not. Readying an implosion weapon required highly trained personnel and large quantities of special gear. Any long-range solution required a much improved implosion bomb. For the immediate future, an obvious tactic was special emphasis on the uranium gun. In the summer of 1946, Groves was actively considering this possibility.[27]

Los Alamos had its bright spots, to be sure. The Chemistry and Metallurgy Research Division devised a much safer plutonium-purification process. A Physics Division team completed design work on a large pressurized Van de Graaff accelerator to replace one returned to the University of Wisconsin. The fast-reactor project progressed rapidly, and the mechanical failure which interrupted critical-assembly measurements in September seemed only a temporary setback. Though heavy personnel losses curtailed studies on the super in June, 1946, the interested theoreticians had found no reason to doubt the weapon could be built if it received the necessary effort. In September, Teller suggested a novel approach that indicated a thermonuclear bomb might lie reasonably within the laboratory's capabilities.[28]

But these achievements brought little sense of accomplishment. On September 24, John H. Manley wrote General Groves a letter. It was Manley's last day at Los Alamos. No one had served the weapons project longer, and he felt duty-bound to report his views. The national security was in jeopardy, he warned. Los Alamos was unable to maintain the position the United States had advertized before the world. Despite an attractive location, a tradition of accomplishment, and a wealth of technical facilities, it was unable to hold enough competent personnel to meet its responsibilities. Many of the old staff had given up the fight. Those who remained were sustained by a slim hope that the AEC would rescue them. Manley thought the difficulty lay in the division of the technical work between immediate needs and future developments. The single objective of the war years was gone. Civilian-military friction was growing. During the war, Oppenheimer had controlled the technical program, and the military had remained a service unit. Since his resignation, Army interference had increased. To correct this situation, Manley had a recommendation that most of his colleagues supported: strengthening and training a military organization that would take over the details of weapons production, stockpiling, and surveillance at some site other than Los Alamos. Manley favored assigning the development of future weapons to a civilian research organization. Los Alamos was the logical place for such an effort if it could be a civilian establishment.[29]

Though Groves bristled at Manley's criticism of the military, he thanked the physicist graciously and invited him to Washington. For different reasons, Groves and Colonel Nichols had come to the same conclusion as Manley some six months earlier. In their view, the military had to exercise the control necessary to use atomic bombs effectively as weapons. This meant assigning metal production and explosives casting to industrial contractors. It meant selecting another firm to turn out standard bomb models. Finally, it meant organizing and training a military unit to take the weapons from the manufacturer and perform any necessary assembly or other work up to the point of hanging a bomb in an airplane. None of these operations should be accomplished at Los Alamos. That installation should be retained for developing new types of bombs. Only by such arrangements could the Army avoid too great a reliance on civilian scientists.[30]

By the time of Manley's letter, Groves had already organized a special Army battalion at Sandia to take over surveillance, field tests, and assembly work. At the end of October, Los Alamos was still processing the Oak Ridge and Hanford product, fabricating normal uranium parts, and producing electric detonators, but Groves was moving on his objectives. He had arranged for Monsanto to assume important responsibilities in the manufacture and development of components at Dayton, Ohio. He was considering the transfer of uranium purification and reduction to Oak Ridge and of pluto-nium operations to Hanford. Los Alamos applauded this trend. The scientists agreed that the laboratory should give up routine production and devote its energies to the weapons of the future.[31]

1946 COMMITMENTS: RESEARCH

While the nation's capacity to produce fissionable material and bombs held first priority, General Groves did not forget research. He recognized its im-portance to national security. He knew it offered the only chance of holding the interest and co-operation of American scientists. Early in February, 1946, he informed Chief of Staff Eisenhower that it was essential to make commit-ments for fiscal year 1947 if the Army was to prevent disintegration of its nuclear research organization.

633

Before Groves could prepare a budget proposal, he needed some guidelines. In September, 1945, the Scientific Panel of the Interim Committee had submitted a comprehensive set of proposals for research and develop-ment. Though this was a splendid effort, it quite properly took the long view. What Groves needed was counsel on definite steps for the coming year. At the suggestion of Colonel Nichols, he appointed an Advisory Committee on Re-search and Development consisting of seven men who had figured promi-nently during the war—Robert F. Bacher, Arthur H. Compton, Warren K. Lewis, John R. Ruhoff, Charles A. Thomas, Richard C. Tolman, and John A. Wheeler.

On March 8 and 9, 1946, the committee met in the Manhattan District's Washington offices with Nichols and representatives from some of the insti-tutions sponsoring proposals. Nichols explained that the Army needed advice on both policies and specific programs. Groves would submit a budget based on the committee's recommendations.

On broad policy, the committee agreed that the Manhattan District should expand its activities to include a larger number of qualified agencies. This expansion was to further research and development in the production of fissionable materials and useful power as well as advance training in nuclear studies and the acquisition of fundamental scientific information. The work undertaken in universities and private laboratories should be limited pri-marily to fundamental research of an unclassified nature. If such investiga-tions led to discoveries which might have direct military application or other-wise affect the national welfare, further development could take place either at universities or private laboratories on a separate classified basis or at Government laboratories where classified work was the norm. National labo-ratories should be established for the primary purpose of pursuing unclassi-fied fundamental research that required equipment too expensive for a uni-versity or private laboratory to underwrite. Government reservations—the

Clinton Engineer Works, for example—were the place for semiworks and other installations associated with commercial exploitation or industrial skill. Enterprises that were hazardous from the medical or legal standpoint should be established at remote federal installations rather than at universities or private laboratories.

The committee envisioned the national laboratories as important channels through which Government funds would flow to nourish nuclear research. Each laboratory should have a board of directors chosen from the universities and other institutions participating. Though some financially responsible and mutually acceptable agency would perform the work of administration, the board of directors would submit research proposals and budgets. Final approval of both must remain with the Manhattan District.

As a start, the Advisory Committee proposed establishing two laboratories—one at Argonne and another somewhere in the northeastern states. Since the preceding November, a regional study group had been at work on a co-operative plan to utilize the Argonne facilities. The Manhattan District should invite the interested institutions to set up a board of directors and seek a satisfactory contract with the University of Chicago for administering Argonne. The northeastern project, not so far advanced, needed preliminary planning and organizing. The Advisory Committee also looked favorably on a national laboratory in the West, but it judged that Groves should take no action until the prospective participants there submitted a definite joint proposal.

For fiscal year 1947, the Advisory Committee recommended fixing the Manhattan District research and development budget at from twenty to forty million, depending on the manpower available. As for specific programs, the committee favored support for two reactor projects. The first was Zinn's fast-fission pile. Qualified reviewers should determine whether it was safe to construct the reactor at Argonne. The second was a high-temperature power pile that Farrington Daniels of the Metallurgical Laboratory had been planning since 1944. Projected as a vertical, helium-cooled unit, it was a lineal descendant of the Moore-Leverett "Mae West" pile of 1942. The Advisory Committee recommended assigning design and construction to Monsanto at Clinton. Believing the project to have broad scope and great importance, the committee urged that Monsanto have the assistance of the Metallurgical Laboratory, the General Electric Company, Westinghouse, the Navy, and such institutions as the Massachusetts Institute of Technology. This would help spread knowledge of nuclear technology.

The committee endorsed the distribution of radioisotopes at cost and advocated Government support for a reasonable health program. It recommended that the Manhattan District continue to subsidize nuclear physics at Berkeley with the understanding that the University of California would assist other American institutions in the design of accelerator equipment. The committee felt the Army should discuss with Lawrence the possibility of giving the Radiation Laboratory status as a special type of national laboratory.[32]

The Manhattan District concurred in these recommendations and developed a budget that went beyond them. Not counting some $19 million set aside for such costs as housing and utilities at Los Alamos and Oak Ridge, Groves scheduled the expenditure of $72.4 million for research. Of this, 68 per cent went for construction—$20 million for Clinton, $10 million for the laboratory General Electric was to operate at Schenectady, $9.4 million for the proposed northeastern national laboratory, $5 million for Argonne, $2.5 million for the University of California, and $2.5 million for miscellaneous laboratories throughout the Manhattan District. The remaining funds—$23 million—were assigned to operating expenses. Argonne and Clinton were to have the lion's share, the northeastern laboratory and the University of California each about half as much, with the rest dispersed among nine other institutions, principally the University of Washington, the University of Rochester, Iowa State, Columbia, the Massachusetts Institute of Technology, and the Battelle Memorial Institute. The Military Appropriation Act of July 16, 1946, marked the first specific appropriation of federal funds for atomic research and development.[33]

635

The summer of 1946 saw the first steps to turn plans to reality. At the Clinton Laboratories, a co-directorship—James H. Lum and Eugene P. Wigner—replaced Whitaker, who had resigned to become president of Lehigh University. Under their leadership, Clinton turned to the development of new piles. On June 15, the Advisory Committee on Research and Development approved a Clinton proposal to build a heterogeneous research reactor fueled by enriched uranium, moderated by heavy water, and cooled by ordinary water. Since this was a very expensive unit from the standpoint of money and critical materials, the Army did not authorize construction. On August 23, the sponsors adopted an alternate design—a reactor moderated as well as cooled with ordinary water and equipped with a beryllium reflector. This decision meant new design studies, which were not likely to be complete before the summer of 1947. Clinton's hope for a power reactor rested on the Daniels pile the Advisory Committee had endorsed in March, 1946. Working on a co-operative basis with specialists from industry, the universities, and Governmental agencies, C. Rogers McCullough's Power Pile Division developed a detailed preliminary design proposal which was ready for Wigner's review on November 1.[34]

Closely associated with the Clinton reactor effort was basic research and a training program. Design work continually demanded fundamental investigations in physics, chemistry, and metallurgy. For biological studies, the laboratory arranged for the United States Public Health Service to furnish qualified personnel and make recommendations on research needs. In August, Monsanto established a school for training a nucleus of technical personnel in the various fields of nuclear science. Originally conceived as a small, postdoctorate seminar, in practice it enrolled well over two hundred individuals—employees of Monsanto and other Oak Ridge contractors as well as Government employees, including a contingent of Army and Navy officers.[35]

The most publicized activity at Oak Ridge was the distribution of radioisotopes. The Clinton air-cooled pile was an ideal tool to produce radioactive materials for research. During the war, it had supplied investigators at Chicago, Hanford, and Los Alamos. Its products had been particularly important at Los Alamos—alone enough to justify its construction. In May, 1946, Groves received a report from his Interim Advisory Committee on Isotope Distribution Policy, a group headed by Lee A. DuBridge, the wartime director of the Radiation Laboratory at MIT. The committee advocated immediate establishment of a major program to prepare and distribute those radioisotopes currently available at prices no greater than the out-of-pocket cost to the Manhattan District. For a start, the committee favored giving priority to publishable research in the fundamental sciences which needed only small samples. Next priority should go to therapeutic applications in humans and fundamental research requiring large samples, followed by education and training and by publishable research in the applied sciences. Groves accepted these recommendations, and the June 14 issue of *Science* carried a formal announcement listing isotopes available, distribution principles, and procurement machinery. On August 2, 1946, Director of Research Wigner and Deputy District Engineer Elmer E. Kirkpatrick stood before the face of the Clinton pile and delivered the first peacetime product of the atomic energy plant, a one-millicurie unit of carbon 14, to Dr. E. V. Cowdry of the Barnard Free Skin and Cancer Hospital of St. Louis.[36]

Groves moved quickly to create the national laboratories advocated by his Advisory Committee on Research and Development. On April 19, 1946, the University of Chicago accepted a letter contract to operate an Argonne National Laboratory. On June 13, representatives of the twenty-four midwestern institutions that desired to participate submitted a statement on organization and operating policy. Gratified that it followed the Advisory Committee recommendations, Groves announced that the Manhattan District intended to negotiate a formal contract with the University of Chicago that would permit Argonne to function in accord with the suggested principles.

Security restrictions delayed active participation of the co-operating universities, but the staff left over from Metallurgical Project days pushed ahead. Argonne continued to support Hanford with research on Redox and graphite expansion. It turned to developing fuel rods for the Daniels pile and continued designing the fast-breeder reactor. Since the latter demanded extensive research and laboratory development, Groves's unwillingness to authorize construction did not inhibit Zinn. Perhaps the most important efforts of his investigators at this stage were those pointing the way to a novel metal coolant, a sodium-potassium alloy which was liquid at room temperatures.[37]

The project for a national laboratory in the Northeast did not proceed so smoothly. After three months of discussion, nine private universities decided to band together and operate the facility as Associated Universities, Inc. On August 1, just two weeks after the New York State Board of Regents granted AUI its charter, Groves announced selection of Camp Upton on Long Island as the site. Christened Brookhaven National Laboratory, the new installation became the subject of hot disagreement. The Argonne planners had agreed that final responsibility for the approval of research programs and budgets rested with the Government. Some of the AUI trustees, however, held out for little or no control. Groves did not believe the federal authorities should pass on detailed laboratory experiments, but he argued that public officials could not abdicate their duty to exercise ultimate approval of research programs, budgets, general administrative practices, wages, and salaries. In November, the issue was still in deadlock.[38]

Groves was unable to carry the national laboratory concept further. A West Coast national laboratory at Berkeley or elsewhere remained only a possibility. Nonetheless, Manhattan District funds for the 184-inch cyclotron, the synchrotron, and a forty-foot linear accelerator strengthened the position of the Radiation Laboratory as a center without equal for the study of high-energy physics. A southeastern national laboratory seemed unnecessary. Led by William G. Pollard, a University of Tennessee physics professor who had worked on gaseous diffusion at Columbia, fourteen universities had organized the Oak Ridge Institute of Nuclear Studies. Representing institutions spread in a great arc from the District of Columbia to Texas, the Oak Ridge Institute proposed to assist Monsanto in scientific staffing and its sponsors in using the Clinton Laboratories for academic research and in gaining federal support. In April, the Manhattan District approved the project in principle. In October, the institute received a Tennessee charter of incorporation. On October 31, just as the Atomic Energy Commission was taking up its duties, Pollard submitted a draft contract to the Army authorities. To a considerable degree, the combination of Clinton and the Oak Ridge Institute gave the Southeast the equivalent of a national laboratory.[39]

At the end of October, 1946, General Groves looked back on a trying year. In many respects, it had been more difficult than the three-year campaign for the bomb. Before Hiroshima and Nagasaki, he had the advantage of leading a great wartime effort. Operating under security wraps with virtually unlimited funds and authority, his word was law. After the war, he had to carry on in a frustrating political environment that permitted no sharp definition of national goals. While the American people returned headlong to peacetime pursuits and values, domestic legislation bogged down in bitter controversy, and negotiations for international control dragged on interminably. The Manhattan District suffered. Yet it would have been unrealistic to expect anything else. The measure of Groves's achievement was not that some segments of the atomic energy project declined from the high standards of the war years but that he had accomplished so much with the cards of circumstance stacked against him.

637

FIRST STEPS

The President's appointments to the Atomic Energy Commission were widely acclaimed. Robert R. Wilson, speaking for the FAS, looked on October 28 as one of the most hopeful days since Hiroshima. "The high caliber of the appointees is an indication of the importance attached to the posts by our Government, and we are gratified that such good men accepted this responsibility." The *New Republic* praised "a set of appointments the like of which the capitol has not seen for 18 months." Arthur Krock in the New York *Times* proclaimed the President's action "a triumph of careful choosing." The Louisville *Courier-Journal* called it "a good commission, drawing diversity and strength of mind from men skilled in organization, in science, in business and in humanity." The Chicago *Times* thought it "an extraordinarily excellent commission." Similar reactions came from other newspapers of every range of opinion from *PM* to the Washington *Times-Herald*. Only the Hearst and the Communist press chose to complain. The Baltimore *News-Post* predicted a "bitter fight" against the confirmation of "certain key members" for their "internationalist, pro-Soviet and leftist affiliation." The *Daily Worker* thought the new commission would retain the American "monopoly of atomic energy." [40]

638

A good press was a valuable asset for a new Government agency, but it was almost the only one the Commission had on the morning of October 29. It had no offices, no funds, no secretaries, no staff, no budget, no files, and no property. To help him slap together the rudimentary administrative machinery, Lilienthal had arranged for the temporary services of three former associates in his recent atomic energy activities. Herbert Marks and Carroll Wilson were his two principal assistants on the Board of Consultants to the Acheson committee. Marks, still serving as Acheson's assistant, had an office in the old State-War-Navy Building, which would serve as the first home of the new Commission. Wilson had just recently returned to Boston after his wartime hitch at OSRD as Bush's assistant. Joseph A. Volpe had served on Groves's legal staff during the war and as his liaison officer with the Acheson and Baruch groups.

Putting first things first, the three young men tackled the prosaic but important housekeeping details. A meeting with Colonel Charles Vanden Bulck from Colonel Nichols' staff on the evening of October 29 opened the way to funds for the Commission's current expenses. The Army agreed to furnish limited office space in the New War Department Building, where General Groves maintained his Washington headquarters. Both the Army and OSRD could provide temporary secretarial and clerical help. [41]

Meanwhile, the Commissioners were trying to .wind up their personal affairs and move to Washington. At the time of their appointments all of them were living outside the capital, though Pike and Strauss had apartments there. Lilienthal had resigned as chairman of TVA but was off fulfilling previous speaking engagements during the last days of October. Strauss had to withdraw from the financial activities to which he had only recently returned after his retirement from active service in the Navy. Bacher had to provide for the future of the nuclear research program he had just established at Cornell. For Waymack, there was unfinished business at the Federal Reserve Bank in Chicago.

The new Commissioners had opportunities to become better acquainted during early November. On the fourth, Lilienthal, Bacher, and Pike arrived at the Manhattan District headquarters in Oak Ridge to snatch a first glimpse of their new domain. The following week, there were meetings with the Attorney General and other Washington officials. On Armistice Day, Senator McMahon entertained the Commissioners at a luncheon at the Metropolitan Club.

By this time, the character of the Commission and its working assumptions had begun to emerge. By temperament and experience, Lilienthal seemed the ideal chairman. He spoke of the Commission as a family representing a variety of talents and points of view. His job was to bring the talents to bear on the immense problems the Commission faced and to develop a strong consensus for action. Leaving the administrative details to his staff, Lilienthal liked to let his mind soar above the work-a-day world in search of the fundamental issues in the human predicament. His sense for publicity, his flair for the dramatic would help him to project the life-and-death issues of atomic energy into the lives of average Americans.

In many respects, Pike was a reverse image of Lilienthal. His folksy manner and appearance seemed to fit the rough isolation of the Maine coast much better than the cosmopolitan atmosphere of Washington. But the facade of a weather-beaten New England fisherman ill concealed his sharp mind, intellectual curiosity, and penetrating wit. An omnivorous reader, Pike was well versed in the life sciences, geology, politics, history, and finance. Impatient with stuffed shirts, he never hesitated to express his opinion of anyone or anything. This he did with a humor that made him a congenial and constructive adviser.

Waymack found that he had much in common with Pike. Both were products of nineteenth-century, rural, Republican America. His honors in journalism testified to his fine judgment of public policy, bolstered by genuine human warmth and common sense. Waymack had an instant pal in Pike and quickly developed a lasting friendship with his young scientific colleague, Robert Bacher.

As the youngest member of the Commission, its only scientist, and its only member with any extensive knowledge of atomic energy, Bacher could not help looking somewhat self-consciously on his position as a representative of the scientists who had built the bomb. Although he had not been directly associated with the scientists' movement during the preceding year (perhaps

639

an important factor in his appointment), Bacher shared the scientists' distrust of the Army. He had not welcomed his appointment but accepted it as a heavy obligation. He would carry his share of the load with quiet, serious determination.

Somehow, Strauss stood apart from his colleagues. A self-made man, he had combined a quick mind with tireless energy and ambition to find success in a variety of careers. During the first World War, he had caught the eye of Herbert Hoover, who asked him to become his personal secretary. While achieving financial independence on Wall Street between the wars, Strauss found time to serve in the Naval Reserve. In 1941, he went on active duty as staff assistant to the Chief of Ordnance. With an interest in science stemming from his philanthropic activities, he became increasingly concerned about the Navy's plans for postwar research and development. In 1945, he had become Forrestal's principal adviser on this subject and had replaced Ralph Bard as a member of the Interim Committee. Beneath his debonair manner was an impatience for action that ran counter to the deliberative spirit of a Lilienthal commission.

Out of the informal meetings of these men in early November came a set of working assumptions which largely determined the Commission's operating philosophy. Never discussed formally, they were more fundamental than many decisions that required hours of debate. There was no need, for example, to argue the wisdom of rigorously separating the Commission from politics. Exclusion of politics had been Lilienthal's cardinal principle at TVA, even though playing the patronage game with Senator McKellar might have made his job easier. Lilienthal was convinced that only by eschewing political entanglements could the Commission maintain the integrity that would permit it to draw on public opinion for support. Despite the bitter fight in Congress on the Act, atomic energy and the Commission still enjoyed a special, nonpartisan status in the minds of most Americans. Most of the problems the Commission faced seemed so far from those of everyday life that the Commission could hope to maintain its preferred status indefinitely if it exercised a little prudence.

Equally implicit was the decision to retain the Army's system of contractor operation. Though the original McMahon bill required Commission employees in the plants, the Act permitted contractor operation as long as the Commission owned the property. In a practical sense, perhaps there was no other choice. It was hard to imagine how the Commission in the midst of all its other concerns could recruit and train the thousands of scientists and technicians then furnished by private industry. There was nothing in the Act, however, requiring the Commission to be practical. That it did make this choice, albeit implicitly, was significant. It meant that the Commission could operate with a small staff in Washington, that most of its work would be performed by universities and private industry, and that a large share of the de-

THE FIRST PEACETIME PRODUCT OF ATOMIC ENERGY / Clinton Laboratories Research Director Eugene P. Wigner delivers one milli-curie of carbon 14 to Dr. E. V. Cowdry, Barnard Free Skin and Cancer Hospital, St. Louis, Missouri, August 2, 1946.

Left to right: Prescott Sandidge, Clinton Laboratories; Wigner; Cowdry; Colonel Elmer E. Kirkpatrick, Deputy District Engineer.

PRESIDENT TRUMAN TRANSFERS CONTROL TO THE ATOMIC ENERGY COMMISSION, DECEMBER 31, 1946 / The President is signing the executive order formally transferring control from the Army, effective 12:01, January 1, 1947. General Manager Carroll L. Wilson is on the President's right; Chairman David E. Lilienthal on his left. Standing, left to right: Commissioner Sumner T. Pike, Colonel Kenneth D. Nichols, Secretary of War Robert P. Patterson, General Leslie R. Groves, Commissioner Lewis L. Strauss, Commissioner William W. Waymack. The fifth Commissioner, Robert F. Bacher, was at Los Alamos.

tailed administrative controls would be decentralized to field operations. All these conditions conformed with Lilienthal's philosophy of public administration.[42]

By the second week in November, the Commission was ready for business. Carroll Wilson had obtained five offices on the sixth floor of the New War Department Building for the Commissioners and three on the second floor for the staff. Though inadequate, they would serve as makeshift headquarters until a permanent home could be found elsewhere in Washington. On November 7, the Treasury transferred the first $1 million from Army to AEC accounts. Temporarily the Manhattan District would manage the account, provide travel authorizations and transportation requests, make personal service contracts for the temporary staff, and pay the Commissioners' salaries. By this time, Lilienthal had borrowed two former TVA employees as consultants—Richard O. Niehoff on organization and personnel and Paul W. Ager on budget and accounting.[43]

641

FIRST VIEW

The Commission's first order of business was to inspect the scattered empire of plants and laboratories to be inherited from the Army. On Tuesday, November 12, the five Commissioners left Washington for Oak Ridge with Wilson, Volpe, and Marks. The next morning, the first formal meeting occurred in the rambling administration building overlooking Black Oak Ridge. After endorsing the preliminary actions which Lilienthal and his assistants had already taken, the Commission adopted five administrative orders. The first appointed Wilson as Acting Administrative Officer. The second gave Alphonso Tammaro, one of Groves's former officers, authority to make personal service contracts, the form of which was prescribed in the third order. The fourth authorized personal service contracts for the existing staff pending FBI investigations. The fifth adopted a system for classifying and handling Restricted Data, as defined in the Atomic Energy Act. Leaving all other decisions until their return to Washington, the Commissioners embarked on their tour.

There was scarcely enough time on Wednesday, November 12, to visit all the production sites in the Clinton Engineer Works, but the Commission saw enough to be tremendously impressed with the gaseous-diffusion plants. They were fascinated to learn that production-control officers had concluded K-25 and K-27 could replace Y-12.[44]

The Commission spent most of Thursday flying in an Army B-25 over the heartland of America to Los Alamos. The Commissioners were up bright and early the next morning for a briefing on weapon research and production. As the day passed, the optimism engendered in Oak Ridge faded away. Bacher, already concerned about the dismal morale among scientists at the

Clinton Laboratories, found the situation at Los Alamos much worse. If the Army's efforts to rehabilitate the laboratory had effected some improvement during the summer of 1946, the esprit de corps was far from that which Bacher remembered in 1945. Worse than that, some of the Commissioners sensed a lack of purpose and vigor in weapon development and production. They left Los Alamos on Saturday morning convinced that the nation's strength in nuclear weapons was far less than they had been led to believe.[45]

Monday, November 18, found the Commissioners in Berkeley. Lawrence, full of confidence and enthusiasm as usual, guided his guests on a tour of the Radiation Laboratory. For the first time, they saw the giant 184-inch magnet operating as a cyclotron after three years of wartime service in the electromagnetic project. They examined the original horizontal tanks still within the jaws of the 37-inch cyclotron, soon to be moved to the Los Angeles campus. Looking to the future, Edwin McMillan explained his electron synchrotron and Luis Alvarez the linear accelerator then under development in the laboratory. Like most visitors to Lawrence's hilltop retreat, the Commissioners left Berkeley with the comforting feeling of having observed a dynamic, firmly directed research enterprise.[46]

The schedule next called for a visit to Hanford, but the mounting pressure of business in Washington forced postponement of that leg of the tour. Instead, the Commissioners climbed into their plane and headed for Chicago. After a harrowing flight through severe icing conditions, the group arrived at Midway Airport tired, hungry, and shaken. That evening there was time only for a dinner with Walter Zinn and his staff at International House. The next morning, the Commission had barely started to review plans for the new Argonne National Laboratory before the plane left for Washington.

FIRST DECISIONS

Back in Washington on November 21, the Commission faced up to the hard decisions involved in assuming its responsibilities under the Act. The first task was to effect the transfer of property, personnel, and records from the Manhattan District. The whirlwind tour through a small portion of the Army project suggested some of the complications to be encountered in transfer. The size and diversity of the Army's holdings made it virtually impossible for the Commissioners to discover in a short time just what they were inheriting.

The Army had approached the transfer with dispatch. As soon as the President announced his appointments, General Groves designated Colonel Nichols as his liaison with the new agency. Nichols began at once to draft a detailed plan, portions of which were waiting for the Commissioners when they returned from their western trip.

Carroll Wilson, who had left the tour at Los Alamos, had already obtained a consultant from the Treasury Department to study the fiscal aspects

642

of transfer. It did not take long to conclude that the Commission would need a detailed audit of all source and fissionable materials. The first general discussion of the mechanics of transfer occurred on the morning of December 3 in preparation for an afternoon session with Groves and Nichols. Most of the talk centered on the manner of transfer and the record of the transaction. The Commissioners assumed there would be a public Executive Order describing the broad terms of the action as well as a detailed classified inventory of property. The Commission thought it "desirable and feasible" that the transfer occur at midnight, December 31, 1946.

The afternoon meeting with the Army started out smoothly. Groves accepted the transfer date and the need for a precise accounting of materials and bomb parts. He warned, however, that only he and Nichols had access to all this information. He urged the Commission to restrict its dissemination as much as possible and suggested that he brief the Commissioners on this subject with the members of the Military Liaison Committee. On two issues there was disagreement. The first, a relatively minor one, arose from the Commission's insistence on a detailed inventory of property other than materials and weapons. Groves held that the Army's accountability records made the inventory unnecessary; in any event such an inventory could not be completed by the end of the year.

643

The second disagreement sprang from the Commission's desire for a precise understanding of the facilities to be transferred. Lilienthal thought the public order should adhere closely to Section 9 of the Act, which specified all fissionable material, weapons and weapon parts, all equipment and processes for producing or utilizing fissionable material, all technical information, patents, and contracts, all research and development facilities, and "such other property owned by or in the custody or control of the Manhattan Engineer District or other Government agencies as the President may determine." Did not the Army wish to except some properties from the transfer? The Commission wanted to know exactly what properties these were. Groves doubted that a detailed list of exceptions could be ready by December 31. He suggested that the order contain general language transferring every item covered in Section 9 "except those which were principally military and were agreed upon by the Secretary of War and the Chairman of the Commission."

Further discussion revealed the General's assumption that all weapons and weapon facilities would be excepted from transfer. This certainly was not the Commission's understanding of the Act. In its view, Section 9 required the transfer of *all* Manhattan District property to the Commission, with any subsequent transfers back to the armed services, as provided in Section 6, to be considered later. Thus did the question of weapon custody first appear in the transfer negotiations. For the moment, neither side hit the issue head-on—the Commission standing on its interpretation of the Act, Groves arguing that Commission custody was impractical without the transfer of military personnel. It was not difficult, however, to detect overtones of the old civilian-military control controversy.

The session with Groves and Nichols helped to define the issues of transfer. On December 5, Wilson told the Commission there was some doubt that the necessary fiscal and administrative procedures could be established for the new agency by December 31. Accepting the possibility of a few weeks' delay, the Commission was determined to plan for a New Year's transfer. Wilson would struggle with the administrative arrangements and draft a letter to Groves formally establishing the December 31 date. Marks would draft an Executive Order to accompany the letter. Meanwhile, the Commission plunged into the bundle of policy questions which Groves had left on its doorstep.[47]

Having to deal with General Groves and his staff surely complicated the Commission's task. The transfer of authority was always an awkward, touchy procedure, but the General's personality and attitude imposed additional obstacles. Whatever the facts, Groves had come to think of the project as his own personal creation. On one occasion he frankly told a Commissioner that he was in the position of a mother hen watching strangers take all her chicks. The Commission could not expect him to be gracious or enthusiastic about the process. The Commissioners respected Groves for his accomplishments and appreciated his position. But their situation was even more difficult. For all their experience and ability, they did not have the basic understanding that had become second nature to Groves and his officers. At best, Groves thought the Commissioners were well-intentioned novices who had wandered into waters far over their heads. Atomic energy was a highly technical, deadly serious business; it was not a subject, as one officer put it, to be entrusted to a group of unrestrained idealists, most of whom had not the slightest comprehension of the technical issues involved. No longer free to act on his own, Groves chafed under what he considered the fumbling indecision of the Commission. In turn, the Commission balked at what they saw as Groves's attempt to force them to ratify his decisions without study. Under the circumstances, it was surprising, not that the Army and the Commission had their differences, but that they accomplished their mission with so little friction.

Though the story had two sides, there was no question of the fact that there were vital questions requiring immediate decision. The Army could decide those issues with a short-term effect, but only the Commission could make those decisions involving a commitment for the years ahead.

One of the first items on the agenda for November 21 was the contract with the General Electric Company for operating the Hanford plant. The initial letter of intent and the contract negotiated in September were due to expire on November 30 unless the Commission approved the contract by that time. The Commission agreed that continued operation of Hanford was essential, but it needed more information about the negotiations between the

Manhattan District and the company. Much to Groves's annoyance, the Commission asked Volpe and Marks to gather the data and report back. They discussed the contract with Nichols and Harry A. Winne and arranged for the Commissioners themselves to talk with Winne on November 27. Still not completely satisfied, the Commission asked Nichols to extend the letter contract for sixty days, to January 30, 1947, to permit the Commission to study the definitive document in greater detail.[48]

Groves was greatly concerned about establishing the new national laboratories. He explained at the meeting on December 3 that the Army was already committed to support the Argonne and Brookhaven laboratories and was contemplating a third in California. It was imperative, he said, that the Commission act soon on approving the contract for Brookhaven and a new site for Argonne.

The shift of the experimental pile to Clinton early in 1943 left the original Argonne site with little more than the few buildings associated with the rebuilt Fermi pile and the CP-3 heavy-water reactor. The site was reasonably well isolated in the Argonne Forest Preserve, but it could not be considered for a permanent laboratory unless the Cook County Commissioners would agree to sell the land or grant a long-term lease. As alternatives the Corps of Engineers had inspected a site farther to the southwest along the Des Plaines River in Du Page County and existing facilities at the Kankakee Ordnance Works near Joliet. At first favoring the Kankakee site, the Engineers had changed their minds when Daniels and Zinn argued that the location was too far from Chicago to make commuting practical to the city and the university campus. Both the Army and Argonne came to the Commission with recommendations for the Du Page site. The Commission's initial reaction on November 26, however, was to favor the original Palos Park location in the Argonne Forest Preserve. No decision would be made until the Commission had satisfied itself that the Palos Park area could not be obtained. Marks and an assistant plunged into the Army's records of the decision and made plans for a trip to Chicago before the Commission agreed to invite Daniels and Zinn to come to Washington to discuss the subject.

645

While the Army simmered with impatience, the Commission turned to other business. The meeting with the Argonne and Army officials on December 12 produced only a commitment from the Commission to approve condemnation proceedings for the Du Page site if the Cook County Commissioners refused to reconsider their decision by December 20. Failing to obtain a favorable decision on the Palos Park land, the Commission continued to postpone condemnation of the Du Page County tract. The issue was still hanging fire at the end of 1946.[49]

General Groves was no more successful in prodding the Commission on the Brookhaven contract. Receiving a copy of the proposed agreement from the Army late in December, the Commission saw no possibility of examining its provisions before the end of the year. The group of universities sponsoring the new laboratory felt handicapped in organizing the enterprise, especially in recruiting scientists, by the lack of a definite commitment from the Government. Bacher learned, however, that the association was also unhappy about some of the provisions the Army negotiators had placed in the contract. Just enough of the scientists' hostility toward the Army had rubbed off on the Commissioners to cause them to give the scientists the benefit of the doubt, at least until the proposed contract could be studied. The Commission would not act on the contract until the Army was out of the picture, but Lilienthal wired the association that the Commission strongly favored the Brookhaven project and was relying on Associated Universities, Inc., "to press ahead with the development of plans and arrangements, including recruitment, for the early establishment of the laboratory." [50]

646

On one Army request the Commission did choose to act. On December 19, Nichols explained the background of a draft letter from General Groves recommending shutdown of Y-12 and use of the gaseous-diffusion plants to produce highly enriched uranium 235. The November-December trials had demonstrated that the electromagnetic plant was no longer necessary. Shutting down Y-12 would permit Tennessee Eastman to cut employment in the area from 8,600 to 1,500 and operating expenses by more than $2 million per month. The next day, the Commission received the formal letter from Groves requesting a decision by December 24. He had to know at once whether to continue operating the gaseous-diffusion plants to produce highly enriched material or to cut them back to their original role of preparing partially enriched feed for Y-12. On December 23, Lilienthal told Groves the Commission would approve closing down all but one Beta track at Y-12. The news broke in Oak Ridge the day after Christmas. A stirring chapter in the history of the wartime project was drawing to a close.[51]

The most unpleasant problem inherited from the Army was personnel security. Groves reported that under the exigencies of war, the Army had granted clearances to certain individuals "despite evidence indicating doubt as to character, associations, and absolute loyalty." The Army had also employed a number of Canadians and British citizens whose continued service would be a technical violation of the Atomic Energy Act. The Commission readily agreed to the Army policy of retaining foreign nationals who had taken out first papers for American citizenship and who were considered loyal and trustworthy. More difficult was the question of how to act on the doubtful security cases. Presumably, these would have to be studied individually. There was no choice but to postpone that onerous task until the transfer period was over.[52]

In some areas, like the declassification of information, the Commission had little choice but to accept the decisions the Army had already made. Any declassification policy worthy of the name required a tortuous analysis of the complexities of nuclear technology. The Army had first tackled these in 1945 and was just beginning to put its plan in operation when the Commission was appointed. There could be no thought of changing the course the Army had set without careful staff study.

Early in November, 1945, when the scientists' campaign for freedom of research was reaching its climax and contractors were clamoring for the Army to declassify reports relating to their wartime work, Groves asked Richard C. Tolman to draft a declassification policy. On November 12, he assembled a committee in his office at the California Institute of Technology in Pasadena. Bacher, Lawrence, Oppenheimer, Spedding, and Urey made up the group. John Ruhoff served as secretary. Though the committee was not convinced that concealing scientific information could long contribute to national security, it seemed inevitable that the Government resort to continued classification in some areas. Using a topical list of production and research activities in the Manhattan project, the committee assigned each subject to one of three categories: information recommended for immediate declassification; information whose declassification would be conducive to the national welfare and to long-term national security; and that not recommended for declassification. The committee suggested that the list serve as a temporary declassification guide. Tolman proposed a procedure whereby directors of laboratories and other organizations would select documents for declassification and submit them to one of several Responsible Reviewers, according to subject matter. The Reviewers would recommend action by the Manhattan District declassification office after checking the documents against the guide and the Army patent regulations.

647

During the last weeks of 1945, Tolman polished his report through correspondence with his committee and met with the heads of thirteen major Manhattan District contractors to learn their views. Discussing the report with Groves in New York on December 29, 1945, Tolman found the General "friendly to a liberal declassification policy" but concerned about the adverse public reaction to release of the Smyth Report. Nonetheless, with firm support from Tolman and his committee, Groves was willing to proceed. Tolman sent a strong letter to Senator McMahon in February to support the Army's declassification policy, and Groves cleared his proposal with Secretary Patterson and President Truman early in March. Colonel Kenneth E. Fields directed the preparation of the formal declassification guide during April and had the organization established by July. Following Fields's recommendation, Groves appointed four Senior Responsible Reviewers: Warren C. Johnson for the pile project, Willard F. Libby for gaseous diffusion, Robert L. Thornton for electromagnetic separation, and John H. Manley for weapons. Before the end of 1946, the committee of reviewers held three meetings and declassified about 500 documents. Scientists outside the project were probably correct in dismissing this accomplishment as an insignificant gesture, but they could not have appreciated the amount of work the reviewers had devoted to studying the great variety of complex technical categories and preparing detailed guides. However meager the first results might seem, the Commission was inheriting a carefully conceived, well organized administrative procedure.[53]

APPOINTMENTS

Creating a new agency involved above all finding the people to operate it. While policy issues held the center of the stage during the last six weeks of the year, the Commission could never escape the nagging demands of selecting men for important positions and then inducing them to accept.

One of the Commission's first acts was to consider possible appointments to the General Advisory Committee. The Act stated the committee would "advise the Commission on scientific and technical matters relating to materials, production, and research and development, to be composed of nine members, who shall be appointed from civilian life by the President." Bacher interpreted this language to mean a committee of chemists, physicists, metallurgists, and engineers. The Commission agreed, but decided to announce at the time of the appointments its intention to establish other advisory committees representing medicine, biology, geology, mining, and the social sciences.

648

By December 5, Bacher and Carroll Wilson had a list of twelve names. From these, the Commission selected the nine it would nominate first. The other three would be held in reserve as alternates. The names sent to the President on the ninth included some of the most experienced and talented participants in the wartime effort—Conant, Oppenheimer, Fermi, Seaborg, Cyril S. Smith, and Hood Worthington, a du Pont official on the Hanford project. The three nominees less closely associated with the Manhattan District were men of undisputed eminence. Lee A. DuBridge was the new president of the California Institute of Technology. Isidor I. Rabi, a Nobel physicist from Columbia, had been an associate director of the MIT Radiation Laboratory. Hartley Rowe had been a consultant at Los Alamos and had directed the development of transportation equipment at OSRD.

Presidential approval came the following day, and Wilson dispatched appointment papers to the new members. Conant, DuBridge, and Oppenheimer received the six-year appointments. Rowe, Fermi, and Seaborg would serve for four years; Worthington, Rabi, and Smith for two. Wilson arranged for the committee to hold its first meeting in Washington immediately after New Year's.[54]

Appointment of the Military Liaison Committee was the responsibility of the Secretaries of War and Navy. As early as July, General Groves had considered possible nominations. When the Commission was finally established in October, Groves was ready to act. On November 4, 1946, the military services announced their appointments. Lieutenant General Lewis H.

Brereton, a veteran air officer of two world wars, was named chairman. Ranking officer on the Navy side was Rear Admiral Thorvald A. Solberg, Admiral Mills's deputy on the Tolman Postwar Policy Committee and long interested in nuclear propulsion for submarines. The only member with extensive experience in the Manhattan District was Rear Admiral William S. Parsons.[55]

Appointment of the Director of Military Application was an overlapping responsibility. By law, he was to be a member of the armed forces. While the Commission would make the final choice, nominations presumably would come from Secretary Patterson. Even before the Act was passed, Groves had decided that Nichols, his right arm on the Manhattan project, should have first priority for any Commission appointment. Thus the Colonel was the War Department's only nominee.

The Commission's encounters with Nichols during the transition period had been pleasant. They found the Colonel a competent, self-confident, businesslike administrator. His experiences with the Manhattan project made him a skilled negotiator with Government officials, scientists, and engineers at any level. And he was a veritable walking encyclopedia on the Manhattan District. Despite his obvious qualifications both professionally and personally, the Commission had second thoughts about making him a key member of its staff. First was the simple need for a fresh start. The transition from Army to civilian control would be difficult at best. A clean break would probably be less painful for both sides. Second, the Commission found itself in fundamental disagreement with Nichols on the function of the statutory division. Nichols explained in a letter to the Commission that he considered the division a "line" organization. By this he presumably meant that the Director of Military Application would be responsible for all activities in this field, which he interpreted to include a large fraction of the Commission's program. The Commissioners agreed on December 10 that they saw the job more as a "staff" function. The director would be expected to concentrate on military planning and policy formulation rather than operating problems.

A week later, Carroll Wilson had spelled out the "staff" and "line" concept more carefully in a memorandum to his superiors. Since the Commission expected to continue the Manhattan District practice of contractor operation, the four statutory divisions should be "staff" units. "The Division of Military Applications," Wilson maintained, "will be concerned with the broad and complicated inter-relationships between military planning and the research, development, and production programs of the Commission."

Acceptance of this view seemed to exclude Nichols, whose experience lay "largely in administration and production." There was some concern that refusal of the nomination might reflect unfairly on Nichols, embitter relations with the Army, or hurt morale among Army officers on the Manhattan project. None of these factors seemed, however, to outweigh the Commission's

649

responsibilities. Lilienthal agreed to ask Patterson and Forrestal for additional nominations. These did not arrive until after Christmas. By that time, it was too late to complete the action before take-over.[56]

Most important of all was the selection of the general manager. At its first meeting in Oak Ridge on November 13, the Commission briefly considered the mechanics for selecting a nominee and asked the temporary staff to canvass top Government officials and leaders in universities and industry. The fourteen men consulted came up with thirty-three suggestions for the job. To narrow down the choice, the Commission appointed an advisory panel consisting of Karl T. Compton, Georges Doriot of the Harvard Business School, Herbert Emmerick, director of the Public Administration Clearing House, and John Lord O'Brian, an eminent Washington lawyer with long Government experience. Starting with the Commission's list and adding suggestions of their own, the panel sifted through dozens of names. The result was a list of about eight contenders, upon whom the Commissioners concentrated their attention. H. Rowan Gaither, Jr., assistant director of the MIT Radiation Laboratory during the war, James R. Killian, Jr., vice president of MIT, and Edwin R. Gilliland, a chemical engineer at MIT, all declined to be considered. Others were eliminated for one reason or another. As Christmas approached the Commission still had no general manager.

One leading contender who remained was Carroll Wilson. Nominated by the advisory panel, Wilson was not at first considered, if only because of his close ties to the Commission as head of the temporary staff. Although Wilson had, for his years, an extraordinary record of experience in academic administration, industry, and Government, he had not at thirty-six held in his own right responsibilities comparable to those of some of the candidates. But as others dropped one by one from the list, Wilson's name looked ever more attractive. As the Commission's Acting Administrative Officer since November 13, he had been efficiently performing many of the duties of a general manager under the most trying conditions. In the last analysis, only his age seemed to be against him, and that hardly seemed a legitimate objection. As one Commissioner remarked when Wilson was asked to accept the post on December 26, the problem was not that Wilson was too young but that the Commissioners were too old to be coping with the problems of the future. Lilienthal wrote the President that the Commission's choice was based on Wilson's strong endorsement by men like Bush and Conant, "the peculiarly relevant experience which he has had, [and] the combination of youth, energy, and mature judgment which he will bring to the office."

The formal announcement of Wilson's appointment as general manager did not come from the White House until December 30. There was little time to think about selecting a staff in the last hours before take-over, but Wilson had already made a start. The temporary staff, the military officers under Colonel Nichols, and the Manhattan District civilian personnel would carry on the essential functions until the new general manager organized his team.[57]

TRANSFER

Within a few days after the December 3 meeting with Groves and Nichols, Wilson and Marks completed the letter and Executive Order reflecting the Commission's position on transfer. The letter, sent to Groves on December 9, noted the transfer would be accomplished by January 1, 1947. The Army would have a complete inventory of all fissionable materials and weapons by that time and would account for all other property as soon as possible. Following his instructions, Marks drafted the Executive Order around Section 9 of the Act. It would require transfer of all atomic energy properties and materials held by the Army and other Government agencies. There was no mention of exceptions or of the administrative details. Wilson planned to include these in a second, highly classified document.

651

Nichols' draft of the transfer papers manifested the disparity of the Army's views. The list of thirty-seven installations to be transferred to the Commission was impressive, but the Commissioners were more interested in the exceptions. These included the Sandia Base near Alburquerque, weapon storage facilities then under construction at various sites, the Naval Ordnance Testing Station at Inyokern, the three Army ordnance works where the heavy-water plants were operating, and an Army installation at Kansas City. Nichols also proposed to except two important activities from the transfer— the raw-materials procurement function of the District's New York office and the Army's special intelligence operation on atomic energy.

Unable to make much sense out of the memorandum at their meeting on December 13, the Commissioners invited Nicholas to join them. He explained that the ordnance works could not be transferred because they were not exclusively Manhattan District property, but he did contemplate transfer of the District's interest in the heavy-water facilities. He confirmed Groves's willingness to surrender the raw-materials function if the Commission accepted membership on the Combined Policy Committee and the Combined Development Trust. This the Commission refused to do pending a review of these activities in light of the Act's provisions on international cooperation. As for intelligence, the Army thought all its operations should be transferred to the new Central Intelligence Group. Here again the Commission wanted more information before making a commitment.

Above all, Nichols emphasized Army retention of Sandia and the new storage sites. The War Department thought it essential to the strategic defense of the United States that the armed services have custody of all weapon stockpiles. This, Nichols explained, meant not only weapons but bomb parts and fabricated fissionable materials ready for assembly. All other items would remain in the custody of the Commission, which might ask the Army to guard the property but would not relinquish control of its disposition and use. Assuming that weapon custody would be the main point of contention in the transfer order, Nichols spared no argument. Actually, he could have saved some of his fire. The Commission agreed among themselves both before and after the meeting with the Colonel to accept the Army's position but only after a full report on the production and stock-piling of materials and weapons. The Commission was much more concerned at the moment about the transfer of the intelligence function.

Events of the next several days, however, heightened the Commission's anxiety over custody. Nichols' own draft of the Executive Order on December 16 was built around Section 9 of the Act, but to every paragraph he had added what General Groves called an "elastic exception." The phrase went: "excepting those functions, facilities, materials, and equipment of a military character which the Secretary of War or Navy and the Commission mutually agree will remain under the custody of the War or Navy Department." The draft also provided that the Army retain $30 million for the excepted functions. The only Army revision the Commission was prepared to accept was that extending to the new agency the armed forces' wartime authority to negotiate contracts without regard to existing laws.

Hard on the heels of Nichols' draft came a set of documents from General Brereton. The chairman of the Military Liaison Committee seemed to assume that the question of weapon custody was already settled. In addition to a proposed charter for the committee, he submitted detailed plans for the division of responsibility for weapon research, development, production, and storage and a set of long-range objectives for producing and stock-piling materials and weapons.

If the Army was trying to convince the Commission of the wisdom of military custody, the effort had precisely the opposite effect. By pressing its suit too insistently, the Army had reawakened the old scruples about civilian control. On December 17, the Commission turned again to the legal requirement for complete transfer under Section 9. The retransfer of weapons to the military, it concluded, was "a matter of political decision to be made by the President," which could not be accomplished by an agreement with the Military Liaison Committee. In any event, the Commission could not come to any understanding even on principle until it had studied production and stockpile statistics. These the Commission hoped the MLC could provide at the first joint conference that afternoon.[58]

This tougher attitude on custody was reflected in the revised draft of the Executive Order which the Commission reviewed on December 19. Fol-lowing Wilson's suggestion, the Commission would insist on two transfer orders. The public order would closely resemble the December 9 draft in sticking close to the language of Section 9 with no exceptions. One change would be a new paragraph providing for automatic transfer of all civilian personnel from the Manhattan District and allowing the detail of military personnel for a limited period. The classified order would authorize retransfer of weapon materials and facilities under Sections 6 and 12.

All the signs of a head-on collision with the Army were apparent when the Commission received General Groves's reply to the December 9 draft. In decidedly angular language, Groves took issue with every major point in the Commission's version. He insisted on military custody of weapons, transfer of the intelligence function to the Central Intelligence Group, no transfer of raw-material operations until the question of the Combined Development Trust membership was resolved, and all the exceptions in Nichols' original list. Groves's letter left the unfortunate impression that the Army's version of the Executive Order and transfer plans was not subject to negotiation.

Time proved, however, that the Commission, not the Army, would prevail. In a second session with Nichols on December 19, the Commission explained its plan for two transfer orders. Nichols was assured that "the transfer orders would preserve the integrity of Sandia and other storage bases as military bases, both in respect to real property and military personnel, and that the initial transfer order was concerned with the transfer of atomic weapons and fissionable materials at these bases." Nichols fought for military custody to no avail. He left the meeting convinced only that he had wrecked any possibility of his appointment as the Commission's first Director of Military Application.[59]

653

With time now running out, Wilson sat down with Marks and the rest of his staff on Saturday, December 21, to lay plans for the last ten days of the year. Marks was to have the Executive Order in final form by Monday noon to send to the Bureau of the Budget and the War and Justice Departments. Although Marks hoped to clear the way by appealing directly to the Budget Director and the Assistant Solicitor General, the order would probably not be signed before December 31. Meanwhile, Ager had completed arrangements to have $500 million transferred from Army accounts to the Commission by Monday evening. Still to be accomplished was processing the appropriation warrant, providing funds for field disbursing officers, extending General Accounting Office activities at field installations, preparing instructions for operating under Treasury disbursement regulations, determining budget allotments for the third quarter of the fiscal year, and printing transportation requests and bills of lading. Niehoff had a long list dealing with personnel matters, including transfer orders for civilian and military officers, and the transfer of records. Tammaro and others had the job of assuring the continuation of essential activities, including communication and real estate services, safety programs, maintenance and procurement of equipment, and contractor operations.

The Commissioners were mostly concerned with the transfer order. On Monday afternoon, the twenty-third, Marks had completed the Executive

Order and a draft letter to Secretary Patterson. The order itself was quickly approved and dispatched to other agencies for clearance. The letter was complicated in that it attempted to define the Commission's position on transferring each of the facilities which the War Department proposed to except from the order. The Commission would not retreat from its demand for a simple transfer order with no exceptions, but it was willing to make some concessions to the Army. It would require that all Manhattan District interests in Sandia, the storage sites, and the ordnance works be transferred, but this would not mean transfer of the bases themselves, physical properties, or military personnel. Likewise, the Commission would insist on transfer of all weapons, parts, and fissionable materials, but would accept the Army demand to submit to the President not later than March 1, 1947, a recommendation for retransfer. The Commission indicated its intention to resolve the question of CDT membership in time to permit appropriate action on that issue. On the intelligence function, the Commission would refuse to act until it had the facts. The major points in the letter were acceptable, but Marks left the meeting with enough minor changes to delay transmittal until after the Christmas holiday.[60]

654

The only remaining issues were raw materials and intelligence. On December 26, the Commission concluded that to maintain control of source materials it would have to participate in the Combined Development Trust. Commission membership in CDT would inevitably reveal to Congress and the public the existence of both CDT and the Combined Policy Committee. Under the circumstances, the Commission thought the Administration would do well to dissolve CPC as quickly as possible, since its continued operation appeared to be illegal under the Atomic Energy Act. If the State Department could assure that the CPC would be disbanded and that Congress would be informed of the wartime arrangement, the Commission was willing to accept membership on the CDT and possibly on the CPC for a temporary period. Four days later, Marks reported the results of his discussions with his former boss at the State Department. Acheson found Secretary Byrnes willing to report the existence of the CPC to Congress but reluctant to put his intention in writing. The Commission then asked Marks to draft a letter to the CPC informing the committee of the Commission's acceptance of membership on the CDT and Byrnes's intention to inform Congress of the wartime arrangement.[61]

On the intelligence question, the Commission decided to insist on complete transfer while reserving the right to determine what phases of the activity might be given to the Central Intelligence Group. The Commission knew, however, that Secretary Patterson had sent the Bureau of the Budget a revision of the Executive Order, which included Army retention of the intelligence function. Anticipating strong opposition from Patterson, the Commission authorized Lilienthal to resort to a compromise which would grant the Commission full access to all the Manhattan District's intelligence files.

Lilienthal's meeting with Patterson late on Monday afternoon, December 30, went about as expected. Patterson agreed to transfer the raw-material function when Lilienthal revealed Marks's discussion with Acheson. Wilson would replace Groves on the CDT, Volpe would fill an existing vacancy on the American side, and Charles K. Leith would continue to serve temporarily. Patterson's position on the intelligence function was so immutable that Lilienthal had to fall back on the compromise. He would agree to leave intelligence temporarily in the War Department if the Secretary would agree to let Wilson, Volpe, and Edwin E. Huddleson examine all the records. Thus were the last issues of transfer resolved.[62]

THE NEW WORLD

On Tuesday afternoon, just a few hours before the New Year's deadline, Lilienthal, Pike, Waymack, Strauss, and Wilson gathered in the President's office to witness the signing of the Executive Order. Patterson, Groves, and Nichols represented the Army. Bacher was in Los Alamos to inventory the weapon stockpile. For the inevitable photograph, Wilson sat at the President's right, Lilienthal on his left. Standing behind were the other Commissioners, the Secretary, and the Army officers.

At midnight, Groves was left with nothing but a paper command. The world had changed since those frenzied days in September, 1942, when he accepted the unenviable task of transforming a few laboratory experiments into the most powerful weapon man had ever seen. By tremendous courage and daring intuition he had accomplished his mission. The victory won, he had held the project together and handed it reasonably intact to his successors. Now he felt history suddenly shove him into the past. He had said as much in his farewell message to the Manhattan project.[63]

Five years ago, the idea of Atomic Power was only a dream. You have made that dream a reality. You have seized upon the most nebulous of ideas and translated them into actualities. You have built cities where none were known before. You have constructed industrial plants of a magnitude and to a precision heretofore deemed impossible. You built the weapon which ended the War and thereby saved countless American lives. With regard to peacetime applications, you have raised the curtain on vistas of a new world.

But what did that new world promise America? A golden age of scientific progress, human betterment, and international understanding or a blackened earth of destruction and death? No one person had the answer, but the nation looked with a hope and a prayer to the five men who would lead them into the new world of the atom.

655

SOURCES

Folklore has it that the United States developed the atomic bomb without benefit of paper work. Striving for speed with security, American leaders forsook the reports and memorandums dear to the bureaucrat. With memories for files, Pullman compartments for offices, crisp spoken commands for directives, and steel and concrete for progress reports, they made the decisions that shook the world. Like all legends, these tales have some basis in fact, but the impression they create is false. The wartime atomic energy program must rank with the most thoroughly documented enterprises in history.

In retrospect, the reasons are apparent. The atomic bomb was a two-billion-dollar gamble. If the wager were lost, Congress would demand an explanation. The men who had staked their reputations on the outcome wanted written evidence to justify their decisions. Farther down the scale of responsibility, scientists of all ranks thought automatically in terms of research reports. The war might preclude the usual ritual of publication, but it could not throttle the inbred urge to write up the experiment. Nor could all the secrecy and hurry of the crisis prevent contract officers from requiring detailed progress reports on the expenditure of public funds.

The records have survived. For this, scholars can thank two much-maligned practices of the bureaucracy: classification and multiple copies. Classified documents endure; they do not disappear from the files as souvenirs. As for copies in sextuplicate, their survival is a matter of simple arithmetic. If the original in one agency is destroyed, the chances are better than even that one of the five carbons will escape the flames in another.

UNPUBLISHED SOURCES

ARCHIVAL COLLECTIONS

The bulk of the manuscript records lie in Government archives. Though large sections remain classified, the number of documents available to independent scholars is rapidly increasing. For those who would study the decision-making process, the most important single collection is the Records of the Manhattan Engineer District at the World War II Records Division of the National Archives, Alexandria, Virginia. Here are the correspondence, general administrative, investigative, fiscal, and foreign intelligence files of General Leslie R. Groves's Washington headquarters. Here are the records accumulated by

George L. Harrison and Harvey H. Bundy, Secretary of War Henry L. Stimson's assistants on atomic energy. The two collections are essential for understanding the Army's role at both the administrative and policy levels.

Another rich storehouse is the Oak Ridge, Tennessee, Operations Office of the United States Atomic Energy Commission. Since Oak Ridge was the headquarters of the Manhattan District Engineer, the central mail and records files there contain data from the entire project. Scores of file drawers are devoted to the Oak Ridge plants: Y-12, K-25, X-10, and S-50. The stacks of periodic status reports are essential for tracing the efforts to design, build, and operate the facilities. Oak Ridge also holds the Records of the SAM Laboratories, the gaseous-diffusion research project at Columbia University.

Oak Ridge maintains a complete file of the research reports prepared at the various Manhattan District laboratories. Many of these reports have been declassified and are available through eighty-five depository libraries in the United States and seventy-nine abroad. To provide a guide, the Atomic Energy Commission has published *Abstracts of Declassified Documents* (1947–48) and *Nuclear Science Abstracts* (1948—). For a quick orientation, the investigator should turn to another Commission publication, *What's Available in the Atomic Energy Literature,* TID-4550 (6th Rev., March 1960).

658

The records of the Hanford Operations Office at Richland, Washington, are not so extensive as those at Oak Ridge, for they are limited to a single installation. Their value lies in data on the construction and operation of the Hanford works. Of signal interest are the personal diary of Colonel Franklin T. Matthias, the Production Office Diary of Major Joseph F. Sally, and the eleven volumes of memorandums on operating experience to July 1, 1945.

Further details on the wartime program lie in the quasi-governmental archives of Atomic Energy Commission contractors. The Argonne National Laboratory, Lemont, Illinois, preserves the files of the Metallurgical Project. These include Director Arthur H. Compton's correspondence with the Oak Ridge and Washington headquarters as well as internal memorandums and other documents. Among the most interesting holdings of the Lawrence Radiation Laboratory at Berkeley, California, are the papers of Ernest O. Lawrence relating to atomic energy, 1940–46. The Los Alamos Scientific Laboratory, Los Alamos, New Mexico, retains a full record of the war years. Each laboratory has its numbered series of research reports.

Though the Atomic Energy Commission did not assume responsibility until January 1, 1947, the Commission has custody of some material dating from earlier years. At its Germantown, Maryland, headquarters are certain technical records transferred from the Manhattan District and a few small collections acquired over the years. Especially useful is the diary of Joseph W. Kennedy, chief of the Chemistry and Metallurgy Division at Los Alamos. The Commission also holds the atomic energy records of the Office of Scientific Research and Development and its predecessor agencies. This collection includes the notes and correspondence of Vannevar Bush and James B. Conant. On the mechanics of transfer from the Manhattan District in 1946, the Commission files are helpful. They include correspondence, draft orders, internal memorandums, and the official minutes and informal notes for the first seventeen meetings.

The United States Department of State is the focal point for any investigation of American policy on international control. The Records of the Special Assistant to the Secretary on Atomic Energy and of the United States Delegation to the United Nations Atomic Energy Commission are indispensable. The Records of the Bureau of the Budget reveal Director Harold D. Smith's part in persuading the White House to withdraw support from the May-Johnson bill and in shaping the McMahon bill. In the National Archives in Washington there are two important sets of records: those of the Senate Special Committee on Atomic Energy and of the OSRD Administrative Office. The legislative records include large amounts of public-opinion mail as well as internal staff memorandums and annotated drafts. The OSRD records consist largely of Vannevar Bush's correspondence on legislation and international control. The Library of Congress Manuscript Division has acquired the Records of the National Committee on Atomic Information.

The principal private archives in the atomic energy field are in the University of Chicago Library, which has specialized in the records of the postwar scientists' movement. The most valuable groups are the Records of the Atomic Scientists of Chicago, of the *Bulletin of the Atomic Scientists*, and of the Federation of American Scientists. The FAS documents, which contain the Washington headquarters files, are especially valuable for the light they throw on the dynamics of an effective pressure group.

PERSONAL MANUSCRIPTS

Despite the relatively short time that has elapsed since World War II, important sets of personal manuscripts have already found places in institutional collections. Most important for the student of atomic energy are the Papers of Henry L. Stimson at the Yale University Library. Stimson's diaries for the war years rank among the great private records of our time. His daily entries, read against the documentary background, make it possible to trace the details of American policy at the highest level. The Papers of Franklin D. Roosevelt at Hyde Park, New York, are disappointing, for Roosevelt usually avoided keeping atomic energy documents in his files. Among those he retained, however, is the American copy of the Hyde Park *Aide-Mémoire*. The most significant atomic energy records at Hyde Park are in the Papers of Harry L. Hopkins. Here is much of the correspondence necessary for an understanding of the Anglo-American controversy on interchange. The materials open to researchers at the Harry S. Truman Library in Independence, Missouri, are not particularly helpful. Mostly incoming correspondence reflecting public opinion, they do not touch the main stream of policy in 1945 and 1946. At the scientific level, the Papers of Ernest O. Lawrence are deposited at the Lawrence Radiation Laboratory and those of Enrico Fermi at the University of Chicago Library. Except for the Lawrence files on atomic energy, these papers are more important for the general history of science than for the details of the wartime enterprise.

Most personal manuscripts are still in private hands. The papers of John R. Dunning reflect the early excitement at Columbia University. John R. Simpson, Jr., has interesting documents that stem from his work with the scientists' lobby; Byron S. Miller has saved what may be the best records on the drafting of the McMahon bill in late 1945. Carroll L. Wilson has fragmentary notes on the November, 1945, interdepartmental study group on international control, and Bernard M. Baruch has preserved extensive files on his role as American representative on the United Nations Atomic Energy Commission. The papers of James F. Byrnes, though they contain several interesting documents, help little in re-creating the evolution of policy.

MANUSCRIPT HISTORIES

Immediately after the war, a number of manuscript histories were prepared. Most important is the voluminous "Manhattan District History" compiled at General Grove's direction to record the project's achievements in research, design, construction, operation, and administration. Though repetitious, compartmentalized, and uneven in quality, the thirty-five volumes assemble much information in a systematic, readily available form. The "Manhattan District History" contains extensive annotations, statistical tables, charts, engineering drawings, maps, and photographs. Its preparation was an act of foresight.

659

The Atomic Energy Commission, the Defense Atomic Support Agency, and the World War II Records Division have copies. An unclassified version of the main volume on Los Alamos has been published recently as Los Alamos Scientific Laboratory Report LAMS-2532. To supplement this historical series, Groves's Washington headquarters drafted a "Diplomatic History of the Manhattan Project." Less historical narrative than special plea, this volume is important for the point of view it reflects. The Atomic Energy Commission, the Department of State, and the World War II Records Division hold copies.

E. I. du Pont de Nemours and Company prepared two multivolumed histories describing its part in the plutonium project: "Construction Hanford Engineer Works" and "Design and Procurement History of Hanford Engineer Works and Clinton Semi-Works." The AEC Hanford Operations Office has a copy of each. Useful but less ambitious is the Tennessee Eastman Corporation's "C.E.W.-T.E.C. History, January 1943 to May 1947" held by the Oak Ridge Operations Office.

660   PUBLISHED SOURCES

BOOKS ON NUCLEAR TECHNOLOGY

First stop on an investigation of nuclear technology in printed sources is Henry D. Smyth's *Atomic Energy for Military Purposes*, preferably the Princeton edition with its additions, corrections, new appendices, and index. The principal shortcomings, as Ambassador Smyth is quick to point out, are the inadequate treatments of the research at Columbia University and of chemistry generally. The reader who wishes to explore the technology further must turn to the *National Nuclear Energy Series*, some one hundred volumes arranged in ten groups. Work on this series started at the end of the war, when the Manhattan District ordered the preparation of a complete record of research accomplished under project contracts and established an Editorial Advisory Board to plan a unified acount. More than half the resulting volumes are unclassified and readily available.

The Atomic Energy Commission's Division of Technical Information has published more than 125 volumes on nuclear science and technology. Several of these—for example, Clement J. Rodden, ed., *Analytical Chemistry of the Manhattan Project* (New York, 1950) and Charles D. Harrington and Archie E. Reuhle, eds., *Uranium Production Technology* (Princeton, 1959)—aid in understanding the developments of the war years. Among independently published volumes on nuclear science, one thinks immediately of Glenn T. Seaborg's *The Transuranium Elements* (New Haven, 1958).

GOVERNMENT PUBLICATIONS

Publications of both the executive and legislative branches of the federal government bring together a great amount of data in convenient form. The career of the wartime director of Los Alamos may be followed in U. S. Atomic Energy Commission, *In the Matter of J. Robert Oppenheimer* (Washington, 1954). A September, 1955, Department of Defense press release, *The Entry of the Soviet Union into the War Against Japan: Military Plans, 1941-1945*, prints several documents that reveal American military thinking in the spring of 1945. On Potsdam, the standard source is the magnificently edited publication of the U. S. Department of State: *Foreign Relations of the United States: Diplomatic Papers. The Conference of Berlin (The Potsdam Conference)* (2 vols., Washington, 1961). The United States Strategic Bombing Survey documented the destruction wrought by the first two nuclear weapons in *The Effects of the Atomic Bomb on Hiroshima, Japan* (3 vols., [Washington], 1947) and *The Effects of the Atomic Bomb on Nagasaki, Japan* (3 vols., [Washington], 1947).

Three publications of the Department of State print the basic documents on international control: *The International Control of Atomic Energy; Growth of a Policy* (Washington, 1946), *The International Control of Atomic Energy; Policy at the Crossroads* (Washington, 1948), and *Documents on Disarmament, 1945–1959* (2 vols., Washington, 1960). For the full record the student should turn to the *Official Records* of the United Nations Atomic Energy Commission and to the mimeographed AEC documents reporting the proceedings of its various committees.

PERSONAL NARRATIVES

Leslie R. Groves, *Now It Can Be Told; The Story of the Manhattan Project* (New York, 1962), reports how the Army discharged its nuclear mission. General Groves is at his best in depicting the atomic strikes of 1945 from the perspective of his Washington headquarters. He is less successful in explaining his contributions to the Manhattan District's achievements in construction and process development.

661

Autobiographies by scientists are rare. Arthur H. Compton's *Atomic Quest; A Personal Narrative* (New York, 1956) complements the Groves memoir by emphasizing scientific research and development. *Atoms in the Family* (Chicago, 1954), Laura Fermi's delightful book, emphasizes the human-interest side of her husband's life and work.

Autobiographical accounts at the policy level are often valuable. Winston Churchill's *The Hinge of Fate* (Boston, 1950) includes fragmentary references to the interchange issue from the British point of view. His *Triumph and Tragedy* (Boston, 1953) reports shrewd insights into the thinking of American leaders at Potsdam. President Harry S. Truman's *Memoirs* (2 vols., Garden City, N. Y., 1955–56) are a forthright record of events as he remembers them. Henry L. Stimson and McGeorge Bundy, *On Active Service in Peace and War* (New York, 1947), records Stimson's preoccupation with the large issues raised by the advent of atomic energy. James F. Byrnes's two volumes, *Speaking Frankly* (New York, 1947) and *All In One Lifetime* (New York, 1958), disappoint in their failure to discuss atomic energy policy in detail. Nevertheless, they contain several illuminating passages. *Baruch: The Public Years* (New York, 1960) is a smooth narrative that softens the clash of personalities. James R. Newman and Byron S. Miller, *The Control of Atomic Energy; A Study of Its Social, Economic, and Political Implications* (New York, 1948), is an analysis by the men who drafted the original McMahon bill. For Miller's account of the legislative fight see "A Law Is Passed: The Atomic Energy Act of 1946." *University of Chicago Law Review*, XV (Summer, 1948), 799–821.

In a different category are *The Forrestal Diaries* (New York, 1951) and *The Private Papers of Senator Vandenberg* (Boston, 1952). Until the Forrestal and Vandenberg papers are open generally to scholars, these printed collections will have to serve. A word of caution: both volumes are frankly selective, and dates in the Vandenberg book are unreliable.

·SECONDARY ACCOUNTS

Despite widespread interest in the nuclear revolution, historians have been reluctant—with good reason—to write about it. While it is possible to discuss the basic science without access to classified materials, no one can proceed to the heart of the technological story without seeing documents still secret. Those who have tried to write on the basis of interviews alone have encountered trouble. Apart from its apparent tendentiousness, Robert Jungk's *Brighter than a Thousand Suns; A Personal History of the Atomic Scientists* (New York, 1958) is hopelessly inaccurate. Ronald W. Clark, *The Birth of the Bomb* (New York, 1961), though more urbane, suffers from dependence on memories twenty years old.

It is around the edges of the atomic energy story that the good work has been done. A. Hunter Dupree, *Science in the Federal Government; A History of Policies and Activities to 1940* (Cambridge, 1957), surveys the relations between the federal government and the scientific community. Irvin Stewart, *Organizing Scientific Research for War* (Boston, 1948) analyzes the administrative organization of the Office of Scientific Research and Development. James P. Baxter, 3rd, *Scientists Against Time* (Boston, 1947), makes it possible to see atomic energy against the backdrop of the entire OSRD scientific offensive. Don K. Price, *Government and Science, Their Dynamic Relation in American Society* (New York, 1954), reviews postwar planning for federal support of science. To understand the priority crisis the Manhattan District faced in the summer of 1942, the student should turn to R. Elberton Smith, *The Army and Economic Mobilization* (Washington, 1959). George O. Robinson, Jr., who was there, re-creates the boomtown spirit of construction days in *The Oak Ridge Story* (Kingsport, Tenn., 1950). Daniel Lang also demonstrates a feel for the excitement that pervaded the war and postwar years in his *Early Tales of the Atomic Age* (New York, 1948).

The climactic summer of 1945 has attracted more scholars than any other period in atomic energy history. The best discussion of policy is Herbert Feis, *Japan Subdued; The Atomic Bomb and the End of the War in the Pacific* (Princeton, 1961). Based on some but not all relevant Manhattan District records, this volume is marred by defects of organization and focus. It should be supplemented by another Feis diplomatic history, *The China Tangle* (Princeton, 1953). John Ehrman had access to official British documents for *Grand Strategy, October 1944-August 1945* (London, 1956), a volume in the United Kingdom *History of the Second World War*. Elting E. Morison's *Turmoil and Tradition; The Life and Times of Henry L. Stimson* (Boston, 1960) would be more satisfying had the author used the pertinent War Department atomic energy files to trace the development of Stimson's position in more detail. The best single volume in Japanese end-the-war maneuvering is Robert J. C. Butow, *Japan's Decision to Surrender* (Stanford, 1954). For the combat delivery of the first weapons, see Wesley F. Craven and James L. Cate, eds., *The Army Air Forces in World War II*; Volume V, *The Pacific: Matterhorn to Nagasaki, June 1944 to August 1945* (Chicago, 1953) and Fletcher Knebel and Charles W. Bailey II, *No High Ground* (New York, 1960).

Surprisingly, historical scholarship has been slow to tackle the postwar fight for domestic and international control. Textbook writers have accepted without question the usual clichés about civilian vs. military control. Margaret L. Coit's pages on international control in *Mr. Baruch* (Boston, 1957) should be used cautiously. Three recent volumes approach American international control policy in scholarly temper: Richard J. Barnet, *Who Wants Disarmament?* (Boston, 1960), Bernhard G. Bechhoefer, *Postwar Negotiations for Arms Control* (Washington, 1961), and Joseph L. Nogee, *Soviet Policy toward International Control of Atomic Energy* (Notre Dame, Ind., 1961). All depend on published sources.

INTERVIEWS

The historian who ventures to write on anything so recent as the development of atomic energy faces formidable obstacles. For one thing, he lacks the perspective that only time can give. For another, he is apt to have difficulty seeing the papers of men still alive and active. Yet the historian of the contemporary scene has a great compensating advantage: he can go behind the documentary record in his search for the ideas and human relationships that bring the records to life. The personal interview is his tool. Recognition of its importance, heightened when death cut short the careers of Enrico Fermi and John von Neumann, played an important part in the Atomic Energy Commission's 1957 decision to establish a history project.

Like all historians, the authors recognized that the memory of man is fallible. We knew that granting the best of memories, an interview is likely to degenerate into random and superficial recollections if the researcher does not ask the right questions. For this reason, we tried to prepare ourselves thoroughly before each appointment. We studied the written record and devised questions that struck at both the central issues and the relevant details. Usually, we conducted the interview jointly, taking what notes seemed appropriate during the course of the conversation and dictating full notes as soon as we departed. Though aware that some scholars have successfully recorded interviews on tape, we concluded that this technique would destroy the atmosphere of informality we desired.

We have talked with substantially more than one hundred individuals who possess special personal knowledge of the events discussed in this volume. Some had been junior scientists or technicians. Others had held posts ranging in responsibility up to the Presidency itself. Despite months of interviewing, we saw only a fraction of those who must have useful recollections. To all who believe they could have provided details and forestalled errors had we but sought them out, we plead only the demands of time and circumstance.

663

For help on the period 1939 to 1941, those years of uncertainty when the United States was groping toward a justifiable program, we talked with Philip H. Abelson, Keith F. Adamson, Samuel K. Allison, Herbert L. Anderson, Gregory Breit, Lyman J. Briggs, Vannevar Bush, Arthur H. Compton, James B. Conant, John R. Dunning, Edwin M. McMillan, Robert S. Mulliken, Robert Oppenheimer, Alexander Sachs, Glenn T. Seaborg, Henry D. Smyth, Leo Szilard, Hugh S. Taylor, Harold C. Urey, John A. Wheeler, and Eugene P. Wigner.

To further our understanding of the Manhattan District and its operations, we turned to Harvey H. Bundy, Vannevar Bush, James B. Conant, John A. Derry, Leslie R. Groves, Kenneth D. Nichols, Samuel R. Sapirie, Harry S. Traynor, James E. Travis, Charles Vanden Bulck, and Joseph A. Volpe, Jr.

Only a few of those we interviewed were in a position to see the wartime technical work as a whole: Vannevar Bush, James B. Conant, Leslie R. Groves, Eger V. Murphree, Kenneth D. Nichols, Henry D. Smyth, and Charles A. Thomas. Compartmentalization prevented most men from knowing even one process through all its stages from research through design and construction to operation. For that reason, we had to consult many individuals on the larger projects in order to obtain an adequate check on our documentary research.

On the electromagnetic process, we interviewed G. M. Banick, Jr., Donald Cooksey, Harold A. Fidler, B. Harmatz, W. H. Hoose, Duncan M. Lang, John P. Murray, Wallace P. Reynolds, Theodore P. Sprague, F. M. Tench, C. D. W. Thornton, Robert L. Thornton, and William K. Whitson, Jr. On gaseous diffusion, we saw Frank P. Baranowski, Harvey A. Bernhardt, Clark E. Center, Lauchlin M. Currie, John R. Dunning, George T. Felbeck, Percival C. Keith, Robert H. Lafferty, Seymour A. Levin, J. A. Marshall, Francis T. Miles, D. A. Overton, J. A. Parsons, H. G. P. Snyder, Hugh S. Taylor, and Harold C. Urey. On liquid thermal diffusion, Philip H. Abelson, Chad J. Raseman, and Arthur E. Ruark provided valuable counsel.

The far-flung plutonium project, which extended from Chicago southeast to Oak Ridge and northwest to Hanford, required many hours of interviewing. We saw Fred W. Albaugh, Edrey S. Albaugh, Samuel K. Allison, Herbert L. Anderson, Joseph W. Baker, E. E. Beauchamp, Howard E. Berg, Arthur H. Compton, Donald D. Deming, Warren K.

Eister, Emery T. Filbey, Charles T. Groswith, Norman Hilberry, Thorfin R. Hogness, F. E. Jochen, Harold F. Lichtenberger, Arthur Z. Lassila, Francis J. McHale, Edward F. Miller, Jr., Robert S. Mulliken, Edgar J. Murphy, B. F. O'Mealy, Harry E. Parker, John R. Parrott, G. S. Sadowski, Glenn T. Seaborg, Morris L. Short, John A. Simpson, Jr., Henry D. Smyth, Leo Szilard, Charles A. Thomas, James E. Travis, John A. Wheeler, Eugene P. Wigner, Roger Williams, Hoylande D. Young, and Walter H. Zinn.

Los Alamos was the capstone of the wartime effort. We had the privilege of discussing the work of the laboratory with Samuel K. Allison, Herbert L. Anderson, Robert F. Bacher, Norris E. Bradbury, John J. Burke, William A. Higinbotham, Robert D. Krohn, Robert Oppenheimer, Charles A. Thomas, Stanislaw M. Ulam, Paul A. Wilson, and John H. Williams.

Moving from the technical program to the vexing international issues it engendered, we sought the guidance of Dean G. Acheson, Robert F. Bacher, Harvey H. Bundy, Vannevar Bush, James F. Byrnes, Benjamin V. Cohen, Arthur H. Compton, James B. Conant, Leslie R. Groves, David E. Lilienthal, John J. McCloy, Herbert S. Marks, Robert Oppenheimer, James T. Shotwell, Charles A. Thomas, Harry S. Traynor, Harry S. Truman, Harold C. Urey, and Carroll L. Wilson. Domestic legislation, related in many ways to the international questions, required assistance from Vannevar Bush, James B. Conant, Leslie R. Groves, Edward H. Levi, John W. McCormack, Byron S. Miller, James R. Newman, Lewis L. Strauss, Harry S. Truman, Joseph A. Volpe, Jr., and Carroll L. Wilson. For the scientists' movement of 1945–1946, we turned to Samuel K. Allison, Herbert L. Anderson, William A. Higinbotham, Norman Hilberry, Thorfin R. Hogness, John A. Simpson, Jr., and Harold C. Urey.

We discussed the transfer of Manhattan District property and responsibilities with the first Commissioners: Robert F. Bacher, David E. Lilienthal, Sumner T. Pike, Lewis L. Strauss, and William W. Waymack. Leslie R. Groves and Kenneth D. Nichols provided further help on the period of transition, as did three members of the original AEC staff: Herbert S. Marks, Joseph A. Volpe, Jr., and Carroll L. Wilson.

PHYSICAL SURVIVALS

More than a century ago, Francis Parkman demonstrated how important it was for the historian to visit the scene of his narrative. We have tried to follow his example and to know not only the geographical setting of the wartime project but also the buildings and equipment that have survived. We located the Washington offices of many project leaders. We visited the campus laboratories at Columbia, Chicago, and Berkeley. In Oak Ridge, we lived for three weeks in the Guest House in sight of the Manhattan District "castle" and Jackson Square. We toured the production sites and clambered through K-25, Y-12, and X-10, studying the converters, the calutrons, the pile, and the separation pilot plant. At Hanford, we savored the desert air, explored the foundations of the dismantled construction camp, and checked our understanding, based on reports and drawings, against the great B pile itself, still in operation as a tribute to the skill of the engineers and craftsmen who built it. We even rode in the huge bridge crane above the concrete canyons where the plutonium for Trinity and Nagasaki was separated. Finally, we went to Los Alamos. Few technical buildings and quarters of the early nineteen-forties still stand, but the mountains, mesas, and canyons endure to help the visitor understand the lives of the men who built the bomb.

We hope that the days spent inspecting the physical survivals add to the value of this book. We know that we write with greater confidence for having extended our research beyond the written and the spoken word.

NOTES

The notes which follow are more a guide to the sources of this volume than a complete documentation of the narrative. From them, the reader can determine quickly the most significant manuscripts and published material which bear on the subjects of his particular interest. He will find, however, that the notes do not identify information that depends on interviews. With the development of atomic energy so charged with controversy, with so many of the participants still active, most witnesses were understandably reluctant to speak for attribution. Forced to choose between a full story and adherence to the accepted canons of scholarly annotation, we selected the first alternative with clear conscience.

One further caveat: the citation of documents does not imply that the materials are unclassified or that they are necessarily available for examination by the public.

665

THE NOTES

AEC   Records of Headquarters, U. S. Atomic Energy Commission, Washington, D. C.

ANL   Records of the Argonne National Laboratory, U. S. Atomic Energy Commission, Lemont, Illinois.

ASC   Records of the Atomic Scientists of Chicago, University of Chicago Library, Chicago, Illinois.

BAS   Records of the Bulletin of the Atomic Scientists, University of Chicago Library, Chicago, Illinois.

BOB   Records of the Bureau of the Budget, Washington, D. C.

BMB   Papers of Bernard M. Baruch, New York, New York.

BSM   Papers of Byron S. Miller, Chicago, Illinois.

DS   Records of the U. S. Department of State, Washington, D. C.

FAS   Records of the Federation of American Scientists, University of Chicago Library, Chicago, Illinois.

FDR   Papers of Franklin D. Roosevelt, Franklin D. Roosevelt Library, Hyde Park, New York.

HLH   Papers of Harry L. Hopkins, Franklin D. Roosevelt Library, Hyde Park, New York.

HOO   Records of the Hanford Operations Office, U. S. Atomic Energy Commission, Richland, Washington.

HST   Papers of Harry S. Truman, Harry S. Truman Library, Independence, Missouri.

JAS   Papers of John A. Simpson, Jr., University of Chicago, Chicago, Illinois.

JRD   Papers of John R. Dunning, Columbia University, New York, New York.

LASL   Records of the Los Alamos Scientific Laboratory, U. S. Atomic Energy Commission, Los Alamos, New Mexico.

LRL   Records of the Lawrence Radiation Laboratory, U. S. Atomic Energy Commission, Berkeley, California.

MD   Records of the Manhattan Engineer District, 1942–48, World War II Records Division, National Archives and Records Service, Alexandria, Virginia.

NCAI   Records of the National Committee on Atomic Information, Manuscript Division, Library of Congress, Washington, D. C.

OROO   Records of the Oak Ridge Operations Office, U. S. Atomic Energy Commission, Oak Ridge, Tennessee.

OSRD   Records of the Office of Scientific Research and Development, Headquarters,

U. S. Atomic Energy Commission, Washington, D. C. A large portion of the OSRD documents are also to be found among the Records of the Manhattan District at Alexandria. In cases of duplication, the footnotes of this volume cite the OSRD collection.

OSRD-NA   Records of the Administrative Office, Office of Scientific Research and Development, National Archives

and Records Service, Washington, D. C.

SAM   Records of the SAM Laboratories at Columbia University, Oak Ridge Operations Office, U. S. Atomic Energy Commission, Oak Ridge, Tennessee.

SCAE   Records of the Senate Special Committee on Atomic Energy, National Archives and Records Service, Washington, D. C.

CHAPTER 1

1. Minutes, Commission Meeting 18, Jan. 2, 1947, AEC.
2. James R. Newman and Byron S. Miller, *The Control of Atomic Energy,* *A Study of Its Social, Economic, and Political Implications* (New York, 1948), pp. 3–4.
3. *Time,* Dec. 30, 1946.

CHAPTER 2

1. Laura Fermi, *Atoms in the Family; My Life with Enrico Fermi* (Chicago, 1954), p. 154; Otto Hahn, "The Discovery of Fission," *Scientific American,* CXCVIII (Feb., 1958), 76–78, 80, 82, 84; Herbert L. Anderson *et al.,* "The Fission of Uranium," *Physical Review,* LV (Mar. 1, 1939), 511.
2. "Resonance in Uranium and Thorium Disintegrations and the Phenomenon of Nuclear Fission," LV, 418–19; C. L. Critchfield, Memorandum, July 6, 1946, FAS.
3. We have drawn freely upon the observations on the history of American physics made by Robert A. Millikan in his *Autobiography* (New York, 1950) and by Isidor I. Rabi in a talk at the New York meeting of the American Historical Association in December, 1957. Lawrence described the invention of the cyclotron in his Nobel Prize address, Dec. 11, 1951. *Les Prix Nobel en 1951* (Stockholm, 1952), pp. 127–34. See also Lawrence to W. Weaver, Feb. 24, 1940, LRL. Abelson reported his work in "Cleavage of the Uranium Nucleus," *Physical Review,* LV (Feb. 15, 1939), 418.
4. LV (Feb. 15, 1939), 416–18 (Mar. 1, 1939), 511–12.
5. *Physical Review,* LVI (Sept. 1, 1939), 426–50.
6. Dunning to A. O. Nier, Apr. 6, 1939, JRD.
7. H. L. Anderson, E. Fermi, and H. B. Hanstein, "Production of Neutrons in Uranium Bombarded by Neutrons," *Physical Review,* LV (Apr. 15, 1939), 797–98; L. Szilard and W. H. Zinn, "Instantaneous Emission of Fast Neutrons in the Interaction of Slow Neutrons with Uranium," *Physical Review,* LV (Apr. 15, 1939), 799–800. Professor Anderson graciously allowed us to read the manuscript of an edition of Fermi documents which he is preparing. His editorial comments are of great value in explaining the experimental work at Columbia. Hereafter this volume is referred to as the Anderson MS.
8. "Neutron Production and Absorption in Uranium," *Physical Review,* LVI (Aug. 1, 1939), 284–86; Szilard to Fermi, July 3, 8, 1939, OSRD.
9. Pegram to Hooper, Mar. 16, 1939, quoted in Fermi, *Atoms in the Family,* pp. 162–63; H. W. Graf, Memorandum for File, Mar. 17, 1939, OSRD.
10. Ross Gunn to Bowen, June 1, 1939, Bowen, Memorandum on Sub-Atomic

Power Sources for Submarine Propulsion, Nov. 13, 1939, OSRD.

11. Szilard to Joliot-Curie, Feb. 2, 1939, OSRD.

12. Copy enclosed as attachment, Alexander Sachs to authors, Sept. 29, 1959.

13. The Einstein letter of Aug. 2, 1939, the Szilard memorandum, and Sachs's covering letter of Oct. 11 are filed in FDR. Sachs has told his story most completely in a typescript manuscript, Early History Atomic Project in Relation to President Roosevelt, 1939–40, which is on file in MD. A somewhat abbreviated version was printed in Senate Special Committee on Atomic Energy, *Atomic Energy. Hearings on S. Res. 179*, Nov. 27, 1945—Feb. 15, 1946 (Washington, 1945–46), pp. 553–58. In his Sept. 29, 1959, letter to the authors he added some new facts and emphases and attached photostatic copies of pages from his diary for February, March, and April, 1939. Col. K. F. Adamson has recalled these events in a statement of Aug. 1, 1947, that is on file in Headquarters, U. S. Atomic Energy Commission. Szilard and Wigner tell somewhat different versions of the events leading up to the Einstein letter.

14. This account depends heavily on A. Hunter Dupree, *Science in the Federal Government; A History of Policies and Activities to 1940* (Cambridge, Massachusetts, 1957).

15. Watson to Einstein, Oct. 17, 1939, FDR; Watson to Briggs, Oct. 13, Szilard to Briggs with attached memorandum, Oct. 26, 1939, OSRD; *Hearings on S. Res. 179*, pp. 559–60.

16. Briggs, Adamson, and Hoover to Roosevelt, Nov. 1, 1939, Watson to Briggs, Nov. 17, 1939, Feb. 8, 1940, Briggs to Watson, Feb. 20, 1940, L. Dennison to Briggs, Feb. 21, 1940, OSRD.

17. Watson to Sachs, Feb. 8, 1940, AEC; Sachs to Watson, Feb. 15, 1940, in Early History Atomic Project, MD.

18. Einstein to Sachs, Mar. 7, 1940, Sachs to Roosevelt, Mar. 15, 1940, Watson to Sachs, Mar. 27, 1940, in Early History Atomic Project, MD.

19. Roosevelt to Sachs, Apr. 5, 1940, Watson to Sachs, Apr. 5, 1940, Watson to Briggs, Apr. 5, 1940, OSRD. In 1945, Sachs stated that he saw the President "at the end of March and early April." *Hearings on S. Res. 179*, p. 565. Roosevelt's letter of Apr. 5 contains no reference to such a meeting.

20. "Nuclear Fission of Separated Uranium Isotopes," *Physical Review*, LVII (Mar. 15, 1940), 546, and "Further Experiments on Fission of Separated Uranium Isotopes," (Apr. 15, 1940), 748. The role of 235 had been predicted by Bohr and Wheeler in the *Physical Review*, LVI (Sept. 1, 1939), 441.

21. Pegram to Briggs, Mar. 11, 1940, Briggs to Watson, Apr. 9, 1940, Gunn to Bowen, May 1, 1940, OSRD.

22. Szilard to Sachs, Apr. 14, 22, 1940, Briggs to Watson, May 9, 1940, OSRD.

23. Pegram to Briggs, May 6, 8, 14, 1940, OSRD.

24. Sachs to Roosevelt, May 11, 1940, Sachs to Watson, May 15, 1940, in Early History Atomic Project, MD; Sachs to Watson, May 23, 1940, OSRD.

25. Gunn to Bowen, May 1, 1940, Tuve, Notes on Atomic Power by Fission of Uranium 235, May 7, 1940, and Uranium Fission and the Separation of Isotopes, May 28, 1940, Bush to Briggs, May 28, 1940, OSRD; Urey to G. B. Kistiakowsky, June 7, 1940, AEC.

26. Briggs to Sachs, June 5, 1940, Briggs to Bush, July 1, 1940, OSRD.

27. Roosevelt to Bush, June 15, 1940, HLH; James P. Baxter, 3rd, *Scientists Against Time* (Boston, 1947), pp. 14–16; Irvin Stewart, *Organizing Scientific Research for War* (Boston, 1948), pp. 7–9; Robert E. Sherwood, *Roosevelt and Hopkins; An Intimate History* (New York, 1948), pp. 153–54.

28. Bush to Briggs, Sept. 19, 1940, Szilard to Joliot-Curie, Feb. 2, 1939, Pegram to Breit, May 27, 1940, OSRD.

29. Sachs to Briggs, June 3, 1940, Briggs to Sachs, June 5, 1940, OSRD.

30. Briggs to Bush, July 1, 1940, OSRD.

31. Bush to Briggs, July 9, 1940, Pegram, Memorandum, July 11, 1940, Pegram and Fermi, Memorandum Report on Proposed Experiments with Uranium, Aug. 14, 1940, Bush to Briggs, Sept. 7, 1940, OSRD.

32. Anderson MS; Anderson and Fermi, Production and Absorption of Slow Neutrons by Carbon, Sept. 25, 1940,

669

Manhattan Engineer District Report A-21, Production of Neutrons by Uranium, Jan. 17, 1941, Report A-6, and Standards in Slow Neutron Measurements, June 5, 1941, Report A-2; Fermi, "The Development of the First Chain Reacting Pile," *Proceedings of the American Philosophical Society*, XC (Jan. 29, 1946), 22; Henry D. Smyth, *Atomic Energy for Military Purposes* (Princeton, 1948), pp. 58–59.

33. Fermi, Memorandum on an Intermediate Experiment for Determining the Possibility of a Chain Reaction with Uranium and Carbon, Dec. 20, 1940, OSRD; Fermi, "The Development of the First Chain Reacting Pile," *APS Proceedings*, XC (Jan. 29, 1946), 22. Supplementing the Columbia results was a four-part theoretical report by James B. Fisk and William B. Shockley: A Study of Uranium as a Source of Power. Fisk and Shockley, Bell Telephone Laboratories physicists, reached conclusions in the late summer of 1940 generally similar to those of official investigators. Mervin J. Kelly, Bell director of research, submitted their report to Frank B. Jewett, who referred it to the NDRC Uranium Committee.

34. Progress Report on Work in connection with the Fission of Uranium, encl., Pegram to Briggs, Feb. 15, 1941, Pegram to Compton, May 3, 1941, OSRD; Szilard to Compton, undated but around Dec., 1942, ANL.

35. Regenerative Fission with Uranium and Beryllium, encl., Compton to Briggs, Nov. 26, 1940, Urey to Briggs, Feb. 4, Mar. 10, 18, 1941, Urey, A. V. Grosse, and G. Walden, Production of D₂O for Use in the Fission of Uranium, June 23, 1941, OSRD.

36. The classic work on the problem is a volume by Karl Cohen in *National Nuclear Energy Series*, Div. III, *Special Separations Project*, Vol. IB, *The Theory of Isotope Separation as Applied to the Large-Scale Production of U²³⁵*.

37. Beams, Report to Briggs, Feb. 5, 1941, Report A-42; Cohen, Theory of the Simple-Process Flow-Through Centrifuge, [Feb. 6, 1941], Report A-50; Cohen, Main Numerical Results on the Separation of UF⁶ by Centrifuges, Mar. 3, 1941, Report A-53; Urey to Briggs, Oct. 21, 1940, Feb. 8, 1941,

Urey to A. H. Compton, May 3, 1941, Briggs to Conant, July 8, 1941, OSRD.

38. Tuve, Uranium Fission and the Separation of Isotopes, May 28, 1940, OSRD; Kistiakowsky to Tuve, May 27, 1940, Kistiakowsky to Urey, May 29, June 10, Oct. 14, 1940, Urey to Kistiakowsky, July 9, 1940, AEC.

39. Urey to Briggs, Feb. 8, 1940, to A. H. Compton, May 3, 1940, Dunning, Uranium Isotope Separation by Diffusion, Nov. 14, 1940, Dunning, Separation of U-235 by Diffusion Methods, July, 1941, OSRD.

40. Briggs to Conant, Sept. 21, 1944, OSRD.

41. L. R. Hafstad, N. P. Heyenburg, and R. B. Roberts, Fission Cross-Sections for Fast Neutrons, July 27, 1940, and Teller to Briggs, Sept. 1, 1940, OSRD.

42. McMillan and Seaborg have told their stories in Nobel Prize addresses. *Les Prix Nobel en 1951* (Stockholm, 1952), pp. 141–73. See also Seaborg, *The Transuranium Elements* (New Haven, 1958), pp. 4–6.

43. "Radioactive Element 93," *Physical Review*, LVII (June 15, 1940), 1185–86; L. A. Turner, Atomic Energy from U-238, May 27, 1940, Report A-5.

44. Abelson to Seaborg, Jan. 16, 1941, Pegram to Briggs, Jan. 27, 1941, OSRD; Fowler to Lawrence, Jan. 28, 1941, [Seaborg] to Briggs, May 29, 1941, McMillan, An Account of the Discovery and Early Study of Element 94, [1942], LRL; Seaborg, *The Transuranium Elements*, pp. 8–10.

45. Lawrence, History Notes on my early activities in connection with the Tubealloy Project Written Mar. 26, 1945, LRL.

46. Compton to Bush, Mar. 17, 1941, OSRD.

47. Bush to Compton, Mar. 21, 1941, to Briggs, Mar. 27, 1941, to F. B. Jewett, June 7, 1941, OSRD.

48. Bush to Jewett, Apr. 15, 19, 1941, OSRD; Jewett to Compton, Apr. 26, 1941, ANL.

49. Minutes of the Advisory Committee of the National Academy on Uranium Disintegration, Apr. 30, May 5, 1941, LRL; Briggs, Work of Uranium Committee, undated, Breit to Nier, Dec. 12, 1941, OSRD; Compton to Briggs, Mar. 5, 1942, ANL.

50. A copy of the report, in the form of a

letter from Compton to Jewett, is filed in OSRD.

51. Bush to Jewett, June 13, 1941, OSRD.
52. A copy of the report is on file in OSRD.
53. Bush to Jewett, July 9, 1941, OSRD.
54. M.A.U.D. Technical Committee. Third meeting held on 9th April, 1941 at the Royal Society, London, OSRD. In early 1941, the MAUD Committee was divided into two units, a Technical Committee and a Policy Committee. An account of early British research based on interviews, not documents, is Ronald W. Clark, *The Birth of the Bomb* (New York, 1961).
55. Briggs to Conant, July 8, 1941, OSRD.
56. Stewart, *Organizing Scientific Research for War*, pp. 35–40; Don K. Price, *Government and Science: Their Dynamic Relation in American Democracy* (New York, 1954), pp. 43–46.
57. Bush to Conant, July 21, 1941, with enclosures, OSRD.
58. Lauritsen to Bush, July 11, 1941, Draft Report by M.A.U.D. Technical Committee on the Release of Atomic Energy from Uranium, encl., F. L. Hovde to C. L. Wilson, July 7, 1941, OSRD.
59. The impact of the news from Britain is clear in Bush's Report of the National Defense Research Committee for the First Year of Operation, encl., Bush to Roosevelt, July 16, 1941, FDR. In this report Bush explained the NDRC policy of not expending public money and valuable scientific talent on what might have been a "wild search" but of making a careful investigation of the fundamental physics.
60. Coolidge to Jewett, Sept. 11, 1941, encl., Jewett to Bush, Sept. 12, 1941, OSRD; History Notes on my early activities in connection with the Tube-alloy Project, LRL; Compton, *Atomic Quest; A Personal Narrative* (New York, 1956), pp. 6–9.
61. Report by M.A.U.D. Committee, encl., Thomson to Conant, Oct. 3, 1941, OSRD.
62. Bush to Compton, Oct. 9, 1941, OSRD.
63. Bush to Conant, Oct. 9, 1941, Bush to Roosevelt, Mar. 9, 1942, OSRD.
64. In *Atomic Quest*, pp. 54–56, Compton states that Fermi's "most conservative estimate showed that the amount of fissionable metal needed to effect a nuclear explosion could hardly be greater than a hundred pounds." This is hardly borne out by Fermi's Remarks on Fast Neutron Reactions, Oct. 6, 1941, Report A-46.
65. Draft report, encl., Compton to members of the National Academy Uranium Committee, Oct. 16, 1941, OSRD; Minutes of Meeting of the Advisory Committee of the National Academy on Atomic Fission at Schenectady on October 21, 1941, letters from Buckley, Chubb, Coolidge, Lawrence, Mulliken, and Slater, OSRD; Lawrence to Compton, Nov. 29, 1941, LRL.
66. The S-1 Section's subcommittee on theory reported on October 28 that it was "reasonable to consider 30 kilograms as sufficient for a fast neutron chain reaction and in round numbers 60 kilograms for a highly explosive bomb." The fission cross section, however, was still uncertain. The amount needed for a bomb might have to be increased to 110 kilograms and possibly might be lowered to 33. Fast neutron chain reactions, encl., Briggs to Conant, Oct. 28, 1941, OSRD. This report was made at Compton's request; presumably, he saw it before he submitted his own report.
67. The results of the first exponential experiment were described in Anderson *et al.*, Neutron Reproduction in a Lattice of Uranium Oxide and Graphite, Mar. 26, 1942, Metallurgical Laboratory Report C-20.
68. The original, with Bush's forwarding letter and Roosevelt's reply, is on file in OSRD.
69. Bush to Compton, Nov. 22, 1941, Bush to Briggs, Nov. 27, 1941, Conant to Bush, undated, but probably late November, 1941, OSRD.
70. Bush to Murphree, Nov. 29, 1941, to Briggs, Dec. 2, 1941, OSRD.
71. Preliminary Report to Dr. V. Bush from Professor Harold C. Urey Relative to his Trip to England in regard to the Uranium Problem, Dec. 1, 1941, OSRD.
72. Lawrence to Compton, Dec. 1, 1941, LRL; Compton to Pegram, Dec. 10, 1941, ANL; Compton, *Atomic Quest*, pp. 70–73.
73. Lawrence, History Notes on my early

activities in connection with the Tube-alloy Project, LRL.

74. Copies of the Bush letters of December 13 are on file in OSRD.

75. Bush to Conant, Dec. 22, 1941, OSRD.
76. Bush to Conant, Dec. 16, 1941, OSRD.
77. Gunn, Memorandum for Director and Files, Dec. 19, 1941, OSRD.

CHAPTER 3

1. Compton to Bush, Conant, and Briggs, Dec. 20, 1941, OSRD.
2. Compton, Progress Report on Physical Measurements, undated, but about Jan. 15, 1942, OSRD.
3. Compton, Progress Report on Project on Physical Measurements, undated, but about Jan. 25, 1942, OSRD.
4. Compton to Coolidge, Chubb, and Buckley, Jan. 14, 1942, OSRD.
5. Compton to Conant, Jan. 22, 1942, Lawrence to Conant, Jan. 24, 1942, OSRD.
6. Compton, Report on Physics Tube-Alloy Project, Feb. 10, 1942, OSRD.
7. Metallurgical Laboratory Weekly Progress Reports, Jan.–Mar., 1942, ANL.
8. Lawrence, Report on Electrical Methods of Isotope Separation, encl., Lawrence to Conant, Oct. 15, 1942, Lawrence, Final Report of Work, encl., P. C. Aebersold to H. T. Wensel, Oct. 21, 1942, OSRD; R. K. Wakerling, Full Energy Receivers Used in the 37″, C1, C2, and R1 Tanks, Lawrence Radiation Laboratory Report RL 34.7.600.
9. Lawrence to Conant, Feb. 21, 1942, OSRD.
10. Best sources on other methods of electromagnetic separation are: the Lawrence report, Oct. 15, 1942, cited above, Henry D. Smyth, *Atomic Energy for Military Purposes* (Princeton, 1948), pp. 197–99, and *National Nuclear Energy Series*, Div. I, *Electromagnetic Separation Project*, Vol. IV, *Electromagnetic Separation of Isotopes in Commercial Quantities*, pp. 321–429.
11. Lawrence to Bush, Mar. 7, 1942, OSRD.
12. Bush to Murphree, Feb. 23, 1942, OSRD.
13. Report to the President, encl., Bush to Roosevelt, Mar. 9, 1942, OSRD.
14. The Destructive Action of Uranium Bombs, encl., Kistiakowsky to Bush, Jan. 3, 1942, OSRD.

15. Minutes, Planning Board, Jan. 7, 1942, OSRD.
16. Dunning, Uranium Isotope Separation By Diffusion, encl., Dunning to Briggs, Nov. 14, 1941, and report by same title, Sept. 29, 1941, OSRD.
17. Dunning to Lewis, Oct. 15, 1941, OSRD.
18. Minutes, Planning Board, May 6, 1942, OSRD.
19. Minutes, Planning Board, Jan. 7, 1942, Murphree to Bush, Jan. 12, 1942, OSRD.
20. Lawrence to Briggs, Jan. 31, 1942, Murphree to Bush, Mar. 3, 1942, OSRD.
21. Abelson to files, Naval Research Laboratory, Mar. 27, 1942, OSRD.
22. Minutes, Planning Board, Jan. 28, Feb. 24, 1942, OSRD.
23. Murphree to Bush, Mar. 3, 1942, OSRD; Smyth to Compton, Jan. 21, 1942, LRL.
24. Murphree to Bush, Mar. 27, 1942, Briggs to Murphree, Jan. 27, 1942, Minutes, Planning Board, May 6, 1942, OSRD; Westinghouse to Compton, Apr. 11, 1942, ANL.
25. A. V. Grosse, Chemical Properties of Uranium Hexafluoride, June 25, 1941, Manhattan Engineer District Report A-83; R. P. Briscoe to Briggs, July 9, 1941 (with enclosure), OSRD; Abelson *et al.*, eds., *Liquid Thermal Diffusion*, AEC Report TID-5229 (Oak Ridge, 1958), pp. 21–22.
26. Gunn to Briggs, Oct. 17, 1941, W. J. Harshaw to Briscoe, Dec. 5, 1941, Minutes, Planning Board, Jan. 7, May 6, 1942, OSRD.
27. Minutes, Planning Board, Jan. 28, Feb. 20, May 6, 1942, OSRD; *Manhattan District History*, Bk. III, *P-9 Project*, pp. 3.1–3.11.
28. Conant to Bush, Apr. 1, 1942, Urey to Conant, Apr. 2, 1942, Compton to Halban, May 11, 1942, OSRD.
29. Metallurgical Laboratory Report for Week Ending March 28, 1942, OSRD.

30. Fermi, Preliminary Report on the Exponential Experiment at Columbia University, March–April 1942, Metallurgical Laboratory Report CP-26.

31. Conant to Bush, May 21, 1942, OSRD.

32. Agenda for S-1 Conference, May 23, 1942, Bush to Conant, May 21, 1942, OSRD.

33. The following reports were among those prepared for, or used at, the meeting: Murphree, Projects Being Handled by the Planning Board, May 22, Lawrence to Conant, May 15, Compton to Conant, May 20, and Urey, Progress on Isotope Separation, May 23, OSRD; Metallurgical Laboratory Report for Week Ending May 16, 1942, C-76.

34. Conant, Notes of Meeting, May 23, 1942, OSRD.

35. Roosevelt to Bush, March 11, 1942, OSRD; Henry L. Stimson Diary, Feb. 21, 1942, Yale University Library; DSM Chronology, Sept. 21, 1942, OROO. This chronology, apparently prepared by members of Groves's staff, provides excellent coverage of the Army program in the period from June to December, 1942.

36. Bush to Conant, June 11, 1942, OSRD.

37. Bush to Styer, June 11, 1942, Clay to Styer, June 10, 1942, Styer to Bush, June 12, 1942, OSRD. Styer noted the results of his second meeting with Marshall on his copy of Bush's memorandum of June 11 on file in OSRD.

38. Bush and Conant to Wallace, Stimson, and Marshall, June 13, 1942, encl., Bush to Roosevelt, June 17, 1942, OSRD. The report called for a pilot plant only for gaseous diffusion and engineering designs of a full-scale plant.

39. R. Elberton Smith, The Army and Economic Mobilization (Washington, 1959), pp. 445–46; Blanche D. Coll, Jean E. Keith, and Herbert H. Rosenthal, The Corps of Engineers: Troops and Equipment (Washington, 1958), pp. 132–36.

40. DSM Chronology, June 18, 1942, OROO; Bush to Styer, June 19, 1942, with first indorsement, and Styer to Chief of Staff, Services of Supply, undated, AEC; Bush to Conant, June 19, 1942, OSRD.

41. Conant to Bush, May 26, 1942, Bush to Conant, June 19, 1942, OSRD.

42. General Leslie R. Groves takes credit for suggesting Stone & Webster in Now It Can Be Told; The Story of the Manhattan Project (New York, 1962), p. 12. Minutes, S-1 Executive Committee, July 9, 1942, OSRD.

43. Deutsch to Murphree, Apr. 29, 1942, OSRD.

44. Conant to Bush, May 26, 1942, Conant to Styer, May 21, 1942, OSRD.

45. Selection of Site for "Power" Project, encl., Compton to Bush, June 13, 1942, OSRD; Bush to Styer, June 15, 1942, MD.

46. DSM Chronology, July 1, 1942, OROO; Stone & Webster Engineering Corp., Report on Proposed Site for Plant, Eastern Tennessee, undated, but probably July 29, 1942, Minutes, S-1 Executive Committee, July 30, 1942, OSRD.

47. DSM Chronology, July 31, 1942, OROO.

48. War Records Section, Bureau of the Budget, The United States At War (Washington, 1946), pp. 103–15.

49. Eliot Janeway, The Struggle for Survival (New Haven, 1951), pp. 299–314; Donald M. Nelson, Arsenal of Democracy (New York, 1946), pp. 368–80; Smith, The Army and Economic Mobilization, pp. 237–78.

50. Richard M. Leighton and Robert W. Coakley, Global Logistics and Strategy (Washington, 1955), pp. 353–82, 417–35.

51. DSM Chronology, OROO, and Minutes, S-1 Executive Committee, OSRD, Aug. 26, 1942.

52. DSM Chronology, Aug. 29, 1942, OROO.

53. Bush to Bundy, Aug. 29, 1942, OSRD.

54. Groves concluded that Bush's displeasure stemmed from the fact that Somervell had not informed Bush of the appointment. While Groves did not favorably impress Bush under the circumstances, Bush's main concern was Somervell's precipitous action. Groves, Now It Can Be Told, p. 20; Bush to Conant, Sept. 17, 1942, OSRD; DSM Chronology, Sept. 17, 1942, OROO.

55. DSM Chronology, June 26, Aug. 11, Aug. 12, Sept. 2, Sept. 7, 1942, OROO.

56. Groves, "Atom General Answers His

673

Critics," *Saturday Evening Post,* June 19, 1948; Somervell to Chief of Engineers, Sept. 17, 1942, MD.

57. DSM Chronology, Sept. 19, 1942, OROO. Groves later wrote that he could not understand why Nelson gave in so quickly. Perhaps Bush's earlier contacts with Nelson had paved the way. Bush to Conant, Sept. 17, 1942, OSRD; Groves, *Now It Can Be Told,* pp. 22–23.

58. Bundy, Record of Meeting, Sept. 23, 1942, MD; Groves, *Now It Can Be Told,* pp. 23–25.

CHAPTER 4

1. Arthur H. Compton, *Atomic Quest* (New York, 1956), p. 68.

2. C. K. Leith to Bush, Apr. 22, 1942, Roosevelt to Bush, July 11, 1942, OSRD; Bush to Roosevelt, June 19, 1942, FDR; C. J. Covington to OSRD files, July 10, 1942, AEC; Bush to C. J. Mackenzie, July 15, 1942, OSRD.

3. Minutes, S-1 Executive Committee, July 9, 1942, C. K. Leith, War Production Board, to Bush, Apr. 22, 1942, OSRD; Groves, *Now It Can Be Told; The Story of the Manhattan Project* (New York, 1962), pp. 34–37; Bush to Styer, Sept. 11, 1942, T. K. Finletter to Bush, Sept. 11, 1942, OSRD.

4. DSM Chronology, Sept. 14, 1942, J. R. Ruhoff to Nichols, Sept. 21, 1942, OROO; Minutes, S-1 Executive Committee, Sept. 26, 1942, OSRD. The initial contract, W-7405-eng 4, signed by Nichols and Sengier on Oct. 19, 1942, is on file in OROO.

5. R. L. Doan to A. C. Klein, Sept. 3, 1942, AEC; P. L. Merritt to MD files, Dec. 21, 1942, MD.

6. Charles D. Harrington and Archie E. Reuhle, *Uranium Production Technology* (Princeton, 1959), pp. 16–20, 126; Henry D. Smyth, *Atomic Energy for Military Purposes* (Princeton, 1948), pp. 92–94; Compton, *Atomic Quest,* pp. 93–96; Metallurgical Laboratory Report for Week Ending April 17, 1942, C-36.

7. DSM Chronology, Sept. 4–5, 1942, OROO.

8. H. A. Wilhelm, A History of Uranium Metal Production in America, Iowa State College Report ISC-1076.

9. T. T. Crenshaw to Nichols, Nov. 18, 1942, OROO.

10. Compton, Progress Report, December 20, 1941 to July 1, 1942, undated, encl., Compton to Briggs, July 31, 1942, OSRD.

11. Metallurgical Laboratory Weekly Reports, July 25–Sept. 15, 1942, C-207, CP-235, CA-247, CP-257; Anderson MS.

12. Conference, Metallurgical Laboratory, Oct. 15, 1942, Report CS-309; Nichols to Files, Oct. 17, 1942, OROO.

13. Seaborg and Wahl, The Chemical Properties of Elements 94 and 93, Mar. 19, 1942, Report A-135.

14. Seaborg, *The Transuranium Elements* (New Haven, 1958), pp. 6–8, 14–17, 34–47.

15. Metallurgical Laboratory Progress Report, Aug. 16–31, 1942, CN-250; Report for Sept. 1–15, 1942, CN-261.

16. Compton, *Atomic Quest,* pp. 108–10.

17. DSM Chronology, June 26, 1942, OROO.

18. DSM Chronology, Sept. 26, Oct. 2, 1942, OROO; Compton, *Atomic Quest,* pp. 132, 151–53; Metallurgical Laboratory Report, Sept. 18, 1942, CS-274; E. I. du Pont de Nemours and Company, Design and Procurement History of Hanford Engineer Works and Clinton Semi-Works (unpublished typescript, Wilmington, 1945), pp. 10–11.

19. Lawrence, Final Report of Work, encl., P. C. Aebersold to R. T. Wensel, Oct. 21, 1942, OSRD; A. C. Mowbray, Sources Used in Tanks C1 and C2, and Early Sources Used in Tanks R1, D1, and XAC, March, 1945, Lawrence Radiation Laboratory Report RL 30.7.602.

20. R. K. Wakerling, Full Energy Receivers Used in the 37″, C1, C2, and R1 Tanks, undated, Report RL 34.7.-600; *National Nuclear Energy Series,* Div. I, *Electromagnetic Separation Project,* Vol. IV, *Electromagnetic Separation of Isotopes in Commercial Quantities,* pp. 59–60; *NNES,* Div. I,

Vol. VII, *Separation of Isotopes in Calutron Units*, p. 36.

21. Bush to Conant, June 19, 1942, Minutes, S-1 Executive Committee, June 26, July 30, Aug. 26, 1942, OSRD.

22. Minutes, S-1 Executive Committee, Sept. 13–14, 1942, OSRD; Lawrence, Multiple Mass Spectrograph, Sept. 13, 1942, LRL.

23. Murphree to Bush, June 23, 1942, Urey to Murphree, June 27, 1942, Murphree to Urey, July 3, 1942, OSRD.

24. Progress reports on centrifuge project, June–Oct., 1942, Abelson, to director, Naval Research Laboratory, July 14, 1942, Westinghouse Research Laboratories, Agenda, S-1 Executive Committee Meeting, Oct. 23, 1942, OSRD.

25. Columbia University, Special Report for Meetings of Executive Committee of Section S-1, Oct. 24, 1942, M. W. Kellogg Co., Industrial Application of the Diffusion Method, Oct. 24, 1942, OSRD.

26. Columbia University, Special Report for Meeting of Executive Committee, Oct. 24, 1942, OSRD. Both Kellogg and Columbia issued during this period regular monthly reports which are in OSRD files.

27. Conant to Bush, Oct. 26, 1942, OSRD.

28. Breit to Briggs, May 18, 1942, OSRD; Compton to Briggs, Mar. 5, 1942, ANL.

29. Oppenheimer to Nichols, Mar. 4, 1954, in U. S. Atomic Energy Commission, *In the Matter of J. Robert Oppenheimer* (Washington, 1954), p. 11.

30. Outline of Fast Neutron Projects, June 11, 1942, OSRD. A fragmentary record of the activities of the group is reflected in correspondence between Oppenheimer, Manley, Compton, Heydenburg, Williams, and others, June–Sept., 1942, AEC.

31. *Manhattan District History*, Bk. VIII, *Los Alamos Project (Y)*, Vol. II, *Technical*, p. I-2.

32. Compton to Conant, Sept. 18, 1942, Oppenheimer, Memorandum on Nuclear Reactions, Aug. 20, 1942, OSRD; Fast Neutron Group Meeting, Sept. 23, 1942, AEC; Compton, *Atomic Quest*, pp. 127–29.

33. DSM Chronology, Aug. 14, Sept. 26, 1942, OROO; Compton, *Atomic Quest*, p. 132.

34. Du Pont, Design and Procurement History, pp. 10–11.

35. Groves, Record of Preliminary Negotiations, undated, MD; du Pont, Design and Procurement History, p. 14; Groves, *Now It Can Be Told*, pp. 46–47.

36. DSM Chronology, Nov. 10, 1942, OROO.

37. DSM Chronology, Nov. 11, 1942, OROO.

38. Minutes, Military Policy Committee, Nov. 12, 1942, MD.

39. Minutes, S-1 Executive Committee, Nov. 14, 1942, and M. W. Kellogg Co., Preliminary Design and Estimate of Full-Scale Diffusion Plant, Nov. 14, 1942, OSRD.

40. Compton, *Atomic Quest*, pp. 137–39; Minutes of Metallurgical Laboratory Technical Council, Nov. 5, 1942, CS-335; J. C. Stearns to Capt. Grafton, Oct. 29, 1942, OROO.

41. Compton to S-1 Executive Committee, Nov. 20, 1942, OSRD; Seaborg to Oppenheimer, Nov. 3, 1942, and reply, Nov. 6, 1942, ANL.

42. Special Committee Report, Nov. 18, 1942, OSRD.

43. James Chadwick, Effect of Impurities on Bomb Material, Nov. 12, 1942, encl., Akers to Conant, Nov. 24, 1942, OSRD.

44. Compton to Conant, Nov. 23, 1942, Lawrence to Conant, Nov. 23, 1942, Oppenheimer to Conant, Nov. 24, 1942, Compton to Conant, Dec. 8, 1942, Compton to Conant, Dec. 9, 1942, E. Teller, Effects of Impurities on Predetonation, Nov. 30, 1942, OSRD.

45. Conant to S-1 Executive Committee, Nov. 20, 1942, OSRD; du Pont, Design and Procurement History, p. 17; Compton, *Atomic Quest*, pp. 132–35; Groves, *Now It Can Be Told*, p. 52.

46. Minutes of Metallurgical Laboratory Technical Council, Nov. 16, 1942, Report CS-352; Compton, *Atomic Quest*, p. 135.

47. Compton, Report on Feasibility of "49" Project, Nov. 26, 1942, OSRD.

48. C. Allardice and E. R. Trapnell, *The First Pile*, AEC Report TID-292; Reports CP-314, CP-297, CP-413, CS-366, CS-368. New York *Times*, Dec. 1, 1946, contains a detailed description of the event by William L. Laurence. The meeting of the Lewis committee

675

is recorded in A. V. Peterson to Nichols, Dec. 4, 1942, OSRD. Compton's recollections are found in *Atomic Quest*, pp. 140–44.

49. Conclusions of Reviewing Committee, Dec. 4, 1942, OSRD. The report was formally transmitted to Groves by letter of December 7, 1942.

50. DSM Chronology, Dec. 9, 1942, OROO; Minutes, S-1 Executive Committee, Dec. 9, 1942, Conant to Groves, Dec. 9, 1942, OSRD.

51. Conant to Bush, Dec. 11, 1942, OSRD; Note, apparently by Groves, attached to Conant to Groves, Dec. 9, 1942, MD.

52. Minutes, Military Policy Committee, Dec. 10, 1942, MD; DSM Chronology, Dec. 10, 1942, OROO.

53. Report on Present Status and Future Program on Atomic Fission Bombs, encl., Bush to Roosevelt, Dec. 16, 1942, OSRD.

CHAPTER 5

1. The construction and operation of the community and central facilities at Oak Ridge are described fully in *Manhattan District History*, Bk. I, *General*, Vol. XII, *Clinton Engineer Works, Central Facilities*.

2. George O. Robinson, Jr., *The Oak Ridge Story* (Kingsport, Tennessee, 1950), p. 54.

3. Henry L. Stimson Diary, Feb. 22, 1943, Yale University Library; Groves to Wallace, Stimson, and Marshall, Aug. 21, 1943, MD.

4. *MD History*, Bk. II, *Gaseous Diffusion*, Vol. III, *Design*, pp. 3.1–3.4; DSM Chronology, Dec. 12, 1942, OROO.

5. *MD History*, Bk. II, Vol. V, *Operations*, p. 2.1; J. F. Gordon, K-25 Process Division Historical Report, 1943–1947, Union Carbide Nuclear Company Records, Oak Ridge; DSM Chronology, Dec. 28, 1942, OROO.

6. A complete file of staff meeting minutes prepared by Kellex is included in SAM. Dunning to group supervisors, Apr. 26, 1943, Dunning, General Program, Diffusion Plant Group, K-25, Columbia University, Apr. 27, 1943, Program, Project K-25, May 11, 1943, SAM; *MD History*, Bk. II, Vol. II, *Research*, pp. 2.2–2.5.

7. Dunning, Diffusion Separation Plants, Jan. 9, 1943, Cohen to Dunning, Dec. 22, 1942, SAM. The best comprehensive description of K-25 design is found in *MD History*, Bk. II. Vol. II, pp. 3.8–3.11 and Vol. III, pp. 7.1–7.8. Kellex Corp., The Diffusion Plant: First Progress Report, Mar. 29, 1943, Manhattan Engineer District Report A-825.

8. A. M. Squires, Minutes of Meeting, Dec. 11, 1942, Intergroup Research and Development Meeting, Jan. 21, 1943, SAM.

9. Minutes, Military Policy Committee, Feb. 5, 1943, MD; DSM Chronology, Jan. 28, 1943, OROO; Special Meeting on Small Centrifuge Pump Pilot Plant, June 8, 1943, SAM; *National Nuclear Energy Series*, Div. II, *Gaseous Diffusion Project*, Vol. XV, *Blowers and Seals*, pp. 25–42, 73–74.

10. Conference at the M. W. Kellogg Office, Dec. 29, 1942, Suggested Program for Powder Nickel Barrier Development, encl., J. H. Arnold to R. H. Burns *et al.*, Jan. 7, 1942, SAM; *MD History*, Bk. II, Vol. II, pp. 4.9–4.16.

11. Dunning, Interim Report, Feb. 27, 1943, Memorandum on Conference Held May 17, 1942, Z. G. Deutsch, Memorandum on Conference, June 10, 1943, IA4 Section Meeting, July 22, 1943, Conference at Columbia on Research Schedule, June 16, 1943, SAM; *NNES*, Div. II, Vol. VIII, *Early Project Barrier Research*, pp. 23–27, 73–75.

12. Dunning, Progress Memorandum, Project K-25, July 14, 1943, SAM.

13. Arnold and Dunning, The Diffusion Plant, Apr. 28, 1943, Minutes of SAM Technical Steering Committee, Aug. 4, 1943, SAM; *MD History*, Bk. II, Vol. II, pp. 7.1–7.3; *NNES*, Div. II, Vol. IV, *Single-Stage and Cascade Pilot Plants*, pp. 188–237.

14. Murphree to Briggs *et al.*, Feb. 18, 1943, OSRD; Minutes of SAM Technical Steering Committee, Aug. 4, 1943, SAM; Minutes, Military Policy

Committee, May 5, Aug. 13, 1943, MD; Minutes of Special Meeting of the Governing Board, Los Alamos, Aug. 31, 1943, AEC. Urey's monthly summary reports are on file in SAM.

15. Virtually all data in this section are derived from *MD History*, Vol. II, *Design*, and Vol. IV, *Construction*.

16. Minutes of steering committee meetings and monthly reports from the Princeton project are on file in SAM.

17. Tolman to Groves, Oct. 7, 9, 1943, OSRD; *MD History*, Bk. II, Vol. II, pp. 4.19–4.27; *NNES*, Div. II, Vol. IX, *Nickel-Powder Barrier*, pp. 21–33, Vol. XIII, *Characterization and Evaluation of Barrier*, pp. 21–25.

18. Memorandum of Kellex Meeting on Barriers, Oct. 20, 1943, Minutes of K-25 Steering Committee Meeting, Nov. 3, 1943, G. Skatchard, Minutes of Meeting at Manhattan District, Nov. 5, 1943, SAM.

19. Urey to Groves, Oct. 20, 1943, Minutes of K-25 Steering Committee Meeting, Nov. 10, 17, Dec. 1, 1943, Urey to Groves, Nov. 10, 1943, Urey to Division Heads, Nov. 28, 1943, SAM.

20. Tolman to Groves, Oct. 2, 1943, OSRD; Tolman Diary, MD; Kellex Weekly Staff Meetings, Nov. 2, 29, 1943, Minutes of Review Conference, Dec. 22, 1943, SAM; *MD History*, Bk. II, Vol. III, p. 15.1. Lauchlin M. Currie is not to be confused with Lauchlin Currie, the Government economist who served as administrative assistant to President Roosevelt from 1939 to 1945.

21. Felbeck and Urey to Groves, Dec. 15, 1943, SAM.

22. Status Report on DSM Project, Dec. 1943, MD; Conant to Groves, Dec. 28, 1943, SAM; Lawrence to Groves, Jan. 1, 8, 1944, OSRD.

23. Encl., Stowers to Groves, Jan. 7, 1944, MD.

24. Keith to Groves, Jan. 4, 1944, MD.

25. Kellex Corp., Minutes of Follow-up Review Conference, Jan. 5, 1944, SAM.

26. Dunning to group supervisors and section leaders, Jan. 6, 1944, Minutes of K-25 Steering Committee Meeting, Jan. 12, 1944, Kellex Corp., Notes on Meeting at Decatur, Jan. 16, 1944, SAM.

27. Tolman to Groves, Mar. 13, Apr. 6, 1944, OSRD; Minutes of K-25 Steering Committee, Mar. 15, 1944, Report, Renewal of Contract W-7405-eng 50, Apr. 14, 1944, SAM.

28. Nichols to Groves, Mar. 2, 1943, MD.

29. Pinner to Taylor, Feb. 5, 15, 1944, E. K. Finlayson to Taylor, June 5, 1944, Johnson, Meeting for Standardization for Procedure for Barrier Research, Feb. 28, 1944, Johnson, Minutes of Meeting on Barrier Processing Held at Decatur, May 5, 1944, SAM.

30. *MD History*, Bk. II, Vol. III, pp. 8.1–8.41; Manhattan District, Narrative Construction Report for K-25 Area, June 1944, AEC.

31. Merrill to Taylor *et al.*, June 1, 1944, A. L. Tinney, Notes on Conference Called by Dr. L. M. Currie, July 8, 1944, SAM.

32. *NNES*, Div. I, *Electromagnetic Separation Project*, Vol. II, *Magnets and Magnetic Measuring Techniques*, pp. 20, 32–33.

33. Factors considered in the basic design of the plant are described in *MD History*, Bk. V, *Electromagnetic Project*, Vol. III, *Design*, pp. 3.5–3.6.

34. *NNES*, Div. I, Vol. II, pp. 144, 154–55.

35. *NNES*, Div. I, Vol. I, *Vacuum Equipment and Techniques*, pp. 59–104, and Vol. XI, *Vacuum Problems and Techniques*, pp. 1–107.

36. *NNES*, Div. I, Vol. IV, *Electromagnetic Separation of Isotopes in Commercial Quantities*, p. 185, and Vol. VI, *Sources and Collectors for Use in Calutrons*, pp. 37–38.

37. DSM Chronology, Nov. 25, Dec. 12, 1942, Minutes of Meeting, Dec. 23, 1942, encl., Fidler to District Engineer, Dec. 31, 1942, OROO.

38. *MD History*, Bk. V, Vol. II, *Research*, pp. 2.3–2.4; Tennessee Eastman Corp., CEW-TEC History, January 1943—May 1947, pp. 6–12, OROO.

39. *MD History*, Bk. V, Vol. III, p. 3.7, and Vol. VI, *Operations*, p. 2.2; Notes on Trip to California, encl., R. C. Blair to A. C. Klein, Jan. 18, 1943, OROO.

40. A full description of the plant may be found in *MD History*, Bk. V, Vol. III, pp. 2.1–2.10, and *NNES*, Div. I, Vol. VII, *Separation of Isotopes in Calutron Units*.

41. A complete set of co-ordination meeting minutes is filed at OROO.

677

42. *MD History*, Bk. V, Vol. VI, pp. 3.1–3.3.

43. Minutes of Berkeley Meetings, Feb. 3, 6, 1943, encl., Fidler to District Engineer, Feb. 18, 1943, OROO.

44. W. E. Kelley to Files, CEW, Mar. 18, 1943, B. K. Hough, Minutes of March 17 Conference, Mar. 19, 1943, OROO; R. L. Thornton, Estimate of Alpha and Beta Operations, undated but undoubtedly Mar. 17, 1943, MD.

45. A full description of construction activities at Y-12 is included in *MD History*, Bk. V, Vol. V, *Construction*.

46. *MD History*, Bk. V, Vol. IV, *Silver Program*, pp. 1.1, 2.1, S3; DSM Chronology, Aug. 3, 1942, OROO.

47. F. H. Belcher to Files, MD, Apr. 26, 1943, General Electric, Minutes of Schenectady Meeting, Apr. 24, 1943, Tennessee Eastman Corp., Minutes of Conference, Apr. 24, 1943, Boston, Minutes, Coordination Meetings, Feb. 27, Apr. 22, Apr. 29, May 10, 1943, OROO; *NNES*, Div. I, Vol. X, *Electrical Equipment for Tanks and Magnets*, pp. 35–50.

48. Minutes, Coordination Meeting, May 6, 1943, OROO.

49. Lawrence to Fidler, Mar. 8, 1943, LRL. The minutes of the co-ordination meetings at Berkeley in OROO for the period Jan.–May, 1943, contain regular references to hot-source development. For an analysis of the relative advantages of cold and hot sources, see W. M. Brobeck, Y-12 Project Proposed Construction and Conversion Program, July 3, 1943, LRL. Details of early hot-source research are described in A. G. Mowbray, R. L. Harris, and R. E. Hurlbert, High Potential Sources Used in Tank R1 Between March 1943 and September 1944, Lawrence Radiation Laboratory Report RL 30.7.600, pp. 4–55.

50. *NNES*, Div. I, Vol. VI, pp. 173–80.

51. The basic design of Beta is described in *MD History*, Bk. V, Vol. III, pp. 3.11–3.12. Alpha and Beta chemistry is analyzed on pp. 3.21–3.32. Beta collectors are fully described in *NNES*, Div. I, Vol. VI, pp. 182–86.

52. History of University of California Radiation Laboratory, Vol. V, Bk. I, p. 29, LRL; *MD History*, Bk. V, Vol. V, pp. 3.7–3.8; A. G. Mowbray, Sources Used in Tanks C1 and C2, and Early Cold Sources Used in Tanks R1, D1, and XAC, Mar. 1945, Report RL 30.7.602, pp. 125–46.

53. *MD History*, Bk. V, Vol. III, p. 3.14; Minutes, Military Policy Committee, May 5, 1943, MD; Conant, S-1 Diary, July 10, 1943, Lawrence to Conant, June 14, 1943, OSRD.

54. The minutes of the Berkeley coordination meetings during this period provide an excellent record of this chain of decisions. Especially useful are the minutes for July 15, Aug. 5, Aug. 12, Aug. 19, 1943, OROO.

55. Minutes, Military Policy Committee, Aug. 13, Sept. 9, 1943, Groves to Wallace, Stimson, and Marshall, Aug. 21, 1943, MD; Minutes, Coordination Meeting, Sept. 2, 1943, OROO.

56. *MD History*, Bk. V, Vol. V, p. 3.9, Bk. V, Vol. VI, pp. 3.3–3.6, 5.2; Tennessee Eastman Corp., CEW-TEC History, January 1943—May 1947, pp. 31–32, OROO; W. B. Reynolds to Lawrence, Nov. 23, 1943, LRL; Status Report on DSM Project, December 1943, MD.

57. Minutes, Coordination Meetings, Oct. 28, 1943, W. E. Kelley to Files, CEW, Dec. 16, 17, 30, 1943, OROO; A. Guthrie to Lawrence, Dec. 22, 1943, LRL; Bush to Groves, Jan. 7, 1944, MD.

58. Minutes, Coordination Meeting, Feb. 3, 1944, OROO; *NNES*, Div. I, Vol. XI, pp. 236–39; *MD History*, Bk. V, Vol. VI, pp. 4.1–4.5; Kelley to Groves, Feb. 27, 1944, MD.

59. Oppenheimer to Groves, Jan. 26, 1944, Groves to Oppenheimer, Feb. 8, 1944, MD; Kelley to Files, CEW, Feb. 7, 1944, OROO.

60. *NNES*, Div. I, Vol. VI, p. 120; *MD History*, Bk. V, Vol. III, pp. 3.10–3.13, 3.35–3.38.

61. Minutes, Military Policy Committee, Mar. 30, Apr. 5, May 10, 1944, MD; Lawrence to Oppenheimer, May 17, 1944, Oppenheimer to Lawrence, May 25, 1944, LASL.

62. Lawrence to Conant, May 31, 1944, OSRD.

63. Lawrence to Oliphant, June 9, 1944, W. M. Brobeck, Why the 5th Track Is So Slow Starting Up, July 4, 1944, LRL; Oliphant to Nichols, June 13, 1944, OROO.

64. Lawrence to Groves, June 30, 1944, LRL; Kelley to Files, CEW, July 4, 1944, A. C. Klein to Groves, July 4, 1944, OROO.
65. *NNES*, Div. I, Vol. VI, pp. 107–8.
66. Oppenheimer to Groves, Apr. 28, 1944, MD.
67. *MD History*, Bk. VI, *Liquid Thermal Diffusion*, pp. 2.1–2.9; P. H. Abelson *et al.*, *Liquid Thermal Diffusion*, AEC Report TID-5229 (Oak Ridge, 1958), pp. 20–27.
68. Urey to Conant, July 27, 1942, Bush to Conant, Aug. 1, 1942, R. Gunn to Files, NRL, Sept. 1, 1942, H. G. Bowen to Briggs, Sept. 2, 1942, Abelson, Progress Report on Liquid Thermal Diffusion Work, Sept. 7, 1942, OSRD.
69. DSM Chronology, Sept. 21, 1942, OROO; Groves, *Now It Can Be Told; The Story of the Manhattan Project* (New York, 1962), p. 23; Harold G. Bowen, *Ships, Machinery, and Mossbacks* (Princeton, 1954), pp. 186–87; Minutes, S-1 Executive Committee, Dec. 9, 19, 1942, Gunn to Files, NRL, Dec. 10, 1942, Bush to Purnell, Dec. 31, 1942, Bush to Conant, Jan. 14, 1943, OSRD.
70. Naval Research Laboratory, Progress Report on Liquid Thermal Diffusion Research, Jan. 4, 1943, NRL Report O-1977, Briggs *et al.*, to Conant, Jan. 23, 1942, Gunn to Files, NRL, undated, Urey, Memorandum on the Liquid Thermal Diffusion, Reports O-1977 and O-1981, Jan. 22, 1943, Cohen to Urey, Jan. 22, 1943, OSRD.
71. Murphree to Briggs, Jan. 25, 1943, Briggs to Conant, Jan. 30, 1943, Groves to Lewis, Feb. 1, 1943, Greenewalt to Groves, Feb. 8, 1943, Minutes, S-1 Executive Committee, Feb. 10, 1943, Gunn to Director, NRL, Feb. 11, 1943, Groves to Purnell, Feb. 27, 1943, OSRD.
72. Conant to Lewis, July 15, 1943, Urey to Lewis, Sept. 4, 1943, Briggs *et al.* to Conant, Sept. 8, 1943, Conant to Purnell, Sept. 15, 1943, OSRD; Ruhoff to Commander R. W. Dole, Oct. 11, 1943, A. H. Van Keuren to Groves, Nov. 10, 1943, Groves to Van Keuren, Nov. 12, 1943, MD.
73. U. S. Atomic Energy Commission, *In the Matter of J. Robert Oppenheimer* (Washington, 1954), pp. 164–65; Groves to Lewis *et al.*, undated draft of letter sent May 31, 1944, Lewis *et al.* to Groves, June 3, 1944, OSRD; Minutes, Military Policy Committee, May 10, 1944, MD.
74. Groves to Murphree, June 12, 1944, Minutes, Military Policy Committee, June 21, 1944, MD; Groves to Fox, July 4, 1944, in *MD History*, Bk. VI, Appendix D.

679

CHAPTER 6

1. The first recorded meeting of the Engineering Council was that of May 28, 1942, Metallurgical Laboratory Report CS-106. Minutes of subsequent meetings are found in the C- report series.
2. Minutes, Engineering Council, June 18, 1942, Report CE-135.
3. Wheeler to E. C. Creutz, Mar. 26, 1942, ANL.
4. Minutes, Engineering Council, June 25, 1942, Report CS-147. M. C. Leverett, Comparison of Proposed Methods of Cooling Power Plant, June 24, 1942, Report CS-138.
5. Metallurgical Project, Monthly Report Ending August 15, 1942, CE-236; For Month Ending September 15, 1942, CE-260.
6. T. V. Moore and M. C. Leverett, Preliminary Process Design for Power Plant, Sept. 25, 1942, Report CE-277.
7. Minutes, Engineering Council, July 2, 1942, Report CS-163.
8. Leo Szilard, "What Is Wrong With Us?," Sept. 21, 1942, ANL.
9. Young and Wigner, A Plant With Water Cooling, Report C-140, undated but probably June 20, 1942. This was followed by C-197, undated but sometime in July, 1942. Minutes, Technical Council, Sept. 4, 1942, CS-251. The name of the Engineering Council was changed to the Technical Council in July, 1942.
10. Szilard's activities on bismuth are described in the memorandum cited above and in Report CE-236.
11. Minutes, Technical Council, Oct. 5, 1942, Report CS-286.

680

12. Minutes of Technical Council, Oct. 13, 1942, Report CS-306; Oct. 15, 1942, CS-309, CS-311.

13. Research on separation processes is described extensively in the following monthly reports from the Metallurgical Laboratory in the summer and fall of 1942: CN-114, CN-239, CN-250, CN-261, CN-299, CN-343, and CN-391. *Manhattan District History*, Bk. IV, *Pile Project (X-10)*, Vol. II, *Research*, pp. 6.1–6.8.

14. Although Seaborg and his associates had been using traces of the 50-year isotope since March, 1942, they did not identify it as 238 until August, as reported in A-135 and CN-261. On early chemistry organization at Chicago, see Seaborg, *The Transuranium Elements* (New Haven, 1958), p. 20.

15. *MD History*, Bk. IV, Vol. III, *Design*, pp. 6.5–6.6.

16. Minutes of Conference, Oct. 15, 1942, Report CS-310.

17. Cooper's work is described in the following monthly reports: CN-359, CN-391, CN-421.

18. Seaborg, *Transuranium Elements*, pp. 21–25. Thompson reported his work in CN-419.

19. Minutes, S-1 Executive Committee, Sept. 13, 26, 1942, OSRD; Minutes, Technical Council, Sept. 18, 1942, Report CS-274.

20. The letter of intent, Dec. 1, 1942, and the subsequent contract, W-7412-eng-1, Nov. 8, 1943, are on file in OROO. R. Elberton Smith, *The Army and Economic Mobilization* (Washington, 1959), pp. 280–83; Richard A. Tybout, *Government Contracting in Atomic Energy* (Ann Arbor, 1956), pp. 53–4.

21. Groves, Record of Preliminary Negotiations, undated, MD.

22. *MD History*, Bk. IV, Vol. III, pp. 10.2–10.3. Minutes, Technical Council, Dec. 28, 1942, Report CS-397. Compton, *Atomic Quest* (New York, 1956), pp. 163–65.

23. E. I. du Pont de Nemours & Co., Design and Procurement History of Hanford Engineer Works and Clinton Semi-Works (unpublished typescript, Wilmington, 1945), p. 18; DSM Chronology, Dec. 14, 1942.

24. *MD History*, Bk. IV, Vol. III, pp. 2.1–2.8. The inspection trip is described

by Matthias in his voluminous diary, on file in HOO.

25. Minutes, Technical Council, Dec. 10, 1942, Report CS-371.

26. Minutes, Technical Council, Dec. 28, 1942, Report CS-397. Du Pont, Design and Procurement History, p. 20.

27. The letter contract, accepted by du Pont on January 8, 1943, was superseded by contract W-7412-eng-23, on file in OROO.

28. DSM Chronology, Jan. 6, 8, 16, 1943, OROO. Williams to Yancey, Jan. 12, 1942, ANL.

29. Compton, *Atomic Quest*, pp. 171–73; *MD History*, Bk. IV, Vol. II, *Research*, Pt. II, *Clinton Laboratories*, pp. 3.1–3.2; Conant to Compton, Mar. 4, 1943, OSRD; Groves to Hutchins, Mar. 10, 1943, ANL.

30. DSM Chronology, Oct. 2, 1942, OROO; Minutes, Technical Council, Oct. 15, 1942, Report CS-311.

31. DSM Chronology, Nov. 10, 25, 1942, OROO; Minutes, Technical Council, Dec. 28, 1942, Report CS-397; du Pont, Design and Procurement History, p. 72.

32. Whitaker, Minutes of Conference at Wilmington, Dec. 17–18, 1942, Report, CS-406; *National Nuclear Energy Series*, Div. IV, *Plutonium Project Record*, Vol. V, *Graphite Uranium Production Piles*, p. 185–88.

33. *NNES*, Div. IV, Vol. V, pp. 189–213, 252–345; *MD History*, Bk. IV, Vol. II, Pt. II, pp. 4.2–4.7.

34. Compton, *Atomic Quest*, pp. 161–67; M. C. J. Boissevain, M. C. Leverett, L. A. Ohlinger, A. M. Weinberg, E. P. Wigner, G. J. Young, Preliminary Process Design of Liquid Cooled Power Plant Producing 5×10^5 Kw., Jan. 9, 1943, Report CE-407.

35. Minutes, Technical Council, Jan. 22, 1943, Report CS-414; du Pont, Design and Procurement History, pp. 74–79; Meeting with Greenewalt, Feb. 24, 1943, Report CS-2644; *MD History*, Book IV, Vol. III, pp. 5.14–5.18; Greenewalt to Groves, July 8, 1943, MD.

36. The University of Chicago contract with OSRD (OEMsr-410) was replaced by War Department contract W-7405-eng-39. Copies of both contracts are on file in OROO. General descriptions of the laboratory are

found in Compton to J. C. Marshall, Mar. 6, 1943, OSRD, *MD History*, Bk. IV, Vol. II, Part I, *Metallurgical Laboratory*, pp. 7.1–7.2, App. B, and Organization of Metallurgical Unit, Feb. 8, 1943, Report CA-436.

37. *MD History*, Bk. IV, Vol. II, Part I, pp. 1.1–1.2; Minutes, Laboratory Council, June 21, 1943, Report CS-731; Minutes, Technical Council, Jan. 28, 1943, Report CS-439; Compton to Groves, Feb. 5, 1943, OSRD; Minutes, Laboratory Council, Feb. 9, 1943, Report CS-461.

38. Minutes, Laboratory Council, April 7, June 21, 23, 1943, Reports CS-557, CS-731, CS-740; *MD History*, Bk. IV, Vol. II, Part I, pp. 3.12–3.13. A summary of research with CP-1 and CP-2 is found in the Anderson MS., described in the notes for Chapter II.

39. Wigner to Compton, Aug. 5, 1943, OSRD; Wigner to Compton, Jan. 7, 1944, MD.

40. *MD History*, Bk. III, *The P-9 Project*, pp. 2.10–2.14; 3.11–3.21. DSM Chronology, Dec. 29, 1942, OROO.

41. Conant to C. J. Mackenzie, Jan. 2, Mar. 13, 1943, Conant to Bush, Mar. 10, 1943, Urey to Conant, Apr. 2, Apr. 16, June 21, 1943, Conant to Urey, Apr. 7, June 29, 1943, OSRD.

42. Minutes Laboratory Council, Feb. 17, 24, Mar. 24, July 28, Aug. 25, 1943, Reports CS-476, CS-492, CS-535, CS-830, CS-886; Minutes, Project Council, Dec. 8, 1943, Report CS-1137; A. V. Peterson to Groves, Aug. 13, 1943, MD.

43. Conant to Bush, July 31, 1943, Bush to Conant, Sept. 22, 1944, OSRD; Margaret L. Coit, *Mr. Baruch* (Boston, 1957) contains a garbled account of the incident on pp. 559–60.

44. Groves to Lewis, Aug. 9, 1943, Urey, memorandum to P-9 Committee, Aug. 9, 1943, Compton to Lewis, Aug. 13, 1943, Report of the Committee on Heavy Water Work, Aug. 19, 1943, OSRD.

45. Notes taken at meeting of reviewing committee, Aug. 19, 1943, Compton to Wigner, July 23, 1943, MD.

46. The following Metallurgical Laboratory reports describe the operation of the semiworks from January to June, 1943: CN-486, CS-495, CS-444, CS-511, CS-531, CN-603.

47. Minutes, Laboratory Council, May 31, July 3, 1943, Report CS-694, CS-749; Chemical Engineering Report, May 31, 1943, CN-698; Seaborg, *The Transuranium Elements*, pp. 26–27; *MD History*, Bk. IV, Vol. III, p. 6.9, Vol. II, Pt. II, p. 5.2.

48. Health Division, Reports for months ending Aug. 15, Sept. 15, 1942, Reports CH-237, CH-259; Compton, *Atomic Quest*, pp. 176–81; *NNES*, Div. IV, Vol. XX, *Industrial Medicine on the Plutonium Project*, pp. 1–16. The organization of the Manhattan District medical section under Col. Stafford L. Warren is described in *MD History*, Bk. I, *General*, Vol. VII, *Medical Program*.

49. The best summary of X-10 construction is found in *NNES*, Div. IV, Vol. V, pp. 213–7. See also *MD History*, Bk. IV, Vol. II, Pt. II, pp. 2.1–2.9. Construction progress was regularly reported in meetings of the Laboratory Council in Chicago, as recorded in Reports CS-534, CS-740, CS-584, CS-637.

50. Du Pont, Design and Procurement History, pp. 94–98. Thomas T. Crenshaw to Groves, Jan. 25, 1943, MD.

51. Du Pont, Design and Procurement History, pp. 357–95.

52. Minutes, Laboratory Council, Feb. 9, Apr. 28, 1943, Report CS-461, CS-602, *MD History*, Bk. II, Vol. II, Pt. II, pp. 3.1–3.6, App. B5–B7.

53. Seaborg, *The Transuranium Elements*, pp. 29–33. A good summary of research activities is included in E. J. Murphy, P Project, Clinton Laboratories (unpublished typescript, 1945), OROO.

54. *MD History*, Bk. IV, Vol. II, Pt. II, pp. 4.7–4.10. Minutes, Project Council, Dec. 8, 1943, Report CS-1137.

55. Monthly Progress Report, Clinton Laboratories, Nov., 1943—July, 1944, OROO; Minutes, Laboratory Council, Jan. 3, Mar. 22, 1944, Reports CS-1226, CS-1522; Compton to Peterson, Jan. 22, 1944, MD. For the effect on weapons development, see Chapter VIII.

56. DSM Chronology, Jan. 23, 1943, OROO.

57. *MD History*, Bk. IV, Vol. IV, *Land Acquisition, Hanford Engineer Works*, pp. 2.1–4.7.

58. *MD History*, Bk. IV, Vol. V, *Construc-*

681

tion, pp. 2.1–2.9, 3.1–3.17, Vol. VI, *Operation*, pp. 2.26–2.27; F. T. Matthias Diary, Feb. 24–Mar. 28, 1943, HOO.

59. *MD History*, Bk. IV, Vol. V, pp. 5.1–5.23, App. B13–B19; Matthias Diary, Apr. 14, 23, 1943, HOO.

60. *MD History*, Bk. IV, Vol. V, pp. 4.1–4.12.

61. *Ibid.*, pp. 6.5–6.22, App. B-38–B-42. Du Pont, Design and Construction History, pp. 66–68. Du Pont, Construction Hanford Engineer Works, U. S. Contract No. W-4412-eng-1, du Pont Project 9536, History of the Project, Aug. 9, 1945, pp. 788–803, 809–10, HOO.

62. *MD History*, Bk. IV, Vol. V, pp. 5.23–5.27, App. B28.

63. *Ibid.*, pp. 6.22–6.31, App. B-44; Bk. IV, Vol. III, pp. 6.8–6.22, App. A53–A74; du Pont, Design and Procurement History, pp. 184–85, 199–200.

64. Seaborg, *The Transuranium Elements*, pp. 28–29.

65. Compton, Memo on State of the Nation, Oct. 20, 1943, OSRD.

66. Du Pont, Design and Procurement History, pp. 388–92; du Pont, Operation of Hanford Engineer Works, Bk. I, p. 70; Minutes, Project Council Meeting, Jan. 18, Apr. 3, 1944, Reports CS-1257, CS-1694.

67. *MD History*, Bk. IV, Vol. V, pp. 6.1–6.4; App. B36, Vol. VI, pp. 2.1–2.5, 4.4–4.6, Vol. IV, pp. 4.1–4.3.

68. Du Pont, Operation of Hanford Engineer Works, Bk. I, pp. 71–81; du Pont, Design and Procurement History, p. 393; Minutes, Project Council, Apr. 5, 18, May 16, June 7, 20, 21, July 5, 18, Reports CS-1574, CS-1600, CS-1726, CS-1769, CS-1822, CS-1815, CS-1913, CS-1933.

69. Manhattan District Status Report, Hanford Engineer Works, June 30, 1944, OSRD.

CHAPTER 7

1. Breit to Briggs, May 18, 1942, Conant to Bush, May 26, 1942, OSRD.

2. Conant and Bush to Wallace, Stimson, and Marshall, June 13, 1942, OSRD; B. B. Somervell to Chief of Engineers, Sept. 17, 1942, H. H. Bundy, Record of Meeting, Sept. 23, 1942, MD.

3. U. S. Atomic Energy Commission, *In the Matter of J. Robert Oppenheimer* (Washington, 1954), pp. 12, 28; Oppenheimer to N. P. Heydenburg, June 10, 1942, OSRD. A number of letters filed in OSRD reflect the deep concern about the secrecy of the hydrogen-bomb possibility.

4. *Manhattan District History*, Bk. VIII, *Los Alamos Project (Y)*, Vol. I, *General*, pp. 2.1–2.7; *MD History*, Bk. VIII, Vol. II, *Technical*, pp. I.3–I.5.

5. *MD History*, Bk. VIII, Vol. I, pp. 4.1–4.2, 5.2, Vol. II, I.5–I.6; Letter contract No. W-7405 eng-36, Jan. 1, 1943, AEC.

6. In *Now It Can Be Told; The Story of the Manhattan Project* (New York, 1962), pp. 61–63, Groves indicates there was more hesitation about Oppenheimer's qualifications than the record suggests.

7. Compton to Conant, Jan. 11, 1943, OSRD.

8. Oppenheimer to Conant, Feb. 1, 1943, OSRD.

9. Conant and Groves to Oppenheimer, Feb. 25, 1943, OSRD.

10. *MD History*, Bk. VIII, Vol. II, pp. I.8–I.10.

11. This discussion is based on the following documents, all in OSRD: Meeting, Oppenheimer and Greenewalt, December 15, 1942; R. C. Tolman, Memorandum on Los Alamos Project as of March 1943; and Lewis *et al.*, Report of Special Reviewing Committee on Los Alamos Project, May 10, 1943. See also *MD History*, Bk. VIII, Vol. II, pp. I.12–I.21.

12. Notes on the Serber lectures by E. U. Condon entitled "The Los Alamos Primer," LASL; Tolman to Groves, Mar. 20, 1943, OSRD; *MD History*, Bk. VIII, Vol. II, p. I.11; The Los Alamos Conference (Reports of Meetings, Apr. 15–24, 1943), Los Alamos Scientific Laboratory Report LA-2.

13. Report of Special Reviewing Committee, May 10, 1943, with attached schedule of experimental program,

OSRD; *MD History*, Bk. VIII, Vol. II, pp. I.23–I.24.

14. Report of Special Reviewing Committee, May 10, 1943, Tolman to Groves, Mar. 20, 1943, OSRD; Oppenheimer, Memorandum on Ordnance, Mar. 15, 1943, MD.

15. Minutes, Governing Board, May 6, May 20, May 31, June 3, June 10, June 17, LASL; Tolman to Groves, July 7, 1943, MD.

16. *MD History*, Bk. VIII, Vol. II, pp. III.1–III.2; Groves, *Now It Can Be Told*, pp. 154–55. Condon subsequently worked at Berkeley on advanced design for the electromagnetic process.

17. Oppenheimer to the Coordinating Council, June 18, 1943, LASL.

18. Minutes, Governing Board, May 6, May 31, Aug. 5, 1943, Oppenheimer to Division Leaders *et al.*, June 23, 1943, LASL; *Oppenheimer Hearing*, pp. 166–67; *MD History*, Bk. VIII, Vol. II, p. III.3.

19. Minutes, Military Policy Committee, June 24, 1943, MD; Bush, Memorandum of Conference with the President, June 24, 1943, OSRD; Roosevelt to Oppenheimer, June 29, 1943, to Groves, June 29, 1943, FDR.

20. *Oppenheimer Hearing*, p. 164.

21. Groves to Compton and Oppenheimer, June 17, 1943, Oppenheimer to Groves, Oct. 4, 1943, OSRD; *MD History*, Bk. VIII, Vol. II, pp. III.4–III.5.

22. Tolman to Groves, May 12, 1944, OSRD; *Oppenheimer Hearing*, p. 949; *MD History*, Bk. VIII, Vol. II, pp. V.19–V.25.

23. Minutes, Governing Board, July 15, 1943, LASL; Oppenheimer to Compton, July 16, 1943, OSRD; Progress Reports of the Experimental Physics Division, July 15, 1943, LAMS-4, Aug. 1, 1943, LAMS-5, Nov. 15, 1943, LAMS-28; Seaborg, *The Transuranium Elements* (New Haven, 1958), p. 55; *MD History*, Bk. VIII, Vol. II, p. IV.4.

24. Minutes, Governing Board, Dec. 1, 1943, Tolman, Report on Status of Ordnance Work at Y (As of March 1, 1944), LASL; Progress Reports of the Experimental Physics Division, Dec. 15, 1943, LAMS-34, Jan. 1, 1944, LAMS-48.

25. For a summary, see *MD History*, Bk. VIII, Vol. II, pp. VI.1–VI.3, VI.27–VI.29. For details, see Progress Reports of the Experimental Physics Division, July, 1943—June, 1944, LAMS reports. Experimental techniques are described in *National Nuclear Energy Series*, Div. V, *Los Alamos Project*, Vol. I, *Electronics*, Vol. II, *Ionization Chambers and Counters*, and Vol. III, *Miscellaneous Physical and Chemical Techniques*.

26. *MD History*, Bk. VIII, Vol. II, pp. V.1–V.6, V.13–V.19; Progress Reports of the Theoretical Physics Division, Jan.–June, 1944, LAMS-47, 61, 74, 92, 102, 110.

27. *MD History*, Bk. VIII, Vol. II, pp. V.25–V.26; Conant, Findings of Trip to L. A., July 4, 1944, OSRD.

28. Groves to Roosevelt, Feb. 4, 1944, Minutes, Military Policy Committee, June 21, 1944, MD.

29. *MD History*, Bk. VIII, Vol. II, pp. VIII.7–VIII.19, and C. S. Smith, "Metallurgy at Los Alamos, 1943–1945," *Metal Progress*, LXV (May, 1954), 81–9, are valuable summaries. Details are recorded in Monthly Progress Reports of the Chemistry and Metallurgy Divisions, Mar.–June, 1944, LAMS reports. For work at the Metallurgical Laboratory see Seaborg, *Transuranium Elements*, pp. 56–67. Joseph W. Kennedy kept a diary for the years 1944–45. A valuable source of information on the chemical and metallurgical work at Los Alamos, it is on file in AEC.

30. Minutes, Military Policy Committee, June 21, 1944, MD. Thomas' report of June 13, as well as others, is to be found in OSRD.

31. *MD History*, Bk. VIII, Vol. II, pp. VII.5, VII.24–VII.25; Kistiakowsky to Conant, Nov. 1, 1943, OSRD.

32. *MD History*, Bk. VIII, Vol. II, pp. VII.5–VII.7; Rose to Parsons, June 16, 1943, OSRD; Minutes, Governing Board, July 1, 1943, LASL.

33. The Critical Mass of Projectiles of Active Material in Guns, Feb. 10, 1944, Report LA-59; Progress Report of the Theoretical Physics Division for the Month ending February 29, 1944, LAMS-61; *MD History*, Bk. VIII, Vol. II, pp. VII.8–VII.10.

34. *Ibid.*, pp. VII.25–VII.26.

35. Minutes, Governing Board, Oct. 28, Nov. 4, LASL; Kistiakowsky to Conant, Nov. 1, 1943, OSRD; Minutes,

683

Military Policy Committee, Nov. 9, 1943, MD.

36. Oppenheimer to Conant, Nov. 1, 1943, Kistiakowsky to Conant, Nov. 1, 1943, OSRD.

37. Tolman, Report on Status of Ordnance Work at Y (As of March 1, 1944), LASL; Progress Reports of the Theoretical Physics Division, Jan.–Feb., 1944, LAMS-47, 61. For the test plans see Minutes, Governing Board, Jan. 27, Feb. 17, 1944, LASL, and Kennedy Diary, May 11, 1944.

38. Tolman, Report on Status of Ordnance Work at Y (As of March 1, 1944), LASL. Kistiakowsky's schedule is in MD.

39. Oppenheimer to Groves, Mar. 25, 1944, AEC; Tolman to Groves, May 12, 1944, OSRD.

40. Oppenheimer to Groves, Feb. 14, 1944, MD; Tolman to Groves, May 12, 1944, OSRD; Progress Reports of the Theoretical Physics Division, Feb.–May, 1944, LAMS-61, 74, 92, 102.

41. Minutes, Governing Board, June 8, 1944, LASL; Tolman to Groves, May 12, 1944, OSRD; Kennedy Diary, June 8, 1944; Report of the Ordnance Division, Mar.–July, 1944, LAMS-73, 80, 94, 106, 116; *MD History*, Bk. VIII, Vol. II, pp. VII.32–VII.34.

42. Conant, Findings of Trip to L. A. July 4, 1944, OSRD.

43. *MD History*, Bk. VIII, Vol. II, pp. VII.2–VII.5, VII.16–VII.26, VII.35–VII.39; Report of the Ordnance Division, Mar.–July, 1944, LAMS-73, 80, 94, 106, 116; N. F. Ramsey and R. L. Brin, compilers, Nuclear Weapons Engineering and Delivery, Report LA-1161, pp. 6–11; Parsons to W. R. Lockridge, July 10, 1944, MD.

44. Minutes, Governing Board, June 17, 1943, R. W. Dodson and E. Segrè, Report of Committee on the Question of Neutrons Accompanying Alpha Decay, Sept. 22, 1943, LAMS-63; *MD History*, Bk. VIII, Vol. II, p. VI.7.

45. Special Chemistry of 94; Report for Month ending March 15, 1943, Metallurgical Laboratory Report CK-514; Progress Reports of the Experimental

Physics Division, June 15, 1944, LAMS-114, July 1, 1944, LAMS-117; Summary of Meeting of Project Y Technical Board on July 13, 1944, Report LAMS-113; O. Chamberlain, G. W. Farwell, and E. Segrè, 94240 and its Spontaneous Fission, Sept. 8, 1944, Report LAMS-131; Oppenheimer to Conant, July 11, 1944, Thomas to Groves, July 21, 1944, OSRD; Oppenheimer to Groves, July 18, 1944, MD; *MD History*, Bk. VIII, Vol. II, pp. IV.17–IV.18.

46. Minutes, Military Policy Committee, May 10, 1944, MD.

47. Groves, undated note on CPC meeting of April 13, 1944, MD; Bush to Conant, June 24, 1943, OSRD.

48. This report to Marshall is in MD.

49. Minutes, Military Policy Committee, May 5, 1943, MD; Ramsey and Brin, Nuclear Weapons Engineering and Delivery, Report LA-1161, pp. 122–25. Groves was not ready to dismiss the German menace in August, 1944. His August 7 report to Marshall carried this warning: "If the enemy has made an active and uninterrupted effort it is a possibility that he could be ready in the near future to use the weapon on a limited scale." In December, 1944, Groves received news that reduced his fears to the vanishing point. Dr. Samuel A. Goudsmit, scientific chief of the Alsos Mission, the Manhattan District's overseas intelligence unit, reported on his findings at Strasbourg (Goudsmit to Tolman, Dec. 8, 1944, OSRD). Captured documents indicated that German scientists were no further along than Americans had been about the end of 1942. In April, 1945, Alsos located about 1,200 tons of Belgian uranium ore the German Army had confiscated in 1940. On April 23, Groves informed General Marshall that this removed any possibility of Germany using an atomic bomb. Groves devotes three chapters in *Now It Can Be Told* to Manhattan District foreign intelligence work. Goudsmit published his story in *Alsos* (New York, [1947]).

CHAPTER 8

1. Lothian to Roosevelt, July 8, 1940, S. Welles to Lothian, July 29, 1940,

Foreign Relations of the United States: Diplomatic Papers, 1940, III

(Washington, 1958), pp. 78–79; James P. Baxter, 3rd, *Scientists Against Time* (Boston, 1947), p. 119.

2. Baxter, *Scientists Against Time*, pp. 120–21; Bush to Marshall and Stark, Sept. 30, 1940, Stimson and Knox to Bush, Oct. 24, 1940, Memorandum on Interchange of Scientific Information between the National Defense Research Committee and Great Britain and Canada, Oct. 25, 1940, Bush to Knox and Stimson, Oct. 30, 1940, HLH.

3. Baxter, *Scientists Against Time*, pp. 121–23; Conant to Bush, Mar. 11, 1943, OSRD.

4. Bush to Wilson, Sept. 30, 1940, Conant to Bush, Apr. 23, 1942, OSRD.

5. Bush to Conant, Oct. 9, 1941, OSRD; Roosevelt to Churchill, Oct. 11, 1941, FDR.

6. Winston S. Churchill, *The Hinge of Fate* (Boston, 1950), pp. 378–79; Churchill to Hopkins, Feb. 27, 1943, HLH.

7. K. Cohen to H. C. Urey, Mar. 3, 1942, SAM; Murphree to Conant, May 7, 1942, Conant to Murphree, May 15, 1942, OSRD.

8. Anderson to Bush, Mar. 23, 1942, Bush to Anderson, Apr. 20, 1942, OSRD.

9. Bush to Anderson, June 19, 1942, OSRD.

10. Churchill, *The Hinge of Fate*, pp. 374–81; Roosevelt to Bush, July 11, 1942, FDR.

11. Churchill, *The Hinge of Fate*, pp. 382–84; Henry L. Stimson and McGeorge Bundy, *On Active Service in Peace and War* (New York, 1947), pp. 423–24.

12. Three letters, Anderson to Bush, Aug. 5, 1942, OSRD.

13. Two letters, Bush to Anderson, Sept. 1, 1942, OSRD.

14. H. H. Bundy, Record of Meeting, Sept. 23, 1942, Suggested Outline for Meeting, Sept. 23, 1942, MD.

15. Bush to Anderson, Oct. 1, 1942, OSRD.

16. Memorandum, H.L.S., Oct. 29, 1942, Annex 5, Diplomatic History of the Manhattan Project, MD.

17. Stimson and Bundy, *On Active Service*, 424–27; Henry L. Stimson Diary, July 12, 1942, Yale University Library.

18. Conant to Bush, Oct. 26, 1942, Bush to Conant, Nov. 2, 1942, OSRD.

19. Minutes, Military Policy Committee, Nov. 12, 1942, MD; Basic Policy Governing Exchange of Information between U. S., Canada and U. K. on S-1, Nov. 13, 1942, Conant to Bush, Nov. 13, 1942, OSRD.

20. Conant to Bush, Dec. 14, 1942, Bush to Conant, Dec. 22, 1942, OSRD; Report on Present Status and Future Program on Atomic Fission Bombs, encl., Bush to Roosevelt, Dec. 16, 1942, OSRD.

21. Stimson Diary, Dec. 26, 27, 1942.

22. Roosevelt to Bush, Dec. 28, 1942, OSRD.

23. Conant to C. J. Mackenzie, Jan. 2, 1943, Memorandum on the Interchange with the British and Canadians on S-1, Jan. 7, 1943, OSRD.

24. Akers, Note on Discussion of the 26th January, 1943, MD.

25. Conant to Mackenzie, Jan. 27, 1943, Conant to Akers, Feb. 6, 1943, Minutes, Military Policy Committee, Mar. 30, 1943, OSRD.

26. Churchill to Hopkins, Feb. 16, 1943, Hopkins to Churchill, Feb. 24, 1943, HLH.

27. Both messages are filed in HLH.

28. Bush to Hopkins, Mar. 31, 1943, HLH. See also Conant to Bush, Mar. 25, 1943, which Bush sent along as an enclosure.

29. Churchill to Hopkins, Apr. 1, 1943, Halifax to Hopkins, Apr. 14, 1943, Hopkins to Eden, Apr. 15, 1943, Bush to Hopkins, Apr. 27, 1943, HLH.

30. Roy F. Harrod, *The Prof; A Personal Memoir of Lord Cherwell* (London, 1959) is a delightful appraisal by a colleague.

31. Bush, Memorandum of Conference with Mr. Harry Hopkins and Lord Cherwell at the White House, May 25, 1943, OSRD.

32. Churchill, *The Hinge of Fate*, p. 809; Cherwell to Hopkins, May 30, 1943, Churchill to Hopkins, June 10, 1943, HLH.

33. Bush, Memorandum of Conference with the President, June 24, 1943, OSRD.

34. Roosevelt to Hopkins, July 14, 1943, FDR; Hopkins to Roosevelt, July 20, 1943, Roosevelt to Churchill, July 20, 1943, HLH; Roosevelt to Bush, July 20, 1943, OSRD.

685

35. Bush, pencilled notes on 10 Downing Street stationery, and Memorandum for the File, Aug. 4, 1943, OSRD.
36. Stimson Diary, attachment to Aug. 10, 1943, entry.
37. Bush, Memorandum for the File, Aug. 4, 1943, OSRD. For the Secretary's attitude toward postwar Anglo-American co-operation, see Stimson Diary, Dec. 18, 1942.
38. Bush, Memorandum for the File, Aug. 4, 1943, OSRD; Bundy, Memorandum of Meeting at 10 Downing Street on July 22, 1943, Annex 11, Diplomatic History of the Manhattan Project, MD; Stimson Diary, July 22, 1943.
39. Bush to Conant, July 23, 1943, Bush to Bundy, July 27, 28, 1943, OSRD.
40. Churchill to Stimson, July 28, 1943, Annex 12, Diplomatic History of the Manhattan Project, MD.
41. Bush, Memorandum for the File, Aug. 4, 1943, OSRD.
42. Anderson to Bush, Aug. 4, 1943, OSRD.
43. Conant to Bush, July 30, 1943, Aug. 3, 6, 1943, OSRD.
44. Bush to Anderson, Aug. 6, 1943, Anderson to Bush, Aug. 6, 1943, OSRD.
45. Bush to Bundy, Aug. 6, 1943, Bush to Roosevelt, Aug. 7, 1943, OSRD; Bundy to Stimson, Aug. 6, 1943, and attached note in Stimson's hand, MD; Stimson Diary, Aug. 10, 1943. The original of the Quebec Agreement is filed in MD. The New York *Times* published the complete text on Apr. 6, 1954.
46. Stimson Diary, Sept. 7, 8, 1943.
47. Minutes of Informal Meeting, Sept. 8, 1943, MD.
48. Extract Minutes, Military Policy Committee, Sept. 9, 1943, Minutes, Subcommittee of the Combined Policy Committee, Sept. 10, 1943, MD.
49. Memorandum by Brigadier General L. R. Groves, 10 December 1943, Annex 19, Diplomatic History of the Manhattan Project, MD.
50. U. S. Atomic Energy Commission, *In the Matter of J. Robert Oppenheimer* (Washington, 1954), pp. 174–75, 177.
51. Urey, Report on Survey of the English Work on Uranium Separation Methods, SAM.
52. Minutes, Combined Policy Committee, Feb. 17, 1944, DS.
53. Report to the Combined Policy Committee from the Sub-Committee on Joint Development of a Heavy Water Pile, Apr. 6, 1944, MD; Minutes, Combined Policy Committee, Apr. 13, 1944, DS.
54. Groves to Compton, May 20, 1944, with encl., OSRD.
55. Mackenzie to Groves, May 25, 1944, MD; Report to Combined Policy Committee on Progress on the Canadian N.R.X. Project, OSRD.
56. C. F. Clarke, Jr., Summary of Information, Sept. 18, 1945, encl., T. R. Mountain to Groves, Sept. 26, 1945, MD.
57. Minutes, Combined Policy Committee, Apr. 13, 1944, Sept. 19, 1944, DS.
58. Groves to Wallace, Stimson, and Marshall, Aug. 21, 1943, MD.
59. Minutes, Military Policy Committee, June 24, 1943, MD. The work of the Manhattan District in the raw-materials field is described in *Manhattan District History*, Bk. VII, *Feed Materials, Special Procurement and Geographical Exploration.*
60. Minutes, Military Policy Committee, Dec. 14, 1943, MD; Minutes, Combined Policy Committee, Dec. 17, 1943, DS.
61. Groves to Roosevelt, Feb. 4, 1944, MD; Bush to Conant, Feb. 15, 1944, Minutes, Combined Policy Committee, Feb. 17, 1944, DS.
62. Articles of Agreement Governing Collaboration Between the Authorities of the United States of America, the Kingdom of Great Britain and the Dominion of Canada in the Matter of Uranium Ore, Draft of Feb. 17, 1944, OSRD.
63. Agreement and Declaration of Trust, June 13, 1944, MD.
64. Tolman to Groves, July 7, 1943, Conant, Historical note on S-1 Developments, May 4, 1944, OSRD.
65. Chronological History of the Negotiations with the Belgian Government, Aug. 25, 1944, H. S. Traynor, Report on Second Trip to London, 6 May to 20 May 1944, Winant to Stimson, May 12, 1944, MD.
66. Stimson to Roosevelt, Aug. 25, 1944, MD; Minutes, Combined Policy Committee, Sept. 19, 1944, DS; History of United States–British and Canadian Atomic Relations, Jan., 1949, AEC.
67. Groves to Stimson, Nov. 24, 1944, with encl., A Survey of the World's

686

Sources of Uranium and Thorium (October 26, 1944), MD.

68. Bush to Anderson, May 15, 1944, OSRD.

CHAPTER 9

1. Henry L. Stimson Diary, Feb. 15, 18, June 9, 1944, Yale University Library; Bush memorandum, June 10, 1944, Bush to Bundy, Feb. 24, 1944, MD. Monthly expenditures and other financial data are included in *Manhattan District History*, Bk. I, *General*, Vol. V, *Fiscal Procedures*, App. B. The S-1 appropriation was part of the unobligated balance of $958,400,-000, which the War Department requested be carried over to fiscal year 1945. Senate Committee on Appropriations, *Military Establishment Appropriation for 1945. Hearing on H. R. 4967*, June 16–17, 1944 (Washington, 1944), pp. 34, 77.

2. The best single source on feed materials is *MD History*, Bk. VII, *Feed Materials, Special Procurement, and Geographical Exploration*, Vol. I, *Feed Materials and Special Procurement*. See also P. L. Merritt to files, Dec. 21, 1942, Apr. 22, 1944, Nichols to J. C. Marshall, June 15, 1943, J. R. Ruhoff to Groves, Oct. 25, Dec. 27, 1943, Ruhoff to Nichols, Apr. 5, 1944, MD; Richard L. Neuberger, "Arctic Cradle of the Atom," *Liberty*, XXII (Nov. 24, 1945), 78–80.

3. Merritt to Nichols, Jan. 26, 1945, Nichols to Groves, Feb. 4, 1944, Production Flow Charts, June 1, 1943, Dec. 1, 1944, in Manhattan District Project Data as of June 1, 1943, W. E. Kelley to Groves, Mar. 6, 1945, Summary of Classified Shipments, June 1, 1945, MD; *MD History*, Bk. VII, Vol. I, pp. 4.1–4.8.

4. W. A. Wilhelm, A History of Uranium Metal Production in America, Iowa State College Report ISC-1076; *MD History*, Bk. VII, Vol. I, pp. 7.1–10.10.

5. *MD History*, Bk. V, *Electromagnetic Project*, Vol. VI, *Operation*, pp. 4.8–4.9; Monthly Report on DSM Project, June, 1944, MD; W. E. Kelley, Notes on Conferences, July 3, 14, 1944, OROO.

6. W. E. Kelley, Notes on Conferences, Aug. 9, 25, 1944, MD. Webb's analysis

is attached to the notes for Aug. 25. *MD History*, Bk. V, Vol. III, *Design*, pp. 3.27–3.31, 3.48–3.50. *National Nuclear Energy Series*, Div. I, *Electromagnetic Process*, Vol. VII, *Separation of Isotopes in Calutron Units*, pp. 118–19, 180–81, 286–89.

7. The section on the S-50 plant is based on *MD History*, Bk. VI, *Liquid Thermal Diffusion*.

8. *MD History*, Bk. II, *Gaseous Diffusion*, Vol. V, *Operation*, p. 3.1. Monthly Reports on DSM Project, July–Oct., 1944, MD.

9. W. E. Kelley, Memo to files, Sept. 23, 1944, K. D. Nichols to J. H. Webb, Nov. 7, 1944, OROO.

10. M. L. Oliphant to Groves, Nov. 13, 1944, Lawrence to Groves, Dec. 14, 1944, LRL; Monthly Reports on DSM Project, Nov.–Dec., 1944, MD; *MD History*, Bk. V, Vol. VI, *Operation*, pp. 4.10–4.11.

11. Monthly Reports on DSM Project, Jan.–Mar., 1946, W. S. Parsons to Nichols, July 9, 1945, MD; J. S. Gordon, K-25 Process Division Historical Report, 1943–1947, in files of Union Carbide Nuclear Co., Oak Ridge.

12. M. Benedict, Production schedule for K-25, Mar. 1, 1945, Notes on conference, Feb. 26, 1945, MD.

13. J. C. Stowers to Nichols, Dec. 12, 1945, A. C. Klein, Minutes of meeting, Jan. 23, 1945, Groves to Lawrence, Feb. 27, 1945, Groves to Stimson, Mar. 17, 1945, Groves, Memo to file, Mar. 27, 1945, MD; Lawrence to Groves, Jan. 6, 1945, OSRD.

14. Stimson Diary, Apr. 11, 1945.

15. Greenewalt to Groves, July 22, 1944, MD.

16. Groves to W. S. Carpenter, Jr., Oct. 11, 1946, Monthly Reports on DSM Project, July, 1944, MD.

17. Production Office Diary, Vol. I, Aug. 16, 17, 1944, du Pont, Operation of Hanford Engineer Works, Bk. I, pp. 91, 113–14, HOO; *MD History*, Bk. IV, *Pile Project*, Vol. VI, *Operation*, pp. 4.7–4.8, 5.57–5.58.

18. Matthias to Groves, Sept. 18, 1944,

687

Franklin T. Matthias Diary, Sept. 13–21, 1944, HOO; *MD History*, Bk. IV, Vol. VI, pp. 5.2–5.5.

19. Hilberry to Compton, Oct. 3, 1944, Production Office Diary, Vol. I, Sept. 26–30, 1944, HOO; *MD History*, Bk. IV, Vol. VI, pp. 4.9–4.12; U. S. Atomic Energy Commission, *In the Matter of J. Robert Oppenheimer* (Washington, 1954), p. 174.

20. Compton to Groves, Oct. 3, 1944, Draft Notes at Meeting at Chicago, Oct. 3, 1944, Zinn to Compton, Oct. 3, 1944, Matthias to Groves, Oct. 3, 1944, MD; Compton to Groves, Oct. 4, 1944, HOO; Minutes, Project Council, Oct. 4, 1944, Metallurgical Laboratory Report CS-2239; *MD History*, Bk. IV, Vol. II, *Research*, Part I, *Metallurgical Laboratory*, pp. 3.13–3.14.

21. Matthias Diary, Oct. 2–10, 12, 1944; Weekly Reports, Hilberry to Compton, Oct. 2–Nov. 27, 1944, HOO; Matthias to Groves, Oct. 17, 1944, MD; Minutes, Project Council, Oct. 18, 1944, Report CS-2272; Minutes, Policy Meeting, Dec. 20, 1944, Report CS-2513.

22. Du Pont, Operation of Hanford Engineer Works, Vol. XII, pp. 56, 63, 69, 86, Weekly Reports, Hilberry to Compton, Oct. 2–Nov. 27, 1944, HOO.

23. A. C. Jones to Groves, Feb. 12, 1945, Minutes, Meeting on Product Specification, Feb. 19, 1945, C. A. Thomas to Groves, Feb. 23, 1945, W. O. Simon to J. N. Tilley, Mar. 19, 1945, MD.

24. Oppenheimer, Memorandum to the U. S. Atomic Energy Commission on participation of the United Kingdom in the wartime development of the atomic bomb, July 15, 1949, AEC.

25. *MD History*, Bk. VIII, *Los Alamos Project (Y)*, Vol. II, *Technical*, pp. I.7, III.17–III.18.

26. P. de Silva to Groves, Aug. 30, 1944, E. K. Clarke to S. L. Warren, Aug. 29, 1944, MD; *Oppenheimer Hearing*, (Washington, 1954), pp. 14, 30.

27. Minutes, Governing Board, June 29, 1944, AEC; Oppenheimer to the Governing Board, July 5, 1944, LASL.

28. Minutes, Administrative Board, July 20, 1944, Oppenheimer to Bacher, Aug. 14, 1944, to Kistiakowsky, Aug. 14, 1944, LASL; *MD History*, Bk. VIII, Vol. II, pp. IX.1–IX.5.

29. Oppenheimer to Groves, Oct. 6, Nov.

14, 1944, MD; Progress Report of the Research Division, Nov. 1, 1944, Los Alamos Scientific Laboratory Report LAMS-163; Serber, Preliminary Report on Multiplication, Nov. 1, 1944, LAMS-154; The Gun, Report LA-1007, Ch. 3, pp. 1–5; *MD History*, Bk. VIII, Vol. II, pp. XIV.3–XIV.5.

30. Kistiakowsky, E-5 Interim Report, Aug. 4, 1944, LASL; Kistiakowsky, ed., Explosives and Detonation Waves, Part I, Report LA-1043, p. III.13.

31. Progress Reports of the Gadget Physics Division, Oct. 1–Dec. 15, 1944, LAMS-150, 158, 169, 170, 186.

32. Conant, Summary of Trip to "Y," December 1944, OSRD.

33. Parsons explained the changing mission of Los Alamos in a letter to Groves via Oppenheimer, Sept. 25, 1944, AEC.

34. N. F. Ramsey and R. L. Brin, compilers, Nuclear Weapons Engineering and Delivery, Report LA-1161, pp. 12–14; *MD History*, Bk. VIII, Vol. II, pp. XIV.2, XIV.7–XIV.8; Wesley F. Craven and James L. Cate, eds., *The Army Air Forces in World War II:* Vol. V, *The Pacific: Matterhorn to Nagasaki, June 1944 to August 1945* (Chicago, 1953), pp. 705–6.

35. Kistiakowsky to Conant, Aug. 30, 1944, OSRD.

36. *MD History*, Bk. VIII, Vol. II, pp. III.27–III.36; *MD History*, Bk. VIII, Vol. III, *Auxiliary Activities*, Chapter 1, *Los Alamos Procurement Office*, pp. 1.1–1.4, 2.1–2.7; *MD History*, Bk. VIII, Vol. III, Ch. 9, *Supplementary Activities*, pp. 9.1–9.3; Minutes, Administrative Board, Aug. 4, 1944, LASL; Conant to Bush, Oct. 20, 1944, OSRD.

37. MD History, Bk. VIII, Vol. II, pp. IX.11, IX.19–IX.20, XVI.14.

38. Rowe to J. A. Derry, Nov. 13, 1944, MD; *Oppenheimer Hearing*, p. 509; *MD History*, Bk. VIII, Vol. II, p. IX.4.

39. *MD History*, Bk. VIII, Vol. III, Ch. 2; Oppenheimer to Bush, Nov. 21, 1944, AEC.

40. Minutes of Technical and Scheduling Conference, Dec. 14, 1944, Report LAMS-178, Dec. 28, 1944, LAMS-183, Jan. 1, 1945, LAMS-185; Progress Report of the Research Division, Mar. 1, 1945, LAMS-222, *MD History*, Bk. VIII, Vol. II, p. XIV.7.

41. Progress Report of the Research Division, Feb. 1, 1945, LAMS-207.
42. Minutes of Technical and Scheduling Conference, Jan. 11, 1945, Report LAMS-191; Progress Report of the Gadget Physics Division, Feb. 15, 1945, LAMS-216.
43. Progress Report of the Gadget Physics Division, Jan. 15, 1945, LAMS-198; Peierls to Chadwick, Jan. 3, 1945, Feb. 7, 1945, AEC.
44. Progress Report of the Gadget Physics Division, Feb. 15, 1945, LAMS-216.
45. Minutes of Technical and Scheduling Conference, Feb. 17, 1945, Report LAMS-210; Allison, Memorandum, Mar. 1, 1945, LASL; Joseph W. Kennedy Diary, Mar. 5, 1945, T. B. Moon to Chadwick, Mar. 7, 1945, AEC; *MD History*, Bk. VIII, Vol. II, p. X.6.
46. Bainbridge, ed., *Trinity*, Report LA-1012, pp. 1–14.
47. Nuclear Weapons Engineering and Delivery, Report LA-1161, pp. 14–16.
48. Monthly Progress Reports of the Chemistry and Metallurgy Division, Sept. 1, 1944—May 1, 1945, LAMS-127, 146, 155, 176, 190, 211, 217, 234, 249; Cyril S. Smith, "Metallurgy at Los Alamos, 1943–1945," *Metal Progress*, LXV (May, 1954), 86–89; *MD History*, Bk. VIII, Vol. II, pp. XVII.5–XVII.10.
49. Kennedy Diary, especially Jan. 18–Feb. 3, Feb. 5–14, 19, Mar. 24, Apr. 5, 1945, AEC.
50. Kennedy Diary, especially Mar. 9, Apr. 5, 18, 27, 1945, Moon to Chadwick, Feb. 28, 1945, Peierls and Moon to Chadwick, Apr. 5, 1945, AEC; Matthias Diary, Apr. 27, 1945, HOO.
51. Progress Report of the Research Division, Apr. 1, 1945, LAMS-233; Minutes of Technical and Scheduling Conference, Apr. 5, 1945, Report LAMS-235; Progress Report of the Gadget Physics Division, Apr. 15, 1945, LAMS-236; Peierls to Chadwick, Apr. 18, 1945, AEC.
52. Oppenheimer to Groves, Apr. 11, 1945, MD; Progress Report of the Gadget Physics Division, Mar. 15, 1945, LAMS-233, Apr. 15, 1945, LAMS-236; Recommendations of the Initiator Advisory Committee, May 1, 1945, Report LAMS-237.
53. Progress Report of the Theoretical Physics Division for April, 1945, LAMS-235.
54. Groves, Memorandum, Mar. 27, 1945, MD.

CHAPTER 10

1. Laboratory Council Policy Meeting, Aug. 25, 1943, Metallurgical Laboratory Report CS-886; Laboratory Council Policy Meeting, Jan. 3, 1944, Report CS-1226; Project Council Policy Meeting, Feb. 16, 1944, Report CS-1354; Compton to Groves, Apr. 10, 1944, OSRD.
2. Conant to Groves, Apr. 6, 1944, OSRD; Project Council Policy Meeting, June 7, 1944, Report CS-1769.
3. Project Council Policy Meeting, July 5, 1944, Report CS-1913; Jeffries to Compton, July 14, 1944, OSRD; Compton, *Atomic Quest* (New York, 1956), p. 232.
4. Compton to Bush, July 22, 1944, with encls., Compton to Bush, July 29, 1944, Bush to Compton, July 31, 1944, Compton, longhand note attached to Bush to Conant, undated, OSRD.
5. Bush to Compton, Aug. 10, 1944, Bush to Franck, Aug. 28, 1944, OSRD. The Military Policy Committee had acted on August 5, two days before Compton's talk with Bush.
6. Prospectus on Nucleonics, Nov. 18, 1944, MD.
7. Report of Committee on Postwar Policy, Dec. 28, 1944, MD.
8. Bush and Conant to Stimson, Sept. 19, 1944, OSRD.
9. Comments by Conant, handwritten on Bush to Conant, Apr. 17, 1944, Conant, Some Thoughts on International Control of Atomic Energy, May 4, 1944, OSRD.
10. Bohr used a memorandum of July 3, 1944, as the basis of his remarks. A copy is filed in MD.
11. Churchill, *Closing the Ring* (Boston, 1951), pp. 146–61; Notes made by John J. McCloy after meeting in Secretary Hull's office, Sept. 20, 1944, attachment to Henry L. Stimson Diary, Sept. 20, 1944, Yale University Library.
12. The American copy is filed in FDR.

690

13. Bush, Memorandum of Conference, Sept. 22, 1944, Bush to Conant, Sept. 23, 1944, OSRD.

14. Bush to Conant, Sept. 25, 1944, OSRD.

15. Bush and Conant to Stimson, with encl., Sept. 30, 1944, OSRD.

16. Bush to Conant, Oct. 24, 1944, OSRD; Memorandum on the Future of Biological Warfare as an International Problem in the Postwar World, encl., Bush and Conant to Stimson, Oct. 27, 1944, OSRD.

17. Bush, Memorandum of Conference, Dec. 8, 1944, Bush to Conant, Dec. 13, 1944, OSRD.

18. Stimson Diary, Dec. 15, 29, 1944; Groves to Stimson, Dec. 14, 26, 1944, Comments on the Aide-Memoire, encl., Groves to Winant, Oct. 31, 1944, MD; Bush to Conant, Oct. 31, 1944, Bush to Groves, Dec. 4, 1944, OSRD.

19. Stimson Diary, Dec. 29, 30, 1944; Groves, Memorandum, Dec. 30, 1944, [Stimson], Memorandum of Conference with the President, Dec. 30, 1944, Groves to Marshall, Dec. 30, 1944, MD. Groves stated in his December 30 memorandum of the conversation at the White House that the report shown the President was one dated August 7. On March 3, 1959, he reviewed the December 30 memorandum and noted that the August 7 date was correct. However, on December 30, 1944, he endorsed the report of that date with the following: "The Sec. of War and the President both read this paper and approved it." In view of this notation and the unlikelihood that Stimson and Groves would give Roosevelt an outdated report almost five months old, it seems certain that the President saw the document described in the text. It is printed in U. S. Department of State, *Foreign Relations of the United States: Diplomatic Papers. The Conferences at Malta and Yalta, 1945* (Washington, 1955), pp. 383–84.

20. Stimson Diary, Dec. 31, 1944.

21. Bush to Conant, Jan. 2, 1945, to Bundy, Jan. 30, 1945, OSRD; Stimson Diary, Jan. 3, 1945.

22. Winant to Bundy, Dec. 31, 1944, MD.

23. H.H.B., Problem with Respect to the French, Jan. 19, 1945, MD; Stimson Diary, Jan. 19, 1945.

24. H.H.B., Memorandum, Jan. 19, 1945,

MD; Stimson Diary, Jan. 22, 1945; Minutes, Combined Policy Committee, Jan. 22, 1945, DS.

25. Minutes, Combined Policy Committee, Mar. 8, 1945, DS.

26. Laboratory Steering Committee, Nov. 29, 1944, Report CS-2460; Policy Meeting, Dec. 6, 1944, Report CS-2463; Nichols to Groves with encls., Feb. 19, 1945, MD.

27. Bush to Bundy, Jan. 30, Feb. 1, 1945, Bush to Conant, Feb. 13, 1945, OSRD.

28. Minutes, Military Policy Committee, Feb. 24, 1945, Groves to Compton, Feb. 27, 1945, MD.

29. Bush to Conant, Feb. 13, 1945, OSRD.

30. Bush to Conant, Feb. 15, 1945, OSRD; Stimson Diary, Feb. 13, 15, 1945. Bush said in a letter to Bundy, Apr. 25, 1945, OSRD, that he had sent his letter to the President.

31. Bundy to Stimson, Mar. 3, 1945, Bundy, undated notes on talk with Stimson, MD; Stimson Diary, Mar. 5, 1945.

32. Engel to Stimson, Feb. 23, 1945, Patterson to Stimson, Feb. 25, 1945, MD; Stimson Diary, Feb. 26, 1945.

33. Byrnes to Roosevelt, Mar. 3, 1945, MD.

34. Stimson Diary, Mar. 15, 1945.

35. Compton to Groves, Mar. 1, 1945, OSRD; Special Meeting of Policy Council, Mar. 20, 1945, Report CS-2863; Minutes of Policy Meeting, Mar. 21, 1945, Report CS-2862.

36. Project Council—Policy Meeting—9:00 A.M. Aug. 23, 1944, Report CS-2087; Allison *et al.* to Compton, Nov. 6, 1944, OSRD.

37. Compton to Groves, Mar. 5, 1945, OSRD.

38. Einstein to Roosevelt, Mar. 25, 1945, FDR. The authors conclude that an unsigned document among the papers of James F. Byrnes is the Szilard memorandum. Excerpts were published in *Bulletin of the Atomic Scientists*, III (Dec., 1947), 351–53.

39. Unsigned memorandum, Apr. 21, 1945, OSRD; Alice K. Smith, "Behind the Decision to Use the Atomic Bomb," *Bulletin of the Atomic Scientists*, XIV (Oct., 1958), 293–95.

40. Truman recalled in his memoirs that Stimson spoke to him in very general terms about the bomb project after his first Cabinet meeting on April 12. *Memoirs* Vol. I, *Year of Decisions*

(Garden City, N. Y., 1955), p. 10. Stimson did not record such a conversation in his diary.

41. Stimson Diary, Apr. 23–25, 1945; Groves to Stimson, Apr. 23, 1945, Stimson, Memorandum Discussed with the President, MD. When Stimson published this memorandum in *Harper's Magazine*, CXCIV (Feb., 1947), 99–100, he omitted the reference to Russia.

42. The addendum, dated Mar. 24, 1945, is filed with the July 3, 1944, memorandum in MD.

43. Bush to Bundy, Apr. 25, 1945, MD.

44. Harrison to Stimson, May 1, 1945, MD; Stimson Diary, May 1, 1945. Stimson did not remain unaware of Bohr's suggestion. Bundy and Harrison almost surely told him of it. If they did not, there was Justice Frankfurter. Frankfurter called on Stimson May 3 and talked over the international implications of S-1. Later, June 12, Frankfurter again talked with Stimson about international matters, specifically mentioning certain Bohr suggestions, Stimson Diary, May 3, June 12, 1945.

45. Stimson Diary, May 2, 3, 1945; Stimson to Bush, May 4, 1945, OSRD.

46. Conant to Stimson, May 5, 1945, OSRD. There were two factors that may have contributed to Conant's heavy stress on notifying the Russians before using the bomb. First, he no doubt knew of Bohr's conversation with Bush. Second, he may well have seen a letter from Smyth to Tolman (Apr. 26, 1945, MD), which argued that telling the Russians about the bomb in general terms might strengthen their motives for cooperating.

47. Stimson to Conant, May 9, 1945, Conant to Harrison, May 9, 1945, MD.

691

CHAPTER 11

1. Henry L. Stimson Diary, Apr. 12, 1945, Yale University Library.

2. *The Entry of the Soviet Union into the War Against Japan: Military Plans, 1941–1945* (U. S. Department of Defense Press Release, September, 1955), pp. 28–30, 46–50; U. S. Department of State, *Foreign Relations of the United States: Diplomatic Papers. The Conferences at Malta and Yalta, 1945* (Washington, 1955), p. 984.

3. *Entry of the Soviet Union into the War Against Japan*, pp. 54–55, 60–68; John R. Deane, *The Strange Alliance; The Story of Our Efforts at Wartime Co-operation with Russia* (New York, 1947), pp. 262–65; Ellis M. Zacharias, *Secret Missions; The Story of an Intelligence Officer* (New York, 1946), pp. 349–50; Truman, *Memoirs*, Vol. I, *Year of Decisions* (Garden City, N. Y., 1955), p. 207. Herbert Feis, *Japan Subdued; the Atomic Bomb and the End of the War in the Pacific* (Princeton, 1961), pp. 5–7, explains the differences among the Joint Chiefs of Staff in detail that space does not permit in this narrative. On pp. 15–17, he narrates the background of the President's May 8 references to Japan.

4. Stimson Diary, Apr. 2, 3, 23, 1945; Walter Millis, ed., *The Forrestal Diaries* (New York, 1951), pp. 50–51.

5. Grew, *Turbulent Era; A Diplomatic Record of Forty Years, 1904–45* (Boston, 1952), II, pp. 1455–57.

6. Stimson Diary, May 13–15, 1945.

7. Stimson to Truman, May 16, 1945, attached to Stimson Diary, May 16, 1945.

8. *Entry of the Soviet Union into the War Against Japan*, p. 68.

9. Stimson to Grew, May 21, 1945, in *Entry of the Soviet Union into the War Against Japan*, pp. 70–71. Forrestal concurred in this reply.

10. Memorandum of 1st Conversation at the Kremlin, 8 PM May 26, *Foreign Relations of the United States: Diplomatic Papers. The Conference of Berlin (The Potsdam Conference), 1945* (Washington, 1961), I, No. 24, pp. 24–31; Memorandum of 3rd Conversation at the Kremlin, 6 PM May 28, *Conference of Berlin*, I, No. 26, pp. 41–52; Robert E. Sherwood, *Roosevelt and Hopkins; An Intimate History* (New York, 1948), pp. 902–4.

692

11. Truman to Hopkins, May 28, 1945, *Conference of Berlin*, I, No. 28, p. 87; Memorandum of 4th Conversation at the Kremlin, 6 PM May 30, *Conference of Berlin*, I, No. 27, pp. 53–57; Herbert Feis, *The China Tangle* (Princeton, 1953), p. 312. Churchill was most distressed at Truman's insistence on July 15. He considered it much too late. *Triumph and Tragedy* (Boston, 1953), p. 599.

12. Grew, *Turbulent Era*, II, pp. 1428–31, 1434; Stimson Diary, May 29, 1945; *Forrestal Diaries*, p. 66.

13. Notes of an Informal Meeting of the Interim Committee, May 9, 1945, MD; Stimson Diary, May 9, 1945.

14. Notes of an Informal Meeting of the Interim Committee, 14 May 1945, MD; Bush to Conant, May 14, 1945, OSRD.

15. Notes of an Informal Meeting of the Interim Committee, Friday, May 18, 1945, Interim Committee Log, May 19, 1945, MD; Conant to Bush, May 18, 1945, OSRD.

16. Stimson Diary, May 18–30, 1945; Brewster to Truman, May 24, 1945, Stimson to Marshall, May 30, 1945, MD.

17. Szilard, "A Personal History of the Atomic Bomb," *The University of Chicago Roundtable*, No. 601 (Sept. 25, 1949), 14–15; Byrnes, *All In One Lifetime* (New York, 1958), pp. 284–85.

18. Notes of the Interim Committee Meeting, 31 May 1945, MD.

19. K. K. Darrow to Lawrence, Aug. 9, 1945, Lawrence to Darrow, Aug. 17, 1945, LRL; Arthur H. Compton, *Atomic Quest*, (New York, 1956), pp. 238–39; Byrnes, *All In One Lifetime*, p. 285. Since Lawrence wrote closest to the event, the account of the luncheon discussion depends heavily on his version.

20. Stimson Diary, May 31, 1945.

21. Notes of the Interim Committee Meeting, Friday, 1 June 1945, MD.

22. A copy of this draft has not been found. An undated, unsigned paper entitled "Objectives" that may be a rough outline for this draft is filed in MD. This document contemplated notifying the world that the United States had the bomb and calling on the Japanese to surrender or accept guilt for all subsequent slaughter.

23. Stimson Diary, June 6, 1945.

24. Truman, *Year of Decisions*, p. 270; Feis, *China Tangle*, pp. 313–14.

25. *Forrestal Diaries*, pp. 68–69.

26. Robert J. C. Butow, *Japan's Decision to Surrender* (Stanford, 1954), pp. 67–72, 75, 78, 90–91, 93–102. The U. S. Strategic Bombing Survey's account of the same events, *Japan's Struggle to End the War* (1946), pp. 4–7, is oversimplified and misleading.

27. *Forrestal Diaries*, p. 69.

28. Grew, *Turbulent Era*, II, pp. 1434–35, 1437.

29. *Entry of the Soviet Union into the War Against Japan*, p. 76; William D. Leahy, *I Was There* (New York, 1950), pp. 383–84.

30. *Entry of the Soviet Union into the War Against Japan*, pp. 77–85; *Forrestal Diaries*, pp. 70–71; McCloy, *The Challenge to American Foreign Policy* (Cambridge, 1953), pp. 40–42.

31. Stimson Diary, June 19, 1945.

32. Notes on Initial Meeting of Target Committee, Apr. 27, 1945, Minutes of Third Target Committee Meeting, May 28, 1945, Groves to L. Norstad, May 30, 1945, Groves to Marshall, June 13, 1945, MD; Groves, *Now It Can Be Told; The Story of the Manhattan Project* (New York, 1962), pp. 266–76. At this time, Stimson was very much concerned over the realization that the Army Air Forces had abandoned precision bombing in attacks on Japan. He saw both Arnold and Truman about this. He was worried, he told the President. He did not want the United States to outdo Hitler in atrocities. He also feared that the Air Forces might bomb out Japan so thoroughly that the atomic weapon would not have a fair background against which to show its strength. Stimson Diary, June 1, 6, 1945.

33. Compton, Statement to the National Policy Committee, May 28, 1945, Compton to Conant, June 2, 1945, Compton to Bush, June 2, 1945, MD; N. Hilberry to Bartky *et al.*, June 4, 1945, ANL.

34. Compton to Stimson, June 12, 1945, with encl., Political and Social Problems, MD; Compton, *Atomic Quest*, p. 236.

35. Interim Committee Log, June 15, 16, 1945, MD.

36. Oppenheimer to Stimson (attention Harrison), June 16, 1945, with encls., MD. Alice K. Smith has expressed doubts that the Scientific Panel saw the Franck report. "Behind the Decision to Use the Atomic Bomb," *Bulletin of the Atomic Scientists,* XIV (Oct., 1958), 306. Her position depends on the assumption that the Scientific Panel met June 9 and 10, while the report was not finished until June 11, and on Oppenheimer's recollection that he did not see the report before it was printed after the war. Mrs. Smith has been led astray by Compton's inexact reference to the date of the meeting. She may still be correct that the panel did not see the report, though this seems most unlikely. There can be no doubt, however, that the four scientists knew the report existed and were familiar with its argument.

37. Notes of the Interim Committee Meeting, 21 June 1945, MD.

38. Bush to Conant, Mar. 9, 1944, Conant to Bush, Mar. 15, 1944, OSRD; Minutes, Military Policy Committee, May 10, 1944, MD.

39. Stimson Diary, June 25, 1945; Harrison to Stimson, June 26, 1945, MD.

40. Bard, Memorandum on the Use of the S-1 Bomb, June 27, 1945, Harrison to Stimson, June 28, 1945, MD. Harrison sent Byrnes a copy of Bard's memorandum on July 2. Interim Committee Log, July 2, 1945, MD. At Forrestal's suggestion, Bard obtained an interview with Truman and argued that the Navy's blockade made invasion unnecessary. Smith, "Behind the Decision to Use the Atomic Bomb," *Bulletin of the Atomic Scientists,* XIV (Oct., 1958), 297.

41. Stimson Diary, June 26, 1945; Minutes of Meeting of the Committee of Three, June 26, 1945, *Conference of Berlin,* I, No. 591, pp. 887–88; Stimson to Truman, July 2, 1945, *Conference of Berlin,* I, No. 592, pp. 889–92.

42. Stimson Diary, July 2, 1945. The draft warning Stimson showed the President is published in *Conference of Berlin,* I, No. 592, pp. 893–94. If the Soviet Union had entered the war, Stalin would join Truman, Churchill, and Chiang in issuing it.

43. Stimson Diary, July 3, 1945.

44. John Ehrman, *Grand Strategy,* Vol.

VI, *October 1944—August 1945* (United Kingdom Military Series, *History of the Second World War*) (London, 1956), pp. 296–99; Interim Committee Log, June 25, 1945, MD.

45. Minutes, Combined Policy Committee, July 4, 1945, DS.

46. London had ordered Wilson's reference to the Prime Minister. Ehrman, *Grand Strategy,* p. 299, concludes that Churchill preferred to acquiesce in the decision to use the bomb and to rely on talks with Truman at Potsdam to learn the reason for it and to influence, if necessary, the manner of carrying it into effect.

47. Monthly Reports on DSM Project, March–July, 1945, Groves, Notes Taken at Meeting at Y, June 27, 1945, MD; Tennessee Eastman Corporation, C.E.W.-T.E.C. History, January 1943 to May 1947 (unpublished typescript, 1947), pp. 73–74; Franklin T. Matthias Diary, July 4, 10, 1945, HOO.

48. Progress Report of the Gadget Physics Division, May 15, 1945, Los Alamos Scientific Laboratory Report LAMS-252; Minutes of Technical and Scheduling Conference, June 4, 1945, Report LAMS-254; Monthly Progress Report of the Chemistry and Metallurgy Division, July 1, 1945, LAMS-266; Joseph W. Kennedy Diary, June 4, 1945, AEC.

49. Progress Report of the Theoretical Physics Division for May, 1945, LAMS-260; Progress Report of the Gadget Physics Division, May 15, 1945, LAMS-252; Progress Report of the Explosives Division for May 1945, LAMS-264; R. C. Tolman to Groves, May 17, 1945, OSRD.

50. Minutes of Technical and Scheduling Conference, May 10, 1945, Report LAMS-240; Monthly Progress Report of the Chemistry and Metallurgy Division, June 1, 1945, LAMS-261; Progress Report of the Theoretical Physics Division for May, 1945, LAMS-260.

51. Progress Report of the Gadget Physics Division, May 15, 1945, LAMS-252; Monthly Progress Report of the Chemistry and Metallurgy Division, June 1, 1945, LAMS-261.

52. Progress Report of the Gadget Physics Division, June 15, 1945, LAMS-262; Samuel K. Allison, Relation between the Various Activities of the Labora-

693

tory, Report LA-1006, Ch. 2, pp. 45–6; Kennedy Diary, June 21, 1945, R. E. Peierls and P. B. Moon to J. Chadwick, June 13, 1945, Peierls to Chadwick, June 7, July 4, 1945, AEC.

53. Progress Report of the Theoretical Physics Division for May, 1945, LAMS-260, for June, 1945, LAMS-267; Relation between the Various Activities of the Laboratory, Report LA-1006, Ch. 1, pp. 32–34, 52; Kennedy Diary, June 25, 1945, Moon to Chadwick, June 20, 1945, Peierls to Chadwick, July 4, 1945, AEC.

54. N. F. Ramsey and R. L. Brin, compilers, Nuclear Weapons Engineering and Delivery, Report LA-1161, pp. 16–17; Ramsey to Oppenheimer, Parsons, and Bradbury, June 23, 1945, LASL; Groves to Conant, May 3, 1945, MD.

55. Nuclear Weapons Engineering and Delivery, Report LA-1161, pp. 17–18, 147–48; Wesley F. Craven and James L. Cate, eds., *The Army Air Forces in World War II:* Vol. V, *The Pacific: Matterhorn to Nagasaki* (Chicago, 1953), pp. 706–7; Groves, *Now It Can Be Told*, pp. 277–87.

56. K. T. Bainbridge, ed., Trinity, Report LA-1012, p. 55.

57. Tolman to Groves, May 13, 1945, OSRD; Trinity, Report LA-1012, pp. 29–32.

58. Trinity, Report LA-1012, pp. 33–49.

59. Tolman to Groves, Apr. 17, 1945, Oppenheimer to Groves, June 27, 1945, Bainbridge, Trinity Experiments for July 1945 Test, July 5, 1945, OSRD.

60. Monthly Progress Report of the Chemistry and Metallurgy Division, Aug. 1, 1945, LAMS-276; Kennedy Diary, July 2, 9, 1945.

61. Nuclear Weapons Engineering and Delivery, Report LA-1161, pp. 30–74; Trinity, LA-1012, pp. 76–78.

62. Trinity, Report LA-1012, p. 79; Kennedy Diary, July 15–16, 1945.

63. Groves to Stimson, July 18, 1945, Thoughts by E. O. Lawrence, July 16, 1945, MD; William L. Laurence, *Dawn Over Zero, The Story of the Atomic Bomb* (New York, 1947), pp. 3–12. An excellent collection of statements by scientists and other observers is filed in OSRD.

64. Progress Report of the Theoretical Physics Division for July, 1945, LAMS-273; Relation between the

Various Activities of the Laboratory, Report LA-1006, Ch. 2, p. 58; Kennedy Diary, July 23, 1945, Oppenheimer to Farrell and Parsons, July 23, 1945, AEC; Notes on Intermediate Scheduling Conference, July 17, 1945, LASL.

65. Interim Committee Log, July 16–17, 1945, MD; Monthly Progress Report of the Chemistry and Metallurgy Division, Aug. 1, 1945, LAMS-276.

66. Harriman to Truman and Byrnes, July 12, 1945, *Conference of Berlin,* I, No. 577, pp. 862–63, July 13, 1945, *Conference of Berlin,* I, No. 578, pp. 863–64.

67. Minutes Secretary's Staff Committee Saturday Morning, July 7, 1945, *Conference of Berlin,* I, No. 595, pp. 900–1. MacLeish sent Byrnes a letter on July 6 which explained his doubts about saving the Emperor and suggested that the American people might resent modification of the unconditional-surrender formula. *Conference of Berlin,* I, No. 593, pp. 895–97.

68. *Entry of the Soviet Union into the War Against Japan,* pp. 87–88; Ray S. Cline, *Washington Command Post: The Operations Division* (Washington, 1951), pp. 345–46.

69. Butow, *Japan's Decision to Surrender,* pp. 116–25; *Forrestal Diaries,* pp. 74–75. Nine messages that passed between Togo and Sato from July 11 through July 15 are printed in *Conference of Berlin,* I, Nos. 580–88, pp. 974–83. The most significant is No. 582.

70. Stimson Diary, July 15, 1945.

71. Stimson to Byrnes, July 17, 1945, with encl., Stimson to Truman, July 16, 1945, *Conference of Berlin,* II, No. 849, pp. 753–57.

72. Stimson to Byrnes, July 16, 1945, with Memorandum for the President, July 16, 1945, *Conference of Berlin,* II, No. 1236, pp. 1265–67.

73. Harrison to Stimson, July 16, 1945, MD; Stimson Diary, July 16, 1945.

74. Stimson Diary, July 17, 1945; *The Memoirs of Cordell Hull* (New York, 1948), II, 1593–94; Grew to Byrnes, July 16, 1945, transmitting Hull to Byrnes, July 16, 1945, *Conference of Berlin,* II, No. 1237, p. 1267; Grew, Memorandum of Telephone Conver-

sation, July 17, 1945, *Conference of Berlin*, II, No. 1238, p. 1268. Grew relayed Byrnes's message to Hull over the telephone. Actually, the two men were not far apart in their views. Grew agreed that it was wise to delay the warning.

75. Stimson Diary, July 17, 1945.

76. Meeting of the Joint Chiefs of Staff, Tuesday, July 17, 1945, *Conference of Berlin*, II, pp. 39–42; Meeting of the Joint Chiefs of Staff, Wednesday, July 18, 1945, *Conference of Berlin*, II, pp. 64–66; Leahy for the Joint Chiefs of Staff, Memorandum for the President, July 18, 1945, *Conference of Berlin*, II, No. 1239, pp. 1268–69.

77. Truman-Stalin Meeting, July 17, 1945, *Conference of Berlin*, II, pp. 43–46. C. E. Bohlen, Memorandum, Mar. 28, 1960, *Conference of Berlin*, II, Doc. 1418, pp. 1582–87; Leahy, *I Was There*, p. 397; Stimson Diary, June 17, 1945.

78. Harrison to Stimson, July 17, 1945, MD; Stimson Diary, July 18, 1945.

79. Churchill, *Triumph and Tragedy*, pp. 640–42; Ehrman, *Grand Strategy*, pp. 302–3. At a meeting of the Combined Chiefs of Staff on July 16, Sir Alan Brooke asked if the United States Chiefs had considered interpreting the unconditional-surrender formula for the Japanese. The American leaders replied that they had, and Admiral Leahy suggested that it would be useful if the Prime Minister explained his views on the subject to the President. Meeting of the Combined Chiefs of Staff, Monday, July 16, 1945, *Conference of Berlin*, II, pp. 35–38.

80. Truman-Stalin Meeting, Wednesday, July 18, 1945, *Conference of Berlin*, II, pp. 86–87; C. E. Bohlen, Memorandum, Mar. 28, 1960, *Conference of Berlin*, II, No. 1419, pp. 1587–88. Truman's reference to Sweden involved an overture from the Japanese military attaché in Stockholm to Prince Carl Bernadotte. *Conference of Berlin*, II, No. 1420, pp. 1589–90. In 1956, Truman told Department of State historians that he was familiar with the Japanese approach to Russia before Stalin mentioned it. Editor's note, *Conference of Berlin*, I, p. 873.

81. Stimson Diary, July 19, 1945; Reflections on the Basic Problems which Confront Us, July 19, 1945, *Confer-*

ence of Berlin, II, No. 1157, pp. 1155–57.

82. Stimson Diary, July 20, 1945.

83. Stimson to Truman, July 20, 1945, *Conference of Berlin*, II, No. 1241, pp. 1271–72.

84. Groves to Stimson, July 18, 1945, MD.

85. Stimson Diary, July 21, 1945.

86. Two messages, Harrison to Stimson, July 21, 1945, and Stimson to Harrison, July 21, 1945, MD. The case for bombing Kyoto rested on the same foundation as Stimson's opposition. The city was an intellectual and cultural center. The people there were most likely to appreciate the significance of the new weapon.

87. Stimson Diary, July 22, 1945.

88. Stimson Diary, July 22, 1945; H. H. Arnold, *Global Mission* (New York, 1949), pp. 588–89; Marshall to Handy, July 22, 1945, MD.

89. No official record of the Truman-Churchill conversation has been found. This account is based on Churchill, *Triumph and Tragedy*, pp. 638–39. Lord Alanbrooke's notes of July 23, 1945, corroborate Churchill's own summary of his views on the bomb. Arthur Bryant, *Triumph in the West: A History of the War Years Based on the Diaries of Field-Marshal Lord Alanbrooke, Chief of the Imperial General Staff* (New York, 1959), pp. 363–64.

90. Truman to P. J. Hurley, July 23, 1945, *Conference of Berlin*, II, No. 1216, p. 1241; Hurley to Truman and Byrnes, July 20, 1945, *Conference of Berlin*, II, No. 1214, pp. 1225–27; Note by Churchill, July 23, 1945, in Ehrman, *Grand Strategy*, p. 272.

91. Stimson Diary, July 23, 1945; Arnold, *Global Mission*, pp. 589–90.

92. Three messages, Harrison to Stimson, July 23, 1945, and Stimson to Harrison, July 23, 1945, MD.

93. Stimson Diary, July 24, 1945.

94. Meeting of the Combined Chiefs of Staff with Truman and Churchill, Tuesday, July 24, 1945, *Conference of Berlin*, II, pp. 339–44. The final version of the report is published in *Conference of Berlin*, II, No. 1381, pp. 1462–73.

95. Tripartite Military Meeting, Tuesday, July 24, 1945, *Conference of Berlin*, II, pp. 344–53.

96. Truman's *Year of Decisions*, p. 416, is

695

the only first-hand account of the conversation. Byrnes, *Speaking Frankly* (New York, 1947), p. 263, Churchill, *Triumph and Tragedy*, pp. 669–70, and Leahy, *I Was There*, p. 429, tell how they watched the conversation and what Truman told them afterwards. According to Byrnes, who talked with the President on the ride back to Babelsberg, Truman told Stalin that the United States planned to use its new bomb very soon unless the Japanese surrendered.

97. Arnold, *Global Mission*, p. 591; Handy to Marshall, July 24, 1945, MD. Groves, *Now It Can Be Told*, pp. 309–10, explains that Nagasaki was added in place of Kyoto.

98. Marshall to Handy, July 24, 1945, Handy to Spaatz, July 25, 1945, MD; Stimson Diary, July 25–28, 1945.

99. *Conference of Berlin*, II, Nos. 1244, 1245, pp. 1275–77; Churchill to Truman, July 25, 1945, *Conference of Berlin*, II, No. 1249, pp. 1279–81.

100. Byrnes, *Speaking Frankly*, pp. 206–7; Hurley to Truman and Byrnes, July 26, 1945, *Conference of Berlin*, II, No. 1251, p. 1282.

101. Proclamation by the Heads of Government, July 26, 1945, *Conference of Berlin*, II, No. 1382, pp. 1474–76.

102. Byrnes to Molotov, July 26, 1945, *Conference of Berlin*, II, No. 1253, p. 1284; Byrnes-Molotov Meeting, Friday, July 27, 1945, *Conference of Berlin*, II, pp. 449–50.

103. Butow, *Japan's Decision to Surrender*, pp. 140–41, 143–49; Press Conference Statement by Prime Minister Suzuki, July 28, 1945, *Conference of Berlin*, II, No. 1258, p. 1293.

104. Tenth Plenary Meeting, Saturday, July 28, 1945, *Conference of Berlin*, II, pp. 459–65.

105. For the Togo-Sato exchanges between July 17 and 25, see *Conference of Berlin*, II, Nos. 1223–35, pp. 1248–64. Truman told Department of State historians in 1956 that he already knew what Stalin reported. Presumably, Washington forwarded the Japanese intercepts to Truman and Byrnes. In any event, Forrestal told Byrnes of the messages in detail when he saw him on July 28.

106. *Forrestal Diaries*, p. 78; Byrnes, *All In One Lifetime*, pp. 297–98.

107. Truman-Molotov Meeting, Sunday, July 29, 1945, *Conference of Berlin*, II, pp. 1333–34.

108. Truman to Stalin, July 31, 1945, *Conference of Berlin*, II, pp. 1333–34; Truman, *Year of Decisions*, pp. 402–3; Byrnes, *All In One Lifetime*, pp. 297–98.

109. Harriman to Byrnes, July 28, 1945, *Conference of Berlin*, II, No. 1218, pp. 1243–44; Byrnes to Hurley, July 28, 1945, *Conference of Berlin*, II, No. 1219, p. 1245; Harriman to Byrnes, July 31, 1945, *Conference of Berlin*, II, No. 1222, pp. 1246–47; Feis, *The China Tangle*, pp. 330–31.

110. Notes of the Interim Committee Meeting, Friday, 6 July 1945, Interim Committee Log, July 7, 10, 11, 20, 25, 28, 1945, MD. The British had submitted the Prime Minister's statement for American approval. On July 20, Harrison told Makins he would recommend it favorably to the Secretary of War. Should the rush of events make it necessary, Harrison favored either party issuing its statements without specific approval at the highest level.

111. Stimson Diary, July 30, 31, 1945; Stimson to Truman, July 31, 1945, MD; Stimson to Truman, July 30, 1945, *Conference of Berlin*, II, No. 1313, pp. 1375–76; *Conference of Berlin*, II, p. 27. In 1953, President Truman wrote Professor James L. Cate that he issued a final order for dropping the bombs on the way back from Potsdam. See Craven and Cate, *Matterhorn to Nagasaki*, letter reproduced between pp. 712 and 713. We have found no contemporary evidence of such an order. Groves has explained that in the minds of leaders in Washington there was no inconsistency between the plans for dropping the bomb as early as August 1 and the "after about 3 August" in the July 25 directive to Spaatz. *Now It Can Be Told*, pp. 311–12.

112. Two messages, Spaatz to Handy, July 31, 1945, and Handy to Spaatz, July 31, 1945, MD.

113. A Petition to the President of the United States, July 17, 1945, MD.

114. Daniels to Compton, July 13, 1945, Compton to Nichols, July 24, 1945, MD; Compton, *Atomic Quest*, pp. 242–45. For an analysis of the mean-

696

ing of the poll, see Smith, "Behind the Decision to Use the Atomic Bomb," *Bulletin of the Atomic Scientists*, XIV (Oct., 1958), 305.

115. Notes for possible use of Secretary Patterson in talking to Mr. Charles Ross, undated, MD.

116. Stimson Diary, Aug. 1–3, 1945; W. H. Kyle, Notes of a Meeting on the Smyth Report in the Office of the Secretary of War, August 2, 1945, Stimson to Truman, Aug. 3, 1945, MD.

117. Nuclear Weapons Engineering and Delivery, Report LA-1161, pp. 147–51; Groves to Marshall, Aug. 6, 1945, MD; Groves, *Now It Can Be Told*, pp. 305–7.

118. Stimson Diary, Aug. 6, 1945; Groves to Marshall, Aug. 6, 1945, MD. The mission against Hiroshima is described in Craven and Cate, *Matterhorn to Nagasaki*, pp. 716–17, and in Fletcher Knebel and Charles W. Bailey II, *No High Ground* (New York, 1960), pp. 158–74, 202–12.

119. Stimson Diary, Aug. 6, 1945. The Truman and Stimson statements were published in the New York *Times*, Aug. 7, 1945; Groves, *Now It Can Be Told*, pp. 327–28. The original releases are included in *Manhattan District History*, Bk. I, *General*, Vol. IV, *Auxiliary Activities*, Ch. 8, *Press Releases*.

120. Stimson Diary, Aug. 6, 1945; Nuclear Weapons Engineering and Delivery, Report LA-1161, p. 153. Farrell's leaflet campaign seems to have been something of an afterthought. The first delivery was made on August 9, the day of the attack on Nagasaki. Farrell cancelled the drops the following day, when Japanese surrender efforts raised doubts about their wisdom. Groves, *Now It Can Be Told*, p. 346.

121. For an account of the attack on Nagasaki, see Craven and Cate, *Matterhorn to Nagasaki*, pp. 718–20.

122. Butow, *Japan's Decision to Surrender*, pp. 150–78; U. S. Strategic Bombing Survey, *Japan's Struggle to End the War*, pp. 8–9.

123. Truman, *Year of Decisions*, pp. 427–32; Byrnes, *All In One Lifetime*, pp. 304–6; *Forrestal Diaries*, p. 84; Stimson Diary, Aug. 9, 1945. On August 10, Groves gave Marshall the schedule for shipping the final components of a second implosion bomb. The same day, Marshall returned Groves's memorandum with the following handwritten notation: "It is not to be released over Japan without express authority from the President." Groves to Marshall, Aug. 10, 1945, MD. This exchange, while not necessarily inconsistent with Groves's account in *Now It Can Be Told*, pp. 352–53, suggests that Groves took less initiative in opposing a third nuclear strike than he later remembered.

124. Butow, *Japan's Decision to Surrender*, pp. 194, 207–8; U. S. Strategic Bombing Survey, *Japan's Struggle to End the War*, p. 9.

125. Butow, *Japan's Decision to Surrender*, pp. 175–77, 224, 233, stresses the unprecedented character of the Emperor's intervention. He points out, pp. 210–13, that even with the imperial will expressed, military fanatics made a last-ditch attempt to block surrender. Samuel E. Morison has argued powerfully that "the atomic bomb was the keystone of a very fragile arch" over which Japan passed to surrender. *Victory in the Pacific, 1945* (*History of United States Naval Operations in World War II*, Vol. XIV) (Boston, 1960), pp. 336–53. Everyman will be his own historian on the merits of American policy on the use of atomic weapons against Japan. Feis discusses many of the issues that have been raised in *Japan Subdued*, pp. 167–87.

126. Stimson Diary, Aug. 9, 1945.

127. *A General Account of The Development of Methods of Using Atomic Energy for Military Purposes under the Auspices of the United States Government, 1940–45* (Washington, 1945), p. 165.

697

CHAPTER 12

1. Truman, *Memoirs*, Vol. I, *Year of Decisions* (Garden City, N. Y., 1955), pp. 334–35.

2. Tolman, Report of Committee on Postwar Policy, Dec. 28, 1944, MD; Hilberry, Suggestions to the Interim

698

Committee on the Subject of Post War Organization, July 17, 1945, Bush to Conant, Apr. 17, 1944, Conant to Bush, July 27, Sept. 15, 1944, Stewart to Bush, Aug. 25, 1944, Bush and Conant to Stimson, Sept. 19, 1944, Bush, Memorandum of conference with President, Sept. 22, 1944, Bush to Harrison and Bush to Conant, May 14, 1945, OSRD.

3. Henry L. Stimson Diary, Nov. 7, 14, 1944, Jan. 4, Apr. 6, 12, 30, 1945, Yale University Library; "Establishing a Research Board for National Security, Hearing before the Senate Committee on Naval Affairs on S. 825," Senate Report, 79 Cong., 1 sess., no. 551 (June 20, 1945); Bush to Conant, Apr. 5, 1945, OSRD.

4. "Legislative Proposals for the Promotion of Science," *Senate Document*, 79 Cong., 1 sess., no. 92 (August, 1945); Don K. Price, *Government and Science* (New York, 1954), pp. 48–51.

5. Bush, *Science, the Endless Frontier* (Washington, 1945) pp. 107–11.

6. Notes of Interim Committee meeting, July 6, 1945, MD; Bush, Federal organization for post-war S-1 activities, July 9, 1945, OSRD.

7. The Magnuson bill was introduced as S. 1285, the Kilgore bill as S. 1297, 79 Cong., 1 sess.

8. Bush and Conant to Interim Committee, July 18, 1945, OSRD; Notes of Interim Committee meeting, July 19, 1945, MD.

9. Draft Bill of July 18, 1945, OSRD. The complete file of legislative records is in MD.

10. Bush to Harrison, July 19, 1945, OSRD; Conant's notes on third draft, July 25, 1945, MD.

11. Interim Committee Log, July 20, 1945, MD. The Interim Committee records indicate at least three subsequent drafts of the bill between July 19 and August 7. The second draft apparently never survived Army review. Marbury gave the third to Harrison on July 25. Bush had the fourth draft on August 7.

12. Royall-Marbury bill, third draft, Sections 3(a) and 10(a).

13. *Ibid.*, Sec. 13(d).

14. Interim Committee Log, July 25, 1945, MD; Bush to Harrison, Aug. 7, 1945, OSRD.

15. Editorials, Des Moines *Register*, Aug. 9, 1945; *PM*, Aug. 13, 1945; Roundtable discussion as reported in New York *Times*, Aug. 13, 1945.

16. Royall and Marbury to Stimson, Aug. 8, 1945, MD.

17. New York *Times*, Aug. 10, 1945.

18. Stimson Diary, Aug. 8, Aug. 12–Sept. 3, 1945; Harrison, Memorandum for the record, Aug. 18, 1945, MD.

19. Oppenheimer to Stimson, Aug. 17, 1945, MD.

20. Cohen to Royall, Aug. 23, 1945, DS.

21. Harrison to Ickes, Aug. 24, 1945, DS; Royall to Stimson, Aug. 24, 31, 1945, Harrison, Memorandum to files, Sept. 8, 1945, MD.

22. Stimson Diary, Sept. 3–5, 1945.

23. G.H.D. to McCloy, Sept. 7, 1945, MD.

24. Proposed Action on Control of Atomic Bombs, encl., Stimson to Truman, Sept. 11, 1945, Interim Committee Log, Sept. 12, 1945, MD; Stimson Diary, Sept. 12, 13, 1945; Henry L. Stimson and McGeorge Bundy, *On Active Service In Peace and War*, (New York, 1947), pp. 642–48.

25. Stimson Diary, Sept. 18, 1945.

26. Stimson Diary, Sept. 21, 1945; Walter Millis, ed., *The Forrestal Diaries*, (New York, 1951), pp. 94–96; Truman, *Year of Decisions*, pp. 525–27.

27. Bush's views were summarized in his memorandum to the President, Sept. 25, 1945, OSRD.

28. Compton to Groves, Aug. 23, 1945; Manley to Groves, Aug. 30, 1945, MD.

29. Chicago *Sun*, Chicago *Sunday Tribune*, Chicago *Herald-American*, Sept. 2, 1945; Dorothy Thompson in Boston *Daily Globe*, Sept. 7, 1945.

30. Draft report of Committee on Social and Political Implications, Aug. 31, 1945, An Attempt to Define the Platform for Our Conversations With Members of the Senate and House of Representatives, Sept. 7, 1945, JAS.

31. *Congressional Record*, 79 Cong., 1 sess., pp. 8336, 8360, 8363.

32. Washington *Evening Star*, New York *Times*, Sept. 10, 1945; Proposed outline of the [Chicago] organization, Sept. 14, 1945, JAS; Memorandum to Chicago scientists, Sept. 21, 1945, Atomic Scientists of Chicago, Educational Questionnaire, Sept. 25, 1945, ASC. Members of the executive committee were: Simpson, chairman; Leo Szilard, Glenn T. Seaborg, J. J. Nick-

son, Austin Brues, David Hill, and Eugene Rabinowitch. See A. K. Smith, "Behind the Decision to Use the Atomic Bomb," *Bulletin of the Atomic Scientists*, XIV (Oct. 1958), 311–2.

33. R. R. Wilson to Oppenheimer, Sept. 7, 1945, Oppenheimer to Harrison, Sept. 9, 1945, Harrison to Oppenheimer, Sept. 24, 1945, L. D. Nordheim *et al.* to Interim Committee, Sept. 24, 1945, MD; W. E. Cohen, Oak Ridge, to Dorothy Thompson, Sept. 12, 1945, ASC.

34. *Congressional Record*, 79 Cong., 1 sess., pp. 8364–76.

35. Harrison, memorandum to files, Sept. 8, 1945, Interim Committee Log, Sept. 11, 12, 1945, MD.

36. Harrison, memorandum to files, Sept. 14, 1945, MD; H. S. Marks, memorandum to D. A. for background in talking to President, Sept., 1945, DS; Interim Committee Log, Sept. 19, 1945; R. B. to Mr. Connally, Sept. 19, 1945, HST; Arthur H. Vandenberg, Jr., ed., *The Private Papers of Senator Vandenberg* (Boston, 1952), pp. 221–22.

37. Interim Committee Log, Sept. 25, 1945, Harrison, memorandum to files, Sept. 25, 1945, MD; Acheson to Truman, Sept. 25, 1945, DS.

38. Notes of a meeting in the Office of the Secretary of War concerning atomic energy legislation, Sept. 28, 1945, Groves to Patterson, Oct. 1, 1945, MD.

39. The first two working drafts, dated Sept. 29 and 30, 1945, with Marks's handwritten changes and notes are on file in DS.

40. Harrison to Rosenman, Oct. 2, 1945, Interim Committee Log, Oct. 1, 1945, Royall to Harrison, Oct. 2, 1945, Groves's handwritten notes for conference with Rosenman, MD; Memorandum of Conversation, the Earl of Halifax and Mr. Acheson, Oct. 1, 1945, with Rosenman redraft, Oct. 2, 1945, Acheson to Byrnes, Oct. 1, 1945, DS.

41. Interim Committee Log, Oct. 3, 1945, MD. The complete text of the message may be found in Truman, *Year of Decisions*, pp. 530–33 and *Congressional Record*, 79 Cong., 1 sess., pp. 9322–23.

699

CHAPTER 13

1. *Congressional Record*, 79 Cong., 1 sess., pp. 9396–9406.

2. *Ibid.*, p. 9325; New York *Times*, Oct. 9, 1945.

3. House Committee or [   ]ary Affairs, *Atomic Energy, H[   ] on H. R.* 4280, Oct. 9, 18, 1[   ] [   ]shington, 1945), especially pp. [   ], 13, 29, 35–39, 51–52, 70.

4. Atomic Scientists of Chicago, Press releases, Oct. 11, 1945, ASC; Chicago *Sun*, Oct. 11, 1945; New York *Times*, Oct. 11, 1945.

5. H. L. Anderson to W. Higinbotham, Oct. 11, 1945, ASC.

6. Interim Committee Log, Oct. 11, 16, 17, 1945; telegram, Oppenheimer, Fermi, and Lawrence to Patterson, Oct. 11, 1945, Lawrence to Patterson, Oct. 13, 1945, MD; U. S. Atomic Energy Commission, *In the Matter of J. Robert Oppenheimer* (Washington, 1954), p. 35.

7. Dubridge to Harrison, Oct. 15, 1945,

Karl T. Compton to Harrison, Oct. 15, 1945, MD.

8. Senate Committee on Military Affairs, Subcommittee on War Mobilization, *Hearings on Science Legislation*, Oct. 8, 1945—Mar. 5, 1946 (Washington, 1945–46), pp. 10, 203–4, 308–9.

9. Truman's attitude was reported by William S. White in the New York *Times*, Oct. 16, 1945. Interim Committee Log, Oct. 17, 1945, MD.

10. Hearings on H. R. 4280, pp. 71, 83–85, 87, 89, 100–104, 109, 115–16, 126–29.

11. F. Aydelotte *et al.* to Patterson, Oct. 23, 1945, MD.

12. *Congressional Record*, 79 Cong., 1 sess., pp. 9403, 9472.

13. Chuck [Charles Calkins] to McMahon, Oct. 12, 1945, Vandenberg to McMahon, Oct. 9, 1945, McMahon to McKellar, Oct. 12, 1945, McKellar to McMahon, Oct. 13, 1945, SCAE. Action on McMahon's resolution (S. Res. 179) is reported in *Congressional*

700

Record, 79 Cong., 1 sess., pp. 9644, 9759, 9785–89, 10068.

14. "Comments on S. 1463 and H. R. 4280," encl., Snyder to Truman, Oct. 15, 1945, BSM. See also Snyder to Truman, Oct. 17, 1945, BSM.

15. Truman to Snyder, Oct. 18, 1945, HST.

16. *Hearings on Science Legislation*, p. 102.

17. Proposed draft, Patterson to May, Oct. 5, 1945, Smith to Truman, Oct. 22, 1945, BOB.

18. Truman to Smith, Oct. 30, 1945, P. H. Appleby to Patterson, Oct. 25, 1945, BOB.

19. G. S. Allan and G. M. Duff to Groves, Oct. 25, 29, 1945, R. G. Arneson to E. O. Lawrence, Oct. 26, 1945, Royall, Statement to House Committee on introduction of amendments, undated, MD; "Atomic Energy Act of 1945," *House Report*, 79 Cong., 1 sess., no. 1186 (Nov. 5, 1945). Rather than submit a revised version of the original bill, H. R. 4280, May introduced a new bill, H. R. 4566. *Congressional Record*, 79 Cong., 1 sess., p. 10320.

20. Vinson to McMahon, Oct. 29, 1945, SCAE.

21. Resolution Adopted in Conference at Rye, N. Y., Oct. 27–28, 1945, ASC.

22. Newman, rough draft of statement explaining committee's role, Oct. 30, 1945, SCAE.

23. The telegrams and letters of recommendation are on file in SCAE. See also New York *Times*, Nov. 7, 1945.

24. Working papers and first draft of atomic energy bill, Nov. 5, 1945, BSM. Factors bearing on the question of removal powers are summarized in Newman and Miller, *The Control of Atomic Energy, A Study of its Social, Economic, and Political Implications* (New York, 1948), pp. 31–33. Patterson to Truman, Oct. 22, 1945, MD.

25. Levi, Analysis of S. 1463, Oct. 16, 1945, Levi, Some suggested changes in proposed legislation, Oct. 16, 1945, ASC; Levi to T. C. Clark, Oct. 25, 1945, SCAE. A copy of the Levi draft bill is on file in BSM.

26. The document referred to is the Newman-Miller draft, Nov. 5, 1945, BSM. Newman and Miller analyze their contention that "fissionable material . . . is the core of the control problem" in *The Control of Atomic Energy*, pp. 48–85.

27. The analysis took the form of a chart, a copy of which is on file in MD. The positions taken by the participants are reflected in Summary of Atomic Energy Meeting, Nov. 7, 1945, encl., Snyder to Truman, Nov. 14, 1945, BSM; Smith to Snyder, Nov. 9, 1945, BOB; Allan and Duff to Groves, Nov. 8, 1945, MD; Wallace to Truman, Nov. 9, 1945, HST.

28. Patterson to Compton, Nov. 9, 1945, MD.

29. New York *Times*, Oct. 31, 1945.

30. Henshaw *et al.*, undated statement on organization meeting, Oct. 31, 1945, Minutes, general meeting of ASC, Nov. 7, 1945, ASC.

31. Simpson, Report on Washington meeting, Nov. 16, 17, 1945, JAS; L. Chalkley to Bush, Nov. 23, 1945, OSRD-NA; Report on November 16 meeting, encl., A. Jaffey to ASC, Nov. 27, 1945, Charter of NCAI, Dec. 18, 1945, ASC.

32. *Newsweek*, XXVI (December 3, 1945), 42.

33. Federation of American Scientists, History-Diary, Nov. 18, 19, 21, 22, 1945, Higinbotham to Henri Corbière, Apr. 29, 1947, FAS.

34. McMahon, Speech at the "Atomic Age Dinner," New York, Nov. 28, 1945, SCAE.

35. FAS, History-Diary, Nov. 21, 1945, FAS; Program for Oak Ridge Meeting, Nov. 20, 1945, ASC.

36. Groves to Patterson, Nov. 23, 1945, with Condon's questions attached, MD; Newman and Condon to McMahon, Nov. 24, Dec. 3, 1945, SCAE.

37. Patterson, Press statement on May-Johnson bill, encl., G. K. Heiss to May, Nov. 19, 1945, MD.

38. Bankhead to McMahon, Nov. 15, 1945, SCAE.

39. McMahon speech at the "Atomic Age Dinner," New York, SCAE.

40. Truman to Patterson and Forrestal, Nov. 28, 1945, MD. The letter was actually signed on Nov. 30 and was cited in later correspondence by that date. Truman, *Memoirs*, Vol. II, *Years of Trial and Hope* (Garden City, N. Y., 1956), p. 3.

41. Walter Millis, ed., *The Forrestal Diaries* (New York, 1951), pp. 123–24. Undated appointment notes on

Dec. 4 meeting, HST. An unverified account of the meeting was reported by Griffing Bancroft in the Chicago *Sun*, Feb. 26, 1946.

42. Interim Committee Log, Nov. 12, 1945, Patterson to Byrnes, Nov. 12, 1945, Conant to Patterson, Dec. 10, 1945, K. T. Compton to Harrison, Dec. 10, 1945, Record of telephone conversation, Oppenheimer to Harrison, undated, O. H. Davis to Royall, Dec. 5, 1945, MD.

43. Draft letter, Patterson to Truman, Dec. 12, 1945, Arneson to Groves, Dec. 21, 1945, Royall to Patterson, Dec. 21, 1945, Groves to Royall, Dec. 27, 1945, Patterson to Truman, Dec. 27, 1945, MD.

44. A. E. Britt to J. W. Martyn, Nov. 7, 1945, Patterson to Association of Oak Ridge Scientists, Dec. 15, 1945, MD; Patterson to Association of Oak Ridge Scientists, Nov. 29, 1945, HST; Bush to Patterson, Nov. 28, 1945, and Patterson to Bush, Dec. 4, 1945, OSRD-Na; Groves, *Now It Can Be Told; The Story of the Manhattan Project* (New York, 1962), pp. 367–72; Washington *Post*, Mar. 14, 1946.

45. Senate Special Committee on Atomic Energy, *Atomic Energy. Hearings on S. Res. 179*, Nov. 27, 1945—Feb. 15, 1946 (Washington, 1945–46); G. S. Allan and G. M. Duff to Groves, Nov. 30, 1945, MD; Simpson to ASC, Dec. 5, 1945, ASC.

46. Minutes, General meeting of ASC, Nov. 28, 1945, ASC; Austin Brues to Simpson, Dec. 2, 1945, JAS; Miller, "Draft 2½," undated but about Dec. 1, 1945, Edward [Levi] to Miller, Dec. 13, 1945, BSM; *Congressional Record*, 79 Cong., 1 sess., p. 12406.

47. New York *Times*, Oct. 8, 1945.

48. New York *Times*, Oct. 9, 1945; Truman, *Memoirs*, Vol. I, *Year of Decisions* (Garden City, N. Y., 1955), pp. 533–34.

49. Meeting of Secretaries of State, War, and Navy, Oct. 10, 16, 1945, MD; *The Forrestal Diaries*, p. 102.

50. Minutes, Combined Policy Committee, Oct. 13, 1945, Attlee to Truman, Oct. 16, 1945, DS.

51. The Office of European Affairs, Department of State, prepared an excellent study: British Attitudes toward Control of the Atomic Bomb, Nov. 7, 1945, DS. Summaries of British opinion appear in New York *Times*, Nov. 1, 4, 1945.

52. Arthur Bryant, *Triumph in the West: A History of the War Years Based on the Diaries of Field-Marshall Lord Alanbrooke, Chief of the Imperial General Staff* (New York, 1959), pp. 371–72; New York *Times*, Oct. 20, Nov. 8, 1945.

53. Clement R. Attlee, *As It Happened* (New York, 1954), pp. 226–27.

54. New York *Times*, Oct. 28, 1945.

55. New York *Times*, Oct. 31, Nov. 1, 1945.

56. Patterson to Byrnes, Nov. 1, 1945, Annex 29, Diplomatic History of the Manhattan Project, MD; Bush to Byrnes, Nov. 5, 1945, OSRD.

57. Bush to Byrnes, Nov. 5, 1945, OSRD.

58. New York *Times*, Nov. 7, 8, 1945.

59. Byrnes, *All In One Lifetime* (New York, 1958), p. 326; Bush and Groves to Byrnes, Nov. 9, 1945, MD.

60. New York *Times*, Nov. 12, 13, 14, 1945; New York *Herald Tribune*, Nov. 12, 13, 1945. The source of the information was Francis Williams, Attlee's press secretary.

61. Bush, Memorandum for the File, Nov. 13, 1945, OSRD. Truman had talked to Attlee and King Sunday morning, when Byrnes was not present. According to Truman's account in *Year of Decisions*, pp. 538–39, he suggested making a start toward international control by advancing the free interchange of scientific knowledge. Attlee and King then gave their views, which were substantially in accord with those of the President.

62. Bush, Memorandum for the File, Nov. 13, 1945, OSRD; Draft attached to note, Bush to Byrnes, Nov. 12, 1945, DS.

63. Bush, Memorandum for the File, Nov. 13, 1945, OSRD.

64. Bush, Memorandum for the File, Nov. 14, 1945, OSRD.

65. *Ibid.*; Draft communiqué, Nov. 14, 1945, DS.

66. Bush, Memorandum for the File, Nov. 15, 1945, OSRD.

67. Atomic Energy Agreed Declaration by the President of the United States, the Prime Minister of the United Kingdom, and the Prime Minister of

Canada, Nov. 15, 1945, HST; New York *Times*, Nov. 16, 1945.

68. Bush, Memorandum for the File, Nov. 13–15, 1945, OSRD; Bush to Truman, Nov. 14, 1945, OSRD.

69. Arneson to Patterson, Apr. 17, 1946, Annex 32, Diplomatic History of the Manhattan Project, MD. The original of the Nov. 16 directive is filed in MD.

70. Anderson and Groves to Chairman, CPC, Nov. 16, 1945, MD; Diplomatic History of the Manhattan Project, pp. 26–28, MD.

71. Bush, Memorandum for the File, Nov. 1, 1945, OSRD.

72. Address by Secretary Byrnes at Charleston, S. C., Nov. 16, 1945, MD; President's Press Conference of Nov. 20, 1945, and Excerpts from the Secretary's Press Conference, Nov. 21, 1945, in Material on Atomic Energy Aspects of Forthcoming Discussions with the Union of Soviet Socialist Republics, DS.

73. A. Harriman to Byrnes, Nov. 17, 1945, DS.

74. Cohen and Pasvolsky to Byrnes, Nov. 24, 1945, DS.

75. *H. Res. 404*, 79 Cong., 1 sess., Nov. 23, 1945; History-Diary, Nov. 27, 1945, FAS; Unsigned, unaddressed memorandum, HST.

76. Byrnes, *All In One Lifetime*, pp. 319, 326–27. Byrnes to Harriman, Nov. 23, 1945, DS.

77. Byrnes to J. G. Winant, Nov. 29, 1945, Memorandum of Conversation, Lord Halifax and Secretary Byrnes, Nov. 29, 1945, *Aide-Mémoire*, Dec. 1, 1945, DS.

78. Rough notes on the December 7 meeting are in the possession of Mr. Carroll L. Wilson.

79. Draft proposals, Dec. 10, 1945, Material on Atomic Energy Aspects of Forthcoming Discussions with the USSR, DS.

80. Groves to Patterson, Patterson to Byrnes, and Forrestal to Byrnes, all Dec. 11, 1945, MD.

81. Arthur H. Vandenberg, Jr., ed., *The Private Papers of Senator Vandenberg* (Boston, 1952), pp. 227–30; Truman, *Year of Decisions*, pp. 547–48; New York *Times*, Dec. 20, 1945; Acheson to Byrnes, Dec. 15, 20, 1945, DS. Vandenberg gives Dec. 11 as the date of the meeting with Truman. Dec. 14 is correct.

82. Acheson to Byrnes, Dec. 21, 1945, DS.

83. Byrnes, *Speaking Frankly* (New York, 1947), pp. 266–68, and *All In One Lifetime*, pp. 332–33, 336–67. The statement that Byrnes presented a modified version of the annex to the December 10 draft proposals is an inference based on a comparison of of that document with the Soviet–Anglo-American communiqué of December 27, 1945.

84. The New York *Times* published the communiqué Dec. 28, 1945.

85. *Private Papers of Senator Vandenberg*, pp. 233–5; Truman, *Year of Decisions*, p. 549; Byrnes, *All in One Lifetime*, pp. 347–48; New York *Times*, Dec. 29, 1945.

86. Bush to Cohen, Jan. 4, 1946, DS.

87. Minutes, Combined Policy Committee, Dec. 4, 1945, DS.

88. Groves to Byrnes, Feb. 13, 1946, Minutes, Combined Policy Committee, Feb. 15, 1946, DS.

89. Minutes, Combined Policy Committee, Apr. 15, 1946, DS.

90. Truman, *Years of Trial and Hope*, p. 12.

91. Truman to Attlee, Apr. 20, 1946, Annex 37, Diplomatic History of the Manhattan Project, MD; Truman, *Years of Trial and Hope*, pp. 12–14.

CHAPTER 14

1. Report of Conference on Domestic Legislation, Dec. 27–28, 1945, ASC. The meeting was described in the *Los Alamos Newsletter*, Jan. 8, 1945, BAS. Miller's notes on the meeting and the views of the Oak Ridge group are in BSM.

2. The sections cited are those of the original bill (see Appendix 1). A copy was printed in Senate Special Committee on Atomic Energy, *Atomic Energy Act of 1946. Hearings on S. 1717*, Jan. 22–Apr. 4, 1946 (Washington, 1946), pp. 1–9. Hereafter cited as *Senate Hearings.*

3. Price to Harold D. Smith, Jan. 2, 9,

1946, Price summary of S. 1717, Jan. 2, 1946, BOB; Price, Suggestions for Revision of S. 1717, Jan. 4, 1946, BSM.

4. FAS, History-Diary, Nov. 1945—Apr. 1946, Minutes, FAS Council, New York, Jan. 5, 6, 1946, FAS; New York *Herald Tribune*, Jan. 7, 1946; Simpson to Executive Committee, ASC, Jan. 22, 1946, JAS; Report on Campaign for Education for Survival in the Atomic Age, May 14, 1946, NCAI. A collection of NCAI releases is included in ASC.

5. FAS, History-Diary, Jan. 27, 1946, FAS.

6. Chuck Calkins, The Senate Committee vs. the Army, undated but apparently between Jan. 14 and Jan. 22, 1946, SCAE.

7. *Senate Hearings*, pp. 73, 74, 79.

8. *Senate Hearings*, pp. 44, 119, 138, 140, 198.

9. A copy of the draft, Jan. 18, 1946, is in BSM. The final memorandum as signed by Truman on Jan. 25, 1946 is in MD and Harry S. Truman, *Memoirs*, Vol. II, *Years of Trial and Hope* (Garden City, N. Y., 1956), pp. 3–4.

10. *Senate Hearings*, pp. 219–45. The final quotation appears on p. 236. Wallace's presence at the September conference in Chicago was reported in the Chicago *Daily News*, Sept. 22, 1945. The Ball bill was introduced as S. 1557 on Nov. 6, 1945, *Congressional Record*, 79 Cong., 1 sess., p. 10406.

11. New York *Times*, Feb. 1, 1946.

12. A copy of the Newman draft is on file in BSM.

13. Truman to McMahon, Feb. 1, 1946, BOB; Washington *Post* and Chicago *Sun*, Feb. 3, 1946. Truman reprinted the letter in his *Years of Trial and Hope*, pp. 4–5.

14. George S. Allan, Groves's observer at the hearings, detected more opposition than detachment among the conservatives. Allan to Groves, Feb. 14, 1946, MD. A less extreme but still pessimistic report is found in Roy Thompson to members of the ASC, Feb. 4, 1946, ASC.

15. Examples of McMahon's tactics are seen in *Senate Hearings*, pp. 38, 40, 78, 100, 140.

16. *Senate Hearings*, pp. 35–43, 117, 126, 130, 147, 202. Johnson introduced his bill as S. 1824. *Congressional Record*, 79 Cong., 2 sess., p. 1193.

17. So meager was the legislative history of the Espionage Act [40 Stat. 217 (1917), 50 U.S.C. § 31 (1940)] and the judicial decisions concerning it that most witnesses wisely refused to state its deficiencies precisely. Secretary Patterson, relying on an extensive study by the War Department legal staff, came closest to discussing the subject in his testimony. *Senate Hearings*, pp. 86, 96, 404; War Department comments on S. 1717, Jan. 18, 1946, MD. Newman and Miller made a detailed analysis of the Espionage Act in their book, *The Control of Atomic Energy* (New York, 1948), pp. 235–47.

18. *Senate Hearings*, pp. 87–88.

19. Newman and Miller, *The Control of Atomic Energy*, p. 64.

20. *Senate Hearings*, pp. 170–71, 297, 318, 324, 439.

21. William H. Davis introduced the "pill in the pail" concept in his testimony. *Senate Hearings*, pp. 60, 68.

22. *Ibid.*, pp. 56–61.

23. *Ibid.*, pp. 332–35, 328–41.

24. *Ibid.*, pp. 344–48.

25. Newman and Miller, *The Control of Atomic Energy*, pp. 142–69, presents an excellent review of the patent issue as seen by the authors of the McMahon bill. Statutory exclusion of inventions from patent protection as applied to atomic energy legislation is described in Casper W. Ooms, "The Patent Provisions of the Atomic Energy Act," *University of Chicago Law Review*, XV (Summer, 1948), 823–28.

26. The two revisions may be found in Senate Special Committee on Atomic Energy, 79 Cong., 2 sess., *Confidential Committee Print No. 1, S. 1717*, Mar. 6, 1946, *Confidential Committee Print No. 2*, Mar. 14, 1946, SCAE.

27. Ooms, pp. 828–29.

28. War Department comments on S. 1717, Jan. 18, 1946, MD.

29. Allan to Groves, Feb. 14, 1946, MD, documents Truman's position on the weapon stockpile. The President's other views are extrapolated from Patterson's prepared statement as it appeared in the hearings.

30. *Senate Hearings*, pp. 389–409.

703

31. *Ibid.*, p. 440.
32. New York *Times*, Feb. 16–21, 1946.
33. Minutes, Executive Committee, ASC, Feb. 19, 23, 1946, ASC; Higinbotham to all sites, Mar. 1, 1946, FAS.
34. Washington *Post*, Feb. 21, 1946; New York *Times*, Feb. 22, 1946; Groves to Eisenhower, Mar. 9, 1946, MD.
35. *Senate Hearings*, 1946, pp. 467–496; Groves to Eisenhower, Mar. 9, 1946, MD.
36. McMahon, Speech before Overseas Press Club, Feb. 28, 1946, SCAE; New York *Times*, Mar. 2, 3, 1946; *Congressional Record*, 79 Cong., 2 sess., p. 1827, A1211; Higinbotham to all sites, Mar. 1, 6, 1946, FAS; *Los Alamos Newsletter*, Mar. 13, 1946, BAS.
37. Byron S. Miller, "A Law Is Passed: The Atomic Energy Act of 1946," *University of Chicago Law Review*, XV (Summer, 1948), 809; Price to Smith, Feb. 26, 1946, BOB.
38. Statement made by Senator Vandenberg at Executive Session, Feb. 28, 1946, SCAE. Two Confidential Committee Prints, Feb. 27, 28, 1946, are in BSM. John W. Snyder to the President, Mar. 6, 1946, BSM. McMahon to Smith, Mar. 8, 1946, Snyder to F. J. Bailey, Mar. 14, 1946, BOB.
39. Special Committee on Atomic Energy, 79 Cong., 2 sess., *Confidential Committee Print No. 1, S. 1717*, Mar. 6, 1946, *Confidential Committee Print No. 2*, Mar. 9, 1946, SCAE; New York *Times*, Mar. 12, 1946. Arthur Krock described the dinner in the New York *Times*, Mar. 19, 1946, reprinted in the *Congressional Record*, 79 Cong., 2 sess., p. 2411.
40. New York *Times*, Mar. 13, 14, 1946, Arthur H. Vandenberg, Jr., ed., *The Private Papers of Senator Vandenberg* (Boston, 1952), pp. 254–57. Washington *Post*, Mar. 13, 14, 1946.
41. Report, Emergency Committee on Atomic Energy, Mar. 13, 1946, New York *Times*, Washington *Post*, Mar. 15, 1946; Truman, *Years of Trial and Hope*, pp. 6–7. The revised version of the Vandenberg amendment with the Austin addition appears in Senate Special Committee on Atomic Energy, 79 Cong., 2 sess., *Confidential Committee Print No. 3, S. 1717*, Mar. 15, 1946, SCAE. Provision for a joint committee first appeared in *Confidential Committee Print No. 2*, Mar. 9, 1946, SCAE. There was an identical print, also number "2," on Mar. 14, 1946. The Hart amendment first appeared in *Confidential Committee Print No. 4*, Mar. 27, 1946, SCAE.
42. Miller, "A Law Is Passed," pp. 811–12. Dean Acheson, *Sketches From Life: Of Men I Have Known* (New York, 1961), pp. 126–30. McMahon's radio address was reprinted in the *Congressional Record*, 79 Cong., 2 sess., Appendix, p. 1467.
43. *Congressional Record*, 79 Cong., 2 sess., pp. 2410–15. New York *Times*, Mar. 20, 1946; Chicago *Herald-American*, Mar. 19, 1946.
44. Washington *Post*, Mar. 20–27, 1946; Minutes, Emergency Conference on Atomic Energy, Mar. 21, 1946, SCAE.
45. A collection of materials sent to Chicago by the Emergency Committee is contained in ASC. The ASC files are also a good record of the activities of the Chicago group. For the effect of the Michigan campaign on Vandenberg, see Vandenberg to Rabbi J. D. Folkman, Mar. 23, 1946, and Beth Olds to Irving Kaplan, Mar. 28, 1946, ASC. Efforts to organize groups in Indiana are described in Melba Phillips to E. A. Akely, Mar. 27, 1946, FAS. An apparently complete file of all correspondence received by the Special Committee and a tabulation of the correspondence is in SCAE.
46. Minutes, ASC, Mar. 27, 1946; Undated, unsigned mimeographed statement from a Washington delegate, ASC; New York *Times*, Mar. 31, 1946.
47. *Town Meeting*, Bulletin of America's Town Meeting of the Air, for broadcast of Mar. 28, 1946 (New York, 1946). Hogness' activities were described in New York *Times*, Apr. 3, 1946. A slightly different version is found in *The Private Papers of Senator Vandenberg*, p. 259.
48. Senate Special Committee on Atomic Energy, 79 Cong., 2 sess., *Confidential Committee Print No. 4, S. 1717*, Mar. 27, 1946, SCAE. This file contains a number of copies of the print on which McMahon made rough notes of the April sessions. These

constitute fragmentary minutes of the executive sessions which have been used to establish the chronology of this section.

49. A copy of the Johnson amendment is included in McMahon's notes for the April 1, 1946, meeting in his copy of *Confidential Committee Print No. 4*, SCAE.

50. McMahon's notes on the April 2, 1946, meeting in the committee print, SCAE.

51. New York *Times*, Apr. 3, 1946; Lindley in Washington *Post*, Apr. 4, 1946; Newman and Miller, *The Control of Atomic Energy*, pp. 42–45.

52. McMahon's notes on April 3 session in his copy of the committee print, SCAE.

53. *Senate Hearings*, pp. 497–539, especially pp. 497–502, 526–27.

54. McMahon's notes on April 9 session, in his copy of the committee print, SCAE. The final version of Section 10 first appeared in *Confidential Committee Print No. 5, S. 1717*, Apr. 11, 1946, SCAE. Only a few minor changes appeared in *Confidential Committee Print No. 6*, Apr. 13, 1946, SCAE. Newman and Miller analyzed the basic problem of information control in *The Control of Atomic Energy*, pp. 205–21.

55. *Congressional Record*, 79 Cong., 2 sess., p. 4031; "Atomic Energy Act of 1946," *Senate Report*, 79 Cong., 2 sess., no. 1211 (Apr. 19, 1946).

56. Higinbotham to all [FAS] associations, Apr. 17, 1946, Statement on revised S. 1717, Apr. 20–21, 1946, FAS; Letter to members, Chicago Committee on Civilian Control of Atomic Energy, Apr. 18, 1946, ASC.

57. R. G. Arneson to W. S. Gaud, Apr. 19, 1946, Draft letter, Patterson to May, Apr. 26, 1946, Marbury to Patterson, Apr. 26, 1946, E. M. Brannon to Royall, Apr. 29, 1946, Arneson to Marbury, May 15, 1946, MD; Report from Washington, Apr. 22, 1946, ASC.

58. Mrs. J. P. Welling to S. W. Lucas, May 21, 1946, Letter from Chicago Committee on Civilian Control, May 24, 1946, ASC; Chicago *Sun*, May 8, 1946.

59. Miller, "A Law Is Passed," p. 813; New York *Times*, June 2, 1946; *Congressional Record*, 79 Cong., 2

sess., pp. 6076–98. Notes for McMahon's floor speech and the committee's loose-leaf notebook, probably prepared for use on the floor, are in SCAE.

60. This analysis is based largely on Miller's excellent statement in "A Law Is Passed," p. 813.

61. Melba Phillips to FAS associations, June 4, 1946, JAS; Jack Merritt to F. J. Bailey, June 12, 1946, Memorandum signed "Winslow," June 13, 1946, BOB. The transcript of May's appearance before the Mead Committee on June 4 in executive session was released by the committee on July 7, 1946. It is printed in Senate Special Committee Investigating the National Defense Program, *Investigation of the National Defense Program, Part 34*, July 1–10, 1946 (Washington, 1946), pp. 18488–502.

62. House Committee on Military Affairs, *Atomic Energy. Hearings on S. 1717*, June 11, 12, 26, 1946 (Washington, 1946).

63. New York *Times*, June 13, 1946.

64. *Congressional Record*, 79 Cong., 2 sess., pp. 9250–51; Miller, "A Law Is Passed," p. 814.

65. Newman to J. R. Steelman, June 26, 1946, HST; Higinbotham, Legislative Memorandum, July 1, 1946, FAS.

66. Miller, "A Law Is Passed," p. 814; On July 2, the Mead Committee received evidence of May's activities, *Defense Investigation Hearings*, pp. 17765–69, 18328–29; New York *Times*, July 3, 1946.

67. "Atomic Energy Act of 1946," *House Report*, 79 Cong., 2 sess., no. 2478 (July 10, 1946); Form letter, Chicago Committee for Civilian Control, July 3, 1946, ASC; Miller to Steelman, July 5, 1946, HST; Washington *Post*, June 27, 1946; Miller, "A Law Is Passed," p. 815.

68. *Congressional Record*, 79 Cong., 2 sess., p. 8602.

69. New York *Times*, July 12, 13, 1946; Chicago *Tribune*, July 12, 1946. The Adamson report was reprinted in *Congressional Record*, 79 Cong., 2 sess., p. 9257. Reactions to the report appeared in newspaper accounts and were introduced by Sabath in the *Record*, pp. 9136–37.

70. *Congressional Record*, 79 Cong., 2 sess., pp. 9135, 9141–42, 9144.

705

71. *Ibid.*, pp. 9249–75, 9340–85; New York *Times*, July 18, 1946.
72. *Congressional Record*, 79 Cong., 2 sess., pp. 9355–57; New York *Times*, July 19, 1946.
73. *Congressional Record*, 79 Cong., 2 sess., pp. 9357–85; New York *Times*, July 19, 1946.
74. *Congressional Record*, 79 Cong., 2 sess., pp. 9464–93; New York *Times*, July 20, 1946.
75. *Congressional Record*, 79 Cong., 2 sess., pp. 9545–63; New York *Times*, July 21, 1946.
76. Higinbotham to Aaron Novick, July 21, 1946, Fermi to McMahon,

July 23, 1946, ASC; Miller to Steelman, July 22, 1946, HST.
77. The conference sessions were covered extensively in the New York *Times*, July 24–26, 1946; Miller, "A Law Is Passed," p. 816; "Atomic Energy Act of 1946," *House Report*, 79 Cong., 2 sess., no. 2670 (July 25, 1946).
78. Miller, "A Law Is Passed," p. 817. *Congressional Record*, 79 Cong., 2 sess., pp. 10167, 10189–99, 10329, 10411.
79. The Atomic Energy Act of 1946 (Public Law 585, 79 Cong., 60 Stat., 755–75; 42 U.S.C., 1801–19); New York *Times*, July 31, Aug. 2, 1946.

706

CHAPTER 15

1. New York *Herald Tribune*, Jan. 8, 1946.
2. Bush to Cohen, Jan. 4, 1946, DS.
3. New York *Herald Tribune*, Jan. 8, 1946.
4. James F. Byrnes, *All In One Lifetime* (New York, 1958), pp. 347–48. Remarks by Connally and Byrnes and text of the resolution were printed in U. S. Department of State, *International Control of Atomic Energy; Growth of a Policy* (Washington, n.d.), pp. 128–33.
5. Encl., Groves to D. D. Eisenhower, Jan. 2, 1946, MD.
6. Minutes, Meeting 1, Secretary of State's Committee on Atomic Energy, Jan. 14, 1946, DS.
7. Minutes, Meeting 2, Secretary of State's Committee on Atomic Energy, Jan. 23, 1946, DS; Notes on Acheson Committee Meeting, Jan. 23, 1946, in possession of C. L. Wilson.
8. C. L. Wilson notes, Meeting of the Board of Consultants, 2:30 P.M. Jan. 23, 1946, DS.
9. Wilson notes, Jan. 28, P.M., Jan. 30, A.M., Jan. 31, 1946, DS.
10. Wilson notes, P.M., Jan. 31, 1946, DS.
11. Wilson notes, A.M. and P.M., Feb. 1, 1946, DS.
12. Board of Consultants Workbook, Feb. 12, 1946, DS.
13. Wilson notes, A.M. and P.M., Feb. 12, P.M., Feb. 13, P.M., Feb. 16, 1946, DS.
14. Wilson notes, A.M. and P.M., Feb. 25, A.M., Feb. 26, 1946, DS.

15. Wilson notes, P.M., Mar. 6, 1946, DS.
16. A Report on the International Control of Atomic Energy, Mar. 7, 1946, DS.
17. Several participants remember that the consultants met alone to consider whether or not to undertake the revision. The records of the Dumbarton Oaks sessions do not reveal when or where the consultants conferred. Since they had planned in advance to meet Thursday night at the Carlton, it seems likely they made the decision then.
18. This section is based on two sources: rough notes by C. L. Wilson and shorthand stenographic notes by Miss Anne Wilson. Both are in DS.
19. Wilson notes, P.M., Mar. 8, A.M., Mar. 9, A.M., Mar. 10, 1946, DS.
20. A Report on the International Control of Atomic Energy, Mar. 16, 1946, DS.
21. Shorthand stenographic notes by Anne Wilson, DS.
22. Acheson *et al.* to Byrnes, Mar. 17, 1946, in *A Report on the International Control of Atomic Energy* (Washington, 1946).
23. F. Eberstadt to B. Baruch, Mar. 28, 29, 1946, DS.
24. Baruch to Byrnes, Mar. 13, 1946, DS.
25. Harry S. Truman, *Memoirs*, Vol. II, *Years of Trial and Hope* (Garden City, N. Y., 1956), pp. 7–8.
26. Washington *Post*, Mar. 18, 1946.
27. McMahon to Byrnes, Mar. 22, 1946, SCAE; Vandenberg to Baruch, Mar.

19, 22, 1946, Baruch to Vandenberg, Mar. 21, 1946, DS.

28. For an attack on the competence of Baruch's aides, see *PM*, Mar. 20, 1946.

29. Byrnes to Baruch, Mar. 21, 1946, Byrnes to Lilienthal, Mar. 23, 1946, DS.

30. New York *Herald Tribune*, Mar. 24, 1946; New York *Times* and Washington *Post*, Mar. 26, 1946. One rumor had it that Acheson had deliberately leaked the plan to Marquis Childs. Childs's column of March 28, however, deplored that the news accounts were garbled and incomplete. He implied that the leak came from members of the Special Committee.

31. Byrnes had called Baruch's attention to the letter of transmittal and said it embodied the Acheson Committee's "unanimous endorsement" and comments. Byrnes had not quoted the letter quite correctly, but Baruch had the full text.

32. Baruch to Truman, Mar. 26, 1946, DS.

33. *Years of Trial and Hope*, pp. 9–10; *Baruch: The Public Years* (New York, 1960), p. 363; New York *Times*, Mar. 28, Apr. 4, 1946.

34. New York *Herald Tribune*, Mar. 28, 1946; *Congressional Record*, 79 Cong., 2 sess., p. 3207.

35. U. S. Department of State, Office of Public Affairs, Report No. 6, U. S. Public Attitudes on Control of Atomic Energy, Apr. 3, 1946, DS; Appleby to Acheson, Apr. 4, 1946, OSRD-NA; New York *Herald Tribune*, Apr. 11, 1946.

36. Baruch to Byrnes, Apr. 4, 1946, Byrnes to Acheson, Apr. 10, 1946, McCloy to Byrnes, Apr. 15, 1946, Bush to Byrnes, Apr. 16, 1946, Conant to Byrnes, Apr. 18, 1946, Hancock, Memorandum for Atomic Energy File, Apr. 19, 1946, Hancock, Memorandum for Files, May 1, 1946, DS.

37. Board of Consultants to Byrnes, Apr. 23, 1946, Lilienthal to Oppenheimer, May 28, 1946, DS.

38. Hancock, Memorandum for Atomic Energy File, Apr. 19, 1946, Byrnes to Baruch, Apr. 19, 1946, DS.

39. Baruch to Byrnes, Apr. 22, 1946, DS.

40. Hancock, Memorandum for Files, May 1, 1946, DS.

41. Baruch to Byrnes, May 6, 1946, DS.

42. Baruch to Groves, Apr. 18, 1946, DS.

43. Hancock, Note on Meeting, Apr. 5, 1946, Hancock to Baruch *et al.*, May 3, 1946, DS; Tolman, Notes on telephone conversations, May 5–9, 1946, OSRD.

44. Draft letter, Baruch to Byrnes, Mar. 31, 1946, Hancock, Notes on Meeting, Apr. 4, 1946, DS.

45. Draft letter, Baruch to Byrnes, Mar. 31, 1946, DS; Baruch to Bush, May 2, 1946, OSRD-NA.

46. Hancock, Memorandum, May 15, 1946, DS. In his book, *The Public Years*, Baruch dated the Cadogan incident shortly after the leak of the Acheson-Lilienthal report. More likely, it occurred early in May, when Byrnes was in Paris. Unsigned memorandum, Notes on Bernard M. Baruch, 1949, BMB.

47. C. L. Wilson, Notes on Blair-Lee Conference, J. P. Davis, Minutes of the Blair-Lee Conference, May 17–18, 1946, DS. Davis was executive secretary to Baruch's staff.

48. Lilienthal *et al.* to Baruch, May 19, 1946, DS.

49. Wilson to Marks, May 24, 1946, DS; Conant to Baruch, May 24, 1946, BMB. The Carnegie draft convention was printed in *International Conciliation*, No. 423 (Sept., 1946), pp. 417–35.

50. Policies for Discussion, May 30, 1946, DS.

51. Hancock, Memorandum of Meeting on May 30, 1946, in the State Department, DS.

52. Hancock, Memorandum of Meeting on the Evening of May 30, 1946, DS.

53. Proposed Statement of United States Policy, May 31, 1946, DS. This document carries a note signed HSM: "Prepared for DA to give JFB for White House Conference."

54. Hancock, Memorandum Written on the Morning of June 1, 1946, DS.

55. *Ibid.*

56. Hancock to Byrnes, June 1, 1946, DS.

57. Comments on "Statement of United States Policy" (Hancock Draft of June 4, 1946), June 6, 1946, DS.

58. Statement of United States Policy with deletions as made by HSM per discussion with DA, June 6, 1946, DS.

59. B.M.B. phone conversation with J.F.B., June 6, 1946, BMB.

60. Memorandum for Conversation with

707

the President and JFB (by BMB), June 6, 1946, DS.

61. B.M.B., Memorandum of meeting on June 7, 1946, with the President and J. F. Byrnes, BMB; Truman to Baruch, June 7, 1946, with encl., Statement of United States Policy, DS.

62. Hancock, Memorandum of Meeting on May 30, 1946, in the State Department, Byrnes, Memorandum of Conversation, June 8, 1946, DS.

63. Nimitz to Baruch, May 27, 1946, DS.

64. D. W. Knoll to R. P. Patterson *et al.*, June 7, 1946, DS.

65. Memorandum of Telephone Conversation, Dean Rusk and John Ross,

June 10, 1946, Memorandum of Conversation, Rusk and Ross, June 12, 1946, Baruch to Eisenhower, May 24, 1946, Spaatz to Baruch, n.d., Nimitz to Baruch, June 11, 1946, Eisenhower to Baruch, June 14, 1946, DS.

66. Washington *Post* and New York *Times*, June 13, 1946; Christopher Boland, Notes on Baruch testimony, June 12, 1946, SCAE.

67. On the evening of June 11, Eberstadt reviewed the draft of this section with Acheson, Lilienthal, and Marks. Eberstadt to Hancock, June 12, 1946, BMB.

68. United Nations Atomic Energy Commission, *Official Records*, First Meeting, June 14, 1946.

CHAPTER 16

1. Laurence described the explosion in the New York *Times* of July 1, 1946. He analyzed its effect on public opinion in the issue of August 4. See Hanson W. Baldwin's remarks on the same theme in the *Times* of August 1.

2. *Congressional Record*, 79 Cong., 2 sess., pp. 624, 2117–31, 2790–95.

3. New York *Times*, July 4, 1946; *Christian Science Monitor*, July 8, 1946.

4. W. A. Shurcliff, *Bombs at Bikini; the Official Report of Operation Crossroads* (New York, 1947), pp. 9–15.

5. Walter Millis, ed., *The Forrestal Diaries* (New York, 1951), p. 150.

6. New York *Times*, June 16, 19, 1946; San Francisco *Examiner*, June 20, 1946; Washington *Post*, June 25, 1946; Chicago *Herald-American*, July 2, 1946; Bush to C. L. Wilson, June 19, 1946, OSRD-NA.

7. United Nations Atomic Energy Commission, *Official Records*, Second Meeting, June 19, 1946.

8. R. G. Arneson to Baruch, June 21, 1946, DS.

9. *AEC Official Records*, Third Meeting, June 25, 1946.

10. Verbatim Record of First Meeting of the Working Committee, June 28, 1946 (Doc. AEC/WC/P.V./1).

11. Summary Record of First Meeting of Sub-Committee I, July 1, 1946 (Doc. AEC/Sub.1/1).

12. "United States Memorandum No. 1,"

U. S. Department of State, *The International Control of Atomic Energy; Growth of a Policy* (Washington, n.d.), pp. 148–51.

13. "United States Memorandum No. 2," *Growth of a Policy*, pp. 152–59; Summary Record of Third Meeting of Sub-Committee I, July 5, 1946 (Doc. AEC/Sub.1/3).

14. "United States Memorandum No. 3," *Growth of a Policy*, pp. 160–65.

15. Summary Record of Fourth Meeting of Sub-Committee I, July 8, 1946 (Doc. AEC/Sub.1/4).

16. Verbatim Record of Second Meeting of the Working Committee, July 12, 1946 (Doc. AEC/WC/P.V./2).

17. Summary Record of First Meeting of Committee 2, July 17, 1946 (Doc. AEC/C.2/1). Hancock to Searls, July 18, 1946, DS.

18. Statement Made by Representative of Union of Soviet Socialist Republics at the Second Meeting of Committee 2 of the Atomic Energy Commission on Wednesday, 24 July 1946, on Questions Contained in United States Memorandum No. 3 (Doc. AEC/WC/2).

19. Summary Record of Third Meeting of Committee 2, July 26, 1946 (Doc. AEC/C.2/3).

20. Summary Record of Fourth Meeting of Committee 2, July 31, 1946 (Doc. AEC/C.2/4).

21. Notes on Staff Conference, Aug. 1, 1946, DS.
22. Hancock to Staff, Aug. 2, 1946, DS.
23. Summary Record of Fifth Meeting of Committee 2, Aug. 6, 1946 (Doc. AEC/C.2/5).
24. The Department of State published these and other reports prepared under the auspices of the American delegation in *The International Control of Atomic Energy; Scientific Information Transmitted to the United Nations Atomic Energy Commission, June 14, 1946—October 14, 1946* (Washington, n.d.)
25. Summary Records of First Meeting of the Scientific and Technical Committee, July 19, 1946 (Doc. AEC/C.3/1); Summary Records of the Informal Discussions of the Scientific and Technical Committee, First through Eighteenth, July 25–Sept. 6, 1946 (Docs. AEC/C.3/W.1–18).
26. Notes of General Staff Meeting, Aug. 23, 1946, DS.
27. Notes of an Informal Meeting with Members of the Canadian Delegation, Aug. 29, 1946, DS.
28. Informal Notes of Staff Meeting, Sept. 10, 1946, Eberstadt to Baruch, Sept. 13, 1946, DS.
29. Baruch to Truman, Sept. 17, 1946, DS.
30. New York *Times*, Sept. 18, 1946.
31. Harry S. Truman, *Memoirs*, Vol. I, *Year of Decisions* (Garden City, N. Y.), pp. 555–58; New York *Times*, Sept. 13–15, 17, 1946. For a detailed account of the release of the Wallace letter see *PM*, Sept. 18, 1946.
32. Where Pearson got the letter remained a mystery. He denied it came from the Department of Commerce. This seemed to point to someone at State.
33. Hancock, Memorandum for the File, Sept. 19, 1946, DS.
34. New York *Times*, Sept. 19, 1946; Truman, *Year of Decisions*, p. 558; William Hillman, *Mr. President* (New York, 1952), p. 128.
35. Hancock, Memorandum for the File, Sept. 19, 1946, DS.
36. Hancock, Memorandum for the File, Sept. 19, 1946, DS; Truman, *Year of Decisions*, pp. 559–60; James F. Byrnes, *All In One Lifetime* (New York, 1958), pp. 374–76; Washington *Daily News*, Sept. 19, 1946.

37. Baruch to Truman, Sept. 24, 1946, DS.
38. Arneson, Memorandum for File, Sept. 19, 1946, DS.
39. The implication of this statement was that the July 23 letter was based on the Acheson-Lilienthal report. While the Acheson Committee's letter of transmittal was not entirely clear on the discretion the United States would exercise, the report itself stated that the sequence and timing of stages would be fixed by negotiation and agreement among the nations.
40. Arneson, Notes of Meeting with Mr. Wallace and his Aide, Mr. Hauser, Sept. 27, 1946, DS. The draft Hauser refused to accept was published in the New York *Times*, Oct. 4, 1946. The draft Hauser accepted was published in the New York *Times*, Oct. 3, 1946.
41. New York *Times*, Oct. 3, 1946.
42. *Ibid.*, Oct. 4, 1946.
43. *Ibid.*, Oct. 3, 1946.
44. *Ibid.*, Oct. 4, 1946.
45. *Ibid.*, Oct. 9, 1946.
46. Baruch to Truman, Sept. 19, 1946, DS.
47. Summary Record of Second Meeting of the Scientific and Technical Committee, Sept. 26, 1946 (Doc. AEC/C.3/2).
48. Summary Record of Seventh Meeting of Committee 2, Oct. 8, 1946 (Doc. AEC/C.2/8).
49. Notes on Informal Discussions of the Second Committee, First through Sixth, Oct. 15–31, 1946 (Docs. AEC/C.2/W.2–7). On Oct. 14, 1946, the U. S. delegation had submitted Technological Control of Atomic Energy Activities, a detailed statement of American views on controls necessary across the whole range of atomic energy production. See *The International Control of Atomic Energy; Scientific Information Transmitted to the United Nations Atomic Energy Commission*, pp. 145–95.
50. *Plenary Meetings of the General Assembly: Verbatim Record 23 October–16 December 1946*, pp. 832–47.
51. *Ibid.*, pp. 893–908.
52. Baruch to Acheson, June 23, 1946, Acheson to Baruch, July 1, 1946, Baruch to Acheson, July 9, Nov. 2, 1946, DS.
53. Baruch to Byrnes, Nov. 4, 1946, DS.

709

54. Byrnes to Baruch, Nov. 5, 1946, BMB; Acheson to Baruch, Nov. 7, 1946, DS. Acheson had misgivings about this decision. He thought it better to seek a report that would point up the basic differences between the United States and the Soviet Union without forcing the Russians to take a public stand against the American proposals. This might make it easier for them to reverse their position at a later date. F. A. Lindsay to Staff, Nov. 21, 1946, DS.

55. *AEC Official Records*, Sixth Meeting, Nov. 13, 1946.

56. Acheson to Byrnes, Nov. 7, 1946, DS.

57. Acheson to Hilldring, Hiss, and Marks, Nov. 8, 1946, DS; *The Forrestal Diaries*, pp. 220–21; *Summary Record of Meetings of First Committee, 2 November–13 December 1946*, pp. 221–24, 343.

58. *Summary Record of Meetings of First Committee, 2 November–13 December 1946*, pp. 221–23, 255–57; New York *Herald Tribune*, Dec. 3, 1946.

59. *Summary Record of Meetings of First Committee, 2 November–13 December 1946*, pp. 307–9.

60. *AEC Official Records*, Seventh Meeting, Dec. 5, 1946, Supplement No. 3, Annex 4.

61. *AEC Official Records*, Eighth Meeting, Dec. 17, 1946.

62. New York *Herald Tribune*, Dec. 21, 1946; New York *Times*, Dec. 22, 1946.

63. *AEC Official Records*, Ninth Meeting, Dec. 20, 1946.

64. Notes on Informal Discussions of the Second Committee, Seventh through Thirteenth, Nov. 4–27, 1946 (Docs. AEC/C.2/W.8–13).

65. Summary Records of Meetings of Committee 2, Tenth through Twelfth, Dec. 18–26, 1946 (Docs. AEC/C.2/11–13).

66. Verbatim Record of Fifth Meeting of the Working Committee, Dec. 27, 1946 (Doc. AEC/WC/P.V./5).

67. Chicago *Herald-American*, San Francisco *Examiner*, New York *Journal-American*, Dec. 28–30, 1946; New York *Herald Tribune*, Dec. 29, 1946.

68. *AEC Official Records*, Tenth Meeting, Dec. 30, 1946; Bernard M. Baruch, *Baruch: The Public Years* (New York, 1960), p. 379.

69. Baruch to Truman, Jan. 4, 1947, HST.

70. For an analysis of Russian motivation, 1945–1953, see Joseph L. Nogee, *Soviet Policy towards International Control of Atomic Energy* (Notre Dame, Ind., 1961), pp. 231–85. Professor Nogee considers Russian opposition to the American plan due basically to determination to avert the threat of foreign penetration of the Soviet economy. He believes that the Soviet negotiators did not expect the United States to agree to "a prohibition without some prior assurance of an effective control system." Bernhard G. Bechhoefer, *Postwar Negotiations for Arms Control* (Washington, 1961), pp. 55–60, criticizes U. S. policy on the veto. For an evaluation of the American control plan, see Richard J. Barnet, *Who Wants Disarmament?* (Boston, 1960), pp. 14–21.

CHAPTER 17

1. *Atomic Energy Act of 1946. Hearings on S. 1717*, Jan. 22–Apr. 4, 1946 (Washington, 1946), p. 172; *Congressional Record*, 79 Cong., 2 sess., p. 9369.

2. Bush to Truman, July 31, 1946, Truman to Bush, Aug. 2, 1946, OSRD-NA.

3. New York *Times*, Oct. 4, 1946.

4. Bush to Truman, Aug. 16, 1946, OSRD-NA.

5. Chicago *Tribune*, Oct. 29, 1946; Truman, *Memoirs*, Vol. II, *Years of Trial and Hope* (Garden City, New York, 1956), p. 296.

6. Clifford to Lilienthal, Oct. 27, 1946, HST; New York *Times*, Oct. 29–30, 1946.

7. Groves to K. D. Nichols, Sept. 1, 1945, Monthly Report on DSM Project, Sept., 1945, MD; E. H. Marsden to T. J. Evans, Sept. 4, 1945, *Manhattan District History*, Bk. VI, *Liquid Thermal Diffusion (S-50) Project*, App. D; J. E. Bigelow, The Contribution of the S-50 Plant to the

Production of Uranium Contained in the First Weapon, June 30, 1961, AEC.

8. Nichols to Groves, Aug. 31, Sept. 17, 1945, Monthly Report on DSM Project, Sept., 1945, MD.

9. Monthly Reports on DSM Project, Aug.–Dec., 1945, MD.

10. Du Pont, Operation of Hanford Engineer Works, Bk. XII, p. 143, HOO; Monthly Reports on DSM Project, Nov.–Dec., 1945, MD.

11. Minutes of Policy Committee Meeting, Project Y, July 26, 1945, LASL; *MD History*, Bk. VIII, *Los Alamos Project (Y)*, Vol. III, *Auxiliary Activities*, Ch. 6, *Sandia*.

12. Joseph W. Kennedy Diary, Aug. 20, Sept. 18, 1944, AEC.

13. "Notes on talks given by Comdr. N. E. Bradbury at Coordinating Council, Oct. 1, 1945," *MD History*, Bk. VIII, *Los Alamos Project (Y)*, *Supplement* to Vol. II, *Technical*, App. 1.

14. Bradbury to S. L. Stewart, Nov. 14, 1945, LASL; Report of the Manager, Santa Fe Operations, U. S. Atomic Energy Commission, July 1947 to July 1950, Bk. I, p. 37.

15. Bradbury to Groves, Nov. 23, 1945, LASL.

16. Bradbury to Groves, Nov. 26, 1945, MD; *MD History*, Bk. VIII, *Supplement* to Vol. II, p. V.3; Progress Report of the Theoretical Physics Division for December, 1945, Los Alamos Scientific Laboratory Report LAMS-349; Morrison, Power Reactor Notes, Report LAMS-320-22.

17. Breeder Pile Discussion, Chicago, June 19–20, 1945, Metallurgical Laboratory Report CF-3199; New Piles Meeting, Oct. 16–17, 1945, Report CF-3352; Technical Division Reports, Nov.–Dec., 1945, Clinton Laboratories Reports MonN-32, MonN-43.

18. Compton to Groves with encl., June 29, 1945, AEC; Nichols to Compton, Nov. 19, 1945, ANL; Metallurgical Laboratory, Argonne Laboratory Division, Report for September, October, November, and December, 1945, Jan. 12, 1946, CF-3403; Zinn, Design of a Fast Breeder Neutron Pile, Jan. 25, 1946, Report CF-3414.

19. Groves to Lawrence, Oct. 15, Dec. 28, 1945, MD; Research Progress Meeting, Dec. 29, 1945, Lawrence Radiation Laboratory Report 28.5.88.

20. Groves to Patterson, Mar. 11, 1946, Patterson to Carpenter, Mar. 15, 1946, MD.

21. Notes for the Secretary of War's Conference with Mr. Carpenter of E. I. du Pont de Nemours & Company, C. E. Wilson to Groves, May 28, 1946, W. J. Williams to Nichols, Aug. 6, 1946, MD; File on Contract W-31-109-eng-52, AEC; U. S. Atomic Energy Commission, *Knolls Atomic Power Laboratory, Schenectady, N. Y.* (Washington, 1951), p. 1.

22. Summary of Progress at K-25 and Y-12, Feb. 21, 1949, Doc. No. KA-37, Union Carbide Nuclear Company Records, Oak Ridge.

23. Monthly Reports on DSM Project, Jan.–Apr., 1946, R. M. Evans to Nichols, Feb. 20, 1946, MD; Minutes of the Graphite Expansion Committee Meetings, 1946, Production Office Diary, II, Apr. 29, 1946, Harvey Brooks, Report, Sept. 17, 1946, HOO.

24. Seaborg, *The Transuranium Elements* (New Haven, 1958), pp. 70–71; Monthly Report on DSM Project, Jan.–Feb. 1945, MD; F. A. Valente, Report, Dec. 13, 1945, HOO; *MD History*, Bk. IV, *Pile Project*, Vol. VI, *Operation*, pp. 4.24–4.25.

25. Groves to Bradbury, Jan. 4, 1946, Groves to Patterson, Apr. 2, 1946, G. L. Williams and R. C. Hill to Col. A. W. Betts, Apr. 16, 1946, MD; Joint Committee on Atomic Energy, *Investigation into the United States Atomic Energy Project.* Hearings, May 26–Oct. 26, 1949, pp. 771–72; Report of the Manager, Santa Fe Operations, I, pp. 38–40; *MD History*, Bk. VIII, Vol. I, *General*, p. 5.21.

26. History of Los Alamos B Division, Apr. 30, 1946, MD; *MD History*, Bk. VIII, *Supplement* to Vol. II, pp. I.14–I.17, V.3, App. 9.

27. Bradbury to Groves, Feb. 12, 1946, LASL; W. F. Schaffer to Lt. Col. E. E. Wilhoyt, Apr. 30, 1946, Wilhoyt to Bradbury, May 6, 1946, L. E. Seeman to Bradbury, Sept. 3, 1946, R. S. Warner to H. W. Russ, Sept. 30, 1946, Groves to CO, Santa Fe Area, CO, Sandia Base, and Bradbury, Oct. 1, 1946, Bradbury to H. C. Gee, Oct. 22, 1946, LASL.

28. *MD History*, Bk. VIII, Vol. II, pp.

711

III.6–III.12, IV.3–IV.5, VI.10–VI.11, App. 9.

29. Manley to Groves, Sept. 24, 1946, A. C. Graves *et al.*, Report, Aug. 9, 1946, LASL.

30. Groves to Manley, Oct. 9, 1946, LASL; Nichols to Groves, Mar. 22, 1946, MD.

31. *MD History*, Bk. IV, Vol. VI, p. 4.25, Bk. VIII, *Supplement* to Vol. II, pp. VIII.6–VIII.7, App. 9; W. J. Williams to Nichols, Sept. 12, 1946, MD; Discussion at Technical Board, Nov. 1, 1946, LASL.

32. Nichols to Groves, Mar. 18, 1946, MD.

33. Supplemental Agenda, Advisory Committee Meeting, June 15, 1946, Tab L, OSRD; 60 Stat. 561.

34. Minutes of the 15 June 1946 Meeting of the Advisory Committee on Research and Development, Nichols to Wilson, Jan. 3, 1947, MD; Technical Division Report for Month Ending September 20, 1946, MonN-175; C. Rogers McCullough, Preliminary Design Proposal—Daniels Experimental Pile, Nov. 1, 1946, Report MonN-188.

35. Proposed Program for Work under Contract No. W-35-058-eng-71 for the Fiscal Year ending June 30, 1947, June 4, 1946, MD; *MD History*, Bk. IV, Vol. II, *Research*, Pt. II, *Clinton Laboratories*, pp. 7.2–7.3.

36. *MD History*, Bk. IV, Vol. II, Pt. 2, pp. 5.9–5.10; DuBridge to Groves, May 1, 1946, MD; "Availability of Radioactive Isotopes," *Science*, CIII (June 14, 1946), 697–705.

37. J. T. Tate to Nichols, June 13, 1946, Groves to Tate, July 15, 1946, AEC; Nichols to C. L. Wilson, Jan. 3, 1947, MD; U. S. Atomic Energy Commission, *Argonne National Laboratory, Chicago, Ill.* (Washington, 1951), p. 4.

38. New York *Times*, July 19, Aug. 2, 1946; Unsigned memorandum, The Founding of the Brookhaven National Laboratory, Jan. 19, 1949, AEC; Groves to the Atomic Energy Commission, Nov. 22, 1946, MD.

39. A. V. Peterson to Pollard, Apr. 12, 1946, MD; *MD History*, Bk. I, *General*, Vol. IV, *Auxiliary Activities*, Ch. 10, *The Oak Ridge Institute of Nuclear Studies*.

40. Newspaper analysis by Department of State, Division of Public Studies, AEC. For a different view, see Harold L. Ickes in the Washington *Evening Star*, Nov. 13, 1946.

41. New York *Times*, Oct. 30, 1946; Bush to Lavender, Oct. 29, 1946, OSRD-NA; Vanden Bulck, Memo to files, Nov. 4, 1946, H. I. Hodes to Lilienthal, Oct. 31, 1946, AEC.

42. David E. Lilienthal, *TVA, Democracy on the March* (New York, 1945), pp. 152–206.

43. Wilson to the Commission, undated but about Nov. 8, 1946, AEC.

44. Minutes, Commission Meeting 1, Nov. 13, 1946, Atomic Energy Commission, Internal Administrative Orders 1–5, Nov. 13, 1946, AEC. Wilson, serving as Acting Secretary to the Commission, prepared memorandums on the seventeen meetings in 1946, from which the brief formal minutes were apparently written. They are hereafter cited as Wilson Memorandums, AEC. Lilienthal and Bacher expressed their impressions of Oak Ridge in Joint Committee on Atomic Energy, *Investigation Into the United States Atomic Energy Project*, pp. 9–10, 773–74.

45. Los Alamos Diary, Nov. 14–15, 1946, LASL. The Lilienthal and Bacher impressions of Los Alamos are found in the hearings of the Joint Committee investigation, pp. 398, 770. A more complete account is found in N. E. Bradbury to AEC, Nov. 14, 1946, in *MD History*, Bk. VIII, *Supplement* to Vol. II, App. 9.

46. New York *Times*, Nov. 19, 1946.

47. F. A. Lindsay, Memorandum, Nov. 4, 1946, DS; Nichols to Strauss, Nov. 22, 1946, Minutes, Commission Meetings 3, 4, 6, 7, Nov. 22, 26, Dec. 3, 5, 1946, and Wilson Memorandums for the same, AEC.

48. Minutes, Commission Meetings 2 and 4, Nov. 21, 26, 27, 1946; and Wilson Memorandums for the same, Lilienthal to Nichols, Nov. 27, 1946, Letter contract W-33-109 Eng 52, AEC; Nichols to Lilienthal, Nov. 4, 1946, MD.

49. Groves to AEC, Nov. 22, 1946, MD; K. E. Fields to Nichols, Oct. 10, 1946, Minutes, Commission Meetings 2, 4, 7, 10, Nov. 21, 26, Dec. 5, 13, 1946, Wilson Memorandums for these same meetings and for Dec. 3, 1946, AEC.

50. Minutes, Commission Meetings 14

and 15, Dec. 23, 26, 1946, and Wilson Memorandums for the same, Lilienthal to E. Reynolds, undated but probably Dec. 27, 1946, P. M. Morse to Bacher, Dec. 30, 1946, AEC.

51. Groves to Lilienthal, Dec. 20, 1946, Minutes, Commission Meetings 12, 13 and 14, Dec. 18, 19, 23, 1946, and Wilson Memorandums for the same, Lilienthal to Groves, Dec. 31, 1946, AEC; Nichols to F. R. Conklin, Dec. 24, 1946, OROO; Nichols to Lilienthal, Dec. 31, 1946, MD; New York *Times*, Dec. 27, 1946.

52. Groves to Lilienthal, Nov. 14, 19, 1946, Lilienthal to Groves, Dec. 4, 1946, MD; Minutes, Commission Meetings 1 and 11, Nov. 13 and Dec. 17, 1946, and Wilson Memorandums for the same, AEC.

53. Tolman to Groves, Nov. 17, 1945, Tolman report on activities of the Committee on Declassification, Nov.–Dec., 1945, Fields to W. S. Hutchinson, June 28, 1946, Groves to District Engineer, July 31, 1946, Reports of meetings of Senior Responsible Reviewers, Aug. 12–14, Oct. 12, Dec. 31, 1946, Groves to AEC, Dec. 9, 1946, AEC; Manual for Declassification of Scientific and Technical Matters, May 1, 1946, Tolman to McMahon, Feb. 1, 1946, Nichols to Groves, Mar. 12, 1946, MD; Baltimore *Evening Sun*, Nov. 7, 1946; New York *Herald Tribune*, Dec. 15, 1946.

54. Minutes, Commission Meetings, 2, 7, 8, 12, Nov. 21, Dec. 5, 10, 18, 1946, and Wilson Memorandums for the same, Lilienthal to Truman, Dec. 9, 1946, AEC Press Release, Dec. 12, 1946, AEC.

55. H. S. Aurand to Patterson, July 5, 1946, MD; New York *Times*, Nov. 5, 1946.

56. Minutes, Commission Meetings 8, 12, 14, Dec. 10, 18, 23, 1946, and Wilson Memorandums for the same, Memo-randum Re Division of Military Applications, Dec. 18, 1946, Lilienthal to Patterson, Dec. 20, 1946, Lilienthal to Forrestal, Dec. 23, 1946, AEC.

57. Minutes, Commission Meetings 1, 5, 6, 8, 17, Nov. 13, Dec. 2, 3, 10, 31, 1946, and Wilson Memorandums for the same, Memorandum to Advisory Panel on Selection of a General Manager, Nov. 25, 1946, Lilienthal to Truman, Dec. 26, 1946, Internal Administrative Order No. 11, Dec. 31, 1946, AEC.

58. Lilienthal to Groves, Dec. 9, 1946, with draft Executive Order, Nichols to Lilienthal, Dec. 9, 1946, with draft Executive Order, Minutes, Commission Meetings 8, 10, 11, Dec. 10, 13, 17, 1946, and Wilson Memorandums for the same, Wilson to the Commissioners, Dec. 17, 1946, AEC; Executive Order 9001, Dec. 27, 1941, 6 FR 6787.

59. Groves to Lilienthal, Dec. 18, 1946, Minutes, Commission Meetings 12, 13, Dec. 18, 19, 1946, and Wilson Memorandums for the same, AEC.

60. Notes on Conference Regarding Transfer Arrangements, Dec. 21, 1946, Minutes, Commission Meeting 14, Dec. 23, 1946, and Wilson Memorandum for the same, Draft letter, Lilienthal to Patterson, Dec. 23, 1946, Final letter, Dec. 27, 1946, AEC.

61. Minutes, Commission Meetings 15, 16, Dec. 26, 30, 1946, and Wilson Memorandums for the same, Lilienthal to Byrnes, Dec. 30, 1946, AEC.

62. Wilson memorandums for Commission Meetings 1, 13, 16, Nov. 13, Dec. 19, 30, 1946, Patterson to Lilienthal, Dec. 30, 1946, Jan. 1, 1947, AEC.

63. Executive Order 9816, Dec. 31, 1946, 12 FR 37; New York *Times*, Jan. 1, 1947; Groves to all members of the Manhattan Project, Dec. 23, 1946, MD; War Department Press Release, Dec. 31, 1946, AEC.

713

THE McMAHON BILL

APPENDIX 1

Brien McMahon introduced his bill in the Senate as S. 1717 on December 20, 1945.

A BILL

For the development and control of atomic energy.
Be it enacted by the Senate and House of Representatives of the United States of America in Congress assembled,

DECLARATION OF POLICY

SECTION 1. (a) FINDINGS AND DECLARATION.—Research and experimentation in the field of nuclear fission have attained the stage at which the release of atomic energy on a large scale is practical. The significance of the atomic bomb for military purposes is evident. The effect of the use of atomic energy for civilian purposes upon the social, economic, and political structures of today cannot now be determined. It is reasonable to anticipate, however, that tapping this new source of energy will cause profound changes in our present way of life. Accordingly, it is hereby declared to be the policy of the people of the United States that the development and utilization of atomic energy shall be directed toward improving the public welfare, increasing the standard of living, strengthening free competition among private enterprises so far as practicable, and cementing world peace.

(b) PURPOSE OF ACT.—It is the purpose of this Act to effectuate these policies by providing, among others, for the following major programs;

(1) A program of assisting and fostering private research and development on a truly independent basis to encourage maximum scientific progress;

(2) A program for the free dissemination of basic scientific information and for maximum liberality in dissemination of related technical information;

(3) A program of federally conducted research to assure the Government of adequate scientific and technical accomplishment;

(4) A program for Government control of the production, ownership, and use of fissionable materials to protect the national security and to insure the broadest possible exploitation of the field;

(5) A program for simultaneous study of the social, political, and economic effects of the utilization of atomic energy; and

(6) A program of administration which will be consistent with international agreements made by the United States, and which will enable the Congress to be currently informed so as to take further legislative action as may hereafter be appropriate.

ATOMIC ENERGY COMMISSION

Sec. 2. (a) There is hereby established an Atomic Energy Commission (herein called the Commission), which shall be composed of five members. Three members shall constitute a quorum of the Commission. The President shall designate one member as Chairman of the Commission.

(b) Members of the Commission shall be appointed by the President, by and with the advice and consent of the Senate, and shall serve at the pleasure of the President. In submitting nominations to the Senate, the President shall set forth the experience and qualifications of each person so nominated. Each member, except the Chairman, shall receive compensation at the rate of $15,000 per annum; the Chairman shall receive compensation at the rate of $20,000 per annum. No member of the Commission shall engage in any other business, vocation, or employment than that of serving as a member of the Commission.

715

(c) The principal office of the Commission shall be in the District of Columbia, but the Commission may exercise any or all of its powers in any place. The Commission shall hold such meetings, conduct such hearings, and receive such reports as will enable it to meet its responsibilities for carrying out the purposes of this Act.

RESEARCH

Sec. 3. (a) Research Assistance.—The Commission is directed to exercise its powers in such manner as to insure the continued conduct of research and developmental activities in the fields specified below by private or public institutions or persons and to assist in the acquisition of an ever-expanding fund of theoretical and practical knowledge in such fields. To this end the Commission is authorized and directed to make contracts, agreements, arrangements, grants-in-aid, and loans—

(1) for the conduct of research and developmental activities relating to (a) nuclear processes; (b) the theory and production of atomic energy, including processes and devices related to such production; (c) utilization of fissionable and radioactive materials for medical or health purposes; (d) utilization of fissionable and radioactive materials for all other purposes, including industrial uses; and (e) the protection of health during research and production activities; and

(2) for studies of the social, political, and economic effects of the availability and utilization of atomic energy.

The Commission may make partial advance payments on such contracts and arrangements. Such contracts or other arrangements may contain provisions to protect health, to minimize danger from explosion, and for reporting and inspection of work performed thereunder as the Commission may determine, but shall not contain any provisions or conditions which prevent the dissemination of scientific or technical information, except to the extent already required by the Espionage Act.

(b) Federal Atomic Research.—The Commission is authorized and directed to conduct research and developmental activities through its own facilities in the fields specified in (a) above.

PRODUCTION OF FISSIONABLE MATERIALS

Sec. 4. (a) Definition.—The term "production of fissionable materials" shall include all methods of manufacturing, producing, refining, or processing fissionable materials, including the process of separating fissionable material from other substances in which such material may be contained, whether by thermal diffusion, electromagnetic separation, or other processes.

(b) Authority to Produce.—The Commission shall be the exclusive producer of fissionable materials, except production incident to research or developmental activities subject to the restrictions provided in subparagraph (d) below. The quantities of fissionable material to be produced in any quarter shall be determined by the President.

(c) PROHIBITION.—It shall be unlawful for any person to produce any fissionable material except as may be incident to the conduct of research or developmental activities.

(d) RESEARCH AND DEVELOPMENT ON PRODUCTION PROCESSES. (1) The Commission shall establish by regulation such requirements for the reporting of research and developmental activities on the production of fissionable materials as will assure the Commission of full knowledge of all such activities, rates of production, and quantities produced.

(2) The Commission shall provide for the frequent inspection of all such activities by employees of the Commission.

(3) No person may in the course of such research or developmental activities possess or operate facilities for the production of fissionable materials in quantities or at a rate sufficient to construct a bomb or other military weapon unless all such facilities are the property of and subject to the control of the Commission. The Commission is authorized, to the extent that it deems such action consistent with the purposes of this Act, to enter into contracts for the conduct of such research or developmental activities involving the use of the Commission's facilities.

(e) EXISTING CONTRACTS.—The Commission is authorized to continue in effect and modify such contracts for the production of fissionable materials as may have been made prior to the effective date of this Act, except that, as rapidly as practicable, and in any event not more than one year after the effective date of this Act, the Commission shall arrange for the exclusive operation of facilities employed in the manufacture of fissionable materials by employees of the Commission.

716

CONTROL OF MATERIALS

SEC. 5. (a) FISSIONABLE MATERIALS.—

(1) DEFINITION.—The term "fissionable materials" shall include plutonium, uranium 235, and such other materials as the Commission may from time to time determine to be capable of releasing substantial quantities of energy through nuclear fission of the material.

(2) PRIVATELY OWNED FISSIONABLE MATERIALS.—Any person owning any right, title, or interest in or to any fissionable material shall forthwith transfer all such right, title, or interest to the Commission.

(3) PROHIBITION.—It shall be unlawful for any person to (a) own any fissionable material; or (b) after sixty days after the effective date of this Act and except as authorized by the Commission possess any fissionable material; or (c) export from or import into the United States any fissionable material, or directly or indirectly be a party to or in any way a beneficiary of, any contract, arrangement, or other activity pertaining to the production, refining, or processing of any fissionable material outside of the United States.

(4) DISTRIBUTION OF FISSIONABLE MATERIALS.—The Commission is authorized and directed to distribute fissionable materials to all applicants requesting such materials for the conduct of research or developmental activities either independently or under contract or other arrangement with the Commission. If sufficient materials are not available to meet all such requests, and applications for licenses under section 7, the Commission shall allocate fissionable materials among all such applicants in the manner best calculated to encourage independent research and development by making adequate fissionable materials available for such purposes. The Commission shall refuse to distribute or allocate any materials to any applicant, or shall recall any materials after distribution or allocation from any applicant, who is not equipped or who fails to observe such safety standards to protect health and to minimize danger from explosion as may be established by the Commission.

(b) SOURCE MATERIALS.—

(1) DEFINITION.—The term "source materials" shall include any ore containing uranium, thorium, or beryllium, and such other materials peculiarly essential to the production of fissionable materials as may be determined by the Commission with the approval of the President.

(2) LICENSE FOR TRANSFERS REQUIRED.—No person may transfer possession or title to

any source material after mining, extraction, or removal from its place of origin, and no person may receive any source material, without a license from the Commission.

(3) Issuance of licenses.—Any person desiring to transfer or receive possession of any source material shall apply for a license therefore in accordance with such procedures as the Commission may by regulation establish. The Commission shall establish such standards for the issuance or refusal of licenses as it may deem necessary to assure adequate source materials for production, research, or developmental activities pursuant to this Act or to prevent the use of such materials in a manner inconsistent with the national welfare.

(4) Reporting.—The Commission is authorized to issue such regulations or orders requiring reports of ownership, possession, extraction, refining, shipment, or other handling of source materials as it may deem necessary.

(c) Byproduct Materials.—

(1) Definition.—The term "byproduct material" shall be deemed to refer to all materials (except fissionable material) yielded in the processes of producing fissionable material.

(2) Distribution.—The Commission is authorized and directed to distribute, with or without charge, byproduct materials to all applicants seeking such materials for research or developmental work, medical therapy, industrial uses, or such other useful applications as may be developed. If sufficient materials to meet all such requests are not available, the Commission shall allocate such materials among applicants therefor, giving preference to the use of such materials in the conduct of research and developmental activity and medical therapy. The Commission shall refuse to distribute or allocate any byproduct materials to any applicant, or recall any materials after distribution or allocation from any applicant, who is not equipped or who fails to observe such safety standards to protect health as may be established by the Commission.

(d) General Provisions.— (1) The Commission is authorized to—

(i) acquire or purchase fissionable or source materials within the United States or elsewhere;

(ii) take, requisition, or condemn within the United States any fissionable or source material and make just compensation therefor. The Commission shall determine such compensation. In the exercise of such rights of eminent domain and condemnation, proceedings may be instituted under the Act of August 1, 1888 (U. S. C. 1940, title 40, sec. 257), or any other applicable Federal statute. Upon or after the filing of the condemnation petition, immediate possession may be taken and the property may be treated by the Commission in the same manner as other similar property owned by it;

(iii) conduct exploratory operations, investigations, inspections to determine the location, extent, mode of occurrence, use, or condition of source materials with or without the consent of the owner of any interest therein, making just compensation for any damage or injury occasioned thereby.

(2) The Commission shall establish by regulation a procedure by which any person who is dissatisfied with its action in allocating, refusing to allocate, or in rescinding any allocation of fissionable, source, or byproduct materials to him may obtain a review of such determination by a board of appeal consisting of two or more members appointed by the Commission and at least one member of the Commission.

717

MILITARY APPLICATIONS OF ATOMIC POWER

Sec. 6. (a) The Commission is authorized and directed to—

(1) conduct experiments and do research and developmental work in the military application of atomic power; and

(2) have custody of all assembled or unassembled atomic bombs, bomb parts, or other atomic military weapons, presently or hereafter produced, except that upon the express finding of the President that such action is required in the interests of national defense, the Commission shall deliver such quantities of weapons to the armed forces as the President may specify.

(b) The Commission shall not conduct any research or developmental work in the military application of atomic power if such research or developmental work is contrary to any international agreement of the United States.

(c) The Commission is authorized to engage in the production of atomic bombs, bomb parts, or other applications of atomic power as military weapons, only to the extent that the express consent and direction of the President of the United States has been obtained, which consent and direction shall be obtained for each quarter.

(d) It shall be unlawful for any person to manufacture, produce, or process any device or equipment designed to utilize fissionable materials as a military weapon, except as authorized by the Commission.

ATOMIC ENERGY DEVICES

SEC. 7. (a) LICENSE REQUIRED.—It shall be unlawful for any person to operate any equipment or device utilizing fissionable materials without a license issued by the Commission authorizing such operation.

(b) ISSUANCE OF LICENSES.—Any person desiring to utilize fissionable materials in any such device or equipment shall apply for a license therefor in accordance with such procedures as the Commission may by regulation establish. The Commission is authorized and directed to issue such a license on a nonexclusive basis and to supply appropriate quantities of fissionable materials to the extent available to any applicant (1) who is equipped to observe such safety standards to protect health and to minimize danger from explosion as the Commission may establish; and (2) who agrees to make available to the Commission such technical information and data concerning the operation of such device as the Commission may determine necessary to encourage the use of such devices by as many licensees as possible. Where any license might serve to maintain or foster the growth of monopoly, restraint of trade, unlawful competition, or other trade position inimical to the entry of new, freely competitive enterprises, the Commission is authorized and directed to refuse to issue such license or to establish such conditions to prevent these results as the Commission, in consultation with the Attorney General, may determine. The Commission shall report promptly to the Attorney General any information it may have of the use of such devices which appears to have these results. No license may be given to a foreign government or to any person who is not under and within the jurisdiction of the United States.

(c) BYPRODUCT POWER.—If in the production of fissionable materials the production processes yield energy capable of utilization, such energy may be used by the Commission, transferred to other Government agencies, sold to public or private utilities under contract providing for reasonable resale prices, or sold to private consumers at reasonable rates and on as broad a basis of eligibility as the Commission may determine to be possible.

(d) REPORTS TO CONGRESS.—Whenever in its opinion industrial, commercial, or other uses of fissionable materials have been sufficiently developed to be of practical value, the Commission shall prepare a report to the Congress stating all the facts, the Commission's estimate of the social, political, and economic effects of such utilization, and the Commission's recommendations for necessary or desirable supplemental legislation. Until such a report has been filed with the Commission and the period of ninety days has elapsed after such filing, within which period the Commission may adopt supplemental legislation, no license for the use of atomic energy devices shall be issued by the Commission.

PROPERTY OF THE COMMISSION

SEC. 8. (a) The President shall direct the transfer to the Commission of the following property owned by the United States or any of its agencies, or any interest in such property held in trust for or on behalf of the United States:

(1) All fissionable materials; all bombs and bomb parts; all plants, facilities, equipment, and materials for the processing or production of fissionable materials, bombs, and bomb parts; all processes and technical information of any kind, and the source thereof (including data, drawings, specifications, patents, patent applications, and other sources, relating to the refining or production of fissionable materials; and all contracts, agreements, leases, patents, applications for patents, inventions and discoveries (whether patented or unpatented), and other rights of any kind concerning any such items;

(2) All facilities and equipment, and materials therein, devoted primarily to atomic energy research and development; and

(3) All property in the custody and control of the Manhattan engineer district.

(b) In order to render financial assistance to those States and local governments in which the activities of the Commission are carried on and in which the Commission, or its agents, have acquired properties previously subject to State and local taxation, the Commission is authorized to make payments to State and local governments in lieu of such taxes. Such payments may be in the amounts, at the times, and upon the terms the Commission deems appropriate, but the Commission shall be guided by the policy of not exceeding the taxes which would have been payable for such property in the condition in which it was acquired, except where special burdens have been cast upon the State or local government by activities of the Commission, the Manhattan engineer district, or their agents, and in such cases any benefits accruing to the States and local governments by reason of these activities shall be considered in the determination of such payments. The Commission and any corporation created by it, and the property and income of the Commission or of such corporation, are hereby expressly exempted from taxation in any manner or form by any State, county, municipality, or any subdivision thereof.

DISSEMINATION OF INFORMATION

719

SEC. 9. (a) BASIC SCIENTIFIC INFORMATION.—Basic scientific information in the fields specified in section 3 may be freely disseminated. The term "basic scientific information" shall include, in addition to theoretical knowledge of nuclear and other physics, chemistry, biology, and therapy, all results capable of accomplishment, as distinguished from the processes or techniques of accomplishing them.

(b) RELATED TECHNICAL INFORMATION.—The Commission shall establish a Board of Atomic Information consisting of one or more employees and at least one member of the Commission. The Board shall, under the direction and supervision of the Commission, provide for the dissemination of related technical information with the utmost liberality as freely as may be consistent with the foreign and domestic policies established by the President and shall have authority to—

(1) establish such information services, publications, libraries, and other registers of available information as may be helpful in effectuating this policy;

(2) designate by regulation the types of related technical information the dissemination of which will effectuate the foregoing policy. Such designations shall constitute an administrative determination that such information is not of value to the national defense and that any person is entitled to receive such information, within the meaning of the Espionage Act. Failure to make any such designation shall not, however, be deemed a determination that such undesignated information is subject to the provisions of said Act;

(3) by regulation or order, require reports of the conduct of independent research or development activities in the fields specified in section 3 and of the operation of atomic energy devices under licenses issued pursuant to section 7;

(4) provide for such inspections of independent research and development activities of the types specified in section 3 and of the operation of atomic energy devices as the Commission or the Board may determine; and

(5) whenever it will facilitate the carrying out of the purposes of the Act, adopt by regulation administrative interpretations of the Espionage Act except that any such interpretation shall, before adoption, receive the express approval of the President.

PATENTS

SEC. 10. (a) Whenever any person invents a device or method for the production, refining, or other processing of fissionable material: (i) he may file a patent application to cover such invention, sending a copy thereof to the Commission; (ii) if the Commissioner of Patents determines that the invention is patentable, he shall issue a patent in the name of the Commission; and (iii) the Commission shall make just compensation to such person. The Commission shall appoint a Patent Royalty Board consisting of one or more employees and at least one member of the Commission, and the Commissioner of Patents.

The Patent Royalty Board shall determine what constitutes just compensation in each such case and whether such compensation is to be paid in periodic payments rather than in a lump sum. Any person to whom any such patent has heretofore been issued shall forthwith transfer all right, title, and interest in and to such patent to the Commission and shall receive therefor just compensation as provided above.

(b) (1) Any patent now or hereafter issued covering any process or device utilizing or peculiarly necessary to the utilization of fissionable materials, or peculiarly necessary to the conduct of research or developmental activities in the fields specified in section 3, is hereby declared to be affected with the public interest and its general availability for such uses is declared to be necessary to effectuate the purposes of this Act.

(2) Any person to whom any such patent has been issued, or any person desiring to use any device or process covered by such patent for such uses, may apply to the Patent Royalty Board, for determination by such Board of a reasonable royalty fee for such use of the patented process or device intended to be used under the Commission's license.

(3) In determining such reasonable royalty fee, the Patent Royalty Board shall take into consideration any defense, general or special, that might be pleaded by a defendant in an action for infringement, the extent to which, if any, such patent was developed through federally financed research, the degree of utility, novelty, and importance of the patent, the cost to the patentee of developing such process or device, and a reasonable rate of return on such research investment by the patentee.

(4) No court, Federal, State, or Territorial, shall have jurisdiction or power to stay, restrain, or otherwise enjoin any such use of any such patented device or process by any person on the ground of infringement of such patent. In any action for infringement of any such patent filed in any such court, the court shall have authority only to order the payment of reasonable royalty fees and attorney's fees and court costs as damages for any such infringement. If the Patent Royalty Board has not previously determined the reasonable royalty fee for the use of the patented device or process involved in any case, the court in such case shall, before entering judgment, obtain from the Patent Royalty Board a report containing its recommendation as to the reasonable royalty fee it would have established had application been made to it as provided in subparagraphs 2 and 3 above.

ORGANIZATION AND GENERAL AUTHORITY

Sec. 11. (a) Organization.—There are hereby established within the Commission a Division of Research, a Division of Production, a Division of Materials, and a Division of Military Application. Each division shall be under the direction of a Director who shall be appointed by the President, by and with the advice and consent of the Senate, and shall receive compensation at the rate of $15,000 per annum. The Commission shall delegate to each such division such of its powers under this Act as in its opinion from time to time will promote the effectuation of the purposes of this Act in an efficient manner. Nothing in this paragraph shall prevent the Commission from establishing such additional divisions or other subordinate organizations as it may deem desirable.

(b) General Authority.—In the performance of its functions the Commission is authorized to—

(1) establish advisory boards to advise with and make recommendations to the Commission on legislation, policies, administration, and research;

(2) establish by regulation or order such standards and instructions to govern the possession and use of fissionable and byproduct materials as the Commission may deem necessary or desirable to protect health or to minimize danger from explosion:

(3) make such studies and investigations, obtain such information, and hold such hearings as the Commission may deem necessary or proper to assist it in exercising any authority provided in this Act, or in the administration or enforcement of this Act, or any regulations or orders issued thereunder. For such purposes the Commission is authorized to require any person to permit the inspection and copying of any records or other documents, to administer oaths and affirmations, and by subpena to require any person to appear and testify, or to appear and produce documents, or both, at any designated place. Witnesses subpenaed under this subsection shall be paid the same fees and mileage as are paid witnesses in the district courts of the United States;

(4) create or organize corporations, the stock of which shall be wholly owned by the United States and controlled by the Commission, to carry out the provisions of this Act;

(5) appoint and fix the compensation of such officers and employees as may be necessary to carry out the functions of the Commission. All such officers and employees shall be appointed in accordance with the civil-service laws and their compensation fixed in accordance with the Classification Act of 1923, as amended, except that expert administrative, technical, and professional personnel may be employed and their compensation fixed without regard to such laws. The Commission shall make adequate provision for administrative review by a board consisting of one or more employees and at least one member of the Commission of any determination to dismiss any scientific or professional employee; and

(6) acquire such materials, property, equipment, and facilities, establish or construct such buildings and facilities, modify such building and facilities from time to time, and construct, acquire, provide, or arrange for such facilities and services for the housing, health, safety, welfare, and recreation of personnel employed by the Commission as it may deem necessary.

ENFORCEMENT

721

SEC. 12. (a) Any person who willfully violates, attempts to violate, or conspires to violate, any of the provisions of this Act or any regulations or orders issued thereunder shall, upon conviction thereof, be punishable by a fine of not more than $10,000, or by imprisonment for a term of not exceeding five years, or both.

(b) Whenever in the judgment of the Commission any person has engaged or is about to engage in any acts or practices which constitute or will constitute a violation of any provision of this Act, it may make application to the appropriate court for an order enjoining such acts or practices, or for an order enforcing compliance with such provision, and upon a showing by the Commission that such person has engaged or is about to engage in any such acts or practices a permanent or temporary injunction, restraining order, or other order shall be granted without bond.

(c) In case of contumacy by, or refusal to obey a subpena served upon, any person pursuant to section 11 (b) (3), the district court for any district in which such person is found or resides or transacts business, upon application by the Commission, shall have jurisdiction to issue an order requiring such person to appear and give testimony or to appear and produce documents, or both; and any failure to obey such order of the court may be punished by such court as a contempt thereof.

REPORTS

SEC. 13. The Commission shall, on the first days of January, April, July, and October, submit reports to the President, to the Senate and to the House of Representatives. Such reports shall summarize and appraise the activities of the Commission and of each division and board therof, and specifically shall contain financial statements; lists of licenses issued, of property acquired, of research contracts and arrangements entered into, and of the amounts of fissionable material and the persons to whom allocated; the Commission's program for the following quarter including lists of research contracts and arrangement proposed to be entered into; conclusions drawn from studies of the social, political, and economic effects of the release of atomic energy; and such recommendations for additional legislation as the Commission may deem necessary or desirable.

DEFINITIONS

SEC. 14. As used in this Act—

(a) The term "atomic energy" shall include all forms of energy liberated in the artificial transmutation of atomic species.

(b) The term "Government agency" means any executive department, board, bureau, commission, or other agency in the executive branch of the Federal Government, or any corporation wholly owned (either directly or through one or more corporations) by the United States.

(c) The term "person" means any individual, corporation, partnership, firm, association, trust, estate, public or private institution, group, any government other than the United States, any political subdivision of any such government, and any legal successor, representative, agent, or agency of the foregoing, or other entity.

(d) The term "United States" includes all Territories and possessions of the United States.

APPROPRIATIONS

SEC. 15. There are hereby authorized to be appropriated such sums as may be necessary and appropriate to carry out the provisions and purposes of this Act. Funds appropriated to the Commission shall, if obligated during the fiscal year for which appropriated, remain available for expenditure for four years following the expiration of the fiscal year for which appropriated. After such four-year period, the unexpended balances of appropriations shall be carried to the surplus fund and covered into the Treasury.

SEPARABILITY OF PROVISIONS

SEC. 16. If any provision of this Act, or the application of such provision to any person or circumstances, is held invalid, the remainder of this Act or the application of such provision to persons or circumstances other than those to which it is held invalid, shall not be affected thereby.

SHORT TITLE

SEC. 17. This Act may be cited as the "Atomic Energy Act of 1946."

FINANCIAL DATA

Cumulative Costs in the Manhattan Engineer District
as of December 31, 1945
(in thousands)

	Plant	Operations
Government overhead	$ 22,567	$ 14,688
Research and development	63,323	6,358
Electromagnetic plant (Y-12)	300,625	177,006
Gaseous-diffusion plant (K-25)	458,316	53,850
Thermal-diffusion plant (S-50)	10,605	5,067
Clinton Laboratories	11,939	14,993
Clinton Engineer Works—headquarters and central utilities	101,193	54,758
Hanford Engineer Works	339,678	50,446
Heavy-water production plants	15,801	10,967
Los Alamos Project	37,176	36,879
Special operating materials	20,810	82,559
TOTALS	$1,382,033	$507,571

Monthly Expenditures in the Manhattan Engineer District
August 1942 through December 1946
(in thousands)

	1942	1943	1944	1945	1946
January	$	$ 2,010	$ 68,984	$ 68,276	$ 19,073
February		6,829	61,336	63,987	18,136
March		6,036	55,269	60,156	18,622
April		8,533	93,041	47,776	16,846
May		14,395	89,283	69,099	18,282
June		23,173	78,459	54,584	18,664
July		25,114	73,539	47,164	11,742
August	15,000*	41,286	111,391	43,414	48,152
September	24	48,344	71,301	51,219	11,791
October	67	54,973	80,779	58,819	17,166
November	138	68,005	81,832	23,885	54,006
December	893	45,889	74,181	21,932	28,563
Annual Totals	$16,122	$344,587	$939,395	$610,311	$281,043
TOTAL					$2,191,458

724

* Transferred to OSRD.

Allis-Chalmers Mfg. Co.: contract for gaseous-diffusion pumps, 124; pump plant, 135–36; pump manufacture, 140; contractor for Y-12, 149; assembles magnets, 153; rebuilds magnet coils, 163

Allison, Samuel K.: beryllium measurements, 29; named to S-1 Section, 144; beryllium pile, 54, 56, 68; directs Met Lab experimentation, 55–56; Met Lab engineering council, 174–75; urges large experimental pile, 181; associate Met Lab director, 200; director, 207; reports Hanford pile poisoning, 306; Los Alamos Technical and Scheduling Conference, 317; implosion design, 317–18; Cowpuncher Comm., 318; questions research limitations, 323; supervises implosion work, 375–76; Trinity test, 379; urges lifting security restrictions, 422

Alpha plant. See *Y-12 plant*

Alsop, Joseph, 485–86, 557

Alsop, Stewart, 557

Aluminum Co. of America, 209

Aluminum-silicon alloy, 223

Alvarez, Luis W., 317, 642

Amagasaki, Japan, 399

American Association for the United Nations, 447

American Association of University Women, 447

American Bar Association, 520, 523

American Brass Co., 99

American Physical Society, April, 1940, meeting of, 22–23

Americans United for World Organization, 448, 451, 506

Ames Laboratory. See *Iowa State College*

Anami, Korechika, 404, 405

Anderson, Herbert L., 13, 14, 377, 432, 434

Anderson, Sir John: presses Bush on interchange, 260, 261–63; concern at limited-interchange policy, 270; attends Churchill-Stimson meeting, 276; negotiates Quebec Agreement, 277–79; sanctions interchange plan, 281; negotiates CDT agreement, 286; negotiates with Belgians, 287; policy on French scientists, 331–33, 335–36; views on Smyth report release, 401; Declaration of Washington, 464; Nov., 1945, interchange talks, 466–68

Andrews, Bert, 485

Anglo-American co-operation. See *Interchange, Anglo-American*

Anglo-American strategy, 255–56, 260, 261, 264, 272, 275–76, 279–80

Antonov, Alexei E., 393

Appleby, Paul H., 559

Appropriations, 73, 289–90, 339, 635

Appropriations Committee (House), 289

Appropriations Committee (Senate), 289–90

Arends, Leslie C., 523–24

Argersinger, Roy E., 149

Argonne Forest Preserve, 91, 645

Argonne Laboratory, 185–86, 207, 306–7, 337–38

Argonne National Laboratory, 634, 635, 636, 645

Army Air Forces, U. S., 365, 581–82. See also individual units and officers

Army and Navy Munitions Board, 79, 154

Army, U. S. See *Manhattan Engineer District; War Department, U. S.*

Arneson, R. Gordon, 354, 399, 464, 471, 515

Arnold, Henry H., 390, 391–92, 581

Arnold, John A., 121, 135

Ashworth, Frederick L., 314, 319, 401

Associated Universities, Inc., 636–37, 645–46

Association of Edison Illuminating Companies, 494

Aston, F. W., 30, 31

Atomic bomb: possibility reported to FDR, 17; Uranium Comm., views, 20, 37; prospects (spring, 1940), 22; not primary objective of early research, 27; 1st NAS report, 37–38; British views on feasibility, 42; Bush briefs FDR, 45; estimated U-235 requirements, 46–47; 3rd NAS report, 47–48; Compton sets schedule, 54–55; early efficiency estimates, 61; production estimate (May, 1942), 71; need for quantity, 91; fast-neutron research reorganized, 103–4; increase in critical-mass estimate, 104; threat of higher Pu purity specifications, 109; Compton's timetable (Nov., 1942), 111; Conant views on need, 113–14; production estimate (Dec., 1942), 115; new estimate of greater critical mass, 159; 1st U-235 shipments, 164; 1st Clinton Pu samples, 212; technical understanding (Mar., 1943), 233–35; Los Alamos work on nuclear specifications, 240–43; chemistry and metallurgy, 243–45; problems of assembly, 245–49; efforts to develop combat model, 249–50; crisis (summer, 1944), 250–51, 290; timetable (Aug., 1944), 252–54; work on gun and implosion (late 1944), 312–13; timetable (Dec., 1944), 313, 334; designs frozen, 317–18; test plans, 318–19; delivery plans, 319; chemistry and metallurgy, 319–20; prospect (Apr., 1945), 320–21, 343; Stimson contemplates role in war against Japan, 347, 350–51; Int. Comm. considers use, 358; Int. Comm. recommendations, 360; Franck comm. recom-

730

731

732

733

735

737

738

741

743

745

747

749

751

Smith, Cyril S., 237, 244, 378, 422
Smith, Harold D.: attends top-policy meeting, 51; postwar research policy, 410, 438; warns Truman on May-Johnson bill, 438; testifies before McMahon comm., 492; action on War Dept. comments to OWMR, 499–500, 504–5
Smith, Howard Alexander, 470
Smith, Lloyd P., 44, 59
Smith, Ronald B., 125
Smith, Waverly Q., 206
Smyth, Henry D.: named to S-1 Section, 44; research on isotron, 59; directs Met Lab research, 202–3; suggests definite research goals, 323; serves on Tolman Postwar Policy Comm., 325; prepares technical summary of wartime program, 368; works on position papers for Moscow talks, 471
Smyth report (*Atomic Energy for Military Purposes*): explained to Int. Comm., 368; British clearance, 373; publication debated, 400–1; release and significance, 406–7; effect on declassification policy, 647
Snyder, John W., 436, 437, 443–44, 505
Sodium-potassium alloy, 636
Solberg, Thorvald A., 649
Solvent extraction, 183
Somervell, Brehon B., 72, 79–82
Soong, T. V., 350, 381
Sources, electromagnetic. See *Calutron sources*
Spaatz, Carl A., 390, 394, 399, 575
Sparkman, John J., 517, 520
Special Committee on Atomic Energy (Senate): established, 435–36; Newman and Condon appointments, 440–41; studies technology, 440, 449; Oak Ridge visit, 449; requests classified data, 449–52; 1st hearings, 454; fears information disclosure at Moscow, 473–75; 2nd hearings, 488–500, 513–14; hears report on Canadian spy case, 501; accepts McMahon bill as basis for legislation, 504; hears Eisenhower and Nimitz on military control, 505–6; Vandenberg amendment, 504–13; discusses revised McMahon bill, 511–13; completes action on McMahon bill, 514–15; witnesses signing of act, 530; hears Baruch, 576
Special Committee Investigating the National Defense Program (Senate), 517
Special Engineer Detachment, 310, 315
Spedding, Frank H., 87, 175, 177, 204, 647
Spontaneous-fission threat to plutonium gun, 251
Stages of international control: Bush proposes, 460–61; Agreed Declaration of

Washington, 465; draft position papers for 1945 Moscow meeting, 472–73; senators' concern, 473–74; Byrnes proposal at Moscow, 475–76; Dec. 27, 1945, Moscow communiqué, 476; Vandenberg reassured, 476–77; General Assembly calls for gradual progress, 532–33; Acheson comm. wants emphasis, 545–46, 548–49; added to Lilienthal board report, 550; Acheson comm. asks for greater emphasis, 551–53; final Lilienthal board report, 553; Acheson comm. transmittal letter, 553–54; discussed at Blair-Lee conference, 564–66; Acheson-Marks-Hancock draft, 572; Truman emphasizes, 574; Baruch reassures senators, 576; Baruch June 14, 1946, speech, 578–79; Baruch-Wallace controversy, 598, 601–2, 602–3, 604, 605–6; Baruch's Dec. 5, 1946, resolution, 613
Stagg Field. See *Metallurgical Laboratory*; *Pile, uranium-graphite*; *Pile, CP-1*
Stalin, Josef V.: sets price for entering Far Eastern war, 348; gives assurances to Hopkins, 351–52; makes stiff demands on China, 381; discusses Far Eastern matters with Truman and Byrnes, 385–86; tells Churchill of Japanese peace feelers, 386–87; tells Truman, 387; told of unusual new weapon, 393–94; reports new Japanese peace feeler, 396
Standard Oil Co. of Louisiana, 67
Standard Oil Development Co., 64
Stanford University, 103, 232
Stassen, Harold E., 3–4
State, U. S. Department of: informed about bomb, 335; thinking about unconditional surrender, 381; plans strategy for domestic legislation, 417–18, 423–27; plans for Moscow conference, 471–73; releases Acheson-Lilienthal report, 558; considers response to USSR disarmament proposal, 609–10; considers future of CPC, 654. See also *Byrnes, James F.*; *Acheson, Dean G.*; *Stettinius, Edward R., Jr.*
Staub, Hans H., 241
Stearns, Joyce C., 336
Steel, stainless, 221
Steelman, John R., 622
Stettinius, Edward R., Jr., 334, 335, 349, 621
Stewart, Irvin, 409, 496
Stimson, Henry L.: assigned S-1 policy consideration, 46; attends top policy meeting, 51; member top policy group, 77; establishes Military Policy Comm., 82–83; reports to FDR on German activity, 119–20; authorizes interchange, 257; proposes going slow on S-1 interchange,

759

761

765